COMPREHENSIVE

ENGLISH–ESPERANTO

DICTIONARY

by Peter J. Benson

esperanto-usa.org

ISBN: 978-1546730644

FIRST EDITION: 1995
PROJECT LEADER: MIKO SLOPER
ESPERANTO LEAGUE FOR NORTH AMERICA. P.O. BOX 1129, EL CERRITO, CA 94530

TABLE OF CONTENTS

About This Dictionary

§ 1. General

(a) Sources. Every effort has been made to make the *Comprehensive English-Esperanto Dictionary* (CEED) the most comprehensive and modern general English-Esperanto dictionary yet to be published. The author has of course consulted existing dictionaries and authorities; however, the translations in the CEED are independent; that is, they have been chosen ordinarily by matching the Esperanto definitions in the Plena Ilustrita Vortaro de Esperanto (PIV) and the Plena Ilustrita Vortaro, Suplemento (PIVS) directly with the definitions in a standard English-language dictionary.

The author is aware of the shortcomings of the PIV and PIVS. The CEED does not blindly follow those sources. Nevertheless, the PIV and PIVS comprise the general authority on Esperanto word-forms and definitions. The CEED diverges from the PIV and PIVS only when common usage differs from them or when there is other good reason to do so (for example, see "**Adelaide**", "**Oregon**", and "**hallucinogen**"). In the case of Esperanto words not in the PIV or PIVS, see § 12.

The authority for the definitions of English-language words used in the CEED is *Webster's Third New International Dictionary of the English Language, Unabridged,* published in 1971 by G. & C. Merriam Company, Springfield, Massachusetts, U.S.A.

(b) Definitions of Esperanto words. For a given word in one language, there is often no *exact* equivalent in another. Therefore, an interlingual dictionary such as the CEED should not be used as the final authority on the *definition* of a word in the language into which the dictionary translates (the target language). For definitions of Esperanto words, refer to the PIV, PIVS, or a specialized glossary.

(c) Compound terms. Compound words and phrases in English consisting either of two or more separate words (e.g., "bulletin board") or terms written as a single word (e.g., "chalkboard") are listed in this dictionary under the more basic or significant part of the expression. Both of the above examples are listed as subentries under the keyword "**board**", because bulletin boards and chalkboards are types of board.

Sometimes no single part of a compound term stands out as primary, or one might disagree as to which part is primary. If a given compound term is not found under one of its component words, it may be found under the other.

Some compound words written as single words are alphabetized as self-standing keywords, especially when the meaning is rather different from that of either of the component words (e.g., **"undertake"**).

Also see § 4.

(d) Dialects of English. Since the author is a native and resident of the U.S.A., this work will inevitably reflect the American branch of the English language. However, whenever an English word or phrase has a substantially different meaning or spelling in one English-speaking country or group of countries than in others, an attempt has been made to include such variants in the CEED.

These usage distinctions among various countries where English is spoken are indicated. For example, compare **"trapezium"** and **"trapezoid"**; also see **"table"**.

It should also be noted that "British" spelling and usage are also widespread in other countries where English is spoken besides Great Britain, such as Australia, South Africa, and Canada. The abbreviation "(Aus)" indicates not only Australian usage, but (in most but not all

cases) that the term was obtained from the *Australian English Dictionary,* by R. L. Harry and V. Gueltling.

§ 2. Parentheses: ( )

(a) To show context. When the English entry being translated has more than one meaning, parentheses enclose approximate synonyms or brief descriptions of context. Parentheses also enclose examples of usage (preceded by the abbreviation "e.g.:").

(b) To show alternate forms. Letter(s) in parentheses within an English word or phrase indicate spelling or phrasing variations involving no difference of meaning; in an Esperanto translation, letter(s) in parentheses indicate nuances of meaning that are apparent from the entry itself, consistent with basic Esperanto grammar and affixes.

§ 3. Square brackets: [ ]

Brackets are used to enclose clarifying comments; or to indicate verb type (see § 7); or to refer to another entry in the CEED; or to refer to one of these numbered sections; or to give guidance for usage.

§ 4. "~" and "/"

A wavy dash ("~") substitutes for the *first* Esperanto translation given, including any affixes, but excluding the final ending "–a", "–e", "–i", or "–o", denoting part of speech. For example, after "fendeto", "~i" stands for "fendeti".

When a slash ("/") appears within an Esperanto translation, the symbol "~" thereafter substitutes for that word only up to the symbol "/". For example, after "dikotom/eco", "~aĵo" stands for "dikotomaĵo".

When "~" stands for an uncapitalized Esperanto word, but a subentry requires capitalization (or vice versa), the initial letter is repeated, capitalized (or decapitalized), immediately preceding the symbol "~". For example, after "kongreso", "K~o" stands for "Kongreso". After "Luno", "l~a" stands for "luna".

See § 1(c) regarding the location of compound terms; see § 6 regarding capitalization.

§ 5. Hyphens

Hyphenation is essentially a matter of grammar and style, and is therefore outside the scope of this type of work. Where English uses a hyphen to join words into, say, a compound adjective (e.g., "a horse–drawn cart"), Esperanto often either joins the words without a hyphen or rephrases to keep the words separate ("ĉevaltirata ĉaro" or "ĉaro tirata de ĉevalo"). However, a hyphen is advisable between word parts in Esperanto if confusion might otherwise result. If in doubt, a hyphen should be used.

§ 6. Capitalization

The most common practice in Esperanto resembles the English convention in most particulars. Unlike English, the usual practice in Esperanto is not to capitalize days of the week or months of the year.

Practice in Esperanto varies concerning capitalization of proper adjectives derived from geographical proper nouns (e.g., "Franca" or "franca") and proper nouns denoting nationality, ethnic or religious association, etc. (e.g., "Judo" or "judo"). The CEED capitalizes all proper nouns and adjectives, as in English. The CEED follows the universal practice in Esperanto (as well as most ethnic languages) in using lowercase for the days of the week and the months of the year. (See § 4 concerning capitalization or decapitalization involving the symbol "~".) However, the user should understand that the usage of capitalization in this dictionary is not definitive.

§ 7. Verbs

Many ethnic languages (including English) often use a verb in the same form in both a transitive and an intransitive sense. Although it is essential to observe this distinction in Esperanto, bilingual Esperanto dictionaries and textbooks often fail to indicate in their translations whether a given Esperanto verb is transitive or intransitive. As a result, one of the most common errors by users of Esperanto is to use a transitive verb root in an intransitive sense, or vice versa, without the appropriate affix "–iĝ–" or "–ig–", or to use one of those affixes redundantly.

Esperanto verbs are therefore marked in the CEED by either "[tr]" or "[int]" to indicate respectively a transitive or intransitive verb. Those few Esperanto verb roots which may be used either transitively or intransitively without adding an affix are marked "[tr, int]". Forms ending in either "–igi" or "–iĝi" are *not* thus marked, however, since these are *always* transitive or intransitive, respectively.

§ 8. Prepositions

Translation of prepositions between any two languages is often perplexingly difficult, because the choice of preposition in a particular context often depends purely on custom, with little or no logical consistency. The definitions of Esperanto prepositions, however, are more precisely established than is usual in ethnic languages. Copious examples of usage are included in the CEED for each preposition.

§ 9. Interjections and onomatopoeias

Interjections and onomatopoeias, by their nature, tend not to vary much from language to language, allowing for spelling variations. Certain common interjections and onomatopoeias have acquired standard forms in Esperanto which vary slightly from English usage; for example, "ho" instead of "oh". All interjections and onomatopoeias found in the PIV are translated herein. Words of this sort not found in the CEED may be spelled in Esperanto as they are sounded.

§ 10. Irregular English word-forms

In the case of an English word which has irregular grammatical inflections (for example, "be", "am", "is", "are", etc.), only the root form (the singular of nouns or the infinitive of verbs) is listed in the CEED. Exceptions are cases in which the singular of a noun is not often known or used (e.g., "datum"/"data"), or in which an irregular verb inflection has some peculiarity of translation which deserves a separate listing (e.g., "had").

§ 11. Slang

There is some temptation to translate slang expressions literally, but the cultural allusions so common in slang are by no means universally understood. This is not to say that Esperanto cannot or should not contain flowery or slangy language; quite the contrary. However, one should consider whether one's hearer will understand the allusion of an English slang or colloquial expression used in literal translation in Esperanto, assuming that the hearer knows only the formal applications for the words in question.

Some common slang expressions and colloquialisms are included in the CEED, especially in those cases lacking a closely equivalent formal expression. Most slang expressions, however, are not included in the CEED, since these expressions tend to become rapidly obsolete.

§ 12. Neologisms

New words, or "neologisms", are constantly being created in Esperanto, as in other living languages, as the need arises in our changing world. The 15th Fundamental Rule of Esperanto grammar permits the coining of new words when necessary, subject to certain criteria.

One should remember that anyone encountering a new word or an existing term that is not in the PIV or PIVS will not be able to look up its meaning in those works. Unless the meaning is *totally* clear from context, a parenthetical or footnote definition would be wise. In books or articles, if many neologisms are used, it may be helpful to include a glossary. To aid in this respect, all Esperanto roots used in the CEED which are not defined in the PIV or PIVS are defined in a separate "Glossary of Neologisms" at the end of this book.

Roots and affixes defined in the CEED "Glossary of Neologisms" are indicated in the body of the CEED by "*". Those taken from the AED are marked "(Aus)". Those taken from PIVS are marked "†".

Further discussion of the use of neologisms in this work can be found at the beginning of the Glossary of Neologisms itself.

§ 13. Non-English phrases in English

English abounds with words and phrases borrowed from other languages. These should not be used untranslated in Esperanto (although Zamenhof himself did so occasionally), since they may not be understood worldwide. Foreign words and phrases which are common in English are translated in the CEED. If a foreign word or phrase is not listed herein, re-express the sense of the foreign term in Esperanto.

§ 14. Plants and animals

The common names of plants and animals are often imprecise

and ambiguous in English. The same flower or insect may have a number of different names in different countries in which English is spoken. Conversely, one name may be applied to several unrelated species. The scientific (taxonomic) nomenclature also shows some variation, but is generally much more consistent and precise.

Since most people know a biological species only by its common name, but since the taxonomic nomenclature is more precise, plants and animals appear in the CEED under both their common and their taxonomic names. The taxonomic names are alphabetized by *genus*—the capitalized part of the taxonomic name. For example, "broccoli" will be found listed under broccoli and under *Brassica* (subentry *Brassica oleracea italica*). Following the usual practice, taxonomic names in the CEED are italicized.

Taxonomic names are themselves international, so they can be used in Esperanto.

When a common name applies to more than one species, the Esperanto name of each species is given, differentiated by the respective taxonomic names in parentheses. However, no attempt has been made to include all minor or local variations in the names.

If a common plant or animal name is not found listed in the CEED, or if there is any question of ambiguity, one should look up the common name in an English-language dictionary to ascertain the corresponding taxonomic genus and species name; then look up the taxonomic genus name in the CEED. If the taxonomic name is not listed in the CEED, then the species is also absent from the PIV and PIVS. Before devising an Esperanto neologism in accordance with the 15th Fundamental Rule of Esperanto grammar, however, one should consult a specialized English-Esperanto glossary for botany, zoology, or some branch thereof. The neologism should be patterned after the taxonomic genus or species name, in accordance with established Esperanto practice. Also see § 12 above regarding neologisms.

§ 15. Abbreviations and symbols

The following abbreviations and symbols are used in the body of this dictionary:

adj	adjective
adv	adverb
AED	*Australian-Esperanto Dictionary (Aŭstralia-Esperanta Vortaro)*
Am	American usage
anat	anatomy, anatomical

arch	architecture, architectural		interj	interjection
ast	astronomy, astronomical; astronautics, astronautical; space		lit	literal(ly); literature
			math	mathematics, mathematical
			med	medicine, medical
Aus	Australian usage (most taken from the AED)		mil	military
			mus	music, musical
Bib	Bible, Biblical		myth	mythology, mythological
bio	biology, biological			
bot	botany, botanical (species)		n	noun
			naut	nautical, marine, sea navigation
Br	British usage (see § 1(d)).			
			neol	neologism
bsns	business, commerce		onom	onomatopoeia, onomatopoetic
CEED	this work: the *Comprehensive English-Esperanto Dictionary*			
			opp	opposite (of), antonym (of)
chem	chemistry, chemical		oth	other; the translation is valid for all senses other than the one(s) previously cited in the same entry
cmptr	computer(s)			
colloq	colloquial, informal usage			
conj	conjunction			
cp	compare with the word indicated, which is similar or related			
			pfx	prefix
			phil	philosophy, philosophical
e.g.	for example			
elec	electricity, electrical, electronic(s)		phon	phonetic(s)
			phot	photography, photographic
esp	especially			
fig	figurative(ly)		phys	physics, physical
gen	general (unspecific) usage; the translation is valid for all meanings of the English word or phrase		PIV	*Plena Ilustrita Vortaro de Esperanto*
			PIVS	*Plena Ilustrita Vortaro de Esperanto, Suplemento*
geol	geology, geological		plur	plural
geom	geometry, geometric		poet	poetical usage
gram	grammar, grammatical		pol	politics, political
inf	infinitive		prep	preposition
int	intransitive verb (see § 7)		pron	pronoun
			psych	psychology, psychiatry

re	regarding, in the context of	§	refers to a section in this Introduction
rel	religion, theology		
rr	railroad		
sci	science, scientific		
sfx	suffix		
sing	singular		
tech	technology, technological		
theat	theater, theatrical, drama		
tr	transitive verb (see § 7)		
TV	television		
vulg	vulgar usage, not used in formal or polite context		
w	with		
w/o	without		
zool	zoology, zoological (species)		
*	Esperanto root or affix is defined in the Glossary of this dictionary (see § 12)		
†	Esperanto root or affix is defined in the PIVS (see § 12) or in "Aldonaĵoj" in the PIV		
( )	indicates context of translation or alternate forms or examples of usage (see § 2)		
[ ]	indicates explanatory note or verb type (see § 3 and § 7)		
~	(see § 4)		
/	(see § 4)		
$	financial; money; economics		

About Esperanto

§ 16. Letters and diacritics

(a) Letters. The Esperanto alphabet consists of the following 28 letters:

Esp. Letter	name	English phonetic equivalent
Aa	a	a (as in "father")
Bb	bo	b
Cc	co	ts
Ĉĉ	ĉo	ch (as in "church")
Dd	do	d
Ee	e	short e (as in "get")
Ff	fo	f
Gg	go	hard g (as in "get")
Ĝĝ	ĝo	soft g (as in "gem")
Hh	ho	h (as in "help")
Ĥĥ	ĥo	kh (guttural "ch" as in "loch")
Ii	i	ee (as in "need")
Jj	jo	y (as in "yes" or "boy")
Ĵĵ	ĵo	zh ("s" as in "leisure")
Kk	ko	k
Ll	lo	l (usually somewhat "dark" or "hard", as in English)
Mm	mo	m
Nn	no	n (or "ng" as in "sing" before "g" or "k")
Oo	o	o (as in "note", without glide to "oo" sound)
Pp	po	p
Rr	ro	r (lightly trilled)
Ss	so	s (unvoiced, as in "set")
Ŝŝ	ŝo	sh
Tt	to	t
Uu	u	oo (as in "food")
Ŭŭ	ŭo	w (as in "now")
Vv	vo	v
Zz	zo	z

The name of each vowel is simply the sound of the vowel itself; the name of each consonant is the sound of that consonant followed by "o". ("J" and "Ŭ" are named like consonants but are technically called semivowels, like English "Y" and "W". For purposes of syllabification they function like consonants; see § 18.)

In forming the plural and accusative forms of letter names, each letter name is treated as a grammatical root. For example: *"En la vorto 'valvo' estas du V–oj* [pronounce 'vooj'] *kaj unu* L ['lo']."

Letters with diacritics are considered to be separate letters from the same letters without diacritics. Thus, for example, "ĉasi" comes later in alphabetical order than "cunamo".

The names of Roman and non-Roman letters, diacritics, punctuation, and other marks, whether or not used in Esperanto, are necessary for spelling ethnic names and words orally. These are listed below.

(b) *Roman letters not used in Esperanto.* The remaining four letters of the standard Roman alphabet occur in Esperanto in proper names, mathematical and chemical formulas, and other contexts. Their Esperanto names follow (with plural forms in parentheses):

Qq   kuo(j)
Ww   ĝermana(j) vo(oj) [not
           "duobla vo"]
Xx   ikso(j)
Yy   ipsilono(j)

(c) *Other Roman letters.* Here are the names of some modified letters of the Roman alphabet used in some languages:
Ææ   a-e-ligaturo
Œœ   o-e-ligaturo
Ðð   do-trastreko
ß   esceto

ı   senpunkta i

(d) *Non-Roman letters.* Letters of non-Roman alphabets retain their native names in Esperanto: (Greek), *alfa, beta, gama;* (Hebrew), *alef, bet, vet, gimel;* (Cyrillic), *a, be, ve, ge;* etc. These names are considered as roots for inflection purposes, like the names of the Esperanto letters. (Examples of plurals: *gamaoj, alefoj, beoj.*) Each letter of the Greek alphabet is also listed in the CEED (under its conventional English spelling) with its Esperanto spelling.

(e) *Diacritics.* Here are the Esperanto names of many diacritics:

X́   akuto
X̀   malakuto
X̋   duakuto
X̂   cirkumflekso
X̌   dukorno
X̆   brevo*
Ẍ   (gen), surdupunkto;
           (functioning as umlaut),
           umlaŭto; (as dieresis),
           dierezo
Ẋ   surpunkto
X̊   ringo
X̃   tildo [cp "ondostreko" in
           § 17]
X̄   surstreko
X̧   cedilo

x̣   subpunkto

ø ł đ   trastreko

The Esperanto name of a letter with a diacritic consists of the name of the unmodified letter followed by the name of the diacritic, hyphenated when written; for example:

á   a-akuto

à   a-malakuto

ä   a-surdupunkto

å   a-ringo

ã   a-tildo

č   co-dukorno

ç   co-cedilo

ł   lo-trastreko

ñ   no-tildo

ø   o-trastreko

ő   o-duakuto

ż   z-surpunkto

§ 17. Punctuation and other symbols

The following table gives the Esperanto names of punctuation marks and other common symbols.

.   punkto

,   komo

;   punktokomo

:   dupunkto

...   tripunkto

/   oblikva streko

\   retroa oblikva streko

| vertikala streko

?   demando-signo

!   kri-signo

¿   surkapa demando-signo

¡   surkapa kri-signo

"   malferma citilo

"   ferma citilo

'   apostrofo; ferma unutreketa citilo

« »   surliniaj citiloj

x-x   streketo, dividostreko

x—x   haltostreko

x̄   superstreko

x̲   substreko

~   ondostreko [cp"tildo" in § 16(e)]

(malferma ronda krampo

)   ferma ronda krampo

[ ]   (ferma, malferma) rektaj krampoj

‹ ›   angulaj krampoj

{ }   kurbaj krampoj

@   po-signo [not used in Esperanto]

numersigno [not used in Esperanto]

$ dolar-signo

¢   cendo-signo

£   pundo-signo

¥   jeno-signo

%   procento-signo

&   kaj-signo [rare in Esperanto]

*   asterisko

†   ponardo-signo

§	paragrafo-signo
¶	alineo-signo [not used in Esperanto]
•	kuglo-signo
°	grado-signo
∧	mank-signo

§ 18. Syllables and accent

Each vowel in an Esperanto word forms its own syllable (with any consonants before and/or after it). In the case of two or more consecutive consonants, syllable division depends primarily on how the word is pronounced. For example, the word "mitrajlo" is divided into syllables as "mi-traj-lo", not "mit-rajl-o". There is no firm rule on this point, and in some cases different divisions can be made.

In words of more than one syllable, the accent, or stress, *always* falls on the next-to-last syllable. For example, the following Esperanto words are hyphenated at each syllable, with the stressed syllable in bold type: **ba**-la, **ba**-laj, ba-**la**-i, ba-la-**i**-lo, mi-**traj**-lo, **ĉir**-kaŭ, ĉir-**kaŭ**-as, pra-**u**-lo.

§ 19. Numbers

(a) Cardinals.

0	nul
1	unu
2	du
3	tri
4	kvar
5	kvin
6	ses
7	sep
8	ok
9	naŭ
10	dek
11	dek unu
12	dek du
13	dek tri
14	dek kvar
20	dudek
21	dudek unu
30	tridek
40	kvardek
100	cent
101	cent unu
136	cent tridek ses
200	ducent
300	tricent
1 000	mil
1 500	mil kvincent [never "dek kvin cent"]
2 000	du mil
10 000	dek mil
100 000	cent mil
1 000 000	miliono (da –oj)
2 000 000	du milionoj
1 000 000 000	[see § 19(b)]

(b) Billions and up. There is ambiguity regarding the name of 1 000 000 000 and larger numbers. The word *biliono* (billion) means a thousand millions in some countries (including the U.S.A.) and a million millions in others (including the U.K.). Esperanto solves this problem by attaching the two suffixes *–iliono* and *–iliardo* to numerals to indicate powers of a thousand, as follows:

A numeral name followed by *–iliono* indicates powers of a million (10^6). Thus, *duiliono* = $(10^6)^2 = 10^{12}$; *triiliono* = $(10^6)^3 = 10^{18}$; *dekiliono* = $(10^6)^{10} = 10^{60}$.

Miliardo = 10^9 (the American "billion", British "thousand million"). For the intermediate powers of a thousand above 10^{12}, a numeral followed by *–iliardo* indicates a thousand of the corresponding *–ilionoj*. Thus, *duiliardo* = 1000 x 10^{12} = 10^{15}; *triiliardo* = 10^{21}; etc.

The following chart provides a quick reference:

10^3	= mil	= 1 000
10^6	= miliono	= 1 000 000
10^9	= miliardo	= 1 000 000 000
10^{12}	= duiliono	= 1 000 000 000 000
10^{15}	= duiliardo	
10^{18}	= triiliono	
10^{21}	= triiliardo	
10^{24}	= kvariliono	
10^{27}	= kvariliardo	
10^{30}	= kviniliono	

(c) Ordinals. Ordinal numbers are formed simply by adding the adjective ending "–a" (including the hyphen) to the cardinal numeral; for example, "third" is (in numerals) "3–a", (spelled out) "tria". (However, each musical interval—"second", "third", etc.—has its own separate root in Esperanto. These are therefore listed individually in the CEED.)

It is customary in Esperanto to hyphenate spelled-out ordinals which involve more than one separate word in the cardinal form: "three hundred sixty-first" is "tri-cent-sesdek-unua" ("361–a"), to show that the whole comprises the ordinal expression. Occasionally (especially with lower numbers), they are written as one word, e.g., "deksesa" ("16–a").

(d) Fractions. Fractions are formed by adding the suffix "–ono" to the cardinal: "a third" (1/3) is "triono"; "42/169" is "kvardek du cent-sesdek-naŭonoj".

(e) Commas and decimal points. International custom varies regarding commas and decimal points in numbers; in most countries a comma is used to mark the division between the unit place and decimal places to the right, while periods are used to mark off thousands, millions, etc. English-speaking countries and some others use the reverse system.

In Esperanto text, following the more international usage, it is advisable to use a comma for the decimal marker. Periods can be used to mark off thousands, millions, etc.; however, to avoid confusion, it is better to leave spaces between thousands, etc., with no punctuation, as in § 19.

§ 20. Units of measure

Since the British Imperial system of units of measure is rarely used outside the U.S.A., one should generally avoid it in Esperanto in favor of the metric or "International" system of units (universally abbreviated "SI" for *Système International*). In fact, Esperanto lacks terms for many of the British units. To assist in converting to the SI system, SI equivalents are given for non-SI units in the body of the CEED along with the Esperanto word for each unit when such a word exists. (For example, see the entries for "furlong" and "quart".) See § 19(e) regarding the decimal point.

§ 21. Proper names and brand names

Many personal given names, geographical names, names of some mythological figures, and the surnames of some famous people in history (for example, Shakespeare, Descartes) have acquired Esperanto equivalents, which may or may not be phonetically identical with their original ethnic forms. These equivalents are given in the CEED.

Brand names can be considered as a type of proper name, and therefore are not generally translated.

Names without established Esperanto equivalents from languages that use the Roman alphabet should retain their original spelling in Esperanto. It is often helpful to show the pronunciation (or the closest approximation renderable in Esperanto orthography) in written Esperanto. For example, when using the name "Clyde" in written Esperanto, the pronunciation can be parenthetically shown ("klajd"). The same holds true for all surnames, which are not translated (with the exception noted for certain famous people), and for untranslated geographical names.

When writing a nontranslatable name from a language that does not use the Roman alphabet, transliterate the name *directly* into the nearest approximation in Esperanto orthography. *Avoid English-language transliterations,* since the transliterated spelling will often be different and therefore misleading or meaningless to those not familiar with English. For example, the name of the Russian composer known in English-speaking lands as "Tchaikovsky" should be spelled in Esperanto as "Ĉajkovskij".

§ 22. Mailing addresses

When referring to geographical names in Esperanto, one should use the Esperanto form if it exists. (See § 21.) However, in addressing mail, the recipient's address should be written in the language of the country of destination. An American letter-carrier might be baffled by "Nov-Jorko, Usono", as would a French letter-carrier by "Kalezo". The return address, of course, should be in the language of that country.

Mail going to countries not using the Roman alphabet can be safely addressed using a transliteration of their local names in the Roman alphabet. If you know the local alphabet or other script, it is advisable to write the address in that script (to facilitate handling at the receiving end), but write the name of the destination country in the language of the country from which the mail is being sent.

YOUR SUGGESTIONS ARE INVITED

How would you improve this dictionary?

Much effort has been invested so that the CEED could live up to its title, "comprehensive". It is inevitable, though, that this work will occasionally fail to offer a satisfactory translation for some English word or phrase. You may also have ideas for a better way to express in Esperanto an English word or phrase included in the CEED. And, in spite of the most careful proofreading by the author and a number of reviewers, some inadvertent errors are likely to have gone unnoticed.

You are encouraged to give feedback on this work for the benefit of users of future editions. The master of this dictionary is in the custody of the Esperanto League for North America (ELNA). ELNA will maintain responsibility for future revisions of this work. Write to:

> Esperanto League for North America
> P.O.B. 1129
> El Cerrito, CA 94530
> U.S.A.

AGNOSKOJ

Multaj amikoj kaj kolegoj helpis min kaj kuraĝigis min en ĉi tiu projektego. Mi estas aparte dankema, tamen, al R. Kent Jones pro la granda helpo kaj kuraĝigado kiun mi ricevis de li en la lastaj stadioj de la evoluigado de la verko. Li reviziis la manuskripton, proponis multajn helpajn sugestojn, kaj provizis multan instigon al la finpretigo kiam mi senkuraĝiĝis kaj mia entuziasmo paneis. Sen tiu daŭra rekuraĝigo kaj instigado lia, mi neniam estus fininta la projekton. Tial mi dediĉas ĉi tiun verkon al li.

Mi ankaŭ volas agnoski tre malavaran anoniman financan donacon, faritan al ELNA por faciligi la eldonon de ĉi tiu verko.

Sen tiu donaco, ĝia apero estus multe pli malfacila.

Mi ricevis tre valoran helpon ne nur je reviziado, sed ankaŭ pri Aŭstrali-Anglaj vortoj kaj esprimoj, de R. L. Harry, kunaŭtoro de la *Aŭstralia-Esperanta Vortaro*. Mia edzino, Diane Alberga, ne nur trasuferis la longajn horojn kiujn mi pasigis sidante antaŭ la komputoro anstataŭ tio, iel rilatadi kun ŝi; ŝi ankaŭ provizis tre valoran helpon deĉifrante la tre potencan sed (pro tio) ankaŭ tre komplikan softvaraĵon en kiu mi kompostis la manuskripton de ĉi tiu verko.

Mi estas elkore dankema al Judith Tarutz kaj David Wolff pro granda, tre utila, kaj tre helpa redakta laboro.

Mi ŝuldas elkoran dankon ankaŭ al pluraj aliaj homoj kiuj volontis revizii la manuskripton de la CEED por elsarki misklavojn kaj aliajn erarojn, por sugesti plibonigojn, kaj por atentigi min pri vortoj kaj esprimoj propraj al siaj diversaj Angla-lingvaj landoj.—*la aŭtoro.*

A

a, (indefinite article), [not expressed in Esperanto (e.g.: *a book:* libro); when necessary to express indefiniteness, "iu" can be used (e.g.: *that is not my book, but it is a book:* tio ne estas mia libro, sed ĝi estas iu libro; *like a wise Solomon:* kvazaŭ iu saĝa Salomono)]; (per), [see "per"]; **A–1**, unuaranga, unuagrada; **from A to Z**, komplete, ĝisfunde, ĝisoste, de komenco ĝis fino

a–, (pfx: in, into, at, to, not, un–, etc.), [sometimes absorbed into Esperanto root as "a–" (see separate entries); if not, translate w pfx per sense expressed (e.g.: *go ashore:* surbordiĝi, albordiĝi; *lie abed:* kuŝi enlite; *acaudal:* senvosta)]

Aachen, Aĥeno

aardvark, orikteropo

Aaron, Aaron; **Aaronic**, ~a

ab–, (gen pfx: from, away, etc.), [usually absorbed into Esperanto root; see separate entries]; (sci pfx), ab– (e.g.: *abampere:* abampero)

aback, (naut), malantaŭe(n); **take aback**, konsterni [tr]

abacus, (gen), abako

Abaddon, Abadono

abaft, (naut adv), ĉepobe; poben; (prep), malantaŭ

abalone, halioto*

abandon, (give up, leave), forlasi [tr]; (totally leave a movement or cause), kabei [int] (de); (unrestrictedness), senbrideco; [not "abandon–"]; **with abandon**, senbride

abase, humiligi

abash, (shame), hont/igi; (embarrass), embarasi [tr]; **unabashed**, sen~a

abasia, abazio; **abasic, abatic**, ~a

abate, (moderate), moder/igi; ~iĝi; (law: nullify), nuligi; (stop), ĉesi [int]; ĉesigi

abatis, abatiso

abattoir, buĉejo

abbacy, abat/eco; **abbatial**, (re monk, nun), ~(in)a; (re monastery), ~(in)eja

abbess, abatino

abbey, (monastery), abat(in)ejo; (monks, nuns), monaĥ(in)aro

abbott, abato

abbreviate, mallongigi; **abbreviation**, ~o

ABC's, (alphabet), aboco, alfabeto; (elements of anything), rudimentoj

Abdias, Obadja

abdicate, abdiki [tr]

abdomen, abdomeno [cp "belly"]; **abdominal**, ~a

abduct, (kidnap), forrabi [tr], forkapti [tr]; (anat), abdukcii [tr]; **abducent**, abdukcia; **abductor**, (muscle), abduktoro

abeam, (naut: across ship), laŭbaŭe(n); (amidship), ŝipmeze(n)

Abel, Habelo

Abélard, Abelardo

aberration, aberrance, (gen), aberacio; **have (show) an aberration**, ~i [int]; **aberrant**, ~a

abet, instigi [tr]

abeyance, suspend/iteco; **in abeyance**, ~ita; ~ite; **hold in abeyance**, ~i [tr]

abhor, abomeni [tr]; **abhorrence**, ~(ad)o; ~aĵo; **abhorrent**, (causing ~rence), ~iga; (feeling ~rence), ~a

abide, (remain), resti [int]; (tolerate), toleri [tr]; **abiding**, daŭra; **abide by**, (follow, as rule), sekvi [tr], observi [tr], respekti [tr], obei [tr]; (fulfill promise etc.), plenumi [tr]

Abidjan, Abiĝano*

ability, (being able), kapablo; (skill), lerteco, kompetenteco; **disability**, mal~o [cp "cripple", "handicap", "invalid"]

–ability, (sfx), –ebleco; –indeco; –endeco; –emo; –ivo; –eco [see "–able"]

ab initio, de la komenco, dekomence

abiogenesis, abiogenezo

abject, mizera; **abject misery**, profunda ~o

abjure, (give up, swear off), forĵuri [tr]; (legally recant), abĵuri [tr]

ablactation, demamigo

ablate, ablacii [tr]; **ablation**, ~o

ablative, (gram), ablativo; ~a; (that ablates), ablacia
ablaze, flamanta
able, (capable), kapabla; (competent), kompetenta; (skillful), lerta; **be able,** (can), povi [tr] (e.g.: *will you be able to do it?:* ĉu vi povos fari ĝin?); (to emphasize capability, not permission), ~i [tr]; (to emphasize permission), rajti [tr]; **able to be –ed,** –ebla [sfx] (e.g.: *able to be bought:* aĉetebla) [see also "–able"]; **disable,** senpovigi, mal~igi; **disabled,** mal~a
–able, (sfx: able to be –ed), –ebla (e.g.: *washable:* lav~a); (worthy to be –ed, that should be –ed), –inda (e.g.: *regrettable:* bedaŭrinda); (which is to be, must be –ed), –enda (e.g.: *payable:* pagenda); (inclined to be), –ema (e.g.: *agreeable:* konsentema); (capable of), –iva (e.g.: *viable:* viviva); (having qualities of), –a (e.g.: *comfortable:* komforta)
abloom, floranta
ablution, (washing), lav(ad)o
abnegate, abnegacii [tr]; **abnegation,** ~o
Abner, Abner
abnormal, (unnatural), nenormala; (nonstandard), nenorma
aboard, (on, in ship, train, etc.), sur, en (e.g.: *a store aboard the ship:* butiko ~ la ŝipo); **all aboard!,** (train etc.), ĉiuj en!; (ship), surŝipen!
abode, loĝejo
abolish, abolicii [tr]; **abolition,** ~o
abomasum, abomaso
abominate, abomeni [tr]; **abominable,** ~inda; **abomination,** ~(ad)o; ~ajo
aborigine, aborigeno; **aboriginal,** ~a, pra(temp)a
abort, aborti [int]; ~igi; **abortion,** ~(ig)o; **abortionist,** ~isto; **abortive,** ~inta; ~iga
abound, abundi [int]; **superabound,** ~egi [int], super~i [int]
about, (around, approximately), ĉirkaŭ (e.g.: *they played about the house:* ili ludis ~ la domo; *I saw about a hundred people:* mi vidis ~ cent homojn) [abb in sense of "approximately": ĉ.]; (regarding), pri (e.g.: *a movie about*

espionage: kino pri spionado; *talk about a problem:* paroli pri problemo [or] priparoli problemon); (adv: here and there, in circles), ~e(n) (e.g.: *look about:* rigardi ~en, ~rigardi; *frolic about:* kaprioli ~e, ~kaprioli); (in all directions), dis– [pfx] (e.g.: *run about* [as in panic]; diskuri); (almost), preskaŭ (e.g.: *just about ready:* preskaŭ preta); (near), proksime, apude (e.g.: *be somewhere about:* esti ie proksime [or] apude); **get about, move about,** (circulate), cirkuli [int]; cirkuligi; **about to,** –onta, baldaŭ –os (e.g.: *I am about to go home:* mi estas (baldaŭ) ironta hejmen [or] mi baldaŭ iros hejmen); **about-face,** ~turno; **be about,** (have to do w), temi pri (e.g.: *what's all that about?:* pri kio temas ĉio tio?); **what are you about?,** kion vi far(aĉ)as?
above, (over), super (e.g.: *soar above the mountains:* ŝvebi ~ la montoj); (higher; previous, in written material), supra; supre (e.g.: *the above paragraph:* la supra alineo); **above-mentioned,** supre menciita; (priority of rank), antaŭ; **above all,** antaŭ ĉio
abracadabra, (magic word), sorĉvorto; (gibberish), galimatio
abrade, (gen), abrazii [tr]; (skin), ekskorii [tr]
Abraham, Abraham
Abramis brama, bramo
abrasion, (gen), abrazio; (skin), ekskoriacio; **abrasive,** ~a; ~ilo
abreast, (side by side), flank-al-flanka; (up to date), ĝisdata; **keep abreast of,** resti ĝisdata pri
abridge, (shorten, gen), mallongigi; (lit), koncizigi, epitomigi; (curtail), limigi, malpliigi; **unabridged,** (e.g., dictionary), nekoncizigita
abroad, (foreign country), eksterlande(n); (broadly, far and wide), vaste(n); (in circulation), cirkulanta (e.g.: *there is a rumor abroad:* estas onidiro cirkulanta [or] onidiro cirkulas)
abrogate, abrogacii [tr]; **abrogation,** ~o
abrupt, abrupta, subita

Abruzzi, (mountains), Abruzoj
Absalom, Absalom
abscess, absceso
abscissa, absciso
abscission, (med), detranĉo; (bot), ~iĝo
abscond, forŝteliĝi
absent, (away, not present), for [adv]; ~estanta (e.g.: *those absent missed it:* la ~estantaj maltrafis ĝin); (lacking), mankanta; **absence**, ~esto; manko; **in the absence of**, je la manko de, mankante; **absentee**, ~estanto; [as adj], de ~estanto [not "~estanta"] (e.g.: *absentee ballot:* balotilo de ~estanto); **absenteeism**, ~estantado, ~estantismo; **absent-minded**, distriĝema, malatenta, vagpensa
absinth(e), (wood or drink), absinto; (essence), ~aĵo
absolute, absoluta; ~o; **absolutism**, ~ismo, despotismo; **absolutely necessary**, (essential), nepra
absolve, absolvi [tr]; **absolution**, ~o
absorb, (soak in and assimilate), sorbi [tr], en~i; (en)~iĝi; (one's thought or attention), absorbi [tr]; **absorbent**, ~a; ~enzo; **nonabsorbent**, ne(en)~a; **absorbing**, absorbiga; **absorption**, ~ado; ~iĝo; **self-absorption**, (psych), memabsorbo; **shock absorber**, sku~ilo, amortizilo
abstain, (refrain from, as vote), sin deteni; (not use, through principle, as alcohol), abstini [int]; **abstention**, sindeteno; **abstinence**, abstin(ad)o
abstemious, abstemia; **abstemiousness**, ~o
abstract, (not concrete), abstrakta; ~aĵo; ~i [tr]; (lit), resumi [tr]; resumo; **abstraction**, ~aĵo; ~eco; resumo
abstruse, malklare kompleksa, malfacile komprenebla, profunda
absurd, absurda; **absurdity**, ~aĵo; ~(ec)o
Abu Dhabi, Abudabo*
abulia, abulio
abundant, abunda; **abundance**, ~o; **overabundant**, tro~a; **overabundance**, troaĵo, tro~o; **superabundance**, ~ego, super~o
abuse, (misuse), misuzi [tr]; ~(ad)o; (mistreat), mistrakti [tr]; mis-

trakt(ad)o; (insult, revile), insulti [tr]; insult(ad)o; **disabuse**, maltrompi [tr], seniluziigi
abut, alfronti [tr], finiĝi ĉe, tuŝi [tr]; **abutment**, (support), abutmento
abutilon, Abutilon, abutilo
abutment, (support), abutmento
abvolt, abvolto
abyss, abismo; **abysmal**, ~a
Abyssinia, Abisenio; **Abyssinian**, ~o; ~a [see "Ethiopia"]
A.C. (abb of "alternating current"), A.K. [abb of "alterna kurento"]
acacia, (*Acacia*), akacio; **rose acacia, false acacia**, (*Robinia*), robinio
Acacia, akacio;   Acacia   catechu, kateĉuo; Acacia senegal, Senegalia ~o
academy, akademio; **academe, academia**, la ~a mondo; **academic**, (of an ~y; scholarly), ~a; (moot, irrelevant), nerilata; (of no practical value), nepraktika, teoria, kleraĉa; **academician**, ~ano
acajou, (mahogany), mahagono; (cashew), akaĵuo
Acanthis cannabina, kanabeno
Acanthopagrus, (Aus), akantopagro*
Acanthopterygii, akantopterigoj
acanthus, Acanthus, akanto
a capella, senakompana; ~e
Acapulco, Akapulko*
acarid, akarulo
Acarina, akaruloj
Acarus, akaro
Accad, [see "Akkad"]
accede, (take on duties), ekdeĵori [int]; (agree), konsenti [int]; (to throne), ekregi [int], surtroniĝi
accelerate, akceli [tr], plirapidigi; ~iĝi; **accelerator**, ~ilo
accelerometer, akcelometro
accent, (stress, emphasize; gram), akcenti [tr]; ~o; (manner of speaking, as foreign accent), akĉento†; **accent mark**, (any diacritical mark), kromsigno [see § 16]; **accentuate**, ~i, emfazi [tr]; **acute accent**, (´), akuto, akuta supersigno, dekstra korno; **grave accent**, (`), malakuto, obtuza supersigno, maldekstra korno [see also "diacritic"]; **tonic accent**, ton~o

accept, (receive willingly; approve), akcepti [tr]; (allow to be, come; admit), allasi [tr]; (take on), alpreni [tr]
access, (ability to reach), aliro (e.g.: *he learned through access to the president:* li sciiĝis per ~o al la prezidento); (way towards), ~ejo (e.g.: *the railroad provided access to the interior:* la fervojo provizis ~ejon al la landinterno); **accessible**, ~ebla, atingebla; **accession**, (taking on duties), ekdejoro; ekrego, surtroniĝo [see "accede"]; (agreement), konsento; **have access to**, (have available), disponi [int] pri
accessory, akcesora; ~aĵo; ~ulo, helpanto, kunfaranto; (criminal), komplico; **accessory before (after) the fact**, antaŭkomplico (postkomplico)
acciacatura, aĉakaturo*
accidence, (gram), fleksio [not "akcidenco"]
accident, (unforeseen misfortune), akcidento; (chance, randomness), hazardo [cp "random"]; (chance happening), hazardaĵo; (nonessential quality), akcidenco; **accidental**, ~a; hazarda; akcidenca; (mus: symbol), kromsigno; (note), kromsignita noto; **by accident**, (by chance), hazarde; (unluckily), malfeliĉe; (fortuitously), ŝance
accipiter, akcipitro
Accipiter, akcipitro; Accipiter nisus, nizo; Accipitridae, ~edoj
acclaim, aklami [tr]; ~o; **acclamation**, ~o
acclimate, acclimatize, alklimat/igi; ~iĝi; aklimatizi [tr]; aklimatiziĝi
acclivity, suprena deklivo
accolade, (conferring knighthood), kavalirigo; (great honor), honorego; (mus), kle-vinkulo
accommodate, (adjust), akomodi [tr]; ~iĝi; (acquiesce), cedi [tr, int] (al); (give lodging), gastigi, loĝigi; **accommodation**, loĝloko; loĝigo; komplezaĵo; **accommodating**, (helpful), komplez(em)a; **easily accommodated**, kompleziĝema
accompany, (gen), akompani [tr]; **accompaniment**, (mus), ~o; ~antaro; **accompanist**, ~isto

accomplice, komplico
accomplish, efektivigi, plenumi [tr]; (reach, as a goal), atingi [tr]; ment, **accomplishment**, atingo; plenumo; **accomplished**, (skilled), lerta
accord, (agreement, harmony of feeling), akordo; **be in accord**, ~i [int]; **bring into accord**, ~igi; **come into accord, reach an accord**, ~iĝi; **of one's own accord**, propravole; **according to**, (so says, by authority of), laŭ (e.g.: *he is right, according to this book:* li pravas, laŭ ĉi tiu libro); **in accordance with**, (in conformity), konforme al, laŭ (e.g.: *I came in accordance with orders:* mi venis konforme al ordonoj [or] laŭ ordonoj); **accordingly**, sekve, pro tio, laŭ tio, tial, do, laŭe; **according as**, laŭ tio ke, tiel kiel
accordion, akordiono
accost, ekparoli [int] (al), aliri al
accouchement, akuŝo
account, ($, lit or fig; adding up, reckoning), konto, kalkulo; (story, description), rakonto, raporto; **accountable**, (responsible), responsa, respondeca; **accountancy, accounting**, (bookkeeping), ~ado; **accountant**, ~isto; **account for, give an accounting for**, doni ~on pri, ekspliki [tr]; **bank account**, bank~o; **checking account**, ĉek~o; **savings account**, ŝpar~o; **enter in one's account**, debeti [tr], enskribi (sumon) en ies ~on; **close (open) an account**, (mal)fermi ~on; **settle one's account**, reguligi sian ~on; **settle accounts with**, (get revenge etc.), reguligi la ~ojn kun [cp "revenge"]; **demand an accounting, call to account**, postuli ~on; **of no account**, senvalora, nekonsiderinda; **on one's account**, (on behalf), por ies ~o; **on one's own account**, (for own benefit), por sia propra ~o; (responsible to self), je sia propra ~o; **on account of**, (because of), pro; **on no account**, nepre ne, tute ne; **take into account**, preni en konsideron, preni en la kalkulon; **turn to good account**, ĉerpi profiton el; utiligi; **accountholder**, ~ulo

accouter, (mil etc.: equip), ekipi [tr]; (provide accessory objects), garnituri [tr] (e.g.: *accouter the desk with a lamp, paper, and pens:* garnituri la skribtablon per lampo, papero, kaj plumoj); accouterments, ~aĵo [note sing]; garnituro
Accra, Akrao*
accredit, (authorize; give credentials), akrediti [tr]; (take as fact), akcepti [tr]; (attribute), atribui [tr]
accrete, alkreski [int]; ~igi; accretion, ~igo; ~aĵo
accrue, ($: earn as interest), lukri [tr], gajni [tr]; ~iĝi, gajniĝi; (be added, gen), aldoniĝi; accrual, ~ado, gajnado; aldoniĝo
acculturate, alkulturigi; acculturation, ~o
accumulate, akumuli [tr]; ~iĝi; amasigi; amasiĝi; accumulation, ~(iĝ)o; ~aĵo; amaso; accumulative, ~a; accumulator, (one who ~es), ~into; ~anto; ~onto; ~isto; (Br: storage battery), akumulatoro; (cmptr: memory circuit), ~ilo
accurate, (precise), preciza, ekzakta, fidela; (on time, as re clock), akurata; accuracy, ~eco; akurateco
accursed, malbenita, abomeninda; (rel: anathema), anatemita
accusative, (gram), akuzativo; ~a; accusative of direction, ~o de almovo; put into the accusative, ~igi
accuse, akuzi [tr], kulpigi; accusation, ~o, kulpigo
accustom, kutim/igi; be(come) accustomed (to), al~iĝi (al); accustomed, (usual), ~a; be accustomed to, ~i [int] (al)
ace, (playing card or oth "one"), aso; (first-rank, expert), unuaranga, lerta; unuarangulo, lertulo; ace in the hole, ace up one's sleeve, avantaĝo en rezervo
–aceae, (bot sfx), –acoj
acephalous, acefala; acephalous organism, ~o
Acer, acero; Acer pseudoplatanus, platan~o; Acer platanoides, platanaca ~o, Norvega ~o; Acer saccar(in)um, suker~o

acerb, acerba; acerbate, ~igi; acerbity, ~eco
Acerina cernua, perĉo
acetabulum, acetabulo
acetate, acetato
acetic, aceta; acetic acid, ~a acido
acet(o)–, (chem pfx), acet(o)–
acetone, acetono
acetyl, acetilo
acetylene, acetileno, etino
acetylsalicylate, acetilsalicilato; acetylsalicylic acid, ~a acido; (aspirin), aspirino
ach, (interj), aĥ!
Achaea, Achaia, Aĥajo
ache, doloro; ~i [int]; achy, ~eca; headache, kap~o; migraine headache, migreno; toothache, dent~o
achene, akeno
Acheron, Akerono
Acherontia, aĥerontio
achieve, (gen), atingi [tr]; achievement, ~o
Achillea, akileo; Achillea ptarmica, ptarmiko
Achilles, Aĥilo
acholia, akolio
Achorion schoenleinii, akorio
achromatic, akromata; achromatism, achromaticity, ~eco
achromatin, akromatino
achromatopsia, akromatopsio
acid, acido; ~a; acid-fast, acid-proof, ~imuna; acid-forming, ~ofara; acidify, ~igi; ~iĝi; acidimeter, ~ometro; acidity, ~eco; acidosis, ~ozo; acidulate, ~izi [tr], acerbigi; acidulous, ~eta, acerba; antacid, kontraŭ~o; kontraŭ~a [for names of specific ~s, see specific names]
Acinonyx, gepardo
acinus, acino
Acipenser, acipensero; Acipenser huso, huzo; Acipenser ruthenus, sterledo; Acipenser stellatus, sevrugo; Acipenser sturio, sturgo
ack-ack, kontraŭavi/a pafilo; ~a pafado
acknowledge, (gen), agnoski [tr]; acknowledgement, ~o
aclinic, senklina
acme, (gen; med), akmeo; (culmination), kulmino

acne, akneo; **acne rosacea**, rozacea ~o, kuperozo
Acnidaria, senkniduloj
acolyte, akolito
Aconcagua, Akonkagvo
aconite, (plant), akonito; (root), ~radiko; **winter aconite**, erantido
Aconitum, akonito; Aconitum napellus, napela ~o
Acontias, akontio
acorn, glano; **acorn barnacle, acornshell**, balano, mar~o
Acorus, akoro; Acorus calamus, kalamo
acoustic, akustika; **acoustics**, (la) ~o [note sing]
acquaint, (personally introduce), kon/atigi; (inform), informi [tr]; **acquaintance**, (person), ~ato; (knowledge), ~o; **acquaintanceship**, ~ateco; **be acquainted with**, (gen), ~i [tr]; **become acquainted with, make one's acquaintance**, ~atiĝi kun, ek~i [tr]
acquiesce, (senentuziasme) konsenti [int]; **acquiescence**, (senentuziasma) konsento
acquire, akiri [tr]; **acquisition**, ~(ad)o; ~aĵo; **acquisitive**, ~ema
acquit, (of guilt), absolvi [tr]; (of debt, duty), kvitigi; **acquitted**, ~ita; kvita; **acquittal, acquittance**, ~o; kvitigo; kvitiĝo
Acrania, senkraniuloj
acre, akreo [0,405 hektaro (see § 20)]; **acreage**, ~aĵo [when not necessary to refer to specific unit, "hektaraĵo" is better (e.g.: *a house with lots of acreage:* domo kun granda hektaraĵo)]
acrid, pikodora, akr(odor)a
Acrida, akrido; Acrididae, ~edoj
acridid, akridedo
acrimonious, amara, kaŭstika; **acrimony**, ~eco, kaŭstikeco
acrobat, akrobato; **acrobatics**, ~aĵoj
acrocephalia, akrocefal/eco; **acrocephalic**, ~a; ~ulo
Acrocephalus, akrocefalo
Acrochordus, akroĥordo
acrocyanosis, akrocianozo
acrogen, akrogen/ulo; **acrogenic, acrogenous**, ~a

acrolein, akroleino propenalo
acromegaly, akromegalio
acromion, akromio
acronym, akronimot, siglo
acrophobia, altecofobio
acropolis, akropolo
across, (prep: from one side to oth), trans [~on]; (upon oth side), trans [~o] (e.g.: *he threw the rock across the road:* li ĵetis la ŝtonon ~ la vojon [from one side to oth], ~ la vojo [he was on oth side and threw it somewhere]); (adv), ~e(n); **across from**, fronte al, vidalvide al, kontraŭ; **put across, get across**, (idea etc.), komuniki [tr]; **across-the-board**, ĉioninkluda
acrostic, akrostiko; ~a
acrylic, akrila; **acrylate**, ~ato; **acrylic acid**, ~a acido, propenacido; **acrylonitrile**, ~onitrilo
act, (do something), agi [int]; (action), ~o, faro; (behave), konduti [int]; (play a theat role), aktori [int]; (division of drama; item of entertainment; decree, law), akto (e.g.: *a play in 3 acts:* dramo en 3 aktoj; *a juggling act:* ĵongla akto; *an act of Congress:* akto de la Kongreso); (serve, function), servi [int], funkcii [int] (e.g.: *she acted as go-between:* ŝi servis kiel peranto); (have effect), efiki [int] (sur) (e.g.: *acid acts on metal:* acido efikas sur metalo); (seem), ŝajni [int] (e.g.: *he acted angry:* li ŝajnis kolera); **acting**, (substitute), anstataŭa; **action**, [see "action"]; **act out**, elaktori [tr]; **act up**, (misbehave), miskonduti [int], malbonkonduti [int]; (malfunction), misfunkcii [int]; (become painful), doloriĝi; inflamiĝi; (become active), (pli)aktiviĝi (e.g.: *the sunspots are acting up:* la sunmakuloj pliaktiviĝas); **counteract**, kontraŭ~i [tr]; **interact**, inter~i [int]; **interaction**, inter~o; interefiko **retroact**, retroefiki [int]
Actaea, akteo
Actaeon, Akteono
ACTH, [see "hormone"]
actinia, aktinio
Actinia, aktinio; Actiniaria, ~uloj

actinic, aktinia
actinide, aktinoido; ~a
Actinistia, celakantuloj†
actinium, aktinio
actinometer, aktinometro
Actinomyces,aktinomicetoj
actinomycete, aktinomiceto
actinomycosis, aktinomicetozo
actinon, aktinono*
Actinopterygii, aktinopterigoj
actinotherapy, aktinoterapio
action, (any deed), ago, faro; (activity),
~ado, funkciado; (activeness), aktive-
co; (effect), efiko; (lawsuit), proceso;
(mil), kombato; **actionable**, procesin-
da; **affirmative action**, (to counteract past discrimination), kompensa
~ado; **bring action**, procesi [int];
take action, ~i [int]; **take necessary
action**, ~i laŭnecese; **in action**, funkcianta; **actions speak louder than
words**, pli efikas ~oj ol blagoj
active, (gen), aktiva; (vigorous), vigla;
(diligent), diligenta, agema; **inactive**,
ne~a, dormanta; **activate**, ~igi; **deactivate**, mal~igi; **activism**, ~ismo; **ac-
tivist**, ~ulo; **activity**, ~eco, agado;
hyperactive, hiper~a; **radioactive**,
radio~a; **retroactive**, retro~a, retro-
efika; **self-activating**, aŭtogena
actor, aktoro; (bad, crude), histriono;
actress, ~ino
actual, efektiva [not "aktuala"]; **self-ac-
tualizing**, aŭtogena; **self-actualiza-
tion**, aŭtogenado, memevoluigado
actuary, aktuario; **actuarial**, ~a
actuate, (re person), agigi; (re machine,
thing), funkciigi
acuity, akreco
acumen, sagaco
acupuncture, akupunkturo
acute, (re angle; sound; accent; med),
akuta; (sharp, re sense perception),
akra; (critical), kriza
acyclic, necikla, senringa
ad, (advertisement), reklamo; (brief personal announcement), anonc(et)o
A.D. (abb of "anno Domini"), p.K. [abb
of "post Kristo" or "post Komunerao"]
adage, sentenco
adagio, adaĝo; ~e

Adam, Adamo; **Adam's apple**, (anat),
~pomo
adamant, adamantine, senceda [not
"adamantin–"]
Adansonia digitata, baobabo
adapt, adapti [tr]; ~iĝi; **adaptable**,
(able to adapt), ~iva; (able to be adap-
ted), ~ebla; **adapter**, ~ilo; **adapta-
tion**, ~(ad)o; ~iĝo; ~aĵo
add, (continue; cause any increase), aldoni [tr], almeti [tr] (e.g.: *add a name
to a list:* ~i nomon al listo; *he added
that he would come:* li ~is ke li
venos); (math), adicii [tr]; **addend**,
adiciato; **addendum**, ~aĵo; **addition**,
~(ad)o; ~aĵo; adicio; **additional**, ~a,
kroma; **additive**, (something added;
chem), ~aĵo; (math: that adds, is added), adicia; adiciebla **add up**, sumigi,
kalkuli [tr]; **add up to**, (total), sumi
[int] al; **adding machine**, kalkulatoro
[cp "calculate: calculator"]; **in addition**, ~e, krome, ankaŭ; **in addition
to**, ~e al, krom
adder, (zool: *Vipera*), vipuro
addict, mani/ulo; ~uligi; **addiction**,
~o; **addictive**, ~iga; **become addicted to**, ~iĝi al; **addicted to**, ~(iĝint)a
al
Addie, (woman's name), Adenjo [cp
"Adele"]
addle, (confuse), konfuzi [tr]; **addle-
brained, addlepated**, ~ita, ~akapa
address, (mail, residence; cmptr),
adreso; ~i [tr] [see § 22]; (speech),
prelego; prelegi [int] (al, antaŭ);
(speak to), alparoli [tr]; (take stance),
alfronti [tr]; (deal w), pritrakti [tr]; **return address**, resenda ~o, resend~o;
forwarding address, plusenda ~o;
self-addressed, mem~ita; **address
oneself to (a problem)**, atenti, pritrakti (problemon), koncerni sin pri
(problemo)
adduce, citi [tr]; **adduction**, ~(aĵ)o
adducent, adukcia
adduct, adukcii [tr]; **adduction**, ~o; **ad-
ductor**, (muscle), aduktoro
Adelaide, Adelajdo*
Adele, Adela
Adélie Coast (Land), Adelilando
Adeline, (woman's name), Adenjo,

Adelina [cp "Adele"]
Aden, Adeno
adenine, adenino
adenitis, adenito
adeno–, (med pfx), adeno–
adenocarcinoma, adenokarcinomo
adenoid, adenoida; **adenoids**, ~aĵoj
adenoma, adenomo
adenopathy, adenopatio
adenosine, adenozino
adept, lerta [not "adepta"]
adequate, adekvata; **adequacy**, ~eco
adhere, adheri [int], kunteniĝi
adherent, (follower), adepto, disĉiplo;
(adhesive), adhera
adhesion, (force), adhero; (object), ~aĵo
adhesive, adhera; (substance), gluo, adherenzo [not "~aĵo"]
ad hoc, porokaza
ad hominem, kontraŭpersona; ~e
adiabatic, adiabata
Adiantum, adianto
Adige, Adiĝo
ad infinitum, ĝis infinito, senlime
adipocere, adipociro
adipose, adipa
adipogenesis, adipogenezo
adiposis, adipozo
Adirondacks, **Adirondack Mountains**,
Adirondakoj*
adjacent, apuda
adjective, adjektivo
adjoin, apud/esti [int] (kun); tuŝi [tr];
(place next to), ~meti [tr]; **adjoining**,
~a
adjourn, (close meeting etc.), fermi [tr]
(la kunvenon); ~iĝi; (move), translokigi, movi [tr]; translokiĝi, moviĝi
adjudge, juĝi [tr], al~i [tr]
adjudicate, juĝi [tr], pri~i [tr] [not "adjudiki"]
adjunct, (thing added; extra), akcesora;
~aĵo; (person), asistanto; (gram), adjekto; (nonessential attribute), akcidenco
adjure, ĵurpeti [tr]
adjust, alĝust/igi, reguligi; ~iĝi, reguliĝi; (accommodate), akomodi [tr];
akomodiĝi; (economics etc.: to remove distorting factor), pondi† [tr]
(e.g.: *seasonally adjusted unemployment:* laŭsezone pondita indico de

senlaboreco); **adjustment**, ~igo, reguligo; (osteopathic manipulation etc.),
manipulo
adjutant, (assistant), adjutanto; (bird),
marabuo
ad-lib, improvizi [tr]; ~a; ~e
administer, (manage), administri [tr];
(give), doni [tr], provizi [tr]; (apply),
apliki [tr] (e.g.: *administer a poultice:*
apliki kataplasmon); **administration**,
(administering), ~(ad)o; (providing),
proviz(ad)o; (government department), administracio; (any governing
board), ~antaro, estraro, administracio; (city government), magistrato;
administrative, ~a; administracia;
administrator, administratoro, ~anto
admiral, admiralo; **admiralty**, (rank),
~eco; (admirals collectively; office;
building), admiraltato; **Admiralty Islands**, Admiraltoj; **rear admiral**,
sub~o; **vice-admiral**, sub~o, kontradmiralo
admire, admiri [tr]; **admirable**, ~inda,
laŭdinda; **admiration**, ~(ad)o; ~aĵo
admissible, allasebla, akceptebla
admit, (confess), konfesi [tr]; (let in),
enlasi [tr]; (allow), allasi [tr]; (hold,
contain), enteni [tr]; (accept), akcepti
[tr]; (grant, concede, acknowledge),
agnoski [tr], konsenti [tr, int]; **admission**, konfeso; enlaso; allaso; akcepto;
agnosko, konsento; **admittedly**, konsentite
admittance, (elec), admitanco
admix, almiksi [tr]; **admixture**, ~(ad)o;
~aĵo
admonish, (gen), admoni [tr]; **admonition**, ~o
ad nauseam, ĝisnaŭze
ado, bruo, ekscitiĝo; **without further
ado**, sen plu
adobe, adobo; ~a
adolescent, adoleska; ~anto; **adolescence**, ~anteco; ~aĝo; **be an adolescent**, ~i [int]
Adolph, Adolfo
Adonai, Adonaj
Adonis, (myth), Adoniso
Adonis, (bot), adonido; Adonis atumnalis, aŭtuna ~o; Adonis vernalis,
printempa ~o; Adonis aestivalis, som-

era ~o

adopt, (gen), adopti [tr]; **adoptee,** ~ito; **adoptive,** ~inta; ~ita; ~a (e.g.: *adoptive father:* ~inta patro; *adoptive son:* ~ita filo; *adoptive brother:* ~a frato)

adore, adori [tr]; **adorable,** ~inda, ĉarmega

adorn, ornami [tr]; **adornment,** ~ado; ~aĵo; **unadorned,** sen~a

adrenal, surrena; **adrenal (gland),** ~a glando

adrenalin, adrenalino

adren(o)–, (med, anat pfx), surren–, surrena

adrenocortical, kortikosurrena

adrenocorticotrop(h)ic, kortiko/tropa; **adrenocorticotropic hormone,** ~surrena hormono

Adrian, Adriano

Adriatic (Sea), Adriatiko; ~a

adrift, drivanta

adroit, lerta; **maladroit,** mal~a; mal~ulo

adsorb, adsorbi [tr]; ~iĝi; **adsorbent,** ~iva; ~ilo; **adsorption,** ~ado; ~iĝo; ~eco

adularia, adulario

adulate, flati [tr]

adult, plenaĝ/ulo, plenkreskulo, adolto; ~a, adolta; [not "adulto"]

adulterate, adulteri [tr]

adultery, adulto; **adulterer,** ~into; **adulterous,** ~eca; **commit adultery,** ~i [int]

adumbrate, antaŭombri [vt]

ad valorem, laŭvalora

advance, (move forward), antaŭ/eniri [int], ~eniĝi; (bring forward), ~enigi, ~enmovi [tr], ~enpuŝi [tr]; (raise rank), promocii [tr]; promociiĝi; (help), helpi [tr], akceli [tr]; (propose, as idea), proponi [tr], sugesti [tr]; (progress), progreso; progresi [int]; progresigi; (make earlier), plifruigi; plifruiĝi; malprokrasti [tr]; malprokrastiĝi; (mil), avanci [int]; ($: prepayment), ~pago; (adj: beforehand), ~a, antaŭ– [pfx] (e.g.: *advance order:* ~a mendo [or] ~mendo); **advanced,** (in front), ~a; (beyond beginner level), progresinta; (old), maljuna; **in advance,** ($), ~page; (gen), ~e, antaŭ–,

anticipe; **advance person, advance agent,** ~ulo, ~isto

advantage, avantaĝo; **advantageous,** favora; **disadvantage,** mal~o; mal~i [tr]; **disadvantageous,** mal~a; **disadvantaged,** malprivilegia, subprivilegia; **take advantage of,** (use, gen, as opportunity), elprofiti [tr], ekspluati [tr]; (treat badly), fiprofiti [tr], fiekspluati [tr]; **mechanical advantage,** (tech), meĥanika gajno

advection, advekcio

advent, (arrival), alveno

Advent, (rel: pre-Christmas), Advento; **Adventism,** ~ismo; **Adventist,** ~isma; ~isto

adventitia, adventico

adventitious, adventiva

adventure, aventuro; **adventurer,** ~ulo; **adventuresome,** (re person), ~ema; (risky), risk(oplen)a, danĝer(plen)a; **misadventure,** malfeliĉo, akcidento

adverb, adverbo

adversary, adversulo†, kontraŭulo, malamiko; ~a, kontraŭa

adverse, (unfavorable), adversa†, kontraŭa, malfavora; (in opp direction), maladirekta; kontraŭa; **adversity,** malfeliĉo, malfavoreco

advertise, advertize, reklami [tr]; **advertisement,** ~(ad)o

advice, konsilo

advise, (give counsel), konsili [tr]; (inform), informi [tr], avizi [tr]; **adviser, advisor,** (gen), ~anto; ~isto; (to a judge), asesoro; **advisory,** ~a; (consultative, not binding), konsultiĝa; **advisory board (committee, etc.),** ~antaro; ~istaro; **advisedly,** intence; **advisable, well-advised,** ~inda, prudenta; **ill-advised,** ne~inda, malprudenta; **one would be well-advised to,** estus ~inde ke oni –u; **take under advisement,** preni por konsidero

advocate, (propose, favor), proponi [tr], rekomendi [tr], subteni [tr]; (lawyer), advokato; **advocacy,** ~(ad)o, rekomend(ad)o, subten(ad)o

adz(e), adzo

Aeacus, Eako

aeci(di)um, ecidio

Aedes aegipti, (zool), stegomijo
aedile, edilo
Aegean, Egea
aegis, egido
Aegisthus, Egisto
Aegopodium, egopodio
–aemia, [see "–emia"]
Aemilianus, Emiliano; **Aemiliana**, ~a
Aemilius, Emilio; **Aemilia**, ~a
Aeneas, Eneo; **Aeneid**, ~ado
aeolian, eola; **aeolian harp**, ~harpo
Aeolis, **Aeolia**, Eol/io; **Aeolian**, ~ia; ~iano
aeon, eono
Aepyornis, epiornito; Aepyornithiformes, ~oformaj (birdoj)
aerate, (ventilate), aerumi [tr], ventoli [tr]; (charge liquid w gas), gasizi [tr]
aeremia, aeremio
aerial, (antenna), anteno; (airy, in air), aera; **aerialist**, altakrobato
aerie, (of eagle), (aglo)nesto
aerobatic, aerobatika; **aerobatics**, ~o
aerobic, aerobia; **anaerobic**, anaerobia; **aerobics**, (exercise), ~aj ekzercoj, ~ajoj
aerodrome, aerodromo
aerodyne, aerodino
aerogram(me), aerogramo
aerolite, aerolito
aerology, aerologio; **aerologist**, aerologo
aerometer, aerometro
aeronautics, aeronaŭtiko; **aeronautical**, ~a
aerophagia, aerofagio
aerophore, aeroforo
aeroplane, [see "airplane"]
aerosol, aerosolo
aerospace, aerokosmo; ~a
aerostat, aerostato
aerostatic, aerostatika; **aerostatics**, ~o
Aeschylus, Esĥilo
Aesculapius, Eskulapo
Aesculus hippocastanum, hipokaŝtano, ĉevalkaŝtano
Aesop, Ezopo
aesthesia, estezo
aesthetic(s), [see "esthetic"]
aestivate, [see "estivate"]
aether, (gen), etero
aethrioscope, etrioskopo

Aethusa, etuzo
aetiology, [see "etiology"]
Aetna, Etno
afar, malproksime(n), for(en)
affable, afabla
affair, (gen), afero; (love affair), am~o; **put one's affairs in order**, ordi siajn ~ojn
affect, (have effect on), influi [tr], efiki [int] sur, tuŝi [tr], rilati [int] al; (stir feelings), afekcii [tr], emocii [tr]; (emotional response), emociiĝo; (pretend), afekti [tr]; **affectation**, afekto; **affective**, afekcia; **disaffect**, malkontentigi; **disaffected**, malkontenta; **become disaffected**, malkontentiĝi
affection, (tendency), tendenco; (warm feeling), kareco, amo; **affectionate**, tenera, am(em)a
affidavit, (gen), ĵurdeklaro; ($: on bill coupon), afidavito; **affiant**, ~into; ~onto; ~onto
affiliate, filio; ~igi; ~iĝi; **affiliation**, ~eco, ~aneco; ~igo; ~iĝo; (membership, gen), aneco
affine, afina
affinity, (chem or oth tendency toward), afineco; (similarity), simileco; (relationship by marriage), boparenceco
affirm, (assert), aserti [tr]; (swear), ĵuri [tr]; (confirm), konfirmi [tr]; (reply "yes", gen), jesi [int]; **affirmative**, (yes), jes; jesa; (positive), pozitiva, definitiva; **by affirmation**, (vote), unuanima; unuanime
affix, (fasten), alfiksi [tr]; (gram), afikso
afflict, aflikti [tr]; **affliction**, ~(iĝ)o
affluent, riĉa; **affluence**, ~eco
afford, ($), elporti la koston de, elporti la elspezon, havi per kio aĉeti [vt] (e.g.: *she cannot afford a car:* ŝi ne povas elporti la koston de aŭto [or] ŝi ne havas per kio aĉeti aŭton); (re time), havi sufiĉan tempon por; (allow self to), permesi al si; (give), doni [tr]; **affordable**, kostelportebla
affricate, afrikato; **affricative**, ~a; ~o
affright, timigi
affront, (insult), insulti [tr], ofendi [vt]; ~o, ofendo; (defy), defii [tr]; defio
afghan, (shawl), Afgana ŝalo
Afghan, (person), Afgano; ~a; (hound),

~a hundo; **Afghanistan,** ~lando
afghani, ($), afganio*
aficionado, adepto
afield, malproksime(n); **far afield,** tre
~e(n)
afire, (lit), brulanta; (fig), arda
aflame, (lit), flamanta; (fig), arda
afloat, flosanta
aflutter, ekscitita; ~e
afoot, (on foot), piede; (in progress),
preparata, leviĝanta, ekmoviĝa
afoul, implik/ita, ~iĝinta; **run (fall)
afoul of,** ~iĝi en
afraid, tim/(ant)a; **be afraid (of),** ~i [tr]
afreet, efrito
afresh, denove, dekomence
Africa, Afriko; **African,** ~a; ~ano;
North Africa, Nord-~o; **South Africa,** (country), Sud-~o; **southern Africa,** (region), suda ~o; **South West
Africa,** Sudokcidenta ~o [cp "Namibia"]
Afrikaans, Afrikanso; ~a; ~e
Afrikaner, Buro
afrit(e), efrito
afro, (hair), Afrikaĵo
Afro–, (pfx: African), Afrik– (e.g.:
Afro-Asian: ~-Azia)
aft, malantaŭe(n); (naut), pobe(n)
after, (prep: behind, later), post (e.g.: *I
came after her:* mi venis ~ ŝi); (manner of), laŭ (e.g.: *a novel patterned after Heinlein:* romano modeligita laŭ
Heinlein); (conj), ~ kiam (e.g.: *I came
after she left:* mi venis ~ kiam ŝi foriris); **aftermath,** (consequence), kon-
sekvenco(j), sekvo(j), postefiko(j);
(crop), ~rikolto; **afternoon,** ~tagme-
zo; ~tagmeza; **in the afternoon,**
~tagmeze; **afterward(s),** ~e; **be (go)
after,** (search), serĉi [tr] (e.g.: *what
are you after?:* kion vi serĉas?); **name
(someone) after,** nomi (iun) ~; **after
all,** ~ ĉio, malgraŭ ĉio
aga, agao
again, (another time), denove, ree;
(amount in addition), aldone (e.g.:
half again as much: aldone duone tiom)
against, kontraŭ; **go against,** ~i [tr],
~iĝi al; **dead (set) against,** senmove
~, senŝancele ~

Agama, agamo; Agamidae, ~edoj
Agamemnon, Agamemnono
agamic, agamous, agamia
Agana, Agano*
Agapanthus, agapanto
agape, (gaping), gapanta; ~e; (rel:
Christian feast; love), agapo
agar-agar, agaragaro
agaric, agariko
Agaricales, himenomicetoj
Agaricus, agariko, lamenfungo [cp
"Psalliota"]; Agaricaceae, ~acoj
agarita, mahonio
agate, (gem), agato
Agatha, Agata
Agathis, damaro; Agathis australis,
kaŭrio
agave, Agave, agavo
age, (time in existence; stage of life),
aĝo; (old age; get old), maljun~o,
maljuneco; **maljunigi;** maljuniĝi; (not
new), malnoveco; malnovigi; malnov-
iĝi; (epoch), epoko, temp~o (e.g.: *the
computer age:* la komputora epoko)
[re geol ages, see "epoch"]; (become
older), pli~i [int] (e.g.: *he aged ten
years while waiting for their return:* li
pli~is dek jarojn dum li atendis ilian
revenon); (make older), pli~igi (e.g.:
*the experience seemed to age her ten
years:* la sperto ŝajnis pli~igi ŝin dek
jarojn; *whiskey aged in the bottle:*
viskio pli~igita en la botelo); **aged,**
maljuna; pli~igita; **ageless,** sen~a,
eterna; **middle-aged,** mez~a; **Middle Aages,** Mezepoko; **of age,** (mature), plen~a; (legal majority),
majoritat(~)a
agency, (position of agent), agent/eco;
(place; office), ~ejo; (distant office of
bsns firm), faktorio; (force), forto;
(means), rimedo
agenda, tagordo [not "agendo"]
agent, (official, gen), agento; (distant
official of bsns firm), faktoro; (any
go-between), peranto; (chem), enzo,
agento†; (mech), efikilo; **agent pro-
vocateur,** kaŝprovokisto
ageratum, Ageratum, agerato
agglomerate, aglomeri [tr]; ~iĝi; ~aĵo
agglutinate, aglutini [tr]; ~iĝi; ~iĝinta
aggrandize, pligrandigi; **self-aggran-**

dizement, mem~o
aggravate, (make worse), plimalbonigi; (annoy), ĉagreni [tr]
aggregate, agregi [tr]; ~ita; ~aĵo, agregato
aggress, agresi [tr]; **aggression**, ~o; ~emo; **aggressive**, ~(em)a; **aggressor**, ~into; ~anto; ~onto
aggrieve, ofendi [tr], aflikti [vt]
agha, agao
aghast, konstern(eg)ita, ŝokita
agile, lertmova, facilmova
agio, aĝio
agiotage, aĝiotado
agitate, (gen), agiti [tr]
Agkistrodon contortrix, agistrodono*
Aglaia, Aglaja
aglitter, scintilanta
agnate, agnato
Agnathi, senmakzeluloj
Agnes, Agnesa
Agni, Agnio
agnosia, agnozio
agnostic, agnostika; ~ulo; **agnosticism**, ~ismo
ago, antaŭ [goes before time expression (e.g.: *two days ago:* ~ du tagoj)]; **long ago**, ~ longe; **not long ago**, ~ nelonge
agog, ekscitite atenda, streĉe atenda; **be agog**, ekscitite atendi [tr] (etc.)
agony, dolorego [not "agonio"]; **agonize**, (hurt), ~i [tr]; ~iĝi [see "hurt"]; (struggle), klopodegi [int]; (torture), torturi [tr]
agora, (gen), agoro
agoraphobia, agorafobio
agouti, agutio
agraf(f)e, agrafo
agraphia, agrafio
agrarian, agrara, kampara
agree, (consent), konsenti [tr, int]; (gram; in gen accord), akordi [int]; (in concord, complete harmony), konkordi [int]; (be same re 2 facts, pieces of evidence, etc.), kongrui [int]; **agreeable**, (easily ~ing), ~ema, komplezema, afabla; (pleasant), plaĉa, agrabla; **agreement**, ~o; akordo; konkordo; kongruo; **disagree**, (differ in opinion), mal~i [tr, int]; (be different), diferenci [int], malsami [int], malkongrui [int]; (cause distress, harm), mal-

konveni [int] (e.g.: *spicy foods disagree with me:* spicaj manĝaĵoj malkonvenas ĉe mi); **disagreeable**, (gen), malagrabla; (re person), malafabla; **mutual agreement**, inter~o
Agricola, Agrikolo
agriculture, agrikulturo; **agricultural**, ~a
Agrigento, **Agrigentum**, Agrigento
Agrimonia, agrimonio
agrimony, agrimonio; **hemp agrimony**, eŭpatorio
Agrippa, Agripo; **Agrippina**, ~ina
agro–, (pfx: field, soil), agro–
agronomy, agronom/io; **agronomist**, ~o
Agropyron, Agropyrum, agropiro; Agropyrum repens, kviko
Agrostemma, agrostemo
Agrostis, agrostido
aground, (naut), grund/inta; **run aground**, ~i [int]; ~igi
ague, (fever), tremfebro
agueweed, eŭpatorio
ah, (gen), ha!; (woe, alas), aĥ!; ve!
aha, aha!, ehe!
Ahab, Aĥab
Ahasuerus, Aĥaŝveroŝ
ahead, antaŭe(n); **ahead of**, antaŭ
ahoy, hoj!, ho hoj!
Ahura-Mazda, Ahura-Mazdo, Mazdao [cp "Ormazd"]
aid, (help), helpi [tr]; ~o; (device), ~ilo; **with the aid of**, ~e de; **first aid**, (initial med help), sukur(ad)o; **give first aid (to)**, sukuri [tr]; **first aid station**, sukurejo
aide, **aide-de-camp**, (gen), adjutanto, subulo; (mil), ~o, servosoldato
AIDS, (acronym of "acquired immune deficiency syndrome"), aideso†
aigret(te), (plume), egreto; (bird), ~birdo
ail, (be ill), malsani [int]; **ailing**, ~a; **ailment**, ~o; **what ails you?**, pro kio vi ~as (suferas)?
ailanthus, Ailanthus, ailanto
aileron, alerono
Ailuropoda melanoleucus, granda pando
Ailurus fulgens, malgranda pando
aim, (goal; act of ~ing), celo; (weapon,

camera, etc.), ~umi [tr]; (ability to ~), ~ivo; **aim at,** ~i [tr]; **aimless,** sen~a
Ainu, Ajnuo; ~a
air, (gas, atmosphere), aero; (expose to ~), ~umi [tr]; (mus), ario; (personal expression), mieno, afekto; (impression in room etc.), impreso; **airboat,** ~boato; **airborne,** ~portata; **airbrush,** ~broso; ~brosi [tr]; **air condition,** klimatizi [tr]; **air conditioner,** klimatizatoro; **aircraft,** aviadilo(j); **antiaircraft,** kontraŭaviadila; **airdrome,** aerodromo; **airdrop,** paraŝutigi; paraŝutigo; **airfield,** flugokampo; **airfoil,** planeo; **airlift,** ~porti [tr]; ~port(ad)o; **airline,** ~linio; **airliner,** pasaĝeraviadilo; **airlock,** ~kluzo; **airman,** ~soldato; **airplane,** avio; **airport,** flughaveno; **airscrew,** (Br), helico; **airship,** ~ŝipo; **airsick,** veturmalsana; **airspace,** ~spaco; **airspeed,** ~rapido; **airstream,** ~fluo; **airstrip,** surteriĝejo; **airtight,** hermet(ik)a; **airwaves,** radiondoj; **midair,** supertera; **in midair,** supertere; **put on airs,** afekti [tr, int]; **on the air,** (broadcasting), dissendanta; dissendata; **be on the air,** dissendi [tr]; **up in the air,** (undecided), nedecidita; **air-to-air,** (mil), ~-al-~a; **air-to-ground,** (mil), ~-al-tera; **surface-to-air,** (mil), ter-al-~a
Aira, airo
aisle, (pass-through), trairejo, koridoro; (side of church), flanknavo
Aix, Aix-en-Provence, Aikso
Aix-la-Chapelle, Añeno
ajar, (open), duonaperta; (inharmonious), malharmonia
Ajax, Ajakso
Ajuga, ajugo
a.k.a. (abb of "also known as"), ankaŭ konata kiel, alinome, kaŝnome [no abb in Esperanto]
akebi, akebio
Akebia, akebio
akimbo, arkigita; ~e
akin, parenca
akinesia, akinezio
Akkad, Akado; ~ano; **Akkadian,** ~a
~al, (chem sfx), –alo
ala, alo

à la, (with), kun (e.g.: *pie à la mode:* torto kun glaciaĵo); (in the manner of), laŭ (stilo) (e.g.: *he was dressed à la New York:* li estis vestita laŭ Nov-Jorko [or] laŭ la Nov-Jorka stilo) [see also separate entries below]
Alabama, Alabamo
alabaster, alabastro; ~a
à la carte, apartapreza, laŭ la menuo; ~e
alack, ho ve!
alacrity, entuziasmo, ĝoja volonteco
Alamanni, [see "Alemanni"]
à la mode, kun glaciaĵo
alar, (wing-like), flugil/eca; (winged), ~hava [cp "ala"]
Alaric, Alariko
alarm, (call to arms; warn; etc.), alarmi [tr]; ~a; ~o; (device, as burglar ~), ~ilo; (signal, as on clock or watch), (vek)signalo; **alarming,** ~a, timiga; **alarmist,** ~emulo; **alarm clock,** vekhorloĝo; **alarm watch,** signalhorloĝo
alas, ve!, ho ve!
Alaska, Alasko; **Alaskan,** ~a; ~ano
alate, flugilhava
Alauda, alaŭdo; Alauda arvensis, kamp~o; Alaudidae, ~edoj
alb, albo
Alba Longa, Albo
Albania, Alban/io; **Albanian,** ~o; ~a
Albany, Albeno*
albatross, albatroso, diomedeo
albedo, albedo
albeit, kvankam
Albert, Alberto
Alberta, (woman's name), Alberta; (province), ~io
Albigensian, Albigenso; ~a; **Albigenses,** ~oj, ~aro
albino, albino; ~a; **albinism,** ~eco
Albion, Albiono
albite, albito
albuginea, albugineo
albugo, (med), albugo
album, albumo
albumen, albumeno
albumin, albumino; **albuminuria,** albuminurio
albumose, albumozo
Alburnus, alburno, blankfiŝo
Alca, aŭko

Alcaeus, Alceo
Alcaic, Alkaja
alcalde, alkado
alcazar, alkazaro
Alcedo, alcedo, alciono; Alcedinidae, ~edoj
Alces, alko
Alcestis, Alcestisa
Alchemilla, alkemilo
alchemy, alĥemio; **alchemist,** ~isto
Alcibiades, Alcibiado
Alcidae, aŭkedoj
Alcmene, Alkmena
alcohol, alkoholo; **alcoholate,** ~ato; **alcoholic,** ~a; ~ulo; **alcoholism,** ~ismo; **alcoholic drink,** ~aĵo; **blood alcohol, alcoholemia,** ~emio
alcove, alkovo
Alcyonaria, alcioniuloj
Alcyone, alcedo, alciono
Alcyonium, alcionio
Aldebaran, Aldebarano
aldehyde, aldehido
alder, alno
alderman, magistratano
Alderney, Aldernejo
aldose, aldozo
ale, elo
aleatory, aleatora, ŝanca
Alec, Aleĉjo
alecost, balzamito
alee, lee(n)
Aleksei, Aleksio
Alemanni, Alemanoj; **Alemannic,** ~a
alembic, alambiko
Alençon, (town), Alensono; (lace), ~a punto
alert, (vigorous), vigla, maldormema; (to danger), averti [tr], alarmi [tr]; (attentive), atenta; (call attention, gen), atentigi
–ales, (bot sfx), –aloj
Aleurites, aleŭrito
Aleut, Aleut/ano [not "Aleŭt–"]; **Aleutian,** ~a; **Aleutian Islands,** ~oj
Alexander, Aleksandro
Alexandra, Aleksandra
Alexandria, Aleksandrio
alexin, aleksino
Alexis, Aleksio
alfalfa, luzerno
Alfilaria, Alfileria, Alfilerilla, erodio

Alfred, Alfredo
alfresco, subĉiela; ~e
alga, algo; **algae,** ~oj; **brown alga,** fuko, brun~o; **red alga,** ruĝ~o; **bluegreen alga,** blu~o
algarroba, karobarbo
algebra, algebro; **algebraic,** ~a
Algeria, Alĝerio; **Algerian,** ~a; ~ano
–algia, (med sfx), –algio
algid, algida
Algiers, Alĝero
Algol, Algolo
algology, algolog/io; **algologist,** ~o
Algonkian, (geol), algonkio; ~a
Algonqui/n, Algonquian, (re Native American tribe; language; etc.), Algonkena*; ~o
algorithm, algoritmo*
Alhambra, Alhambro
Ali, Alio
alias, kaŝnomo; ~e
alibi, alibio
Alice, Alica
alidade, alidado
alien, (foreign), fremda; ~ulo; (extraterrestrial), ekstertera; eksterterulo; **alienate,** (transfer ownership), alieni† [tr]; (psych), ~igi; mallogi [tr]; **alienation,** ~igo; (psych), alieneco; **alienist,** (psych), alienisto; **inalienable,** neforprenebla, neforigebla
alight, (from vehicle), elaŭtiĝi; elbusiĝi; elvagoniĝi; elaviadiliĝi (etc.); (from saddle), elseliĝi; (settle to ground), descendi [int], surteriĝi; (lit up), lumigata; (burning), brulanta, flamanta
align, (line up), liniigi, al~i, kun~i; (put in one row), vicigi; (pol), alianci [tr]; alianciĝi
alike, simila
aliment, (food), nutr/aĵo; (means of support), alimento; **alimentary canal,** ~okanalo
alimony, alimento
aliphatic, alifata, senringa
aliquant, alikvanto
aliquot, alikvoto
Alisma, alismo; Alisma plantago-aquatica, plantag~o, akvoplantago; Alismaceae, ~acoj
alison, aliso
alive, viva, ~anta; **be alive,** ~i [int]; **be**

alive with, svarmi je
alizarin, alizarino
alkali, alkalo; **alkaline**, ~a; **alkalinity**, ~eco; **antalkali**, kontraŭ~o; kontraŭ~a; **alkali metal**, alkalio; **alkaline-earth metal**, ter-alkalio
alkaloid, alkaloido
alkalosis, alkalozo
alkanet, (*Anchusa*), ankuzo
all, (entirely), tute; (entirety), ~o (e.g.: *it is all gone:* ĝi estas ~e for; *he gave his all:* li donis sian ~on); (everything), ĉio; (none lacking), ĉiuj (e.g.: *we all came:* ni ĉiuj venis); (every, each), ĉiu (e.g.: *beyond all doubt:* preter ĉiu dubo); (apiece, in scores), po (e.g.: *the score is 30 all:* la poentaro estas po 30); (as pfx: everything), ĉio– (e.g.: *all-powerful:* ĉiopova; *all-seeing:* ĉiovida); (as pfx: every sort), ĉia– (e.g.: *all-weather:* ĉiavetera); (as pfx: for every), ĉiu– (e.g.: *all-purpose:* ĉiumotiva); **all of**, (re number of items), ĉiuj el (e.g.: *I found all of them:* mi trovis ĉiujn el ili); (re liquids, %age of whole, etc.), ĉiom el, da (e.g.: *all of it:* ĉiom el ĝi; *all of our water:* ĉiom da nia akvo); **all (of) that**, (as pron), ĉio tio (e.g.: *we did all of that:* ni faris ĉion tion); **all (of) this**, ĉio ĉi; **all (of) these**, ĉiuj ĉi; **all of those**, ĉiuj tiuj; **all of us (them, etc.)**, ni (ili, etc.) ĉiuj, ĉiuj el ni (etc.); **all along**, dum la ~a tempo; **all-around, all-round**, multkapabla, multtalenta; **all at once**, subite; **all but**, (all except), ĉiuj krom; ĉiom krom; ĉio krom; (almost), preskaŭ; **all in**, (tired out), ellaciĝinta; **all in all**, (all things considered), ĉion konsiderinte; (as a whole, generally), en~e; **all manner of**, ĉia(j); **all over**, (finished), ~e finita; (everywhere), ĉie, ~e ĉie; **be all over**, (finished), esti (~e) finita; **all right**, (okay), en ordo; **all the more (less)**, des (mal)pli (e.g.: *I liked him all the more because of that:* mi ŝatis lin des pli pro tio); **all the same**, (nevertheless), malgraŭ tio, tamen; **at all**, (to any extent), ajn (e.g.: *anything at all:* io ajn); **not at all**, tute ne (neniom, etc.) (e.g.: *that doesn't bother me at all:* tio ~e ne ĝenas min;

we didn't find any at all: ni trovis ~e neniom); **in all**, (inclusive), en~e; **the be-all and end-all**, la nepra esenco; **first of all**, antaŭ ĉio
Allah, Alaho
allay, malakrigi, mildigi
allege, aserti [tr]; **allegation**, ~o; **alleged**, (unproved), laŭdira, ~ita
Alleghenies, Allegheny Mountains, Aleganoj
allegiance, lojaleco, fideleco
allegory, alegorio; **allegorical**, ~a
allegro, (mus: lively), alegre; (mus work or movement), ~o; **allegretto**, ~ete; ~eto
alleluia, (interj), haleluja
allergy, alergio; **allergen**, ~genaĵo; **allergic**, ~a; **allergist**, ~isto
alleviate, mildigi, moderigi
alley, (street), strateto; (narrow space; e.g., tennis), koridoro; **bowling alley**, kuglejo
allheal, (bot: *Prunella*), brunelo; (Br: *Valeriana*), valeriano
alliance, alianco; **misalliance**, mezalianco
Alliaria, aliario
allied, [see "ally"]
alligator, Alligator, aligatoro
alliteration, aliteracio; **alliterative**, ~a
Allium, ajlo; Allium ampeloprasum, Allium holmense, ampeloprazo; Allium ascalonicum, askalono, ŝaloto; Allium cepa, cepo; Allium porrum, poreo; Allium schoenoprasum, ŝenoprazo
allocate, (assign), asigni [tr]; (specify), specifi [tr]; (distribute), distribui [tr], disdoni [vt]
allopath, alopato; **allopathy**, ~io
allophone, alofono
allorhythmia, aloritmio
allot, asigni [tr]; **allotment**, ~o; ~aĵo
allotrophy, allotrophism, alotrop/io; **allotrophic**, ~a
allow, (permit), permesi [tr] [cp "let"]; (enable), ebligi; (admit, accept, leave room for), allasi [tr]; **allowance**, ~o; ebligo; allaso; ($), monasignaĵo, alimento; **disallow**, mal~i [tr]; malakcepti [tr], rifuzi [tr]; **disallowance**,

mal~o; malakcepto, rifuzo; **make allowances for**, preni en konsideron, allasi por, kalkuli kun
alloy, (gen), alojo; ~i [tr]; (including mercury), amalgamo
allspice, (spice or tree), pimento
allude, allude to, aludi [tr] [not "aludi al"] (e.g.: *she alluded to that fact:* ŝi ~is tiun fakton)
allure, (attract), allogi [tr]; ~o; (charm), ĉarmo; **alluring**, ~a; ĉarma
allusion, aludo
alluvium, aluvio; **alluvial**, ~a
ally, (pol), alianci [tr]; ~iĝi; ~ano; (relate, gen), rilatigi; **allied**, ~ita; rilata; (similar), simila
allyl, alilo; ~a
alma, almeo
almagest, almagesto
almah, almeo
alma mater, ĉeestita universitato (kolegio, lernejo, etc.); hejma universitato (etc.)
almanac, almanako
alme(h), almeo
almighty, ĉiopova
almond, (nut), migdalo; (tree), ~arbo; **earth almond, ground almond**, ter~o
almost, preskaŭ
alms, almozo [note sing] [cp "charity"]
alnico, alniko*; ~a
Alnus, alno
Alocasia, alokazio
alodium, alodo
aloe, aloo; **aloe(s)**, (laxative resin), ~aĵo
Aloë, aloo
aloft, alte(n), supre(n), en la aero(n)
alone, sola; ~e; **let alone**, (not to mention), sen mencii [tr]; **leave well enough alone**, ne inciti abelujon; **"alone together"**, (man and woman ~), ge~aĵ; ge~e
along, (following length of, conforming to), laŭ, ~longe (de) (e.g.: *she bicycled along the road:* ŝi biciklis ~ la vojo; *I walked along the river:* mi marŝis ~ [or: ~longe de] la rivero; *he spoke along the lines of her report:* li prelegis ~ ŝia raporto); (onward), plu, ~adi (e.g.: *we sang as we walked along:* ni kantis dum ni plu marŝis [or]

ni marŝadis); (with), kune, kun– (e.g.: *she took her camera along:* ŝi kunportis sian fotilon); (advanced), progresinta (e.g.: *the work is well along:* la laboro estas bone progresinta); **all along**, (the whole time), la tutan tempon; **alongside**, ~longe (de), apud, apude (de), flanke (de); **get along**, (be compatible), akordiĝi, harmoniiĝi; **along with**, kune kun
aloof, distanc(em)a, apart(em)a, malintimema
alopecia, alopecio, kalveco
Alopecurus, alopekuro
Alopex lagopus, monta vulpo; (in bluefur stage), izatiso
Alosa, alozo
Alouatta, aluato
aloud, laŭte; **read aloud**, ~legi [tr], voĉlegi [tr]
alp, alpo; **the Alps**, la Alpoj; **alpenglow**, alpardo; **alp(en)horn**, ~a korno; **alpenstock**, montbastono; **alpine**, ~a; **cisalpine**, cis~a; **transalpine**, trans~a
alpaca, alpako
alpha, alfa [see § 16]; **the alpha and omega**, la komenco kaj fino
alphabet, alfabeto [cp "ABC's"] [see § 16]; **alphabetical**, (using ~), ~a; (order), abocorda; **alphabetize**, ~igi, abocordi [tr]; **analphabetic**, analfabeto; analfabeta; **Arabic, Cyrillic, Greek, Hebrew, Roman alphabet**, Araba, Cirila, Greka, Hebrea, Romana ~o
alphanumeric, litercifera
Alphonso, Alfonso
Alpinia, galango
Alps, [see "alp"]
already, jam
Alsace, Alzaco†; **Alsace-Lorraine**, ~o-Loreno
also, ankaŭ [always goes before word modified (e.g.: *I want to come also:* ~ mi volas veni)]; **also-ran**, sensukcesa konkurinto
Altaic, Altaja
Altai (Mountains), Altajo
Altair, Altairo
altar, altaro
alter, (change, gen), ŝanĝi [tr]; ~iĝi; ali-

igi; (make minor adjustment of fit of suit etc.), retuŝi [tr]; (castrate), kastri [tr]; (spay), inkastri [tr]; **alteration,** ~o; ~aĵo; retuŝo; **alter ego,** intima kunulo
altercation, kverelo, disputo, malpaco
alternate, alterni [int]; ~igi; ~a; (substitute), anstataŭa; anstataŭaĵo; **alternation,** (gen), ~(ad)o; ~ig(ad)o; ~eco; (elec etc.: half cycle), alternanco; **alternative,** alternativo; alternativa; **alternator,** alternatoro
Althaea, (bot), alteo; Althaea rosea, roz~o
althea, alteo
although, kvankam
altimeter, altometro, altimetro
altiplano, altebenaĵo
altitude, altitudo
alto, (singing voice), aldo; (singer), ~ulino; **alto clef,** ~a kleo
altogether, (wholly), entute; (all added, considered), sume (e.g.: *$25 for gas, $50 for a motel room, $30 for meals; altogether, the trip cost $105:* $25 por benzino, $50 por motelĉambro, $30 por manĝoj; sume, la vojaĝo kostis $105); **in the altogether,** tute nuda; tute nude
altruism, altruismo; **altruistic,** ~a; **altruist,** altruisto
alum, aluno
alumina, (aluminum oxide), alumino, aluminia oksido
alumin(i)um, aluminio
alumnus, diplomito; **alumna,** ~ino
alunite, alunito
alveolus, alveolo; **alveolar,** (anat), ~a; (phon), alveolaro; alveolara
always, ĉiam
alyssum, Alyssum,aliso
a.m. (abb of "ante meridiem"), atm. [abb of "antaŭtagmeze"]
Amadeus, Amadeo
Amalek, Amaleko; **Amalekite,** ~ido
amalgam, (alloy w mercury), amalgamo; (gen mixture), miksaĵo; **amalgamate,** (alloy), ~i [tr]; (combine), kombini [tr]; kombiniĝi
Amalia, Amalia
Amanita, amanito
amanitine, amanitino

amanuensis, sekretario
amaranth, (flower), amaranto; (color), ~a (koloro)
Amaranthus, amaranto
amarelle, grioto
amaryllis, Amaryllis, amarilido
amass, amasigi
amateur, diletanto, amatoro; ~a, amatora; **amateurish,** ~eca; **radio amateur,** (ham), radioamatoro
amatory, amora
amaurosis, amaŭrozo
amaze, mir/igi; **be amazed,** ~i [int]; **amazing,** ~iga; **amazement,** ~o
amazon, (woman), amazono
Amazon, (river), Amazono; **Upper Amazon,** (Marañón), Maranjo
ambassador, ambasadoro; **ambassadorial staff,** ambasado
amber, sukceno; ~a [not "ambro"]
ambergris, ambro
ambi–, (pfx: both), ambaŭ– (e.g.: *ambidextrous:* ~dekstra) [sometimes absorbed into Esperanto root as "ambi–"; see separate entries]
ambiance, medio
ambidextrous, ambaŭdekstra, ambaŭmana; **ambidexterity,** ~eco, ambaŭmaneco
ambient, ĉirkaŭa, media
ambiguous, ambigua, dubasenca; **ambiguity,** ~eco; ~aĵo
ambition, ambicio; **ambitius,** ~a; **have ambitin,** ~i [tr]
ambivalence, ambivalenco; **ambivalent,** ~a
ambivert, ambiverti* [tr]; ~ito; **ambiversion,** ~iteco
amble, ambli [int]; ~o
amblyopic, ambliopa; **amblyopia,** ~eco
Amblystoma,amblistomo
ambo, ambono
Ambrose, Ambrozio
ambrosia, (food of gods), ambrozio
Ambrosia, (bot), ambrosio
ambulance, ambulanco
ambulate, (walk), marŝi [int]; **ambulant,** (walking), ~anta; **ambulatory,** (able to walk), ~iva; (covered walkway), ambulatorio
ambush, embusko; ~igi; **lie (wait) in ambush,** ~i [int]; **set up an ambush,**

~iĝi
ameba, [see "amoeba"]
ameer, emiro
ameliorate, plibon/igi; ~iĝi
amen, (interj), amen; (n), ~o
Amen, Amono
amenable, influebla, cedema, inklina
amend, (improve, gen), plibonigi; (correct, gen), korekti [tr]; (change law etc.), amendi [tr]; **amendment**, ~o, korekto; amendo; **amends**, kompenso; **make amends for**, kompensi [tr]
ameni/ty, agrabl/aĵo; ~eco; (courtesies), ĝentilaĵoj
amenorrhea, amenoreo
ament, (bot), amento
America, (entire western hemisphere), Ameriko; (USA), Usono; **American**, ~a; Usona; ~ano; Usonano; **Americana**, Usonaĵoj; **Americanism**, ~anismo; Usonanismo; **North America**, Nord-~o; **Central America**, Centr-~o; **South America**, Sud-~o; **Latin America**, Latin-~o; **Native American**, aborigena ~no; aborigen-~na
americium, americio
Amerind(ian), Indiano; ~a
amethyst, ametisto
ametropic, ametropa; **ametropia**, ~eco
Amharic, Amharo; ~a
amiable, amik(ec)a, komplez(em)a
amid, inter, meze de
amide, amido
amidships, ŝipmeze
amine, amino
amino, amina
amino–, (chem pfx), amino–
aminophenol, aminofenolo
amir, emiro
Amish, Pensilvangermano; ~a
amiss, misa; **be amiss**, ~i [int] (e.g.: *something is amiss:* io ~as) [cp "awry"]
amitosis, amitozo
amity, amikeco
Amman, Amano
ammeter, ampermetro
Ammi majus,amio
Ammon, Amono
ammonia, amoniako; **ammoniacal**, ~a; ~eca; **ammoniate**, (mix w ~), ~izi [tr]
ammonite, (mollusk), amonito

ammonium, amonio
Ammophila,amofilo
ammunition, municio; **ammunition dump**, ~ejo
amnesia, amnezio; **amnesiac**, ~a; ~ulo
amnesty, amnestio
amniocentesis, amniocentezo*
amnion, amnio; **amniotic**, ~a
amoeba, amebo; **amoebic**, ~a; **amoebozoa**, ~uloj
amok, amoko; ~a; **run amok**, kuri ~e
Amomum,amomo
Amon, Amono
among(st), (between, within), inter, meze de; (by, w many), ĉe (e.g.: *a favorite among students:* favorito ĉe studentoj); **among other things**, ~alie [abb: i.a.]
amoral, nemorala
amorous, amora; ~ema
amorphous, amorfa
amortize, amortizi [tr]
Amos, Amos
amount, kvanto; (sum), sumo; **any, some amount**, iom [adv]; **what amount**, kiom; **that amount**, tiom, **this amount**, ĉi tiom; **the full amount**, ĉiom; **no amount**, neniom; **amount to**, (be equivalent to, add up to) sumiĝi al, kalkuliĝi al; (be equivalent), esti ekvivalenta al; **amount to the same thing**, esti ekvivalenta; **amount to something**, fariĝi indulo; **amount to nothing**, rezulti vana, rezulti senvalora
amour, (affair), amafero; (person), amant(in)o
amp, [see "ampere"]
Ampelopsis,ampelopso
ampere, ampero; **amperage**, kurent-intenso [not "~aĵo"]; **ampere-hour**, ~horo; **ampere turn**, ~volvo; **abampere**, ab~o; **milliampere**, mili~o; **microampere**, mikro~o
ampersand, kajsigno [note: "k" is more common abb for "kaj" than is "&"]
amphetamine, amfetamino†
amphiarthrosis, amfiartro
Amphibia, amfibioj
amphibian, amfibio; ~a; **amphibious**, ~a
amphibole, amfibolo

amphibology, amfibologio
amphibrach, amfibrako
Amphimallus solstitialis, solstica skarabo
Amphineura, amfineŭroj
amphioxus, amfiokso, brankiostomo
amphitheater, amfiteatro
Amphitrite, Amfitrita
Amphitryon, Amfitriono
amphora, amforo
amphoteric, amfotera
ample, (large), granda, plenforma; (vast), ampleksa, vasta; (abundant), abunda
amplify, (elec), amplifi [tr]; (broaden), ampleksigi, plivastigi; (increase, gen), pliigi; (give more details, explain further), pluklarigi, pludetali [tr]; amplifier, (elec), ~atoro; amplification, (elec), ~(ad)o; preamplifier, antaŭ~atoro
amplitude, amplitudo
ampul, ampule, ampulla, ampoule, ampolo
amputate, amputi [tr]; amputee, ~ito
Amsterdam, Amsterdamo
amuck, [see "amok"]
amulet, amuleto
Amur (River), Amuro
amuse, amuzi [tr]; amusing, ~a; amusement, ~(ad)o; ~iĝo; ~aĵo
Amygdalus communis, migdalo; Amygdalus persica, persikarbo, persikujo
amyl, amilo
amylase, amelazo
amylum, amelo
Amyris, amirido
an–, (pfx: not), [see "a–"]
–an, (sfx: member, follower, inhabitant, etc.), –ano [cp "–ist"]
Anabaptist, Anabaptisto; ~a
anabatic, anabata
anabolism, anabolo
Anacardium, anakardiarbo; Anacardium occidentale, okcidenta ~o, akajuarbo
anachronism, anakronismo; anachronistic, ~a
anacoluthon, anakoluto
anaconda, anakondo
Anacreon, Anakreono

anacrusis, anakruzo
anaemia, [see "anemia"]
anaerobic, anaerobia
anaesthesia, [see "anesthesia"]
Anagallis, anagalo; Anagallis arvensis, kamp~o; (w red flowers), ruĝa kamp~o
anaglyph, anaglifo
anagram, anagramo
anakinesis, anakinezo
anal, anusa
analects, analecta, elektitaj legaĵoj
analeptic, analeptiko; ~a
analgesia, analgezio; analgesic, ~a; (drug), analgeziko
analog, (analogous thing), analog/aĵo; (cmptr, tech: not digital), ~at; analogous, ~a
analogy, analogio, analogeco
analyze, analizi [tr]; analysis, ~o; analyst, ~isto; analytical, ~a; analytics, (math), analitiko; psychoanalyze, psik~i [tr]; combinatorial analysis, kombinatoriko
Anam, Anamo
Anamirta, anamirto
anamorphosis, anamorfozo
Ananas, ananasujo
anapest, anapesto; anapestic, ~a
anaphora, anaforo
anaphylaxis, anafilaksio
anarchy, anarkio; anarchism, ~ismo; anarchist, ~isto; anarchistic, ~isma
Anas, anaso; Anas penelope, fajf~o; Anas querquedula, marĉ~o, kerkedulo; Anas clypeata, kuler~o
anasarca, anasarko
Anastasius, Anastazio; Anastasia, ~a
Anastatica hierochuntica, anastatiko, jerikorozo
anastigmatic, anastigmata
anastomosis, anastomozo
anastrophe, anastrofo
anathema, anatemo
Anatole, Anatolo
Anatolia, Anatolio
anatomy, anatom/io; anatomical, ~ia; anatomist, ~o
Anaxagoras, Anaksagoro
–ance, (sfx: quality, condition of), –eco; (thing showing that quality, –aĵo; (elec), –anco

ancestor, praulo, prapatro; **ancestral**, ~a; **ancestry**, deveno
Anchises, Anĥizo
anchor, (of ship, or similar device), ankro; ~i [tr]; ~iĝi; (of molly bolt), dubelo; **anchorage**, (act), ~iĝo; ~ado; (place), ~ejo; (fee), ~otarifo; (area outside harbor, shielded against wind etc.), rodo; **weigh anchor**, mal~i [tr]; mal~iĝi
anchovy, (species), engraŭlo; (spiced), anĉovo; (pickled and canned), sardelo
Anchusa, ankuzo
ancient, antikva; ~ulo
ancillary, akcesora; helpa
ancon, konzolo
anconeus, (muscle), ankoneo
and, kaj [note: "k" is more common abb than is "&"]; **and/or**, kaj/aŭ
Andalusia, Andaluz/io; **Andalusian**, ~o; ~a
andante, (mus: tempo), andante; (mus movement or work), ~o; **andantino**, ~ine; ~ino
Andes (Mountains), Andoj; **Andean**, ~a
andiron, morelo, fajrohundo
Andorra, Andoro
André, Andreo
Andrea, Andrea
Andrew, Andreo
androgen, androgen†; **androgenic**, **androgenous**, ~a
androgyne, androgino; **androgynous**, ~a
android, homaŭtomato, homroboto
Andromache, Andromaĥa
Andromeda, (ast; myth), Andromeda
Andromeda, (bot), andromedo; **Andromeda polyfolia**, marĉa ~o
Andropogon sorghum, sorgo
–ane, (chem sfx), –ano
anecdote, anekdoto
anechoic, seneĥa
anemia, anemio; **anemic**, ~a; **sicle-cell anemia**, falĉil-forma ~o
anemograph, anemogramo
anemometer, anemometro
anemone, (bot), anemono; **sea anemone**, (zool), mar~o, aktinio
Anemone, anemono; **Anemone pulsatilla**, pulsatilo

aneroid, aneroida*
anesthesia, anestezo
anesthesiology, anestezolog/io; **anesthesiologist**, ~o
anesthetic, anesteza; ~enzo; **anesthetist**, ~isto; **anesthetize**, ~i [tr]
Anethus, aneto
aneurysm, **aneurism**, aneŭrismo
anew, denove, dekomence
anfractuous, anfrakta; **anfractuosity**, ~o
angel, anĝelo; **angelic**, ~eca; **archangel**, arki~o, ĉef~o; **guardian angel**, gard~o
Angel, (man's name), Anĝelo
Angela, **Angeline**, **Angelica**, (woman's names), Anĝela, Angela, Angelino
Angeleno, Los-Anĝeles/ano; ~a; ~ana
angelfish, skvateno
angelica, Angelica, (bot), angeliko
Angelus, **Angelus bell**, (rel), anĝeluso
anger, kolero; ~igi; [see also "angry"]
angina, angino; **angina pectoris**, brust~o
angiosperm, angiospermo
angle, (geom; any corner), angulo; (measured in radians), arkuso; (point of view), vidpunkto, starpunkto; (motive), (fi)motivo; (tricky method), ruzo; (bend in ~), ~igi; ~iĝi; (fish), fiŝi [tr]; **right angle**, orto; **angle iron**, ~fero
Angle, Engl/ano; **Angles**, (tribe), ~o
angler, (fish), lofio
Anglia, Englujo
Anglican, Anglikano; ~a
Anglicism, Angl/ismo; **Anglicist**, ~isto; **Anglicize**, ~igi
Anglo, blankulo; ~a
Anglo–, (pfx: England), Anglo–
Anglomania, Anglomanio
Anglophone, Anglaparola; ~anto
Anglo-Saxon, Anglosakso; ~a
Angola, Angolo
angophora, Angophora, (Aus), angoforo
angora, Angora, angura; (cat), ~a kato; (goat), ~a kapro; (wool), ~a lano, mohajro
angostura, angusturo
Angrecum, Angraecum, angreko

angry, kolera; be angry (with), ~i [int] (kontraŭ); get angry, ~igi; ~iĝi
angstrom, anstromo
Anguilla, (zool), angilo; Anguilliformes, ~oformaj (fiŝoj)
Anguis, angviso, vitroserpento
anguish, angoro; ~i [int]; ~igi; anguished, ~a
angular, angula [see "angle"]
Anhwei, Anhuj
anhydride, anhidrido
anhydrite, anhidrito
anhydrous, anhidra, [or as pfx], anhidro–
anil, anilo
aniline, anilino
animal, (common usage), besto; (sci: including humans), animalo
animate, animi [tr]; viv(ant)a; animation, ~ado; vivanteco; inanimate, senviva; suspended animation, suspendita animado
animism, animismo
animosity, malamikeco, malamo
animus, (animating force), animilo; (animosity), malamo
anion, anjono
anise, (seed), anizo; (plant), ~planto; Chinese anise, star anise, ilicio
aniseed, anizo
aniso–, (tech pfx: not equal), neizo– [sometimes absorbed into Esperanto root as "anizo–"; see separate entries; also see "a–"]
anisocoria, anizokorio
anisometropia, anizometropio
anisosphygmia, anizosfigmio
anisotropia, anizotropio; anisotropic, ~a
Anita, Anneta
Anjou, Anĵuo
Ankara, Ankaro
ankh, maŝkruco
ankle, ankle-bone, maleolo [cp "tarsus", "malleolus", "talus", "astragalus", "navicular", "cuboid"]
anklet, (ornament), (krur)braceleto; (sock), ŝtrumpeto
ankylosis, ankilozo
Ann, Anna, Anne, Anna; Annette, ~eta
anna, anao

annals, kroniko [note sing], analoj
Annam, Anamo
Annapurna, Anapurno
annatto, (tree), bikso; (dye), rokuo
anneal, malhardi [tr]
annelid, anelido
Annelida, anelidoj
annex, aneksi [tr]; ~aĵo
annihilate, neniigi, ekstermi [tr]
anniversary, datreveno
Anno Domini, (abb: A.D.), post Kristo, post Komunerao [abb: p.K.]
Annona, anono; Annona cherimola, ĉerimoliarbo; Annona muricata, graviolarbo; Annona squamosa, sukerpomarbo
annotate, prinoti [tr]; annotation, ~ado; ~aĵo
announce, anonci [tr]; announcement, ~o; wedding announcement, geedziĝ~o; birth announcement, naskiĝ~o; announcer, ~isto
annoy, ĝeni [tr], ĉagreni [tr]
annual, (once a year), jara, ĉiu~a; (re plant), ~daŭra; ~daŭrulo; (yearbook), ~libro; biannual, semiannual, duon~a
annuity, (pension), pensio; (from investment etc.), rento; [not "anuitato"];
annuitant, ~ulo; rentulo
annul, (nullify, gen), nuligi; (law), kasacii [tr]; annulment, ~o; kasacio
annular, ring(ec)a
Annunciation, Anunciacio
Anobium, anobio
anode, anodo; anodize, ~izi [tr]
Anodonta, anodono
anodyne, sendolor/iga; ~enzo
anoint, sanktolei [tr]; (poet), unkti [tr]; anointing, (act of), ~ado
anomaly, anomalio; anomalous, ~a
anomie, senidenteco, senmotiveco, malorganiziteco
anon, (bot), [see "sweetsop"]
Anona, [see "Annona"]
anonymous, anonima; anonymity, ~eco
anopheles, Anopheles, anofelo
anopsia, anopsio
anorak, anorako
anorexia, anoreksio
anosmia, anosmio

another, (one more; additional), alia; (still more), ankoraŭ (e.g.: *another two people:* ankoraŭ du homoj); **another one**, ~a; **one another**, unu la ~an; si(n) reciproke (e.g.: *they congratulated one another:* ili gratulis sin unu la alian [or] sin reciproke)

anoxemia, anoksemio

anoxia, anoksio

ansate, anshava

Ansel(m), Anselmo

Anser, ansero

Anshan, Anŝan

answer, (gen), respondi [tr, int]; ~o; (reply to demand or assertion), repliki [tr, int]; repliko; **be answerable to**, devi ~i al

ant, formiko; **anthill**, ~ejo; **anteater**, (gen), ~manĝanto; **scaly anteater**, (pangolin, genus *Manis*), maniso; **spiny anteater**, (*Tachyglossus*), eĥidno [see also "aardvark", "bear: ant bear"]

–ant, (sfx: one who did, does, or will do), –into; –anto; –onto [cp "–ist"]; (chem agent, drug, etc.), –enzo (e.g.: *antidepressant:* kontraŭdeprimenzo)

antagonism, antagonismo; **antagonistic**, ~a; **antagonist**, antagonisto; **antagonize**, (oppose), kontraŭi [tr]; (incur antagonism), antagonistigi

antarctic, antarkta; ~o; **Antarctica**, A~io

Antares, Antareso

ante, (poker etc.), antaŭveto; ~i [tr]; **ante up**, (colloq: pay), pagi [tr]

ante–, (pfx: before, in front), antaŭ– (e.g.: *anteroom:* ~ĉambro)

antebellum, antaŭmilita

antecede, antaŭi [int] (al); **antecedence**, (being before), ~eco; (ast: retrograde motion), retroiro; **antecedent**, ~a; ~aĵo; **antecedents**, (life history), antecedentoj

Antedon, antedono

antefix, antefikso

antelope, antilopo

ante meridiem, (abb: a.m.), antaŭtagmeze [abb: atm.]

antenna, (gen), anteno

Antennaria, antenario

anterior, antaŭa

anthelion, anthelio

anthem, himno

Anthemis, antemido; Anthemis tinctoria, farbo~o

anther, antero

antheridium, anteridio

anthology, antologio

Anthony, Antonio

Anthoxanthum, antoksanto

Anthozoa, koraluloj

anthozoan, koralulo

anthracene, antraceno

anthracite, antracito

anthracosis, antrakozo

anthraquinone, antrakinono

anthrax, antrakso

anthropo–, antropo–

anthropocentric, antropocentra

anthropoid, antropoida; ~ulo

anthropology, antropolog/io; **anthropologist**, ~o

anthropometry, antropometrio

anthropomorphism, antropomorfismo; **anthropomorphic**, ~a; **anthropomorphize**, ~igi

anthropomorphosis, homform/iĝo; **anthropomorphous**, ~a

anthropophagus, anthropophagite, antropofago; **anthropophagy**, ~ismo

Anthropopithecus troglodytes, ĉimpanzo

Anthurium, anturio; Anthurium scherzerianum, flamengofloro

Anthus, pipio

Anthyllis, antilido

anti–, (gen pfx), kontraŭ–; (sci, tech), anti–, kontraŭ– [often absorbed into Esperanto root as "anti–"; see separate entries]

antiar, antiarrezino

Antiaris, antiaro; Antiaris toxicaria, upasarbo

antibiotic, antibiotiko; ~a

antic, kapriolaĵo, klaŭnaĵo, burleskaĵo

antichlor, kontraŭkloraĵo

anticipate, anticipi [tr]

anticline, antiklinalo

Antidorcas, saltantilopo

antidote, antidoto

antigen, antigeno, kseno

Antigone, Antigona

Antigua, Antigvo†; **Antigua and Bar-**

buda, ~o-Barbudo
Antilles, Antiloj; **Lesser Antilles**, Malgrandaj ~oj
antimony, antimono
antinomy, antinomio
Antioch, Antioĥo
Antiochus, Antioĥo†
antipathy, antipatio, malsimpatio
antiphon, antiphony, antifono; **antiphonal**, ~a
antiphrasis, antifrazo
antipode, antipodo
antipyrine, antipirino
antiquarian, antikvaĵa; ~isto; ~ista; **antiquary**, ~isto
antiquate, arkaik/igi; **antiquated**, ~a, eksmoda
antique, antikva; ~aĵo; **antiquity**, ~eco; **antiquities**, ~aĵoj, ~aĵaro
antirrhinum, Antirrhinum, antirino
antisepsis, antisepso
antistrophe, antistrofo
antitartaric, antitartrata
antithesis, antitezo; **antithetical**, ~a
antitussant, antitussive, kontraŭtusa; ~enzo
antivenin, kontraŭveneno
antler(s), kornaro
Antoine, Antono [cp "Anthony']; **Antoinette**, ~eta
Anton, Antono [cp "Anthony"]
Antoninus, Antoneno
antonomasia, antonomazio
antonym, antonimo
antrum, antro
Antwerp, Antverpeno
Anubis, Anubo
Anura, batrakoj
anuria, anurio
anus, anuso
anvil, (in forge), amboso; (bone), inkudo
anxious, (disturbed), anksia; (desirous), dezir(ant)a; **anxiety**, ~eco; **be anxious to**, (desire to), deziri [tr]
any, (some unspecified one(s)), iu (e.g.: *any member absent may not vote:* iu forestanta membro ne rajtas voĉdoni); (any whatever), iu ajn, ajna (e.g.: *any member may vote:* iu ajn [or: ajna] membro rajtas voĉdoni); (some kind of), ia; (any kind whatever), ia ajn;

(possible future), eventuala (e.g.: *I will answer any letter that comes:* mi respondos eventualan leteron kiu venos); [note: in negative and interrogative expressions, "any" is not translated (e.g.: *do you have any milk?:* ĉu vi havas lakton?; *I don't have any milk:* mi ne havas lakton)]; **hardly any**, preskaŭ neniu(j), preskaŭ neniom (da) (e.g.: *hardly any members came:* preskaŭ neniuj membroj venis; *I have hardly any milk:* mi havas preskaŭ neniom da lakto)
anybody, [see "anyone"]
anyhow, (any way at all), iel ajn; (in any event), ĉiuokaze
anymore, (still, in negative expressions), plu (e.g.: *she doesn't live here anymore:* ŝi ne plu loĝas ĉi tie); (nowadays), nuntempe (e.g.: *it's hard to get that anymore:* estas malfacile akiri tion nuntempe)
anyone, (someone), iu; (anyone at all), iu ajn; (whoever), kiu ajn (e.g.: *anyone you choose will be okay:* kiun ajn vi elektos estos en ordo); **not anyone**, neniu [not "ne iu"] (e.g.: *I don't see anyone:* mi vidas neniun); **hardly anyone**, preskaŭ neniu [cp "any"]; **anyone's**, ies; (anyone's at all), ies ajn; **hardly anyone's**, preskaŭ nenies
anyplace, [see "anywhere"]
anything, (something), io; (anything at all), io ajn; (whatever), kio ajn (e.g.: *anything you do will be okay:* kion ajn vi faros estos en ordo); **not anything**, nenio [not "ne io"; see "anybody"]; **hardly anything**, preskaŭ nenio [cp "any"]
anytime, (sometime), iam; (anytime at all), iam ajn; (whenever), kiam ajn (e.g.: *anytime you want to go will be okay:* kiam ajn vi volos iri estos en ordo)
anyway, (in some manner), iel; (in any manner at all), iel ajn; (in whatever manner), kiel ajn (e.g.: *anyway you want to do it will be okay:* kiel ajn vi volos fari ĝin estos en ordo); (in any event), ĉiuokaze; (at least), almenaŭ
anywhere, (at someplace), ie; (to someplace), ien; (anywhere at all), ie(n)

ajn; (wherever), kie(n) ajn (e.g.: *anywhere you want to go is okay:* kien ajn vi volas iri estas en ordo); **not anywhere**, nenie(n) [not "ne ie(n)"] (e.g.: *I don't see it anywhere:* mi vidas ĝin nenie); **not get anywhere**, (not progress), ne progresi [int]
aorist, aoristo
aorta, aorto
Aosta, Aosto
Aotes, Aotus,aoto
apace, rapide
Apache, (gen), Apaĉo; ~a
apart, (separate), aparta; ~e; disa; dise; (into pieces), dis– [pfx] (e.g.: *tear apart:* disŝiri); (at stated interval of time or space), je intervalo(j) de (e.g.: *three trips two years apart:* tri vojaĝoj je intervaloj de du jaroj; *cities a thousand kilometers apart:* urboj je intervalo de mil kilometroj); **apart from**, (besides), krom; **break apart**, disrompi [tr]; disrompiĝi; diseriĝi; **take apart**, dispecigi, diserigi; (dismantle), malmunti [tr]; **tear apart**, disŝiri [tr]; disŝiriĝi
apartheid, (ras)apartigo
apartment, apartamento; **mother-in-law apartment**, avinejo
apaster, apastro*
apathy, apatio; **apathetic**, ~a
apatite, apatito
Apatosaurus, brontosaŭro
ape, (any monkey; mimicking person), simio; (gross, uncouth person), ~aĉo; (imitate), ~i [tr]
Apelles, Apelo
Apennines, Apeninoj
apepsia, apepsio
aperitif, aperitivo
aperture, aperturo
apex, (culmination; climax), kulmino; klimakso; (anat), apekso; (highest point), pinto, zenito
aphaeresis, aferezo
Aphaniptera, afanipteroj
aphasia, afazio
aphelion, afelio
apheresis, aferezo
aphid, afido
Aphis, afido; Aphididae, ~edoj
aphonia, afonio

aphorism, aforismo
aphotic, senluma
aphrodisia, afrodizio;   **aphrodisiac**, ~iga; ~igenzo
Aphrodita, afrodito
Aphrodite, Afrodita
aphtha, afto
Apia, Apio*
apiary, abelejo
apical, (phon), apeksa; ~aĵo; (re apex in oth senses), [see "apex"]
apiculture, abelbredado
Apidae, abeledoj
apiece, po [goes before expression of quantity (e.g.: *we ate two apples apiece:* ni manĝis po du pomojn)] [see also "each" for more examples]
Apios, apioso
Apis, (myth), Apiso
Apis, (zool), abelo
Apium,apio; Apium graveolens, celerio
Aplacentalia, senplacentuloj
aplanatic, aplanata
aplenty, abunda; ~e
aplomb, aplombo
apnea, apneo
apocalypse, apokalipso;   **apocalyptic**, ~a
apocope, apokopo; **apocopate**, ~igi
apocrypha, apokrif/aĵoj;   **apocryphal**, ~a
Apocrypha, (Bib), Apokrifaĵoj
Apocynum,apocino
apod, apodo; **apodal**, ~a
Apodiformes,apusoformaj (birdoj)
apogee, apogeo
Apollo, (myth), Apolonio
Apollonius, Apolonio
Apollyon, Abadono
apologia, apologio
apology, (begging pardon), pardonpeto; (apologia), apologio; **apologetic**, ~a; apologia; **apologetics**, (rel etc.), apologetiko; **apologize**, ~i [int]; apologii [int]; **apologist**, apologiisto
aponeurosis, aponeŭrozo
apophysis, apofizo
apoplexy, apopleksio; **apoplectic**, ~a
aposiopesis, aposiopezo
apostate, apostato;   **apostacy**, ~iĝo; ~eco; **apostatize**, ~iĝi, kabei [int]

a posteriori, aposteriora; ~e
apostle, apostolo; **apostolic,** ~a
apostrophe, (gen), apostrofo; **apostrophize,** ~i [tr]
apothecary, apotek/isto;   **apothecary shop,** ~o [cp "drug", "pharmacy"]
apothem, apotemo
apotheosis, apoteozo; **apotheosize,** ~i [tr]
appal, konsterni [tr]
Appalachia, Apalaĉ/io*; **Appalachian,** (re region), ~ia; **Appalachians,** **Appalachian Mountains,** ~oj
appall, konsterni [tr]
appanage, apanaĝo
apparatchik, aparat/ulo†, ~isto
apparatus, aparato
apparel, vesto(j)
apparent, (seeming), ŝajna; (visible), videbla; (obvious), evidenta; (in manner of, as it were), kvazaŭa; **apparently,** ~e; videble; evidente
apparition, (anything   appearing), aper/aĵo; ~anto; (ghost), fantomo
apparitor, pedelo
appeal, (decision to higher court; to public opinion; etc.), apelacii [tr] (pri io al io); ~o; (implore), petegi [tr]; petego; **appeal to,** (attract, impress favorably), tuŝi [tr], logi [tr]; (invoke), ~i al, alvoki [tr], envoki [tr]; **court of appeals,** kasacia kortumo; **sex appeal,** sekslogo
appear, (become visible), aperi [int]; (display aspect, mien), aspekti [int], mieni [int]; (seem similar, but not be same), ŝajni [int]; **appearance,** ~o; aspekto, mieno; ŝajno [cp "look"]; **disappear,** mal~i [int]; **disappearance,** mal~o; **disappeared (person),** mal~into
appease, (calm), kvietigi, trankviligi; (give in), komplezi [int] (al); **appeasement,** ~o, trankviligo; komplez(ad)o; (as pol policy), komplezismo
appellate, (re appeal), apelacia; **appellate court,** kasacia kortumo; **appellant,** ~into; ~anto; ~onto
appellation, (name), nomo; (naming), ~igo
append, (fasten, add, gen), alfiksi [tr],

aldoni [tr]; (hang on), alpendigi; **appendage,** ~aĵo, aldonaĵo; alpendigaĵo [cp "appendix"]
appendix, (gen), apendico; **appendectomy,** apendektomio; **appendicitis,** ~ito
apperceive, apercepti [tr]; **apperception,** ~o
appertain, aparteni [int]
appetency, apetenco
appetite, apetito
appetizer, aperitivo, almanĝaĵo; **appetizing,** apetitiga
Appian, Appia*
applaud, aplaŭdi [tr]; **applause,** ~(ad)o
apple, (fruit of any tree of genus *Malus*), pomo; **applejack,** ~brando; **applesauce,** ~saŭco; **apple tree,** ~arbo; **Adam's apple,** Adam~o; **balsam apple,** momordiko; momordika frukto; **colocynth apple, bitter apple,** kolocinto; kolocinta frukto; **crab apple,** amara ~(arb)o; **custard apple, sugar apple,** suker~(arb)o; **reinette apple,** renedo; reneda frukto; **rose apple,** jamboso; jambosfrukto; **apple of Peru, thorn apple,** (*Datura stramonium*), stramonio
appliance, aparato
applicable, (can be applied), aplikebla; (appropriate), konvena, taŭga; (relevant), rilata, koncerna
applicant, (seeker, as of job), petanto, aspiranto, kandidato; (claimant), pretendanto
application, [see "apply"]
apply, (use, gen), apliki [tr]; (fasten, stick on), alfiksi [tr]; (be relevant), rilati [int]; (be valid), validi [int]; (go to), sin turni (al) (e.g.: *for information, apply at:* por informo, turnu vin al); (spread, as butter, paint, medication, etc.), ŝmiri [tr]; **apply for,** (seek, request, as job etc.), peti [tr], sin proponi por, aspiri [int] (al, pri); (claim right, as pension etc.), pretendi [tr]; **apply oneself,** diligenti [int]; **applied,** (practical, not theoretical), ~ita; ~ata; **application,** alfiks(ad)o; rilateco; ŝmir(ad)o; (for job etc.: act of), pet(ad)o; (for pension etc.), pretend(ad)o; (form for so doing), petilo;

pretendilo; (form for joining, registering, etc.), aliĝilo; (diligence), diligenteco

appoggiatura, apoĝaturo

appoint, (designate, name), asigni [tr], nomumi [tr]; (fix, as date), fiksi [tr]; (commission), komisii [tr]; **appointee**, ~ito; komisiito; **appointive**, ~a; **appointment**, ~o; komisiiĝo; komisio; (agreed time or place to meet person), rendevuo; **self-appointed**, memdeklarita; **well-appointed**, (furnished), bone meblita, bone ekipita

apportion, distribui [tr], dispartigi

apposition, apozicio; **put in apposition**, ~i [tr]; **be in apposition**, ~iĝi

appraise, taksi [tr], apreci [tr]

appreciable, konsiderinda, perceptebla, sentebla, rimarkebla

appreciate, (esteem), estimi [tr], valortaksi [vt], alte taksi [tr]; (realize), kompreni [tr], konscii [int] (pri, de); (understand), kompreni [tr]; (raise $ value), plivalorigi; plivaloriĝi

apprehend, (catch), kapti [tr]; (understand), kompreni [tr]; (await w anxiety), anksie atendi [tr]; **apprehension**, ~o; kompreno; anksieco; **apprehensive**, anksia; **misapprehend**, miskompreni [tr]; **misapprehension**, miskompreno

apprentice, (young boy, as in former times), lern/oknabo; (of any age and sex), meti~anto, ~observanto; (make an ~), meti~antigi, ~observantigi; **be apprenticed to**, ~oservi ĉe; **apprenticeship**, (condition), meti~anteco, ~oservo; (time of), ~ojaroj, ~otempo, provjaroj, provtempo

apprise, (inform), informi [tr], avizi [tr], sciigi

approach, (go toward), aliri [tr]; ~o; (way through), ~ejo; (get closer), (al)proksimiĝi al; (al)proksimiĝo; (approximate), proksimumiĝi al; (math), aproksimi [tr]

approbation, aprobo

appropriate, (proper), taŭga, konvena; (take for self, gen), proprigi al si; (take possession of by law), evikcii [tr]; (assign $, budget), monasigni [tr], buĝeti [tr]; **be appropriate**, ~i [int],

konveni [int]; **appropriation**, proprigo; evikcio; monasigno; buĝetiĝo; **misappropriate**, prifraŭdi [tr], misalproprigi, fiproprigi al si

approve, **approve of**, aprobi [tr]; **approval**, ~o; **disapprove**, mal~i [tr]

approximate, proksimuma; ~igi; ~iĝi al; (math, gen), aproksimi [tr]; (math: compute approximate value of *a* approximately equal to $f(x)$ by expressing $f(a)$ as approximate function of oth known values of x), poli [tr]; **approximately**, ~e, rondcifere, ĉirkaŭ [abb: ĉ.]; **approximation**, ~igo; ~iĝo; ~aĵo; aproksim(ad)o; aproksimaĵo; polado; polaĵo

appurtenance, (thing belonging), aparten/aĵo; (accessory), akcesoraĵo; **appurtenant**, ~a; akcesora

après, post (e.g.: *après-ski:* ~skiada)

apricot, abrikoto

April, aprilo

a priori, apriora; ~e

apron, (to protect clothing), antaŭtuko; (in front of hangar; driveway; etc.), manovrejo; (protecting shield), ŝirmilo; (of stage), rivalto

apropos, rilata; **apropos of**, ~e al, kiel koncernas [tr]

apse, absido

apsis, (ast), apsido; (apse), absido; **lower apsis**, malsupera ~o; **upper apsis**, supera ~o; **line of apsides**, ~a linio

apt, (appropriate), taŭga; (quick to learn), lerta, inteligenta, talenta; (prone to), ema; **be apt to**, emi [tr, int]

Apterygota, senpterigulojt

apteryx, apterigo

Apteryx, apterigo, kivio; Apterygiformes, ~oformaj (birdoj)

aptitude, (fitness), taŭgeco; (talent), lerteco, talento, inteligenteco

Apulia, Apulio

Apus, (ast), Apuso

Apus, (zool), apuso, murhirundo

Aqaba, Akabo

aquaculture, akvokultivado

aqua fortis, (nitric acid), nitrata acido

aqualung, akvopulmo

aquamarine, akvamarino; ~a

aquaplane, akvoplaneo

aqua regia, reĝakvo
aquarium, akvario
Aquarius, (ast), Amforo
aquatic, (watery), akva, akvo– [pfx]; (in
water), en~a [cp "aqueous"]
aquatint, akvatinto; ~a
aqueduct, akvedukto
aqueous, akva; ~eca (e.g.: *aqueous solution:* ~a solvaĵo) [cp "aquatic"]
aquiculture, akvokultivado
Aquifoliaceae, akvifoliacoj
Aquila, (ast), Aglo
Aquilegia, akvilegio
Ara, (zool), arao
Arab, Arabo; ~a; Arabia, ~io; Saudi
Arabia, Saudi-~io [not "Saŭdi–"];
Arabic, ~a; Arabic numerals, ~aj
ciferoj
arabesque, arabesko; ~a
arabinose, arabinozo
arable, erpebla, plugebla
Arachis, arakido
Arachne, Arakna
arachnid, araneoido
Arachnida, araneoidoj
arachnoid, (anat), araknoido; (zool),
araneoido; arachnoiditis, ~ito
Arachnoidea, araneoidoj
Aragón, Aragono; Aragonese, ~a;
~ano
aragonite, aragonito
Aral (Sea), Aralo
Aralia, aralio
Aramaic, Arameo; ~a
Aranea, araneo; Araneida, ~uloj
Ararat, Ararato
Aratinga, konuro
araucaria, Araucaria, araŭkario
arbiter, arbitraci/into; ~anto; ~onto;
~isto
arbitrage, (arbitration), arbitracio; ($:
buying and selling bills), arbitraĝo
arbitrary, arbitra; arbitrariness, ~o,
~eco
arbitrate, arbitracii [tr]; arbitration,
~o; arbitrator, [see "arbiter"]
arbor, (bower), laŭbo
arboretum, arboĝardeno
arboriculture, arbokultivado
arborvitae, tujo
arbour, (bower), laŭbo
arbutus, Arbutus, arbutujo

arc, (gen), arko; ~igi; ~iĝi
arcade, arkado
Arcadia, Arkadio
arcane, arkana; arcanum, ~o
arch, (gen), arko; ~igi; ~iĝi; arched,
~a; arched roof, volbo; archway,
(one ~), ~opasejo; (series), arkado
arch–, (pfx: chief), arki–, ĉef–
archaeology, arkeolog/io; archaeolo-
gist, ~o
archaeopteryx, arkeopterigo
archaic, arkaika
archaism, (gen), arkaismo
archeology, arkeolog/io; archeologist,
~o
archer, ark/isto, paf~isto; archery,
~pafado
archetype, arketipo; archetypical, ~a
archi–, (pfx: original, primitive), pra–
[often absorbed into Esperanto root as
"arki–"; see separate entries]
archiepiscopal, arkiepiskopa; archi-
episcopy, ~ismo
archil, (dye), lakmuso; (plant), ~a rocelo
archimandrite, arkimandrito
Archimedes, Arkimedo
archipelago, arkipelago, insularo
Archipelago, (Aegean), Arkipelago
Archiptera, arkipteroj
architect, arkitekto; architecture, ar-
kitekturo
Architeuthis, arkiteŭto
architrave, arkitravo
archive, arkivo; archivist, ~isto
archivolt, arkivolto
archon, arkonto
Arctia, arktio; Arctia caja, bruna ~o;
Arctia villica, nigra ~o
arctic, arkta; ~o
Arctium, arktio, lapo
Arctocephalus, marurso
Arcturus, Arkturo
Ardea, ardeo; Ardeidae, ~edoj
Ardennes, Ardeno
ardent, arda; be ardent, ~i [int]
ardor, ardo
arduous, peniga, malfacila, laboriga
are, (100 m²), aro; deciare, deci~o; de-
care, deka~o; hectare, hekt~o
area, (surface extent), areo; (region,
field), regiono, kampo (e.g.: *she is*

adept in the area of physical sciences:
ŝi estas lerta en la kampo de la fizikaj
sciencoj; *the southern area:* la suda
regiono; *area code:* regionkodo)
Areca, areko; Areca catechu, ka-
teĉu~o, betelpalmo
arena, (gen), areno
Arenaria, arenario
Arenga, sukerpalmo
Areopagus, Areopago
Ares, Areso
Argemone, argemono
Argentina, Argentino; **Argentine,** ~a;
~ano
argil, (pot)argilo
Argolis, Argolando
argon, argono
Argonaut, Argonaŭto
Argonauta, argonaŭto
Argos, Argo
argot, ĵargono
argue, (dispute), disputi [int] (pri), prid-
isputi [tr]; (make point, reason), argumenti [int]; **argument,** ~o;
argument(ad)o; **argumentative,**
~ema
Argus, Arguso
argyle, romba
Argyroneta, argironeto
aria, ario
Ariadne, Ariadna
arian, (of Arius), ariano; ~isma; (Aryan), arja; arjano; **arianism,** ~ismo
arid, arida
Ariel, (ast), Arielo*
Aries, (ast), Arieso, Ŝafo
aright, ĝuste; **set aright,** re~igi
aril, arilo
arioso, arieca; ~e; ~aĵo
Ariosto, Ariosto
arise, (rise up), leviĝi; (come to be), ~i,
estiĝi; (ascend), ascendi [int], supreniri [int]; **arise from,** (result from), rezulti el, naskiĝi de, folti el
arista, aristo
Aristarchus, Aristarko
Aristides, Aristido
aristocracy, aristokrat/io; **aristocrat,**
~o; **aristocratic,** ~ia
Aristolochia, aristolokio
Aristophanes, Aristofano
Aristotle, Aristotelo; **Aristotelian,** ~is-

ma; ~isto
arithmetic, aritmetiko; ~a; **arithmetic
mean,** aritmo
Arius, Ario [see also "Arian"]
Arizona, Arizono
ark, (Noah's), arkeo; **Ark of the Covenant,** Kesto de la Interligo, Toraujo
Arkansas, Arkansaso
Arles, Arlezo
arm, (anat; any extension, gen), brako;
(provide weapons), armi [tr]; (of balance scales or similar device), vekto;
arms, (weapons), armiloj; **armament,** armaĵo, armilaro; (armor etc.),
ŝirmarmaĵo; **armchair,** fotelo, ~seĝo;
armlet, (~)braceleto; **armpit,** akselo;
cross-arm, kruc~o; **disarm,** malarmi
[tr]; (re one person), senarmigi; **disar-
mament,** malarm(ad)o; malarmiĝo;
disarming, sentimiga, sensuspektiga;
forearm, (anat), antaŭ~o; **lever arm,**
levil~o; **overarm,** superŝultra; **tone-
arm,** (of record player), son~o; **up in
arms,** batalpreta, batalvola
armada, militŝiparo
Armadilla officinalis, armadelo
armadillidium, Armadillidium, arma-
dilo† [cp "armadillo"]
armadillo, (any of *Dasypodidae*), armadelo [cp *"Dasypus",* "armadillidium"]
Armageddon, Har-Magedon
armament, [see "arm"]
Armand, Armando
armature, (gen), armaturo; **provide armature,** ~i [tr]
Armenia, Armen/io; **Armenian,** ~o;
~a; ~ia
Armeria, armerio
armistice, armistico
armor, (metal or oth shielding), kiraso;
~i [tr]; **armored,** ~ita
Armoracia rusticana, Armoracia lap-
athifolia, kreno
armorial, armoria
Armorica, Armoriko; **Armorican,** ~a
armory, arsenalo, armilejo
armour, [see "armor"]
army, armeo; **Salvation Army,** Sav~o
arnatta, arnatto, [see "annatto"]
arnica, Arnica, arniko
Arno, Arno

Arnotta, Arnotto, [see "annatto"]
aroma, aromo: **aromatic,** (odorous), ~a: (chem), aromata: **have, emit aroma,** ~i [int]
around, (moving in circles; in vicinity; approximately; etc.), ĉirkaŭ; ~e (e.g.: *run around the house:* kuri ~ la domo; *they are somewhere around:* ili estas ie ~e; *around a hundred people:* ~ cent homoj); [note: in expressions of motion toward, "around" can often be omitted (e.g.: *come around and see us:* venu kaj vizitu nin; *I don't get around there often:* mi ne ofte iras tien)]; **get aroma,** [see under "get"]; **move aroma,** cirkuli [int]
arouse, (waken), veki [tr]; (stir, excite), ~i, eksciti [tr]; (evoke), elvoki [tr]; (incite anger), inciti [tr]
arpeggio, arpeĝo; **play arpeggios,** ~i [int]
arpent, arpento
arquebus, arkebuzo
arrack, arako
arraign, (bring to court), venigi antaŭ tribunalo
arrange, (gen), aranĝi [tr]; **disarrange,** konfuzi [tr], malordi [tr], ĥaosigi, mal~i [tr]
arras, Arasa murtapiŝo
Arras, Araso
array, (arrange), aranĝi [tr]; ~o: (clothe), vesti [tr]; vestoj; (math), matrico, vicaro; **disarray,** (disorder), konfuzi [tr], malordi, ĥaosigi; konfuzo, malordo, ĥaoso: (ruffle, rumple), taŭzi [tr]; **in disarray,** konfuzita; malordita, ĥaosa; taŭzita
arrears, postmatura(j) ŝuldo(j); **in arrears,** ne akurate paginta; ne akurate pagita; **arrearage,** postmaturaĵo(j)
arrest, (law), aresti [tr]; ~o; ~iĝo; (halt), haltigi; haltigo; **under arrest,** ~ita; **house arrest,** dom~o
arrhythmia, misritmo
arrive, alveni [int]; **arrival,** ~o; **arrive at,** atingi [tr]
arrogant, aroganta; **arrogance,** ~eco
arrogate, arogi [tr]
arrondissement, arondismento
arrow, (gen), sago; **arrowhead,** (of arrow), ~pinto; (bot), sagitario; **arrow-**
root, aroruto; **arrowwood,** viburno
arroyo, ravino
arse, (Br colloq: buttocks), pugo
arsenal, arsenalo
arsenate, arsenato
arsenic, (element), arseno; (in compound w valence 5), arsenika; (arsenic trioxide, "white arsenic"), arseniko; **arsenic acid,** ~ata acido
arsenious, arsen/oza; **arsenious acid,** ~ita acido
arsenite, arsenito
arsenous, arsenoza
arshin(e), arŝino [71,12 cm (see § 20)]
arsine, arsino
arsis, (poet: accented syllable), ikto; (unaccented), sen~o
arson, krimbruligo; **arsonist,** ~into; ~isto; **commit arson,** ~i
arsphenamine, salvarsano
art, (gen), arto; **artist,** ~isto; **artistic,** ~(ec)a; **artistry,** ~ismo; **fine arts,** bel~o; **work of art, objet d'art,** ~aĵo, ~verko, ~objekto
Artaxerxes, Artakserkso
artefact, artefakto†
Artemis, Artemisa
Artemisia, artemizio; Artemisia abrotanum, abrotano; Artemisia dracunculus, drakunkolo; Artemisia officina, verm~o
arteriosclerosis, arteriosklerozo
artery, (gen), arterio; **arterial,** ~a
artesian, arteza
arthralgia, artralgio
arthritis, artrito; **arthritic,** ~a; ~ulo
arthro–, (med, anat pfx), artro–
arthrology, artrologio
arthropod, artropodo
arthrosis, artrozo
Arthur, Arturuo; **Port Arthur,** Port-~o [now "Ljuŝun"]
artichoke, artiŝoko; **Jerusalem artichoke,** topinamburo, tubera helianto, terpiro
article, (gram; written piece; section of law etc.; item in dictionary etc.), artikolo; (item of commerce, goods), artiklo, varo; **article of faith,** kred~o
articulate, (pronounce), artikulacii [tr]; (clearly expressed), klar~a, klaresprima; (jointed), artikita; **articulation,**

~o; artik(ad)o; **inarticulate**, (w/o speech), ne~ita (e.g.: *inarticulate cry:* ne~ita krio); (unclear, incoherent), malklaresprima, malkohera, balbuta, malelokventa; (zool: w/o joints), senartika
artifact, artefakto†
artifice, artifiko
artificial, art(efarit)a
artillery, artilerio, kanonaro
artiodactyl, parhufulo
Artiodactyla, parhufuloj
artisan, artlaboristo, metilaboristo, metiisto
Artocarpus, panarbo; Artocarpus heterophyllus, Artocarpus integrifolia, jakvarbo, jakvujo
Artois, Artezo
arum, arumo; **water arum**, kalao
Arum, arumo
Arundo, Arundinaria, kano
Arvicola, arvikolo
Aryan, Arja; ~ano; **Aryanism**, ~anismo
aryl, arilo
arytenoid, aritenoido; ~a
as, (in same manner; like; for example), kiel (e.g.: *as one sows, so one reaps:* ~ oni semas, tiel oni falĉas; *a playwright, as Shakespeare:* dramverkisto, ~ Ŝekspiro); (to same degree), egale (e.g.: *it will be just as hot tomorrow:* estos egale varme morgaŭ); (in manner of), kvazaŭ (e.g.: *he treated me as a brother:* li traktis min kvazaŭ fraton); (in accordance w), laŭ (e.g.: *as you wish:* laŭ via plaĉo; *treat people as they deserve:* trakti homojn laŭ ilia merito [note that verb becomes n]); (because), ĉar (e.g.: *as it is raining, we won't go:* ĉar pluvas, ni ne iros); (to be), por (e.g.: *I took it as [to be] a joke:* mi prenis ĝin por ŝerco); (while), dum (e.g.: *we talked as we ate:* ni parolis dum ni manĝis); (when), kiam (e.g.: *as she reached the door, the phone rang:* kiam ŝi atingis la pordon, la telefono sonoris); **as ... as**, (to same extent, gen), tiel ... kiel (e.g.: *it is as hot today as it was yesterday:* estas tiel varme hodiaŭ ~ estis hieraŭ [also see specific subentries below; also subentries under middle word]; **as ... as possible**, ~ eble plej [abb: k.e.p.], plej eble (e.g.: *come as soon as possible:* venu ~ eble plej baldaŭ [k.e.p. baldaŭ], plejeble baldaŭ); **as far as**, (to extent that), (tiom) kiom; laŭ (e.g.: *as far as I know:* laŭ mia scio; tiom kiom mi scias; *I will continue as far as time allows:* mi daŭros tiom kiom la tempo permesos); (re distance), ĝis (e.g.: *travel as far as Philadelphia:* veturi ĝis Filadelfio); **as much as, as many as**, [see "much: as much as"]; **twice (... times) as much (many) as**, duoble (...oble) tiom (da) ... kiom; ... fojojn tiom (da) ... kiom (e.g.: *I have twice as many problems as I had yesterday:* mi havas duoble tiom da problemoj kiom mi havis hieraŭ; *this book has two and a half times as many pages as that one:* ĉi tiu libro havas du kaj duonan fojojn tiom da paĝoj kiom havas tiu); **as soon as**, tuj kiam (e.g.: *we will leave as soon as John arrives:* ni ekiros tuj kiam Johano alvenos); **as for**, (regarding), pri, ~ koncernas [tr]; **as if**, kvazaŭ –us (e.g.: *he dropped the book as if it were a glowing coal:* li faligis la libron kvazaŭ ĝi estus ardanta karbo); **as is**, (in present condition, gen), tiel ~ ĝi (vi, li, ŝi, etc.) estas; (re purchased item: that the buyer must accept w/o guarantee; etc.), telkela; telkele; **as it were**, (so to speak), kvazaŭ, kvazaŭa, por tiel diri (e.g.: *we swam home, as it were:* ni kvazaŭ naĝis hejmen [or] ni naĝis hejmen, por tiel diri; *arrows fell in a torrent, as it were:* sagoj falis en kvazaŭa torento); **as of**, (at time, date), je (e.g.: *we had sold ten of them as of eleven o'clock:* ni estis vendintaj dek el ili je la dekunua horo); (starting from), ekde (e.g.: *as of last month we are open on Saturday:* ekde la pasinta monato ni estas malfermitaj je sabato) **as though**, [see "as if"]; **as well**, (also, besides), ankaŭ, krome (e.g.: *he is intelligent, and a good athlete as well:* li estas inteligenta, kaj ankaŭ bona atleto [or] kaj bona atleto krome); **just as**, (in the same way), sam~, same ~

(e.g.: *he sings that just as his father did:* li kantas tion sam~ [or] same ~ ĝin kantis lia patro); (equally much), egale; **so as to,** por (e.g.: *she sent the memo so as to inform us:* ŝi sendis la memorandon por informi nin)
asabaracca, azaro
asafetida, asafetido
asak, aŝoko
asarum, azaraĵo
Asarum, azaro
asbestos, asbesto; **asbestosis,** ~ozo
ascarid, askarido
ascaris, Ascaris, askarido
ascend, (rise), ascendi [int], supreniri; (climb), supreniri [vt]; **ascent,** ~o; supreniro **ascendancy, ascendency, ascendance, ascendence,** (superiority), supereco; (domination), reg(ad)o, aŭtoritateco; **ascendant, ascendent,** (rising), ~anta; ~anto; (dominant), supera, reganta; (ancestor), praulo; (ast), ~anto; ~anta; **ascension,** (ast), ascensio; **right ascension,** rekta ascensio
ascertain, konstati [tr], certiĝi pri
ascetic,asketo; **asceticism,** ~ismo
ascidian, ascidio
ascites, ascito
Asclepius, (myth), Asklepio
ascomycete, askomiceto
Ascomycetes,askomicetoj, askofungoj
ascorbate, askorb/ato; **ascorbic,** ~a; **ascorbic acid,** ~a acido
ascot, askoto*
ascribe, imputi [tr], atribui [tr]
ascus, asko
–ase, (enzyme sfx), –azo
asepsis, asepsio; **aseptic,** ~a; **use asepsis (in, on),** ~i [tr]
ash, (from fire), cindro; (tree), frakseno; **ashtray,** ~ujo; **manna ash, flowering ash,** orno
ashamed, honta; **be ashamed,** ~i [int]; **you should be ashamed!,** ~u!
Ashkenaz, Ashkenazi, Aŝkenazo; ~a; **Ashkenazim,** ~oj; **Ashkenazic,** ~a
ashrafi, tomano
ashram, aŝramo*
Ashtaroth, Aŝtarot [cp "Ashtoreth"]
Ashtoreth, Aŝtar [cp "Ashtaroth"]
Ashur, Aŝur
Asia, Azio; **Asian, Asiatic,** ~a; **Asia**

Minor, Malgrandazio; **Southeast Asia,** Sudorient–~o; **Southwest Asia,** Sudokcident–~o
aside, (at, to one side), flanke(n) [often as pfx (e.g.: *put the matter aside:* ~enmeti la aferon)]; (thing done or said aside), ~aĵo; **aside from,** (except), escepte [–on], escepte de [–o], ekster [–o], krom [–o]
Asimina triloba, papaŭo
asinine, azen(ec)a
–asis, (med sfx), –ozo
ask, (a question), demandi [tr]; (request), peti [tr]; **ask for,** peti; **ask a question,** fari ~on, meti ~on [not "~i ~on"]
askance, straba; **look askance,** ~i [int]; **look askance at,** (fig: disapprove), malaprobi [tr], malfavori [tr]
askew, oblikva, malrekta
aslant, oblikva
asleep, dorm/anta; **be asleep,** ~i [int]; **sound asleep, fast asleep,** profunde ~anta
asok(a), aŝoko
asp, (zool), aspido
asparagus, Asparagus, asparago
Aspasia, Aspazia
aspect, (gen), aspekto
aspen, tremolo
aspergillosis, aspergilozo
aspergillum, aspergilo
aspergillus, Aspergillus, (bot), aspergilo
aspersion, (slander etc.), malaŭdo; **cast aspersions on,** ~i [tr], suspektigi
Asperula, asperulo; Asperula odorata, odora ~o
asphalt, asfalto; ~i [tr]
asphodel, asfodelo
Asphodelus, asfodelo
asphyxia, asfiksio; **asphyxiate,** ~i [tr]; **asphyxiation,** ~(iĝ)o [cp "suffocate"]
aspic, (snake), aspido; (food), aspiko
aspidistra, Aspidistra, aspidistro
Aspidius alburnus, alburno, blankfiŝo
Aspidosperma quebracho, blanka kebraĉo
aspirate, (phon), aspiraci/igi; (inhale), enspiri [tr]; (med: suck out), elsuĉi [tr]; **aspiration,** ~o; enspiro; elsuĉo [see also "aspire"]

aspiration, [see "aspirate" or "aspire", per sense]
aspirator, aspiratoro
aspire, aspiri [tr]; **aspirant**, ~anto; **aspiration**, ~(ad)o [see also "aspirate"]
aspirin, aspirino
Aspis cornutus, cerasto
Asplenium, asplenio; Asplenium nidus, nest~o; Asplenium rutamuraria, mororuto; Asplenium trichomanes, har~o, mura ~o
ass, (donkey), azeno; (colloq: buttocks), pugo; **half-assed**, fuŝ(it)a, faraĉita; **smart ass**, impertinentulo, senhontulo
assail, ataki [tr]; **assailant**, ~into; ~anto; ~onto
assassin, murd/into; ~isto; (hired), sikurio; **assassinate**, ~i [tr]; **assassination**, ~o
assault, (attack, gen), ataki [tr]; ~o; (upon chastity or virtue, lit or fig; e.g., by pollution against environment), malĉastigi; malĉastigo; **assault and battery**, ~o kaj bato
assay, (analyze, gen), analizi [tr], provi [vt]; ~o; (esp re precious metal), titri [tr]; titr(ad)o
assemble, (put together, gen), kun/igi; ~meti [tr]; (get together), ~iĝi; (meet), ~veni [int]; (parts of machine etc.), munti [tr]; muntiĝi; (connect), konekti [tr]; konektiĝi; **assemblage**, (act of), ~veniĝo; (group), ~venintaro; (art), ~metajo; **assembly**, ~igo, ~meto; ~iĝo; muntado; (thing ~ed), muntaĵo; (legal body etc.), asembleo; **assembly line**, ĉenstablo; **assembly(wo)man**, asemblean(in)o; **disassemble**, (take apart), malmunti [tr]
assent, konsenti [tr, int]; ~o
assert, (state), aserti [tr]; (insist on, demand), postuli [tr], trudi [tr]; **assertion**, ~o; (sin)trudo; **assertive**, ~ema; postulema, insistema
assess, (gen), taksi [tr]; **assessment**, ~o; **assessor**, ~isto
assiduous, asidua, diligenta
assign, (designate, appoint), asigni [tr]; (give work), taski [tr]; (ascribe, attribute), atribui [tr], alskribi [tr];

(transfer), cedi [tr], transdoni [tr]; **assignment, assignation**, ~o; taskado; atribuo; cedo, transdono; (task), tasko; (tryst), amrendevuo; **homework assignment**, hejmtasko
assignat, asignato
assimilate, (gen), asimili [tr]
Assisi, Asizo
assist, (help, gen), helpi [tr]; (through duty, officially), asisti [int] al; **assistance**, ~o; asist(ad)o; (welfare grant), mon~o; **assistant**, (helper), ~into; ~anto; ~onto; ~isto; asistinto (etc.); (to a judge), asesoro; (clerk etc.), komizo; (subordinate to any official), adjunkto [cp "adjutant"]
assize, (court session), asizo; **court of assizes**, ~a tribunalo
associate, (form formal ~ion), asocii [tr]; (group together; relate), ~iĝi, kunesti [int]; (member of ~ion), ~ito; ~ano; (any comrade, colleague), kamarado, kolego; (deputy), asista; adjunkta [see "assist: ~ant"]; **association**, (formal organization), ~o; (grouping together), ~igo; ~iĝo
assonance, asonanco; **assonant**, ~a; be **assonant**, ~iĝi; **make assonant**, ~i [tr]
assort, sortimenti [tr]; **assorted**, ~ita(j), diversa(j); **assortment**, ~o
assuage, (moderate), moderigi; (calm), kvietigi, trankviligi; (satisfy, satiate), satigi
assume, (suppose), supozi [tr]; (require, presume, presuppose, take as premise), premisi [vt]; (take on), alpreni [tr]; ŝarĝi sin per; **assumption**, ~o; premiso; alpreno; (rel), ĉieliro
assure, (make sure), certigi; (insure against loss), asekuri [tr]; **assurance**, ~o; askur(ad)o; **reassure**, trankviligi, rekuraĝigi, sendubigi; **self-assurance**, aplombo, memfido
Assyria, Asirio; **Assyrian**, ~a; ~ano
Astacus, astako, kankro
Astarte, Astarta
astatic, astata
astatine, astateno
aster, (bot), astero; **China aster**, kalistefo
Aster, astero

Asterias, asterio
asterisk, asterisko
astern, pobe(n)
asteroid, asteroido
Asteroidea, asteriedoj
asthenia, astenio
asthma, astmo; **asthmatic**, ~a; ~ulo
astigmatic, astigmata;   **astigmatism**,
~eco; **anastigmatic**, anastigmata
Astilbe, astilbo
astir, moviĝanta
astonish, mireg/igi, mirfrapi [vt]; **aston-
ishing**, ~iga; **astonishment**, ~o; be
astonished, ~i [int]
astound, konsterni [tr], miregigi; **as-
tounding**, ~a, miregiga
astrachan, astrakano
astragalus, (bone), astragalo, talo
Astragalus, (bot), astragalo
astrakhan, astrakano
Astrakhan, Astrañano
astral, (ast, phil, rel), astra
astray, devojiĝ/inta; **go astray**, ~i, erar-
vagi [int]; **lead astray**, delogi [tr]
astride, rajde sur
astringent, (constricting),   adstringa;
~enzo; (re flavor), acerba
astro–, (sci pfx), astro– (e.g.: *astrophysics:* ~fiziko)
astrodome, astrokupolo
astrogate, kosmonavigi [int]; **astroga-
tion**, ~ado; **astrogator**, ~isto
astrolabe, astrolabo
astrology, astrolog/io;   **astrological**,
~ia; **astrologer**, ~o
astronaut, kosmonaŭto,   astronaŭto
[note: "astronaŭto" implies traveler to
oth bodies in space; "kosmonaŭto"
implies traveler through space and is
therefore the preferable general term]
astronautics, astronaŭtiko; **astronauti-
cal**, ~a; **bioastronautics**, bio~o
astronomy, astronom/io;   **astronomi-
cal**, ~ia; **astronomer**, ~o; **radio astronomy**, radio~io
Asturias, Asturio; **Asturian**, ~a; ~ano
astute, sagaca
Asunción, Asunciono
asunder, dise(n), dis– [pfx]
asylum, azilo
asymptote, asimptoto; **asymptotic**, ~a
asyndeton, asindeto

asystole, missistolo
asystolia, asistolio
at, (near a thing or place; re simultaneous events), ĉe (e.g.: *sit at the table:*
sidi ~ la tablo; *I awoke at the sound of
her footsteps:* mi vekiĝis ~ la sono de
ŝiaj paŝoj); [note: re person's home
etc., omit "home" etc. (e.g.: *we met at
Mr. Smith's house:* ni kunvenis ~ s–ro
Smith); however, see "*at* home" be-
low]; (re clock time), je (e.g.: *at six
o'clock:* je la sesa horo); (in), en (e.g.:
I did it at school: mi faris ĝin en la
lernejo); (at rate of, "@"), po (e.g.: *5
books at $7 [each]:* 5 libroj po $7);
(according to), laŭ (e.g.: *fire at will:*
pafu laŭ via plaĉo); (during), dum
(e.g.: *at night:* dum la nokto, dumnokte); **at home**, hejme; **keep at it**,
resti ~ la tasko
Atalanta, Atalanta
ataman, hetmano
ataractic, ataraksienzo
ataraxia, ataraksio; **ataraxic**, ~enzo
atavism, atavismo; **atavistic**, ~a
ataxia, ataksio
–ate, (sfx: cause to become; produce),
–igi (e.g.: *renovate:* renovigi); (become), –iĝi (e.g.: *evaporate:* vapor-
iĝi); (infuse, treat w), –izi [tr] (e.g.:
oxygenate: oksigenizi); (characteristic
of), –eca (e.g.: *collegiate:* universitat-
eca); (having), –hava (e.g.: *caudate:*
vosthava); (rank), –eco (e.g.: *directorate:* direktoreco); (chem: salt), –ato
Ateles, atelo
atelier, ateliero
atheism, ateismo; **atheistic**, ~a; **athe-
ist**, ateisto
Athena, Athene, (myth), Atena
Athanasius, Atanazio; **Athanasian**, ~a
Athene noctua, (zool), noktuo
atheneum, ateneo
Athens, Ateno; **Athenian**, ~a; ~ano
Atheroma, ateromo
atherosclerosis, aterosklerozo
athlete, atleto; **athletic**, ~a; ~ika, ~is-
ma; **athletics**, ~iko, ~ismo
athrepsia, atrepsio
athwart, transverse(n) de
–ation, (sfx: act of, after verb), –o (e.g.:
after your recommendation: post via

rekomendo); (causing to be, after adj, n, etc.), –igo (e.g.: *renovation:* renovigo); (concrete example of), –aĵo (e.g.: *compilation:* kompilaĵo)

–ative, (sfx: serving to), –a (e.g.: *informative:* informa); (tending to), –ema (e.g.: *talkative:* parolema, babilema)

Atlanta, Atlanto*

atlantes, atlantoj

Atlantic, Atlantiko; ~a; **transatlantic,** transatlantika

Atlantis, Atlantido; **Atlantean,** ~a; ~ano

atlas, (maps), atlaso; (arch [plur: "atlantes"]; anat), atlanto†

Atlas, (myth; geog), Atlaso

atman, (rel: individual soul), atmo

Atman, (rel: cosmic soul), atmano

atmosphere, (gen), atmosfero; (milieu), etoso, ~o; **atmospheric,** ~a

atoll, atolo

atom, atomo; **atomic,** ~a; **atomic energy,** ~energio; **atomic number,** ~numero; **atomic mass, atomic weight,** ~maso; **atomism,** ~ismo; **atomist,** ~isma; ~isto; **atomize,** (reduce to ~s), ~igi; (to small pieces), diserigi; (spray), ŝprucetigi; **atomizer,** ŝprucflakolo; **monatomic,** unu~a; **diatomic,** du~a; **triatomic,** tri~a; **subatomic,** sub~a; **split the atom,** dis~i [tr]

atonal, atonala

atone, (gen), kompensi [tr]; (rel: for sin etc.), pekliberiĝi

atony, atonio; **atonic,** ~a

atop, (prep: on top of), supre de, sur

–ator, [see "–er"]

atrabilious, atrabila; **atrabiliousness,** ~o

atresia, atrezio

Atreus, Atreo

Atriplex, atriplo; Atriplex hortensis, ĝarden~o

atrium, (gen), atrio

atrocious, abomena; terura; kruelega; besteca; **atrocity,** ~aĵo; ~eco; teruro; teruraĵo

Atropa belladona, beladono

atrophy, atrofio; ~i [tr]; ~iĝi

atropine, atropino

atropism, atropismo

Atropos, Atropa

attach, (fasten, gen), fiksi [tr]; al~i [tr]; (al)~iĝi; (tie to, lit or through emotion etc.), alligi [tr]; (ascribe), atribui [tr]; (connect), konekti [tr]; (legally seize property, as to pay debt), tradi [tr]

attaché ataŝeo; **attaché case,** ~a teko

attack, (strike against, criticize, etc., gen), ataki [tr]; ~o; (med), ikto

attain, atingi [tr]; **attainment,** ~o

attar, floroleo; **attar of roses,** rozoleo

attempt, (try, gen), peni [tr], provi [vt]; (stronger), klopodi [tr]; ~o, provo; klopodo; (attack on one's life), atenci [tr]; atenco

attend, (be present), ĉeesti [tr]; (serve), servi [tr]; (look after, care for), prizorgi [tr]; (be w), akompani [tr]; **attendance,** ~(ad)o; serv(ad)o; prizorg(ad)o; akompan(ad)o; (total of those ~ing), ~antaro; **attendant,** servisto; akompan(ant)a; **attend to,** priatenti [tr]

attention, (attentiveness), atento; (mil command), rektiĝ'!; **pay attention (to),** ~i [tr]; **call (one's) attention to,** ~igi (iun) pri, al; **undivided attention,** nedistrita ~o; **inattention,** distriĝo; **at attention,** (mil), rekta, en rekteco; rekte; **come to attention,** (mil), rektiĝi

attentive, atenta; **be attentive (to),** ~i [tr]; **inattentive,** mal~(em)a, distriĝema

attenuat/e, atenui [tr]; ~iĝi; **attenuator,** ~atoro

attest, atesti [tr]; (document), ~ilo

attic, (below roof, gen), subtegmento; (mansard), mansardo; (arch: above façade; anat), atiko

Attic, (of Athens), Atika

Attica, Atiko

Attila, Atilo

attire, (clothes, gen), vesti [tr]; ~oj; (grooming), tualeto

attitude, (emotion), sinteno; (physical position of plane etc.), pozicio; (pose), pozo

attorney, (lawyer), advokato; **power of attorney,** prokuro; **attorney-in-fact,** prokuranto; prokuristo; **attorney general,** prokuroro; **district attorney,** (ĉef)prosekutisto

attract, (emotionally etc.), allogi [tr]; (w phys force, as gravity etc.), altiri [tr]; **attraction**, ~o; ~aĵo; altiro, altirforto; (of show, movie, etc.), atrakcio†; **attractive**, ~a; altira; **attractiveness**, ~eco, ~ivo
attribute, (ascribe), atribui [tr]; ~(aĵ)o; (charge, impute), imputi [tr]; (n: characteristic quality; symbolic essence), atributo; (quality, gen), eco
attrition, (wearing away, lit or fig), forfrot/iĝo, forŝlifiĝo; (diminution), malkreskado; (rel), atricio; **war of attrition**, ~–milito
attune, (gen), agordi [tr]; **attunement**, ~o
au, [see "à la"; also see separate entries below]
aubade, aŭbado
aubergine, (bot), melongeno
aubr(i)etia, aŭbrietio
Aubrietia, aŭbrietio
auburn, ruĝbruna; ~o; (~–colored horse, mule, etc.), alzano†
Auckland, Aŭklando; **Auckland Islands**, Insuloj ~aj
au contraire, male
auction, aŭkcio; ~i [tr]; **auctioneer**, ~into; ~anto; ~onto; ~isto; **at auction**, ~e
aucuba, Aucuba, aŭkubo
audacious, aŭdaca; **audacity**, ~o
audible, aŭdebla
audience, (persons assembled to hear), aŭdantaro, ĉeestantaro; (hearing before person of high rank), aŭdienco
audio, (sound), son(signal)o [cp "audio–"]
audio–, (pfx: re hearing), aŭd(o)– (e.g.: *audio-visual:* ~vida) [cp "audio"]
audiogram, aŭdogramo
audiology, aŭdolog/io; **audiologist**, ~o
audiometer, aŭdometro; **audiometry**, ~io
audiophile, aŭdamanto
audio-visual, aŭdvida
audit, (kont)revizori [tr]; **auditor**, ~o; (judicial official in some countries), aŭditoro
audition, (trial of actor, musician, etc.), prov–aŭdo; ~i [tr]
auditorium, aŭditorio

auditory, aŭda
Augeas, Aŭgio; **Augean**, ~a
auger, borilo
augite, aŭgito
augment, (increase, gen), pli/igi; ~iĝi; ~grandigi; ~grandiĝi; (gram), aŭmento; aŭmentigi; **augmented interval (chord)**, (mus), diesigita intervalo (akordo)
au gratin, gratenita; ~e; (with cheese), fromaĝigita; fromaĝigite
augur, aŭguri [tr]; **augury**, (act of), ~ado; (omen), ~o; **augur well (ill)**, (be good, bad omen), esti (mal)bona ~o
august, eminenta, majesta
August, (month), aŭgusto; (man's name), A~o
Augusta, (woman's name), Aŭgusta; (city), ~o
Augustine, Aŭgusteno; **Augustinian**, ~a; **Augustinism**, ~ismo
Augustus, Aŭgusto
au jus, kun suko
auk, aŭko
aunt, onklino; **great-aunt**, pra~o
aura, (radiance around person etc.; med: sign of impending attack), aŭro†; (impression, quality), impreso
aural, (re aura), aŭreola; aŭra [see "aura"]; (auditory), aŭda
aurate, orato
Aurelia, (woman's name), Aŭrelia
Aurelia, (zool), aŭrelio, vitromeduzo
Aurelian, Aŭreliano
Aurelius, Aŭrelio
aureole, aŭreolo [cp "aureolus"]
aureolus, areolo [cp "aureole"]
auric, (re gold, gen), ora; (w valence 3), ~ika; **auric acid**, ~ata acido
auricle, aŭriklo
auricula, (bot: *Primula auricula*), aŭrikulo; (anat: auricle), aŭriklo
Auricularia, aŭrikulario, orelfungo
Auriculus, aŭrikulo
Auriga, (ast), Koĉero
aurochs, (*Bos bonasus*), uro
aurora, aŭroro; **aurora borealis**, Arkta ~o; **aurora australis**, Antarkta ~o
Aurora, (myth; woman's name), Aŭrora
aurous, oroza
auscultate, aŭskulti [tr]; **auscultation**,

~(ad)o

auspice, (sponsorship), aŭspicio, egido; (omen), aŭguro; **under the auspices of**, ~ata de; ~ate de

auspicious, bonaŭgura, favora

Aussie, (colloq), Aŭstralia; ~ano

austere, aŭstera; **austerity**, ~eco

austral, (southern), aŭstrala; (Argentine $), ~o

Australasia, Aŭstralazio

Australia, Aŭstralio; **Australian**, ~a; ~ano; **South Australia**, Sud-~o; **Western Australia**, Okcident-~o; **Australian Capital Territory**, ~a ĉefurba Teritorio

Australoid, Aŭstraloida; ~ulo

Austria, Aŭstrio; **Austrian**, ~a; ~ano; **Austro-Hungary**, ~o-Hungario

Austronesia, Aŭstronezio

australopithecine, aŭstralopitekeno Australopithecus, aŭstralopiteko†; Australopithecinae, ~enoj

autarchy, aŭtarcio

authentic, aŭtentika; **authenticate**, ~igi; **authenticity**, ~eco

author, (of a specific work, gen), aŭtoro; (professional writer; write professionally), verkisto; verki [tr], ~i [tr]; **authorship**, ~eco

authoritarian, aŭtoritatisma, aŭtokrati(ec)a; aŭtokratulo; aŭtokratisto; **authoritarianism**, aŭtokrato

authority, (power, condition), aŭtoritato; (person), ~ulo; (degree of power to judge; person having such power), instanco; **authoritative**, ~a

authorize, (permit, gen), rajtigi, permesi [tr]; (by official authority), licenci [tr]; (approve), aprobi [tr]; (commission), komisii [tr]; **authorization**, ~o, permeso; licenco; aprobo; komisio

autism, aŭtismo; **autistic**, ~a

auto, (automobile), aŭto [cp "automobile"]

auto–, (pfx), aŭto–, mem–

autocatalysis, memkatalizo

autochthon, aŭtoktono; **autochthonous**, ~a

autoclave, aŭtoklavo; ~i [tr]

autocracy, aŭtokrat/io; **autocrat**, ~o

auto-da-fé aŭtodafeo

audodidact, aŭtodidakto, memlernan-

to; **audodidactic**, ~a, memlerna

autogenous, aŭtogena

autogiro, aŭtogiro

autograph, aŭtografo; ~i [tr]

autography, (type of lithography), aŭtografio

autogyro, aŭtogiro

autoharp, aŭtoharpo*

autolysis, aŭtolizo

automat, aŭtomatejo

automate, aŭtomacii [tr]; **automation**, ~o

automatic, aŭtomata

automatism, (automatic condition), aŭtomat/eco; (phil), ~ismo; (automatic action, thing, etc.), ~aĵo

automaton, aŭtomato

automobile, aŭtomobilo [cp "auto"]

autonomy, (self-governing), aŭtonomo; (bio etc.; evolving and functioning independently), aŭtonomio, memstareco; **autonomic**, aŭtonomia, memstara; **autonomous**, ~a; aŭtonomia, memstara

autopsy, nekropsio; ~i [tr]

autosome, aŭtosomo†

autotrophic, aŭtotrofa

autumn, aŭtuno; **autumnal**, ~a

Auvergne, Aŭvernjo

aux, [see "à la"]

auxiliary, (helping), helpa; ~anto; ~antaro; (extra, reserve), rezerva; rezervaĵo

auxin, aŭksino

auxochrome, aŭksokromo; **auxochromic**, ~a

avail, helpi [tr], utili [int] (al) (e.g.: *that will avail you nothing:* tio neniel ~os vin [or] utilos al vi); **avail oneself of**, utiligi, elprofiti [tr]; **to no avail**, vane, senefike

available, dispon/ebla, havebla; **be available**, ~iĝi; **have available**, ~i [tr, int] (pri); **make available**, ~igi

aval, avalo

avalanche, lavango; ~i [int]

avant-garde, avangardo; ~a

avarice, avaro; **avaricious**, ~a

avatar, avataro

Avena, aveno

avenge, venĝi [tr]

avens, geumo

Aventine, Aventino; ~a
aventurine, aventurino
avenue, avenuo
aver, aserti [tr]
average, (math), averaĝo, mezvaloro, meznombro; ~a; ~i [int]; ~igi; (gen), mezo; meza; (loss to ship or cargo), averio; (suffer such loss), averii [int]; **on the average,** ~e, meze, meznombre, rondcifere
Avernus, Averno, Averno†
Averr(h)oës, Averoeso
averse, (disinclined), malinklina, antipatia; (bot), forklinita; **aversion,** ~o, antipatio; forkliniĝo
avert, (avoid), eviti [tr]; (deflect), forturni [tr]
Aves, birdoj
Avesta, Avesto
aviary, birdejo
aviation, aviado; **aviator,** ~isto
Avicenna, Aviceno
Avicularia, avikulario, birdaraneo
aviculture, birdobredado
avid, avida
Avignon, Avinjono
aviso, (boat), aviso
avocado, (fruit), avokado; (tree), ~arbo
avocation, ŝatokupo, hobio
avocet, avoceto
avoid, eviti [tr]
avow, (admit), konfesi [tr]; (acknowledge), agnoski [tr]; **avowed,** ~inta; **disavow,** mal~i [tr]; malagnoski [tr]; (disclaim, repudiate), malakcepti [tr], malaprobi [tr], malapogi [tr]
avuncular, onkl(ec)a
await, atendi [tr]
awake, veki [tr]; ~iĝi; (not asleep), maldorma; **awaken,** ~i; ~iĝi; **awakening,** ~iĝo; (disillusionment), seniluziiĝo
award, (grant, gen), aljuĝi [tr] (ion al iu); ~o; (prize), premii [tr] (ion al iu); premio
aware, konscia; **be aware of,** ~i [tr]; **become aware of,** ek~i [tr], ~iĝi pri; **awareness,** ~o; **make (one) aware (of something),** ~igi (iun pri io); **take one unawares,** surprizi iun
awash, (at water level), akvonivela; (floating), flosanta; (flooded), inundita

away, for [adv], for– [pfx] (e.g.: *put it away:* meti ĝin ~ [or] ~meti ĝin; *I will be away:* mi estos ~ [or] mi ~estos); (at distance of), for, je distanco de (e.g.: *the bomb fell 100 meters away from us:* la bombo falis 100 metrojn ~ [or] je distanco de 100 metroj de ni); (out, in all directions), dis– [pfx] (e.g.: *chase away birds:* dispeli birdojn); **do away with,** (get rid of), ~igi; (kill), mortigi
awe, miro, respektego, admirego; **feel awe (about),** ~i [int] (pri); **awesome,** **awe-inspiring,** ~iga; impona; **overawe,** ~egigi, imponegi [tr]
awful, (terrible), terura; (awesome), impona, miriga; (extremely), treege
awhile, iom, ~ da tempo
awkward, (clumsy), malgracia, mallerta; (inconvenient), maloportuna, embarasa; (difficult, delicate, re situation etc.), delikata
awl, aleno
awn, aristo
awning, (of translucent material), markezo; (canvas etc.), tol~o (etc.)
AWOL, (abb of "absent without leave"), dizert/inta, for sen permeso [no abb in Esperanto]; **go AWOL,** ~i [int], foriri sen permeso
awry, (askew), oblikva, malrekta; (amiss), misa; **go awry,** misiri [int], misiĝi, iri mise [cp "amiss"]
ax(e), (gen), hakilo; (w broad blade, short handle), toporo; **battle-ax,** milit~o [cp "halberd"]; **broadax,** toporo; **pickax,** pioĉo; **poleax,** stango~o; **ax to grind,** privata intereso
axial, aksa; **biaxial,** du~a; **coaxial,** sam~a [not "koaksa"]
axil, akselo
axilla, (gen), akselo
axiom, aksiomo; **axiomatic,** ~a
axis, (line, center of rotation, etc., gen), akso; (anat: vertebra), aksoido†; **semimajor axis,** (geom, ast), duonmaĵora ~o; **semiminor axis,** duonminora ~o
axle, akso
axolotl, aksolotlo
axon, aksono
axseed, koronilo

ayapana, ajapano
aye, (yes), jes; (always), ĉiam
Aythya,merganaso; Aythya fuligula,
 fuligulo
azalea, Azalea, azaleo
azarole, azarolo
Azerbaijan, Azerbajĝano; **Azerbaija-**
 ni, ~a; ~ano
azimuth, azimuto
azo–, (chem pfx), azo–
azoic, azoiko; ~a
Azores, Acoroj
Azov, Azovo; **Sea of Azov,** Maro ~a
azoxy–, (chem pfx), azoksi–
Aztec, Azteko; ~a
Azukia angularis, azukio
azulejo, azuleño
azure, lazuro; ~a [not "aĵura"]
azurite, lazurito
azygous, malpara

B

baa, (sheep noise), be!, be-e-e!; (goat),
mek-mek-mek!; bei [int]; meki [int]
Baal, Baalo
baaskaap, blankulregado
baba au rhum, babao
babble, (talk), babili [int]; ~(ad)o; (onom), tra-ra-ra; (re stream), murmuri
[int]; murmur(ad)o
babe, bebo
Babel, Babelo
babirusa, Babirusa, (zool), babiruso
baboon, paviano; **sacred baboon, ha-
madryas baboon,** hamadriado
babouche, babuŝo
baby, bebo; **babysit,** varti [tr], ~varti
[int], infanvarti [int]; **babysitter,** in-
fanvartanto; infanvartisto; **bush baby,**
(zool), galago
Babylon, Babilono; **Babylonia,** ~io;
Babylonian, ~ia; ~iano
baccalaureate, bakalaŭro; ~a
baccara(t), bakarato
bacchanal, bakña; (person), ~an(in)o;
(party etc.), ~ofesto
bacchanalia, bakñanalio
bacchant, bakñanto; **bacchante,** ~ino
Bacchus, Bakño
bachelor, (unmarried man), fraŭlo;
(university degree), bakalaŭro; (graduate), bakalaŭrulo, diplomito (kun
bakalaŭro); **bachelor woman,** ~ino
Bacillaria diatomea, diatomeo
bacillus, (gen), bacilo; **comma bacillus,**
komoforma ~o; **Koch's bacillus,** ~o
de Koch
Bacillus, bacilo; Bacillus coli communis, kojlo~o, kolibacilo; Bacillus
malleus, maleo
back, (anat: rear side of person or animal; corresponding part of garment
etc.), dorso; ~a; ~e(n); (rear of building or any object; opp front), malantaŭo; malantaŭa; malantaŭe(n);
(spine), spino; spina (e.g.: *break one's
back:* rompi la spinon; *back problem:*
spina problemo); (of chair etc.),
apogilo; (roof of mine), tegmento;
(football etc.: in rear position), ariera;

arierulo; (after verb: returning), re-
[pfx], returne (e.g.: *go back home:* reiri hejmen; *send a present back:* resendi donacon; *cut the weeds back:*
retranĉi la trudherbojn); (adv: at or toward former place or time), ree(n)
(e.g.: *back to the salt mine:* reen al la
salminejo); (rear, backward), retro-
[pfx] (e.g.: *step back:* retropaŝi; *lean
one's head back:* retroklini la kapon);
(support), apogi [tr], subteni [tr], sub-
stari [tr]; (bet on), priveti [tr]; (provide a backing, covering), tegi [tr];
(back up, go backward), retroiri [int];
(having returned), reveninta; **be back,**
(returned), reveni [int] (e.g.: *are you
back already?:* ĉu vi jam revenis?);
backing, (support), apogo, subteno;
(covering layer), tegaĵo; **backache,**
~doloro; **back and forth,** tien kaj re-
en; **backbencher,** (Br), senpostena
parlamentano; **backbend,** retroflekso;
backbite, (slander), kalumnii [tr]; kalumnio; **backboard,** ~tabulo; **backbone,** (lit or fig), spino; **backdate,**
antaŭdatigi; **back down, back off,**
(withdraw), retiri sin, retiriĝi; **back-
door,** (secret, underhanded), postkulisa; **backdrop,** (theat), fonkuliso;
(background, gen), fono; **backfield,**
(football etc.), ariero; **backfire,** (re
motor), knali [int]; knalo; (re gun,
plan, etc.), retropafi [int]; retropafo;
backlash, (gen), retrofrapi [int]; ret-
rofrapo; **backlog,** (accumulation of
work etc.), retroakumuli [tr]; retroa-
kumuliĝi; retroakumulaĵo, retrolabo-
ro, farotaĵoj; (reserve), rezervi [tr];
rezervaĵo; **back out (of),** (withdraw),
eksigi sin, eksiĝi, retiri sin, retiriĝi;
(not fulfill promise etc.), ne plenumi
[tr]; **backside,** (gen), postaĵo; **backslide,** (morally etc.), refali [int];
backspace, (cmptr, typewriter, etc.),
retroigi; retroiri [int]; (cmptr: delete
~wards), retroviŝi [tr]; **backspin,**
retrorotacii [int]; retrorotaciigi; ret-
rorotacio; **backstage,** postkulisa;

backstitch, retrostebi [tr]; retrostebo; **backstop**, postekrano; **backstroke**, (swimming), ~naĝado; **back-to-back**, (Am: consecutive), sinsekva(j); sinsekve; **backtrack**, retroiĝi, retiri sin, retiriĝi; **back up**, (go backward), retroiri [int]; (support), apogi [tr], subteni [tr]; (accumulate due to stoppage, as traffic etc.), (ŝtop)akumuli [tr]; (ŝtop)akumuliĝi; [cp "backup"]; **backup**, (reserve, alternate), rezerva; rezervo; rezervulo; (piling up, as traffic etc.), (retro)akumuliĝo, ŝtop-akumuliĝo; **backward(s)**, (to rear), retroa, retroira; retro(ir)en, malantaŭen, retro– [pfx] (e.g.: *a backward step:* retro(ir)a paŝo, retropaŝo); (reverse), inversa; (behind the times), neprogresinta; neprogresema; eksmoda; (turned around; wrong), retroturnita (e.g.: *backward thinking:* retroturnita pensado); **backwardation**, ($), diporto; **backwash**, retrofrapo; **back water**, (row backward), retroremi [tr]; (w boat propeller), retropeli [tr]; **backwater**, (behind dam etc.), retroakvo; eddy in stream etc.), akvokirleto; (stagnant place, re culture, stream, etc.), stagnejo; **backwoods**, malproksimejo; arbar(ec)a; **bareback**, sensela; sensele; **behind one's back**, malantaŭ ies ~o; **be (flat) on one's back**, kuŝi (senhelpe) sur la ~o; **fullback**, (football etc.), plenarierulo; **halfback**, halfo; **hatchback**, [see under "hatch"]; **quarterback**, kvaronarierulo; **get one's back up**, kolerigi iun; koleriĝi; **go back on**, perfidi [tr]; **in back**, malantaŭe; **(in) back of**, malantaŭ; **turn one's back on**, forturni sin de
backgammon, triktrako
backsheesh, bakŝiŝo
bacon, lardo; **chipped bacon**, grivoj [note plur]; **bacon-rind**, ~haŭto; **bring home the bacon**, gajni vivrimedon
bacterium, bakterio; **bacteria**, ~oj; **bacterial**, ~a; **bactericide**, ~cido; **bacteriology**, ~ologio; **bacteriologist**, ~ologo; **antibacterial**, kontraŭ~a

Bacterium, bakterio
Bactria, (ancient Balkh), Baktro; (Persian satrapy), ~io
bad, (not good, gen), malbona; ~e; ~o; ~aĵo; (poet), mava; (rotten), putra; (not valid), falsa (e.g.: *bad check:* falsa ĉeko); (severe), severa; (serious), grava; (naughty), ~konduta, miskonduta; (not tasty), ~gusta; **be bad**, (behavior), ~konduti [int], miskonduti [int], konduti [int] ~e; **go from bad to worse**, de ~o pli~iĝi
Baden, (district), Baden/io, ~lando; **Baden-Baden**, (city), ~o
badge, insigno
badger, (zool), melo; (hassle, gen), molesti [tr]; (put-down), ĉikani [tr]; (hassle w requests), tropetadi [tr]
badian, ilicia frukto
badinage, ŝercbabilado
badminton, volanludo
Baelt, (strait), Belto
Baffin, Bafina; **Baffin Bay**, Golfo ~a; **Baffin Island**, Insulo ~a
baffle, (confuse), konfuzi [tr]; (hinder), malhelpi [tr]; (deflector), obstaklo
bag, (sack etc.), sako; en~igi; (luggage), valizo; (catch), kapti [tr]; kaptaĵo; (frumpy woman), plumpulino; **baggy**, (re clothing etc.), vasta, loza; **airbag**, (as in car), aer~o; **handbag**, (purse), retikulo, monujo; (small valise), valizeto; **mailbag**, poŝt~o; **punching bag**, boksopilko; **ratbag**, (Aus), strangulo, frenezeta entuziasmulo; **saddlebag**, sel~o; **shopping bag**, (Am), **carrier bag**, (Br), aĉet~o; **sleeping bag**, dorm~o, lit~o; **be in the bag**, esti certaĵo; **leave (be left) holding the bag**, las(iĝ)i kun la sekvoj
bagatelle, (trifle), bagatelo; (game), Japanbilardo
Bagdad, Bagdado
bagel, kringo
baggage, (trunks, bags, etc.), bagaĝot, pakaĵo [cp "package"]
Baghdad, Bagdado
bagpipe, sakŝalmo
bah, (interj), ba!
Bahai, Bahaa*; ~ano; **Bahaism**, ~ismo
Bahamas, Bahamoj; **Bahamian**, ~a; ~ano

Bahía, Bahio
Bahrain, Bahrein (Islands), Barejno
Baikal, Bajkalo
bail, ($), kaŭcio; ~i [tr]; (water etc.), ĉerpi [tr]; ĉerpilo; (cricket), bastoneto; bail out, (boat), priĉerpi [tr]; (from jail or oth difficult situation), ~e liberigi, liberigi per ~o; (from plane), paraŝuti [int]; (fig: get out), elsalti [int]
bailiff, (Am: deputy sheriff), subŝerifo; (officer of court etc.), pedelo; (overseer of estate etc.), intendanto, ekonomo; (Br: head of district), distriktestro
bailiwick, (district), distrikto; (area of activity etc.), kampo, regiono (de agado, intereso, etc.)
Bairam, Bajramo
bairn, infano
bait, (lure, gen), logi [tr]; ~ilo; (live, as for fishing), ~aĵo; (goad, harass), ĉikani [tr]; bait a trap, ~ilizi kaptilon
baize, felto
Baja California, Basa Kalifornio
bake, baki [tr]; ~iĝi; baker, ~isto; bakery, ~ejo; half-baked, (lit or fig), duonmatura, duon~ita, nov~ita
bakelite, bakelito
baksheesh, bakŝiŝo
Balaam, (Bib), Bileam
balaclava, balaklavo*
Balaena, baleno; Balaenidae, ~edoj
Balaenoptera, balenoptero; Balaenopteridae, ~edoj
balalaika, balalajko
balance, (equilibrium), ekvilibro; ~i [int]; ~igi; (scales), pesilo; (remainder), restaĵo, cetero; ($), saldo; saldi [tr]; (stabilize), stabiligi; stabiliĝi; (an equation), bilanci [tr]; balance sheet, bilanco; balance wheel, balanciero; balance brought forward, (balance at bottom of page and reentered at top of next), transporto; balance of payments, ~o de pagoj; balance of power, ~o de potenco; balance of trade, ~o de komerco; counterbalance, kontraŭpezi [tr]; kontraŭpezo; hang in the balance, dependi de tio, resti dependa de tio
balantidium, balantidio; balantidiasis, ~ozo
Balantidium coli, balantidio

Balanus, balano, marglano
balaphone, balafono†
balata, (gum), balato; (tree), ~arbo
Balaton, Balatono
balcony, balkono
bald, kalva; baldness, ~eco, alopecio
baldachin, baldaquin, baldakeno
Bald(er), Balduro
balderdash, sensencaĵo, galimatio
baldric, balteo
Baldwin, Baldueno
bale, garbo; ~igi; baler, ~igatoro
Balearic (Islands), Balearoj
baleen, barto [not "baleno"]
baleful, sinistra; malbonaŭgura, misaŭgura
Bali, Balio†
balk, (hesitate, stop), heziti [int], kalcitri [int], (fig), baŭmi [int], panei [int]; (thwart), obstrukci [tr], malsukcesigi; (between furrows), intersulko; (beam), trab(eg)o
Balkan, Balkana; Balkan States, ~io; Balkan Mountains, ~oj
balkanize, balkanigi
Balkh, Balĥo
Balkhash, Balkaŝo
ball, (round or oval etc. object used in any game), pilko; (as part of name of specific game), ~ado (e.g.: basketball: korbo~ado) [note: some game names end w "~balo"; see separate entries]; (any oth round or approximately round object), bulo (e.g.: snowball: neĝbulo; ball of wax: bulo de vakso); (throw of ball in game), ~oĵeto; (baseball: wide pitch), misĵeto; (globe), globo; (dance), balo; (of dust etc.), floko; (cover plant roots w dirt and burlap before planting), ĵosi [tr]; ĵosaĵo; (colloq: testicle), kojono; ball up, (form balls), buligi; buliĝi; (mess up), fuŝi [tr]; ball of string, fadenbulo; ball and chain, globo kaj kateno; ball and socket, ball-and-socket joint, globartiko; ball bearing, globlagro; ballroom, balejo; cannon ball, kuglego; behind the 8–ball, en dilemo, en embaraso, en malfacilaĵo [see § 11]; keep the ball rolling, ne halti [int], resti aktiva, (fig), ne panei [int]; be on the ball, esti (resti) vigla

ballad, ballade, balado
ballast, balasto; ~i [tr]
ballerina, baletistino
ballet, baleto
ballista, balisto
ballistic, balistika; **ballistics,** ~o; **anti-
ballistic,** kontraŭ~a
balloon, (gen), balono [cp "dirigible",
"airship"]
ballot, (vote), baloti [int]; (paper, object, etc., used for ballot), ~ilo; (right
to vote), ~rajto; **ballot-box,** ~ilujo
Ballota, baloteo
ballyhoo, bruo, pomp(aĉ)o, ekscit(aĉ)o
balm, (resin, ointment; also fig), balzamo; **balm of Gilead,** (tree), ~arbo;
(lemon) balm, (bot: *Melissa*), meliso;
bee balm, fragrant balm, monardo
balmy, (gen), balzama
baloney, (bologna), bolonjo*; (nonsense), sensencaĵo, galimatio
balsa, (tree), balzo; (wood), ~a ligno
balsam, (resin, oil, etc.), balzamo; (tree:
Commiphora, Balsamodendron, or
Myroxylon), ~arbo; (shrub: *Impatiens*), balzamio; **balsam of Peru,** pe-
ru~o; **balsam of Tolu,** tolu~o
Balsamina, balzamino
Balsamodendron, balzamarbo
balsamweed, gnafalio
Balthazar, (man's name), Baltazaro [cp
"Belshazzar"]
Baltic, Balto; ~a; **Baltic Sea,** Maro ~a;
Baltic States, Ŝtatoj ~aj
Baltimore, Baltimoro
baluster, balustro
balustrade, balustrado
bamboo, bambuo; ~a
bamboozle, tromp(log)i [tr]; ~o
Bambusa, bambuso
ban, (prohibit), malpermesi [tr]; ~o;
(exile, exclude), ekzili [tr], ekskludi
[tr]; ekzilo, ekskludo; (rel condemnation), interdikto; (Hungarian etc. mil
ruler), banuso
banal, banala; **banality,** ~ajo; ~eco
banana, banano; **banana tree,** ~arbo
band, (any long, narrow object; strip;
radio etc. frequency range), bendo; ~i
[tr]; (stripe), strio; strii [tr]; (ribbon or
similar object), rubando; (of cigar;
mailing wrapper), banderolo; (musi-

cians or oth group), bando; (any group
moving, acting together), roto, aro;
(organized brigade, gang), brigado;
banded, ~ita; striita; ringizita, ringo-
hava; **bandstand,** (outdoor), muzik-
kiosko; (indoor), muzikpodio; **band
together,** ariĝi; bandiĝi; rotiĝi; (tie
up), ligi [tr]; **bandwagon,** (lit), ban-
doĉaro; **jump on the bandwagon,**
(fig: join the winners), aliĝi al la ven-
kotajdo; **armband,** brak~o; **disband,**
disigi; disiĝi; **hatband,** ĉapelruban-
do; **interference bands,** interferaj
~oj; **rubber band,** kaŭĉuka ringo,
kaŭĉuka ~o; **sideband,** (radio etc.),
flank~o
bandage, bandaĝo, pansbendo; ~i [tr];
(wrap, as w elastic bandage), vindi
[tr]; vindo; **elastic bandage, "Ace"
bandage,** vindo
bandan(n)a, kaptuko
Bandar Seri Begawan, Bandar-Seri-
Begavano*
bandeau, (ribbon), harbendo
banderilla, banderilo;   **banderillero,**
~isto
banderol(e), (pennant),   standardeto
[not "banderolo"]
bandicoot, (Aus: any of *Paramelidae*),
paramelo*; (India: *Bandicota*), bandikoto
Bandicota, bandikoto
bandit, bandito
bandoleer, bandolier, (to hold sword
etc.), balteo, bandoliero; (for ammunition), kartoĉozono
Bandung, Bandungo
bandy, reĵetadi [tr]
bane, (cause of ruin etc.), ruinigo
baneberry, (plant), aketo; (berry), ~a
bero
bang, (any loud noise), krako, knalo,
bruego; ~i [int], knali [int]; ~igi, knaligi; (shut, knock, etc.), brue fermi [tr]
(frapi [tr] etc.); (gunfire etc.), pafbruo;
(hit hard), frapegi [tr]; (onom), bam!,
krak!; **the Big Bang (Theory),** (ast),
(la Teorio de) la Granda K~o
Bangkok, Bankoko
Bangladesh, Bangladeŝo†
bangle, braceleto
Bangui, Bangvio*

banian, (tree), banjano
banish, ekzili [tr]
banister, balustrado
banjo, banĝo
bank, ($ institution), banko; (of river etc.), (river)bordo; (any rise of ground, clouds, etc.), altaĵeto; (slope of earthfill, trench, etc.), taluso; talusi [tr, int]; (lean for curve), (turn)klini [tr]; (turn)kliniĝi; (turn)kliniĝo; (med: storage place), rezervejo (e.g.: *blood bank:* sangorezervejo); (blood, organs, etc., thus stored), rezervaĵo; (deposit in bank), deponi [tr]; (shallow area of water), malprofundejo; (billiards), resaltigi; resalti [int]; (row, tier), vico; (set fire etc. to burn low), malhejti [tr]; **banker**, (owner or manager), bankiero; **bankbook**, **~libro**; **bank note**, **~**bileto; **bank on**, (anticipate), anticipi [tr]; (trust), fidi [tr], dependi [int] de; **bankroll**, monprovizo; monprovizi [tr], financi [tr]; **piggy bank**, (or similar bank in oth form), ŝparmonujo; **soil bank**, noval(ar)o; **come out of its banks**, (re river etc.), superbordiĝi
bankrupt, bankrot/inta; **~**ulo; **~**igi; **go bankrupt**, **~**i [int]; **bankruptcy**, **~**o; **bankruptcy proceedings**, **~**oproceso
banksia, Banksia, (Aus), banksio*
banner, (flag), standardo; (headline), tutpaĝa titolo
bannister, balustrado
banns, geedziĝoanonco
banquet, bankedo; **banquet hall**, **~**ejo
banshee, mortaŭgura feino
bantam, (bird), bantamo
banter, priŝerci [int]; **~**ado
Bantu, Bantuo; **~**a
banus, banuso
banyan, banjano
baobab, baobabo
baptism, bapto; **baptismal** (**font**), **~**ujo; **baptist(e)ry**, **~**ejo; (esp outside church), baptisterio
Baptist, Baptisto; **~**a
baptize, bapti [tr]
bar, (prevent), bari [tr]; **~**o; (thing which prevents), **~**aĵo; **~**ilo; (pole, rod, etc.), stango; (soap, candy, etc.), briko, tabuleto; (tavern), drinkejo; (al-

so serving food), taverno; (counter as in tavern), verŝtabulo; (mus: measure), mezuro; (door bolt etc.), rigli [tr]; riglilo; (law, by statute of limitations), preskripti [tr]; preskripto; (rock or sand outcropping etc.), **~**o; (stripe), strio; (hinder), malhelpi [tr]; malhelpo; (legal profession), advokataro; (exclude), ekskludi [tr]; ekskludo; **bar line**, (mus), taktostreko; **bartender**, drinkejmastro; **fraction bar**, **diagonal bar**, ("/"), oblikva streketo; **horizontal bars**, (gymnastics), reko; **milk bar**, laktotrinkejo; **space bar**, (on cmptr, typewriter keyboard etc.), spacetostango
Barabbas, Barabaso
barb, pikilo; (thorn), dorno
Barbados, Barbado†
Barbara, Barbara
barbarian, barbaro; **~**a; **barbaric**, **barbarous**, **~**a; **barbarity**, **barbarism**, **~**aĵo; **~**eco; **~**ismo; **barbarize**, **~**igi
Barbarossa, Barbaroso
barbecue, fajrrosti [tr]; (food **~**d), **~**aĵo; (grill), **~**ilo; (party etc.), **~**ofesto; **barbecue sauce**, **~**saŭco
barbel, (thread on fish), barb/fadeno; (fish: *Barbus*), **~**fiŝo
barbell, halterego [cp "dumbbell"]
barber, barbiro; (cut one's hair), pritondi [tr]; **barbershop**, **~**ejo
barberry, (shrub), berberiso; (berry), **~**bero; **holly-leaved barberry**, mahonio
barbette, barbedo
barbican, barbakano
barbital, veronalo
barbiton, barbitono
barbiturate, barbituraĵo, barbiturato
barbituric, barbitura; **barbituric acid**, **~**a acido
barcarol(l)e, barkarolo
Barcelona, Barcelono
bard, bardo
bare, (naked; plain, unadorned), nuda, senvesta; **~**igi; (not more than), nura, apenaŭa; (reveal), malkaŝi [tr], riveli [tr]; malkaŝ(it)a, rivelita; **barely**, apenaŭ; **lay bare**, **~**igi, malkaŝi, riveli
barège, bareĝo
Barents (Sea), (Maro) Barenca

barf, (colloq: vomit), vomi [tr]; ~aĵo
bargain, (agree), interkonsenti [int]; ~o; (discuss terms; haggle), marĉandi [int]; (thing bought after bargaining), marĉandaĵo; (good buy), bonaĉeto; (offer), mir~oferto
barge, (boat), barĝo; **barge in(to),** enpuŝegi sin, entrud(eg)i sin
bargee, (Br), barĝisto
barilla, salsolo
barite, baria spato, baria sulfato [not "barito"]
baritone, (mus range; voice), baritono; (singer), ~ulo
barium, bario; **barium oxide,** (BaO), barito, ~a oksido [cp "barite"]
bark, (of tree or plant), ŝelo (arb~o, plant~o); (dog), boji [int]; bojo; (fig: shout words like dog ~), elboji [tr]; (boat), barko; **barker,** (circus etc.), ĉarlatano; **cassia bark,** kasio; **stringy bark,** (Aus: *Eucalyptus macrorhyncha*), fibro~arbo
barley, hordeo
barm, biergisto
bar mitzvah, (rite), barmicvo*; (boy), ~ulo
barn, (farm storage building, gen), tenejo; (for animals), stalo; (for grain, hay, etc.), garbejo, grenejo, pajlejo (etc.); (Am: for busses, trolleys, etc.), garaĝo
Barnaby, Barnabas, Barnabo
barnacle, balano, marglano
barograph, barografo
barometer, barometro; aneroid barometer, aneroida* ~o
baron, barono; **baronage,** (rank), ~eco; (all barons), ~aro; **baroness,** ~ino; **baronet,** ~eto; **baronial,** ~(ec)a; **barony,** (domain), ~ejo
baroque, baroko; ~a
baroscope, baroskopo
barque, barko
barrack(s), (temporary), barako; ~aro; en~igi; (permanent), kazerno; enkazernigi
barrage, (mil), pafbaraĵo; (fig, as of words etc.), pafadego, mitralado
barramunda, barramundi, (Aus), baramundo*
barrel, (container), barelo; en~igi; (unit of measure, gen), ~pleno [liquid mea-

sure: (Am: water), 119,2 litroj; (Br: water), 163,7 litroj; (oil, gen), 159,0 litroj; dry measure: (flour), 88,9 kilogramoj; (pork or fish), 90,74 kilogramoj; (see § 20)]; (of gun), (paf)tubo; (of padlock), ŝlostubo; **double-barreled,** dutuba; **rain-barrel,** (pluv)cisterno
barren, (not fertile), malfekunda; (w/o result), ~a, senfrukta, senrezulta; (desert), dezerta; (lifeless), senviva
barricade, barikado; ~i [tr]
barrier, (movable, across road etc.), bariero; (obstacle), obstaklo; (dike), digo; **sound barrier,** son~o
barrio, (section of city, gen), kvartalo; (tin shack slum), ladvilaĝo
barrister, advokato
barrow, (burial mound), tumulo; (cart), puŝĉaro
barter, (var)interŝanĝi [tr]; ~ado
Bartholomew, Bartolomeo
Bartonellosis, verugao
Baruch, Baruĥo
baryon, barjono†
Baryta, barito
barytes, [see "barite"]
barytone, [see "baritone"]
basal, baza
basalt, bazalto
bascule, baskulo
base, (bottom, support, basis, essence, etc.; mil; math; geom; chem), bazo; ~a; ~i [tr]; (low, menial, ignoble, etc.), maldeca, malnobla; (counterfeit), falsa; (of pedestal, statue, light bulb, electron tube, etc.), soklo [cp "basement"]; **be based on,** ~iĝi sur, esti fundamentita sur; **baseless,** sen~a; **base level,** ~nivelo; **base line,** ~linio; **touch base with,** kontakti [tr], konsulti [tr]
baseball, (game), basbalo; (ball), ~pilko
Basel, Bazelo
basement, (gen), subetaĝo†; (cellar), kelo; (arch base, as of monument etc.), bazamento [cp "base"]
bash, (hit), bategi [tr]; ~o; (party), festego
bashful, modesta, singena
basic, (fundamental), baza, fundamenta; (chem), ~a, alkala; **basics,** fundamen-

to(j), rudimentoj
basidiomycete, bazidiomiceto
Basidiomycetes, bazidiomicetoj
basidium, bazidio
basil, (bot), bazilio; **sweet basil**, ~o;
wild basil, kalaminto
Basil, (man's name), Bazilo
basilica, baziliko
Basiliscus, bazilisko
basilisk, (gen), bazilisko
basin, (pan, bowl, etc.), kuv/eto, pelvo;
(for expectoration), sputujo; (pool, as
of fountain etc.; geol; harbor, as yacht
basin), baseno; **washbasin**, lav~o
basis, bazo, fundamento; **on the basis
of**, sur~e de
bask, ripozi [int], sin varmigi, sunĝui
[int]
basket, korbo
basketball, (game), basketbalo†; (ball),
~a pilko
bas mitzvah, [see "bat mitzvah"]
basoche, (former legal group in Paris),
bazoĉo
Basque, Vasko; ~a; **Basque Provinces**,
~io
bas-relief, bareliefo
bass, (mus range; voice), baso; ~a;
(singer), ~ulo; (bass fiddle), kontrabaso; (tuba), tubjo; (fish: any variety
of *Centrarchidae*), centrarkedo*;
(fish: any variety of *Serranus* or *Serranidae*), seran(ed)o*; (fish: *Labrax*),
labrako; (tree), [see "basswood"];
contrabass, double bass, kontrabaso
Bass (Strait), (Markolo) Bassa
Bassia, basio
bassinet, korbliteto
bassoon, fagoto; **contrabassoon, double bassoon**, kontrafagoto
basswood, (tree), tilio; (wood), ~a ligno
bast, (phloem), basto, floemo; (fiber),
~aĵo
bastard, (lit: born out of wedlock), bastardo; ~a; (fig: mean), ~o, kanajlo;
bastardy, ~eco
baste, (sew), duonkudri [tr]; (in cooking), priverŝi [tr]
Bastian, (man's name), Bastiano
Bastille, Bastilo; **Bastille Day**, ~tago
bastion, bastiono
bat, (baseball, cricket, etc.: any club),

klabo; (cricket batsman), batanto;
(hit), bati [tr]; (zool), vesperto; **bat-
man**, (Br), oficirservisto; **batsman**,
(cricket), batanto; **batter**, [see "batter"]; **at bat**, ~anta; **fruit bat**, pteropo; **javelin bat**, filostomo;
pipistrel(le) bat, pipistrelo; **vampire
bat**, (*Desmodus*, true blood-sucking
bat), desmodo; (*Vampirus*, not blood-
sucking), vampiro; **go to bat for**, (fig:
defend), defendi [tr]; **right off the
bat**, tuj, senprokraste; **he has bats in
his belfry**, li havas muŝon en la cerbo; muŝo zumas en lia cerbo
Batavia, (old name of Jakarta), Batavio;
(re ancient Germanic people), Batavo;
Batava
batch, (amount baked at one time),
fornpleno; (amount of anything used
at one time), ŝarĝo; (amount made at
one time; any oth lot, set, group), aro,
opo, aropo
bateau, (river)boato
bath, (gen), bano; (Bib: unit of volume),
bat'o; **bathe**, (gen), ~i [tr], sin ~i, baniĝi; (swim), naĝi [int]; **bathing suit**,
(for men), ~kalsono; (woman's), ~ko-
stumo; **bathing cap**, ~ĉapo; **bath-
house**, ~ejo; **bathinette**, beb~ujeto;
bathmat, ~mato; **take a bath**, sin ~i,
baniĝi; **acid bath**, acido~o; **birdbath**,
bird~ujo; **fixing bath**, (phot), fiks~o;
(public) baths, (publika) ~ejo; **show-
er-bath**, duŝo [see "shower"]; **sitz
bath**, sid~o; **sun-bath**, sun~o; **steam-
bath, Turkish bath**, vapor~o [cp
"sauna"]
bathochromic, batokroma
bathometer, batometro
Bathsheba, Bat-Ŝeba
bathyscaphe, batiskafo
bathysphere, batisfero
batik, batiko
batiste, batisto
bat mitzvah, (rite), batmicvo*; (girl),
~ulino
baton, (any stick, rod), bastono; (of mus
conductor), ~o, takto~o
Batrachia, (*Salientia*), batrakoj; (*Amphibia*), amfibioj
battalion, bataliono
batten, (wood strip etc.), lato; (strength-

en or fasten w battens), ~izi [tr]; (fatten), grasigi; grasiĝi; **batten down**, fiksfermi [tr]
batter, (baseball, cricket), bat/anto; (pound), ~adi [tr]; (injure), ~vundi [tr]; (smash), frakasi [tr]; (cooking, for cakes, pancakes, etc.), farunmiksaĵo; **battering ram**, murrompilo
battery, (elec; mil), baterio; (beating), bat(ad)o; **storage battery**, akumulatoro
battik, batiko
batting, (cotton etc.), vato
battle, batalo; ~i [int]; ~i kontraŭ, kontraŭ~i [tr]; **battle-axe**, milithakilo [cp "halberd"]; **battlefield**, ~ejo, ~kampo; **battlement**, krenelaro
battledore, (volan)rakedo
battue, batuo
batz, baco
bauble, breloko, brikabrakero
Baucis, Baŭcisa
baud, baŭdo
Baudelaire, Bodlero
baulk, [see "balk"]
bauxite, baŭksito
Bavaria, Bavario; **Bavarian**, ~a; ~o
bawdy, lasciva, malpruda
bawl, (yell), kriegi [int]; el~i [tr]; (cry), ploregi [int]
bay, (arm of ocean etc.), golfo; (small), ~eto, kreko; (alcove, wing of building), alkovo; (bin), kuvego; (compartment), fako; (bark, as dog), boji [int]; (howl, as wolf etc.), hurli [int], hojli [int]; (bot: laurel), laŭro; (color), ruĝbruna; (horse etc.), ruĝbrunulo; **bay leaf**, laŭrofolio; **at bay**, enangulita; **sick bay**, flegejo; **bring to bay**, enanguligi; **keep at bay**, forteni [tr]; **embayment**, (small inlet), kreko
bayadere, **bayadeer**, (dancer), bajadero; (fabric), ~aĵo
bayonet, bajoneto; ~i [tr]
bayou, marĉkreko
bazaar, bazaro
bazooka, bazuko
B.C., **B.C.E.**, (abb of "Before Christ" or "Before Common Era"), a.K. [abb of "antaŭ Kristo" or "antaŭ Komunerao"]
bdelium, (Bib jewel), bedelio

be, esti [int] [note: as auxiliary verb, "esti" is most often omitted (e.g.: *we are coming:* ni venas); but if needed for emphasis, add "ja" (e.g.: *we are [indeed] coming:* ni ja venas); in questions, add "ĉu" before phrase (e.g.: *are you coming?:* ĉu vi venas?); when followed by adj, the adj is occasionally made into verb (esp poet) in place of "esti –a" (e.g.: *the light is red:* la lumo ~as ruĝa [or] la lumo ruĝas)]; **being**, (entity), ~aĵo; ~ulo; ento; **there is (are)**, **there was (were)**, (etc.), ~as, ~is (etc.) (e.g.: *there is a book on the table:* ~as libro sur la tablo); **there is (are, etc.) no(t)**, (insufficient, lacking), mankas (~is, etc.) [int], ne ~as (~is, etc.) (e.g.: *there is not enough time to finish:* mankas sufiĉa tempo [or] ne estas sufiĉa tempo por fini; *there were no people in the room:* mankis homoj en la ĉambro); **which is to be –ed**, (must be –ed), –enda [sfx] (e.g.: *those are the problems which are to be solved:* jen la solvendaj problemoj); (will be –ed), –ota [sfx] (e.g.: *that package is yet to be sent:* tiu pako ~as ankoraŭ sendota); **be (distance) (away) from**, distanci [int] de (e.g.: *New York is 4500 kilometers from Los Angeles:* Nov-Jorko distancas 4500 kilometrojn de Los-Anĝeleso); **be that as it may**, ~u (tio) kiel ajn
Bea, (short for "Beatrice"), Beanjo
beach, plaĝo; (land boat etc.), albordigi; albordiĝi
beacon, (light), gvidlumo; (radio etc.), gvidsignalo; (fire), signalfajro
bead, (pierced), bido; (any small round object), globeto; (of tire), flanĝo; (on gun), celgrajno
beadle, pedelo
beagle, biglo
beak, beko
beaker, (goblet), pokalo; (chem etc.), (laboratoria) kruĉeto
beam, (of wood, metal, etc., for structural support), trabo (e.g.: *I-beam:* I-trabo); (support, as in mine, archway, etc.), stego; (horizontal, to keep spacing between vertical parts), ŝpalo;

(crossbeam of ship), baŭo; (arm of scales), vekto; (shine), brili [int] [cp "gleam"]; (radiate), radii [int]; elradii [tr]; (ray of light etc.), (lum)fasko, radio; (guide signal, beacon), gvidsignalo [cp "beacon"]; (show joy), ĝojbrili [int] **bean**, (seed or food, gen), fabo; (plant), ~oplanto; (genus *Phaseolus*), fazeolo; **beanbag**, ~osako; **beanery**, restoraciaĉo; **beanie**, vertoĉapo; **bean trefoil**, anagiro; **bogbean, buckbean**, menianto; **butter bean, Lima bean, sieva bean, mung bean, kidney bean**, fazeolo; **carob bean, locust bean**, (fruit), karobo; (tree), karobarbo, karobujo; **castor bean**, ricina semo; **chestnut bean**, kikero; **green bean**, verda fazeolo; **Indian bean**, katalpo; **mescal bean, coral bean**, (plant), soforo; (seed), soforsemo; **tonka bean, tonca bean, tonga bean, tonqua bean**, tonka* fabo; **full of beans**, viglega, plena de energio; **spill the beans**, malkaŝi la sekreton **bear**, (zool, gen: *Ursus*), urso; (carry), porti [tr]; (support weight), subporti [tr]; (take upon self; withstand), elporti [tr] (e.g.: *bear the guilt:* elporti la kulpon); (resist), rezisti [tr]; (suffer through), trasuferi [tr]; (tolerate), toleri [tr], elporti [tr]; (give birth to, lit or fig), naski [tr]; (give forth), produkti [tr] [not "eldoni"]; ($, re stock market etc.), (prez)basiĝa; basiĝisto; (require, call for), postuli [tr] (e.g.: *his actions bear watching:* liaj agoj postulas kontroladon); (face), fronti [int] (al, ~en) (e.g.: *the house bears east:* la domo frontas al la oriento [or] frontas orienten); (aim at), celi [tr, int] (e.g.: *artillery bearing on the base:* artilerio celanta la bazon); (turn in given direction), turniĝi (e.g.: *bear right at the corner:* turniĝu dekstren ĉe la angulo); (relate to), rilati [int] al (e.g.: *your question doesn't bear on the subject:* via demando ne rilatas al la temo); **unbearable**, neelportebla, netolerebla, neelportebla; **bearing**, [see "bearing"]; **bear's-breech**, (bot), akanto; **bear's-ear**, (bot), aŭrikulo; **bear

down (on), (forte) premi [tr]; **bear on**, (relate to), rilati al (e.g.: *this doesn't bear on the problem:* ĉi tio ne rilatas al la problemo); (aim at), celi [tr, int]; **bear out**, (confirm), konfirmi [tr]; **bear up (with, under, etc.)**, elteni [tr]; **bear up!**, (take heart!), kuraĝon!; **bear with**, pacienci [int] kun; **ant bear**, mirmekofago, formik~o; **black bear**, nigra ~o; **brown bear**, bruna ~o; **cat bear**, pando; **forebear**, antaŭulo, praulo; **grizzly bear**, griza ~o; **koala bear, kangaroo bear, native bear**, koalo; **offbear**, forporti [tr]; **overbearing**, aroganta; **polar bear**, polusa ~o; **Teddy bear**, (remburita) ludil~o; **woolly bear (caterpillar)**, arktia raŭpo **beard**, (on man or animal), barbo; (re grains), aristo; **bearded**, ~(hav)a; **bearded man**, ~ulo **bearing**, (mech), lagro [cp "bushing", "hub"]; (direction), direkto, orientiĝo; direction fix), biro; (manner, mien), mieno; (act of bearing), [see "bear"]; **ball bearing**, (the ball), ~oglobo; (the bearing), glob~o; **blade bearing**, eĝo~o; **journal bearing**, glit~o; **pivot bearing**, pied~o; **roller bearing**, rul~o, cilindra ~o; **get a bearing on**, biri [tr]; **get (lose) one's bearings**, (mal)orientiĝi **Béarn**, Bearno; **Béarnaise**, ~a **beast**, (gen), besto; (esp wild), bestio; (brute), bruto; **beastial**, ~(ec)a; besti(ec)a; bruta **beat**, (strike or pound, gen; flap; etc.), bati [tr, int]; (conquer), venki [tr]; (exceed, overcome), superi [tr]; (win game etc.), gajni [tr] (ludon) super (kontraŭulo); (mix by beating), ~miksi [tr]; (pulse, as between 2 slightly unequal sound frequencies), pulsi [int]; puls(o~)o; (mus: rhythm), takto; (baffle, puzzle), konfuzi [tr]; (trick, cheat), superruzi [tr]; (escape, avoid, as criminal charge), eskapi [int] de; (route, as of police officer, reporter, etc.), kurso; (naut: progress by tacking), boardi [int]; boardo [cp "tack"]; (pre-hippie), prahipia*; prahipiulo*; (Bohemian, gen), bohemia; bohemiulo; **beating**, ~ado; **beat around the bush**, ĉirkaŭmarĉandi [int]; **beat to death**, mort~i [tr]; **beat one to the punch**, antaŭfrapi iun; **beat in**, en~i [tr]; **beat out**, el~i [tr]; **beat time**, (mus), ~i la takton; **beat up**, dis~i [tr], draŝi [tr]; **beat-up**, (worn, battered), kaduka, ŝlifita, dis~ita; (re clothes), ĉifona; **dead-beat**, ŝuldrifuzanto; **downbeat**, (mus), ĉeftakto, ĉefpulso; **heartbeat**, kor~(ad)o; **offbeat**, (mus), flanktakto; flanktakta; (odd), stranga, kurioza, originala, nekonvencia; **upbeat**, (mus), antaŭtakto, malĉeftakto, antaŭpulso, malĉefpulso; (lively, cheerful), gaja, vigla

beatific, (blissful), beata; (making blissful), ~iga; **beatification**, ~igo; ~iĝo

beatify, beatigi

beatitude, beateco

beatnik, (pre-hippie), bitniko; ~a; (Bohemian, gen), Bohemiano; Bohemia

Beatrice, Beatrica

beau, amato

Beaufort, Boforto; **Beaufort scale**, ~a skalo; **Beaufort Sea**, Maro ~a

Beaufront, Bofronto

beauty, (condition), belo, ~eco; (thing), ~ajo; (person), ~ul(in)o; (charm), ĉarmo; **beautiful**, ~a; **beautify**, ~igi; **beautician**, kosmetikist(in)o; **beauty shop**, **beauty parlor**, kosmetikejo

beaux-arts, belartoj

beaver, (zool), kastoro; **muskrat beaver**, ondatro

becalm, (calm), kvietigi; **be becalmed**, (re ship), senventiĝi

because, ĉar, tial ke; **because of**, pro (e.g.: *because of the fact that:* pro tio ke [more emphatic than "ĉar"])

béchamel, beŝamelo

bêche-de-mer, (zool: *Holothuria;* food), holoturio, markolbaso; (language), piĝino

beck, (Br), rivereto

beckon, (gesture), gestvoki [tr], geste alvoki [tr]; (lure, gen), logi [tr]

Becky, Renjo [cp "Rebecca"]

becloud, malklarigi, nubigi

become, (get to be), fariĝi, iĝi, ~iĝi

[sfx] (e.g.: *become hot:* varmiĝi, (far)iĝi varma; *become an actor:* aktoriĝi, (far)iĝi aktoro)

becoming, (proper), konvena, deca; (attractive), alloga, bela

bed, (furniture; sleeping place of animals etc.), lito; en~igi; en~iĝi; (of flowers etc.), bedo; (of lake, ocean), fundo; (of river), fluejo; (of truck etc.), ŝarĝplato; (any place for lying, resting), kuŝejo; (geol), kuŝujo; **bedding**, (blankets etc.), ~ajo; (straw), pajlo~o; **bedframe**, **bedstead**, ~kadro; **bedridden**, ~malsana; **bedroll**, ~rulaĵo; **bedside**, ~flanko; ~flanka; **bed-sitter**, (Br), unuĉambra apartamento; **bedtime**, en~iĝa tempo; en~iĝotempa; **deathbed**, mort~o; **double bed**, duloka ~o; **hotbed**, (lit or fig), varmbedo; **kingsize bed**, grandformata ~o; **Murphy bed**, klap~o; **oyster bed**, ostrejo; **queensize bed**, plenformata ~o; **single bed**, "twin" bed, unuloka ~o; **sofa bed**, sofo~o; **straw bed**, pajlo~o; **truckle bed**, **trundle bed**, subŝovebla ~o; **go to bed**, en~iĝi; **put to bed**, en~igi; **bed and board**, (boarding house), pensiono; **bed and breakfast**, (for overnight), tranokta pensiono; **get up on the wrong side of bed**, miskomenci la tagon

bedeck, ornami [tr]

bedlam, (any chaotic place, situation), pandemonio, ĥaosejo

Bedouin, Bedueno; ~a

bedraggled, malsekaĉa, kotita

bee, (zool, gen), abelo; (contest), konkurso (e.g.: *spelling bee:* literuma konkurso); (any gathering), kunveno (e.g.: *sewing bee:* kudra kunveno); **bee-eater**, (zool), meropo; **beehive**, ~ujo; **beeswax**, ~vakso; **bumblebee**, burdo; **honey bee**, miel~o; **beekeeper**, ~bredisto; **beekeeping**, ~bredado; **beeline**, rektlinio

beech, (tree), fago; (wood), ~ligno; **copper beech**, **purple beech**, sango~o; **beechnut**, ~nukso

beef, bov/aĵo; **beefalo**, (animal), ~bizono; (meat), ~bizonaĵo; **beefcake**, (re show or photo of attractive man),

(vir)figurmontr(ad)o; (vir)figurmontra [cp "cheese: cheesecake"]; **roast beef**, rostbefo, ~-rostaĵo; **corned beef**, spicita ~aĵo
Beelzebub, Baal-Zebub
beep, (honk car horn etc.), hupi [int]; ~(ad)o; (small sound, as by digital watch alarm), pepi [int]; pep(ad)o
beer, biero; **root beer**, sasafras–sodo, radik–sodo
beet, beto; **red beet**, ruĝa ~o; **sugar-beet**, suker~o
Beethoven, Betoveno
beetle, (zool, gen), skarabo, koleoptero; **black beetle**, blato; **bombardier beetle**, brahino; **burying beetle**, nekroforo; **calosoma beetle**, kalosomo; **carpet beetle, larder beetle, museum beetle**, *(Dermestes)*, dermesto; **churchyard beetle**, blapto; **click beetle**, elatero; **cockchafer beetle**, melolonto, maj~o; **Colorado potato beetle**, leptinotarso; **darkling beetle, darkling ground beetle**, tenebrio; **death-watch beetle**, anobio; **diving beetle**, ditisko; **dung beetle**, *(Scarabaeus)*, ~o; *(Geogrupes)*, geotrupo, sterko~o; **furniture beetle**, anobio; **goliath beetle**, *(Cetonia)*, cetonio; *(Goliathus)*, goliato; **ground beetle**, karabo; **lady(bird) beetle**, kokcinelo; **leaf beetle**, krizomelo, or~o; **long-horn(ed) beetle**, cerambiko; **oil beetle**, meloo; **sap chafer beetle**, cetonio; **stag beetle**, lukano, cerv~o; **tiger beetle**, cicindelo
befall, trafi [tr], okazi [int] al
befit, konveni [int] al, deci [int] al; **befitting**, ~a, deca
before, (prep, re time or place), antaŭ (e.g.: *before your arrival:* ~ via alveno; *she stood before the house:* ŝi staris ~ la domo); (conj), ~ ol (e.g.: *read it before you come:* legu ĝin ~ ol vi venos); (adv), ~e (e.g.: *I've never done that before:* mi neniam ~e faris tion); **beforehand**, ~e; **before long**, post nelonge
befuddle, (confuse), konfuzi [tr], perpleksigi, mistifiki [tr]; (stupefy, as w alcohol), stuporigi; **befuddlement**, ~o, perplekseco; stuporo

beg, (implore), pet/egi [tr]; (ask charity), almozi [int], almoz~i [int]; **beggar**, almozulo; **go begging**, resti ne~ita; **beggar('s)-sticks**, (bot), bidento
begam, begamo
beget, (re man), generi [tr], naskigi; (re woman), naski [tr]; (fig), ~i
begin, komenci [tr]; ~iĝi, (colloq), eki [int]; **begin to**, komenc(iĝ)i, ek– [pfx] (e.g.: *she began to sing:* ŝi ~is kanti [or] ŝi ekkantis; *it's beginning to rain:* ekpluvas) [cp "start"]; **beginning**, ~o; **beginner**, ~anto; **from the beginning**, de~e, de la ~o
begone, for!
begonia, Begonia, begonio
begrudge, domaĝi [tr]
beguile, (trick), trompi [tr], superruzi [tr]; (lure, attract), logi [tr]; (charm), ĉarmi [tr]
beguine, (dance), begindanco
Beguine, (rel), begino
begum, begamo
behalf, intereso; **in (on) behalf of**, por; en la nomo de, nome de
behave, (conduct self, gen), konduti [int]; (behave well, properly), bon~i [int], ~i bone; **behave oneself**, ~i bone; **misbehave**, malbon~i [int], mis~i [int]
behavior, (gen), konduto; **behaviorism**, behaviorismo; **behaviorist**, behaviorisma; behavioristo*; **misbehavior**, mis~o
behemoth, behemoto
behest, (order), ordono; (request), peto
behind, (prep: re place), malantaŭ (e.g.: *she sat behind me:* ŝi sidis ~ mi; *the sun went behind a cloud:* la suno iris ~ nubon); (remaining after), post (e.g.: *he left little behind him when he died:* li lasis malmulton post si kiam li mortis); (beyond), preter (e.g.: *behind the hill:* preter la monteto); (supporting), subtenanta (e.g.: *the group behind the proposal:* la grupo subtenanta la proponon); (adv), ~e(n); poste(n); (slow, re time), malfrue (e.g.: *the train is running behind:* la trajno kuras malfrue); (not current), malakurata (e.g.: *I am behind in my*

work: mi estas malakurata en mia laboro); (buttocks), postaĵo, (colloq), pugo; **be behind,** (support), subteni [tr]; (be late, slow), malfrui [int]; **behind the 8-ball,** en embaraso, en malfacilaĵo [see § 11]
behold, (see), rigardi [tr]; (interj), jen; **lo and behold,** jen
beholden, (danko)ŝulda
behoove, behove, endi [int] al, konveni [int] al, necesi [int] al, endi [int] al
beige, grizbruneta; ~o
Beijing, Pekino; **Beijingese,** ~a; ~ano
Beirut, Bejruto; ~a
bejewel, juvelizi [tr]
beka(h), bek'o
bel, belo; **decibel,** deci~o
Bel, Belo
belabor, (beat), bati [tr]; (scold; overemphasize; etc.), draŝi [tr], troknedi [tr]
Belarus, Belarus/iot; **Belarussian,** ~o; ~a; ~ia
belated, malakurata, malfrua
Belau, Belaŭot
belay, fiksi [tr], ligi [tr]; ~(iĝ)o, lig(iĝ)o; **belaying pin,** bito
belch, rukti [int]; el~i [tr] (e.g.: *belch smoke:* el~i fumon); ~o
beleaguer, (gen), sieĝi [tr]
belemnite, belemnito
Belfast, Belfasto
belfry, (gen), sonorilejo; (for spying), belfrido
Belgium, Belg/io; **Belgian,** ~o; ~a; ~ia
Belgrade, Beogrado
Belial, Belialo
belie, malkonfirmi [tr], malpruvi [tr], dementi [tr]
belief, (gen), kredo; **disbelief,** mal~o; **belief in,** [see "believe"]
believe, kredi [tr, int] (e.g.: *I don't believe that tale:* mi ne ~as tiun rakonton; *do you believe her when she says that?:* ĉu vi ~as al ŝi [or] ~as ŝin kiam ŝi diras tion?; *I believe [that] it will rain:* mi ~as ke pluvos); (have opinion), ~i, opinii [int]; **believe in,** (believe veracity of person), ~i al; (believe existence of; have faith in), ~i je (e.g.: *believe in God, in ghosts:* ~i je Dio, je fantomoj; *believe in de-*

mocracy: ~i je la demokratio); **believable,** ~inda; **believably,** ~inde [not "~ebla", "~eble"; see "course: of course"]; **disbelieve,** mal~i [tr, int]
Belisarius, Belizaro
belittle, mallaŭdi [tr], subtaksi [tr], maltroigi
Belize, (country), Beliz/iot; **Belize City,** ~o
bell, (w clapper, gen), sonorilo; (handheld, or of that size), ~eto; (bell jar, cloche), kloŝo; **bell-bottom(ed),** larĝbaza; **bellhop, bellman,** grumo; **bellwether,** (lit or fig), estroŝafo; **bellwort,** (*Campanula*), kampanulo; (*Uvularia*), uvulario*; **bluebell,** blua kampanulo; **Canterbury bell,** (bot), kampanulo; **cathedral bells,** (bot), kobeo; **diving bell,** mergokloŝo; **doorbell,** pord~o; **jingle bell, sleigh bell,** (or similar-sounding bell), tintilo
belladonna, (plant), beladono; (drug), atropino
belle, belulino
Belle-Isle, (French island), Bel-Insulot
Bellerophon, Belerofono
belles-lettres, beletr(istik)o
bellicose, militema, atakema
belligerent, (at war), milit/anta; ~anto; (quarrelsome; warlike), kverelema, ~ema, atakema; **belligerence,** atakemo, ~emo; **belligerency,** ~anteco; atakemo; **cobelligerent,** kunbatalanto, kun~o; kunbatalanta, kun~a
Bellis perennis, lekanteto
Bellona, Belona
bellow, muĝegi [int], kr/ egi [int]; ~o, kriego
bellows, balgo [note sing]
belly, (gen), ventro [cp "abdomen"]; **bellyache,** ~odoloro; (colloq: grumble, complain), grumbli [int], plend(aĉ)i [int]; **bellybutton,** umbiliko; **belly-flop,** ~ofrapo; **potbellied,** (re person), dik~a, ~aĉa, ~ega, dik~a; (re stove etc.), ~ega
Belone, belono
belong, aparteni [int]; **belongings,** posedaĵoj, havaĵoj
Belorussia, [see "Belarus"]
beloved, amata; ~o
below, (prep: under), sub (e.g.: *below*

the horizon: ~ la horizonto); (adv: under), ~e(n); (lower; later, as in written material), malsupre(n), infre(n) (e.g.: *the list given below:* la malsupre [or] infre donita listo)
Belshazzar, Belŝacaro [cp "Balthazar"]
belt, (garment, or any similar-shaped thing; zone; etc.), zono; ~i [tr]; (colloq: hit), bati [tr]; **beltway,** ~vojo; **chastity belt,** ĉasteco~o; **life-belt, seat-belt,** sav~o; **hit below the belt,** kanajlumi [int] (al); kajnalaĵo; **tighten the belt,** (lit or fig), streĉi la ~on
beluga, *(Husa),* huzo
belvedere, belvedero
bemoan, lamenti [int] (pri), pri~i [tr]
bemuse, (stupefy), stupor/igi; (distract), distri [tr]; **bemusement,** ~o; distriĝo; **bemused,** ~igita; distrita, sensobtuzigita
Benares, Benareso
bench, (seat), benko; (place for judges), juĝistejo; (office of judge), juĝisteco; (all judges), juĝistaro; **benchmark,** (termezura) fiksnivela punkto; **workbench,** stablo
bend, (flex), fleksi [tr]; ~iĝi; ~(aĵ)o; (curve), kurbigi; kurbiĝi; kurbaĵo; kurbiĝo; (in road), (voj)turno; (incline), klini [tr]; kliniĝi; kliniĝo; (twist, wind), sinui [int]; sinuo; (yield), cedi [int]; **bending,** (sinuous), sinua; **unbending,** (rigid), rigida; (unyielding), necedema; **the bends,** (decompression disease), kasonmalsano; [see "bent"]
beneath, (prep: below, under), sub; (adj, adv), ~a; ~e; (unworthy of), malinda de (e.g.: *such behavior is beneath him:* tia konduto estas malinda de li)
Benedict, Benedikto
benedictine, Benediktana likvoro
Benedictine, Benediktana; **Benedictine monk,** ~o; **Benedictine nun,** ~ino
benediction, beno
benefactor, bonfar/into; ~anto; ~onto
benefice, benefico
beneficence, bonfaro; **beneficent,** ~(em)a
beneficial, utila; bonfara
beneficiary, (receiver of insurance,

pension, gift, etc.), profitanto; (of bequest), heredanto; (holder of benefice), beneficulo
benefit, (help, advantage), helpi [tr], esti avantaĝo al; ~o; avantaĝo; (payment from insurance, pension, welfare, etc.), profito; (public performance, event, etc., for charity, specific person or organization etc.), benefico; **benefit of the doubt,** fido malgraŭ duboj
Benelux, Belelukso; ~a
benevolent, (charitable), karitata; (inclined to good), bonfarema; (beneficent), bonfara; **benevolence,** ~o; bonfar(em)o
Bengal, Bengalo; **Bay of Bengal,** Golfo ~a; **Bengalese, Bengali,** ~a; ~ano
benign, benigna
Benin, Beninoṭ
Benjamin, Benjamino
bent, (inclination), inklino, emo; (not straight), [see "bend"]; (grass), agrostido
benzedrine, benzedrinoṭ
benzene, (C_6H_6), benzeno [cp "gasoline"]
benzidine, benzidino
benzo–, (chem pfx), benzo–
benzoic, benzoa; **benzoic acid,** ~-karbonacido
benzoin, benzoo
benzol, (benzene: C_6H_6), benzeno; (mixture of aromatics), benzolo
benzyl, benzilo
Beograd, Beogrado
bequeath, testamenti [tr], heredigi; **bequest,** (act), ~o, heredigo; (thing bequeathed), ~aĵo, heredaĵo
berate, riproĉ(eg)i [tr]
Berber, Berbero; ~a
Berberis, berberiso
bereave, (cause to mourn), funebr/igi; (deprive), senigi; **bereaved,** ~anta; ~anto; **be bereaved,** (mourn), ~i [int]; **bereavement,** ~o
bereft, senigita
Berenice, Berenica
beret, bereto
bergamot, (orange: fruit of *Citrus bergamia*), bergamoto; (tree), ~arbo; (oil), ~oleo; (herb: *Monarda*), monar-

do; **wild bergamot**, monardo
beriberi, beribero
Bering, Beringa; **Bering Sea**, Maro ~a;
   Bering Strait, Markolo ~a
berkelium, berkelio
Berlin, Berlino
berm, bermo
Bermuda, (la) Bermudoj [note plur]
Bern, Berno
Bernard, (man's name), Bernardo;
   Saint Bernard, (dog), hundo de San-
   ~o; **(Great) Saint Bernard Pass**, la
   (Granda) Trapasejo de San--o
Berne, Berno
Bernice, Berenica
berry, (gen), bero; **blackberry**, (plant),
   rubuso; (berry), rubus~o; **blueberry**,
   mirtelo; mirtel~o; **china berry**, (plant
   or berry), melio; **cranberry**, oksikoko; **cranberry tree, highbush
   cranberry**, viburno; **huckleberry**,
   loganberry, logan~ujo; logan~o;
   raspberry, frambujo; frambo; (derisive noise), mokbruo; **strawberry**,
   fragujo; frago; **strawberry mark**,
   fragmarko; **strawberry pigweed,
   strawberry spinach, strawberry
   blite**, fragspinaco, blito; **whortleber-
   ry**, mirtelo
berserk, berserk/eca; **berserker**, ~o;
   go berserk, ~iĝi
berth, (room to maneuver), manovrejo;
   (place to anchor), ankrejo; (bunk etc.),
   litbenko, kuŝbenko, kuŝejo; (anchor),
   ankri [tr]; **give a wide berth to**, ne tro
   proksimiĝi al
Bertha, Berta
Bertholletia excelsa, Bertholletia nobi-
   lis, Brazila nukso
Bertrand, Bertrando
beryl, berilo
beryllium, berilio
besant, bizanto
beseech, petegi [tr]
beset, sieĝi [tr]
beside, (next to), apud; (in addition, oth
   than), krom; **beside the point**, ne rilata; **be beside the point**, ne rilati [int];
   beside oneself, ekstaza, ekscitegita
besides, (prep: in addition to), krom
   (e.g.: *besides Esperanto, he also
   knows Spanish:* ~ Esperanto, li ankaŭ

scipovas la Hispanan); (conj, adv), ~e
   (e.g.: *it rained, and besides, it was
   windy:* pluvis, kaj ~e, ventis)
besiege, sieĝi [tr]
besmirch, (soil), makuli [tr], malpurigi; (dishonor), malhonori [tr]
Bessarabia, Besarabio
best, plej bona; plej bone; plejbono; **at
   best**, plej favore; **as best one can, to
   the best of one's ability**, laŭ (ies, sia)
   plejeblo, laŭeble; **had best**, devus
   prefere –us [see "better"]; **get the
   best of**, superi [tr], venki [tr]; **do
   one's (level) best**, fari sian plejeblon;
   make the best of, aranĝi sin laŭeble;
   next best, second best, dua plej bona, duagrada, duaranga
bestow, (give gift), donaci [tr]; (grant,
   adjudicate), aljuĝi [tr]; (devote, apply), dediĉi [tr]
bet, veti [tr, int]; (act of), ~o; ($ etc. at
   stake), ~ajo; betting office, betting
   shop, ~oficejo; bet on, pri~i [tr] (e.g.:
   I bet on that horse: mi pri~is tiun
   ĉevalon); a good bet, bona ~o; it's a
   good bet that, (likely), probable,
   verŝajne; you bet!, sendube!, certe!
beta, beta [see § 16]; **beta-rays**, betara-
   dioj
Beta, (bot), beto; Beta vulgaris, suk-
   er~o
betatron, betatrono
betel, betelo
Betelgeuse, Betelĝuzo
Beth, (short for "Elizabeth"), Elinjo [cp
   "Eliza", "Elizabeth"]
Bethany, Betanio
Bethlehem, Bet-Leĥem
betide, trafi [tr], okazi [int] al
Betonica, betoniko
betony, betoniko; **purple betony**, purpura ~o
betray, perfidi [tr]; **betrayal**, ~o
betroth, fianĉ/iĝi; **betrothal**, ~iĝo; **be-
   trothed**, ~igita; ~iĝinta; ~(in)o
better, pli bona; pli bone; (improve,
   gen), plibonigi; (must, should), prefere –u (e.g.: *you better not do that:* vi
   prefere ne faru tion; *I beter go home
   soon:* mi prefere iru hejmen baldaŭ);
   (as stronger admonishment), ja devus,
   nepre –u (e.g.: *you had better not for-*

get!: vi nepre ne forgesu!); **betters**, (persons), plibonuloj, superuloj; **get better**, (improve, gen), pliboniĝi; (re health), resaniĝi; **get the better of**, (overcome), superi [tr], venki [tr]; (outwit), superruzi [tr], dupigi; **had better**, (should), [see "(must, should)" above]; **all the better**, des pli bone (e.g.: *if the sun shines tomorrow, that's all the better:* se la suno brilos morgaŭ, des pli bone); **better than**, (more), pli ol; **the better part of**, pli granda parto de, la plejmulto de (da); **for the better**, por la pli granda bono; **betterment**, plibonigo

Betty, (short for "Elizabeth"), Elinjo [cp "Eliza", "Elizabeth"]

Betula, betulo

between, (gen), inter; **go-between**, peranto

bevel, (cut), bevelo; ~i [tr]; (tool), ~ilo

beverage, (gen), trinkaĵo; (alcoholic), drinkaĵo

bevy, bando, aro; (of birds), svarmo

bewail, lamenti [int] (pri), pri~i [tr]

beware, zorgi [int], esti gardema; **beware of**, sin gardi kontraŭ; **beware!**, ~u!, atentu!

bewilder, mistifiki [tr], perpleksigi

bewitch, sorĉi [tr]

bey, bejo; **beylic, beylik**, ~ejo

beyond, (farther), preter; ~e(n) (e.g.: *beyond the limits:* ~ la limoj); (after), post; poste(n) (e.g.: *beyond the time limit:* post la limtempo); (besides), krom (e.g.: *no help beyond her own wits:* nenia helpo krom sia propra sagaco); (the hereafter), ~ejo

Beyrouth, Bejruto

bezant, bizanto

bezoar, bezoaro

Bhagavad-Gita, Bagavadgito

Bharat, (king), Barato; (land), ~io

Bhutan, Butano†

bi–, (pfx: two), du–, bi–; (half), duon– [note: "bi–" is often absorbed into Esperanto root as "bi–" or "di–"; see separate entries]

Biafra, Biafro*

Bialystok, Bjalistoko

bias, (prejudice), antaŭjuĝo; ~igi; (diagonal), diagonalo; diagonala; (tenden-cy), inklino, tendenco, emo; influi [tr], inklinigi, tendencigi, emigi; (elec), biaso†; biasi† [tr]; (math), taksdevio; **biased**, ~a, partizana, partiema; inklina, partiema; **unbiased**, ne~a, nepartizana, nepartiema

biaxial, duaksa

bib, (for child), salivtuko; (for overalls etc.), brusttuko

bibcock, kurbkrano

bible, biblio; **the Bible**, la B~o; **Biblical**, B~a; **bible leaf**, (bot), balzamito

bibliography, bibliograf/io; **bibliographer**, ~o; **bibliographical**, ~ia

bibliomania, bibliomanio; **bibliomaniac**, ~a; ~ulo

bibliophile, bibliofilo, libro–amanto

Bibos gaurus, gaŭro

bicameral, duĉambra

bicarbonate, hidrokarbonato, hidrogena karbonato; **sodium bicarbonate**, **bicarbonate of soda**, natria ~o

biceps, bicepso

bichir, poliptero

bicker, (quarrel), kvereli [int], ĉikani [int]; (re stream), plaŭdi [int]

bicron, mikromikrono

bicycle, biciklo; ~i [int]; (antique, w huge front wheel), pra~o; **bicyclist**, ~isto

bid, (request), peti [tr]; ~o; (at auction etc.: offer, gen), proponi [tr]; propono; (attempt), peni [tr]; peno; (offer price in competition for bsns contract etc.), prezkonkuri [int]; prezkonkuro; (card games), anonci [tr]; anonco; **out-bid**, pliproponi [tr]; **let bids on**, adjudiki [tr]; **take bids on**, meti en prezkonkurado; **sacrifice bid**, (bridge), ofera anonco, ofera oferto

bide, (wait), atendi [tr]; **bide one's time**, pacience ~adi, ~i sian oportunon, ~i la ĝustan momenton

Bidens, bidento

bidet, bideo

biennial, (once in 2 years; lasting 2 years), dujara; (plant), ~ulo

bier, mort/platformo, ~estrado

bifid, bifida

bifilar, bifilara

bifurcate, (dis)forkiĝi; **bifurcation**, ~o

big, granda

bigamy, bigamio; **bigamist,** ~ulo; **bigamous,** ~a
bight, (loop), maŝo; (bend, as in river), kurbiĝo; (bay), golfo
bignonia, Bigonia, bignonio
bigot, prejudiced), antaŭjuĝ/anto; (hypocritically pious), bigoto [cp "zealot"]; **bigoted,** ~a; bigota; **bigotry,** ~(ad)o; bigoteco
bike, [see "bicycle" or "motor: motorcycle"]; **motorbike,** motorbiciklo
bikini, (swimsuit), bikino
Bikini, (island), Bikini*
bilabial, (having 2 lips), dulipa; (phon), bilabialo
Bilbao, Bilbao
bilberry, mirtelo
bilboquet, bilboko
bile, galo; **bile duct,** koledoko
bilge, (bottom of ship), bilĝo; (water), ~akvo
bilharzia, bilharzio;   **bilharziasis,** ~ozo, skistosomozo
bilious, gal(ec)a
bilk, (swindle),   fraŭdi   [tr];   (avoid, elude), eviti [tr]
bill, (invoice),   fakturo,   kalkulo;   [tr]; (paper $), bileto (e.g.: *five–dollar bill:* kvindolara bileto); (proposed law), bilo, leĝprojekto; (legal document), akto (e.g.: *bill of sale:* vendakto); (sunshade on hat etc.), viziero; (beak), beko; (poster), afiŝo; (mus, theat program), programo; enprogramigi; **billfold,** monbilujo; **billhook,** serpo; **bill of exchange,** kambio; **bill of fare,** manĝokarto, menuo; **bill of lading,** (gen),   frajtletero;   (esp on ship), konosamento,   ŝarĝatesto;   **bill of rights,** akto de rajtoj; **bill and coo,** kolombumi [int]; **fill the bill,** plenumi la bezonon; **top billing,** (mus, theat), (la) plej alta enprogramigo; **waybill,** frajtletero
Bill, (short for "William"), Vilĉjo
billabong, (Aus), bilabongo*
billet, (lodging), loĝ/ejo; ~igi; (order), ~igasigno; (wood), ŝtipo; (metal rod), stango
billet-doux, amletero
billiard, bilarda; **billiards,** ~o [note sing]

billion, (Am: 10^9), miliardo; (Br: 10^{12}), duiliono [see § 19(b)]
billow, ondego; ~(ad)i [int]; **billowing,** ~a, pufa
billy, (club), klabo; (pot), gamelo; **billycan,** gamelo; **billyclub,** ~o
biltong, viandostrio(j)
bimetallic, bimetala, dumetala; **bimetalism,** ~ismo
bimonthly, dumonata; ~e
bin, (gen), kuvo, ujo; (for specific purpose), –ujo [sfx] (e.g.: *coal bin:* karbuj(eg)o; *dustbin,* rubujo)
binary, (math: base 2),duaria†; (having 2 elements, 2 parts), binara
binaural, (2 ears), duorela; (stereophonic), stereofonia
bind, (tie, gen), ligi [tr], kun~i [tr]; (kun)~o; (wrap, bandage), vindi [tr] [see "bandage"]; (stick together), kunglui [tr]; kungluiĝi; (obligate), devigi; (make unfree, gen), malliberigi; (constrict, as re garment), esti malloza; (books), bindi [tr]; (freeze up, stick, as metal parts w/o oil), rajpi [int]; (dilemma), dilemo, embaraso, malfacilaĵo;   **binder,**   (notebook),   kajero; **binding,** (of book), bindaĵo; (obligatory), deviga; **clothbound,** tolbindita; **paperbound,** broŝurita; **double bind,** senelira dilemo
bine, sarmento
binge, (gen), diboĉo
bingo, (game), bingo*
binnacle, kompasujo
binocular, (re 2 eyes), duokula; **binoculars,** binoklo [note sing]
binomial, binomo, dutermo; ~a, duterma
bio–, (pfx: life), bio–
biocenosis, biocenozo†
biography,   biograf/io;   **biographer,** ~o; **biographical,** ~ia; **autobiography,** aŭto~io; **autobiographical,** aŭto~ia
biology, biolog/io, biontologio; **biologist,** ~o, biontologo; **biological,** ~ia, biontologia; **astrobiology,** astro~io; **exobiology,** ekzobiologio*; **microbiology,** mikro~io
biomass, biomaso†
biopsy, biopsio

biosphere, biosferot
biotite, biotito
biotope, biotopot
bipartisan, dupartia
bipartite, (w 2 parts), duparta; (2 parties, bipartisan), dupartia
biped, dupieda; ~ulo
biplane, biplano
bipod, dupiedo
birch, (tree), betulo; **silver birch**, arĝenta ~o
bird, (gen), birdo; (middle-finger insult), mezfingro; **bird's-eye**, (bot: *Veronica*), veroniko; (*Primula*), primolo; **bird('s)-foot**, (bot: *Ornithopus*), ornitopo; **bird of paradise**, paradiz~o, paradizeo; **adjutant bird**, marabuo; **apostle bird**, (Aus), apostol~o; **blackbird**, (*Turdus merula*), merlo; **bluebird**, (*Sialia*), sialio*; **catbird**, kat~o; **frigate bird**, **man-o'-war bird**, fregato; **lyrebird**, menuro, lirvostulo; **mockingbird**, mok~o; **rain bird**, (Aus), ŝanelbeka kukolo; **reedbird**, **ricebird**, bobolinko; **rifle bird**, (Aus), paradiza pafil~o; **scrub bird**, (Aus: *Atrichornis rufescens*), rufa arbustar-birdo; **thunderbird**, tondro~o; **bird in the hand**, certaĵo; **bird in the bush**, necertaĵo; **birds of a feather**, similuloj; **for the birds**, ridinda; **the birds and the bees**, la rudimentoj de sekso; **give one the bird**, (middle-finger insult), mezfingri [tr]
birdie, (golf), minusŝoto; ~i [int]; (bird), birdĉjo, birdeto
biretta, bireto
birgus, Birgus, birgo
Birmingham, Birmingamo
biro, (Br), globkrajono
birth, nask/iĝo [see "bear"]; **give birth to**, ~i [tr]; **birth control**, ~olimigo, ~oregulado; **birthday**, ~iĝtago; **birthmark**, haŭtmakulo, nevuso; **birthplace**, ~iĝloko; **birthrate**, ~okvanto, natalitato; **birthright**, ~iĝorajto; **birthstone**, ~iĝoŝtono; **birthwort**, aristolokio; **afterbirth**, post~aĵo; **childbirth**, (labor), akuŝo; **be in childbirth**, akuŝi [tr]; **premature birth**, fru~iĝo; **stillbirth**,

mort~o
Biscay, (province), Biskajo; **Bay of Biscay**, Golfo ~a
biscuit, (Am: bread roll), panbuleto; (unglazed pottery; Br: crisp cracker), biskvito; (Br: cookie), kekso [cp "scone"; (re-toasted, as zweiback), biskoto
bise, bizo
bisect, (geom: divide equally), bisekci [tr]; (med etc.: cut), sekci [tr]
bishop, (rel), episkopo; (chess), kuriero; **bishopric**, (diocese), ~ejo; (rank, office), ~eco; **archbishop**, arki~o; **bishop('s)-weed**, amio
bismuth, bismuto
bison, bizono
bisque, (ceramics), biskvito; (soup), kremsupo
bister, bistro; ~a
bistort, bistorto
bistoury, bisturio
bistre, bistro; ~a
bistro, drinkejeto [not "bistro"]
bit, (small piece), peceto; (small amount), iometo, ĉerpeto; (cmptr unit), bitot; (for bridle), mordaĵo; (of pipe etc.), buŝaĵo; (drill), borilo; **a (little) bit**, iomete (e.g.: *I'm a little bit tired:* mi iomete lacas); **a (little) bit of a**, iometa (e.g.: *I have a bit of a headache:* mi havas iometan kapdoloron); **quite a bit**, **a good bit**, (much), ja multe (e.g.: *quite a bit of rain fell:* ja multe da pluvo falis); **not a bit**, tute ne; tute neniom (e.g.: *Are you tired? Not a bit:* Ĉu vi lacas? Tute ne; *there's not a bit of milk left:* restas tute neniom da lakto); **a bit much**, iom tro; **bit by bit**, iom post iom; **every bit**, (altogether), entute; **do one's bit**, fari sian parton; **bit part**, (theat), roleto, malĉefa rolo
bitch, (dog), hundino; (woman), inaĉo [cp "shrew"]; (unpleasant thing), aferaĉo, ajaĉo, aĉaĵo
bite, (w teeth, lit or fig), mordi [tr]; (act of), ~o; (piece bitten), ~aĵo; (wound), ~ovundo; (sting, as by insect etc.), piki [tr]; piko; **bite off more than one can chew**, alpreni al si tro multe, entrepreni tro multe

bitt, bito
bitter, amara, maldolĉa; **bitters,** ~aĵo [note sing]; **bittersweet,** (taste; expression etc.), dolĉacida; dolĉacido; (bot: *Solanum*), dolĉamaro; **climbing bittersweet, false bittersweet,** celastro
bittern, botaŭro
bitumen, bitumo; **bituminous,** ~a
biuret, biureto
bivouac, bivako; ~i [int]
Bixa, bikso
bizarre, bizara
blab, blabber, klaĉi [int]; el~i [tr]; ~(ad)o; **blabbermouth,** ~anto; ~emulo
bla-bla-bla, (onom: babble), tra-ra-ra
black, (color), nigra; ~o; (thing), ~aĵo; (person), ~ulo; ~ula [cp "Negro"]; (shoe polish etc.), ciri [tr]; (evil), fia; **blacken,** (gen), ~igi; ~iĝi; (w soot etc.), fulgizi [tr]; **black-and-blue,** livida [cp "bruise"]; **black-and-blue spot,** lividaĵo, ekimozo; **blackball,** (by vote), malakcepti [tr]; (ostracize, gen), ostracismi [tr]; **black-out,** (all lights off), ~umi [tr]; ~umo; (lose consciousness), senkonsciiĝi; senkonsciiĝo; (temporary blindness), blindumo; blindumiĝo; **lamp-black,** lampfulgo; **Black Sea,** Maro N~a
blackguard, kanajlo
blackjack, (bludgeon), klabeto; (game), (kartludo) dudek unu
bladder, (gen), veziko; **gall bladder,** kolecisto; **bladderwort,** utrikulario
blade, (cutting), klingo; (of grass), tigo, herbero; (of oar, propeller, turbine, etc.), padelo; **roller blade,** linia sketŝuo; **switchblade,** (blade), faldo~o; (knife), faldotranĉilo
blah, (nonsense), sensencaĵo; (dull etc.), malinteresa, malvigla
Blaise, (man's name), Blazo, ~io
blame, kulpo; ~igi; **to blame,** (guilty), ~a; (responsible), respondeca; **be to blame,** ~i [int]; respondeci [int] (e.g.: *we are not to blame:* ni ne ~as; *the snow is to blame for my lateness:* la neĝo respondecas por mia malakurateco); **blameless,** sen~a
blanch, pal/igi; ~iĝi; (scald), brogi [tr];

(treat metal w acid), acidizi [tr]; (treat w tin), stanizi [tr]
Blanche, (woman's name), Blanka
bland, (flavorless), sapor/manka, sen~a; (mild), milda
blandish, kaĵoli [tr]
blank, (empty, plain, etc.), blanka; (form), [see "form"]; (w/o expression), senesprima; (gun cartridge), ~a kartoĉo; **blank out,** (line out written material), forstreki [tr]; (lose consciousness), senkonsciiĝi; **draw a blank,** rikolti nenion, trovi nenion
blanket, (for bed), (lit)kovrilo; (spread over surface, as snow etc.), sterni [tr]; (cover surface), pristerni [tr] (e.g.: *snow blanketed the city:* neĝo pristernis la urbon); sternaĵo, tavolo
blanquette, blanketo
Blaps, blapto
blare, sonegi [int], bruegi [int]; ~o, bruego
blarney, kaĵol/ado; ~aĵo
blasé, indiferenta
blaspheme, blasfemi [int]; **blasphemy,** ~o; **blasphemous,** ~a
blast, (steady flow, as in blast furnace, jet), blovegi [int]; ~igi; ~(ig)o; (gust, sudden air rush), ek~i [int]; ek~igi; ek~(ig)o; (noise), ekbruegi [int]; ekbruego; (explode), eksplodi [int]; eksplodigi; eksplod(ig)o; (colloq: good time), festego; (intense fire), brulegi [int]; brulego, fajrego, incendio; (of gunfire etc.), pafaro; (squall), skualo
blastema, blastemo
Blastocerus, blastocero
blastoderm, blastodermo
blastomycete, blastomiceto
Blastomycetes, blastomicetoj
blastomycosis, blastomikozo
blastula, blastulo
blatant, (noisy), bruaĉa; (conspicuous, obvious), okulfrapa, evidenta; (unjust), krianta, indigniga
blather, babilaĉi [int]; ~(ad)o
Blatta, blato
blaze, flamegi [int]; ~o; incendio; (fig: be ardent), ardi [int]; ardo; (hack out trail etc.), elhaki [tr] (padon, vojon); (trail marker), (pado)marko; **blazer,** (jacket), sportjako; **blazing,** ~anta; ar-

da; **ablaze**, flamanta; **blaze the way**, elhaki la vojon, pioniri [int]
bleach, blank/igi; ~iĝi; ~igenzo; **bleachers**, (subĉiela) benkaro
bleak, (w/o shelter, exposed), senŝirma; (harsh), malmilda; (gloomy), morna, malgaja, tenebra; (unpromising), senesperiga; (fish), alburno, blankfiŝo
bleary(-eyed), nebulokula
bleat, (goat noise), meki [int]; ~o; (sheep), bei [int]; beo [see "baa"]
bleb, flikteno
bleed, (blood), sangi [int]; ~igi; (ooze, exude, as sap etc.), eksudi [int]; eksudigi; (draw off oth gas or liquid, as from pipeline, or elec from wire), deĉerpi [tr], likigi; **bleeding**, ~ado; **nose-bleed**, epistakso, nazosangado
blemish, (spot, mark, on skin or oth), makulo; ~i [tr]; ~iĝi; (damaged spot), difekteto, ~o
blend, (mix, gen), kunmiksi [tr]; ~iĝi; ~(iĝ)o; ~ajo; (melt together, lit or fig, as ingredients, colors, influences), kunfandi [tr]; kunfandiĝi; kunfand(iĝ)o; kunfandajo; **blender**, ~ilo
blende, blendo
Blennius, blenio; Blenniidae, ~edoj; Blenniiformes, ~oformaj (fiŝoj)
Blennorrhagia, blenoragio
blennorrhea, blenoreo
blenny, (*Blennius*), blenio; (*Zoarces*), zoarco
blepharitis, blefarito
bless, beni [tr]; **blessing**, ~o; **blessed**, ~ita; (rel: beatific), beata
Bletia, bletio
blight, (any withering condition), velk/igi; ~iĝi; ~igo; ~iĝo; (plant disease, gen), plantmalsano; (causing spots on leaves), folimakulozo; (stigma), stigmato
blighter, (Br colloq), ulaĉo
blimp, aerŝipo [cp "dirigible", "balloon"]
blin, blino
blind, (w/o sight, lit or fig; invisible; opaque; dead–end), blinda; ~igi; (hiding place, as for hunter), kaŝejo; **blinder**, (for horse), okulŝirmilo; **blindfold**, okulbandaĝi [tr]; okulban-

daĝo; **blinds**, (windowshade, rolling up on rod), rulkurteno; **Persian blind(s)**, persieno; **Venetian blind(s)**, latkurteno; **blindman's-b(l)uff**, ~ludo; **blind alley**, (lit or fig), senelirejo; **color-blind**, kolor~a, daltonisma; **color-blindness**, kolor~eco, daltonismo
blini, blinoj
blink, (eyes), palpebrumi [int]; ~o; (light), flagri [int]; flagrigi; **blinker (light)**, flagrolumo
blintz, blin/eto; (Juda) ~o
blip, pulso
bliss, (blessedness, rapture), beat/eco; (great happiness), feliĉego; **blissful**, ~a; feliĉega
blister, (on skin, filled w clear liquid), flikteno; ~igi; ~iĝi; (w gas or any liquid), blazo; blazigi; blaziĝi; (any similar-shaped object), blazo; **blood blister**, sangoblazo
blite, blito, fragspinaco
blithe, gaja, senzorga
blithering, galimati(ant)a
Blitum, blito
blitz, fulm/ataki [tr]; ~atako; **blitzkrieg**, ~milito
blizzard, blizardo
bloat, puf/igi, ŝveligi; ~iĝi; ~ulo; ~ajo; **bloated**, ~a, ŝvela
blob, maso, bulo
bloc, bloko
block, (any chunk or solid piece of wood, stone, etc.), bloko; (bar, obstruct), ~i [tr], obstrukci [tr]; (city), (dom)~o; (pulley, in block and tackle), rul~o; (of wood, for chopping, supporting something, etc.), ŝtipo; (plug up), ŝtopi [tr]; ŝtopiĝo; ŝtopaĵo; **block and tackle**, (w only 2 pulleys, one fixed), takelo; (w blocks of multiple pulleys), puliaro; **blockbuster**, (lit or fig), ~rompilo; **blockhead**, stultulo, ventkapulo, azeno; **block letter**, diklitero; **in block letters**, diklitere; **block out**, (cut off, blot out), for~i [tr] (e.g.: *block out the memory*: for~i la memoron); (sketch, lit or fig), skizi [tr]; **building block**, (lit or fig), konstrubriko; **concrete block**, beton~o; **mental block**, mensa ~o; **motor-**

block, motorframo [not "motor~o"];
stumbling-block, obstaklo, stumb-
loŝtono
blockade, blokado; ~i [tr]
Blois, (city), Blezo; (region), ~io
bloke, ulo
blond(e), blonda; ~ul(in)o
blood, (body fluid, lit or fig), sango;
(ancestry, lineage), deveno; **bloody,**
~a; **blood bank,** ~orezervejo [see under "bank"]; **blood bath,** masakro;
blood brother, (gen), ~ofrato; **blood
count,** globulnombro; **bloodcurdling,**
horora, terurega; **bloodhound,** spurhundo; **bloodmobile,** ~aŭto; **blood
poisoning,** ~oveneniĝo; **bloodshed,**
~overŝ(ad)o, mortig(ad)o; **bloodshot,**
~ostria; **bloodstain,** ~omakulo; ~i
[tr]; **bloodstream,** ~kurento, ~ofluo;
bloodthirsty, ~avida; **cold-blooded,**
senkompata; **in cold blood,** senkom-
pate; **hot-blooded,** ekscitiĝema;
blue-blood, aristokrato; **pure-blood,**
purrasulo; **pure-blooded,** purrasa;
half-blood, miksrasulo; miksrasa;
bad blood, malamo
bloom, (flower), floro; ~i [int]; (blos-
soming, lit or fig), ~iĝo; (coating on
some fruits etc.), lanugo; (spongy
iron), ferspongo; **abloom,** ~anta
bloomer, (Br colloq: mistake), fuŝaĵo,
maltrafo; **bloomers,** (pants), pufpantalono [note sing]; (undergarment),
pufkalsono
blossom, (flower, lit or fig), floro; ~i
[int]
blot, (spot, stain, lit or fig), makulo; ~i
[tr]; ~iĝi; **blot out,** neniigi, forbloki
[tr]; **blot up,** forsorbi [tr]
blotch, makulo; ~i [tr]; ~iĝi; **blotchy,**
~(hav)a
blotter, (for desk, holder for blotter paper), skribsubaĵo; **blotter paper,** sor-
bopapero
blouse, (like shirt), bluzo; (like jacket),
~jako
blow, (move air), blovi [tr, int]; (pant),
anheli [int]; (explode), eksplodi [int];
eksplodo; (sound, as wind instrument), sonigi; (bungle, mess up), fuŝi
[tr]; (melt, re fuse etc.), fandi [tr]; fan-
diĝi; (hit), bato; (on a fire), ~eksciti

[tr]; **blower,** ~ilo [cp "bellows"];
blow away, for~i [tr, int]; dis~i [tr,
int]; **blow out,** (explode, as tire), krevi
[int]; krevo; (extinguish), ~estingi
[tr]; ~estingiĝi; (plug etc.), el~i [tr,
int]; malŝtopi [tr]; malŝtopiĝi; **blow
over,** (storm etc.), for~i [tr, int]; **blow
up,** (inflate), plen~i [tr]; (explode),
eksplodi [int]; eksplodigi; (intensify),
leviĝi, intensiĝi; levi [tr], intensigi;
(phot), pligrandigi; (exaggerate), troigi; (get angry), koleriĝi, furioziĝi;
blow one's nose, mungi [int]; **blow
one's own horn (trumpet),** fanfaroni
[int], laŭdi sin mem; **dirty blow, blow
below the belt,** kanajlaĵo; **come to
blows,** ekbatali [int]; **blow-by-blow,**
plendetala
blowzy, (ruddy), ruĝvanga; (slovenly),
plumpa
blubber, (fat), (balen)graso; (cry), plo-
raĉi [int]
bludgeon, klabo; ~i [tr]
blue, (color), blua; ~o; ("bluing", actu-
ally a bleach), blankigenzo, lav–blu-
aĵo; **navy blue,** marista ~o; **bluegreen,** ~verda, (poet), glaŭka; **the
blues,** (mood), melankolio; (mus),
bluso; **rhythm and blues,** ritmenblu-
so†
bluff, (deceive), blufi [int] (al); ~o;
(cliff), klifo; **call one's bluff,** kontesti
ies ~on
blunder, (mistake), fuŝi [tr]; ~o; (stumble about), stumbladi [int]
blunderbuss, blunderbuzo
blunt, (not sharp, gen), malakra; ~igi;
(outspoken), malsubtila
blur, (blot, smudge), makulo; ~i [tr];
(hazy), nebuligi; (dull), malakrigi;
blurred, blurry, ~ita; nebula; malakra
blurb, (ad), (puf)reklamo; ~i [tr]
blurt (out), elverŝi [tr]
blush, roziĝi, ruĝiĝi; ~o, ruĝiĝo
bluster, (gen), tempesto; ~i [int]
boa, Boa, boao; **boa constrictor,** konstriktoro
boar, (male pig), virporko; **wild boar,**
apro
board, (wood piece, gen; flat surface
for specific use; any similar object),

tabulo; ~i [tr] [cp "plank"]; (cardboard), kartono; (meals), nutrado; (executive, managing group), estraro, administrantaro, direktoraro; (council), konsilio; (commission), komisio; (get on train, ship, etc.), entrajniĝi, enŝipiĝi (etc.); eniri [tr] (trajnon, ŝipon, etc.); (cmptr: circuit module), ico†, cirkvito~o; **boarder,** (in boarding house), pensionulo; **boarding house,** pensiono; **boarding school,** pensionlernejo; **boardwalk,** ~promenejo; **above-board,** senruza; **across-the-board,** ĉioninkluda; **baseboard,** plankoplinto; **billboard,** reklampanelo, afiŝ~o; **blackboard, chalkboard,** (of any color, as modern green chalkboards), kreto~o; (of black color), nigra ~o; **breadboard,** pan~o; **bulletin board,** afiŝ~o; **cardboard,** kartono; kartona; **chessboard, checkerboard,** ŝak~o; **chopping board,** hak~o; **clapboard,** kojn~o; **dashboard,** (of car etc.), panelo; **diving board,** plonĝo~o; **drawing board,** desegno~o, desegnostablo; **inboard,** enboata, enŝipa; **on board,** (in train, etc.), en (la trajno etc.); **get on board,** [see "(get on ...)" above]; **outboard,** eksterboata; eksterboate; eksterboata motoro; **overboard,** (from ship), elŝipe(n); **fall overboard,** fali elŝipen; **go overboard,** (go too far), troigi; troiĝi; **pasteboard,** pastokartono; **pegboard,** kejl~o; **plasterboard,** gipso~o; **running-board,** piedbreto; **sailboard,** vel~o; **sounding board,** (mus or fig), son~o; **springboard,** (for gymnastics), salt~o; (diving ~), plonĝo~o; **surfboard,** surf~o; **switchboard,** (telephone etc.), konekto~o, ŝalto~o; **wallboard,** gipsopanelo(j); **washboard,** lav~o; **weatherboard,** teg~o; **go by the board,** perdiĝi, ruiniĝi

boast, (brag), fanfaroni [int]; ~o; **boastful,** ~(em)a

boat, (gen), boato; **boathook,** hokstango; **boathouse,** ~remizo; **longboat,** long~o; **motorboat,** motor~o; **paddlewheel boat,** radŝipo; **rowboat,** rem~o; **sailboat,** vel~o; **surfboat,**

surf~o; **tugboat,** puŝŝipo, trenŝipo; **be in the same boat,** (fig), havi la saman sorton; **rock the boat,** (fig), inciti abelujon, kirli la koton

Boaz, Boazo

bob, (cluster, ball), bulo; (move as cork on water), balanciĝi, ĵetiĝadi; (cut, re hair etc.), tondi [tr]; (cut, re tail etc.), pritondi [tr]; (Br colloq: shilling), ŝilingo; (sled), bobo†

Bob, (short for "Robert"), Roĉjo

bobbin, bobeno

bobble, (mistake), fuŝi [tr]; erari [int]; ~o, eraro; (fringe), franĝbulo

bobolink, bobolinko

bode, aŭguri [tr]

bodhisattva, bodisatvo

bodice, korsaĵo

Bodoni, (type), bodonio

body, (main structural part of person or animal, gen; quantity of matter; etc.), korpo; (object in free space), astro; (of car etc.), karosiero; (torso), torso; (corpse), kadavro; (main part), ĉefparto; ~o; **bodyguard,** ~ogardisto; **able-bodied,** ~osana, laborkapabla; **antibody,** anti~o, antikseno; **blackbody,** nigra ~o

Boehmeria, bemerio; Boehmeria nivea, ramio

Boeotia, Beot/io; **Boeotian,** ~a; ~o; ~ia

Boer, Buro; ~a

boffin, (Br), (esplor)sciencisto

bog, marĉo; **bog down,** (lit or fig), en~igi; en~iĝi

bogey, (goblin), koboldo; (golf: par), normo; normŝoti [int]; (one over par), plusŝoto; plusŝoti [int]

boggle, (startle, stun), konsterni [tr], kapturni [tr]; ~iĝi; (hezitate), heziti [int], sin ĝeni pri

bogie, (train wheel assembly), boĝio

Bogotá Bogoto

bogy, [see "bogie"]

Bohemia, Bohem/io; **Bohemian,** (re region), ~ia; (person from region), ~o; (re unconventional lifestyle), ~ia; ~ia-no; **Bohemianism,** (lifestyle), b~io

boil, (vaporize), boli [int]; ~igi; (cook by boiling), ~kuiri [tr]; ~kuiriĝi; (skin sore), furunko; **boiler,** ~ujo, kaldron(eg)o; **soft (hard) boil,**

(mal)mole ~kuiri; **hard-boiled**, (fig. re person), hardita; **parboil**, duon~igi; **boiling point**, ~punkto; **boil down**, (fig: summarize), resumi [tr] **boisterous**, brua, tumulta, malkvieta, ŝtorma, tempesta **bold**, (courageous), kuraĝa; (valiant), brava; (audacious), aŭdaca; (fearless), sentima; (resolute), rezoluta; **boldface**, grasa tipo, grasliteroj; **boldfaced**, grastipa, graslitera **bole**, trunko **bolero**, bolero **bolete**, **boletus**, boleto Boletus, boleto, tubfungo; Boletus luteus, buterfungo **bolide**, bolido **Bolivia**, Bolivio; **Bolivian**, ~a; ~ano **boll**, kapsulo **bollix (up)**, fuŝi [tr] **bollard**, bolardo **bologna**, (meat), bolonjo* **Bologna**, (city), Bolonjo* **bolometer**, bolometro **bolshevik**, bolŝevisma; bolŝevisto; **bolshevism**, ~o **bolster**, (small pad), kusen/eto; (long cushion), cilindra ~o; (prop up), apogi [tr] **bolt**, (screw w flat end), bolto; ~i [tr]; (door latch, pivoted; or similar device), klinko; (door-fastening rod), rigli [tr]; riglilo; (of fabric), (ŝtof)bloko; (of lightning), fulmo; (withdraw from party, group, etc.), kabei [int]; (swallow fast), glutegi [tr]; (run), ekkuregi [int]; (sift), bluti [tr]; **molly bolt**, dubel~o; **stop-bolt**, haltiga kejlo **bolus**, (lump), buleto; (pill), boluso **bomb**, bombo; ~i [tr]; **bomber**, ~aviadilo; **bombshell**, (bomb), ~o; (surprise), surprizego; **bombsight**, ~ocelilo; **atom(ic) bomb**, **A-bomb**, atom~o; **hydrogen bomb**, **H-bomb**, hidrogen~o, H-~o; **incendiary bomb**, brul~o; **nuclear bomb**, nuklea ~o; **neutron bomb**, neŭtron~o [see also "nucleus", "nuke"] **bombard**, (gen), bombardi [tr]; **bombardier**, (in charge of bombs), bombisto; (Br officer), kaporalo; **bombardment**, ~(ad)o

bombast, bombasto; **bombastic**, ~a **bombax**, Bombax, bombako **Bombay**, Bombajo Bombinator, bombinatoro Bombus, burdo Bombycilla, bombicilo **bona fide**, (in good faith), bonfida, bonintenca; (genuine), aŭtentika, vera; **bona fides**, ~o **bonanza**, (lit: ore vein), riĉega vejno; (fig), riĉigilo, ormonto **Bonaparte**, Bonaparto Bonasa, bonazio **Bonaventura**, **Bonaventure**, Bonaventuro **bonbon**, bombono **bond**, (chem; any tying), ligi [tr]; ~iĝi; ~o; (as glue), aglutini [tr]; aglutiniĝi; aglutino; ($: obligation, as savings bond), obligacio; ($: security, as for accused person), kaŭcio; kaŭcii [tr]; (any contract), kontrakto; **bondage**, (gen), servuto; **bonded**, **on bond**, kaŭciita **bone**, osto; ~a; (remove bones from meat), sen~igi; **bony**, ~(ec)a; **boneset**, (bot), eŭpatorio; **backbone**, (spine), spino; **cuttlefish bone**, sepi~o; **jawbone**, (lower jaw), mandiblo; **temporal bone**, temporalo; **thighbone**, femur~o; **wishbone**, fork~o; **zygomatic bone**, zigomo; [for oth ~s, see separate entries]; **to the bone**, (thoroughly), ĝis~e **Boniface**, Bonifaco **bonito**, bonito **bon mot**, spritajo **Bonn**, Bonno **bonnet**, (for head), kufo; (Br: car hood), kapoto; (naut), bonedo; **bluebonnet**, (bot: *Lupinus*), lupino **bonus**, bonifiko **bon vivant**, bonvivanto **bon voyage**, bonan vojaĝon! **bonze**, bonzo **boo**, (interj), hu! **boob**, (stupid person), bubo; (colloq: breast), mam(glob)o **booboo**, bubaĵo **booby**, (stupid person), bubo; (colloq: breast), mal(glob)o; (zool: *Sula*), sulo; **booby prize**, ~opremio; **booby trap**,

~okaptilo
book, (gen), libro; ~a; (set appointment, reserve), rezervi [tr]; (record, list), registri [tr]; (charge w crime), imputi [tr]; (**all**) **booked up**, plene rezervita; **booking agent**, rezervagento; **bookbinding**, bindado; **bookcase**, ~oŝranko; **bookend**, ~apogilo, ~okrampo; **bookkeep, keep books**, kontadi [int], ~oteni [int]; **bookkeeper**, kontisto, ~otenisto; **bookkeeping**, kontado, ~otenado; **booklet**, (brochure), broŝuro; (any small book), ~eto; **bookmaker**, (publisher), eldonisto; (bookie), bukmekro; **bookmark**, legosigno; **bookmobile**, ~aŭto; **bookplate**, ekslibriso; **bookworm**, (person), legemulo; (insect), ~overmo; **appointment book**, agendo; **cookbook**, receptaro, kuir~o; **guide book**, gvid~o; **handbook**, man~o; **notebook**, (small book for making notes), not~o; (unbound, ringbound, etc.), kajero; (for appointments), agendo; **pocket notebook**, kajereto; **ringbinder notebook**, ringokajero, ringo~o; **prayer book**, preĝo~o; **passbook**, (for bank), bank~o; **phrasebook**, esprim~o; **pocketbook**, (purse), monujo; (wallet), (mon)bilujo; **pocket(-sized) book**, poŝ~o; **scrapbook**, (eltond)albumo, kolekto-libro; **textbook**, lerno~o; **workbook**, (student's), laborkajero, labor~o; (book of instructions), instrukciaro; (work record book), (labora) registrokajero; **yearbook**, jar~o; **bring to book**, postuli konton; **by the book**, laŭregule; **in one's book**, laŭ ies opinio; **one for the books**, notindaĵo; **throw the book at**, imputi [tr] kiel eble maksimume, imputi (iun) pri ĉio
bookie, bukmekro
boom, (loud sound), tondri [int]; el~i [int]; ~o; (onom), bum!, pum!; (mast), bumo; (prosperity), prospero; pros-pera; (growth), kreskego
boomerang, bumerango
boon, (blessing), beno
boor, (crude person), krud/ulo; **boorish**, ~a

boost, (lift), levi [tr]; ~o; (support), subteni [tr]; (elec: amplify), amplifi [tr]; (revaccinate), revakcini [tr]; **booster**, subtenanto; amplifatoro; revakcino; (rocket), kromraketo
boot, (shoe, esp reaching knee), boto; (partway up calf), ~eto; (kick), piedbati [tr]; piedbato; (Br: car trunk), kofrujo; **bootblack**, ciristo; **bootee, bootie**, (small boot), ~eto; (baby shoe), ŝueto; **bootjack**, ~otirilo; **bootleg**, kontrabandi [tr]; kontrabandita; kontrabandaĵo; **bootlegger**, kontrabandisto; **bootlegging**, (act), kontrabando; **bootstrap**, (lit), ~rimeno; (progress by building on prior efforts), progresi [int] (progresigi) pere de antaŭatingoj; **boot up**, (cmptr), startigi; **lift oneself up by one's own bootstraps**, sukcesi [int] per sia propra penado; **wading boots**, vad~oj; **to boot**, (besides), krome, aldone
Boötes, la Bovisto
booth, (small compartment, stall, gen), budo, kiosko (e.g.: *telephone booth:* telefon~o); (in restaurant, bar, etc.), separeo; (display stall at fair, exhibition, etc.), stando, kiosko
booty, rabaĵo, kaptaĵo, predo
booze, (colloq), alkoholaĵo; **booze it up**, drink(ad)i [int]
bop, (hit), bati [tr]; (mus), bopo
borage, borago
Borago, borago; Boraginaceae, ~acoj
borate, borato
borax, borakso
borborygmus, borborigmo
Bordeaux, Bordozo; **Bordeaux mixture**, ~likvaĵo
bordello, bordelo
border, (boundary, gen), limo; ~igi; ~iĝi; apud~a; (between countries, states, provinces, etc.), land~o, ŝtat~o provinc~o (etc.); (decorative), border(aĵ)o; borderi [tr]; (edge), [see "edge"]; **borderland**, ~ejo; **borderline, ~o; **border town, border city**, ~urb(et)o
bordun, borduno
bore, (cut hole into, through), bori [tr]; (smooth inside of bored hole), alezi [tr]; (caliber), kalibro; (tidal), mask-

areto; (cause tedium), tedi [tr]; (boring person), tedulo; (be uninteresting), enuigi; **boring**, teda; enuiga; **bored**, enua; **be bored**, enui [int]; **get bored**, enuiĝi; **boredom**, tedo; enuo; **ship borer**, (zool), teredo
boreal, boreala
Boreas, Boreo
Borellia, borelio
borelliosis, boreliozo
boric, (having boron, gen), bora; (of borate), ~ata; **boric acid**, ~ata acido
born, nask/ita [see "bear"]; (since birth), de~a (e.g.: *a born leader:* de~a estro); **be born**, ~iĝi, esti ~ita (e.g.: *when were you born?* kiam vi ~iĝis?);
aborning, ~iĝante; **first-born**, unue~ita; unua~ito; **inborn**, de~a; **newborn**, nov~ita; nov~ito; **stillborn**, mort~ita
Borneo, Borneo
borneol, borneolo
boron, boro
borough, (district), (urbo)distrikto; (Br: chartered town), municipo
borrow, prunt/epreni [tr], de~i [tr], ~i [tr] de
borsch, barĉo
borzoi, Rusa luphundo
Bos, (zool, gen), bovo; Bos bison, bizono; Bos bubalis, bubalo; Bos fruntalis gaurus, gaŭro; Bos grunniens, poefago, grunt~o; Bos indicus, zebuo; Bos primigenius, Bos urus, uro
boscage, kopso
Boselaphus, boselafo
bosket, bosko
Bosnia, Bosnio†
bosom, (inner part, middle), sino; (breast), mamo; **bosom buddy, bosom friend**, koramiko
boson, bosono
Bosporus, Bosporo
boss, (person in charge), mastro; ~i [tr]; (raised area), boso; bosi [tr]; **strawboss**, sub~o, vokto; **bossy**, ~ema
bossa nova, bosanovo†
boston, (dance), bostono
Boston, (city), Bostono
Bostrychus, bostriko
Bostryx, bostriko
Boswellia carteri, olibanarbo

botany, botaniko; **botanist**, ~isto; **botanical**, ~a; **Botany Bay**, Golfo B~a
Botaurus, botaŭro
botch, fuŝi [tr]
both, ambaŭ [not "~aj"]; **both of (them)**, ~ el (ili); **both ... and**, kaj ... kaj (e.g.: *both Mary and Bob received prizes:* kaj Maria kaj Roĉjo ricevis premiojn)
bother, (inconvenience, disturb), ĝeni [tr]; ~o; (bore), tedi [tr]; (worry, disquiet), ĉagreni [tr]; ĉagreno; (uncalm; e.g., re emotion etc.), malkvietigi; malkvietigo; malkvieteco; **bothered**, ~ita; ĉagrenita; **go to the bother (to)**, fari al si la ~on [or] klopodon (–i) [not "sin ~i"]; **bothersome**, ~a; ĉagrena
Bothnia, Botnio
Bothrops, botropo
Bothus rhombus, rombo
Botswana, Bocvano†
bottle, botelo; en~igi; (from animal hide), felsako; **bottleneck**, (lit), ~kolo; (fig: constriction, blockage in flow of traffic, production process, etc.), ŝtopiĝo†; stopaĵo; **hot water bottle**, varmakva ~o; **siphon bottle**, sifon~o; **squeeze bottle**, prem~o
bottom, (lowest point), fundo; (underneath side), malsupro; (buttocks), postaĵo [cp "ass"]
botulism, botulismo*
boudoir, buduaro
bouffant, pufita
bougainvillea, Bougainvillea, bugenvilo
bough, branĉo
bougie, buĝio
bouillabaisse, bujabeso
bouillon, boljono
boulder, roko, ŝtonego
boulevard, bulvardo
Boulogne, Bulono; **Boulogne-sur-Mer**, ~o ĉe Maro
bounce, resalti [int]; ~igi; ~(ig)o; **bouncer**, elpelisto
bound, (bounce), resalt(ad)i [int]; ~igi; ~o; (resolute), rezoluta; (boundary), limo; limigi; [see "bind"]; **bounds**, (boundary in football, tennis, etc.), taĉo; **inbound**, enir(ant)a; **in bounds**, ene de taĉoj; **out of bounds**, ekster

taĉoj; **be bound for,** celi [tr, int], esti
survoje al; **within the bounds of,** interne de la limoj de; **clothbound,**
hardbound, (etc., re books), [see under "bind"]
boundary, limo
bounden, devig(it)a
bounder, kanajlo
bounteous, bountiful, (giving freely),
malavara; (plentiful), abunda
bounty, (generosity), malavar/eco;
(generous gift), ~ajo; (prize, reward),
premio
bouquet, bukedo
bourbon, (whiskey), burbono, ~a viskio
Bourbon, (re French family etc.), Burbono
bourdon, borduno
bourgeois, burĝo; ~a; **bourgeoise,**
~ino; **bourgeoisie,** ~aro
Bourgogne, Burgonjo
Bourkina Fasso, Burkina-Faso†
bourse, borso
boustrophedon, plugskriba; ~ado
bout, (struggle), lukto; (of illness), atako
boutique, (shop, gen), butiko; (esp for
fashionable things), mod~o
boutonnière, roversofloro
bovine, bova; ~o
Bovista, bovisteo, polvofungo
bow, (lower head etc. in respect), riverenci [int]; ~o; (yield, as to authority),
cedi [tr, int]; (bend, be bent, as by
weight), klini [tr]; kliniĝi; (of ship or
boat), pruo; (any arc), arko; (weapon,
w arrows), pafarko; (mus: for string
instrument), arĉo; arĉi [tr]; (of eyeglasses), orelumo; (ornamental knot),
bulennodo; **bowman,** (archer), pafarkisto; **bowsprit,** busprito; **bowstring,**
arĉkordo; **crossbow,** arbalesto; **bow**
one's head, klini la kapon; **bow out,**
sin retiri; **take a bow,** fari ~on; **bow**
and scrape, flataĉi [tr], lakei [tr]
bowel, (intestine), intesto; (inner part,
gen), internajo; (lower part), subaĵo;
disembowel, sen~igi
bower, (arbor), laŭbo; **virgin's bower,**
(bot), klematido
bowl, (soup etc.), bovlo, pelvo; (wash
basin etc.), kuveto; (chalice), kaliko;

(game), ludi keglojn, kegli [int];
(cricket: throw ball), ĵeti [tr]; (go fast),
rapidegi [int]; **bowler,** (hat), bulĉapelo; **bowling,** (game), kegloludo;
bowling alley, keglejo; **bowling ball,**
keglopilko; **bowling pin,** keglo;
(lawn) bowls, lawn bowling, gazonkegloludo; **washbowl,** lavkuvo;
bowl (one) over, konstern(eg)i (iun),
stuporigi (iun)
bow-wow, (onom: dog sound), boj-boj
[see "bark"]
box, (container, gen), skatolo; en~igi;
(for specific use), ~ujo [sfx] (e.g.:
jewel box: juvelujo); (sport), boksi
[int] (kontraŭ, kun); (shrub), bukso;
(in theater), loĝio; (booth, for sentry
etc.), budo; **boxer,** boksisto; **boxing,**
bokso; **box spring,** (for bed), somiero; **boxwood,** (shrub), bukso; (wood),
buksligno; **ballot-box,** urno; **bandbox,** (for hats), ĉapelujo; **breadbox,**
panujo; **junction box,** (elec wall outlet), kontakto~o; (elec: large underground box), junktokesto; **lunch box,**
manĝo~o; **music box,** muzik~o; **Post**
Office box, poŝtkesto [abb: pk.] [see
§ 22]; **sentry box,** gardista budo;
sound box, (of mus instrument),
sonkesto; **strongbox,** monkesto [cp
"safe"]; **voice box,** laringo; **window**
box, ~ĝardeno
Box, (zool), bokso
boy, knabo; **boyhood,** ~aĝo; **tomboy,**
~ulino
boyar, bojaro
boycott, bojkoti [tr]; ~o
Bozcaada, Tenedo
br, br!, brr!
bra, mamzono
Brabant, Brabanto
brace, (tighten), streĉi [tr]; (fasten), fiksi [tr]; (support, gen), apogi [tr];
apogilo; (support during construction
etc.), armaturi [tr]; armaturo; (to
strengthen mech part etc.), stegi [tr];
stego; (stimulate), stimuli [tr]; (make
firm), firmigi, fortikigi; (metal bracket
etc.), krampo; (punctuation: ( )), kurba(j) krampo(j); (pair), paro; (naut:
rope for yard), braso; brasi [tr]; **brace**
and bit, krankborilo; **braces,** (den-

tal), dent–agrafaro [note sing]; (Br:
suspenders), ŝelko [note sing]
bracelet, braceleto
brachialis, brakialo
Brachinus, braĥino
brachiopod, brakpiedulo
Brachiopoda, brakpieduloj
brachycephalic, brachycephalous,
brakicefala; **brachycephaly,** ~eco;
brachycephalic person, ~o
Brachynus, braĥino
Brachyura, krabo
bracken, bracken fern, pterido
bracket, (metal brace etc.), krampo;
(punctuation: [ ]), rekta(j) ~o(j);
(range), rango; ĉirkaŭrangigi; **right-
angle bracket,** ortaĵo
brackish, saleta, sal–amara
bract, brakteo
brad, (drat)najleto; **bradawl,** aleno
bradycardia, bradikardio
bradypepsia, bradipepsio
Bradypus, bradipo
brae, deklivo
brag, fanfaroni [int]; ~o; **braggart,**
~ulo
Brahma, (god), Bramo; (basic principle of universe), b~o, brameno
Brahman, (person), bramano; (re cattle), ~a bov(in)o; **Brahmani, Brah-
manee,** ~ino; **Brahmanic,** ~a; ~isma;
Brahmanism, ~ismo
Brahmaputra, Bramaputro
Brahmin, [see "Brahman"]
braid, (hair etc.), plekti [tr]; ~aĵo; (ornament on clothing or furniture),
pasamento; (ribbon, cordon), kordono; **upbraid,** riproĉi [tr]
brail, brajl/ŝnuro; **brail up,** ~i [tr]
braille, Braille, brajlo; **in braille,** ~e
brain, (anat), cerbo; (knock brains out),
sen~igi; (hit on head), kapobati [tr];
(colloq: intelligent person), ~ulo; (animal brain as food), ~aĵo; **brains,**
(brain), ~o; (intelligence), inteligenteco; **braincase,** ~ujo; **brainchild,**
~umaĵo; **brain drain,** ~ulforfuĝo;
brainpan, ~ujo; **brainstorm,**
fulm–idei [int] (pri); fulm–ide(ad)o;
~umaĵo; **brain trust,** ~ularo, ~umko-
mitato; **birdbrain, lame-brain, hare-
brain,** stultulo, ventkapulo, sen~ulo;

**lame-brained, hare-brained, scat-
ter-brained,** facil-anima, malsaĝa,
ventkapa, sen~a
braise, brezi [tr]
brake, (mech), bremso; ~i [tr]; (fern),
pterido; **brake band,** ~bendo; **brake
drum,** ~otamburo; **brake lining,**
~otegaĵo; **brake shoe,** ~oŝuo
bramble, (gen), dorn/arbusto; (Rubus),
rubuso; **bramble-patch,** ~ejo
brambling, montofringo
bran, brano
branch, (of tree or oth plant; division,
gen), branĉo; (dis)~iĝi; (of company,
organization, etc.), filio; (area of
study), fako; (fork), forkiĝi; forkiĝo;
branch off, for~iĝi; forforkiĝi;
branch out, (gen), dis~iĝi
Branchiostoma, brankiostomo, amfiokso
brand, (sign, gen; bsns name), marko;
~i [tr]; (re cattle etc.), ~o; brul~i [tr],
brulstampi [tr]; **branding iron,**
brul~ilo; **brand name,** varnomo
Brandenburg, (city), Brandenburgo;
(province), ~io
brandish, (minace) svingi [tr]; ~o
brandy, brando; **rice brandy,** arako
brant, (zool), berniklo
Branta bernicla, berniklo
brash, (hasty, impetuous), impeta;
(bold, audacious), aŭdaca
Brasilia, Brazilio
brass, (metal), latuno; (mus instruments), ~instrumentoj; (object of
brass) ~aĵo
Brassica, brasiko; Brassica campestris
rapigera, kampa rapo; Brassica napus, ~napo, napo; Brassica napus sativa biennis, kolzo; Brassica oleracea
acephala, Brassica oleracia crispa,
krispa ~a; Brassica oleracia botrytis,
flor~o; Brassica oleracia capitata,
kapo~o; (w white head), blanka ~o;
(w red head), ruĝa ~o; Brassica oleracia gemmifera, brusel~o; Brassica
oleracia gongyloides, tigo~o; Brassica oleracea italica, brokolo
brassidic, brasida; **brassidic acid,** ~a
acido
brassiere, mamzono
brat, bub(in)aĉo

Braunschweig, Brunsviko
bravado, falskuraĝo, temeraro
brave, kuraĝa,sentima; (defy), defii [tr];
(native American), (Indiana) militisto;
bravery, ~o, sentimeco
bravo, (interj), brave!
bravura, bravuro
brawl, kverelego, tumulto, miksbatalo;
~i [int], miksbatali [int]
brawn, muskoloj, ~aro, ~forto
bray, (as donkey), iai [tr]; ~o, azenble-
ko
braze, (solder w zinc-copper), brazi [tr];
(coat w brass), latunizi [tr]
brazen, (of brass), latuna; (shameless),
senhonta
brazier, (for coals), braĝujo; (brass
worker), latunisto
brazil, (wood), cesalpini/a ligno; (dye),
~a farbo
Brazil, (country), Brazilo
brazilwood, cesalpinia ligno
Brazzaville, Brazavilo*
breach, (opening, crack, etc.), breĉo;
~i [tr]; (breaking, as of promise), rompi [tr]; rompo; (interrupt), interrompi
[tr]; interrompo
bread, (gen), pano; ~umi [tr] (e.g.:
breaded veal: ~umita bovidaĵo); (soft
center part), ~molo; **breadbasket**,
(basket), ~korbo; (grain-producing region), grenprovizejo; **breadboard**,
~tabulo; **breadbox**, ~ujo; **bread
crumb**, ~ero; **bread line**, ~vico;
breadwinner, ĉefgajnanto; **black
bread**, nigra ~o; **cornbread**, maiz~o;
raisin bread, rosin~o; **rye bread**,
sekal~o; **shortbread**, graskuko,
buterkuko [cp "cake: shortcake"];
sowbread, (bot), ciklameno; **sweet-
bread**, (thymus, as food), timusaĵo;
(pancreas), pankreataĵo; **white bread**,
blanka ~o; **whole-wheat bread**, plen-
tritika ~o; **loaf of bread**, ~o (e.g.:
three loaves of bread: tri ~oj); **slice of
bread**, ~tranĉo; **bread and butter**,
buter~o; **bread-and-butter**, (re earn-
ing living), vivgajna; (practical, everyday), praktika, ĉiutaga; (re letter
expressing thanks), dankesprima
breadfruit, (tree), panarbo; (fruit), ~a
frukto

breadth, larĝo; **along the length and
breadth (of)**, laŭlonge kaj laŭ~e (de)
break, (rupture, snap, come apart, etc.),
go against [promise, rule, etc.]; interrupt [silence etc.]; overcome [will,
bondage, etc.]), rompi [tr]; ~iĝi;
~(iĝ)o; (bankrupt), bankrotiĝi; (surpass record), superi [tr]; (open, enter
by force), perforti [tr]; (escape), eskapi [int] (de); eskapo; (interrupt), in-
ter~i [tr]; (reduce force of, weaken, as
re fall, wind, etc.), malfortigi; (penetrate), penetri [tr]; (reveal, disclose),
malkaŝi [tr], riveli [tr]; (decipher),
deĉifri [tr]; (solve criminal case etc.),
solvi [tr]; (disprove), malpruvi [tr];
(begin, start), ekiri [int], komenciĝi;
(reduce $ to smaller bills, coins), eri-
gi; (burst), krevi [int]; krevigi; (scatter
in all directions, as a crowd; move
apart, as fighters), disiĝi; (stop work
etc. for rest), paŭzi [int]; paŭzo (e.g.:
coffee break: kafpaŭzo); (occur), okazi [int] (e.g.: *things broke badly:* aferoj okazis malbone); (luck), ŝanco
(e.g.: *get a (good) break:* ricevi
(bon)ŝancon; *that's the breaks!:* jen la
ŝanco!); (take down camp), malstarigi; (destroy), detrui [tr]; (sudden
change, as in weather), ekŝanĝiĝi;
ekŝanĝiĝo; **breakage**, ~iĝado; ~aĵo;
breaker, (wave), ŝaŭmondo; **circuit-
breaker**, cirkvit~ilo; **ice-breaker**,
(ship), glaci~ulo; (fig, as game at party, comment to start conversation,
etc.), glaci~ilo; **break apart**, dis~i
[tr], diserigi; dis~iĝi, diseriĝi; **break
down**, (go out of order, re machine
etc.; cease, as relationship, talk, etc.),
~i; ~iĝi; (collapse, gen), disfali [int];
disfaligi; (nervous or oth med collapse), kolapsi [int]; kolapso; (stall, lit
or fig), panei [int]; paneigi; (overcome), superi [tr]; (separate into
parts), diserigi; diseriĝi; (analyze), analizi [tr]; (categorize), kategoriigi, erigi; **break even**, finiĝi kvita; **break
in**, (enter forcibly), en~iĝi en (~on),
perforti [tr]; (interrupt), inter~i [tr];
(tame animal), malsovaĝigi; (train animal), dresi [tr]; (train person), trejni
[tr], spertigi; (smooth up, re machine),

(ek)glatigi; (ek)glatiĝi; (soften, re
shoes etc.), moligi; moliĝi; **break in
(up)on**, inter~i [tr], trudi sin ĉe, trudiĝi ĉe; **break into**, (start), [see
"break out" below]; (break in), [see
"break in" above]; **breakneck**,
danĝerega; **break off**, (stop), ĉesigi,
inter~i [tr]; ĉesi [int], inter~iĝi; (snap,
shear), deŝiri [tr], de~i [tr]; deŝiriĝi,
de~iĝi; **break open**, krevi [int]; krevigi, enbati [tr]; **break out**, (begin),
ek– [pfx] (e.g.: *break out singing* [or]
in song: ekkanti); (escape), eskapi
[int]; (rupture), el~iĝi; (explode, as
war), eksplodi [int]; (in pimples),
akniĝi; (in rash), raŝiĝi; (appear, as
sun from behind cloud), ekaperi [int];
(show in greater detail), detali [tr]; de-
tal(ad)o (e.g.: *a break-out of these cumulative totals:* detalo de ĉi tiuj
amasiĝaj sumoj); **breakthrough**,
(gen), tra~o; **break up**, (cease relationship), ~i; ~iĝi; (thing into pieces),
dis~i [tr]; dis~iĝi; (cease, as fight, discussion, etc.), ĉesi [int]; ĉesigi; (disperse), disigi; disiĝi; (chem etc.:
uncombine), malkombini [tr]; mal-
kombiniĝi; **breakwater**, moleo;
heartbreak, [see under "heart"]; **out-
break**, el~iĝo, ekapero, eksplodo;
break it up!, ĉesu!, disiĝu!; **breaking
point**, ~opunkto; **daybreak**, tagiĝo;
day is breaking, tagiĝas; **break (a,
the) habit (of)**, dekutimiĝi (je) (e.g.:
*it is difficult to break the smoking
habit:* estas malfacile dekutimiĝi je
fumado); **break (a person or animal) of (doing) something**, deku-
timigi (iun) je (fari) io(n) (e.g.: *break
a dog of urinating on the rug:* de-
kutimigi hundon je urinado sur la tapiŝo); **broken down**, (not working),
[see "break down" above]; (decrepit),
kaduka
breakfast, matenmanĝo
bream, (European, Am fish: *Abramis
brama*), bramo; (Aus: *Acanthopagrus*), akantropago*
breast, (mammary), mamo; (entire
chest), brusto; (clothing part), brustaĵo; (bosom, lap, lit or fig), sino;
(face), alfronti [tr]; **make a clean**

breast, plene konfesi [tr]; **breast-
feed**, ~nutri [tr]; **breast stroke**,
brustnaĝado
breath, (single breath), spiro; (process
of breathing), ~ado; (air breathed),
~aĵo; **breathe**, ~i [int]; en~i [tr];
breathe in, en~i [tr]; **breathe out**,
el~i [tr]; **breather**, (brief rest),
~paŭzo, ek~o; **take a breather**,
~paŭzi [int]; **breathless, short of
breath**, ~manka, sen~a, anhelanta;
breathalyzer, ~analizatoro; **breath-
taking**, sen~iga; **be out of breath**,
anheli [int]; **lose one's breath**,
sen~iĝi, ekanheli [int]; **recover one's
breath**, ĉesi anheli [int]; **hold one's
breath**, reteni la ~on; **in the same
breath**, sam~e; **take one's breath
away**, sen~igi, mirigi, konsterni [tr];
below (under) one's breath, flustre,
murmure; **with bated breath**, ~re-
tene, kun retenita ~o; **baby's breath**,
(bot), gipsofolio
breccia, brecĉio
bred, [see "breed"]
breech, (rear, back side, gen), postaĵo
breeches, (pants, gen), pantalono [note
sing]; (to below knee and tapered),
kuloto
breed, (generate), generi [tr]; (raise animals), bredi [tr]; (rear, train), eduki
[tr]; (race), raso; (reproduce), reprodukti [tr]; **breeding**, ~ado; bredado; edukado; reproduktado; (re
manners etc.), bonedukiteco; **in-
breed**, endogamii [tr], enbredi [tr];
inbred, (innate), denaska; (bred in),
enbredita; **inbreeding**, endogamio;
outbreeding, ekzogamio; **well–
(ill–)bred**, (mal)bonedukita
breeze, (light wind), zefiro; (vertical
convection current), brizo; **breeze
through**, facile fari [tr]; facile trairi
[tr]; **shoot the breeze**, babil(ad)i [int]
bregma, bregmo; **bregmatic**, ~a
Bremen, Bremeno
brethren, (ge)fratoj
Breton, Bretono; ~a
breve, (diacritical mark: [˘]), brevo*,
hoketo, ŭo-signo; (papal letter, judicial writ), brevo; (mus), duobla noto;
semibreve, plena noto

brevet, breveto
breviary, breviero
brevity, (shortness), mallongeco; (conciseness), koncizeco
brew, (beer), fari (bieron); bier~i [int]; (ferment, gen), fermenti [int]; fermentigi; (steep tea etc.), infuzi [tr]; infuziĝi; infuzaĵo; (plot), komploti [int] (pri); (arise), leviĝi (e.g.: *a storm is brewing:* ŝtormo leviĝas); brewer, bier~isto; brewery, bier~ejo
briar, [see "brier"]
Briareus, Briareo
bribe, subaĉeti [tr]; ~o; ($ given), ŝmir~mono, ~a mono; bribery, ~ado
bric-a-brac, brikabrako
brick, briko; brickbat, ~peco; bricklayer, masonisto; bricklaying, masonado; brickwork, ~aĵo; brickyard, ~ejo
bride, (before wedding), fianĉ/ino; (during, after), novedzino; bridal, (re bride), novedzina; (re wedding, gen), nupta (e.g.: *bridal shower:* nupta donacofesto); bridegroom, (before wedding), ~o; (during, after), novedzo; bridesmaid, ~inamiko
bridge, (for crossing or connecting, gen), ponto; super~i [tr], trans~i [tr]; (game), briĝo; bridgehead, ~kapo; bridgework, (dental), dento~aĵo; drawbridge, (over river etc., to let ships pass), baskul~o; (over castle moat), lev~o; footbridge, ~eto; pontoon bridge, flos~o, ponton~o; rope bridge, ŝnur~o; suspension bridge, suspensia ~o, pendo~o; Wheatstone bridge, (or oth similar elec measuring device), mezur~o, ~o de Wheatstone
Bridgetown, (capital of Barbados, or oth city), Briĝtaŭno*
bridle, brido; ~i [tr]; unbridled, sen~a
brief, (short), mallonga; (concise), konciza; (abrupt), abrupta; (legal), akto; (papal letter), brevo; (summarize), resumi [tr]; (summary), resumo; (inform, report), raporti [tr]; (instruct), instrukcii [tr]; briefs, (underpants), kalsoneto [note sing]; debrief, postkonsulti [tr]; briefing, raporto; instrukcio; debriefing, postkonsulto; in brief, ~e; resume

brier, (any thorny bush), dornarbusto; (bot: *Erica*), eriko; (pipe), erika pipo; brierroot, erikradiko; sweetbrier, eglanterio
brig, (prison), prizono; (2-masted ship), brigo
brigade, brigado; brigadier, ~estro
brigand, bandito, rabisto
brigandine, skvamkiraso
brigantine, brigskuno, brigantino
bright, (shining, clear, vivid, etc., re light or sound), hela, brila; (lively), vigla; (cheerful), gaja; (favorable), favora; (intelligent), inteligenta
Brigit, Brigita
brill, rombo
brilliant, (very shiny), bril(eg)a, hel(eg)a; (very intelligent), inteligentega; (very well done, as performance etc.), bravega; (diamond), brilianto; brilliance, ~eco, hel(eg)eco; inteligenteco; bravegeco
brilliantine, (hair dressing), harbriligaĵo
brim, (edge, as of cup etc.), rando; (be brim-full), plenpleni [int]; brimming, plenplena; brim-full, full to the brim, plenplena, ĝis~e plena; fill to the brim, ĝis~e plenigi
brine, (sea water), marakvo; (salt water, gen), salakvo
bring, (take, carry, etc.), porti [tr], preni [tr] (e.g.: *bring me the flower:* portu al mi la floron); (take to), al~i [tr] (e.g.: *bring the flower here:* al~u la floron ĉi tien); (take with), kun~i [tr] (e.g.: *bring your umbrella:* kun~u vian ombrelon); (lead), konduki [tr]; (accompany, make come, re person), venigi (e.g.: *bring your child to the doctor:* venigu vian infanon al la kuracisto); bring about, bring into being, estigi, okazigi, efektivigi, rezultigi [tr]; bring around, (persuade), persvadi [tr]; (awaken), rekonsciigi, veki [tr]; bring back, re~i [tr]; revenigi; rekonduki [tr]; bring down, faligi; bring forth, (give birth), naski [tr]; (produce), produkti [tr]; bring forward, ($), transporti [tr] [see "balance"]; (suggest, propose), sugesti [tr], proponi [tr]; (show), montri [tr];

(advance, promote), antaŭigi; **bring off**, sukcesigi; **bring it off**, sukcesi [int], sukcesigi ĝin; **bring on**, kaŭzi [tr], aperigi, estigi; **bring out**, (reveal), riveli [tr], malkaŝi [tr]; (in relief), reliefigi; **bring over**, (persuade), persvadi [tr]; **bring to**, (awaken), rekonsciigi, veki [tr]; (stop ship), haltigi; **bring together**, (gen), kunigi; (in a meeting), kunvenigi; **bring up**, (raise, educate), eduki [tr]; (mention), mencii [tr]; (for discussion), diskutigi, proponi [tr], levi [tr]; (vomit), elvomi [tr]; (stop short), abrupte halti [int]; abrupte haltigi; **bring to an end**, fini [tr], ĉesigi; **bring to bear**, (invoke), envoki [tr]; (use), utiligi, uzi [tr], apliki [tr]; **upbringing**, edukado; **bring someone around to**, persvadi iun pri, konvinki iun pri; **he cannot bring himself to do it**, li ne sukcesas fari ĝin [or] ne povas igi sin fari ĝin
brink, rando; **brinksmanship**, ĝis~ismo
brioche, brioĉo
briquette, briketo
Brisbane, Brisbano
Briseis, Brizeisa
brisk, (active, quick), vigla; (cool), malvarmeta, freska
brisket, brustaĵo
bristle, (stiff hair), harego, keto; (on insect, plant), aristo; (stand on end like bristle), hirtigi; hirtiĝi; **bristly**, **bristling**, hirta
Bristol, Bristolo
Britain, **Great Britain**, Britio
British, Brita; **Britisher**, ~o; **British Columbia**, ~a Kolumbio; **British Thermal Unit**, (abb: B.T.U.), ~a Termika Unuo [252 (malgrandaj) kalorioj, 1,055 kiloĵuloj; avoid abb in Esperanto (see § 20)]
Briton, (modern), Brito; (ancient), Britono
Brittany, Bretonio
brittle, frakasiĝema
broach, (roasting spit), trapikilo; (tap keg etc.), spili [tr]; (tool for this), spililo; (introduce subject), enkonduki [tr], levi [tr]
broad, (wide), larĝa; (vast), vasta;

broaden, (pli)~igi; pli~iĝi; plivastigi; plivastiĝi; **broadside**, (side, as of ship), (ŝip)flanko; (flier), flugfolio; (ballad), flugfolia balado; (gunfire), (tutflanka) salvo; (alongside), laŭ~e, flanke
broadcast, (radio), dissendi [tr], disaŭdigi; ~(ad)o, disaŭdig(ad)o; (TV), telesendi [tr]; telesend(ad)o; (spread news, rumor, etc.), diskonigi
brocade, broki [tr]; ~aĵo
brocatel(le), remburbrokaĵo [not "brokatelo"]
broccoli, brokolo
brochure, broŝuro, libreto
brock, melo
brocket, (zool: *Mazama*), mazamo
brogue, (accent), (Irlanda) akcento; (shoe), fortika ŝuo
broil, (cook or heat), rosti [tr]; ~iĝi; (get angry), koleriĝi; (squabble), kverelego, tumulto; **broiler**, (device, oven compartment), ~ilo; (chicken), ~kokido; **charcoal-broil**, karbonadigi; **charcoal-broiled meat**, karbonado
broke, (w/o $), senmona; (bankrupt), bankrotinta; **go broke**, bankroti [int]; **go for broke**, riski ĉion; **stone broke**, tute ~a
broker, makler/isto; **serve as broker**, ~i [int] **brokerage**, (work), ~ado; (fee), kurtaĝo; **marriage broker**, svatisto; **serve as marriage broker**, svati [tr]
brolga, (Aus), brolgo*
bromelia, Bromelia, bromelio; **bromeliad**, ~ado
bromide, (chem), bromido; (trite saying), banalaĵo
bromine, bromo
bromoform, bromoformo, tribrometano
bronchial, bronka; **bronchial tube**, ~o
bronchiole, bronketo
broncho–, (med, anat pfx), bronko–
bronchus, bronko; **bronchitis**, ~ito; **bronchoscope**, ~oskopo; **bronchoscopy**, ~oskopio
bronco, sovaĝa ĉevalo, nedresita ĉevalo
brontosaurus, brontosaŭro
bronze, bronzo; ~a; ~i [tr]; ~aĵo
brooch, broĉo; (w spring clip fastener), klipo

brood, (offspring), idaro; (hatch, incubate), kovi [tr]; (meditate), mediti [int]; **brooding**, meditema; **brood over**, primediti [tr]
brook, (small stream), rojo; (tolerate), toleri [tr]
broom, (for sweeping), balailo; (bot: *Cytisus*), citizo; **whisk-broom**, ~eto; **Spanish broom**, (bot), spartio
Brosmius, brosmo
broth, (water in which only meat cooked), brogaĵo; (in which vegetables w or w/o meat cooked), buljono
brothel, bordelo
brother, frato; (intimate form), fraĉjo; **brotherhood**, (brotherliness), ~eco; (organization), ~aro; **brotherly**, ~eca; **half-brother**, duon~o; **brother-in-law**, bo~o; **brother(s) and sister(s)**, ge~oj
Broussonetia, brusonetio
brow, brovo; **browbeat**, mienminaci [tr], parole minaci [tr]; **highbrow**, altkultura, intelekta; altkulturulo, intelektulo; **lowbrow**, malaltkultura, malintelekta; malaltkulturulo, malintelektulo; **knit one's brows**, kuntiri la ~ojn
brown, (color), bruna; ~o; ~igi; ~iĝi; (roast, grill until ~ color appears), subrosti [tr]; subrostiĝi; **brownie**, (elf), elfo; (young girl scout), skoltineto; (of chocolate), (ia Usona) ĉokoladaĵo; **brown-nose**, flataĉi [tr]
browse, (glance casually, as in shop, library, etc.), abeli [int], vagrigardi [tr, int]; (graze), paŝtiĝi; (leaves etc. for grazing), paŝtaĵo
brr, brr!
brucella, Brucella, brucelo
brucellosis, brucelozo
brucine, brucino
Bruges, **Brugge**, Bruĝo
bruise, (gen), kontuzi [tr]; ~iĝi; (act), ~o; (~d spot, gen), ~aĵo; (black and blue spot), lividaĵo, ekimozo; **bruiser**, (strong man), fortulo
bruit, disbabili [tr], disklaĉ(ad)i [tr]
Brumaire, Brumero
brumal, vintreca
brume, brumo
brunch, matenlunĉo; ~i [int]

Brunei, Brunejo†
brunet(te), brun/hara; ~ul(in)o
Brunfelsia, brunfelsio
Bruno, Bruno
Brunswick, Brunsviko; **New Brunswick**, Nov-~o
brunt, ĉef/forto, ~puŝo, ~skuo; **bear the brunt**, [~on] trafi la ~forto, la ~forto trafi [~on] (e.g.: *our town bore the brunt of the hurricane:* nian urbeton trafis la ~forto de la uragano)
brush, (for hair or similar brush), broso; ~i [tr]; (paint brush or similar brush), peniko; peniki [tr]; (of carbon, in elec motor etc.), karbopinto; (graze, barely touch), tanĝi [tr]; tanĝo; (wild, scraggly vegetation), vepro; (skirmish), bataleto; **brush aside**, **brush away**, forŝovi [tr], flankenŝovi [tr]; **brush country**, veprejo; **brush off**, bruski [tr]; **brush up**, (renew skill, knowledge), refreŝiĝi (sin), renovigi (sin); **bear brush**, (bot), gario; **bottle brush**, (or any cylindrical brush), skovelo; skoveli [tr]; **paint brush**, peniko; peniki [tr]; **scrub brush**, frot~o, lav~o; **shaving brush**, razpeniko; **toothbrush**, dento~o; **underbrush**, (shrubs etc. growing under larger trees), subkreskaĵo; (scrub plants growing alone), vepro; **vegetable brush**, legom~o
brusque, bruska; **treat brusquely**, ~i [tr]
Brussels, Bruselo; **Brussels sprouts**, ~brasikoj
brutal, brutala, brut(ec)a; **brutal person**, ~o; **brutality**, ~eco, bruteco; ~aĵo
brute, bruto; ~(ec)a
Brutus, Bruto
Bryophyta, briofitoj*
bryophyte, briofito*
Bryozoa, briozooj
Bryum, brio
B.T.U., [see under "British"]
Bubalus, bubalo
bubble, bobelo; ~i [int]; (bead, as of air, water), globeto
bubo, bubono [not "bubo"; cp *Bubo bubo*]
Bubo bubo, (zool), gufo [cp "bubo"]

bubonic, bubona
buccal, (re cheeks), vanga; (re mouth), buŝa
buccaneer, flibustro
buccina, bukceno
buccinator, bukcinatoro
Buccinum, bukceno
Bucephalus, Bucefalo
Buceros, bucero
Bucharest, Bukareŝto
buck, (male deer or oth ruminant), boko; (to specify animal), vir– [+ generic name] (e.g.: *buck antelope:* virantilopo); (dandy), dando; (rear up), baŭmi [int]; (resist), rezisti [tr]; (marker, for poker etc.), ĵetono; (dollar), dolaro; **buck for**, celi [tr, int]; **buckskin**, (leather), cervledo; cervleda; **buck up**, (cheer up), gajiĝi; **pass the buck**, pludoni la responsecon
bucket, (pail), sitelo; (of dredge, waterwheel, etc.), trogo; **bucketful**, ~o
buckeye, (tree), hipokaŝtano; (nut), ~onukso
buckhorn, (horn of buck), bokkorno; (lawn weed), plantago
buckle, (fasten), buki [tr]; ~iĝi; ~o; (warp, as from pressure or heat), kniki* [int], (prem)tordiĝi, (varm)tordiĝi; knikigi*, (prem–, varm)tordi [tr]; **turnbuckle**, streĉoŝraŭbo; **buckle down**, (energie) eklabori [int], ekatenti [tr]; **buckle down!**, (get to it!), ek al (la laboro etc.)!
buckler, ŝild(et)o
buckram, gumtolo
buckshee, gratifiko [cp "baksheesh"]
bucolic, (rustic, rural), kampara, paŝtista; (poem), bukoliko
Bucorax, bukorako
bud, (gen), burĝono; ~i [int] |not "budo"]; (of leaf etc.: poet), sproso; sprosi [int]; **taste bud**, gusto~o
Budapest, Budapesto, Budapeŝto
Buddha, Budho; **Buddhism**, ~ismo; **Buddhist**, ~isma; ~ano, ~isto; **Buddhahood**, ~eco
buddy, kamarado, amiko, kunulo, fraĉjo
budge, (move), ekmovi [tr]; ~iĝi; (yield), cedi [tr, int]
budgerigar, (Aus), buĝerigo*
budget, bu(d)ĝeto; ~igi

budgie, (Aus), buĝerigo*
Buenos Aires, Buenos-Ajreso
buff, (color), ĉamkolora; ~o; (polish), poluri [tr]; (devotee), adepto; **in the buff**, nuda; nude
buffalo, (true buffalo, gen), bubalo [cp "bison"]
buffer, (to absorb shocks, phys or fig; cmptr; chem), bufro; ~i [tr]; (polisher), polurilo; **buffer state**, ~oŝtato
buffet, (shake, hit), taŭzi [tr], skubat(ad)i [tr]; ~o, skubato; (re food), bufedo
buffoon, bufono; **buffoonery**, ~ado
Bufo, bufo; Bufonidae, ~edoj
bug, (small animal, gen), besteto; (specifically of order *Hemiptera*), hemiptero; (microbe), mikrobo; (minor illness), malsaneto; (minor cmptr, mech, elec etc. problem), misaĵeto; (hidden microphone), kaŝmikrofono, kaŝaŭdilo; kaŝmikrofoni [tr]; (annoy), ĝeni [tr]; (worry, upset), ĉagreni [tr]; **bugbane**, cimicifugo; **bugbear**, teruraĵo; **bug off**, foriri [int]; **bug off!**, for!; **bug out**, forkuri [int]; **bedbug**, cimo; **boat bug**, korikso; **buffalo bug**, dermesto; **harvest bug**, (larva of *Trombiculidae*), lepto; **lady bug**, kokcinelo; **red bug**, ĉiko; **scale bug**, koĉo; **sow bug**, **pill bug**, onisko; **stinkbug**, **shield bug**, pentatomo; [for names of oth bugs, see specific name if single word]
bugaboo, terurajo
bugger, (sodomy), bugri [tr]; ~ulo
buggy, (4 wheels), kaleŝo; (Br: 2 wheels), kabrioleto; **dune buggy**, (Am), **beach buggy**, (Aus), plaĝoĵipo
bugle, (mus), klariono; ~i [int]; (bot), ajugo
bugloss, ankuzo; **viper's bugloss**, ekio
build, (erect, set up, gen), konstrui [tr]; (grow), kreski [int]; kreskigi; (stature), staturo; **building**, ~aĵo; **outbuilding**, krom~aĵo, kromdomo; **build up**, (increase), pliigi; pliiĝi; (erect), pri~i [tr] (e.g.: *a built-up area:* pri~ita regiono); (amass), amasigi; amasiĝi; (propagandize, as by advertising), reputaciigi, propagandi [tr], fanfaroni [int] pri; **jerry-build**, provi-

zore ~i, ~aĉi [tr], fuŝ~i [tr]
Bujumbura, Bujumburo*
bulb, (of plant, or similar-shaped object), bulbo; (of thermometer etc.), ampolo; **light bulb**, lum–ampolo; **squeeze bulb**, (rubber, w tube, as for basting etc.), pilko
bulbil, bulbilo
Bulgaria, Bulgar/io; **Bulgarian**, ~a; ~o; ~ia
bulge, ŝveli [int]; ~igi; ~aĵo
bulimia, bulimio
bulk, (mass), maso; (size), grandeco, volumeno; (aggregate, not individually packaged), amasa; (majority), plejmulto; **bulkhead**, (divider), septo, vando; **bulky**, ~a; **in bulk**, amase; (not packed), loza
bull, (male bovine), virbovo, taŭro; (papal decree), buleo; ($), prezaltiĝa; (bluff), blufi [int]; blufo; **bullseye**, celpunkto; **bullfight**, taŭrbatalo; **bullfighter**, taŭrbatalisto; **bullhead**, (*Cottus*), ĉoto; **bullock**, (castrated), kastrita bovo; **bullshit**, taŭrmerdo [vulg], blago, sensencaĵo
bulla, (med), bullo
bulldoze, buldozi [tr]; **bulldozer**, ~o
bullet, (for gun), kuglo; (symbol [•]), ~o–signo; **tracer bullet**, spur~o
bulletin, bulteno; **bulletin-board**, (gen), afiŝ–tabulo
bullion, ingoto(j)
bully, tirani [tr]; ~o
bulwark, (rampart), bastiono; (breakwater), moleo; (of ship), pavezo
bum, (tramp, beggar), pigr/ulo; (live as bum), paraziti [int], ~adi [int]; (Br colloq: buttocks), pugo; (mooch), deprunt(aĉ)i [tr]; paraziti [int]
bumblebee, burdo
bump, (knock, jar), skui [tr]; ~iĝi; ~(iĝ)o; (collide w), kunpuŝiĝi (kun), kun~iĝi (kun); (swelling), ŝvelaĵo; (any unevenness sticking up, as in road etc.), tubero; **bumper**, (of car etc.), bufro; (abundant, as crop etc.), abunda; **bumpy**, tuber(plen)a, malglata; **bump into**, (meet), hazarde renkonti [tr]; **bump off**, (kill), mortigi
bumpkin, bub(eg)o
bun, (baked), bulko; (hair), hartubero;

(buttock), pug(glob)o, gluteo
buna, arta kaŭĉuko
bunch, (gen), aro; (bouquet), bukedo; (of flowers, fruit, etc.), grapolo; (of sticks etc.; bundle), fasko [cp "bundle"]
bundle, (package etc.), pako; ~i [tr]; (bale, as of grain, cut vegetables, etc.), garbo; garbigi; (of sticks etc.), fasko; faskigi; **bundle up**, (dress warmly), varme vesti [tr]; varme vestiĝi
bung, ŝtopi [tr]; (stopper), ~kejlo; **bunghole**, kejltruo
bungalow, bengalo
Bungarus, bungaro
bungle, fuŝi [tr]; ~o
bunion, piedbursito
bunk, (bed), kuŝbenko, litbenko; ~e tranokti [int]; (nonsense), blago, sensencaĵo; **debunk**, senblagigi; **bunkhouse**, ~ejo
bunker, (mil), bunkro; (bin, tank), kuvego, ujego; (refuel), brulaĵizi [tr]
bunny, kuniĉjo
bunt, (baseball), bateti [tr]; ~o
bunting, (cloth), stamino; (flag), flago; (flag-like decorations), ~aĵoj; (zool), emberizo; **snow bunting**, neĝemberizo
buoy, buo; **buoyage**, ~aro; **buoy up**, (float), flosigi; (encourage), kuraĝigi; **sonobuoy**, sonamplifa ~o
buoyant, (floats), flosiva; (re upward force of lighter fluid), levema; (cheerful), gaja; **buoyancy**, ~o; gajeco
Buphagus, bufago
Buphthalum, buftalmo
Bupleurum, bupleŭro
buplever, bupleŭro
buprestid, bupresto
Buprestis, bupresto
bur, (pod), lapo; (plant on which these grow: *Xanthium*), ksantio [cp "burr"]
burble, (gurgle), glugli [int]; ~o; (babble), babili [int]; babil(ad)o
burbot, lojto
burden, ŝarĝi [tr]; ~o; **unburden**, mal~i [tr]
burdock, arktio
bureau, (admin), buroo; (chest of drawers), ŝranko, komodo; (Br: writing table), skribtablo

bureaucrat, burokrato; **bureaucracy**, (bureaucrats), ~aro; (system), ~ismo
buret(te), bureto
burg, urbeto, vilaĝo
burgeon, burĝoni [int]
burger, (gen: bun w any chopped meat filling), burgo* [specify filling by source animal name (e.g.: *hamburger:* bov~o [because made of beef, not ham]; *chickenburger:* kokin~o)]
burgess, burĝo
burglar, (dom)ŝtel/isto; **burglary**, ~(ad)o; **burglarize**, priŝteli [tr]
burgomaster, urbestro
burgrave, burgrafo
Burgundy, Burgonjo; **Burgundian**, (of province), ~a; ~ano; (of early people), Burgundo; **Burgundy wine**, ~a vino
burial, enterigo, entombigo; **burial ground**, ~ejo [cp "cemetery"]
burka, (Russian cloak), burko
burl, (wood), nodo, ligno~o; (fabric), ~eto; sen~igi
burlap, paktolo
burlesque, burleska; ~igi; ~aĵo
burly, solidkorpa
Burma, Birmo; **Burmese**, ~a; ~ano
burn, (consume by fire, gen; have hot or stinging feeling, etc., gen), bruli [int]; ~igi; (wound), ~vundi [tr]; ~vundo; (damage), ~difekti [tr]; ~difekto; (rocket, jet firing), ~igi; ~igo; **burner**, (of gas stove etc.), flamingo; **Bunsen burner**, ~ilo de Bunsen; **burning**, (ardent), arda; (caustic), kaŭstika; **be burning**, (ardent), ardi [int]; **afterburner**, post~ilo; **sideburns**, vangoharoj; **burn at the stake**, ŝtiparumi [tr]; ŝtiparumiĝi; **burn to cinders (ashes)**, cindrigi
burnet, (*Sanguisorba*), sangvisorbo
burnish, brilpoluri [tr]
burnoose, burnous, burnuso
burp, rukti [int]; ~igi; ~o; **burp up**, el~i [tr]
burr, (bur), [see "bur"]; (metal), krest(et)o; (trill R's), kartavi [int]; kartavo
burro, azeno
bursa, burso
bursar, (treasurer), kas/isto; **bursary**, (treasury), ~o; (scholarship), stipen-

dio
Bursera, bursero; **Burseraceae**, ~acoj
bursitis, bursito
burst, (explode), eksplodi [int], knali [int]; ~igi, knaligi; ~o, knalo; (split open), krevi [int]; krevo; (gunfire), salvo; (seed pod), dehiski [int]; **burst out**, ~i (e.g.: *burst out laughing:* ~i en ridado); **outburst**, ~o
Burundi, Burundo†
bury, (lit or fig), enterigi; (in grave), entombigi
bus, (vehicle), buso, aŭtobuso; en~igi; (elec), buso†; (clear dirty dishes in restaurant etc.), grumi [tr]; **busboy, busser**, grumo; **trolley bus**, trole~o
busby, husara ĉapo
bush, (plant, gen), arb/eto; (w woody stem branching at base), arbedo; (trunk woody at base, herbaceous at top), arbusto; (brush: scraggly vegetation), vepro; (land where this grows), veprejo; **bushland**, (Canadian), ~arlando; **bushranger**, veprulo; **bushy**, fruteska; vepra; **benjamin bush**, benzo~o; **burning bush**, (*Dictamnus*), diktamno, fraksinelo; **ringworm bush**, fistulkasio; **salt bush**, (Aus), kenopodio; **beat around the bush**, ĉirkaŭmarĉandi [int]
bushel, (unit of measure), buŝelo [(Am), 35,2 litroj; (Br), 36,5 litroj; (French), 10 [or] 13 litroj (see § 20)]; (basket), ~korbo
bushing, (mech), kusineto
Bushman, (African), Boŝmano
business, ($ activity; commercial firm), negoco; ~a; (commerce), komerco; komerca; (any matter, concern), afero; **be in business**, komerci [int]; **businessman, businessperson**, ~isto, komercisto; **agribusiness**, agrokomerco; **be the business of**, (concern), koncerni [tr] (e.g.: *that's my business:* tio koncernas min); **be none of one's business**, ne koncerni iun; **do business with**, ~i [int] (kun), komerci [int] (kun); **mind one's own business**, atenti siajn proprajn aferojn; **mean business**, esti serioza
buskin, kotorno
buss, kis(eg)i [tr]; ~o

bust, (anat), busto; (burst), [see "burst"]; (breasts), mamaj; mama; (clothing part), brustaĵo; (hit), bati [tr]; bato; (arrest), aresti [tr]; aresto; ($ crash etc.), kraŝi [int]; kraŝo; (bankrupt), bankroti [int]; bankrotigi; **go bust**, bankroti [int]

bustard, otido

bustle, (hurry about), ĉirkaŭhasti [int]; ~ado; (to puff out skirt), juppufilo

busy, (gen), okup/ata; **busybody**, klaĉemulo; **busywork**, ~olaboro; **busy oneself with**, ~iĝi pri

but, (conj: yet, still, however), sed; (adv: except), krom; (only), nur [see also "can: cannot (help) but"]

butadiene, butadieno

butane, butano; **butanol**, ~olo; **butanone**, ~ono

butcher, buĉi [tr]; ~isto; **butcher shop**, viandejo; **butcher's-broom**, (bot), rusko

butene, buteno

buteo, Buteo, buteo

butler, ĉefservisto

Butomus, butomo

butt, (of cigarette or cigar, or remaining stump of anything), stumpo; (of rifle), kolbo; (mount behind target), celfono; (colloq: buttocks), pugo; (knock w head, as goat), kornofrapi [tr], kapfrapi [tr]; (bump, gen), kunpuŝiĝi (kun, kontraŭ); (abut), apudesti [tr], finiĝi ĉe; (barrel), barel(eg)o; **butt in**, entrudi sin, trudiĝi

butte, platmont(et)o

butter, butero; ~i [tr]; **butter-and-eggs**, (bot), linario; **buttercup**, (bot), ranunkolo; **butterfat**, ~graso; **buttermilk**, ~lakto; **butterscotch**, ~karamelo; **kokum butter**, **Goa butter**, garcinia oleo; **witch's butter**, (bot), nostoko

buttock, gluteo; **buttocks**, ~oj, postaĵo; (colloq), pugo

button, (gen), butono; ~i [tr]; **button-down**, ~ata; **buttonhole**, ~truo; **buttonhole stitch**, ~trua stebo; **buttonhook**, ~tirilo; **push-button**, prem~o; prem~a; **unbutton**, mal~i [tr]

buttress, (support, gen), apogi [tr]; ~o; (projection from wall etc.), ~(o)pilastro

butyl, butilo; **butyl alcohol**, ~a alkoholo

butyne, butino

butyric acid, butanacido

buxom, plenfigura

Buxus, bukso

buy, ($), aĉeti [tr]; ~o; (bargain), bon~o; (accept), akcepti [tr] (e.g.: *I don't buy his reasoning:* mi ne akceptas lian rezonadon); **buy up**, (monopolize), akapari [tr]

buzz, (gen humming sound, like bee), zumi [int]; ~(ad)o; (sibilant, like saw), ~sibli [int]; ~sibl(ad)o

buzzard, (gen), buteo; **honey buzzard**, vespo~o, perniso; **turkey buzzard**, katarto

buzzword, fulmĵargon/aĵo; **buzzwords**, ~o

by, (authorship; doer of any action), de, far (e.g.: *a drama by Shakespeare:* dramo de [or] far Ŝekspiro [note: "far" avoids confusion w oth senses of "de"]); (during), dum, dum– [pfx] (e.g.: *travel by night:* veturi dumnokte [or] dum la nokto); (next to), apud (e.g.: *sit by me:* sidu apud mi); (past, beyond), preter, preter– [pfx]; pretere (e.g.: *she went by me:* ŝi iris preter min [or] preteriris min; *he went by:* li iris pretere [or] preteriris); (not later than), ĝis (e.g.: *finish it by Saturday:* fini ĝin ĝis sabato); (to extent of; by means of); per (e.g.: *succeed by hard work:* sukcesi per forta laboro; *by hand:* per mano, permane; *you are taller than I by 5 centimeters:* vi estas pli alta ol mi per [or: je] 5 centimetroj); (in units of), po (e.g.: *work by the hour:* labori pohore; *work by 2-hour shifts:* labori po 2-horaj skipoj; *sell by the liter:* vendi po litro, politre); (according to; through, via), laŭ, (e.g.: *know a tree by its fruits:* koni arbon laŭ ĝiaj fruktoj; *act by law:* agi laŭ la leĝo, laŭleĝe; *go north by the tunnel:* iri norden laŭ la tunelo); (on authority of; invoking), je (e.g.: *swear by God:* ĵuri je Dio); (at), apud, ĉe (e.g.: *stand by the tree:* stari apud la arbo); (next to, across from), kontraŭ;

(in oth dimension), kontraŭ, per (e.g.:
a board 20 centimeters by 3 meters:
tabulo 20 centimetrojn kontraŭ 3
metroj); (multiplied by), multiplikita
de, oble (e.g.: *3 by 4 is 12:* 3 multiplikita de 4 [or: 3 oble 4] estas 12 [see also "time: times"]); (at a time), –ope
[sfx] (e.g.: *they strolled past two by
two:* ili preterpromenis duope; *do not
translate word by word:* ne traduku
vortope; *they arrived by the busload:*
ili alvenis busplenope); (increments
of, after), post (e.g.: *little by little:* iom
post iom; *step by step:* paŝon post
paŝo [or] paŝope); (on behalf of), por
(e.g.: *do well by a friend:* agi bone por
amiko); **by and by,** baldaŭ, post iom
da tempo, iom poste; **by and large,**
plejparte, ĉion konsiderinte; **by oneself,** sola; sole; **by the way, by the
by,** parenteze, flanke
by–, (pfx: side), flank–, apud– [pfx]
(e.g.: *bystander:* apudstaranto); (secondary), krom– (e.g.: *byproduct:*
kromprodukto)
Byelorus, Byelorussia, [see "Belarus"]
bygone, pasinta; ~ajo: **let bygones be
bygones,** la ~aĵoj estu ~aj
byline, aŭtorindiko
B.Y.O., (abb: "bring your own"), kunportu vian propran [no abb in Espe-
ranto]; **B.Y.O.B.,** kunportu vian
propran botelon (alkoholaĵon)
Byron, (poet), Bajrono
byssus, bisino
byte, bitoko†; **kilobyte,** kilo~o; **mega-
byte,** mega~o; **gigabyte,** giga~o
Byzantium, Bizanco; **Byzantine,** ~a

C

c. (abb of "circa"), ĉ. [abb of "ĉirkaŭ"]
Caaba, Kaabo
cab, (taxi), kabo [cp "taxi"]; (control
compartment of truck, crane, etc.), kajuto; (Hebrew measure), kab'o
cabal, (plot, intrigue), kabalo; (secret
group), ~istaro
cabala, kabalo
cabana, kabano
cabaret, kabareto
cabbage, (gen), brasiko; (garden vegetable), ~o, kap~o; (w white head),
blanka ~o; (w red head), ruĝa ~o;
cabbage tree, cabbage palm, (Aus:
Livistona australis), ~arbo; savoy
cabbage, sabeliko
cabbala, kabalo
cabin, (modest house), kabano; (private
room on ship etc.), ĉambreto; (passenger compartment in plane etc.),
pasaĝerejo; (pilot's compartment), kajuto
cabinet, (cupboard), ŝranko; (pol), kabineto; china cabinet, teler~o; medicine cabinet, medikamento~o
cable, (rope, wire), kablo; (fasten), ~izi
[tr]; (~gram), ~ogramo; ~ogrami [tr];
cablegram, ~ogramo; ~ogrami [tr]
cabochon, kapolo
caboose, (of train), vostvagono; (Br:
galley), (ŝip)kuirejo
cabriolet, kabrioleto
cacao, (bean), kakao; (tree), ~arbo
Cacatua, kakatuo
cachalot, kaĉaloto, makrocefalo
cache, kaŝi [tr]; (place), ~ejo; (things),
~aĵo
cachet, (stamp), stampo; (capsule), kapsulo
cachexia, cachexy, kakeksio, kaĥeksio
cacique, (leader), kaciko
cackle, gaki [int]; ~o
cacodyl, kakodilo
cacography, kakografio
cacophony, kakofonio; cacophonous,
~a
cacosmia, kakosmio
cactus, (gen), kakto; prickly-pear cac-

tus, opuntio, nopalo; Russian cactus,
salsolo
cacuminal, kakuminalo; ~a
cad, kanajlo
cadastre, cadaster, katastro; cadastral,
~a
cadaver, kadavro
cadaverine, kadavrino
caddie, portisto
caddis, caddice, caddisworm, frigan-
larvo [cp "fly: caddis fly"]
caddy, (golf caddie), portisto; (for tea),
teujo; (container for oth objects), ~ujo
[sfx] (e.g.: disk caddy: diskujo)
cade, (tree), oksicedra junipero; (oil),
kadoleo
cadence, kadenco
cadet, kadeto
cadge, almozpeti [tr]
cadi, kadio
Cádiz, Kadizo
cadmium, kadmio
Cadmus, Kadmo; Cadmean, ~a; ~ano
cadre, kadro
caduceus, kaduceo
Caecilius, Cecilio
caecum, cekumo
Caesar, Cezaro; Caesarean, c~a (e.g.:
Caesarean section: c~a operacio)
Caesarea, Cezareo
caesium, cezio
caesura, cezuro
cafe, kafejo
café au lait, (coffee w cream), kafo kun
kremo; (color), kremkafkolora; krem-
kafkoloro
cafeteria, kafeterio [cp "canteen"]
caffeine, kafeino; caffeine-free, sen~a;
decaffeinated, sen~igita
caftan, kaftano
cage, kaĝo; en~igi
cagey, ruza
cahier, kajero
cahoots, komploto, konspiro
Caiaphas, Kajafas
caiman, Caiman, kajmano
Cain, Kaino
caique, kaiko

cairn, kairno
Cairo, Kairo
caisson, (for work under water), kasono;
(mil), municia ĉaro; **caisson disease,**
~malsano
Caius, Kajo
cajeput, [see "cajuput"]
cajole, kaĵoli [tr]
Cajun, Franc-Luiziana; ~ano
cajuput, (oil), kajeputo; (tree), ~arbo
cake, (baked), kuko; (soap etc.), briko;
(crust, deposit), krusto; krustigi;
krustiĝi; (pack, stick, as mud on shoe
etc.), aglomeri [tr]; aglomeriĝi; aglo-
meraĵo; **cupcake,** ~eto; **layer cake,**
tavol~o; **pancake,** pat~o, krespo;
shortcake, savarino [cp "bread: short
bread"]; **spice cake,** miel~o, spic~o;
that takes the cake, tio ĉion superas
Calabar, (town), Kalabaro; (river), Rivero ~a; **Calabar bean,** ~a fabo
calabash, (fruit), kalabaso; (tree), ~ar-
bo; (gourd), ~kukurbo
Calabria, Kalabrio
Calais, Kalezo
calamine, kalamino
calamint, kalaminto
Calamintha, kalaminto
calamity, katastrofo; **calamitous,** ~a
calamus, (bot: *Acorus calamus*), akoro;
(*Calamus*), kalamo
Calamus, kalamo; Calamus rostang,
rotango
calander, kalandro
Calandra, kalandrao
calash, kaleŝo
Calathea, kalateo
calcaneus, (bone), kalkaneo
canceolaria, Canceolaria, kalceolario
Calchas, Kalĥaso
calciferol, kalciferolo
calcify, (gen), kalci/igi; ~iĝi; (med),
sklerozigi; skleroziĝi
calcine, kalcini [tr]
calcino, muskardino [not "kalcino"]
calcitrate, kalcitri [int]
calcium, kalcio
calculate, (compute), kalkuli [tr];
(count, determine quantity of), komp-
ti† [tr]; [cp "compute", "count"];
(plan), plani [tr]; **calculator, calculat-
ing machine,** (small, pocket–sized),

~ilo; (large, table–top), ~atoro [not
"~ilo"; see "count"]; **incalculable,**
ne~ebla; **miscalculate,** (compute
wrong), mis~i [tr]; (misjudge), mistaksi [tr], misjuĝi [tr]
calculus, (math), infinitezima kalkulo
[cp "analytics"]; (med: stony mass),
kalkuluso; **differential calculus,**
diferenciala kalkulo; **integral calculus,** integrala kalkulo
Calcutta, Kalikato, Kalkuto
caldron, kaldrono
calèche, kaleŝo
Caledonia, Kaledonio; **Caledonian**
Canal, Kanalo ~a; **New Caledonia,**
Nov-~o
calefaction, hejtado [not "kalefakcio"]
calendar, kalendaro; **appointment calendar,** agendo; **Gregorian calendar,**
Gregoria ~o; **Islamic calendar,** Islama ~o; **Jewish calendar,** Hebrea ~o;
Julian calendar, Julia ~o; **perpetual
calendar,** porĉiama ~o
calender, kalandri [tr]; ~ilo
Calendra, kalandrao
calends, Kalendoj
calendula, Calendula, kalendulo
calenture, kalenturo
calf, (young cattle), bovido; (of leg), suro
Caliban, Kalibano
caliber, (measure, gradation), kalibro;
(quality), kvalito; **calibrate,** (set measuring instrument; measure ~er of), ~i
[tr]; (give precise diameter to), ~igi;
(mark gradations on), gradigi
calico, (Br: unprinted; uncolored or solid color), kalikoto; (Am: printed), indieno
Calidris, kalidro
California, Kalifornio; **Gulf of California,** Golfo de ~o
californium, kalifornio
Caligula, Kaligulo
caliper, calipers, kalibr/ilo, ~ocirkelo
[note sing]; **inside calipers,** interna
~ilo; **outside calipers,** caliper rule,
ekstera ~ilo
caliph, kalifo; **caliphate,** (rank), ~eco;
(land), ~ejo
calisthenics, (korpaj) ekzercoj
calix, kaliko

calk, (on horseshoe), piedbuteo; (caulk), kalfatri [tr]; kalfatraĵo

call, (summon; say loudly, as to get attention; square and contra dancing; etc.), voki [tr]; ~o (e.g.: *call out the names on the list:* ~i la nomojn en la listo; *call her to supper:* ~i ŝin al la vespermanĝo); (name), nomi [tr] (e.g.: *what is that called?:* kiel oni nomas tion? [or] kiel tio nomiĝas?; *I call that stupid:* mi nomas tion stulta); (re court witness), invoki [tr]; (on telephone), ~i, telefoni [tr], telefon~i [tr]; (telefon)~o; (re pool shot), nomi (la pafon); (stop), haltigi (e.g.: *the game was called due to rain:* la ludo estis haltigita pro pluvo); (characteristic cry of animal), bleki [int]; bleko; (hunting whistle etc.), logfajfi [int]; logfajfilo; **calling,** (profession), profesio; (inner urging etc.), al~o; **call back,** (gen), re~i [tr]; **call down,** (invoke), en~i [tr]; (rebuke), riproĉi [tr]; **call for,** (demand, require), postuli [tr]; (go get), iri havigi; venigi havigi; (re person), veni por (e.g.: *I will call for you at 8:* mi venos por vi je la 8–a); **call forth,** el~i [tr]; **call in,** (invoke), en~i [tr]; (call back, revoke), re~i [tr]; **call into question,** pridubigi; **call letters,** (radio, TV), ~signalo; **call off,** (order away), for~i [tr], forordoni [tr], forsendi [tr]; (cancel), nuligi; **call on, call upon,** (visit), viziti [tr]; **call (up)on one to do something,** peti iun fari ion, peti ke iu faru ion; **call out,** (shout), krii [tr]; (read aloud), laŭtlegi [tr]; (summon as to action), al~i [tr]; **call up,** summon, as to mil duty), al~i [tr]; (remind), rememorigi (iun) pri (io); (phone), ~i, telefoni [tr], telefon~i [tr]; **call to order, call together,** (meeting etc.), kun~i [tr]; **catcall,** prifajfi [tr]; prifajfo; **on call,** ~e deĵoranta; **roll call,** kontrol~o; **call the roll,** kontrol~i [int]; **so-called,** tiel nomata [abb: t.n.]; **within call,** ~ebla, en ~ebla distanco

Calla, kalao

Callicebus, kalicebo

calligraph, (write in calligraphy), kali-

grafi [tr]; **calligrapher,** ~o; **calligraphic,** ~a; **calligraphy,** ~io

Calliope, (myth), Kaliopa

calliper, [see "caliper"]

callipygian, belpuga

Callistephus, kalistefo

callisthenics, (korpaj) ekzercoj

Callisto, (myth), Kalistoa; (ast), ~o*

Callitriche, kalitriko

Callocalia, salangano

Callorhinus, marurso

callosum, kalozo

callous, (unfeeling, merciless), senkompata, hardita

callow, nematura

Calluna, kaluno

callus, (hardened skin), kalo; (of broken bone), kaluso; **callused,** (skin), ~a

calm, (serene, quiet), serena, kalma†; kalmigi; kalmiĝi; kalmo; (tranquil), trankvila; **calm down,** ~igi; ~iĝi; trankviligi; trankviliĝi; **becalm,** enkalmigi; **become becalmed,** enkalmiĝi

calomel, kalomelo

calorie, (gen), kalorio; **large calorie, great calorie, kilogram calorie, kilocalorie,** granda ~o, kilo~o; **small calorie, gram calorie,** malgranda ~o; **caloric,** (re calories), ~a

calorimeter, kalorimetro; **calorimetry,** ~io

calosma, Calosma, kalosmo

calpac(k), kalpako

Caltha, kalto

calumet, kalumeto

calumny, kalumnio; **calumniate,** ~i [tr]; **calumnious,** ~a

calvarium, kalvario

Calvary, Kalvario

calve, (gen), naski [tr]

Calvin, Kalvino; **Calvinism,** ~ismo; **Calvinist,** ~isma; ~isto, ~ano

calx, kalcinaĵo

calypso, (mus), kalipso*

Calypso, (myth), Kalipsoa

Calystegia, kalistegio

calyx, kaliko

cam, kamo; **camshaft,** ~ŝafto

camaraderie, kamaradeco

camber, konveks/eco, arkeco; ~igi; ~iĝi

Cambodia, Kamboĝo [cp "Kampuchea"]
camboge, gumiguto
Cambrian, (geol), kambria; ~o; (Welsh), Kimra; Cambrian Period, ~o; **Pre-Cambrian,** antaŭ~a; antaŭ~o
cambric, batisto
Cambridge, Kembriĝo
cambrium, kambriumo
came, (lead strip), plumbostrio
camel, kamelo; **two-humped camel,** duĝiba ~o; **one-humped camel,** (dromedary), dromedaro
camellia, *Camellia,* kamelio
Camelus, kamelo; Camelus dromedarius, dromedaro
Camembert, (cheese), kamemberto
cameo, kameo
camera, (phot, gen), fotilo, fotografilo; (movie or TV), kamerao; camera oscura, senluma kamero; camera-ready, (re copy), fotopreta; in camera, (law), private, sekrete; camera person, cameraman, ~isto; kameraisto
Cameroun, Cameroon, (mountain), (Monto) Kameruno; (region), ~io; (country), ~ia Respubliko
Camille, (man's name), Kamilo; (woman's), ~a; Camilla, ~a
camisole, kamizolo
camlet, kamloto
camomile, [see "chamomile"]
camouflage, kamufli [tr]; ~ado; ~aĵo; camoufleur, ~isto
camp, (place for camping, gen, as in tents, campers), kamp/adejo; (for tents alone), tendejo; (stay in tent or camper), ~(ad)i [int]; (in tent), tendumi [int]; (in camper trailer), remorkumi [int]; (barracks), barakaro; (barracks area), barakejo; (bivouac), bivaki [int]; bivako; (group supporting a cause, pol position, etc.), partio; **camp out, go camping,** ~(ad)i; **camper,** (person), ~adanto; (trailer), ~ada remorko; (motorized), ~adaŭto, ~ada veturilo; **campground,** ~adejo; tendejo; **campsite,** (for one tent or camper), ~adloko; **decamp,** el~iĝi; **encampment,** ~ado; tendaro
campaign, (gen), kampanjo; ~i [int]
Campania, Kampanio

campanile, kampanilo
campanology, sonorilologio
Campanula, kampanulo; Campanula rapunculus, rapunkolo; Campanula rotundifolia, rondfolia ~o; Campanula trachelium, trakelio
campeachy, [see "logwood"]
camphire, kofero
camphor, kamforo; camphor tree, ~arbo; camphorated oil, ~oleo
campion, (bot: *Lychnis*), likniko; (*Silene*), sileno; corn campion, agrostemo
campus, (universitata) tereno
can, (is able), povas [see "able"]; (hermetically sealed metal container), ladskatolo [cp "canister"]; (seal into cans), enladigi; (seal hermetically in any container, as jar etc.), hermetikigi; **canned,** (in cans), lad– [pfx] (e.g.: *canned milk:* ladlakto); **cannery,** enladigejo; **cannot (help) but,** ne ~i ne (e.g.: *I cannot help laughing* [or] *I cannot help but laugh:* mi ne ~as ne ridi); **can opener,** ladskatola malfermilo; **jerrycan,** benzinkruĉo
Canaan, (gen), Kanaano; **Canaanite,** ~ido; **Canaanitic,** ~a
Canada, Kanado; **Canadian,** ~ano; ~a
canal, (gen), kanalo; **alimentary canal,** nutro~o; **Canal Zone,** K~zono
canapé kanapo
canard, (false report), falsfamo
canary, (zool), kanario
Canary Islands, Kanarioj
Canberra, Kanbero
cancan, kankano
cancel, (line through, strike out), forstreki [tr]; (invalidate), malvalidigi; (re purchase order; public performance; meeting; etc.; call off), nuligi; (postage), stampi [tr]; **precancel,** antaŭstampi [tr]
cancer, (disease), kancero [cp "carcinoma"]
Cancer, (ast), Kankro; **Tropic of Cancer,** Tropiko de la ~o
Cancer, (zool), kancero
candela, kandlo*
candelabrum, kandelabro
Candia, Kandio [cp "Krete"]
candid, (not secretive), malkaŝema;

(honest, fair), honesta, justa; (informal, as photo), neformala, nepozita
candidate, kandidato;   **candidacy**, ~eco; **be a candidate**, ~i [int]
Candide, Kandido
candle, (gen), kandelo [cp "candela"]; **candle-stick, candle-holder**, ~ingo; **candle power**, ~povo
Candlemas, Kandelfesto
cando(u)r, malkaŝemo, honesteco, verdiremo [see "candid"]
candy, (any sugary, sweet food), dolĉaĵo; (bonbon), bombono; (crystallized sugar), kando; (coat fruit etc. w sugar), kandizi [tr]
cane, (bot: *Arundo, Arundinaria;* any hollow-stemmed plant; walking stick etc.), kano; **sugar cane**, suker~o; **canebrake**, ~ejo; **cane-bottomed chair**, ~plektita seĝo
canephoros, kaneforo
canine, (dog), hundo; ~(ec)a; (tooth), kanino
Canis, Canis Major, (ast), Hundo; **Caniss Minor**, Malgranda Hundo
Canis, (zool), kaniso [cp "dog"]; Canidae, ~edoj; Canis aureus, ŝakalo; Canis dingo, dingo; Canis familiaris, hundo; Canis familiaris laniarius, laniario; Canis lagopus, [see "Alopex lagopus"]; Canis latrans, kojoto; Canis lupus, lupo; Canis vulpes, vulpo
canister, kanistro [cp "can"]
canker, (open sore), ŝankro; ~igi; ~iĝi; cankerous, ~a
canna, Canna, kanao
cannabis, Cannabis, kanabo
Cannae, Kanno
Cannes, Kanno
cannibal, kanibalo; **cannibalism**, ~ismo; **cannibalize**, (mech), ~izi [tr]
cannon, kanono; ~i [tr]; **cannonade**, ~ado; **cannon-ball**, ~kuglo; **cannoneer**, ~isto, kanoniero
cannula, kanulo
canny, (careful), zorga; (shrewd, clever), sagaca, ruzeta
canoe, kanuo; ~i [int]
canon, (rel law; book list; part of mass; mus), kanono; (person), kanoniko; **canoness**, kanonikino; **canonic**, ~a; ca-

nonical, ~a; kanonika; **canonize**, ~izi [tr]; **canonical hour**, kanonika horo
canopic, kanopa; **canopic urn (jar, vase)**, ~o
canopy, baldakeno
Canossa, Kanoso; **go to Canossa**, iri al ~o
cant, (jargon), ĵargono; (bevel), bevelo; (tilt, jerk), ŝanceli [tr]; ŝanceliĝi; ŝanceliĝo; (lean), klini [tr]; kliniĝi; kliniĝo
Cantal, (department),   Kantalo; (cheese), ~fromaĝo
cantaloup(e), (*Cucumis melo cantalupensis*), kantalupo; (muskmelon: *C. m. reticulatus*), retmelono
cantankerous, kverelema
cantata, kantato
canteen, (cafe, recreation center, etc.), kantino [cp "cafeteria"]; (water flask), akvobotelo
canter, galopeti [int]; ~igi; ~o
Cantharellus, kantarelo; Cantharellus cibarius, manĝebla ~o, ovofungo
cantharides, kantaridaĵo
cantharis, Cantharis, (insect), kantarido; (powder), ~aĵo
canticle, kantiko
cantilever, kantilevro; ~izi [tr]; cantilever bridge, ~a ponto
canto, kanto
canton, kantono; **cantonment**, kvartiro, kantonmento
Canton, Kantono
cantor, kantoro
canvas, (close-mesh, for tents, sails, paintings, etc.), dreliko; ~aĵo; (open-mesh, for embroidery etc.), kanvaso; **canvasback**, (zool), merganaso
canvass, (examine, look over), kontroli [tr]; ~(ad)o; (ask for, solicit), varbi [tr]; varb(ad)o
canyon, kanjono; **Grand Canyon**, K~o Granda
canzone, canzona, kanzono
caoutchouc, (kruda) kaŭĉuko
cap, (any brimless hat, or similar-shaped object), ĉapo; (w bill or visor), ~o, kaskedo; (put cap on), en~igi; en~kapsuligi; (exceed), superi [tr]; (limit), limigi; (for toy gun), prajmeto; **blasting cap**, prajmo, eksplodiga kap-

sulo; **bottle cap**, kapsulo; **dynamite cap**, eksplodigilo; **hubcap**, nabo~o; **(polar) icecap**, bankizo; **redcap**, (rr porter), (fervoja) portisto; **skullcap**, verto~o; **skycap**, (flughavena) portisto
capable, (able), kapabla; (competent), kompetenta; **be capable**, ~i [int]; kompetenti [int]; **capability**, ~o; kompetenteco
capacious, (re volume), mult/kapacita; (re scope), ~ampleksa
capacitance, (elec), kapacitanco
capacitor, (elec), kondensilo
capacity, (volume), kapacito; (load capacity of truck, ship, etc.), ŝarĝokapablo, ŝarĝomaksimumo; (ability, gen), kapablo; (role, function), rolo; have a capacity of, (volume), kubi [int] (e.g.: *the bottle has a capacity of 2 liters:* la botelo kubas je 2 litroj [or] kubas 2 litrojn); **incapacity**, nekapablo; **incapacitate**, malkapabligi
caparison, (for horse), ornami [tr] (ĉevalon); ĉeval~ajo; (clothing, equipment, etc.), ekipaĵo
cape, (cloak), mantelo, pelerino; (land), kabo; **Cape Breton Island**, Insulo Kabo Bretona; **Cape Horn**, Kabo Horna; **Cape of Good Hope**, Kabo Bonespera; **Cape (of Good Hope) Province**, Kablando; **Cape Town**, Kab-urbo; **Cape Verde**, Kabo Verda; **Cape Verde Islands**, Insularo Verdakaba; **Cape Verde Republic**, Verdakaba Respubliko; **Cape York Peninsula**, Duoninsulo Kabo Jorka; **North Cape**, Kabo Norda
Capella, (ast), Kaprino
Capella gallinago, (zool), galinago
caper, (jump, prance), kaprioli [int]; ~o; (spice; plant), kaporo; (illegal job), fitasko
capercaillie, capercailzie, urogalo
Capernaum, Kapernaŭmo
Capet, Kapeto
capillary, (gen), kapilara; (blood vessel), ~o; **capillary action**, ~eco; **capillary tube**, ~a tubo
capital, ($), kapitalo; ~a; (primary; most important; most serious), ĉefa; (first-rate), unuaranga; (seat of gov-

ernment), ĉefurbo; (capital letter), majusklo; majuskla; (arch), kapitelo; **capitalism**, ~ismo; **state capitalism**, ŝtat~ismo; **capitalist**, ~isma; ~isto; **capitalize**, (convert to capital), ~igi; (letters), majuskligi; **capitalize on**, **make capital of**, ekspluati [tr], elprofiti [tr]; **operating capital**, spez~o; **venture capital**, riskhava ~o
capitate, kap/forma; ~hava
capitation, (tax), kap/imposto; (oth fee), ~opago
capitol, (gen), kapitolo
Capitoline, Kapitolo
capitulate, kapitulaci [int]
capitulum, kapitulo
capo, gamkapo
capon, kapono
capote, kapoto
Cappadocia, Kapadocio
Capparis, kaporo
cappucino, elpremita kafo kun kremo [cp "espresso"]
Capra aegagrus, Capra ibex, ibekso
Capreolus, kapreolo
Capri, Kapreo
capriccio, kapriĉo
caprice, kaprico; **capricious**, ~a; **be capricious**, ~i [int]
Capricorn, Kaprikorno; **Tropic of Capricorn**, Tropiko de la ~o
Caprimulgus, kaprimulgo
capriole, kapriolo; ~i [int]
Capsella, kapselo; Capsella bursa-pastoris, paŝtista ~o
capsicum, Capsicum, kapsiko
capsize, renversi [tr]; ~iĝi
capstan, kapstano
capsule, (gen), kapsulo
captain, (mil), kapitano; (ship), ŝipestro; (leader, gen), estro; estri [tr]
caption, (title), titolo; ~i [tr]; (heading), kapvorto(j), rubriko
captious, disputema
captivate, (capture), kapti [tr]; (delight, charm), ĉarmi [tr], ravi [tr]
captive, kaptito; ~a; **captivity**, ~eco
captor, kaptinto
capture, (gen), kapti [tr]; ~o; (by corsair), kaperi [tr]
Capua, Kapuo
capuche, kapuĉo

capuchin, (monk), kapuceno
capybara, hidrohñero
car, (auto), aŭto; (any vehicle), veturilo;
(rr), vagono; (of elevator), liftokaĝo;
(of balloon, airship), kajuto; **carhop,**
~okelner(in)o; **carjack,** ~o-pirati [tr];
carjacker, ~o-pirato; **carjacking,**
~o-piratado; **carload,** (rr), vagonple-
no; **carpool,** ~okomunaĵo; iri (veturi
etc.) per ~okomunaĵo; **carport,**
~oŝedo; **carwash,** ~olavejo; **baggage
car,** pakvagono; **compact car,** kompakta ~o; **dining car,** manĝovago-
no; **flatcar,** platvagono; **freight car,**
varvagono; **handcar,** drezino; **mail
car,** poŝtvagono; **motorcar,** aŭtomobilo, ~o; **Pullman car,** litvagono;
sidecar, flankĉaro; **streetcar,** tramo;
tank car, cisternvagono; **turbocar,**
(any vehicle riding on turbo air cushion), teraplano
carabineer, carabinier, karabenisto
Carabus, karabo; Carabidae, ~edoj
caracal, Caracal, karakalo
Caracalla, Karakalo
Caracas, Karakaso
carack, karako
caracole, karakoli [int]; ~o
caracul, karakulo
carafe, karafo
caragana, Caragana, karagano
caramel, karamelo
carapace, karapaco
Carassius, karaso
carat, karato (e.g.: *24-carat gold:* oro je
24 ~oj)
caravan, (company of travelers etc.),
karavano; (Br: house trailer), domveturilo
caravel(le), karavelo
caraway, (plant or seed), karvio
carbamate, karbam(in)/ato; **carbamic
acid,** ~a acido, aminometanacido
carbazole, karbazolo
carbide, karbido
carbine, karabeno; **carbineer,** ~isto
carbinol, karbinolo
carbo–, (chem pfx), karbo–
carbohydrate, karbohidrato
carbolated, karbolizita; **carbolic acid,**
fenolo, karbola acido [cp "phenol"]
carbon, (chem element), karbono;

(powdered, for adhesion), norito; **car-
bonate,** ~ato; ~atizi [tr] (e.g.: *carbonated beverage:* ~ata trinkaĵo);
decarbonate, sen~atigi; **carbonic,**
~ata; **carbonic acid,** ~ata acido; **car-
boniferous,** (coal-bearing), karboha-
va; (geol era), karbonio; **carbonize,**
~igi; karbigi; **decarbonize,** sen~igi;
carbon dioxide, ~a dioksido; **carbon
monoxide,** ~a monoksido; **carbon
disulfide,** ~a disulfido; **carbon paper,** karbonpapero; **carbon copy,** tra-
kopio, ~kopio; **radiocarbon, carbon
14,** radio~o, ~o 14
carbonado, (gen), karbonado
Carbonari, Karbonaroj
carborundum, karborundo
carboxyl, karboksilo
carboy, kirasbotelo
carbuncle, (gem), karbunkolo; (boil;
plant disease), karbunklo
carburet, karburi [tr]; **carburetor,**
~atoro
carcajou, mustelvulpo
carcass, kadavro
Carcinidae, karcinoj
carcinogen, kancerogen/enzo; **carcino-
genic,** ~a
carcinoma, karcinomo; **squamous-cell
carcinoma,** skvamĉela ~o; **carcino-
matosis,** ~ozo
Carcinus, karcino
card, (piece of thick paper, gen), karto;
(comb wool etc.), kardi [tr]; **carder,**
(comb), kardilo; (person), kardisto;
(machine), kardomaŝino; **card shark,**
~ruzulo; **business card, calling card,**
~eto, vizit~o; **credit card, charge
card,** kredit~o; **(key)punch card, data card,** (cmptr), tru~o; **scorecard,**
poent~o; **deck of cards,** (gen), ~aro;
index card (or oth similar card or paper slip), slipo; **playing card,** lud~o;
tarot card, [see "tarot"]
cardamom, cardamum, (plant), kardamomo; (spice; med), ~aĵo
cardia, (ostium cardiacum), kardjo
cardiac, kardia [cp "heart"]
cardialgia, kardjalgio
cardigan, apertosvetero
cardinal, (primary), ĉefa; (rel), kardina-
lo; (bird), kardinalbirdo

cardi(o)–, (med: heart), kardi(o)–
cardiogram, kardi/ogramo; **cardiograph**, ~ografo; **cardiography**, ~ografio; **cardiographer**, ~ografiisto; **electrocardiogram**, elektro~ogramo
cardioid, (heart-shaped), korforma; (math), kardioido
cardiology, kardiolog/io; **cardiologist**, ~o
cardiopathy, kardiopatio
cardiotomy, (re heart), kardiotomio; (re ostium cardiacum), kardjotomio
cardiovascular, kardiovaskula
carditis, kardiito
Cardium, kardio*
cardoon, kardono, Hispana artiŝoko
Carduelis, kardelo; Carduelis cannabina, kanabeno; Carduelis spinus, fringelo
Carduus, karduo
care, (care for, look after; caution etc.), zorgi [tr, int]; ~o; (woe, worry, concern), ĉagreno; **care for**, (like), ŝati [tr] (e.g.: *I don't care for apricots:* mi ne ŝatas abrikotojn); (love), ami [tr] (e.g.: *I care for you a great deal:* mi tre amas vin); (treat, look after, be responsible for), pri~i [tr]; varti [tr]; **carefree**, sen~a, senĉagrena; **careful**, ~(em)a, atent(em)a (e.g.: *careful handling:* ~a traktado; *a careful driver:* ~ema gvidanto); (diligent), diligenta; **be careful**, ~i, atenti [int] (e.g.: *be careful of the ice!:* ~u [or] atentu pri la glacio!); **careless**, mal~(em)a; **carelessness**, mal~emo; **be careless (about)**, mal~i [tr, int]; **take care**, ~i, singardi [int], gardemi [int]; **take care of**, (care for), [see "care for" above]; (deal w), trakti [tr]; **caretaker**, ~anto; ~isto; (government), transira; **(in) care of**, (in mailing address: "c/o"), ~e de [abb: z/d] [see § 22]; **after-care**, (med), postflegado; **I don't care**, ne gravas al mi, estas indiferente al mi, estas egale al mi; **for all I care**, ne gravas al mi; **I couldn't care less (about that)**, al mi (tio) ne povus gravi malpli; **do you care (if)** ...?, ĉu gravas al vi (se) ...?
careen, (part of ship below water), kareno; (tilt for cleaning), ~i [tr]; (speed swayingly), ŝanceliĝe rapidegi [int]
career, kariero; ~a
caress, karesi [tr]; ~o
caret, manksigno [not "kareto"]
Caretta, kareto
Carex, karekso
cargo, kargo
Caria, Kario
Carib, Karibo; ~a
Caribbean, Kariba; la ~a regiono; **Caribbean Sea**, Maro ~a
caribe, piranjo
caribou, karibuo
Carica papaya, papajo
caricature, karikaturo; ~i [tr]
caries, kario
carillon, kariljono; ~i [int]; **carilloneur**, ~isto
carina, (any keel-shaped anat or bot part; lower petals), kareno; (crest on breast of bird or similar object), karino
Carinata, karinuloj
carinate, karenforma
Carinthia, Karintio
Carioca, Rio-de-Ĵaneirano
cariole, (carriage), kariolo; (dog-sled), hundosledo
Carl, Karlo; **Carla**, ~a
Carlina, karlino
carmagnole, (dance or song), karmanjolo
Carmel, (mountain or rel order), Karmelo; **Carmelite**, ~an(in)o
Carmen, Karmena
carminative, karminativa; ~aĵo
carmine, karmino; ~a
carnage, masakro, buĉado
carnal, karneca
carnassial, tranĉa; ~a dento
carnation, (bot), kariofildianto
carnelian, karneolo
carnet, (customs certificate), duanakto; (ticket book), biletolibro
carnival, karnavalo
Carnivora, karnovoruloj
carnivorous, karnovora; **carnivore**, ~ulo
carob, (fruit), karobo; (tree), ~arbo, ceratonio
carol, karolo

Carolina:, North Carolina, Nord-Karolino; South Carolina, Sud-Karolino
Caroline, Karola; ~ino; Caroline Islands, ~ino
Carolingian, Karolido; ~a
Carolyn, Karola, ~ino
carom, resalti [int]; ~o
carotene, karoteno
carotid, karotido
carouse, diboĉi [int]
carousel, karuselo
carp, (bicker, complain), ĉikani [tr]; (zool), karpo; crucian carp, karaso
carpal, karpa; ~a osto
Carpathian, Karpata; Carpathians, Carpathian Mountains, ~oj
carpel, karpelo
Carpentaria, Gulf of, Golfo Karpentaria
carpenter, ĉarpenti [tr]; ~isto; carpentry, ~ado; ~aĵo
carpet, (gen), tapiŝo; ~i [tr]; call on the carpet, (reprimand), riproĉi [tr]
Carpinus, karpeno
carpology, karpologio
carpus, karpo; carpal, ~a; ~a osto
carrack, karako
Carrara, Kararo
carriage, (horse-drawn), kaleŝo; (baby), infanĉareto; (roller assembly in typewriter, cmptr printer), ĉareto; (carrying), port(ad)o; (transportation), transport(ad)o; (cost), frajtoprezo; (posture), sinteno; (Br: rr car), vagono; (of gun), afusto
carrier, (person), port/isto (e.g.: letter-carrier: leter~isto); (device), ~ilo; (med: disease carrier: chem), vehiklo; (elec: signal), ~anta ondo; (freight company), frajtisto, frajtokompanio; aircraft carrier, (ship), aviadilŝipo; [see also "carry"]
carrion, kadavraĵo
carrot, karoto
carrousel, karuselo
carry, (hold, support, etc., and move), porti [tr]; (lead), konduki [tr]; (impel), peli [tr]; (support weight), sub~i [tr]; ($ support), subteni [tr]; (transport; $: transfer sum from one column etc. to oth), trans~i [tr] [see also "balance"];

(be pregnant w), esti graveda kun; (hold self, have posture), sin teni; (behave), konduki [int]; (include in radio or TV program etc.), prezenti [tr]; (include in newspaper, magazine, etc.), aperigi, prezenti [tr]; (win, gain support, etc.), gajni [tr]; (withstand), el~i [tr], elteni [tr]; (be affirmed in voting), akceptiĝi; (chem; med; phil medium for thought etc.), vehikli [tr]; carrier, [see "carrier"]; carry forward, ($), trans~i [tr]; (proceed w), daŭrigi; balance carried forward, trans~o; carry off, for~i [tr]; (make succeed), sukcesigi; (kill), mortigi; carry on, (proceed, continue), daŭri [int]; daŭrigi; (engage in activity), konduki [tr]; (behave badly), miskonduti [int]; (debauch), diboĉi [int]; carry out, el~i [tr]; (effectuate), efektivigi, realigi; (for taking out, as food), el~a; carry over, (remain), resti [int]; restigi; (postpone), prokrasti [tr]; carry through, (accomplish), plenumi [tr]; (support, as through difficulty), sub~i [tr]; miscarry, (gen), aborti [int]; (fig: go astray), devojiĝi; miscarriage, aborto; devojiĝo; be (get) carried away, be carried off one's feet, for~iĝi (de entuziasmo, ekscitiĝo); carrying charge, debetinterezo
cart, (gen), ĉaro; (small handcart, as grocery cart), (puŝ)~eto; (move by cart), ~porti [tr]; pushcart, puŝ~o
Cartagena, Kartageno
carte blanche, blanketo
cartel, kartelo
Cartesian, Kartezia; ~ano; Cartesianism, ~anismo
Carthage, Kartago
Carthamus, kartamo
Carthusian, Kartuzian(in)o
cartilage, kartilago; cartilaginous, ~(ec)a
cartography, kartograf/io; cartographer, ~o
carton, (cardboard box), karton/skatolo; (of cigarettes etc.), pako; carton pierre, ŝton~o
cartoon, (ŝerc)desegnaĵo, karikaturo; (film), trukfilmo
cartouch(e), kartuŝo

cartridge, (gen), kartoĉo; **cartridge clip**, ~ujo
Carum carvi, karvio
caruncle, karunkolo
carve, (wood, stone, etc.), ĉizi [tr]; (meat), distranĉi [tr]
Carya, hikorio; Carya illlinoensis, Carya pecan, pekanarbo
caryatid, kariatido
Caryophyll/us aromaticus, kariofil/arbo, ~mirto; Caryophyllaceae, ~acoj
casava, [see "cassava"]
cascade, kaskado; ~i [int]; ~igi
case, (example; individual matter; gram form), kazo; (occurrence, instance), ~o, okazo; (set of legal arguments for suit etc.), argumentaro (e.g.: *build a strong case for the defense:* starigi fortan argumentaron por la defendo); (basis, grounds), bazo (e.g.: *you have no case to sue him:* vi havas neniun bazon por procesi kontraŭ li); (coating, covering), tegaĵo; (any container), ujo, –ujo [sfx] (e.g.: *glasses case:* okulvitrujo); (box), skatolo (e.g.: *a case of beer:* skatolo da biero); (small suitcase), valizeto; (chest), kesto; (cabinet), ŝranko; (book cover), kovrilo; (type tray), tipkesto; **casebook**, ~olibro; **caseharden**, surface hardi [tr]; **case history**, ~a historio; **caseload**, ~oŝarĝo; **case of conscience**, (casuistry), kazuo; **bookcase**, libroŝranko; **briefcase**, (porto)teko; **display case**, vitrino, montrokesto; **encase**, tegi [tr]; **in case**, (if, in the event), se, por se, okaze ke (e.g.: *we won't go in case it rains:* ni ne iros se pluvos; *we'll take an umbrella in case it rains:* ni prenos ombrelon por se pluvos); **in case of**, okaze de; **in the case of**, (relative to), rilate [–on], rilate al [–o]; **in that case**, tiuokaze; **in any case**, ĉiuokaze; **as the case may be**, laŭokaze, kiel estu la ~o; **a case in point**, ekzempla ~o, ilustra ~o; **upper case**, (capital letter), majusklo; majuskla; (type chest), supera tipkesto; **lower case**, minusklo; minuskla; malsupera tipkesto; **make a case for (against)**, (bone) argumenti por (kontraŭ), fari (starigi) argumentaron por (kontraŭ)

casein, kazeino
casemate, kazemato
casement, (window), fenestroklapo
casern(e), kazerno
cash, (ready $: bills, coins, checks), kontanta; ~aĵo; (convert check etc. to bills and coins), ~igi, monigi; (sapek coin), sapeko; [cp "change"]; **(in) cash**, (immediate payment, not credit), ~a; ~e; **cash register**, kasregistrilo; **cash-box**, kaso; **cash discount**, ~a rabato; **cash reserve**, monrezervo; **petty cash**, poŝmono; **cash on delivery**, [see "C.O.D."]
cashew, (nut), akaĵuo; (tree), ~arbo, okcidenta anakardiujo
cashier, ($), kasisto; (dismiss), eksigi; (reject), forĵeti [tr], malakcepti [tr]
cashmere, (gen), kaŝmiro
cashoo, kateĉuo
Casimir, Kazimiro
casing, tegaĵo
casino, kazino
cask, barelo
casket, (coffin), ĉerko; (small box), kesteto
Caspian, Kaspia; **Caspian Sea**, Maro ~a
Cassandra, Kasandra
cassation, kasacio
cassava, (bot: Manihot, gen), manihoto; (Manihot utilissima), manioko, kasavo
casserole, (pot), kaserolo; (food), ~aĵo
cassette, kasedo†; **video cassette**, video~o [cp "tape: videotape"]
cassia, Cassia, (tree: Cinnamomum cassia), kasio; (bark), ~aĵo; ringworm cassia, fistul~o; Cassia fistula, fistul~o; Cassia acutifolia, Cassia angustifolia, sena~o
Cassiopeia, Kasiopeo
cassique, kaciko
cassiterite, kasiterito
Cassius, Kasio
cassock, (robe), sutano
cassowary, kazuaro
cast, (throw, fling, lit or fig), ĵeti [tr]; ~o; (throw out, as anchor, fishing line, etc.), el~i [tr]; el~o; (calculate, as horoscope etc.), kalkuli [tr]; (mold), muldi [tr]; muldiĝi; muldaĵo; (of ac-

tors), rolularo; (choose actors), roligi; (twist, warp), tordi [tr]; tordiĝi; (med, for broken bone), (splint)muldaĵo; (coloration), koloretiĝo, nuanco (e.g.: *blue with a reddish cast:* blua kun ruĝeca nuanco); (eyes not coordinated), strabismo [see "strabismus"]; **casting,** (molded), muldaĵo; **cast about (for),** (search for), ĉirkaŭserĉi [tr]; (plan), plani [tr]; **cast aside, cast away,** for~i [tr], flanken~i [tr]; **castaway,** ŝiprompulo; **cast a ballot,** baloti [int]; **cast a vote,** voĉdoni [int]; **cast off,** (throw away), for~i [tr]; (knitting), fintriki [tr]; (boat from shore), debordiĝi; **cast on,** (knitting). ektriki [tr]; **cast out,** el~i [tr], elpeli [tr]; **outcast,** elpelita; elpelito; **overcast,** (clouds), plennuba, nubkovrita; nubkovraĵo; (sewing), faldokudri [tr]; **cast a glance,** ~i rigardon [cp "askance"]

Castanea, kaŝtanarbo

castanet, kastanjeto

caste, kasto

castellated, krenela

caster, (small bottle), flakono; (stand to hold these), ~ujo; (roller), rulilo, svingrado

castigate, riproĉ(eg)i [tr], mallaŭd(eg)i [tr]

Castile, Castilla, Kastilio; **Castilian,** ~a; ~ano; **New Castile,** Castilla la Nueva, Nov-~o; **Old Castile,** Castilla la Vieja, Malnov-~o

castle, (gen), kastelo; (medieval fortified), burgo†; (chess piece), turo; (chess: move ~ and king), aroki [tr]; castle in the air (clouds), ĥimer~o, nub~o

castor, (oil from beaver), kastoreo; (bottle; roller), [see "caster"]; **castor oil,** (from castor bean), ricinoleo; **castor bean,** ricina semo; **castor-oil plant,** ricino

Castor, (myth), K~o

Castor, (zool), kastoro

castoreum, kastoreo

castrate, kastri [tr]

castrato, kastrito

Castries, Kastrio*

casual, (random), hazarda; (occasional), ~a, neregula; (careless), senzorga; (superficial), surfaca; (informal), neformala, senceremonia; **casuals,** (clothing etc.), neformalaĵoj

casualty, (victim of accident, mil death, etc.), viktimo, trafito; (any loss), perdo

Casuarius, kazuaro; Casuariiformes, ~oformaj (birdoj)

casuist, kazuisto

casuistry, kazuistiko

casus belli, militkaŭzo

cat, (domestic), kato; (any of genus *Felis*), feliso; **catty,** malica, spitema; **catmint, catnip,** katario; **cat's-eye,** (quartz, glass, etc.), ~okulo; **cat's-foot,** (bot), antenario; **cat's-paw,** (dupe, fool), ilulo; (light breeze), zefireto; **cattail,** (bot), tifao*; **catwalk,** pontopaŝejo; **tomcat,** vir~o; **bear cat,** pando; **civet cat,** cibeto; **polecat,** putoro; **snow cat,** neĝtraktoro; **wildcat,** (zool: gen, unspecific term), sovaĝa ~o; (lynx), linko; (unsound, risky), riskoplena; (unofficial, unauthorized, as strike), neoficiala, nepermesita, neaprobita; **cat-o'-nine-tails,** skurĝo; **let the cat out of the bag,** malkaŝi la sekreton

catabolism, katabolo; catabolic, ~a

cataclysm, kataklismo

catacomb, katakombo

catafalque, katafalko

Catalán, Kataluna; ~o

catalectic, katalekta

catalepsy, katalepsio; **cataleptic,** ~a; ~ulo

catalog(ue), katalogo; ~i [tr]

Catalonia, Katalun/io; **Catalonian,** ~o; ~a; ~ia

catalpa, *Catalpa,* katalpo

Cataluña, [see "Catalonia"]

catalysis, katalizo; **catalyst,** ~enzo; **catalyze,** ~i [tr]; **catalytic,** ~a; **anticatalyst,** anti~enzo

catamaran, katamarano

catamite, njo-knabo

cataphoresis, kataforezo

cataplasm, kataplasmo

catapult, (gen), katapulto; ~i [tr]; ~iĝi

cataract, (med), katarakto; (waterfall), ~o, kaskadego

catarrh, kataro
catastrophe, katastrofo; **catastrophic,** ~a
catatonia, katatonio; **catatonic,** ~a; ~ulo
catawba, (vine: *Vitis labruscana*), labruskano* [cp "grape: wild grape"]; (grape), ~a vinbero; (wine), ~a vino
catbrier, smilako
catch, (seize, capture, trap, take, etc.), kapti [tr]; ~o; ~ito; ~aĵo; (understand), (ek)kompreni [tr]; (get on bus, plane, etc.; hit), trafi [tr] (e.g.: *catch the bus:* trafi la buson; *the shot caught him in the leg:* la pafo trafis lin en la kruro); (see), vidi [tr]; (hear), aŭdi [tr]; (med: contract disease), malsaniĝi de, (malsano) trafi (iun) (e.g.: *I caught the flu:* mi malsaniĝis de gripo [or] gripo trafis min); (hook onto, grasp), kroĉi [tr], kroĉiĝi al (e.g.: *the thorn caught my shirt:* la dorno kroĉis mian ĉemizon [or] kroĉiĝis al mia ĉemizo); (pawl), kliko; (start to burn), ekbruli [int] (e.g.: *the fire won't catch in that damp wood:* la fajro ne ekbrulos en tiu humida ligno); (tricky, hidden condition), ruzo (e.g.: *there must be a catch in that offer:* devas esti ruzo en tiu propono); (child's game of catching and touching), tuŝludo; **catching,** (contagious), kontaĝa; **catchy,** loga; **catch-all,** ĉioninkluda, ĉion~a; ĉion~ilo; ĉionujo; **catchword,** frapvorto, frapfrazo; **catch–22 (situation),** senelira dilemo; **catch as catch can,** ajnmaniere, iel ajn; **catch on,** (understand), ekkompreni [tr]; (become popular), populariĝi, modiĝi; **catch oneself,** ekhalti [int], ekhaltigi sin; **catch up,** (overtake), (kur)atingi [tr]; (become current), reakuratiĝi; **play catch,** tuŝludi [int]; **get caught in,** (involved in, tangled in), implikiĝi en; **oyster catcher,** (zool), hematopo, marpigo
catechesis, kateĥizado, katekizado
catechetical, kateĥiza, katekiza
catechism, kateĥismo, katekismo
catechist, kateĥisto, katekisto
catechize, kateĥizi, katekizi [tr]
catechol, katekolo

catechu, kateĉuo
catechumen, kateĥumeno, katekumeno
category, kategorio; **categorical,** (gen), ~a; **categorize,** ~igi, klasifiki [tr]
catenary, (curve), ĉenlinio; ~a
cater, (provide food), provianti [tr]; **caterer,** ~isto; **cater to,** (seek to fulfill desires), komplezemi [int] al
caterpillar, (zool; machine tread), raŭpo; (vehicle w caterpillar tread), ~aŭto; ~okamiono; ~otraktoro; **woolly bear caterpillar,** arktia ~o
caterwaul, kathojli [int]; ~o
catgut, katguto
catharsis, (of bowels), laksigo; (purifying, as of emotions), elpurigo; **cathartic,** ~a; ~enzo; elpuriga; elpurigenzo [cp "enema"]
Cathartes, katarto; Cathartidae, ~edoj
cathect(icize), koncentriĝi pri
cathedra, (gen), kadedro
cathedral, katedralo
Catherine, Katarina
catheter, katetero; **catheterize,** ~i [tr]
cathexis, prikoncentriĝo
cathode, katodo; **cathode rays,** ~radioj; **cathode-ray tube,** ~radia tubo; **anticathode,** anti~o
catholic, (universal), universala
Catholic, (rel), Katolika; ~o; **Catholicism,** ~ismo; **Roman Catholic,** Rom~a; Rom~~o
Catiline, Katilinio
cation, katjono
catkin, amento
Cato, Cato the Elder, Cato the Censor, Katono; Cato Uticensis, Cato the Younger, ~o el Utiko
Catocala, katokalo
catoptrics, katoptriko; **catoptrical,** ~a
Catskills, Catskill Mountains, Katskiloj*
catsup, keĉupo*
cattle, brutoj, gebovoj; **scrub cattle,** (Aus), eskapintaj ~oj
cattleya, *Cattleya,* katlejo
Catulla, Katulo
Caucalis, kaŭkalido
Caucasia, Kaŭkaz/io; **Caucasian,** (re Caucasia), ~ia; (re race etc.), ~a; ~ulo; **Caucasus,** (mountains), ~o

caucus, (meeting), kunsido; (Br: pol committee), regokomitato
caudad, ĝisvosta
caudal, vost(ec)a
caudate, vosthava
caudillo, (milit)estro
caul, (fetal membrane), kufo; (great omentum), granda epiploo
cauldron, kaldrono
cauliflower, florbrasiko
caulk, (gen), ŝtopgarni [tr]; (re ship, w oakum, tar, etc.), kalfatri [tr], stupi [tr]; caulking, ~aĵo; kalfatraĵo
causal, kaŭza; **causality**, ~eco
causalgia, kaŭsalgio
cause, (bring into existence; reason behind), kaŭzi [tr], estigi, elvoki [tr]; ~o; (purpose; social goal), motivo (e.g.: *the cause of justice:* la motivo de justeco; *for a good cause:* por bona motivo); (cause to be, render), igi (e.g.: *cause one to do something:* igi ke iu faru ion [or] igi iun fari ion); (law: issue), demando, afero [cp "case"]; **causeway**, digvojo; **cause and effect**, ~o kaj efiko; **show cause (for)**, motivi [tr]; **cause célèbre**, famafero
caustic, (corrosive), kaŭstika; ~aĵo; **lunar caustic**, lapiso
cauterize, (w heat), kaŭteri [tr]; (w caustic chemical), kaŭstikizi [tr]; (gen), ~izi [tr]
cautery, (tool), kaŭtero; (act), ~ado
caution, (carefulness, attentiveness), singardo, zorg(em)o [not "kaŭcio"]; (warn), averti [tr]; averto; cautious, ~a, zorg(em)a; (discreet), diskreta; **precaution**, antaŭzorgo; **take precautions (for, about)**, antaŭzorgi [tr, int]
cava, kavao
cavalcade, kavalkado
cavalier, kavaliro; ~eca
cavalry, kavalerio
cavatina, kavatino
cave, kaverno [cp "grotto"]; **cave in**, kavigi; kaviĝi; enfaligi; enfali [int]; **cave-in**, (of ground), terenfalo; **cave man**, ~ulo, ~homo
caveat, averto; **caveat emptor**, sin gardu la aĉetonto
cavern, kaverno; **cavernous**, ~a

Cavia, kavio; Cavia cobaya, Cavia porcellus, kobajo
caviar(e), kaviaro
cavil (at), ĉikani [tr]; ~o
cavitation, kaviĝ(ad)o
cavity, (any hollow place), kavo; (bot, zool, anat), alveolo (e.g.: *dental cavity:* denta alveolo) [cp "caries"]
cavort, kaprioli [int]
cavy, kavio
caw, graki [int]; ~o; (onom), grak!
cay, insuleto [not "kajo"]
cayenne, cayenne pepper, papriko, kajena pipro, ruĝa pipro
Cayenne, (town), Kajeno; **Cayenne River**, Rivero ~a
cayman, kajmano
CD-ROM, [see under "disk"]
C.E. (abb of "(year of the) Common Era"), p.K. [abb of "post Komunerao" or "post Kristo"]
cease, ĉesi [int]; ~igi; ~o (e.g.: *the rain ceased:* la pluvo ~is; *he ceased talking:* li ~is paroli; *we ceased our discussion:* ni ~igis nian diskuton); [cp "halt"]; **cease-fire**, batalhalto; **ceaseless**, sen~a
Cebus, cebo
Cecidomyia, cecidomio
Cecil, Cecilo; **Cecile, Cecilia, Cecily**, ~a
Cecrops, Cekropso
cecum, cekumo
cedar, (tree), cedro; (wood), ~oligno; **cedar of Lebanon**, Lebanona ~o; **Spanish cedar, cigar-box cedar**, cedrelo
cede, cedi [tr, int]
cedilla, cedilo
Cedrela, cedrelo
Cedrus, cedro; Cedrus deodara, Himalaja ~o, deodaro; Cedrus liban(on)i, Lebanona ~o
ceiba, (bot: *Bombax*), kapok/arbo; (kapok), ~o
Ceiba pendandra, kapokarbo
ceil, plafoni [tr]
ceiling, (gen), plafono; ~i [tr]
celandine, (bot: *Chelidonium majus*), kelidonio; (*Impatiens, Balsamina*), balzamino; **lesser celandine**, (*Ranunculus ficaria*), fikario

Celastrus, celastro
Celebes, Celebeso
celebrate, (perform rel ceremony), celebri [tr]; (observe festive occasion), festi [tr]; (solemnize), soleni [tr]; celebrant, ~anto; celebrated, (famous), fama, renoma; celebration, ~(ad)o; fest(ad)o; solen(ad)o
celebrity, (renown), renomo; (famous person), ~ulo, famulo
celery, celerio
celesta, celeste, celesto
celestial, ĉiela
celestine, celestino
Celestine, Celesteno; ~a
celestite, celestino
celibacy, seksabstino; celibate, ~a; ~ul(in)o
cell, (of prison, or oth small room; anat; elec tube etc.; of honeycomb etc.), ĉelo; (elec battery), pilo; cellular, ~(ec)a; ~hava; red blood cell, ruĝa globulo; white blood cell, blanka globulo, leŭkocito; cells of Leydig, ~oj de Lejdigo; dry cell, seka pilo; photoelectric cell, photocell, lumelektra ~o; solar energy cell, sunenergia ~o
cella, naoso
cellar, kelo
cello, violonĉelo [not "ĉelo"]; cellist, ~isto
cellobiose, celobiozo
cellophane, celofano
cellule, (small compartmental division of bone or oth tissue), celulo; (any small cell), ĉeleto
celluloid, celuloido
cellulose, celulozo
celom, celomo
Celsius, Celsius [abb: C]
Celt, Kelto; Celtic, ~a; Celt-Iberian, ~-Ibero; ~-Ibera
cement, (of mortar, sand, etc.; any agglutinant, lit or fig), cemento; ~i [tr]; (metallurgy; tooth layer), ĉemento; ĉementi [tr]; cementation, ĉementado; Portland cement, Portlanda ~o; [cp "concrete", "mortar"]
cementum, ĉemento
cemetery, tombejo
cenobite, cenobito
cenotaph, cenotafo

Cenozoic, kenozoiko; ~a
censer, incens/ujo, ~ilo
censor, (prohibit book, newspaper, movie, etc., or portions of), cenzuri [tr]; ~isto, cenzoro; (Roman official), censisto, cenzoro; censorship, ~(ad)o; censorious, malaproba, kondamna; [cp "censure"]
censure, malaprobi [tr], kondamni [tr]; ~o, kondamno [cp "censor"]
census, censo†; ~a; census-taker, ~isto
cent, cendo
centaur, (myth), centaŭro
Centaur, (ast), Centaŭro
centaurea, centaŭreo
Centaurea, centaŭreo; Centaurea calcitrapa, stelkardo; Centaurea cyanus, cejano
Centaurus, (ast), Centaŭro
centavo, centavo
centenarian, centjara; ~ulo
centenary, jarcento; ~a [cp "centennial"]
centennial, centjara jubileo; sesquicentennial, cent-kvindek-jara jubileo; bicentennial, ducentjara jubileo; tricentennial, tricentjara jubileo
center, (midpoint, gen), centro; ~i [tr]; ~iĝi; (sport player), ~ulo; (place, as for special studies, higher learning, oth activity), ~ejo; center of gravity, pezo~o; center of mass, mas~o; centerpiece, tablomamaĵo; off-center, ekster~a; self-centered, egoisma; shopping center, butik—~o [cp "mall"]
centesimal, centezimala
centi-, (pfx), centi–
Centigrade, centezimala; ~e, Celsius [abb: C] [note: "Celsius" is the official international term]
centime, centimo, centimo
centipede, (any of Chilopoda), skolopendro
cento, ĉentono
central, centra; (in geog names), Mez– [pfx]; centralize, (pol, bsns, etc.), centralizi [tr]; decentralize, malcentralizi [tr]; centralism, centralizismo; centralist, centralizisma; centralizisto; Central African Republic, Centrafrika Respubliko

centranth, centranto
Centranthus, centranto
Centrarchidae, centrarkedoj*
centre, [see "center"]
centrifugal, centrifuga; **centrifugalize**,
~i [tr]; **centrifugation**, ~ado; **centrifuge**, ~atoro
centripetal, centripeta
centrist, centristo
centuple, cent/obla, ~obla [see "double"]
centurion, centuriestro
century, jarcento; **century plant**, agavo
cephalad, ĝiskapa
cephalic, cefala; **cephalic index**, ~a indico
–cephalic, (anat sfx: head), –cefala
cephal(o)–, (anat pfx: head), cefal(o)–
Cephalonia, Cefalonio
cephalopod, cefalopodo
Cephalopoda, cefalopodoj
cephalous, kaphava
–cephalous, (anat sfx: –headed), –cefala
Cepheus, (myth; ast), Cefeo; **Cepheid** (variable), ~ido
Cerambyx, cerambiko
ceramic, ceramika; ~aĵo; **ceramics**, ~o
cerastes, Cerastes, cerasto
Cerastium, cerastio
Cerasus, ĉerizarbo
Ceratonia, karobarbo, ceratonio
Cerberus, Cerbero
Cercidiphyllum japonicum, kacuro
Cercopithecus, cerkopiteko; Cercopithecidae, ~edoj
cereal, (grain, gen), cerealo; (processed, e.g., breakfast food), ~aĵo
cerebellum, cerebelo
cerebral, cerba
cerebrate, cerbumi [int]
cerebro–, (anat pfx: brain), cerbo– (e.g.: *cerebrospinal:* ~ospina)
cerebrum, cerebro
ceremony, (gen), ceremonio; (rite), ~o, rito; **ceremonial**, ~a; ~aro; **ceremonious**, ~a; **unceremonious**, sen~a; **stand on ceremony**, fari ~ojn; **not stand on ceremony**, lasi ~ojn
Ceres, Ceresa
ceresin, cerezino
Cerigo, Cerigo

cerise, ĉerizkolora
cerium, cerio
cerotic, cerotina; **cerotic acid**, ~a acido
certain, (sure, definite), certa (e.g.: *she's a certain winner:* ŝi estas ~a gajnonto); (some unspecified), iu, difinita (e.g.: *a certain member told me:* iu membro diris al mi; *certain mushrooms are poisonous:* iuj fungoj estas venenaj); (some kind of a), ia (e.g.: *it gives off a certain odor:* ĝi eligas ian odoron); (to a certain extent), ioma (e.g.: *one expects a certain honesty:* oni anticipas ioman honestecon); **certainly**, (assuredly), ja, ~e (e.g.: *it certainly is hot today:* ja estas varme hodiaŭ); **certainty**, ~aĵo; ~eco; **to a certain extent**, iom, iomgrade, iagrade, ~agrade; **a certain amount of**, ioma, iom da
Certhia, certio
certificate, (legal document), akto (e.g.: *birth certificate:* naskiĝ~o); (attestation), atestilo; (diploma), diplomo
certify, (declare true, affirm), atesti [tr]; (declare person insane), deklari (iun) freneza; (authorize), rajtigi; aprobi [tr]
certitude, certeco
cerulean, lazura
cerumen, cerumeno
Cervantes (Saavedra), Cervanto†
cervix, (gen), cerviko; **cervical**, ~a
Cervus, cervo; Cervidae, ~edoj; Cervinae, ~enoj
cesium, cezio
cessation, (by self), ĉeso; (being stopped), ~igo
cession, cedo
cesspit, kloak/fosaĵo; (fig: evil place), ~o; **cesspool**, ~cisterno
Cestoda, *Cestodes,* cestodoj
cestode, cestodo
cestus, cesto
cesura, cezuro
Cetacea, cetacoj
cetacean, cetaco; ~a
Ceterach, ceterako
cetology, cetacologio
Cetonia, cetonio
Cettia diphone, ugviso
Cetus, (ast), Baleno

cetyl, cetílo; ~a
Cévennes, Cevenoj
Ceylon, Cejlono [cp "Sri Lanka"]
cf. (abb for "compare"), komparu [abb: kp.]
CGS (system), (sistemo)   CGS   [see "centimeter"]
chablis, (wine), ŝablizo*
cha-cha(-cha), ĉaĉaĉao*; ~i [int]
Chaco, Granĉako
Chad, (lake), Ĉado; (country), ~io, ~lando
chaeta, ĥeto
chaetognath, ĥetognato
Chaetognatha, ĥetognatoj
chaetopod, ĥetulo
Chaetopoda, ĥetuloj
chafe, (rub), froti [tr]; ~o; (irritate), ~iriti [tr]; ~irito; **chafe at the bit**, malpacienci [int]; **sap chafer, rose chafer**, (zool: *Cetonia*), cetonio [see also "beetle"]; **chafing dish**, fondupoto* [see "fondue"]
chaff, (of grain, lit or fig), brano; (tease), ŝerci [int]; priŝerci [tr]
chaffinch, fringo
chagrin, ĉagreni [tr]; ~o
chain, (of links, gen, lit or fig; any series or group, as of businesses), ĉeno; ~i [tr]; (shackles, fetters), kateno; kateni [tr]; (hinged, for bicycle, motorcycle, etc.), artik~o; (unit of length: surveyor's), 20,12 metroj; (engineer's), 30,48 metroj [see § 20]; **enchain**, kateni [tr]; **unchain**, mal~i [tr], de~igi, el~igi; malkateni [tr], senkatenigi; **chain-guard**, (bicycle etc.), ~ujo; **chain gang**, katenbrigado; **chain letter**, ~letero; **chain mail**, maŝkiraso; **chaincarrier, chainman**, (surveying), ~isto; **chain reaction**, ~reakcio; **chain saw**, ~segilo; **chain-smoke**, ~fumi [tr]; **chain-smoker**, ~fumanto; **chain stitch**, ~stebi [tr]; ~stebo; **chain store**, ~butiko; **golden chain**, (bot), laburno, orpluvo
chair, (furniture, gen), seĝo; (speaker's, on platform; university position etc.), katedro; (rr: rail fastener), relingo; (preside), prezidi [int] (ĉe); (chairperson), prezidanto; **chairlift**, ~otelfero; **chairperson, chair(wo)man**, prez-

idant(in)o; **chair(man)ship**, prezidanteco; **armchair**, fotelo, brak~o; **deck chair**, ferdek~o; **easy chair**, komfort~o; **electric chair**, elektra ~o; **folding chair**, fald~o; **lawnchair**, gazon~o; **office chair**, (chair w rollers), rul~o; **rocking chair**, lul~o; **swivel chair**, gir~o; **wheelchair**, rad~o
chaise longue, chaise lounge, kuŝoseĝo
chakra, ĉakro*
chalazion, kalazio
chalcedony, kalcedono
Chalcidice, Kalcidiko
Chaldea, Ĥalde/ujo,   Kaldeo;   **Chaldean**, ~o; ~a; ~uja
chalet, ĉaleto
chalice, kaliko
chalk, (gen), kreto; ~i [tr]; **chalkboard**, [see under "board"]; **French chalk**, talko; **chalk it up to**, atribui ĝin al
challenge, (call into question, dispute, etc.), kontesti [tr]; ~o; (defy), defii [tr]; defio; (make demands on), pripostuli [tr]; postulo; (call to duel, battle, etc.), provoki [tr]; provoko; (inspire, urge, instigate), instigi [tr]; instigo
Chamaeleon, (ast), Ĥameleono
Chamaeleon, (zool), ĥameleono
chamber, (small compartment; room w/o windows; closed hollow volume in machine or apparatus), kamero; (any room), ĉambro; (of gun), kulaso; **chamber-servant, chamber-maid**, ĉambrist(in)o; **Chamber of Commerce**, Komerca ĉambro; **antechamber**, antaŭĉambro; **cloud chamber**, nubo~o, ~o de Wilson; **combustion chamber**, (of motor), kulaso; **gas chamber**, gas~o; **judge's chamber(s)**, juĝista(j) ĉambro(j); **lead chamber**, plumboĉambro, plumbo~o; **Second Chamber**, (Aus), Senato
chamberlain, (servant), ĉambelano; (Br: treasurer), trezoristo
chameleon, ĥameleono
chamfer, bevelo; ~i [tr]
chammy, chamois, (animal), ĉamo; (skin), ŝamo
chamomile, (*Anthemis*), antemido;

(Matricaria), kamomilo, matrikario
champ, (chew), (ŝmace) maĉi [tr]; (champion), ĉampiono
champagne, (drink), ĉampano
Champagne, (region), Ĉampanjo
champion, (gen), ĉampiono; ~i [tr]; championship, ~eco
chance, (random; w/o apparent cause), hazarda; ~o (e.g.: *leave things to chance:* lasi aferojn al ~o; *a chance meeting:* ~a renkontiĝo); (opportunity), oportuno; (likelihood; odds; luck), ŝanco (e.g.: *you have a good chance of being chosen:* vi havas bonan ŝancon, ke vi estos elektita); (math: random), aleatora; aleatoreco (e.g.: *chance alone would yield a rate of 25% right answers:* aleatoreco sola rezultigus proporcion je 25% da ĝustaj respondoj); (risk), riski [tr]; risko (e.g.: *I do not want to chance being rained on:* mi ne volas riski esti surpluvata); **chancy**, risk(ec)a, riskoplena; **mischance**, malfeliĉo, akcidento; **there is an off chance that**, estas ioma ŝanco ke; **on the off chance that**, por la eventualajo ke; **not have a snowball's chance in hell**, ne havi la ŝancon de neĝbulo en infero; havi nenioman ŝancon; **take a chance**, fari riskon
chancel, ĥorejo
chancellor, kanceliero; **chancellery**, (place), ~ejo; (rank), ~eco; **Lord (High) Chancellor**, Lordo-K~o; **Chancellor of the Exchequer**, Financa Ministro
chancery, (office), kancelario; (court), ~a kortumo
chancre, ŝankro
chandelier, lustro
chandler, (of candles), kandelisto; (retail supplier, gen), provizisto
Changchun, Ĉangĉun
change, (alter, exchange, gen), ŝanĝi [tr]; ~iĝi; ~(iĝ)o; (coins and/or bills to round a sum), apunto (e.g.: *give $5 for a $3.74 purchase and receive $1.26 in change:* doni $5 por aĉeto de $3,74 kaj ricevi apunton de $1,26; *please have exact change:* bonvolu havi precizan apunton) [cp "cash"]; **change-**

over, tra~o; **interchange**, inter~i [tr]; inter~o; (of highways, gen), inter-kruciĝo; (highway cloverleaf), tref-kruciĝo; **shortchange**, (give insufficient $ in change), subapunti [tr]; (cheat, deprive of, gen), forruzi [tr]; **change of life**, menopaŭzo
Changteh, Changte, Changtu, Ĉangdu
channel, (TV etc.; any means of communication; canal; way through), kanalo; (groove), kanelo; (deeper part of river), ŝanelo; (of sea), markolo; (direct), direkti [tr], en~igi; **English Channel**, Maniko
chanson, kanzono
chant, ĉanti [tr]; ~o; **chanter**, (person), ~isto; (of bagpipe), meloditubo
chanterelle, chantarelle, (bot), manĝebla kantarelo, ovofungo
chantey, markanzono
chaos, ĥaoso; **chaotic**, ~a
Chanukah, Ĥanukao*
chap, (fellow), ulo; (split, re skin), fendeti [tr]; fendetiĝi; chapped, fendeta; **chaps**, (worn by cowboys), vep-roŝirmiloj
chaparral, veprejo
chapel, kapelo
chaperon(e), (vart)akompan/ant(in)o; ~i [tr]
chaplain, kapelano
chapter, (of book etc.), ĉapitro; (local branch of organization), filio
char, (charcoal; half-burn), braĝo; ~igi; ~iĝi [see also "charcoal"]; (clean), (dom)purigi; **charwoman**, (dom)purigistino
Chara, karao
character, (traits; morals), karaktero; (written, printed symbol), karaktro† [cp "symbol"]; (any person), ulo; (unusual person), originalulo; (theat), rolo; (in book etc.), persono; **characteristic**, (typical), tipa; (distinguishing), distinga; (trait), trajto, eco; (distinguishing feature), distingaĵo; (math), karakteristiko; **characterize**, (gen), karakterizi [tr]
charade, ŝarado
Charadrius, ĥaradrio; Charadriidae, ~edoj; Charadriiformes, ~oformaj (birdoj)

charcoal, braĝo, lignokarbo [see also "char"]; **charcoal-broil**, karbonadi [tr]; **charcoal-broiled meat**, karbonado **charge**, (load), ŝarĝi [tr]; ~iĝi; ~(iĝ)o; ~ajo; (battery w elec; gun w ammunition; dynamite etc.; any apparatus w necessary part, fuel, etc.), ŝargi [tr]; ŝargiĝi; ŝarg(iĝ)o; ŝargaĵo; (set price), postuli [tr]; postulo (e.g.: *he charged $20 for his services:* li postulis $20 por siaj servoj); (cause to pay), pagigi; (assess debt), debeti [tr]; debet(iĝ)o; (add to any account; accuse person of crime or oth act), imputi [tr] (iun pri io, ion al iu); imput(iĝ)o; (buy item on credit), debetigi; (commission), komisii [tr]; komisio; (assign task to), taski† [tr]; (attack), sturmi [tr]; sturmo; (order), ordoni [tr]; ordono; **charge account**, debetkonto; **charge card**, kreditkarto; **charge off**, (as $ loss), forimputi [tr]; **in charge**, reganta, estranta; **be in charge (of)**, estri [tr]; **person in charge**, estro; C.O.D. **charges**, remburso [see also "C.O.D."]; **supercharger**, (mech), kunprematoro; **surcharge**, (extra charge), kromdebeti [tr], kromimputi [tr]; kromdebeto, kromimputo; (overcharge), trodebeti [tr]; trodebeto; (overload), tro~i [tr]; (revaluation, as of postage stamp), revalorigi; revalorigo; **take charge of**, (control), ekestri [tr], ekregi [tr]; (look after), ekprizorgi [tr]; (take into protection), preni (ion, iun) sub sian protekton; (take responsibility for), ekrespondeci [int] pri; **charge whatever the traffic will bear**, postuli kiom ajn toleros la merkato
chargé d'affaires, aferŝarĝito
chariot, ĉaro; **charioteer**, ~isto
charisma, karismo†; **charismatic**, ~a
charity, ($ donated), almozo; (charitable organization), ~fondaĵo; (love, good will), karitato; **charitable**, ~a; (generous), ~donema; (loving), karitata
charlatan, ĉarlatano
Charlemagne, Karlo la Granda
Charles, Karolo, Karlo; **Charles Mar-**

tel, ~-Martelo
Charleston, Ĉarlestono*
charlock, sovaĝa sinapo
charlotte, (food), pandeserto
Charlotte, (woman's name), Ĉarlota, Karlota [nickname: Lonjo]
charm, (delight; physics), ĉarmi [tr]; ~o; (bewitch), sorĉi [tr]; sorĉo; (for charm bracelet), breloko; (talisman), talismano; **charming**, ~a
charnel (house), ostejo
Charon, (myth; ast), Karono*
chart, (map), mapo; ~i [tr]; (marine), mar~o; (diagram), diagramo, skemo; (graphic), grafikajo [cp "table"]; **flow chart**, (cmptr; fig), fluskemo†
charter, (grant; document), ĉarto; ~izi [tr]; (rent from), ~i [tr]; (rent to), ~igi (e.g.: *we chartered a bus for the trip:* ni ~is buson por la vojaĝo; *the company chartered it to us for $2000:* la kompanio ~igis ĝin al ni por $2000)
chartreuse, (color), kartuzian/kolora, verdflaveta; (liquor), ~a likvoro
chary, (cautious), singard(em)a; (not generous), avara
Charybdis, Karibda
chase, (drive away, out), peli [tr]; ~o; for~i [tr]; el~i [tr]; (pursue), postkuri [tr]; postkur(ad)o; (hunt), ĉasi [tr]; ĉaso; (groove), foldo; foldi [tr]; **wild goose chase**, vana elserĉo, vana entrepreno
chasm, abismo
Chassid, Ĥasido†; **Chassidim**, ~oj; **Chassidic**, ~a
chassis, (gen), ĉasio
chaste, ĉasta; **chastity**, ~(ec)o [cp "celibate"]
chasten, (humiliate), humiligi; (punish, gen), puni [tr]
chastise, (beat), punbati [tr]; (scold), riproĉi [tr]
chasuble, kazublo
chat, babili [tr, int]; ~(ad)o
chateaubriand, ĉatobriando
chatelain(e), kastelestr(in)o
chattel, (movebla) posedaĵo
chatter, (babble), babil(aĉ)(ad)i [tr, int]; ~o; (clatter, clack, as teeth, machinery, etc.), klak(et)adi [int]; klak(et)ado

chauffeur, ŝoforo; ~i [tr]
chauvinism, (gen), ŝovinismo; **chauvinist**, ~a; ŝovinisto; **male (female) chauvinism**, maskla (femala) ~o [cp "sex: sexism; sexist"]
cheap, (inexpensive), malmultekosta, ĉipa†; (of little value), malaltvalora; (contemptible), malestiminda, aĉa, fia; **cheapskate**, avarulo; **dirtcheap**, tre ~a, tre ĉipa†; preskaŭ senpaga
cheat, fripono; ~i [int]; pri~i [tr]; cheating, (pri)~ado [cp "trick", "fraud", "charlatan", "dupe"]
check, (supervise, observe, verify, etc.), kontroli [tr]; ~o; (stop motion, halt), haltigi; haltigo; (stop activity, cease), ĉesigi; ĉesigo; (restrain), bridi [tr]; brido; (moderate), moderigi; (hook-shaped symbol), hoksigni [tr]; hoksigno; (payment order), ĉeko; (invoice, bill), fakturo, kalkulo; (deposit for safekeeping), deponi [tr]; (ticket, gen), bileto; (square, as in checkerboard pattern), kvadrato [see also "checker"]; (in chess), ŝako; ŝakigi; (said when opponent's king is checked), ŝak!, ŝakon!; (look over text, group of people, etc., for correctness, fitness, etc.), revizii [tr]; revizio; **checkbook**, ĉeklibro; **check in**, (at hotel etc.), enskribi [tr], registri [tr]; enskribiĝi, registriĝi; (return a book etc. to library), malprunti [tr]; **check off**, (mark as verified etc.), ~signi [tr], ~marki [tr], hoksigni [tr]; **check out**, (from hotel etc.), elskribi [tr]; elskribiĝi; (from grocery etc.), kont~i [tr]; kont~iĝi; (verify, gen), ~i; (borrow book etc. from library), prunti [tr]; **checklist**, ~listo; **checkmate**, (chess), [see under "mate"]; **checkpoint**, ~punkto; **check ticket**, **check receipt**, (for check-room), deponatesto; **check person**, deponprenisto; **checkroom**, deponejo; **check up**, ~i; **checkup**, (eg, med exam), (~)ekzameno; **blank check**, blanketo; **cashier's check**, **bank check**, bankĉeko; **traveler's check**, vojaĝa ĉeko; **be in check**, (chess), ŝaki [int]; **in check**, (restrained), bridita

checker, (game piece), dam/peco; **checkers**, (the game), ~ludo; **checkerboard**, ~tabulo; ~tabula, ŝaktabula; **checkered**, (pattern), ŝaktabula; **checkered pattern**, ŝaktabulaĵo, kvadrataĵo
cheek, (of face), vango; (gluteus), sid~o, gluteo; (impertinence), impertinenteco, aŭdaco, aroganteco; **cheekbone**, zigomo
cheep, (as bird), pepi [int], kviviti [int], kviki [int]; ~o, kvivito, kviko; (onom, as bird), kvivit!; (as cricket etc.), ĉirpi [int]; ĉirpo
cheer, (gaity), gaj/eco; (approving acclaim), hurai [tr, int]; hurao; aklami [tr]; **cheerful, cheery,** ~a; **cheerless,** mal~a, morna; **cheers!,** (je via) sano!; **cheer up,** ~igi, konsoli [tr]; ~iĝi, konsoliĝi
cheerio, (goodbye), ĝis!, adiaŭ!
cheese, (gen), fromaĝo; **cheeseburger,** fromaĝobovburgo* [cp "burger", "hamburger"]; **cheesecake,** (food), ~okuko; (re photo, pose of attractive woman), (in)figurmontr(ad)o; (in)figurmontra [cp "beef: beefcake"]; **cheesecloth,** stamino; **cheese spread,** ŝmir~o; **cottage cheese, Dutch cheese, pot cheese, curd cheese,** kazea ~o; **cream cheese,** (Am), krem~o; (Br), kazea ~o; **Parmesan cheese,** Parma ~o; **Roquefort cheese,** rokforto; **Swiss cheese,** Svisa ~o
cheetah, gepardo
chef, (ĉef)kuiristo [not "ĉefo"]
Cheiranthus, keiranto
Chekiang, Ĝegiang
Chelidon urbica, urbhirundo
Chelidonium, kelidonio
Chelonia, ĥelonio; *Cheloniidae,* ~edoj
chemical, kemia; ~aĵo; **biochemical,** bio~a; bio~aĵo; **petrochemical,** petrol~a; petrol~aĵo [see also "chemistry"]
chemise, inĉemizo [cp "shirt", "blouse"]
chemist, (re chemistry), kemiisto; (Br: druggist), drogisto, apotekisto, farmaciisto; **biochemist,** bio~o; **chemist's shop,** (Br), apoteko, drogejo

chemistry, (gen), kemio; **analytical chemistry**, analiza ~o: **biochemistry**, bio~o; **electrochemistry**, elektro~o; **histochemistry**, histo~o; **(in)organic chemistry**, (ne)organika ~o; **physical chemistry**, fizika ~o; **stereochemistry**, stereo~o; **thermochemistry**, termo~o [see also "chemist", "chemical"]
chemo–, (pfx: chemical, re chemistry), kemio–
chemotropism, kemiotropismo
Chengdu, Ĝengĝoŭ
chenile, ĉenilo
chenopod, kenopodio
Chenopodium, kenopodio
Cheops, Keopso
cheque, [see "check"]
chequeen, zekino
Cherbourg, Ĉerburgo
cherimoya, (fruit), ĉerimolio; (tree), ~arbo
cherish, (love), ami [tr]; (look after lovingly), dorloti [tr]
Cherkessk, (person), Ĉerkeso; (region), ~io
cheroot, tubcigaro
cherry, (fruit, gen), ĉerizo; (tree), ~arbo; (red to white variety w firm flesh), bigarelo; **European bird cherry**, (fruit or tree), paduso; **ground cherry, winter cherry**, (*Physalis*), fizalìdo; (*Physalis alkekengi*), alkekengo; **maraschino cherry**, maraskina ~o; **sour cherry**, grioto; **Surinam cherry**, (*Eugenia uniflora*), pitango; pitangarbo; **sweet cherry**, merizo; merizarbo
cherub, (gen), kerubo
chervil, cerefolio
chervonets, ĉervonco
Chesapeake Bay, Golfo Ĉesapika*
chess, ŝak/ludo; **chessboard**, ~tabulo; **chesspiece, chessman**, ~peco
chest, (anat), brusto; (large trunk), kofro; (smaller, lidded box etc.), kesto; (storage cabinet), ŝranko; **chest of drawers**, komodo; **medicine chest**, medikamentoŝranko
chesterfield, (any sofa), sofo
cheval vapeur, (metra) ĉevalpovo
chevin, leŭcisko

cheviot, (fabric), ŝevioto
Cheviot, (sheep), Ŝeviota ŝafo; Cheviot Hills, Montaro Ĉeviota
chevron, ĉevrono
chevrotain, tragolo
chew, maĉi [tr]; **chewy**, malmola, karameleca; kaŭĉukeca; **chewing gum**, ~gumo
chi, ĥi [see § 16]
chiaroscuro, klaroskuro
chiasm(a), kiasmo; **chiasma opticum**, optika ~o
chibouk, ĉibuko
chic, ŝika
Chicago, Ĉikago
chicane, (trick), ĉikani [tr]; (racing obstacle), obstaklo
chicanery, ĉikanado
Chicano, Meksik-Usona; ~ano
chich, kikero
chichi, ŝikaĉa
chick, (young chicken), kokido; (of any bird), birdido; (colloq: woman), ulino
chickadee, nigrakapa paruo
chicken, (generic), koko; ge~oj; (hen), ~ino; (meat), ~aĵo; (colloq: cowardly), malkuraĝa; malkuraĝulo
chicle, ĉiklo
chicory, cikorio
chide, riproĉeti [tr]
chief, ĉefo; ~a, precipa; (as part of title), ĉef– [pfx] (e.g.: *chief justice:* ~juĝisto); **chieftain**, tribestro, klanestro; **chief of state, chief executive**, landestro
chiffchaff, ĉifĉafo
chiffon, (fabric), gazo; (re food), ŝaŭma (e.g.: *lemon chiffon pie:* limonŝaŭma torto)
chigger, (larva of *Trombiculidae*), lepto; (chigoe: *Tunga penetrans*), ĉiko
chignon, hartubero
chigoe, (*Tunga penetrans*), ĉiko; (chigger: larva of *Trombiculidae*), lepto
chilblain, pernio
child, infano; **childbearing, childbirth**, (labor), akuŝo; (birth), nasko; **be in childbirth**, akuŝi [tr]; **childhood**, ~eco; ~aĝo; ~aĝa; **childish**, ~eca; **childlike**, ~simila; **stepchild**, duonfil(in)o; duonfil(in)a; **stepchildren**, duongefiloj; **wonder-child**, mir~o

Chile, Ĉilio; **Chilean,** ~a; ~ano
chili, (pepper pod), kapsiko; (dish w
this), ~aĵo; **chili con carne,** ~aĵo kun
viando
chill, (cool), malvarm/eto; ~a; ~igi, fridigi; ~iĝi, fridiĝi; **chilly,** (cold), friska
[cp "cold", "cool"]; (aloof), distanca
chimaera, *Chimaera,* (zool), ĥimero
Chimborazo, Ĉimborazo
chime, (ring), sonori [int]; ~igi; (bell),
~ilo; (set of tuned bells), ~ilaro;
chime in, (agree, fig), kun~i [int]; (interrupt), interrompi [tr]
chimera, (gen), ĥimero
chimney, (gen), fumtubo; (esp for fireplace), kamentubo; **chimney-sweep,**
kamentubisto
chimp(anzee), ĉimpanzo
chin, mentono; **chin-ups,** (exercise),
~umoj; **do chin-ups, chin oneself,**
~umi sin
china, (pottery), fajenco
China, (country), Ĉin/io; **Chinese,** ~o;
~a; ~ia; **Chinatown,** (la) Ĉinkvartalo;
Indo-China, Hindoĉinio; **Chinese
lantern plant,** alkekengo
chinchilla, *Chinchilla,* (animal),
ĉinĉilo; (pelt), ~pelto
chinc(h)ona, kinkono
chine, (meat), spinaĵo; (Br: ravine),
ravino
Chinghai, Kuku-Noro
chink, (crack), fendeto; ~i [tr]; (clink
sound), tinti [int]; tintigi; tinto
chinkapin, (dwarf chestnut), nan-
kaŝtanarbo
chinook, (wind), feno
chinquapin, [see "chinkapin"]
chintz, indieno
Chios, Ĥio†
chip, (notch, small missing piece in
dish, knife, etc.), breĉeto; ~i [tr]; (the
broken-off piece), ereto; (of wood),
lignero; (in cmptr, calculator, etc.),
blato†; (of dung), sterkero; (hack at),
haketi [tr]; **chipboard,** lignertabulo;
chocolate chips, ĉokoladeroj; **micro-
chip,** mikrofloko; **poker chip,** (poker)ĵetono; **chips,** (of potatoes: Br),
terpomfingroj; (potato) chips, terpom-
flokoj; **cash in one's chips,** (lit),
monigi siajn ĵetonojn; (colloq: die),

morti [int]; **chip off the old block,**
fil(in)o laŭ sia patr(in)o; **have a chip
on one's shoulder,** esti kverelema;
let the chips fall where they may,
okazu kio ajn; **when the chips are
down,** en testa krizo
chipmunk, *(Eutamias),* eŭtamio*
chipper, gaja, bonhumora
chirimoya, [see "cherimoya"]
chiromancy, kiromancio; **chiromancer,**
~isto
Chiron, (myth; ast), Kirono
Chironectes, ĥironekto
chiropody, [see "podiatry"]
chiropracty, kiropraktiko;   chiroprac-
tor, ~isto
Chiroptera, ĥiropteroj
chirp, (as bird), pepi [int], kviviti [int],
kviki [int]; ~o, kviviko, kviko; (onom,
as bird), kvivit!; (as cricket), ĉirpi
[int]; ĉirpo
chirr(up), ĉirpadi [int]
chirurgical, kirurgia
chisel, ĉizi [tr]; ~ilo; (for metal– and
jewel-workers), ~ileto; (for sculptor),
skulptilo; **cold chisel,** frido~ilo
chit, (small note), slipo; (voucher for
small $ sum), pag~o; (token), ĵetono
chitchat, babilado
chitin, kitino
chitlin(g)s, tripaĵo
chiton, (tunic), kitono; (zool), ĥitono
Chiton, (zool), ĥitono
chitterlings, tripaĵo
chivalry, kavalireco; **chivalrous,** ~a
chives, ŝenoprazo
chiv(v)y, ĝeni [tr], ĉagreni [tr]
chlamys, klamido
Chloë, Kloa
chloral, kloralo; **chloral hydrate,** ~a
hidrato
chloramphenicol, kloramfenikolo
chlorate, klorato
chloremia, kloremio
chlorhydria, hiperklorhidreco
chloric, klorata; **chloric acid,** ~a acido
chloride, klor/ido; **carbon tetrachlor-
ide,** tetra~metano, karbona tetra~ido
chloridemia, kloridemio
chlorinate, klorizi [tr]
chlorine, kloro
chlorite, (gen), klorito

chloro–, (chem pfx: chlorine), klor(o)–
chloroform, kloroformo, triklormeta-
no; ~i [tr]
chlorophyl(l), klorofilo
chloroplast, kloroplasto
chloroprene, kloropreno
chlorosis, klorozo
chlorous, klorita; chlorous acid, ~a acido
chlortetracycline, klortetraciklino
choana, ĥoano
chock, kojnbloko; ~i [tr]
chocolate, ĉokolado; ~a; ~aĵo
choice, elekto; ~inda, preferinda, rara
choir, ĥoro; choir loft, ~ejo
choke, (strangle), strangoli [tr]; ~iĝi;
(suffocate), sufoki [tr]; (sufokiĝi);
(constrict tightly, gen; re motor),
stringi [tr]; stringilo; (elec), amortizi
[tr]; amortizilo; choke back, retro-
premi [tr]; choke down, pengluti [tr];
choke off, for~i [tr]; choke up, (from
emotion etc.), ~i; ~iĝi; (clog), ŝtopi
[tr]; ŝtopiĝi
cholagogue, kolagogo
cholate, koleato
cholecyst, kolecisto; cholecystectomy,
~ektomio; cholecystitis, ~ito
choledochal, koledoka
cholehemia, koleemio, kolemio
cholelith, gala kalkuluso; cholelithia-
sis, kolelitiazo
cholera, ĥolero
choleric, kolerika, kolerema
cholesterol, cholesterin, kolesterolo,
kolesterino; cholesterolemia, ~emio
cholic, kole/ata; cholic acid, ~a acido
cholla, opuntio
Choloepus, unaŭo
chomer, ĥomero
chomp, maĉegi [tr]; ~o
chondrectomy, kondrektomio
Chondrichthyes, elasmobrankoj
chondritis, kondrito
chondr(o)–, (anat, med pfx), kondr(o)–
chodroma, kondromo
Chondrostei, ĥondrosteoj, kondrosteoj
Chondrostoma, ĥondrostomo
Chongging, Ĉongking
choose, elekti [tr]; choosy, ~ema
chop, (hack, slice), haki [tr]; ~o; (meat
slice), kotleto (e.g.: pork chop: pork-

kotleto; lamb chop: ŝafidokotleto);
chopper, (person), ~isto; (tool; elec),
~ilo; (helicopter), helikoptero; choppy, turbula; chophouse, kotletejo;
chopstick, manĝobastono; chop suey, rizkaĉo [cp "chow: chow mein"]
Chopin, Ŝopeno
choral, ĥora
chorale, ĥoralo
chord, (mus), akordo; (geom; anat),
kordo; augmented chord, (mus),
diesigita ~o; diminished chord, bemoligita ~o; spinal chord, mjelo; vocal chords, voĉkordoj [cp "cord"]
chorda, kordo; chorda dorsalis, ĥordo
chordal, korda
chordate, ĥord/ohava; ~ulo; ~ula
chorditis, kordito
chore, (small, routine task), task/eto;
(unpleasant task), ~aĉo
chorea, koreo; chronic chorea, Huntington's chorea, ~o de Huntington
choreograph, koregrafii [tr]; choreog-
raphy, ~o; choreographer, koregra-
fo
chorion, korio; chorion frondosum,
shaggy chorion, vila ~o; chorion
laeve, glata ~o
chorister, ĥorano
chortle, ĝojkluki [int]; ~o
chorus, (choir; Greek theat), ĥoro; (mus
refrain), refreno
Chosid, [see "Chasid"]
chough, pirokorako, montkorvo
chow, (food), manĝaĵo; (dog), ĉaŭo*;
chow mein, nudelkaĉo [cp "chop:
chop suey"]
chowder, ~supo [name after main flavoring ingredient (e.g.: clam chowder: pekten~o; pork chowder:
pork~o)]
chrestomathy, krestomatio
chrism, krismo
Chris, (man's nickname), Kri(s)ĉjo;
(woman's), Krinjo
Christ, Kristo; antichrist, antikristo;
before Christ, (abb: B.C.), antaŭ ~o
[abb: a.K.]
christen, bapti [tr]
Christendom, (all Christians), la Kris-
tanaro; (Christian countries), la Kris-
tanlandoj

Christian, (rel), Kristano; ~a; (man's name), Kristiano; Christianity, ~ismo; la ~aro: Christiana, (woman's name), Kristina, Kristiana; Christian name, [see under "name"]
Christiania, (ski turn), kristianio; (Oslo), K~o
christie, christy, kristianio
Christine, Christina.
Kristina
Christmas, Kristnasko; ~a
Christopher, Kristoforo
chromate, kromato
chromatic, (gen), kromata
chromatin, kromatino
chromatography, kromatografio
chrome, kromo [note: in combined forms, include final "o" to avoid confusion w prep "krom"]: chrome yellow, ~oflavo; chrome (plate), ~i [tr]
chromic, kromata; chromic acid, ~a acido
chromium, kromio; chromium steel, ~ita ŝtalo; [see also "chrome"]
chromo, kromolitografiaĵo [not "kromo"]
chrom(o)–, (chem pfx) kromo– [not "krom–"; see note under "chrome"]
chromolithograph, kromolitografi/aĵo; chromolithography, ~o
chromophore, kromoforo; chromophoric, ~a
chromophotograph, kromofotografi/aĵo; chromophotography, ~o
chromosome, kromosomo
chromosphere, kromosfero
chromyl, kromilo
chronaxia, chronaxie, chronaxy, kronaksio
chronic, kronika
chronicle, kroniko; ~i [tr]; chronicler, ~isto; Chronicles, (Bib), K~o [note sing]
chronograph, kronografo
chronology, kronologio; chronological, ~a
chronometer, kronometro; chronometry, ~io; chronometric, ~ia; measure by chronometer, ~i [tr]
chrysalis, krizalido; chrysalid, ~a; ~o
chrysanthemum, Chrysanthemum, krizantemo; Chrysanthemum balsamita, balzamito; Chrysanthemum

leucanthemum, lekanto
Chryseis, Krizeisa
Chrysippus, Krizipo
chrysoberyl, krizoberilo
Chrysocolla, krizokalo
Chrysocyon brachiurus, aguarao
chrysolite, krizolito, oloveno
Chrysomela, krizomelo, orskarabo
Chrysopa, krizopo
Chrysopogon, (Aus), krisopogono*
Chrysoprase, krizoprazo
Chrysostom, Krizostomo
chub, (zool: Leucichthys), leŭcisko
chubby, kompakta, dik(et)a
chuck, (pat, tap), frapeti [tr]; ~o; (throw), ĵeti [tr]; (discard), forĵeti [tr], forĵasi [tr]; (meat), ŝultraĵo; (block, chock), (kojn)bloko; (kojn)bloki [tr]; (as on lathe, drill, air hose, etc.), ĉuko;
chuckhole, vojtruo
chuckle, rid/kluki [int], sub~i [int]; ~kluko, sub~o
Chudskoye, (lake), Pejpuso
chufa, cipero
chugalug, glugloglugi [tr], unuglute eltrinki [tr]
chum, kamarado, kunulo
chump, (block), bloko; (person), malsaĝulo, stultulo, simplulo
Chungking, Ĉongking
chunk, bloko, dikaĵo; chunky, kompakta, dikkorpa, blok(ec)a
church, (Christian denomination), eklezio; (building), kirko; (any house of worship), preĝejo; church-goer, ~ano; churchwarden, laik–estro; churchyard, (ground around church), preĝejkorto, kirkkorto; (as cemetery), tombejo
churl, krud/ulo; churlish, ~(ul)eca
churn, (make butter), buterigi, fari [tr] (buteron); ~ilo; (stir, gen), kirl(eg)i [tr]; kirl(eg)iĝi
chute, (pour through sloping trough, as coal, grain, etc.), ŝuti [tr]; ~ilo; (shaft for mail, garbage, etc.), ŝakto; mail chute, poŝtoŝakto; garbage chute, ruboŝakto
chutney, ĉatnio*
chutzpah, aŭdacego
chyle, ĉilo
chyme, ĉimo

chymosin, ĉimozino
ciborium, (for Eucharist), ciborio, hostiujo; (baldachin), baldakeno
cicada, Cicada, cikado
cicatrix, cikatro; cicatrize, ~iĝi
cicely,**sweet cicely**, (bot), mirido
Cicer, kikero
Cicero, Cicerono
cicerone, ĉiĉerono
Cichorium, cikorio; Cichorium endivium, endivio
Cicindela, cicindelo
Ciconia, cikonio
Cicuta, cikuto; Cicuta virosa, akvo~o
Cid, Cido
–cide, (sfx: killing), –mortigo [note: often absorbed into Esperanto root as "–cido"; see separate entries]
cider, (fermented, "hard"), cidro; (sweet), dolĉa ~o, pom–mosto; (hot), punĉo
cigar, cigaro; **cigar holder**, ~ingo; **cigar box**, ~ujo
cigarette, cigaredo; **cigarette holder**, ~ingo
cigarillo, cigareto
cilia, [see "cilium"]
Ciliata, ciliuloj
Cilicia, Cilicio
cilium, cilio; cilia, ~oj; **ciliate(d)**, ~ohava
cimbalom, cimbalon, zimbalono
Cimbri, Cimbroj
cimex, cimo
Cimex, cimo; Cimex lectularius, lit~o, litlaŭso
Cimicifuga, cimicifugo
cinch, (saddle strap), selzono; ~i [tr]; (easy, sure thing), certaĵo; (assure), certigi
cinchona, Cinchona, kinkono
cinchonine, kinkonino
cinchonism, kininismo
Cinclus, cinklo; Cinclidae, ~edoj
cinder, (ash), cindro; (slag from coal or ore), skoriero; (burning coal), braĝo; **cinders**, (slag), skorio
cinema, (movie), kino; (theater), ~ejo, ~(o)teatro; (art form), ~arto; **cinematograph**, kinematografo; **cinema verité**, vereco~arto
cineraria, cinerario

cinglum, (anat), cingulo; (zool: color band), kolorzono
cinnabar, cinabro
cinnamomum, (tree), cinamarbo; **Chinese cinnamomum**, kasio
Cinnamomum, cinamo
cipher, (symbol for zero: "0"), nulo [cp "zero"]; (unimportant person, nonentity), neniulo; (code), ĉifro; ĉifri [tr]; [not "cifer–"]
circa, ĉirkaŭ [abb: ĉ.]
circadian, cirkadiurna†
Circaea, circeo
circaetus, Circaetus, cirkaeto
Circassia, Ĉirkes/io; **Circassian**, ~o; ~a; ~ia
Circe, Circa
circle, (geom), cirklo; (anything more or less round; loose group, as of friends), rondo (e.g.: walk in circles: marŝi en rondoj; study circle: studrondo); (go around), en~igi, ĉirkaŭi [tr]; (go in circles), rondiri [int], ĉirkaŭiri [int]; **encircle**, en~igi, ĉirkaŭi [tr]; **semicircle**, duon~o; **vicious circle**, neelirebla ~o; **come full circle**, kompletigi la ciklon
circuit, (elec), cirkvito; (going around), rondiro, ĉirkaŭiro; (regular route), itinero; (district), distrikto; (group of theaters), teatraro; (of nightclubs etc.), klubaro; **circuitry**, ~aro; **circuitous**, malrekta, rondira; **circuit breaker**, interuptoro; **integrated circuit**, ico†; **printed circuit(ry)**, presita konduktilaro†; distrikta tribunalo; **shortcircuit**, (lit or fig), korta ~o; kurt~i [tr]
circular, (round), cirkla, ronda; (notice, bulletin, flier), cirkulero [cp "brochure"]; **semicircular**, duon~a
circulate, (as $, blood, rumor, etc.), cirkuli [int], rondiri [int]; ~igi; (spread word), diskonigi; diskoniĝi; **circulation**, ~(ad)o; **put into circulation**, ($ etc.), emisii [tr], enkursigi, en~igi; **remove from circulation**, elkursigi, el~igi
circum–, (pfx: around), ĉirkaŭ– [note: absorbed into many Esperanto roots as "cirkon–" or "cirkum–"; see separate entries]
circumambient, ĉirkaŭanta

circumcise, cirkumcidi [tr]; **circumcision**, ~o
circumference, cirkonferenco
circumflex, cirkumflekso
circumlocution, ĉirkaŭparolo
circumscribe, ĉirkaŭskribi [tr]
circumspect, singarda, diskreta
circumstance, cirkonstanco; **circumstantial**, ~a
circumvallate, cirkonvalaci/igi; ~a; **circumvallation**, ~o
circumvent, (avoid), eviti [tr]; (get around, lit or fig), ĉirkaŭiri [tr]
circus, (gen), cirko
Circus, (zool), cirkuo
Cirenaica, Cirenio
cirrhosis, cirozo
cirrus, (cloud), ciruso; (bot and zool: tendril, tentacle), ĉiro; **cirrocumulus**, ~okumuluso; **cirrostratus**, ~ostratuso
Cirsium, cirsio
cis–, (pfx: near side), cis–
Cistercian, Cistercia; ~ano
cistern, cisterno
cistus, Cistus, cisto
citadel, citadelo
cite, (summon), alvoki [tr]; (quote; give reference for legal or scholarly authority etc.), referenci [tr], citi [tr]; (charge w crime etc.), imputi [tr] (iun pri io, ion al iu); (credit w good act, accomplishment, etc.), krediti [tr] (iun je io); **citation**, ~o; citaĵo; imputo; kredito
Cîteaux, Cistercio
Citellus, zizelo
cithara, citro
cither, citro
citizen, (person w civil rights), civit/ano; **citizenry**, ~o; **citizenship**, ~aneco, ŝtataneco; ~aneca, ŝtataneca
citral, citralo
citric, citr(at)a; **citric acid**, ~a acido
citron, (fruit), cedrato; (tree), ~arbo
citronella, (grass), citronelo; **citronella oil**, ~a oleo
citronellal, citronelalo
citrous, citrusa
Citrullus, citrolo; Citrullus colocynthis, kolocinto; Citrullus vulgaris, akvomelono
citrus, (tree), citruso; ~a; (fruit), ~fruk-

to
Citrus, (bot), citruso; Citrus aurantifolia, Citrus aurantium, limetarbo; Citrus aurantium amara, bigarado; Citrus bergamia, bergamotarbo; Citrus maxima, Citrus decumana, Citrus grandis, pampelmusarbo; Citrus medica, cedratarbo; Citrus medica limonium, Citrus limonia, limonarbo
city, (any large urban area), urbo; (chartered municipality; gen term), municipo; **citified**, ~ecigita; **city father**, ~ĉefo [cp "mayor"]; **city hall**, ~(o)domo; **city manager**, ~administristo; **cityscape**, ~opejzaĝo; **city slicker**, ~an(aĉ)o; **holy city**, (e.g., Jerusalem, Mecca), sankt~o
civet, (cat: *Viverra civetta*), civeto; (*Civettictis zibetha*), zibeto; (substance), cibeto
Civettictis zibetha, zibeto
civic, (re a city), civita; (re citizenship), ~ana; **civics**, ~ismo
civil, (re citizenship; not mil, not rel, not criminal, etc.), civila; (polite), ĝentila; **civil death**, ~a morto; **civil defense**, ~a defendado; **civil disobedience**, ~a malobeo; **civil law**, ~a juro; **civil liberties**, ~aj liberecoj; **civil rights**, ~aj rajtoj; **civil servant**, ŝtatoficisto; **civil service**, ŝtatoficaro; **civil war**, enlanda milito; **civility**, ĝentileco
civilian, civila; ~ulo
civilize, civilizi [tr]; **civilization**, civilizacio; (un)civilized, (ne)~ita
civvies, civilaj vestoj
clabber, kazeo; ~igi; ~iĝi
clack, klaki [int]; ~igi; ~o
Cladonia, kladonio
claim, (assert right to [e.g., pension, throne] allege), pretendi [tr]; ~o; (demand from someone), depostuli [tr]; depostulo; (register complaint re loss, shipment not received, etc.), reklamacii [tr]; reklamacio; (assert), aserti [tr]; aserto; **claimant**, ~anto; reklamacianto; **disclaim**, forkonfesi [tr], fornei [tr]; **disclaimer**, forkonfeso, fornego; **reclaim**, (gen), regajni [tr], revalorigi, reutiligi
clairaudient, klaraŭda; **clairaudience**, ~ado

Claire, Klara
clairsentient, klarsenta; ~anto; **clairsentience,** ~ado
clairvoyant, klarvida; ~anto; **clairvoyance,** ~ado
clam, (ordinary edible clam), pekteno; **clambake,** ~festo; **giant clam,** tridakno
clamber, grimpi [int]
clammy, humidaĉa
clamor, kriadi [int], bruadi [int]; (poet), klami [int]; ~o, bruado, klam(ad)o; **clamorous,** brua
clamp, (bracket; holder), krampo; ~i [tr]; (grip), kroĉi [tr]; **clamp down on,** sur~i [tr], surpremi [tr]; **hoseclamp,** pinĉkrano
clan, klano; **clannish,** ~ema; **clansman,** ~ano
clandestine, kaŝ– [pfx], ~ita, sekreta (e.g.: *clandestine operations:* ~operacioj; *we worked clandestinely:* ni laboris ~(it)e [or] sekrete)
clang, sonor(eg)i [int]; ~o; **clangor,** ~ado
Clangula, klangulo, glaci-anaso
clank, tint/egi [int], klak~i [int]; ~ego, klak~o
clap, (hands), aplaŭdi [tr]; ~o; (slapping sound), plaŭdi [int]; plaŭdigi; plaŭdo; (of thunder), ektondro; **clapper,** (of bell), frapilo; **claptrap,** blago
claque, aplaŭdistaro
Clara, Klara
claret, klareto
clarify, klar/igi; ~iĝi
clarinet, klarneto
clarion, klariono; ~a; ~i [tr, int]
clarity, klareco
clary, (bot: *Salvia*), salvio; (*S. sclarea*), sklareo
clash, konflikti [int], kunfrapiĝi; ~o, kunfrapiĝo
clasp, (grip by hand), manpremi [tr]; ~o; (clothes hook), agrafi [tr]; agrafo
class, (division; type; school group; etc.), klaso; ~a; ~i [tr] [cp "classify", "kind"]; (course in school), ~o, kurso; (good style), bonstilo; (rank), rango; **classmate,** sam~ano, samkursano; **classroom,** ~ĉambro; **classy,** bonstila, unua~a; **first (second) class,** (rank,

order), unua~a, unuaranga (dua~a, duaranga); **lower-class,** malalt~a; **middle-class,** mez~a, burĝa; burĝaro; **upper-class,** alt~a
classic, klasika; ~ajo; **classical,** ~a
classify, klasi [tr], klasifiki [tr]
Clathrus, klatro
clatter, klakadi [int]; ~igi; ~o
Claude, Klaŭdo; **Claudette,** ~ino, ~a
Claudia, Klaŭda, ~ino
Claudian, Klaŭdiano
claudication, lameco
Claudius, Klaŭdio
clause, (phrase of sentence), propozicio (e.g.: *subordinate clause:* subordigita ~o [or] sub~o); (legal stipulation; condition), klaŭzo
claustrophobia, klaŭstrofobio
Clavaria, klavario
Claviceps, ergotfungo
clavichord, klavikordo
clavicle, klaviklo
clavier, (any keyboard mus instrument), klavinstrumento
claw, (of animal, bird, etc.), ung/ego; (poet), krifo; (rooster spur), ergoto; (wound w claw), ~i [tr]
clay, argilo
clean, (pure, not dirty, gen), pura; ~igi; ~iĝi; (neat, tidy), neta; netigi; (a wound), detergi [tr]; (remove organs etc. from animal for cooking), sentripigi; (remove scales from fish), senskvamigi; (entirely), entute; **cleanly,** ~ema; **cleanliness,** ~emo; ~eco; **cleaner,** (any cleaning device), ~igilo; (substance), ~igenzo; **vacuum cleaner,** polvosuĉilo; **clean out,** el~igi; **clean up,** ~igi; netigi; **dry-clean,** sek~igi; **cleaners,** (laundry), ~igistejo; **clean-cut,** (trim, neat), neta; (w sharp outline), akralinia, akr–eĝa; **clean room,** ~ĉambro
cleanse, purigi, el~i; **cleanser,** ~enzo
Cleanthes, Kleanto
clear, (transparent; understandable; distinct, sharp, re view, sound, etc.), klara; ~igi; ~iĝi; (unblemished, pure), senmakula; senmakuligi; senmakuliĝi; (obvious), evidenta; (free of guilt), senkulpa; senkulpigi; (free of suspicion), sensuspekta; sensuspekti-

gi; (free of debt), kvita; kvitigi; (remove encumbrances, as dishes from
table), prilevi [tr]; (free, liberate), libera; liberigi; (bright), hela; (entirely),
tute; (unimpeded), senobstrukca; malobstrukci [tr]; malobstrukciĝi;
(empty), malplena; malplenigi; malpleniĝi; (pass w/o touching), transpasi
[tr], subpasi [tr] (e.g.: *the truck
cleared the wall:* la kamiono transpa-
sis la muron; *the boat cleared the
bridge:* la boato subpasis la ponton);
(approve), aprobi [tr]; (allow), allasi
[tr]; (go through), trairi [tr]; (let
through), tralasi [tr]; (make as profit),
(profite) gajni [tr]; (remove trees),
senarbigi; (remove brush etc.), senve-
prigi; **clearance,** (act or state of clearing), ~igo; ~iĝo; senkulpigo; kvitigo;
kvitiĝo; liberigo; liberiĝo; malob-
strukc(iĝ)o; malplenigo; malpleniĝo;
transpaso; subpaso; aprobo; allaso;
trairo; (space between moving parts or
moving object and obstruction), inter-
spaco [cp "play"]; (sale), elvend(ad)o;
(through customs), eldoganigo; **clear
away,** malobstrukci [tr], forigi; **clear-
cut,** tute ~a; **clear-eyed,** ~okula;
clear-headed, ~kapa; **clearing,** (in
forest etc.), placo, maldensejo, senar-
bejo; **clearinghouse,** ($), trapasoficejo;
jo; (any central office for collection
and dissemination, as of information),
perantoficejo; **clear off,** (make, become clear), ~igi; ~iĝi; (remove obstruction), malobstrukci [tr]; (remove
objects, as dishes from table), prilevi
[tr]; **clear out,** (drive out people, animals, etc.), elpeli [tr]; (empty, gen),
malplenigi; malpleniĝi; (leave), foriri
[int]; (sell), elvendi [tr]; **clear-sight-
ed,** ~e vidanta, kun ~a vido [avoid
"~vida"; see "clairvoyant"]; **clear the
air (atmosphere),** forigi la miskom-
prenojn; retrankviligi la situacion;
clear up, (make, become clear), ~igi;
~iĝi; (clarify, explain), ~igi, ekspliki
[tr]; (cure), resanigi (iun de io); resaniĝi (iu de io); **in the clear,** (unobstructed), senobstrukca, libera; (free
from suspicion etc.), senkulpa, nesus-
pektata; (free from debt), kvita; **get**

clear of, (disentangle, get out of
way), malimpliki [tr]; malimplikiĝi de
cleat, buteo
cleave, (split), fendi [tr]; ~iĝi; (re gem,
mineral), klivi [tr]; kliviĝi; **cleavage,**
(split), ~o; ~ado; ~iĝo; kliv(ad)o;
kliv(iĝ)o; ~aĵo; (of woman's breasts),
~o, intermamo; (of buttocks), ~o, in-
tergluteo; **cleavage plane,** (gem etc.),
klivebeno; **cleaver,** ~ilo
cleavers, (bot), galio
clef, kleo
cleft, fendo
cleistogamy, klejstogam/io; cleistogam-
ic, **cleistogamous,** ~a
Clelia, Klelia
clematis, Clematis, klematido
clemency, (pardon), pardono; (leniency), ~emo, indulgo; (mildness, as re
weather), mildeco; clement, ~ema, in-
dulgema; milda
Clement, Klemento; **Clementina,**
Clementine, ~a, ~ino. Klemencia
clench, (grip, clinch), kroĉi [tr], kunpremi [tr]; (make fist), pugnigi (la
manon)
cleome, Cleome, kleomo
Cleon, Kleono
Cleopatra, Kleopatra
clepsydra, klepsidro
cleptomania, [see "kleptomania"]
clergy, (one person), kleriko; (collective), ~aro; **clergyman,** ~o
cleric, kleriko; ~(ar)a
clerical, (re clergy), klerika; (re office
duties etc., as typing, filing, etc.),
sekretario; sekretari(ec)a; (favoring
clericalism), klerikala; klerikalisma;
klerikalisto; **clericalism,** klerikalismo
clerk, (in office, hotel, store, bank, etc.),
komizo; court clerk, aktuaro
cleveite, kleveito
Cleveland, (city), Klevlando
clever, (skillful, adroit, witty), lerta;
(sprightly), sprita; cleverness, ~eco;
sprito
clew, (ball of yarn etc.), bulo; (clue), indico; (corner of sail), velangulo; clew
line, angula brajlilo
cliché kliŝaĵo
click, (sound), klaketi [int]; ~igi; ~o;
(mech: catch, pawl), kliko; (onom),

klik!; **clicketyclack**, ~ado
client, kliento; **clientele**, ~aro
cliff, klifo; **cliff dweller**, ~loĝanto
climacteric, klimaktero [cp "menopause"]
climate, klimato; **climatic**, ~a; **climatology**, ~ologio; **climatologist**, ~ologo
climax, (high point, gen), kulmino, klimakso; ~i [int]; ~igi; (orgasm), orgasmo, klimakso; orgasmi [int], klimaksi [int]; **climactic**, ~a, klimaksa; **anticlimax**, antiklimakso; **anticlimactic**, antiklimaksa
climb, (esp on all 4's; w tendrils etc., re plants), grimpi [int] (sur); (ascend, gen), ascendi [tr]; (twist round, as plant), volvrampi [int] (sur); (rise), leviĝi; (increase), pliiĝi
clime, regiono
clinch, fasten), fiksi [tr]; (make certain, settle, decide, as argument, doubt), certigi; **clincher**, ~ilo; certigaĵo
cline, kontinuaĵo
cling, (fasten self to, lit or fig), alkroĉiĝi; (hang ~ingly), kroĉpendi [int]
clinic, (gen), kliniko; **out-patient clinic**, ambulatorio; **clinical**, ~a; **clinician**, ~isto
clink, tinti [int]; ~igi; ~o; (onom), tint!
clinker, (of coal slag), skori/ero; (brick), klinkero; (mistake), fuŝo; **clinkers**, (slag), ~o; **Dutch clinkers**, Nederlandaj klinkeroj; **clinker-built**, (ship), ŝinde konstruita
clinometer, klinometro
Clio, Klioa
clip, (cut as w scissors), tondi [tr]; (cut out, as article from newspaper), el~i [tr]; (shorten, elide, re word), elizii [tr]; (clamp), krampo; krampi [tr]; (hit), frapi [tr]; (cheat), superruzi [tr]; (move fast), rapidi [int]; (trim, prune), stuci [tr]; **clipboard**, kliptabulo; **clippers**, ~ilo [note sing]; stucilo; **nailclippers**, ungo~ilo; **hair-clippers**, (elec), ~omaŝino; **cartridge clip**, (for gun etc.), ŝargilo; **paper clip**, paperklipo†
clipper, (ship, plane), klipero
clique, kliko
Clitoria, klitorio
clitoris, klitoro

clivers, galio
cloaca, (gen), kloako
cloak, (coat), mantelo; ~igi; (hide), kaŝi [tr]; **cloakroom**, deponejo; **cloak-and-dagger**, spioneca
clobber, bategi [tr]
cloche, kloŝo
clock, (device), horloĝo; (measure duration), tempomezuri [tr]; **clock radio**, ~oradiofono; **clockwise**, dekstruma; dekstrume; **counterclockwise**, **anticlockwise**, livuma; livume; **clockwork**, ~a meĥanismo; (go) **like clockwork**, (iri, funkcii) tre glate; **alarm clock**, vek~o; **digital clock**, cifer~o; **time clock**, registra ~o; **wall clock**, mur~o; **water clock**, klepsidro; **wind-up clock**, risorta ~o
clod, (dirt), glebo; (person), bubego, stultulo; **clodhopper**, (boot), ~saltilo
Cloelia, Klelia
clog, (stop up), ŝtopi [tr], obstrukci [tr]; ~iĝi, obstrukciĝi; ~aĵo, obstrukco; ~iĝo, obstrukciĝo; (shoe), lignoŝuo; (dance), stamfdanci [int]
cloisonné klozoneo
cloister, klostro; en~igi
clone, klono; ~igi; **clonal**, ~a
clonus, klono
clop, huffrapi [int]; ~o
Clorissa, Klorisa
close, (shut, confine), fermi [tr]; ~iĝi; ~ita; (near), proksima; proksime(n); proksimiĝi; (soon), baldaŭa; (intimate), intima; (dense, crowded), densa, homplena; (narrow, gen; phon), malvasta; (hidden), kaŝita; (compact), kompakta; (secretive, reserved), kaŝema, sekretema; (miserly), avara; (stuffy, re air), sufoka, malfreŝa; (unite), unuigi, kunigi; unuiĝi, kuniĝi; (finish), fini [tr]; finiĝi; fino; (finalize, effectuate, as $ deal), efektivigi; (contact), kontakti [tr], tuŝi [tr]; kontaktiĝi, tuŝiĝi; (Br: enclosed yard etc.), placo; **close by**, apud, apude al, proksime al; **close down**, (stop), ĉesigi; ĉesi [int]; (cease operations), ~i; ~iĝi; **close in (on)**, **close on**, proksimiĝi (al); **close off**, (seal), obturi [tr]; **close out**, elvendi [tr]; **close round**, ĉirkaŭi [tr]; **close up**, ~i; ~iĝi;

(draw together), kunpremi [tr]; kunpremiĝi; **close-up**, (phot etc.), unuaplana (bildo, foto, sceno); la unua plano; **close-fitting**, malloza, strikta; **(come, be) close to**, (almost), preskaŭ (e.g.: *we came close to solving the problem:* ni preskaŭ solvis la problemon)

closet, (to store clothing etc., or fig), kamero; en~igi; **water closet**, klozeto; **come out of the closet**, el~iĝi

clostridium, *Clostridium,* klostridio

closure, (closing, gen), fermo; ~iĝo; unuigo, kunigo; unuiĝo, kuniĝo; fin(iĝ)o; efektivigo; kontakt(iĝ)o, tuŝ(iĝ)o [see "close"]; (thing that closes), ~ilo

clot, koaguli [tr]; ~iĝi; ~aĵo

Clotar, Klotaro

cloth, (fabric, gen), tolo; (any fabric used for garments), ŝtofo; (for specific use), -tuko [sfx] (e.g.: *tablecloth:* tablotuko) [see also "towel", "napkin", "sheet", etc.]; **broadcloth**, drapo; **cheesecloth**, stamino; **communion cloth**, korporalo; **dropcloth**, gutotuko; **oilcloth**, lak~o, vaks~o; **sailcloth**, vel~o; **tablecloth**, tablotuko; **washcloth**, lavtuko; **terrycloth**, viŝ(tuk)~o [cp "towel"]

clothe, vesti [tr]; **clothes, clothing**, ~oj; **article of clothing**, ~(aĵ)o; **clothes hanger**, ~arko; **clothes hook**, ~hoko; **clotheshorse**, ~framo; **clothesline**, ~oŝnuro; **clothespin**, **clothespeg**, ~pinĉilo; **clothier**, ~isto; **bedclothes**, litaĵo [note sing]; **put one's clothes on**, ~i sin, ~iĝi; **take one's clothes off**, mal~i sin, mal~iĝi; **change clothes**, trans~i sin, trans~iĝi; **plainclothes**, civil~a; **plainclothes police officer**, kaŝpolicano

Clot(h)ilda, Klotilda

cloture, debatfermo

cloud, nubo; (shade, cast shadow), ombri [tr]; (make unclear, obfuscate), malklarigi; **clouded**, (unclear), malklara; **cloudy**, ~(ec)a; **cloudburst**, ekpluvego; **cloud-cover**, ~kovraĵo; **cloud up**, ~iĝi; **mushroom cloud**, fumfungo

clout, (hit), (man)frapi [tr]; ~o; (power),

potenco, influo (e.g.: *great political clout:* granda politika influo)

clove, (spice), kariofilo; (tree), ~arbo, ~mirto; (segment of bulb, as garlic), bulbero

cloven, [see "cleave"]

clover, trifolio; **subterranean clover**, (Aus: *Trifolium subterraneum*), subtera ~o; **(yellow) sweet clover**, meliloto; **cloverleaf**, (highway intersection), trefkruciĝo

clown, klaŭno; ~i [int], kaprioli [int]

cloy, trosati [tr]

club, (organization; building etc.), klubo; (weapon), klabo; klabi [tr]; (card emblem), trefo; **nightclub**, nokto~o; **billy club**, (police stick), polica klabo; **club-foot**, bulpiedo

cluck, (by or like chicken), kluki [int]; ~o

clue, indico, ŝlosilo; **clue in**, informi [tr]

clump, (of grass etc.), tufo; ~igi; ~iĝi; (lump), bulo; buligi; buliĝi; (cluster), [see "cluster"]; (stomp), stamfi [int], paŝegi [int], botfrapi [int]

clumsy, (awkward), malgracia, mallerta; (crude, uncouth), maldelikata

Cluny, Klunizo

Clupea, klupeo; Clupea alosa, alozo; Clupea harengus, haringo; Clupea sprattus, sproto; Clupeidae, ~edoj; Clupeiformes, ~oformaj (fiŝoj)

clupeid, klupeedo; ~a

Clupes pilchardus, pilĉardo

cluster, (bunch, gen), amaso; ~igi; ~iĝi; (bundle of sticks etc.), fasko; (of flowers, fruits, etc., on one stem, as grapes), grapolo; (group), grupo

clutch, (mech), kluĉi [tr]; ~ilo; (grab), kapti [tr]; (hold tight), kroĉi [tr]; kroĉo; **clutch at**, ekkapti [tr], ekkroĉi [tr]; **clutch pedal**, ~opedalo

clutter, malordo, ĥaoso; ~i [tr]

Clytemnestra, Klitemnestra

Cnicus, kniko

Cnidaria, kniduloj

Cnidus, Knido

Cnossus, Knoso

Co. (abb of "Company"), K-io [abb of "Kompanio"]

co–, (pfx: together, joint), kun– (e.g.: *coauthor:* ~aŭtoro) [note: sometimes absorbed into Esperanto root as "ko–"; see separate entries]

c/o, (abb of "care of" in mailing addresses), z/d [abb of "zorge de"] [see § 22]

coach, (instruct, train, rehearse), trejni [tr]; ~isto; (rr car), vagono; (low class, re airline accommodations etc.), malaltklasa; (bus), buso; (carriage), diligenco, kaleŝo; **coachman**, (carriage driver), koĉero; **stagecoach**, diligenco

coadjutor, koadjutoro

coagulate, koaguli [tr]; ~igi; **coagulant**, ~enzo; **anticoagulant**, anti~a; anti~enzo

coal, collectively, gen), karbo; (Br: one lump), ~ero; **coals**, (burning embers), brago [note sing]; (Br: coal collectively), ~o [note sing]; **coal dust**, ~polvo; **anthracite coal**, antracito; **bituminous coal**, **soft coal**, bitum(hav)a ~o, fulgo~o; **brown coal**, lignito

coala, koalo

coalesce, kunfandigi, kunkreski [int], unuigi

coalition, koalicio; **form a coalition**, ~i [int]

coarse, (rough, crude, gen), kruda, maldelikata; (not smooth), malglata; (thick, large particles, re sand, powder, etc.), malfajna, malsubtila; (re adjustment of microscope etc.), makrometra; **coarsen**, ~igi; ~igi; malglatigi; malglatigi; **coarsely ground**, dike muelita, malfajne muelita

coast, (of sea), marbordo; ~a; (go w/o power), senpele iri (gliti, ruligi, ŝvebi, etc.) [int]; **coastal**, ~a; **coast guard**, ~a gardistaro; **coastland**, ~a tero, ~ejo; **coastline**, ~o; **seacoast**, ~o

coaster, (mat etc. for glass, bottle), subglaso, subbotelo

coat, (garment, gen), jako; (outdoor, gen), palto; (long, w or w/o sleeves), mantelo; (man's or woman's formal jacket), jaketo; (overcoat), surtuto; (frock coat, w full skirt, worn in 19th Century), redingoto; (frock coat, open over front of thighs), frako; (of animal), felo; (spread layer, as paint, grease, etc.), ŝmiri [tr]; ŝmirigi; (spread solid layer, as veneer, gold,

cloth, etc.), tegi [tr]; (layer, gen), tegajo; **coating**, (layer), tegajo; **coat hanger**, vestarko; **coatroom**, (palto)deponejo; **coattail**, basko; **overcoat**, palto, surtuto; **turncoat**, apostato, renegato; **waistcoat**, veŝto; coat of arms, blazono

coati, **coati-mundi**, **coati-mondi**, nazuo

coax, kajoli [tr]

cob, (corn), (maizo)spiko; (swan), vircigno

Cobaea, kobeo

cobalt, kobalto

cobbler, (re shoes), ŝuflikisto; (pie), pantorto

Cobitis, kobitido

cobnut, (nut), avelo; (tree), ~arbo

cobra, (any of genus *Naja*), najo; (*N. tripudians*), kobro

cobweb, araneajo

coca, kokao

cocaine, kokaino

Coccaceae, kokacoj

Coccidia, kokcidioj

coccidiosis, kokcidiozo

Coccinella, kokcinelo

cocco–, (med pfx), koko–

Coccoloba, kokolobo

Coccothraustes, kokotraŭsto

cocculus (indicus), kokianamirto

coccus, (bacterium), mikrokoko, koko; (carpel), karpelo; (insect), koĉo

–coccus, (med sfx), –koko

Coccus cacti, koĉo

coccyx, kokcigo; **coccygeal**, ~a

Cochin-China, Koĉinĉin/io; **Cochin-Chinese**, ~o; ~a; ~ia

cochineal, (insect), koĉenilo; (dye), ~ajo

cochlea, kokleo

Cochlearea, kokleario; Cochlearea armoracia, kreno; Cochlearea officinalis, skorbut~o

cock, (rooster), vir/koko; (male of any bird), ~birdo; (of gun), ĉano; (faucet), krano; (vulg slang: penis), kaco; (raise gun cock), levi (la ĉanon); (tilt), klini [tr]; **cock-eyed**, (askew), oblikva, malrekta, klinita; (wrong), misa (e.g.: *there's something cock-eyed in that:* io misas [or] estas io misa en tio); **cock of the wood**, (*Tetrao urogallus*),

urogalo
cockade, kokardo
cock-a-doodle-doo, (rooster sound, onom), kokeriko; ~i [int]
cockatoo, kakatuo
cockatrice, bazilisko
cockchafer, melolonto, majskarabo
cocker, (dog), spanielo
cockerel, virkokido
cockle, (shellfish), kardio*; (wrinkle), foldo; **corn cockle,** agrostemo
cocklebur(r), ksantio
Cockney, orient-Londona; ~ano
cockpit, (of plane etc.), kajuto; (for cockfights), kokluktejo
cockroach, blato
cockscomb, (of rooster), kresto [cp "tuft"]
cocktail, (food or drink, gen), koktelo; **Molotov cocktail,** benzinbombo
cocky, (overconfident), memfiera, tromemfida; (Aus: farmer), farmisto, bientenanto; (Aus: cockatoo), kakatu(cĵ)o
cocoa, (drink or powder), kakao; (tree), ~arbo; **cocoa butter,** ~obutero; **cocoa milk,** ~olakto; **cocoa oil,** ~oleo; **shredded cocoa,** ~eroj
cocoon, kokono
Cocos, kokosarbo
Cocytus, Kocito
cod, (any fish of *Gadus*), gado; (*G. morrhua*), moruo; **salted cod,** laberdano
C.O.D. (abb of "collect on delivery"), remburse, per ~o [no abb] (e.g.: *mail a package C.O.D.:* enpoŝtigi pakon ~e) [see § 22]; **C.O.D. charges,** ~o
coda, vosto [cp "fine", "finale"]
coddle, (treat gently), dorloti [tr]
code, (body of laws etc.; set of symbols or signals; genetic etc.), kodo; ~i [tr] [cp "codex"]; (text etc. written in code), ~aĵo; (secret), ĉifro; ĉifri [tr]; ĉifraĵo; **area code,** (phone), region~o; **bar code,** streko~o; **Morse code,** morsa ~o; **signal by Morse code,** morsi [tr]; **ZIP Code, postal code,** poŝt~o† [not "ZIP—o"]
codeine, kodeino
codex, kodekso [cp "code"]
codger, maljunulo, oldulo
codicil, kodicilo, alpendaĵo

codify, kodigi
codon, kodono†
coed, (having or for both sexes), gea; (female student), studentino
coefficient, (gen), koeficiento
coelacanth, celakanto†
Coelacanthus, celakanto†;   Coelacanthini, ~uloj
Coelenterata, celenteruloj
coelenterate, celenterulo
coelenteron, celentero
coelom, celomo
Coelomata, celomuloj
Coendou, koenduo
coerce, premdevigi, truddevigi
coeval, (of same period), samepoka; (same age), samaĝa
coffee, kafo; **coffee bean,** ~grajno; **coffee break,** ~paŭzo; **coffeebush,** ~arbo; **coffee can,** ~ujo, ~skatolo; **coffee cup,** ~taso; **coffee grounds,** ~rekremento; **coffeehouse,** ~ejo; **coffee pot,** ~kruĉo; **coffee shop,** lunĉejo; **coffee table,** ~tablo
coffer, (chest), kesto, kofro; (treasury, funds), kaso; (cofferdam), koferdamo
coffin, ĉerko
cog, (rado)dento; **cog-wheel,** dentrado
cogent, konvinka, forta
cogitate, cerbumi [int]
cognac, konjako
Cognac, Konjako*
cognate, (any blood relative), parenco; (relative by female descent), kognato; (re words, languages), ~a (vorto, lingvo) (e.g.: *English "fire" and Esperanto "fajro" are cognates:* la Angla "fire" kaj la Esperanta "fajro" estas ~aj vortoj; *English "fire" is a cognate of Esperanto "fajro":* la Angla "fire" estas ~a al la Esperanta "fajro")
cognition, sciado
cognizance, (knowledge), scio; (recognition), rekono; (authority, jurisdiction), jurisdikcio, aŭtoritato
cognizant, konscia; **be cognizant of,** ~i [tr]
cognoscente, spertulo
cohabit, kunloĝi [int]; **cohabitation,** ~ado
cohere, koheri [int]; **coherent,** ~a; coherence, ~(ec)o

cohesion, kohero, ~eco; **cohesive**, ~a
cohort, (tenth of legion; gang; statistics), kohorto; (companion), kompano, kamarado, kunulo
coif, (cap), kufo
coiffure, hararangô
coil, (spiral), spiralo; ~i [int]; (spool), bobeno; (one turn, as of elec wire), volvo; (wind into coil, gen), volvi [tr]; volvîgi; (loop, as rope etc.), buklo; bukli [tr]; [not "kojlo"]
coin, ($), mon/ero; (stamp out coins), stampi [tr]; (devise, make up; manufacture, gen), fabriki [tr] [cp "invent"]; **coinage**, (all coins), metal~o; (process), (~er)stampado; (device; thing made up), fabrikajô; (devising), fabrikado
coincide, koincidi [int]; **coincidence**, ~o; coincident(al), ~a
coitus, koito; **engage in coitus**, ~i [int]; **coitus incompletus**, **coitus interruptus**, interrompita ~o
coke, (fuel), koakso
col, intermonto
cola, (tree or extract), kolao; (drink), ~ajô, ~-sodo; **cola nut**, ~onukso
colander, kribrilo
colchicine, kolĉikino
colchicum, kolĉiko
Colchicum, kolĉiko; *Colchicum autumnale*, aŭtuna ~o
Colchis, Kolĉido, Kolĥido
colcothar, kolkotaro
cold, (temperature, lit or fig), malvarma; ~o; (esp in compound words), frida, frid– [see "refrigerator"]; (virus), ~umo; **cold chisel**, fridoĉizilo; **cold cream**, koldkremo; **cold cuts**, fridotranĉajôj; **cold duck**, (drink), burgonjoĉampano; **cold pack**, fridoterapio; **(the) cold shoulder**, indiferenteco; **give one the cold shoulder**, montri al iu indiferentecon; **cold sore**, herpeto; **cold sweat**, ~a ŝvito; **cold turkey**, abrupte; **cold war**, ~a milito; **catch a cold**, ~umi [int]; **leave one cold**, tute ne impresi iun
cole, brasiko; **sea cole**, mar~o
colectomy, kojlektomio
Coleoptera, koleopteroj
coleopteron, koleoptero; **coleoptera**,

~oj
coleoptile, koleoptilo
coleslaw, brasiksalato
coleus, Coleus, koleo
colewort, senkapa brasiko
colic, koliko
coliseum, koloseo
colitis, kojlito
collaborate, kunlabori [int]
collage, glubildo
collagen, kolageno
collapse, (fall apart, gen), disfali [int]; ~o; (fold), faldi [tr]; faldîgi; (med), kolapsi [int]; kolapsigi; kolapso; **collapsible**, (folding, as chair etc.), faldebla
collar, (clothing), kol/umo; (for animal), ~ringo; (catch), kapti [tr]; **collarbone**, klaviklo
collard, senkapa brasiko
collate, (pages, as of book), kolacii* [tr]; (compare texts), kontrole kompari [tr]
collateral, (security for loan), ristorno; (subordinate, accessory), akcesora
colleague, kolego
collect, (gather, accumulate, gen), kolekti [tr]; ~îgi; (for rel or oth worthy cause), kvesti [int] (por); **collection**, ~o; ~îgo; kvesto; (anthology), antologio; (gathering, as of people), aro; (things), amaso; **collector**, ~anto; ~isto; ~ilo; **collect on delivery**, [see "C.O.D."]
collective, (gen), kolektivo; ~a; **collectivism**, ~ismo [cp "cooperative", "commune", "kibbutz", "moshav", "kolkhoz"]
college, (independent school; special group), kolegio (e.g.: *Howard Community College*: la Komunuma K~o Howard; *College of Cardinals*: K~o de la Kardinaloj); (subdivision of university), fakultato (e.g.: *College of Engineering of the University of Maryland*: Fakultato de Inĝenier–arto de la Universitato de Marilando)
collegiate, kolegia; universitata [see "college"]
colleculus, koliklo; **colleculus seminalis**, verumontano
collide, kolizii [int]; (rebounding, as bil-

liard balls), karamboli [int]; **collision,**
~o; karambolo
collie, (Skota) ŝafhundo
collier, (miner), karb/oministo; (ship),
~oŝipo; **colliery,** (Br), ~ominejo
collimate, kolimati [tr]; collimator, ~ilo
collision, [see "collide"]
collodion, kolodio
colloid, koloido; **colloidal,** ~a
colloquial, familiara;   **colloquialism,**
~aĵo
colloquium, kolokvo
colloquy, kolokvo
collusion, koluzio
collutory, kolutorio
coloboma, kolobomo
Colocasia, kolokasio; Colocasia anti-
quorum, taro
colocynth, kolocinto
cologne, Kolonj/a akvo, ~akvo
Cologne, (city), Kolonjo; **eau de Co-**
logne, ~a akvo, ~akvo
Colombia, Kolombio
Colombo, Kolombo
colon, (symbol ":"), dupunkto; (anat),
kojlo; [not "kolono"]; **semicolon,**
(";"), punktokomo; **sigmoid colon,**
sigmoido
colonnade, kolonaro
colonel, kolonelo
colony, kolonio; **colonial,** ~a; ~ano;
colonize, ~i [tr]; **colonialism,** ~ismo;
colonialist, ~isma; ~isto; **colonist,**
~ano, ~anto [not "~isto"] [cp "settle"]; **penal colony,** pun~o
colophon, kolofono
colophony, kolofono
color, (gen), koloro; ~i [tr]; ~iĝi; (give
color to, as by dye, paint), farbi [tr];
coloration, ~eco; ~igo; ~aĵo; **col-**
ored, ~(hav)a; **colorfast,** paliĝimuna; **colorful,** (lit or fig), mult~a;
coloring, ~igo; ~aĵo; **colorless,**
sen~a; **discolor,** mis~igi; mis~iĝi;
discoloration, mis~igo; mis~iĝo;
mis~aĵo; **multicolored,** bunta; **off-**
color, (wrong color), mis~a; (poor
taste), triviala, misgusta; **tricolor,**
tri~o; **varicolored,** vari~a, bunta; **wa-**
ter-color, (paint), akvarela farbo;
(painting), akvarelo
Colorado, (river), Kolorado; (state), ~io

coloratura, (voice, style), koloraturo;
~a; (singer), ~ist(in)o
Colossae, Koloso
colossal, kolosa
colosseum, koloseo
Colossians, (Bib), Kolosanoj
colossus, koloso
colostomy, kojlostomio
colostrum, kolostro
colour, [see "color"]
colporteur, kolportisto
colt, (of horse), ĉevalido; (donkey),
azenido (etc.); **coltsfoot,** (bot), tusilago
Coluber, kolubro; Colubridae, ~edoj
Columba, (zool), kolombo; Columba
livia, livio, rok~o; Columba oenas,
enado; Columba palumbus, palumbo,
arbo~o; Columbidae, ~edoj; Colum-
biformes, ~oformaj (birdoj)
columbarium, kolumbario
columbary, kolumbejo
Columbia, Kolumbio; **British Colum-**
bia, Brita ~o; **District of Columbia,**
Distrikto de ~o [no abb]
columbine, (zool), akvilegio
Columbine, (theat), Kolombina
columbium, niobio
Columbus, Kolumbo;   **Christopher**
Columbus, Kristoforo ~o
columella, kolumelo
column, (cylindrical building support,
or anything of similar shape), kolono;
(on page; row of objects or persons;
knitting), kolumno; (row, queue, series), vico; (section of newspaper,
magazine, etc., devoted to one topic),
rubriko, angulo; **columnist,** publicisto, rubrikisto
colure, koluro
Colutea, koluteo
Colymbus, kolimbo;   Colymbiformes,
~oformaj (birdoj)
colza, (plant), kolzo; (oil), ~oleo
coma, (med), komato; (ast), nebulo; **co-**
matose, ~a; **comatogenic,** ~ogena
comb, (for hair), kombi [tr]; ~ilo; (bird
crest), kresto; **comb out,** el~i [tr];
el~iĝi; **curry-comb,** striglilo; **Ve-**
nus's-comb, (zool: *Murex*), murekso
combat, batalo; ~ado; ~i [int] (kontraŭ),
kontraŭ~i [tr]; **combative,** ~ema;

combatant, ~anto
combine, (put together), kombini [tr], kunigi; ~iĝi, kuniĝi; (bsns, pol, etc.: cartel), kartelo; (farm machine), kombajno; **combination,** ~o; (clothing), kombineo; (math), kombinacio; **combinatorial analysis,** (math). kombinatoriko
combo, bando, trupo (e.g.: *jazz combo:* ĝaz~o)
combust, ekbruli [int]; ~igi; **combustion,** (active: causing to burn), bruligo; (passive), brulado; **combustible,** bruliva; **combustion point,** ekflama punkto; **incombustible,** nebruliva, fajrimuna; **heat of combustion,** brulvarmo
come, (gen), veni [int]; come about, (happen), okazi [int], estiĝi; (turn), giri [int]; come across, (meet by chance), (hazarde) renkonti [tr], (hazarde) trovi [tr]; (have effect), efiki [int]; **come again?,** ripetu, mi petas!; **come along,** (arrive), al~i [int]; (progress), progresi [int]; **come and go,** cirkuli [int], ~i kaj re~i; **come around,** (revive), rekonsciiĝi; (turn), giri [int]; (acquiesce, yield), cedi [tr, int]; (come by, visit), al~i [int]; viziti [tr]; **come back,** (return), re~i [int]; (retort), repliki [tr]; **come-back,** (retort, rebuttal), repliko; (returned stroke), rebato; (revival), reviviĝo; (sports, pol, as actor, etc.), revigliĝo; **make a come–back,** revigliĝi (e.g.: *She was defeated in 1990 but made a come–back in the 1992 election:* ŝi estis venkita en 1990 sed revigliĝis en la elekto de 1992); **come by,** (get), akiri [tr]; (visit), al~i [int]; viziti [tr]; **come down (up)on,** (scold), riproĉi [tr]; **come forward,** (volunteer), sin proponi; **come in,** (enter), en~i [tr, int]; (finish, as in race), finiĝi; **come into,** (inherit), heredi [tr]; **come into being,** ekesti [int], estiĝi; **come now!,** mi ne kredas vin! [or] tion!; nekredeble!; **come off,** (come unfastened), malfiksiĝi; (happen), okazi [int]; (end up), finiĝi; (succeed), sukcesi [int]; (turn out), rezulti [int] (e.g.: *the concert came off well:* la koncerto rezultis bo-

na); **come off it!,** ĉesigu tion!; **come on,** (progress), progresi [int]; (find), (hazarde) trovi [tr]; **come-on,** (lure), logilo; (talk etc.), logado; **come on!,** (get going, hurry), rapidu!, ek!; (please), mi petas!; **come one's way,** ~i ĉe iu; **come on strong,** forte efiki [int] (sur); **come out,** (become evident), evidentiĝi; (appear, as on market for sale), aperi [int]; (turn out), rezulti [int] [see "come off" above]; (by gay, lesbian), elkameriĝi (see also "out"); **come out for,** (support, as candidate etc.), subteni [tr], anonci (sian) subtenon por; **come out with,** (bring out), aperigi; (utter), eldiri [tr]; (produce), produkti [tr]; (publish), eldoni [tr]; **come over,** (happen to), trafi [tr] (e.g.: *fear came over me:* timo trafis min); **come round,** [see "come around" above]; **come through,** (live through, endure), travivi [tr]; **come to,** (revive), rekonsciiĝi; (arrive at), al~i ĉe; (eventually begin to), fine ek– (e.g.: *she came to love him:* ŝi fine ekamis lin); **come to an end,** ĉesi [int], finiĝi; **come to be,** (become), estiĝi, fariĝi (e.g.: *come to be an expert:* fariĝi spertulo); **come to think of it,** nun kiam mi pensas pri ĝi; **come together,** kuniĝi [avoid "kun~i"; see "meet"]; **come under,** (be classified w), klasifikiĝi, klasiĝi kun (sub, kiel); **come up,** (arise, begin, be mentioned), leviĝi; **come up to,** etendiĝi ĝis, egali [tr]; **come up with,** prezenti [tr], proponi [tr]; **come upon,** [see "come across" above]; **come what may,** okazu kio ajn; **how come?,** kial?, pro kio?; **newcomer,** nov~into, novulo; **outcome,** sekvo, rezulto, konsekvenco; **overcome,** superi [tr], venki [tr]; **shortcoming,** (deficiency), manko, nesufiĉo; (defect), difekto, neperfektaĵo; **upcoming,** (baldaŭ) ~onta, okazonta, baldaŭa; **as ... as they come,** tiel ... kiel estas, treege ... (e.g.: *the day was as hot as they come:* la tago estis tiel varma kiel estas [or] estis treege varma)
comedo, komedono
comedy, komedio; **comedian,** ~isto,

komikisto
comely, bela, pimpa, alloga
comet, kometo
comfort, ease), komforto; ~igi; (console), konsoli [tr]; (soothe), karesi [tr]; **comfortable**, ~a; **comforting**, ~iga; konsola; **comforter**, (quilt), peplomo; (scarf), skarpo; **discomfort**, mal~o; mal~igi
comfrey, simfito
comic, komika; ~isto [cp "comedy"]; **comical**, ~a; **comics**, bildstrioj; **comic book**, bildstria gazeto; **comic strip**, bildstrio
comma, komo
command, komandi [tr], ordoni [tr]; ~o, ordono; **commandant**, ~anto; **commander**, (rank), komandoro; **commandment**, ~o, ordono; **at one's command**, (available), je ies dispono; **the Ten Commandments**, la Dek Ordonoj
commandeer, rekvizicii [tr]
commando, sturmisto; ~aro; ~a
commassation, komasacio
Commelina, komelino
commemorate, (remind), memor/honori [tr], re~igi; (by ceremony), ~festi [tr], soleni [tr]; **commemoration**, re~igo; ~festo; **commemorative**, ~honora, re~iga; ~festa; (stamp, coin, etc.), re~iga poŝtmarko (monero etc.)
commence, komenci [tr]; ~iĝi; **commencement**, (beginning), ~o; (graduation), diplomceremonio
commend, (praise), laŭdi [tr]; (entrust), konfidi [tr]; **commendable**, ~inda
commensurable, kunmezurebla
commensurate, (equal), egala; (proportionate), proporcia
comment, komento; ~i [tr]; **commentary**, komentario(j); **commentator**, komentariisto
commerce, komerco; **do commerce**, **be in commerce**, ~i [int]; **commercial**, ~a; (~a) reklamo; **commercialism**, ~ismo; **commercialize**, ~igi
commingle, kunmiksi [tr]
comminute, eretigi
Commiphora, balzamarbo; Commiphora myrrha, Commiphora abyssinica, mirhoarbo

commiserate, kompati [tr], kondolenci [tr]
commisar, komisaro; **commisariat**, komisariato
commissary, (person), komisaro; (office), ~ejo; (place w food etc.), provizejo
commission, (request to do task, art, etc.), komisii [tr]; ~o; (group commissioned to do task), komisiono; (%age, as of profit), procentaĵo; **commissioner**, ~ito, komisaro; **out of commission**, ne funkcianta, ne servopreta; **put (back) in commission**, servopretigi
commit, (do), fari [tr] [note: "commit" + n often expressed as verb in Esperanto (e.g.: *commit murder:* murdi; "fari murdon" correct but not best style)]; (devote, dedicate), dediĉi [tr]; (entrust), konfidi [tr]; (commission), komisii [tr]; (make obligatory), devontigi (e.g.: *I am committed to doing it:* mi estas devontigita fari ĝin); (confine to hospital), enhospitaligi, enigi (iun) en (mensan hospitalon, psikiatrian institucion, etc.); **commitment**, devontigo, sinligo; (sin)dediĉo; enhospitaligo; (duty), devo; (promise), promeso; (between 2 or more people), interdediĉo, interpromeso; **commit to memory**, parkerigi, parkere (el)lerni [tr]; **commit to paper (writing)**, surpaperigi; **noncommittal**, senpromesa, nedefinitiva
committee, komitato; **ad hoc committee**, portempa ~o; **standing committee**, konstanta ~o; **subcommittee**, sub~o
commode, (room), klozeto; (toilet fixture), fekseĝo; (chest), komodo
commodious, vasta, ampleksa
commodity, varo; **food commodity**, nutro~o
commodore, komodoro
common, (frequent), ofta; (joint, cooperative, shared), komuna; (ordinary, vernacular), vulgara [cp "vulgar"]; (banal), banala; (math: belonging to 2 or more quantities), komunona; **commons**, (common people), popolamaso, plebanoj, ordinaruloj,

nenobeloj; (land tract), komunejo; **common denominator**, komunono; **House of Commons**, Ĉambro de Deputitoj; **commoner**, nenobelo; **Common Era**, [see "C.E."]; **Before the Common Era**, [see "B.C.E."]; **common people**, popolamaso, ordinaruloj, plebanoj; **commonplace**, (ordinary), ordinara, rutina; (banal), banala; **in common**, komune **commonwealth**, (nation, state, etc.), regno; (people of), regnanaro; (confederation, group of nations), konfederacio; **Commonwealth of Independent States**, Konfederacio de Sendependaj Ŝtatoj; **British Commonwealth**, Brita Konfederacio); **Commonwealth Day**, Konfederacia Tago

commotion, (bru)konfuzo [not "komocio"]

commune, (residential cooperative), komjuno* [cp "collective", "cooperative", "community"]; (be one w. associate w), komuniiĝi (e.g.: *commune with nature:* komuniiĝi kun la naturo); (district, community, as in China), komunumo; **The Commune**, (French), La Komunumo; **communal**, ~a; komuna; komunuma; **communalism**, ~ismo; (socialism), socialismo; **communard**, ~ano; **Communard**, Komunumano

communicable, (can be communicated), komunikebla; (contagious), kontaĝa

communicant, (rel), komuniiĝanto

communicate, (pass on, impart; give message, meaning), komuniki [tr] (ion al iu); (receive communion), komuniiĝi; **communication**, ~(ad)o; ~aĵo; **communicative**, ~ema; **telecommunications**, tele~oj, tele~ado; tele~a

communion, (rel), komunio; (sharing, gen), komuneco; (intimacy), intimeco; [cp "commune"]; **give communion**, ~i [tr]; **intercommunion**, inter~o; **receive communion**, ~iĝi

communiqué komunikaĵo

communism, komun/ismo; **communist**, ~isma; ~isto; ~ista; **Communist Party**, K~ista Partio; (short form),

Kompartio

community, (being in common), komun/eco; (district, area; group of people w common interests etc.), ~umo; (neighborhood), najbarejo; **European Community**, Eŭropea K~umo

communize, (make common), komunigi; (make communistic), komunismigi

commutate, komuti [tr]; **commutator**, ~atoro

commutation, (substitution), anstataŭ/iĝo; ~aĵo; (exchange), interŝanĝo; (act of commut(at)ing), [see "commutate", "commute"]

commute, (travel back and forth, as to work), naveti [int]; (substitute), anstataŭi [tr]; (make [punishment] less severe), plimildigi; **commuter**, ~a; (traveler), ~anto; **telecommute**, tele~i [int]

Comoro, Comores Islands, Komoroj

compact, (re car; dense; close-fitted), kompakta; ~igi; ~iĝi; (car), ~a aŭto; (cosmetic powder case), pudrujo; (pact), interkonsento, pakto; **compact disc**, [see under "disc"]; **trash compacter**, rubo~igatoro

companion, akompan/anto, kompano, kunulo, kamarado; **companionable**, amikema, kompanema; **companionship**, kamaradeco, kompanio; **companionway**, ŝtuparo; **be companion for**, ~i [tr]

company, (bsns; mil; being together), kompanio, firmao [see also "Co."]; (visitor), vizitanto(j), gasto(j); (theat), aktoraro; (any band, as of robbers, travelers, etc.), roto; **holding company**, holdingo; **in company with**, akompanata (–e) de; **part company with**, disiĝi de, lasi [tr]

comparative, (comparing), kompara; (relative), relativa (e.g.: *a comparative success:* relativa sukceso); (gram), komparativo [cp "comparison"]

compare, kompari [tr]; **comparable**, ~ebla; ~inda; **incomparable**, ne~ebla, sen~a

comparison, (comparing), kompar(ad)o; (gram), komparacio [cp "comparative"]

compartment, (any division; pigeonhole; field, category), fako; (of train, car, etc.), kupeo; **compartmental**, ~a; compartmentalize, (dis)~igi
compass, (to find north), kompaso; (to draw circle), cirkelo; (range, scope), amplekso, atingo; (go round), ĉirkaŭi [tr]; (encompass, include), ampleksi [tr]
compassion, kompato; **feel compassion for**, ~i [tr]; **compassionate**, ~(em)a
compatible, (non–tech), akorda; ~igebla; (cmptr. med, etc.), kompatibila† (e.g.: *IBM–compatible computer:* IBM-kompatibila komputoro); **incompatible**, ne~(igebl)a; nekompatibila†; **(in)compatibility**, (ne)~(igebl)eco; (ne)kompatibilecot
compatriot, sampatrujano, samlandano
compeer, (of same class), samklasano; (companion), kamarado, kompano, kunulo
compel, devigi, prem~i, trud~i
compendium, kompendio
compensate, (gen), kompensi [tr]; **compensation**, ~(ad)o; (pay), pago; (legal, as court judgment), ~odevo; **compensatory**, ~a
compère, anoncisto, prezentisto
compete, (contend, gen), konkuri [int]; (bsns), konkurenci [int]; (in contest), konkursi [int]; **competition**, (act), ~(ad)o; konkurenco; konkursado; (those ~ing), ~ant(ar)o; konkurencant(ar)o; konkursant(ar)o; (a contest), konkurso; **competitor**, ~anto; konkurencanto; konkursanto; **competitive**, ~a; ~ema; konkurenc(em)a
competent, kompetenta; **competence**, **competency**, ~eco; **incompetent**, mal~a; mal~ulo
competition, [see "compete"]
compile, (gen), kompili [tr]; ~iĝi; (cmptr), kompileri†; kompileriĝi†; **compiler**, (cmptr), kompilero†
complacent, memkontenta; **complacency**, ~eco
complain, plendi [int]; **complaint**, ~o; (disease), malsano
complaisant, komplezema; **complaisance**, ~o

complement, (gen), komplemento; ~igi; **complementary**, ~a, kompletiga
complete, kompleta; ~igi
completorium, kompletorio
complex, (gen), kompleksa; ~o
complexion, (gen), kompleksio
complicate, kompliki [tr]; **complicated**, ~a; **complication**, ~aĵo; ~eco
complicity, kompliceco
compliment, komplimento; ~i [tr]; **complimentary**, (~ing), ~(em)a; (free), senpaga; **left-handed compliment**, dutranĉa ~o
complin(e), kompletorio
comply, konform/iĝi, ~igi sin; **comply with**, ~iĝi al, ~igi sin al; **compliance**, ~iĝo, obeo; **compliant**, ~ema; **in compliance with**, ~a kun; ~e kun
component, (part), elemento, komponanto; (ingredient), ingredienco; (particle), ero
comportment, konduto
compose, (mus etc.), komponi [tr]; (set type; cmptr), komposti [tr]; (calm), trankviligi, kvietigi; **composed**, (calm), trankvila, kvieta; **composer**, (mus), ~isto; **composition**, ~(ad)o; ~aĵo; kompozicio; kompostado; kunmetado; kunmetaĵo; **composing machine**, kompostatoro; **composing room**, kompostoĉambro; **composing stick**, kompostujo
Compositae, kompozitacoj
composite, (compound), kompunda, kunmetita; (bot: re family *Compositae*), kompozitaca; kompozitaco
compositor, kompostisto
compos mentis, mense sana
compost, (for fertilizer), kompoŝto; ~i [tr]; (any mixture), miksaĵo
composure, trankvilo
compote, (fruit preserve), kompoto
compound, (combine, gen), kunmeti [tr]; ~ita; ~aĵo (e.g.: *compound interest:* ~ita interezo); (chem), kombinaĵo; (mix), kunmiksi [tr]; kunmiksita; (kun)miksaĵo; (tech), kompunda (e.g.: *compound engine:* kompunda motoro); (enclosed area), remparzono
comprehend, (understand), kompreni

[tr]; (comprise), ampleksi [tr], konstitui [tr], konsistigi; **comprehension**, ~o; amplekso, konsisto; **comprehensible**, ~ebla
comprehensive, (wide scope), ampleksa, inkluziva; (all), tut~a, ĉion~a, ĉioninkluda; (much), mult~a
compress, (press together; apply pressure, reduce volume), kunpremi [tr]; ~iĝi; (summarize), koncizigi, resumi [tr]; (med: pad), kompreso; (med: warm pad), fomentaĵo; (poultice), kataplasmo; **compression**, ~(ad)o; ~iĝo; **compressor**, kompresoro; **decompress**, mal~i [tr]; mal~iĝi; **warm compress**, fomentaĵo
comprise, ampleksi [tr], konstitui [tr], konsistigi
compromise, (agree, settle), kompromisi [int]; ~igi; ~o; (endanger etc.), kompromíti [tr]; kompromito
comptometer, kalkulilo
compulsion, (requirement), devigo, prem~o, trud~o; (psych), impulso; **compulsive**, (psych), impulsa; impulsulo; **compulsory**, ~a
compunction, pentosento
compute, (gen: count, calculate, measure number or quantity), komputi† [tr]; (count, calculate), kalkuli [tr]; (re any activity of cmptr), komputori† [int]; **computation**, ~(ad)o; kalkulado; komputorado
computer, komputoro†; **lap-top computer**, surgenua ~o; **main-frame computer**, centra ~(eg)o; **microcomputer**, mikro~o; **personal computer**, persona ~o
comrade, kamarado [abb. as for title: k–do]; **comrade in arms**, kunbatalanto
comsat, komunika satelito
con, (swindle), fraŭdi [tr] [cp "swindle"]; (against), kontraŭ (e.g.: *arguments pro and con:* argumentoj por kaj kontraŭ); (study), studi [tr]; **con man, con artist**, ~isto
con–, (pfx: together, joint, w), kun– [note: often absorbed into Esperanto root as "kon–", "kom–", etc.; see separate entries]
conation, penado

concatenation, ĉeno; kun~ado
concave, konkava; **biconcave**, bi~a
conceal, kaŝi [tr], maski [tr]
concede, koncedi [tr]; **concession**, [see "concession"]
conceit, vanity), orgojlo; **conceited**, ~a
conceive, (idea), koncepti [tr]; (child), koncipi [tr], gravediĝi (kun); **misconceive**, miskompreni [tr]; **preconceive**, antaŭjuĝi [tr]; **preconceived notion (idea etc.)**, antaŭ~o [see also "concept", "conception"]
concentrate, (gen), koncentri [tr]; ~iĝi; ~aĵo; **concentration**, ~ado; ~iĝo; ~eco (e.g.: *a high concentration of mercury compounds in water:* alta ~eco de hidrargaj kombinaĵoj en akvo)]; **concentration camp**, ~ejo
concentric, samcentra [not "koncentra"]
concept, koncepto; **conceptual**, ~a; **conceptualize**, ~i [tr]
conception, (of child), koncipo; (idea), koncepto; **misconception**, miskompreno; **preconception**, antaŭjuĝo; **the Immaculate Conception**, (rel), la Senpeka K~o
concern, (relate to), koncerni [tr], rilati [int] (al); (worry), zorgo, ĉagreno; (bsns), firmo [cp "company", "conglomerate"]; **concerning**, (about, regarding), ~e [–on, al –o], rilate [–on, al –o], pri [–o] (e.g.: *your letter concerning our up-coming visit:* via letero ~e [or: rilate] nian baldaŭan viziton [or] pri nia baldaŭa vizito); **as far as ... is concerned**, (w regard to), ~e, kiel ~as [–on, al –o]; (in opinion), laŭ (ies) opinion, laŭ (iu) (e.g.: *it is good enough, as far as I am concerned:* ĝi estas sufiĉe bona, laŭ mia opinio [or] laŭ mi)
concert, (mus), koncerto; (accord), akordo; **concerted**, (mutual, joint), komuna; (strong), forta, intensa; **concert hall**, ~ejo; **concertize, give a concert**, ~i [int]; **concertmaster**, ~estro
concertina, koncertino
concerto, konĉerto; **concertino**, ~eto; **concerto grosso**, granda ~o
concession, (bsns franchise), koncesio; (act of conceding), koncedo; **conces-**

sionaire, ~ito; **grant a concession to,** (bsns), ~i [tr]
conch, konko
concha, konko
conchoid, konkoido
conchology, konkolog/io;   **conchologist,** ~o
concierge, pordist(in)o
conciliate, akord/igi, repacigi, (re)konkordigi;   **conciliatory,** ~igema; ~iĝema
concise, konciza
conclave, (meeting), konklavo; (room), ~ejo
conclude, (decide, infer), konkludi [tr] [cp "infer"]; (end, close), fini [tr], fermi [tr]; finiĝi, fermiĝi; **conclusion,** ~o; fino, fermo; conclusive, decidiga, ~iga; **foregone conclusion,** decidita ~o
concoct, fabriki [tr], kunfari [tr], kunmiksi [tr]
concomitant, akompana, ~anta; ~aĵo; **concomitance,** ~anteco
concord, harmony), konkordo; (gram agreement), akordo; **be in concord,** ~i [int]; akordi [int]; **bring into concord,** ~igi; akordigi; **concordant,** ~a
concordance, (agreement), konkordo; (index), konkordanco
concordat, konkordato
concourse, (flowing together), kunfluo; (crowd), homamaso; (open space), placo; (broad boulevard or walkway), korso
concrescence, (concretion), konkremento; (any growing together), kunkresk(ad)o
concrete, (of cement, sand, etc.), betono; ~a; ~i [tr]; (not abstract; math), konkreta; (formed into solid mass), konkrementa; **reinforced concrete,** fer~o, ŝtal~o, armita ~o; **concrete mixer,** ~miksatoro
concretion, konkremento
concubine, konkub(in)o
concupiscence, voluptem(eg)o
concur, (agree), konsenti [int], akordi [int], samopinii [int]; (coincide), koincidi [int]
concurrence, (agreement), konsento, akordo; (happening together), kuno-

kazo, koincido; **concurrent,** samtempa
concussion, (med), komocio
condemn, kondamni [tr]; **condemnation,** ~o
condense, (gen), kondensi [tr]; ~iĝi; (summarize), ~i, resumi [tr]; **condenser,** (elec, chem, mech), ~atoro; (optic), kondensoro; **condensation,** ~ado; ~iĝo; ~aĵo
condescend, degni [tr]; **condescending,** ~(em)a; **condescension,** ~ado, ~emo
condiment, kondimento; ~i [tr]
condition, (state, circumstance), kondiĉo, stato, cirkonstanco; (prerequisite, requirement), ~o; (set as a precondition, stipulate), ~i [tr]; (influence), influi [tr]; (put into proper condition, state), bonstatigi; (psych: develop conditioned reflex, create inclination, tendency), influi [tr], emigi, tendencigi; (accustom), kutimigi; **conditional,** (having conditions), ~a; (gram), kondicionalo; kondicionala; **unconditional,** sen~a; **air-condition,** klimatizi [tr]; **air-conditioner,** klimatizatoro; **precondition,** antaŭ~o, stipulo, premiso; (prepare), antaŭprepari [tr]; **recondition,** rebonstatigi; **on condition that,** ~e ke
condole, kondolenci [tr]; **condolence,** ~o; **letter of condolence,** ~a letero
condom, kondomo
condominium, (building), kundomaro; (one home), ~a loĝejo, ~a hejmo; (pol), kunsuvereneco
condone, (tolerate), toleri [tr]; (excuse), pardoni [tr], malkondamni [tr]
condor, kondoro
condottiere, kondotiero
conducive, favora, kondukema
conduct, (heat, elec, light, etc.), kondukti [tr]; (lead, guide, direct), konduki [tr]; (carry out, do), efektivigi, fari [tr], plenumi [tr], realigi; (behave), [see "behave"]; (be in charge of, leader of), estri [tr]; **conductance,** (elec), konduktanco; **conduction,** ~ado; kondukado; **conductive,** ~iva; **conductivity,** (ability to conduct, gen), ~ivo; (elec: inverse of resistivity), ~eco;

photoconductive, foto~a; **superconductive,** super~iva; **superconductivity,** super~eco; **conductor,** (of heat, elec, light, etc.), ~anto; (one specific wire, glass rod, etc.), ~ilo; (cable, etc.), ~aĵo; (on train etc.), konduktoro; (mus), kondukisto; **nonconductor,** (elec), ne~anto; **semiconductor,** duon~anto; **misconduct,** (misbehavior), miskonduto; (mismanagement, malfeasance), misadministrado

conduit, (gen), dukto

condyle, kondilo

condyloma, kondilomo

cone, (geom etc.; of tree), konuso; (crust for ice cream cone), vafleto; **conic(al),** ~(form)a; **ice cream cone,** glaciaĵ~o; **retinal cone,** ~eto

coney, (rabbit), kuniklo; (fur), ~ofelo; (zool: *Procavia*), prokavio

confection, frandaĵo [not "konfekcio"]; **confectioner,** ~isto; **confectionery,** (shop), ~ejo

confederate, (pol), konfederacii [tr], konfederi [tr]; ~a; ~ita; ~iĝinta; ~ito, ~iĝinto; (accomplice), komplico; (any comrade), kamarado; **confederacy,** ~o; **confederation,** (league), ~o; (ac| of), ~ado; ~iĝo; **the Confederate States of America,** la K~itaj Ŝtatoj de Ameriko

confer, (consult), konsult/iĝi, konsiliĝi, konferenci [int]; (give, bestow), doni [tr], aljuĝi [int] (al) [cp "invest"]; **confer with,** ~i [tr]; **conferee,** (in conference), konferencanto; (on whom honor etc. is conferred), investito

conference, (meeting, consultation), konferenco; (bestowal), dono [cp "invest"]; **hold a conference,** ~i [int]

conferva, *Conferva,* konvervo

confess, (admit), konfesi [tr]; (declare rel faith), kred~i [tr]; **confession,** ~o; kred~o; [cp "faith"]; **confessional,** ~ejo; **confessed,** ~inta; **confessor,** (one who confesses), ~anto; (priest), ~prenanto

confetti, konfetoj

confidant(e), konfidencul(in)o

confide, (entrust, gen), konfidi [tr]; (secrets), konfidenci [tr]

confident, (trusting), fida (e.g.: *a confident step upon the ice:* ~a paŝo sur la glacio); (self-assured), mem~a, certa (e.g.: *a confident tone of voice:* mem~a voĉtono; *I am confident that you will win:* mi estas certa ke vi gajnos); confidence, (trust), ~o; (self-assurance), mem~o; (entrusted secret knowledge), konfidenco; **confidential,** (secret), konfidenca; **confidence artist,** fraŭdisto; **self-confidence,** aplombo, mem~o

configuration, (arrangement), aranĝo; (form, outline), formo, aspekto; (chem structure, (molekula) strukturo

confine, (close up, enclose, gen), enfermi [tr], enŝlosi [tr]; (limit), limigi; limo; **confinement,** ~o; limigo; (for childbirth), akuŝo; **be in confinement (with),** akuŝi [tr]

confirm, (validate, verify), konfirmi [tr]; (rel), konfirmacii [tr]; **confirmation,** ~(ad)o; konfirmacio; **confirmed,** (habitual, persistent), persista (e.g.: *confirmed bachelor:* persista fraŭlo)

confiscate, konfiski [tr]

conflagration, konflagracio

conflict, konflikti [int]; ~o; come into conflict, ek~i [int]

confluence, conflux, (flowing together), kunfluo; (place), ~ejo; **confluent,** (gen), ~a

conform, konform/igi; ~iĝi; **conformity, conformance,** ~eco; **conformist,** ~ema; ~emulo; **nonconformist,** ne~ema; ne~emulo; **in conformance with,** ~a al; ~e al

confound, (confuse), konfuzi [tr]; (mix), intermiksi [tr]

confrere, kolego

confront, (face, gen), alfronti [tr]; (law: witnesses in court etc.), konfronti [tr]; **confrontation,** ~(ad)o; konfront(ad)o

Confucius, Konfuceo; **Confucian,** ~a; ~ano; **Confucianism,** ~anismo

confuse, konfuzi [tr]; **confusion,** ~o; ~aĵo; **confusing,** ~a; ~iva; ~ema

confute, refuti [tr]

congeal, (thicken), koaguliĝi, ĝeliĝi; (become solid), malfandiĝi, solidiĝi, firmiĝi

congener, samspec/ulo; ~aĵo

congenial, simpatia, afabla, amikema
congenital, denaska
conger, *Conger*, kongro
congest, (gen), troplen/igi, ŝtopi [tr];
(med), kongesti [tr]; congested, ~a,
ŝtopita; kongestiga; congestion,
~igo, ~iĝo, ŝtop(ad)o, ŝtopiĝo; kon-
gesto; decongest, (med), malkonges-
ti [tr]; decongestant, malkongesta;
malkongestenzo
conglomerate, (gen), konglomeri [tr];
~iĝi; ~a; ~aĵo, konglomerato; (bsns),
konzerno
Congo, (river), Kongo; (former colonies), (Franca, Belga) ~olando; (country), Kongolo [cp "Zaire"];
Congolese, ~a; Kongola; Kongolano;
Congo red, k~o
congratulate, gratuli [tr]; congratula-
tion, ~o; congratulations!, ~on!
[note sing]; congratulatory, ~a
congregate, amasiĝi, kolektiĝi, ariĝi
congregation, (rel order), kongregacio;
(members of one house of worship),
kirkanaro, sinagoganaro, moskeanaro
(etc., depending on faith); (of any
faith), preĝejanaro; (not rel), ĉeestantaro; congregational, ~a; kirkanara,
preĝejanara (etc.); Congregational,
(denomination), Kirkanara; Con-
gregationalism, Kirkanarismo;
Congregationalist, Kirkanarisma;
Kirkanaristo
congress, (legislature; convention, large
gathering), kongreso; (any coming together), kuniĝo; Congress, (U.S. legislature), K~o; Member of
Congress, Congressperson, Con-
gress(wo)man, K~an(in)o
congruent, kongrua; congruence,
~eco; be congruent with, ~i [int] kun
conic, koniko
conical, konusa
conicoid, konikoido
conidiophore, konidioforo
conidium, konidio
conifer, konifero
Coniferae, Coniferales, koniferoj
conine, conin, coniine, koniino
Conium, konio; Conium maculatum,
makula ~o
conjecture, konjekti [tr]; ~o, ~aĵo

conjoin, kunigi, kombini [tr]; conjoint,
komuna, ~ita, kombinita
conjugal, gepara
conjugate, (gen), konjugi [tr]; (math),
~i; ~ito; conjugation, (gram: reciting
of verb forms), ~(ad)o; (system of
verb inflection), konjugacio
conjunct, komuna, kombinita; (person), asociito
conjunction, (gen), konjunkcio; coordi-
nating conjunction, kunordiga ~o;
subordinating conjunction, (gram),
subjunkcio; be in conjunction
(with), (ast), ~i [tr]
conjunctiva, konjunktivo; conjunctivi-
tis, ~ito
conjunctive, (joining), kuniga, kombi-
na; (gram), konjunkcia
conjuncture, (gen), kuniĝo; ~ado; ~aĵo;
(crisis), krizo
conjure, ĵurvoki [tr]
conk, (colloq: hit on head), kapobati
[tr]; ~o; conk out, panei [int]
conker, (horse chestnut), hipokaŝtano
con moto, (mus), vigle
conn, (naut), direkti [tr]; conning tower, ~okajuto, blokhaŭso
connect, (join, gen), kontakt/igi, ligi
[tr]; ~iĝi, ligiĝi; (between chambers,
rooms, etc.), komunikigi; komunikiĝi;
(elec, phone, etc.), konekti [tr]; konektiĝi; (link machinery), kupli [tr];
kupliĝi; (have some relationship),
rilati [int]; connection, ~(iĝ)o,
lig(iĝ)o; konekt(iĝ)o; kupl(iĝ)o; rilato;
connector, ~ilo; konektilo; kuplilo;
connective tissue, (anat), konektivo;
disconnect, mal~igi; malkonekti [tr];
malkupli [tr]; malfiksi [tr], malligi
[tr]; disconnected, malkontinua, interrompita; in this connection, ĉi-
rilate; in that connection, tiurilate; in
connection with, (about), pri, koncerne [–on, al –o], rilate [–on, al –o],
konekse kun
Connecticut, Konektikuto*
connexion, [see "connect: connection"]
connive, fihelpi [tr], esti komplico
(kun); connivance, kompliceco
Connochaetes gnu, gnuo
connoisseur, spertulo, adepto, aprecan-
to

connote, implici [tr]; **connotation**, ~(aĵ)o
connubial, gepara, geedz(ec)a
conoid, konoido
conquer, konkeri [tr]; **conquest**, ~(ad)o
Conrad, Konrado
consanguineous, (sango)parenca; **consanguinity**, ~eco
conscience, konscienco; **clear conscience**, senŝarĝa ~o; **troubled conscience**, **bad conscience**, ŝarĝita ~o, maltrankvila ~o; **conscience-stricken**, trafita de (sia) ~o
conscientious, konscienca; **conscientious objector**, ~a sindetenanto
conscious, konscia; **be conscious of**, ~i [tr]; **consciousness**, ~o; **lose consciousness**, sen~iĝi; **regain consciousness**, re~iĝi; **self-conscious**, embarasita, senaplomba, ĉagrenita, ĝenita; (psych: aware of self), mem~a; **unconscious**, sen~a; (psych), ne~o; **unconsciousness**, sen~eco; **subconscious**, sub~o; sub~a; **superconscious**, super~o
conscript, konskripcii [tr]; konskripto; **conscription**, ~o
consecrate, konsekri [tr]
consecutive, sinsekva(j); **consecutively**, ~e
consensus, (ĝenerala) konsento
consent, konsenti [int]; ~o; **mutual consent**, inter~o
consequence, konsekvenco, sekvo, rezulto; **consequent**, ~a, rezulta; ~o; **consequential**, (resulting), ~a, sekva, rezulta; (important), grava; **inconsequential**, sen~a, negrava; **consequently**, sekve, ~e
conservancy, (conservation), konservo, ~ado; (Br: commission), ~a komisiono
conservation, konservo, ~ado; **conservationist**, ~adisma; ~adisto
conservative, (pol), konservativa; ~ulo; (inclined to conserve), konservema; **conservatism**, ~ismo
conservator, (guardian), kuratoro; **conservatorship**, ~eco
conservatory, konservatorio
conserve, (keep, save), konservi [tr]; (fruit jam), konfiti [tr]; konfitaĵo

consider, konsideri [tr]; **consideration**, ~(ad)o; **considerable**, (noteworthy), ~inda; **considerate**, ~ema, komplezema; **inconsiderate**, sen~a; **considered**, ~ita, (zorge) elpensita; **considering**, (in view of), ~ante; **reconsider**, (judicial or administrative decision), revizii [tr] [cp "annul"]; **all things considered**, ĉion ~inte; **take into consideration**, kalkuli kun, preni en la kalkulon, preni en ~on
consign, konsigni [tr]; **consignment**, ~o; ~aĵo; **consignee**, ~ito; ~ato; ~oto; **consignor**, ~into; ~anto; ~onto
consist, konsisti [int]; **consist of**, (be made up of), ~i el (e.g.: *an hour consists of 60 minutes:* horo ~as el 60 minutoj); (have as main ingredient), ~i en (e.g.: *music consists of more than notes:* muziko ~as en pli ol notoj); **consistency**, (make-up, gen), ~o; (chem), konsistenco; (conformity), konformeco; **consistent**, konforma; konsekvenca
consistory, konsistorio
console, (comfort, soothe), konsoli [tr]; (keyboard of cmptr, organ, etc.), klavaro; (cabinet for radio etc. standing on floor), plankŝranko; (instrument panel), panelo; (ornamental wall bracket), konzolo; **consolation**, ~o; **disconsolate**, sen~a; **inconsolable**, ne~ebla
consolidate, (unite), unuigi; (strengthen), fortikigi, firmigi, firme establi [tr]; (create solidarity), solidarigi
consols, (Br), solidaraj fondusoj
consommé konsomeo
consonance, consonancy, konsonanco
consonant, (gram), konsonanto; (agreeing), akorda; (re consonance), konsonanca; **consonantal**, ~a; **consonant shift**, ~oŝoviĝo
consort, (spouse), edz(in)o; **consort with**, akompan(ad)i [tr], asociiĝ(ad)i kun
consortium, konsorcio
conspectus, (summary), resumo
conspicuous, okulfrapa, elstara
conspire, konspiri [int]; **conspiracy**, ~o; **conspirator**, ~anto

con spirito, (mus), sprite
constable, (Br, Am law officer), konstablo; (medieval mil officer), konestablo
Constance, (woman's name), Konstanca; (city in Germany), ~o; Lake Constance, Lago ~a
constant, konstanta; (math), ~o; constancy, ~eco
Constanta, Konstanco
constantan, konstantano
Constantine, (man's name), Konstancio, Konstanto, Konstanteno; (emperor), Konstanteno; (city), Konstantino
Constantinople, Konstantinopolo
constellation, konstelacio
consternate, konsterni [tr]; consternation, ~(iĝ)o
constipate, konstipi [tr]; constipation, ~o; be(come) constipated, ~iĝi
constituent, (part), konsistiga; ~aĵo, ~a parto, elemento, ingredienco; (citizen), civitano; constituency, (makeup), konsisto; (citizens), civito
constitute, konstitui [tr], konsistigi; reconstitute, (reconstruct), rekonstrui [tr], restarigi, reorganizi [tr]; (rehydrate), reakvizi [tr]
constitution, (basic law, esp pol; state of health), konstitucio; (basic rules, structure of organization etc.), statuto; (content, make-up, gen), konsisto; constitutional, ~a; constitutionality, ~eco; unconstitutional, kontraŭ~a
constrain, (obligate), devigi; (limit), limigi; constraint, ~o; limigo; (thing that constrains), retenilo
constrict, konstrikti [tr], stringi [tr]; ~iĝi, stringiĝi; constriction, ~(iĝ)o, string(iĝ)o; ~aĵo; constrictor, (muscle etc.), ~anto; ~ilo; (snake), konstriktoro
construct, (gen), konstrui [tr]; ~o [not "~aĵo"; see "building"; not "konstrukci–"; se "design"]; construction, ~(ad)o; (structure), ~aĵo; (construing, interpretation), interpreto; (gram: word arrangement), ~o, vortaranĝo; reconstruct, re~i [tr]; construction contractor, ~entreprenisto; construction site, ~ejo; under construction, ~ata

constructive, (positive), pozitiva, krea (e.g.: constructive criticism: ~a kritiko); (inferential, construed), implicita (e.g.: constructive fraud: implicita fraŭdo)
construe, (interpret), interpreti [tr]; (gram), konstrui [tr]; misconstrue, mis~i [tr]
consubstantial, samsubstanca; consubstantiate, ~igi; consubstantiation, ~eco; ~igo
consul, (gen), konsulo; consular, ~a; consulate, (position, rank), ~eco; (place), ~ejo
consult, konsulti [tr]; consultant, (one who consults), ~into; ~anto; ~onto; (person consulted), konsilisto, ekspertizisto; ~ito; ~ato; ~oto; consultative, (advisory, not binding), ~iĝa; consultation, ~o
consume, konsumi [tr]; consumption, ~(ad)o; ~iĝo; (tuberculosis), ftizo; consumer, ~anto
consummate, (supreme), perfekta, zenita; (effectuate), efektivigi, plenumi [tr]
consumption, [see "consume"]
contact, kontakti [tr]; ~iĝi; (elec), ~ilo; (oth), ~o; contact point, (elec), ~aĵo; bad (poor) contact, (elec), mis~o
contagion, kontaĝo; contagious, ~a
contain, (hold inside), enhavi [tr], enteni [tr]; (hold back, keep from spreading), reteni [tr]; container, (gen), ujo [used as sfx to specify contents; as separate word to specify what made of (e.g.: container made of glass: vitra ujo; container for glass: vitrujo)]; (large, for shipping; pallet), kontenero; container ship, kontenerŝipo; containerize, kontenerizi [tr]; containment, reten(ad)o; self-contained, memstara, sendependa
contaminate, (infect), infekti [tr]; (chem etc.: introduce impurity), malpurigi; contamination, ~(ad)o; ~iĝo; ~aĵo; malpurig(ad)o; contaminant, ~aĵo; decontaminate, mal~i [tr], sen~igi; senmalpurigi
contemplate, kontempli [tr]; contemplative, ~ema
contemporaneous, samtempa

contemporary, (of same era), samepoka; ~ulo; (of same age), samaĝa; samaĝulo; (of present time), nuntempa, moderna, aktuala
contempt, malestimo; contemptible, ~inda, fia; contemptuous, ~a
contend, (struggle), lukti [tr], batali [int]; (argue), argumenti [int]; disputi [int] [see "argue"]; (compete), konkuri [int]; (assert), aserti [tr]; contention, ~o, batalo; argumento; disputo, kverelo; contentious, kverelema, disputema; bone of contention, disputopunkto, punkto de disputo
content, (happy), kontenta; ~igi; content(s), (quantity contained), enhavo, enteno; contented, ~a; contentment, ~eco; discontent, mal~eco; discontented, mal~a; malcontent, mal~a; mal~ulo
contention, [see "contend"]
contest, (race, game, etc.), konkurso; ~a; (struggle), lukto; (call into question), kontesti [tr]; contestant, ~anto; participate in (a, the) contest, ~i [int]
context, (words), kunteksto, ĉirkaŭteksto; (milieu), situacio, ĉirkaŭaĵo
contiguous, apuda, tuŝanta, kontaktanta
continence, ĉasteco
continent, (geog), kontinento; (abstaining), ĉasta; (withholding, as urine), reten(iv)a; continental, ~a; incontinent, nereten(iv)a; intercontinental, inter~a; subcontinent, sub~o; transcontinental, trans~a
contingent, (uncertain), kontingenca; (portion, as of troops), kontingento; (possible), eventuala; (dependent), dependa; contingency, ~aĵo; ~eco; eventualaĵo; dependeco
continue, daŭri [int]; ~igi (e.g.: the rain continued 2 days: la pluvo ~is 2 tagojn; continue one's efforts: ~igi siajn penojn); continual, ~a, ripetada, senĉesa; continuance, (duration), ~o; (postponement), prokrasto; continuation, (~ed action), ~ado; ~ig(ad)o; (extension, supplement), plilongigo, suplemento; continuity, kontinuaĵo; kontinueco; continuous, kontinua; be continuous, kontinui

[int]; discontinue, ĉesigi; (a subscription), malaboni [tr]; discontinuation, discontinuance, ĉesigo; discontinuity, malkontinuaĵo, kontinurompo; malkontinueco; discontinuous, malkontinua, nekontinua, intermita, interrompita
continuo, (mus), (bas)kontinuaĵo
continuum, kontinuaĵo
contoid, kontoido
contort, distordi [tr]; contortion, ~(ad)o; ~iĝo; contortionist, sintordisto
contour, (outline), konturo; ~i [tr]; (level), nivelo; (French "galbe": convex curve of chair, artwork, etc.), galbo; contour line, izohipso†; contour map, izohipsa† mapo; contour plowing, nivelkurba plugado
contra-, (pfx), kontraŭ– [note: sometimes absorbed into Esperanto root as "kontra–"; see separate entries]
contraband, kontrabando; ~aĵo; contrabandist, ~isto [see also "smuggle"]
contrabass(o), (instrument, voice part), kontrabaso; (singer), ~ulo
contraception, kontraŭkoncipo; contraceptive, ~a; (drug), ~enzo; (device, e.g., condom, IUD), ~ilo ["~ilo" may be used as gen term including both chemical and mechanical contraceptives]
contract, (legal agreement), kontrakto; ~i [int]; (shrink), malekspansii [int], maldilatiĝi; malekspansiigi, maldilati [tr] [cp "shrink"]; (re muscle), kontrahi [tr]; kontrahiĝi; (catch disease), malsaniĝi de, (malsano) trafi (iun), atakiĝi de, trafiĝi de (e.g.: I contracted the flu: mi malsaniĝis de gripo [or] gripo trafis min); (gram), elizii [tr]; (acquire, as debt), akiri [tr]; contraction, malekspansi(iĝ)o, maldilat(iĝ)o; kontrah(iĝ)o; elizi(aĵ)o; contractor, entreprenisto (e.g.: construction contractor: konstruentreprenisto); contractual, ~a; subcontract, sub~o, subentreprenisto
contracture, kontrakturo
contradance, kontradanci [int]; ~o
contradict, kontraŭdiri [tr]; contradic-

tion, ~o, antinomio; **contradictory,**
~a, antinomia; **self-contradictory,**
mem~a
contrail, vaporspuro
contralto, (voice part), kontralto; ~a;
(singer), ~ulino
contrapposto, kontraposto
contraption, aparat(aĉ)o, umilo
contrapuntal, kontrapunkta
contrary, (against), kontraŭa; (opposite), mala; (inclined to disagree; perverse), ~ema; **contrary to,** ~kontraŭ;
mala al; male al; **on (to) the contrary,** male; **be contrary to,** ~i [tr]
contrast, kontrasto; ~i [int]; ~igi, kon-
traŭmeti [tr]; **contrasty,** (phot), ~eca
contravene, (act against), kontraŭ/agi
[tr], konflikti [int] kun; (contradict),
~diri [tr]; **contravention,** ~ago; ~diro
contredanse, kontradanco
contretemps, maloportunaĵo
contribute, kontribui [int] (per, al), kotizi [int] (per, al) (e.g.: *contribute
money to the fund:* ~i per mono al la
fonduso; **contribution,** (act), ~o;
(thing, $), ~aĵo, kotizo; **contributor,**
~into; ~anto; ~onto; **contributory,** ~a
contrite, kontricia, pentema, pentople-
na; **contrition,** ~o
contrive, elpensi [tr], aranĝi [tr]; **con-
trivance,** ~aĵo, aranĝaĵo; **contrived,**
(not spontaneous), (tro)~ita
control, (regulate, rule), regi [tr, int];
(act of), ~(ad)o; (device for control-
ling), ~ilo; (verify, check against standard), kontroli [tr]; kontrol(ad)o;
kontrolilo; (regulate machinery etc.),
komandi [tr]; komand(ad)o (e.g.: *that
switch controls the lights:* tiu ŝaltilo
komandas la lumojn); (direct), direkti
[tr]; direkt(ad)o; (administer), administri [tr]; administr(ad)o; (restrain),
bridi [tr]; brid(ad)o; **control room
(booth, area, panel),** komandoĉam-
bro (komandobudo, komandokajuto,
komandejo, komandopanelo); **birth
control,** naskolimig(ad)o, naskoregu-
lado; **decontrol,** sen~igi; sen~igo; **remote control,** telekomandi [tr];
telekomand(ad)o; **self-control,**
mem~ado; **take control of,** ek~i [tr]
controversy, (debate), debat/ado, pole-

miko, vortbatalo; (dispute), disputo;
controversial, ~ata, ~inda, ~ebla
controvert, refuti [tr], kontraŭdiri [tr],
kontraŭargumenti [tr], nei [tr], kontesti [tr]
contumacy, kontumaco; contumacious,
~a
contuse, kontuzi [tr]; **contusion,** (act),
~o; (blue spot), ~aĵo
conundrum, (kalembur)enigmo
conurbation, urbokomplekso
conure, konuro
Conurus, konuro
convalesce, konvaleski [int]; **convales-
cence,** ~o; **convalescent,** ~a; **convalescent home,** ~ejo
Convallaria, konvalo, majfloro
convect, konvekti [tr]; **convection,** ~o,
konvekcio†; **convective,** ~a
convene, kunvoki [tr]; kunveni [int],
~iĝi [not "konveni"]
convenient, oportuna [not "konvena"];
convenience, ~aĵo; ~eco; **inconvenient,** mal~a; **inconvenience,**
mal~aĵo; mal~eco; (bother), ĝeni [tr];
ĝeno; **convenience store,** krakbutiko,
~butiko
convent, monaĥinejo, inkonvento
convention, (assembly), kongreso;
(pact, as between countries; social
custom; accepted usage, device;
assembly of Am pol party; French
constitutional assembly); konvencio;
conventional, konvencia; **conven-
tioneer,** ~ano; **hold a convention,** ~i
[int]
converge, konverĝi [int]; ~igi; **conver-
gence,** ~eco; **convergent,** ~a(j)
conversazione, (lit, art, etc.) konver-
skunveno
converse, (talk), konvers(aci)i [int], in-
terparoli [int]; (reverse), mala; malo;
conversation, konversacio, interparo-
lo; **conversant with,** sperta pri, ko-
nanta; **be conversant with,** havi
sperton pri, sperti [int] pri, koni [tr]
convert, (rel, phil, etc.: chem; $), kon-
verti [tr]; ~iĝi; ~ito; (change, gen),
ŝanĝi [tr]; ŝanĝiĝi; **conversion,** ~o;
~ado; ~iĝo; ŝanĝ(iĝ)o; **converter,**
convertor, (person), ~into; ~anto;
~onto; ~isto; (machine, Bessemer

etc.), konvertoro; **nuclear converter**, nuklea konvertoro; **motor converter**, konvertora kompleto; **convertible**, (car), kapuĉaŭto **convex**, konveksa; **biconvex**, bi~a **convey**, (communicate), komuniki [tr], transdiri [tr], peri [tr]; (lead), konduki [tr]; (give), (trans)doni [tr]; (send), transporti [tr], sendi [tr]; **conveyance**, (act of), ~(ad)o; konduk(ad)o; (trans)don(ad)o; transport(ad)o; send(ad)o; (vehicle), veturilo; (deed), transdonatesto; **conveyor** (**belt**), transportilo (transportzono, transportoĉeno) **convict**, konvikti [tr]; ~ito **conviction**, (of crime), konvikto; (convincing; belief), konvinko **convince**, konvinki [tr]; **convincing**, ~a **convivial**, amikema, afabla, festena, gaja **convoke**, kunvoki [tr]; **convocation**, (gen), ~o; (rel assembly), sinodo **convolute**, (wind), volvi [tr]; ~iĝi; ~ita; **convoluted**, (wound), ~ita; (twisted, tangled), implikita; **convolution**, ~aĵo; implikaĵo **convolvulus**, Convolvulus, konvolvulo; Convolvulus soldanella, soldanelo **convoy**, konvojo; ~i [tr] **convulse**, konvulsii [int]; ~igi; convulsion, ~o; convulsive, ~a **cony**, [see "coney"] Conyza, konizo **coo**, (as dove; speak lovingly), rukuli [int], kveri [int] **cook**, kuiri [tr]; ~iĝi; ~ist(in)o; **cookie**, kekso [see "biscuit"]; **cookbook**, receptaro, ~libro; **cook out**, ~pikniki [int]; **cookout**, ~pikniko; **cook up**, (concoct plan etc.), fabriki [tr], kunfari [tr], kunmiksi [tr], elpensi [tr]; **pressure cooker**, premmarmito **Cook Islands**, Kuk-Insularo **cool**, (not warm, gen), malvarma, frida; ~igi, fridigi; ~iĝi, fridiĝi; (warmer than cold), ~eta (e.g.: *the soup cooled off:* la supo ~iĝis; *feel a cool breeze:* senti ~etan zefiron); (chilly), friska; (cool-headed), aplomba; (aloof), distanca; (tranquil), trankvila; coolant, fridigenzo; **supercool**, (phys), subfri-

digi; **keep cool**, (calm), konservi sian aplombon, ne konfuziĝi, resti trankvila **coolabah**, coolibah, (Aus), kulabao* **coolie**, kulio **coon**, prociono; **coonskin**, ~felo; ~fela **coop**, (cage), kaĝo; (building), ~ejo; **coop up**, enfermi [tr]; **fly the coop**, fuĝi [int], eskapi [int] **co-op**, [see "cooperative"] **cooper**, barelisto **cooperate**, (work together), kunlabori [int]; (help), kunhelpi [int]; (participate in a cooperative), kooperi [int] **cooperative**, (working, helping together), kunlabora, kunhelpa; ($), koopera; (joint economic etc. enterprise, gen), kooperativo; **cooperativism**, kooperativismo **co-opt**, koopti [tr]; co-optation, ~(ad)o **coordinate**, (put order in, adjust, organize), kunordigi; (geom), koordinato; **coordination**, ~(ad)o; **coordinates**, (as unit), koordinataro; **coordinate system**, koordinatsistemo; **rectangular coordinate system**, orta koordinatsistemo; **polar coordinate system**, polusa koordinatsistemo **coot**, (zool), fuliko **cootie**, laŭso **cop**, (catch), kapti [tr]; (colloq: police officer), sbiro [tr]; **cop out**, (colloq: renege; leave a movement or cause), kabei [int] **copaiba**, (resin), kopaivo Copaiba, (bot), kopaivarbo Copaifera, kopaivarbo **copal**, kopalo **cope**, (deal w), (sukcese) trakti [int] (kun); (struggle), lukti [int], batali [int] (kun, kontraŭ); (bear up, tolerate), elteni [int] (e.g.: *I can't cope when the children are yelling:* mi ne povas elteni kiam la infanoj krias); (cape), mantelo **Copenhagen**, Kopenhago **Copernicus**, Koperniko; **Copernican**, ~a **coping**, (arch), supr/otavolo, mur~o **copper**, (metal), kupro; ~a; (small coin), ~ero; (colloq: police), sbiro; **copper-plate**, ~i [tr]; **coppersmith**,

~isto
copperah, kopro
copperhead, (snake), agistrodono*
coppice, kopso
coppra, copra(h), kopro
Copris, kopriso
coprolalia, koprolalio
coprolite, koprolito
coprophagous, koprofagia;   **coprophagy**, ~o
copse, kopso
Copt, Kopto; **Coptic**, ~a
copula, (gram), kopulo
copulate, kopulacii [int]; **copulation**, ~o
copy, (reproduce, gen), kopii [tr]; ~iĝi; ~o; (of book, magazine, etc.), ekzemplero; (material printed), presitaĵo; (to be printed), presotaĵo; (written draft), malneto; (advertising), reklammaterialo; (imitate), imiti [tr]; **copyreader**, provlegisto; **copyright**, ~rajto, aŭtorrajto; ~rajtigi; **copywriter**, reklamverkisto; **hard copy**, paper~o; **photocopy**, foto~i [tr]; foto~iĝi; foto~o
coquet, koketi [int]; **coquetry**, ~ado; **coquette**, ~ulino; **coquettish**, ~a
Coracius, koracio; Coraciidae, ~edoj; Coraciiformes, ~oformaj (birdoj)
coracle, koraklo
coracoid, korakoida
coral, (skeletal colonies), koralo; ~a; (single animal), ~ulo; **coralroot**, koraliorizo; **soft coral**, alciono; **Coral Sea**, Maro K~a
Corallina, koralino
coralline, (re coral), koral/(ec)a; ~kolora; (zool), koralino
Coralliorhiza, koraliorizo
corbel, korbelo
Corchorus, juto
cord, (string, gen), ŝnuro; (2– or 3–strand wire, insulated, for any elec device), ~o, ~konduktilo; (lace), laĉo; laĉi [tr]; (firewood measure), 3,62 steroj [see § 20]; [see "chord"]; **extension cord**, (elec), plilongiga ŝnuro; **cordless**, sen~a
cordate, korforma
Cordelier, kordeliero
cordial, (friendly, hearty), (el)kora, afa-

bla; (drink), kordialo
cordillera, kordilero
cordite, kordito
cordoba, kordovo
Córdoba, Córdova, Kordovo
cordon, (gen), kordono
corduroy, kordurojo
core, (gen), kerno; sen~igi; **corer**, sen~igilo
Coregonus, koregono
coreopsis, *Coreopsis*, koreopso
corespondent, kunadultinto
Corfu, Korfuo [cp "Kerkyra"]
coriander, koriandro
Coriandrum, koriandro
Corinth, Korinto; **Corinthian**, ~a; ~ano; **Corinthians**, (Bib), ~anoj
Coriolanus, Koriolano
corium, dermo
Corixa, korikso
cork, (gen), korko; ~a; ~i [tr]; **uncork**, mal~i [tr]; **corkscrew**, ~tirilo
corm, kormo
cormophyte, kormofito
cormorant, kormorano
corn, (maize: *Zea mays*), maizo; (Br: any grain), greno; (wheat), tritiko; (oats), aveno; (med: callus), (pied)kalo; (shallow humor), banaleco; **corny**, banala; **cornbread**, ~pano; **corncob**, ~ospadiko; **corn cockle, corn campion**, agrostemo; **corncrake**, krekso; **cornflakes**, ~flokoj; **cornflower**, (*Agrostemma*), agrostemo; (*Centaurea*), cejano; **popcorn**, krak~o
cornea, korneo; **corneitis**, ~ito, keratito
Corneille, (Pierre), (Petro) Kornelio
cornel, kornuso
Cornelius, Kornelio; **Cornelia**, ~a
cornemeuse, kornemuzo
corner, (angle), angulo; (back into a corner), en~igi; (of market), akaparo; akapari [tr]; (turn corner), turniĝi, ĝiri [int]; **(just) around the corner**, baldaŭa, baldaŭ venonta; **cut corners**, (lit), transtranĉi ~ojn; (economize), ŝpari [tr]; corner of the earth, mondflanko; **cater-corner(ed)**, diagonala; diagonale (de)
cornet, (mus instrument), korneto [root: "kornet–"]; (cone of paper), korneto ["eta korno"]; (nun's headdress; cav-

alry flag-carrier), kornedo
cornice, (gen), kornico
cornucopia, abundokorno
Cornus, kornuso
Cornwall, Kornvalo; **Cornish**, ~a
corolla, korolo
corollary, korolario
corona, (of sun), korono; (any halo), aŭreolo; (any crownlike object), krono; (bot), koronulo
coronary, (anat), koronaria; (crownlike), kron(ec)a; **coronary insufficiency**, kora nesufiĉeco; **coronary thrombosis**, kora trombozo
coronation, kronado
Coronella, koronelo
coroner, mort–enketisto
coronet, (small crown), kroneto; (diadem), diademo
Coronilla, koronilo
corporal, (mil), kaporalo; (re body), korpa; (communion cloth), korporalo
corporation, korporacio; **corporate**, ~a
corporeal, korpa, materia
corps, korpuso
corpse, kadavro
corpulent, korpulenta, dikventra; **corpulence**, ~eco
corpus, (anat etc. body), korpo; (collection, as of works), kolekto, verkaro; **Corpus Christi**, Eŭkaristia Festo; **corpus ciliare**, ciliaro; **corpus delicti**, krimfaktoj; **corpus juris**, leĝaro; **corpus luteum**, lutea ~o; **corpus pineale**, [see "pineal"]; **corpus striatum**, striato
corpuscle, (small particle, gen), korpusklo; (of blood, lymph), globulo; **corpuscular**, ~a; globula; **red (blood) corpuscle**, hematio, ruĝa globulo; **white (blood) corpuscle**, blanka globulo; **Pacini's corpuscle**, pacinian corpuscle, paĉinia ~o
correct, (not wrong), ĝusta [not "korekta"]; (rectify error), korekti [tr]; (re opinion, statement, etc.), prava; (decent), deca; (appropriate), konvena; **correction**, korekt(ad)o; korektiĝo; **corrective**, korekta; **correctness**, ~eco; **incorrect**, mal~a, erara; malprava; **be correct**, pravi [int] (e.g.: *she is correct in her description of the*

situation: ŝi pravas en sia priskribo de la situacio; *is that assertion correct?:* ĉu tiu aserto pravas?); **I stand corrected**, mi agnoskas la korekton
corregidor, koregidoro
correlate, korelativ/igi; ~iĝi; ~a; ~o; **correlation**, ~eco, korelacio
correspond, (exchange letters), korespondi [int]; (relate), respondi [int] (e.g.: *the movements of a barometer correspond to changes in the weather:* la moviĝoj de barometro respondas al ŝanĝiĝoj en la vetero; *inflation and corresponding price increases:* inflacio kaj respondaj prezaltiĝoj); (interrelate), interrespondi [int]; (be in harmony, agreement w; relate correctly to), akordi [int]; **correspondence**, ~(ad)o; ~aĵo; (inter)respondo, (inter)rilato; akordo; **correspondent**, ~into; ~anto; ~onto; ~isto
corridor, (gen), koridoro; **air corridor**, aer~o
corroborate, konfirmi [tr]
corroboree, koroborio*
corrode, korodi [tr]; ~iĝi; **corrosive**, ~a; (caustic), · kaŭstika; **corrosive agent**, ~enzo; kaŭstikaĵo; **corrosion**, ~o [cp "rust"]
corrugate, ond/umi [tr]; **corrugated sheet metal**, ~olado; **corrugated paper**, **corrugated cardboard**, ~okartono
corrupt, korupti [tr]; ~ita; **corruption**, ~o; ~ado
corsage, (bodice), korsaĵo; (bouquet), (~)bukedo
corsair, (gen), korsaro
corset, korseto
Corsica, Korsik/io; **Corsican**, ~o; ~a; ~ia
cortège, (any retinue), akompantaro; (funeral), funebrantaro
Cortes, (Spanish, Portuguese legislature), Kortesoj
cortex, (cerebral), kortekso; (of oth organ), kortiko; **cortical**, ~a; kortika
cortico–, (med, anat root), kortiko–
cortisone, kortizono
corundrum, korundo
corvette, korveto
Corvus, (ast), Korvo

Corvus, (zool), korvo; Corvus corax, korako; Corvus cornix, korniko; Corvus frugilegus, frugilego; Corvus monedula, monedo; Corvidae, ~edoj
Coryanthe yohimbe, johimbo
Corybant, koribanto
Corylus, avelujo
corymb, korimbo
Coryphaena, korifeno
coryphaeus, korife(in)o
coryphée, korife(in)o
coryza, korizo
cosign, kunsubskribi [tr]
cosmetic, kosmetika; ~o, ŝminko; **use, apply cosmetics**, ŝminki [tr] (sin)
cosmic, kosma
cosmo–, (pfx: space), kosmo–
cosmogony, kosmogonio
cosmography, kosmograf/io; **cosmographer**, ~o
cosmology, kosmologio
cosmonaut, kosmonaŭto [see "astronaut"]
cosmopolitan, kosmopolito; ~a; **cosmopolitanism**, ~eco; ~ismo
cosmos, kosmo
Cossack, Kozako; ~a
cost, kosto; ~i [tr, int] (e.g.: *they cost 2 dollars each:* ili ~as (po) 2 dolarojn; *it costs 50 pence a liter:* ĝi ~as po 50 pencojn por litro); **costly**, (multe)~a; **at the cost of**, ~e de, je ~o de; **at all costs**, ĉiariske; **cost of living**, viv~o; **cost of living index**, viv~a indico; **cost-plus**, ~plusa
Costa Rica, Kosta-Riko; **Costa Rican**, Kosta-Rika; Kosta-Rikano
costermonger, (Br), stratvendisto
costmary, balzamito
costume, kostumo; ~i [tr]
cosy, gemuta†, komforta
cot, faldlito
coterie, koterio
cotillion, kotiljono
cottage, (any small house), dom/eto; (summer, holiday home etc.), somer~o
cotter, (any bolt etc.), stifto; **cotter pin, cotter key**, (w spread ends), duobla ~o
cotton, (fiber), kotono; ~a; (plant), ~planto; (fabric), katuno; **lavender**

cotton, (*Santolina*), santolino
Cottus, ĉoto
Coturnix, koturno
cotyledon, kotiledono
couch, (sofa), kanapo, sofo; (express), esprimi [tr]
cougar, pumo
cough, (from throat tickle), tusi [int]; ~o; (clearing throat as of phlegm), graki [int]; grako; **cough drop**, (kontraŭ~a) lozanĝo; **cough up**, el~i [tr]; **whooping cough**, kokluŝo
could, (past tense: was able), povis (e.g.: *I could see the moon last night* [I did see it]: mi ~is vidi la lunon hieraŭ nokte); (conditional: would be able; would have been able), ~us (e.g.: *I could see the moon* [now or last night] *if the sky were clear:* mi ~us vidi la lunon se la ĉielo estus klara); **could not (help) but**, [see "can"]
coulee, (lava), lafofluo; (ravine), uedo
coulisse, (theat), kuliso
coulomb, kulombo; **abcoulomb**, ab~o
coumarate, kumar/ato; **coumaric acid**, ~a acido
coumarin, kumarino
council, (gen), konsilio; (rel), koncilio; **Security Council**, (of UN), K~o de Sekureco; **councilmember, councilman, councilor**, ~ano
counsel, (advise), konsili [tr]; ~o; (lawyer), advokato
count, (recite numbers), kalkuli [tr] (e.g.: *count to ten:* ~i ĝis dek); (determine quantity of, number), komptit† [tr], nombri [tr]; ~o, nombro (e.g.: *count the books on the shelf:* kompti la librojn sur la breto); (be of value, to be considered), validi [int], gravi [int] (e.g.: *his opinions don't count:* liaj opinioj ne validas; *your experience counts for little:* via sperto malmulte gravas); (consider), konsideri [tr] (e.g.: *count oneself fortunate:* konsideri sin feliĉa); (criminal charge), imputo; (title), grafo; **countess**, grafino; **countless**, sennombraj, nenombreblaj; **count off**, nombri (sin); **count on**, (rely on), fidi (al, je, –on), dependi de, kalkuli je (e.g.: *I am counting on you to come:* mi fidas vin [or: al vi] ke vi

venos; *we must count on the weather not to change:* ni devas fidi ke la vetero ne ŝanĝiĝos); **count-down**, retro~i [int]; retro~o; **miscount**, mis~i [tr]; mis~o
countenance, (facial expression), mieno; (approve), aprobi [tr], apogi [tr]
counter, (machine for counting a quantity), kompt/ilo†; (disk etc. for counting, as in games), ĵetono; (table, cabinet, etc., as in store for display), vendotablo; (any table-top surface, as in kitchen), tablo; (act against), kontraŭi [tr], kontraŭagi [tr]; (opposing), kontraŭa; **Geiger counter**, ~ilo de Geiger; **lunch counter**, lunĉejo
counter–, (pfx), kontraŭ– [note: sometimes absorbed into Esperanto root as "kontra–"; see separate entries]
counterfeit, falsi [tr]; ~ita; ~aĵo; **counterfeiter**, (mon)~isto
countermand, (orders to person), kontraŭ/ordoni [tr]; (to machine, cmptr, etc.), ~komandi [tr] [see "command"]; ~ordono; ~komando
counterpart, kontraŭparto
counterpoint, kontrapunkto
counterpoise, kontraŭpezo; ~i [tr]
country, (rural area), kamparo; ~a; (rural area, poet), ruro; rura; (nation), lando; **countryman**, (rural resident), ~ano; **(fellow) countryman**, samlandano; **country dance**, popoldanco [cp "contradance"]; **countrified**, ~ecigita; **countryside**, ~o, ~a regiono; **countrywide**, tutlanda; **cross-country**, transgrunda; **upcountry**, landinterna; landinterne(n)
county, (division of U.S. state or Canadian province), konteo*; (division of country, as in U.K., Ireland), provinco; (land ruled by count or earl), graflando
coup, (any blow), bato; **coup de grâce**, mort~o; **coup d'état**, ŝtatrenverso; **attempted coup d'état**, puĉo
coupé (in Br and European rr cars), kupeo
couple, (pair, gen), paro, duopo; ~igi; ~iĝi; (mech: join), kupli [tr]; kupliĝi; (flexible or rotating joint), artiki [tr]; artikiĝi; **uncouple**, malkupli [tr]; mal-

kupliĝi; elartiki [tr]; elartikiĝi; **coupler**, bufro†; **coupling**, (on rr cars), kuplilo; (pipe fitting), niplo; **a couple of**, (colloq), unu-du, ~o da (e.g.: *we'll stay there a couple of weeks:* ni restos tie unu-du semajnojn); **thermocouple, thermoelectric couple**, termoelemento, termo~o
couplet, koplo, distiko
coupon, kupono; **international reply coupon**, (internacia) respond~o [abb: IRK, irk]
courage, kuraĝo; **courageous**, ~a
courbaril, himeneo
courier, kuriero; ~a
Courland, Kurlando
course, (of study; route), kurso; (movement, progress), ~ado, irado; (direction), direkto; (duration), daŭro; (of meal), manĝmeto; (for golf etc.), tereno; (raceway), kurejo; (layer, as of bricks), tavolo; **course of action**, ~o de agado, agmaniero; **in due course**, siatempe, ĝustatempe; **in the course of**, (during), dum; **in the course of time**, dum la tempo pasis (~as, ~os); **of course**, kompreneble, ja vere; **on course**, sur~a; **off course**, el~iĝinta
courser, (bird), kurbirdo
court, (open space), korto; (area for game, e.g., tennis), tereno; (of royalty), ~ego; (high tribunal), ~umo; (low tribunal), tribunalo; (woo), amindumi [tr]; (invite, ask for), inviti [tr] (e.g.: *court disaster:* inviti katastrofon); **court clerk**, aktuaro; **courtly**, (befitting court), ~ega, eleganta; (re troubadors, as courtly love), korteza; **court martial**, milittribunalo; milҩtprocesi [tr]; **courtship**, amindumado; **courtyard**, ~o; **appeals court**, kasacia ~umo; **circuit court**, distrikta ~o; **supreme court**, ĉef~umo
courtesan, amoristino, hetajro
courtesy, (politeness), ĝentil/eco; (favor to another), komplezo; **courteous**, ~a; **do (one) a courtesy**, komplezi [int] (al iu)
courtier, kortegano
Courtrai, Kortrejko
cousin, (male), kuzo; (female), ~ino
cove, (inlet), kreko; (valley), val(et)o

coven, (sorĉistina) rondo
covenant, interligo, kontrakto; ~iĝi, kontrakti [int]
cover, (lie or lay over, gen), kovri [tr]; ~(ad)o; (layer etc.), ~aĵo; (lid etc.), ~ilo; (bell– or bowl–shaped, for food, display, etc.), kloŝo; (cover charge, entrance charge), enirkosto; (attach outer covering, as on cushion), tegi [tr]; (hide), kaŝi [tr]; (shield, protect), ŝirmi [tr], protekti [tr]; (include), ampleksi [tr], inkludi [tr]; (brood, incubate), kovi [tr]; (insure), asekuri [tr]; (pay off debt etc.), kvitigi; (deal w), trakti [tr] (kun), pritrakti [tr]; (report as news, feature, etc.), raporti [tr]; **covering,** ~aĵo; tegaĵo; **coverall,** kombineo; **cover up,** ruzkaŝi [tr], fikaŝi [tr]; **air cover,** aerprotektado, aerŝirmado; **bedcover,** lit~ilo; **slipcover,** seĝo~ilo; **undercover,** kaŝa, sekreta, spiona; **under separate cover,** en aparta koverto; (in mailing wrapper), sub aparta banderolo; **covering letter,** akompana letero
covert, (hidden), kaŝ/ita, kaŝ– [pfx] (e.g.: _covert activities:_ ~itaj agadoj [or] ~agadoj); (shelter), ŝirmejo, ~ejo
covet, avidi [tr]; covetous, ~a
covey, greg(et)o
cow, (female of cattle), bov/ino; (intimidate), timigi, malkuraĝigi; **cowbane,** (water hemlock), akvocikuto; **cowberry,** (_Vaccinium_), vakcinio; **cowboy,** vakero [cp "gaucho"]; **cowlick,** (hair), harfasketo; **cow-pie, cow-pat,** ~ofekaĵo, (vulg), ~kako*; **cowpox,** kaŭpokso; **cowslip,** primolo; **cowwheat,** melampiro, ~intritiko; **sea cow,** dugongo, manato
coward, malkuraĝ/ulo, poltrono; **cowardice, cowardliness,** ~o; **cowardly,** ~a
cower, kaŭri [int]
cowl, kapuĉo; cowling, kapoto
cowrie, cowry, cipreo; **money cowrie,** mon~o, kaŭrio
coxcomb, (dandy), dando
coxswain, stiristo
coy, modesta, sinĝena
coyote, kojoto
coyp(o)u, kojpo

cozen, tromplogi [tr]
cozy, gemutaǂ, komforta
cozymase, kozimazo
crab, (zool: any of _Brachyura_), krabo; (ill-tempered person), plendulo, malbonhumorulo, malafablulo; **crabby,** plendema, mishumora, malbonhumora, malafabla; **green crab,** karcino; **hermit crab,** paguro; **king crab,** limulo; **purse crab, palm crab, robber crab, thief crab, tree crab,** birgo; **crab apple,** [see under "apple"]
crack, (sound of snapping wood etc.; chem: break down hydrocarbons etc.), kraki [int]; ~iĝi; ~o; (onom), krak!; (sound of whip, gun, etc.), knali [int]; knaligi; knalo; [cp "crackle", "clack", "click"]; (burst), krevi [int]; krevigi; (break, as wood, pottery, glass, etc.), fendi [tr]; fendiĝi; fendo; (expert), majstra; (joke), ŝerco; (cocaine), superkokaino; **crack apart, crack open,** fendi [tr]; fendiĝi; **crackpot,** freneza; frenezulo; **crack down on,** striktiĝi kun, severiĝi kun; **crack up,** (accident), suferi akcidenton, akcidentiĝi; (go crazy), freneziĝi; **crack-up,** akcidento; freneziĝo; **cracked up to be,** supozata esti, pretendata esti; **crack a joke,** eligi ŝercon; **crack a smile,** ekrideti [int]; **have a crack at,** provi [tr]; **nutcracker,** nuksrompilo
cracker, (soda cracker, saltine), (sal)biskvito; (sweet), krakeno; (unsweetened), kringo; (firecracker), petardo; **graham cracker,** krakeno
crackle, krepiti [int], kraketadi [int]; ~o, kraketado
crackling, (pork rind), (pork)haŭtaĵo
cracknel, (crisp biscuit), kringo; (sugared), krakeno; (cracklings), (pork)haŭtaĵo
Cracow, Krakovo
Cractes, krakto
cradle, luli [tr]; (gen), ~ilo
craft, (manual art, skill, trade), metio; (deceit), ruzo; (ship), ŝipo; (smaller boat), boato, barko; (plane), aviadilo, avio; **craftsperson, craftsman, craftworker,** ~isto; **craft(sman)ship,** ~lerteco; **crafty,** ruza
crag, apik/aĵo, ~a roko; **craggy,** ~a

crake, krekso
cram, (stuff), farĉi [tr]; (fig: study hurriedly), ~i sin (e.g.: *I crammed for the exam:* mi ~is min por la ekzameno) Crambe, krambo; Crambe maritima, marbrasiko
cramp, (of muscle), kramfo; (of organ), koliko (e.g.: *kidney cramp:* rena koliko); (metal bracket), krampo; **cramped,** (w little space), spacomanka, malvasta, premita
crampon, (gen), krampo
crane, (zool; mech), gruo [cp "derrick"]; **cranesbill,** (bot), geranio; **overhead crane,** rulponto; **crane one's neck,** streĉi la kolon
cranium, kranio; **cranial,** ~a; **craniology,** ~ologio; **craniometry,** ~ometrio; **craniotomy,** ~otomio
crank, (mech), kranko; ~i [tr]; (colloq: complainer), plendulo; (eccentric), strangulo; **cranky,** plendema; **crankcase,** ŝaftingo; **crankshaft,** ~ŝafto
cranny, breĉeto
crap, (nonsense), galimatio; (junk), fatraso; (vulg: shit), merdo; kaki [int]
crape, [see "crêpe"]
crash, (collision etc.), kolizii [int], akcidenti [int]; ~igi, akcidentigi; ~o, akcidento; (plane crash etc.; $ crisis), kraŝi [int]; kraŝigi; kraŝo; (ruin, gen), ruinigi; ruiniĝi; ruiniĝo; (enter party uninvited, concert w/o pay, etc.), entrudi sin (en, ĉe); (urgently hasty), urĝ(eg)a
crasis, krazo
crass, senhonta, kruda
Crassus, Krasso
crassula, Crassula, krasulo
Crataegus, kratago; Crataegus azarolus, azarolo
crate, latkesto; en~igi, enkestigi
crater, (gen), kratero
cravat, (neckcloth), fulardo; (necktie), kravato
crave, avidi [tr]; **craving,** ~o
craven, malkuraĝ(eg)a
crawdad, crawfish, astako, kankro
crawl, gen), rampi [int]; ~(ad)o; (as many-legged animal), krabli [int]; (swim), kraŭli [int]; kraŭlo; **be crawling with,** svarmi [int] (je, per)
crayfish, (European, Am: *Astacus*), as-

tako; (Aus: *Parastacidae*), parastacedo*
crayon, paŝtelo [not "krajono"]
craze, (mania), manio; (fad), furoro
crazy, freneza; **drive (one) crazy,** ~igi (iun); **go crazy,** ~iĝi; **be crazy for (about),** (greatly love), amegi [tr], ~e (furore, pasie) ami [tr]
creak, (sharp squeak), grinci [int]; ~o; (duller scraping sound), knari [int]; knaro
cream, (gen), kremo; ~a; ~kolora; ~igi; ~iĝi; sen~igi; **creamery,** laktejo; **beauty cream,** beleco~o; **cold cream,** koldkremo; **ice cream,** glaciaĵo; **shaving cream,** raz~o; **whipped cream,** kirlita (lakto)~o
crease, (fold), faldi [tr]; ~iĝi; ~o; (wrinkle, wad up), ĉifi [tr]; ĉifiĝi; (graze by bullet etc.), tanĝvundi [tr]; tanĝvundo; (dagger), kriso
create, krei [tr]; **creation,** ~(ad)o; ~aĵo; **creative,** ~iva, ~ema; **creativity,** ~ivo, ~emo
creature, kreito, estaĵo
crèche, (Christmas scene), stalsceno; (Br: nursery), (infan)vartejo
credence, (belief), kredo; (rel: table etc.), kredenco
credential(s), akreditaĵo(j), legitimaĵo(j)
credenza, kredenco
credible, kredinda; **credibility,** ~eco; **credibly,** ~e [not "kredeble"; see "course: of course"]; **incredible,** ne~a
credit, (trust; right to charge purchase; add to account), kredito; ~i [tr]; (recognize), rekoni [tr]; rekono; (acknowledge), agnoski [tr]; agnosko; (positive $ balance), aktivo; **creditable,** ~inda, laŭdinda; atribuebla; **creditor,** kreditoro; **credit card,** ~karto; **credit union,** ~unio; **discredit,** dis~i [tr], sen~igi; dis~o; **credit one with (something),** atribui (ion) al iu; **do credit to,** honori [tr]; **give credit to (one), give (one) credit,** ~i (iun); **on credit,** nekontante
credulity, kredemo, tro~o; **credulous,** (tro)~a; **incredulous,** ne~a
creed, kredo, ~konfeso; **Nicene Creed,**

Nicea K~o; **Apostles' Creed,** K~o de la Apostoloj
creek, (stream), rojo, rivereto; (Br: inlet), kreko
creel, fiŝkorbo
creep, (crawl), rampi [int]; ~o; (as many-legged animal), krabli [int]; **creepy,** (fearsome), hirtiga; **creeper,** (zool: *Certhia*), certio; **canary creeper,** (bot: *Tropaeolum*), tropeolo; **Virginia creeper,** (*Parthenocissus quinquefolia* or *Ampelopsis*), ampelopso
creese, kriso
cremate, kremacii [tr]; **cremation,** ~o; **crematorium,** krematorio
crème, (liquor), likvoro; (any cream), kremo; **crème de cacao,** kakao~o; **crème de menthe,** mento~o
crenate, krenela
crenel, crenelle, krenelo; **crenel(l)ate,** ~i [tr]; crenel(l)ated, ~a
crenulate(d), kreneleta
Creodontia, kreodontoj†
creole, Kreolo; ~a
Creon, Kreono
creosote, kreozoto; ~i [tr]
crêpe, (cloth), krepo; (pancake), krespo; **crêpe paper,** ~a papero; **crêpe rubber,** ~a kaŭĉuko; **crêpe de Chine,** Ĉina ~o; **crêpes suzette,** krespovolvaĵoj
Crepis, krepido
crepitate, krepiti [int]; **crepitation,** ~ado
crepuscle, crepuscule, krepusko; **crepuscular,** ~a
crescendo, kresĉendo; ~e; **decrescendo,** diminuendo, mal~o; diminuende
crescent, krescento; ~a
Crescentia cujete, kalabasarbo
cresol, krezolo, hidroksimetil–benzeno
cress, kreso; **water cress,** akvo~o, nasturcio; **garden (pepper) cress,** lepidio
crest, (gen), kresto; ~i [int]; (small tuft), hupo; (of roof, mountain, etc.), firsto; **crest-fallen,** senkuraĝa, (fig), malpufita
cretaceous, (chalky), kret(ec)a
Cretaceous, (geol), kretaco; ~a
Crete, Kreto

cretin, kreteno; **cretinism,** ~ismo
cretonne, kretono
Creüsa, Kreuza
crevasse, fendego
crevice, fendo
crew, (of ship), ŝipanaro; (any working group), laboristaro, deĵorantaro, taĉmento [cp "shift"]
Crex, krekso
crib, (baby bed), beblito; (manger), kripo; (framework etc.), kadro
cribbage, (game), kribaĝo*
Cricetus, hamstro
crick, kolkramfo
cricket, (insect), grilo; (game), kriketo; **(be) not cricket,** (Br, Aus colloq: improper, unfair), ne lica; ne lici [int] (e.g.: *that's not cricket!:* tio ne licas!)
crico-, (med pfx), kriko–
cricoid, krikoido; ~a
crime, krimo; **capital crime,** mortpuna ~o; **criminal,** ~a; ~ulo; (re law, court, etc.), kriminala; **criminology,** kriminalologio
Crimea, Krimeo
crimp, krispo; ~igi; ~iĝi; **crimped,** ~a
crimson, karmezina; ~o
cringe, timkaŭri [int]
cringle, koŝo
crinkle, ĉifi [tr]; ~iĝi; ~(iĝ)o; ~aĵo
Crinoidea, krinoidoj
crinoline, krinolino
crinum, Crinum, krinumo
cripple, kripl/igi; ~ulo; **crippled,** ~a; **crippling condition,** ~aĵo
cris, kriso
crisis, (gen), krizo
crisp, (crunchy), krusta; ~igi; (fresh), freŝa; (curly), krispa; (lively), vigla
crisscross, (X–mark), ikso; (cross repeatedly), transiradi [tr], interkrucigi, interkruciĝi (kun); interkruciĝo; (hachure), kruc–haĉado
criterion, kriterio
critic, (professional), kritik/isto, recenzisto; (fault-finder), ~anto; **critical,** (re crisis), kriza; (phys; math; geom), krita†; (criticizing), ~(em)a; (analytical), analiz(em)a; **criticize,** (gen), ~i [tr]; **criticism,** (act), ~(ad)o; (phil system), ~ismo, kriticismo
critique, kritiko

croak, (re frog etc.), kvaki [int]; ~o; (onom: frog), kva! kvak!; (toad), kŭaks!, kŭaks, kŭaks, brekekekeks!
Croat, Kroato; **Croatia,** ~io; **Croatian,** ~o; ~a; ~ia
crochet, kroĉeti [tr]; ~aĵo; **crochet hook,** ~ilo
crock, argil/aĵo, ~a poto; **crockery,** ~aĵoj, ~aĵaro
crocodile, krokodilo
Crocodilus, krokodilo
crocus, krokuso; **autumn crocus,** aŭtuna kolĉiko
Crocus, krokuso; Crocus sativus, safrano
Croesus, Krezo
cromlech, kromleño, dolmeno
Cromwell, Kromvelo
crone, maljunulinaĉo, oldulinaĉo
Cronus, Cronos, Krono
crony, kamarado
crook, (criminal), krim/ulo; (rascal, gen), fripono, kanajlo; (shepherd's), hokstango; (bend), flekso, kurbo; fleksi [tr]; (bent thing, hook), hoko; **crooked,** zigzaga, kurbita, hokforma, malrekta; malhonesta, ~a, fripona, kanajla
croon, dolkanti [tr]
crop, (reaped), rikolto; (trim, prune), stuci [tr]; (of bird), kropo; **crop up,** leviĝi, (ek)aperi [int]; **outcropping,** elstaraĵo
croquet, kroketo
crosier, hokbastono
cross, (any X–shaped thing or symbol), kruco; (make any cross; cross-breed), ~i [tr]; (go across), transiri [tr], transpasi [tr] (e.g.: *cross the street:* transiri la straton); (go through), trairi [tr], trapasi [tr], travojaĝi [tr] (e.g.: *cross the prairies:* trairi [or: travojaĝi etc.] la preriojn); (line across), transstreki [tr]; (oppose), kontraŭi [tr]; (contrary), kontraŭa; (angry), kolera; [see also "cross–"]; crossing, (roads etc.), ~ejo; (cross-breeding), ~aĵo, hibrido; **crossbar,** (any transverse bar), transstango; **crossbars,** (latticework), krado; **crossbill,** (zool), loksio, ~bekulo; **crossbow,** arbalesto; **cross-country,** (not on roads), trakampa; (across

nation), translanda; **crosscurrent,** ~kurento; **crosscut,** transtranĉa; transtranĉi [tr]; **cross-examine,** kontraŭekzameni [tr]; **cross-eye,** konverĝa strabismo; **cross-eyed,** konverĝastraba; **cross-fire,** ~pafado, transpafado; **cross-hairs,** faden~o; **crosshatch,** ~haĉi [tr]; ~haĉo; **cross-hatching,** ~haĉaĵo; **cross off, cross out,** (delete), forstreki [tr]; **cross one's mind,** veni en la (ies) kapon; **cross one's t's,** trastreki siajn t-ojn; **cross oneself,** (rel), ~i sin; **cross over,** transiri [tr]; **crossover,** (act), transiro; (place), transirejo; **crosspiece,** transaĵo; **cross-refer,** ~referenci [tr]; **cross-reference,** ~referenco; **crossroad,** (side road), flankvojo; **crossroads,** (road crossing), voj~iĝo, ~iĝejo; **cross section,** kversekco; **cross-stitch,** ~ostebi [tr]; ~ostebo; **cross-town,** transurba; **cross-trees,** transtraboj; **crosswalk,** transpaŝejo; **crosswind,** flankvento; **crossways, crosswise,** transversa; **crossword (puzzle),** ~vort(enigm)o; **double-cross,** perfidi [tr]; perfido; **grade crossing,** (road & rr track at same level), traknivelpasejo; **Maltese cross,** Malta ~o; **Red Cross,** Ruĝa K~o; **Southern Cross,** (ast), Suda K~o; **zebra crossing,** transpaŝejo; **sign of the cross,** ~osigno
cross–, (pfx: across), trans– (e.g.: *crosstown:* ~urba); (against), kontraŭ– (e.g.: *cross-check:* kontraŭkontroli); (tech: transverse), kver– (e.g.: *cross-section:* kversekco)
Crossopterygii, krosopterigoj
Crotalus, krotalo, sonserpento
crotch, (forked object), forko; (forking), ~iĝo; (groin), ingveno; (of garment), ingvenumo
crotchet, (quarter note), kvaronnoto
croton, Croton, krotono
crotonate, kroton/ato; **crotonic acid,** ~a acido, 1–butenacido
crouch, kaŭri [int]; ~o
croup, (disease), krupo; (animal rump), gropo
croupier, krupiero
crouton, krusteto

crow, (zool), korvo; (rooster sound), kokeriki [int]; kokeriko; crowbar, levstango [cp "lever"]; crowberry, (bot), empetro; crowfoot, (bot), ranunkolo; hooded crow, gray crow, korniko; as the crow flies, rektlinie, fluglinie; eat crow, sin humiligi, malfieriĝi; something (nothing) to crow about, io (nenio) prifajfinda

crowd, amaso, hom~o, ~igi, kunpremi [tr]; ~iĝi, kunpremiĝi; crowded, densa; dense loĝata; homplena; overcrowd, tro(hom)plenigi; overcrowded, tro(hom)plena

crown, (gen), krono; ~i [tr]; (top of head), verto; crownbeard, (bot), verbesino; crown-of-the-field, agrostemo

crozier, hokbastono

crucial, gravega; decidiga, kriza

crucible, krisolo

crucifer, (bot), krucifero

Cruciferae, kruciferoj

crucifix, krucifikso

crucify, krucumi [tr]; crucifixion, ~(ad)o

crud, (stuff), aĉaĵo; (person), aĉulo

crude, (gen), kruda; (rough, uncouth), maldelikata, nekulturita, ~a; (vulgar), triviala

cruel, kruela; cruelty, ~aĵo; ~eco

cruet, kruĉeto, karafeto

cruise, (gen), krozi [int]; ~(ad)o; cruiser, (ship), ~isto, ~oŝipo; (pleasure boat), plezurŝipo; battle cruiser, batal~isto

cruller, tordbulo

crumb, (of bread; lit or fig), panero; (of cake), kukero (etc.)

crumble, (into pieces), (dis)pec/igi; ~iĝi

crummy, aĉa

crumpet, (pat)kringo

crumple, ĉifi [tr]; ~iĝi

crunch, (chew), krak/maĉi [tr]; (noise), knari [int]; knaro; (showdown, tight situation), kulmino, krizo; crunchy, ~eta, ~ema [cp "crisp"]

cruor, kruoro

crupper, (strap), vostrimeno; (rump), gropo

crusade, krucmilito; ~i [int]; Crusad-

er, Krucisto

crush, (break), prem/rompi [tr], dis~i [tr], ~frakasi [tr]; ~rompiĝi, ~frakasiĝi; (press hard), ~egi [tr]; ~ego; (pound, grind), pisti [tr]; (great crowd), (hom)amasego; have a crush on (someone), furorami [tr] (iun)

crust, (gen), krusto; (of pie), flano; crusty, ~eca; crust over, ~iĝi

Crustaceae, krustuloj, krustacoj

crustacean, krustulo, krustaco

crutch, lambastono

crux, kerno, nodo

Crux, (ast), Suda Kruco

cruzeiro, kruzejro

cry, (call out), krii [int]; ~o; (weep), plori [int]; ploro; (any animal sound), bleki [int], ~i; bleko, ~o; crybaby, ploremulo; cry off, kabei [int], sin retiri; cry out, el~i [int]; outcry, ~ego, protestego; a far cry from, (far), tre malproksima (–e) de; (different), tre malsama de

cryo–, (pfx), krio–

cryogenic, kriogenika; cryogenics, ~o

cryolite, kriolito

cryophorus, krioforo

cryoscopy, krioskopio

cryotherapy, krioterapio

crypt, (gen), kripto

cryptic, kripta

crypt(o)–, (pfx), kripto–

cryptogam, kriptogamo

cryptogram, kriptaĵo

cryptonym, kriptonimo

crystal, kristalo; ~a; crystallize, ~igi; ~iĝi; crystalline, ~a; crystallize out, (of solution), el~iĝi; crystallography, ~ografio; crystallographer, ~ografo; crystalloid, ~oido; ~oida; crystallose, ~ozo; liquid crystal, likva ~o; likva~a

csárdás, ĉardaŝo

Ctenomys, tukuo

Ctenophora, ktenoforoj†

cub, ido, –ido [sfx] (e.g.: wolf cub: lup~o; a lion and her cubs: leonino kaj ŝiaj idoj)

Cuba, Kubo; Cuban, ~a; ~ano

cube, kubo; ~igi; cubic, ~a, kub– [pfx] (e.g.: cubic meter: ~metro); cubism, ~ismo; cubist, ~isma; ~isto

cubeb, kubebo
cubicle, ĉelo
cubit, ulno [length imprecise]
cuboid, (bone), kuboido
cuckold, kokri [tr]; ~ito
cuckoo, kukolo
Cuculus, kukolo
cucumber, (plant or fruit), kukumo; **bitter cucumber,** kolocinto; **sea cucumber,** holoturio, markolbaso; **squirting cucumber,** elaterio
Cucumis, kukumo; Cucumis melo, melono; Cucumis melo cantalupensis, kantalupo; Cucumis melo reticulatus, retmelono
cucurbit, kukurbo
Cucurbita, kukurbo
cud, remaĉ/aĵo; **chew the cud, chew one's cud,** (lit or fig), ~i [tr, int]
cuddle, cuddle with, premkaresi [tr], brakumi [tr]; **cuddle up with,** ekkaresi [tr], komfortiĝi kun
cudgel, klabo; ~i [tr]
cudweed, gnafalio
cue, (to actor etc.), repliki [tr]; ~o, vostvorto; **cue ball,** celpilko; **cue card,** ~okarto; **cue stick,** (billiards), bilardbastono
cuff, (of shirt etc.), man/umo; (hit), ~frapi [tr]; ~frapo; **cuff link,** ~umbutono; **off the cuff,** senpripensa; **on the cuff,** kredite
cuirass, (gen), kiraso; ~i [tr]
cuisine, (art), kuir/arto; (style of cooking), ~ado; (food), ~aĵo [cp "culinary"]
cul-de-sac, (street), senelirejo, sakstrato; (situation), ~o; (anat), saketo
culex, *Culex,* kulo
Culicidae, kuledoj
culinary, kulinara [cp "cuisine"]
cull, (select), selekti [tr]; (pluck), pluki [tr]; (eliminate, weed out, lit or fig), elsarki [tr]
culm, (grass), kulmo
culminate, kulmini [int], apogei [int]; **culmination,** ~o
culotte, (like short pants; e.g., old-fashioned), kuloto; (resembling skirt, for women), jup~o
culpable, kulpa
culprit, kulpulo

cult, (worship), kulto; (sect), sekto
cultivar, kultivaro
cultivate, (agriculture), kultivi [tr]; (gen), kulturi [tr]; **cultivator,** (machine), ~atoro
culture, (refined ways; social customs; art; etc.), kulturo; ~i [tr]; (of microbes etc.), ~aĵo; (cultivation), kultivado; **cultural,** ~a; **cultured,** ~ita, klera; **counterculture,** kontraŭ~o; **subculture,** sub~o; **culture medium,** ~medio
culvert, kulverto
cumbersome, ĝenpeza, maloportuna, ŝarĝa
cumin, kumino
cum laude, kun laŭdo; **magna cum laude,** kun granda laŭdo; **summa cum laude,** kun plej granda laŭdo
cummerbund, vastzono, larĝa zono
cummin, kumino
cumulate, (law), kumuli [tr]
cumulative, akumuliĝa, amasiĝa
cumulus, kumuluso; **cumulonimbus,** ~onimbo
Cunegunde, Cunegonde, Kunegunda
cuneiform, kojn/forma; ~skribado
Cuniculus, kuniklo
cunnilingus, vulvolekado
cunning, ruzo; ~a
cunt, (vulg), piĉo
cup, (container or contents of), taso; (unit of volume), 237 mililitroj [see § 20]; (as prize), pokalo (e.g.: *the Davis Cup:* La Davisa Pokalo); (chalice), kaliko; (make hollow, as hands), kavigi; (cupping glass), kupo; **cupping,** kupado; **cupcake,** kuketo, ~kuko
cupboard, (teler)ŝranko; **china cupboard,** servico~o
cupel, kupeli [tr]; ~ujo; **cupellation,** ~ado
Cupid, Kupido
cupidity, avareco
cupola, kupolo
Cupressus, cipreso
cupric, kuprika
cuprous, kuproza
cupule, kupulo; **cupulate,** ~forma; ~hava
Cupuliferae, kupuliferacoj

cur, hundaĉo

curaçao, (drink), kuracao

Curaçao, (geog), Kuracao*

curare, kuraro; **curarize,** ~izi [tr]

curate, vikario

curative, saniga [not "kuraca"]

curator, kuratoro

curb, (on sidewalk), trotuarrando; (restrain, moderate), bridi [tr], modeigi; bridado, moderigo; (on bridle), mentonĉeno; **curb service,** ĉeaŭta servado

curculio, *Curculio,* kurkulio

curcuma, *Curcuma,* kurkumo

curd(s), kazeo [note sing]

curdle, kaze/igi; ~iĝi

cure, (heal), sanigi [not "kuraci"]; ~o; (a drug), ~enzo; (correct, as situation), korekti [tr]; (preserve, as meat, tobacco, etc.), prezervi [tr], konservi [tr]; (process, as leather etc.), prepari [tr]; (harden), hardi [tr]

curette, kureto; ~i [tr]; **curettage,** ~ado

curfew, (modern), elirmalpermeso; (medieval), vespersignalo

curia, (gen), kurio; curial, ~a

curie, (unit), kurio*

Curie, (Marie and Pierre), (Maria kaj Petro) Kuri

curio, kuriozaĵo

curious, (desiring to know), scivola, ~ema; (strange, peculiar), kurioza; **be curious,** ~i [tr] (e.g.: *I am curious about who she is:* mi ~as, kiu ŝi estas); **curiosity,** ~(em)o; kuriozaĵo; kuriozeco

curium, kuriumo

curl, (hair etc.; wavy), frizi [tr], krispigi; ~iĝi, krispiĝi; (spirals, ringlets), bukli [tr]; (single lock of hair), buklo; (wind, gen), volvi [tr]; volviĝi; volv(aĵ)o; **curly,** krispa; bukla; **(hair) curler,** buklilo; **curl up,** (as in bed), buliĝi; (as re leaf), volviĝi

curlew, numenio, kurlo

curlicue, volvaĵeto

curling, (game), glitŝton/ludo; **curling stone,** ~o

curmudgeon, grumblulo, malagrablulo, malafablulo

currant, (*Ribes:* plant or berry), ribo; **black currant,** nigra ~o; **red cur-**

rant, ruĝa ~o; **white currant,** blanka ~o

currency, (cash, not checks etc.), kontant/aĵo, ~a mono; (official $ of a country), valuto; (current validity), aktualeco; (circulation), cirkulado; **unit of currency,** monunuo

current, (elec), kurento; (any flow), fluo; (air draft), trablovo; (now in effect), aktuala, kuranta, nuna; (circulating), cirkulanta; **alternating current,** (abb: A.C.), alterna ~o [abb: A.K.]; **direct current,** (abb: D.C.), kontinua ~o [abb: K.K.]; **eddy current,** (elec), kirlo~o; (oth), kirlofluo; **Japan Current,** Kuroŝio; [name oth ocean currents by "fluo" (e.g.: *Humboldt Current:* Fluo de Humboldt); see also "stream"]

curriculum, kursaro

currier, (leatherworker), ledpretigisto

curry, (rub down [horse etc.], comb), strigli [tr]; (food), kareo; **currycomb,** ~ilo; **curry favor,** kultivi favoron

curse, (opp "bless"), malbeni [tr]; ~o; (blaspheme), blasfemi [int]; blasfemo; (use vulgar language), sakri [int] [see "word: 'four-letter' word"]

cursive, kursiva

cursor, kursoro†

Cursorius cursor, kurbirdo

cursory, traglita, supraĵa

curt, abrupta

curtail, mallongigi, malpliigi

curtain, (on window; theat; lit or fig), kurteno; ~i [tr]; (parapet), kurtino; **Iron Curtain,** Fer~o; **Bamboo Curtain,** Bambu~o

curtsey, (genua) riverenco; (genue) riverenci [int]

curve, kurbo; ~igi; ~iĝi; **curved,** ~a; **curvature,** ~eco; **curvy, curvaceous,** ~oplena; **curvilinear,** ~linia

Cuscuta, kuskuto

Cush, Kuŝ; **Cushitic,** ~ida

cushion, (gen), kuseno; ~i [tr]; **pincushion,** ~eto

cushy, (soft, as job etc.), dorlota

cusp, (math; ast; arch), kuspo; (anat: e.g., re heart valve), kuspido

cuspid, kanido; **bicuspid,** premolaro;

tricuspid, tripinta dento
cuspidate, kusphava
cuspidor, kraĉujo
cuss, (curse), [see "curse"]; (person), perversulo, aĉulo; **cussed,** perversa, aĉa
custody, (guarding, care, gen), vart/ado, prizorgado; (detention), malliberigo, gardo; **custodial,** ~a, prizorga; **custodian,** ~into; ~anto; ~onto; ~isto; (janitor), purigisto
custom, (habit, usage), kutimo, uzanco; (social convention, mores), ~o, moro; **customary,** ~a; **custom-made, custom-built,** laŭmende farita (konstruita, tajlita, etc.); **customize,** laŭmendigi, individuecigi; **customs,** (at border: tax or bureau), dogano; **go through customs, clear customs,** tradoganiĝi, trapasi la doganon; **customs house (office),** doganejo; **customs official,** doganisto; **customs union,** doganunio
customer, kliento
cut, (as w knife, gen, lit or fig; sever, incise; divide card deck; hit [tennis etc.] ball certain way), tranĉi [tr]; ~iĝi; ~o; (as w scissors, shears), tondi [tr]; tondiĝi; tondo; (stab, pierce), piki [tr]; (pierce through, as new tooth), trapiki [tr]; (cut into parts), dis~i [tr]; (hew), haki [tr]; (mow, reap), falĉi [tr]; (pass through, intersect), tra~i [tr], sekci [tr]; (snub), malrekoni [tr], malagnoski [tr]; (not attend, as class etc.), malĉeesti [tr]; (turn off: mech), haltigi, malstarti [tr], malfunkciigi; (turn off: elec), malŝalti [tr]; (stop any activity), ĉesigi; (reduce, lessen), redukti [tr], malpliigi; (facet gem), klivi [tr], faceti [tr]; faceto; (fabric for garment), tajli [tr], fasoni [tr]; tajl(ad)o; (style of garment), fasono; (haircut style), tondofasono; (dilute), dilui [tr]; (dissolve), solvi [tr]; (edit out, as from movie, written material), elredakti [tr]; (turn as wheels), turni [tr] (e.g.: *cut the wheels sharply:* turni la radojn akute); (make sound or video recording), registri [tr]; registro; (pass, go), pasi [int] (e.g.: *let's cut through the library:* ni pasu tra la biblioteko); (part,

slice cut off), ~aĵo; (share), dividaĵo; **cutting,** (anything cut off), (de)~aĵo; **cutter,** (any cutting tool), ~ilo; tondilo; ~maŝino, tondmaŝino; (person), ~isto; tondisto; (boat), kutro; **a cut above,** iom pli bona ol, (en) tavolo super; **cut across,** (go across, take shortcut), transiri [tr]; (traffic on cross street etc.), krucpasi [tr]; **cut and dried,** (simple), simpla, senproblema, rutina; (prearranged), antaŭaranĝita; (dull), malsprita; **cut and run,** forkuri [int]; **cutaway,** (coat), frako; cut back, (shorten, gen), mallongigi; (lessen, gen), malpliigi; (re bush etc., to near ground), recepi [tr]; **cut both ways,** ~i duflanke; **cut down,** (reduce), redukti [tr], malpliigi; (chop off, lit or fig), dehaki [tr]; **cut (someone) down to size,** senpompigi, malpufigi; **cut in,** (into line, as traffic or queue), enviciĝi, envicigi (sin); (interrupt), interrompi [tr]; (to couple dancing), entrudi (sin); (connect into elec circuit), konektiĝi, encirkvitiĝi; (share w), dividi [tr] kun; **cut it out,** ĉesi [int] [see "cut out" below]; **cut it out!,** ĉesigu tion!; **cut loose,** senbridiĝi (sin); **cut no ice (with),** neniel impresi [tr], tute ne impresi, neniel efiki [int] (sur, ĉe); **cut off,** (break off, sever), de~i [tr]; (limit), limigi; (stop abruptly), ĉesigi; (interrupt), interrompi [tr]; (intercept), interkapti [tr]; (disconnect, as phone etc.), malkonekti [tr]; (obstruct), obstrukci [tr], bari [tr]; (deprive of), senigi de, sen...igi, forbari [tr], forfermi [tr], forŝlosi [tr] (e.g.: *the besieging army cut off the city's food supplies:* la sieĝanta armeo senigis la urbon de ĝiaj nutroprovizoj; *he cut his son off from his inheritance:* li senheredigis sian filon); **cut out,** (w knife), el~i [tr]; (w scissors), eltondi [tr]; (eliminate), elimini [tr]; (leave out, omit), ellasi [tr]; (stall, re motor etc.), panei [int]; (leave), foriri [int]; (stop activity), ĉesigi (e.g.: *cut that out!:* ĉesigu tion!); (deprive of), [see "cut off" above]; **cut out for,** (fit for), taŭga por; **cut-rate,** malaltpreza, malmultekosta, ĉipa; **cut short**, (stop), abrupte halt(ig)i; abrupte ĉes(ig)i [see "stop"]; (interrupt), interrompi [tr]; **cutthroat**, (murderer), murdisto, murdinto; (murderous), murd(ec)a; (ruthless), senkompata; (w/o partner), unuopa, senpara; **cut through**, tra~i [tr], penetri [tr]; **cut up**, (into pieces), dis~i [tr], dispecigi; distondi [tr]; dishaki [tr]; (misbehave), miskonduti [int]; **cold cut**, fridkotleto; **shortcut**, (lit or fig), kurtvojo

cutaneous, haŭta; **subcutaneous**, sub~a

cutch, kateĉuo

cute, (pretty), beleta, bonaspekta; (witty), sprita; **cutesy**, ~aĉa

cuticle, (gen), kutiklo

cutireaction, kutireakcio

cutis, dermo

cutlas(s), sabreto

cutler, trančil/isto; **cutlery**, ~aro

cutlet, (gen), kotleto; (veal), ~o, eskalopo

-cy, (sfx: quality, condition of; rank), ~eco

cyanate, cianato; **cyanic acid**, ~a acido

Cyanea, cianeo, brulmeduzo

cyanide, cianido; ~izi [tr]

cyan(o)–, (chem radical: CN), cian(o)–

cyanogen, ciano

Cyanophyta, blualgoj

cyanosis, cianozo; **cyanotic**, ~a

cyanurate, cianur/(at)o; **cyanuric acid**, ~a acido

Cybele, Cibela

cybernate, aŭtomatizi [tr]; **cybernation**, ~ado

cybernetic, cibernetika; **cybernetics**, ~o

Cyclades, Cikladoj

cyclamate, cikloheksilsulfamato

cyclamen, *Cyclamen*, ciklameno

cyclane, ciklano

cycl/e, (gen), ciklo; (bicycle), biciklo; bicikli [int]; (move through cycle), ~i [int]; **cyclic(al)**, ~a, perioda [cp "period"]; **cyclist**, biciklisto; motor~isto; **acyclic**, acikla; **recycle**, re~igi; re~iĝi; **kilocycle**, kilo~o; **megacycle**, mega~o; **motorcycle**, motor~o; **vicious cycle**, neelirebla cirklo

cyclo–, (pfx), ciklo–

cycloid, cikloido

cyclometer, ciklometro

cyclone, ciklono; **anticyclone**, anti~o

cycloparaffin, cikloparafino

Cyclops, Ciklopo

cyclorama, ciklopejzaĝo

cyclostome, ciklostomo

cyclostomi, **cyclostomata**, ciklostomoj

cyclotron, ciklotrono; **synchrocyclotron**, sinkro~o

cyder, cidro

Cydonia, cidonio

cygnet, cignido

Cygnus, (ast), Cigno

Cygnus, (zool), cigno; *Cygnus cygnus*, kanto~o

cylinder, cilindro; **cylindrical**, ~a; **cylinder head**, (motor), kulaso

cyma(tium), cimatio

cymbal, cimbalo

Cymbalaria muralis, cimbalario

cymbalom, cymbalon, zimbalono

Cymbopogon nardus, citronelo

cyme, cumo

Cymric, Kimra

Cynara, artiŝoko; Cynara cardunculus, Hispana ~o, kardono

cynic, (modern skeptic), skeptik/ulo; (of ancient phil school), cinikulo; **cynical**, ~a; cinika; **cynicism**, ~ismo; cinikismo

Cynips, cinipo

Cynocephalus, galeopiteko

Cynodon, cinodonto

Cynoglossum, cinogloso; Cynoglossum officinale, hundolango

cynosurus, cinozuro, hundovosto

Cyperus esculentus, termigdalo

cypher, [see "cipher"]

Cypraea, cipreo

cypress, cipreso

Cyprian, (of Cyprus), Cipra; (man's name), Cipriano

Cyprinus, ciprino; Cyprinus carassius, karaso; Cyprinus carpio, karpo; Cyprinidae, ~edoj; Cypriniformes, ~oformaj (fiŝoj)

cypripedium, Cypripedium, cipripedio

Cyprus, Cipro; **Cypriot**, ~a; ~ano

Cyrenaica, Cirenio

Cyrene, Cireno

Cyril, Cirilo
Cyrillic, cirila
Cyrus, Ciro
cyst, (sac), cisto; (tumor), kisto; **cystitis**,
~ito; **cystocele**, cistocelo
cysteine, cisteino
Cystercian, Cistercia
cysticercus, cisticerko;   **cysticercosis**,
~ozo
cystine, cistino
Cystopteris, cistopterido
Cythera, Citera
Cytherea, Citerea
Cytinus, citino
Cytisus, citizo
cytochrome, citokromo
cytology, citolog/io; **cytologist**, ~o
cytophylaxis, citofilakto
cytoplasm, citoplasmo
cytotropic, citotropa
czar, caro; **czarina**, ~ino
czárdás, ĉardaŝo
Czech, Ĉeĥo; ~a; **the Czech Republic**,
la ~a Respubliko
Czechoslovak, Ĉeĥoslovaka;   **Czecho-**
slovakia, ~io

D

dab, (pat lightly), dabi [tr]; ~o; (zool: *Limanda*), limando
dabble, (dip), trempeti [tr]; (deal slightly w), diletanti [int]
da capo, (mus), dekomence
dace, leŭcisko
dachshund, vertago, melhundo
Dacia, Dacio; Dacian, ~o; ~a
dacron, sinteza poliestro
dacryoadenitis, dakrioadenito
dacryocyst, dakriocisto; dacryocystitis, ~ito
dactyl, daktilo
dactylography, daktiloskopio   [not "daktilograf–"]
dad, paĉjo
dada, dadaism, dadaismo; dadaist, dadaisto
daddy, paĉjo; daddy-longlegs, (zool: *Phalangida*), falangio; (*Tipula*), tipulo
dado, panelo
Daedalus, Dedalo
daemon, dajmono
daffodil, dafodilo; sea daffodil, pankracio
daffy, daft, frenezeta, ventkapa
dagger, (weapon), ponardo; ~i [tr]; (symbol "†"), ~osigno
Daghestan, Dagestano
Dagobert, Dagoberto
daguerrotype, (picture), dagerotipo; (process), ~io
dahlia, Dahlia, dalio, georgino
Dahomey, Dahomeo [cp "Benin"]
daily, ĉiutaga; ~e; (newspaper), (~a) ĵurnalo
daimio, daimio
dainty, delikata
daiquiri, dajkirio*
Dairen, Dajren
dairy, lakt/ejo; dairy cow (cattle), melkobovino(j); dairy farm, ~ejo; dairy product, ~aĵo, ~oprodukto
dais, podio
daisy, (common wild daisy, English daisy: *Bellis perennis*), lekant/eto; Michaelmas daisy, astero; oxeye

daisy, white daisy, (*Chrysanthemum leucanthemum*), ~o
Dakar, Dakaro*
Dakota, (Native American), Dakoto; North Dakota, Nord-~o; South Dakota, Sud-~o
Dalai Lama, Dalai-lamao
dale, valo
dally, (flirt), flirti [int]; (loiter, dawdle), lanti [int], malrapidi [int]; dalliance, ~ado
Dalmatia, Dalmatio; Dalmatian, ~o; ~a; ~ia; (dog), ~a hundo
dalmatic, dalmatiko
dalo, kolokasio
dal segno, (mus), de l' signo
dam, (on river), digo; ~i [tr]; (animal mother), patrino; cofferdam, koferdamo
Dama, damao
damage, (harm, cause defect), difekti [tr]; ~o; ($ etc. loss), damaĝo; damaĝi [tr]; (re ship or its cargo), averio; damages, (law: $ awarded for loss suffered), reparacio
daman, Siria prokavio
damar, [see "dammar"]
damascene, damaskeni [tr]
Damascus, Damasko
damask, (fabric), damasko
damaskeen, damaskeni [tr]
dame, (noble title, gen), damo; (vulg), ino, virinaĉo
Damian, Damiano
dammar, dammer, damarrezino [see "pine"]
damn, damni [tr]; ~ita, diabla; (interj), diable!; damned, damnable, ~inda, ~ita, diabla; God damn!, goddamn!, (interj), Dio ~u!; goddamn(ed), di~ita; I don't give a damn, tute ne gravas al mi; estas tute indiferente al mi; not worth a damn, tute senvalora
damnify, (law), damaĝi [tr]
Damocles, Damoklo
damp, (moist), humida; ~eco; ~igi; (mus: mute stringed instrument), dampi [tr]; (lessen any vibration), am-

ortizi [tr]; (spontaneous diminution of phys quantity, as voltage, sound, or oth vibration, etc.), rilaksiĝi; rilakso; **dampen**, ~igi; ~iĝi; **damper**, (mech), flapo; (for sound or oth vibration), amortizilo, obtuzilo
damsel, fraŭlino, knabino
Danae, Danaa
Danaides, Danaidinoj
Danaus, Danao
dance, (gen), danci [tr, int]; ~o; (formal ball), balo; **contradance**, kontra~i [int]; kontra~o; **folk dance**, popol~i [int]; popol~o; **square dance**, kvadrato~i [int]; kvadrato~o; **step dance**, stamf~i [int]; stamf~o; **St. Vitus's dance**, koreo, ~o de Sankta Vito [cp "disease: Parkinson's disease"]
dandelion, leontodo, buterfloro; **fall dandelion**, leontodono
dander, floketoj [note plur]; **get one's dander up**, ekkoleri [int], koleriĝi; ekkolerigi
dandle, balanci [tr]
dandruff, harflokoj, haŭteroj [note plur]
dandy, (fop), dando; (very good), unuaranga, bonega
Dane, Dano
danewort, ebulo
danger, danĝero; **dangerous**, ~a; **endanger**, en~igi
Daniel, Danielo
dank, mucida
dangle, (svinge) pendi [int]; (svinge) pendigi
danish, (pastry), dolĉebulo
Danish, (re Danes, Denmark), Dana; ~ia, ~landa
Danube, Danubo
Danzig, Dancigo
Daphne, (myth; woman's name), Dafna Daphne, (bot), dafno; Daphne mezereum, Daphne mezereon, mezereo
daphnia, Daphnia, dafnia, akvopulo
daphnid, dafnio, akvopulo
Daphnis, Dafniso
dapper, eleganta
dapple(d), makulhara
Dardanelles, Dardaneloj
dare, (have audacity), aŭdaci [tr]; (have courage), kuraĝi [tr]; (defy), defii [tr]; (exhort), instigi [tr]; instigo; **daring**,

~a; ~o; kuraĝa; kuraĝo; **dare-devil**, ĉioriskulo; **not dare**, (fear to), timi [tr], ne kuraĝi [tr] (e.g.: *I didn't dare try that:* mi timis provi tion [or] mi ne kuraĝis provi tion)
Dar es Salaam, Dar-es-salamo*
daric, darkemono
dariole, dariolo
Darius, Dario
dark, (not light), mallumo; ~a, obskura; (swarthy, dark-skinned), nigreta; (unclear), malklara; (evil), fia; (ominous), sinistra; (re colors), malhela, malhel– [pfx] (e.g.: *dark blue:* malhelblua); **darken**, ~igi; ~iĝi; malheliĝi; malheliĝi; **in the dark**, (ignorant), senscia, neinformita
darling, kara; ~ul(in)o
darn, (patch), fadenfliki [tr]; (damn), diabla; (interj), diable!, aĥ!, oj!
darnel, lolo
d'arsonvalize, darsonvalizi [tr]; **d'arsonvalism**, ~ado
dart, (little arrow), sag/eto; (fly like arrow), ~i [int]; (in garment), pinĉfaldo; **darts**, (game), ĵet~ludo
Darwin, (person or city), Darvino; **Darwinian**, ~(ism)a; ~isto; **Darwinism**, ~ismo
das, prokavio
dash, (smash), frakasi [tr]; ~iĝi; (splash); ĵetverŝi [tr]; (destroy), detrui [tr] (e.g.: *dash one's hopes:* detrui ies esperojn); (rush), hasti [int]; (run), kuri [int]; kuro; (verve, spirit), vigleco, spriteco; (long hyphen: "—"), (halto)streko; (small amount), iometo, iomete (da); **dashboard**, (of car etc.), panelo
dashiki, daŝiko*
dassie, prokavio
dastard, kovard/ulo; **dastardly**, ~a
dasymeter, dasimetro
Dasyprocta aguti, agutio
Dasypus, dazipo; Dasypus sexcinctus, armadelo; Dasypodidae, ~edoj
data, (tech), datenoj [note sing]; (nontech), donitaĵoj, informoj; **database**, ~bazo; **electronic data processing**, komputorado
date, (day), dato; ~i [tr]; ~iĝi (e.g.: *date a letter:* ~i leteron; *the style of the*

painting dates it from the 17th Century: la stilo de la pentrajô ĝin ~as de la 17-a Jarcento; *that fossil dates from the Pleistocene:* tiu fosilio ~iĝas de la Plejstoceno); (appointment, social engagement), rendevuo; rendevu(ad)i kun, rendevuig(ad)i; (fruit), daktilo; **Chinese date**, (fruit), jujubo; (tree), jujubarbo; **date-stamp**, ~ilo; ~i per ~ilo; **date palm**, daktilarbo, daktilujo; **antedate**, (precede), antaŭi [tr]; **due date**, matur~o; **misdate**, mis~i [tr]; **outdated**, **out of date**, eksmoda, eks~a, malvalidiĝinta, malaktuala; **go out of date**, eksmodiĝi, eks~iĝi, malvalidiĝi, malaktualiĝi; **postdate**, post~i [tr]; **predate**, (precede), antaŭi [tr]; (mark earlier date), antau~i [tr]; **to date**, (adv), ĝis nun; (adj), ĝis-nuna; **update**, ĝis~igi; ĝis~igo; **up to date**, laŭmoda, aktuala, moderna; **bring up to date**, ĝis~igi, aktualigi, modernigi; **International Date Line**, Internacia D~linio
dative, dativo
datum, datenero† [see "data"]
datura, daturo
Datura, daturo; Datura stramonium, stramonio
daub, ŝmiri [tr]; ~o; ~ajô
Daucus carota, karoto
daughter, filino; **daughter-in-law**, bo~o; **stepdaughter**, duon~o; **goddaughter**, bapto~o
daunt, timigi, senkuraĝigi; **daunting**, ~a, senkuraĝiga; **undaunted**, **dauntless**, ne~ita, ne~ebla, sentima, kuraĝa
dauphin, daŭfeno; **dauphine**, ~ino
davenport, (couch), kanapo; (Br: table), skribotablo
David, Davido
davit, davito
dawdle, lanti [int], malrapidi [int]
dawn, aŭroro, tagiĝo; (begin, lit or fig), ~i [int], tagiĝi; **it dawned on me**, mi ekkomprenis, mi ekkonstatis, venis en mian kapon
day, (period of ~light or 24 hours), tago; ~a; (diurnal), diurno; (time, era), tempo, epoko (e.g.: *in this day of instant communication:* en ĉi tiu tempo [or] epoko de tuja komunikado); (work

shift), skipo (e.g.: *work an 8-hour day:* labori 8-horan skipon); **day-break**, ~iĝo; **day is breaking**, ~iĝas; **day-care**, ~~vartado; ~~varta; **day-care center**, ~~vartejo; **daydream**, revi [int]; rev(ad)o; **daylight**, ~lumo; ~luma; **daylong**, tut~a, ~odaŭra; **day off**, (w/o work), liber~o, ferio; **an off day**, (unfavorable), malfavora ~o; **leap-year day**, (29 Feb.), super~o; **midday**, (noon), ~mezo; ~meza; **name day**, nomfesto; **weekday**, **workday**, labor~o; labor~a; **the other day**, (a few days ago), antaŭ kelkaj ~oj; **one of these days**, iun ~on, iam baldaŭ; **these days**, **nowadays**, nuntempe; **present-day**, nuntempa; **latter-day**, lastatempa; **day-to-day**, ĉiu~a
daze, stuporo; ~igi; **dazed**, ~a
dazzle, (w too much light, lit or fig), blindumi [tr]; ~o; (amaze), mirigi
D.C. (abb of "direct current"), K.K. [abb of "kontinua kurento"]; (abb of "District of Columbia"), [see under "Columbia"]
DDT, (abb of "dichlorodiphenyltrichloroethane"), DDT [abb of "diklordifenil–trikloretano"]
de–, (pfx: separation), de– (e.g.: *derail:* dereliĝi); (opp), mal– (e.g.: *deactivate:* malaktivigi); (removal), des–, sen– (e.g.: *deodorize:* desodori; *debug:* senbestetigi)
deacon, (in charge of rel district), dekano; (lay church assistant), diakono; **deaconess**, ~ino; **archdeacon**, arki~o
dead, (w/o life, lit or fig), morta; (certain), certa, tutcerta (e.g.: *a dead shot:* certa pafisto); (exact), preciza (e.g.: *dead center:* preciza centro); (complete), kompleta (e.g.: *dead stop:* kompleta halto); **deaden**, (sound, feeling), obtuzigi, malakrigi [cp "damp"]; **dead-end**, senelira; senelirejo; **deadbeat**, (person), nepagemulo, ŝuldrifuzanto; **dead heat**, (in race), kunvenko; **deadline**, (date), limdato; (time), limtempo, limhoro; **deadlock**, plenhalto, senvenko; plenhalti [int]; plenhaltigi; **deadly**, (lethal), letala, ~iga, pereiga; (deathly),

~(ec)a; **deadly nightshade,** (bot), beladono; **Dead Sea,** Maro M~a; **the dead of the night (winter),** la plej profunda nokto (vintro); **be a dead ringer for,** mirinde simili [tr, int] (al), esti mirinde simila al; **be dead set (on, against),** senmove, senŝancele (intenci [tr], kontraŭi [tr])

deaf, surda; **deafen,** ~igi; **deafness,** ~eco; **deaf-mute,** ~amuta; ~amutulo; **go deaf,** ~iĝi

deal, (give out), distribui [tr], disdoni [tr]; (bsns), komerci [int]; (bsns, $ transaction), transakcio; (deal in used or cheap items), brokanti [int]; (deal in illegal drugs etc.), ŝakri [tr]; (bsns or oth agreement), (inter)konsento; **deal with,** (act toward), trakti [tr] (e.g.: *we'll deal with that problem tomorrow:* ni traktos tiun problemon morgaŭ); (cope w), elteni [tr] (e.g.: *I cannot deal with their opposition:* mi ne povas elteni ilian kontraŭadon); (have to do w, have as theme), temi pri (e.g.: *my question deals with your position:* mia demando temas pri via pozicio); **dealer,** (bsns), komercisto; (card game), disdonisto; (peddler etc.), brokantisto; (drug pusher etc.), ŝakristo; **cut a deal,** kontrakti [int], fari kontrakton; **a good deal (of),** (much, many), multa(j) (el); multe (da) (e.g.: *a good deal of the members came:* multaj el la membroj venis; *a good deal of rain fell:* multe da pluvo falis); **a great deal (of),** multega(j) (el); multege (da); **a big deal,** granda afero

dean, (university etc.), dekano; (oldest in group), dojeno

dear, (beloved; informal letter greeting), kara; ~ul(in)o (e.g.: *yes, my dear:* jes, mia ~a; *Dear Pete:* K~a Peĉjo); (formal letter greeting), estimata (e.g.: *Dr. Mr. Ivanov:* Estimata s-ro Ivanov; *Dear Sirs (Sir or Madam):* Estimataj (ge)s-roj); (expensive), multekosta, altpreza, ~a; **dear me!,** ho ve!; **endear,** amatigi, ~igi

dearth, manko, nesufiĉo, malabundo

death, morto; **deathly,** ~(ec)a; ~(ec)e; **deathbed,** ~lito; **death blow,** ~bato;

death duty, (Br), heredimposto; **death rate,** ~okvanto; **death rattle,** ~ostertoro; **death throes,** agonio; **death warrant,** ekzekutordono; **put to death,** (kill, gen), ~igi; (execute), ekzekuti [tr]; **deathly ill, at death's door,** ~malsana

debacle, (defeat), malvenkego; (failure), fiaskego, malsukcesego

debar, elbari [tr], malpermesi [tr]

debark, (from ship), elŝip/igi; ~iĝi; (plane), elaviigi; elaviiĝi

debase, degenerigi; ($), malnobligi

debate, debati [tr]; ~o; **debateable,** ~inda

debauch, diboĉi [int]; ~igi; **debauched,** ~a; **debauchery,** ~(ad)o

debenture, obligacio

debilitate, debil/igi; **debilitated,** ~a, ~igita; **debility,** ~eco

debit, debeto; ~i [tr]

debonair(e), afabla, sprita

Deborah, Debora

debouch, eliri [int]

debris, rubo, disrompaĵoj

debt, ŝuldo; **in debt, indebted,** ~a; **be in debt, be indebted,** ~i [tr, int]; **indebtedness,** ~o; **debtor,** ~anto; **national debt,** ŝtat~o; **go into debt,** en~iĝi; **get out of debt,** kviti̇ĝi; **clear from debt,** kvitigi

debut, debuti [int]; ~igi; ~o

debutant(e), debutant(in)o

deca–, (pfx), deka–

decade, (10 years), jardeko; (10 days), dekado; (any group of 10), dekopo

decadent, dekadenca; **be decadent,** ~i [int]; **decadence,** ~o

decagon, dekangulo, dekagono

decahedron, dekedro

decal, glu/bildo, trans~ebla bildo; ~etikedo

decalin, dekaleno

Decalog(ue), dekalogo

Decameron, Dekamerono

decanal, dekana

decane, dekano

decant, dekanti [tr], deverŝi [tr]

decanter, karafo

decapitate, senkapigi

decapod, dekapodo

Decapolis, Dekapolo

decate, dekati [tr]
decathlon, dekatlono
decatize, dekati [tr]
decay, (rot), putri [int]; ~iĝi; ~(ad)o; ~(aĵ)o; (decompose, gen), malkomponi [tr], diserigi; malkomponiĝi, diseriĝi; (lessen, re any phys quantity, as vibration, radioactivity, etc.), amortiziĝi; amortiziĝo; (become decadent), dekadenci [int]; dekadenco; (re tooth), kariiĝi; kariiĝo [cp "cavity"]
Deccan (Plateau), Dekkano
decease, morti [int]; **deceased**, ~a; **predecease**, antaŭ~i [tr]
decedent, mortinta; ~o
deceive, trompi [tr]; **deceit**, ~o; **deceitful**, ~(em)a
decelerate, malakceli [tr]; ~iĝi
December, decembro
decemvir, decemviro
decennium, jar/deko; **decennary**, ~deko; dek~a; **decennial**, dek~a
decent, deca; **be decent**, ~i [int]; **decency**, ~o
deception, trompo; **deceptive**, ~(em)a; **self-deception**, mem~o
deci–, (pfx), deci–
decibel, decibelo
decide, (conclude), decidi [tr]; (determine), determini [tr]; **decided**, (definite, clear-cut), definitiva, klara, evidenta
decidua, deciduo
deciduous, decidua
decillion, (Am: 10^{33}), kviniliardo; (Br: 10^{60}), dekiliono [see § 19(b)]
decimal, (re fractions etc.), decimala; ~o; (math: base 10), dekaria†; **decimal point**, ~a markilo [avoid "~a punkto" or "~a komo", as these may be ambiguous: see § 19(e)]
decimate, dekumi [tr]
decipher, deĉifri [tr]
decision, decido; **decisive**, (causing decision), ~iga; (firmly deciding), ~(em)a
deck, (of ship), ferdeko; (of cards), kartaro; (ornament), ornami [tr]; **deckhouse**, rufo; **afterdeck**, post~o; **flightdeck**, flug~o; **poop deck**, **quarter deck**, pobo, poŭpo; **deck with flags**, flagi [tr]

declaim, deklami [tr]; **declamation**, ~o; **declamatory**, ~a
declare, deklari [tr]; **declaration**, (act), ~o; (thing declared), ~aĵo, deklaracio
declension, deklinacio
declination, deklinacio
decline, (refuse), rifuzi [tr], malakcepti [tr]; (gram), deklinacii [tr]; (decadence), dekadenci [int]; (wane, lessen), malpliiĝi, malkreski [int]; malpliiĝo, malkresko
declivity, (malsuprena) deklivo; **declivitous**, kruta
decoct, dekokti [tr]
decode, deĉifri [tr]
décolletage, dekolt/aĵo; **décolleté**, ~ita
decompose, (break up), malkombini [tr], disigi; ~iĝi, disiĝi; (rot), putri [int]; putrigi
décor, dekoro
decorate, (ornament), ornami [tr]; (re decor), dekori [tr]; (medal), medali [tr]; (give honorary title to), ordeni [tr]; **decoration**, ~o; ~ado; dekorado; medalo; ordeno; **decorative**, ~a; **decorator**, ~isto; dekoristo
decorticate, senŝeligi
decorum, deco; **decorous**, ~a
découpage, eltond/aĵo; ~ado
decoy, (gen), forlogi [tr]; ~ilo; (bird etc. in hunting), logbirdo
decrease, (gen), malpli/igi, malkreskigi; ~iĝi, malkreski [int]; ~iĝo, malkresko; (re specific quantity), ~...igi; ~...iĝi; ~...iĝo (e.g.: *decrease in size*: ~grandigi (etc.); *decrease in value*: ~valorigi (etc.))
decree, dekreti [tr]; ~o
decrement, (decrease), [see "decrease"]; (loss), perdiĝo; (waste), malŝpariĝo; (math), dekremento
decrepit, kaduka
decrepitate, (heat), dekrepit/igi; (crackle due to heating), ~i [int]; **decrepitation**, (heating process), ~igo; (crackling sound), ~o
decry, mallaŭdi [tr]
decubitus, dekubito
dedicate, dediĉi [tr]; **dedicated**, (fervent), fervora, sin~a
deduce, dedukti [tr]; **deduction**, ~(ad)o
deduct, (subtract, gen), subrahi [tr]; ($

from pay), depagi [tr]; (from account etc.), dekalkuli [tr], elkalkuli [tr]; [not "dedukti"]; **deduction**, ~o; depago; dekalkulo; **deductible**, (insurance), franĉizo

deed, (act), faro, ago; (document), akto; (transfer ownership), donatesti [tr]; **misdeed**, mis~o, misago; **transfer deed**, donatesto

deejay, diskludisto

deem, (declare, presume, treat as if), supozi [tr] (e.g.: *a child living with its parents is deemed dependent on them:* infano loĝanta kun siaj gepatroj estas ~ata esti dependa de ili); (think, opine), opinii [tr]

deep, (gen), profunda; ~(aĵ)o; **deepen**, ~igi; ~iĝi; (darken), malheligi; malheliĝi; **deep-freeze**, ~e frostigi, frostegigi; frostegigilo; **deep-fry**, trempfriti [tr]; **deep-rooted**, **deep-seated**, ~radika; **deep-sea**, ~amara

deer, cervo; **fallow deer**, damao; **mouse deer**, tragolo; **musk deer**, moskulo; **pudu deer**, puduo; **roe deer**, kapreolo

deface, profani [tr], difekti [tr]

de facto, laŭfakta, efektiva

defalcate, malversacii [tr]

defame, kalumnii [tr]

default, (failure to fulfill obligation etc.), malplenumi [tr]; ~o; (failure to appear), neapero; (lack, absence), manko; (cmptr etc.: assumed value), defaŭltot

defeat, venki [tr]; (act of conquering), ~(ad)o; (state of being defeated), mal~o; **be defeated**, mal~i [int], esti ~ita; **defeatism**, defetismo; **defeatist**, defetisma; defetisto; **self-defeating**, sinkontraŭa

defecate, feki [int]; (vulg), kaki* [int]

defect, (imperfection), difekto; (blemish), makulo; ~eto; (leave country, party, etc., for another), transiri [int]; (leave a movement, gen), kabei [int]; **defective**, ~ita

defend, defendi [tr]; **defendant**, ~anto; akuzito; **defense, defence**, ~(ad)o; **defensible**, ~ebla; **defensive**, (defending), ~a; (mil, pol policy etc.), defensivo; defensiva; **self-defense**,

sin~o; **on the defensive**, je la defensivo

defer, (delay), prokrasti [tr]; (yield), cedi [tr, int]

deference, respekto, cedemo; **deferential**, ~(oplen)a, cedema

deferent, (sperm duct), deferenta kanalo

defiant, defia, spita

deficiency, nesufiĉo, manko; (med), karenco; **deficient**, neadekvata, ~a; **be deficient in**, havi ~an (neadekvatan), manki al (iu, io) (e.g.: *her diet is deficient in vitamins:* ŝia dieto havas neadekvatajn vitaminojn [or] mankas al ŝia ŝia dieto adekvataj vitaminoj; *his French is deficient:* lia Franca estas neadekvata)

deficit, deficito; ~a

de fide, laŭfida

defilade, desfili [tr]; ~iĝi; ~o

defile, (march single-file), defili [int]; (narrow passage), ~ejo; (profane), profani [tr], malsanktigi

define, (give meaning, describe), difini [tr]; (determine, set), determini [tr], fiksi [tr], establi [tr]; (delineate), dislimi [tr]; **definition**, ~o; determino, fikso, establo; dislimo; (re lens, TV, phot, etc.), akreco, klareco, fokus(iv)o

definite, (certain), definitiva; (exact, sharply defined), difinita; **definitely**, ~e; **definite article**, (gram), difina artikolo; **indefinite article**, nedifina artikolo

definitive, definitiva

deflagrate, deflagracii [int]; **deflagration**, ~o

deflate, (let air out), malpuf/igi; ~iĝi, malŝveli [int]; ($), deflaciigi; deflaciiĝi; **deflation**, ~igo; ~iĝo; deflacio

deflect, devi/igi; **deflection**, ~o; ~igo; **angle of deflection**, ~a angulo

deflower, deflori [tr], (law), stupri [tr]; **defloration**, ~o, stupro

defoliate, senfoliigi; **defoliant**, ~enzo

deform, deformi [tr], misformi [tr]; ~iĝi, misformiĝi; **deformity**, (gen), ~aĵo, misformaĵo; (crippling), kriplaĵo

defraud, fraŭdi [tr]

defray, pagi [tr], re~i [tr], rekompenci [tr]

deft, lerta
defunct, (gen), morta; (ceased, former), ĉesinta, eksa
defy, defii [tr], spiti [tr]
degenerate, degeneri [int]; ~inta; ~into; degeneracy, ~inteco; degeneration, ~ado; degenerative, ~a; ~iga
degrade, (decompose, gen), degrad/iĝi; (dishonor), malhonori [tr], malnobligi; (demote), ~i [tr]; (chem), malkomponi [tr] [cp "decadent", "degenerate", "deprave"]; degradation, malhonoro, malnobleco; malkompon(iĝ)o; biodegradable, bio~a
degree, (of temperature, angle, or oth extent), grado; (diploma), diplomo [see also "graduate"]; degrees Celsius, degrees Centigrade, ~oj (de) Celsius [abb: °C]; degrees Fahrenheit, ~oj (de) Fahrenheit, ~oj Farenhejte [abb: °F] [see § 20]; degrees Kelvin, ~oj (de) Kelvin, ~oj Kelvine [abb: °K]; Celsius degree, Celsius~o; Fahrenheit degree, Farenhejta ~o; to a high degree, ege, treege, ĝis alta ~o; to a slight degree, iomete; give one the third degree, turmenti iun
dehisce, dehiski [int]
dehydrate, deshidrat/igi, senakvigi; ~iĝi, senakviĝi
Deianira, Dejanira
deify, apoteozi [tr], diigi
deign, degni [tr]
Deimos, Dejmoso*
Deinotherium, dinoterio
deism, deismo; deist, ~a; deisto
deity, (a god), dio; (godliness), ~eco
Dejanira, Dejanira
déjà vu, jamvidaĵo
deject,deprimi [tr]; dejected, ~ita; dejection, ~o
de jure, laŭjura; ~e
Delaware, (river; Native American), Delavaro; (state), ~io
delay, prokrasti [tr], malfruigi; ~(ad)o, malfruigo
del credere, delkredera; ~o
delectable, delektinda, delica
delegate, delegi [tr]; ~ito; delegation, ~o; ~itaro, delegacio
delete, forstreki [tr]

deleterious, malutila, malhelpa, noca
Delft, Delfto
delftware, delftaĵo
Delhi, Delhio; New Delhi, Nov-~o
deli, [see "delicatessen"]
deliberate, (intentional), intenca; (careful), zorga; (ponder, consider), konsiliĝi, mediti [int]
delicate, (slight, fine, gentle, fragile, etc.), delikata; (discreet), diskreta; (re paintings etc.), morbida; delicacy, ~aĵo; ~eco; diskreteco; morbideco; (food), frandaĵo; indelicate, kruda, mal~a, malkonvena, maldeca
delicatessen, (food), gastronomi/aĵo; (shop), ~ejo
delicious, delica, bongusta, franda
delict, delikto
delight, delekti [tr], ĝojigi, ravi [tr]; ~iĝi, sin ~i; ~o, delico; delighted, ~ita; delightful, ~inda, delica; Turkish delight, lukumo
Delilah, Delila
delineate, (sketch, draw), skizi [tr], desegni [tr]; (mark off), dislimi [tr]
delinquent, (guilty), delikta; ~ulo, kulpulo; (late), malakurata; delinquency, ~o; malakurateco; juvenile delinquent, juna ~ulo
deliquesce, (chem), delikveski [int]; deliquescent, ~a
delirium, deliro; delirious, ~a; be delirious, ~i [int]; delirium tremens, trema ~o
deliver, (give over, gen), liveri [tr]; (save), savi [tr]; (give birth), naski [tr]; (help woman or animal give birth), akuŝigi [cp "labor"]; deliverance, savo; delivery, ~(ad)o; ~aĵo; nasko; general delivery, (mailing address), poŝtrestante [see § 22]; special delivery, (mail etc.), ekspreso; ekspresa; eksprese
dell, valeto
Delos, Deloso
Delphi, Delfo(j); Delphic, ~a
delphinium, Delphinium, delfinio
Delphinus, (ast), Delfeno
Delphinus, (zool), delfeno
delta, (of river), delto; (letter), delta [see § 16]
deltoid, deltoido; ~a

delude, trompi [tr], erarigi; **delusion,** (act of ~ding), ~o; (error, illusion), iluzio
deluge, diluvo; ~i [int]
deluxe, luksa
delve, (gen), fosi [tr]
demagog, demagogue, demagogo; **demagogy,** ~io
demand, (insist on), postuli [tr]; ~o; [not "demandi"]; (bsns, $), mendado (e.g.: *supply and demand:* ofertado kaj mendado); **demanding,** ~ema; (difficult), ~a, malfacila; **in demand,** ~ata; **on demand,** je ~o
demarcate, dislimi [tr]; **demarcation,** ~o; (pol), demarkacio
demean, malnobligi, humiligi
demeanor, konduto
demented, demenca, psikoza [cp "sane", "crazy"]
dementia, demenco
Demeter, Demetera
demi–, (pfx: half, partial, less), duon–
demijohn, flasko
demimonde, demimondo; **demimondaine,** ~anino
demise, morto, forpaso
demitasse, taseto
demiurge, demiurgo
democrat, demokrato; **democratic,** ~a; **democracy,** (a government), ~io; (theory, ism), ~eco; **Democrat,** D~o; **Democratic,** D~a; **social democrat,** social~o
Democritus, Demokrito; **Democritean,** ~a
demodex, Demodex, demodekso
demography, demografio; **demographer,** demografo*
demolish, (destroy, gen), detrui [tr]; (a building etc.), malkonstrui [tr]; **demolition,** detruo; malkonstruo
demon, demono
demonstrate, (prove), demonstri [tr]; (exhibit, show), montri [tr], ekspozicii [tr]; (public mass protest), manifestacii [int]; **demonstraion,** ~o; ekspozicio; manifestacio; **demonstrable,** ~ebla; **demonstrative,** (self-expressive), sinesprim(em)a; (gram), demonstrativo; demonstrativa
demoralize, demoralizi [tr]

Demosthenes, Demosteno
demote, degradi [tr]
demotic, demotika
demur, heziti [int]
demure, modesta, sinĝena
den, (lair), kuŝejo, kaŝejo, ternesto; (room), kabineto
denarius, denaro
dendrite, dendrito
Dendrocalamus, bambuso
Dendrolagus, dendrolago
dendrology, dendrologio
dengue, dengo
denial, [see "deny"]
denier, ($), denaro
denigrate, kalumnii [tr], mallaŭdi [tr]
denim, dreliko; ~a
Denis, Denizo; **Denise,** ~a; **Saint Denis, St-Denis,** (city), Sankta-~o
denizen, loĝanto
Denmark, Dan/io, ~lando
Dennis, Denizo
denominate, nomi [tr]; **denomination,** (Christian sect), konfesio; (rel, gen), religio (e.g.: *person of another denomination:* alireligiano; *interdenominational:* interreligia); (value, as of $, stamp), valoro
denominator, (math), denominatoro
denote, indiki [tr], signi [tr], kvalifiki [tr]
dénouement, elnodiĝo
denounce, (formally accuse), denunci [tr]; (condemn), kondamni [tr]
Denpasar, Denpasaro*
dense, densa; **density,** ~eco
dent, kaveto; ~igi; **make a dent in,** (have small effect), iomete (minimume) efiki [int] sur
dental, (re teeth), denta; (phon), dentalo; dentala
dentate, (w teeth), dent/hava; (re leaves etc.), ~randa
dentifrice, dentopasto
dentin(e), dentino
dentist, dent/isto; **dentistry,** ~(o)medicino
dentition, (teething), dent/okreskado; (teeth and their condition etc.), ~ostato
denture(s), dent/a protezo, art-~aro [note sing]

denude, (person), nudigi; (geol), denudi [tr]

denunciation, denunco;   kondamno [see "denounce"]

Denver, Denvero*

deny, (say no), nei [tr], negi [tr]; (reject, as accusation, truth, God, etc.), for~i [tr], fornegi [tr], rifuzi [tr]; (not admit), malkonfesi [tr]; **denial**, neo, nego; fornego, rifuzo; **self-denial**, abnegacio; **undeniable**, preterduba, certa

deodar, deodaro, Himalaja cedro

deodorize, desodori [tr], senodorigi; **deodorant**, ~enzo

deontology, deontologio

deoxyribonucleic, [see "desoxyribonucleic"]

depart, foriri [int] (de), (for)lasi [tr]; **departed**, (dead), forpasinta, formortinta; forpasinto, formortinto

department, (administrative division; French or oth pol subdivision), departemento; (branch of study etc.), fako; **departmental**, ~a; faka

depend, (gen), dependi [int]; **depend on**, ~i de; **dependable**, fidinda, kredinda; **dependent**, ~a; ~into; ~anto; ~onto; **depending on**, (according to), ~e de; **dependency**, ~aĵo; ~eco; **independent**, sen~a; **independence**, sen~eco

depict, bildigi, pentri [tr]

depilate, senharigi; **depilatory**, ~a; ~enzo

deplete, forkonsumi [tr]

deplore, bedaŭri [tr], ~egi [tr]; **deplorable**, ~ind(eg)a

deploy, deploji [tr], dismeti [tr], disloki [tr]

deponent, depozicianto [not "deponanto"]

deport, deporti [tr]; **deportation**, ~o; **deportee**, ~ito; ~ato; ~oto

deportment, konduto

depose, (make legal statement), depozicii [tr]; (remove from office), eloficigi; (from throne), detronigi

deposit, (for safekeeping, as $ in bank etc.; minerals, soil, etc., by river†), deponi [tr]; ~(aĵ)o; (prepayment), antaŭpago; (leave behind), delasi [tr];

delasaĵo; (crust), krusto; (dregs etc.), feĉo; **depositor**, ~anto; **depository**, ~ejo; **on deposit**, (deposited), ~ita; (payment), antaŭpage

deposition, (law), depozicio

depot, (rr, bus station), stacidomo; (storage), magazeno, deponejo

deprave, depravici/igi; **depraved**, ~a; **depravity**, **depravation**, ~o

deprecate, mallaŭdi [tr]; **deprecation**, ~o; **deprecatory**, ~a

depreciate, depreci [tr]; ~iĝi; **depreciation**, ~ado [cp "devalue"]

depredation, rabo

depress, (psych), deprimi [tr]; (push down, gen; $), depremi [tr]; (make cavity), kavigi; **depressant**, ~a; ~enzo; **depression**, ~o; depremo; kavigo; kavaĵo; ($; psych; geol), depresio†; **depressor**, (med: nerve), depresora (nervo); **antidepressant**, anti~a; anti~enzo

deprive, senigi (e.g.: *deprive one of life:* ~i iun je la vivo); **deprivation**, ~(ad)o

depth, profundo; ~aĵo; ~eco; **depth of field**, (phot), kampa ~o

depute, deputi [tr]; **deputation**, delegacio, ~it(ar)o; **deputize**, ~i [tr]; **deputy**, ~ito

derange, (make insane), frenez/igi, psikozigi; (disorder), malordi [tr]; **deranged**, (insane), ~a, psikoza

derby, (horse race), ĉevalvetkuro; (bowler hat), bovloĉapelo

derelict, (negligent), neglektinta; (abandoned), forlasita; forlasitaĵo; (person), senhejmulo

deride, moki [tr], priridi [tr]; **derision**, ~ado; **derisive**, ~(em)a

derive, derivi [tr]; ~iĝi; (math), derivei† [tr]; **derivative**, (gen), ~aĵo; (math), deriveo

derma, (skin), dermo [cp "skin", "dermat(o)–"]

dermat(o)–, (pfx), dermat(o)–

dermatitis, dermatito

dermatology, dermatolog/io; **dermatologist**, ~o

dermatosis, dermatozo

Dermestes, dermesto

dermis, dermo

derogatory, mallaŭda
derrick, argano [cp "crane"]
dervish, derviŝo; **whirling dervish,**
turniĝanta ~o
des–, (chem pfx), des–
descant, (mus), diskanto; ~a
Descartes, Kartezio
descend, (go down), descendi [int],
malsupreniri [int]; (re ancestry), deveni [int]; **descent,** ~o; deveno; **descendant,** posteulo, (pra)ido; **of mixed
descent,** miksdevena
describe, (esp in writing, but also gen),
priskribi [tr]; (orally), priparoli [tr];
(draw), desegni [tr] [cp "trace", "depict"]; **description,** ~o; priparolo; desegn(aĵ)o; **descriptive,** ~a
Desdemona, Desdemona
desecrate, profani [tr], malsanktigi
desert, (arid), dezerto; (mil etc.), dizerti
[tr]; **deserted,** ~a, forlasita, senhoma;
deserter, dizertinto; **desertion,** dizerto; **deserts,** (thing deserved), merit(aĵ)o; **get one's just deserts,** ricevi
laŭ sia merito
deserve, meriti [tr], esti inda je, esti
–inda (e.g.: *her proposal deserves attention:* ŝia propono ~as atenton [or]
ŝi estas atentinda); **deserving (of),**
~anta, inda (je), –inda (e.g.: *those deserving (of) respect:* tiuj ~antaj respekton [or] la respektindaj)
desiccate, (plen)sekigi; **desiccator,**
~ujo; **desiccant,** ~enzo
Desiderata, (woman's name), Deziderata
Desiderio, Dezidero
design, (detailed shape of artificial object; develop same), dezajno†; ~i [tr];
(draw, gen), desegni [tr]; desegnado;
desegnaĵo; desegnarto; (plan), celi
[tr], projekti [tr], intenci [tr]; celo, intenco; (devise, plan, develop engineering project), konstrukcii [tr];
designer, ~isto; desegnisto; konstrukciisto; **by design,** intence, laŭ intenco
designate, (nominate), nomumi [tr];
(specify), specifi [tr]; (indicate), indiki [tr], signi [tr]
desire, deziri [tr]; ~o; **desirable,** ~inda;
if you so desire, se vi tion ~as
desist, ĉesi [int]

desk, skribtablo
Desmodium, desmotropio
desmotrope, desmotropio
desolate, (desert), dezerta; ~igi, ruinigi; (forlorn, wretched), afliktita; aflikti [tr]; **desolation,** ~eco; ~igo; aflikto;
afliktiĝo
desoxyribonucleic, desoksiribonuklea;
desoxyribonucleic acid, (abb: DNA),
~a acido [abb: DNA]
despair, malesperi [int]; ~o
despatch, [see "dispatch"]
desperado, bandit(eg)o
desperate, (having little hope), senespera (e.g.: *desperate criminal:* ~a
krimulo; (offering little hope), ~iga
(e.g.: *desperate illness:* ~iga malsano); (drastic, urgent), urĝa (e.g.:
desperate need: urĝa bezono); **desperation,** ~o; **be desperate for,** bezonegi [tr], urĝe bezoni [tr]; deziregi
[tr]
despise, malamegi [tr], malestimegi [tr]
despite, (in spite of), malgraŭ (e.g.: *we
came despite the rain:* ni venis ~ la
pluvo); (scorn), malestimego
despoil, rabi [tr]
despondent, senespera, senkuraĝa, deprimita; **despondency,** ~o, senkuraĝo,
depresio
despot, despoto; **despotism,** ~ismo
dessert, deserto
destination, (place), (ir)celo; (address),
adreso
destine, destini [tr]; **destiny,** (fate), sorto; (purpose), ~o; **destined for,**
(bound for), survoja al; **predestine,**
antaŭ~i [tr]; **predestination,** antaŭ~ismo
destitute, (poor), malriĉega, senposeda, senhava; (w/o, lacking), sen, manki [int] (e.g.: *the region is destitute of
trees:* la regiono estas sen arboj [or]
mankas arboj en la regiono)
destroy, detrui [tr]; **destroyer,** (ship),
destrojero
destruct, detruo; ~iĝi; **destructible,**
~ebla; **destruction,** ~o; ~iĝo; **destructive,** ~a; ~ema; **destructor,**
~ilo; (Br), rubbrulilo; **self–destruct,**
sin~iĝi
desuetude, neuzateco

desultory, sencela, senmetoda
detach, malfiksi [tr], malligi [tr], apartigi; ~iĝi, malligiĝi, apartiĝi; (mech), malkonekti [tr]; malkonektiĝi; [see "fasten"]; detached, (separate), aparta; (aloof), indiferenta, nepersona, nepartizana
detachment, (mil), taĉmento
detail, (item, small part), detalo; ~i [tr]; (send on special mission etc., esp mil), taĉmenti [tr]; taĉmento; detailed, ~a; go into detail, ~i, prezenti ~ojn
detain, (confine, keep in custody), malliberigi, enfermi [tr]; (hold back, gen), deteni [tr]
detect, (notice, gen), rimarki [tr]; (elec, tech), detekti [tr]; detector, ~ilo, detektoro
detective, detektivo
détente, malstreĉiĝo
detention, malliberigo, enfermo; deteno [see "detain"]
deter, deturni [tr], malinstigi [tr]; deterrent, ~a; ~ilo; (repellent), forpela, malloga; mallogilo
deterge, (med), detergi [tr]
detergent, deterga; detergento†
deteriorate, degeneri [int], malpliboniĝi, (pli)malboniĝi
determine, (ascertain, establish facts), determini [tr]; (decide, fix), decidi [tr], fiksi [tr]; determined, (resolute), rezoluta, firma, insista, neŝancelebla; determinant, (math etc.), ~anto; determination, ~(ad)o; ~aĵo; decido; rezoluteco, firmeco, insisto, neŝancelebleco; determinism, (phil), ~ismo; determinist, ~isma; ~isto; indeterminate, ne~a, nepreciza; predetermine, antaŭ~i [tr]; self-determination, aŭtonomeco
detest, abomeni [tr]; detestable, ~inda
detonate, detonacii [tr], eksplodigi; detonation, ~o; detonator, ~ilo; ~enzo
detour, ĉirkaŭiri [tr]; ~o
detract, forpreni [tr], fortiri [tr]; detract from, malpliigi; detractor, mallaŭdanto
detriment, noco, malutilo; detrimental, ~a, malutila
detritus, (rock debris), ŝtoneroj, dis-

rompaĵoj [note plur]; (junk, trash), fatraso, rubo
Detroit, Detrojto
Deucalion, Deŭkaliono
deuce, (two), duo
deuterium, deŭterio
deuteromyces, deŭteromicetoj
deuteron, deŭterono
Deuteronomy, (Bib), Readmono
devastate, ruinigi, dezertigi
develop, (built up, evolve, etc.), evolui [int], disvolviĝi; ~igi, disvolvi [tr]; (work on), prilabori [tr]; (phot), riveli [tr]; riveliĝi; (build up land area), prikonstrui [tr]; development, ~(ad)o, disvolviĝ(ad)o; ~ig(ad)o, disvolv(ad)o; rivelado; prikonstruado; (built-up area), prikonstruita regiono, vorkejo†; developer, (construction), konstruentreprenisto; (phot), rivelenzo; under development, ~igata, disvolvata; developing, (country etc.), ~anta
deviate, devii [int], devojiĝi, deflankiĝi; ~anto; ~a; (from pol etc. orthodoxy), deviaciulo; deviation, ~o, devojiĝo, deflankiĝo; deviacio; (between apparent or approximate and exact, between measured and real, between aimed-at and achieved, etc.), ekarto; deviationism, (pol), deviaciismo; deviant, ~anto; ~a; deviaciulo; standard deviation, (math), varianca radiko
device, (simple machine, tool), ilo; (apparatus), aparato; (means, plan), rimedo; (motto), devizo
devil, (gen), diablo; the Devil, (la) D~o, Satano; devilish, ~a; deviltry, ~ajo(j); devil's-fig, (bot), argemono; bedevil, turmenti [tr]; between the devil and the deep blue sea, inter martelo kaj amboso; play devil's advocate, ludi rolon de kontraŭulo; devil-may-care, senzorga
devious, (indirect), malrekta; (scheming), ruz(em)a
devise, (think up, work out), elpensi [tr], ellabori [tr]; (bequeath), testamenti [tr]
devoid of, (tute) sen, (tute) malplena je
devolve, (re property), herediĝi; (re pol

power etc.), malcentralizi [tr]; (delegate authority), transpasi [tr]; (degenerate, opp "evolve"), degeneri [int], malevolui [int]; **devolution,** ~o; malcentralizo; transpaso; degenerado, malevoluado

Devonian, (geol), devonio; ~a

devote, (set aside, dedicate), dediĉi [tr] (e.g.: *devote two hours to study:* ~i du horojn al studado); **devoted,** ~ita; (loving etc.), sindona; **devotee,** adepto, amanto, –amanto [sfx] (e.g.: *devotee of music:* adepto (amanto) de la muziko [or] muzikamanto); **devotion,** ~o; (self-dedication), sin~o; (love), am(eg)o; (rel: devoutness), devoteco, pietato; (rel act, object), devotaĵo

devour, vori [tr]

devout, pia, devota; ~ulo(j)

dew, roso; **dew is forming,** ~as; **dewdrop,** ~ero; **dew point,** ~opunkto

dewclaw, ergoto

dexterous, manlerta; **dexterity,** ~eco

dextrin, dekstrino

dextro–, (tech pfx), dekstro–

dextrorota(to)ry, dekstroĝira

dextrorse, dekstruma

dextrose, dekstroglukozo, dekstrozo*

dextrous, manlerta

dey, dejo

dharma, darmo

dhow, daŭo

di–, (tech pfx: 2), di–, du–

diabase, diabazo

diabetes, diabeto; **diabetic,** ~a; ~ulo; **diabetes insipidus,** hidruria ~o; **diabetes mellitus,** sukera ~o

diabolic, diabla

diabolo, diabolo

diachronic, diakrona

diachylon, diakilo

diaclase, diaklazo

diaconal, diakona; **archidiaconal,** arki~a

diaconate, (office), diakon/eco; (group), ~aro

diacritic, diacritical mark, diakrit/aĵo. ~a signo, kromsigno; (above letter, as "ĉ"), supersigno; (below, as "ç"), subsigno [see § 16]; **diacritical,** (re mark, gen; med), ~a

diadem, diademo

diaeresis, dierezo

diagnose, diagnozi [tr]; **diagnosis,** ~o; **diagnostic,** ~a; **diagnostician,** diagnostiko; **serodiagnosis,** sero~o

diagonal, diagonalo; ~a

diagram, (gen), diagramo; ~i [tr]; (tech, elec, etc., showing parts etc.), skemo; skemi [tr]; (of any complex organism), organigramo; **schematic diagram,** konektoskemo

dial, (of analog clock or gauge, rotary phone, gauge, etc., gen), ciferplato; (call on any phone, including pushbutton), ciferi [tr] [cp "call"]; (call on rotary phone), diski [tr]; **dial tone,** voktono

dialect, dialekto

dialectic, dialektiko; ~a; **dialectics,** ~o; **dialectical,** ~a; **dialectician,** ~isto

dialog(ue), (gen), dialogo; ~i [int]; ~igi

dialyze, dializi [tr]; **dialysis,** ~o; **dialyzer,** ~ilo

diamagnetic, diamagneto; ~a; **diamagnetism,** (gen), ~ismo, ~eco

diameter, diametro; **diametrical,** ~a; **conjugate diameters,** konjugitaj ~oj

diamond, (gem, gen), diamanto; ~a; (faceted), brilianto; (lozenge shape), lozanĝo; (on playing card), karoo

Diana, Diane, Diana

dianoetic, perrezona

dianthus, dianto

Dianthus, dianto; Dianthus caryophyllus, kariofil~o

diapason, (gen), diapazono

diapedesis, diapedezo

diaper, bebtuko

diaphanous, (transparent), travidebla; (translucent), diafana

diaphragm, (gen), diafragmo

diaphysis, diafizo; **diaphysial,** ~a

diarrhea, (colloq), lakso; (med), diareo

diarthrosis, diartro

diary, taglibro

diaspora, diasporo

diaspore, diasporo

diastase, diastazo

diastole, diastolo; **diastolic,** ~a

diathermy, diatermio; **diathermic,** ~a

diathesis, diatezo

diatom, diatomeo; **diatom ooze, diato-**

maceous earth, diatomite, ~a tero, kiselguro
diatonic, diatona
diatribe, denunc(eg)o, filipiko
diazo, diazo
diazonium, diazonio; ~a
diazotate, diazotato
diazotize, diazoti [tr], diazoigi, diazoizi [tr]
dibble, plantilo
dibs, (claim), pretendo; (interj), mia!; (mi la) unua!; have first dibs on, havi la unuan rajton pri
dice, (for games), ĵetkuboj; (chop food), kubigi (e.g.: diced carrots: kubigitaj karotoj)
dichloride, diklorido
dichlorodiethyl sulfide, iperito, mustarda gaso, dikloro–dietil–sulfido
dichotomy, dikotom/eco, ~io; ~aĵo; dichotomous, ~a; dichotomize, ~iĝi
dichroism, dikroismo; dichroic, ~a
dicker, marĉandi [int]
dickey, (shirt, blouse front), frustumo
diclinous, diklina; diclinism, dicliny, ~eco
dicot(yledon), dukotiledono
Dicotyledoneae, Dicotyledones, dukotiledonoj
Dictamnus, diktamno; Dictamnus albus, Dictamnus fraxinella, fraksinelo
dictaphone, diktafono
dictate, dikti [tr]; ~aĵo, diktato; dictation, ~ado; ~aĵo; dictator, (pol), diktatoro; (gives dictation), ~into; ~anto; dictatorial, diktatoreca, diktatorema; dictatorship, diktaturo, diktatoreco
diction, (wording), vort/elekto, (~)stilo, lingvaĵo; (enunciation), elparolo, parolmaniero
dictionary, vortaro
dictum, diraĵo
did, [see "do"]
didactic, didaktika; didactics, ~o
diddle, (cheat), superruzi [tr], prifriponi [tr]
Didelphis, didelfo; Didelphidae, ~edoj
Diderot, Dideroto
Dido, Didona
Didus, dido
didymium, didimo

die, (cease life, lit or fig, gen), morti [int] [see also "death"]; (sing of "dice", for games), ĵetkubo; (for stamping coins, metal parts, etc.), patrico; die down, moderiĝi, kvietiĝi; die-hard, ĝisosta, obstina; ĝisostulo, obstinulo; die off, for~i [int]; be dying to, avide voli [tr], sopiri [int] (al); the die is cast, la decido estas farita; (fig), la kubo estas ĵetita; never say die, neniam rezignu
diecious, dioika
Diego, Diego
dielectric, dielektriko; ~a
diene, dieno
dieresis, dierezo [cp "umlaut"]
diesel, dizelo; ~a; diesel fuel, ~oleo
diet, (food; legislature), dieto; dietary, ~o; ~a; dietetic, ~a; dietetics, ~istiko; dietitian, dietician, ~isto
differ, (not same), diferenci [int], malsami [int]; (disagree), malkonsenti [int]; malakordi [int] [see "agree"]; difference, ~o; malkonsento; malakordo; different, (not same), ~a, malsama, malsam– [pfx] (e.g.: in a different way: laŭ malsama maniero [or] malsammaniere; a different kind of: malsamspeca); (another), alia; (various), diversaj; make a difference, gravi [int]; make no difference, ne gravi [int], esti tute egale, ne efiki [int]; split the difference, kompromisi [int]; dividi la ~on
differential, (re difference), diferenca; ~iga; ~igaĵo; (math), diferencialo; diferenciala; (extra pay for night, hazardous duty, etc.), supersalajro; (gear), ~iga dentradaro
differentiate, (differ, distinguish), diferenc/igi, distingi [tr]; ~iĝi, distingiĝi; (math), diferenciali [tr], diferencii [tr]
difficult, malfacila; difficulty, (gen), ~aĵo; ~eco; (impediment, complications, $ problems, etc.), embaraso
diffident, senmemfida; diffidence, ~o
diffract, difrakti [tr]; diffraction, ~o
diffuse, difuzi [tr]; ~iĝi; ~ita; diffusion, ~(iĝ)o
dig, fosi [tr]; ~aĵo; ~ejo; (colloq; critical remark), pika kritiko, piko; dig up, (disinter, lit or fig), elterigi, elfosi [tr];

take a dig at someone, pike kritiki iun

digamma, digamo†

digest, (re food; assimilate, gen), digesti [tr]; (summary), diĝesto, resumo; **digestion**, ~o; **digestive**, ~a; **indigestion**, dispepsio, mis~o

digit, (numeral), diĝito†; (finger), fingro; (toe), piedfingro; **digital**, ~a; fingra; **digitate**, fingrohava; fingreca

digitalin, digitalino

digitalis, (gen), digitalo

Digitalis, digitalo

Digitaria, digitario

digitoxin, digitoksino

dignify, dign/igi; **dignified**, ~a

dignitary, dignulo, altrangulo

dignity, digno

digraph, digramo

digress, devii [int], deflankiĝi; **digression**, digresio†, ~o

dihedral, duedro; ~a

Dijon, (city), Diĵono; (region), ~io

dike, (dam), digo

dilapidated, kaduka

dilate, dilati [tr]; ~iĝi; **dilator**, (med), ~atoro; (oth), ~ilo; ~enzo

dilatory, prokrast/ema; ~iĝ(em)a

dilemma, dilemo; **on the horns of a dilemma**, kaptita en ~o

dilettante, diletanto; **dilettantism**, ~ismo

diligent, diligenta; **diligence**, ~eco; (coach), diliĝenco

dill, (bot), aneto

Dillenia, dilenio

dillydally, lanti [int], malŝpari tempon

dilute, dilui [tr]; ~ita; **diluent**, ~a; ~enzo; **dilution**, ~(aĵ)o

diluvium, diluvo; **diluvial, diluvian**, ~a; **antediluviian**, antaŭ~a; antaŭ~ulo; antaŭ~aĵo

dim, (not bright), malhela, duonhela, duonluma; ~igi; ~iĝi; (unclear), malklara; (pale), pala; paligi; paliĝi; (dull, not lustrous), malbrila; malbriligi; malbriliĝi; (dusky), krepuska

dime, dekcendo; **a dime a dozen**, tre malmultekosta, preskaŭ senpaga, ĉipega

dimension, dimensio; (extent), ampleksso; **dimensional**, ~a; **unidimension-**

al, unu~a; **two-dimensional (three-dimensional etc.)**, du~a (tri~a etc.); **multidimensional**, plur~a

diminish, (lessen, reduce, gen), redukti [tr], malgrandigi; ~iĝi, malgrandiĝi; (phot; knitting), diminui [tr]; (mus), bemoligi; **diminished interval (chord)**, (mus), bemoligita intervalo (akordo)

diminuendo, (mus), diminuendo; ~e

diminution, (lessening, gen), redukt(iĝ)o, malgrand(iĝ)o; malgrandigo; (spontaneous damping of phys quantity, as voltage, vibration, etc.), rilakso [cp "damp"]

diminutive, (small), eta; (gram), diminutivo

Dimitri, Demetrio

dimorphic, dimorfa; **dimorphism**, ~ismo

dimple, kaveto

din, bruego

dinar, dinaro

Dinaric, Dinara

dine, manĝi [tr], tag~i [int], vesper~i [int] [see "dinner"]; **dining room**, ~oĉambro; **diner**, (person), ~anto; (restaurant), ~ejo; (rr car), ~o-vagono; **dinette**, ~alkovo

ding, ding-dong, ding-a-ling, (jingling sound, onom), tin tin tin, gilinggilang, ging-gang

dinghy, (rowboat), remboato; (rubber raft), kaŭĉukboato

dingo, dingo

dingy, (dim), malhela, malbrila; (dirty), malpura; (gloomy), morna

dinner, (in evening), vespermanĝo; (midday), tagmanĝo

Dinornis, dinornito; Dinornithidae, ~edoj; Dinornithiformes, ~oformaj (birdoj)

dinosaur, dinosaŭro

Dinosauria, dinosaŭroj

dinothere, dinoterio

dint: by dint of, per, ~e de

diocese, (Catholic, Protestant), diocezo; (Greek), eparkio

Diocletian, Diokleciano

diode, diodo; **light-emitting diode**, (abb: LED), lum–elsenda ~o [abb: LED; LED-a]; **liquid-crystal diode**,

(abb: LCD), likvakristala ~o [abb:
LKD; LKD-a]
Diodon, diodonto
Diodorus, Diodoro
dioecious, dioika
Diogenes, Diogeno
dioicous, dioika
Diomedea exulans, albatroso,   diomedeo
Diomedes, Diomedo
Dion, Diono
dionaea, Dionacea, dioneo, muŝkaptulo
Dion(n)e, (ast, myth), Diono
dionin, dionino
Dionysius, Dionizio; **Dionysia**, ~ofesto
Dionysus, **Dionysos**, Dionizo
Diophantine, diofanta
diopter, dioptrio
dioptric, dioptrika; **dioptrics**, ~o
diorama, dioramo
diorite, diorito
Dioscorea, dioskoreo
Dioscuri, Dioskuroj
Diospyros kaki, Diospyros   virginiana,
(fruit or tree), persimono
dioxane, dioksano
dioxide, dioksido; **carbon dioxide**, karbona ~o
dip, (into liquid), mergi [tr]; ~iĝi;
~(iĝ)o; (ladle out), ĉerpi [tr]; (lower,
gen), mallevi [tr]; malleviĝi, descendi
[int]; (sauce), (~)saŭco; **dipper**, (ladle), kulerego; (zool: *Cinclus*), cinklo;
dipstick, (to measure oil etc.), stangogaŭĝo; **Big Dipper**, **Little Dipper**,
(ast), [see "Ursa"]; **sheep dip**, (liquid), ŝaftrempaĵo; (basin), ŝaftrempejo
diphtheria, difterio
diphthong, diftongo
diplococcus, diplokoko
diplodocus, Diplodocus, diplodoko
diploe, diploo
diploid, duobla
diploma, (gen), diplomo; **diplomate**,
~ito; **high school diploma**, (Am),
mezlerneja ~o; (in Europe), abiturienta ~o; **grant a diploma (to)**, ~i [tr]
diplomacy, diplomat/io; **diplomat**, ~o;
diplomatic, ~a; ~ia
diplomatics, (re old documents), diplomatiko, diplomistiko
diplopia, diplopio

dipnoan, pulmofiŝo; ~a
Dipnoi, pulmofiŝoj
Dipodidae, dipodedoj
dipole, dipolo
Dipsacus, dipsako; Dipsacus   fullonum, feltkardo, fulkardo
dipsomania, dipsomanio; **dipsomaniac**, ~a; ~ulo
diptera, Diptera, dipteroj
dipteran, diptero; **dipterous**, ~a
diptych, diptiko
Dipus, dipodo
dire, (urgent), urĝa; (terrible, dreadful),
terura
direct, (straight; elec: w/o relay, as contact, TV transmission, etc.), rekta;
(w/o intermediary), senpera; (manage,
conduct; set in given direction), direkti [tr]; (aim), celi [tr]; (movie, theat),
reĝisori [tr]; (mus), konduki [tr]; **direction**, (compass etc.), direkto; (act
of directing), direktado; celado;
reĝisorado; kondukado; (instruction),
instrukcio; **directional**,   direkta;
unidirectional, unudirekta; **multidirectional**, plurdirekta; **director**, direktoro; reĝisoro; (mus), dirigento†;
directorate, **directors**, (collectively),
direkcio
directive, direktivo
directoire, **Directoire**, direktorio, D~o
directory, (phone), telefonlibro; (address book), adresaro; (any listing),
listo
directrix, (math), direktrico
dirge, funebra kanto, lamentokanto
dirigible, (airship), aerŝipo; (steerable),
direktebla ~o
dirk, ponardo; ~i [tr]
dirt, (soil, earth), tero, grundo; (dirtiness, filth), malpuraĵo; (maliciousness), fiaĵo; fieco; **paydirt**, (lit or fig),
riĉa erco; **dirty**, (unclean), malpura;
malpurigi; (unfair), fia, maldeca, maljusta; **do (one) dirt**, fitrakti [tr] (iun);
hit the dirt, fali sur~en
dis–, (pfx: away, apart), dis– (e.g.: *disintegrate:* ~eriĝi; *disseminate:*
~semi); (opp. un–), mal– (e.g.: *disconnect:* malkonekti; *disapprove:*
malaprobi); (removal), des– (e.g.: *disinfect:* desinfekti) [see also separate

entries]
disagio, disaĝio
disappoint, (not satisfy hopes, expectations, etc.; let down, cause disappointed feeling), desaponti† [tr]; (thwart),
trompi [tr]; **disappointed,** ~ita; **dis-
appointment,** ~o
disaster, katastrofo; **disastous,** ~a
disburse, elspezi [tr]; **disbursement,**
~o
disc, (gen), disko; (w disc harrow),
~plugi [tr]; **disc harrow,** ~plugilo;
disc jockey, ~ludisto; [see also
"disk"]; **discography,** (listing), ~aro;
(catalog), ~okatalog(ad)o; **discophile,**
~amanto; **discotheque,** ~oklubo;
compact disc, kompakta ~o [abb:
KD]; **compact disc, read-only memory** [abb: CD–ROM], codoroma*
(~o)
discant, diskanto
discard, (gen), forĵeti [tr], formeti [tr];
(card games), deĵeti [tr]
discarnate, elkarniĝi; ~inta; [cp "skin:
skinny"]; **discarnate entity,** ~into
discern, (perceive), percepti [tr]; (distinguish, see difference), distingi [tr];
discerning, ~ema, ~iva; distingema,
distingiva
discharge, (fire from job), maldungi
[tr]; ~(iĝ)o; (flow), flu-kvanto; (gun,
elec battery, etc.), malŝargi [tr];
malŝargiĝi; malŝarg(iĝ)o; (give off,
give out, gen), eligi; eliĝi; eligaĵo;
(unload, as cargo), malŝarĝi [tr]; (free,
release), liberigi; (from debt, duty),
kvitigi; kvitigo; (mil document), kvit-
atesto; (fulfill, as duty), plenumi [tr];
plenumo; (ooze, exude), eksudigi; eksudi [int]; eksudaĵo; (elec radiation),
efluvo; **discharge tube,** malŝargotu-
bo
disciple, disĉiplo
discipline, (gen), disciplini [tr]; ~o;
(field of study), fako; **disciplinary,**
~a; **interdisciplinary,** inter~a, inter-
faka; **disciplinarian,** ~isto; **self-disci-
pline,** sin~ado; **undisciplined,** sen~a
disclose, riveli [tr], malkaŝi [tr]; **disclos-
ure,** ~o; ~ado; ~aĵo
disco, diskoteko†
discombobulate, maltrankviligi, ĝeni

[tr], konsterni [tr]
discomfit, (thwart), obstrukci [tr], malhelpi [tr]; (make uneasy, disconcert),
maltrankviligi, ĝeni [tr], konsterni
[tr]; **discomfiture,** ~o, malhelpo;
maltrankvileco, ĝeno; (frustration),
frustracio
discommode, maloportunigi
discompose, konsterni [tr], maltrankviligi
disconcert, konsterni [tr], konfuzi [tr],
maltrankviligi
discord, (disagreement), malakordo,
malkonkordo, (poet), diskordo;
(dissension, conflict), malpaco, konflikto; (dissonance), disonanco; **discordant,** ~a, malkonkorda, diskorda;
malpaca, konflikta; disonanca; **be in
discord,** ~i [int], malkonkordi [int],
diskordi [int]; malpaci [int], konflikti
[int]; disonanci [int]
discothèque, diskoteko†
discount, ($, gen), diskonti [tr]; ~o; (re-
bate), rabati [tr]; rabato; (reject, disbelieve), malakcepti [tr], malkredi [tr]
discourage, (dishearten), senkuraĝigi;
(dissuade), malinstigi [tr]; (hinder),
malhelpi [tr]
discourse, (conversation, communication, gen), komuniki [tr]; ~ado; (dissertation), diserti [int]; diserto; (pol
speech), diskursi [int]; diskurso
discover, (gen), malkovri [tr]; (find out,
invent, etc.), eltrovi [tr]; **discovery,**
~(aĵ)o; eltrov(aĵ)o; **discoverer,** ~into
discreet, diskreta
discrepancy, (lack of accord, gen), malakordo; (between apparent or approximate and exact, between measured
and real, between aimed-at and
achieved, etc.), ekarto; **discrepant,**
~a
discrete, diskreta
discretion, (discreteness), diskreteco;
(own choice), plaĉo, bontrovo (e.g.:
do it at your discretion: faru ĝin laŭ
via plaĉo [or] bontrovo); (law), dis-
krecio; (prudence), prudento; **discre-
tionary,** laŭplaĉa; diskrecia
discriminate, (differentiate), distingi
[tr]; ~igi, diferencigi; (treat unequally
and unfairly), diskriminacii [int]; **dis-**

crimination, ~o; ~ivo; diskriminacio; **discriminatory**, diskriminacia; **indiscriminate**, sen~a
discursive, (wandering), vagema, neligita; (phil), diskursiva
discus, (ĵet)disko
discuss, diskuti [tr, int] (pri); **discussion**, ~o
disdain, disdegni† [tr], malŝati [tr]; ~o; **disdainful**, ~a
disease, malsano; (med), morbo, afekcio; **diseased**, ~a; [note: specific diseases, as those below, may be named either "~o" or "morbo"]; **Addison's disease**, ~o de Addison; **Basedow's disease**, ~o de Basedow; **Bright's disease**, ~o de Bright; **caisson disease**, **decompression disease**, kason~o; **Carrion's disease**, verugao; **foot-and-mouth disease**, afta febro; **Parkinson's disease**, Parkinsona ~o; **Pott's disease**, Potta ~o; **tsutsugamushi disease**, cucugamuŝio
disgorge, (gen), elverŝi [tr], elvomi [tr], elsputi [tr]
disgrace, (dishonor), malhonori [tr]; (make ashamed), hontigi; ~o, malfavoro; **disgraceful**, hontinda, malind(eg)a, ~a
disgruntle, malafabligi, malplaĉi [tr], malbonhumorigi; **disgruntled**, malafabla, malbonhumora, malkontenta, grumblema
disguise, alivesti [tr], maskvesti [tr]; ~aĵo; (hide), kaŝi [tr]; **thinly disguised**, apenaŭ kaŝita [cp "camouflage", "incognito"]
disgust, naŭzo; ~igi; **disgusting**, ~iga; **disgusted**, ~igita
dish, (plate, bowl, platter, etc.; any similar-shaped object), telero (e.g.: *wash the dishes:* lavi la ~ojn; *dish antenna:* ~a anteno); (plate, or plateful of food), plado; (course of meal), manĝmeto; **dishcloth**, **dishrag**, (~)lavtuko; **dishpan**, ~lavujo; **dish towel**, (~)viŝtuko; **dishwasher**, (machine), ~lavatoro; (person), ~lavisto; **dishwater**, ~lavakvo
dishabille, senvesteco
dishevel, taŭzi [tr]
disingenuous, malsincera

disintegrat/e, diser/igi; ~iĝi; **disintegrator**, (mech), desintegratoro
disk, (gen), disko; **diskette**, (cmptr), ~eto; **floppy disk**, mol~o; **hard disk**, dur~o; **disk drive**, ~odrajvo†; **slipped disk**, (med), ~a hernio [see also "disc"]
dislodge, elpeli [tr], delokigi
dismal, morna, malgaja
dismantle, malmunti [tr]
dismay, konsterni [tr]; ~o
dismiss, (send away), forsendi [tr], forigi; (give leave, as in mil), forpermesi [tr]; (not consider), malakcepti [tr], rifuzi [tr], elmensigi; (fire from job), maldungi [tr]
disparage, (discredit), diskrediti [tr]; (slight, belittle), mallaŭdi [tr], malestimigi
disparate, malsama, neegala; **disparity**, ~eco, neegaleco, diferenco
dispatch, (send), ekspedi [tr], (for)sendi [tr]; ~o, (for)sendo; (message), depeŝo; (kill), mortigi; (end), fini [tr]; (speed), rapido; **by dispatch mail**, depeŝe
dispel, dispeli [tr]
dispensary, dispensario
dispensation, (exemption, permission), permeso
dispense, (distribute, give out), disdoni [tr], distribui [tr]; (administer), administri [tr]; **dispense with**, formeti [tr], forigi, senigi sin je; **dispenser**, ~ilo
disperse, (spread, scatter, gen), sterni [tr], dismeti [tr], disloki [tr], disĵeti [tr], disigi; ~iĝi, dismetiĝi, dislokiĝi, disĵetiĝi, disiĝi; (re light, chem solution, etc.), dispersi [tr]; dispersiĝi [cp "diaspora"]; **dispersion**, (light, chem, etc.), dispersado; dispersiĝo; dispersaĵo;
dispirit, malĝojigi, senkuraĝigi, deprimi [tr]
display, (show), montri [tr], aperigi; ~(ad)o, aperig(ad)o; (more emphatic), el~i [tr]; el~(ad)o; (on cmptr screen, LCD read-out, etc.), videbligi; videbligo; (exhibit), eksponi [tr], ekspozicii [tr]; ekspozicio; (manifest, make visible), manifesti [tr]; manifestado; manifestaĵo; (spectacle), spek-

taklo
disport, distri [tr]; ~iĝi, ~i sin
dispose, (arrange, settle), aranĝi [tr]; (incline one), inklinigi; **dispose of**, (give away), fordoni [tr]; (get rid of), forigi, forĵeti [tr], senigi sin je; (settle affairs), fin~i [tr] (e.g.: *let's dispose of that problem now:* ni fin~u tiun problemon nun); (consume), forkonsumi [tr]; **disposal**, ~o; fin~o; fordono; forigo, forĵeto; **at one's disposal**, (available), je ies dispono (e.g.: *my services are at your disposal:* miaj servoj estas je via dispono); **have at one's disposal**, disponi [int] pri (e.g.: *we had 3 rooms at our disposal:* ni disponis pri 3 ĉambroj); **disposed**, inklina (e.g.: *she is well-disposed to do it:* ŝi estas bone inklina [or] ŝi bone inklinas ĝin fari); **be disposed to**, (have feeling re), inklini [int]; **become disposed to**, inkliniĝi; **disposer**, (for garbage in sink), rubforigilo; **disposition**, (arrangement), dispozicio, ~o; fordono; forigo, forĵeto; inklino; (tendency, temperament), dispozicio, temperamento; **indispose**, (disincline), malinklinigi; (make unfit), maltaŭgigi; (make ill), malsan(et)igi; **indisposed**, malinklina; maltaŭga; malsan(et)a; **predispose**, predispozicii [tr]; **predisposition**, predispozicio
dispute, (quarrel, discuss hotly), disputi [int] (pri); kontesti [tr], pri~i [tr]; ~o; (doubt), pridubi [tr]; (pri)dubo; (oppose), kontraŭi [tr]; **in dispute**, pri~ata; pridubata; **indisputable**, nekontestebla
disquisition, disertaĵo
disrupt, disrompi [tr]; **disruption**, ~(iĝ)o; **disruptive**, ~(em)a
dissect, dissekci [tr]
disseminate, (spread, gen), disvastigi, dispersi [tr]; (seed, lit or fig), dissemi [tr]
dissension, malpaco, disputado, malkonkordo
dissent, malkonsenti [int]; ~o; **dissenter**, ~anto
dissertate, diserti [int]; **dissertation**, disertacio
dissever, dis/igi, distranĉi [tr]; ~iĝi, dis-

dissidence, (gen), disident/eco†; **dissident**, ~o; ~a
dissimilate, malsimil/igi; ~iĝi
dissipate, disipi [tr]; ~iĝi [cp "debauch"]
dissociate, (opp "associate"), malasocii [tr]; ~iĝi; (separate, gen), apartigi; apartiĝi; (chem), disocii [tr]; disociiĝi
dissolute, (debauched), diboĉema
dissolve, (chem), solvi [tr]; ~iĝi; (break up, scatter, gen), dis~i [tr]; dis~iĝi (e.g.: *his hopes dissolved with the news:* liaj esperoj dis~iĝis kun la novaĵoj); **dissolution**, (dis)~(iĝ)o; **indissoluble**, nedisigebla
dissonance, disonanco; **dissonant**, ~a
dissuade, malinstigi [tr], malpersvadi [tr]
distaff, (spinning stick), konuklo, ŝpinbastono
distance, (interval), distanco; (farness), malproksimeco; **distant**, (far), malproksima, fora; (far, poet), dista, lontana; (aloof), malintimema, sinĝena, modesta, ~a; **from a distance**, de malproksime; **be distance from, be distant**, ~i [int] (e.g.: *New York is 4500 kilometers distant from Los Angeles:* Nov-Jorko ~as 4500 kilometrojn [or] je 4500 kilometroj de Los-Anĝeleso); **out-distance**, preter~i [tr]; **equidistant**, egal~a
distemper, (paint), temperi [tr]; ~ita farbo; (painting method), ~o; (disease), tempro*
distend, disstreĉi [tr], ŝveligi, pufigi; ~iĝi, ŝveli [int], pufiĝi; **distention, distension**, (distending), ~(ad)o, ŝvelig(ad)o, pufig(ad)o, ~iĝ(ad)o, ŝvel(ad)o, pufiĝ(ad)o; (distended state), ~iteco, ŝvelinteco, pufeco
distich, distiko; **distichous**, ~a
distill, distili [tr]; ~iĝi; **distillate**, ~aĵo; **distillation**, ~(iĝ)ado; **distiller**, (person), ~isto; (still), ~ilo; **distillery**, ~ejo
distinct, (sharp, clearly distinguishable), klara, distinga; (different, separate), aparta, malsama; **distinction**, (separateness), aparteco, diferenco; (differentiation), diferencigo; (distin-

guished or distinguishing thing), distingaĵo; (eminence), eminenteco; (honor), honoro; **distinctive**, distinga; **contradistinction**, kontrasto; **in contradistinction to**, kontraste al; **as distinct from**, (considered separate from), disde, distingita de
distinguish, (make or note difference, perceive), distingi [tr]; (differentiate), diferencigi; **distinguished**, (eminent), eminenta; **distinguishing**, ~a; diferenciga; **distinguishing mark**, ~ilo; **as distinguished from**, (considered separate from), disde, ~ita de
distome, distomo
distort, distordi [tr]; **distortion**, ~o
distract, (divert attention), distri [tr]; (draw in opp directions), distiri [tr]; **distraction**, ~(ad)o; ~aĵo; distir(ad)o
distrain, ristornigi
distrait, distriĝema, malatent(em)a
distraught, frenezigita, ĉagrenita, afliktita
distress, aflikti [tr], suferigi, ĉagreni [tr]; ~o, sufer(ad)o, ĉagreno; **distressed**, ĉagrenita, suferanta, ~ita
distribute, distribui [tr], dispartigi; **distribution**, ~(ad)o; **distributive**, ~a; **distributor**, (person, bsns), ~isto; (device, as in motor), ~ilo
district, distrikto; ~a; **district attorney**, ~a prokuroro
disturb, (bother), ĝeni [tr]; (agitate), agiti [tr]; (make uncalm), malkvietigi, maltrankviligi; (upset, cause med disorder etc.), perturbigi; (interrupt), interrompi [tr]; **disturbance**, ĝeno; agito; malkvietigo, maltrankviligo; malkvieteco, maltrankvil(ec)o; perturbo; perturbigo; (riot, public commotion), tumulto, malpaco; **disturbed**, ~ita; agitita; malkvieta, maltrankvila; perturb(igit)a
disulfate, pirosulfato; **disulfuric acid**, ~a acido
ditch, (trench), fosaĵo; ~izi [tr] (e.g.: *ditch a tent:* ~izi tendon); (crash plane on sea), markraŝi [tr]; markraŝiĝi; (get rid of, gen), senigi sin je
dither, tremekscito
dithionic, dition/ata; **dithionic acid**, ~a acido

dithyramb, ditirambo
ditto, same; **ditto mark**, (desupra) ripetsigno
dittography, ditografioꝉ
ditty, kanzoneto
diuresis, diurezo; **diuretic**, ~(ig)a; ~enzo
diurnal, (24 hours, on Earth; one revolution of any planet), diurna, tagnokta; (daytime), dumtaga; **diurnal period (span)**, ~o
divalent, [see "bivalent"]
divan, (couch), divano [cp "couch", "sofa"]; (coffee etc. room), kafĉambro, fumĉambro
divaricate, disbranĉ/igi; ~iĝi
dive, (gen), plonĝi [int]; ~igi; ~o; **dive-bomb**, ~bombi [tr]; **dive bomber**, ~bombanto; **power dive**, flug~i [int]; flug~o; **diving suit**, (mar)skafandro; **diving bell**, akvokloŝo [cp "bathyscaphe", "bathysphere"]; **deep-sea diver**, (mar)skafandristo
diverge, diverĝi [int]; **divergence**, ~o; (math), diverĝenco; **divergent**, ~a
divers, diversaj
diverse, diversa; **diversify**, ~igi; ~iĝi; **diversity**, ~eco
diversion, (diverting), devi(ig)o, deturn(iĝ)o; (amusement; distraction), distr(iĝ)o; distraĵo
divert, (turn away), deturni [tr], deviigi; (amuse, distract), distri [tr]
diverticulum, divertikulo
divertimento, distraĵo
divertissement, distraĵo
divest, senigi; **divest oneself of (something)**, ~i sin je (io)
divide, (math; separate, gen), dividi [tr]; ~iĝi; (math: divide evenly w no remainder), divizori [tr]; divizoriĝi; (room, desk drawer, etc., by partition), septi [tr]; (mountain crest), firstolinio; (between watersheds), akvodislimo; **divider**, (room etc. partition), septo; **dividers**, (compass), cirkelo; **divide out**, (distribute), distribui [tr], disdoni [tr], porciumi [tr]; **subdivide**, (gen), sub~i [tr]; (land into lots), parceligi
dividend, ($), dividendo; (math), dividato

divine › 170 ‹ do

divine, (godly), dia; (guess, figure out),
diveni [tr]; (foretell, prophesy), aŭguri
[tr]; (search for water etc. w divining
rod), rabdi [int] (por), radiestezi [int]
(por); (clergy), ekleziulo; (theologian), teologo; divination,
aŭgur(ad)o; diviner, (user of divining rod), rabdisto; divining rod, rab-
do; divinity, (godliness), ~eco; (a
god), ~o, ~aĵo; (theology), teologio
divisible, divizorebla [see "divisor"]
division, (math), divid/(ad)o; ~iĝo;
(mil; admin; bot), divizio; subdivision, sub~(ad)o; (house lots), parcela-
ro
divisive, divid(em)a
divisor, (any number divided into another), dividanto; (number which di-
vides another evenly), divizoro
divorce, (gen), divorco, eksedziĝo; ~i
[int] disde (e.g.: he divorced her: li
~is disde ŝi); (by repudiation, as per
Arab etc. custom), repudii [tr]; repu-
dio; divorcé(e), ~ul(in)o, ~int(in)o
divot, gazonero
divulge, riveli [tr], malkaŝi [tr]
Dixie, Sud-Usono
dizzy, (giddy feeling), kapturn/iĝa; ~i
[tr]; (dizzying), ~a (e.g.: dizzy
heights: ~aj altaĵoj); be(come) dizzy,
~iĝi; dizziness, ~o; dizzying, ~a
Djibouti, Ĝibutio
Dmitri, Demetrio
DNA, (abb of "desoxyribonucleic acid"), DNA [abb of "desoksiribo-
nukleata acido"] [note: PIVS lists abb
as "D.A.N.", alphabetized through ty-
pographic error after "divorco"]
Dnepr, Dnepro
Dnestr, Dnestro
do, (perform an act, fulfill, carry out,
produce, deal w, etc.), fari [tr] [note:
English expressions w "do" and the
abstraction or action indicated are
usually expressed in Esperanto by
simple verb (e.g.: it does no harm to
try: neniel malutilas provi)]; (complete, finish), fini [tr] (e.g.: the hot sun
did me in: la varma suno min finis;
are you done yet [have you fin-
ished]?: ĉu vi ankoraŭ finis?); (work
at as job, profession), ofici [int] (en,

kiel) (e.g.: what do you do [what is
your profession]?: kiel vi oficas? [or]
kio estas via ofico?; I do social work:
mi oficas en socia laboro); (suffice),
sufiĉi [int] (e.g.: that one isn't good,
but it'll do: tiu ne estas bona, sed ĝi
sufiĉos); (work out, solve, as problem), solvi [tr]; (move at speed), iri
(flugi etc.) je (po) (rapido) (e.g.: that
car does 200 kilometers per hour: tiu
aŭto iras po 200 kilometroj hore [or]
je 200 kilometroj en horo); (travel distance), iri (veturi, vojaĝi, etc.) (distancon) (e.g.: we did 1000 kilometers
yesterday: ni vojaĝis 1000 kilometrojn hieraŭ); (visit, tour), viziti [tr]
(e.g.: we did three museums and a cathedral: ni vizitis tri muzeojn kaj kat-
edralon); (get along, fare), farti [int]
(e.g.: mother and baby are doing well:
patrino kaj bebo fartas bone); (occur),
okazi [int] (e.g.: what's doing tonight?: kio okazas ĉi-nokte?); (mus
note), do [root (e.g.: sing the lower
do: kantu la pli malaltan doon)]; (party, social affair), festeno; [note: when
"do" substitutes for oth verb in ellip-
sis, translate as "fari" or "jes" or repeat oth verb (e.g.: I wonder if you
have an extra pen. Do you?: Mi scivolas ĉu vi havas ekstran plumon. Ĉu
vi havas? [or] Ĉu jes?; I asked you to
mow the lawn. Did you? Yes, I did: Mi
petis vin tondi la gazonon. Ĉu vi ~is
(ĝin)? Jes, mi ~is)]; [when "do"
serves as auxiliary verb in questions
etc., omit in Esperanto (e.g.: what do
you see?: kion vi vidas?); as an auxiliary verb to give emphasis, translate
as "ja" (e.g.: I do have an extra pen:
mi ja havas ekstran plumon; I did
mow the lawn: mi ja tondis la gazonon)]; do away with, forigi; do by,
(treat), trakti [tr] (e.g.: I'll do right by
you: mi juste traktos vin); do in, (kill),
mortigi; (trick, cheat), trompi [tr], superruzi [tr]; (exhaust), ellacigi, (fig),
fini [tr]; be(come) done in, ellaciĝi;
do-it-yourself, mem~a; do-nothing,
neni~anto; neni~anta; do one's (level) best, ~i sian plejeblon; do over,
(rearrange), rearanĝi [tr]; (redecorate),

reornami [tr]; (refurnish), remebli [tr]; **do up right (brown)**, bone ~i; **do with**, utiligi (e.g.: *I could do with a beer:* mi povus utiligi bieron); **do without**, kontentigi sin sen, esti kontenta sen; **outdo**, superi [tr]; **overdo**, troigi; troiĝi; **undo**, (unfasten), malfiksi [tr], malligi [tr]; (reverse, cancel, annul), mal~i [tr], nuligi; (bring downfall, ruin), pereigi, ruinigi; **done for**, (finished), finita; (ruined), ruinigita; **how do you do?**, kiel vi fartas?; **have to do with**, temi pri, koncerni [tr], rilati al (e.g.: *our discussion has to do with religion:* nia diskuto temas pri religio; *what does that have to do with the problem?:* kiel tio koncernas la problemon [or] rilatas al la problemo?); **have nothing to do with**, (not relate, not be relevant), neniel koncerni [tr], neniel rilati al; (deal w. treat), neniel trakti [tr] (e.g.: *she won't have anything* [or] *will have nothing to do with him:* ŝi neniel traktos lin [or] rilatos al li); **make do with(out)**, kontentigi sin kun (sen), kontentiĝi kun (sen); **have done with**, finiĝi kun, pri; ne plu koncerni sin pri; **that is not done**, (one should not act thus), oni ne agas tiel; tio ne decas; **well done**, (cooked), bone kuirita, funde kuirita; **what can I do for you?**, kiel mi povas servi vin?
dobro, dobro*
docent, docento
Docetism, docetismo†
docile, obeema, kondukebla
dock, (naut), doko; en~igi; en~iĝi; (for trucks, trains), kajo; (ast), kupli [tr]; kupliĝi; (bot: *Rumex*), rumekso; (for accused in court), akuzitejo; (body of tail), vostkorpo; (clip, bob, as tail), tranĉi [tr]; (deduct from pay), depagi [tr]; **dockage**, (dock fee), ~pago; **dock(work)er**, ~isto; **dockyard**, ~ejo; **drydock**, sek~o; **loading dock**, (for trucks, trains), ŝarĝkajo
dockmackie, viburno
doctor, (anyone w doctorate degree), doktoro; (M.D. or oth med doctor), kuracisto [title before name is "~o" (abb: d-ro) for med or any oth doctor,

as in English]; (treat as by doctor), kuraci [tr]; (tamper w. alter), falsi [tr], aliigi; **doctoral**, ~a; **doctorate**, (degree), ~a diplomo; ~eco; **postdoctoral**, post~iĝa; **witch doctor**, sorĉkuracisto
doctrine, doktrino; **doctrinaire**, ~ema, dogmema; **doctrinal**, ~a; **indoctrinate**, ~izi [tr]
document, dokumento; ~i [tr]; **documentary**, ~a; (film), informfilmo; (video tape), imformbendo
dodder, trem/ŝanceliĝi, (kaduke) ~i [int]; (bot), kuskuto; **doddering**, kaduka
dodecagon, dekduangulo
dodecahedron, dodekaedro, dekduedro
dodge, (avoid), (tord)eviti [tr]; (ruse), ruzo; (phot), priombri [tr]
dodo, dido
doe, ino, –ino [sfx] (e.g.: [re deer], cervino; [re antelope], antilopino)
does, [see "do"]
doff, demeti [tr]
dog, (any of *Canis*), hundo [cp "Canis"]; (track, follow, as a dog), spuri [tr]; **dogged**, (obstinate), obstina, insista; **dogbane**, apocino; **dogcart**, kariolo; **dogear**, (fold page corner), korni [tr]; **dogeared**, kornita; **dog-eat-dog**, (ruthless), sovaĝa, senkompata; **dogleg**, zigzago; **dog('s)-tail**, (bot), cinozuro, ~ovosto; **dog('s)-tongue**, (bot), cinogloso, ~olango; **dogtooth**, (bot), eritronio; **bulldog**, buldogo; **firedog**, (andiron), morelo, fajro~o; **hot dog**, [see "frankfurter"]; **sheep dog**, (*Canis familiaris laniarius*), laniario, ŝaf~o; **top dog**, superulo, ĉefulo; **underdog**, malavantaĝulo, subpremato, subulo; **watchdog**, gardo~o; **a dog's life**, vivaĉo, mizera vivo; **every dog has its day**, ĉiu ricevas sian ŝancon; **go to the dogs**, ruiniĝi; **let sleeping dogs lie**, lasi dormanta la ~on, ne blovi en abelujon
doge, doĝo
doggerel, poeziaĉo, versaĉoj
dogma, dogmo; **dogmatic**, ~ema; **dogmatize**, ~umi [int]; **dogmatics**, ~ismo; **dogmatism**, ~emo
Doha, Dohao*

doily, puntmateto
doldrums, (low spirits, inactivity), spleno; (fig), marasmo; (no wind), senventaj zonoj
dole, (welfare $), almozo, senlaboreca pago; [cp "welfare"]; (give out), disdoni [tr]; **on the dole**, pri~ata
doleful, morna, malgaja
dolichocephalic, dolichocephalous, dolikocefala; **dolichocephalic person**, ~o; **dolichocephaly**, ~eco
Dolichonyx oryzivorus, bobolinko
Dolichotis, doliñoto
doll, pupo; **get dolled up**, pimpiĝi
dollar, dolaro
dollop, maseto
dolly, (platform for moving heavy objects, camera, etc.), dolio†; [cp "truck: hand truck"]; (for rivets), nittenilo; (doll), pupeto; **crane dolly**, gruo—~o
dolman, dolmano
dolmen, dolmeno
dolomite, dolomito
Dolomites, Dolomitoj
dolorous, dolora, morna
dolphin, (*Delphinus*), delfeno; (*Coryphaena*), korefeno
dolt, azeno, stultulo, ventkapulo
domain, (gen), regno; **eminent domain**, ŝtata posedrajto
dome, (arch), kupolo; (geol), altaĵo
domestic, (re home; tame animal), hejma; (re housecleaning etc.), mastruma (e.g.: *domestic chores:* mastrumaj taskoj): (person hired for domestic work), mastrumist(in)o; (internal, re country), enlanda (e.g.: *domestic politics:* enlanda politiko); **domestic animal**, ~besto; **domesticate**, malsovaĝigi; **domesticity**, ~eco
domicile, domicilo
dominate, domini† [tr], (super)regi [tr. int]; **dominance**, ~ado, reg(ad)o; **dominant**, (mus; genetic or oth main trait etc.), dominanto; dominanta; (ruling), ~a, reganta; **predominate**, superregi; **predominant**, ĉefa, precipa, ~a, reganta; **subdominant**, (less than or partly dominant; bio), subreg(ant)a; (mus), subdominanto; **dominant trait**, dominanto
domineer, tirani [tr]; **domineering**,

~(ec)a, ~ema
Dominic, Dominiko
Dominica, Dominikio
Dominican, (monk), Dominikano; ~a; **Dominican Republic**, San-Domingo
dominion, (rule), reg(iv)o; (country), dominio; **Dominion Day**, Dominia Tago
domino, domen/peco; **dominoes**, (the game), ~o
Domitian, Domiciano
don, (put on), surmeti [tr]; (Br university official), asociito, docento
Don, (river), Dono; (man's name), Donêjo, Doĉjo
Donald, Donaldo
donate, donaci [tr]; **donation**, ~o
done, [see "do"]
Donets, Doneco
donga, uedo
Don Juan, Donjuano
donkey, azeno
donneybrook, tumulto, kverelego
donor, don/into; ~anto; ~onto
Don Quixote, Donkiñoto
donut, pastoringo
doodad, umo
doodle, desegnet/adi [tr]; ~o
doohickey, umo
doom, (fate), sorto; (ruin, tragic end), pereo; (condemn), kondamni [tr]; **doomsday**, (la) Lasta Juĝo; **doomed**, pereonta; kondamnita
door, (gen), pordo; **doorbell**, ~sonorilo; **doorjamb**, (~)framflanko; **doorsill**, sojlo; **doorstep**, ~ŝtupo [cp "porch"]; **doorway**, ~o; **closed-door**, (closed to public), malpublika, privata; **double door**, duklapa ~o; **front door**, ĉef~o [not "antaŭ~o"]; **indoor**, endoma; **indoors**, endome(n); **next-door**, najbara; apuda; **next-door neighbor**, apuda najbaro; **open-door**, (open to public), publika; **outdoor**, subĉiela, liberaera; **outdoors**, subĉiele(n), ekstere(n), eksterdome(n); **the outdoors**, la liberaero; **sliding door**, ŝov~o; (sliding vertically, as in garage, castle, etc.), herso; **swinging door**, svingo~o; **trap-door**, klap~o
dope, (smear thick substance), ŝmiri [tr]; ~aĵo; (drug, gen), [see "drug"];

(use drugs to enhance sports performance etc.), dopi† [tr]; dopiĝi
Doppler, Doppler†; **Doppler effect**, ~–efekto†; **Doppler shift**, ~–ŝoviĝo
Dorian, Doria; ~ano
Doric, Dorika
Doris, (woman's name), Dora; (Greek), ~io
Doris, (zool), dorido
dorm, dormejo
dormant, dormanta
dormer, gablofenestro
dormitory, dormejo
dormouse, gliro
Doros, Doro
Dorothy, **Dorothea**, Dorotea
dorsal, dorsa
Dorus, Doro
dory, (boat), doriso; (fish), zeo
dose, dozo; ~i [tr]; **dosage**, ~o; **overdose**, super~o; super~i [tr]; **dosimeter**, ~ometro
dossier, dosiero
dot, punkto; ~i [tr]; **dotted**, (scattered), disa; dise; **polka dot**, piz~o
dotage, senileco
dote, (be foolish, senile), senili [int]; **dote (up)on**, dorloti [tr]
douar, duaro
double, (w 2 combined; twice normal; dual), duobla; ~e; ~o; ~igi; ~iĝi (e.g.: *double consonant:* ~a konsonanto; *the price doubled:* la prezo ~iĝis); (2-by-2, paired), duopa; duope (e.g.: *ride double:* rajdi duope); (substitute for actor etc.), dubli [tr]; dublanto; (any look-alike person), sozio; (mus: octave lower), kontra– [pfx] (e.g.: *double bassoon:* kontrafagoto); **double back**, (fold), refaldi [tr]; refaldiĝi; (turn), reĝiri [tr]; reĝiriĝi; **double-cross**, perfidi [tr]; perfido; **double-decker**, (re boat, bus, etc.), duetaĝa; (layers, as sandwich), dutavola; **double-edged**, dutranĉa; ambaŭtranĉa; **double entendre**, dusencaĵo [cp "ambiguous"]; **double-header**, (gen), ~aĵo; (baseball or oth game), ~a ludo; **double-jointed**, ambaŭdirekte artikigita; **double-space**, [see under "space"]; **double-take**, dofoja rigardo; **double-talk**, galimatio; **redou-**

ble, (double), ~igi; ~iĝi; (double twice), re~igi; re~iĝi; (fold back), kuspi [tr], refaldi [tr]; kuspiĝi, refaldiĝi; (turn back), returniĝi; **play doubles**, (tennis etc.), ludi ~e
doublé dubleo
doubt, dubo; ~i [int] (pri), pri~i [tr]; **doubtful**, ~inda; **doubtless**, **beyond doubt**, **without a doubt**, sen~e; **cast doubt on**, **raise doubts about**, ~indigi, pri~igi; **self-doubt**, sin~o, nememfido
douche, duŝi [tr]; ~o; (device), ~ilo
dough, pasto; **doughnut**, ~oringo
dour, severa, malmilda
douse, (put out light, fire), estingi [tr]; (soak, immerse), trempi [tr]; (w divining rod), [see "dowse"]
dove, kolombo; **dovecot(e)**, ~ejo; **dovetail**, hirundovosta; hirundovostaĵo; hirundovostigi; hirundovostiĝi; **ringdove**, palumbo, arbo~o; **rock dove**, livio, rok~o; **stock dove**, enado
Dover, Dovero; **Strait of Dover**, Markolo ~a
Dovre(fjeld), Dovro
dowager, (noble), nobelvidvino; (rich), riĉulino
dowdy, plumpa
dowel, dubelo; ~izi [tr]
dower, (vidvina) heredaĵo
down, (adv), malsupre; ~en, sob (e.g.: *go down:* iri ~en; *it's down there:* ĝi estas tie malsupre); [note: in expressions like "go downstairs", "go downhill", etc., "stairs" etc. is usually omitted ("iri ~en"), but may be included for emphasis or to be specific ("iri ~en la ŝtuparon", "iri ~en la deklivon")]; (prep: following along), laŭ (e.g.: *go down that road:* iri laŭ tiu vojo); (adj: directed downward), ~en(ir)a (e.g.: *the down escalator:* la ~enira eskalatoro); (less, smaller, lower, etc.), malpli (granda, alta, etc.) (e.g.: *prices are down:* prezoj estas malpli altaj); (not functioning), ne funkcianta (e.g.: *the system is down:* la sistemo ne estas funkcianta [or] la sistemo ne funkcias); (psych: depressed), deprimita (e.g.: *I feel down:* mi sentas min deprimita; *don't let that*

get you down: ne lasu tion deprimi vin); (feathers), lanugo; (hill), monteto; ($), kontanta; kontante (e.g.: *down payment:* kontanta pago; *pay $500 down:* pagi $500 kontante); (let go of), de– [pfx] (e.g.: *put it down:* demeti ĝin, delasi ĝin); (become), –iĝi [sfx] (e.g.: *calm down:* trankviliĝi; *cool down:* malvarmiĝi); (finished, completed), finita (e.g.: *two down, three to go:* du finitaj, tri farotaj); (defeat), venki [tr]; (make fall, by knocking, chopping, etc.), faligi (e.g.: *down a tree:* faligi arbon); **downbeat,** ĉefpulso; **downcast,** (looking down), vizaĝaltera; vizaĝaltere; (sad, discouraged), malgaja, senkuraĝa, morna; **downer,** (drug), depremenzo; (fig, depressing experience), depremilo; **downfall,** (fall), falo; (ruin), ruinigo; **downgrade,** (degrade, demote), degradi [tr]; (slope down), (~ena) deklivo; **downhearted,** senkuraĝa, malgaja; **downhill,** ~en (la deklivon) [see note above]; **downpour,** pluvego, pluvtorento; **downrange,** subtrajektoria; subtrajektorie(n); **downright,** absoluta, entuta; abso lute, entute; **downspout,** pluvodukto; **downstairs,** ~en (la ŝtuparon) [see note above]; **downstream,** laŭflua; laŭflue(n); **downtime,** nefunkcianta tempo; **downtrodden,** tiranata, subpremata; **downward(s),** (adv) ~en, sob (e.g.: *the road leads downward:* la vojo kondukas ~en); (adj: leading downward), ~en(ir)a (e.g.: *a downward slope:* ~ena deklivo); **downwind,** laŭventa; laŭvente(n); **down with ...!** (protest slogan), for ...!, sob ...!; **down the street (hall, river, etc.),** laŭ la strato (koridoro, rivero, etc.); **down and out,** malfeliĉega. mizerega, plenvenkita; **down-to-earth,** realisma, praktik(em)a; **bring down,** (lower), malaltigi; (make fall), faligi; **come down,** malaltiĝi; fali [int]; **go down,** ~eniri [int]; **keep down,** (restrain), bridi [tr]; **let down, set down,** demeti [tr], delasi [tr]; **get down to,** (start to deal w bsns at hand), ekatenti [tr]; **take down, put down, get**

down, (on paper), surpaperigi; (on tape), surbendigi; **upside down,** [see under "up"]; [see also subentries under verbs followed by "down"]
dowry, doto
dowse, (search for water etc. w dowsing rod), rabdi [tr], radiestezi [int]; **dowser,** (person), ~isto; **dowsing rod,** ~o
doxology, doksologio
doyen, dojeno; **doyenne,** ~ino
doze, somnoli [int]; ~o
dozen, dekduo; ~o(j) da (e.g.: *three dozen eggs:* tri ~oj da ovoj); **dozens,** (imprecise number), dekoj (e.g.: *there were dozens of people in the pool:* estis dekoj da homoj en la naĝejo); **a half dozen, half a dozen,** (imprecise number), kvin-ses, ses-sep, ĉirkaŭ ses, pluraj [less awkward than "duono de ~o da"]
Dr. (abb of "Doctor", as title), d–ro [abb of "doktoro"]
drab, (dull color), malhela; (not lively), malsprita, malvigla; (yellowish brown), flavbruna; **olive drab,** olive ca
Draba, drabo
dracaena, Dracaena, draceno
drachma, draĥmo, drakmo
Draco, (Greek), Drakono; (ast), Drako; **Draconian,** ~a
Draco, (bot), drako
Dracocephalum, drakocefalo; Dracocephalum moldavica, moldaviko
Dracunculus medinensis, medina filario
draff, feĉo
draft, (of air), trablovo; (check, gen), ĉeko [see "check"]; ($: by one person requiring oth to pay), trato; (money order), mandato; (payment order), asigno; (conscription), konskripcio; konskripcii [tr]; (pulling, as of vehicle), tiro; (drink), trinko; (portion for drinking), ĉerpo; (available to be drawn from cask, as beer), ĉerpebla (e.g.: *draft beer, beer on draft:* ĉerpebla biero); (test writing or drawing, unpolished), malneto; malneta; malnetigi, malnete verki [tr], skizi [tr]; (mech: taper), bevelo; (displacement of ship), enakviĝo; **drafts,** (Br: game

of checkers), damludo; **draftee,** konskripto; **draftsperson, draftsman,** desegnisto; **drafty,** ~a; **draft animal,** tirbesto; **draft dodger,** konskripcievitanto; **indraft,** enblovo, entiro; **overdraft,** ($), troretrato; **rough draft,** malneto; **final draft,** neto
drag, (pull trailing object; trail; resist etc.), treni [tr]; ~iĝi; ~(iĝ)o; (dredge), dragi [tr]; (draw, pull, as on cigarette or drink), tiri [tr]; tiro; (brake), bremso; (swallow), gluto; (bore), tedulo; **drag on, drag out,** trodaŭri [int]; trodaŭrigi; **drag one's feet,** rezisti [tr], malkunlabori [int]
dragée, drageo
dragnet, dragneto
dragoman, dragomano
dragon, drako; **dragonfly,** (*Odonata*), odonato; (*Libellula*), libelo; **dragonhead,** (bot), drakocefalo
dragoon, dragono
drain, (carry off excess liquid, gen, lit or fig), dreni [tr]; ~iĝi; ~(iĝ)o; (pipe), ~ilo, defluilo; (drink up), eltrinki [tr]; **drainage,** ~aĵo; ~ado; **drainpipe,** ~ilo [cp "sewer"]
drake, viranaso
dram, (1/8 ounce apothecary), 3,89 gramoj [see § 20]; (1/16 ounce avoirdupois), 1,77 gramoj; (fluid), 3,70 mililitroj; (small drink), trinketo
drama, (theat work), dramo; (art of theat), teatro; **dramatic,** ~a, teatra; **dramatize,** ~igi; **dramatist,** ~verkisto [cp "dramaturgy"]; **psychodrama,** psiko~o
dramatis personae, roluloj
dramaturgy, dramaturg/io; **dramaturge, dramaturgist,** ~o†; **dramaturgic,** ~ia
drape, drapiri [tr]; ~aĵo; **draper,** drapisto; **drapery,** (draped cloth, as curtains etc.), ~aĵo(j); (Br: fabric), drapo; **drapes,** (curtains), kurtenoj
drastic, drasta
Drau, Dravo
draught, [see "draft"]
Drava, Dravo
Dravidian, Dravidic, Dravido; ~a
draw, (picture, design), desegni [tr] [cp "sketch"]; (drag), treni [tr]; (pull), tiri

[tr]; tiriĝi; (float in depth, re ship), enakviĝi (je) (e.g.: *that ship draws ten meters:* tiu ŝipo enakviĝas dek metrojn [or] je dek metroj); (attract, entice), allogi [tr]; (elicit, bring out), estigi, eltiri [tr]; (bring to self, attract), altiri [tr]; (naut: pull sail to yardarm or mast), brajli [tr]; (take out, pull out), eltiri [tr], elpreni [tr]; (take liquid), ĉerpi [tr]; (get, receive), ricevi [tr]; (withdraw $), depreni [tr], maldeponi [tr]; ($: accrue interest), gajni [tr], lukri [tr]; (disembowel), sentripigi; (deduce), dedukti [tr]; (infer), indukti [tr]; (derive), derivi [tr]; (tie in game, contest, etc.), egalvenko; (stretch), streĉi [tr]; streĉiĝi; (distort, distend), distordi [tr]; distordiĝi; (constrict), stringi [tr]; stringiĝi; (become), ~iĝi [sfx] (e.g.: *the time is drawing near:* la tempo proksimiĝas); (move), moviĝi (e.g.: *she drew off a bit from us:* ŝi moviĝis iomete for de ni); (track game), spuri [tr]; (gully, ravine), ravino; (dry ravine, as wadi), uedo; **drawing,** (design, picture), ~aĵo; **drawing board,** (for drafter, artist, etc.), ~ostablo; **draw away,** formoviĝi; **draw back,** retiri [tr]; retiriĝi; **drawback,** (disadvantage), malavantaĝo; (rebate), rabato; **drawbar,** kuplostango; **drawbridge,** [see under "bridge"]; **draw off,** (liquid from container, pipe), deĉerpi [tr]; (move away), formoviĝi; **draw on,** (utilize), utiligi, uzi [tr]; **draw out,** (prolong), trodaŭrigi; (extract), eltiri [tr]; (get person to talk), parolemigi; **drawstring,** stringoŝnureto; **draw up,** (draw together, gather), kuntiri [tr]; kuntiriĝi; (halt), halti [int]; haltigi; (approach), proksimiĝi; (write), skribi [tr]; verki [tr] [see "write"]; (compile list), kompili [tr]; **draw oneself up,** rektiĝi, rektigi sin; **overdraw,** ($), troretrati [tr]
drawer, (in desk, chest, etc.), tirkesto; **drawers,** (old-style underwear), kalsono [note sing]
drawl, trenparoli [tr]; ~o
dray, platĉaro
dread, timegi [tr]; ~o; **dreadful,** ~inda,

terura
dreadnought, dreadnaught, (coat),
drappalto; (ship), drednaŭto
dream, (in sleep), songî [tr]; ~o; (aspire), revi [int]; revo; **daydream,** revi
[int]; revo; **pipe dream,** pip~o
dreary, morna
dredge, dragi [tr]; (apparatus), ~ilo;
(barge equipped w dredge), ~ŝipo;
(sprinkle flour etc. on food), surŝuti
[tr], farunizi [tr]
dregs, feĉo [note sing]
drench, saturi [tr]
Dresden, Dresdeno
dress, (clothe), vesti [tr]; ~i sin, ~igî;
(clothing, gen), ~o; (woman's garment), robo; (usual clothing style),
kostumo (e.g.: *Japanese dress:* Japana
kostumo); (re formal attire), formala
(e.g.: *dress uniform:* formala uniformo); (trim, adorn), ornami [tr], garni
[tr]; (bandage wound), pansi [tr] [cp
"bandage"]; (mil: line up), vicigi;
viciĝi (e.g. [mil command]: *dress
right!:* viciĝu dekstren!); (eviscerate),
sentripigi; **dresser,** (chest of drawers), komodo; (Aus: dish, china cabinet), telerŝranko; **dressing,** (for
wound), pansaĵo; **dressing gown,** tualeta robo; **dressing room,** vestoĉambro; **dressy,** formala, eleganta; **dress
down,** riproĉi [tr]; **dressmaker,** robtajloro; **dress up,** (in formal attire),
formale ~igî; (in disguise costume),
masko~i [tr]; masko~i sin, masko~igî; (in costume or otherwise, for
amusement), travestii (sin); **dressed
up,** (formally), formale ~ita; **pantdress,** pantalonrobo; **get dressed,** ~i
sin, ~igî; **undress, get undressed,**
mal~i [tr]; mal~i sin, mal~igî
dressage, (ĉeval)dresado
dribble, (drool), bavi [int]; ~o; (drip),
guti [int]; guto; gutado; (sports), dribli
[int]
drier, [see under "dry"]
drift, drivi [int]; ~o; (gist of meaning),
senco; (tendency), tendenco; (of
snow, sand, etc.), ~aĵo, ~amaso [cp
"dune"]; (wander), vagi [int]; **drift
ice,** ~glacio; **driftwood,** ~ligno; **get
the drift of,** kapti la sencon de

drill, (bore), frezi [tr], bori [tr]; (machine), drilo; (large, w derrick, as for
oil well), drilego; (train, rehearse),
trejni [tr]; trejniĝi; trejn(ad)o; (exercise), ekzerci [tr]; ekzerciĝi; ekzerc(ad)o; (fabric), dreliko; **drill-bit,**
~ilo; **drill instructor,** trejninstruisto;
drill press, ~maŝino
Drimys, drimiso
drink, (gen), trinki [tr]; (act), ~o; (beverage), ~aĵo; (alcoholic beverage), alkoholaĵo; (drink alcoholic beverages,
esp to excess), drinki [int] [cp
"drunk"]; **drink in,** (avidly consume,
lit or fig), sorbi [tr]; **drink to,** (toast),
tosti [tr]; **drink up,** el~i [tr]; **drinking
fountain,** ~fontaneto; **drinking
song,** drinkkanzono; **drinking water,** ~akvo
drip, guti [int]; ~igi (e.g.: *the faucet
drips:* la krano ~as; *the car drips oil:*
la aŭto ~igas oleon); ~o; ~ado; **dripdry,** neĉifiĝema; ~sekigi; ~sekiĝi
(e.g.: *drip-dry the drip-dry shirt:*
~sekigi la neĉifiĝeman ĉemizon);
postnasal drip, postnaza ~ado
drive, (make go, urge on, re animals,
machinery, passions, etc.), peli [tr];
~o (e.g.: *the motor drives the front
wheels:* la motoro ~as la antaŭajn radojn; *driven by hate:* ~ata de malamo); (guide vehicle etc.), stiri [tr],
konduki [tr]; (travel by car, as driver
or passenger), veturi [int]; veturo;
(take someone by car), veturigi (e.g.:
I'll drive you home: mi veturigos vin
hejmen); (cause to be), ~igi [sfx] (e.g.:
you drive me mad: vi frenezigas min);
(cmptr; sports), drajvi† [tr]; drajvo†;
(force through, into), trabati [tr], enbati [tr] (e.g.: *she drove her point
home:* ŝi enbatis sian punkton); (selfmotivation), sin~ado; (psych urge),
urĝo; (campaign), kampanjo; (power
train, as of car, machinery), transmisiilo (e.g.: *chain drive:* ĉena transmisiilo); (propulsion system, as in rocket),
~sistemo (e.g.: *ion drive:* jona ~sistemo); (drift), drivi [int]; (driveway),
alirvojo; **drive at,** (aim at), celi [tr];
(hint, allude to), aludi [tr]; **drive
away,** for~i [tr]; **drive in,** (hit), enbati

[tr]; **drive-in**, (restaurant, bank, etc.), envetura; **drive shaft**, transmisia ŝafto; **driveway**, alirvojo; **driver's license**, stirlicenco, konduklicenco; **disk drive**, (cmptr), diskodrajvo†; **mass driver**, (linia) mas–akcelatoro; **overdrive**, superrapidumo; **pile driver**, ramo

drivel, (drool), bavi [int]; ~o; (nonsense), galimatio; paroli galimatie

drizzle, nebulpluvo; ~i [int]

droll, drola

–drome, (sfx), –dromo

dromedary, dromedaro

Dromia, dromio

Dromiceus, dromiceo

drone, (bee), virabelo; (any nonworker), nelaboranto, parazito, nenifaranto; (plane, spaceship, etc.), telestirata avio (ŝipo, etc.); (hum, buzz), zumadi [int]; zumado; (bagpipe pipe), zumtubo

drool, bavi [int]; ~o

droop, velki [int]; ~igi; ~o

drop, (fall; let fall), fali [int]; ~igi, lasi ~i; ~o; (decrease), malpliiĝi, ~i; malpliiĝo, ~o; (lower), mallevi [tr]; mallevîĝi; (descend), descendi [int]; descendo; (steep slope), krutaĵo; (of liquid), guto; (drip), guti [int]; gutigi; (chute, as mail drop), ŝutilo; (give birth), naski [tr]; (give out, as hint), eligi, ellasi [tr]; (leave; no longer deal w), lasi [tr]; lasiĝi (e.g.: *I'll drop you at the station:* mi lasos vin ĉe la stacidomo; *let's drop the matter:* ni lasu la aferon; *the matter droped there:* la afero lasiĝis tie); **drop back**, posteniri [int], retroiri [int]; **dropcloth**, guttuko; **drop in (to visit)**, hazarde viziti [tr]; **droplet**, guteto; **droplight**, levebla lumo; **drop off**, (decrease), malpliiĝi, de~i [int]; (fall asleep), ekdormi [int]; **drop-off**, (decrease), malpliiĝo, de~o; (steep slope), krutaĵo; **drop out**, (quit), retiri sin, retiriĝi; (from school etc.), el~i [int]; **dropout**, (student etc.), el~into; **dropper**, gutigilo; **droppings**, (dung), fekaĵo, sterko

dropsy, hidropso

dropwort, felandrio

drosera, Drosera, drozero

droshky, droŝko

drosophila, Drosophila, drozofilo

dross, (on metal), skorio; (rubbish), rubo; (junk), fatraso

drought, drouth, senpluveco

drove, (of animals), brutaro, grego; ~r, (Aus), brutpelisto

drown, droni [int]; ~igi; **drown out**, (by noise), superbrui [tr]

drowsy, somnola

drub, bati [tr]

drudge, servut/ulo; **drudgery**, ~o; **do drudgery**, ~i [int]

drug, (medicinal), drogo; ~i [tr]; (narcotic), narkoti [tr]; toksiko†, narkotaĵo; **druggist**, ~isto; **drugstore**, ~ejo [cp "apothecary", "pharmacy"]

druid, Druid, Druido; ~a; **druidism**, ~ismo

drum, (mus, gen; or similar-shaped cylindrical object), tamburo; ~i [tr, int]; (for cable etc.), ~o, bobenego; **drummer**, ~isto; **drum major**, bandestro; **drumstick**, (for drum), ~bastono; (meat), suraĵo; **bass drum**, ~ego; **eardrum**, timpana membrano [cp "ear: middle ear"]; **kettledrum**, timbalo; **snare drum**, drat~o

drunk, (intoxicated), ebria; ~ulo; **drunken**, ~a; **drunkard**, drink(em)ulo; ~emulo; **get drunk**, ~igi; ~iĝi [cp "drink"]

drupe, drupo

druse, druzo

Druse, Druze, Druzo; **Drusian**, ~a

druthers, prefero

dry, (gen), seka; ~igi; ~iĝi; **dryer**, (gen), ~igilo; **dry out**, (dry fully), el~igi; el~iĝi; **freeze dry**, liofilizi† [tr]; **hair dryer**, [or any dryer blowing hot air], feno, harsekigilo†

dryad, driado

dual, (gen), duala; ~o; **duality**, ~eco; **dualism**, ~ismo

dub, (movie or oth recorded sound etc.), dubli [tr]; (make a knight), kavalirigi; **overdub**, sur~i [tr]

dubious, (inclined to doubt), dub/ema; (improbable), ~inda

Dublin, Dublino

ducal, duka

ducat, dukato
duchess, dukino
duchy, duk/ejo, ~lando
duck, (zool), anaso; (bend down), ekkaŭri [int]; (avoid, gen), eviti [tr]; (push under water), mergi [tr]; (fabric), tiko; **duckmole,** ornitorinko; **duckweed,** lemno; **lame duck,** (pol), nereelektito; **old-squaw duck, old injun duck, oldwife duck, long-tailed duck,** klangulo, glaci~o; **spoon-bill duck,** kuler~o; **tufted duck,** fuligulo
duct, (tube, channel, gen), dukto; **bile duct,** koledukto; **milk duct,** lakto~o; **sperm duct,** spermato~o
ductile, duktila
ductus, (anat), dukto; **ductus deferens,** spermato~o
dud, (bomb, shell, etc.), mispafo; (worthless, gen), senvalora; senvaloraĵo; (person), sentaŭgulo
dude, (any man), ulo; (dandy, fop), dando; (city fellow), urbano
duds, (colloq), vestoj
due, (payable), pagenda (e.g.: *the debt is due tomorrow:* la ŝuldo estos ~a morgaŭ); (owed, gen), ŝuldata; (to be submitted, presented), submetenda, prezentenda (e.g.: *the report is due in two weeks:* la raporto estos prezentenda post du semajnoj); (expected at given time), atendata (e.g.: *the train is due at 7:00:* la trajno estas atendata je la 7.00 [see "(be) past due" below]); (fitting, proper), deca, justa (e.g.: *give her her due credit:* doni al ŝi ŝian justan krediton; *with all due respect:* kun ĉia deca respekto); (thing merited), meritaĵo (e.g.: *give him his due:* doni al li lian meritaĵon); (exactly, as re compass direction), rekte, precize (e.g.: *we went due south:* ni iris rekte suden); **dues,** ($), kotizo [note sing]; **pay one's dues,** kotizi [int]; **due to,** (caused by, because of), pro, kaŭze de [see "because: because of"]; **(be) past due, overdue,** (arriving late), malakurata, malfrua; malfrui [int] (e.g.: *the train is ten minutes past due:* la trajno estas malakurata [or] la trajno malfruas je dek minutoj); (not paid, not presented, etc.), postmatura, posttempa

(e.g.: *a pile of overdue bills:* amaso da postmaturaj fakturoj); **undue,** (excessive), ekscesa; (improper), nekonvena; **become due, fall due,** (re bill, loan, etc.), maturiĝi, ~iĝi; **in due time, in due course,** siatempe, ĝustatempe
duel, duelo; ~i [int]
duet, (any group of 2), duopo; (mus composition), dueto
duffel, duffle, kapotŝtofo; **duffel bag,** dreliksako; **duffel coat,** duflot
duffer, fuŝulo
dugong, Dugong, dugongo
dugout, (canoe), pirogo; (any shelter), ŝirmejo
duke, duko; **archduke,** arki~o
dulcet, dolĉa
dulcimer, (hammered), dulcimero, martel~o; **mountain, dulcimer, fretted dulcimer, lap dulcimer, Appalachian dulcimer,** freto~o
Dulcinea, Dulcinea
dull, (not sharp, re blade, senses, etc.), mal/akra; ~akrigi; ~akriĝi; (not bright, re color etc.), ~hela; (unwitty, unclever), ~sprita; (unintelligent), ~inteligenta, stulta; (boring), teda, enuiga; (obtuse), obtuza; obtuzigi; **dullard,** ~spritulo; ~inteligentulo, stultulo
duly, taŭge, dece
dumb, (mute), muta; (stupid), stulta, malinteligenta; **dumbfound,** konsterni [tr]; **dumbstruck,** konsternita; **dumbwaiter,** (elevator), lifteto
dumbbell, haltero [cp "barbell"]
dumdum, dumduma (kuglo)
Dumetella carolinensis, katbirdo
dummy, (cards), fantomo; ~a; (any substitute), anstataŭaĵo; (puppet, lit or fig), pupo; (man of straw), pajlohomo; (mannikin), manekeno; (effigy etc.), figuraĵo
dump, (spill), renversi [tr]; ~iĝi; ~(aj)o; (chute, as coal etc.), ŝuti [tr]; ŝutiĝi; (throw away), forĵeti [tr]; (bsns, $), dumpingi [tr]; **dumping,** (bsns, $), dumpingo; **dumpy,** (inelegant), plumpa; **garbage dump,** rubejo; **supply dump,** provizejo; **down in the dumps,** deprimita, melankolia

dumpling, pastbuleto; (Chinese: wonton), huntuno
dun, (gray-brown), grizbruna; ($), pagpostuli [tr]
dunce, stultulo
dune, duno; **dune buggy**, ~aŭto
dung, (manure), sterko; (any feces), fekaĵo; **dunghill, dungheap**, ~amaso
dungarees, drelik/pantalono; ~aĵo [note sing]
dungeon, karcero [cp "prison", "jail"]
dunk, trempi [tr]
Dunkirk, Dunkirko
duo, duo
duodecimal, dekduaria†
duodecimo, dozavo†
duodenum, duodeno; **duodenal**, ~a; **duodenitis**, ~ito
dupe, dupo; ~igi
duple, duopa
duplex, (twofold, double), duobla; (elec), dupleksa; (house), ~a (domo)
duplicate, (reproduce, copy), kopii [tr], multobligi, duobligi; ~o [cp "photocopy"]; (facsimile of document etc.), duplikato; (double), duobla; (corresponding exactly), precize responda; **reduplicate**, (re)duobligi, ripeti [tr] [see also "double: redouble"]
duplicity, ruzemo
dura (mater), duramatro
durable, daŭr/ema, ~iva, fortika
duralumin, duralumino
duramen, kernligno
duration, daŭro
durative, durativo
duress, premdevigo, perforto; **under duress**, sub ~o
durian, (tree), durio; (fruit), ~a frukto
during, dum
Durio, durio
durion, [see "durian"]
duro, duro
dusk, krepusko, vesper~o; **dusky**, ~a
dust, polvo; sen~igi; (powder lightly), ŝuteti [tr]; **dusty**, ~a; **dustbin**, (Br), rubujo; **dust bowl**, ~oregiono; **dust jacket**, librojaketo; **dustpan**, ~oŝovelilo; **dust particle**, ~ero; **dust storm**, ~oŝtormo; **feather-duster**, plumviŝilo; **bite the dust**, morti [int]
Dutch, Nederlanda; ~ano; **Dutchman**,

~ano; **Pennsylvania Dutch**, Pensilvan-Germana; Pensilvan-Germano; **go Dutch**, iri mempage; **in Dutch**, en embaraso; **get one(self) in Dutch**, embarasi [tr] (sin)
dutiful, obeema
duty, (obligation), devo; (period of official service), deĵoro; (tax), dogano; **duty-free**, doganlibera; **dutiable**, doganata; **on duty**, deĵoranta; **off duty**, ne deĵoranta; **be on (off) duty**, (ne) deĵori [int] [cp "watch"]
Dvina, Dvino
dwarf, nano; ~a; ~igi; ~iĝi; **dwarfism**, ~eco, ~ismo
dwell, reside), loĝi [int]; **dwelling**, ~ejo; **dwell on**, emfazi [tr], insisti pri; **indwell**, en~i [int]
dwindle, ŝrumpi [int]
dyad, duopo; **dyadic**, ~a
dye, tinkturi [tr]; ~o; **dyed-in-the-wool**, ĝisosta
dyke, [see "dike"]
dynamic, dinamika; **dynamics**, ~o; **aerodynamic**, aero~a; **astrodynamic**, astro~a; **electrodynamic**, elektro~a; **isodynamic**, izodinama; **thermodynamic**, termo~a
dynamism, dinamismo
dynamite, dinamito; ~i [tr]
dynamo, dinamo
dynamometer, dinamometro; **electrodynamometer**, elektro~o
dynamotor, dinamotoro
dynasty, dinastio; **dynastic**, ~a
dynatron, dinatrono
dyne, dino
dys–, (med pfx), dis–, mis–
dysentery, disenterio; **dysenteric**, ~a
dysfunction, misfunkcio
dyslexia, disleksio; **dyslectic**, ~a; ~ulo
dysmenorrhea, dismenoreo
dyspepsia, dispepsio; **dyspeptic**, ~a
dyspnea, dispneo
dysprosium, disprozio
dystrophy, distrofio*
dysuria, disurio
dytiscid, ditisko
Dytiscus, ditisko

E

each, (every), ĉiu (e.g.: *read each book:* legi ĉiun libron); (at rate of, "@", for each one), po [followed by "-o" or "-on" same as if "po" were not used] (e.g.: *we ate two apples each:* ni manĝis po du pomojn; *they cost $2 each:* ili kostas po $2 [du dolarojn]; *mix one spoonful per [in each liter of water:* miksu po unu kulerplenon en ĉiu litro da akvo; *two books were in the chairs [in each chair]:* po du libroj estis en la seĝoj) [note that "po" goes in front of numerical expression]; **each one**, ĉiu (e.g.: *each one of them:* ĉiu el ili); **each and every (one)**, ĉiu ajn; **each other**, (one another), si(n) reciproke, unu la alian (e.g.: *they kissed each other:* ili kisis unu la alian [or] sin reciproke)

eager, avida

eagle, aglo; **bald eagle, sea eagle, harpy eagle**, harpio; **white-tailed (sea) eagle**, haliaeto

ear, (anat), orelo; (of cap etc., to cover ears), ~umo; (grain spike, as corn), spiko; **earache**, ~doloro; **eardrum**, timpana membrano; **earflap**, ~umo; **earmark**, (set aside, reserve), rezervi [tr], asigni [tr], destini [tr]; (sign, indicator), indiko (e.g.: *this shows earmarks of wrongdoing:* ĉi tio montras indikojn de misfarado); **earphone**, kapaŭdilo; **earplug**, ~ŝtopilo; **earring**, ~ringo; **earshot**, aŭdatingo; **inner ear**, interna ~o; **middle ear**, timpano, meza ~o; **outer ear**, ekstera ~o; **be all ears**, atente aŭskulti [tr]; **be up to one's ears in**, troviĝi ĝis la ~oj en, droni en; **bend someone's ear**, aŭskultigi iun; **turn a deaf ear to**, rifuzi atenti [tr]; **fall on deaf ears**, resti neatentita; **give (lend) an ear (to)**, atenti [tr], klini ~on (al); **keep an ear to the ground**, resti atenta; **it went in one ear and out the other**, tra unu ~o ĝi eniris, tra la dua eliris; resti aŭdita sed ne atentita; **(play) by ear**, (mus; fig), (ludi) laŭ ~o; **play it**

by ear, (mus: improvise; fig), improvizi [tr]; **prick up one's ears**, streĉi la ~ojn

earl, grafo

early, frua; ~e

earn, ($, gen), lukri [tr], gajni [tr] (e.g.: *deposits earn interest:* deponoj ~as [or] gajnas interezon); (wages, salary), ~i, perlabori [tr]; (gain, win, gen), gajni (e.g.: *earn respect:* gajni respekton); **earnings**, ~aĵo(j), gajnaĵo(j); **earn a living**, vivi [int], vivgajni [int], gajni (la) vivon

earnest, (serious, deliberate), serioza; **in earnest**, ~e; **earnest (money)**, garantiaĵo

earth, (ground, gen), tero; ~a; (soil), grundo; (elec), ~konekto; ~konekti [tr]; ~konektiĝi; **earthbound**, (confined to ground, gen), ~ligita; **earthen**, (of clay), argila; **earthenware**, argilaĵo(j), argilaĵaro [cp "crock"]; **earthlight**, **earthshine**, ~lumo; **earthly**, (re material plane, not spiritual), materia, sur~a, nespirita, fizika; **earthmover**, (digging machine), elkavatoro; **earthquake**, sismo, ~tremo; **earthstar**, (bot), geastro; **earthwork**, (fortification), remparo; (re embankments, gen), ~aĵo [cp "bank"]; **earthworm**, lumbriko, ~vermo; **unearth**, el~igi, elfosi [tr]; **unearthly**, ne~(ec)a; **down-to-earth**, praktika; **come down to earth**, elreviĝi; reveni el aero al ~o; **what on earth?**, kio diable?

Earth, (planet), Tero

earwig, forfikulo

ease, (easy-ness), facil/eco; ~igi; ~iĝi; (repose), ripozo; (relax, loosen), malstreĉi [tr]; malstreĉiĝi; (make milder, as pain etc.), mildigi; mildiĝi; **at ease!**, (mil command), ripozu!, ripoz'!; **ill-at-ease**, maltrankvila; **put at ease**, (re)trankviligi

easel, stablo

easement, (easing), [see "ease"]; (legal right of way), pasrajto

east, oriento; ~a; ~e(n); (esp re compass point), eosto; **eastern**, ~a; **easterner**, ~ano; **eastward**, ~e(n); ~en(ir)a; **easterly**, (eastern), ~a; (toward east), ~e(n); ~en(ir)a; (from east), de~a; de~e; **eastbound**, ~en(ir)a; **Near East**, Proksim-O~o; **Middle East**, Mez-O~o; **Far East**, Malproksim-O~o

Easter, Pasko; ~a; **Easter Island**, ~insulo

easy, (not difficult, gen), facila; (unhurried), malhasta; **easy-going**, komplezema; **uneasy**, maltrankvila; **easy come, easy go**, ~a akiro, ~a perdo; **easy does it!**, zorgu!, ne hastu!

eat, (re food), manĝi [tr]; (corrode, as re acid), mordi [tr] [cp "corrode"]; **maneater**, hom~ulo; **eat one's fill (of)**, ĝissate ~i, sat~i [tr]; **what's eating you?**, kio vin ĝenas?; **eat one's words**, maldiri [tr]; repreni siajn dirojn

eave, alero; **eavesdrop**, subaŭskulti [tr]

ebb, malflusi [int]; ~o; **ebb-tide**, ~o

ebonite, ebonito

ebony, ebono; ~a; **ebony tree**, ~arbo

Ebro, Ebro

ebullient, entuziasma, verva

ebullioscope, ebulioskopo

Ecballium, ekbalio; Ecballium elaterium, elaterio

eccentric, (mech: off-center), ekscentrika; ~o; (odd, strange), originala, stranga; originalulo, strangulo

ecchymosis, ekimozo

Ecclesiastes, (Bib), Predikanto

ecclesiastic, eklezi/ulo; **ecclesiastical**, ~a; **ecclesiasticism**, ~ismo

echelon, eskalono; ~igi; ~iĝi

echevin, skabeno

echidna, Echidna, eĥidno

echinococcus, ekinokoko

echinoderm, eĥinodermo

Echinoderm(at)a, eĥinodermoj

echinoid, eĥinoido

Echinops, kardo

echinorhynchus, Echinorhynchus, eĥinorinko

echinus, Echinus, eĥino

Echium, ekio

echo, eĥo; ~i [tr]; ~iĝi

Echo, (myth), Eĥoa

echolalia, eĥolalio

éclair, krembulko

eclampsia, eklampsio

eclectic, eklektika

eclipse, eklipso; ~i [tr]; **total eclipse**, plena ~o; **partial eclipse**, parta ~o; **annular eclipse**, ringa ~o

ecliptic, ekliptiko

eclogue, eklogo

ecology, ekolog/io; **ecological**, ~ia; **ecologist**, (scientist specializing in ecology), ~o [cp "environment"]

econometrics, ekonometrio†

economy, (gen), ekonomio; **economic**, (re sci of economics), ekonomika; (re economy), ~a; **economical**, (re economics), ekonomika; (thrifty, sparing), ~a; **economics**, ekonomiko; **economist**, ekonomikisto; **economize**, ŝpari [tr]

ecosystem, ekosistemo*

ecstasy, ekstazo; **ecstatic**, ~a

ectasia, ektazio; **ectatic**, ~a

ectoderm, ektodermo

–ectomy, (med sfx), –ektomio

ectopia, ektopio; **ectopic** ~a

ectoplasm, ektoplasmo

ectropion, ektropio

Ecuador, Ekvadoro

ecumenical, ekumena; **ecumenism**, ~ismo

eczema, ekzemo

Edam, Edamo; ~a

Edda, Eddo

eddy, (in water), kirl/akvo; (in any fluid), ~fluo; (gen), ~iĝi [cp "whirlpool"]

edelweiss, edelvejso, neĝfloro

edema, edemo; **edematous**, ~a

Eden, Edeno

Edentata, edentatoj

edentate, (toothless), sendenta; (zool), edentato

edentulous, sendenta

Edgar, Edgaro

edge, (rim, brink, etc.; limit of any surface, lit or fig, as re table, knife, desert, fear, etc.), rando; (border around edge, as on hat, curtain, etc.), ~aĵo; (narrow surface around edge, as on coin), ~umo; (sharp, as on blade;

math), eĝo; (of river), bordo; (put an edge on), ~izi [tr]; ~umizi [tr]; (trim edge, as lawn etc.), ~ostuci [tr]; (move slowly), movetiĝi, rampi [int]; **edgeways, edgewise**, (edge foremost), flanka; flanke(n); (on edge), sur~a; sur~e; **double-edged**, (sword etc., lit or fig), dutranĉa; **straightedge**, liniilo; **on edge, edgy**, (nervous), nervoza, agaciĝema; **put on edge**, agaci [tr]; **have an edge on** **(over)**, havi avantaĝon super; **take the edge off**, (gen), obtuzigi, malakrigi; **get a word in edgewise**, interkojni vorton
edible, manĝebla; **inedible**, ne~a
edict, dekreto, edikto
edifice, konstruaĵo
edify, edifi [tr]; **edification**, ~ado
edile, edilo
Edinburgh, Edinburgo
edit, manage magazine etc.; polish anything written), redakti [tr]; **editor**, redaktoro, ~isto; **editial staff, editial office**, redakcio
Edith, Edita
edition, eldono
Edmond, Edmund, Edmondo
Edom, (gen), Edomo
EDP, (abb of "electronic data processing"), komputor/ado; ~a
educate, eduki [tr], klerigi; **education**, (teaching, gen), ~(ad)o; (of children), ~(ad)o, pedagogio; (learned state), klereco, ~iteco; **educator**, ~isto; pedagogo; **educated**, (learned), klera; **educable**, ~ebla; **coeducation**, ge~ado; **coeducational**, ge~ada, gea; **self-educated**, memlerninta, aŭtodidakta
Edward, Eduardo
–ee, (sfx: person, object of action indicated by root), –ito; –ato; –oto (e.g.: *appointee:* asignito); (person to whom or for whom action done), al...ito; al...ato; al...oto (e.g.: *payee:* alpagoto)
eel, angilo; (as food), ~aĵo; **eelgrass**, zostero; **eelpout**, zoarco; **conger eel**, kongro; **electric eel**, gimnoto; **mud eel**, sireno
eerie, eery, mistera
efface, (rub out, erase), forviŝi [tr], ne-

niigi; (make inconspicuous, withdraw), retiri (sin); **self-effacing**, sinretirema, malegoisma
effect, (thing brought about, caused), efiko; (efficacy), ~eco; (impression, as on spirit, senses), efekto; (sci phenomenon), ~o, fenomeno (e.g.: *the Hall effect:* la ~o [or] fenomeno de Hall); (bring about), estigi, efektivigi, kaŭzi [tr]; **effects**, (possessions), havaĵoj, posedaĵoj; **effective**, (having effect, operative, active), ~a; (real, actual), efektiva; **effectiveness**, ~eco; **effectual**, ~a; **effectuate**, efektivigi; **aftereffect**, post~o; **sound effects**, sonefektoj; **have an effect (on)**, ~i [int] (sur –on, ĉe –o); **in effect**, efektiva, valida; efektive; **go into effect, take effect**, ek~i [int], efektiviĝi, validiĝi; **put into effect, give effect to**, efektivigi, realigi, validigi; **to the effect (that)**, (w the meaning, sense), kun la senco (ke) (e.g.: *an indication to the effect that the plan is approved:* indiko kun la senco ke la plano estas aprobita; *words to that effect:* vortoj kun tiu senco)
effeminate, ineca; **effeminacy**, ~o
effervesce, eferveski [int]; **effervescent**, ~a; **effervescence**, ~o
effete, (decadent, unvigorous), dekadenca; (sterile), sterila
efficacious, efika; **efficacy**, ~eco
efficient, (producing effect w little effort or waste), efika; (mech: high ratio of work done to energy consumed), alt~a, altrendimenta; **efficiency**, (gen), ~eco; (mech), rendimento
effigy, figuraĵo; **hang (someone) in effigy**, pendigi ~on de (iu)
effloresce, (bloom), ekflori [int]; (chem), efloreski [int]; **efflorescence**, ~ado; efloresk(ad)o; **efflorescent**, ~ada; efloreska
effluence, elflu/(ad)o; ~aĵo; **effluent**, ~aĵo
effluvium, efluvo
efflux, elflu/(ad)o; ~aĵo
effort, pen/(ad)o, fortostreĉ(ad)o; **effortless**, sen~a; **make an (the) effort**, klopodi [int]; **make every effort**, klopodi laŭeble

effrontery, aŭdaco, impertinenteco
effusive, sinverŝa, emociverŝa
efreet, **efrit**, **efrite**, efrito
eft, trituro
egalitarian, egal/isma; ~isto; **egalitarianism**, ~ismo
Egeria, Egeria
egg, (gen), ovo; **egg(s)**, (as food), ~aĵo [note sing]; **egg-cup**, ~ingo; **eggnog**, ~laktaĵo; **eggplant**, melongeno; **egg roll**, ~rulaĵo; **egg-white**, ~blanko, albumino; **egg-yolk**, ~oflavo; **nest egg**, ŝparaĵo; **scrambled eggs**, ~kirlaĵo, kirlitaj ~oj; **lay egg(s)**, ~umi [int]; **lay an egg**, (flop), fiaski [int]; **egg on**, (incite), instigi [tr]; (goad), inciti [tr]
egis, [see "aegis"]
eglantine, eglanterio
ego, egoo; **egocentric**, ~centra; **egomania**, ~manio; **egomaniac**, ~mania; ~maniulo; **ego(t)ism**, ~ismo; **ego(t)ist**, ~isto; **egotistic(al)**, ~isma; **superego**, super~o
egress, (act), eliro; (right), ~rajto; (place), ~ejo
egret, egretbirdo [cp "aigrette"]
Egypt, Egipt/io; **Egyptian**, ~o; ~a; ~ia
eh, (interj), ej
Eichhornia crassipes, akvohiacinto
eicosane, ejkosano
eider, somaterio, solanaso; **eiderdown**, ~a lanugo
Eiffel, Ejfelo; **Eiffel Tower**, ~turo
eight, ok; **eighth**, (8th), ~a; (1/8), ~ono [see § 19]
eightvo, oktavo
eikosane, ejkosano
Einstein, Ejnstejn
einsteinium, ejnstejnio
Eire, Ejro
either, (one or the oth of 2), iu (ajn) (e.g.: *use either hand:* uzu iun [or] iun ajn manon); (each), ĉiu (e.g.: *she had a tool in either hand:* ŝi havis ilon en ĉiu mano); **either ... or**, aŭ ... aŭ (e.g.: *take either the cookies or the cake:* prenu aŭ la keksojn aŭ la kukon; *either he'll do it or he won't:* aŭ li faros ĝin aŭ li ne faros; *either go or stay:* aŭ iru aŭ restu); **not either**, (also not), nek, ankaŭ ne (e.g.: *if you don't go, I*

won't either: se vi ne iros, nek mi iros [or] ankaŭ mi ne iros; *he has no friends, and no family either:* li havas neniujn amikojn, nek familion [or] li havas nek amikojn nek familion); (colloq: indeed not), ja ne (e.g.: *It's mine. It isn't either!:* Ĝi estas mia. Ĝi ja ne estas!); **either-or**, (consisting of 2 alternatives), duera (e.g.: *a black-and-white, either-or situation:* nigra-blanka, duera situacio)
ejaculate, (sperm), ejakuli [int]; ~aĵo; (cry out), ekkrii [tr]
eject, eljeti [tr], elpeli [tr]; **ejection seat**, ~ilo
ejective, (phon), ejektivo
eke, pliigi; **eke out**, (living), pene gajni (vivon), pene vivadi [int]; (use frugally), ŝpare uzi [tr]
el, (elevated urban train), (supertera) metroo
elaborate, ellabori [tr], kompliki [tr]; ~ita, komplika
Elaeagnus, eleagno; **Elaeagnus angustifolia**, oleastro
elaidate, elaidato; **elaidatic**, ~a
Elaine, Helena
Elam, Elamo
élan, vervo [not "elano"]; **élan vital**, vitala elano
Elaphrus, elafro
elapid, elapo
Elaps, elapo; **Elaps corallinus**, koralserpento; **Elapinae**, ~enoj
elapse, pasi [int]; **elapsed time**, ~inta tempo
elasmobranch, elasmobranko
Elasmobranchii, elasmobrankoj
elastic, elasta; ~aĵo; **elasticity**, ~eco; **elasticize**, ~igi
elastin, elastino
elastomer, elastomero
elate, ekzalti [tr]
elater, elatero
Elater, elatero; **Elateridae**, ~edoj
elaterium, elaterio
Elatine, elatino
Elba, (Insulo) Elbo
Elbe, (Rivero) Elbo
elbow, (gen), kubuto; ~umi [tr]; (pipe), genutubo
Elbrus, Elbruso

elder, (older), pli aĝa; pliaĝulo; (rel), presbitero; (bot: *Sambucus*), sambuko; **elderly**, maljuna; maljunuloj; **eldest**, plej aĝa; **dwarf elder**, (*S. ebulus*), ebulo
elderberry, (plant), sambuko; (berry), sambuka bero
El Dorado, Eldorado
Eleagnus, [see *"Elaeagnus"*]
Eleanor, Eleonora
elecampane, inulo
elect, (choose, approve by vote, gen), elekti [tr]; (to parliament etc.; depute), deputi [tr]; **election**, ~o; **byelection, primary election**, krom~o; **elective**, (re office to which one is elected), ~a; (optional, gen), ~ebla; ~eblaĵo; (esp re school subject), fakultativo; fakultativa; **elector**, ~anto; **Elector**, (of emperor), princo~~isto; **electorate**, ~antaro; **electoral**, ~a; **electoral college**, kolegio de ~antoj
electret, elektreto
electric, electrical, elektra; **electricity**, ~o; **electrician**, ~isto; **electrify**, (give electric charge, as to a fence), ~i [tr] [cp "charge"]; (provide electricity, as to a city), ~izi [tr]; **isoelectric**, izo~a; **photoelectric**, lum~a; **piezoelectric**, piezo~a; **static electricity**, statika ~o; **thermoelectric**, termo~a; **thermoelectric couple, thermoelectric pile**, termo~a pilo; **triboelectric**, tribo~a
electro–, (pfx: elec), elektro–
electrocute, (gen), elektrokuti [tr]
electrode, elektrodo
electrolysis, elektrolizo; **electrolytic**, ~a; **electrolyze**, ~i [tr]
electrolyte, elektrolito
electrometer, elektrometro; **electrometric**, ~a
electromotive, elektromova
electron, elektrono; **electron-volt**, ~-volto
electronic, elektronika; **electronics**, ~o; **electronic data processing**, (abb: EDP), komputorado
electrophoresis, kataforezo
electrophorus, elektroforo, plat–kondensilo
Electrophorus, (zool), gimnoto

electroplate, galvanizi [tr]
electroscope, elektroskopo
electrotropism, elektrotropismo
electrotype, elektrotipo; ~igi; **electrotypic**, ~a; **electrotypy**, ~io
electrum, elektrumo†
electuary, elektuario
eleemosynary, (charitable), karitata; (supported by charity), ~apogata
elegant, eleganta; **elegance**, ~eco; **inelegant**, mal~a, kruda
elegy, elegio
element, (gen), elemento; **elemental, elementary**, ~a; **elements**, (weather), vetero; (basics), aboco, rudimentoj; **thermoelement**, termo~o; **trace element**, (in organism), oligo~o, spur~o; **be out of one's element**, esti ekster sia medio
eleo–, (chem pfx), eleo–
elephant, elefanto; **elephantiasis**, elefantiazo; **sea elephant**, mar~o; **white elephant**, senutilaĵo, multekosta balasto
Elephantine, Elefantino
Elephas, elefanto; **Elephas** primigenius, mamuto; **Elephantidae**, ~edoj
Eletteria cardamomum, kardamomo
Eleusis, Eleŭziso; **Eleusinian**, ~a
elevate, (lift, raise, gen), levi [tr]; **elevation**, (lifting), ~(ad)o; (height, as above sea level, ground level, etc.), alteco; **elevated**, ~ita; (dignified), digna; **elevator**, (for people etc.), lifto; (hoist), elevatoro; (of plane), empenerono; (for grain storage), grenprovizejo
elf, elfo
Eli, Elio
Eliana, Eliana
Elias, (modern name), Eliĝo; (Bib), Elija
elicit, elvoki [tr], eltiri [tr]
elide, elizii [tr]
Eliezer, Eliezero
eligible, (fit to be chosen), elektebla; (having right), rajtanta; **eligible person**, ~ulo; rajtanto
Elijah, (modern name), Eliĝo; (Bib), Elija
eliminate, elimini [tr]
Elinor, Eleonora

Elisabeth, Elizabeta
Elisha, Eliŝa
elision, elizio
elite, elito; ~a
elixir, eliksiro
Eliza, Eliza
Elizabeth, Elizabeto
elk, (Eŭropea) alko
ell, (L-shaped pipe joint etc.), genu(tub)o; (unit of measure), ulno [length varies]
Ellen, Helena
ellipse, elipso; **elliptical,** ~a
ellipsoid, elipsoido
Ellis, Eliŝa
elm, ulmo
elocution, elokucio
Elohim, Elohim; **Elohist,** ~isto; **Elohistic,** ~a
Eloise, Heloiza
elongate, (pli)long/igi; ~iĝi
elope, (kun)forkuri [int]; **elopement,** ~o
eloquent, elokventa; **eloquence,** ~eco
Elsa, Ilza
El Salvador, Salvadoro
else, (different, other; otherwise), alia; ~e (e.g.: *someone else:* iu ~a; *where else could it be?:* kie ~e ĝi povus esti?; *eat, or else you'll be hungry:* manĝu, aŭ ~e vi malsatos); (still more), ~a, ankoraŭ (e.g.: *do you want anything else?:* ĉu vi volas ion ~an [or] ankoraŭ ion?); **else's,** (possessive), [rephrase w "de" (e.g.: *that is someone else's umbrella:* tiu ombrelo estas de iu ~a)]; **elsewhere,** ~loke(n); **or else!,** (threat), aŭ ve! (e.g.: *clean your room or else!:* purigu vian ĉambron aŭ ve!)
Elsinore, Elsinoro
elucidate, klarigi, prilumi [tr]
elude, eviti [tr], eskapi [tr, int] (–on, de –o); **elusive,** eskapema, nekaptebla
elutriate, elui [tr]
elver, angilido
Elvira, Elvira
Elymus, elimo
Elysium, Elizeo; **Elysian,** ~a
elytron, elitro
Elzevir, elzevira; **Elzevir type, Elzevir book,** ~o

em, (unit of font or type size), kadrato; (pica, 1/6 inch), sesoncolo
emaciate, marasm/igi; **emaciated,** ~a; **emaciation,** ~o
emanate, emani [int]; ~igi
emancipate, emancipi [tr]
emancipist, (Aus), ekspunlaborulo
Emanuel, Emanuelo
emasculate, (castrate), kastri [tr]; (weaken), debiligi
embalm, balzami [tr], en~igi
embankment, (dike), digo; (slope of road fill, trench, etc.), taluso
embargo, embargo; ~i [tr]
embark, (get on ship), enŝipiĝi; (on plane), enaviiĝi; (start out, as on journey, gen), ekiri [int]; **disembark,** elŝipiĝi; elaviiĝi; **embark upon,** (undertake, begin), entrepreni [tr], komenci [tr]
embarrass, (gen), embarasi [tr]; **embarrassment,** ~o; **embarrassing,** ~a
embassy, ambasado
embattle, fortikigi
embayment, kreko
embed, (set in, gen), enfiksi [tr]; (ornament, as jewel etc.), inkrusti [tr]
embellish, ornami [tr]
ember, braĝ/ero; **embers,** ~o [note sing]
Emberiza, emberizo; **Emberiza** hortulana, hortulano ?
embezzle, malversacii [tr]; **embezzlement,** ~o; **embezzler,** ~into
embitter, amarigi
emblazon, blazoni [tr]
emblem, emblemo
embody, enkorpigi; **disembody,** elkorpigi [cp "discarnate"]
embolism, embolio
embolus, embolo
emboss, reliefigi; (by chiseling), bosi [tr]
embouchure, (mus: mouthpiece), buŝ/aĵo; (method of applying mouth to mus instrument), ~tekniko
embrace, (clasp in arms, hug), brakumi [tr]; ~o; (enclose, gen), ĉirkaŭpreni [tr]; (w some pressure), ĉirkaŭpremi [tr]; (include, extend to), ampleksi [tr]; amplekso
embrasure, embrazuro [cp "crenel"]

embrocate, embrokacii [tr]; **embrocation,** ~o
embroider, brodi [tr]; **embroidery,** ~ado; ~aĵo; **embroidery hoop,** (~aĵa) tamburino
embroil, impliki [tr]
embryo, embrio; **embryogeny, embryogenesis,** ~ogenezo; **embryogenetic, embryogenic,** ~ogeneza; **embryology,** ~ologio; **embryological,** ~ologia; **embryologist,** ~ologo; **embryonic,** ~a; ~eca
emcee, programestro; ~i [tr]
emeer, emiro
emend, revizii [tr]; **emendation,** ~o; ~aĵo
emerald, smeraldo; ~a
emerge, (come out of, gen), eliĝi (de); (from specific medium or state), eliĝi (e.g.: [from water], elakviĝi; [from chaos], elĥaosiĝi); (from any liquid; opp "submerge"), emerĝi† [int], malmergiĝi; (re light, as from transparent medium), emerĝi [int]; (appear, lit or fig), aperi [int]; **emergence,** ~o; emerĝo†; apero
emergency, kriz(okaz)o; ~a; **state of emergency,** ~ostato
emeritus, emerito; ~a
emersed, malmergiĝ/inta; **emersion,** ~o [see "emerge"]
emery, (mineral), smirgo; **emery paper,** ~a papero; **emery wheel,** ~a rado
Emery, (man's name), Emeriko
emesis, vom/ado; **emesis basin,** ~ujo
emetic, emetiko, vomigenzo; ~a
emetine, emetino
emeu, emuo
–emia, (med sfx), –emio; **–emic,** ~a
emigrate, (gen), elmigri [int]; (for pol reason), emigri [int]; **emigration,** ~(ad)o; (pol), emigracio, emigr(ad)o; **emigrant,** ~into; emigrinto
émigré (gen), elmigrinto; (for pol reason), emigrinto
Emil, Émile, Emilo
Emilia, Emila, ~ino
eminent, (outstanding, noteworthy), eminenta; (rising above), elstara; **eminence,** ~eco; elstaraĵo; elstareco; (title of cardinal), eminenco; **preemi-**

nent, supera, super~a, (super)elstara; **be eminent,** ~i† [int]
emir, emiro; **emirate,** ~lando; **United Arab Emirates,** Unuiĝintaj Arabaj E~landoj
emissary, reprezentanto, sendito
emit, (give off, gen), eligi, ellasi [tr], elsendi [tr]; ($: issue), emisii [tr]; **emission,** ~(aĵ)o, ellas(aĵ)o, elsend(aĵ)o; emisiaĵo; **emitter,** (tech), elsendilo; **nocturnal emission,** dumdorma ejakulo
Emma, Emma
Emmanuel, Emanuelo
Emmaus, Emauso
Emmery, Emeriko
emmetropia, eŭmetrop/eco; **emmetropic,** ~a
Emmy, Eminjo
emollient, moliga; ~enzo
emolument, lukraĵo
Emory, Emeriko
emotion, emocio; **emotional,** ~a, ~iĝema; **emotionalism,** ~emo; ~eco; **emote,** ~umi [int]; **emotive,** ~a
empale, [see "impale"]
empanel, [see "impanel"]
empath, klarsent/ulo; **empathy,** (having feeling for), kunsentado; kunsentemo; (psychic), ~ado; **empathize,** kunsenti [int]; **empathic,** ~a; kunsentema; **empathethic,** kunsentema
Empedocles, Empedoklo
empennage, empeno
emperor, imperiestro [cp "imperator"]
Empetrum, empetro
emphasis, emfazo; **emphatic,** ~a; **emphasize,** ~i [tr]
emphysema, emfizemo; **emphysematous,** ~a
empire, (pol), imperio; (furniture), empiro; empira
empiric, empiri/ulo; **empirical,** ~a; **empirical experi ence,** ~o; **empiricism,** ~ismo; **empiricist,** ~isto
emplacement, (mil), (kanona) nesto, sidejo
employ, (hire person), dungi [tr]; (use), uzi [tr], utiligi, apliki [tr]; **employe(e),** ~ito; **employer,** ~into; ~anto; **employment,** (hiring), ~ado; ~eco; (a job), ofico; (profession), pro-

fesio; (number, %age of employed persons), ~iteco (e.g.: *a period of high employment:* periodo de alta ~iteco); **employment agent,** ~agento; **employment agency,** ~agentejo; **self-employed,** mem~ita; **unemployed,** senofica, senlabora; **unemployed person,** senlaborulo, senoficulo; **unemployment,** senlaboreco; **unemployment compensation,** mal~a kompenso, mal~a mono; **be employed (in, as),** ofici [int] (en, kiel) [see "do"]
emporium, (bsns center), emporio; (large store, department store), magazeno
empower, (give right, authorize), rajtigi; (commission), komisii [tr]
empress, imperiestrino
empty, (not full), malplena; ~igi; ~iĝi; (vacant), vaka
empyema, empiemo
empyrean, empireo; ~a; **empyreal,** ~a
empyreuma, empireŭmo
emu, emuo
emulate, (imitate), imiti [tr]; (rival), rivali [int] (kun)
emulsion, emulsio; **emulsify,** ~igi
Emys, emido; Emydinae, ~enoj
en, (printing: half em), kadrateto; dekduoncolo [see "em"]
en–, (pfx: in, onto), en–
–en, (sfx: made of), –a (e.g.: *wooden:* ligna); (cause to be), –igi (e.g.: *strengthen:* fortikigi)
enable, ebligi
enact, (law), leĝdoni [tr]; (theat), ludi [tr]; roli [int] (kiel); **enactment,** ~o; ludado
enallage, enalago
enamel, (gen), emajlo; ~i [tr]; (dental), adamantino
enamo(u)r, enam/igi; **be(come) enamored of,** ~iĝi al
enantiomorph, enantiomorf/aĵo; **enantiomorphic,** ~a; **enantiomorphism,** ~eco
enantiosis, enantiozo
enantiotropy, enantiotrop/eco; **enantiotropic,** ~a
encaustic, enkaŭstiko; ~a; **paint with encaustic,** ~i [tr]

Enceladus, Encelado
encephalitis, encefalito
encephalogram, encefal/ogramo; **encephalograph,** ~ografo; **encephalography,** ~ografio; **encephalographer,** ~ografiisto; **electroencephalogram,** elektro~ogramo
encephalon, encefalo
enchant, (bewitch), sorĉi [tr]; (charm), ĉarmi [tr]; (delight, rapture), ravi [tr]; **enchanting,** ĉarma; rava; **enchantment,** ĉarmo; ravo; **disenchant,** seniluziigi
enchilada, kapsikofaldaĵo
enclave, enklavo
enclitic, enklitiko; ~a
enclose, enfermi [tr]; (in mail), kunsendi [tr]
encomium, panegiro
encompass, ampleksi [tr]
encore, (mus work etc.), bis/aĵo; (shout), ~i [tr]; ~o; (interj), bis!
encounter, (gen), renkonti [tr]; ~iĝi; ~(iĝ)o
encourage, instigi [tr], kuraĝigi; **be(come) encouraged,** kuraĝiĝi; **encouragement,** ~o, kuraĝigo
encroach, sin trudi; **encroachment,** sintrudo
encrust, [see "incrust"]
encumber, (hinder), malhelpi [tr], embarasi [tr]; (block), obstrukci [tr]; (load down), ŝarĝi [tr]; **encumbrance,** ~o, embaraso; obstrukco; ŝarĝado; ŝarĝo
encyclical, encikliko
encyclopedia, enciklopedio
end, (cease, stop, limit, etc.), fini [tr]; ~iĝi; ~(iĝ)o; ~aĵo; (goal), celo; (extremity), ekstremaĵo; **ending,** ~(aĵ)o; (gram), ~aĵo, sufikso; **end up,** ~e esti [int], ~e troviĝi, rezultiĝi; **in the end,** post ĉio, ~e, ~~e; **on end,** (standing, vertical), vertikala; vertikale; (continuous), sinsekvaj; sinsekve (e.g.: *for three days on end:* dum tri sinsekvaj tagoj [or] tri tagoj sinsekve); **upend,** (stand on end), starigi; stariĝi; (topple, turn over), renversi [tr]; renversiĝi; **come to an end,** ~iĝi, ĉesi [int]; **bring to an end, put an end to,** ~i, ĉesigi; **to that end,** tiucele; **to the bit-**

ter end, ĝis la ~a ekstremo; **at loose ends**, senokupa; senokupe; **be no end to**, abundi [int]; **be at the end of one's rope (tether)**, be at wit's end, ne plu povi elteni [tr]; **make ends meet**, sufiĉigi la enspezojn; **end for end**, renversite; **end to end**, vic(apud)e; **hold one's end up**, fari sian parton; **to end all**, super ĉiuj. superantaj ĉiujn (e.g.: *a trip to end all trips:* vojaĝo super ĉiuj vojaĝoj [or] superanta ĉiujn vojaĝojn)
endeavor, klopodi [tr], peni [tr]; ~(ad)o, pen(ad)o
endemic, endemia; ~o
endive, endivio
endo–, (sci pfx), endo–
endocardium, endokardio; **endocardiitis**, ~ito
endocarp, endokarpo
endocrine, endokrina; **endocrinology**, ~ologio; **endocrinologist**, ~ologo
endoderm, endodermo
endogamy, endogamio
endogenous, **endogenic**, endo/gena; **endogeny**, ~genezo
endoplasm, endoplasmo
Endor, En-Doro
endorse, (check etc.), ĝiri [tr], endosi [tr]; (support), subteni [tr]; **endorsement**, ~o, endoso; subteno; (on insurance policy etc.), krompoliso
endoscope, endoskopo
endosmosis, endosmozo
endothelium, endotelio
endothermic, endoterma
endow, **endue**, doti [tr]
endure, (last, remain), daŭri [int]; (bear pain, suffer, etc.), elteni [tr], elporti [tr], suferi [tr], rezisti [tr]; **endurance**, ~(ad)o; ~ivo; elten(ad)o, elport(ad)o, sufer(ad)o, rezist(ad)o; **enduring**, ~a, persista
Endymion, Endimiono
–ene, (chem sfx), –eno
enema, klistero [cp "catharsis"]
enemy, malamiko; ~a
energy, (phys), energio; (vigor), vigleco; **energetic**, ~a; vigla; **energetics**, (sci), energetiko; **energize**, ~izi [tr]
enervate, senfortigi, debiligi
enfilade, enfili [tr]; ~o

enfold, (wrap), envolvi [tr]; (embrace), brakumi [tr]
enforce, (make law etc. effective), efikigi; (impose by force), perforti [tr]; **enforced**, ~ita; ~ata; perforta
enfranchise, (re vote right), voĉdonrajt/igi, doni ~on al
Engadine, Engadino
engage, (hire person), dungi [tr]; (performers for show etc.; involve someone in plot etc.), engaĝi [tr]; (mech: connect, mesh), kupli [tr]; kupliĝi [see "connect"]; (reserve), rezervi [tr]; (attract), altiri [tr]; (keep busy, occupy), okupi [tr]; (mil: attack), ataki [tr]; (take part), partopreni [tr]; **engaged**, (not available), nedisponebla, okupata; (to marry), fianĉ(in)iĝinta; gefianĉiĝintaj; **get engaged**, (to marry), fianĉ(in)iĝi; gefianĉiĝi; **engage upon**, **engage in**, (undertake, begin), entrepreni [tr], komenci [tr]; **engagement**, ~(iĝ)o; engaĝ(iĝ)o; kupl(iĝ)o; rezerv(iĝ)o; altir(iĝ)o; okup(iĝ)o; atako; partopreno; fianĉ(in)iĝo; gefianĉiĝo
en garde, (position), singardo; (interj), gardu vin!
engender, estigi, kaŭzi [tr], generi [tr]
engine, (motor), motoro; (any machine), maŝino; (rr locomotive), lokomotivo; **engine room**, maŝinejo; **diesel engine**, dizelo; **gasoline engine**, benzin~o; **internal combustion engine**, eksplod~o; **steam engine**, vapor~o
engineer, (does engineering), inĝeniero; ~i [tr]; (operator of engines etc.), maŝinisto; (in charge of building), flegisto; (rr), lokomotivestro; **engineering**, ~arto; **reengineer**, re~i [tr]
English, (of England), Angla; ~o; la ~a (lingvo); (spin), rotaciigi; rotacio; **Englishman**, ~o; **(the) English Channel**, Maniko [note no "la"]; **body English**, postmoviĝo
England, Anglio; **New England**, (Am; Aus), Nov-~o
engorge, (devour), vori [tr]; (med: congest), kongesti [tr]; kongestiĝi
Engraulis, engraŭlo
engrave, gravuri [tr]; **engraving**, ~aĵo

engulf, engluti [tr]
enharmonic, enharmona
enigma, enigmo; **enigmatic,** ~a
enjoin, (prohibit), malpermesi [tr]; (order), ordoni [tr]
enjoy, ĝui [tr]; **enjoyable,** ~inda, ~iga; **enjoyment,** ~o; **enjoy oneself,** amuziĝi
enlarge, (make larger, gen), pligrand/igi; ~iĝi; (dilate), dilati [tr]; dilatiĝi; (go into detail), detali [tr]; (increase scope, extent), pliampleksigi; **enlarger,** (phot), ~igilo
enlighten, lumigi, klarigi; **enlightened,** (learned, educated), klera; **enlightenment,** ~o, klarigo; ~iteco, klereco; **Enlightenment,** (18th-Century school of philosophy), Klerismo
enlist, (mil), rekruti [tr]; ~iĝi; (gen), varbi [tr]; varbiĝi; (enroll), enlistigi; enlistiĝi; **enlistee, enlisted (wo)man,** ~(in)o
enliven, vigligi, animi [tr], gajigi
en masse, amase
enmesh, impliki [tr]
enmity, malamikeco
ennoble, (re noble qualities), nobligi; (re nobleman), nobeligi
ennui, enuo
Enoch, Ĥanoĥ
enol, enolo
enology, enolog/io; **enologist,** ~o
enormous, enorma, grandega, mamuta; **enormity,** (size), ~eco, grandegeco; (wicked, outra geous), fiegeco, ekscesego
enough, sufiĉa; ~e (de, da); **be enough,** ~i [int]
en passant, pasante
enquire, [see "inquire"]
enrage, furioz/igi; **enraged,** ~a
en rapport, en raporto, en akordo
enrapture, ravi [tr], ekstazigi
enrich, (gen), (pli)riĉigi
enroll, (in school), matrikuli [tr]; ~iĝi; (put on any list), registri [tr], listigi; registriĝi, listiĝi; **enrollment,** ~(iĝ)o; registr(iĝ)o, listigo, listiĝo; (number enrolled), ~itaro, registritaro
en route, survoja; ~e
ens, ento
ensconce, ennestigi

ensemble, (gen), ensemblo
enshrine, sankt/igi, en~ejigi
ensign, (badge), insigno; (banner), standardo; (naval officer), suboficiro
ensile, insili [tr]; **ensilage,** ~ado; ~i; (silage), ~aĵo, silaĵo
enslave, sklavigi
ensnare, kapti [tr], en~iligi
ensue, sekvi [tr]
ensure, (make sure), certigi; (make safe), sekurigi
–ent, (sfx), [see "–ant"]
entablature, entablemento
entail, (involve), koncerni [tr]; (bring about, necessitate), necesigi, sekvigi, estigi, rezultigi; (limit inheritance), majoratigi
entangle, impliki [tr]; **disentangle,** mal~i [tr]
entelechy, enteleksio
entellus, entelo
entente, entento; **entente cordiale,** kora ~o
enter, (go in), eniri [tr]; (come in), enveni [tr]; (travel into), enveturi [tr]; (into cmptr, calculator), enmeti [tr]; (write into list, $ account, etc.; register), enskribi [tr], registri [tr]; **entry,** ~o; enveno; enveturo; enskrib(aĵ)o, registr(aĵ)o; **enter upon,** (undertake, start), entrepreni [tr], komenci [tr]
enteralgia, enteralgio
enteric, entera
enteritis, enterito
enter(o)–, (med pfx), enter(o)–
enterococcus, enterokoko
enterocolitis, enterokojlito
enterokinase, enterokinazo
enteron, entero
enteropneust, enteropneŭsto
Enteropneusta, enteropneŭstoj
enterostomy, enterostomio
enterovaccine, enterovakcino
enterprise, entrepreno; **enterprising,** ~ema, ambicia
entertain, (amuse), amuzi [tr], distri [tr]; (be host), gastigi; (regale), regali [tr]; **entertainment,** (show etc.), distraĵo; **entertainer,** distristo
enthalpy, entalpio
enthrall, fascini [tr], ravi [tr]
enthrone, surtronigi

enthuse, entuziasm/igi; **enthusiasm**, ~o; **enthusiast**, ~ulo, adepto; **enthusiastic**, ~a; **be enthusiastic**, ~i [int]
enthymeme, entimemo
entice, logi [tr]; **enticement**, ~o; ~aĵo
entire, (all of), tuta; (whole, undivided), integra; **entirely**, ~e; **entirety**, ~o
entitle, (give right), rajt/igi; (give title), titoli [tr]; **entitlement**, ~igo; ~iĝo; **be entitled to**, havi ~on (al)
entity, (being, gen), ento, estaĵo; (essence), esenco; **nonentity**, (nonexistence), neekzisto; (unimportant person), neniulo, nulo; **incarnate entity**, enkarniĝinto; **discarnate entity**, elkarniĝinto
entoderm, endodermo
entomology, entomolog/io; **entomologist**, ~o
Entomostraca, entomostrakoj
entourage, sekvantaro, ĉirkaŭantaro
Entozoa, entozooj
entozoon, entozoo; **entozoa**, ~oj; **entozoal**, **entozoan**, **entozoic**, ~a
entr'acte, interakto
entrails, intestoj, ~aro [cp "tripe"]
entrance, (act of entering), eniro; enveno; [see "enter"]; (place), ~ejo; envenejo; (right to enter), ~rajto; envenrajto; (put into trance), trancigi; (rapture), ravi [tr]
entrant, (in contest), konkursanto
entrap, kapti [tr], en~iligi
entreat, pet/egi [tr], ĵur~i [tr]; **entreaty**, ~ego, ĵur~o
entrée, (main dish), ĉef/manĝaĵo, ~plado; (dish between soup etc. and main dish), entreo; (entrance), [see "entrance"]
entrench, (fortify w trenches), trancĉeizi [tr]; **be(come) entrenched**, (firmly established), firmiĝi, firme fiksiĝi [not "establiĝi"; see "establish"]
entrepreneur, entreprenisto
entropy, entropio
entrust, (confide in; assign care of), konfidi [tr]; (commission to do something), komisii [tr]
entry, (going in; place etc.), eniro; enveno; ~ejo; envenejo; [see "enter", "entrance"]
entwine, enplekti [tr]; ~iĝi

enucleate, enuklei [tr]; **enucleation**, ~(ad)o
enumerate, (count), nombri [tr], kompti [tr]; (list), listigi; (detail), detali [tr]
enunciate, (pronounce), elparoli [tr]; (state, declare), deklari [tr]
enuresis, enurezo
envelop, (wrap), envolvi [tr]; (cover), tegi [tr]; (hide), kaŝi [tr]
envelope, (for mail etc.), koverto; (covering), tegaĵo; (math), envelopo
environment, (surroundings, gen), medio, ĉirkaŭaĵo; (biosphere), viv~o, natur~o; (sci study of), ~ologio; **environmental**, viv~(ologi)a; **environmentalist**, (scientist specializing in environment), viv~ologo; (person favoring protection of ecology), (viv)~aktivulo
environs, ĉirkaŭaĵo
envisage, (envision), imagi [tr]
envision, imagi [tr]
envoy, sendito
envy, envii [tr]; ~o; **enviable**, ~inda; **envious**, (gen trait), ~ema; **be envious of**, ~i
enzyme, enzimo
Eocene, eoceno; ~a
Eolian, [see "Aeolian"]
eolithic, eolitika; ~o
eon, eono
eosin, eozino
epacris, Epacris, epakrido
epact, epakto
Epaminondas, Epaminondo
epanorthosis, epanortozo
eparch, eparki/estro; **eparchy**, ~o
epaulet(te), epoleto
épée, spado
ependyma, ependimo; **ependymitis**, ~ito
epenthesis, epentezo
epha(h), efo
ephebus, **ephebos**, efebo
ephedrine, efedrino
ephemeral, efemera
ephemeris, efemerido
Ephesus, Efezo; **Ephesian**, ~a; ~ano; **Ephesians**, (Bib), ~anoj
ephod, efodo
Ephraim, Efraimo
Ephrata, Efrato

epic, epopeo; epikat, ~a
epicalyx, epicaliko
epicanthus, epikanto; epicanthic, ~a
epicarp, epikarpo
epicene, ambaüseksa
epicenter, epicentrot
epicondyle, epikondilo
Epictetus, Epikteto
epicure, epikur/ano; epicurean, ~a;
~ano; epicureanism, epicurism, ~is-
mo
Epicurus, Epikuro; Epicurean, ~ano;
Epicureanism, ~ismo
epicycle, epiciklo*
epicycloid, epicikloido
Epidaurus, Epidaüro
epidemic, epidemio; ~a; epidemiolo-
gy, ~ologio; epidemiologist, ~ologo
epidendrum, epidendron, Epidendrum, epidendro
epidermis, epidermo
epidiascope, epidiaskopo
epididymis, epididimo
epigastrium, epigastro; epigastric, ~a
epiglottis, epigloto
epigram, epigramo
epigraph, epigrafo
epigynous, epigina
epilepsy, epilepsio; epileptic, ~a;
~ulo; grand mal epilepsy, majora
~o; petit mal epilepsy, minora ~o
Epilobium, epilobio
epilogue, epilogo
epinephrine, adrenalino
Epiphany, Epifanio
epiphenomenon, epifenomeno
epiphonema, epifonemo
epiphysis, epifizo
epiphyte, epifito
epiploon, epiploo
Epirus, Epiro
episcopal, episkopa; Episcopal(ian),
E~a; E~ano; Episcopalianism, E~an-
ismo [cp "Anglican"]
episcopate, (rank), episkop/eco; (all
bishops), ~aro
episiotomy, perineotomio
episode, epizodo
epispastic, epispastika; ~ilo
epistaxis, epistakso
epistemology, epistemologio
epistle, epistolo

epitaph, epitafo
epitaxy, epitaksiot; epitaxial, epitaxic,
~a
epithalamion, epithalamium, epitala-
mo
epithelium, epitelio
epithet, epiteto
epitome, epitomo; epitomize, ~igi
epizootic, epizootio; ~a
epoch, epoko
epode, (gen), epodo
epopee, epopeo
epos, eposot
epoxide, epoksiido, alkena oksido
epoxy, epoksio; ~a
epoxy-, (chem pfx), epoksi-
EPROM, (cmptr: acronym for "eras-
able programmable read-only memory"), epromot
epsilon, epsila [see § 16]
epulis, epuliso
equable, (calm, serene), egalanima
equal, egala; ~i [tr]; equalize, ~igi;
equality, ~eco; coequal, ~a; ~ulo;
unequal, mal~a, ne~a; unequaled,
sen~a; of equal ..., sam...a, ~...a (e.g.:
of equal rank: samranga); be equal
to, (math), ~i; (be capable, sufficient
for), kapabli [tr], povi [tr], sufiĉi por
(e.g.: my knowledge is not equal to the
task: mia scio ne sufiĉas por la tasko;
is he equal to that assignment?: ĉu li
kapablas [or] povas fari tiun asignon?)
equanimity, egalanimeco
equate, egaligi
equation, (equating), egaligo; (math,
chem), ekvacio
equator, ekvatoro; equatorial, ~a;
(telescope), ekvatorialo
equerry, eskviro
equestrian, (re horses), ĉevala; (horse
rider), ~isto, ~rajdanto
equi-, (pfx: equal), egal– (e.g.: equidistant: ~distanca)
equilateral, egallatera; ~o
equilibrist, ekvilibristo
equilibrium, ekvilibro; be in equilibrium, ~i [int]; put into equilibrium,
~igi
equine, ĉeval(ec)a
equinox, ekvinokso; equinoctial, ~a
equip, (supply, provide), ekipi [tr] (per)

(e.g.: *equip them with boots:* ~i ilin
per botoj); **equipage,** ~aĵo; **equipment,** (provisions), ~aĵo; (machinery), aparataro, maŝinaro; (cmptr
hardware), hardvarot
equipoise, egalpezo, ekvilibro
equipollent, ekvipolenta
equisetum, Equisetum, ekvizeto
equitable, justa
equity, (fairness), justeco; (value of
property above amount owed), posedumo, posedvaloro
equivalent, ekvivalento, egalvaloro; ~a,
egalvalora; **equivalence,** ~eco
equivocal, dubasenca; **equivocate,**
~umi [int], ~e paroli [tr]; ~e skribi
[tr]; **unequivocal,** ne~a, klar(senc)a,
eksplicita
Equus, ekvo; Equus asinus, azeno; Equus caballus, ĉevalo; Equus hemionus, Equus kiang, hemiono, kiango;
Equus zebra, zebro
er, (vocalized pause in speaking), aa, ah
-er, (sfx: person who does), -into; -anto; -onto; -isto (e.g.: *seller:* (before
closing deal), vendinto; (during settlement), vendanto; (later), vendinto;
(sales agent), vendisto); (simple tool),
-ilo (e.g.: *scraper:* skrapilo); (more
complex machinery), -ilo, -atoro
(e.g.: *photocopier:* fotokopiilo; *transformer:* transformatoro); (chem
agent), -enzo; (more), pli (e.g.: *higher:* pli alta)
era, erao, epoko
eradicate, elradikigi, elimini [tr]
Eranthis, erantido
erase, (rub out, as something written),
for/skrapi [tr], ~gumi [tr], ~viŝi [tr];
(delete from cmptr memory etc.),
~viŝi [tr], ~streki [tr]; (eradicate), elradikigi, elimini [tr]; **eraser,** (rubber,
for pencil or ink), skrapgumo; (for
chalk), viŝilo; **erasure,** ~skrap(ad)o,
~viŝ(ad)o; ~skrapaĵo, ~viŝaĵo
Erasmus, Erasmo
Erato, Eratoa
Eratosthenes, Eratosteno
erbium, erbio
ere, [see "before"]
Erebus, Erebo
erect, (build), konstrui [tr]; (set up,

gen), starigi; (put together, assemble), munti [tr]; (anat, e.g., re penis),
erekti [tr]; erektiĝinta; (upright), rekta, vertikala; **erection,** ~o; starigo;
munto; erektiĝo
erepsin, erepsino
ereptase, ereptazo
erethism, eretismo
erg, ergo; **erg(o)meter,** ~ometro; **ergograph,** ~ografo
ergonomic, ergonomiat; **ergonomics,**
~o
ergosterol, ergosterolo
ergot, (plant disease; drug), ergoto;
(fungus), ~fungo
Eric, Eriko
Erica, (woman's name), Erika
Erica, (bot), eriko
ericaceous, erikaca
Erycina, (zool), ericinot
Eridanus, Eridano
Erie, (gen), Erio; **Lake Erie,** Lago ~o
erigeron, Erigeron, erigerono
Erik, Eriko
Erin, Erino
Erinaceus, erinaco
eringo, eringio
Erinys, Erinio; **Erinyes,** ~oj
Eriodendron anfractuosum, kapokarbo
Eriophorum, erioforo
Erithacus rubecola, rubekolo
Eritrea, Eritreo
ermine, (animal or fur), ermeno
Ernest, Ernesto; **Ernestine,** ~a, ~ino
erode, erozii [tr]; ~iĝi [not "erodi"; see
"wear"]
Erodium, erodio
erogenous, erotogena
Eros, Eroso
erosion, erozio
erotic, erotika, erota; **erotica,** ~aĵoj;
eroticism, erotismo
erotism, erotismo
erotogenic, erotogena
erotology, erotologio
erotomania, erotomanio
erotophobia, erotofobio
err, erari [int], misi [int]; malpravi [int]
[see "error"]
errand, irtasko; **run an errand,** fari
~on
errant, (roving), vaganta; (erring), erar-

anta
errata, (pres)eraroj, erar-tabelo [note sing]; **errata page**, eratumo
erratic, vaganta, neregula; (geol), eratika
erroneous, erara, malprava [see "error"]
error, (incorrectness, gen), eraro; (re opinion, statement, etc.), malpraveco; (between apparent or approximate and exact; between measured and real; between aimed-at and hit; etc.), ekarto; **trial and error**, provo kaj ~o
ersatz, postiĉa, surogata; ~aĵo, surogato [cp "substitute", "surrogate"]
erstwhile, antaŭa, iama
Eruca, eruko
erucic, eruka; **erucic acid**, ~a acido
eruct(ate), rukti [int]
erudite, erudicia; **erudition**, ~o; **erudite person**, ~ulo, erudito
erupt, (spew forth, gen), elsputi [tr]; ~iĝi; (med; volcanic), erupcii [int], erupti [int]; erupciigi, eruptigi; **eruption**, ~(iĝ)o; erupcio, erupto
–ery, (sfx: place), –ejo
Eryngium, eringio
eryngo, (plant), eringio; (candied root), kandizita ~a radiko
Erysimum, erizimo
erysipelas, erizipelo; **erysipelatous**, ~a
Erythea, eritio
erythema, eritemo
erythrocyte, eritrocito
erythronium, eritronio
erythrose, eritrozo
erythrosis, eritrozo
Erythroxylon coca, kokao
Esau, Esavo
escadrille, eskadro
escalade, eskalado; ~i [tr]
escalate, ekspansii [int]; ~igi
escalator, eskalatoro; **escalator clause**, (bsns, $), ekspansia klaŭzo
escapade, (frolic, romp, prank), petolaĵo, kapriolaĵo
escape, eskapi [tr, int] (–on, el –o, de –o); ~o; **escapism**, ~ismo; **escapist**, ~isma; **escape artist**, ~emulo; **fire-escape**, saveskalo, sav~ejo; **narrow escape**, apenaŭa ~o; **have a narrow escape**, apenaŭ ~i

escapement, (clock etc.), klikaĵo, ellasilo [cp "pawl"]
escarole, endivio
escarp, (mil), eskarpo; ~igi; (geol), krutaĵo; **escarpment**, (geol), krutaĵo; (mil), kontraŭ~o
eschar, eskaro
eschatology, eskatologio
Escherichia coli, kojlobacilo
eschew, eviti [tr]
escort, eskorti [tr]; (escorting group), ~o; (individual), ~anto
escrow, fidita; ~a dokumento; **in escrow**, ~a; ~e; **escrow account**, fidkonto
escudo, eskudo
esculent, mangebla
escutcheon, blazonŝildo
Eskimo, Eskimo; ~a [term now pejorative; see "Inuit"]
Esocidae, ezok/edoj; Esociformes, ~oformaj (fiŝoj)
esophagus, ezofago; **esophageal**, ~a
esoteric, esotera
Esox, ezoko [see *"Esocidae"*]
espagnolette, espanjoleto
espalier, spaliro; ~i [tr]
esparto, (*Stipa tenacissima*), alfo; (gen name covering several similar grasses), esparto
especially, (mainly), precipe, aparte, ĉefe
Esperanto, Esperanto; ~a; **Esperantist**, ~isto; ~ista; **Esperantologist**, ~ologo; **Esperantology**, ~ologio; **translate into Esperanto**, ~igi; **the Esperanto world, the world of Esperantists**, ~ujo, la ~istaro
espionage, spionado
esplanade, esplanado
espouse, (advocate), subteni [tr], akcepti [tr], favori [tr]
espresso, espreso†
esprit, spirito; **esprit de corps**, grup~o
espy, ekvidi [tr]
–esque, (sfx), –eska, –eca
Esquiline, Eskvilino
esquire, (gen), eskviro
essay, (lit), eseo; (test, try out), provi [tr]; provo
essence, esenco
Essene, Eseno; **Essenic**, ~a

essential, (basic; re essence), esenca;
(obligatory), deviga; (absolutely necessary), nepra
–est, (sfx: most), plej (e.g.: *highest:* ~
alta)
establish, (bring about, settle, gen), estigi, stabiligi, firmigi; (show, demonstrate), demonstri [tr]; (found an
organization, bsns, etc.), establi [tr],
starigi; [cp "settle"]; (officialize state
rel), ŝtatigi, oficialigi; establish-
ment, ~o, stabiligo, firmigo;
demonstro; establ(iĝ)o; establaĵo; dis-
establish, (gen), malestabli [tr], malstarigi; (re state rel), malŝtatigi,
maloficialigi
estancia, latifundio
estate, (large grounds w building(s)),
bieno, grand~o; (possessions, gen),
posedaĵoj; (of deceased person), heredaĵo; real estate, terenaĵo(j); real estate broker, terenomakleristo
esteem, estimi [tr], respekti [tr]; ~o; es-
teemed, ~inda; self–esteem, memrespekto
ester, estero
Esther, Estera
esthesia, estezo
esthetic, estetika; esthetics, ~o; es-
thete, ~ulo
estimable, (esteemable),   estiminda;
(calculable), kalkulebla, taksebla
estimate, taksi [tr]; ~o; estimation,
~o; overestimate, super~i [tr]; un-
derestimate, sub~i [tr]
estivate, somerumi [int]; estivation,
(manner of passing summer), ~o;
(bot: petal arrangement), estivacio
Estonia, Eston/io; Estonian, ~o; ~a;
~ia
estrange, (remove), forpreni [tr]; (alienate), fremdigi, malamikigi; (separate,
re spouses), separi [tr]; estranged,
(separated spouses), separiĝinta
estrogen, oestrogen/aĵo, ~a hormono;
estrogenic, ~a
estrone, oestrono
estrus, oestro; estrous, estrual, ~a
estuary, estuaro
eta, eta [see § 16]
etc. et cetera, (and so forth), kaj tiel plu
[abb: k.t.p., ktp.]; (and the like), kaj

simile [abb: k.s.]; (and the remainder),
kaj cetere [abb: k.c.]; (and others), kaj
aliaj [abb: k.a.]
etch, akvaforti [tr], gravuri [tr]; etch-
ing, ~o [cp "engrave", "eat"]
Eteocles, Eteoklo
eternal, eterna; eternity, ~eco; for
eternity, por~e
ethanal, etanalo
ethane, etano
ethanol, etanolo
ethene, eteno
ether, (gen), etero; ethereal, ~(ec)a
ethic, etiko; ~a; ethical, ~a; ethics, ~o
Ethiopia, Etiop/io; Ethiopian, ~o; ~a;
~ia
ethmoid, (bone), etmoido; ~a
ethnic, etna; ~ulo; ethnic group, ~o,
gento
ethnocentric, etnocentra;   ethnocen-
trism, ~ismo
ethnography, etnograf/io;   ethnogra-
pher, ~o
ethnolog/y, etnolog/io; ~ist, ~o
ethnos, etno
ethology, etolog/io; ethologist, ~o
ethos, etoso
ethoxy–, (chem pfx), etoksi–
ethyl, etilo; ~a; ethylate, ~izi [tr]; eth-
ylene, etileno, eteno
–etin, (chem sfx), –etino
etiolate, etiola; ~igi; ~iĝi
etiology, etiolog/io; etiologist, ~o
etiquette, etiketo
Etna, (mountain), Etno
Etruria, Etrurio
Etruscan, Etrusko; ~a; ~ia
et seq. (abb of "et sequens"), k.sekv.
[abb of "kaj sekvantaj"]
Etta, Henjo
étude, etudo
etymology, etimolog/io;   etymologist,
~o
etymon, etimo
eu–, (sci pfx: good, normal, etc.), eŭ–
Euboea, Eŭbeo
eucalyptus, eŭkalipto
Eucalyptus, eŭkalipto;   Eucalyptus
macrorhyncha, (Aus), fibroŝelarbo;
Eucalyptus microtheca, (Aus), kulabao*; Eucalyptus phellandra, felandrio

eucharist, eŭkaristo; eucharistic, ~a; eucharistial, ciborio, hostiujo
Euclid, Eŭklido; Euclidean, Euclidian, ~a
eud(a)emonism, eŭdajmonismo
eudiometer, eŭdiometro; eudiometry, ~io
Eugene, (man's name), Eŭgeno
Eugenia, (woman's name), Eŭgena
Eugenia, (bot), eŭgenio*; Eugenia brasiliensis, grumiksamarbo; Eugenia caryophyllata, kariofilarbo, kariofilmirto; Eugenia jambos, jamboso; Eugenia pimenta, pimento; Eugenia uniflora, pitangarbo
eugenic, eŭgenika; eugenics, ~o
euhemerism, evemerismo
Euhemerus, Evemero
Eulabes religiosa, majno*
Eulalia, Eŭlalia
eulogy, oracio; eulogize, pri~i [tr]
Eumenides, Eŭmenidoj
Eumetopias otaria, marleono
eumycetes, eŭmicetoj
Eunectes, anakondo
euonymus, Euonymus, evonimo
Euopatorium, eŭpatorio; Euopatorium ayapana, ajapano
eupatory, eŭpatorio
eupepsia, eŭpepsio
euphemism, eŭfemismo; euphemistic, ~a; euphemize, ~igi
euphony, eŭfonio; euphonic, euphonious, ~a
euphorbia, Euphorbia, eŭforbio
euphoria, eŭforio; euphoric, ~a
Euphoria litchi, liĉiujo
Euphrasia, eŭfrazio
Euphrates, Eŭfrato
Euphrosyne, Eŭfrozina
eupnea, eŭpneo
Eurasia, Eŭrazio
Euratom, Eŭratomo†
eurhythmia, eurhythmy, eŭritmo
Euripides, Eŭripido
Eur(o)–, (pfx: Europe(an)), Eŭr(o)–†
Europa, Eŭropa
Europe, Eŭropo; European, ~a; ~ano; Indo-European, Hind-~a
europium, eŭropio
Europort, Eŭroporto†
Eurovision, Eŭrovizio†

Eurydice, Eŭridica
Eustace, Eŭstakio
Eustachian, eŭstakia; Eustachian tube, ~a tubo, otosalpingo
Eutamias, (zool), eŭtamio*
eutectic, eŭtekta; ~o
Euterpe, Eŭterpa
euthanasia, eŭtanazio
Euthynnus pelamys, bonito
Eutremia wasabi, vasabio
euxenite, eŭksenito
Eva, Eva
evacuate, (leave place: remove people from place), evakui [tr]; (tech: make vacuum), vakuigi; (defecate), feki [int]
evade, eviti [tr]; evasion, ~o; evasive, ~(em)a
evaluate, apreci [tr], elvalorigi, (pri)juĝi [tr]
Evan, Johano
evanesce, malaperi [int]; evanescence, ~(em)o; evanescent, ~ema, efemera
evangel, evangelio; evangelic(al), ~a; ~ano; evangelicalism, ~ismo [cp "evangelism"]
Evangeline, Evangelina
evangelism, evangeliz/ado; evangelist, (preacher), ~isto; (Bib: author of Gospel), evangeliisto; evangelize, ~i [tr] [cp "evangel"]
evaporate, vapor/igi; ~iĝi
evasion, [see "evade"]
eve, (day before), antaŭ/vespero, ~tago
Eve, (woman's name), Eva
even, (not only, but also), eĉ (e.g.: even a child can do it: ~ infano povas fari ĝin; he ate it all, and even took another one: li manĝis ĝin tute, kaj ~ prenis alian); (level), ebena; ebenigi; (math: divisible by 2), para; (w/o odd amounts), ekzakta; ekzakte (e.g.: ten dollars even: dek dolaroj ekzakte); (equal), egala; (free of debt), kvita; evenhanded, justa; even so, tamen; malgraŭ tio; not even, eĉ ne (not "ne eĉ"); get even (with), (gen), kvitiĝi (kun); even up, ebenigi; ebeniĝi; egaligi; egaliĝi
evening, vespero; ~a; it is evening, ~as; this evening, ĉi-~e, hodiaŭ ~e; tomorrow evening, morgaŭ ~e; yes-

terday evening, hieraŭ ~e

event, evento, okazo; in any event, ĉiuokaze; in the event of, okaze de; in the event that, okaze ke; se okazos ke; in that event, tiuokaze

eventual, (consequent, ultimate), rezulta, fina [not "eventuala"]; eventually, fine, iam (e.g.: she will eventually come: Ŝi iam venos); eventuality, eventualaĵo

ever, (at any time), iam (e.g.: have you ever gone there?: ĉu vi ~ iris tien?); (always), ĉiam (e.g.: they are ever ready: ili ĉiam pretas; ever after: ĉiam poste); ever since, ekde (kiam, tiam, la tempo de, etc.) (e.g.: ever since you came: ekde kiam vi venis; ever since the flood: ekde (la tempo de) la inundo; ever since (then): ekde tiam); everglade, marĉo; evergreen, ĉiamverda, folidaŭra; ĉiamverda arbo; everlasting, eterna, ĉiamdaŭra; (bot), imortelo; evermore, ĉiam, (por)eterne; ever so, (extremely), ~ega [sfx], (tre)ege (e.g.: the cake was ever so good: la kuko estis bongustega [or] treege bongusta); ever so much (many), multegaj, multege (da); (tre)ege (e.g.: I liked it ever so much: mi treege ŝatis ĝin; ever so much rain fell: multege da pluvo falis; ever so many reasons: multegaj kialoj [or] multege da kialoj); hardly ever, preskaŭ neniam

~ever, (sfx: any at all), ajn (e.g.: whenever: kiam ~; whatever: kio ~)

Everest, (mountain), Everesto

Eversmanni furo, furo

every, ĉiu; every one, ĉiu (e.g.: he gave away every one of them: li fordonis ĉiun el ili); everyday, ĉiutaga; everyone, everybody, ĉiu [for e.g.'s, see "any" and subsequent entries]; everyone at all, ĉiu ajn; everyone and his brother, absolute ĉiu, ĉiu ajn; everyone's, ĉies; everyone's at all, ĉies ajn; everything, ĉio; everything at all, ĉio ajn; everywhere, everyplace, (at every place), ĉie; (to every place), ĉien; every other (third, fourth, etc.), ĉiu dua (tria, kvara, etc.) (e.g.: I cook every other week: mi

kuiras ĉiun duan semajnon); every now and then, every so often, de tempo al tempo, fojfoje, iam kaj iam; every Sunday (day, year, etc.), ĉiudimanĉe (ĉiutage, ĉiujare, etc.)

evict, evikcii [tr]

evidence, (sign, indication), indico, indikaĵo [cp "testimony", "proof"]; (things evident), evidentaĵo(j); (make evident), evidentigi, montri [tr]; (indicate), indiki [tr]; in evidence, (visible), videbla, evidenta

evident, evidenta; evidential, evidentiary, indika; self-evident, (mem)~a, memklara

evil, malico, fieco, malbon(eg)o; ~a, fia, malbon(eg)a

evince, manifesti [tr], montri [tr], evidentigi

eviscerate, (disembowel, gen), senintestigi; (clean animal, as for cooking), sentripigi

evocative, elvok/ema, ~iva

evoke, elvoki [tr]

evolute, evoluto

evolve, evolui [int]; ~igi; evolution, ~(ad)o

Evonymus, evonimo

Evvoia, Eŭbeo

ewe, ŝafino

ewer, kruĉo

ex–, (pfx: former), eks–, eksa

exacerbate, pliseverigi, plimalbonigi, pliakrigi

exact, (precise), ekzakta, preciza; (demand), postuli [tr]; exacting, severa, postulema

exaggerate, troigi

exalt, (praise), laŭdegi [tr]; (elevate), altigi [tr]; (elate, lift feelings), ekzalti [tr]

exam, ekzameno; examine, (gen), ~i [tr] [cp "test"]; examination, ~o; (investigation, inspection), kontrol-esploro; cross-examine, kontraŭ~i [tr]

example, (gen), ekzemplo; for example, ~e [abb: ekz-e]

exanthema, ekzantemo

exarch, (pol, rel), ekzarko

exasperate, kolerigi, iriti [tr], agaci [tr]

ex cathedra, elkatedra; ~e

excavate, elfosi [tr], elkavigi; excava-

tor, (earth-moving machine), skrapatoro
exceed, superi [tr]; **exceedingly,** treege, –eg– [sfx] (e.g.: *exceedingly hot:* varmega [or] treege varma)
excel, superi [tr]; eminenti [int]
excellent, bonega; **excellence, excellency,** ~(ec)o; (title), ekscelenco
excelsior, (packing material), pakmaterialo
except, (prep), krom, escepte de (e.g.: *I have all except that one:* mi havas ĉiujn ~ tiu; *I found none except that one:* mi trovis neniun ~ tiu); (conj), ~ tio ke (e.g.: *it was a nice day, except it rained:* estis agrabla tago, ~ tio ke pluvis); (exclude, make exception), escepti [tr]; **exception,** (gen), escepto; (law), ekscepcio; **exceptional,** escepta; **with the exception of,** escepte de; **without exception,** senescepte; **take exception to,** kontraŭi [tr], kontraŭstari [tr]
excerpt, ekstrakti [tr]; ~o, eltiraĵo
excess, (too much, gen), tro/aĵo; ~eco; (overabundance), ~abundaĵo; ~abundeco, superfluo; (indecency, immoderateness), eksceso; (extra, surplus), restaĵo, ekstraĵo; **excessive,** ~a, ekscesa, superflua; **excessively, to excess,** tro, ekscese; **in excess of,** pli ol
exchange, (swap), interŝanĝi [tr]; ~o; (phone), centralo; (stock market), borso; ($ or bill exchange fee), aĝio; **in exchange for,** ~e por; **exchange rate,** ($), valuto, kurzo; **exchange stocks,** aĝioti [int]
exchequer, fisko
excise, (tax), akciza; ~o; (med: cut out), ekscizi [tr]
excite, (gen), eksciti [tr]; **excitable,** ~iĝema; **excitation, excitement,** ~o
exclaim, ekkrii [tr, int]; **exclamation,** ~o; (in a speech, etc.), eksklamacio; **exclamation mark, exclamation point,** ("!"), kri–signo [see § 17]
exclude, ekskludi [tr], ekskluzivi [tr], ellasi [tr]; **exclusive,** ekskluziva, senescepta; **exclusion,** ~o, ekskluzivo; **mutually exclusive,** alternativa(j), reciproke ekskluziva(j)
excommunicate, ekskomuniki [tr]

excoriate, ekskorii [tr]; **excoriation,** ~aĵo
excrement, ekskremento [cp "excrete"]
excrescence, elkreskaĵo
excrete, ekskrecii [tr]; **excretion,** (substance), ~o; (act), ~ado; **excretory,** ~a [cp "excrement", "feces", "urine"]
excruciate, turmenti [tr], doloregi [tr]; **excruciating,** ~a, dolorega; **excruciating pain,** ekstrema doloro
exculpate, absolvi [tr], senkulpigi
excursion, ekskurso
excuse, (pardon), pardoni [tr], senkulpigi; ~o; (make excuses, alibi), ekskuzi (sin pri); ekskuzo; **excuse me!,** ~u min!, ~on!
execrate, (loathe), abomeni [tr]; (curse), malbeni [tr], denunci [tr]; **execrable,** ~inda
execute, (carry out, fulfill, gen), plenumi [tr], efektivigi; (carry out legal order), ekzekucii [tr]; (law: kill), ekzekuti [tr]; (create, produce, as art etc.), krei [tr], produkti [tr]; (perform, as mus, theat), ludi [tr], prezenti [tr]; **execution,** ~o, efektivigo; ekzekucio; ekzekuto; kreo, produktado; ludado, prezentado; **executioner,** ekzekutisto; **executor,** (law), ekzekuciinto; ekzekucianto; ekzekucionto; **coexecutor,** kunekzekuciinto (etc.)
executive, (any manager etc.), direktoro, administratoro; administra, plenuma; (branch of government), ekzekutivo; ekzekutiva
exegesis, ekzegezo; **exegete,** ~isto; **exegetic(al),** ~a; **exegetics,** ~ismo
exemplar, modelo; **exemplary,** ~a
exemplify, (show by example, be example of), ekzempli [tr]
exempt, escepti [tr]; ~ita, libera; **exemption,** ~o; liberigo
exequatur, ekzekvaturo
exercise, (to improve skill, tone muscles), ekzerco; ~i [tr]; ~i sin, ~iĝi; (use, as judgment), praktiki [tr]; ~o
exergue, ekzergo
exert, (use, apply), apliki [tr], uzi [tr] (e.g.: *exert influence:* ~i influon); (phys, chem), efiki [int] (per io sur ion) (e.g.: *the gas exerts a pressure on the container:* la gaso efikas per pre-

mo sur la ujon); **exert oneself,** (try, make effort), peni [tr], streĉi sin; **exertion,** pen(ad)o, streĉ(ad)o, laboro; **overexert (oneself)**, trostreĉi (sin)
exeunt, (theat), (ili) eliras; **exeunt omnes,** ĉiuj eliras
exhale, elspiri [tr, int]
exhaust, (fatigue), ellac/igi, lacegigi; (use up), forkonsumi [tr], eluzi [tr], elĉerpi [tr]; (make vacuum), vakuigi; (gas from motor etc.), ellas-gaso, ellasaĵo; **exhausted,** ~iĝinta; forkonsumita, eluzita, elĉerpita; vakuigita; **exhaustion,** ~iĝo; **exhaustive,** ĝisfunda; **exhaust pipe,** ellastubo
exhibit, (show, gen), montri [tr], el~i [tr]; ~(aĵ)o; (have certain visible characteristics), ~i, prezenti [tr]; (manifest), manifesti [tr]; manifest(aĵ)o; (public display), eksponi [tr], ekspozicii [tr]; ekspozicio; (in court), (konvinka) ~aĵo; **exhibition,** ~(ad)o; prezent(ad)o; manifest(ad)o; ekspozici(ad)o; (Br: stipend), stipendio; **exhibitionism,** (psych), ekshibicio; **exhibitionist,** ekshibicia; ekshibiciulo
exhilarate, gajigi, vigligi, stimuli [tr]
exhort, (urge), instigi [tr], sproni [tr]; (warn), ~i, admoni [tr]
exhume, (dig up, gen), elterigi; (from grave), eltombigi
exigent, kriza, urĝa; **exigency,** ~(okaz)o
exile, ekzili [tr]; (condition), ~o; (person), ~ito
exist, ekzisti [int]; **existence,** ~(ad)o; **coexist,** kun~i [int]; **self-existent,** mem~a
existential, ekzistencialisma; **existentialism,** ~o; **existentialist,** ~a; ekzistencialisto
exit, eliri [int]; (act), ~o; (doorway etc.; highway ramp), ~ejo; (theat), (li, ŝi) ~as; **emergency exit,** sav~ejo
ex libris, ekslibriso
exo–, (sfx: outer), ekzo–*
exocarp, epikarpo
Exocoetus, ekzoceto, flugfiŝo
exodus, elir(ad)o; **Exodus,** (Bib), Eliro
ex officio, proofica
exogamy, ekzogamio
exogenous, ekzogena

Exogonium purga, jalap/ujo, ~planto
exonerate, absolvi [tr], senkulpigi
exophthalmia, exophthalmos, exophthalmus, ekzoftalmio
exorbitant, ekscesa
exorcise, exorcize, ekzorci [tr]; **exorcism,** (act), ~o; (ritual, formula, etc.), ~aĵo; **exorcist,** ~isto
exordium, komenco
exoskeleton, ekzoskeleto*
exosmosis, ekzosmozo
exoteric, ekzotera
exothermic, ekzoterma
exotic, ekzota, ekzotika
expand, (gen), ekspansii [int]; ~igi; (chem, phys), dilati [tr]; ~iĝi
expanse, (extent), amplekso; (vast area), vastaĵo; **vast expanse,** granda vastaĵo
expansion, ekspansio, dilat(iĝ)o; **expansion bolt,** dubelbolto; **expansion case,** (for expansion bolt), dubelo; **expansionism,** ~ismo
expansive, (expanding), ekspansia, ~ema; ~iva; (broad), vasta; (comprehensive), ampleksa; (psych: open), malkaŝ(em)a
ex parte, unupartia; ~e
expatiate, ellabori [tr], detali [tr]
expatriate, ekzili [tr], elpatrujigi; ~ita; ~ito
expect, (await), atendi [tr]; (anticipate), anticipi [tr]; (look for as proper, due), esperi [tr]; (suppose), supozi [tr]; **expectancy, expectation,** ~o; anticipo; espero; (math: probability), ekspekto; **expectant,** ~anta; **come up to (meet) expectations,** plenumi esperojn; **life expectancy,** vivekspekto
expectorate, ekspektori [int]; **expectorant,** ~iga; ~enzo [cp "spit"]
expedient, (convenient), oportuna; ~aĵo; (goal-oriented), laŭcela; (means), rimedo; **expediency,** ~aĵo; ~eco; laŭceleco
expedite, akceli [tr], rapidigi
expedition, ekspedicio
expeditious, rapid(ag)a, senprokrasta, hasta
expel, (drive out, eject), elpeli [tr]; (remove from membership etc.), eksigi
expend, ($), elspezi [tr]; (consume),

konsumi [tr], eluzi [tr]; **expendable,** konsumebla, nenepra; konsumeblaĵo, neneprajô; **expenditure,** ~o; konsumo
expense, (expenditure), elspezo; (cost), kosto; (cost payment), kostpago (e.g.: *at the expense of the company:* je la kostpago de la kompanio); **expense account,** ~konto; **at the expense of,** (accompanied by loss), je kosto de, koste de (e.g.: *he won the argument at the expense of their friendship:* li gajnis la disputon je kosto de ilia amikeco); **out-of-pocket expense,** proprapoŝa ~o
expensive, multekosta; **inexpensive,** mal~a, ĉipa
experience, sperti [tr]; ~(ad)o; **experienced,** ~a; **inexperience,** sen~eco; **inexperienced,** ne~a, sen~a
experiment, eksperimento; ~i [int]; **experimental,** ~a; **experimentation,** ~ado
expert, sperta, lerta; ~ulo, eksperto, lertulo; **inexpert,** sen~a
expertise, ekspertizo; **use expertise,** ~i [tr]
expiate, pentopagi [tr]
expire, (exhale), elspiri [tr, int]; (die), morti [int]; (run out, terminate), eksvalidiĝi, finiĝi
explain, (gen), klarigi; (explicate), ekspliki [tr], komentarii [tr]; **explanation,** ~o; ekspliko, komentario; **explanatory,** ~a; **self-explanatory,** mem~a
expletive, sakr/aĵo; **utter expletives,** ~i [int]
explicate, ekspliki [tr]
explicit, (gen), eksplicita
explode, eksplodi [int]; ~igi; **explosion,** ~o; **explosive,** (substance), ~enzo; (device), ~ilo; (able to ~de), ~iva; (causing), ~iga; (tending to), ~ema
exploit, (utilize), ekspluati [tr], utiligi; (for own gain), ~i, elprofiti [tr]; (bold deed), bravaĵo, heroaĵo
explore, (gen), esplori [tr]; **exploration,** ~(ad)o; **exploreer,** ~isto, ~anto
exponent, (expounder), ekspon/into; ~anto; ~onto; ~isto; (math), eksponento; **exponential,** eksponencialo;

eksponenciala
export, eksporti [tr]; ~(ad)o; ~aĵo
expose, (exhibit; phot), eksponi [tr]; (uncover, reveal), elmeti [tr], malkaŝi [tr], malŝirmi [tr], riveli [tr], videbligi; **exposé,** ~o; **exposition,** (explanation), klarigo, ekspliko [see "explain"]; (exhibition), ekspozicio; **exposure,** ~(ad)o, elmeto; malkaŝo, malŝirmo, rivelo, malkovro, videbligo; **exposure meter,** (phot), ~metro; **overexpose,** super~i [tr]; **underexpose,** sub~i [tr]
ex post facto, postokaza
expostulate, protesti [tr]
expound, (set forth, present), (detale) prezenti [tr]; (explain), ekspliki [tr]
express, (say, communicate), esprimi [tr]; (show), montri [tr]; (signify), signifi [tr]; (press out), elpremi [tr];; (fast train, bus, etc.), ekspreso; ekspresa; (explicit), eksplicita; **expression,** ~o; ~ado; montr(ad)o; elprem(ad)o; **expressionism,** ekspresionismo; **expressionist,** ekspresionisma; ekspresionisto; **expressive,** ~ema; ~plena; **expressway,** aŭtovojo
expropriate, eksproprietigi
expulsion, elpelo; eksigo [see "expel"]
expunge, forviŝi [tr], forstreki [tr]; forigi, neniigi
expurgate, cenzuri [tr]
exquisite, ekskvizita
extant, ekzistanta
extemporaneous, ekstemporala; **extempore,** ~e; **extemporize,** improvizi [tr]
extend, (reach, stretch out, lengthen), etendi [tr], pluigi; ~iĝi; (cover, include), ampleksi [tr]; (delay expiration), pluvalidigi (e.g.: *extend the contract 30 days:* pluvalidigi la kontrakton 30 tagojn); (delay any event), prokrasti [tr] (e.g.: *extend the deadline:* prokrasti la limdaton); **extension,** ~(iĝ)o; pluvalidigo; prokrasto
extensive, vasta, (mult)ampleksa
extensor, (anat, re muscle), ekstensoro
extent, (degree, amount), amplekso, etendo, grado (e.g.: *the extent of one's influence:* la ~o de ies influo); **to the extent that,** ĝis tiom ke, tiomgrade ke

(e.g.: *we succeeded to the extent that no one was hungry:* ni sukcesis ĝis tiom ke [or: tiomgrade ke] neniu malsatis); **to a certain extent**, certagrade; **to some extent**, iom, iomgrade; **to that extent**, tiom, tiomgrade; **to what extent**, kiom, kiomgrade
extenuate, mildigi
exterior, ekstera; ~aĵo
exterminate, ekstermi [tr]
extern, eksterulo
external, estera
extinct, formort/inta; **become extinct**, ~i [int]
extinguish, estingi [tr]
extirpate, elradikigi, ekstermi [tr]
extol(l), glori [tr], laŭdegi [tr]
extort, eltrudi [tr], eldevigi, elpremi [tr] [cp "blackmail"]
extra, ekstra; ~aĵo; (theat), figuranto; (very), tre
extra–, (pfx: outside, beyond), ekster– (e.g.: *extraterrestrial:* ~tera); (additional), krom– (e.g.: *extrasystole:* kromsistolo)
extract, (take part from whole; draw conclusion; etc.), ekstrakti [tr], eltiri [tr]; ~o, eltiro; (pull out), eltiri [tr], elpreni [tr]
extradite, ekstradicii [tr]; **extradition**, ~o
extrados, ekstradoso
extraneous, (outside), ekstera, fremda; (irrelevant), nerilata
extraordinary, eksterordinara
extrapolate, ekstrapoli [tr], eksterpoli [tr]
extrasystole, kromsistolo
extravagance, ekstravaganco; **extravagant**, ~a; **extravaganza**, ~o
extravert, [see "extrovert"]
extreme, (gen), ekstrema; ~aĵo; **extremely**, ~e, (tre)ege, –eg– [sfx] (e.g.: *extremely hot:* varmega [or] treege varma); **extremism**, ~ismo; **extremist**, ~isma; ~isto; **extremity**, ~eco; (anat etc.), ~aĵo
extricate, malimpliki [tr]; **inextricable**, ne~ebla
extrinsic, malmanenta, malesenca
extrorse, ekstrorsa
extrovert, ekstroverti* [tr]; ~ito; **extro-**

version, ~iteco; **extrovertive**, **extroverted**, ~it(ec)o
extrude, elpremi [tr]; **extrusion**, ~(aĵ)o
exuberant, (joyous), gaj(eg)a, ĝoj(eg)a, gaj-anima; (profuse), abunda; **exuberance**, ~(ec)o, ĝojo; abundo
exude, eksudi [int]; ~igi; **exudate**, ~aĵo
exult, ĝojegi [int]; **exultation**, ~o
eye, (anat; any similar object), okulo; (look, glance at), ~umi [tr], rigardi [tr]; **eyeball**, ~globo; **eyebright**, (bot), eŭfrazio; **eyebrow**, brovo; **eyecatching**, ~frapa; **eyelash**, ~haro; **eyelet**, (ring), koŝo; (in shoe etc. for lace), laĉtruo; **eyelid**, palpebro; **eyepiece**, okulario; **eye shadow**, ~ŝminko; **eyeshot**, ~atingo; **eyesight**, vidivo; **eyesore**, ~dorno, malbelaĵo; **eyestrain**, ~laciĝo; **eyetooth**, supera kanino; **eyewash**, (med), kolirio; (nonsense), ĉarlatanaĵo, galimatio; **eyewitness**, vidatestanto; **black eye**, livida ~o; **evil eye**, (spell cast by malevolent look), maligna ~o; **pinkeye**, (kontaĝa) konjunktivito; **private eye**, detektivo; **in the eyes of**, laŭ (e.g.: *improper in the eyes of the law:* maldeca laŭ la leĝo); **catch one's eye**, allogi ies atenton; **keep an eye on**, prizorg(ad)i [tr]; **make eyes at**, (flirte) ~umi [tr]; **see eye to eye**, plene akordi [int]; **with an eye to**, cele al, kun la intenco
eyrie, agl/ejo, ~onesto
Ezekiel, Jeĥezkel, Ezekielo
Ezra, Ezrao

F

fa, (mus), fa
Fabian, (man's name), Fabiano; (re Society), ~isma; ~isto; **Fabianism**, ~ismo
fabism, fabismo
Fabius, Fabio
fable, fablo; **fabled**, ~a
fabric, (any woven material, lit or fig), teksaĵo; (for clothing), ŝtofo
fabricate, (make), fabriki [tr]; (make up, invent, as explanation, lie, etc.), inventi [tr], elfari [tr]; **prefabricate**, pretkonstrui [tr]; **prefabricated**, pretkonstruita [see also "prefab"]
Fabricius, Fabricio
Fabrizio, Fabricio
fabulous, fabela
façade, fasado
face, (front of head), vizaĝo; (expression thereon), ~o, mieno; (crude expression, as leer etc.), ~aĉo; (flat surface), faco; (front side, as of coin, card, etc.), averso†; (turn to, confront, present face toward), fronti [int] (al), alfronti [tr]; (appearance, semblance), ŝajno; (apply facing, as garment lining), tegi [tr]; **facial**, ~a; **facing**, (garment lining etc.), tegaĵo; (treatment), ~aĵo; **face-to-face**, ~-al-~a; ~-al-~e; **face up to**, alfronti [tr]; **face value**, nominala valoro; **bare-faced**, (shameless), senhonta; **interface**, interfaco; **interface with**, interfaci [tr]; **in the face of**, (in spite of), malgraŭ; (confronted w), alfrontita (–e) de; **fly in the face of**, defii [tr]; **make a face**, **make faces**, fari ~aĉo(j)n; **on the face of it**, laŭŝajne, ŝajne; **lose (save) face**, (mal)embarasiĝi, perdi (konservi) reputacion; **two-faced**, du~a, hipokrita
facet, faceto; ~i [tr]; **many-faceted**, mult~a
facetious, ŝercema, malserioza
facia, (Br: dashboard), panelo
facies, facio
facile, facila
facilitate, faciligi

facility, (ease), facileco; (skill, talent), lerteco, talento; (means), rimedo(j); (building, place), instalaĵo, ejo, ~ejo [sfx] (e.g.: *eating facility:* manĝejo)
facsimile, faksimilo [see also "fax"]
fact, fakto; **in fact, as a matter of fact**, ~e, efektive
factice, faktiso
faction, kliko, partieto
factitious, artefarita
factitive, faktitivo
factor, (gen), faktoro; (math), ~igi
factorial, (math), faktorialo
factory, (gen), fabriko; (mill, plant), uzino [cp "manufacture"]
factotum, faktoto
facultative, (optional), fakultativa, nedeviga; (contingent), kontingenca
faculty, (ability), kapablo; (division of school, or all instructors), fakultato
fad, furoro; **faddism**, ~emo; **faddist**, ~emulo, snobo
fade, (pale), pal/igi; ~iĝi; (wither), velki [int]; velkigi; (radio etc.), fado; fadi [int]; **fade in**, (sound, video, etc.), enfadi [int]; enfadigi; **fade out**, forfadi [int]; forfadigi
fado, (Portuguese song), faduo†
faeces, feko; **faecal**, ~a
faerie, faery, feujo
Faeroes, Faeroe Islands, (Insuloj) Feroa(j); **Faeroese**, Feroa; Feroano
fag, (fatigue), lac/eco; ~iĝi; (Br: servant boy), servojunulo
Fagopyrum, fagopiro; Fagopyrum sagittatum, poligono
fagot, (bundle), fasko [not "fagoto"]; ~igi
Fagus, fago; Fagus sylvatica, sango~o
Fahrenheit, Farenhejta; ~e; (de) Fahrenheit [see also "degree"; see § 20]
faience, fajenco
fail, (not succeed), fiaski [int] (en), fiaski [int] (en) (e.g.: *our efforts failed:* niaj klopodoj ~is [or] fiaskis; *he failed the test:* li ~is en la testo); (be lacking), manki [int]; (be insufficient), nesufiĉi [int]; (not function,

malfunction), misfunkcii [int] (e.g.:
the brakes failed: la bremsoj mis-
funkciis); (stall), panei [int] (e.g.: *the
motor failed:* la motoro paneis); (become damaged), difektiĝi; (not do, not
be), ne, mal– [pfx] (e.g.: *I failed to answer your letter:* mi ne respondis vian
leteron; *he failed to fulfill his duties:* li
malplenumis siajn devojn; *it failed to
rain:* ne pluvis); **failure,** ~o; manko;
nesufiĉo; misfunkcio; paneo; ne...o,
mal...o (e.g.: *because of your failure
to come:* pro via neveno [or] ĉar vi ne
venis); **without fail,** nepre (e.g.: *do it
without fail:* nepre faru ĝin); **fail-safe,**
misfunkciimuna; misfunkciimunaĵo
faille, fajo
fainéant, nenifaranto
faint, (swoon), sveni [int]; ~o; (weak),
malforta; (pale), pala
fair, (exhibition; carnival), foiro (e.g.:
world's fair: mondo~o) [cp "festival"]; (attractive; clear and sunny),
bela; (light color, blond), blonda;
(just), justa, honesta, senpartia; (in accord w rules), laŭregula; (mediocre,
somewhat), mez(bon)a; certagrada;
(favorable), favora; **fairground,** ~ejo;
fairway, (navigation), ŝanelo; (golf),
meztereno; **fair and square,** juste kaj
ĝuste
fairy, fe(in)o; ~a; **fairy tale,** fefabelo
fait accompli, plenumitaĵo, efektivaĵo
faith, (trust, belief), fido; (rel group or
dogma etc.), religio, kredo; **faithful,**
fidela; (rel), kredantaro; **interfaith,**
interreligia; **article of faith,** kred–artikolo **have faith in,** ~i [tr]; **in good
(bad) faith,** (mal)sincere, (mal)bonin-
tence
fake, (imitation, false), falsi [tr]; ~a;
~aĵo [cp "imitate: imitation"; "improvise"]
fakir, fakiro
Falange, Falango
Falco, falko; Falco peregrinus, migra
~o; Falco rusticolus, ĉas~o; Falco
subbuteo, alaŭd~o; Falco tinnuncu-
lus, tur~o; Falco vespertinus,
vesper~o; Falconidae, ~edoj; Falconiformes, ~oformaj (birdoj)
falcon, falko; **falconer,** ~(obred)isto;

falconry, ~oĉasado; **peregrine falcon,** migra ~o
Falerii, Falerno
Falerno, Falerna (vino)
fall, (drop, go down, gen), fali [int];
~igi; ~(ig)o; (autumn), aŭtuno; aŭtuna; (occur), okazi [int] (e.g.: *Christmas fell on Wednesday:* Kristnasko
okazis je merkredo); (be divided), dividiĝi (e.g.: *fall into 3 types:* dividiĝi
en 3 specojn); (become), (far)iĝi, –iĝi
[sfx] (e.g.: *fall behind:* malantaŭiĝi;
fall due: pagendiĝi) [see also "become"]; (waterfall), akvo~o; **fall
back,** (withdraw), sin retiri, retiriĝi;
fall back on, sin turni al; **fall for,** (fall
in love w), enamiĝi (je, por); (be
fooled by), trompiĝi (de, far); esti
trompita de; **fall afoul of,** implikiĝi
en; **fall in,** (collapse), en~i [int]; (mil
etc.: into formation), enviciĝi; **fall in
with,** kuniĝi kun; **fall off,** (decrease),
malpliiĝi; **fall (up)on,** (attack), ataki
[tr]; (come upon), (al)veni al; **fall out,**
(quarrel), kvereli [int]; (pass out), senkonsciiĝi; (mil), elviciĝi; **fallout,**
(e.g., radioactive), el~aĵo; **fall short,**
(be not enough), nesufiĉi [int]; malsu-
peri [tr], maltrafi [tr] [see also "fail"];
fall through, (fail), malsukcesi [int];
freefall, liber~o; **shortfall,** nesufiĉo
fallacious, (erroneous), erara; (deceptive), ~iga, trompa; **fallacy,** ~o
fallible, erariva; **infallible,** ne~a
fallow, novala; **fallow ground,** ~o; **lie
fallow,** ~i [int]
false, falsa; **falsify,** ~i [tr]; **falsehood,**
(lie), mensogo; **falsies,** ~mamoj
falsetto, falseto; ~a; ~e
falter, (stumble, lit or fig), stumbli [int];
(waver), ŝanceliĝi; ŝanceliĝo; (hesitate), heziti [int]; hezito
Faluns, faluno
fame, renomo, famo
familiar, (well-known), kon/ata; (informal), neformala, hejm(ec)a; (com-
mon, often), ofta; **familiar with,**
~anta; **be familiar with,** ~i [tr]
family, familio; ~a; **familial,** ~a
famine, malsatego
famish, malsategi [int]; ~igi; **be fam-
ished,** ~i

famous, fama, renoma; **infamous**, ~aĉa, mis~a, fi~a; **infamy**, ~aĉo, mis~o, fi~o; (poet), infamio
fan, (move air, gen), ventumi [tr]; (ventilate), ventoli [tr]; (simple device or machine), ~ilo; (ventilator), ventolatoro; (devotee), amanto, adepto, fervorulo; **fanjet**, turbinojeto; **fantail**, (fan-shaped tail or similar object), ~vosto
fanatic, fanatika; ~ulo; **fanatical**, ~a [cp "zealot"]
fancy, (image; imagine), imago, fantazio; ~i [tr], fantazii [tr]; (caprice, whim), kaprico; (fondness), ŝato; (extravagant), ekstravaganca; (decorated), ornamita; (elaborate), ellaborita; (skillful), lerta; **strike one's fancy**, plaĉi ies kapricon
fandango, fandango
fanfare, fanfaro
fang, dent(eg)o
fantasia, fantazio
fantastic, (amazing), miriga; (re fantasy), fantazia; (incredible), nekredebla; (re lit style), fantasta
fantasy, (imagination, fancy; creation of same; mus), fantazio; (psych: esp to escape reality), fantasmo†; (lit style), fantasto
far, (distant), malproksima, fora, (poet), lontana; ~e(n); ~e(n), for(en), lontane(n); (adj: more distant), pli ~a (e.g.: *the far side of the room:* la pli ~a flanko de la ĉambro); (beyond), pretera (e.g.: *the far side of Luna:* la pretera flanko de Luno); (much), multe (e.g.: *far better:* multe pli bona); **faraway**, tre ~a; **farfetched**, malprobabla, nekredinda; **far-off**, tre ~a; **farsighted**, (of good judgment), sagaca; (re eyes), hipermetropa; **farther**, (more distant), pli ~a; pli ~e(n); (beyond), transa, pretera; (in addition, further), plu; **farthest**, plej ~a; plej ~e(n); **as far as**, [see under "as"]; **by far**, je multo; **far and wide**, vaste kaj dise; **how far (away) is** ...?, kiom longe for estas ...?; **so far**, (to now), ĝis nun; (to then), ĝis tiam; **that far**, tiom; tien; **this far**, ĉi tiom; ĉi tien; **far be it from me to**, mi eĉ ne pensus

pri, mi eĉ ne konsiderus
farad, farado; **faradize**, faradizi [tr]; **abfarad**, ab~o; **microfarad**, mikro~o
farandole, farandolo
farce, farso; **farcical**, ~(ec)a
fare, (travel cost), veturprezo; (do, get along), farti [int] (e.g.: *how did you fare on your trip?:* kiel vi fartis dum via vojaĝo?); (passenger), pasaĝero, (vetur)kliento; (food), nutraĵo; **farewell**, adiaŭo; adiaŭa; (interj), adiaŭ!; fartu bone! [see also "good: goodbye"]
farina, (as cereal etc.), farun/aĵo; **farinaceous**, ~a
farm, (land and buildings, gen), bieno; (rented), farm~o; (small, one-family), et~o; (large), grand~o [cp "plantation"]; (cultivate, gen), kultivi [tr]; (on land rented from oth person), farmi [tr]; **farmer**, (ter)kultivisto; (renter), farmisto; **farming**, (ter)kultivado; farm(ad)o; **farm out**, (lit), farmigi; (fig: delegate), delegi [tr]
faro, farao [cp "pharaoh"]
Faroe, [see "Faeroes"]
farouche, sovaĝa, senkultura
farrago, miksamaso
farrier, hufferisto
farrow, (pig litter), porkidaro
Farsi, (la) Persa (lingvo) [cp "Parsee"]
fart, furzi [int]; el~i [tr]; ~o
farthing, kvaronpenco
fasces, fasko
fascia, (strip, band), strio; (anat), fascio
fascicle, (of book), fasko; (bot), ~eto
fascicule, **fasciculus**, kajero
fascinate, fascini [tr]; **fascination**, ~ado; **fascinating**, ~a
fascine, fasĉino
Fasciola, fasciolo
fascism, faŝismo; **fascist**, ~a; faŝisto
fashion, (make, form, gen), formi [tr]; (shape a garment), fasoni [tr]; (shape garment or oth object by cutting etc.), tajli [tr]; (manner), maniero; (style), modo; **fashionable**, **in fashion**, laŭmoda; **out of fashion**, **old-fashioned**, eksmoda, malmoderna; **after a fashion**, (somewhat), iom; ioma
fast, (rapid), rapida; ~e; (firm, stuck), firma, fiksita; (resistant, ~proof), imu-

na, eltena (e.g.: *fast color:* paliĝimuna koloro; *acid-fast bacilli:* acidimunaj baciloj); (loyal), lojala; (re clock), frua (e.g.: *the clock is 5 minutes fast:* la horloĝo estas 5 minutojn frua [or] la horloĝo fruas 5 minutojn); (promiscuous), malĉasta, diboĉema; (deep), profunda (e.g.: *fast asleep:* profunde dormanta; *ocean fastnesses:* oceanaj profundoj); (not eat), fasti [int]; fasto; **fastness,** (stronghold), fortikaĵo; (depth), profund(aĵ)o; **make fast,** (fasten), fiksi [tr]
fasten, (attach, gen), fiksi [tr]; (tie), ligi [tr] [cp "lock", "buckle", "glue", etc.]; **fastener, fastening,** ~ilo
fastidious, precioza, elektema, neplaĉiĝema
fat, (grease, fatty tissue), graso; ~a; (thick, corpulent, obese), dika, korpulenta; (fertile), fekunda; fekundeco (e.g.: *the fat of the land:* la fekundeco de la tero); (lucrative), lukra; **fatback,** dors~o
fatal, (of or causing death), morta, pereiga; (of fate), fatala; **fatalism,** fatalismo; **fatalist,** fatalisma; fatalisto; **fatality,** (death), ~o; (causing death), ~igivo; (fate), fatalo [see also "fate"]
fata morgana, fatamorgano
fate, (power determining events), fatalo (e.g.: *fate seemed to thwart her efforts:* la ~o ŝajnis obstrukci ŝiajn penojn); (individual outcome, lot, luck), sorto (e.g.: *he met a terrible fate:* li trafis teruran sorton); (destine), destini [tr] (e.g.: *she was fated to inherit the house:* ŝi estis destinita heredi la domon); **Fate,** (myth), F~o; **fateful,** ~a
father, patro; (beget, become father of), generi [tr], naskigi; (act like father toward), ~umi [tr], ~i [int] al; **forefather,** pra~o, praulo; **stepfather,** duon~o; **father-in-law,** bo~o; **fatherland,** ~io, ~olando; **godfather,** bapto~o
fathom, (unit), klafto [1,83 metroj; see § 20]; (measure depth), sondi [tr]
fatigue, (tire), lac/igi; ~iĝi; ~eco; **fatigued,** ~a; **fatigues,** (mil clothing), batalvestoj

fatuous, malsaĝa, stulta, idiota, ventkapa
faucet, krano
fault, (blame), kulpo; ~igi; (flaw), difekto, misaĵo; (geol), faŭlto; **faulty,** misa, difektita, neperfekta; **faultless,** perfekta, sendifekta; **at fault,** ~a; **find fault (with),** ~igi; **to a fault,** ekscese, tro
faun, faŭno
fauna, faŭno
Faunus, Faŭno
Faust(us), Faŭsto
fauvism, faŭvismo
faux pas, misfaro, mispaŝo, sentaktaĵo
favo(u)r, favoro; ~i [tr]; **favorable,** ~a; **unfavorable,** mal~a; **favored,** ~ata; **disfavor,** mal~o; **in favor of,** ~e al; **out of favor,** ne~ata, ne plu ~ata
favo(u)rite, (preferred), prefer/ata; ~aĵo; ~ato; (favored person, thing), favorato; **favoritism,** favoratismo
favus, favo
fawn, (young deer), cervido; (yellowish brown), flavbruneta; (act servilely), lakei [int], flataĉi [tr]
fax, faksi* [tr]; (faxed copy), ~aĵo; **fax machine,** ~atoro [cp "facsimile"]
fear, timi [tr]; ~o; **fearful,** ~anta; ~iga; **fearsome,** ~iga, terura
feasible, (practicable), praktikebla, efektivigebla, farebla; (suitable), taŭga
feast, (banquet), festeno; ~i [int]; (festival, celebration), festo [cp "festival"]
feat, atingo, bravaĵo, heroaĵo
feather, (of bird), plumo; ~izi [tr]; (turn blade of oar, propeller), platigi; **featherbedding,** laborremburado
feature, (appearance), aspekto; (outstanding, salient aspect), trajto; elstaraĵo; (main event, item, etc.), ĉef–[pfx] (e.g.: *feature event:* ĉefevento; *feature film:* ĉeffilmo); (display), reliefigi, emfazi [tr], elstarigi; (present as a feature), prezenti [tr]; (section of newspaper, magazine, etc., on certain subject), rubriko, felieton(aĵ)o; **feature-length,** plenlonga
febrifuge, kontraŭfebra; ~aĵo
febrile, febra; **be febrile,** ~i [int]
February, februaro

feces, feko; **fecal,** ~a
feckless, (ineffective), senefika, malforta; (irresponsible), malzorgema
fecund, fekunda
federal, federacia, (esp re U.S.), federala; [cp "federate"]; **federalism,** ~ismo; **federalist,** ~isma; ~isto
federate, federi [tr]; ~iĝi; **federation,** (act), ~(iĝ)o; (pol unit), federacio [cp "federal"]
fee, (honorarium), honorario (e.g.: *we offer a fee of $100 for your talk:* ni proponas ~on de $100 por via prelego); (toll; fee for service), takso (e.g.: *the park requires an entrance fee:* la parko postulas enirtakson) **fee simple,** absoluta posedrajto; **fee tail,** limigita posedrajto
feeble, febla, malforta
feed, (give food, or provide in manner of food), nutri [tr]; ~(ad)o (e.g.: *feed the cat:* ~i la katon; *the event fed his anger:* la evento ~is lian koleron; *feed the engine more gas:* ~i al la motoro pli da benzino; *feed data to the computer:* ~i datenon† al la komputoro; *paper feed:* paper ~o); (eat), sin ~i, manĝi [tr]; (food, or analogous act, substance), ~ado; ~aĵo; (provide, gen), provizi [tr]; **feeder,** (tube, elec cable etc.), fidro; (that feedss, e.g., tributary stream), ~a; **feedback,** (elec or fig), retro~o, retrokupl(ad)o; **biofeedback,** bioretrokuplo; **feed bag,** ~osako; **force-feed,** ŝtop~i [tr]; **fed up,** trosatigita, senpacienciĝi
feel, (have sensation or emotion), senti [tr]; ~o (e.g.: *I feel sand in my shoes:* mi ~as sablon en miaj ŝuoj; *how do you feel about that idea?:* kiel vi ~as pri tiu ideo?; *I feel sick:* mi ~as (min) malsana); (give impression), impresi [tr] (~e) (e.g.: *the air feels cold:* la aero impresas malvarme) [see also "feel like" below]; (grope, palpate), palpi [tr]; palp(ad)o (e.g.: *feel one's way through the dark:* palpi sian vojon tra la mallumo; *do it by feel:* fari ĝin per palpado); **feeler,** (as on insect), palpilo; (to sound out opinion, reaction, etc.), sondilo; **feeling,** (a sensation), ~o; (basic sense), ~ivo;

(emotion), ~emo, emocio; **feel like,** (give impression of), impresi kiel (e.g.: *that feels like rubber:* tio impresas kiel kaŭĉuko); (be inclined to), emi [tr], inklini [int] (al) (e.g.: *Do you feel like taking a walk?:* Ĉu vi emas [or] inklinas fari promenon?; *No, I don't feel like it:* Ne, mi ne emas tion [or] ne inklinas al tio; *I feel like [eating] a sandwich:* mi inklinas al sandviĉo); **feel out,** (sound out opinion etc.), sondi [tr], opinisondi [tr]; **feel up to,** ~i sin kapabla; **hurt one's feelings,** dolorigi ies ~ojn
feign, ŝajnigi
feint, (fake attack), finti [int]; ~o; (sham), ŝajnigo
feldspar, feldspato
Felicia, Feliksa
felicitate, gratuli [tr]
felicitous, taŭga
felicity, (happiness, good fortune), feliĉo
feline, (any animal of *Felidae*), feliso; ~a; (informal: re cats, gen), kato; kata **Felis,** feliso; **Felidae,** ~edoj
Felix, Felikso
fell, (knock, cut down), faligi; (terrible), terura, kruela; (hide), felo; (hill), monteto, altaĵo
fellah, felaho
fellatio, penislekado
fellow, (man or person, gen, colloq), ulo; (comrade), kunulo, kamarado; (one of several similar), kun–, sam– [pfx] (e.g.: *fellow artists:* kunartistoj; *our fellow countrymen:* niaj samlandanoj); (member of learned society etc.), asociito, ano; **fellowship,** (companionship), kamaradeco, kunuleco; (group), societo, (ge)frataro; **bedfellow,** litkunulo
felon, (ĉef)krim/ulo; **felony,** ~o; **felonious,** ~a
felspar, feldspato
felt, (fabric), felto; ~a; (make into felt), ~i [tr]; (cover w felt), ~izi [tr]
felucca, feluko
female, (gen), ina; ~ulo; (bot, zool), femala; femalo
feminine, (womanly), virin(ec)a; (gram gen der; of female sex gen), in(seks)a,

femala; **femininism**, feminismo; **femininist**, feminisma; feministo
femur, femurosto, femuralo [not "femuro"]
fen, marĉo
fence, (barrier), bari [tr]; ĉirkaŭ~i [tr]; ~ilo; (sport), skermi [int]; (deal in stolen goods), riceli [tr]; ricelisto; ricelejo; **fencing**, ~ilaĵo; skermado; ricela
fend, fend off, rezisti [tr], forturni [tr]; **fend for (oneself)**, provizi por (si mem)
fender, (over vehicle wheel), kotŝirmilo; (on ship, wharf, front of streetcar, etc.; any buffer), bufro; (firescreen), fendro
fennel, fenkolo
fennelflower, nigelo
fenugreek, fenugreko
feral, sovaĝa
Ferdinand, Ferdinando
fermata, fermato
ferment, (lit or fig), fermenti [int]; ~igi; (substance), ~o; (process), ~(ig)ado
fermi, mikronanometro [not "fermio"]
fermion, fermiono
fermium, fermio
fern, filiko
Fernando, Fernando
ferocious, kruel(eg)a, (poet), feroca; **ferocity**, ~eco, feroceco
Ferrara, Feraro
ferrate, ferato
ferret, (zool), mustelo; (search out), elserĉi [tr]
ferric, (of iron, gen), fera; (valence 3), ~ika
ferricyanide, fericianido [cp "ferrocyanide"]; **ferricyanic acid**, ~ida acido
ferriferous, ferhava
ferrite, (chem, gen), ferito
ferro-, (chem pfx), fer(o)–
ferrocyanide, ferocianido [cp "ferricyanide"]; **ferrocyanic acid**, ~a acido
ferrous, (re iron, gen), fera; (valence 2), ~oza
ferrule, metalpinto
ferry, (boat or analogous spacecraft), pramo; (large), ~ŝipo; (carry in or as in a ferry), ~i [tr]
fertile, fekunda; **fertility**, ~eco; **fertilize**, (gen), ~igi; (treat soil w fertiliz-

er), grasumi [tr]; (w manure), sterki [tr]; **fertilizer**, grasumo; (manure), sterko; **infertile**, mal~a
Ferula, ferolo
fervent, fervid, fervora, arda; **fervor**, ~o, ardo
fescue, festuko
fester, (form pus), pusi [int]; ~igi; (fig: embitter), amarigi; amariĝi
festival, festivalo; ~a; (festive), festa [cp "fair", "party"]
festive, festa; **festivity**, ~o
festoon, festono; ~i [tr]
Festuca, festuko
fetch, (bring object), (al)porti [tr]; (bring person), venigi [see "bring"]; **fetching**, (attractive), ĉarma, alloga, pimpa
fête, festo; ~i [tr]
fetid, fetora; **fetid odor**, ~o
fetish, fetiĉo; **fetishism**, ~ismo; **fetishist**, ~isma; ~isto
fetlock, superhufaĵo
fetor, fetoro
fetter, (pied)kateno; ~i [tr]
fetus, feto; **fetal**, ~a
feud, kverel/(ad)i [int]   ~ado [not "feŭd–"]; (blood feud), vendetto
feudal, feŭda; **feudalism**, ~ismo
fever, febro; **feverish**, (having fever), ~a; (frenetic), freneza; **be feverish**, ~i [int]; **aphthous fever**, afta ~o; **boutonneuse fever**, butona ~o; **hay fever**, fojnkataro, fojn~o; **parrot fever**, psitakozo; **puerperal fever**, puerpera ~o; **quartan fever**, kvartana ~o; **rheumatic fever**, reŭmata ~o; **scarlet fever**, skarlata ~o; **tertian fever**, terciana ~o; **typhoid fever**, tifoida ~o; **undulent fever**, brucelozo; **yellow fever**, flava ~o
few, malmultaj; **a few**, kelkaj; **few and far between**, ~aj kaj maloftaj   ·
fez, fezo
fiancé(e), fianĉ(in)o
fiasco, fiasko; **be a fiasco**, ~i [int]
fiat, dekreto
fib, mensog(et)o; ~i [int]
fiber, fibro; **fibrous**, ~eca; **fiberboard**, ~otabulo; **fiberglass**, vitro~o; **muscle fiber**, miono
Fiber, (zool), fibero, ondatro

fibre, [see "fiber"]
fibril, fibreto
fibrillate, fibrilacii [int]; fibrillation, ~o
fibrin, fibrino; fibrinogen, ~ogeno; plant fibrin, vegetable fibrin, vegetaĵa ~o
fibroid, fibra
fibroin, fibroino
fibroma, fibromo
fibroscope, fibroskopo†; fibroscopy, ~io
fibrosis, fibrozo
fibrositis, fibrito
fibula, (bone), fibulo; (clasp), fibolo
Ficaria, fikario
fickle, facilanima
fiction, fikcio; fictional, fictitious, ~a, fiktiva; science fiction, scienc~o
Ficus, figarbo; Ficus indica, banjano; Ficus sycamorus, sikamoro
fiddle, (mus), violono; ~i [int]; (dawdle), lanti [int]; fiddle with, (mess w inexpertly), (fuŝ)fingrumi [tr]; play second fiddle, (fig), ludi la duan rolon
fideicommissum, fideikomiso
fidelity, fidel/eco; high fidelity, alt~a; alt~eco
fidget, barakteti [int]
fiduciary, komisia; ~ito
fie, (interj), fi; fie on you!, ~ al vi!
fieff, feŭdo
field, (gen), kampo; (of study etc.), fako; (tillable), agro; (those competing), konkurantaro; konkurencantaro; konkursantaro [see "compete"]; (catch), kapti [tr]; field day, festotago; fieldfare, (zool), litorno; field of vision, vid~o; depth of field, (phot, optics), ~a profundo; electromagnetic field, elektromagneta ~o; gravitational field, gravita ~o; infield, (sports), internakorta; interna korto; outfield, eksterakorta; ekstera korto
fiend, diablo, demono; fiendish, ~(ec)a
fierce, (savage), feroca, sovaĝa, kruel(eg)a; (violent, furious), furioza; (ardent), arda
fiery, fajra; (ardent), arda
fiesta, festo
fife, fifro; ~i [int]

fifth, (5th), kvina; (1/5), ~ono [see § 19]; (mus), kvinto
fig, (fruit), figo; (tree), ~arbo; figwort, skrofulario
Figaro, Figaro
fight, (gen), batali [int] (kontraŭ); kontraŭ~i [tr]; ~o; (w/o weapons; struggle), lukti [int]; lukto; fighter, ~isto; (plane), ĉasaviadilo, ĉasavio; bullfight, torei [int]; tore(ad)o; bullfighter, toreisto; prizefighter, boksisto
figment, imag/(aĵ)o; figment of one's imagination, kreaĵo de ies ~o
figure, (shape; picture; etc.), figuro, formo [cp "form"] (numeral), cifero; (sum of $), (mon)sumo; (calculate), kalkuli [tr]; (estimate, reason), taksi [tr], rezoni [tr] (e.g.: I figure it's about another hour's drive home: mi taksas ke estos ĉirkaŭ unu pluan horon hejmen) [also see "figure out" below]; (to be expected), esti atendenda (-e) (e.g.: since it's snowing, it figures that they'll be late: ĉar neĝas, estas atendende ke ili malfruos); figurative, ~a; figurhead, (gen), antaŭ ~o; ("straw man", having little authority), pajlohomo; figurine, ~eto; figure in(to), (include), inkludi [tr], enkalkuli [tr]; (play a part), inkludiĝi, ~i en, roli [int] en, havi rolon en; figure on, (trust, depend on), fidi [tr], dependi [int] je; (plan), plani [tr], intenci [tr]; figure out, (deduce), dedukti [tr]; (conclude), konkludi [tr], ekkompreni [tr]; (guess), diveni [tr]; (solve), solvi [tr]; (calculate), kalkuli [tr]; figure up, (add), sumi [tr]; figure of speech, dirmaniero; disfigure, mutili [tr], difekti [tr]; prefigur, antaŭ~i [tr]; transfigure, transformi [tr], aliformi [tr]; fine figure of a, bonstatura
Fiji (Islands), Fiĝioj
filament, (gen), filamento
filaria, Filaria, filario [see "Dracunculos", "Wucheria"]; filariasis, ~ozo
filbert, (nut), avelo; (tree), ~arbo
filch, marodi [tr] [cp "maraud"]
file, (dossier; cmptr; folder w information on person, subject), dosiero, teko; (collection of items), teko (e.g.: address file: adresoteko); (file away in

dossier, cabinet, etc.), enarkivigi; (column, row), vico; (march etc. in rows), defili [int]; (to distinguish from rank, as in mil formation), laŭvico [cp "rank"]; (scraping tool), fajli [tr]; fajlilo; (register, record), registri [tr]; **file (filing) cabinet**, ~ŝranko [not "~ujo"; see "folder"]; **files**, (archives), arkivo(j); **filings**, fajlajo(j); **card file**, (collection of cards, as index etc.), sliparo; (cabinet for these), slipujo

filet, [see "fillet"]; **filet mignon**, fileeto
filial, fil(in)a
filiation, (relationship), fil(in)eco; gefileco; (descent), deveno; (formation of branch of association), filiigo
filibuster, filibustro*; ~i [int]
Filic(al)es, filikoj
filigree, filigrano; ~i [tr]
Filipendula ulmaria, ulmario
Filipine, [see "Philippine"]
Filix, cistopterido
fill, (gen), plen/igi; ~iĝi; ~igo; ~iĝo; (eating, drinking), satigi; satiĝi; sato; (tooth), plombi [tr]; (earthfill for road over valley etc.), talusi [tr, int]; taluso; **filler**, ~igaĵo; ~igenzo; **filling**, (gen), ~igaĵo; (dental: substance used), plombo; (act of), plombado; (result), plombaĵo; **fill in**, ~igi; ~iĝi; (complete), kompletigi; kompletiĝi; (plug up), ŝtopi [tr]; ŝtopiĝi; **fill out**, ~igi; ~iĝi; kompletigi; kompletiĝi; (take shape), (~)formi [tr]; (~)formiĝi; dikigi; dikiĝi; ŝveligi; ŝveli [int]; (mature), elkreskigi; elkreski [int]; maturigi; maturiĝi; **fill up**, ~igi, ~~igi; (~)~iĝi; **fill with**, ~igi je; ~iĝi je; **refill**, (any ~ing), re~igi; re~igo; re~aĵo; (reloading, as in ball-point pen), reŝargi [tr]; reŝargo; **fill one in on**, informi iun pri; **eat (drink) one's fill**, ĝissate manĝi [tr] (trinki [tr])
fillet, (headband), diademo; (stripe), strio; (meat; arch), fileo; (listel), listelo; (piece to fill groove in tongue-and-groove, rabbet, etc.), foldolistelo
fillip, frapeti [tr]
filly, ĉevalidino
film, (phot; a movie), filmo; ~a; ~i [tr]; (any layer), tavolo; (coating), tegaĵo;

filmy, (hazy), neklara, nebuleca; **filmstrip**, ~strio; **microfilm**, mikro~o; mikro~i [tr]
filter, filtri [tr]; ~iĝi; ~ilo; **filtrate**, ~aĵo; **filter (tip)**, (cigarette), ~a (cigaredo)
filth, (dirt etc.), malpuraĵo; (fig: words, actions, etc.), fiaĵo, aĉaĵo; **filthy**, malpura(eg); fia, aĉa
filum, filamento
fimbria, fimbrio
fin, (of fish), naĝilo; (object of similar shape, as on plane, radiator, turbine), alo; **finback (whale)**, balenoptero
finagle, ruzarانĝi [tr]
final, (last), fina; (exam), ~ekzameno, ~testo; **final(s)**, (contest etc.), finalo(j); finala; **finalist**, finalulo; **final (draft)**, (as of written material), neto; **semifinal(s)**, antaŭfinalo(j); antaŭfinala; **semifinalist**, antaŭfinalulo
finale, (mus), finalo [cp "fine", "coda"]
finance, financo; ~i [tr]; **financial**, ~a; **financier**, ~isto
finch, (*Fringilla*), fringo; (any of *Fringillidae*), ~edo; **bramble finch**, monto~o; **bullfinch**, pirolo; **pine bullfinch**, pinikolo
find, (locate, discover), trovi [tr]; ~o; ~aĵo; (notice to be true), konstati [tr] (e.g.: *we found it was raining:* ni konstatis ke pluvas); (determine, adjudge), juĝi [tr], decidi [tr], determini [tr] (e.g.: *the judge found him guilty:* la juĝisto juĝis lin kulpa); **finding(s)**, ~aĵo(j); **find out**, (discover, learn), sciiĝi (pri), el~i [tr], malkovri [tr]
fine, (pure, high-quality; close, as fine tuning), fajna; (in very small particles, re dust etc.), subtila; (of good character), brava; (refined, delicate), delikata; ($ punishment), monpuni [tr]; monpuno; (mus: end), fino [cp "finale"]; (good, excellent), bon(eg)a; **finery**, galanterio
finesse, (skill), lerteco; (cards), fineso
finger, (anat), fingro; (of glove etc.), ~umo; (similar-shaped object), ~aĵo; (touch w fingers), ~umi [tr]; (mus), ~i [tr]; **fingering**, (mus), ~ado; **fingerflower**, **fingerroot**, (bot), digitalo; **fingernail**, [see under "nail"]; **finger-**

print, ~opremi [tr]; ~opremaĵo; **fore-finger**, **index finger**, montro~o; **little finger**, orel~o; **middle finger**, mez~o; mez~i [tr]; **ring finger**, ringo~o; **have a finger in**, implikiĝi en, sin miksi en; **light-fingered**, **stickyfingered**, ŝtelema

finial, finialo†

finicky, (tro)elektema

finish, (end), fini [tr]; ~iĝi; ~(iĝ)o; (final preparation), ~pretigi; ~pretigo; (final effort in race or oth sporting event), finiŝo†; finiŝi [int]; (polish paper, leather, etc.), apreti [tr]; (substance used to polish paper etc.), apreturo; (coating on any oth material, as wood etc.), tegi [tr]; tegaĵo [cp "polish", "glaze", "lacquer", etc.]; **photofinishing**, fotorivelado; **photofinisher**, fotorivelisto

Finisterre, Finistero

finite, (math), finia, fajnajta†; ~o, fajnajto†; (gen), limigita, nesenfina; (gram, re verb), finitiva; **infinite**, (gen), nefinia, nefajnajta†; (non-tech), senlima; **infinity**, infinito

finitive, finitivo

Finland, Finn/lando, Suomio; **Finn**, ~o; **Finnish**, ~a; ~landa; **Finno-Ugric**, ~o-Ugra

Finnmark, Finnmarko

fiord, fjordo

fir, abio; **cluster fir**, pinastro; **ground fir**, likopodio

fire, (flames), fajro; (set fire to), ~igi; (large), incendio; (ardor), ardo; (opp "hire"), maldungi [tr]; (shoot gun etc.), pafi [tr]; pafiĝi; (re rocket, jet engine), bruligi; ekbruli [int]; (bake, as bricks, pottery, etc.), baki [tr]; bakiĝi; (excite), eksciti [tr]; ardigi; (explode), eksplodi [int]; eksplodigi; **fire alarm**, ~alarm(il)o; brulalarm(il)o; **firearm**, pafarmilo; **fire away (at)**, ekpafadi [tr]; **fireball**, (meteor), bolido; **firebox**, ~ujo; **firebrand**, (wood), brulŝtipo; (agitator), agitanto; **firebreak**, ~oizolejo; **firebug**, piromaniulo; **firecracker**, petardo; **firedamp**, grizuo [cp "methane"]; **fire department**, ~obrigado; **firedog**, morelo, ~ohundo; **fire engine**,

fire truck, ~okamiono; **fire escape**, saveskapejo; **fire extinguisher**, ~estingilo; **firefighter**, **fireman**, ~obrigadisto; **firefly**, lampiro; **fire irons**, (fireplace tools), ~opreniloj; **fireplace**, kameno; **fireplug**, ~okranego; **firepower**, pafkapablo; **fireside**, (hearth), ~ejo; (by the fire), apudkamena, apud~a; **firestorm**, incendiego; **firetail**, (*Phoenicurus*), fenikuro; **fireweed**, epilobio; **firewood**, brulligno; **fireworks**, ~aĵo(j), piroteknikaĵo(j); **misfire**, (engine), misbruli [int]; misbrulo; (gun), mispafiĝi; mispafo; (malfunction, gen), misfunkciі [int]; misfunkcio; **bonfire**, fest~o, ĝoj~o; **campfire**, kampado~o; **be on fire**, bruli [int]; **catch fire**, ekbruli [int]; **cease-fire**, batalhalto, militpaŭzo; **cross-fire**, enfil(ad)o; **put under cross-fire**, enfili [tr]; **line of fire**, paflinio; **set on fire**, ekbruligi; **surefire**, nemaltrafebla; **wildfire**, incendio, ~ego; **spread like wildfire**, disfulmiĝi

firkin, tineto

firm, (steady, fixed, unyielding, gen), firma; (bsns), ~o; **firm up**, ~igi; ~iĝi

firmament, firmamento

firmware, (cmptr), firmvaro†

firn, firno

first, unua; ~e [see § 19]; **first aid**, [see under "aid"]; **at first**, komence, ~e; **first of all**, antaŭ ĉio; **first come first served**, ~a venas, ~a prenas; **on a first-come-first-served basis**, laŭ tio ke ~a venas, ~a prenas; **first things first**, ~ajojn ~e

firth, fjordo, estuaro

fiscal, fiska

fish, (zool, gen), fiŝo; (as food), ~aĵo; (catch), ~i [tr]; (young, for restocking river etc.), alvuso; **fisher**, (person), ~isto; (zool), marteso; **fisherman**, ~isto; **fishery**, ~ado; ~ejo; **fishy**, (colloq: dubious), dubinda; **fish ball**, **fish cake**, ~bulo; **fishhook**, ~hoko; **fishplate**, relkunigilo; **fishing line**, ~fadeno; **fishing pole**, ~kano; **fish story**, nekredindaĵo, blagaĵo; **fishtail**, (car skid etc.), jori [int]; joro; **bandfish**, cepolo; **catfish**, (gen), barb~o; (Euro-

pean catfish: *Silurus*), siluro; **crayfish**, astako, kankro; **cuttlefish**, sepio; **cuttlefish bone**, sepiosto; **flatfish**, ekzoceto, flug~o; **goldfish**, or~o; **lungfish**, pulmo~o; **monkfish**, skvateno; **needlefish**, belono; **pilotfish**, pilot~o; **porcupine fish**, diodonto; **ribbonfish**, (*Cepola*), cepolo; **rockfish**, (gen, imprecise term), ŝton~o; (*Scorpaenidae*), skorpeno; (*Sebastodes*), sebasto; **sawfish**, pristo, seg~o; **scorpion fish**, skorpeno; **sheatfish**, siluro; **shellfish**, konkulo; **starfish**, asterio, marstelo; **swordfish**, spad~o, ksifio; **tunafish**, tinuso; **whitefish**, koregono; **like a fish out of water**, ekster sia medio
fissile, (splittable, gen), fendebla; (phys: fissionable), fisiebla
fission, (split, gen), fend(iĝ)o; (phys: nuclear), fisio
fissure, fend(iĝ)o
fist, pugno; **make a fist**, ~igi la manon; **fist-fight**, **fisticuffs**, ~ado
fistula, fistulo
fit, (have right size; go into, onto), (bone) sidi [int] (al, en); sidigi; sidigo (e.g.: *this shirt fits me (well)*: ĉi tiu ĉemizo ~as al mi (bone); *that blouse doesn't fit her well:* tiu bluzo malbone ~as al ŝi; *the screw fits in that hole:* la ŝraŭbo ~as en tiu truo); be appropriate; etc.), taŭgi [int] (al), akordi [int] (kun), taŭgigi; taŭg(ig)o; taŭgeco (e.g.: *his answser did not fit the question:* lia respondo ne taŭgis al [or] ne akordis kun la demando); (decent), deca; (capable), kapabla; (healthy), sana; (med: seizure), ikto; (equip), ekipi [tr]; **fitful**, maltrankvila; **fitting**, (proper), konvena; (decent), deca; (suitable, appropriate), taŭga; (measurement for fit of clothing), taŭgigo; (mech, as for pipe), fitingo; **be fitting**, konveni [int]; deci [int]; taŭgi; **misfit**, sentaŭgulo; **fit in**, akordiĝi; **fit out**, (equip), ekipi [tr]; (garnish), garni [tr]; **outfit**, (kit, set of tools, things, clothing, equipment), kompleto; (organization), organizo, societo; **not fit for man nor beast**, taŭga nek por homo nek besto; **in fits and spurts**, panee-

me
five, kvin [see § 19]
fix, (fasten; make fast; phot), fiksi [tr]; (repair), ripari [tr]; (determine), determini [tr]; (arrange), aranĝi [tr]; (prepare), prepari [tr]; (dilemma), dilemo, embaraso; (direction bearing), biro; (drug), (drog)dozo; **fixed**, (unmoving, unchanging), ~a; **fixer**, (phot), ~enzo; **fixings**, (accessories, as for food), garnaĵo(j); **fix (up)on**, (choose), elekti [tr]; **fix up**, ripari [tr], (re)bonigi; aranĝi [tr]; organizi [tr]; **get a fix on**, (bearing), biri [tr]
fixate, fiksi [tr]; ~iĝi; **fixation**, ~iĝo; **fixative**, ~enzo
fixture, fiksaĵo
fizz, (hiss), sibli [int], fuzi [int]; (foam), ŝaŭmi [int]; (bubble), eferveski [int]; eferveskaĵo
fizzle, (hiss), sibli [int], fuzi [int]; (fiasco), fiasko; fiaski [int]
fjord, fjordo
flab, grasaĉo; **flabby**, ~a, molaĉa
flabbergast, konfuzegi [tr], konsterni [tr]
flaccid, molaĉa, malfirma
flacon, flakono
Flacourtia, flakurtio
flag, (as of nation), flago; (standard, banner), standardo; (iris), irido; (tire), laciĝi, malvigliĝi; **flag down**, signali [tr]; **flagship**, ~ŝipo; **flagstone**, pavimŝtono; **sweet flag**, (bot), kalamo
Flagellatae, flageluloj
flagellate, (whip), vipi [tr], skurĝi [tr]; (bot), flagelforma; flagelhava; **flagellant**, flagelanto
flagellum, flagelo
flageolet, flaĝoleto
flagon, flakono
flagrant, senhonta, fifama, skandala
flail, draŝi [tr]; ~ilo
flak, (gen), kontraŭpafado
flake, (as of snow etc.),floko; ~igi; ~iĝi; (Aus: shark meat), ŝarkaĵo
flambé flamanta; ~e; ~aĵo
flamborough, (sword), flambergo; (dance), ~a danco
flamboyant, (showy, extravagant), (grand)efekta, ekstravavanca, puca, pava, vanta; (bright), brila, hela

flame, flamo; ~i [int]; **flame up**, ek~i [int], ~iĝi; **inflame**, (excite), ek~igi, inciti [tr]; (med), inflamigi; (set on fire), ~igi, ekbruligi; (arouse passion etc.), ardigi; **inflamed**, inflama; arda; **inflammation**, (med), inflamo; **inflammatory**, inflamiga; ardiga, incita
flamen, flamino
flamenco, flamenko*; ~a
flamingo, flamengo, fenikoptero
Flaminius, Flaminio; **Flaminian**, ~a
flammable, brulema;   **nonflammable**, ne~a
flan, (Br: tart), torteto [not "flano"]
Flanders, Flandrio
flange, flanĝo
flank, (side, gen), flanko; (of army), alo; (mil etc.: cover, protect, occupy side), ~i [tr]; (side part), ~aĵo; (go alongside), ~pasi [tr], al~iĝi
flannel, flanelo; ~a
flap, (covering), klapo; (of plane), post~o; (sound), klaki [int]; klako
flapjack, krespo, patkuko
flare, (blaze up), ekflamegi [int]; (burn irregularly), flagri [int]; (curve out), elkurbigi; elkurbiĝi; (phot), lummakulo; (torch, gen), torĉo; (torch for road emergencies), krizotorĉo;   **signal flare, distress flare**, (rocket, for boat etc.), lumraketo, alarmraketo
flash, (shine), ekbrili [int]; ~o; (sparkle: blink on and off), flagri [int]; flagro; (move through like lightning), fulmi [int]; fulmigi; (intuit), intui [tr]; (show), montri [tr]; (moment), momento; (phot light), fulmlumo; **flasher**, (exhibitionist), ekshibiciulo; **flasher (light)**, (as on vehicle), flagrolumo; **flashing**, (arch), gutlado; **flashy**, brilaĉa, puca; **flashback**, retrosceno†; **flashcard**, ekzercokarto; **flash gun**, fulmlumilo; **flashlight**, poŝlampo; **flash point**, ekflama punkto, ekflama temperaturo
flask, (gen), flakono [not "flasko"]; **Erlenmeyer flask**, konusa ~o; **Florence flask**, platfunda ~o
flat, (smooth), plata; (level), ebena; (re color, style, etc.), malbrila; (monotonous), monotona, senreliefa; (categorical), kategoria; (decarbonated),

senŝaŭma; (constant), konstanta; (deflated, re tire etc.), malpufa, krevinta; (mus), bemolo; bemola (e.g.: *my guitar is flat:* mia gitaro estas bemola; *Symphony in B-flat Major:* Simfonio en B-bemolo Maĵora); (apartment), apartamento; **flatbed**, (truck), ~kamiono; (rr car), ~vagono; **flatboat**, ~boato; **flatfish**, pleŭronekto, ~fiŝo; **flatfoot**, ~piedo; **flatfooted**, ~piede; **flatware**, manĝilaro; **double-flat**, (mus), dubemolo; **granny flat**, (Br, Aus), avinejo
flatter, flati [tr]; **flattery**, ~(ad)o
flatulate, furzi [int]; **flatulent**, ~a; ~ema; ~iga; **flatulence**, ~emo; ~igo; **flatus**, ~ogaso, ventrogaso
flaunt, paradi [int] (en, per, kun), pavi [int]
flautist, flutisto
Flavian, Flaviano
Flavius, Flavio
flavone, flavono
flavo(u)r, saporo,   gusto;   ~igi [cp "taste", "spice"]; **flavorful**, ~plena, bongusta; **flavoring**, ~igenzo
flaw, difekto; ~i [tr]; **flawless**, sen~a, perfekta
flax, lino; **flaxen**, ~kolora, ~hara; **New Zealand flax**, formio
flay, (strip skin), senhaŭtigi; (hide), senfeligi; (whip, gen), vipi [tr], skurĝi [tr]
flea, pulo; **beach flea**, talitro; **water flea**, akvo~o, dafnio
fleabane, daisy fleabane, erigerono
fleck, (spot), punkto; ~i [tr]
fledge, plumizi [tr]; ~iĝi; **fledgling**, (bird), birdido; (fig, gen: new), novmatura, freŝmatura; **full-fledged**, (lit or fig), plenforma, plensuka
flee, fuĝi [int] (de, el)
fleece, (wool), lano; sen~igi; (swindle), fraŭdi [tr], prifriponi [tr]; **fleecy**, ~eca
fleet, (of ships, or gen), floto; (planes), aer~o; (space), kosmo~o; (cars etc.), aŭto~o (kamion~o etc.); (fast), rapida; **fleeting**, efemera, maldaŭra
Flemish, Flandra; **Fleming**, ~o
flesh, karno [cp "tissue", "meat"]; **fleshy**, ~odika, ~ohava, ~oriĉa [cp "corpulent", "fat"]
fleur-de-lis, lilifloro

flex, (bend), fleksi [tr]; ~iĝi; ~(iĝ)o; (Br: elec cord), ŝnur(konduktil)o [see "cord"]; **flexible**, ~ebla, supla; **flexion**, ~(ad)o; **flexor**, (anat: any flexor muscle), ~anto; (in specific name of muscle), fleksoro; **flexure**, ~(iĝ)o

flick, (flip), frapeti [tr]; ~o; (sound), kraketi [int]; kraketo; **flick (on)**, (switch, elec device), ŝalti [tr]; **flick off**, malŝalti [tr]

flicker, flagreti [int], tremeti [int]; ~(ad)o, tremet(ad)o

flier, (aviator), aviadisto; (express), ekspresa (trajno, buso, etc.); (step), ŝtupo; (handbill), flugfolio

flight, (flying), flug/(ad)o; (group of planes or spaceships), eskadreto; (of stairs), ŝtuparo; (fleeing), fuĝo; **flighty**, facilanima; **flight deck**, ek~a ferdeko; **flight-path**, ~itinero; **put to flight**, fuĝigi

flimflam, fripon/ado; pri~i [tr]

flimsy, malfortika, rompiĝema

flinch, ekretir/iĝi, sin ~i; **flinching**, tuŝotima; **unflinching**, nekonsternebla, resoluta, neŝancelebla

fling, (throw), ĵeti [tr]; ~iĝi; ~o; (swing), svingi [tr]; svingiĝi; svingo; (debauchery), diboĉaĵo; **have a fling**, diboĉi [int]; **have a fling at**, (try), provi [tr]

flint, siliko; **flint glass**, flinto

flip, (knock, flick), frapeti [tr]; ~o; (jump), salti [int]; salto; (turn over, rotate), renversi [tr]; renversiĝi; renvers(iĝ)o [cp "flop"]; (turn, as pages), turn(ad)i [tr]; turn(ad)o; (flip pant), frivola, impertinenta; **flipper**, (as of whale, or similar object), palmopiedo; **flip-flop**, (footwear), (senkalkanuma) sandalo; (human swimming aid, artificial flipper), naĝilo; (be indecisive), ŝanceliĝaĉi [int]

flippant, frivola, impertinenta

flirt, koketi [int], flirti [int]; ~ul(in)o, flirtul(in)o; **flirty, flirtatious**, ~ema, flirtema

flit, flirti [int]; ~o

float, (on top of, as raft), flosi [int]; ~igi; (through, as balloon, fish, idea), ŝvebi [int]; ŝvebigi; (raft etc.), ~o; (floating support, as cork, barrel, etc.).

~ilo

floc, floko; **floccose**, ~eca

floccule, floko; **flocculate**, ~iĝi; **flocculence**, ~eco; **flocculent**, ~eca

flock, (of animals), grego, –aro [sfx] (e.g.: [re sheep]: ŝaf~o [or] ŝafaro); (gather), amasigi; amasiĝi; (fluff), floko

floe, bankizero [cp "cap: icecap"]

flog, skurĝi [tr], vergi [tr], bategi [tr]

flood, (inundate), inundi [tr]; ~iĝi; ~o; (tide), flusi [int]; fluso; (gasoline motor etc.), supernutri [tr]; supernutriĝi; **the Flood**, (Bib), (la) diluvo; **floodgate**, kluzpordo; **floodlight**, verŝlumilo; verŝlumigi; [cp "light: spotlight"]; **flood-tide**, fluso

floor, (of room etc.; platform), planko; (bottom surface or limit, gen, as of ocean, wages, etc.), fundo; (level of building), etaĝo; (right to speak at meeting), parolo (e.g.: *I yield the floor to Mr. Jones:* mi cedas la parolon al s–ro Jones); (put floor in building), ~i [tr]; (stun, surprise), konsterni [tr]; (press to floor), sur~igi (e.g.: *floor the accelerator:* sur~igi la akcelilon); **flooring**, ~aĵo

flop, (flip over), renversi [tr]; ~iĝi; ~(iĝ)o; (writhe), barakti [int]; barakto; (flap noisily), klaki [int]; klako; (fail), fiaski [int]; fiasko; **floppy**, (flexible), fleksebla; (loose, unfirm), loza, malfirma; **flophouse**, hotelaĉo, pensionaĉo; **flopy disk**, (cmptr), moldisko

flora, (bot), flaŭro

Flora, (woman's name), Flora

floral, flora

Floréal, Florealo

Florence, (city), Florenco; (woman's name), ~a; **Florentine**, ~a; ~ano

florescence, florado

floret, floreto

Florian, Floriano

florid, (ruddy), ruĝ(vang)a; (gaudy), puca

Florida, Florido

florin, floreno

florist, floristo

floss, (fluff), floko; (of cocoon), kokonlanugo; (clean teeth w dental floss), fadenpurigi (la dentojn); **flossflower**,

agerato; **dental floss**, dent-fadeno
flotation, flos/ado; ~igo; ~il(ar)o
flotilla, floteto
flotsam, flosantajô(j)
flounce, (jump), sin jeti; (clothing trim), falbalo
flounder, (struggle), barakti [int]; (opp "prosper"), malprosperi [int]; (fish), fleso
flour, faruno; ~izi [tr]
flourish, (prosper), prosperi [int], flori [int]; (wave), svingi [tr]; (fanfare), fanfaro
flout, moki [tr], ridindigi
flow, (gen), flui [int]; ~o; (tide in, opp "ebb"), fluso; flusi [int]; **overflow**, (of water), superakvi [tr]; superakviĝi, superbordiĝi; superakv(iĝ)o, superbordiĝo (any flow; people; etc.), super~i [int]; super~o (e.g.: *the crowd overflowed into the garden:* la homamaso super~is en la ĝardenon)
flower, floro; ~i [int]; **flowery**, (lit), ~riĉa; (speech), ~a, deklama; use **flowery speech**, deklami [tr]; **bellflower**, kampanulo; **butterflower**, ranunkolo; **canarybird flower**, tropeolo; **cardinal flower**, lobelio kardinala; **carrion flower**, (gen), kadavro~o; (*Smilax*), smilako; (*Stapelia*), stapelio; **fennel-flower**, nigelo; **flamingo flower**, flamengo~o; **mayflower**, (nonspecific), maj~o; **mistflower**, eŭpatorio; **monkey flower**, mimulo; **pasque flower**, (*Anemone pulsatilla*), pulsatilo; **passion flower**, pasi~o; **shadflower**, drabo; **spiderflower**, (*Cleome*), kleomo; **spoonflower**, ksantosomo; **strawflower**, helikrizo; **sunflower**, sun~o, helianto; **trumpet flower**, (*Bibnonia*), bignonio; **wallflower**, (*Cheiranthus*), keiranto; (*Erysimum*), erizimo; (colloq: nonparticipant at dance etc.), murstaranto; **wildflower**, sovaĝa ~o; **windflower**, anemono
flu, gripo
flub, fuŝi [tr]; ~o
fluctuate, fluktui [int], ondi [int]
flue, fumtubo
fluegelhorn, flugilkorno
fluent, flua; **fluency**, ~eco; **be fluent**

in, ~e paroli [tr] (e.g.: *he is fluent in French and Russian:* li ~e parolas la Francan kaj Rusan lingvojn)
fluff, (down), lanugo; (err), fuŝi [tr]; fuŝo; (loosen, as pillow), moligi; **fluffy**, ~a
flügelhorn, flugilkorno
fluid, fluida; ~o; (accumulating in tissues in dropsy, edema, etc.), seraĵo; **amniotic fluid**, amnia ~o; **(cerebro)spinal fluid**, (cerbo)spina ~o
fluke, (flatworm: *Distoma*), distomo; (*Fasciola*), fasciolo; (flatfish), pleŭronekto, flatfiŝo; (anchor point), ŝpato; (chance happening), hazardo
flume, klintrogo
flunk, malsukcesi [int] (en), fiaski [int] (en) [see "fail"]
flunky, lakeo
fluoresce, fluoreski [int]; **fluorescence**, ~eco; **fluorescent**, ~a
fluorescein(e), fluoresceino
fluoride, fluorido; **fluoridate**, ~izi [tr]
fluorine, fluoro; **fluorinate**, ~izi [tr]
fluoroscope, fluoresko-ekrano; **fluoroscopy**, ~ado
fluorspar, fluorito
flurry, (snow), neĝeto; ~i [int]; (agitate), agiti [tr]; agitiĝi; agitiĝo; (gust), ventpuŝo
flush, (wash out w water, as toilet or wound), akvumi [tr]; ~iĝi; ~o; (wash away), forlavi [tr] (e.g.: *flush the pills down the toilet:* forlavi la pilolojn malsupren la fekseĝon); (rinse), gargari [tr]; (blush), ruĝiĝi; ruĝ(vang)a; (put to flight), ekflugigi; (make flee), fuĝigi; (excite), eksciti [tr]; (full), plena; (to brim), plenplena; (level, even), ebena; ebene; (having $), monhava; (abundant), abunda; (cards), samemblemaro
fluster, konfuzi [tr]; ~o
Flustra, flustro
flute, (mus), fluto; ~i [int]; (groove), kanelo; kaneli [tr]; **fluting**, kanelaĵo
flutter, (as flag), flirti [int]; ~o; (as butterfly), papiliumi [tr, int]; (as eyes), palpebrum(ad)i [int]; (quiver, tremble), tremi [int]; (radio), flagra fado; flagre fadi [int]; (heart), flutero; fluteri [int]; (Br: bet), veteto

flux, (flow, gen), fluo; (math, sci), flukso; (for soldering etc.), fandigenzo; (med: loose bowels), lakso

fly, (as bird, aircraft, spacecraft), flugi [int]; ~igi; (in aircraft), aviadi [int]; [see also "flier", "flight"]; (hasten), rapidegi [int], hast(eg)i [int]; (as flag), flirti [int]; flirtigi; (insect, gen), muŝo; (of pants), pantalonfendeto; (of man's pants, slang), kacujo [see "penis"]; **flyer,** [see "flier"]; **fly at,** furioze ataki [tr]; **fly-by,** preter~o; **fly-by-night,** nefidinda; **flycatcher,** (bird), muŝkaptulo; **flyleaf,** ŝirmopaĝo; **fly open,** krevi [int]; **flywheel,** inercirado; **fly in the ointment,** io misa, tubero en la afro; **let fly,** elĵeti [tr]; **botfly,** (horse botfly: *Gasterophilidae*), gastrofilo; (sheep botfly: *Oestridae*), ojstro; **butterfly,** (gen), papilio; **cabbage butterfly,** pieriso; **swallowtail butterfly,** papiliono; **caddis fly,** frigano; **catch fly,** (bot), sileno; **crane fly,** tipulo; **fruit fly, banana fly,** drozofilo, bananmuŝo; **gadfly,** tabano; **golden-eyed fly,** krizopo; **harvest fly,** cikado; **horsefly,** tabano; **lantern fly,** fulgoro; **May fly,** efemero; **sand fly,** (*Phlebotoma*), flebotomo; (*Simulium*), simulio; **Spanish fly,** (insect), kantarido; (powder), kantaridaĵo; **tsetse fly,** ceceo; (sci), glosino

foal, (of horse), ĉevalido; naski (~on); (of donkey etc.), azenido (etc.)

foam, ŝaŭmo; ~i [int]; ~igi

fob, (watch pocket), (horloĝa) poŝeto; (swindle), prifriponi [tr], trompi [tr]

F.O.B. fri [prep] (e.g.: *F.O.B. Chicago:* fri Ĉikago) [see "free"]

focal, fokusa; **focal distance,** inter~a distanco; **bifocal,** du~a; **bifocals,** du~aj okulvitroj; **trifocal,** tri~a; **trifocals,** tri~aj okulvitroj

focus, fokuso; en~igi

fodder, furaĝo

foe, malamiko, adversulo†, kontraŭulo

foehn, feno

Foeniculum, fenkolo

foetus, [see "fetus"]

fog, (in air, or analogous unclarity), nebulo; (condensation on cold surface, as window, glass or ice water, etc.), ro-

sumo; **foggy,** ~a; rosuma; **fog up,** ~igi; ~iĝi; rosumigi; rosumiĝi; **defogger,** (e.g., for car window), senrosumilo; **pea-soup fog,** ~supo†

fogy, kadukulaĉo, eksmodulo

foible, malfortaĵeto

foil, (thwart), malsukcesigi, vanigi; (metal leaf), folio; (rapier), rapiro; **aluminum foil,** aluminia folio; **tin foil,** staniolo

foist, (tromp)trudi [tr]

fold, (crease, bend over), faldi [tr]; ~(aĵ)o; (put together), as wings, tent, etc.), kunmeti [tr]; (fail), malsukcesi [int]; (herd of sheep etc.), grego; (sheep pen), gregejo, ŝafejo; **folding,** (foldable), ~ebla

–fold, (sfx: multiplied by), ~obla; ~~e (e.g.: *a tenfold increase:* dek~a pliiĝo); (number of parts), ~opa; ~ope (e.g.: *our task is threefold:* nia tasko estas triopa); **multiply (increase)** ...**fold,** ~~igi; ~iĝi (e.g.: *increase fivefold:* kvin~igi; kvin~iĝi)

folder, (of heavy paper for file), dosierujo; (pamphlet), broŝuro; (cmptr), baĉot†

foliaceous, (like leaf), foli/eca; (having leaves), ~hava

foliage, foliaro

foliar, folieca

foliate, (gen), foli/igi; ~iĝi; **defoliate,** sen~igi

folio, (sheet folded once), folio; (folded twice, for 4 pages; book of this format), folianto

folk, (a people, ethnic group), popolo, gento; (persons, gen), homoj; (re folklore), folklora, ~a (e.g.: *folk dance:* ~danco [or] folklora ~o); **folks,** homoj; **folksy,** neformala, familiara; **folklore,** folkloro; folklora

follicle, foliklo

folliculin, oestrono, folikulino

follow, (go after, gen), sekvi [tr]; (go along, as coast, road, etc.), ~i, laŭiri [tr]; (result as consequence), ~i, rezulti [int]; (obey), obei [tr]; **follower,** (of an idea, doctrine, etc.), ano, adepto, ~anto, disĉiplo; **following,** (group of followers), ~antaro, anaro, adeptaro; (prep: after), post; **the following,** (introducing an item or list), la jena(j); **as follows, in the following manner,** jene, jenmaniere, laŭ la jena maniero, kiel ~e; **it follows that,** ~as ke; ~e; tial; **follow through (on),** kompletigi; **follow up,** (check, proceed, try further), plu~i [tr]

folly, malsaĝ/aĵo; ~eco

Fomalhaut, Fomalhoto

foment, (incite), inciti [tr]; (med), fomenti [tr]

Fomes fomentarius, tindrofungo, fajrofungo

fond, (loving), ama, ~ema; (gentle, tender), tenera; **be fond of,** ŝati [tr], ~i [tr]

fondle, karesi [tr]; ~o

fondu(e), fonduo*

font, (type), karaktraro; (basin), kuvo; **baptismal font,** baptujo

Fontainebleau, Fontanbelo

fontanel(le), fontanelo

food, manĝaĵo, nutraĵo; **fast food,** krak~o; krakmanĝa; **junk food,** sub~o; **food for thought,** pripensindaĵo

fool, (deceive), trompi [tr]; (cause to err), erarigi; (unwise person), malsaĝulo; (stupid person), stultulo; (jester), arlekeno; (joke), ŝerci [int]; priŝerci [tr]; **foolhardy,** malprudenta, troriskema; **foolish,** (unwise), malsaĝa; (silly), fola; (stupid), stulta; (imprudent), malprudenta; **foolproof,** nefuŝebla; **fool around,** (loaf), lanti [int]; **fool around with,** (mess with carelessly or inexpertly), fuŝfingrumi [tr]; **make a fool of,** ridindigi; **tomfool,** stulta, malsaĝa; stultulo, malsaĝulo; **tomfoolery,** stulteco, malsaĝo

foot, (anat; similar object; unit of verse meter), piedo; (lowest point, as of mountain etc.), bazo, malsupro; (unit of length), futo [0,3048 metro (see § 20)]; **footer,** (at bottom of document), ~strio **footing,** (firm place to stand), starejo; (building foundation), ~aĵo; **football,** (soccer: game), futbalo; (ball), futbalpilko; (Am), Usona futbalo; Usona futbalpilko; **foothill,** antaŭmont(et)o; **footlocker,** kofro; **footman,** lakeo; **footnote,** ~noto;

footpath, pado; **footprint,** ~signo; **footstep,** paŝo; **footstool,** skabelo; **footwear,** ~vestoj [note plur]; **footwork,** ~umado; **barefoot(ed),** nud(a)~a; **Blackfoot,** (Native American), Nigra~ulo; Nigra~ula; **clubfoot,** bul~o; **flat-footed,** plat~a; **fleet-footed,** facil~a; **sure-footed,** firm~a; **tenderfoot,** novbakito; **web-footed,** palmo~a; **on foot,** ~ira; ~ire; sur~a; sur~e; **go on foot,** ~iri [int]; **get off on the right (wrong) foot,** (mal)bone komenci [tr]; (mal)bone komenciĝi; **get cold foot,** (lose courage), malkuraĝiĝi; **put one's foot down,** (ek)kontraŭi [tr]; **put one's best foot forward,** prezenti sian plej favoran flankon; **put one's foot in one's mouth,** fuŝparoli [int]; **set foot in,** enpaŝi [tr]; **set foot on,** surpaŝi [tr]

fop, dando; **foppish,** ~a

for, (re purpose, goal; person or thing to whom given, done; future duration), por (e.g.: *for what purpose:* ~ kiu celo; *prepare for the trip:* prepari ~ la vojaĝo; *that glass is for water:* tiu glaso estas ~ akvo; *that gift is for you:* tiu donaco estas ~ vi; *I paid $15 for that book:* mi pagis $15 ~ tiu libro; *pay for one's mistakes:* pagi ~ siaj eraroj; *I took you for [to be] someone else:* mi prenis vin ~ iu alia; *enough food for a week:* sufiĉa nutraĵo ~ semajno); (against, in exchange for, re price), kontraŭ (e.g.: *I sold it for $200:* mi vendis ĝin kontraŭ $200; *a medicine for fever:* medikamento kontraŭ febro); (because), ĉar (e.g.: *I can't come, for I am sick:* mi ne povas veni, ĉar mi estas malsana); (because of), pro (e.g.: *I couldn't come for lack of money:* mi ne povis veni pro manko de mono; *thank you for your letter:* dankon pro via letero; *an eye for an eye:* okulo pro okulo); (instead of), anstataŭ (e.g.: *use coats for blankets:* uzi paltojn anstataŭ litkovriloj); (as, to be), kiel (e.g.: *I know that for a fact:* mi scias tion kiel fakton); (during), dum (e.g.: *we were there for a month:* ni estis tie dum monato; *for a long time:* dum longa tempo); (one by

one), –opa; –ope [sfx] (e.g.: *avoid translating word for word:* evitu vortopan tradukadon): **for all**, (in spite of), malgraŭ (ĉiom el, ĉiuj el, etc.) (e.g.: *for all her courage, the experience frightened her:* malgraŭ (ĉiom el) ŝia kuraĝo, la sperto timigis ŝin; *a man's a man, for all that:* homo estas homo, malgraŭ ĉio tio); **what for**, (more emphatic than "why"), pro kio (e.g.: *what did you do that for?:* pro kio vi faris tion?); **what ... is for**, ~ kio ... estas, la motivo de ... (e.g.: *she explained what the meeting is for:* ŝi klarigis tion, por kio estas la kunveno [or] ŝi klarigis la motivon de la kunveno); **for ... to (do)**, ~ ke ... –u (e.g.: *he baked a cake for us to eat:* li bakis kukon ~ ke ni manĝu)
forage, furaĝo; ~i [int]
foramen, truo
Foraminifera, foraminiferoj
forbear, (refrain, avoid), sin deteni (de), eviti [tr]; (resign self to), rezignacii [int] (pri); **forbearance**, sindeteno; rezignacio; **forbearing**, sindetena; rezignaci(em)a; sindetenemo; rezignaciemo; (not severe), malsevera, milda
forbid, malpermesi [tr]
force, (strength, vigor, intensity of power, etc.), forto; (enforce, obligate by force, do violence on), per~i [tr]; (obligate, gen), devigi, trud(pel)i [tr]; (re plants, as in greenhouse), forci [tr]; (validity, effectiveness), valideco; **forceful**, ~a; **forcible**, per~a; **brute force**, kruda ~o; **in force**, (in effect, valid), valida; (in great number), grandnombre, multnombre; **be in force**, validi [int]; **armed forces**, armeo(j), milit~o(j); **ground forces**, terarmeo; **air force**, aerarmeo; **force oneself on**, trudi sin al; **labor force**, **work force**, labor~o
forceps, forcepso [note sing]
ford, travadi [tr]; ~ejo
fore, antaŭa; ~(aĵ)o; **foremost**, ĉefa, unu(arang)a, plej ~a; **come to the fore**, ~iĝi, evidentiĝi; **bring to the fore**, ~igi, evidentigi
fore–, (pfx: in front), antaŭ– (e.g.: *forearm:* ~brako); (earlier), antaŭ–, pra–

(e.g.: *forebear:* ~ulo [or] praulo) [see also separate entries below]
forebode, aŭguri [tr]; **foreboding**, (malbon)~o; (malbon)~a
forecast, prognozi [tr]; ~o [cp "predict"]
forecastle, teŭgo
foreclose, (exclude, bar), ekskludi [tr], ekskluzivi [tr]; (re mortgage), eksvalidigi (hipotekon)
foreign, (gen), fremda; (of oth country), ~a, eksterlanda, alilanda; **foreigner**, ~ulo, alilandano; **foreign body**, **foreign substance**, (med: antigen), antigeno, kseno, ~a korpo
foreman, (gen), submastro, vokto, ĉefo; (of jury), (ĵuri)ĉefo; (in printing shop), proto
forensic, jura
forest, arbaro; ~a; ~igi; (methodically tended), forsto; **forested**, ~eca; **forester**, ~isto; forstisto; **forestry**, ~kulturo, silvikulturo; forstokulturo; **deforest**, sen~igi, senarbigi; **reforest**, re~igi; **Forest Service**, ~administracio; forstadministracio; **Black Forest**, Ŝvarcvaldo
forestall, antaŭeviti [tr]
forever, por ĉiam; porĉiama; **forever after**, ĉiam poste
forfeit, rezigni [tr]; ~aĵo; ~ita; (against will, e.g. as fine, punishment), pun–perdi [tr]; pun–perdaĵo; **forfeiture**, ~o; ~aĵo; pun–perdo
Forficula, forfikulo
forge, (counterfeit), falsi [tr]; (hammer metal, lit or fig), forĝi [tr]; (press metal), pregi [tr]; (machine), forĝatoro; pregatoro; (plant), forĝejo; pregejo; **forger**, ~into; ~isto; **forgery**, ~ado; ~aĵo; **cold-forge**, fridmarteli [tr]
forget, forgesi [tr]; **forgetful**, ~ema; **forget-me-not**, (bot), miozoto, ne~umino
forgive, pardoni [tr]; **forgiving**, ~ema; **forgiveness**, ~emo
forint, forinto
fork, (gen), forko; ~i [tr]; (split, divide), ~iĝi, branĉiĝi; ~iĝo, branĉiĝo; (large, as pitchfork), ~ego; **forked**, ~a; **pitchfork**, ~ego; ~egi [tr]; **tuning fork**, diapazono

forlorn, forlasita, mizera, senespera
form, (shape, figure; make; take shape), formo; ~i [tr]; ~iĝi [cp "figure"]; (model), modelo; (condition, state), stato (e.g.: *in good form:* en bona stato); (manners), konduto; (arrangement), aranĝo; (style, technique), stilo, tekniko; (formula, order), formulo; (printed blank), formularo; (for specific purpose), [purpose]–ilo (e.g.: *subscription form:* abonilo; *membership form,* *enrollment form:* aliĝilo); (kind, variety), speco; (lair), kuŝejo; (Br: school class), klaso; (for molding concrete, building arch, etc.), cintro, muldilo [cp "frame"]; **formation,** (arrangement), aranĝo; (geol), formacio; (mil etc.), kunvicigo; kunviciĝo; kunvicaro; **formative,** ~dona
–form, (sfx: –shaped), –forma (e.g.: *dentiform:* dento~a)
formal, formala; **informal,** ne~a, familiara, senceremonia
formaldehyde, metanalo, formaldehido
formalin, formalino
format, formato; ~i [tr]
formate, formiato; **methyl formate,** metila ~o
former, eks– [pfx], eksa, eks– [pfx], antaŭa (e.g.: *former husband:* ~edzo [or] ~a edzo [or] antaŭa edzo); **the former,** (first of 2 cited), tiu, la unua [see "latter"]
formic, (chem), formi/ata; **formic acid,** ~a acido, metanacido
Formica, (zool), formiko
formication, formikado
formidable, terura, timiga, imponega
Formosa, Formozo [now "Tajvan"]
formula, formulo; **formulate,** ~i [tr]; **formulation,** ~ado; ~iĝo
formyl, formilo
fornicate, malĉasti [int], (nelice) kopulacii [int]; **fornication,** ~ado, (nelica) kopulacio
fornix, formikso
forsake, forlasi [tr]
forsythia, Forsythia, forsitio
fort, fuorto [cp "fortress"]
forte, (mus: loud), laŭte; (strong point), fortaĵo; **fortissimo,** ~ege
forth, (out), el– [pfx] (e.g.: *go forth:*

~iri; *send forth:* ~sendi); **forthcoming,** (baldaŭ) venonta, (baldaŭ) aperonta; **forthright,** rekta, malkaŝema; **forthwith,** (w/o delay), senprokraste; (immediately), tuj; **and so forth,** [see "etc."]; **put forth, set forth,** (suggest, propose), antaŭmeti [tr], proponi [tr], sugesti [tr]
fortify, fortik/igi; fortigi [see "strong"]; **fortification,** ~igo; fortigo; fortikaĵo [cp "fort", "fortress"]
fortitude, kuraĝo, animforto
fortnight, semajnduo, du semajnoj
fortress, fortreso, burgo†
fortuitous, hazarda; **fortuity,** ~o; ~eco
Fortunato, Fortunato
fortune, (good luck), fortuno, feliĉo, bonŝanco; (fate), sorto; (riches), riĉaĵoj; **fortunate,** feliĉa, bonŝanca; **unfortunate,** malfeliĉa, malbonŝanca, bedaŭrinda; **misfortune,** malfeliĉo, mal~o; mis~o; **tell fortune(s),** sortodiveni [int]; **fortune-teller,** sortodivenist(in)o, aŭgurist(in)o
Fortune, (myth), Fortuna
forum, forumo
forward, (ahead), antaŭa, ~ena; ~e(n); (readdress mail), plusendi [tr], transsendi [tr]; (dispatch), ekspedi [tr], sendi [tr]; (sport), avanulo; (arrogant), aroganta, malmodesta; **look forward to,** ~ĝui [tr]; **carry forward,** ~enigi, progresigi, pluigi; **forward-looking,** ~enema, progresema
fossil, (gen), fosilio; ~a: (of animal), zoolito; **fossilize,** ~igi; zoolitigi; ~iĝi; zoolitiĝi
foster, (care for), varti [tr] (stimulate), stimuli [tr]; **foster father (mother),** ~opatr(in)o; **foster child,** ~infano; **foster home,** ~ejo, ~odomo
foul, (disgusting), abomena, aĉa; (wicked), fia; (dirty), malpura; malpurigi; (stinking), fetora, haladza, miasma, stinka; (rotten), putra; (sport), faŭli [int]; prifaŭli [tr]; faŭlo: faŭla; **foul up,** (botch), fuŝi [tr]
foulard, fulardo
found, (set up, originate), fondi [tr]; (give firm foundation), fundamenti [tr]; (mold, cast), muldi [tr]; **unfounded,** sen~a, senbaza; **foundation,**

~ado; ~aĵo; ~iĝo; ($), ~aĵo; (of building or oth base), fundamento
founder, (stumble), stumbli [int]; (sink), eksinki [int]; (bog down, lit or fig), enmarĉiĝi; (fail), malsukcesi [int], fiaski [int]
foundling, (baby), trovito†
foundry, fandejo, muldejo
fount, (source), fonto; (Br: type font), tiparo
fountain, fontano; **fountainhead**, fonto; **fountain pen**, fontoplumo
four, kvar; **fourth**, (4th), ~a; (1/4), ~ono [see § 19]; (mus interval), kvarto; **four-o'clock**, (bot), niktago
fovea, foveo
fowl, (any bird), birdo; (domestic), korto~o; (hunt), ~oĉasi [int]; **guinea fowl**, numido; **jungle fowl**, galino
fox, (zool, gen), vulpo; (bewilder), mistifiki [tr]; **foxy**, (attractive), alloga, pimpa; (sneaky), ruza; **foxglove**, (bot), digitalo; **foxtail**, (bot), alopekuro; **foxtrot**, (dance), fokstroto; fokstroti [int]; **arctic fox**, **white fox**, (*Alopex lagopus*), monta ~o; **blue fox**, (*A. lagopus* in blue-fur stage), izatiso; **flying fox**, (*Pteropus*), pteropo; (Aus: cable car), telfero; **outfox**, superruzi [tr]
foyer, vestiblo
fracas, bruego, kverelego, malpaco
fractal, fraktalo*; ~a
fraction, (math; chem), frakcio; (lesser part, gen), ~o, ono (e.g.: *just a fraction of its former size:* nur ono de ĝia antaŭa grando); **fractional**, ~a; **complex fraction**, **compound fraction**, ĉen~o
fracto–, (pfx), frakto–
fracture, (break, gen), rompi [tr]; ~iĝi; ~(iĝ)o; (of bone), frakturo; (geol), diaklazo; **simple fracture**, fermita frakturo; **compound fracture**, aperta frakturo; **comminuted fracture**, splita frakturo
fraenum, frenulo
Fragaria, fragujo
fragile, rompiĝema, (poet), fragila
fragment, fragmento; ~igi; ~iĝi; **fragmented**, **fragmentary**, ~a
fragrant, aroma; **fragrance**, ~o; be

fragrant, have fragrance, ~i [int]
frail, delikata, malforta, debila
fraktur, frakturo
frambesia, frambezio
frame, (structure, framework), framo; en~igi; (border; of movie etc.), kadro; kadri [tr] (e.g.: *a view framed by trees:* vidaĵo kadrita de arboj); (shape, formulate), formi [tr]; (fit, adjust), taŭgigi, alĝustigi; (false evidence), falskulpigi; (wooden framework, as re house), ligno~o; **frame-up**, fals-kulpigo; **framework**, ~o; kadro; **A-frame**, A-~o; **frame of mind**, animstato; **frame of reference**, referencokadro
framea, frameo
franc, franko
France, Francio
Frances, Franciska
Franche-Comté Franĉkonteo
franchise, (right to vote), balotrajto; ~igi; (bsns), koncesio, agenturo; koncesii [tr]; [not "franĉizo"]; **franchised**, ~a; koncesiita; **enfranchise**, ~igi; **disenfranchise**, (gen), senrajtigi; (of vote), senigi je la ~o, sen ~igi
Francis, Francisko
Franciscan, Franciskano; ~a
francium, francio
Franco–, (pfx: French), Franc– (e.g.: *Franco-German:* ~–Germana)
francolin, frankolino
Francolinus, frankolino
Franconia, (ancient), Frankulo; (modern), Frankonio
Francophone, Francparola; ~anto
frangipani, (pastry), franĝipano
frank, (sincere), sincera, honestadira, malkaŝema; (mail), afranki [tr]; afranko; afrankrajto
Frank, (man's name), Francisko; (re German tribe), Franko; **Frankish**, Franka
Frankfurt, Frankfurto; **Frankfurt am Main**, ~o ĉe Majno; **Frankfurt an der Oder**, ~o ĉe Odro
frankfurter, (meat), frankfurto*; (w bun), ~a bulko
frankincense, olibano
frantic, freneza, furioza
Franz Josef Land, Insuloj Franc-Joze-

faj
Fratercula, fraterkulo
fraternal, frat/(ec)a; **fraternity,** ~eco;
~aro; **fraternalize,** ~iĝi
fratricide, fratmortigo
fraud, fraŭdo; **defraud,** ~i [tr]; **fraudulent,** ~a
fraught, ŝarĝita
fraxinella, fraksinelo
Fraxinus, frakseno; Fraxinus ornus,
orno
fray, (wear), ĉifon/igi; ~iĝi; (brawl),
bruego, kverelego, malpaco, tumulto
frazil (ice), kirloglacio
frazzle, ĉifon/igi; ~iĝi; ~iĝo; (colloq:
tire out), (plene ellacigi, elĉerpi [tr]
freak, (monstrosity), monstro; ~a;
(odd), kurioza, stranga; kuriozulo,
strangulo; kuriozaĵo, strangaĵo; (caprice), kaprico; kaprica; **freaky,
freakish,** kurioza, stranga; kaprica
freckle, efelido
Fred, Freĉjo
Frederica, Frederika
Frederick, Frederiko
free, (not restricted, not controlled, not
in use, not limited, etc.), libera; ~igi;
(no cost), senpaga; senpage; (of debt,
duty), kvita; kvitigi; kvitiĝi; (vacant),
vaka; vakigi; (untie), malligi [tr]; (unfasten), malfiksi [tr]; (release), ellasi
[tr]; (remove, deprive of), senigi (je);
(freight cost paid to specified place),
fri [prep] (e.g.: *free alongside ship:* fri
kajo; **freebie,** senpagaĵo; **freeboard,**
(superakva) flankalto; **freebooter,**
flibustro; **freedom,** ~(ec)o; **freedom
of speech (press, thought, etc.),** pa-
rol~(ec)o, pres~(ec)o, pens~(ec)o
(etc.); **free-for-all,** bruego, malpaco,
tumulto; **freehand,** ~mana; ~mane;
freehold, plenproprieto; **freeholder,**
plenproprietulo, burĝo; **free-lance,**
aŭtonoma, sendependa; aŭtonomulo,
sendependulo; **freeman,** civitano,
burĝo; **Freemason,** framasono; **Free-
masonry,** framasonismo; **free on
board,** [see "F.O.B."]; **freeway,** aŭtovojo; **freewill,** ~vola; **scot-free,** (w/o
punishment), (tute) senpune; (w/o injury), (tute) senvunde
freeze, (become very cold, lit or fig,

gen), frost/igi; ~iĝi; ~igo; ~iĝo;
(freeze food to –20°, –30°C), konge-
li† [tr]; (be, feel cold), ~i [int] (e.g.:
I'm freezing: mi ~as; *it's freezing in
here:* ~as ĉi tie); (poet), gelo; (turn to
ice), glaciigi; glaciiĝi; (re wages, prices, etc.), bloki [tr]; blok(ad)o; (stop all
motion), (plen)halti [int], senmoviĝi;
(plen)haltigi, senmovigi; (re machine,
as from lack of lubrication), rajpi
[int]; **freezing,** (below 0°C), ~a;
freezer, (any device for freezing),
~atoro; (deep freeze: appliance to
keep food etc. at about –20°C), kon-
gelatoro; **freeze dry,** liofilizi† [tr];
freezing compartment, (as in refrigerator), ~fako; **freezing point,**
~opunkto; **antifreeze,** kontraŭglaci-
enzo
Fregata, fregato
freight, (goods shipped; charge), frajto;
(ship, transport), transporti [tr] [not
"~i"]; (load), ŝarĝi [tr]; **freighter,**
~ŝipo; ~avio; **freight car,** (rr), ~vago-
no; **freight train,** ~trajno
French, Franca; ~o; la ~a (lingvo);
Frenchman, ~o
frenetic, freneza
frenum, frenumo; **frenulum,** ~eto
frenzy, frenezo, deliro; **frenzied,** ~a
frequent, (often), ofta; (visit), frekventi [tr], vizitadi [tr]; **frequency,** (often-
ness), ~eco; (phys), frekvenco;
infrequent, mal~a; **audio-frequen-
cy,** aŭdo-frekvenca
fresco, fresko
fresh, (not stale), freŝa; (re water: not
salty), nesala; (bold), aŭdaca; **fresh-
en,** ~igi; ~iĝi; **freshen up,** re~igi sin;
freshman, unuajara; unuajarulo;
freshwater, nesalakva; **refresh,**
re~igi; **refreshment,** re~igaĵo; **be
fresh out of,** ĵus elĉerpiĝi de (e.g.:
we're fresh out of milk: ni ĵus elĉer-
piĝis de lakto)
fret, (worry), ĉagreni [tr]; ~iĝi; ~o;
(wear, gnaw), mordi [tr]; mordiĝi; (on
mus instrument; decoration), freto;
(mus: finger), fingri [tr]; **fretful,** malkvieta, maltrankvila; ~ita; **fretwork,**
fretaĵo
Freud, Freŭdo; **Freudian,** ~a; **Freud-**

ianism, ~ismo
Frey(j)a, Freja
friable, dispecîĝema
friar, monaño; **friary,** ~ejo; ~aro;
    White **Friar,** karmelano
fricandeau, fricando, frikando
fricassee, frikasi [tr]; ~aĵo
fricative, frikativo; ~a
friction, (rubbing, gen), frot(ad)o; (discord), malakordo
Friday, vendredo; ~a; ~e; **Good Friday,** la Sankta V~o
Fridtjof Nansen Land, Insuloj Franc-Jozefaj
friend, amiko; **friendly,** ~a; **friendship,** ~eco; **befriend,** ~iĝi kun, ~e
    helpi [tr]; **boyfriend, (girlfriend),** karul(in)o; **make friends (with),** ~iĝi
    (kun); **Society of Friends,** Societo de
    A~oj [cp "Quaker"]
Friesland, Frisio; **Friesian,** ~o; ~a; ~ia
frieze, (decoration), friso
frigate, fregato; **frigate bird,** ~o
fright, timo; **frighten,** ~igi; **frightening,** ~iga; **frightful,** ~iga, ~inda;
    stage fright, kulis~o
frigid, (cold), malvarmega, fridega [see
    "cold"]; (psych), frigida; **frigidity,**
    ~eco; frigideco
frill, (ruffle), krispo, falbalo; ~igi; ~iĝi;
    (fringe), franĝo; (decoration), ornamaĵo; (extra), bagatelo, ekstraĵo; **frilly,**
    ~a; **no-frills,** senornama
Frimaire, Frimero
fringe, franĝo; ~i [tr]; ~a
Fringilla, fringo; Fringilla montifringilla, monto~o; Fringillidae, ~edoj
frippery, puc/aĵo(j); ~eco
frisbee, flugdisko
Frisian, Friso; ~a; ~ia
frisk, (frolic), kaprioli [int], petoli [int];
    ~o; (search), priserĉi [tr]; **frisky,**
    ~ema, petolema
Fritillaria, fritilario, imperiestra krono
fritillary, (bot), fritilario, imperiestra
    krono
fritter, (food), benjeto; **fritter away,**
    miskonsumi [tr], forlanti [tr], formalŝpari [tr], frivole malŝpari [tr];
    corn fritter, maiz~o
Friuli, Friulo
frivolous, frivola; **frivolity,** ~eco; ~aĵo

frizz, frizi [tr]; ~o
frock, (robe), frako; ~vesti [tr]; (of
    monk etc.), froko; **defrock, unfrock,**
    sen~igi; senfrokigi; **frock coat,** redingoto, kitelo
frog, (zool), rano; (rr), frogo; (looped
    clothing fastener), maŝagrafo; (to hold
    flowers in vase), flortenilo; **frogman,**
    ~homo; **bullfrog,** ~ego; **tree frog,** hilo
frogbit, hidrokarido
frolic, kaprioli [int], petoli [int]; ~o;
    frolicsome, ~ema, petolema
from, (motion away; opp "to"; origin),
    de (e.g.: *hang, bounce from the wall:*
    pendi, resalti de la muro; *a letter from
    Mary:* letero de Maria) [note: to distinguish "de" in these senses from
    sense of "by", "of", etc., "for de",
    "ekde", "disde" may be used (e.g.:
    take the Anderson book from him:
    preni la libron de Anderson for de li;
    start Ms. Smith's term from January:
    komenci la deĵoron de s-ino Smith
    ekde januaro; *separate Mr. Brown's
    records from mine:* apartigi la registraĵojn de s-ro Brown disde la miaj)];
    (out of; part of whole; from geog
    place), el (e.g.: *she is from Washington:* ŝi estas el Vaŝingtono; *leave from
    the house:* eliri el la domo; *drink from
    a glass:* trinki el la glaso; *three from seven:* tri el sep); (because of), pro (e.g.:
    tremble from fear: tremi pro timo);
    across from, kontraŭ; **be ... from,**
    (distance away), [see under "be"];
    made from, farita el; **(a month, year,
    etc.) from now,** de nun post (monato,
    jaro, etc.)
frond, (as of fern, palm), frondo; (any
    leaf), folio
Fronde, Frondo
front, (forward part, gen; pol action organization), fronto; (organization etc.
    w hidden purpose), fasadorganizo;
    (face, confront), ~i [int] (al), al~i [tr];
    (face in direction), rigardi [tr] (e.g.:
    the building fronts to the north: la
    konstruaĵo rigardas norden); **frontage,** ~o; **frontal,** (of front, gen), ~a;
    (med), frontala; (bone), fruntalo; **in
    front,** antaŭe; **in front of,** antaŭ; **fore-**

front, avangardo, antaŭajô, unua rango

frontier, (any limit), limo; (national boundary), land~o; (between inhabited and uninhabited regions), loĝ~o, setlo~o*; ekloĝata, setlata*; (limit of explored area, volume), esplorlimo

frontispiece, frontispico

frost, (icy condensation), prujno; ~i [int]; (cold), frosto; (cover cake etc. w icing), glazuri [tr] sukerumi [tr]; **frosting,** (icing, as on cake), glazuro, sukerumo; **frosty,** ~a; frosta; **frostbite,** frostvundo; **defrost,** (remove frost), sen~igi; (thaw), malfrostigi; **defroster,** (as in car), sen~igilo

froth, ŝaŭmi [int]; ~o; **frothy,** ~a

frown, malrideti [int], kuntiri la brovojn; ~o

frowsty, (Br: stuffy), sufoka, malfreŝa

frozen, [see "freeze"]

Fructidor, Fruktidoro

fructify, frukti [int]; ~igi

fructose, fruktozo, levulozo

frugal, malluks(em)a, ŝparema

fruit, (gen), frukto; **fruitful,** ~odona; **bear fruit, be fruitful,** ~i [int]; **fruitless,** (w/o result), vana, senrezulta, sen~a; **first fruits,** (rel), primicoj; **stone fruit,** drupo

fruition, (realization), realiĝo, efektiviĝo; (bearing fruit), fruktado

frump, plump/ulino; **frumpy,** ~a

frustrate,frustri† **[tr],** malhelpi [tr], bloki [tr], vanigi; **frustration,** (condition), frustracio; (act), frustr(ad)o†, malhelp(ad)o, blokado

frustum, frusto*

fry, (cook), friti [tr]; ~iĝi; (party), ~festo (e.g.: *fish fry:* fiŝ~festo); (spawn), frajo; **French fry,** tremp~i [tr]; **French-fried potatoes, French fries,** terpomfingroj; **frying pan,** ~ilo; **small fry,** etuloj

fuchsia, Fuchsia, fuksio

fuchsin, fuksino

fuck, (vulg), fiki [tr]; ~o; **fuck up,** fuŝi [tr]

Fucus, fuko; Fucus vesiculosus, vezik~o

fuddle, stuporo; ~igi

fuddy-duddy, eksmodulo

fudge, (candy), molbombono; (fake), falsi [tr]; (cheat), friponi [int]

fuel, (gen), fuelo†; ~izi [tr]; (for heat), hejtaĵo; hejtaĵizi [tr]; (gaseous), karburaĵo; **fuel oil,** mazuto; **diesel fuel,** dizeleleo, dizel~o; **add fuel to the fire,** (fig), intensigi la situacion

fugitive, fuĝa, efemera; ~into; ~anto

fugue, fugo

Fuji(yama), Fuĵi-monto

Fukien, Fugian

–ful, (sfx: re quantity), –pleno (e.g.: *spoonful:* kuler~o; *handful:* man~o); ("full of"), –plena, –oza (e.g.: *flavorful:* sapor~a)

fulcrum, apogpunkto

fulfill, plenumi [tr]; **fulfillment,** ~o

Fulgora, fulgoro

Fulica, fuliko

full, (filled, gen), plena; ~e [see "fill"]; (sated), sata; (complete), tuta, kompleta; (re cloth), fuli [tr]; **fullback,** (football etc.), ~arierulo; **brim-full, chock-full,** ~~a, ĝisrande ~a; **in full,** komplete, ~e, tute, (~)detale; **full-fledged,** ~forma, ~suka; **full stop,** (period), punkto

fulmar, fulmaro

Fulmarus, fulmaro

fulminate, (gen), fulmini [int]; (chem), fulminato

fulsome, naŭza, ofenda

fumarate, fumar/ato; **fumaric acid,** ~a acido, trans-buten-diacido

Fumaria, fumario

fumarole, fumarolo†

fumble, (grope), palpi [int]; ~(ad)o; (bungle), fuŝi [tr]; fuŝo; (lose grasp), miskapti [tr]; miskapto; misporto

fume, (gas), haladzo; ~i [int]; en~igi; (be angry), koleri [int]

fumerolo, fumarolo

fumigate, fumizi [tr]; **fumigation,** ~(ad)o

fumitory, fumario

fun, amuzo; ~a; (tease), moki [tr]; **funny,** [see "funny"]; **poke fun at, make fun of,** moki

Funafuti, Fanafutio*

function, (operate; math), funkcii [int]; ~o; (social occasion), aranĝo, ceremonio; **functional,** ~a; **functionary,**

~ulo; **malfunction**, mis~i [int]; mis~o
fund, ($), fonduso; monprovizi [tr], financi [tr]; (any supply), provizo;
funds, ($), mono, monprovizo(j);
slush **fund**, fi~o
fundamental, fundamenta; ~o
fundus, fundo (e.g.: *ocular fundus:*
okul~o)
funeral, funebra; ~aĵoj, ~a ceremonio;
~a procesio; **funeral director**, ~aĵisto, sepult(entrepren)isto; **funeral
home**, ~aĵejo, sepultistejo
funereal, funebra
Fungi, fungoj; **Fungi** imperfecti, ~oj
neperfektaj
fungicide, fungicido
fungus, fungo; milk (cap) **fungus**, laktario, lakto~o, laktagariko; pore **fungus**, poliporo; tinder **fungus**,
tindro~o, fajro~o
funicular, (cable rr), funikularo†
funiculus, (umbilical cord), funiklo
funk, (depression), deprimo; (fear), timo; **funky**, ~ita; (mus), blusa
funnel, funelo; ~i [tr]
funny, (amusing), amuza, komika;
(odd), kurioza, stranga; (tricky, suspicious), suspektinda, ruza
fur, (animal skin and hair), pelto; ~a [cp
"hide"]; (garment), ~aĵo; (coating on
tongue etc.), tartro; **furrier**, ~isto
furan, furano
furbelow, falbalo
furbish, renovigi, (re)poluri [tr]
furfural, furalo
furious, furioza, kolerega
furl, ferli [tr]; ~aĵo
furlong, 201,2 metroj [see § 20]
furlough, forpermeso; ~i [tr]
furnace, (gen), forno; (for smelting),
alt~o [cp "stove", "oven"]
furnish, (provide), provizi [tr]; (deliver), liveri [tr]; (equip), ekipi [tr];
(give), doni [tr]; (provide furniture),
mebli [tr]; **furnished**, (w furniture),
meblita; **unfurnished**, senmebla,
nemeblita; **furnishings**, (furniture),
meblaro; (any accessories), garnituro,
akcesoraĵoj
furniture, mebl/aro, ~oj [note plur]; ~a;
piece of furniture, ~o
furor(e), furoro

furrow, sulko; ~i [tr]; ~iĝi
further, (moreover, yet more), plu; ~a
(e.g.: *I can go no further:* mi ne povas
iri ~; *further progress:* ~a progreso);
[cp "far: farther"]; (promote), antaŭenigi, akceli [tr]; **furthermore**,
krome, plu; **furthest**, plej (malproksima)
furtive, ŝtelema, kaŝema, sekretema
furuncle, furunko
fury, (anger), furiozo
Fury, (myth), Furio
furze, (*Ulex*), ulekso [not "furzo"]; needle **furze**, genisto
fuse, (of explosive), meĉo; (oth types,
as chem, percussion), fuzeo; (elec, to
break circuit), fandodrato [cp "circuit:
circuit breaker"]; (melt), (kun)fandi
[tr]; (kun)fandiĝi; **defuse**, (lit or fig),
sen~igi
fusel (oil), fuzelo
fuselage, fuzelaĝo
Fushun, Fuŝun
fusilier, fuziliero
fusillade, pafado
fusion, (nuclear), fuzio; (any melting together), kunfandiĝo
fuss, (bustle), ekscitiĝi, brui [int]; ~o,
bruo; (quarrel), kvereli [int]; kverelo;
fussy, (choosy), elektema; (quarrelsome), kverelema; (bothered), malkvieta, maltrankvila, ĉagrenita; **make
a fuss over**, dorloti [tr]; **without a
fuss**, sengene, facile, trankvile
fustian, (cloth), fusteno
fusty, mucida
futile, vana; **futility**, ~eco
future, estonta; ~eco, futuro [not "~o"];
futurism, futurismo; **futurist**, futurisma; futuristo; **futurology**, futurologio; **futurologist**, ~ologo; **future
tense**, (gram), futuro; **futures**, (bsns),
liverotaĵoj, liverotaj akcioj [see
"stock", "share"]
fuze, [see "fuse"]
Fuzhou, Fuĝou
fuzz, (fine hair), lanugo, vilo; **fuzzy**, vila; (imprecise), malpreciza; (not
sharply focussed etc.), neenfokusigita,
malbone enfokusigita, malklara, malakra, nebula, nuba

G

g, (short for "gravity", as unit), goo, gravito
gab, babili [tr, int]; ~(ad)o
gabardine, gabardino
gabble, babili [tr, int]; ~(ad)o
gabbro, gabro
gabion, gabio
gable, (gen), gablo
Gabon, Gabono
Gabriel, Gabrielo; **Gabriella, Gabrielle,** ~a
Gabun, Gabono
gad, (interj), Dio!; **gad about,** ĉirkaŭvagi [int]; **gadabout,** vagemulo
Gad, (Bib), Gado
gadfly, (lit or fig), tabano
gadget, umo; ~ilo; **gadgetry,** ~(il)aro
gadolinium, gadolinio
Gadus, gado; Gadus aeglefinus, eglefino; Gadus merlangus, merlango; Gadus morrhua, moruo; Gadidae, ~edoj; Gadiformes, ~oformaj (fiŝoj)
Gael, Gaelo; **Gaelic,** ~a; la ~a (lingvo); **Scots Gaelic,** la Skot-~a (lingvo)
gaff, (hooked pole), hokstango; (for sail), gafo
gaffe, (error), malkonvenaĵo, misdiro, misfaro; (chief electrician), ĉefelektristo; (any foreman), ĉefo, vokto
gag, (choke), strangoli [tr]; ~iĝi; (in mouth to prevent talking), buŝoŝtopi [tr]; buŝoŝtopilo; (joke), gago
gaga, freneza
gage, [see "gauge"]
Gagea, gageo, orstelo
gaggle, aro
gaity, gajeco
gain, (increase), pliiĝi; ~o; (progress), progresi [int]; progreso; (acquire), akiri [tr]; akiro; (earn), lukri [tr], gajni [tr]; lukro, gajno, profito; (win), gajni; (reach, attain), atingi [tr]; (become fast, re clock), fruiĝi; (elec), amplifo; **gainful,** lukra; **regain,** (recover), regajni [tr], reakiri [tr]; (get back to), reatingi [tr]
gainly, gracia; **ungainly,** mal~a
gainsay, kontraŭdiri [tr]

gait, irmaniero
gaiter, gamaŝo
Gaius, Gajo
gal, (colloq: woman, girl), ulino, ino
gala, festo; ~a
galactose, galaktozo
Galago, galago
galalith, galalito
Galanthus, galanto; Galanthus nivalis, neĝborulo
galantine, galantino
Galápagos (Islands), (Insuloj) Galapagoj
Galatea, (myth), Galatea
Galatia, Galat/io; **Galatian,** ~o; ~a; ~ia; **Galatians,** (Bib), ~oj
galaxy, galaksio; **galactic,** ~a; **intergalactic,** inter~a
Galba, Galbo
galbanum, galbano
Galbula, galbulo; Galbulidae, ~edoj
gale, (wind), ventego; **sweet gale, Scotch gale,** (bot), miriko
galena, galeno; **false galena,** zinkoblendo
galenite, galeno
Galeopithecus, galeopiteko
Galeopsis, galeopso
Galeoscoptes carolinensis, katbirdo
Galicia, (Spanish), Galeg/io; (Polish), Galicio; **Galician,** ~o; ~a; ~ia; Galiciano; Galicia
Galilee, Galileo; **Galilean,** ~ano; ~a
Galileo, Galilejo
galingale, (*Alpinia*), galango; (*Cyperus*), cipero
galimatias, galimatio
galiot, galioto
gall, (bile), galo; (annoy), ĉagreni [tr]; (audacity), aŭdaco; (plant tumor), gajlo; **gallbladder,** ~a veziko, ~veziko; **gallstone,** (~a) kalkuluso
gallant, (brave, noble), brava; (courtly), galanta; **gallantry,** ~eco; galanteco
galleass, galeaso
galleon, galiono
gallery, (gen), galerio
galley, (ship), galero; (kitchen), kuirejo;

(printing), galeo; **galley proof**, galeprovaĵo
Gallic, (re modern France), Franca; (re ancient Gaul), Galla
Gallican, Galikano; ~a; ~isma; **Gallicanism**, ~ismo
gallicism, galicismo
Galliformes, galinoformaj (birdoj)
Gallinula, galinolo, akvokoko
gallinule, galinolo, akvokoko
galliot, galioto
gallium, galio
gallnut, gajlo
Gallo–, (pfx), Franc–; Gallo– [see "Gallic"]
gallon, galjono [see § 20]; U.S. **gallon**, Usona ~o [3,7853 litroj]; **Imperial gallon**, Brita ~o [4,5460 litroj]
galloon, galono; ~i [tr]
gallop, galopi [int]; ~igi; ~o
gallows, pendumilo
Gallus, galino
galop, galopo; ~i [int]
galore, abunde
galosh, galoŝo
galvanic, galvana; **galvanism**, ~ismo; **galvanize**, ~izi [tr]
galvano–, (pfx), galvano–
galvanometer, galvanometro
galvanoscope, galvanoskopo
Gambia, (river), Gambio; (country), ~lando
gambit, gambito
gamble, (bet), veti [tr]; ~o; (play game of chance), ~ludi [int]; (risk), riski [tr]; risko; (speculate), spekuli [int]; spekulaĵo; **gambler**, ~ludisto
gamboge, gumiguto
gambol, kaprioli [int], petoli [int]; ~o, petolo
gambrel, (roof), duonmansardo; ~a
game, (sport, play, etc.), ludo; (scheme), komploto, projekto, intenco; (hunted animals), ĉasaĵo; (courageous), kuraĝa; (willing, ready), preta, volonta; (lame), lama; **gamecock**, batalkoko; **gamekeeper**, ĉasgardisto; **video game**, video~o; **game of chance**, hazard~o; **fair game**, licaĵo; **ahead of the game**, gajnanta
gamelan, gamelano†
gamete, gameto; **gametophyte**, ~ofito

gamma, gama [see § 16]; **gamma rays**, gama-radioj; **gamma quantum**, gama-kvantumo
gamopetalous, gamopetala
gamosepalous, gamosepala
gamut, gamo
gander, viransero
gang, (any band, group, etc.), roto, bando, aro; (organized group), taĉmento, brigado; **gang up on**, are ataki [tr]
Ganges, Gango
ganglion, ganglio
gangplank, pas–tabulo
gangrene, gangreno
gangster, gangstero
gangue, gango
gangway, (passageway), pasejo; (gangplank), pastabulo; (Br: aisle), koridoro
gannet, (*Sula*), sulo
gantry, gantro†
Ganymede, (gen), Ganimedo*
gaol, [see "jail"]
gap, (breach, hole), breĉo; (crack), fendo; (in mountains), intermonto; (narrow water gap), kluso; (missing item, blank space, lack), mankloko; **stopgap**, mankŝtopa; mankŝtopilo
gape, (stare blankly, mouth open), gapi [int]; (open mouth or hole wide), faŭki [int] [cp "gaze"]
garage, (private shelter for car etc.), remizo; ~i [tr]; (commercial, for many cars, or to repair), garaĝo; garaĝi [tr]
garavance, kikero
garb, vesto, kostumo; ~i [tr]
garbage, rubo, forĵetaĵo; **garbage can**, ~ujo
garbanzo, kikero
garble, (mix up, confuse), galimatiigi, konfuzi [tr]
Garcinia, garcinio; Garcinia mangostana, Garcinia morella, gumigutarbo, mangostano
garden, ĝardeno; ~i [tr]; **gardener**, ~isto; **gardening**, ~ado; **gardener's-garters**, (bot), falaro
gardenia, Gardenia, gardenio
garganey, kerkedulo, marĉanaso
Gargantua, Gargantuo
gargantuan, gargantua, enorma
gargle, gargari [tr]; ~aĵo
gargoyle, gargojlo

garish, helaĉa, puca, afektaĉa
garland, girlando; ~i [tr]
garlic, ajlo; garlic mustard, hedge garlic, aliario
garment, vesto
garner, (for grain), grenejo; en~igi; (gather, gen), (kun)kolekti [tr]
garnet, (gem), grenato; ~kolora
garnish, (embellish), garni [tr]; ~aĵo; (law), [see "garnishee"]
garnishee, tradi [tr]; pri~ito; garnishment, ~(ad)o; ~atesto
garniture, garnaĵo [not "garnituro"]
Garonne, Garono
garret, (gen), subtegmento; (mansard), mansardo
garrison, garnizono; ~igi
garrote, (ŝnur)strangoli [tr]
garrulous, babilema
Garrulus, garolo
Garrya, gario; Garryaceae, ~oj
garter, ĝartero, ĵartelo; garter belt, ~zono; Order of the Garter, Ordeno de la Ĝ~o
gas, (any vapor), gaso; (gasoline), benzino [see "gasoline"]; (kill by gas), ~umi [tr]; gaseous, ~a; gas oil, gasojlo; gasometer, ~ometro; illuminating gas, lum~o; laughing gas, rid~o; marsh gas, marĉ~o, metano; mustard gas, iperito, mustarda ~o; natural gas, natura ~o, ter~o; pass gas, furzi [int]
gascon, gaskono
Gascon, Gaskono; ~a; ~ia; Gascony, ~io
gash, tranĉi [tr]; ~vundi [tr]; ~(vund)o
gasket, (for motor, pipe joint, etc.), garnaĵo; (naut: rope), brajlilo
gasogene, gasogeno
gasohol, benzinolo
gasoline, benzino; regular gasoline, regula ~o, ordinara ~o; lead-free gasoline, senplomba ~o; high-test gasoline, supera ~o
gasp, anheli [int]; ~o
Gaspar, Gasparo
Gaspé (Peninsula), Gaspeo*, la Duoninsulo ~a
Gasterophilus, gastrofilo
Gasterosteus, gasterosteo, dornfiŝo; Gasterosteiformes, ~oformaj (fiŝoj)

Gaston, Gastono
gastralgia, gastralgio
gastrectomy, gastrektomio
gastric, gastra
gastritis, gastrito
gastr(o)-, (med, anat pfx), gastr(o)-
gastrocnemius, gastroknemio
gastroenteritis, gastroenterito
gastronome, gastronomist, gastronomo; gastronomy, ~io
Gastrophilus, gastrofilo
gastropod, gastropodo
Gastropoda, gastropodoj
gastroscope, gastroskopo; gastroscopy, ~io
gastrostomy, gastrostomio
gastrotomy, gastrotomio
gastrula, gastrulo
gate, (any opening through), pordo; (large, as in city wall etc.), ~ego; (small, as in fence), (baril)~o; (sliding in grooves, as for irrigation, dam sluice), herso; (any barrier), bariero; gate-crash, ŝteltrudi [int] (en); gateway, ~o, portalo; flood-gate, herso; tailgate, postklapo; (drive close behind), vostsekvi [int], vostveturi [int]; tailgater, vostsekvanto
gather, (collect), kolekti [tr], en~i [tr], kun~i [tr]; (conclude), konkludi [tr]; (gather together, assemble), amasigi; amasiĝi; (pull close), kuntiri [tr], altiri [tr]; kuntiriĝi, altiriĝi; (fold), faldi [tr]; faldiĝi; faldo; gathering, homamaso
gauche, sentakta, malgracia, kruda
gaucho, gaŭĉo
gaudy, puca
gauge, (tech), gaŭĝo; ~i [tr]; [cp "meter"]; (measure, assess, gen), taksi [tr], mezuri [tr]; takso, mezuro; (determine quantity of), komptit [tr]; (specific measuring device), [thing measured] + ~metro (e.g.: rain gauge: pluvometro); (rr track width), ŝpuro; narrow-gauge, (rr), mallarĝaŝpura; standard-gauge, normŝpura; wide-gauge, larĝaŝpura; tube-gauge, tub~o
Gaul, (person), Gallo; (region), ~io
gaunt, marasma
gauntlet, (armored glove), ferganto; run the gauntlet, trairi la krucpafa-

don
gaur, gaŭro
gauss, gaŭso
Gaussian, gaŭsa
Gautama, Gotamo
gauze, gazo
gavel, maleo; ~i [tr]
gavial, gavialo
Gavialis, gavialo
gavotte, gavoto
gawk, gapi [int]; ~anto, stultulo, idioto;
gawky, malgracia, mallerta
gay, (homosexual), samseksema; ~ulo;
(joyous), gaja; **gaywings**, (bot), poligalo
Gaza, Gaza; **Gaza Strip**, ~astrio
gazal, gazalo
gaze (at), rigard/adi [tr], fiks~i [tr],
spektadi [tr]; ~(ad)o, fiks~o [cp
"gape"]
gazebo, kiosko
gazel, gazalo
Gazella, gazelo
gazelle, gazelo
gazette, gazeto
Gdansk, Dancigo
gean, (fruit), merizo; (tree), ~arbo
gear, (gear-wheel), dentrado; (gear arrangement), rapido (e.g.: *second gear:*
la dua rapido); (equipment), ekipaĵo;
(machinery), aparat(ar)o; **gearing**,
~aro; **gearbox**, intertransmisiilo;
gear down, malaltigi la rapidon;
gearshift (lever), kluĉostango; **gear-
tooth**, (rado)dento; **gear up**, (shift
gears up), altigi la rapidon; (prepare),
pretigi sin, pretiĝi, prepariĝi; **gear-
wheel**, ~o; **planetary gear**, satelita
~o; **spur gear**, sprona ~o; **worm
gear**, helica ~o; **put into gear**, kupli
la ~ojn (de); **shift gears**, ŝanĝi la rapidon; **take (put) out of gear**, malkupli
la ~ojn (de)
Geastrum, Geaster, geastro
gecko, **gecco**, geko
gee, (short for "gravity", as unit), goo,
gravito; (interj), nu!
Gehenna, Geheno
geisha, gejŝo
Gekko, geko
gel, ĝelo; ~iĝi
gelatine, gelateno; **gelatinous**, ~eca

geld, kastri [tr]; **gelding**, ~ito
gem, gemo; **gemstone**, ~ŝtono
geminate, ĝemina; ~igi; ~iĝi
Gemini, (ast), Ĝemeloj
gemul, guemulo
–gen, (med, tech sfx: generating), –geno
[cp "–genic", "agent"]
gendarme, ĝendarmo
gender, sekso; **the opposite gender**,
la alia ~o
gene, geno, cistrono†
Gene, (man's name), Eŭĝeĉjo,
Eŭĝenĉjo
genealogy, genealog/io; **genealogical**,
~ia; **genealogist**, ~o
general, (not specific), ĝenerala; (common, shared), komuna; (mil rank), ge-
neralo; **generality**, ~aĵo; **generalize**,
~igi; ~iĝi; **generalissimo**, generalisi-
mo
generate, (produce, gen), generi [tr];
(math, as loci generate curve), naski
[tr], estigi; **generation**, ~(ad)o;
nask(ad)o; (those born about same
time), generacio; **spontaneous generation**, abiogenezo; **generator**,
(elec, gen), generatoro; (hand-
cranked), induktoro; **turbogenerator**,
turbingeneratoro; **Van de Graaf generator**, generatoro de Van de Graaf
generic, (general, common), komuna;
(of genus), genra
generous, malavara, grandanima, sindona, donacema; **generosity**, ~eco,
grandanimeco, sindonemo, donacemo
genesis, genezo; **biogenesis**, bio~o;
thermogenesis, termo~o
Genesis, (Bib), Genezo
genet, (*Genetta*), genoto
genetic, genetika; **genetics**, ~o
Genetta, genoto
Geneva, Ĝenevo; **Lake Geneva**, Lago
~a, Lago Lemano
Genevieve, Ĝenoveva
Genghis Khan, Ĝingis-Ĥano
genial, afabla, bonhumora, varmkora,
simpatia
–genic, (sfx: producing), –gena; (produced by), –genea
genie, ĝino
Genista, genisto
genital, genera; **genitals**, genitalia, ~aj

organoj
genitive, (gram), genitivo; ~a
genitourinary, generurina
genius, (mental power), genio; (person), ~ulo
Genoa, Ĝenovo
genocide, genocido
genotype, genotipo–
genous, (sfx: producing), –gena; (produced by), –genea
genre, ĝenro
gens, gento
genteel, rafinita, eleganta [not "ĝentila"]
gentian, genciano
Gentiana, genciano
gentile, (not Jew), ne-Judo; ne-Juda [cp "goy"]; (not Mormon), ne-Mormono; ne-Mormona [not "ĝentil–"]
gentle, (mild), milda, delikata; (light), leĝera; (not loud), mallaŭta; (not steep), malkruta; (genteel), rafinita; **gentleman,** (respectful term for man), sinjoro; (well-mannered, genteel), ĝentlemano, ĝentilhomo; **gentlewoman,** sinjorino; ĝentlemanino; **ladies and gentlemen!**, (in speech), gesinjoroj!
gentry, etnobelaro
genu, genuo
genuflect, genufleksi [int]
genuine, aŭtentika
genus, genro
–geny, (tech sfx), –genado
geo–, (pfx), geo–
geocentric, geocentra
geode, geodo
geodesy, geodezio; **geodesic, geodetic,** ~a
Geoffrey, Ĝofredo
geography, geograf/io; **geographer,** ~o; **geographical,** ~ia
geology, geolog/io; **geologist,** ~o; **geological,** ~ia; **astrogeology,** astro~io
geomancy, geomancio
Geometra, geometro
geometry, geometr/io; **geometrician, geometer,** ~o; **geometric,** ~ia; **plane geometry,** ebeno~io; **solid geometry,** solida ~o, stereometrio; **non-Euclidean geometry,** ne-Eŭklida ~o
geophagy, geophagism, geofagio

geophysics, geofiziko; **geophysical,** ~a; **geophysicist,** ~isto
geopolitics, geopolitiko; **geopolitical,** ~a
George, Georgo; **Georgette,** ~(et)a
Georgetown, Georgtaŭno*
Georgia, (woman's name), Georga; (U.S. state), ~io; (in Eurasia), Gruzio, Gruzujo
Georgics, Georgikoj
geosynchronous, geosinkrona
geotropism, geotropismo
Geotrupes, geotrupo; Geotrupidae, ~edoj
Gephyrea, gefireoj
gerah, gero
Gerald, Ĝeraldo
geraniol, geraniolo
geranium, (*Geranium*), geranio; (*Pelargonium*), pelargonio
Geranium, geranio
Gerard, Gerardo
gerbil, gerbilo
Gerbillus, gerbilo
gerfalcon, girfalko
geriatric, geriatria; **geriatrics,** ~o
germ, (microbe), mikrobo; (earliest stage of anything), ĝermo; **germicide,** ~icido; **germinal,** (embryonic), ĝerma, embria; **germinate,** ĝermi [int]
German, Germano; ~a; ~ia; **Germanic,** Ĝermana; Ĝermano [cp "Teuton"]; **Germany,** ~io; **High German,** Alt~a; **Low German,** Malalt~a; **Old High German,** Malnov~a; **German Democratic Republic,** ~a Demokratia Respubliko [abb: ~a D.R., G.D.R.]; **Federal Republic of Germany,** ~a Federacia Respubliko, Federacia Respubliko ~io [abb: F.R. ~io, F.R.G.]
germander, teŭkrio
germane, rilata
Germanicus, Germaniko
germanium, germanio
germen, ĝermeno
Germinal, (month), Ĝerminalo
gerontocracy, gerontokratio*
gerontology, gerontolog/io*; **gerontological,** ~ia; **gerontologist,** ~o
gerrymander, fi–dislimi [tr]
Gertrude, Gertruda

gerund, gerundio
Gervais, Gervazo
gest, (poem), ĝesto
gestalt, spertomatrico; ~a
Gestapo, Gestapo
gestation, graved/eco; **gestate,** esti ~a
kun
geste, (poem), ĝesto
gesticulate, gest(ad)i [int]
gesture, (body movement), gesti [int];
~o; (token, sign), signo
gesundheit! (interj after sneeze), sanon!
get, (obtain, acquire, gen), havigi, akiri
[tr] (e.g.: *go get some coffee:* iri ~i
iom da kafo); (receive; pick up, re radio, TV), ricevi [tr] (e.g.: *that radio
gets Moscow:* tiu radiofono ricevas
Moskvon; *get a worried look:* ricevi
ĉagrenitan mienon); (cause to), igi,
~igi [sfx] (e.g.: *get it hot:* varmigi ĝin;
get the radio repaired: riparigi la radiofonon; *get him to write a letter:* igi
lin skribi leteron [or] igi ke li skribu
leteron); (become), (far)iĝi, ~iĝi [sfx]
(e.g.: *get in touch:* kontaktiĝi; *he got
suspiciously nervous:* li fariĝis [or]
iĝis suspektinde nervoza); (catch, capture, gen), kapti [tr]; (catch disease),
[see under "catch"]; (bring), [see under "bring"]; (arrive), alveni [int]
(e.g.: *I'll get home late:* mi alvenos
hejmen malfrue); (start), ek~ [pfx]
(e.g.: *get going:* ekiri); (understand),
kompreni [tr] (e.g.: *I don't get it:* mi
ne komprenas); (learn), lerni [tr];
(prepare), prepari [tr] (e.g.: *get breakfast:* prepari matenmanĝon); (give
birth), naski [tr]; (beget, re man or
male animal), generi [tr]; (overpower), superi [tr] (e.g.: *her illness got
her:* ŝia malsano ŝin superis); (baffle),
mistifiki [tr] (e.g.: *that problem gets
me:* tiu problemo min mistifikas);
(hit), trafi [tr]; (notice), rimarki [tr];
get about, (move about), cirkul(ad)i
[int], ĉirkaŭmoviĝ(ad)i; **get across,**
(go across), transiri [tr]; (make understood), komprenigi; (be understandable), esti komprenebla, esti klara; **get
after,** (attack), ataki [tr]; (goad), inciti
[tr]; **get along,** (manage, do okay),
elteni [int], sukcesi [int]; (relate

peaceably), (pace) interrilati [int]; **get
along with,** pace rilati kun; **get
around,** (move about), cirkul(ad)i
[int], ĉirkaŭmoviĝ(ad)i; (avoid), eviti
[tr]; (overcome), superi [tr]; **get
around to,** fine ek~, fine komenci
[tr], fine ~i (e.g.: *get around to it:* fine
komenci ĝin; *get around to writing:*
fine (ek)skribi); **not get around to**
(yet), ankoraŭ ne ek~, ankoraŭ ne komenci (e.g.: *I haven't done it simply
because I didn't get around to it yet:*
mi ne faris ĝin simple ĉar mi ankoraŭ
ne komencis ĝin); **get at,** (reach),
atingi [tr]; (aim at, have as goal), celi
[tr]; (allude to), aludi [tr]; **get away,**
(go away), foriri [int]; (escape), eskapi [tr, int]; **get away with,** (a misdeed), eskapi [tr, int] senpune; **get
back,** (return), reveni [int]; revenigi;
reiri [int]; resendi [tr] [see "return"];
(recover), re~i, reakiri [tr], rericevi
[tr]; **get back at,** (revenge), venĝi [tr];
get behind, (move back), iri malantaŭ(en); (support), apogi [tr], subteni
[tr]; (become late, as in payments),
malakuratiĝi; **get by,** (survive w meager amenities), magre postviv(ad)i
[int], magre (apenaŭ) sukcesi [int];
(be adequate), esti mezbona, esti (meze) adekvata; (get away with), eskapi
senpune; **get down,** (descend), descendi [int], malsupreniri [int]; (record), registri [tr]; surpaperigi;
surbendigi; (dismount), elseligi; elseliĝi; (bother), ĝeni [tr], ĉagreni [tr];
get down to, (begin to consider), ekkonsideri [tr], ekprilabori [tr], ektrakti
[tr]; **get here,** (arrive), alveni [int];
get in, (enter), eniri [tr]; (join), aliĝi
al, en; membriĝi en; (arrive), alveni
[int]; (put in), enmeti [tr]; **get in with,**
asociiĝi kun; **get it,** (understand), kompreni [tr]; (be punished), esti punita;
(be hit by, gen), trafiĝi, esti trafita
(de); **get it over with,** finfari [tr]; **get
nowhere, not get anywhere,** neniom
progresi [int], atingi nenion; **get off,**
(from a bus etc.), eliri [tr, int] el;
(from a horse, bike, etc.), elseliĝi de;
(from any surface, object), deiri [int]
de; (go free), eskapi [tr, int] (sen-

pune); (have leave, time off), havi forpermeson, ricevi forpermeson; **get off on**, ekscitiĝi per; **get on**, (bus etc.), eniri [tr]; (horse, bike, etc.), suriri [tr]; (put on, as garment), surmeti [tr]; (progress), progresi [int]; (agree, relate well), bone (inter)rilati [int]; **get out**, (leave, go out), eliri [tr, int]; (become known, as secret), koniĝi; (publish), eldoni [tr]; (interj: go away!), for!; **get out of**, eliri el; eliri de; (escape), eskapi [tr, int]; (avoid), eviti [tr]; (resign from), eksiĝi de; (free of duty, debt), kvitigi (sin) de, kvitiĝi de; (free, gen), liberigi (sin) de, liberiĝi de; (untangle), malimpliki (sin) de, malimplikiĝi de; (force out), eligi de, el; **get over**, (illness), resaniĝi de; (overcome, gen), superi [tr]; (live through), travivi [tr]; (stop marveling at), ĉesi miri pri (e.g.: *I can't get over his behavior:* mi ne povas ĉesi miri pri lia konduto); (forget), forgesi [tr]; (make understood), komprenigi; **get somewhere**, sukcesi [int], progresi [int]; **get there**, (arrive), alveni [int]; (succeed), sukcesi [int]; **be getting there**, (progress), progresi [int]; **get through**, (finish), fini [tr]; (go through), trairi [tr]; (live through, survive), travivi [tr], postvivi [tr]; (make succeed, enact, etc.), efektivigi, sukcesigi; (communicate), komuniki [tr] (kun); **get to**, (reach, gen), atingi [tr]; (be able), povi [tr] (e.g.: *the rain stopped, so we got to go outside:* la pluvo ĉesis, do ni povis eliri); (be allowed), rajti [tr] (e.g.: *if you finish your homework, you'll get to stay up late:* se vi finos viajn hejmtaskojn, vi rajtos resti ellite malfrue); **get together**, (bring together), kun igi, kunvenigi; (come together), kuniĝi, kunveni [int]; (amass), amasigi; amasiĝi; (agree), akordiĝi; **get-together**, kunsido, kuniĝo; **get up**, (raise, rise, gen), levi [tr]; leviĝi; (from bed), ellitigi; ellitiĝi; (arrange, contrive), aranĝi [tr]; **get-up**, (costume), kostumo; **ill-gotten**, fiakirita; **let's get going!**, let's get started!, ek al!; **(have) got**, (have), havi [tr] (e.g.: *I've got* [or] *I*

got an idea: mi havas ideon); **have got to**, (must), devas [tr] (e.g.: *I've got to leave now:* mi devas foriri nun)
geta, getao
Gethsemane, Getsemano
Geum, geumo
gewgaw, breloko, brikabrakero, strasero
geyser, gejsero
Ghana, Ganao
gharial, gavialo
ghasel, gazalo
ghastly, (awful, macabre), makabra; (ghostly pale in appearance), kadavre pala, palaĉa
ghazel, **ghazal**, gazalo
Gheber, **Ghebre**, gebro [cp "Zoroaster: Zoroastrian"]
Ghent, Gento
gherkin, kukumeto
ghetto, getto
Ghibelline, Gibelino; ~a
ghost, fantomo; **ghostly**, ~(ec)a; **ghostwrite**, komisiverki [tr]; **ghostwriter**, ~a verkisto, komisiverkinto; komisiverkisto
giant, giganto; ~a
Giardia, lamblio
giardiasis, lambliozo
gibber, galimatio; paroli ~on; **gibberish**, ~o; (in joke), halanĝo
gibbet, pendumilo
gibbon, gibono
gibbous, ŝvela
gibbsite, hidrargilito
gibe, moki [tr]
giblet, detranĉaĵo, organaĵo (de birdo)
Gibraltar, Ĝibraltaro; **Straits of Gibraltar**, Markolo ~a
giddy, vertiĝa; **giddiness**, ~o
giddyap! (interj to horse), hot!, hoto!
Gideon, Gideono
gift, (thing given), donaco; (talent), talento; **gifted**, talenta, dotita; **be gifted with**, esti talenta je (e.g.: *he is gifted with great insight:* li estas talenta je granda envido)
gig, (mus etc.), prezento; (boat), gigo; (carriage), kabrioleto
giga-, (pfx), giga–
gigantic, giganta
giggle, subridi [int]; ~o
gigolo, ĝigolo

gigue, ĝigo
Gilbert, (man's name), Gilberto
gild, ori [tr]
Gilead, Gileado
Giles, Ĝilo
gill, (of fish), branko
gilt, (gilded), or/ita; ~aĵo; **gilt-edged,** randa—~ita
gimbals, kardano [note sing]
gimlet, borileto
gimmick, (trick, ruse), artifiko, ruzo; (gadget), umo, aĵo
gin, (drink), ĝino; (for cotton), sensematoro; sensemigi; (trap), kaptilo
Gina, Ĝina
ginger, (plant or spice), zingibro; ~a; ~i [tr]; **gingerly,** (delicate touch), delikata, zorga; **ginger ale,** ~a sodo; **gingerbread,** (cake), ~okuko; (gaudy ornamentation), pucaĵo; **wind ginger,** azaro
gingham, gingamo*; ~a
gingiva, gingivo; **gingival,** ~a; (phon), gingivalo; gingivala; **gingivitis,** ~ito
ginkgo, Ginkgo, ginko
ginseng, ginsengo
gipsy, [see "gypsy"]
Giraffa, ĝirafo; **Giraffidae,** ~edoj
giraffe, ĝirafo
gird, (belt), zoni [tr]
girder, solivo, (apog)trabo
girdle, (belt; encircle, gen), zoni [tr]; ~o; (undergarment), tali~o
girl, knabino
Gironde, (river), Ĝirondo; (dept), ~io; **Girondist,** ~isto
girth, (saddle belt), selzono; (circumference), ĉirkaŭmezuro
Giselle, Gizela
gist, esenco, kerno
give, (turn over possession; hand over; impart, imbue), doni [tr] (e.g.: *give her the report:* ~i al ŝi la raporton; *give him a kiss:* ~i al li kison; *cows give milk:* bovinoj ~as lakton); (donate, give as gift), donaci [tr]; (present, perform), prezenti [tr] (e.g.: *give a concert:* prezenti koncerton; *give a reception:* prezenti akcepton); (concede, yield; give way, collapse), cedi [tr, int]; cedemo; (show, exhibit), montri [tr], eksponi [tr], ekspozicii

[tr]; (make movement etc.), fari [tr] (e.g.: *give a leap:* fari salton); (impart), komuni ki [tr]; **give and take,** reciproki [tr]; reciprokado; **give away,** fordonaci [tr]; for~i [tr]; (reveal), elperfidi [tr], malkaŝi [tr], riveli [tr]; (betray), perfidi [tr]; **give back,** re~i [tr]; redonaci [tr]; **give forth,** (emit), eligi; **give or take,** pli-malpli, plus aŭ minus; **give out,** (emit), eligi; (make known), diskonigi; (distribute), dis~i [tr], distribui [tr]; (be used up), eluziĝi, elkonsumiĝi, elĉerpiĝi; (break down), misfunkcii [int]; (stall), panei [int]; (become exhausted), ellaciĝi; **give over,** (hand over), trans~i [tr]; (cease), ĉesi [int]; (set apart, reserve), rezervi [tr]; **give rise to,** estigi, levi [tr], kaŭzi [tr], naski [tr]; **give up,** (hand over), trans~i [tr]; (cease), ĉesi [int]; (stop trying, admit failure; abandon claim to), rezigni [tr]; (surrender), kapitulaci [int]; (yield), cedi [tr, int]; (renounce), forkonfesi [tr]; **give way,** (yield), cedi [tr, int]; (collapse), disfali [int]; **given,** (as premise), ~ata, ~ita; ~itaĵo, premiso; (datum), datenero†, ~itaĵo; **be given to,** (tend to), tendenci [tr] (al), emi [int] (al), kutimi [int] (al)
gizmo, umo
gizzard, maĉostomako
glabella, glabelo
glacé glacea; ~o
glacial, (re ice, gen), glacia; (re glacier, icecap), glaĉera
glacier, glacirivero [not "glaĉero"; cp "ice: ice cap"]
glacis, glaciso
glad, ĝoja; **be glad,** ~i [int]; **gladly,** (willingly), volonte (e.g.: *I would gladly help you:* mi volonte helpus vin)
glade, (clearing), placo, maldensejo; (marsh), marĉo
gladiator, gladiatoro
gladiolus, Gladiolus, gladiolo
Glagolitsa, Glagolico; **Glagolitic,** ~a
glamo(u)r, ĉarmo, logo; **glamorous,** ~a, (al)loga
glance, (look), ekrigardi [tr]; ~o; (ricochet), resalti [int]; resalto; **glance at,** ~i; **glance off,** resalti de; **at first**

glance, unuavide; **cast a sidelong glance, glance askance**, strabi [int]
gland, (anat, gen), glando; **glandular**, ~a; **adrenal gland**, surrena ~o; **endocrine gland, ductless gland**, endokrina ~o, sendukta ~o; **exocrine gland**, ekzokrina ~o, ekskrecia ~o; **meibomian gland**, mejboma ~o; **pineal gland**, pineala ~o; **pituitary gland**, pituitario, pituitaria ~o; **prostate gland**, prostato; **salivary gland**, saliva ~o; **sweat gland**, ŝvit~o; **thyroid gland**, tiroido
glans, glano; **glans clitoridis**, klitora ~o; **glans penis**, penisa ~o
glare, (angry look), rigard/ego, (kolera, furioza) ~o, kolergrimaco; (light), brilego; **glare at**, ~egi [tr], (kolere, furioze) ~i [tr], kolergrimaci [int] al; **glaring**, (obvious), okulfrapa, krianta
Glareola, glareolo, marhirundo
Glasgow, Glasgovo
glasnost, aperteco, malfermeco
glass, (substance), vitro; ~a; (container for drinking), glaso; (mirror), spegulo; **glasses**, (eyeglasses), okul~oj; **glassy**, ~eca; **glasswort**, (*Salsola*), salsolo; **crown glass**, kraŭno; **cupping glass**, kupo; **fiberglass**, ~ofibro; **field glass(es)**, binoklo [note sing]; **flint glass**, flinto; **looking glass**, spegulo; **magnifying glass**, lupeo; **plate glass**, glaco; **safety glass**, sendanĝera ~o, sekureco~o; **safety glasses**, sekurecokul~oj; **stained glass (window)**, vitralo; **sunglasses**, sun~oj, ŝirmokul~oj
Glaucium, glaŭcio
glaucoma, glaŭkomo
glauconite, glaŭkonito
glaucous, glaŭka, bluverda
glaze, (pottery, etc.; icing for baked goods etc.), glazuro; ~i [tr]; (leather etc.), glaceigi; (wood etc., by covering w shellac etc. and polishing), polituri [tr]; (install glass), vitri [tr]; (ice due to freezing rain etc.), glatiso; **glazed paper**, glacea papero
glazier, vitristo
gleam, glimi [int], brileti [int]; ~brilo [not "~o"]
glean, (harvest), spikumi [tr]; (fig: pick

out, sift ideas etc.), kribri [tr]
Glec(h)oma, glekomo
Gleditsia, glediĉio
glee, (joy), gajo, ĝojo; (song), glio; **glee club**, gliklubo
glen, valeto
glib, ŝajnparola, facilparola
glide, glisi [int]; **glider**, (plane), ~ilo
glimmer, glimeti [int], lumeti [int]; ~o
glimpse, ekvidi [tr]; ~o; **catch a glimpse of**, ~i
glint, rebrili [int]; ~o
Glis, gliro; Gliridae, ~edoj
glissade, gliti [int]; ~o
glissando, glito; ~a; ~e
glisten, bril/eti [int], re~i [int], scintili [int]; (re)~(et)o, scintilo
glitch, difekteto, problemeto
glitter, scintili [int]; ~ado; ~aĵo
gloaming, krepusko
gloat, ĝoj/aĉi [int], avar~i [int]; (avar)~(aĉ)o
glob, bulo, amaso [not "globo"; cp "globe", "glop"]
globe, (gen), globo; (Earth), ter~o; (round map), globuso; **global**, (worldwide), tutmonda; **global warming**, tutmonda varmiĝo; **globeflower**, (*Trollius*), trolio
globin, globino
Globularia, globulario
globule, glob/eto; (anat), globulo; **globular**, ~a, ~eta
globulin, globulino; **gamma-globulin**, gama~o
glockenspiel, kampaneto
glomerule, (med, anat; bot†), glomerulo; **glomerulus**, ~o; **glomerulonephritis**, ~onefrito
gloom, (dimness), krepusko, mallumo, tenebro; (sadness), melankolio, malgajo, malĝojo, tenebro; (sadness, poet), morno; **gloomy**, ~a, malluma, tenebra; malgaja, malĝoja, morna
glop, (food), kaĉo; (any goo, ooze, etc.), ŝlimo [cp "glob"]
glory, (honor etc.; rel), gloro; (halo), aŭreolo; **glorify**, ~i [tr]; **glorious**, ~a; **inglorious**, mal~a, hont(ind)a
gloss, (shiny, gen), glaceo; ~igi; (re cloth), katizi [tr]; (comment), gloso; glosi [tr]; **glossy**, ~a; katizita; **gloss**

over, (cover up), maski [tr]; (ignore), ignori [tr]
glossa, lango
glossary, glosaro
Glossina, glosino, ceceo
glossitis, glosito
glossolalia, glosolalio
glossopharyngeal, glosofaringa; **glossopharyngeus,** ~a muskolo
glossotomy, glosotomio
glottis, gloto; **glottal,** ~a
glove, ganto; ~i [tr]; **boxing glove,** boks~o; **cycling glove,** biciklo~o
glow, (as red-hot or similar light), ardi [int]; (any low light), lumeti [int]; lumet(ad)o; (smolder), bruleti [int]; (elec discharge), efluvo; **afterglow,** post~o; **glowworm,** lampiro, lumvermo
glower, (koler)grimaci [int]; ~o
gluco–, (chem pfx), gluko–
glucose, glukozo; **glucosuria,** ~urio
glue, gluo; ~i [tr]; **gluey,** ~eca
glug, (bottle noise), glugli [int]; ~o
glum, malgaja
glume, glumo
glut, supersato, superabundo, troaĵo; ~igi; **glutted,** ~a
glutamine, glutamino
glutaric, glutar/ata; **glutaric acid,** ~a acido, pentandiacido
glutathione, glutationo
gluten, gluteno
gluteus, gluteo; **gluteal,** ~a
glutinous, glueca
glutton, (eater), manĝegem/ulo, voremulo; (zool: *Gulo*), gulo; (*Icticyon*), mustelvulpo; **gluttonous,** ~a, vorema; **gluttony,** ~o
glycemia, glukozemio; **hyperglycemia,** hiper~o; **hypoglycemia,** hipo~o
Glyceria, glicerio
glyceride, glicerido
glycerine, glicerolo, glicerino
glycerol, glicerolo
glyceryl, glicerilo
glycine, glicino
Glycine, (bot), glicino; Glycine hispida, sojfabo
glyco–, (chem sfx), gliko–
glycogen, glikogeno
glycol, glikolo

Glycyrrhiza, glicirizo
glyoxal, glioksalo
glyoxyl, glioksilo; **glyoxylic, acid,** ~a acido
glyph, piktogramo
glyptics, gliptiko [note sing]
glyptodont, gliptodonto
glyptography, gliptiko
Gnaphalium, gnafalio; Gnaphalium leontopodium, edelvejso, neĝfloro
gnarled, tubereca, nodeca, tordita
gnash, grinci [int]; ~igi (la dentojn)
gnat, (*Culex*), kulo; (any bug), besteto; **gall gnat,** cecidomio
gnaw, ronĝi [tr]
gneiss, gnejso
gnome, gnomo
gnomic(al), gnomika
gnomon, gnomono
gnosis, gnostiko
gnostic, gnostika
Gnostic, gnostik/ulo; **Gnosticism,** ~ismo
gnu, gnuo
go, (move, travel, proceed, progress, gen), iri [int] (e.g.: *where are you going?*: kien vi ~as?; *things are going well:* aferoj ~as bone; *go fast:* ~i rapide); (function, operate), funkcii [int] (e.g.: *the motor won't go:* la motoro ne funkcios); (become), –iĝi [sfx], (far)iĝi (e.g.: *go mad:* freneziĝi) [see "become", "get"]; (fit, be appropriate), taŭgi [int] (e.g.: *that shirt doesn't go with the pants:* tiu ĉemizo ne taŭgas kun la pantalono); (be appropriate, proper), deci [int], konveni [int] (e.g.: *that kind of behavior doesn't go here:* tia konduto ne decas [or] ne konvenas ĉi tie); (be worded), teksti [int] (e.g.: *how does the poem go?:* kiel tekstas la poemo?); (~ away, leave), ~i, for~i [int]; (make sound, action), fari [tr] (e.g.: *the balloon went "pop!":* la balono faris "krak!"); (belong in place), aparteni [int] (e.g.: *the socks go in that drawer:* la ŝtrumpetoj apartenas en tiu tirkesto); (bet), veti [tr]; (all right, okay), en ordo (e.g.: *all systems are go:* ĉiuj sistemoj estas en ordo); (Japanese game), goo, go-ludo; **go about,** (occupy self), okupiĝi pri

(e.g.: *go about one's business:* okupiĝi pri sia afero); (get about, circulate), cirkul(ad)i [int], ĉirkaŭmoviĝ(ad)i; **go after**, (pursue), sekvi [tr], celi [tr, int]; (hunt), ĉasi [tr]; **go against**, kontraŭi [tr], oponi [tr]; **go ahead**, (proceed), procedi [int]; (continue), daŭri [int]; **go-ahead**, (approval), aprobo, permeso; **go all out**, ~i plenforte, ~i plenstrebe; **go along**, (continue), daŭri [int], progresi [int]; (agree), akordiĝi; (follow, as road etc.), sekvi [tr], ~i laŭ, laŭ~i; **go and**, (colloq, to emphasize oth verb), ja [or may be omitted] (e.g.: *what did you go and do that for?:* pro kio vi ja faris tion?); **go around**, (surround), ĉirkaŭi [tr]; (be shared), dividiĝi (e.g.: *we don't have enough to go around:* ni ne havas sufiĉe por dividiĝi); (circulate), cirkuli [int]; **go at**, ataki [tr]; **go back on**, (betray), perfidi [tr]; (be disloyal), esti mallojala al; **go-between**, peranto; **act as go-between**, peri [int]; **go beyond**, (exceed), superi [tr]; **go by**, (rely on), sekvi [tr], fidi [tr] (al); (pass by), preter~i [tr], devanci [tr], preterpasi [tr]; (be known), esti konata per (e.g.: *his name is Gordon but he goes by "Bud":* lia nomo estas Gordon sed li estas konata per "Bud"); **go down**, (descend), descendi [int], malsupren~i [tr] (e.g.: *go down the stairs:* malsupren~i la ŝtuparon); (set, re sun etc.), sub~i [int]; (lose), malgajni [int], malvenki [int]; (be recorded, as in history), registriĝi; **go for**, (as goal), celi [tr, int] (al); (support), subteni [tr]; (attack), ataki [tr]; (like), ŝati [tr]; (be valid), validi [int] por (e.g.: *stop it, and that goes for you too:* ĉesigu tion, kaj tio validas ankaŭ por vi); **go in for**, (participate), partopreni [tr] en, okupiĝi pri; (under take), entrepreni [tr]; (tend toward), emi [int] al, tendenci [int] al; **go in with**, (share), dividi [tr] kun; **go into**, (explore, inquire), esplori [tr], enketi [int] pri, demandi [tr] pri; (undertake), entrepreni [tr], okupiĝi pri; (divide), dividiĝi en (e.g.: *6 goes into 12 twice:* 6 dividiĝas en 12 du fojojn); (discuss, talk about),

diskuti [tr], paroli [int] pri; **go off**, (re gun etc.), malŝargiĝi; (explode, as bomb etc.), eksplodi [int]; knali [int]; (elec: turn off), malŝaltiĝi; (leave), for~i [int]; **go on**, (happen), okazi [int] (e.g.: *what's going on here?:* kio okazas ĉi tie?); (elec: turn on), ŝaltiĝi; (rely on), sekvi [tr], fidi [tr] (al); (behave), konduti [int]; (babble), babili [int]; **oh, go on!**, (nonsense!), nekredeble!, sensence!, blago!; **go (a person) one better**, superi tion (al iu); **go out**, (elec: turn off), malŝaltiĝi; (re fire, candle, etc.), estingiĝi; (leave), el~i [tr]; (socialize, have dates), societumi [int], rendevu(ad)i [tr]; **go out for**, (try out for theat role, sport, mus group, etc.), proviĝi por; (involve self in sport, activity), okupiĝi pri; **go out with**, (have date(s)), rendevu(ad)i [tr] (kun); **go over**, (check), kontroli [tr]; (try), provi [tr]; (read), tralegi [tr]; (do again), refari [tr]; (succeed), sukcesi [int], atingi la celon; **go through (with)**, (endure), travivi [tr], sperti [tr]; (search through), traserĉi [tr]; (get approval), ricevi, akiri aprobon de; (spend), elspezi [tr]; (complete, finish), fini [tr], kompletigi, daŭri ĝisfine kun, persisti [int] kun; **go to**, (attend), ĉeesti [tr]; (serve to), servi [tr] por (e.g.: *that goes to show:* tio servas por montri); **go to the bother, go to the trouble**, fari al si la ĝenon; **go together**, (match), akordiĝi, taŭgi [int]; (date), rendevuadi [tr] (kun), kun~adi [int] kun; **go too far**, troiĝi, tro~i [int]; **go under**, (fail, gen), fiaski [int], malsukcesi [int]; (bankrupt), bankroti [int]; **go without**, (make do w/o), resti sen, kontentiĝi sen, kontentigi sin sen; **forgo**, (do w/o), rezigni [tr], kontentigi sin sen; **forego**, (precede), antaŭi [tr]; (forgo, do w/o), rezigni [tr], kontentigi sin sen; **foregoing**, antaŭa; **foregone**, (previous), antaŭa; (decided), (antraŭ)decidita; **ongoing**, daŭra, progresanta; **outgo**, (going out), el~o; (expenditure), elspezo; (surpass), superi [tr]; **outgoing**, (leaving), el~anta; (retiring), eksiĝanta; (friendly), amikema, sociema,

ekstravertita; **undergo,** (suffer unpleasant experience), suferi [tr]; (go through any experience, process, chem reaction, etc.), sperti [tr], suferigi; **as (things) go,** relative ~a, kiel koncernas ~o(j)n (e.g.: *it was an interesting meeting, as meetings go:* ĝi estis relative interesa kunveno; *a pretty town, as seaports go:* bela urbo, kiel koncernas havenurbojn); **let go,** (free, release), delasi [tr], malkroĉi [tr], liberigi; **let oneself go,** senbridi sin, senbridiĝi, liberigi sin, malstreĉi sin; **go so far as to,** etendi sin ĝis [~o] (e.g.: *I would not go so far as to approve their actions:* mi ne etendus min ĝis aprobo de iliaj agoj); **have a go at,** (try), (ek)provi [tr]; **make a go of (it),** sukcesigi (ĝin, la aferon); **on the go,** aktiva, vigla; **to go,** (to be carried out, re food from restaurant etc.), elportota; (remaining), restanta(j); **too far gone,** preter helpo; **be going to,** (to indicate future tense), ~os (e.g.: *I'm going to see her soon:* mi vidos ŝin baldaŭ); **(one) who is going to,** ~onta [sfx]; ~onto (e.g.: *the students who are going to graduate:* la diplomiĝontaj studentoj; *those who are going to attend:* la ĉeestontoj); **(thing) that is going to,** ~ontaĵo; **get going,** ek~i [int]; ek~igi; **(let's) get going!,** ek al!
goad, piki [tr], (~)inciti [tr]; ~ilo, incitilo
goal, (target, aim, gen), celo; (sport: point(s) scored), golo; (sport: target), golejo; **goalie, goalkeeper,** golulo; **toward that goal, with that goal in mind,** tiu~e
goat, kapro; **goatee,** ~obarbo; **goatfish,** surmuleto; **goatherd,** ~isto; **goatsbeard,** (bot: *Tragopogon*), tragopogo, bokbarbo; **false goatsbeard,** astilbo; **goatsucker,** kaprimulgo; **billy-goat,** vir~o; **nanny-goat,** ~ino; **scapegoat,** propeka ~o
goban(g), gobango
gobbet, peco, bulo
gobble, (turkey sound), glu-glui [int]; (onom), glu-glu-glu!; (eat), manĝegi [tr], vori [tr]
gobbledygook, (burokrata) ĵargon(aĉ)o

Gobelin, Gobelino; ~a
Gobi, Gobio
Gobio fluviatilis, gobio
Gobius, gobiuso; Gobiidae, ~edoj; Gobiiformes, ~oformaj (fiŝoj)
goblet, pokalo
goblin, koboldo
goby, gobiuso
god, dio; **God,** Dio; **goddess,** ~ino; **godchild,** baptinfano; **goddam(n),** ~damnita [see also "damn"]; **goddaughter,** baptofilino; **godfather,** baptopatro; **godhead,** ~eco; **godmother,** baptopatrino; **godparent,** baptopatro, baptopatr(in)o; **godparents,** baptogepatroj; **godsend,** beno; **godson,** baptofilo; **godwit,** (zool), limozo; **demigod,** duon~o; **ungodly,** (terrible), terura, infereca (impious), malpia; (sinful), peka, malvirta
Goethe, Goeto, Gete
goffer, gofri [tr]; ~ilo
goggle, (stare), rigardegi [tr], okulum(eg)i [tr]; **goggles,** (glasses), ŝirmvitroj, protektaj okulvitroj; **swimming (skiing, etc.) goggles,** naĝ(okul)vitroj (ski(okul)vitroj, etc.)
Gogol, Gogolo
goiter, strumo; **exophthalmic goiter,** bazedova malsano, ekzoftalmia ~o
gold, oro; ~a; **golden,** (gen), ~a; ~kolora; **goldbrick,** (loaf, freeload), paraziti [int]; **goldbricker,** parazito, nenifaranto; **goldcup,** (bot), ranunkolo; **goldeneye,** (insect), krizopo; **goldenrod,** (bot), solidago; **goldenseal,** (bot), hidrasto; **goldfinch,** (*Carduelis*), kardelo; (*Spinus*), fringelo; **goldfish,** ~fiŝo; **goldrush,** ~ĉaso; **fool's gold,** pirito; **not all that glitters is gold,** ne ĉio utilas kiu brilas
golf, golfludo; **golf club,** (stick), ~a klabo; (organization), ~a klubo; **golf course, golf links,** ~ejo
Golgotha, Golgoto
goliard, goliardo
Goliath, Goljato
Goliathus, goliato
golosh(e), (Br), galoŝo
Gomorrah, Gomoro
gomuti, sagu/arbo, ~palmo

–gon, (sfx: side(s)), –gono
gonad, gonado
gondola, gondolo; **gondolier**, ~isto
gong, gongo
Gongora, Gongora y Argote, Gongoro; **Gongorism**, ~ismo
goniometer, goniometro
gonococcus, gonokoko
gonorrhea, gonoreo, blenoreo
goo, ŝlimo, gluaĵo; **gooey**, ~a, glueca
good, (desirable, proper, suitable, high quality, etc., gen), bona; ~e; ~o; ~aĵo; ~eco; (tasty), ~gusta; (well-mannered), ~konduta; **goods**, (wares), varoj; (possessions), posedaĵoj, havaĵoj; **household goods**, mebloj, meblaro; **worldly goods**, mondaĵoj; **second-hand goods**, brokantaĵoj; **goodies**, (sweets), frandaĵoj; (pleasant result, nice thing), ~aĵo(j); **goodly**, (ample), abunda, sufiĉ(eg)a, konsiderinda; (good-looking), bela; **be good**, (behave), konduti [int] ~e, ~konduti [int]; **good and**, (very), tre, tute; **good at**, (talented, skillful), lerta, talenta (pri, kun, ĉe); **goodbye**, (interj), adiaŭ, ĝis revido, ĝis la, ĝis; **say goodbye to**, adiaŭi [tr]; **good for**, (worth), valida por, utila por; **be good for**, (useful), utili [int] por; **good-for-nothing**, sentaŭga; sentaŭgulo; **good-hearted**, ~kora; **good-looking**, bela, ~aspekta; **good morning (afternoon, evening, night, day)**, (greeting or farewell), ~an matenon (posttagmezon, vesperon, nokton, tagon); **goodwill**, ~volo; **as good as**, (virtually), kvazaŭ, virtuale; **for good**, (forever), por ĉiam; **make good**, (compensate), kompensi [tr] (iun pro io) (e.g.: *if you will pay the cost, we will make it good to you:* se vi pagos la koston, ni kompensos vin pro ĝi); (fulfill), plenumi [tr] (e.g.: *make good on a promise:* plenumi promeson); (succeed, do well), sukcesi [int]; **no good**, (worthless), senvalora; (not valid), nevalida; ne validi [int]; **it's no good**, (in vain), estas vane; **do any good (for, to)**, helpi [tr]
goof, (mistake), erari [int], misi [int], fuŝi [tr]; ~o, miso, fuŝo; (person),

fuŝemulo; **goof off**, lanti [int], malŝpari tempon, maldiligenti [int]
gook, ŝlimo
goon, gangstero
goop, glu/aĵo; **goopy**, ~eca
goose, ansero; **gooseberry**, (berry), groso; (plant), grosarbusto, grosujo; **Cape gooseberry**, fizalido; **goosefoot**, (bot), kenopodio; **barnacle goose**, berniklo; **Canada goose**, Kanada ~o; **solan goose**, sulo; **cook one's goose**, ruinigi iun (sin); **his goose was cooked**, li ruiniĝis
gopher, terrato; **gopherwood**, gofero
Gordius, Gordio; **Gordian knot**, ~a nodo
gore, (blood), sango; (stab w horn), kornopiki [tr]; **gory**, ~a
gorge, (throat), gorĝo; (narrow pass), interkrutejo; (maw, big opening), faŭko; (eat), supersatigi (sin); **disgorge**, el~igi, elfaŭkigi; **gorge oneself on**, manĝegi [tr], supersatigi sin per
gorgeous, belega, rava
Gorgon, Gorgono
gorilla, Gorilla, gorilo
gorse, (*Ulex*), ulekso
gosh, (interj), Dio!, nu!
goshawk, akcipitro
gosling, anserido
gospel, evangelio; ~a
gossamer, filandro; ~(ec)a
gossip, klaĉi [int]; ~o; ~emul(in)o
Gossypium, kotonujo
Goth, Goto; **Gothic**, (re ~s), ~a; (arch; printing; story style), gotika; **early Gothic**, frugotika
Gottfried, Gotfredo
gouache, guaŝo
gouge, guĝo; ~i [tr]; **gouge out**, el~i [tr]
goulash, gulaŝo
goumi, eleagno
gourd, (any plant of *Cucurbita;* fruit), kukurbo; (calabash: *Crescentia cujete*), kalabaso; kalabasarbo; **(bottle) gourd**, (plant: *Lagenaria*), kalabas~o, botel~o, lagenario; (fruit, or bottle etc. made from), kalabaso
gourmand, manĝemulo, gastronomo
gourmet, gastronomo; ~ia
gout, podagro; **goutweed**, egopodio

govern, (gen), regi [tr]; (child, living w), guverni [tr]; (rule absolutely), diktatori [tr]; **governess,** guvernistino; **government,** (process), ~ado; (institution), ~istaro; **governor,** (of state), ŝtatestro; (of province), provincestro [cp "premier"]; (of colony or oth district), guberniestro; (mech: speed regulator), bremso, regulilo; **self-government,** mem~ado, aŭtonomio
gown, (gen), robo; (of judge etc.), talaro; **dressing gown,** ĉambro~o, negliĝa ~o
goy, (non-Jew), gojo [cp "gentile"]
grab, (snatch), ekkapti [tr], kroĉi [tr]; ~o; (Br: re power shovel), ŝovelfaŭko
Graccus, Grakko
grace, (attractive quality, beauty), gracio; (divine favor), graco; (prayer at meal), tablopreĝo; (delay), prokrasto; **graceful,** ~a; **grace period,** prokrastoperiodo; **scapegrace,** kanajlo, bubego; **in one's good (bad) graces,** en ies (mal)favoro
Graces, (myth), Gracioj
gracile, gracila
gracious, (kind, charming, courteous), favora, ĉarma, bonkora, bonvola, afabla; (compassionate), kompata; (polite), ĝentila; (luxurious, tasteful), luksa, bongusta
grade, (degree), grado; ~igi; (quality), kvalito; (school class), klaso; (slope), deklivo; (level), nivelo; (rank), rango; (score, as on test, course), noto; noti [tr]; **gradation,** ~igo; ~iĝo; **grader,** (road-working vehicle w scraper blade), skrapmaŝino; **upgrade,** (upward, uphill), supre(n); supre na; (upward slope), suprena deklivo; (improve), plibonigi; plibonig(aĵ)o; (promote to higher job, position), promocii [tr]; (raise in importance, value, etc.), pligravigi, plivalorigi; (etc.); **grade crossing,** (rr), nivelpasejo
gradient, (math, sci, tech), gradiento; (any slope), deklivo
gradual, (slow changing), grada, po~a, laŭ~a; (rel), gradualo
graduate, (from university), diplomi [tr]; ~iĝi; ~ito; (from high school, secondary school), abiturientigi; abituri-

entiĝi; abituriento; (calibrate), gradizi [tr]; **postgraduate,** ~ito; ~ita, post~a; **postgraduate degree,** supera ~o; **undergraduate,** ne~a; ne~ito, ne~a studento
gradus, (Latin dictionary), graduso
Graf, grafo
graffito, murskribaĉo; **graffiti,** ~oj
graft, (limb, skin, plant, etc.), grefti [tr]; ~iĝi; ~o; ~aĵo; (corrupt $), fiprofiti [tr]; fiprofito
Grail, Gralo
grain, (seed; any small particle), grajno; (kernel), kerno; (cereal plant, gen; Br: corn), greno; (basic element of something), ~ero [sfx] (e.g.: *grain of sand:* sablero); (of wood etc.), vejno(j); (unit of mass), grano [64,8 miligramoj (see § 20)]; **go against the grain,** kontraŭi la inklinon
gram, (mass), gramo; **gram-mass,** ~maso; **gram-negative,** ~negativa; **gram-positive,** ~pozitiva; (Bengal) **gram,** (chickpea), kikero; **microgram,** mikro~o; **milligram,** mili~o; **decigram,** deci~o; **kilogram,** kilo~o [not "kilo"]
Graminaceae, graminacoj
Gramineae, graminacoj
grammar, gramatiko; **grammatical,** ~a; **ungrammatical,** kontraŭ~a
gramme, [see "gram"]
gramophone, gramofono
Gram's method, Gram's stain, (iodine-iodide solution), gramaĵo
Granada, Granado
granadilla, (passionflower), grenadilo
Gran Chaco, Granĉako
grand, (primary, higher), ĉefa; (luxurious), luksa; (very good), bonega; (complete, comprehensive), tuta, kompleta, plena; (grandiose, imposing), grandioza, impona; (piano), horizontala (piano); **grandchild(ren),** genepo(j); **great-grandchild(ren),** pragenepo(j); **granddaughter,** nepino; **great-granddaughter,** pranepino; **grandee,** (gen), magnato; **grandeur,** majesto, grandiozo; **grandfather,** avo; **great-grandfather,** praavo; **grandfather (grandmother) on the father's (mother's)**

side, patroflanka (patrinflanka) av(in)o; **grandmother**, avino; **great-grandmother**, praavino; **grandparent(s)**, geavo(j); **great-grandparent(s)**, prageavo(j); **grandson**, nepo; **great-grandson**, pranepo
grand–, (pfx, re relative), pra– [see subentries under "grand"]
grandiloquent, bombasta, pompa
grandiose, grandioza, bombasta
grandioso, (mus), grandioze
grandstand, benkaro
grange, bieno [cp "farm"]
granite, granito
granola, granolo*
grant, (approve), aprobi [tr], jesi [tr] (e.g.: *grant one's request:* ~i ies peton); (concede), cedi [tr, int]; (give), doni [tr]; (accept as fact), akcepti [tr]; ($ for certain purpose), donacio [cp "subsidy", "gift"]; **take for granted**, senplue akcepti [tr]
granule, (anat, med), granulo; (any small grain), grajneto; **granular**, ~(ec)a; grajna; **granulate**, ~igi; ~iĝi; grajnetigi; grajnetiĝi
granulocyte, granulocito
granuloma, granulomo; **granulomatosis**, ~ozo
grape, (gen), vinbero; (esp as food), uvo; **grapevine**, vito; (trunk), rebo; **Oregon grape**, mahonio; **sea grape**, (*Coccoloba*), kokolobo; **wild grape**, labrusko† [cp "catawba"]
grapefruit, (fruit), grapfrukto; (tree), ~arbo
graph, grafik/aĵo; ~igi–
graph, (sfx), –grafo
–grapher, (sfx: person who), –grafo [however, see "telegraph", "photograph"; see separate entries]
graphic, (re graphic arts), grafika; (vivid), brila, viva; **graphics**, ~o
graphite, grafito
graphology, grafolog/io; **graphologist**, ~o
–graphy, (sfx), –grafio
grapnel, graplo
grapple, (small anchor, grapnel; fish for w grapple), graplo; ~i [tr]; **grapple (with)**, (struggle), lukti [int] (kun)
Graptolitha, graptolitoj†

grasp, (take hold, seize), kapti [tr], ekpreni [tr], kroĉi [tr]; ~o, kroĉo, teno; (understand), kompreni [tr]; kompreno, intuo; **grasp at**, ek~i [tr], ekkroĉi [tr]; **grasping**, (greedy), avara, monavida; **within (beyond) one's grasp**, en (preter) ies atingo
grass, (collective), herbo, greso; (single plant or blade), ~ero, gresero; (put to pasture), engresigi; (marijuana), mariñuano; **grassy**, ~(oriĉ)a, gresa; **grasshopper**, akrido; **Bahama grass**, cinodonto; **beach grass**, amofilo; **beard grass**, (Aus: *Chrysopogon*), krisopogono*; **bentgrass**, agrostido; **Bermuda grass**, cinodonto; **bluegrass**, (grass), blu~o; (mus), blu~a muziko; **bunchgrass**, (*Stipa*), stipo; **canary grass**, (*Phalaris*), falaro; (*Lepidium*), lepidio; **China grass**, (plant), ramio; (fiber from), ramiaĵo; **citronella grass**, citronelo; **cotton grass**, erioforo; **couch grass**, kviko; **crabgrass**, digitario; **feather grass**, (*Stipa*), stipo; **fescue grass**, festuko; **guinea grass**, paniko; **herd's grass**, fleo; **ichu grass**, stipo; **knotgrass**, poligono; **lyme grass**, elimo; **marram grass**, amofilo; **millet grass**, [see "millet"]; **moor grass**, (*Molinia*), molinio; **needlegrass**, (*Stipa*), stipo; **painted grass**, falaro; **panic grass**, **Pará grass**, **porcupine grass**, paniko; **quack grass**, **quick grass**, **quitch grass**, kviko; **ribbon grass**, falaro; **ryegrass**, lolo; **scorpion grass**, miozoto, neforgesumino; **scurvy grass**, koklcario; **scutch grass**, (*Agropyrum*), kviko; (*Cynodon*), cinodonto; **sea grass**, (*Zostera*), zostero; **sleepy grass**, stipo; **soft grass**, holko; **stipa grass**, stipo; **timothy grass**, fleo; **tumble grass**, paniko; **twitch grass**, kviko; **velvet grass**, holko; **(sweet) vernal grass**, antoksanto; **viper's-grass**, skorzonero; **whitlow grass**, drabo; **witch grass**, (*Agropyrum*), kviko; (*Panicum*), paniko
grate, (scrape food etc.), raspi [tr]; (scratch), grati [tr]; (on nerves), agaci [tr]; (scraping sound), knari [int]; (creak), grinci [int]; (metal lattice),

krado; **grater,** ~ilo; **grating,** krado
grateful, dankema; **gratefulness,** ~o
gratify, plaĉi [tr], kontentigi [not "grati-
fiki"]
gratin, graten/aĵo; **au gratin,** ~ita; ~ite;
prepare (food) au gratin, ~i [tr]
Gratiola, gratiolo
gratis, senpaga; ~e
gratitude, dankemo; **ingratitude,** ne~o
gratuity, gratifiko; **gratuitous,** ~a; **give
a gratuity (to someone),** ~i [tr] (iun)
Graubünden, Grizono
grave, (important), grava; (serious), ~a,
serioza; (critical), kriza; (for burial),
tombo; (carve), ĉizi [tr]; **graveyard,**
tombejo; **grave-digger,** tombisto;
mass grave, amastombejo; **beyond
the grave,** transmorta, transtomba;
gravestone, tomboŝtono; **auto
graveyard,** aŭtovrakejo
gravel, (gen), gruzo, ŝotro†; ~izi [tr];
gravelweed, (*Verbesina*), verbesino
gravimetry, gravimetro
gravity, (phys force), gravito; (unit of
force: gee), goo, ~o; (seriousness),
graveco; **gravitate,** ~i [int]; **gravita-
tion,** ~o; **gravitational,** ~a; **center of
gravity,** masocentro; **microgravity,**
mikro~o; **null-gravity, zero gravity,**
nul~o; **specific gravity,** relativa dens-
eco, specifa maso
gravure, (plate), intajlo; (process),
~ado [cp "engrave"]
gravy, viandosaŭco
gray, (color), grizo; ~a; **grayhound,**
grejhundo; **grayling,** (fish), timalo;
African gray, (zool), papago
graze, (feed), paŝti [tr]; ~i sin, ~iĝi;
(barely touch), tanĝi [tr]; tanĝo;
(wound), tanĝovundi [tr]; tanĝovundo
grease, (gen), graso; ~i [tr], ŝmiri [tr];
(tallow), sebo; **elbow grease,** fizika
klopodo
great, (large; of high degree; eminent;
etc.), granda; (excellent), bonega, brava; **greater,** (more, larger), plia (e.g.:
the greater Washington area: la regiono de plia Vaŝingtono); **Great
Lakes,** (la) Lagoj G~aj
great–, (re relationship), pra– (e.g.:
great-aunt: ~onklino; *great-great-
grandfather:* ~~avo; *great-grandson:*

~nepo) [see also under "grand"]
grebe, kolimbo, podicipo
Grecian, Greko; ~a; ~ia
Greco-, (pfx: Greek), Grek(o)–
Greece, Grek/io [cp "Hellas"]; **Greek,**
~o; ~a; ~ia; (Hellene), Heleno; Helena
greed, avar/eco; **greedy,** ~a
green, (color; pol), verda; ~o; ~igi;
~iĝi; (immature), nematura; (inexperienced), sensperta; (public area), herbejo; (golf), gazonpeco [cp "common;
commons"]; (pol: follower of Green
Party), ~ulo†; **greenfly,** afido; **greengage,** renklodo; **greenhorn,** novico,
novbakito, flavbekulo; **greenhouse,**
forcejo, oranĝerio; **greenweed,** genisto
Greenland, Groenlando
Greenwich, Grenviĉo;   **Greenwich
Mean Time,** ~a Meza Tempo [see also under "time"]
greet, saluti [tr]; **greeting,** ~o; **greet-
ings!,** ~on! [note sing]
gregarious, ariĝema, gregema
Gregory, (Pope), Gregorio;   (man's
name), Gregoro; **Gregorian,** ~a
gremlin, koboldo
grenade, grenado; **grenadier,** ~isto
grenadilla, grenadillo, grenadilo
grenadine, granataĵo
Grenoble, Grenoblo
Greta, Greta
grey, [see "gray"]
grid, (gen), krado; **gridwork,** ~aĵo;
screen grid, ekrana ~o, ŝirma ~o
griddle, platpato
gridiron, rostkrado
grief, (as from death), funebro, lamenta-
do; (sorrow, gen), aflikto, malĝojo,
doloro; **come to grief,** fiaski [int], ruiniĝi; **give one grief,** ĉagreni [tr],
riproĉi [tr]
grievance, (complaint),   plendo;
(grounds for), ~omotivo
grieve, (as from death), funebri [tr, int],
lamenti [int] (pri), prilamenti [tr];
(distress), ĉagreni [tr]; **grievous,** la-
mentinda, dolora
griffin, grifo
griffon, (griffin), grifo; (dog), grifono
grill, (any lattice of metal etc.), krado;

(for cooking), rost~o; (cook), rosti
[tr]; rostiĝi; (restaurant), rostejo;
(question), pridemandegi [tr]; **grille**,
~o; **grillwork**, ~aĵo
grim, (savage, cruel), kruela, sovaĝa;
(gruesome), makabra; (insistent), insista; (joyless), senĝoja, malgaja, serioza
grimace, grimaco; ~i [int]
grime, malpur/aĵo, fulgo; **grimy**, ~a,
fulga
grin, larĝe rideti [int]; larĝa rideto
grind, (as in mill), mueli [tr]; ~iĝi; ~aĵo;
(pulverize), pisti [tr]; pistiĝi; (wear
smooth, erode), ŝlifi [tr]; ŝlifiĝi;
(glass), smirgi [tr]; (creak), grinci
[int]; (scraping sound), knari [int];
grinder, ~ilo; pistilo; smirgilo;
(large, for minerals, ore, etc.), pisto-
maŝino; **grindstone**, (millstone),
~ŝtono; (to sharpen tools etc.), akrigilo
grindelia, Grindelia, grindelio
grip, (clutch), kroĉi [tr], stringi [tr]; ~o,
stringo; (of pistol etc.), kolbo; (satchel), valizo
gripe, (complain), plendi [int]; ~o,
ve--esprimo; (annoy), ĉagreni [tr]
grippe, gripo
grisaille, grizaĵlo
Griselda, Grizelda
grisly, horora, makabra
Grisons, Grizono
grist, muel/otaĵo; **gristmill**, gren~ejo
gristle, kartilago
grit, (sand), sablo; (courage), kuraĝo;
grits, (food), griaĵo [note sing]; **grit
one's teeth**, kunpremi la dentojn
grivet, cerkopiteko
grizzle, (gray), griz/igi; ~iĝi; (grumble),
grumbli [int]; **grizzled**, ~(iĝint)a
grizzly, griza; ~a urso
groan, ĝemi [int]; ~o
grocer, nutrovar/isto; **grocery**, ~a;
~ejo; **groceries**, ~oj; **grocery store**,
~ejo
grog, (drink), grogo; (fired refractory
material), ŝamoto
groggy, stupora, ŝanceliĝa, nespiritopreta
groin, ingveno
grommet, koŝo

groom, (husband), novedzo; (horse tender), grumo; (curry), strigli [tr];
(dress, use cosmetics), tualeti [int]; tu-
aletigi; (train), trejni [tr]; **grooming**,
tualeto
groove, (gen), foldo; ~i [tr]; (mech,
arch, etc.; re phonograph record), kanelo; kaneli [tr]; **microgroove**, mik-
rokanelo
grope, palpi [tr]
grosbeak, (*Coccothraustes*),
kokotraŭsto; **pine grosbeak**, (*Pinicola*), pinikolo
groschen, groŝo
gross, (before deductions, re weight,
salary, etc.), malneta; ~o; (w tare, re
weight), brutta; (144), groco; (rough),
maldelikata, malfajna; (uncouth), kruda, triviala
grotesque, groteska
grotto, groto
grouch, grumbli [int]; (person), ~emu-
lo; (complaint), plendo; **grouchy**,
~ema, plendema
ground, (earth, solid land), tero; ~a;
(soil; piece of ground; fig: subject of
discussion etc.; ground surface under
body of water), grundo; (base, basis),
bazo; bazi [tr]; (land for specific purpose), tereno (e.g.: *parade ground*:
paradotereno; *training ground(s)*: tre-
jntereno; *gain ground*: gajni terenon);
(elec), ~o; ~konekti [tr]; ~konektiĝi;
~konekto; (elec: conductive parts in
contact w actual ground), maso; al-
masigi; almasiĝi; (mus or oth background), fono; (land plane, spacecraft,
etc.), sur~igi; sur~iĝi; (run ship
aground; keep plane, pilot, etc., from
flying; etc.), grundi [int]; grundigi;
(give foundation, as to argument),
fundamenti [tr], bazi [tr]; **grounds**,
(basis, reason), bazo, kialo, motivo;
(estate), bieno; (dregs), rekremento
(e.g.: *coffee grounds*: kafrekremento);
groundcloth (Am), subtenda tuko;
ground floor, ~etaĝo; **groundhog**,
marmoto; **groundnut**, (*Apios*), apioso; (Br: peanut), arakido; **groundsel**,
senecio; **groundsheet**, (Aus), subtenda tuko; **groundskeeper**, terenisto;
groundswell, (gen), ondego; **ground-**

work, fundamento; **above-ground**, super~a; **background**, (gen), fono; fona; **break ground**, ekfosi [tr]; **groundbreaking**, ekfoso; **cover ground**, transiri distancon; (fig: progress), progresi [int]; **foreground**, unua plano, malfono, antaŭo; **cut the ground from under one**, subfosi iun; **from the ground up**, dekomence ĝisfine; **gain ground**, gajni terenon, progresi [int]; **get off the ground**, ekprogresi [int]; ekprogresigi; **give ground**, cedi terenon; **lose ground**, perdi terenon, malprogresi [int]; **on grounds of**, pro, surbaze de; **stand one's ground**, ne cedi [tr, int], persisti [int]; **underground**, (lit: under ground), sub~a; sub~aĵo; (people), sub~ularo; (Br: subway), (sub~a) metroo; **be on firm (shaky) ground**, havi (mal)firman fundamenton
group, grupo; ~igi; ~iĝi; **study group**, stud~o, studrondo; **pressure group**, prem~o
grouse, (zool: *Tetrao*), tetraono; (grumble, complain), grumbli [int], plendi [int]; **black grouse**, (*Lyrurus*), tetro; **hazel grouse, ruffed grouse**, (*Tetrastes*), tetrao, bonazio; **red grouse, willow grouse**, (*Lagopus*), lagopo
grout, likva mortero
grove, bosko
grovel, lakei [int], humilaĉi [int]
grow, (gen), kreski [int]; ~igi; (cultivate), kultivi [tr]; (become), -iĝi [sfx], (far)iĝi [see "become", "get"]; **growth**, ~(ad)o; ~aĵo; (as wart etc.), (el)~aĵo, tubero; **grow up**, maturiĝi, elkreski [int]; **grown up**, matura, elkreskinta; **grown-up**, maturulo, plenkreskulo, adolto; **grow on one**, oni laŭgrade ekŝati [tr] (e.g.: *the idea will grow on you:* vi laŭgrade ekŝatos la ideon); **grow out of**, (result), rezulti de, el; **ingrown, ingrowing**, (as toenail, hair), enkarniĝinta; **outgrow**, (gen), preter~i [tr]; **outgrowth**, ~(aĵ)o; (result), rezulto, konsekvenco; **overgrown**, super~inta, tro~inta; **undergrowth**, (shrubs etc.), [see "brush"]
growl, graŭli† [int]; ~o [cp "roar"]

grub, (dig), fosi [tr]; (drudge), servuti [int]; (food), nutraĵo; (larva), larvo; **grubby**, malpuraĉa
grudge, (begrudge), domaĝi [tr]; (ill will), rankoro, malbonvolo; **grudging**, malbonvola
gruel, kaĉo, poriĝo
grueling, peniga, ellaciga
gruesome, makabra
gruff, bruska, raŭka
grumble, grumbli [int], murmuri [int]; ~o
grumichama, grumixama, (fruit), grumiksamo; (tree), ~arbo
grummet, koŝo
grump, malafabl/ulo, grumblemulo; **grumpy**, ~a, grumblema
grunt, grunti [int]; ~o
Grus, gruo; Grus rubicunda, (Aus), brolgo*
Gruyère, (cheese), grujero
Gryllus, grilo; Gryllidae, ~edoj
gryphon, [see "griffon"]
guacamole, avokadaĵo
Guadalquivir, Gvadalkiviro
Guadeloupe, Gvadelupo
guaiacol, gvajakolo
guaiacum, guaiocum, (tree), gvajako; (resin), ~a rezino, rezino de ~o
Guajacum, gvajako
Guam, Gvamo*
guana, igvano
guanaco, guanako
guano, guano
guarana, gvarano
Guaraní, Gvaranio; ~a
guarantee, guaranty, garantii [tr, int]; ~o; **guarantor**, ~anto
guard, (gen), gardi [tr]; ~isto; (screen, shield), ŝirmi [tr]; ŝirmilo; (mil: special detachment), gvardio; (prison), provoso; (Br: rr conductor), konduktoro; **guarded**, (discreet), diskreta, kaŝema; (uncertain), necerta; **National Guard**, Nacia Gvardio; **off guard**, nesin~a; **on guard**, sin~a; **rearguard**, arier~o; arier~a; **stand guard**, ~estari [int]
guardian, (legal), kuratoro; (any guard), gardisto; **guardianship**, ~eco; **guardian angel**, gardanĝelo
Guatemala, Gvatemalo

guava, (fruit), gujavo; (tree), ~arbo
guayacan, gvajako
gubernatorial, štatestra; provincestra;
guberniestra [see "governor"]
gudgeon, (mech: pin), stifto, akso~o;
(socket), ~ingo; (fish), gobio
Guelph, (Italy), Gelfo
guemal, guemul, guemulo
Guenever, Ginevra
guenon, cerkopiteko
guerilla, [see "guerrilla"]
Guernsey, (Island), Gernezejo; (cattle), ~a bov(in)o
guerrilla, geril/ano; ~isto; guerrilla
war, ~o; guerrilla warfare, ~ado
guess, (gen), konjekti [tr]; ~o; ~aĵo;
(correctly figure out), diveni [tr]; di-
veno; guesstimate, ~otaksi [tr];
~otakso; guesswork, ~ado; second-
guess, postkritiki [tr]
guest, gasto
Guglielmo, Gulielmo
guffaw, ridegi [int]; ~o
Guiana, (gen region), Gvajano; British
Guiana, Brita ~io; French Guiana,
Franca ~io
guide, (gen), gvidi [tr]; ~into; ~anto;
~onto; ~isto; ~ilo; guidance, ~ado;
guidance counselor, ~okonsilisto [cp
"mentor"]; guidance system, ~siste-
mo; guidebook, ~libro; guide dog,
~hundo; guideline, (standard, norm),
(~)normo; (lit: a line), ~linio; guide-
post, (post), indikfosto, ~fosto;
(guideline, standard), (~)normo; girl
guide, (scout), skoltino
Guienne, Gujeno
guild, gildo
guilder, guldeno
guile, artifiko, ruz(em)o, trompemo;
guileless, sen~a, sincera
guillemot, (Uria), urio
guillotine, gilotino; ~i [tr]
guilt, kulpo; guilty (of), ~a (pri); be
guilty, ~i [int]; plead guilty (of),
konfesi [tr] (~on)
guinea, ($), gineo
Guinea, (geog), Gvineo; Guinea–Bis-
sau, Bisaŭ–~o†; Equatorial Guinea,
Ekvatora ~o†; New Guinea, Nov–~o
[see "Papua"]
Guinever(e), Ginevra

guipure, gipuro
guisard, geŭzo; ~a
guise, (pretense), ŝajno; (aspect), aspekto; under the guise of, sub la mantelo
de, sub la ~o de
guitar, gitaro; guitarrón, kontragitaro*
Guiyang, Gujjang
gulag, gulago†
gulch, ravino
gulden, guldeno
gulf, (as of sea), golfo; (abyss), abismo;
Gulf Stream, G~a Fluo
gull, (zool: gen, common term), mevo;
(Larus), laro; (dupe), dupigi, trompi
[tr] ĉarlatani [tr]; dupo
gullet, (esophagus), ezofago; (throat),
gorĝo
gullible, dupiĝema, naiva, trompebla
gully, ravineto
Gulo, gulo
gulose, gulozo
gulp, (swallow hastily, much), glut/egi
[tr]; ~ego; (choke back, catch breath,
etc.), ek~i [int]; ek~o
gum, (rubbery substance, gen), gumo;
~i [tr]; (glue), gluo; gluaĵi [tr]; (anat),
gingivo; (chew w/o teeth), gingivumi
[tr]; (eraser), skrap~o; (galosh), galoŝo; gummed, gluaĵita, glu– [pfx]
(e.g.: gummed label: gluetikedo, glumarko); gummy, ~eca, glueca; gum
arabic, Araba ~o; gumboil, gingiva
absceso; gumdrop, ~–bombono,
~–buleto; gummosis, ~ozo; gum-
weed, grindelio; chewing gum,
maĉ~o; red gum, (Aus), ruĝligna
eŭkalipto
gumption, entreprenemo, iniciatemo
gun, (weapon, gen), paf/ilo; (for spraying liquid under pressure), pistolo
(e.g.: grease gun: graspistolo);
(shoot), ~i [tr]; (open throttle), brulaĵi
[tr]; gunboat, kanonboato; guncot-
ton, fulmokotono; gunfight, ~batalo;
gunfire, ~ado; gun for, ĉasi [tr]; gun-
man, ~isto; hired gun(man), sikario;
gunner, (mil), artileriisto; gunnery,
kanonaro; kanonado; gunpowder,
pulvo; gunshot, ~o; gunsmith, ~ilis-
to; gunsmoke, ~fumo; air gun,
aer~ilo; BB gun, globeto~ilo; blowgun, blov~ilo; handgun, man~ilo; la-

sergun, laser~ilo; **machine gun,** mitralo; **popgun,** kork~ilo; **shotgun,** kugletar–fusilo; **squirtgun,** špruc~ilo; **submachine gun, Tommy gun,** mitraleto; **at gunpoint,** je ~minaco; **jump the gun,** tro frue komenci [tr]
gung-ho, entuziasm(eg)a, verva
gunk, šlimgraso
gunnel, gunwale, boatrando
guppy, gupio*
gurgle, murmuri [int], glugli [int]; ~o, gluglo
Gurkha, Gurko
gurnard, gurnardo
guru, guruo
gush, šprucegi [int]; ~o
gusset, vastigpeco
gust, ventpušo; ~iĝ(ad)i [cp "squall"]; **gusty,** ~a; **gusty winds,** ekpušaj ventoj
Gustav, Gustave, Gustavus, Gustavo
gusto, vervo, entuziasmo [not "gusto"]
gut, (intestines), intesto; sen~igi; (any internal organs), viscero, internaĵoj; (belly), ventro; (catgut), katguto; (burn out), finbruligi, elbruligi; (emotional), emocia (e.g.: *a gut reaction:* emocia reago); **guts,** ~oj; (innards, gen), internaĵoj; (courage), kuraĝo; **gutsy,** kuraĝa, aŭdaca
Gutenberg, Gutenbergo
gutta, (drop), guto; (gutta-percha), gutaperko; (ingredient of gutta-percha), gutao
gutta-percha, gutaperko
gutter, (of roof), gutujo; (street etc.), defluilo
guttural, velaro, guturalo; ~a, guturala; **pronounce r's gutturally,** (in throat), kartavi [int]
guy, (fellow; colloq, of either gender), ulo; (guy-wire; rope, cable, etc., to steady, guide, etc.), stajo; (provide with guy), stajizi [tr]
Guyana, Gvajano
Guyenne, Gujeno
guzzle, trinkegi [tr]
gybe, gibi [tr]; ~iĝi
gym, gimnastikejo
gymkhana, ĝinkano
gymnasium, (gym), gimnastikejo; (European high school), gimnazio

gymnast, gimnasto; **gymnastic,** ~ika; **gymnastics,** ~iko
gymn(o)–, (pfx), gimn(o)–
Gymnophiona, gimnofionoj
gymnosperm, gimnospermo
Gymnotus, gimnoto;   Gymnotidae, ~edoj
gyn(a)ecium, gineceo
gynecology, ginekolog/io; **gynecologist,** ~o
gynoecium, gineceo
gyp, fraŭdi [tr]; ~o; ~into
Gypaetus, gipaeto
Gyps, gipo
Gypsophila, gipsofilo
gypsum, gipso
gypsy, Cigano, Romo*; ~a, Roma*
gyrate, giri [int]
gyrfalcon, girfalko
gyro, (gyroscope), giroskopo
gyro–, (pfx), giro–
Gyromitra, giromitro
gyroscope, giroskopo
gyrus, giro

H

ha, (interj), ha!
Habakkuk, Habacuc, (Bib), Ĥabakuko
haberdasher, (dealer in clothing accessories), galanteri/isto; (Br: dealer in sewing supplies), merceristo; haberdashery, (objects), ~o; mercero; (shop), ~ejo; mercerejo
habergeon, maŝkuteto [cp "hauberk"]
habit, (custom), kutimo [cp "inertia"]; (costume), kostumo; habitual, ~a; habit-forming, ~iga [cp "addict"]; be in the habit of, ~i [tr]; break the habit (of), de~iĝi (je); break (someone) of a habit, de~igi (iun je io); get into the habit of, ~iĝi (al)
habitable, loĝ/ebla; habitat, (re animal; any habitable place), ~loko; (of plant), kreskejo; habitation, ~ejo
habitué frekventanto
Habroxylon cembra, cembro
Habsburg, Habsburgo
habutai, habutajo
hachure, haĉi [tr]; ~o
hacienda, latifundio, bienego; ~a dom(eg)o
hack, (chop, lit or fig), haki [tr]; (throat noise, bringing up mucus), graki [int]; grako; (routine writer), soldoverkisto, gurdverkisto; (cmptr programmer, user), gurd(komputor)isto; (hackney, gen), gurdi [tr]; (any drudge), servutulo; hackberry, celtido; hacksaw, metalsegilo
hackle, (feathers), kol/plumoj; (fur), ~haroj; get one's hackles up, kolerigi; koleriĝi
hackney, (make trite), gurdi [tr]; ~ita; (carriage), fiakro; hackneyed, ~ita
had, (if ... had), se ... -us (e.g.: had I wings to fly with: se mi havus flugilojn por flugi; had you gone: se vi estus irinta)
haddock, eglefino
Hades, (gen), Hadeso
hadron, hadrono†
hadj, haĝo; hadji, ~ulo
Hadrian, Hadriano; Hadrian's Wall, la ~a Murego

haem–, [see "hem–"]
Haemanthus, hemanto, sangofloro
Haematopus, hematopo, marpigo
Haematoxylon, kampeĉo
Hafiz, Hafizo
hafnium, hafnio
haft, tenilo
hag, virinaĉo; hagfish, miksino
haggada(h), hagado
Haggai, Ĥagajo
haggard, (gaunt), marasma, malgrasaĉa
haggis, organaĵo
haggle, marĉandi [int]
Hagiographa, Hagiography, hagiograf/io; Hagiographer, Hagiographist, ~o
Hague, (The), Hago [note no "La"]
haiduk, hajduko
haiku, hajko
hail, (ice), hajli [int]; ~o; (acclaim), aklami [tr]; aklamo; hailstone, ~ero; hailstorm, ~ŝtormo
Hainan, Hajnano
Hainaut, Henegovio
Haiphong, Hajfongo
hair, (single strand), haro; (collective), ~aro, ~oj; (of horse, poet), krino; hair('s)-breadth, apenaŭa; haircut, ~tondo; get a haircut, tondigi la ~aron; hairdo, ~aranĝo; hairdresser, frizisto; have one's hair done, frizigi la ~aron; hairdryer, (har)feno; hairnet, ~reto; hairpiece, peruko; hairpin, ~pinglo; ~pingla; hair-raising, hirtiga; hair-splitting, ~fend(em)a; ~fendado; split hairs, fendi ~ojn; hairspring, spiralrisorto; cross-hairs, kruc~oj
Haiti, Haitio; Haitian, ~a; ~ano
Hajj, haĝo; Hajji, ~ulo
hake, merluĉo
halation, haloo
halberd, halebardo
hale, sana, fortika
half, duono; ~a; ~e; duon– [pfx] (e.g.: half of the cake: ~o de la kuko; a half hour: ~a horo [or] ~horo; half dead: ~e morta [or] ~morta); half a, ~o de

(e.g.: *I drank half a liter of milk:* mi trinkis ~on de litro da lakto); (**number**) **and a half**, [number] kaj ~o (~a) (e.g.: *I read three and a half pages:* mi legis tri kaj ~an [not "~ajn"] paĝojn); **halfback**, (football etc.), halfo; **half-blood**, ~parenco; **half-brother** (**half-sister**), ~frat(in)o; **half-breed**, miksrasa; miksrasulo; **half-hearted**, indiferenta, senentuziasma; **half-life**, ~iĝa daŭro, ~vivo; (**at**) **half-mast**, ~hisita; ~hisite; **halfpenny**, ~penco; **halftime**, (game), ludmezo; **halftrack**, ~raŭpa kamiono; **halfway**, meze, egaldistance; **halfway house**, ~liberejo; **cut** (**divide**) **in half**, ~igi; ~iĝi; **meet one halfway**, kompromisi [int]
Haliaëtus, haliaeto
halibut, hipogloso
Halichoerus, haliñero, grizfoko
Halicore dugong, dugongo
halide, halogenido
Haliotis, halioto*
halitosis, miasma spiraĵo
hall, (large room), halo; (for festive occasions), aŭlo; (corridor), koridoro; (building), domo, konstruajo; **hallmark**, karat–stampo, titro–stampo; **hallway**, (vestibule), vestiblo; (corridor), koridoro; **hall of fame**, aŭlo de famo; **city hall**, urbodomo
hallelujah, (interj), haleluja!
halloo, voki [tr]
hallow, sankt/igi, konsekri [tr]; **hallowed**, ~a
Halloween, Halovino*, Antaŭvespero de Ĉiuj Sanktuloj
hallucinate, halucini [tr]; ~iĝi; **hallucination**, ~o; **hallucinatory**, ~a; **hallucinogen**, ~enzo; **hallucinogenic**, ~iga; **hallucinosis**, ~ozo
hallux, halukso, dika piedfingro
halo, (around sun etc.), nimbo, aŭreolo, haloo; (in painting of saint etc.), ~o, aŭreolo; (phot), haloo
halochromism, halokromio
halogen, halogeno
haloid, haloido
halt, (stop), halti [int]; ~igi, stopi [tr]; ~o; (lame), lama
halter, (for horse), kaprimeno [cp "bri-

dle"]; (woman's garment), mamvesto [not "haltero"; cp "bra"]; (for hanging), pendumilo
halvah, halvao
halve, duonigi
halyard, hisilo
ham, (meat), ŝinko; (radio), radioamatoro; (anat), poplito, genua kavo; (overact), histrioni [int]; (actor), histriono; **hamstring**, poplita tendeno; tranĉi la popliton (al)
Ham, (Bib), Ĥam; **Hamite**, ~ido; **Hamitic**, ~ida
hamadryad, hamadriado
Hamamelis, hamamelido
Haman, Hamano
Hamburg, Hamburgo
hamburger, (sandwich), bov/burgo†; (meat), hak~aĵo; (patty), hak~a platbulo
Hamilcar, Hamilkaro
Hamiltonian, (math), hamiltoniana; ~o
hamlet, vilaĝeto
Hamlet, (theat), Hamleto
hammer, (gen), martelo; ~i [tr]; **ball-peen hammer**, bulbeka ~o; **cross-peen hammer**, kojnbeka ~o; **claw hammer**, forkbeka ~o; **drop hammer**, fal~o; **jack-hammer**, manramo; **sledgehammer**, ~ego; **hammer throw**, (sports), ~ĵeto
hammock, hamako
Hammurabi, Hamurabo
hamper, (hinder), malhelpi [tr]; (basket), korbego
Hampshire, Hampŝiro*; **New Hampshire**, Nov-~o
hamster, hamstro
Han, Hano
hanap, hanapo
hand, (anat etc.; action of hand, lit or fig; cards given out in card game), mano; ~a; (of clock etc.), montrilo; (help), helpo (e.g.: *I could use a hand with that:* mi povus uzi helpon kun tio); (hired helper), helpisto, laboristo; (handwriting), ~skribado; (give), doni [tr]; **handbag**, (purse), retikulo, monujo; (small valise), valizeto; **handball**, (game: Am), (Usona) handbalo†; (oth), (Eŭropa) handbalo†; (ball), handbala† pilko; **handbill**,

flugfolio; **handbook,** ~libro; **handcar,** drezino; **handclasp,** ~premo; **handcraft,** [see "handicraft"]; **handcuff,** ~kateni [tr]; **handcuffs,** ~kateno [note sing]; **hand down,** (give on), transdoni [tr], pludoni [tr]; (bequeath), heredigi, testamenti [tr]; **handful,** ~pleno; **hand in,** submeti [tr], prezenti [tr]; **hand-in-hand,** ~-en-~e; **handmake,** ~e fari [tr], ~fari [tr]; **hand-me-down,** uzita; uzitaĵo [cp "secondhand" below]; **hands-off,** (not interfering), neentruda; **hand on,** transdoni [tr], pludoni [tr]; **hands-on,** praktika, memfara; **hand out,** disdoni [tr], distribui [tr]; **handout,** (alms), almozo; (flier), flugfolio; **hand over,** transdoni [tr], liveri [tr]; **handrail,** balustrado; **handset,** (of phone), aŭdilo; **handshake,** ~premo; **handspike,** ~levstango; **hand-to-hand,** ~-al-~a; ~-al-~e; **handwriting,** ~skribado; **handwritten,** ~skribita; **at hand,** ĉe~a; ĉe~e; **at first hand,** senpere; **at the hands of,** ĉe, sub la ~oj de; **backhand,** (re handwriting), livklina; (tennis etc.), ~dorso; ~dorsa (bato); **backhanded,** (sarcastic, insincere), dutranĉa, malsincera; **back of the hand,** ~dorso; **barehanded,** senarmile; **by hand,** (per)~e; **change hands,** transdoniĝi; **clubhand,** bul~o; **cupped hand,** ~kavo; **force one's hand,** devigi iun (agi); **forehand,** (tennis etc.), ~antaŭa (bato); **highhanded,** aroganta; **hour hand,** hormontrilo; **left-handed,** maldekstra~a, liv~a; (re screw thread etc.), livuma; **minute hand,** minutomontrilo; **off-hand,** tuja, senpripensa, improviza; **old hand,** (expert), spertulo; **on hand,** ĉe~a; ĉe~e; (in stock), en stoko; **on every hand,** ĉie, ĉiuflanke; **on the one hand,** unuflanke; **on the other hand,** aliflanke; **out of hand,** (out of control), neregebla; **overhand,** ~supra; ~supre; **palm of the hand,** polmo, ~plato; **place in (one's) hands,** (for safekeeping, action, etc.), en~igi; **right hand,** (main assistant), ĉefa asistanto; **right-handed,** (dextrous w right hand), dekstra~a; (re

screw thread etc.), dekstruma; **second-hand,** (gen, as re information, etc.), dua~a; dua~e; (used), uzita; (resold wares), brokanta; (indirect), malrekta, (nesen)pera; **second-hand goods (merchandise),** brokantaĵo(j); **deal in second-hand goods,** brokanti [tr, int]; **shake hands,** ~premiĝi [tr]; **shake hands with,** ~premi [tr]; **shorthand,** stenografio, steno; **take shorthand, write in shorthand,** stenografi [tr]; **single-ed,** (w/o help), propra~a, senhelpa; **underhand,** (w hand below elbow), ~suba; ~sube; **underhanded,** (secret, deceitful), fi~kaŝa, ruza, insida, artifika; **live from hand to mouth,** vivi iele-trapele; **my hands are clean,** mi ne kulpas, mi estas senkulpa, mi ne responsas [or] respondecas; **take (something) off one's hands,** malŝarĝi iun de (io); **wash one's hands of,** senigi sin de responseco [or] respondeco pri; **play into the hands of,** sin kompromiti favore al, agi al la avantaĝo de; **fall into the hands of,** kaptiĝi de, esti kaptita de; **have (take) a hand in,** partopreni [tr]; **hand-in-glove with,** intima kun; **have the upper hand,** esti supera (al); **get the upper hand (over),** superi [tr]; **give (lend) a hand (to),** helpi [tr]; **try one's hand at,** provi [tr]; **be a good hand at,** esti lerta pri; **catch one red-handed,** kapti iun kun la peko en la ~o, kapti iun kun la freŝa faro; **in the hands of,** sub la rego de, sub la ~oj de

handicap, (disabling med condition; sports etc.), handikapo†; ~i [tr]; (disadvantage), malavantaĝi [tr]; malavantaĝo; (hinder, gen), malhelpi [tr]; (contest), ~o; (difficulty imposed), ~(aĵ)o; malhelpo; **handicapped person,** ~ulo

handicraft, (skill), lerteco; (occupation; e.g., pottery, weaving), (man)metio; **handicrafter, handicraftsperson, handicraftsman,** (man)metiisto

handiwork, (man)faraĵo

handkerchief, naztuko

handle, (for holding, pulling, etc., gen,

lit or fig), tenilo [cp "knob"]; (curved
piece of door handle on which hand
closes), manilo; (use by handle, manipulate), manuzi [tr], trakti [tr], manipuli [tr]; (touch), tuŝi [tr]; (tolerate),
toleri [tr]; **handlebar,** stirilo
handsome, bela, bonaspekta
handy, (skillful), lerta; (convenient),
oportuna; (useful), utila; **handyman,**
faktoto; **come in handy,** montriĝi utila, utiliĝi
hang, (suspend), pendi [int]; ~igi; (execute by hanging), ~umi [tr]; (by hook,
as picture), kroĉi [tr]; kroĉiĝi; (re
wallpaper), tapeti [tr]; tapetiĝi; **hang
around,** frekventi [tr], ariĝi ĉirkaŭ;
hang back, heziti [int]; **hangglide,**
~oglisi [int]; **hangglider,** ~oglisilo;
hangnail, haŭtŝirajo; **hang out (at),**
(frequent), frekventi [tr]; **hang-out,**
frekventejo; **hangover,** postebrio;
hang together, (gen), kunteniĝi, koheri [int]; **hang up,** ~igi; kroĉi [tr];
(phone), remeti la aŭdilon; (delay, as
car in traffic), prokrasti [tr]; **hang-up,**
(psych), obsed(et)o; **(clothes) hanger,** vestarko; **overhang,** superelstari
[int], kornice elstari [int], superstari
[int]; superelstarajo; **get the hang of,**
akiri komprenon (povoscion) de
hangar, hangaro
Hangzhow, Hangĝoŭ
hank, buklaro
hanker, sopiri [int]; **hanker for, hanker after,** ~i al, ~i pri, deziri [tr], avidi [tr]; **hankering,** ~o, deziro
Hankow, Hankoŭ
hanky-panky, (kaŝ)ruzado
Hannibal, Hanibalo
Hanoi, Hanojo
Hanover, (city; family), Hanovro;
(province), ~io
Hanse, Hanso; **Hanseatic,** ~a
hansom, kabrioleto
Hanuka, Ĥanukao*
hanuman, entelo
Hanumant, Hanumanto
haoma, haomo
hap, sorto, hazardo, ŝanco
Hapale, hapalo, silksimio; Hapalidae,
~edoj
hapax legomenon, hapaksot

haphazard, hazarda
hapless, malfeliĉa, fatala
haplography, haplografiot
happen, okazi [int]; **happening,** ~(aĵ)o;
happen to, (by chance), hazarde –i
(e.g.: *it happens to be raining:* hazarde pluvas; *if you happen to see her:* se
hazarde vi vidos ŝin); **happen across,**
happen on(to), hazarde trovi [tr], hazarde renkonti [tr]; **it happens that,**
hazarde; **happenstance,** hazardo
happy, (contented), kontenta, feliĉa;
(lucky), feliĉa; **happy-go-lucky,** facilanima
Hapsburg, Habsburgo
hara-kiri, harakiro; **commit hara-kiri,**
~i [int]
harangue, bombastadi [int]; ~o
harass, ĉagreni [tr], turment(ad)i [tr],
ĝenadi [tr], molestadi [tr]; **sexual ha-
rassment,** seksa molestado
Harbin, Harbin
harbinger, (thing), antaŭsigno; (person), ~anto; **be a harbinger (of),** ~i
[tr]
harbo(u)r, haveno; (shield, hide), ŝirmi
[tr], kaŝi [tr]
hard, (not soft; having minerals, re water), malmola, dura; (firm), firma;
(powerful, vigorous), forta, vigla;
(difficult), malfacila; (severe), severa, rigora; (rigid), rigida; (obstinate),
obstina, hardiĝinta, maldorlot(em)a,
malcedema; (phon), dura; **harden,**
~igi; ~iĝi; (re steel; feelings), hardi
[tr]; hardiĝi; **hardly,** apenaŭ; **hard-
board,** fibrotabulo; **hardship,** sufera-
do, manko; **hardwood,** (wood),
durligno; durligna; (tree), durligna arbo; **hard and fast,** (inflexible), ne-
fleksebla, firma; **hard up,** senmona,
malriĉa; **hard-working,** laborema, diligenta; **be hard on,** maldorloti [tr],
esti severa kun, al; **be hard put to,**
malfacile povi [tr], apenaŭ povi
hardware, (metal items, gen), metal-
aĵoj; (cmptr), hardvaro
hardy, (robust, strong), fortika, hardita
hare, leporo; **hare's-ear,** (bot), bupleŭro; **hare's-tail(s),** (*Eriophorum*),
eriforo
harem, haremo

haricot, (bean), fazeolo
hari-kari, [see "hara-kiri"]
hark, (listen), aŭskulti [tr]; **hark back**, reveni [int]
harlequin, arlekeno
harlot, prostituitino, putino
harm, (hurt, damage), difekti [tr], damaĝi [tr]; ~(iĝ)o, damaĝo; (hinder, work against), noci [tr], malhelpi [tr]; (wrong), malutilo; malutili [int] (e.g.: *there's no harm in that:* tio neniel malutilas); **harmful**, noca, danĝera, malutila (e.g.: *harmful drug:* noca toksiko†); **harmless**, sendanĝera; **come to harm**, trafi malfeliĉon
harmonic, (multiple frequency of base tone), harmono; (harmonious), harmonia; **harmonics**, harmoniko
harmonica, harmoniko, buŝ~o; **glass harmonica**, glas~o
harmonium, harmoniumo
harmony, (mus etc.), harmonio; (agreement), akordo; **harmonious**, ~a; akorda; **harmonize**, ~i [int]; ~igi; akordi [int]; akordigi; (be appropriate), konveni [int]; **inharmonious**, mal~a; malakorda
harness, (horse etc.), jungi [tr]; ~ilaro; (for loom), harneso
Harold, Haroldo
harp, harpo; ~i [int]; **harper**, **harpist**, ~isto; **harp on**, gurdi [tr], ripetaĉi [tr], ĝiskaĉe remaĉi [tr]; **aeolian harp**, eol~o
Harpalus, harpalo
Harpia harpyja, harpio
harpoon, harpuno; ~i [tr]
harpsichord, klaviceno
harpy, (gen), harpio
Harpy, (myth), Harpio
harquebus, arkebuzo
harridan, megero
harrier, (hawk), cirkuo
harrow, erpi [tr]; ~iĝi; ~ilo; **harrowing**, hirtiga, korŝira, terura
harry, (harass), ĉagren(ad)i [tr], turment(ad)i [tr]; (pillage), rab(ad)i [tr]
Hasid, [see "Chasid"]
harsh, (opp "mild"), malmilda, severa, rigora, bruska akra; (raw, crude), kruda; (raucous), raŭka, raspa; (w/o compassion), senkompata, maldorlot(em)a

hart, vircervo; **hart's-tongue**, (*Phyllitis*), skolopendrio
harum-scarum, malzorgema
Harun Al-Rashid, Harun-al-Raŝido
haruspex, haruspekso
harvest, rikolti [tr]; ~o; ~ado; ~aĵo; **harvestman**, (insect), falangio
Harz (Mountains), Harco
has, [see "have"]; **has-been**, eksulo
Hasdrubal, Hasdrubalo
hash, (food), haketaĵo; (bungle), fuŝi [tr]; fuŝo; (hashish), haŝiŝo; **hash out**, **hash over**, diskutadi [tr]; **make hash of**, fuŝi [tr]
hashish, haŝiŝo
Hasid, [see "Chasid"]
hasp, klinko
hassle, (quarrel), kvereli [int]; ~o; (bother, harrass), ĉagren(ad)i [tr], ĝen(ad)i [tr]; ĉagreno
hassock, piedkuseno
haste, hasto; **hasten**, ~i [int]; ~igi; **hasty**, ~a; (rash), tro~a, senpripensa, senkonsidera, maldiskreta, tro hasta
hat, ĉapelo; **hatter**, ~isto; **hat-check person**, ~deponisto; **cocked hat**, trikorna ~o; **top-hat**, cilindra ~o; **keep under one's hat**, konservi [tr] sekreta; **throw one's hat in the ring**, kandidatiĝi, anonci sian kandidatecon
hatch, (re egg, lit or fig), elkovi [tr]; ~iĝi; (in ship deck), luko; (lines), haĉi [tr]; haĉo; (floodgate), kluzpordo; **hatchback**, (rear door, as of car), luko; (rear of car), lukdorso; (the car), lukdorsa aŭto [cp "wagon: station wagon","van"]; **hatchery**, (poultry), ~ejo; (fish), frajejo; **hatchway**, luko
hatchet, hakileto
hate, malami [tr]; ~o; **hateful**, ~ema; ~inda; **hatred**, ~o
hauberk, maŝkuto [cp "habergeon"]
haughty, aroganta, fieraĉa, orgojlaĉa
haul, (pull, gen), tiri [tr]; ~iĝi; ~o; (w effort), haŭli [tr]; (drag, tow), treni [tr]; (ship freight), ekspedi [tr], transporti [tr]; (catch, as fish), kaptaĵo; **haul up**, (naut), brajli [tr]; **overhaul**, revizii [tr]; revizio
haunch, (anat), kokso; (as food), ~aĵo
haunt, (frequent), frekventi [tr]; ~ejo; (as ghost), hanti [tr]; fantomi [int];

(ghost), fantomo
hausen, huzo
Hausmannite, Haŭsmanito
Havana, Havano
have, (possess, gen), havi [tr]; (as auxiliary verb), esti [int] (e.g.: *it has been raining:* estas pluvinte) [note: usually expressed as simple verb tense unless necessary to show continued action (e.g.: *I have waited for you two hours:* mi atendis vin du horojn; *have you seen that movie?:* ĉu vi vidis tiun filmon?)]; (to emphasize following verb), ja [see "do"]; (trick), trompi [tr] (e.g.: *I've been had!:* mi estas trompita!); (give birth), naski [tr] (e.g.: *she had a boy:* ŝi naskis knabon); (tolerate), toleri [tr] (e.g.: *I won't have that kind of behavior!:* mi ne toleros tian konduton!); **have someone do something**, igi iun fari ion (e.g.: *I'll have her send a report:* mi igos ŝin sendi raporton); **have (something, somebody) -ed**, (w transitive verb), –igi [sfx on verb] (e.g.: *have the radio repaired:* riparigi la radiofonon; *have him fired:* maldungigi lin); **having –ed**, –inte [sfx] (e.g.: *having finished the book, I went to bed:* fininte la libron, mi enlitiĝis); **have at**, ataki [tr]; **have got**, ~i [see under "get"]; **have had it**, ne plu povi elteni [tr]; **have it out with**, findecidi (ĝin, la aferon) kun; **have on**, (be wearing), porti [tr]; **have to**, (must), devi [tr] (e.g.: *we have to go now:* ni devas iri nun); **have to do with**, (have as theme, deal w, relate to), temi [int] pri; **the haves and the have-nots**, la ~uloj kaj la sen~uloj; **let one have it**, (reproach), riproĉegi [tr]; (hit, beat), bategi [tr]
haven, haveno, azilo, rifuĝejo
haversack, tornistro
havoc, detruego, ruinigo; **play havoc with**, ĥaosigi
Havre, Havro
haw, (crataegus), kratago; **black haw**, (*Viburnum*), viburno
Hawaii, (island), Havajo; (state), ~io
hawfinch, kokotraŭsto
hawk, (any bird of *Falconiformes*), falko; (peddle), kolporti [tr]; (advertise

by shouting), prikrii [tr]; (cough), tusi [int]; **hawkbit**, (bot), leontodono; **hawkmoth**, sfingo; **hawk's-beard**, (bot), krepido; **hawkweed**, hieracio; **Cooper's hawk**, **sharp-shinned hawk**, akcipitro; **sparrow hawk**, nizo
hawse, (area of ship), klus/ejo; (hawsehole), ~o; **hawser**, haŭsero; **hawsehole**, ~o
hawthorn, kratago
hay, fojno; **haystack**, ~amaso; **haywire**, ĥaosa, konfuza, freneza
hazard, (danger), danĝero; (risk), riski [tr]; risko; [not "hazard–"]; **hazardous**, ~a, riskoplena
haze, (light fog), brumo, nebuleto; (oth un clarity, as from smoke, smog), malklarajeto, fumajeto, brumo; (humiliate), ĉikani [tr]; **hazy**, ~a; malklareta, fumeta
hazel, avel/arbo; (color), ~kolora; **hazelnut**, ~o; **witch hazel**, hamamelido
he, li; (pfx to indicate male gender), vir– (e.g.: *he-dog:* virhundo); **heman**, virviro
head, (anat; any similar object, e.g. on tape recorder), kapo; (lead), estri [tr]; estro; (main, chief), ĉefa, ĉef– [pfx] (e.g.: *head waiter:* ĉefkelnero); (top), supro; supra; (front), antaŭo; antaŭa; (foam), ŝaŭmo; (of hammer), martel~o; (promontory, headland), promontoro; (source, as of river), fonto; (pressure, as of steam, water), prem(ŝarg)o, premalteco; (direct), direkti [tr]; direktiĝi, direkti sin (e.g.: *head the car east:* direkti la aŭton orienten; *head home:* direkti sin hejmen); **header**, (top of document), ~strio; **heading**, (in newspaper, magazine, etc.), titolo, rubriko; (in dictionary etc.), ~vorto; **heads**, face of coin etc.), aversot; **heady**, (impetuous), impeta; (intoxicating), ebriiga; **headache**, ~doloro; **I have a headache**, mi havas ~doloron, mia ~o (min) doloras; **headband**, diademo; **headboard**, ~tabulo; **headdress**, ~ornamo; **head-first**, ~antaŭe; **head for**, direkti sin al, direktiĝi al; **headgear**, (gen), ~vesto(j); **headland**, promontoro, kabo; **headlight**, lum–jetilo;

headline, kaplinio, titolo, frap–vorto; **banner headline**, tutpaĝa titolo; **headlong**, impeta; **headmaster** **(headmistress)**, lernejestr(in)o; **head off**, forturni [tr], deturni [tr], antaŭeviti [tr]; **head-on**, fronta; fronte; **headphone**, ~aŭdilo; **headquarters**, stabejo, estrejo; **headrest**, ~apogilo; **headroom**, ~spaco; **headset**, ~aŭdilo; **headstone**, tomboŝtono; **headstrong**, obstina; **heads up!**, atentu!; **headwaters**, fontoj; **headway**, (progress), progreso; **make headway**, progresi [int]; **behead**, sen~igi; **head and shoulders above**, tre supera al; **head of the household**, domestro, dommastro [cp "house: househusband"]; **blockhead**, stultulo, vent~ulo, azeno; **bubble-headed**, vent~a; **forehead**, frunto; **hot–head**, flamiĝulo, ekkoleremulo; **hot-head-ed**, ekkolerema, koleriĝema, flamiĝema; **overhead**, (above), supera; supere; (in air), aera, en la ĉielo; (bsns cost), ĝeneralaj kostoj; **pig-headed**, mule-headed, obstinaĉa; **towhead**, stuphara; stupharulo; **keep one's head**, konservi sian trankvilon, resti trankvila; **lose one's head**, perdi sian trankvilon, maltrankviliĝi; **(fall)** **head over heels**, (fali) trans~iĝe; **be able to make neither heads nor tails of**, tute ne kompreni [tr], neniom kompreni; **come to a head**, (re crisis), atingi krizon, kriziĝi; (re boil), maturiĝi; **come to one's head**, veni en ies (sian) ~on, en~iĝi; **go to one's head**, (make conceited), orgojligi iun, iu orgojliĝi pro (e.g.: *his success went to his head:* lia sukceso orgojligis lin [or] li orgojliĝis pro sia sukceso); (make drunk), ebriigi; **get it into one's head**, konvinki iun (sin); konvinkiĝi; **be over one's head**, esti preter ies (sia) kompetenteco (kompreno, kapablo); **go over one's head**, (to higher authority), pretersalti iun; **hold one's head high**, fiere konduti [int], resti fiera
heal, resan/igi; ~iĝi [cp "cure"]; **healer**, (spiritual or oth), ~igisto; **healing**, ~igo

health, (healthy state), sano, bonfarto; (toast), tosto; **healthy**, ~a; **healthful**, ~iga; **health worker**, ~isto [cp "heal: healer"]; **in good (poor) health**, en (mal)bona ~stato; **to your health!**, je via ~o!; **drink a health to**, tosti [tr]
heap, amaso; ~igi; ~iĝi
hear, (w ears), aŭdi [tr]; (try case in court etc.), juĝi [tr] **hearing**, (sense), ~ado; (formal meeting), aŭdienco; **hearing aid**, fonoforo; **hearsay**, onidiro; onidira; **hear tell of**, ~i pri; **hear one out**, finaŭskulti iun; **overhear**, sub~i [tr]; **hard of hearing**, malbon~a, duonsurda; **unheard-of**, neniam ~ita; **hear, hear!**, hura!; brave!
hearken, aŭskulti [tr]
hearse, ĉerkveturilo
heart, (anat; similar–shaped object or figure; re feelings etc. associated w heart), koro [cp "cardiac"]; (courage), kuraĝo; (compassion), kompato; (cards), kero; **hearten**, kuraĝigi; **dishearten**, senkuraĝigi, malkuraĝigi; **be(come) (dis)heartened**, (mal)kuraĝiĝi; **hearty**, (cordial), (el)~a; (ebullient), verva, entuziasma; **heartache**, malĝojo, ~pezo; **heartbeat**, ~bato; **heartbreak**, ~ŝiro, ~krevo; **heartbreaking**, ~ŝira, ~kreviga; **break one's heart**, krevigi ies ~on; **my heart broke**, mia ~o krevis; **heartburn**, pirozo; **heart-felt**, el~a; **heartsease**, (bot), violego, trikoloreto; **heart-to-heart**, ~-al-~a; **by heart**, parkere; **learn by heart**, parkerigi, lerni [tr] parkere; **down-hearted**, malgaja, pez~a; **half-hearted**, sentuziasma; **light-hearted**, gaja, leĝer~a; **sweetheart**, dolĉul(in)o, karul(in)o, amat(in)o; **from the bottom of one's heart**, tut~e; **put one's heart into (it, something)**, entuziasme ~i; havi entuziasmon; **lose heart**, senkuraĝiĝi, malkuraĝiĝi; **eat one's heart out**, konsumiĝi de envio; **to one's heart's content**, ĉiom kiom oni deziras; **take heart**, kuraĝiĝi; **take to heart**, serioze akcepti [tr]; **lose one's heart to**, enamiĝi al; **not have the heart to**, ne havi la kuraĝon por

hearth, fajrejo [cp "fire: ~place"]
heat, (hotness), varmo; ~igi; ~iĝi;
(warm a room etc., as by furnace,
stove), hejti [tr]; (sex drive), seksardo;
(any ardor, strong feeling), ardo; (fertile period), oestro; (preliminary race),
antaŭkonkurso; **heater**, hejtilo; **immersion heater**, merghejtilo; **super-
heat**, (phys), super~igi; **dead heat**,
(race), egalvenko; **in heat**, en oestro,
seksarda
heath, (plant: *Erica*), eriko; (*Calluna*),
kaluno; (moor), ~ejo
heathen, pagano; ~a
heather, (bot: *Erica*), eriko; (*Calluna*),
kaluno
heave, (pull), haŭli [tr], tiregi [tr]; ~o,
tirego; (push), puŝ(eg)i [tr]; puŝ(eg)o;
(vomit), vomi [tr]; vomo; **heave ho!**,
ruk!, ho ruk!; **heave in sight**, ekaperi
[int]; **heave to**, kapeigi (la ŝipon),
kapei [int]; **dry heave**, senprodukte
vomi; senprodukta vomo; **upheaval**,
renversiĝo, revolucio, revolucia ŝanĝo
heaven, ĉielo; **heavenly**, ~a; **(good)
heavens!**, je Dio!, je l' ~o!; **for heav-
en's sake!**, pro l' ~o!
heavy, (of great weight, import, etc.,
gen), peza; (massive), masa, masiva;
(intense), forta (e.g.: *heavy rain:* forta
pluvo); (ungentle, rough), maldelikata, malmilda; **heavy-duty**, fortika,
~labora; **heavy-footed**, ~paŝa;
heavy-handed, ~mana; **heavy-
hearted**, ~kora; **heavyweight**,
grand~a; grand~ulo; **top-heavy**, su-
per~a
Hebe, (myth), Heba
Hebe, (bot: *Veronica*), veroniko
hebephrenia, hebefrenio
hebetate, hebeta; **hebetude**, ~eco
Hebrew, Hebreo; ~a; **Hebraic**, ~a;
~eca; **Hebrews**, (Bib), ~oj
Hebrides, Hebridoj; **New Hebrides**,
Nov-~oj [cp "Vanuatu"]
Hecate, Hekata
hecatomb, hekatombo
heckle, interkrii [int]; **heckler**, ~anto
hectare, hektaro
hectic, (rushed, excited), ekscitita, furioza, hasta, konfuza; (med), hektika
hect(o)–, (pfx), hekt(o)–

hectograph, hektografo
hector, (bully), tirani [tr]
Hector, (man's name), Hektoro
Hecuba, Hekuba
Hedera, hedero
hedge, row of shrubs), heĝo; (hide,
shield self), sin ŝirmi, rifuĝi [int];
(protection, shield), ŝirm(il)o; **hedge-
hog**, erinaco
Hedjaz, Heĝazo
hedonism, hedonismo; **hedonist**, ~a;
hedonisto
–hedr/on, (sfx), –edro; **–hedral**, ~a
Hedwig, Hedviga
Hedysarum, hedisaro
heed, atenti [tr]; ~o
hee-haw, (donkey sound), iai [int]; (onom), ia! ia!
heel, (anat), kalkano; (shoe), ~umo;
~umi [tr]; (lean, re ship), klini [tr];
kliniĝi; **heel-bone**, kalkaneo; **high-
heeled**, (shoe), pik~uma; **Achilles's
heel**, vundebla loko; **cool one's
heels**, devige atendadi [tr]; **cool your
heels!**, paciencu!; **take to one's
heels**, forkuri [int], (for)fuĝi [int];
well-heeled, monhava; **down at the
heels**, kaduka, ĉifona
heft, (weight), pezo; (lift), levi [tr];
hefty, ~a; (powerful), forta, impona
Hegel, Hegelo; **Hegelian**, ~a; ~ano;
Hegelianism, ~ismo
hegemony, hegemonio
hegira, heĝiro
heifer, guno
height, (vertical dimension; high state,
gen), alt/eco; ~aĵo; (top), supro; (zenith, apex), zenito; **heighten**, (raise),
levi [tr], ~igi; (emphasize), emfazi
[tr], elstarigi, substreki [tr]
Heilungkiang, Hejlonggiang
heinous, abomena, fiega, horora
heir, hered/into; ~anto; ~onto; **heir-
loom**, (familia) ~aĵo; **heir apparent**,
rekta ~onto; **heir presumptive**, kondiĉa ~onto
Hejaz, Heĝazo
hejira, heĝiro
Hekate, Hekata
Hekla, Mount, Monto Hekla
Helen, Helena; **Saint Helen**, (island),
Sankta-~o

Helgoland, Helgolando
Helianthemum, heliantemo
Helianthus, helianto, sunfloro; Helianthus tuberosus, tubera ~o, terpiro
Helichrysum, helikrizo
Helicon, Helikono
helicopter, helikoptero
Heligoland, Helgolando
helio–, (pfx), helio–
heliocentric, heliocentra
heliograph, heliografo;   heliography, ~io
heliogravure, heliogravuro
Heliopolis, Heliopolo
helioscope, helioskopo
heliostat, heliostato
heliotrope, heliotropo
heliotropism, heliotropismo; heliotropic, ~a
Heliotropium, heliotropo
heliport, helikopter/haveno, ~a haveno
helium, heliumo
helix, (any spiral), helico; (anat), helikso; helical, ~a; helicoid, ~a; (geom), helicoido
Helix, (zool), heliko
hell, infero; hellish, ~a; raise hell, ~umi [int]; (a) hell of a, (extremely), ja –ega (e.g.: campers use a hell of a lot of gas: kampadaŭtoj uzas ja multege da benzino); (hellish), ~a (e.g.: what a hell of a situation!: kia ~a situacio!); what the hell (is that?), kio diable (estas tio)?; (just) for the hell of it, pro ĝia amuzo, (nur) por amuzo; hell-bent for leather, impetege, furiozege
Hellas, Helaso [cp "Greece"]
hellebore, (Helleborus), heleboro; (Veratrum), veratro; black hellebore, nigra ~o, Kristo-rozo; white hellebore, blanka ~o
Helleborus, heleboro; Helleborus niger, nigra ~o, Kristo-rozo
Hellene, Heleno; Hellenic, ~a; Hellenism, ~ismo; ~eco; Hellenist, ~isma; ~isto; Hellenistic, ~eca; Hellenize, ~igi
heller, (coin), helero
Hellespont, Helesponto
hello, (greeting), saluton!; (phone greeting), lo!, ha lo!; (expression of sur-

prise), aha!; say hello to, ~i [tr]; wave hello to, man~i [tr]
helm, (helm wheel on ship, lit or fig), rudr/orado; (tiller pole), ~ilo [not "~ostango"; see "rudder"]; (steer at helm), ~i [tr]; (helmet), helmo
Helma, Helma
helmet, kasko; crash helmet, kraŝ~o; pith helmet, sun~o
helminth, helminto
Helodea, helodeo; Helodea canadensis, akvopesto
Heloise, Heloiza
helot, heloto
help, (assist, gen), helpi [tr]; ~o; (be useful), utili [int] (e.g.: money won't help with that problem: mono ne utilos por tiu problemo); (serve), servi [tr] (e.g.: help yourself: servu vin mem); (servants), servistaro; helpful, ~a; ~ema; utila; helping, (serving of food at meal), servo (e.g.: a large helping, second helping: granda, dua servo); helpless, sen~a; self-help, sin~o; sin~a; cannot help (but), ne povi ne (e.g.: I cannot help but laugh: mi ne povas ne ridi); cannot help it, ne povi alie (e.g.: I shouldn't laugh, but I can't help it: mi ne devus ridi, sed mi ne povas alie); cannot be helped, estas neevitebla; with the help of, ~e de
Helsingør, Elsinoro
Helsinki, Helsinki
helter-skelter, iele   trapele,   pelmele; pelmelo
Helvella, helvelo
Helvetia, Helvet/io;   Helvetian,   ~o; ~a; ~ia; Helvetii, ~oj
hem, (of garment), orlo; ~i [tr]; hem and haw, balbuti [int], ŝanceliĝi
hematemesis, hatematemezo
hematin, hematino
hematite, hematito
hemat(o)–, (pfx), hemat(o)– [see also "hem(o)–"]
hematogenous, hemato/genea;   hematogenesis, ~genezo
hematology, hematologio
hematoma, hematomo
hematosis, (formation), hemat/ogenezo; (aeration), ~ozo

hematozoon, hematozoo
hematuria, hematurio
heme, hemo
hemi–, (pfx), hemi–
hemianopia, hemianopsia, hemianopsio; **binasal hemianopia**, binaza ~o; **bitemporal hemianopia**, bitempia ~o; **lateral hemianopia**, samflanka ~o
hemicellulose, hemicelulozo
hemicrania, hemikranio
hemihedron, hemiedro; **hemihedral**, ~a
hemiplegia, hemiplegio; **hemiplegic**, ~a
Hemiptera, hemipteroj
hemisphere, (gen), hemisfero
hemistitch, hemistiko
hemlock, (*Conium*), konio; (*Cicuta*), cikuto; **poison hemlock**, (*Conium maculata*), makula ~o; **water hemlock**, cikuto
hem(o)–, (pfx: blood), hemat(o)– [note: sometimes absorbed into Esperanto root as "hemo–"; check separate entries]
hemodialysis, hematodializo
hemoglobin, hemoglobino
hemolysin, hemolizino
hemolysis, hematolizo, hemolizo
hemophilia, hemofilio; **hemophiliac**, ~a; ~ulo
hemopoiesis, hematiopoezo
hemoptysis, hemoptizo
hemorrhage, hemoragio; ~i [int]
hemorrhoid, hemoroido
hemostasis, hemostazo
hemostat, angiopinĉilo
hemp, kanabo; **Bengal hemp, Bombay hemp, Indian hemp**, (*Apocynum*), apocino; (*Crotalaria*), krotalario; **New Zealand hemp**, (*Phormium*), formio
hen, kokino; **henbane**, hiskiamo; **henpecked**, inregata; **(rock) Cornish hen**, Kornvala ~o; **hazel hen**, tetrao, bonazio; **marsh hen, swamp hen, water hen, moor hen**, galinolo, akvokoko
henbit, lamio
hence, (therefore), tial, sekve; (from now), de nun; (interj), for!; **hence-**

forth, de nun
henchman, gangstero
Hendyadis, hendiadino
henna, (dye), henao; (bush), ~a arbedo
Henrietta, Henrieta
henry, (elec), henro; **abhenry**, ab~o; **stathenry**, stat~o
Henry, (man's name), Henriko
heparin, heparino
hepatic, hepata
Hepatica, hepatiko
hepatitis, hepatito
Hephaestus, Hephaistos, Hefesto
hepta–, (pfx), hept(o)–, sep–
heptagon, heptagono, sepangulo
heptahedron, sepedro
heptane, heptano
hept(o)–, (pfx), hept(o)–
heptode, heptodo
heptose, heptozo
her, ŝi(n); ŝia (e.g.: *she saw her:* ŝi vidis ŝin; *she saw her* [someone else's] *book:* ŝi vidis ŝian libron); (reflexive), si(n); sia (e.g.: *she found her* [own] *book:* ŝi trovis sian libron); **herself**, [see "self"]; **her –ing (something, someone)**, (fact that she –ed, –s, etc.), ŝia –o (de io, iu) (e.g.: *I viewed her doing the job as a favor:* mi konsideris ŝian faron de la tasko kiel favoron); **of her –ing**, (that she –ed, –s, etc.), ke ŝi –is (–as, etc.) (e.g.: *there is no indication of her having gone:* estas neniu indiko ke ŝi iris); **of her being –ed**, ke ŝi estis (–as, etc.) –ita, ke oni –is (–as, etc.) ŝin (e.g.: *we have proof of her being murdered:* ni havas pruvon ke ŝi estis murdita [or] ke oni murdis ŝin)
Hera, Hera
Heracles, Heraklo
Heracleum, herakleo
Heraclitus, Heraklito
herald, heroldo; ~i [tr]; **heraldry**, heraldiko; **heraldric**, heraldika
herb, (med), drogherbo; (spice), aromherbo; **herbal**, herba; **herbalist**, ~isto; **herbarium**, herbario; **herbicide**, herbicido; **herbivorous**, herbovora; **herbivore**, herbovorulo; **herb Bennett**, geumo; **herb Christopher**, ekteo, Kristoforherbo; **herb Gerard**,

egopodio; **fuller's herb**, saponario;
willow herb, epilobio
Herbert, Herberto
Hercegovina, Hercegovino
Herculaneum, Herkulano
Hercules, Herkulo; **Herculean**, ~a
herd, (gen), grego; ~igi; ~iĝi; ~a; (of
deer etc.), herdo; **herdsman**, ~isto
here, (at this place), ĉi tie, tie ĉi; (to this
place), ĉi tien, tien ĉi; (behold, look),
jen (e.g.: *here is the house:* jen la domo [or] jen estas la domo; *here lies
John Smith:* jen kuŝas John Smith;
here, I'll do that: jen, mi faros tion;
here! [giving something to someone]:
jen!); **hereabouts**, ĉi-proksime, ie ĉi
tie; **hereafter**, estonte, ekde nun; estonteco; **hereby**, ĉi-pere; **hereof**, de
tio ĉi; **hereto**, al tio ĉi; **heretofore**,
ĝisnuna, jama; ĝis nun, jam; **hereun-
der**, ĉi-sube, sube; **herewith**, (along
w), ĉi-kune; (hereby), ĉi-pere; **here
and there**, (scattered), tie kaj tie, diversloke, dise; **neither here nor
there**, (all the same, doesn't matter),
tute egale
Here, (myth), Hera
heredity, hered/eco; **hereditary**, ~a
heresy, herezo; **heretic**, ~ulo; **hereti-
cal**, ~a
heritable, (can be inherited), hered/eb-
la; (may inherit), ~iva
heritage, heredaĵo
herm(a), hermo
Herman, Hermano
hermaphrodite, hermafrodita;　　~aĵo;
~ulo
Hermaphroditus, Hermafrodito
hermeneutic, hermeneŭtika;　　herme-
neutics, ~o
Hermes, Hemeso, Hermo
hermetic, (re seal), hermetika; **hermetically seal**, ~igi; **hermetically
sealed**, ~a; **hermetic seal**, ~aĵo
Hermetic, (of Hermes), Hermesa
Herminia, herminio
Hermione, Hermiona
hermit, ermito; **hermitage**, ~ejo
hernia, hernio; **herniate**, ~igi; ~iĝi
Herniaria, herniario
hero, heroo; **heroine**, ~ino; **heroic**, ~a;
heroic deed, ~aĵo

Herod, Herodo; **Herod the Great**, ~o
la Granda
Herodias, Herodiasa
Herodotus, Herodoto
heroin, heroino
heron, ardeo; **heron's-bill**, (bot), erodio
herpes, herpeto; **herpes zoster**, zostero
Herpestes, mungo
herpetology, serpentolog/io; **herpetol-
ogist**, ~o
herring, haringo; **red herring**, (diversion), erarigilo
hertz, herco; **kilohertz**, kilo~o(j); **megahertz**, mega~o(j); **gigahertz**, gi-
ga~o(j)
Herzegovina, Hercegovino
Hesiod, Heziodo
hesitate, heziti [int]; **hesitant**, ~(em)a;
hesitancy, ~(em)o
Hesperia, Hesperio
Hesperis, hesperido
Hesse, Hes/io; **Hessian**, ~o; ~a; ~ia
hetaera, hetajro
heter(o)-, (pfx), heter(o)-
heterocyclic, heterocikla
heterodox, heterodoksa;　　**heterodoxy**,
~eco
heterodyne, heterodino; ~a; ~igi; **superheterodyne**, super~o
heterogeneous, heterogena
heteronomous, heteronomia; **heteron-
omy**, ~o
heteropolar, heteropolara
heteropolyacid, heteropoliacido
Heteroptera, cimoj
heterosexual, aliseksema; ~ulo; **het-
erosexism**, ~ismo
heterosome, heterosomo†
heterotrophic, heterotrofa
heterozygote, heterozigoto; **heterozy-
gosis**, ~eco
hetman, hetmano
Hetty, Henjo
heuristic, heŭristika; **heuristics**, ~o
hew, (chop, gen), haki [tr]; (carve, fashion), tajli [tr]
hex, (cast spell), sorĉi [tr]; ~o; (hexadecimal), deksesaria†
hexa-, (pfx), ses- [note: sometimes absorbed into Esperanto root as "hek-
sa-"; see separate entries]
Hexacorallia, seskoraluloj

hexadecimal, deksesaria†
hexagon, heksagono, sesangulo
hexagram, sespinta stelo
hexahedron, heksaedro, sesedro
hexameter, heksametro
hexane, heksano
hexenbesen, fefasko
hexitol, heksitolo
hexode, heksodo
hexonate, heksonato
hexose, heksozo
hey, (interj), he!, ej!, hej!
heyday, florado, apogeo
Hezekiah, Ĥizkija
hi, (interj), saluton!, hej! [see "hello",
   "hey"]
hiatus, (any gap), breĉo; (hole), truo;
   (phon), hiato
hibachi, hibaĉo
hibernate, vintrodormi [int]; **hiberna-**
   tion, ~(ad)o
Hibernia, Hibernio
hibiscus, Hibiscus, hibisko
hiccup, hiccough, singulti [int]; ~o
hickory, (tree), hikorio; (wood), ~a ligno
hidalgo, hidalgo
hide, (conceal), kaŝi [tr]; ~i sin, ~iĝi;
   (of animal), felo; (land measure), [no
   exact equivalent; if desired to use obsolete term, as for lit effect, use "hu-
   bo" (about 10 to 15 hectares)]; **hide-**
   and-seek, ~ludo; **hideaway**, ~ejo;
   hidebound, (narrow-minded), mal-
   larĝanima, etanima; **rawhide**, kruda
   ledo
hideous, malbelega, terura; (poet), hida
Hieracium, hieracio
hierarchy, hierarkio; **hierarchical**, ~a
hieratic, hieratika
hierodule, hierodul(in)o
hieroglyph, hieroglifo; **hieroglyphic**,
   ~a; ~o; **hieroglyphs**, ~o(j)
Hieronymus, Hieronimo
hierophant, hierofanto
higgle, marĉandi [int]
higgledy-piggledy, senorda, ĥaosa,
   konfuza
high, (lofty; tall; advanced; more; etc.),
   alta; ~e(n); (chief; primary), ĉefa
   (e.g.: *high priest:* ĉefpastro); (re mus
   pitch), akuta; (loud), laŭta; (intoxicat-

ed, gen), ebria; (stale, re meat etc.),
malfreŝa; (maximum), maksimumo;
maksimuma; (zenith), zenito; **higher**,
(upper, superior), supera (e.g.: *higher
math:* supera matematiko); **highball**,
koktelo; **highbrow**, intelekt(aĉ)a; in-
telektul(aĉ)o; **highfalutin(g)**, **high-
flown**, (flowery, re speech etc.), bombasta, ~efluga; **highland**, montaro,
~aĵo, ~aĵejo; montara; **highlight**, emfazi [tr], akcenti [tr], substreki [tr];
(main, basic part), kulmino, zenito,
ĉefparto; (summary), resumi [tr]; resumo; **highness**, (term of address for
royalty), moŝto (e.g.: *your royal highness:* via reĝa moŝto); **high point**,
(acme, zenith), zenito; **high-rise**,
(building), domturo; **hightail**, forhasti
[int], forkuri [int]; **high and mighty**,
aroganta (kaj fieranta); **leave high
and dry**, lasi senhelpa
highway, ŝoseo; **highwayman**, vojrab-
isto; **superhighway**, aŭtovojo, ekspresa ~o, ekspresvojo; **superhighway**
~o, ekspresvojo; **superhighway**,
datuma ekspresvojo
hijack, pirati [tr, int]; **hijacker**, ~o
hike, (walk), marŝadi [int]; ~o; (increase), altigi; altigo; **hitchhike**, [see
under "hitch"]
hilarious, amuzega, gajega
Hilary, Hilario
Hilda, Hilda
hill, mont/eto, holmo†; **hilly**, malebena,
~eta; **hillbilly**, ~arano; ~arana; **hill-
ock**, teramaso, altaĵeto; **downhill**, **uphill**, [see under "up"]; **the Hill**, (Am),
Kongreso
Hillel, Hilelo; **Hillelism, school of Hillel**, ~ismo
hilt, manŝirmilo; **(up) to the hilt**, ĝis-
lime, ĝisrande
hilum, hilumo
him, li(n); si(n) [see "her"]
Himalayas, Himalaya Mountains, Hi-
malajo, Montaro ~a
himation, himatio
hin, hino
hinayana, hinajano
hind, (rear), malantaŭa, posta; (doe),
cervino; **hindmost**, lasta, plej ~a;
hindquarter(s), postaĵo; **hindsight**,
postvidado

hinder, malhelpi [tr]; hindrance, ~o
Hindi, Hindia
Hindu, Hindoo, Hinduo; ~a; Hinduism, ~ismo; Hindu Kush, Hindukuŝo; Hindustan, Hindustano; Hindustani, Hindustana; Hindustanano
hinge, (gen), ĉarniro; ~i [tr]; ~iĝi [cp "joint"]; (bookbinding), ongleto; hinge on, dependi de, pivoti sur, ~iĝi sur
hinny, (animal), hino; (whinny), heni [int]; heno
hint, aludi [tr], sugesti [tr] [cp "clue"]; ~o, sugesto
hinterland, landinterno
hip, (anat), kokso; hip measurement, (as for clothes), pugmezuro; rose hip, rozbero
hippie, hipio†; ~a
Hippocamelus, guemulo
Hippocampus, (gen), hipokampo
Hippocrates, Hipokrato; Hippocratic, ~a
Hippocrene, Hipokreno
hippodrome, hipodromo
Hippoglossus, hipogloso
hippogriff, hippogryph, hipogrifo
Hippolais, hipolao
Hippolytus, Hipolito
Hippomenes, Hipomeno
hippophagy, hipofagio; hippophagous, ~a
hippopotamus, Hippopotamus, hipopotamo
hippurate, hipur/ato; hippuric acid, ~a acido
Hiram, Ĥiram
hire, (employ person), dungi [tr]; (Br: rent object, place), lui [tr] [see "rent"]; for hire, ~ebla; (Br), luebla; hire (oneself) out, sin ~igi; hireling, ~ito, soldulo
Hirneola, aŭrikulario
Hiroshima, Hiroŝimo
hirsute, hara, vila
Hirudo, hirudo
Hirundo, hirundo; Hirundo rustica, dom~o; Hirundinidae, ~edoj
his, lia; sia [see "her"]
Hispanic, Hispana; ~devena; ~(deven-int)o

Hispaniola, Dominikinsulo
hiss, sibli [int]; ~(ad)o; (onom), sss!
histamine, histamino; antihistamine, anti~o
histogenesis, histogenezo
histogram, blok/grafikaĵo, ~diagramo
histology, histolog/io; histologist, ~o
histone, histono
historiography, historiograf/io; historiographer, ~o
history, (gen), historio; (med; life history, gen), antecedentoj; historian, ~isto; historic(al), ~a; prehistoric, pra~a; prehistoric times, pra~o; natural history, natur~o
histrionic, (gen), drameca; (bad, crude, overacted), histrioneca; histrionics, ~o; histrionado
hit, (come upon, reach, bump, make goal, affect, gen), trafi [tr]; ~o; (strike, knock), frapi [tr]; frapo; (success), sukceso, furoro; hit it off, akordiĝi, amikiĝi; hit on, (guess right), diveni [tr]; hit-and-run, kolizifuĝa; hit-and-run driver, kolizifuĝinto; hit-or-miss, hazarda; hazarde, ~e-mal~e
hitch, (hook), kroĉi [tr]; ~iĝi; ~o; ~ilo; (trailer, plow, etc.), jungi [tr]; jungiĝi; jungilo; (limp), lami [int]; lamo; (problem), problemo, obstaklo, kontraŭaĵo; hitchhike, petveturi [int]; hitchhiker, petveturanto; hitch a ride, peti veturon
hither, ĉi tien, tien ĉi; hitherto, ĝis nun [adv]; ĝisnuna
Hitler, Hitlero; Hitlerism, ~ismo; Hitlerite, ~a; ~ano
Hittite, Hitito; ~a
hive, (gen), abel/ujo; (beekeeper's, w trays), ~kesto; hives, (med), urtikario
hm, hmm, (interj), hm!
ho, (interj), ho!
hoard, hamstri [tr], akapari [tr]; ~aĵo, akaparaĵo; hoarding, (Br: billboard), reklampanelo
hoarfrost, (frost, gen), prujno; (rime on trees etc. from fog), nebul~o
hoarhound, [see "horehound"]
hoarse, raŭka
hoary, (gray-white, as from age), blanka, griz~a, aĝo~a; (old), antikva
hoax, mistifiki [tr]; ~o, ruzo

hob, (in fireplace), kamenbreto
Hobart, Hobarto*
hobble, (limp), lami [int]; ~igi; ~ado; (tie horse's feet), piedkateni [tr]; piedkateno; (hinder, gen), malhelpi [tr]
hobby, (activity), hobio*, ŝatokupo; (zool), subuteo, alaŭdfalko; **hobby-horse,** ludĉevalo; **favorite hobby,** maroto; **as a hobby,** amatore, diletante, ~e
hobnail, plandnajlo; ~izi [tr]
hobo, trampo, vagabondo
Ho Chi Minh City, Ho-Ĉi-Min-Urbo
hock, (pawn), lombardi [tr]; (anat), kalkano; **hockshop,** ~ejo
hockey, hokeo; **hockey stick,** ~ilo; **ice hockey,** glaci~o
hocus-pocus, ĉarlatanaĵo, sorĉgalimatio
hod, morterportilo, brikportilo
hodgepodge, (of things, ideas, etc.), miksamaso; (words), galimatio
hoe, (gen), sarki [tr]; ~ilo; (w solid blade, like pick-ax), hojo; hoji [tr]; **hoedown,** (party), dancfesto; **back hoe,** trentranĉeatoro
hog, (pig, gen), porko; (male), vir~o; (grab, hoard), akapari [tr]; **hogshead,** (approximate unit of measure), okshofto [see § 20]; (barrel), okshofta barelo; **hogwash,** sensencaĵo, blago; **warthog,** fakoĉero
hogan, terdomo
Hogmanay, (Br), silvestra vespero
Hohenstaufen, Hohenstaŭfoj
Hohenzollern, Hohencolernoj
hoi polloi, plebo, popolamaso, popolaĉo
hoist, (lift by rope etc.), hisi [tr]; ~ilo; (mech), ŝarĝlifto
Hokkaido, Hokajdo
Holcus, holko
hold, (have, keep, hang onto), teni [tr]; ~iĝi; ~o (e.g.: *hold a candle:* ~i kandelon; *hold a job:* ~i oficon; *hold one responsible:* ~i iun responsa; *a strong hold on the public:* forta ~o sur la publiko); (support), apogi [tr], sub~i [tr]; (possess), posedi [tr], havi [tr]; (restrain), bridi [tr]; (maintain, continue), daŭri [int]; daŭrigi; (keep, retain), konservi [tr]; (make happen, as meeting, party), okazigi; (reserve), rezervi [tr]; (bind, obligate), devigi; (contain,

gen), en~i [tr]; (have volume of), kubi [int] (e.g.: *the bottle holds 2 liters:* la botelo kubas 2 litrojn); (have opinion), opinii [tr]; (adjudge), juĝi [tr]; (decree), dekreti [tr]; (hold out, not yield), el~i [int]; (be valid, in effect), validi [int]; (halt), halti [int]; haltigi; halt(ig)o, paŭzo; (mus: fermata), fermato; (of ship), holdo; **holder,** (gen), ~ilo; ~into; ~anto; ~onto; (like a socket), –ingo [sfx] (e.g.: *cigarette holder:* cigaredingo); **holdings,** posedaĵoj, havaĵoj; **hold back,** (withhold), re~i [tr]; (restrain), bridi [tr] (sin), de~i [tr] (sin); (reserve), rezervi [tr]; **hold down,** bridi [tr], regi [tr]; (have, as job), ~i; **hold forth,** (talk), paroladi [int], deklami [int]; (propose), prezenti [tr], proponi [tr]; **hold in,** de~i [tr], bridi [tr]; **hold it!,** atendu!; **hold it down,** (moderate), moderigi (ĝin); **hold off,** (keep away), for~i [tr]; (delay), prokrasti [tr]; prokrastiĝi; **hold on,** (hang on), ~adi [tr]; (continue, persist), daŭri [int], persisti [int]; (wait), atendi [int]; **hold onto,** ~adi [tr], kroĉi [tr]; **hold one's own,** konservi sian lokon, ne sinki [int], el~i [int]; **hold out,** (last), daŭri [int]; (against difficulty), el~i [int]; (offer), prezenti [tr]; (put out, as hand etc.), etendi [tr], elmeti [tr]; **holdout,** el~anto; **hold out for,** (demand), persiste postul(ad)i [tr]; **hold oneself out (as, to be),** prezenti sin (kiel, esti); **hold over,** (postpone), prokrasti [tr]; (keep longer, as movie etc.), restigi, (plu)daŭrigi; **holdover,** (person), postrestinto; (thing), postrestaĵo; **hold together,** kun~i [tr]; kun~iĝi; **hold up,** (support), apogi [tr], sub~i [tr]; (show), montri [tr], elmontri [tr]; (delay), prokrasti [tr]; (rob), prirabi [tr]; **holdup,** (stall), paneo, prokrast(iĝ)o; (hindrance), malhelpo, obstaklo; (robbery), rabo; **hold with,** (agree), konsenti kun, akordiĝi kun; **foothold,** piedo~o; **handhold,** man~o; **take hold,** (take effect), ekefiki [int]; **take (grab, lay) hold of,** ekkroĉi [tr], kapti [tr], ekpreni [tr]; **uphold,** (defend), defendi [tr]; (support), apogi [tr], sub-

teni [tr]; **withhold,** (hold back, retain), re~i [tr]; ($ from pay), depagi [tr]; ($ from any account etc.), dekalkuli [tr], elkalkuli [tr]; (refuse), rifuzi [tr]; **withholding,** re~o; depago; dekalkulo, elkalkulo; **no holds barred,** senregula, ĉio permesata
hole, (gen), truo; (hollow), kavo; (dug out), elfosaĵo; (breach, gap), breĉo; (item missing, blank space), mankloko; **hole-puncher,** (to punch tickets, paper for notebook, etc.), ~ilo; **hole up,** sin kaŝi; **armhole,** (as in garment), brak~o; **blowhole,** (in whale etc.), blov~o; (in ice, or any airhole), aer~o; **buttonhole,** buton~o; **chuckhole,** (in road), voj~o, kratereto; **cubby-hole,** faketo; **keyhole,** ŝlosil~o; **manhole, workhole,** luko, laborŝakto; **neckhole,** kol~o; **peephole,** luketo; **pigeonhole,** faketo; **porthole,** (naut), luko; (any window-like opening), fenestro; (embrasure), embrazuro; **pothole,** (in road), voj~o, kratereto; (in river), kirlakvo; **sinkhole,** (hollow in ground), kavo; **in the hole,** (in debt), ŝulda; ŝulde
holiday, (special day, usually w businesses closed), ferio; ~a; (Br, Canadian: vacation, personal longer time off), ~oj, libertempo
holism, tutismo; **holistic,** ~a
holla, (interj), hola!
Holland, Nederlando
holler, (yell), krii [tr, int]; ~o; (song), laborkanto
hollo, (interj), hola!
hollow, kavo; ~a; **hollow out,** ~igi
holly, ilekso; **hollyhock,** rozalteo; **sea holly,** eringio
Hollywood, Holivudo
holmium, holmio
holocaust, (genocide), holokaŭsto†; (catastrophe), katastrofego, detruego; (fire), incendiego
Holocene, holoceno; ~a
Holocephali, holocefaloj
Holofernes, Holoferno
hologram, hologramo; **holograph,** holografo; **holography,** holografio
holohedral, holoedro; ~a; **holohedrism,** ~io

Holosteum, holosteo; Holostei, ~oj
Holstein, Holstinio; ~a
holster, pistolingo; eningigi (sian pistolon)
holy, sankta; **holiness,** ~eco; **your holiness,** (title of address), via ~a moŝto; **holy of holies,** plej~ejo; plej~aĵo; **holier-than-thou,** aroganta, fieraĉa
homage, omaĝo; **pay homage (to),** ~i [int] (al)
Homarus, omaro
home, (residence, dwelling, or oth base), hejmo; ~a; ~e(n); (Br: internal to nation), enlanda; **(at) home,** ~e; **(to) home, homeward(s),** ~en (e.g.: *go home:* iri ~en); **homing,** (finding home, as pigeon), ~trova; (finding target, as missile), celtrova; **homey,** ~eca; **homely,** (unattractive), malbela; (Br: re home), ~eca; **homecoming,** (arrival), ~reveno; (welcome), ~bonvenigo; **homeland,** patrio, patrujo; **homemade,** ~farita; **homemaker,** dommastr(in)o; **Home Office,** (Br), Ministerio pri Internaj Aferoj; **home rule,** aŭtonomio, memregado; **homesick,** ~sopira; **homesickness,** ~sopirado; **homespun,** (rustic, simple), rustika; **homestead,** (home and land), ~bieno; (settle previously empty place), setli† [tr], loĝigi; setliĝi†; ekloĝi [int]; setlobieno†; **homesteader,** setlinto†; **(the) home stretch,** la fina vojero; **homework,** ~tasko(j); **feel at home,** senti sin kiel ~e; **make oneself at home,** sentigi sin kiel ~e; **home in on,** celtrovi [tr]; **bring home (the fact),** atentigi, konstatigi, substreki [tr], emfazi [tr]; **strike home,** trafi la celon; **mobile home,** ruldomo, domveturilo; **convalescent home,** kuracejo; **nursing home,** (Am), kuracejo; (Br), akuŝejo; **retirement home, rest home, old folks' home,** maljunulejo
homeopath, homeopato; **homeopathy,** homeopatio; **homeopathic,** homeopatia
homer, (Bib), ĥomero [364 litroj (see § 20)]
Homer, (man's name), Homero; **Homeric(al),** ~a
homicide, hommortigo [cp "murder"];

homicidal, ~(em)a
homily, homilio; homiletic, ~a
hominid, homedo†
Hominidae, homedoj†
homo, Homo sapiens, homo
homo–, (sci pfx), homo–
homoeopath, homeopato; homoeopathy, homeopatio; homoeopathic, homeopatia
homogeneous, homogenous, homogena; homogenize, ~igi
homologous, homologa
homonym, homonimo
homophobia, samseksemofobio; homophobe, ~ulo
homophone, homofono
homopolar, homopolara
homosexual, (gen), samseks/ema, ~ama, homoseksuala; ~emulo, ~amanto, homoseksualulo; (re 2 men), uranisma; (re 2 women), safisma, lesba
homoteleuton, homeoteleŭto
homothetic, homotetia
homozygote, homozigoto; homozygosis, ~eco
homunculus, homunkolo
Honan, Henan
Honduras, Honduraso; Honduran, ~a; ~ano
hone, fajnakrigi; ~ilo
honest, honesta; honesty, ~eco; (bot), lunario; dishonest, mal~a
honey, mielo; honeycomb, ~ĉelaro; honeycomb cell, ~ĉelo; honeycombed, ~ĉel(hav)a; honeyflower, (Protea), proteo; honeymoon, ~monato; ~i [int]; honeymyrtle, kajeputarbo; honeysuckle, (Lonicera), lonicero; French honeysuckle, centranto
Hong Kong, Hongkongo
Honiara, Honiaro*
honk, (horn), hupi [int]; ~(ad)o; (goose), gaki [int]; gak(ad)o
honor, honori [tr]; ~o; honorable, honorary, ~a; honorarium, honorario; your honor, (title of address), via moŝto
Honoratus, Honorato, Honorato
Honore, Honorio
honour, [see "honor"]

Honshu, Honŝuo
hood, (on coat, over fire, etc.), kapuĉo; (over car motor), kapoto; hood(lum), gangstero, bandito; hoodwink, mistifiki [tr]
–hood, (sfx), ~eco (e.g.: childhood: infaneco)
hoof, hufo; (kick), ~bati [tr]
hook, (fastener, gen, or similar-shaped object), hoko; ~i [tr], kroĉi [tr]; ~iĝi, kroĉiĝi; (in clothing), agrafo; agrafi [tr]; (of door or window), kardino; hook up, (elec), konekti [tr]; konektiĝi; (mech), kupli [tr]; kupliĝi; hook-up, konekto; kuplo; hookworm, nematodo; pothook, noĉostango; tenterhook, streĉo~o; on tenterhooks, (fig), streĉe senpacienca, senpacience streĉita; hook and eye, agrafo kaj agrafingo; hook and ladder, eskalkamiono; by hook or by crook, iele trapele, juste aŭ maljuste; off the hook, malembarasiĝinta; get off the hook, malembarasiĝi; get (one) off the hook, malembarasi [tr] (iun)
hookah, nargileo
hooligan, huligano
hoop, (of barrel etc.), ring/ego; (child's toy for rolling), rul~o
hoopla, pompo
hoopoe, upupo
hooray, hurai [int]; ~o; (interj), hura!
hoot, (as owl etc.), ululi [int]; ~o; (onom), hu! hu!; (honk horn), hupi [int]; hupado; (mock performer etc.), prifajfi [tr]; (pri)fajfo
hop, hopi [int], salteti [int]; ~o, salteto; (bot), lupolo; hopscotch, paradizludo
hope, esperi [tr]; ~o; hopeful, ~(plen)a; (aspirant), ~ulo; ~anto; be hopeful, hope for, ~i; hopeless, sen~a; (no chance of success), senŝanca†, vana; get one's hopes up, levi siajn (ies) ~ojn; there may be hope for one yet, ankoraŭ restas iom da ~o por iu; lose hope, sen~iĝi
hoplite, hoplito
hopper, (container), funelego; (rr car), ~a vagono
hops, (bot), lupolo
Horace, (modern name), Horaco; (Roman poet), Horacio

Horatio, Horacio
horde, (gen), hordo; **Golden Horde,** Ora H~o
hordeolum, hordeolo
Hordeum, hordeo
Horeb, Ĥorebo
horehound, marubio;   **black**   **horehound,** nigra baloteo
horizon, horizonto
horizontal, horizontala
Hormium, hormino
hormone, hormono; **hormonal,** ~a; **adrenocorticotropic**   **hormone,** (abb: ACTH), adrenalo-kortikotropa* ~o [abb: AKTH]
horn, (of animal; similar mus instrument; oth similar object), korno; (auto etc.), hupo; **horny,** (sexually aroused), amorema, seksema; (re horns), ~eca; ~hava; (tough, callused), kala; **hornbeam,** karpeno; **hornbill,** bucero; **hornpipe,** (instrument), ~tubo; (dance), ~tuba danco; (tune), ~tuba melodio; **hornwort,** (*Ceratophyllum*), ceratofilo; **honk the horn,** hupi [int]; **English horn,** aldohobojo; **foghorn,** nebul~o; **French horn,** orkestra ~o; **saxhorn,** saks~o; **shoehorn,** ŝu~o
hornet, krabro
horoscope, horoskopo
horrendous, terura, horora
horrible, horora
horrid, (terrible), terura, abomena
horrify, horor/igi; **horrific,** ~a
horror, hororo; **feel horror,** ~i [int]
hors-d'oeuvre, almanĝaĵo,   antaŭmanĝaĵo
horse, ĉevalo;   **horsefly,** tabano; **horsemint,** (*Monarda*), monardo; **horseplay,** petolado, kapriolado; **horsepower,** ~povo [0.746 kilovatoj (see § 20)]; **horseradish,** kreno; **horseshoe,** huffero; **horsetail,** (bot), ekvizeto; **charley horse,** kramfo; **dark horse,** (candidate etc.), nekonata; nekonato; **draft horse,** tir~o; **racehorse,** kur~o; **rocking horse,** balanc~o; **saddle horse,** sel~o; **sea horse,** hipokampo; **stock horse,** (Aus), vaker~o; **horse of another color,** alispeca afero; **hold your hors-**

es!, paciencu!, ne rapidu!; **right from the horse's mouth,** rekte de la fonto; **up on one's high horse,** aroganta, fieraĉa
Hortense, Hortensa
Hortensius, Hortensio
horticulture, hortikulturo; **horticultural,** ~a
Horus, Horuso
hosanna, (interj), hosana!; (n), hosanao
hose, (flexible pipe), hoso†; (stockings), ŝtrumpoj
Hosea, Hoŝea
hosier, ŝtrump/isto; **hosiery,** ~oj
hospice, hospico
hospitable, gastama; **inhospitable,** (no hospitality), ne~a; (forbidding, barren, harsh), malfavora, severa, maldorlota
hospital, hospitalo; ~a; **hospitalize,** en~igi; **maternity hospital, lying-in hospital,** akuŝejo; **military field hospital,** ambulanco
hospitality, gastamo
host, (to guests, gen), gastig/into; ~anto; ~onto; ~i; (to guests in home, hotel, etc.; to parasites in plant, animal), mastro; (rel), hostio; (army or oth large group), armeo; **elevation of the host,** (rel), hosti-levado
hostage, ostaĝo; **be hostage,** ~i [int]; **hold (someone) hostage,** ~igi (iun)
hostel, hostelry, gastejo; **youth hostel,** junular~o
hostile, malamika; **hostility,** ~eco; **hostilities,** (mil), militado
hot, (gen), varma; **red-hot,** ruĝarda; **white-hot,** blankarda; **hotbed,** (for plants), ~bedo; (place of activity), ardejo; (interj), bonege!; **hothouse,** forcejo; **hotline,** rektlinio
hotel, hotelo; ~a
Hottentot, Hotentoto; ~a
hound, (any dog), hundo; (for hunting), ĉas~o; (chase, hunt), (~o)ĉasi [tr]; (hassle w requests), tropedati [tr]; **hound's-tongue,** (bot), cinogloso, ~olango; **rabbit hound,** lepor~o, levrelo; **wolfhound,** lup~o
hour, horo; **hourly,** ĉiu~a; ĉiu~e; **hourly (pay), paid by the hour,** ~paga; ~page; **hourglass,** sablohorloĝo; sa-

blohorloĝu; **during the wee hours,** frumatene; **rush hour, peak hour,** pinto~o(j)†; **at the eleventh hour,** last~e, lastmomente
houri, hurio
house, (building, gen; family; ast), domo; (legislative body), ĉambro; (specialized place), –ejo [sfx] (e.g.: *publishing house:* eldonejo; *monkey house:* simiejo; *meeting house:* kunvenejo); (give lodging to), loĝigi (e.g.: *refugees were housed in the school:* oni loĝigis fuĝintojn en la lernejo); **housing,** loĝig(ad)o (e.g.: *housing shortage:* loĝiga nesufiĉo); **housebreak,** (break in), ~ŝteli [int]; (train animal), hejmtrejni [tr]; **housebreaker,** ~ŝtelinto; **house-cleaning,** mastrumado, ~purigado; **do housecleaning,** mastrumi [int]; **household,** (persons), ~anaro; (home), hejmo; hejma; **householder,** ~posedanto; **member of the (same) household,** ~ano; **head of the household,** ~estro [cp "househusband", "housewife" below]; **househusband,** ~mastro; **housekeeper,** mastrumist(in)o; **housekeeping,** mastrumado; **houseleek,** sempervivo; **housemaid,** (~)servistino; **housemother,** ~estrino; **housewarming (party),** fajrej–inaŭguro; **housewife,** ~mastrino; **house of cards,** (lit or fig), karto~o; **House of Commons, House of Deputies,** Ĉambro de Deputitoj; **House of Lords,** Ĉambro de Lordoj; **House of Representatives,** Ĉambro de Reprezentantoj; **blockhouse,** blokhaŭso; **boarding house, rooming house,** pensiono; **deckhouse,** rufo; **outhouse,** (any outbuilding), krom~o; (privy), ekstera necesejo; **poorhouse,** malriĉulejo; **storehouse, warehouse,** staplo; stapli [tr]; **wheelhouse,** navigejo; **whorehouse,** bordelo, putinejo; **workhouse,** (prison), bagno; (poorhouse), malriĉulejo; **bring down the house,** (theat), instigi aplaŭdegon; **on the house,** regale de l' ~o; **put one's house in order,** ordi siajn aferojn
hovel, domaĉo

hover, ŝvebi [int]; **hovercraft,** teraplano
how, (in what way, to what extent, etc.), kiel; (more intense), kiamaniere; **how much, how many,** kiom (da) [see also "much"]; **no matter how,** ~ ajn; **no matter how much (many),** kiom ajn (da); **how are you?, how do you do?,** ~ vi fartas?
howdah, baldakenselo
however, (nevertheless), tamen; (no matter how, whatever way), kiel ajn; **however much, however many,** kiom ajn (da)
howitzer, haŭbizo
howl, hurli [int], ululi [int], hojli [int], kriegi [int]; ~o, ululo, hojlo, kriego
hoyden, bubino
Hsinking, Ĉangĉun
huanaco, guanako
hub, nabo; **hubcap,** ~oĉapo
hubbub, bru(ad)o
Hubert, Huberto
hubris, orgojlo
huckleberry, (bush), gajlusaco*; (berry), ~bero
huckster, kolportisto
huddle, (gen), kunpremi [tr]; ~iĝi; ~o; (football), kunkapiĝo
Hudson, (river), Hudsono; **Hudson Bay,** Golfo ~a
hue, (color, gen), koloro; (nuance of color), (~)nuanco, (~)tono; **hue and cry,** (clamor), diskriego, muĝego, bruado; (chase), persekutado
huemul, guemulo
huff, (offend), ofendi [tr]; ~iĝi; ~(iĝ)o; **huffy,** ~ita; **in a huff,** ~ite; **get in a huff,** ~iĝi
hug, brakumi [tr], ĉirkaŭpremi [tr]; ~o, ĉirkaŭpremo
huge, enorma, grandega
Hugo, Hugo
Huguenot, Hugenoto
huh, (exclamatory interj), ha!; (questioning), eh?, ej?
hula(-hula), hulahulo
hulk, (of ship), ŝipkorpo; (person), bubego; (any large body, shell), korpego, ŝelego, kolosaĵo; **hulking,** malgracia
hull, (pod), guŝo; (any shell), ŝelo; (ship), ŝipkorpo; (part below water),

kareno
hullabaloo, tumulto, bruego
hullo, (interj), hola! [cp "hello"]
hum, zumi [tr, int]; ~(ad)o; (interj),
hmm!
human, homa; ~o; [not "humana"]; **humanism**, humanismo; **humanist**, humanisma; humanisto; **humanity**,
(humanness), ~eco; (humaneness),
humaneco; (humankind), (la) ~aro;
(the) humanities, (la) ~araj studoj;
~arstuda; **humanize**, ~ecigi; **humankind**, (la) ~aro; **dehumanize**,
mal~ecigi; **inhuman**, (not human),
ne~a; (not humane), nehumana, barbara, kruela; **superhuman**, super~a
humane, humana; **humanity**, ~eco; **inhumane**, ne~a, barbara, kruela; **inhumanity**, ne~eco, barbareco, krueleco
humanitarian, homama; ~anto; **humanitarianism**, ~o
humble, humila; ~igi; **humble oneself**, **eat humble pie**, ~iĝi, sin ~igi
humblebee, burdo
humbug, (empty talk), blago; (trickster), ĉarlatano
humdrum, enuiga, monotona; ~o, monotoneco
humerus, humero
humid, humida; **humidity**, ~o; **(de)humidify**, (mal)~igi; **(de)humidifier**,
(mal)~igilo
humiliate, humil/igi; **humility**, ~eco
hummingbird, kolibro, muŝbirdo
hummock, terĝibo, altaĵeto
humor, (funny), humuro; (emotional state, whim), humoro; (indulge), indulgi [tr]; **humorous**, ~a; **humorist**,
~isto; **sense of humor**, senso de ~o
humoresque, humoresko
humour, [see "humor"]
hump, (as on camel), ĝibo; (hummock),
ter~o; (arch back, as cat), ĝibigi, arkigi (la dorson), ĝibiĝi, arkiĝi; **humped**,
~a; **humpback**, (back), ~o; (person),
~ulo; **humpbacked**, ~a
Humulus lupulus, lupolo
humus, humo
Hun, huno
Hunan, Hunan
hunch, (premonition), antaŭsento, intuo; (hump), ĝibo; (jerk, shove),

ŝoviĝi; (arch back), arkigi la dorson,
arkiĝi; **hunchback**, ĝibulo; **have a
hunch (about)**, ~i [tr], intui [tr]
hundred, cent [see § 19]; **hundredweight**, (Am), 45,4 kilogramoj; (Br),
50,8 kilogramoj [see § 20]
Hungary, Hungar/io; **Hungarian**, ~o;
~a; ~ia
hunger, malsato; ~i [int]; **hungry**, ~a;
be hungy, ~i; **go hungry**, resti ~a
hunk, pec(eg)o, maso, bulo
hunker, kaŭri [int]
hunt, (chase animals etc.), ĉasi [tr]; ~o;
(search), serĉi [tr]; serĉo; **hunter**,
(person or animal), ~anto; ~isto;
(dog), ~hundo; **manhunt**, hom~o
huntun, huntuno
Hupeh, **Hupei**, Hubej
Huram, Ĥuram
hurdle, (racing), hurdo; (any obstacle),
obstaklo; (overcome), superi [tr]
hurdy-gurdy, gurdo
hurl, ĵet(eg)i [tr], impetegi [tr]; ~o
Huron, (Native American), Hurono;
Lake Huron, Lago ~a
hurrah, hurai [int]; ~o; (interj), hura!
hurricane, uragano
hurry, rapidi [int], hasti [int]; ~igi, hastigi; ~(em)o, hasto; **hurried**, ~(em)a,
hast(em)a
hurt, (pain), dolori [tr] (iun) (e.g.: *my
finger hurts:* mia fingro min ~as); ~iĝi
(e.g.: *I hurt from the injury:* mi ~iĝas
pro la vundo); (to others), ~igi (e.g.:
did I hurt you?: ĉu mi ~igis vin?);
(wound), vundi [tr], lezi [tr]; vundo,
lezo; (damage), difekti [tr]; (offend),
ofendi [tr]; (interfere, hinder), malutili
[int] (al), malhelpi [tr]; **hurt one's
feelings**, ~igi ies sentojn
hurtle, (throw), ĵetegi [tr]; (go fast), impeti [int]
Hus, [see "Huss"]
husband, (spouse), edzo; (manage, conserve), ŝpari [tr], konservi [tr]; **husbandry**, (farming), kultivado;
animal husbandry, bestkultivado;
co-husband, kun~o; **househusband**,
dommastro
hush, silento; ~igi; ek~i [int], ~iĝi; ~u!;
hush up, ~igi; ~iĝi; (suppress, keep
secret), subpremi [tr], kaŝi [tr], kon-

servi sekreta; **hush-hush**, kaŝ-kaŝa, sekretega; **hush-puppy**, maizbenjeto
husk, (seed shell), semŝelo; senŝeligi
husky, (strong), forta; (hoarse), raüketa; (dog), sledhundo
huso, huzo
Huss, (Jan Hus), Hus; **Hussite**, ~ano
hussar, husaro
hussy, kanajlino, friponino
hustings, (campaign route), kampanja itinero
hustle, (shove, jostle), ŝanceli [tr]; (expel), elpeli [tr]; (deal in any shady, illegal bsns), ŝakri [tr]; (hurry), hast〡 [int], rapidi [int]; **hustler**, ŝakristo; hastemulo
hut, kaban(et)o; (thatched; poet), ĥato
hutch, (bin), kesto; (cabinet), bret~o; (hut), kaban(et)o; (animal coop), kaĝo
hutments, barakaro
hyacinth, (bot), hiacinto; (gem), jacinto; **water hyacinth**, akvo~o
hydrodynamic, hidrodinamika; **hydrodynamics**, ~o
hydroelectric, hidroelektra
hydrofoil, akvoplaneo
hydrogen, hidrogeno; **hydrogenate**, ~izi [tr]; **hydrogen peroxide**, (chem), ~a peroksido; (as commercial preparation), perhidrolo
hydrography, hidrografio
hydroid, (hydrozoan), hidredo
hydrolysis, hidrolizo; **hydrolytic**, ~a; **hydrolyze**, ~i [tr]
hydrometer, piknometro [not "hidrometro"]
hydrophilic, hidrofila
hydrophobia, hidrofobio
hydrophone, hidrofono
hydroplane, hidroplano
hydroponic, hidrokultiva; **hydroponics**, ~ado
hydrops, hidropso
hydroquinone, kinolo
hydrorrhea, hidroreo
hydrosol, hidrosolo
hydrosphere, hidrosfero
hydrostatic, hidrostatika; **hydrostatics**, ~o
hydrosulfite, hidrosulfito
hydrous, hidrata, akvoza
hydroxide, hidroksido

hydroxy, hidroksilo
hydroxy–, (chem pfx), hidroksi–
hydroxyl, hidroksilo
Hydrus, (ast), Vira Hidro
hyena, hieno
Hygeia, Higiea
hygiene, higieno; **hygienic**, ~a; **hygienist**, ~isto
hygrograph, higrografo
hygrometer, higrometro
hygroscope, higroskopo
Hyksos, Hiksosoj
Hyla, hilo; Hylidae, ~edoj
Hylobates, gibono
hylozoism, hilozoismo; **hylozoic**, ~a
hymen, (anat), himeno
Hymen, (myth), Himeno
hymenomycete, himenomiceto
Hymenomycetes,himenomicetoj
Hymenoptera, himenopteroj
hymn, himno; **hymnal**, ~aro
hyoglossus, hiogloso
hyoid, hioido
hyoscyamine, hiosciamino
Hyoscyamus, hiskiamo
hypallage, hipalago
hyper–, (pfx), hiper–
hyperbaton, hiperbato
hyperbola, hiperbolo
hyperbole, hiperbolo
hyperbolic, (gen), hiperbola
hyperboloid, hiperboloido
hyperborean, hiperboreo; ~a
hyperchloremia, hiperkloridemio
hyperchlorhydria, hiperklorhidreco
hyperemia, hiperemio
hyperesthesia, hiperestezio
hyperglycemia, hiperglukozemio
hypergranulocytemia, hipergranulocitemio
Hypericum, hiperiko
hypermetropia, hipermetrop/eco; **hypermetropic**, ~a
hyperon, hiperono
hyperplasia, hiperplazio
hypertension, hipertensio; **hypertensive**, ~a; **antihypertensive**, kontraŭ~iga; kontraŭ~igenzo
hyperthyroid, hipertiroida; ~ulo; **hyperthyroidism**, ~ismo
hypertonia, hipertonio; **hypertonic**, ~a
hypertrophy, hipertropio

hypesthesia, hipoestezo
hypha, hifo
hyphen, strek/eto, divid~o; **hyphenate**, ~eti [tr], divid~i [tr]
hypnosis, hipnoto [not "hipnozo"]; **hypnotic**, ~a; **hypnotism**, ~ismo; **hypnotist**, ~isto; **posthypnotic**, post~a; **hypnotic trance**, ~o; **hypnotize**, ~igi
Hypnum, hipno
hyp(o)–, (pfx), hipo–
hypocaust, hipokaŭsto
hypocenter, hipocentro†
hypochlorite, hipoklorito
hypochlorous, hipoklorita; **hypochlorous acid**, ~a acido
hypochondria, **hypochondriasis**, hipokondrio; **hypochondriac**, (re illness), ~a; ~ulo; (re hypochondrium), hipokondra
hypochondrium, hipokondro
hypocotyl, hipokotiledono
hypocrisy, hipokrito; ~ado; ~eco; **hypocrite**, ~ulo; **hypocritical**, ~a
hypocycloid, hipocikloido
hypoderma, hipodermo
hypodermic, subhaŭta [not "hipoderma"]
hypodermis, hipodermo
hypogastrium, hipogastro; **hypogastric**, ~a
hypogeum, hipogeo
hypoglossal, (nerve), hipogloso; (oth), sublanga
hypoglycemia, hipoglukozemio
hypogranulocytemia, hipogranulocitemio
hypogynous, hipogina; **hypogyny**, ~eco
hypoiodite, hipojodito
hypophysis, hipofizo
hypoplasia, hipoplazio
hypospadias, hipospadio
hypostasis, (gen), hipostazo; **hypostatic**, ~a; **hypostatize**, ~igi
hypostyle, hipostilo; ~a
hyposulf/ite, hiposulfito
hypotension, hipotensio; **hypotensive**, ~a; ~ulo; ~igulo
hypotenuse, hipotenuzo
hypothalamus, hipotalamo
hypothec, hipoteko; **hypothecary**, ~a;

~ita; **hypothecate**, ~i [tr]
hypothenar, hipotenaro
hypothesis, hipotezo; **hypothesize**, ~i [tr]; **hypothetical**, ~a
hypothyroid, hipotiroida; ~ulo; **hypothyroidism**, ~o
hypotonia, hipotonio; **hypotonic**, ~a
hypsochromic, hipsokroma
hypsometer, hipsometro
hyrax, prokavio
Hyrcania, Hirkanio
hyssop, hisopo; **hedge hyssop**, gratiolo
Hyssopus, hisopo
hyster–, (med, anat pfx: uterus), uter–
hysterectomy, uterektomio
hysteresis, histerezo; **hysteresis curve**, ~a ciklokurbo
hysteria, histerio; **hysterical**, ~a
hysteroptosis, uteroptozo
hysterotomy, uterotomio
Hystrix, histriko

I

I, (pron), mi
iamb, iambus, jambo; **iambic**, ~a
Iapetus, Jafeto*
–iasis, (med sfx), –ozo
Iberia, Iber/ujo; **Iberian**, ~o; ~a; ~uja
ibex, ibekso
ibis, Ibis, ibiso
–ible, (sfx), [see "–able"]
–ic, (sfx: of, re), –a; (having quality of), –eca; (chem: higher valence; tech), –ika; (chem: inorganic acid of –ate), –ata
Icaria, Ikario
Icarus, Ikaro
ice, (gen), glacio; ~igi; ~iĝi; (on cake), glazuri [tr]; [cp "glaze", "frost", "sleet", "hail"]; **icing**, (cake), glazuro; **icy**, (frigid), ~a, frosta, malvarmega; **iceberg**, ~monto; **icebox**, ~ujo; **icebreaker**, (ship), ~rompatoro; **icecap**, **ice field**, (on land), glaĉero; (on sea), bankizo; **ice cream**, ~aĵo; **ice floe**, bankizero, ~insulo; **ice-pack**, (on sea), bankizo; **break the ice (with)**, iniciati [tr] (konversacion, rilaton, aferon kun); **cut no ice**, ne efiki [int]
Iceland, Islando; **Icelander**, ~ano; **Icelandic**, ~a; **Old Icelandic**, (la) Norena (lingvo)
ichneumon, (mongoose), ikneŭmono; **ichneumon fly**, ~oido
ichor, ikoro
ichthyology, iĥtiolog/io; **ichthyological**, ~ia; **ichthyologist**, ~o
ichthyophagy, iĥtiofagio; **ichthyophagous**, ~a
ichthyosaur, iĥtiosaŭro
Ichthyosaurus, iĥtiosaŭro
ichthyosis, iktiozo
ichu, stipo
icicle, pendoglacio
–icide, (sfx), [see "–cide"]
icky, aĉa
icon, ikono; **iconoclasm**, ikonoklastis-

mo; **iconoclast**, ikonoklasto; **iconography**, ikonografio; **iconographic(al)**, ikonografia; **iconology**, ~ologio; **iconoscope**, ~oskopo; **iconostas, iconostasion, iconostasis**, ikonostazo
icosahedron, ikosaedro; **icosahedral**, ~a
icosane, ikozano
–ics, (tech sfx), –iko
Icticyon, mustelvulpo
ictus, (gen), ikto
id, ĝio
ID, identiga; ~aĵo
Ida, Ida; **Mount Ida**, Monto ~a
–idae, (bot, zool sfx), –edoj
Idaho, Idaho
–ide, (chem sfx), –ido
idea, ideo; **ideation**, ~igado; **have no idea**, tute ne scii [tr]
ideal, ideala; ~o; **idealism**, ~ismo; **idealist**, ~isto; **idealistic**, ~isma; **idealize**, ~igi
identify, ident/igi; ~iĝi; **identification**, ~igo; ~iĝo; **identical**, ~a; **identity**, (gen), ~eco
ideogram, ideogramo; **ideography**, ideografio
ideology, ideolog/io; **ideological**, ~ia; **ideologist, ideologue**, ~o
Ides, Iduoj
idioblast, idioblasto
idiom
(local dialect), idiomo; (non-literal phrase), lokucio†; **idiomatic**, ~a; lokutisma†
idiopathy, idiopatio; **idiopathic**, ~a
idiosyncrasy, idiosinkrazio; **idiosyncratic**, ~a
idiot, idioto; **idiotic**, ~eca; **idiocy**, ~eco; ~aĵo; **idiotism**, ~eco [not "~ismo"]
idle, (inactive), sen/okupa, ~labora, dormanta, neuzata; (useless), ~utila, vana; (unimportant), vanta; (lazy),

maldiligenta, mallaborema; (unfounded), ~baza; (re machine, wheel), idli [int]; **idler,** (wheel), idlilo; **sit idle,** resti ~okupa (etc.)
Ido, Ido
idol, idolo; **idolater,** ~isto; **idolatrous,** ~ista; **idolatry,** ~isteco, ~kulto, ~servo; **idolize,** ~igi
Idomeneus, Idomeneo
Idum(a)ea, Idumeo
idyll, idilio; **idyllic,** ~(ec)a
i.e. (abb of "id est"), t.e. [abb of "tio estas"]
if, (in case that), se (e.g.: *if you come, bring it:* ~ vi venos, alportu ĝin; *if I were you:* ~ mi estus vi); (whether), ĉu (e.g.: *ask her if she knows him:* demandu de ŝi ĉu ŝi konas lin); (uncertainty), seo (e.g.: *that's a big if:* tio estas granda seo); **iffy,** (uncertain), ŝanca, necerta; **as if,** [see under "as"]; **if it weren't for,** ~ ne temus pri
–ification, (sfx), [see "–ify" and "–ation"]
–ify, (sfx: cause to be), –igi [see also "–ation"]
igloo, iglo
Ignatius, Ignaco
igneous, (rock), magma
ignite, ekbruli [int]; ~igi; **ignition,** ~(ig)o; (for motor), ~igilo; **ignition point,** ekflama punkto, ~a punkto
ignoble, malnobla
ignominy, malhonoro, honto; **ignominious,** ~a, hontinda
ignoramus, stultulo, sensciulo
ignorant, senscia, malklera; **ignorance,** ~o, malklereco
ignore, ignori [tr], malatenti [tr]
iguana, igvano
Iguana, igvano; Iguanidae, ~edoj
Iguanadon, igvanodonto
–ile, (math sfx: equal division), –ilo (e.g.: *quartile:* kvar~o)
ileac, ilea
Île de France, Parizio
ileum, ileo; **ileitis,** ~ito
Ilex, ilekso; Ilex paraguayensis, mate-

arbo
iliac, iliaka
Iliad, Iliado
Ilion, Iliono
iliopsoas, (muscle), iliopsoaso
ilium, ilio, iliako
Ilium, Iliono
ilk, speco
ill, (sick), malsana; (bad), malbona; malbono; malbone; **illness,** ~o [cp "disease"]; **deathly ill,** mort~a; **be ill,** ~i [int]
ill–, (pfx: improperly, poorly, etc.), mis– (e.g.: *ill-fitting:* ~taŭga)
Illicium, ilicio
illinium, [see "prometheum"]
Illinois, Ilinojso
–illion, (number sfx), [see § 19(b)]
illiterate, analfabeto; ~a; **illiteracy,** ~eco
illuminate, (shine light), lumigi; (clarify; decorate w festive lights; decorate manuscript), ilumini [tr]; **illumination,** ~ado; iluminado; iluminaĵo
illusion, iluzio; **illusory,** ~a; **disillusion,** sen~igi; **become disillusioned,** sen~iĝi
illustrate, (gen), ilustri [tr]; **illustration,** ~ado; ~aĵo; **illustrative,** ~a
illustrious, eminenta, fama
Illyria, Ilirio
ilmenite, ilmenito
im–, (pfx), [see "in–"]
image, (any picture, form), bildo, figuro; (in imagination), imago; **imagery,** ~ig(ad)o, figurado; imagado; **self-image,** memkoncepto
imagine, imagi [tr]; **imaginary,** ~a; (math), imaginara; **imagination,** ~(ad)o; **imaginative,** ~ema; ~iga
imago, (zool), imagino; (psych), imago
imam, imamo
imbecile, imbecilo; **imbecility,** ~eco
imbed, [see "embed"]
imbibe, (drink), trinki [tr]; (absorb), (en)sorbi [tr]
imbricate, imbriki† [tr]; ~ita
imbroglio, konfuzaĵo, implikaĵo

imbue, (permeate), penetri [tr], prisorbi [tr]; (inspire), inspiri [tr]
imidazole, imidazolo
imide, imido
imine, imino
imitate, imiti [tr]; **imitation,** ~(ad)o; ~aĵo; (not genuine), malaŭtentika, falsa; malaŭtentikaĵo, straso
immaculate, senmakula; **immaculate conception,** (rel), ~a koncip(itec)o
immanent, imanenta
immediate, tuja; **immediately,** tuj; **immediacy,** ~eco
immemorial, praa, pra– [pfx], pretermemora (e.g.: *time immemorial:* ~tempo)
immense, enorma, grandega, vast(eg)a
immerse, (gen), mergi [tr]; (to wetten), trempi [tr]; (in specific medium), en...igi (e.g.: *immerse the car in paint:* enfarbigi la aŭton); **be(come) immersed,** ~iĝi, trempiĝi; en...iĝi; **immersion,** ~(iĝ)o; tremp(iĝ)o; en...igo; en...iĝo; (ast; microscope), imersio; **immersion heater,** ~hejtilo
immigrate, enmigri [int]; **immigration,** ~(ad)o; **immigrant,** ~into; ~anto
imminent, tuja, ~okazanta, minacanta, baldaŭa; **imminence,** ~eco, (~a) okazonteco
immiscible, nemiksebla
immolate, (burnt offering), oferbuĉi [tr]; (self), sinbruligi
immortelle, imortelo
immune, imuna; **immunize,** ~igi; **immunity,** ~eco
immure, enmurigi
immutable, senŝanĝa, neŝanĝebla
imp, koboldo, diableto; **impish,** ~a, petolema
impact, (strike), ekfrapi [tr]; ~o; kolizii [int]; kolizio; (wedge, press together), kunpremi [tr]; kunpremo; (effect), efiko, influo; **impacted,** kunpremita
impair, difekti [tr]; **impairment,** ~o
impale, palisumi [tr]
impart, doni [tr], komuniki [tr]
impasse, (gen), senelirejo

impassive, (insensible), nesentiva, sensenta, sensufera; (w/o emotion, calm), senemocia, serena, kvieta
impatiens, balzamino
Impatiens, balzamino; Impatiens nolitangere, netuŝumino, ĝardena ~o
impeach, (indict), (formale) akuzi [tr]; (denounce), denunci [tr]; (cast doubt, challenge), kontesti [tr], dubigi; **impeachment,** (formala) ~o; **impeachable,** akuzinda; **unimpeachable,** nekontestebla
impeccable, (flawless), sendifekta, perfekta
impecunious, senmona
impede, malhelpi [tr], obstrukci [tr]; **impedance,** (elec), impedanco; **impediment,** ~o, obstrukco
impel, (push, drive), peli [tr]; (urge, incite), instigi [tr], impulsi [tr]
impend, minaci [tr], esti okazonta; **impending,** ~anta, okazonta, baldaŭa
imperative, (gram), imperativo; ~a; (obligatory), ~o; ~a, deviga
imperator, imperatoro
imperial, imperia; **imperialism,** ~ismo; **imperialist,** ~isma; ~isto
imperious, aroganta, ordonema, tiranema
imperium, imperatoreco
impersonate, (mimic), imiti [tr], enpersonigi; (as fraud), fraŭd~i [tr]
impervious, nepenetrebla
impetigo, impetigino; **impetiginous,** ~a
impetuous, impet(em)a
impetus, impeto; **give impetus to,** ~igi; **thrust, move with impetus,** ~i [int]
impinge, (have effect), efiki [int] (sur); (contact, as light ray on surface etc.), incidi [int] (sur)
implacable, neplaĉebla, nepacigebla
implement, (carry out), efektivigi; (tool), ilo; (apparatus), aparato, maŝino
implicate, (accuse w), kunkulpigi; (entwine), impliki [tr]; **implication,** ~o; impliko; (thing implied), implico
implicit, implicita

implode, implodi [int]; **implosion**, ~o
implore, pet/egi [tr], plor~i [tr]
implosive, (gram), injektivo
imply, (logically), implici [tr]; (suggest, hint), sugesti [tr]
import, (bring into country; cmptr), importi [tr]; ~a; ~aĵo; (importance), graveco, signifo
important, grava; **importance**, ~eco; **unimportant**, mal~a, bagatela
importune, petadi [tr], ĝeni [tr]; **importunate**, ~ema, persista, ĝena
impose, (force on), trudi [tr]; (more emphatic), al~i [tr]; (printing), impozi [tr]; **imposisition**, (al)~(ad)o; impoz(ad)o; **imposing**, (impressive), impona; **self-imposed**, mem~ita; **superimpose**, (print), surpresi [tr]; (put object over), surmeti [tr], supermeti [tr]; (assert will), sur~i [tr]
impost, (arch), impoŝto
impostor, fraŭdimitanto
impound, (confiscate), konfiski [tr]; (dam up), digi [tr]
impoverish, malriĉ/igi; **impoverished**, ~(iĝint)a
imprecate, malbeni [tr]
impregnable, nekaptebla, neskuebla, nepenetrebla
impregnate, (gen), impregni [tr]
impresario, impresario
impress, (on mind), imponi [tr]; (cause feel ing; phot), impresi [tr]; (print, emboss, etc.; fig, make mark on memory etc.), stampi [tr]; **impression**, ~o; impreso; stampo; (on spirit etc.), efekto; (of hard material in soft by pressure), premsigno; **impressionable**, impresiĝema; **impressionism**, impresionismo; **impressionist**, impresionisma; impresionisto; **impressive**, ~a
imprimatur, imprimaturo
imprint, surpremi [tr]; ~o
impromptu, improvizita; ~e
improve, plibon/igi; ~iĝi; **improvement**, ~igo; ~iĝo
improvise, improvizi [tr]
impudent, impertinenta, aroganta

impugn, kontesti [tr], ataki [tr], kontraŭi [tr], dubigi
impulse, impulso; **impulsive**, ~iĝema, senpripensa
impunity, senpun/eco; **with impunity**, ~e
impute, (ascribe), atribui [tr]; (charge, accuse), imputi [tr]
in, (inside, within; into), en (e.g.: *the cat is in the room:* la kato estas ~ la ĉambro; *the meeting in July:* la kunveno ~ julio; *the cat came in [into] the room:* la kato venis ~ la ĉambron); (through), tra (e.g.: *the cat jumped in the window:* la kato (en)saltis tra la fenestro); (by means of), per (e.g.: *dressed in silk:* vestita per silko); (after), post (e.g.: *I'll be there in a week [a week from now]:* mi estos tie post semajno); (in range of sense), ~ebla [sfx] (e.g.: *in sight:* videbla); (according to; concerning), laŭ (e.g.: *in my opinion:* laŭ mia opinio; *high in cost, low in value:* alta laŭ kosto, malalta laŭ valoro); (part out of whole; medium of which made; etc.), el (e.g.: *one in ten will succeed:* unu el dek sukcesos; *a statue in marble:* statuo el marmoro); (for sake of), por (e.g.: *in her honor:* por ŝia honoro); (at home), hejme (e.g.: *will you be in this evening?:* ĉu vi estos hejme ĉi-vespere?); (at oth place), en (ĉe, etc.); (re inward direction), ~ira (e.g.: *the in door:* la ~ira pordo); (re inside condition), ~a (e.g.: *the in crowd:* la ~a grupo); (fashionable, in vogue), laŭmoda (e.g.: *hats are in this year:* ĉapeloj estas laŭmodaj ĉi-jare); (inner), interna; (complete), kompleta (e.g.: *the results are in:* la rezultoj estas kompletaj); **inasmuch as**, ĉar; pro tio ke; **in camera**, malpublika; ~e; **in for**, (sure to receive), (nepre) ricevonta; **in for it**, ricevonta ĉagrenon, embarason; esti ĉagrenota, embarasota, esti en amaso de embaraso; **in on**, inkludita ~; **the ins and outs**, (details), detaloj; in

that, (because), ĉar; (in the sense that), laŭ tio ke: **inward,** interna; interne(n); internenira; **in with,** (close w), intima kun

in–, (pfx: in, into, etc.), en– (e.g.: *intake:* ~preno); (not), ne– (e.g.: *insufferable:* netolerebla); (opp), mal– (e.g.: *inauspicious:* malfavora); (w/o), sen– (e.g.: *insignificant:* sensignifa)

–in, (sfx: type of strike), –striko (e.g.: *sit-in:* sid~o; *stall-in* [blocking roads]: pane~o); (chem etc.), –ino

in absentia, dum foresto

Inachus, Inaĥo

inadvertent, senintenca; **inadvertence,** ~aĵo; ~eco

–inae, (zool sfx), –enoj

inane, (foolish, meaningless), vanta, sensenca, absurda, ventkapa

inanition, inanicio

inaugurate, inaŭguri [tr]; **inauguration,** ~o; **inaugural,** ~a

Inc. [see "incorporate"]

Inca, Inkao; ~a

incandesce, inkandeski [int]; ~igi; **incandescent,** ~a; **incandescence,** ~(ig)o

incantation, sorĉkanto

incarcerate, (jail), enprizonigi

incarnate, enkarniĝi; ~inta; **incarnation,** ~o; **reincarnate,** re~i; **reincarnation,** re~o; **incarnate entity,** ~into

incendiary, incendia

incense, (for odor), incenso; (anger), kolerigi; **burn incense before,** ~i [tr]; **be incensed,** koleri [int]

incentive, stimula; ~ilo

inception, komenco

incessant, senĉesa

incest, incesto, sang-adulto; **incestuous,** ~a

inch, colo [2,54 centimetroj (see § 20)]; (move slowly), rampi [int]; **inchworm,** geometra larvo; **inch by inch,** iom post iom, gradon post grado, gradope

inchoate, (rudimentary), rudimenta

incidence, (occurrence), okazo; ~ado;

(phys), incido; **angle of incidence,** incida angulo

incident, incidento, okazo; **incidental,** akcesora, flanka, hazarda; **incidentally,** (by the way), parenteze, flanke

incinerate, cindrigi; **incinerator,** ~atoro

incipient, komenca

incise, incizi [tr]; **incision,** ~(ad)o; ~aĵo; **incisive,** ~a, tranĉa

incisor, incizivo

incisure, incisura, incizuro

incite, provoki [tr] [not "inciti"]

inclement, (re weather), malfavora, ŝtorma; (harsh), senkompata, severa

incline, (lean), klini [tr]; ~iĝi; (tend), inklini [int], emi [int]; inklinigi, emigi; (slope), deklivo; **inclination,** ~(iĝ)o; deklivo; inklino, emo, tendenco; (from horizontal), inklinacio; **inclined,** ~ita; inklina, ema; **be inclined to,** inklini [int], emi [int]; **disincline,** malinklinigi; **disinclined,** malinklina; **be disinclined,** malinklini [int], ne emi [int]; **disinclination,** malinklino; **steep incline,** krutaĵo

include, inkludi [tr], inkluzivi [tr]; (comprise), ampleksi [tr]; **inclusion,** ~o, inkluzivo; **inclusive,** inkluziva; inkluzive

incognito, inkognita; ~e; (person), ~ulo; (state), ~o; **incognita,** ~ulino

income, ($, gen), enspezo(j); (from rental, interest, investment, etc.), rento; **income tax,** ~imposto

incommode, ĝeni [tr]; **incommodious,** ~a, maloportuna

incommunicado, senkomunika; ~e

incorporate, (bsns), korporaci/igi; ~iĝi; (embody), enkorpigi; enkorpiĝi; (include), inkludi [tr], inkluzivi [tr]; **incorporated,** (bsns), ~igita [abb: Korp.]

incorrigible, nekorektebla

increase, (gen), pli/igi, kreskigi; ~iĝi, kreski [int]; ~igo; ~iĝo, kresko; (re specific quantity), ~...igi (etc.) (e.g.: *increase (in) size:* ~grandigi; ~gran-

diĝi; *increase (in) value:* ~valorigi; ~valoriĝi); **increasingly,** ~ kaj ~, laŭgrade ~
increment, (increase, gen), pli/igo; ~iĝo, kresko [see "increase"]; (math: small change), ŝanĝero; **incremental,** eropa
incriminate, kulpigi; **self-incrimination,** mem~o
incrust, inkrusti [tr]; **incrustation,** ~aĵo
incubate, (gen), kovi [tr]; ~iĝi; (by machine), inkubatori [tr]; **incubation,** (med), inkubacio; **incubator,** inkubatoro
incubus, inkubo
inculcate, inokuli [tr]
incumbent, (in office), posten-tenanta; ~o; (lying), kuŝanta; **incumbency,** postenperiodo; (duty), devo; **be incumbent on (one),** devi [tr], al iu endi [int] (e.g.: *it is incumbent on us to be careful:* ni devas zorgi [or] endas al ni zorgi)
incunabulum, (book), inkunablo
incur, akiri [tr]; (al)tiri sur sin
incursion, invado
incus, inkudo
indanthrene (blue), indantreno
indeed, ja [adv]; **yes indeed,** jes ja, certe; **no indeed,** ja ne, certe ne
indefatigable, nelacigebla
indelible, neforigebla
indemnify, (insure), asekuri [tr]; (compensate, repay), kompensi [tr]; **indemnity,** ~o; kompenso
indene, indeno
indent, (paragraph), aline/igi; (notch, give "teeth"), denti [tr], noĉi [tr]; (indenture), servodevigi; **indentation,** ~o; noĉo; **be indented,** (paragraph), ~i [int]
indenture, (servant), servodev/igi; (any contract), kontrakti [tr]; kontrakto; **indentured,** ~a
index, (as in book, cmptr menu, etc.; phys; refractive; Latin list), indekso; (math, phys, chem, med, anat: ratio; number to right and below), indico;

(statistics: base number), ~nombro; (any indicator), indikilo
India, Hind/io; **Indian,** (of India), ~o; ~a; ~ia [see also "Indian"]; **Indian Ocean,** Oceano ~ia
Indian, (native American), Indiano; ~a; (Asian), [see "India"]
Indiana, Indianio
Indianapolis, Indianopolo
Indic, Hinda
indican, indikozido
indicate, (gen), indiki [tr]; **indication,** ~o; **indicative,** ~a; (gram), indikativo; indikativa; **indicator,** ~ilo; (chem), ~enzo; (mech), ~atoro; **contraindicate,** kontraŭ~i [tr]; **contraindication,** kontraŭ~o
indict, akuzi [tr]; **indictment,** ~o
Indies: East Indies, Indonezio; **West Indies,** Antiloj
indifferent, indiferenta; **indifference,** ~eco, apatio
indigenous, indiĝena
indigent, malriĉa, senmona; ~ulo(j)
indignant, indigna; **indignation,** ~o; **be indignant,** ~i [int]
indignity, humiligo, insulto, indignindaĵo
indigo, (color; dye), indigo; ~a; **indigoplant,** (gen), ~oplanto; (*Indigofera tinctoria*), anilo
Indigofera, indigoplanto; Indigofera tinctoria, anilo
indispensable, nepra, nemalhavebla
indium, indiumo
individual, individuo; ~a; **individuality,** ~eco; **individualism,** ~ismo; **individualist,** ~isma; ~isto
Indo–, (pfx), Hindo–
Indochina, Hindoĉin/io; **Indochinese,** ~a; ~o
indol(e), indolo
indolent, maldiligenta, mallaborema, apatia; **be indolent,** mallabori [int]; **indolence,** mallaboremo, apatio
indomitable, nebridebla, neregebla
Indonesia, Indonezio; **Indonesian,** ~a; ~ano

indoxyl, indoksilo
Indra, Indro
indri, indrio
Indri(s), indrio
indubitable, senduba, nedubebla, nekontestebla
induce, (persuade), persvadi [tr]; (bring
  about), estigi, instigi [tr]; (infer), indukti [tr]; (phys, elec), induki [tr]; **in-**
  ducement, ~(il)o; estigo; (incentive),
  stimulilo; **self-induced**, (gen), mem-
  produktita; (elec), meminduktita
induct, (draft), konskripcii [tr]; (install
  in office), enoficigi; (initiate, as to
  knowledge), inici [tr]; **inductance**,
  (elec), induktanco; **induction**, (mil
  draft), ~ado; ~iĝo; (installation), eno-
  ficigo; (elec), induko; (inference), indukto; **inductive**, ~a; induka; indukta
indulge, indulgi [tr], dorloti [tr]; **in-**
  dulge (oneself), sin ~i; **indulgent**,
  ~ema, dorlotema; **indulgence**,
  ~(em)o; (rel), indulgenco; **self-indul-**
  gence, sin~o, sindorlot(ad)o
indult, indulto
Indus, Induso
indusium, indusio
industry, (bsns), industrio; (diligence),
  diligenteco; **industrial**, ~a; **industri-**
  alize, ~igi; **industrialist**, ~isto;
  industrious, diligenta, laborema; **pri-**
  mary industry, (Aus), agrara kaj mina produktado; **secondary industry**,
  (Aus), manufaktura ~o
–ine, (chem sfx), –ino
inebriate, ebria; ~igi; ~ulo; **inebriat-**
  ed, ~a; **inebriant**, ~igenzo
ineffable, neesprimebla
ineluctable, neevitebla, nepra, certa
inept, (unsuited), mal/trafa, ~taŭga;
  (clumsy), ~lerta, ~gracia, fuŝa; **inept-**
  itude, ~trafeco, ~taŭgeco; ~lerteco,
  ~gracio
inert, inerta
inertia, (gen), inercio
inevitable, neevitebla, nepra
inexorable, neŝanĝebla, nedeturnebla,
  nepra

inexplicable, neklarigebla
infant, bebo, infaneto; **infancy**, ~eco;
  infanticide, infanmortigo; **infantile**,
  infan(ec)a
infante, infanto; **infanta**, ~ino
infantry, infanterio; **infantryman**,
  ~ano
infarct, infarkto; **infarction**, ~iĝo; **inf-**
  arctogenic, ~ogena
infatuation, furoramo; **be infatuated**
  with, ~i [tr]
infect, infekti [tr]; **infection**, ~o; **infec-**
  tious, ~a, kontaĝa; **disinfect**, des~i
  [tr]; **disinfectant**, des~enzo
infer, (conclude, deduce), inferenci [tr],
  indukti [tr] [cp "deduce", "imply"];
  inference, ~o, indukto
inferior, (lower, gen), malsupera, suba;
  (psych; less value, gen), malplivalora;
  (person), subulo; **inferiority**, ~eco;
  malplivaloreco; **inferiority complex**,
  (psych), komplekso de malplivaloreco
inferno, (hell), infero; (fire), incendio;
  infernal, ~a
infest, infesti [tr]
infidel, nekredanto
infiltrate, infiltri [tr]; ~iĝi; ~aĵo
infinite, (gen), infinita; (non-tech), senlima; **infinity**, ~o; **infinitesimal**,
  infinitezima; **infinitesimal size**, infi-
  nitezimo
infinitive, infinitivo; ~a
infirm, (weak, feeble), malfortika, febla; (unstable), malstabila; (decrepit),
  kaduka; **infirmity**, ~aĵo; ~eco; mal-
  stabileco; kadukeco
infirmary, flegejo, hospital(et)o
infix, infikso
in flagrante delicto, kun la peko en la
  mano, kun la freŝa faro
inflate, (w air), aeri [tr]; ~iĝi; (swell,
  puff up), ŝveli [int], pufiĝi; ŝveligi,
  pufigi; ($), inflaciigi; **inflated**, ~ita;
  (swollen), ŝvela, pufa; (pompous),
  bombasta, pompa; ($), inflaciigita; **in-**
  flation, ~(iz)(ad)o; ŝvel(ig)(ad)o, pu-
  fig(ad)o, pufiĝ(ad)o; ($), inflacio;
  inflationary, inflaci(ig)a

inflect, (gram), fleksii [tr]; ~iĝi; (modulate voice etc.), moduligi; moduliĝi; inflected, inflectional, ~a; uninflected, sen~a; inflection, ~o; (change of internal vowel, as "foot"/"feet"), infleksio
inflexion, [see "inflect"]
inflict, trudi [tr]; infliction, ~o; (suffering, punishment, etc.), sufer(ad)o, pun(ad)o; self-inflicted, sin~ita
inflorescence, infloresko
influence, (gen), influi [tr]; ~o; (elec), influenco; influential, ~a
influenza, gripo
influx, enfluo
inform, informi [tr], sciigi; informant, ~into; ~anto; information, (report, communication, gen), informo(j); ~a; (criminal), akuzo; informative, ~a; informer, denuncinto; denuncanto; inform on, (report criminal), denunci [tr]; (well-)informed, klera, (bone) ~ita; ill-informed, malklera, ne~ita, senscia; disinformation, mal~o [not "dis~o"]; misinform, mis~i [tr]; misinformation, mis~o
infra-, (pfx), infra-
infraction, romp(et)o, malobeo
infrastructure, vorkaro†, infrastrukturo
infringe, rompi [tr], malobei [tr]; infringe on, (intrude), sin trudi (sur, al, ĉe); infringement, altrudo, surtrudo
infundibulum, infundiblo
infuriate, furioz/igi; infuriated, ~a; become infuriated, ~iĝi
infuse, (imbue, impart), impregni [tr], plenigi; (inspire), inspiri [tr]; (steep, as tea), infuzi [tr]; infusion, ~o, plenigo; inspiro; infuzo
Infusoria, infuzorioj
infusorium, infuzorio
ingenious, inĝenia, genia
ingenue, senspertulino
ingenuity, inĝenieco
ingenuous, malkaŝema, simpla, naiva, senartifika
ingest, ingesti [tr]
ingot, ingoto

ingrained, enradikiĝinta, ĝisosta
ingrate, nedankema; ~ulo
ingratiate, favorigi
ingredient, ingredienco
ingress, (entering), eniro; (right), ~rajto; (place), ~ejo
inguinal, ingvena
inhabit, (reside in), loĝi [int] (en); (take up residence), ek~i [int] (en); inhabitant, ~anto; inhabitable, ~ebla; inhabited, ~ata; uninhabitable, ne~ebla; uninhabited, ne~ata, senhoma
inhale, enspiri [tr, int]; (med: draw in medication), inhali [tr]; inhalant, inhala; inhalaĵo; inhalator, inhalatoro
inherent, imanenta
inherit, heredi [tr]; inheritance, ~aĵo; disinherit, sen~igi
inhibit, (chem: psych), inhibi† [tr], inhibicii [tr]; (hinder, gen), malhelpi [tr], bridi [tr]; inhibition, ~o; inhibiter, ~ilo; ~anto; (chem), inhibenzo; uninhibited, sen~a
inimical, malamika
inimitable, neimitebla
iniquitous, maljusta, fia; iniquity, ~eco, fieco
initial, (first), unua, komenca; (letter), inicialo; (sign initials), parafi [tr]; initialize, (cmptr), initi† [tr]; initials, (signed), parafo
initiate, (into club, private knowledge, etc.), inici [tr]; ~ito; ~ato; ~oto; (start), iniciati [tr]; initiation, ~o; iniciato
initiative, (first action), iniciato; (enterprise, tendency to act first), ~emo, iniciativo
inject, (force into, lit or fig, as into body, motor, discussion), injekti [tr]; (ast: into orbit), enorbitigi; injection, ~o; enorbitigo; injector, (in motor), injektoro
injective, injektivo
injunction, (malpermes)ordono
injure, (wound), vundi [tr], lezi [tr]; (damage), difekti [tr]; (offend; do in-

justice to, wrong), ofendi [tr]; (hinder, gen), malhelpi [tr], malutili [int] (al); **injurious**, ~a; difekt(em)a; malutila; **injury**, ~o, lezo; difekto; ofendo; malhelpo, malutilo
ink, inko; ~i [tr]; **inky**, ~(ec)a; **inkblot**, ~makulo; **ink brush**, (for Oriental writing, art), tuĉopeniko; **ink stick**, tuĉobastoneto; **inkwell**, ~ujo; **India ink**, Ĉina inko, tuĉo; (draw, write w India ink), tuĉi [int]
inkling, ideeto
inlaid, inkrustita [cp "marquetry"]
in-law, boparenco [see also sfx "-in-law"]
-in-law, (sfx), bo– [pfx] (e.g.: *father-in-law:* bopatro) [see also n "in-law"]
inlay, inkrusti [tr]; ~aĵo [cp "marquetry"]
inlet, (small bay), kreko
in loco parentis, anstataŭ gepatroj
in memoriam, memorige (al)
inn, hotelo, gastejo; (esp rural), albergo†; **innkeeper**, mastro
innards, (gen), internaĵoj; (viscera), visceroj
innate, denaska, natura
inner, (inside), interna; (farther in), pli ~a; **innermost**, plej ~a
innervate, nervizi [tr]
inning, (lud)periodo
innocent, (blameless), senkulpa; (guileless, naïve), naiva, senartifika; (ignorant), senscia; **innocence**, ~eco; naiveco; senscio
Innocent, (pope), Inocento
innocuous, (harmless), sendanĝera; (dull, uninspiring), seninspira
innovate, novenkonduki [tr], (en)novigi; **innovation**, ~o; ~aĵo; **innovative**, ~ema
innuendo, subsugesto
innumerable, sennombraj
Ino, Inoa
inoculate, inokuli [tr]
inordinate, malmodera, ekscesa
inquest, enketo
inquire, enketi [int] (pri), demandi [tr]

(pri), esplori [tr]; **inquiry**, ~o, demando, esploro
inquisition, (gen inquiry), enketo; (rel), inkvizicio
inquisitive, scivolema, demandema
inquisitor, inkvizitoro
in re, pri
inroad, (invasion; any penetration), invado, enrompo, penetro; (erosion), erozio
inscribe, (write on, gen; over door etc.), surskribi [tr]; (write in book, list, etc.; geom: draw in), enskribi [tr]; (enroll, record), registri [tr]; **inscription**, ~o; enskribo; registro; (epigraph), epigrafo
inscrutable, nekomprenebla,   mistera, nepenetrebla, enigma
insect, insekto; **insecticide**, ~icido; **insectivora**, ~ovoruloj; **insectivore**, ~ovorulo; **insectivorous**, ~ovora; **scale insect**, koĉo; **stick insect**, fasmo; **winged insect**, flugilulo; **wingless insect**, senflugilulo
inseminate, (impregnate),   impregni [tr]; (sow seeds in, gen), prisemi [tr]; **insemination**, ~(ad)o; **artificial insemination**, art~(ad)o
insert, enmeti [tr]; ~aĵo; **insertion**, ~o
inside, interno; ~a; ~e de; ~en; **insider**, ~ulo; **inside-out**, (thoroughly), ĝisfunde; (sides reversed), ~o-ekstera; ~o-ekstere; **turn (something) inside-out**, eksterigi la ~on (de io)
insidious, insida
insight, (perceptiveness),   sagac/eco, perceptivo, akravido; (understanding of specific situation), ekkompreno; **insightful**, ~a, percepta, akravida
insignia, insigno(j)
insinuate, (hint), subsugesti [tr], implici [tr]; (worm way into), enŝovi (sin en)
insipid, (w/o flavor), sen/sapora; (dull, lifeless), ~viva, malinteresa, banala
insist, insisti [int]; **insistent**, ~a; **insistence**, ~(ad)o
insofar as, [see "as: as far as"]
insole, interna plandumo

insolent, insolenta, impertinenta, malre-
spekta; insolence, ~eco
insoluble, (gen), nesolvebla
insolvent, nesolventa; insolvency, ~eco
insomnia, sendormeco
insouciant, trankvila, senzorga
inspan, jungi [tr]
inspect, inspekti [tr]; inspector, ~into;
~anto; ~onto; ~isto, inspektoro; (government official), revizoro
inspire, inspiri [tr]; inspiration, ~o; in-
spirational, ~a
install, instali [tr]; installation, ~(ad)o;
~aĵo; installment, ($), partopago;
(any part), parto; yearly installment,
($), anuitato
instance, (example, case), kazo, ekzemplo; (step of legal procedure), instanco; (legal suit), proceso
instant, (moment), momento; (present),
nuna; (immediate), tuja; (instantly
dissolving, as coffee, tea, etc.), tuj-
solvebla instantly, instantaneously,
tuj; instantaneous, tuja
instate, (in office etc.), enoficigi, instali [tr], enpostenigi
instead, anstataŭe; instead of, anstataŭ
[prep]
instep, instepo
instigate, instigi [tr]
instill, semi [tr], inspiri [tr], infuzi [tr]
instinct, instinkto; instinctive, instinctual, ~a
institute, (institution), instituto; (begin),
iniciati [tr], estigi, komenci [tr], starigi
institution, institucio; institutional,
~a; institutionalize, (create institution), ~igi; (put into institution),
en~igi
instruct, instrui [tr, int]; instruction,
(gen), ~(ad)o; ~aĵo; (regulations;
cmptr), instrukcio; instructive, ~a;
instructor, (gen), ~into; ~anto; ~on-
to; ~isto; (university, not professor),
docento
instrument, (gen), instrumento; (tool),
ilo; instrumental, (mus), ~a; (help-

ful), helpa, utila; (gram), instrumenta-
lo; instrumentalist, (mus), ~isto;
instrumentation, ~ado; ~aro; brass
instrument, latun~o; percussion instrument, perkut~o; string(ed) instrument, kord~o; wind instrument,
blov~o; woodwind instrument, ligna
blov~o
insular, insula; ~eca; (isolated), izolita;
insularity, ~eco
insulate, (gen), izoli [tr]; (against heat,
cold), varm~i [tr]; insulation, ~ado;
~aĵo; insulating, ~a; insulator, ~ilo;
~aĵo; (dielectric), dielektriko
insulin, insulino
insult, insulti [tr]; ~o; insulting, ~a
insuperable, nesuperebla, nevenkebla
insure, (against loss, misfortune), asekuri [tr]; (make sure), certigi; insurance, ~o; coinsure, kun~i [tr];
insurance agent, ~agento
insurgent, insurgento; insurgence, insurekcio, ribelo
insurrection, insurekcio
intact, integra, sendifekta, senmanka,
tuta
intaglio, intajlo; ~igi
integer, entjero
integral, (math: integrated function), in-
tegral/ato; ~a; (re integer), entjera;
(whole), integra; (basic), esenca, baza
integrate, (math), integrali [tr]; (make
whole, unite, gen), ~igi; ~iĝi
integrity, (sound, whole, gen), integre-
co; (honesty), honesteco
integument, tegumento
intellect, intelekto; intellectual, ~a;
~ulo; intellectualism, ~isma; intellectualize, (think intellectually),
~umi [int]
intelligent, inteligenta; intelligence,
(intelligent condition), ~eco; (spying),
spionado; (news), novaĵo, informo;
intelligentsia, inteligencio
intelligible, komprenebla, klara
intend, (plan, have intent), intenci [tr];
(set time, purpose, etc.), destini [tr]
intendant, intendanto

intense, intensa; **intensify**, ~igi; ~iĝi; **intensity**, ~eco; **intensive**, (intense), ~a, intensiva; (making intense, as in gram), ~iga

intent, (purpose, plan), intenco; (law: to commit crime), dolo; (firmly attentive), (firm)atenta; (intense), intensa; **intention**, ~o; **intentional**, ~a; **well-intentioned**, bon~a

inter, enterigi, entombigi; **disinter**, elterigi, eltombigi

inter–, (pfx), inter–

intercede, propeti [int]; **intercession**, ~o

intercept, (stop, catch), interkapti [tr]; (math etc.: intersect), sekci [tr], tranĉi [tr]

intercom, interkomo†

intercourse, (social), rilatoj, ~ado, komunikado; (sexual), koito, kopulacio, seks~o(j)

interdict, interdikto; ~i [tr]; **interdiction**, ~o

interest, (desire, concern about), interesi [tr]; ~o; ($), interezo; (concern), koncerni [tr]; koncerno; (right, claim), rajto; (advantage), avantaĝo, profito; **interested**, ~ita; (having concern in), koncerna; **interests**, (persons involved in something), ~uloj; koncernuloj; **be(come) interested (in)**, (iu) ~iĝi (pri), ~i (iun) (e.g.: *he's interested in music:* li ~iĝas pri la muziko [or] muziko ~as lin); **interesting**, ~a; **disinterest**, indiferenteco, mal~o; **disinterested**, indiferenta; (impartial), nepartizana, neŭtrala; **self-interest**, mem~o

interface, (cmptr; tech; fig), interfaco†; ~i [int]

interfere, (conflict), konflikti [tr]; (intervene), interveni [int]; (hinder), malhelpi [tr]; (meddle), sin trudi, sin intermiksi, sin intermeti; (mus, optics, etc.), interferi [int]; (radio etc.: disturbance as from atmospheric conditions), perturbi [tr] [cp "jam"]; **interference**, ~o; interveno; malhel-

po; sintrudo; interfero; perturbo

interferon, interferono†

interim, intertempo, intervalo; ~a, provizora; **in the interim**, ~e, dum(temp)e, provizore

interior, (inside, gen), interna; ~o; (of country), land~o; (of picture), interioro; **Department (Ministry) of the Interior**, Departemento (Ministerio) pri I~aj Aferoj

interject, intermeti [tr]; **interjection**, (gram), interjekcio

interlocutor, konversaci/anto, kunparolanto; **interlocutory**, ~a; (law: not final), provizora

interlope, sin trudi; **interloper**, sintrudanto, entrudanto

interlude, interludo

intermediary, pera; ~into; ~anto; ~onto; ~isto; interulo; ~ilo

intermediate, (in middle), intera, meza; ~ajo

intermezzo, intermezo

intermission, (theat etc.), interakto; (interruption, pause), intermito, interrompo, paŭzo

intermit, intermiti [int]; **intermittent**, ~a; **be intermittent**, ~i

intermontane, intermonta

intern, (doctor etc.), intern/ulo; (any apprentice), metilernanto, studento-asistanto; (detain), ~igi, reteni [tr]; **internist**, ~aĵisto; **internship**, ~servo

internal, interna; **internalize**, ~igi

interne, [see "intern"]

internecine, interdetrua, intereksterma

interpellate, interpelacii [tr]; **interpellation**, ~o

interpolate, interpoli [tr]

interpose, intermeti [tr]

interpret, interpreti [tr]; **interpretation**, ~o; ~ado; **interpreter**, ~isto; **interpretive**, ~a; **misinterpret**, mis~i [tr]

interregnum, inter/regado, ~reĝado [not "~regno"]

interrogate, pridemandi [tr], ekzameni [tr]; **interrogation**, ~ado, ekzamena-

do; **interrogative, interrogatory**, demanda; (law), demandaro
interrupt, interrompi [tr]; **interruption,** ~o
inter se, inter si
intersect, intersekci [tr], kruci [tr]; ~iĝi, kruciĝi; **intersection,** (gen), ~(iĝ)o, kruc(iĝ)o; (roads), vojkruco, stratkruco
intersperse, interŝuti [tr], intersterni [tr], traplekti [tr]
interstice, interstico; (of mesh etc.), maŝo; **interstitial,** ~a
intertrigo, intertrigo
interval, (space), inter/spaco; (time), ~tempo; (mus; math), intervalo
intervene, interveni [int]; **intervenion,** ~o
interview, intervjuo; ~i [tr]
intestate, sentestamenta
intestine, intesto; **intestinal,** ~a; **gastrointestinal,** gastroentera
intimate, intima; ~ulo; (hint), implici [tr], sugesti [tr]; **intimacy,** ~eco; ~aĵo; **intimation,** implico, sugesto
intimidate, timigi, minaci [tr]
into, en (–on) (e.g.: *into the house:* ~ la domon) [cp "in"]; **be into,** (colloq; involve self in, be interested in), koncerni sin pri, envolvi sin en, interesiĝi pri
intone, (as chant), psalmi [tr], ĉanti [tr]; (give intonation, set tone), tonigi; **intonation,** ~ado, ĉantado; tonigo; (phon), intonacio
in toto, entute
intoxicate, (drunk), ebri/igi; (med; re any toxin), toksi [tr]; **intoxicated,** ~a; toksita; **intoxicating,** ~iga; toksa; **intoxication,** ~o; toks(iĝ)o; **intoxicant,** ~enzo; tokso; toksino [see "toxin"]
intra–, (pfx), intra–
intractable, nepritraktebla, neregebla, nebridebla
intramural, (same school), samlerneja
intransigent, malcedema
intravenous, intravejna
intrepid, sentima, kuraĝa, brava
intricate, komplika, labirint(ec)a; **intri-**

cacy, ~eco, labirinteco
intrigue, (plot), intrigi [int], komploti [int]; ~o, komploto; (interest), fascini [tr], interes(eg)i [tr]; **intriguing,** fascina, interes(eg)a
intrinsic, esenca, imanenta, propra
introduce, (re thing), enkonduki [tr]; (re person), prezenti [tr], konatigi; **introduction,** ~o; prezento, konatigo; **introductory,** ~a; prezenta, konatiga
introit, enirkanto
introject, internigi
introrse, introrsa
introspection, introspekto; **introspective,** ~a
introvert, introverti* [tr]; ~ito; **introversion,** ~iteco; **introvertive, introverted,** ~it(ec)a
intrude, entrud/iĝi, sin ~i; **intrusion,** ~o; **intrusive,** ~(em)a
intuit, intui [tr]; **intuition,** intuicio, ~ado; **intuitive,** intuicia, ~a
intumesce, ŝveli [int], pufiĝi
Inuit, Inuito†; ~a
inundate, inundi [tr]
inure, hardi [tr], alkutimigi
in utero, enutera; ~e
invade, invadi [tr]; **invasion,** ~o
invalid, (cripple), invalido; ~a
invar, invaro
invective, insult(ad)o, denunc(eg)o
inveigh, ataki [tr], denunci [tr]
inveigle, forlogi [tr], mistifiki [tr], kaĵol(log)i [tr]
invent, inventi [tr]; (think up), elpensi [tr] **invention,** ~ado; ~aĵo; **inventive,** ~(em)a
inventory, inventaro; ~i [tr]
inverse, inversa; ~o
inversion, inversigo; (gram; of atmosphere), inversio
invert, (mus; chem; psych), inverti [tr]; ~iĝi; ~ito; (reverse, gen), inversigi; **invert sugar,** ~sukero
invertase, invertazo
invest, (gen), investi [tr]; (esp for purpose of saving), plasi [tr]; **investment,** ~ado; ~aĵo

investigate, espalori [tr], enketi [tr] (pri), sondi [tr]; **investigation**, ~o, enketo, sondo
inveterate, enradikiĝinta, ĝisosta
investiture, investituro
invidious, (causing envy), enviiga; (offensive), ofenda
invigorate, (pli)vigligi; **invigorating**, ~a
invincible, nevenkebla
inviolate, netuŝ/ita, sankta, neperfidita; **inviolable**, ~ebla, sankta, neperfidebla
invite, (give invitation), inviti [tr]; (attract), logi [tr]; **invitation**, ~o; **invitational**, ~a; **inviting**, loga
invocation, alpreĝo; ~ado
invoice, fakturo
invoke, (call on, gen), envoki [tr]; (pray to), alpreĝi [tr]; (law etc. to defend action), invoki [tr]
involute, (curved in), envolv/ita; **involution**, ~(aĵ)o
involve, (concern, have to do w), koncerni [tr], temi pri; (entangle), impliki [tr]; **involved**, (complex), komplika, kompleksa; (tangled), implikita; (busy), okupita; **be involved (in, with)**, (occupy self with), engaĝiĝi (en, pri)
invultation, envulto; **perform invultation on**, (doll etc.), ~i [tr]
Io, (ast), Ioo*; (myth), Ioa
iodine, jodo; **iodate**, ~ato; **iodide**, ~ido; **iodize**, ~i [tr]
iodo–, (chem pfx), jodo–
iodoform, jodoformo
iodol, jodolo
iodometry, jodometrio
ion, jono; **ionic**, ~a; **ionize**, ~igi; **ionosphere**, ~osfero; **zwitterion**, ambaŭ~o
Ionia, Ionio; **Ionian**, ~a
Ioni/c, (re Ionia), Ionia; (arch), Ionika
ionium, ionio
iota, joto, jota [see § 16]
I.O.U. pagpromeso
Iowa, Iovao

ipecac(uanha), ipeko, ipekakuano
Ips, (zool), ipo†
IQ, intelekta kvociento† [no abb established in Esperanto]
Iphigenia, Ifigenia
Ipomoea batatas, batato
Iran, Irano; **Iranian**, ~a; ~ano
Iraq, Irako; **Iraqi**, ~a; ~ano
irascible, kolerema
ire, kolero; **irate**, ~a
Ireland, Irlando [cp "Eire"]; **Northern Ireland**, Nord-~o; **Irish**, ~a; ~ana [cp "Gaelic"]; **Irish(man)**, ~ano
Irene, Irena
iridectomy, irisektomio
iridesce, iriz/iĝi; **iridescence**, ~eco; **iridescent**, ~a; **make iridescent**, ~i [tr]
iriditis, irisito
iridium, iridio
iridotomy, irisotomio
iris, (bot), irido; (anat), iriso
Iris, (myth; woman's name), Irisa; (bot), irido
Irish, [see under "Ireland"]
iritis, irisito
irk, ĝeni [tr], ĉagreni [tr], koleretigi; **irksome**, ~a, ĉagrena
Irma, Irma
iron, (metal), fero; ~a; (clothes), gladi [tr]; gladilo; **ironing board**, gladotabulo; **iron-clad**, kirasita; **ironweed**, veroniko; **ironwood**, (tree), karpeno; (wood), karpenligno; **ironworker**, **ironmonger**, ~aĵisto; **cast iron**, giso; **cast-iron plant**, (bot), aspidistro; **pig iron**, kruda ~o [cp "pig"]; **steam iron**, vaporgladigilo; **strike while the iron is hot**, forĝi ~on dum ĝi estas varmega; elprofiti oportunon; **have too many irons in the fire**, havi tro da okupoj
irony, ironio; **ironic**, ~a
Iroquois, Irokezo; ~a; **Iroquoian**, ~o; ~a; ~lingva
Irrawady, Iravadio
irredentism, iredent/ismo; **irredentist**, ~isma; ~isto
irrevocable, nerevokebla, nemalfareb-

la, nenuligebla
irrigate, (land), irigacii [tr]; (flush, as eyes), akvumi [tr]; **irrigation**, ~o; akvumo
irritate, iriti [tr], agaci [tr], inciti [tr]; **irritable**, ~iĝema; **irritation**, ~o, agaco, incito; **irritant**, ~enzo; ~ilo
Isaac, Isaako
Isabel, **Isabella**, **Isabelle**, Izabela
Isador, **Isadore**, Izidoro; **Isadora**, ~a
Isaiah, **Isaias**, (Bib), Jesaja
isatin, izatino
Isatis, izatido
Iscariot, Iskarioto
ischemia, iskemio
ischium, iskio
Isegrim, Izengrino
Isengrim, **Isengrin**, Izengrino
isentropic, izentropa
–ish, (sfx: like), –eca (e.g.: *devilish:* diableca); (somewhat), iom (e.g.: *largish:* iom granda)
Ishmael, Iŝmael
Ishtar, Iŝtar
Isidor(e), Izidoro
isinglass, (fish glue), iĥtiokolo; (mica), glimo
Isis, Izisa
Islam, Islamo; **Islamic**, ~a
Islamabad, Islamabado*
island, insulo; ~a; **islander**, ~ano; **traffic island**, **pedestrian island**, rifuĝejo; **Long Island**, I~o Longa; **Long Island Sound**, Markolo Long–I~a
isle, insul(et)o
islet, insuleto; **islets of Langerhans**, ~oj de Langerhans
ism, ismo
–ism, (sfx: doctrine, theory; manner of speaking; med condition; etc.), –ismo (e.g.: *capitalism:* kapital~o; *Americanism:* Uson~o; *alcoholism:* alkohol~o); (condition), –eco (e.g.: *heroism:* heroeco)
Ismail, Ismailo; **Ismailian**, ~ano
Ismene, Ismena
is(o)–, (pfx), izo–

isobar, izobaro
isobath, isobato†
isochronal, **isochronous**, izokrona
Isocrates, Izodrato
isodimorphous, **isodimorphic**, izodimorfa; **isodimorphism**, ~ismo
isogeotherm, izogeotermo
isogloss, izogloso
isolate, (gen), izoli [tr]; **isolation**, ~ado; ~eco; **isolationism**, ~ismo; **isolationist**, ~isma; ~isto
Isolde, Izolda
isomer, izomero; **structural isomer**, struktura ~o; **structural isomerism**, struktura ~eco
isomorph, (structure), izomorf/aĵo; (organism), ~ulo; **isomorphic**, ~a; **isomorphism**, ~eco
isonym, izonimo
isoprene, izopreno
isosceles, simetria
isotherm, izotermo; **isothermal**, **isothermic**, ~a
isotonic, izotona
isotope, izotopo; **radioisotope**, radio~o
isotropic, izotropa
Israel, (man's name; Jewish people), Izraelo; (country), Israelo; **Israeli**, Israelano; ~a, Israela; **Israelite**, ~ido
Israfil, **Israfel**, **Israfeel**, Israfilo
Issachar, Isaĥar
issue, (question), demando; (of publication), numero (e.g.: *the May issue:* la numero de majo); (publish), eldoni [tr], aperigi; (emit, give out, gen), eligi, disdoni [tr], eldoni [tr]; eliĝi; (distribute), distribui [tr]; ($), emisii [tr]; emisio; (outflow), elflui [int]; elfluo; (come out), elveni [int]; (result), rezulti [int]; rezulto; (offspring), id(ar)o; (profit), profito; **at issue**, diskutata, diskutota, decidenda; **take issue with**, malkonsenti kun, pri~i [tr]
Issus, Isso
–ist, (adj sfx: re "–ism"), –isma (e.g.: *a socialist country:* socialisma lando); (n sfx: follower of "–ism"), –isto [cp "–ant"]

Istanbul, Istanbulo
isthmus, istmo
–istic, [see "–ist"]
Istria, Istrio
it, ĝi; (reflexive), si [see "her"]; [note: not translated when impersonal, when verb has no subject (e.g.: *it is raining:* pluvas; *it doesn't matter:* ne gravas)]; **its,** ~a; sia; **itself,** si(n) mem
italic, (type), kursiva; **italics,** ~o; **italicize,** ~igi
Italy, Ital/io; **Italian,** ~o; ~a; ~ia
itch, juki [int]; ~o; **itchy,** ~(ig)a; **itchweed,** blanka veratro; **make (one) itch,** ~igi (e.g.: *grass makes me itch:* herbo min ~igas)
–ite, (chem, mineral etc. sfx), –ito; (descendant), –ido (e.g.: *Israelite:* Israelido); (follower), –ano, –isto (e.g.: *Hitlerite:* Hitlerano)
item, ero; **itemize,** detali [tr]
iterate, (repeat, gen), ripeti [tr]; (math), iteracii [tr]; **iteration,** ~(ad)o; iteracio
Ithaca, (gen), Itako
itinerant, migra; **itinerancy,** ~ado; ~antaro
itinerary, itinero
–ition, (sfx), [see "–ation"]
–itis, (med sfx), –ito
itty-bitty, eteta
–itude, (sfx), –eco (e.g.: *pulchritude:* beleco)
–ity, (sfx), –eco (e.g.: *stupidity:* stulteco)
IUD, (abb of "intrauterine device"), intrautera kontraŭkoncipilo [no abb established in Esperanto]
Ivan, Ivano
–ive, (sfx: of, relating to), –a (e.g.: *substantive:* substanca); (tending to), –ema (e.g.: *creative:* kreema)
Ivo, Ivo
ivory, eburo; ~a; **Ivory Coast,** E~io; **vegetable ivory,** korozo, vegetaĵa ~o
ivy, hedero; **ground ivy,** nepeto; **Kenilworth ivy,** cimbalario; **poison ivy,** venen~o
Ixia, iksio

Ixion, Iksiono
Ixodes, iksodo
–ize, (sfx: apply substance; use method of), –izi [always tr] (e.g.: *pasteurize:* pasteŭrizi); (make into [n], make [adj]), –igi (e.g.: *fossilize:* fosiliigi; *publicize:* publikigi); (become), –iĝi (e.g.: *crystallize:* kristaliĝi); (act in manner of), –umi (e.g.: *intellectualize:* intelektumi)
Izmir, Izmiro

J

jab, (w sharp object), piki [tr]; ~o; (hit), bati [tr]; bato
jabber, babil(aĉ)i [int]; ~(ad)o
jaborandi, jaborando
jabot, ĵaboto
jacamar, galbulo
jacaranda, Jacaranda, jakarando
jacare, kajmano
jacinth, jacinto
jack, (lifting tool), kriko [cp "jack-screw" below]; (lift w jack), ~i [tr], ~levi [tr]; (cards), fanto, bubo; (elec: male plug), ĵako; (female plug), ĵakingo; (fish: pike), ezoko; (lawn bowling), celglobo; (flag), flago; **jack(ass),** (lit or as insult), (vir)azeno; **jackboot,** kavaleria boto; **jackdaw,** monedo; **jackfruit,** (fruit), jakvo; (tree), jakvarbo; **jackhammer,** manramo; **jack-in-the-box,** saltpupo; **jackknife,** poŝtranĉilo; (dive), faldplongo; faldplongi [int]; (fold, as truck), kunfaldi [tr]; kunfaldigi; kunfaldigo; **jack-of-all-trades,** (gen), ĉiufakulo; (esp as employee), faktoto; **jack-o'-lantern,** (pumpkin), citrolulo; **jackpot,** ĉefpremio; **hit the jackpot,** (lit or fig), gajni la ĉefpremion; **jackscrew,** ŝraŭblevilo
Jack, (man's name), [see "John"]; **Jacky, Jackie,** (short for "Jacqueline"), Jakenjo, Janjo; **Jack-by-the-hedge,** (bot), aliario
jackal, ŝakalo
jacket, (coat), jako; (of book), ~eto; (of cmptr or recording disk), (disk)koverto; (any covering, as of bullet, pipe, etc.), kovri [tr]; kovraĵo, volvaĵo, tegaĵo; (folder), dosierujo; **life jacket,** sav~o; **smoking jacket,** smokingo; **straight-jacket,** frenez~o
Jackson:, Port Jackson, Porto Jackson
Jacob, Jakobo; **Jacobite,** ~isto; **Jacob's-ladder,** (bot: *Polemonium*), polemonio
Jacobin, jakobeno; **Jacobinism,** ~ismo
Jacquard, [see "loom", "weave"]
Jacqueline, Jakelino, Ĵakvino; **Jacquie,**

Jakenjo, Janjo
Jacques, Ĵakvo
jade, (stone), jado; (weary), tedi [tr], lacigi, supersatigi, enuigi; **jaded,** supersata, enua
jaeger, rabmevo
Jaffa, Jafo
jag, noĉo; ~i [tr]; **jagged,** ~ita, neregula, zigzaga
Jag(i)ello, jagelono
jaguar, jaguaro
jai alai, pelotot
jail, prizono, malliberejo; en~igi, malliberigi; **jailbird,** ~ulo; **jailbreak,** ~eskapo
Jain, Jaina, Ĝaino; ~a; **Jainism,** ~ismo
Jakarta, Ĝakarto
jalap, (root, drug), jalapo; ~ujo, ~planto
jalopy, aŭtaĉo
jalousie, ĵaluzio
jam, (plug, clog), ŝtopi [tr], obstrukci [tr]; ~igi, obstrukcigi; ~(ig)o, obstrukc(ig)o; (radio etc.), ĵami [tr] [cp "interfere"]; (fruit preserve), konfitaĵo; (stuff, shove in), farĉi [tr], enŝovi [tr]; (mus), improvizi [int]; improviz(ad)o; (predicament), embaraso, malfacilaĵo; **jampacked,** (plen)farĉita, plen~ita; **jam session,** improviza sesio; **in a jam,** embarasita, en embaraso, en malfacilaĵo
Jamaica, Jamaiko; **Jamaican,** ~a; ~ano
jamb, framflanko
jamboree, ĵamboreo
Jambosa, jamboso; Jambosa caryophyllus, kariofilarbo, kariofilmirto
James, Jakobo
Jane, Johana; **Janie,** Janjo
Janet, Johana
jangle, (clanging sound), klaktinti [int]; ~igi; ~(ad)o; [cp "jingle"]; (on nerves), agaci [tr], malkvietigi, maltrankviligi
janitor, purigisto; **janitorial,** ~a
janizary, janiĉaro
Jansen, (Cornelis), Janseno; **Jansenism,** ~ismo; **Jansenist,** ~isma; ~isto
January, januaro

Janus, Jano
Japan, Japan/io; **Japanese**, ~o; ~a; ~ia
Japheth, Jafeto; **Japhetic**, (language), ~ida
japonica, (*Camellia*), kamelio
jar, (pot), jaro, poto; (on nerves), agaci [tr]; (be dissonant), disonanci [int]; (shake), skui [tr]; **jarring**, agaca; disonanca; skua; **bell jar**, (for vacuum), recipiento; (for storage, display), klošo
jargon, jargono
jarrah, eŭkalipto
Jarvis, Gervazo
Jasione, jaziono
jasmine, jasmeno; **Cape jasmine**, gardenio; **night jasmine**, (*Cestrum*), cestro
Jasmium, jasmeno
Jason, Jazono
jasper, jaspo, jaspiso
jaundice, iktaro; **jaundiced**, ~a; (jealous), jaluza; (envious), envia
jaunt, ekskurso; **jaunty**, gaja
Java, Javo; **Javanese**, ~a; ~ano
Javan, Javan
javelin, jetlanco
jaw, (anat, gen; or similar object), makzelo; (maxilla), maksilo; (of wild animal, or analogous opening), faŭko
jay(bird), garolo
jazz, jazo; **jazzy**, (mus), ~(ec)a; (lively), gaja, vigla; **jazz band, jazz combo**, ~trupo
jealous, jaluza [cp "envy"]; **be jealous (of)**, ~i [int] (pri); **jealousy**, ~o
Jean, (woman's name), Jana, Johana; (French man's name), ~o; **Jeanette**, ~eta; **Jean-Jacques**, ~-Jakvo
jeans, ĝinzo [note sing]
jeep, jipo
jeer, moki [tr]; ~krii [int]; ~(kri)o
Jeff, Ĝoĉjo
Jeffrey, Gofredo
Jehoash, Jehoašo
Jehoiada, Jehojada
Jehoshaphat, Jehošafat
Jehova, Jehovo†; **Jehova's Witness(es)**, (rel), Atestanto(j) de ~o
Jehu, Jehu
jejunum, jejuno
jell, ĝel/iĝi; ~iĝi

jelly, (food), jeleo; (any gelatinous substance), gelatenajo; **jellyfish**, meduzo; **stinging jellyfish**, cianeo, brulmeduzo; **star jelly**, (bot), nostoko
Jenghiz Khan, Ĝingiz-Ĥano
Jenna, Jennie, Jenny, Janjo, Ginjo [see also "Jane", "Jennifer"]
Jennifer, Ginevra
jenny, (donkey), azenino
Jenny, (woman's name), [see "Jenna"]
jeopardy, danĝero; (law), akuzateco; **jeopardize, put in jeopardy**, en~igi
jerboa, dipodo
Jeremiad, Jeremiado
Jeremiah, Jeremias, Jeremy, Jeremia, ~o
Jericho, Jeriĥo, Jeriko
jerk, (pull), ektiri [tr]; ~iĝi; ~o; (shake, push), ekskui [tr], ekšovi [tr], šanceli [tr]; ekskuiĝi, ekšoviĝi, šanceliĝi; (spasm), spasmiĝi; spasmo; (colloq: foolish person), stultulo, folulo
jerky, (beef), sekbovajo
Jeroboam, Jerobeam
Jerome, Jeromo
jersey, (gen), jerzo
Jersey, (island), Jerzeo; (cattle), ~a(j) (gebovoj); **New Jersey**, Nov-~o
Jerusalem, Jerusalemo
Jervis, Gervazo
jessamine, [see "jasmine"]
jest, (joke), šerci [int]; ~o; (lie jokingly), blagi [int]; blago; **jester**, klaŭno
Jesuit, Jezuito; **Jesuitism, Jesuitry**, ~ismo
Jesus, Jesuo; **Jesus Christ**, ~o Kristo
jet, (spurt, stream), špruci [int]; ~(aj)o; (nozzle), (~)ajuto; (plane), jeto; (mineral), gagato; **jet engine**, reaktoro; **jetliner**, jeto; **jet-propelled**, reakcipelita; **jet propulsion**, reakcipelado; **jet stream**, (in atmosphere), ~fluo; (behind rocket etc.), reakcifluo; **ramjet**, ramreaktoro; ramjeto; **propjet**, helicojeto; **turbojet**, turbinreaktoro; turbinjeto
jetsam, forjetajo
jettison, forjeti [tr]
jetty, ĝeto
Jew, Judo; **Jewish**, ~a; **Jew's-ear**, (bot), aŭrikulario; **Jew's-harp**, zumfero; **Wandering Jew**, (myth), Ahas-

vero
jewel, juvelo; **jewelry,** ~aro; **jeweler,** ~isto; **jewelweed,** balzamino; **costume (paste, imitation) jewelry,** straso
jezebel, diablino
Jezebel, Izebel
jib, (sail), ĵibo; (boom), bumo; (balk), kalcitri [int]; **flying jib,** for~o; **jib boom,** buspritbumo
jibe, (naut), gibi [tr]; ~iĝi; (conform), konformiĝi [cp "gibe"]
Jibuti, Ĝibutio
jiffy, (moment), moment(et)o, sekundo
jig, (tune, dance), ĵigo; (template), ŝablono
jigger, (chigger), ĉiko; (glass), glaseto
jiggle, skueti [tr]; ~iĝi; ~o
jigsaw, ĵigsegilo; **jigsaw puzzle,** puzlo
jillion, umiliono [see § 19(b)]
jilt, forlasi [tr], amtrompi [tr]
Jim, Jaĉjo
jimmy, levstang/eto; ~umi [tr]
Jina, (founder of Jainism), Ĝino
jingle, (plink, tinkle), tinti [int]; ~igi; ~(ad)o; (song), kanzoneto
jingo, ŝovinisto; **jingoism,** ŝovinismo; **jingoistic,** ŝovinisma
jinn, jinni, jinnee, ĝino
jinri(c)k(i)sha(w), rikiŝo, ĵinrikŝo
jinx, sorĉo; ~i [tr]
jitney, buseto
jitter, anksii [int], esti nervoza, barakteti [int]; **jittery,** nervoza, ~a
jive, blago; ~i [int] (al)
Jo, (woman's name), Jonjo
Joab, Joab
Joachim, Joakimo
Joan, Johana, Ĵana; **Joan of Arc,** ~a Dark
Joash, Jehoaŝo
job, (employment), ofico; (task), tasko, laboro, okupo; **jobless,** sen~a, sendunga, senlabora
Job, (Bib), Ijobo
Jocasta, Jokasta
jock, (jockey), ĵokeo; (jockstrap), ingvenzono; (athlete), atleto
jockey, (rider), ĵokeo; (maneuver), manovrigi
jockstrap, ingvenumo; (athlete), atleto
jocose, jocular, ŝerc(em)a, gaja

jodhpur(s), rajdopantalono [note sing]
Joel, Joel
joey, (kangaroo), kanguruido
jog, (trot), trot(et)i [int]; ~o; (jerk, nudge, as memory), skueti [tr]; skueto; (sharp turn), angulo; anguli [int]; **jogger,** ~anto
joggle, (shake), skueti [tr]; ~o
john, (colloq: toilet, restroom), necesejo
John, Johano; **Johnny,** Joĉjo, Johanĉjo, Hanĉjo; **Johnnie,** Johana, Janjo [see also "Ivan", "Jean", "Jacques", "Jane", "Jacqueline"]; **John Dory,** (zool), zeo; **St.-John's-bread,** (fruit), karobo; (tree), karobarbo; **St.-John's-wort,** hiperiko
joie de vivre, vivĝojo
join, (put, come together, gen), kun/igi, ~meti [tr]; ~iĝi, ~metiĝi; (mech: connect), kupli [tr]; kupliĝi; (w hinged or oth flexing joint), artiki [tr]; artikiĝi [see also "joint", "junction"]; (become member), aliĝi al; membriĝi al, en; aniĝi en; **subjoin,** aldoni [tr]; **join together, join up,** (~)ligi [tr]; (~)ligiĝi
joint, (mech; anat), artiko [see also "join", "junction"]; (of meat), (viando)peco; (between bricks, metal pieces, etc.), junto; (marijuana), mariĥuana cigaredo; (cheap bar), drinkejaĉo; (restaurant), manĝejaĉo, restoraciaĉo; (in common), komuna, kuna; **jointed,** (w joints), ~ita; **ball(-and-socket) joint,** glob~o; **mortise and tenon joint,** junto per tenono kaj mortezo; **rabbet joint,** rabeto, duonuma junto; **scarf joint,** fiksita junto; **tongue and groove joint,** junto per faldo kaj lango; **universal joint,** kardan~o; **out of joint,** (amiss), misa; (mech), el~igita
joist, solivo; ~izi [tr]
joke, ŝerci [int]; ~o; (lie in jest), blago; blagi [int]; **joker,** (card), ĵokero; **practical joke,** tromp~o; **no joke,** sen~e, serioze
jolly, gaja
jolt, (bump), ekskuegi [tr]; ~o; (shock, gen), ŝoki [tr]; ŝoko
Jonah, Jonas, Jona
Jonathan, Jonatano

Jonesia asoka, aŝoko
jonquil, jonkvilo
Jordan, (river), Jordano; (country), ~io;
  Jordanian, ~iano; ~iana; ~ia
Joseph, Jozefo; **Josephine,** ~a, ~ino
josh, (joke), priserĉi [int]
Josh, (man's name), Josĉjo, Josuĉjo
Joshua, Josuo
Josiah, Josias, Joŝija
jostle, ŝanceli [tr]; ~iĝi; ~o
Josue, Josuo
jot, (iota, bit), joto; (note), noti [tr]
jota, (dance), ĥoto
joule, ĵulo
jounce, skusalti [int]; ~igi; ~o
journal, (newspaper), ĵurnalo; (periodical), gazeto; (diary, record, log),
  taglibro; (mech: axle bearing), apogpunkto, lagropunkto; **journal box,** lagro; **journalese,** ~ĵargono
journey, vojaĝi [int]; ~o; **journeyman,**
  (person completing apprenticeship),
  submajstro
joust, turniri [int]; ~o
Jove, Jovo
jovial, joviala, gaja
Jovian, (re Jove, myth), Jova; (re planet
  Jupiter), Jupitera; (man's name), Jovi-
  ano
jowl, vangego
joy, ĝojo; **joyous,** ~a; **overjoy,** ravi [tr];
  overjoyed, ravita, ekstaza
jube, jubeo
jubilate, jubili [int]; **jubilation, jubi-
  lance,** ~o; **jubilant,** ~a
jubilee, jubileo
Judah, Jehudo, ~a
Judaic, Juda; **Judaism,** ~ismo; **Juda-
  ize,** (follow Jewish custom), judaizi
  [int]; (make Jewish), ~ecigi
Jude, Judas, Judaso
Judea, Judeo
Judeo–, (pfx), Jud(o)– (e.g.: *Judeo-
  Christian:* Jud-Kristana)
judge, (gen), juĝi [tr]; ~anto; ~isto;
  judgment, ~o; (discretion), diskreto,
  ~opovo; (prudence), prudento; **misjudge,** mistaksi [tr], mis~i [tr]; **pre-
  judge,** antaŭ~i [tr]
judicial, juĝista
judiciary, juĝa; ~ista; ~istaro
judicious, (discreet), diskreta, saĝa, pru-

denta; (moderate), modera; **injudi-
  cious,** mal~a, malsaĝa; malmodera
Judith, Judita
judo, ĵudo
Judy, Judinjo, Junjo
jug, vazo [cp "pitcher"]
Juggernaut, (rel) Ĝaganato†
juggle, ĵongli [tr] (per); **juggler,** ~isto
Juglans, juglandarbo
Jugoslavia, [see "Yugoslavia"]
jugular, jugularo; ~a
juice, suko; **juicy,** ~(plen)a
jujube, (fruit), jujubo; (tree), ~arbo
jukebox, diskogurdo
julep, julepo; **mint julep,** ment~o
Jules, Julino
Julian, Juliano; ~a
Julie, Julino
Juliette, Julieta
Julius, Julio
July, julio
jumble, miksi [tr], malordi [tr], malaranĝi [tr], ĥaosigi; ~amaso, senor-
  daĵo, ĥaoso; (words), galimatio;
  jumble (sale), (Br), brokantobazaro
jumbo, grandega, giganta
jump, (gen), salti [int]; (make jump),
  ~igi (e.g.: *jump a horse:* ~igi ĉevalon); (jump over), super~i [tr] (e.g.:
  the horse jumped the fence: la ĉevalo
  super~is la barilon); ~o; **jumpy,** nervoza; **jumper,** (blouse), bluzo; (elec
  cable), konektokablo; **jump rope,**
  ŝnur~i [int]; **jump-rope,** ~ŝnuro;
  broad jump, (sport), longo~o†; **high
  jump,** alto~o†; **jump off the deep
  end,** entrepreni tro multe; **jump to
  one's feet,** (subite) ekstari [int]; **jump
  the gun,** (lit or fig), antaŭ~i la pa-
  filon; **jump the track,** (lit or fig), dereliĝi
junction, (joining), kun/igo, ~meto;
  ~iĝo, ~metiĝo; [cp "join", "joint"];
  (elec, mech, etc.: contact), junto;
  (roads etc.), vojkruco; (rr) relkruco;
  junction box, (elec), juntejo
juncture, kun(met)iĝo; vojkruco; relkruco [see "junction"]; (crisis), krizo
Juncus, (bot), junko
June, (month), junio; (woman's name),
  J~a
jungle, ĝangalo

junior, (younger), pli juna; plijunulo; (after name), Juna, la Juna (e.g.: *John Smith, Jr.:* John Smith (la) Juna); (lower, subordinate), suba; subulo; sub– [pfx] (e.g.: *junior high school:* submezlernejo); (later date), pli lasta
juniper, junipero
Juniperus, junipero; Juniperus oxycedrus, oksicedra ~o
junk, (useless material), fatraso; ~igi; (Chinese boat), ĵonko; **junker**, (car etc.), ~aĵo, aŭtaĉo
junket, (trip), (plezura) ekskurso; (food), kaseaĵo
junkie, narkotulo
Juno, Junona
junta, konsilio, regantaro; (after coup d'état), puĉ-registaro
jupati, **jupaty** (**palm**), rafio
Jupiter, (gen), Jupitero [cp "Jove"]
Jura, (gen), Ĵuraso
Jurassic, Ĵuraso; ~a
juridical, jura
jurisdiction, (gen), jurisdikcio
jurisprudence, (gen), jurisprudenco; **jurisprudent**, juristo
jurist, (law expert), juristo; (member of jury), ĵuriano
jury, (law), ĵurio; (naut etc.: improvized), improvizita; **juror**, **member of the jury**, ~ano; **jury-rigged**, improvizita
just, (exact), ĝusta; ~e; (fair, lawful, proper), justa; (deserved), meritita; (near in time), ĵus (e.g.: *they just left:* ili ĵus foriris; *I'm just leaving:* mi ĵus foriras); (only), nur; (barely), apenaŭ; (next to, immediately), tuj (e.g.: *just beyond the tree:* tuj preter la arbo); (quite), tute; **just as much**, egale; **just right**, ~ega, preciza ~a, tute ~a
justice, (fairness; proper legal action), just/eco; (judge), juĝisto; (government department or ministry), justico (e.g.: *Department of Justice:* Departemento de Justico); **justice of the peace**, juĝisto de la paco; **do justice to**, dece trakti [tr], ~e trakti; **bring to justice**, venigi al ~eco, venigi antaŭ tribunalo
justify, (vindicate; show to be proper), pravigi; (give reason for), motivi [tr];

(type, page margin), ĝustigi; **justification**, ~o; ĝustigo
Justin, Justeno
Justinian, Justiniano; **Justinian Code**, ~a Kodo
jut, (project, stick out), elstari [int], korbeli [int]
jute, juto
Jutland, Jutlando
Juvenal, Juvenalo
juvenile, (young), juna; (childish), infaneca; (immature), nematura; (person), ~ulo, infano
juxtapose, apudigi; **juxtaposition**, ~o
Jylland, Jutlando
Jynx, jingo

K

Kaaba, Kaabo
kab, kab'o
kabala, kabalo
Kabul, Kabulo
Kabyle, (person), Kabilo; (region), ~io
Kaffir, Kafro; Kaffraria, ~io
kainite, kainito
kaiser, (Germana) imperiestro
Kakatoe, kakatuo
kakemono, kakemono
kala-azar, kala-azaro, nigra febro
Kalahari, Kalaharo
kale, krispa brasiko; sea kale, marbrasiko
kaleidoscope, kalejdoskopo
Kalends, Kalendoj
Kali, Kalia
kalif, kalifo
Kaliningrad, Kaliningrado
Kalmuk, Kalmyk, Kalmuko; ~a
kalpak, kalpako
Kamchatka, Kamĉatko
kamikaze, kamikazo†
Kampuchea, Kampuĉeo† [cp "Cambodia"]
Kanaka, Kanako
kangaroo, kanguruo; tree kangaroo, dendrolago
Kansas, Kansaso; Kansas City, ~urbo
Kansu, Gansu
Kant, Kantio; Kantian, ~a; ~ano; Kant(ian)ism, ~anismo
kaolin, kaolino
kaori, kaŭrio
kapok, kapoko
kappa, kapa [see § 16]
kaput, kaputa
Karachi, Karaĉio
Karakoram, Karakorumo
karakul, karakulo
karat, [see "carat"]
karate, karateo
Karelia, Karelio
Karen, Katarina
Karl, Karlo
karma, karmo; karmic, ~a
karst, karsto
karyokinesis, karjokinezo†, mitozo

karyoplasm, karjoplasmo†
karyotype, karjotipo†
Kashmir, Kaŝmiro
Katherine, Katarina
Katmandu, Katmanduo
Kattegat, Kategato
Katy, Kanjo
Kaunas, Kovno
kauri, kaurie, kaury, kaŭrio
kava, kavao
kawrie, kawry, kaŭrio
kayak, kajako
kayo, (k)nokaŭto; ~i [tr]
Kazakh, Kazaño; ~a; Kazakhstan, ~lando
Kazan, Kazano
kazoo, mirlitono
kea, keo
Kedron, Kidrono
keel, (gen), kilo; keelhaul, ~umi [tr]; keel over, fali [int], renversiĝi; on an even keel, stabila, senŝancela, ebena
keelson, kilsono
keen, (sharp, gen), akra; (enthused), entuziasma, vigla, fervora; (witty), sprita
keep, (save, conserve), konservi [tr]; ~iĝi (e.g.: she kept it as a souvenir: ŝi ~is ĝin kiel memoraĵon); (not spoil), ~iĝi; (observe, celebrate, as holiday, rite, etc.), celebri [tr]; (fulfill, follow, as promise, duty, etc.), plenumi [tr]; (maintain, hold in a place), teni [tr] (e.g.: keep a bird in a cage: teni birdon en kaĝo; keep one's feet warm: teni siajn piedojn varmaj); (retain), reteni [tr]; (last), daŭri [int]; (continue action), daŭre (e.g.: we kept running: ni daŭre kuris); (further, still), plu (e.g.: I changed her diaper, but she kept crying: mi aliigis ŝian bebtukon, sed ŝi plu ploris); (stay, remain), resti [int] (e.g.: keep right: resti dekstre; keep warm: resti varma); (take care of), varti [tr], gardi [tr], prizorgi [tr]; (lodging), loĝigi; loĝigo; (food), manĝigo; (prevent), malebligi, malhelpi [tr] (e.g.: keep him from talking:

malebligi ke li parolu); (stronghold), fortikaĵo; (support, livelihood), vivrimedo; **keeper**, (guard), gardisto; **keep at**, persisti en; **keep back**, (restrain), bridi [tr], reteni [tr]; (set aside, reserve), rezervi [tr]; **keep (it) down**, (quiet, calm), moderigi (ĝin); **keep it up**, daŭri [int]; daŭrigi; **keepsake**, memoraĵo; **keep the books**, kontadi [int]; **keep to**, persisti en; **keep to oneself**, (stay alone), (emi) resti sola; (keep secret), ~i sekreta; **keep up (with)**, (continue, maintain), daŭrigi; (not lag), resti flank-al-flanka (kun); resti ĝisdata (kun); **bookkeeper**, kontisto; **upkeep**, (on machinery etc.), reviziado; (on building etc.; any caring for), prizorgado; ($ support, gen), vivtenado; **in keeping with**, konforme al, kun; **for keeps**, (forever), por ĉiam; (in game), ~onte

keg, bareleto
keloid, keloido
kelp, *(Laminaria)*, laminario; *(Fucus)*, fuko
kelson, kilsono
Kelt, [see "Celt"]
ken, koni [tr]; ~o
kennel, (for dogs), hundejo; (for any pet), hejmbestejo
Kentucky, Kentukio
Kenya, Kenjo
kepi, kepo
keratin, keratino
keratitis, keratito
kerat(o)–, (anat. med pfx), kerat(o)–
keratoconus, keratokonuso
keratolysis, keratolizo
keratosis, keratozo
kerb, [see "curb"]
kerchief, (for head), kaptuko; (shawl), ŝalo; (handkerchief), naztuko, poŝtuko
Kerguelen, Kergeleno(j)
Kerkyra, Korciro [cp "Corfu"]
kermes, (dye), kirmeso
kermis, kermess, kermeso
kernel, kerno
kerosene, kerosine, keroseno
kestrel, kestrelo, tinunkolo, turfalko
ketch, keĉo†
ketchup, keĉupo*
ketene, keteno

ket(o)–, (chem pfx), ket(o)–
ketogenic, keto/gena;   **ketogenesis**, ~genezo
ketone, ketono; **ketonuria**, ~urio
ketose, ketozo
ketosis, ketonozo
kettle, kaldrono; **kettledrum**, timbano
key, (for lock, or similar, analogous object or person), ŝlosilo; ~a; (chief, main), ĉefa, ~a; (on piano, cmptr, typewriter, etc.), klavo; (enter in cmptr by keys), klavi [tr]; (mech: pin etc.), stifto; (mus), tonalo (e.g.: *major key:* maĵora tonalo; *in the key of F-sharp minor:* en la tonalo F-diesa minora) [cp "scale"]; (connect, be operated by), klavigi; **keyboard**, klavaro; **keyboard instrument**, klavinstrumento; **keyhole**, ~truo; **key in**, (cmptr input), klavi [tr]; (connect, gen), klavligi [tr]; klavligo; **keynote**, (gen), toniko; tonika; **keystone**, ĉefŝtono, ~ŝtono; **key up**, stimuli [tr]; **church key**, (colloq: can opener), ladotruilo; **Cotter key**, duobla stifto; **master key, passkey**, ĉef~o; **off-key**, (mus), misagorda; misagorde; (not appropriate), nekonvena; **turnkey**, uzopreta
Keynes, (economist J. M.), Kejnso†; **Keynesian**, ~isma; ~isto; **Keynesianism**, ~ismo
Khaibar, Khaiber, Kajbaro
khaki, (color), kakia; (cloth), ~ŝtofo
khalif, kalifo
khamsin, khamseen, ĥamsino
khan, ĥano; **khanate**, (region), ~ejo; (position), ~eco
Khartoum, Khartum, Kartumo
khedive, kedivo
Khíos, Ĥio†
Khmer, Ĥmero; ~a
Khorasan, Khurasan, Ĥorasano
Khyber, Kajbaro
kiang, kiango
Kiangsi, Gianghi
Kiangsu, Giangsu
kibbutz, kibuco; **kibbutznik**, ~ano
kibitz, kibici [int]; **kibitzer**, ~o; **kibitzing**, ~ado
kiblah, kiblo
kick, (w feet), piedbati [tr]; ~o; (w hind

legs, as mule etc.; fig: balk), kalcitri [int]; kalcitro; (esp sports), ŝoti [tr]; ŝoto; (complain), plendi [int]; plendo; (excitement), ekscito; **kick around,** (gen), ĉirkaŭbati [tr]; **kick back,** (gen), rebati [tr]; ($), firabati [tr]; **kickback,** firabato; **kick in,** kontribui [int] (per) [see "contribute"]; **kick off,** (start), komenci [tr]; (sports), ekŝoti [int]; ekŝoto; **kick out,** forpeli [tr], elpeli [tr]; **kickstand,** batstarigilo; **kick up,** batlevi [tr]; **sidekick,** kamarado, kunulo; **get a kick from,** ekscitiĝi pro; **give (one) a kick,** (excite), eksciti [tr]
kid, (child), infano; (goat), kaprido; (leather), kaproledo; (joke), ŝerci [int]; priŝerci [tr]; **kidnap,** (child), ~ŝteli [tr]; (any person), forkapti [tr]; **no kidding,** senŝerce, serioze
kidney, reno
Kidron, Kidrono
kieselgu(h)r, kiselguro, diatomea tero
Kiev, Kievo
Kigali, Kigalo†
kill, (gen), mortigi; ~o; **kill off,** for~i [tr]; **overkill,** super~ivo
kiln, bakforno
kilo, (kilogram), kilogramo [not "kilo"]
kilo-, (pfx), kilo–
kilt, kilto
kilter, bonstato; **out of kilter,** ne~a
kimono, kimono
kin, (relative), parenca; ~o; ~aro; (ethnic group), gento; **kinfolk,** ~aro; **next of kin,** plej proksima ~o
–kin, (diminutive sfx), –eto (e.g.: *lambkin:* ŝafideto)
kind, (sort, type), speco; (helping others), komplez(em)a, helpema, bonkora, afabla; (tender), tenera; **kindly,** (polite), afabla, ĝentila; (please), afable, bonvolu –i, bonvole –u [see "please"]; **kindness,** komplez(em)o, helpemo, bonkoreco, afableco; tenereco; **kind of,** (somewhat), iom (e.g.: *that light is kind of hot:* tiu lumo estas iom varma); **kind of a,** iom; ioma, kvazaŭa; **some kind of (a),** ia; **any kind (at all) of (a),** ia ajn; **what(ever) kind of (a),** kia (ajn); **that kind of (a),** tia; **this kind of (a),** ĉi tia, tia ĉi;

every kind of (a), ĉia; **no kind (at all) of (a),** not any kind (at all) of (a),** nenia (ajn); **(pay) in kind,** nemona (pago); nemone (pagi [tr]); **do (one) a kindness,** komplezi (iun); **of a kind,** sam~a
kindergarten, infanĝardeno
kindle, (ignite), ekbruligi; (arouse), ardigi, eksciti [tr], inciti [tr]; **kindling,** ~a ligno, ~aĵo
kindred, (similar), simila; (related), parenca; parencaro; **kindred spirit, kindred soul,** ~ulo
kinematics, kinematiko
–kinesis, (sfx), –kinezo
kinesitherapy, kinezoterapio; **kinesitherapist,** kinezoterapeŭto, ~isto
kinesthesia, kinesthesis, kinestezo; **kinesthetic,** ~a
kinetic, kineta; **kinetics,** ~iko
kinetotherapy, [see "kinesitherapy"]
king, (monarch; chess), reĝo; (checkers), damo; **Kings,** (Bib), R~oj; **kingbolt,** pivotstifto; **kingcup,** (bot), ranunkolo; **kingdom,** regno, ~lando; **United Kingdom,** Unuiĝinta Regno; **kingfisher,** (zool), alcedo, alciono; **kinglet,** (zool), regolo; **king-sized,** (Am), grand-formata
Kingstown, Kingstaŭno*
kink, (twist), tordi [tr]; ~iĝi; ~aĵo [cp "buckle"]; (curl), krispigi; krispiĝi; krispaĵo; (crick, spasm), kramfo; (whim, quirk), kaprico, ~aĵo; **kinky,** ~ita; krispa; kaprica
kino, (gum), pterokarpaĵo [not "kino"]
Kinshasa, Kinŝasa*
kiosk, kiosko
kipper, kipr/igi; **kippered herring,** (or oth fish), ~o
Kirghiz, Kirgizo; ~a
Kiribati, Kiribato†
Kirin, (gen), Gilin
kirsch(wasser), kirŝo
kiss, kisi [tr]; ~o
kit, (set, as of parts), kompleto (e.g.: *first-aid kit:* sukur~o; *build a radio from a kit:* konstrui radiofonon el ~o); (equipment), ekipaĵo; (tools), ilaro; (accessories), akcesoraĵoj, garnituro
kitchen, kuirejo; **kitchenette,** ~eto
kite, (flying), kajto; (zool), milvo; **hon-**

ey kite, (zool), perniso, vespobuteo
kitten, katido
kittiwake, kitio
kitty, (kitten), katido; ($), kaso
kiwi, kivio, apterigo
kiyang, kiango
klaxon, hup(eg)o
kleptomania, kleptomanio; **kleptomaniac,** ~a; ~ulo
klicka, dukorno [see § 16(e)]
knack, lertajo; **get the knack of,** akiri ~on (komprenon, povoscion) de, pri
knacker, (Br: horse butcher), ĉevalbuĉisto
knapsack, tornistro
knapweed, centaŭreo
knave, (rascal),   kanajlo,   fripono; (cards), fanto
knawel, skleranto
knead, knedi [tr]
knee, (anat, or similar object), genuo; (hit w), ~umi [tr]; **kneecap,** patelo; **knee-deep,** ĝis~a; **knee-jerk,** senpripensa; **knock-kneed,** iks-krura, X-krura
kneel, (stand on knees), genui [int]; (get onto knees), ~iĝi
Kneiffia, enotero
knell, mortsonori [tr]; ~o
knicker(bocker)s, kuloto [note sing]
knickknack, brikabrak/ero;   **knickknacks,** ~o [note sing]
knife, (gen), tranĉ/ilo; ~i [tr]; **penknife, pocket knife,** poŝ~ilo; **pruning knife,** serpeto; **switchblade knife,** faldo~ilo
knight, (noble), kavaliro; ~igi; (medieval horseman, esp one famous for courage etc.), prodo; (chess), ĉevalo; **Knights Templar,** (of 12th Century), Templo
knit, (sew), triki [tr]; (re wound etc.), kun~iĝi; (pull together, as eyebrows), kuntiri [tr]; **knitting needle,** ~ilo
knob, (handle), anso; (bump), tubero; (mountain), montopinto
knock, (hit), frapi [tr]; ~iĝi; ~o; (rap), perkuti [tr], marteli [tr]; perkutiĝi; marteliĝi; perkut(ad)o, martelado; (criticize), kritiki [tr]; kritiko; **knocker,** (as on door), ~ilo; **knock about, knock around,** (wander), (sencele)

vagi [int]; **knock down,** (make fall), (~)faligi; (dismantle), malmunti [tr]; **knock off,** (finish), fini [tr]; (stop), ĉesi [int]; (deduct), dekalkuli [tr]; **knock it off!,** ĉesigu tion!; **knock out,** (pound out), el~i [tr], elbati [tr]; (make quickly, badly), faraĉi [tr]; (make unconscious, gen), senkonsciigi; (boxing), (k)nokaŭti [tr]; (tire out), ellacigi; (defeat), venki [tr]; **antiknock,** kontraŭbata; kontraŭbatenzo
knoll, teraltajo
Knossos, Knoso
knot, (as in rope; anything analogous), nodo; ~i [tr]; (knitting), maŝo; (bump), tubero; (speed), knoto [1,852 kilometroj hore (see § 20)]; **knotty,** ~eca, ~oplena, ~hava; (complicated), komplika; **tie a knot (in),** ~i; **bow knot,** (as in shoelaces etc.), banto; **granny knot,** fuŝkvadrat~o; **sheepshank knot,** krur~o; **slipknot,** glit~o; **square knot,** kvadrat~o; **topknot,** kaptufo
knout, knuti [tr]; ~o
know, (have knowledge of fact; have idea, awareness), scii [tr] [cp "aware", "recognize"]; (be acquainted, familiar w person, thing, idea), koni [tr]; (be competent in, have know-how about), povo~i [tr]; **knowledge,** ~o; kono; **knowledgeable,** informita, klera, multe~a; **foreknowledge,** antaŭ~o; **self-knowledge,** memkonscio; **well-known,** (bone) konata; **unknown,** nekonata; (person), nekonato, senfamulo; **get to know,** ekkoni [tr]; **know how to,** ~povi [tr], ~i (e.g.: _he doesn't know how to read:_ li ne ~poas legi [or] ne ~as legi); **knowhow,** ~povo; **make known,** informi [tr], ~igi, komuniki [tr]; **all-knowing,** ĉio~a
knuckle, fingrartiko; (of toe), pied~o; **knuckle under,** (lakee) cedi [int]
knurl, (groove etc.), ikskaneli [tr]; (bump), tubero; **knurled,** ~ita
Knut, Knuto
KO, (abb of "knockout"), (k)nokaŭti [tr]; ~o
koala, koalo
Kobe, Kobeo

kobold, koboldo
Koh-i-noor, Kohinuro
kohlrabi, brasikrapo
Koko Nor, Kuku-Noro
kola, [see "cola"]
kolkhoz, kolĥozo
kombinat, (Russian industrial collective), kombinato
Königsberg, Kenigsbergo [cp "Kaliningrad"]
Konrad, Konrado
kook, frenezet/ulo; **kooky**, ~a
kopek, kopeko
kopher, kofero
kor, kor'o
Korah, Koraĥo
Koran, Korano
Korea, Koreo; **Korean**, ~a; ~ano; **North Korea**, Nord-~o; **South Korea**, Sud~o
koruna, ($), (Ĉeĥa) krono
kosher, koŝera
koto, kotoo
koulan, hemiono
koumis, **koumiss**, **koumyss**, kumiso
Kovno, Kovno
kowhai, soforo
kowtow, adorsterniĝi, lakeiĝi
kraal, (village), (indiĝena) vilaĝo; (pen), kralo†
krait, bungaro
Krakow, Krakovo
krater, kratero
Kraunia, visterio
Kremlin, Kremlo
kreu(t)zer, krejcero
Kriemhild, Krimhilda
kris, kriso
Krishna, Kriŝno
krona, ($), krono
krummhorn, kurbkorno
krypton, kriptono
Kshatriya, kŝatrio
Kuala-Lumpur, Kuala-Lumpuro
kudos, laŭdo, gloro, renomo
Ku Klux Klan, Ku-Kluks-Klano
kulak, kulako
kulan, hemiono
kumiss, kumiso
kundalini, kundalina*
Kunigunde, Kunegunda

Kunlun (Mountains), Kun-Luno
Kunming, Kunming
Kuomintang, Kuomintango
Kurd, Kurdo; **Kurdish**, ~a; **Kurdistan**, ~io; (rug), ~ia tapiŝo
Kurile (Islands), Kuriloj
Kurland, Kurlando
Kuroshio, Kuroŝio
Kush, Kuŝ
Kuwait, (city), Kuvajto†; (country), ~io
kvas(s), kvaso
Kwangsi, Guanghi
Kwangtung, Guangdongo
kwashiorkor, senproteinozo
Kweichow, Gujĝoŭ
kyang, kiango
Kyoto, Kioto
kyphoscoliosis, cifoskoliozo
kyphosis, cifozo; **kyphotic**, ~a

L

la, (mus note), la
laager, (fortikigita) tendaro
lab, (laboratory), labo
labarum, labaro
label, etikedo; ~i [tr]; (arch), lambelo; **gummed label**, glu~o, glumarko
labellum, labio
labia, [see "labium"]
labial, (phon), labialo; ~a; (of lip, labium), labia
Labiatae, labiacoj
labiate, labiata
labile, labila
labiodental, labiodentalo; ~a
labium, labio; **labia**, ~oj; **labia majora**, majˆoraj ~oj; **labia minora**, minoraj ~oj
labor, (work, gen; all workers, workforce), laboro; ~i [int]; (childbirth), akuˆso; **labored**, (difficult), peniga; **laborer**, ~isto; **laborious**, (difficult), peniga, malfacila; (industrious), ~ema; **day-labor**, tag~o; **do day-labor**, tag~i [int]; **day-laborer**, tag~isto; **forced labor**, trud~o; **hard labor**, (as punishment), pun~o; **manual labor**, man~o; **be in labor** (with), (childbirth), akuˆsi [tr]; **go into labor**, ekakuˆsi [tr]
laboratory, laboratorio, labo; **pharmaceutical laboratory**, oficino
Labrador, Labradoro
Labrax, labrako
Labrus, labro; Labridae, ~edoj
laburnum, Laburnum, laburno, orpluvo
labyrinth, labirinto; **labyrinthine**, ~(ec)a
Labyrinth, Labirinto
lace, (fabric), punto; ~a; (shoestring etc.), laĉo; laĉi [tr]; (weave in), enplekti [tr], interplekti [tr]; (trimming), pasamento; **lacy**, ~(ec)a; **lacewing**, neŭroptero; **interlace**, interplekti [tr]; interplektiĝi
Lacedaemon, Lacedemono; **Lacedaemonian**, ~a; ~ano
lacerate, (gen), ˆsir(vund)i [tr]; **lacera-**

tion, ~ado; ~(aĵ)o
Lacerta, lacerto; Lacertidae, ~edoj; Lacertilia, ~uloj
laches, malplenumo
lachrymal, (tears), larma; (bone), lakrimalo
lack, manko; ne havi [tr], malhavi [tr]; **be lacking**, ~i [int]; **I lack something**, ~as al mi io
lackadaisical, malvigla, senspirita, langvora
lackey, lakeo; ~i [tr]; ~iĝi
Laconia, Lakon/ujo; **Laconian**, ~o; ~a; ~uja
laconic, lakona; **laconism**, ~ismo
lacquer, (substance), lako; ~i [tr]; (lacquered furniture etc.), ~aĵo; **spray lacquer**, ˆspruc~i [tr]
lacrimal, [see "lachrymal"]
lacrosse, (poˆs)bastonludo
lactalbumin, laktalbumino
Lactarius, laktario, laktofungo, laktagariko
lactase, laktazo
lactate, (secrete milk), lakti [int]; (nurse young), suĉigi; (chem), laktato; **lactation**, ~ado
lactic, (chem), lakt/(at)a; (of milk), lakta; **lactic acid**, ~ata acido, 2-hidroksipropan-acido
lactoflavin, laktoflavino
lactone, laktono
lactose, laktozo
Lactuca, laktuko
lactucarium, laktukario
lacuna, (missing place), mankloko; (gap), breĉo; (anat etc.: cavity), lakuno
lad, junulo, knabo
ladder, (steps), eskalo; ~izi [tr]; (Br: run in stocking), ˆstupetaro, dismaˆsiĝo; ˆstupetarizi [tr], dismaˆsigi; ˆstupetariĝi; **stepladder**, ˆstup~o
lade, (load), ˆsarĝi [tr]; (ladle), ĉerpi [tr]; **laden**, ~ita; **lading**, (load), ~o; **bill of lading**, ~atesto
la-di-da, (interj), dirlididi!
Ladino, (la) Judhispana (lingvo)

Ladislav, Ladislao
ladle, kuler/ego, ĉerp~o; ĉerpi [tr]
Ladoga, **(Lake)**, (Lago) Ladoga
Ladrones, Ladrone Islands, Insuloj
   Marianaj
lady, (respectful term for woman), sin-
   jor/ino; (noble), damo, lordino; (female counterpart of gentleman),
   ĝentlemanino; **ladylike,** ~ineca, ĝent-
   lemanineca; **ladybird, ladybug,** (beetle), kokcinelo; **lady's-comb,** (bot),
   skandiko; **lady's-finger,** (kidney
   vetch), antilido; **lady's-laces,** (bot),
   falaro; **lady's-mantle,** (bot), alkemilo; **lady-slipper,** (bot), cipripedio;
   lady's-tresses, (bot), spiranto; **lady-
   in-waiting,** ĉambristino; **ladies and
   gentlemen!,** (as in speech), ge~oj!;
   first lady, (wife of president), prezi-
   dent-edzino
Laertes, Laerto
La Fontaine, Lafonteno
lag, (delay), prokrasto; ~a; ~iĝi; ~operi-
   odo; (fall behind), malrapidi [int];
   (wane), malkreski [int], malvigliĝi;
   (stave), daŭbo; (insulation etc.), tegi
   [tr]; tegaĵo; (Br: arrest), aresti [tr];
   (Br: convict), konvikto; **lag behind,**
   maldevanci [tr]; postiĝi, maldevan-
   ciĝi; **jet lag,** jetismo
Lagenaria, kalabaskukurbo
lager (beer), hela biero
laggard, lanta,   ~ema,   postiĝema;
   ~(em)ulo, postiĝinto
lagoon, laguno
lagophthalmos, lagoftalmo
Lagopus, lagopo
Lagorchestes, valabio
Lagostomus, lagostomo
Lagothrix, lagotriko
Lagrange, Lagranĝo; **Lagrangian,** ~a
Lagria, lagrio
Lahore, Lahoro
lair, kuŝejo
laissez-faire, neinterveno;   ~ismo;
   ~(em)a, ~isma
laity, laikaro
Laius, Lajo
lake, (water), lago; (color), karmino;
   karmina; **the Great Lakes,** la Grandaj L~oj; **the Lake District,** la L~re-
   giono

lallate, lambdacizi [int]; **lallation,** ~o
lama, (priest), lamao; **Dalai Lama,** Da-
   lai-~o; **lamasery,** (~a) monaĥejo
Lama, (zool), lamo; Lama guanicoe,
   Lama huanachus, guanako; Lama
   pacos, alpako; Lama vicugna, vikuno
lamb, (animal), ŝafido; (as meat), ~aĵo;
   lamb's-lettuce, (bot), valerianelo;
   lamb's-quarters, (bot), kenopodio;
   Lamb of God, (rel), Ŝ~o de Dio
lambaste, (beat), bat(eg)i [tr]; (scold),
   riproĉ(eg)i [tr]
lambda, (Greek letter), lambda [see
   § 16]; (anat), lambdo
lambdacize, lambdacizi [int]; **lambda-
   cism,** ~o
lambdoid, lambdoida
Lambert, Lamberto
Lamblia, lamblio
lambiosis, lambliozo
lambrequin, lambrekino
lame, (gen), lama; ~igi; **be lame,** (limp
   etc.), ~i [int]
lamé brok/aĵo; ~ita; **weave a lamé (into),** ~i [tr]
lamella, lamelo; **lamellate, lamellar,**
   ~hava; ~eca
lamellibranch, lamenbrankulo
Lamellibranchi(at)a, lamenbrankuloj
lamellicorn, lamenkornulo
Lamellicornia, lamenkornuloj
lament, lamenti [int] (pri); pri~i [tr]; **la-
   mentable,** ~inda;   **lamentation,**
   ~(ad)o; **Lamentations,** (Bib), Plor-
   kantoj
lamia, lamio
lamina, lameno; **laminate,** ~igi; **lami-
   nated,** ~a; **lamina orbitalis,** planumo
Laminaria, laminario
Lamium, lamio
lammergeier, gipaeto
Lamna, lamno
lamp, (light, gen; elec bulb), lampo;
   (lantern), lanterno; (hanging, globed,
   etc., as in church, temple, etc.), lucerno; **lampblack,** ~fulgo; **lamp shade,**
   ~ŝirmilo; **hurricane lamp,** uragana
   lanterno; **slush lamp,** (Aus), gras~o;
   oil lamp, meĉujo; **sunlamp,** sun~o
lampoon, satiro; ~i [tr]
lamprey, petromizo
Lampyris, lampiro, lumvermo

Lancaster, (gen), Lankastro; **Lancastrian**, ~a; ~ano
lance, (weapon), lanco; ~i [tr]; (sport), ĵet~o; (med: puncture cavity to drain liquid), punkcii [tr]; lanceto; **lance corporal**, subkaporalo; **free-lance**, sendependa, aŭtonoma; labori [int] sendepende, aŭtonome
lancelet, brankiostomo, amfiokso
Lancelot, Lanceloto
lanceolate, lancforma
lancet, (med), lanceto
Lanchow, Langoŭ
lancinating, lancina; **have lancinating pain**, ~i [int]
land, (country, nation), lando; (dry land), tero; (ground), grundo; (estate), bieno; (re ocean ship), alterigi; alteriĝi; (plane, space ship), surterigi, alterigi; surteriĝi, alteriĝi; (disembark), elŝipiĝi; **landed**, (owning land), bienhava; **landed immigrant**, (Canada), enloĝa enmigrinto; **landfall**, alteriĝo; **landgrave**, ~grafo; **landlocked**, senmarborda, terĉirkaŭita; **landlady**, mastrino, luigantino; **landlord**, mastro, luigantino; **landmark**, orientilo, gvidosigno; **landmass**, termaso; **landowner**, bienulo; **landscape**, pejzaĝo; **landslide**, **landslip**, (gen), lavango; (earth, rocks, etc.), terlavango; **foreland**, (promontory), promontoro; **homeland**, **fatherland**, **motherland**, hejm~o, patro~o, patrujo; **inland**, ~interno; ~interna [not "en~a"]; **mainland**, ĉeftero; ĉeftera; **midland**, ~mezo; ~meza; **no-man's-land**, nenies~o; **outlandish**, strangega, kuriozega; **overland**, transtera; transtere(n); **upland**, altejo; alteja; **wetland**, marĉejo; **wonderland**, mir~o; **land of milk and honey**, Kuk~o
landau, landaŭo
lane, (of highway, or similar way), leno†; (narrow road), vojeto; (street), strateto; **air lane**, aer~o; **space lane**, kosmo~o
Langerhans, [see under "islet"]
langouste, palinuro, langusto
language, (formalized), lingvo (e.g.: *the*

English language: la Angla ~o) [cp "idiom"]; (individual manner of speech), ~aĵo (e.g.: *eloquent language:* elokventa ~aĵo); **bridge language**, (intermediate language in two-step translation), pont~o†; **sign language**, gest~o; **source language**, (from which text translated), font~o†; **target language**, (into which translated), cel~o†
Languedoc, Langvedoko [cp "langue d'oc"]
langue d'oc, (la) Okcitana (lingvo) [cp "Languedoc"]
languor, langvoro; **languorous**, **languid**, ~a, malvigla; **languish**, ~i [int]
langur, presbito
Lanius, lanio
lank, (lean), magra; (re hair), malkrispa
lanky, altmagra
lanolin, lanolino
Lantana, lantano
lantern, lanterno; **Chinese lantern**, (for decoration), lampiono; **Chinese lantern (plant)**, alkekengo; **Japanese lantern**, andono; **magic lantern**, magia ~o
lanthanum, lantano; **lanthanide (element)**, ~ido; **lanthanide series**, ~ida serio
lanugo, lanugo
lanyard, ligŝnuro
Laocoon, Laokoono
Laodamia, Laodamia
Laodicea, Laodikeo; **Laodicean**, ~a; ~ano
Laos, Laoso; **Laotian**, ~a; ~ano
Lao-Tse, **Lao-Tsu**, Laŭzi
lap, (of sitting person, lit or fig), sino; (one turn around racecourse etc.), rondiro; (drink), lektrinki [tr]; (splash, as waves), plaŭdi [tr]; **overlap**, superkuŝi [tr] (unu la alian); superkuŝiĝi; superkuŝ(aĵ)o
laparo–, (med root), laparo–
laparoscopy, laparoskopio
laparotomy, laparotomio
La Paz, La-Pazo
lapel, roverso
lapidary, lapidara; ~isto
lapis, lapiso; **lapis lazuli**, lazurŝtono
Lapith, Lapito

Lapland, Laponio
La Plata, La-Plato
Lapp, Lapono; ~a; ~ia
Lapsana, lapsano
lapse, (error, slip), erar(et)o; ~i [int];
(expire), malvalidiĝi, eksvalidiĝi;
(fall, backslide), (re)fali [int]; (pass,
as time), pasi [int]; **lapsed,** malvalida,
eksvalida; (re)falinta; pasinta
lapwing, vanelo
larceny, ŝtel/(ad)o; **larcenous,** ~a;
grand larceny, ~ego; **petit larceny,**
~eto
larch, (tree), lariko; (wood), ~ligno
lard, (fat), porkograso; (add bacon; fig:
garnish talk etc.), lardi [tr]; **interlard,**
traplekti [tr], interplekti [tr]
larder, manĝoŝranko
Lares, Laroj
largando, (mus), largigante; ~aĵo
large, (big), granda; (naut), large;
largely, ~parte, plejparte; **at large,**
(not captured), libera, nekaptita; (general, re whole), ĝenerala
largess, malavaro
larghetto, (mus), largete; ~o
lariat, lazo
Larix, lariko
lark, (zool), alaŭdo; (frolic), petoli [int];
petolaĵo; **calandra lark,** kalandro;
skylark, kamp~o
larkspur, delfinio
La Rochelle, Roĉelo
Larus, laro; Larus ridibundus, ridme-
vo; Laridae, ~edoj; Lariformes,
~oformaj (birdoj)
larva, larvo; **larval,** ~(ec)a
larynx, laringo; **laryng(e)al,** ~a; **laryn-
gectomee,** ~ektomiulo; **laryngecto-
my,** ~ektomio; **laryngismus,** ~ismo;
laryngitis, ~ito; **laryngology,** ~olo-
gio; **laryngologist,** ~ologo; **laryngo-
scope,** ~oskopo; **laryngoscopy,**
~oskopio; **laryngotomy,** ~otomio
lasagna, lasanjo†
lascivious, lasciva
laser, lasero; ~a; **laser beam,** ~fasko
lash, (whip), vipo; ~i [tr]; ~obato; (eyelash), okulharo; (tie), (ŝnur)ligi [tr];
lash out, ekataki [tr]
lass, knabino, junulino
lassitude, langvorfo, laceco

lasso, lazo
last, (opp "first"; most recent), lasta; ~e
(e.g.: *the last car of the train:* la ~a
vagono de la trajno; *I came last Monday:* mi venis la ~an lundon; *she came
last:* ŝi venis ~e); (final), fina; (continue, persist), daŭri [int] (e.g.: *the storm
lasted two hours:* la ŝtormo daŭris du
horojn); (unit of weight), laŝto [value
varies]; (cobbler's), ŝuformilo; **lasting,** daŭr(em)a; **last year (month,**
etc.), pasintjare (pasintmonate, etc.),
la pasintan jaron (monaton, etc.); **last
but not least,** ~e sed ne malplej
grave; ~vice sed ne ~range; **at last,**
fine; (more emphatic), finfine; **next to
last,** antaŭ~a; **second from last,**
praantaŭ~a; **third (etc.) from last,**
tria (etc.) antaŭ la ~a
latch, klinko; ~i [tr]; **latch onto,** (get),
akiri [tr]; (grab), alkroĉi [tr]
late, (not early), malfrua; ~e; (poet), tar-
da; (not on time), neakurata; (recent),
last(atemp)a; (dead), mortinta, forpasinta; **be late,** ~i [int]; **lately,** lastatempe; **later,** (subsequent), posta;
poste; **at the latest,** plej ~e
latent, latenta
lateral, (side), flanka; ~aĵo; (geom), la-
tera; (phon), laterala; **bilateral,** (gen),
du~a, dupartia; (geom), dulatera; **tri-
lateral,** tri~a, tripartia; trilatera; trilat-
ero; **multilateral,** plur~a, plurpartia;
plurlatera; **unilateral,** unu~a, unupartia
Lateran, Laterano
laterite, laterito
latex, latekso
lath, lato; ~i [tr]
lathe, tornilo
lather, ŝaŭmo; ~umi [tr]
Lathraea, latreo
lathyrism, latirismo
Lathyrus, latiro; Lathyrus odoratus,
bonodorpizo
latifundium, latifundio, latifondo, latifundio
Latimeria, latimerio†
Latin, (language; re Catholic Church;
etc.), Latina; (citizen of Latium), Lati-
ano, ~o
latissimus dorsi, (muscle), latisimo

latitude, (angle from equator), latitudo; (width), larĝeco; (fig: leeway), drivspaco, liberspaco; colatitude, kolatitudo
Latium, Latio
Latona, Latona
latrine, latrino
latter, ĉi lasta, ĉi tiu; latter-day, lastatempa [cp "former"]
lattice, (any grid), krado; (of metal rods or wire), latiso; (of wood lath), latlatiso, latajo; latticework, ~ajo
Latvia, Latv/io [see "Letono" in PIVS]; Latvian, ~o; ~a; ~ia
laud, laŭdi [tr]; ~o; laudable, ~inda; laudatory, ~a
laudanum, laŭdano
laugh, ridi [int]; ~o; laughter, ~ado; (choked off: onom), fu! fu!; laughable, ~inda, komika; laugh at, pri~i [tr]; laughing-stock, mokato; laugh up one's sleeve, sub~i [int], kaŝ~i [int], ~i en sia barbo
launch, (set off, gen), lanĉi [tr]; ~(ad)o; (gen-purpose motorboat), ŝalupo; launching pad, ~ejo
launder, (wash, gen), lavi [tr]; ~iĝi; ($), fi-~i [tr], ĵongli [tr]; laundry, (shop), ~butiko; (place, gen), ~ejo; (clothes), ~itajo; ~atajo; ~otajo; laundromat, ~aŭtomatejo
Laura, Laŭra
laureate, laŭreato; ~a; Nobel laureate, Nobel-premiito
laurel, (bot), laŭro; camphor laurel, kamforarbo; spurge laurel, dafno
Laurence, Laŭrenco
Laurus, laŭro
Lausanne, Laŭzano
lava, lafo
lavage, lavo
Lavandula, lavendo
lavatory, (basin), lav/ujo; (room), ~ejo
lave, (wash, gen), lavi [tr], bani [tr]
lavender, (bot), lavendo; (color), ~okolora; lavender oil, ~a oleo
lavish, ekstravaganca, luksa, abunda; superŝuti [tr]; ~e (etc.) doni [tr]
law, (statute; natural principal etc.), leĝo; (study; legal system), juro; lawful, laŭ~a; lawless, sen~a; lawsuit, proceso; lawyer, (any attorney), ad-

vokato; (for the defense), defendisto; (jurist, specialist in law), juristo; criminal lawyer, kriminalisto; bylaw, (krom)regulo; bylaws, (as a set), (krom)regularo; common law, kadro~o; kadro~a; in-law, [see "in-law", "-in-law"]; military law, milit~o; outlaw, (person), bandito, ekster~ulo; (make illegal, ban), mallegalizi [tr], kontraŭ~igi; statutory law, statut~o; in the eyes of the law, laŭ~e, laŭ (la takso de) la ~o; lay down the law, arogante ordoni (pri)
lawn, (yard), gazono; (cloth), batisto; lawn mower, ~tondilo
Lawrence, Laŭrenco; St. Lawrence, (river), Rivero Sankta-~o; Gulf of St. Lawrence, Golfo de Sankta-~o; St. Lawrence Seaway, Markanalo Sankta-~o
lawrencium, laŭrencio
lax, (not rigid), malrigida; (not strict), malstrikta; (loose, slack), mola, malstreĉa; (undisciplined), sendisciplina, maldiligenta; (re bowels), laksa
laxative, laks/iga; ~enzo; (mild, as olive oil), ~etiga; ~etenzo; laxative condition, ~o
lay, (put), meti [tr], kuŝigi; (place, locate), loki [tr]; (sexually), kuŝi [int] (kun); kuŝigi; kuŝ(ig)o; (make fall), faligi; (spread out), sterni [tr]; sterniĝi; (masonry), masoni [tr]; (eggs), de~i [tr]; (table), pri~i [tr]; (bet), veti [tr]; (not clerical; not professional), laika; lay aside, lay away, lay by, lay up, flanken~i [tr], rezervi [tr] (store), stapli [tr]; lay-away plan, rezerva plano; (put) in lay-away, (~i) en rezerviteco(n); lay down, (assert), aserti [tr], deklari [tr]; (establish), establi [tr]; (spread), sterni [tr]; (store), stapli [tr]; (bet), veti [tr]; lay off, (fire), maldungi [tr]; (mark boundaries), dislimi [tr], limmarki [tr]; (stop), ĉesi [int]; lay out, ($), elspezi [tr]; (arrange), aranĝi [tr]; (spread), sterni [tr]; (knock out), senkonsciigi; lay oneself open to, sin el~i al; lay over, veturpaŭzi [int]; layover, veturpaŭzo; layperson, layman, laiko; lay to, (ascribe), atribui [tr] (al); (naut), halti [int]; mis-

lay, misloki [tr], perdi [tr]; **outlay**, ($), elspezo; **overlay**, (gen), super~i [tr]; (spread), supersterni [tr]; (cover, layer), supertegi [tr]; supertegaĵo; (print), superpresi [tr]; superpresaĵo; **lay to rest**, (bury, lit or fig), enterigi **layer**, (gen), tavolo; ~igi; ~iĝi; (lamina), lameno; (plant shoot), markoto; markoti [tr]; **layered**, ~iĝinta; **Heaviside layer**, ~o de Heaviside
layette, bebogarnituro
lazaret, lazarette, lazaretto, lazareto
Lazarus, Lazaro
laze, lanti [int]
lazy, maldiligenta, mallaborema, pigra
lazzarone, lazarono
LCD, [see under "diode"]
leach, perkoli [tr]; ~iĝi
lead, (conduct, direct, guide), konduki [tr] [cp "manage", "guide"]; (be head of), estri [tr]; (ahead of), antaŭi [tr]; antaŭa; antaŭeco; (live, follow), vivi [tr], sekvi [tr]; (begin), komenciĝi; (initiate), iniciati [tr]; (elec), (en)~a drato; (theat: main role), ĉefrolo; (actor playing same), korife(in)o, ĉefrolul(in)o; (mus), ĉefparto; ĉefludanto; ĉefkantanto; (metal: Pb), plumbo; plumba; plumbi [tr]; (clue), indiko; indiki [tr]; **leader**, (one who leads, chief), estro, ĉefo; (at beginning of tape, film, cord, etc.), antaŭbendo; antaŭfilmo; antaŭŝnuro [etc.]; **leadership**, estrado; estreco; estrivo; estraro; **crew leader**, submastro; **leading**, (main), ĉefa, supera; (in front), antaŭa; **leading man (lady)**, (theat etc.), korife(in)o, ĉefrolul(in)o; **leading question**, sugesta demando; **lead to**, (cause), kaŭzi [tr], ~i al, rezultigi, estigi; **lead poisoning**, plumbismo; **leadwort**, plumbago; **mislead**, ruzi [tr] (kontraŭ, al), devojigi
leaf, (of plant, book), folio; (hinged), klapo; (bear leaves), ~i [int]; **leafy**, ~ara; ~eca; **leaflet**, (printed, gen), ~o, flug~o; (w propaganda etc.), agit~o; (part of compound leaf), ~ero; **leaf out**, ek~i [int]; **leafstalk**, petiolo; **leaf through**, (book etc.), ~umi [tr]; **figleaf**, fig~o; **flyleaf**, ŝirmopaĝo; **gold leaf**, or~o; **interleaf**, inter~o;

interleave, inter~izi [tr]; **overleaf**, dorsflanka; dorsflanke
league, (compact; alliance, organization, etc.), ligo; (unit of length), leŭgo† [value imprecise]; **League of Nations**, L~o de Nacioj
Leah, Lea
leak, liki [int]; ~igi; ~o; **leakage**, ~aĵo; **leaky**, ~ema; **spring a leak**, ek~i [int]
lean, (incline), klini [tr]; ~iĝi; ~(iĝ)o; (support self), apogi sin; (not fat), magra, malgrasa; (meat), magra viando; **lean-to**, apogŝedo, duonŝedo
Leander, Leandro
leap, (jump), salti [int], ~(eg)i [int]; ~(eg)igi; ~(eg)o; (gaily, like goat), kaprioli [int]; kapriolo; (surge forward), impeti [int]; impeto; **leapfrog**, (jump over, gen), ran~i [int] (super, trans, preter, etc.); (child's game), ŝaf~ado; **by leaps and bounds**, per ~egoj, mirige rapide, fulmorapide
learn, (increase gen knowledge; study; acquire skill; etc.), lerni [tr]; (find out), informiĝi (pri), sciiĝi (pri); (learn thoroughly), el~i [tr]; **learned**, klera, multescia, (poet), dokta; **learning**, klereco; **learn how (to)**, povosciiĝi [see "know"]; **learn the hard way**, ~i per tuŝo kaj fuŝo, ~i per sperto
lease, (receive for $), lui [tr]; (give for $), ~igi; (contract), ~atesto, ~kontrakto; ~kontrakti [tr, int]; **sublease**, vic~i [int]; vic~igi; **for lease**, ~igota
leash, rimeno; ~i [tr]
least, malplej; ~ da [see "less"]; (smallest), ~ granda, plej malgranda; (minimum), minimumo, ~o; minimuma; **at least**, almenaŭ; **at the very least**, minimume; **not in the least**, tute ne; tute neniom
leather, ledo; ~a; **leathery**, ~eca; **leatherette**, art~o; **leather goods**, ~aĵoj; **leather worker**, ~pretigisto; **artificial leather**, (of various substances), art~o; **Morocco leather**, marokeno; **patent leather**, bril~o
leave, (go away from), for/iri [int] (de); (go out of, as room), eliri [int] (de); (travel from), elveturi [int], ~veturi [int]; (not take w; tolerate as is; re-

ject), lasi [tr] (e.g.: *leave the book on the table:* lasi la libron sur la tablo; *leave me alone:* lasu min sola; *leave a light on:* lasi lumon ŝaltita; *take it or leave it:* prenu ĝin aŭ lasu ĝin); (leave behind, gen), postlasi [tr]; (bequeath), heredigi; (permission), permeso; (permission to be absent), ~permeso; **leavings**, lasitaĵo(j); **leave aside**, flankenlasi [tr]; **leave behind**, ~lasi [tr], postlasi [tr]; **leave off**, (cease), ĉesi [int]; (omit), ellasi [tr]; **leave out**, ellasi [tr]; **take leave**, preni ~permeson; **take leave of**, adiaŭi [tr]; **on leave**, en ~permeso; **leave of absence**, ~permeso; **absent without leave**, ~ sen permeso; **leave well enough alone**, ne inciti abelujon

leaven, ferment/igi; ~aĵo; **leavening**, ~aĵo

Lebanon, (country), Libano; **Lebanese**, ~ano; ~a; **Lebanon Mountains**, Lebanono; **Anti-Lebanon**, Antilebanono

Lebistes reticulatus, gupio*

lecher, lasciv/ulo; **lecherous**, ~a; **lechery**, ~eco

lecithin, lecitino

lectern, legpupitro

lector, lektoro

lecture, (speech, gen), prelegi [int]; ~o; (formal, as in university), lekcii [int]; lekcio; (scold), skoldi [tr], riproĉi [tr]; skoldo, riproĉo

lectus, lekto

Lecythis, lecitido

LED, [see under "diode"]

Leda, Leda

lederhosen, ledkuloto

ledge, (of window, or anything like shelf), breto; (anything jutting out, as of rock), kornico

ledger, (bookkeeping), kontlibro

lee, leo; **leeward, alee**, ~a; ~e(n); **leeway**, drivspaco, liberspaco; **Leeward Islands**, Insuloj L~aj

leech, (zool; fig: parasitic person), hirudo; (cling, suck), ~umi [int]

leechee, [see "litchi"]

leek, poreo; **wild leek**, (Eurasian), ampeloprazo

leer, vizaĝaĉi [int]; ~o

leery, suspektema

lees, feĉo [note sing]

left, (lefthanded; at or to that side; pol), maldekstra; ~o; ~e(n); (counterclockwise), ~uma; ~ume(n); (left behind), (for)lasita; (remaining), restanta; restante; **leftist**, (pol), ~a; ~ano [avoid "~ulo"]; **left-handed**, ~a, ~amana; **left-handed person**, ~ulo; **leftover**, restanta; restaĵo; **left-overs**, (food), manĝorestaĵoj

leg, (anat, or similar object, as of table), kruro; (of pants etc.), ~umo; (entire extremity), gambo; (geom: side of triangle adjacent to right angle), ĉeorta latero; (segment, as of trip), parto, stadio; **legging**, ~ingo; **leggy**, (re woman etc.), bel~a; **legwork**, irlaboro; **bowlegged**, kurba~a; **cross-legged**, ~kruca; ~kruce; **on one's last legs**, kaduk(iĝant)a; **pull one's leg**, blagi [int] al iu; **not have a leg to stand on**, esti tute sen pravigo, esti tute malprava, tute malpravi [int]

legacy, legaco; **leave a legacy (to)**, ~i [tr] (ion al iu)

legal, (stated in, required by law), leĝa; (proper, not illegal), laŭ~a; (re study of law), jura; **legalism**, (tro)laŭ~emo; **legality**, ~aĵo; laŭ~eco; **legalize**, ~igi, legalizi [tr]; **illegal**, kontraŭ~a, nelica; **paralegal**, parajura; parajuristo

legate, legato

legatee, allegacito, heredanto

legation, legacio

legato, (mus), ligite

legend, (folk tale), legendo; (text), teksto, skribaĵo; (key on map etc.), simbolklarigo; **legendary**, ~a

leger, (mus), eksterklea; **leger line**, ~a streko

legerdemain, prestidigit/ado; **perform legerdemain**, ~i [int]

Leghorn, (city), Livorno

legible, legebla; **illegible**, ne~a

legion, legio; **legionary**, ~a; ~ano; **legionnaire**, ~ano

legislate, leĝ/doni [int] (pri), ~fari [tr]; **legislation**, ~donado; ~o(j); **legislative**, ~dona; **legislator**, ~donanto, parlamentano; **legislature**, parlamento

legitimate, legitimi [tr]; lica, laŭleĝa; **legitimacy**, liceco; **legitimating**, ~a; **legitimism**, ~ismo; **legitimist**, ~isma; ~isto; **illegitimate**, (bastard), bastarda; eksteredzeca; (illegal), kontraŭleĝa, mallica; (illogical), mallogika; **legitimating documents**, ~aĵoj, legitimacio
legume, legumenaco [not "legomo"]
legumin, legumino
Leguminosae, legumenacoj
leguminous, legumenaca
lei, (Havaja) girlando
Leibnitz, Lejbnico; **Leibnitzian**, ~a; ~ano; **Leibnitzianism**, ~ismo
Leiden, Lejdeno; **Leiden jar**, ~a botelo
Leie, (river), Liso
Leipzig, Lepsiko
Leishmania, leiŝmanio
leishmaniasis, leiŝmaniozo;   **visceral leishmaniasis**, kala-azaro
leisure, libertempo; ~a; nelabordeva (e.g.: *the leisure class:* la nelabordeva klaso); **leisurely**, malhasta, malrapida, malurĝa, lanta, langvora
leitmotif, gvidmotivo
Leman, (Lake), Lago Lemano, Lago Ĝeneva
Le Mans, Manso
lemma, (logic, math), lemo
lemming, lemo, lemingo
Lemmus, lemo, lemingo
Lemna, lemno
lemniscate, lemniskato
lemniscus, lemnisko
lemon, (fruit: common name), citrono; (sci), limono; (tree), ~arbo, limonarbo; **lemonade**, limonado
lemur, Lemur, lemuro
Lemures, lemuroj
Lena, (river), Leno
lend, prunt/edoni [tr], ~i [tr] (al); **lend itself to**, utili [int] por
length, (longness, gen), longo; (duration), ~o, daŭro; (long stretch), etendo, amplekso; **lengthy**, ~edaŭra; **lengthen**, (pli)~igi; (pli)~iĝi; **lengthwise**, laŭ~e (de); **full-length**, (portrait, mirror, etc.), piedostara; **to what lengths**, kiomgrade; **along the length and breadth of**, laŭ~e kaj laŭlarĝe de –**length**, (sfx: as long as), –longa (e.g.:

a book-length report: libro~a raporto); (reaching), ĝis– [pfx] (e.g.: *floor-length dress:* ĝisplanka vesto)
lenient, indulga, malsevera; **leniency**, ~(em)o; **be lenient (toward)**, ~i [tr]
Lenin, Lenino; **Leninism**, ~ismo; **Leninist**, ~isma; ~isto
Leningrad, Leningrado
Lenore, Lenora, Lenora
lens, (gen), lenso; (in microscope, telescope, etc.; lens or combination of lenses closest to thing viewed), objektivo; **lensometer**, ~ometro; **contact lens**, kontakto~o; **crystalline lens**, (eye lens), kristalino; **fish-eye lens**, (phot), fiŝokula objektivo; **telephoto lens**, telefota objektivo; **wide-angle lens**, larĝangula objektivo; **zoom lens**, zomobjektivo
Lens, (bot), lento
Lent, Karesmo; **Lenten**, ~a
lenticel, lenticelo
lenticular, lensa; ~oforma
lentil, (plant or seed), lento
lento, (mus), malrapida; ~e [not "lent-"]
Leo, (ast; man's name), Leono
Leon, Leono; **Leona**, ~a
Leonard, Leonardo
Leonidas, Leonido
leonine, leon(ec)a
Leonora, Leonore, Lenora
Leontine, Leontina
Leontodon, leontodono
Leontopodium, leontopodo; Leontopodium alpinum, edelvejso, neĝfloro
leopard, leopardo; **snow leopard**, uncio
Leopold, Leopoldo
leotard, striktaĵo
leper, leprulo
Lepidium, lepidio
Lepidoptera, lepidopteroj
Lepisma, lepismo
leprechaun, (Irlanda) koboldo
leprosy, lepro
Leptinotarsa, leptinotarso
leptocephalus, leptocefalo
lepton, leptono†
Leptopilus crumeniferus, marabuo
Lepus, leporo; Lepus cuniculus, kuniklo
Le Puy, (city in France), Podo

lesbian, lesba, safisma; ~anino, safismulino; **lesbianism**, ~ismo, safismo
Lesbos, Lesbo
lesion, lezo; **cause a lesion**, (injure), ~i [tr]
Lesotho, Lesoto†
less, (adv), malpli (e.g.: *less hot:* ~ varma); (adj), ~ da (e.g.: *less smoke:* ~ da fumo); (minus), minus (e.g.: *$1000 less taxes:* $1000 minus impostoj); **lessen**, ~igi; ~iĝi; **lesser**, ~a; ~ granda; **the less ..., the less (more)**, ju ~ ..., des ~ (pli) (e.g.: *the less said, the better:* ju ~ dirite, des pli bone); **all the less**, des ~ [see "all"]; **(all) the less because (of)**, des ~ ĉar (pro)
–less, (sfx: w/o), sen– [pfx] (e.g.: *endless:* ~fina; *tireless:* ~laca)
lessee, luanto
lesson, leciono; **object lesson**, praktika ~o
lessor, luiganto
lest, por ke ... ne, pro timo ke (e.g.: *be careful, lest you be seen:* zorgu, por ke oni ne vidu vin; *we were careful, lest we be seen:* ni zorgis, pro timo ke oni vidu nin)
let, (allow, permit), lasi [tr], permesi [tr] (e.g.: *let me go:* ~u min iri; *let him in the house:* ~i lin en la domon; *let one do something:* ~i al iu [or] ~i iun fari ion; *let oneself be caught:* ~i sin esti kaptita); (in subjunctive expressions, indicating desire or command; math given), –u (e.g.: *let them eat cake:* ili manĝu kukojn; *let N = 1:* N egalu 1); (rent out), luigi; **let's (do something)**, ni –u (e.g.: *let's dance:* ni dancu); **let down**, (lower), mallevi [tr]; (disappoint), malkomplezi [tr], trompi [tr], senesperigi; (leave helpless, abandon), forlasi [tr]; **let go (of)**, (from job), maldungi [tr]; (release, gen), de~i [tr], malteni [tr], liberigi; malfiksiĝi (de), malkroĉiĝi (de), malligiĝi (de); **let go by, let pass**, preter~i [tr]; **let go through**, tra~i [tr]; **let off**, (emit), eligi, el~i [tr]; (pardon), pardoni [tr]; (excuse, free, as from duty), liberigi, sendevigi; (punish mildly), milde puni [tr]; **let out**, (release), eligi, liberigi; el~i [tr]; (reveal), riveli

[tr], malkaŝi [tr]; **let up**, (relax), malstreĉiĝi; (cease), ĉesi [int]; **outlet**, (for any fluid), elfluejo; (elec), ingo; (mouth, gen), buŝo; (bsns: market), merkato; (retail shop etc.), vendejo
–let, (diminutive sfx), –eto (e.g.: *hamlet:* vilaĝeto); (offspring), –ido (e.g.: *piglet:* porkido)
lethal, letala, pereiga
lethargy, letargio; **lethargic**, ~a
Lethe, Leteo
Leto, Letoa
Lett, Letono
letter, (correspondence), letero; (of alphabet), litero [see § 16]; (draw letters on, as poster, sign, etc.), literigi; **letter carrier**, ~portisto; **letter box**, [see under "mail"]; **letterhead**, ~kapo; **letter of application**, peta ~o; **letter of credit**, akreditivo, kredit~o; **letter of security**, sekur~o; **the letter of the law**, la litero de la leĝo; **call letters**, (radio, TV), voksignalo; **capital (upper-case) letter**, majusklo; **lower-case (small) letter**, minusklo; **chain letter**, ĉen~o; **open letter**, nefermita ~o; **red-letter day**, ruĝlitera tago; **to the letter**, (literal, precise), laŭlitera; laŭlitere
Lettish, Letona
lettuce, laktuko
Leucas, Leŭkado
leucine, leŭcino
Leuciscus, leŭcisko; Leuciscus idus, iduso, alando; Leuciscus rutilus, ploto
leuco–, (sci pfx), leŭk(o)–
leucocyte, leŭkocito; **leucocytic**, ~a; **leucocytosis**, ~ozo
Leucojum, leŭkojo
leucoma, leŭkomo
leucomaine, leŭkomaino
leucoplast, leŭkoplasto
leucopoiesis, leŭkopoezo
leucorrhea, leŭkoreo
leucosis, leŭkozo
Leukas, Leŭkado
leuk–, (sci pfx), leŭk(o)–
leukemia, leŭkemio
lev, levo
Levantine, Levanteno
levator, levatoro

levee, (dike), digo; ~i [tr]
level, (degree of height etc., gen), nivelo (e.g.: *sea level:* mar~o; *high-level conference:* alt~a konferenco); (flat, even, horizontal), ebena; (make level), ~i [tr]; ebenigi; (tool), ~ilo; (aim), celumi [tr]; (flat land), ebenaĵo; **levelfull**, ebenplena, plenplena; **levelheaded**, trankvila, neekscitiĝema, neĉagreniĝema; **level off**, ebenigi; ebeniĝi; **on the level**, (open, honest), honesta, justa, senartifika; **on a level with**, sam~a kun
lever, (to lift), lev/ilo [cp "crow: crowbar"]; (on machine, to control, shift, engage, etc.), regstango; **leverage**, ~oforto, ~povo; **gear-shift lever**, kluĉostango
Levi, Levi
leviathan, levjatano, L~o
levirate, levirato
Levisticum, levistiko
levitate, levitacii [int]; ~igi; **levitation**, ~o
Levite, Levido
Leviticus, (Bib), Levidoj
levity, malseriozeco, ŝercemo, spriteco, gajeco
Levkas, Leŭkado
levorotatory, livoĝira
levulose, levulozo
levy, (tax), imposto; imputi [tr] (~on); (collect, seize), kolekti [tr]
lewd, lasciva
Lewis, Luiso, Luizo
lexical, vortara, leksikona
lexicography, leksikograf/io; **lexicographer**, ~o
lexicology, leksikolog/io; **lexicologist**, ~o
lexicon, leksikono
Leyden, [see "Leiden"]
Lhasa, Lasso
li, (Chinese measure), lio [536,33 metroj (see § 20)]
liable, (legally obligated; mutually responsible), solidara (kun), respondeca (e.g.: *liable for another's debts:* ~a kun alia pri ŝuldoj); (inclined to), ema (al), inklina (al); **liability**, ~eco, respondeco; inklino, emo; (debt), ŝuldo, kompensodevo

liaison, (gen), interligo, interrilato; (love affair), amligo
liana, **liane**, liano
Liao(he), Liaŭ
Liaoning, Liaŭning
liar, mensog/anto; ~(em)ulo
Lias, liaso
libation, (rel), oferverŝo; (drink), trink(aĵ)o
libel, skribe) kalumnii [tr]; (skriba) kalumnio [not "libel–"]; **libelous**, kalumnia
liberal, (free), libera; (pol etc.), liberala; (generous; freely giving, given), donacema, malavara, grandanima; (tolerant), tolerema; **liberalism**, liberalismo
liberate, liberigi; **liberation**, ~o; **liberator**, ~into
Liberia, Liberio; **Liberian**, ~ano; ~a
libertine, (gen), libertino; ~a; **libertinism**, ~ismo; ~eco
liberty, libero, ~eco; **at liberty**, ~a; **take liberties with**, esti tro ~a kun
libido, libido; **libidinal**, ~a; **libidinous**, lasciva
Libra, (ast), Pesilo
library, (more formal; institution; cmptr software), biblioteko; (any collection of books etc., as by one person or publisher), libraro; (collection of audio, cmptr, or oth disks), diskaro; (of tapes), bendaro; **librarian**, ~isto
librate, (ast), oscili [int]; **libration**, ~ado; **libration point**, ~opunkto
libretto, libreto
Libya, Libio; **Libyan**, ~ano; ~a
license, (gen), licenco; ~i [tr]; **license plate**, numerplato
licentiate, (person w license), licencito; (European university degree), licencio
licentious, lasciva, libertina, malĉasta, diboĉ(em)a
lichee, [see "litchi"]
lichen, likeno; **cup lichen**, (Cladonia), kladonio
Lichenes, likenoj
lichi, [see "litchi"]
licit, lica; **be licit**, ~i [int]; **illicit**, ne~a, mal~a; **be illicit**, ne ~i [int]
lick, (w tongue), leki [tr]; ~o; (win over), venki [tr]

licorice, (gen), glicirizo; licorice root, ~a radiko; wild licorice, (*Galium*), galio
lictor, liktoro
lid, (any top, cover), kovrilo; (hinged), klapo; eyelid, palpebro
lie, (be horizontal), kuŝi [int] (e.g.: *lie in bed:* ~i en la lito); (be located), ~i, situi [int] (e.g.: *England lies between the European continent and the Atlantic:* Anglio situas inter la Eŭropa kontinento kaj la Atlantiko; *here is where the problem lies:* jen kie ~as la problemo); (untruth), mensogo; mensogi [int]; lie down, ~iĝi; take lying down, akcepti [tr] senproteste; underlie, sub~i [tr]; give the lie to, montri la mensogon en, de
Liechtenstein, Liĥtenŝtejno
lied, (German art song), lido; lieder, ~oj
liege, (master), feŭd/mastro, ~estro; (vassel), vasalo, ~ulo; (loyal), lojala
Liege, Lieĝo
lien, retenrajto, konfiskrajto
lienectomy, splenektomio, lienektomio
lien(o)–, (med root), lien(o)–
lientery, lienterio
lieu, loko; in lieu of, anstataŭ, vic' al
lieutenant, leŭtenanto; sublieutenant, sub~o
life, (gen), vivo; ~a; (lasting lifetime), dum~a, ~daŭra; (e.g.: *life member:* dum~a membro); life belt, savzono; lifeboat, savboato; lifeguard, savgardisto; life jacket, savjako; lifeline, (rope), savŝnuro; (fig, as important trade route), savlinio; lifelong, dum~a, ~daŭra; life preserver, lifesaver, savoflosilo; life-size, naturgranda; life span, ~daŭro; lifestyle, ~stilo; lifetime, ~daŭro; dum~a, ~daŭra; lifework, dum~a laboro; afterlife, post~o; change of life, (menopause), menopaŭzo; a dog's life, mizera ~o; wildlife, sovaĝularo, sovaĝuloj; sovaĝula; flee (hang on, etc.) for dear life, fuĝi (kroĉiĝi, k.t.p.) pro mortotimo; take one's life in one's hands, riski sian ~on; a matter of life and death, ~grava afero; bring to life, (make conscious),

(re)konsciigi; (make lively), vigligi, animi [tr], ~igi; come to life, (re)konsciiĝi; vigliĝi, animiĝi, ~iĝi; for life, dum~e; for the life of me, neniel ajn; malgraŭ ĉio; make life worth living, indigi la ~adon; not on your life, nepre ne, absolute ne; take (a) life, mortigi; true to life, ~overa
lift, (raise, rise, gen), levi [tr]; ~iĝi; ~(iĝ)o; (force for lifting), ~oforto; (pilfer), marodi [tr] [cp "maraud"]; (Br: elevator), lifto; (end, revoke), revoki [tr], nuligi (e.g.: *the storm warnings have been lifted:* la ŝtormavertoj estas revokitaj); (ride), veturigo; (dispel), forigi; (be dispelled), foriĝi, disiĝi, malaperi [int]; lift-off, (rocket etc.), lanĉiĝi; lanĉiĝo; (plane, balloon, etc.), de~iĝi; de~iĝo; chairlift, seĝotelfero; forklift, ĉarelot; skilift, skitelfero; uplift, (raise, lift, gen), ~i; ~o; ~a (e.g.: *uplift bra:* ~a mamzono); (inspire, raise to higher moral etc. level), edifi [tr]; edifo; give one a lift, (give ride to), veturigi iun
ligament, ligamento
ligate, (gen), ligi [tr]; (med), ligaturi [tr]
ligature, (any tie), ligo; ~ado; ~aĵo; (med, mus), ligaturo*; ligaturi* [tr]
light, (radiation, gen; en~enment, illumination, lit or fig), lumo; ~i [int] (sur), ~igi (e.g.: *visible light:* videbla ~o; *light the way:* ~i sur la vojo [or] ~igi la vojon; *the light of knowledge:* la ~o de la scio); (decorative), ilumini [tr]; iluminilo (e.g.: *Christmas lights:* Kristnaskaj iluminiloj); (source of light), ~o, ~ilo; (give light to), ~igi (e.g.: *light a candle:* ~igi kandelon; *light a room with a candle:* ~igi ĉambron per kandelo); (lighter, as match etc.), fajrilo; (set afire), ekbruligi; (animate), animi [tr]; (aspect), aspekto (e.g.: *in a favorable light:* en favora aspekto); (bright, not dark), ~a, hela; (pale), pala, pal–, –eta (e.g.: *light green:* palverda, verdeta); (not heavy, gen), malpeza, leĝera; (not dense), maldensa; (gentle, delicate), delikata; (not difficult, not intense), leĝera, malintensa, facila, nepeniga; (graceful), gracia; (soft, muted, re sound etc.),

mallaŭta; (not serious), leĝera, malserioza, malgrava; (happy, light-spirited), gaja, bonhumora, kontenta; (flighty, frivolous), facilanima, frivola; (dizzy), kapturniĝa; (land, alight), surteriĝi; **lighten**, (pli)~igi, (pli)heligi; (pli)paligi; malpezigi; leĝerigi; maldensigi; delikatigi; faciligi; gajigi; kontentigi; (lessen load), malŝarĝi [tr]; (remove ballast), senbalastigi; **lighter**, (cigarette etc.), fajrilo; (barge), gabaro, ŝarĝpramo; **light-headed**, kapturniĝa; **light into**, ekataki [tr]; **light out**, ekiri [int]; **light up**, (give light to), ~igi; (start to give light), ek~i [int]; (light cigarette etc.), ekbruligi; (start to smoke cigarette etc.), ekfumi [int]; (beam, radiate), ekradii [int] (e.g.: *her face lit up:* ŝia vizaĝo ekradiis); **light upon**, (come across), hazarde trovi [tr], hazarde renkonti [tr]; **lightweight**, malpeza, leĝera; malpezulo; **blinker light**, flagro~o; **daylight**, tag~o; **Earthlight**, Ter~o; **flashlight**, poŝlampo; **floodlight**, verŝ~ilo; **footlights**, plank~oj; **half-light**, (as dusk), krepusko, duon~o; **headlight**, (of car etc.), reflektoro; **limelight**, kalk~o; (any spotlight, lit or fig), spoto; **moonlight**, (light from Luna or oth moon), lun~o; (hold 2nd job), duaofici [int]; duaofica; **moonlighting**, duaoficado; **moonlight job**, dua ofico, krom-ofico; **night light**, dormlampo; **northern lights**, nord~o [cp "aurora"]; **penlight**, poŝlampeto; **recessed light(ing)**, (flush w ceiling), plafon~o(j); **safelight**, sekur~o; **searchlight**, serĉ~ilo; **sidelight**, (lateral illumination), flank~o; (light on side of ship etc.), flanklampo; (incidental information), krominformo; **skylight**, luko; **spotlight**, spoto; spoti [tr]; **starlight**, stel~o; **stoplight**, semaforo, trafik~o, halt~o; **sunlight**, sun~o; **taillight**, (on car etc.), post~o; **traffic light**, semaforo, trafik~o, halt~o; **bring to light**, ĵeti ~on sur; **give light**, ~i; **make light of**, priridi [tr]

lightning, fulmo; **lightning arrester**, ~olikilo; **lightning rod**, ~osuĉilo,

~oŝirmilo
ligneous, lign(ec)a
lignin, lignino
lignite, lignito
lignum vitae, gvajako
ligroine, ligroino
ligule, ligula, ligulo
ligure, ligurio
Liguria, Ligur/io; **Ligurian**, ~o; ~a; ~ia
Ligustrum, ligustro
like, (similar), simila (al); ~e (al), kiel (e.g.: *a like situation:* ~a situacio; *it is like a pencil:* ĝi estas ~a al krajono; *I want a car like that one:* mi volas aŭton ~an al tiu [or] aŭton kiel tiun); (as), kiel (e.g.: *that sounds like thunder:* tio sonas kiel tondro); (in manner of, as if it were), kvazaŭ; (have warm feelings for, appreciate), ŝati [tr], ami [tr], (io, iu) plaĉi [int] al (iu) (e.g.: *I like it:* mi ŝatas ĝin [or] ĝi plaĉas al mi); **be like**, (resemble), ~i [tr]; **likeable**, plaĉa, agrabla, afabla; **likely**, [see "likely"]; **likeness**, (similarity), ~aĵo; ~eco; (similar form), formo, ~aĵo; **likewise**, ~e, same, sammaniere; **liking**, ŝato, plaĉo; **be to one's liking**, plaĉi al iu (e.g.: *their actions were not to my liking:* iliaj agoj ne plaĉis al mi); **dislike**, malŝati [tr], malami [tr]; malŝato, malamo; **unlike**, (dissimilar), mal~a (al); (in different way), mal~e (al), malkiel (e.g.: *he has long hair, unlike his brother:* li havas longan hararon, malkiel sia frato); **like that**, (in that way), tiel, tiumaniere (e.g.: *don't do it like that:* ne faru ĝin tiel [or] tiumaniere); (such as that one), tia (e.g.: *there has never been a day like that one since:* neniam poste estis tia tago); **like this**, ĉi tiel, ĉi-maniere (e.g.: *do it like this:* faru ĝin ĉi tiel [or] ĉi-maniere); **as you like**, laŭ via plaĉo; **and the like, and such like**, kaj ~e [see also "etc."]; **that's more like it!**, jen pli bone!; **what is it like?**, kia ĝi estas?; **it is like that**, ĝi estas tia; **I would like to (do something)**, mi ŝatus (fari ion)
−like, (sfx), −eca (e.g.: *desertlike:* dezerteca)
likely, verŝajna, probabla, kredebla; ~e

(e.g.: *it is likely that I will go:* ~e mi iros; *a likely story:* ~a rakonto); **likelihood,** ~o, probableco; **in all likelihood,** plej probable; **unlikely,** ne~a, malprobabla; **it seems likely that,** ~e [avoid "ŝajnas ~e"]
liken, kompari [tr], similigi
lilac, (plant, flower), lilako; (color), lila
Lilian, Liliana
Lilium, lilio; Lilium martagon, martagono
Lilliput, Liliputo; **Lilliputian,** ~ano; ~a
Lilongwe, Lilongvo*
lilt, leĝer/a ritmo; **lilting,** ~ritma
lily, lilio; **lily-white,** ~a; **lily of the valley,** konvalo, majfloro; **African lily,** agapanto; **blood lily,** hemanto, sangofloro; **corn lily,** iksio; **day lily,** hemerokalo, tag~o; **Turk's-cap lily,** martagono; **water lily,** nimfeo, akvo~o; **yellow water lily,** nufaro, flava akvo~o, flava nimfeo
Lima, (city), Limo
Lima, (zool), limao
Limanda, limando
Limax, limako
limb, (branch, gen), branĉo; (anat), membro; (bot; ast), limbo
limber, supla, facilmova; **limber up,** ~igi; ~iĝi
limbo, (rel), limbo, L~o
Limburg, Limbourg, Limburgo; **Limburger,** (person), ~ano; (cheese), ~a fromaĝo
limbus, limbo
lime, (chem), kalko; (fruit), limeto; (tree), limetarbo; (linden tree), tilio; **limeade,** limetado*; **lime kiln,** ~forno; **birdlime,** birdogluo; **brooklime,** bekabungo; **quicklime,** kalcia oksido, kaŭstika kalko
limerick, limeriko
Limerick, Limeriko*
liminal, limina; **subliminal,** sub~a
limit, (gen), limo; ~igi; (math), limeso; (determine), determini [tr]; (delimit), dis~i [tr]; **limitation,** ~igo; **off limits,** ekster~a, ekster ~oj; **within limits,** iomgrade, certagrade, ĝis ia ~o; **within the limits of,** ene de la ~oj de; **statute of limitations,** preskriptostatuto; **the statute of limitations (to) run**

(on), preskriptiĝi (e.g.: *the statute of limitations runs on taxable income after three years:* impostado de enspezoj preskriptiĝas post tri jaroj)
Limoges, Limoĝo
limonite, limonito
Limosa, limozo
Limousin, Limoĝio
limousine, limuzino
limp, (walk lamely; fig: any crippled action), lami [int]; (unrigid), malrigida, supla; (flabby), molaĉa
limpet, patelo
limpid, klara
Limulus, limulo
Linaria, linario; Linaria cymbalaria, cimbalario
linden, (tree), tilio; (wood), ~a ligno
line, (math; any series of points, persons, objects, etc.; mark showing this; pipes etc., as gas line; line of words on page; bus line, shipping or airline, etc.; line of defense, attack, etc.), linio; ~i [tr]; (elec; 1/12 inch), lineo; (single short line, stroke, mark, etc.), streko; streki [tr]; (cord, rope, etc.), ŝnuro; (thread), fadeno; (row, queue, column), vico; (series, chain), ĉeno; (limit, boundary), limo; (skin wrinkle), falto; (course, sequence), sinsekvo; (occupation), okupo; (type of goods), varspeco; (field of knowledge etc.), fako; (short letter, note), noto; (flattering, boastful talk etc.), blago; (be, put along, as border), borderi [tr]; bordero (e.g.: *trees lined the street:* arboj borderis la straton); (put layer, lining in, on), tegi [tr]; (of descendents), deveno, sango~o; **lineage,** (ancestry), deveno, sango~o; **linear,** (re any line), ~a; (math), lineara; **lineworker, lineman,** (elec etc.), lineisto; (surveying), ĉenisto; **linesman,** (sport, gen), ~isto; **line of fire,** paf~o; **line of sight,** cel~o; **line out, line through,** (delete), forstreki [tr], trastreki [tr]; **line up, get into line,** ~igi; ~iĝi; vicigi; viciĝi; **lineup,** (gen), vico; **assembly line,** ĉenstablo; **bar line,** (mus), taktostreko; **clothesline,** sekiga ŝnuro; **contour line,** izohipsot, nivel~o [cp "isobath"];

dotted line, (as to guide writing or tearing on paper), punkto~o; fishing line, fiŝfadeno; hard line, necedema sinteno, fera sinteno; fer-sintena; interline, (re written lines), inter~i [tr]; interlineal, interlinear, inter~a; lifeline, savŝnuro; mainline, (road etc.), ĉefvojo; ĉefvoja; midline, mez~o; off-line, (elec. cmptr: not connected), nekonektita; nekonektite; on-line, (elec: connected), konektita; konektite; (cmptr), en-linea; en-linee; outline, (contour), konturi [tr]; konturo; (sketch), skizi [tr]; skizo; (detail), detali [tr]; detalado; detalaro; (list of main ideas etc.; schema), skemo; (summary), resumi [tr]; resumo; out of line, nekonforma, neakorda, nekongrua; plumbline, plumbofadeno; sideline, (side boundary in sport), taĉo, tuŝ~o; (take out of play, lit or fig), malaktivigi; (incidental work), kromlaboro; skyline, horizonto; straight line, rekto; underline, (lit or fig), substreki [tr], sub~i [tr]; substreko; bring into line, (make conform), konformigi; toe the line, konformiĝi, submetiĝi; draw the line (at), starigi la limon (ĉe); in the line of duty, dum (en) devoplenumo

linen, (of flax), linaĵo; (cloth, gen), tolo; (article of), tolaĵo (e.g.: *bed linens:* littolaĵoj)

liner, (ship), pasaĝer/ŝipo; (plane). ~avio; (cosmetic), liniŝminko; (lining), interna tegaĵo; (cover), kovrilo

ling, (fish), molvo; (heather), kaluno

lingam, lingamo

linger, (dawdle), lanti [int], malrapidi [int]; (persist, hang on), restadi [int], daŭri [int]

lingerie, (virinaj) subvestoj

lingua franca, interlingvo

lingual, (anat), langa; bilingual, dulingva; trilingual, trilingva; multilingual, plurlingva; sublingual, sub~a

linguist, (re sci of linguistics), lingvistik/isto; (one who knows languages), lingvisto; linguistic, ~a; linguistics, ~o; interlinguistics, inter~o

liniment, linimento

lining, (interna) tegaĵo

link, (of chain, lit or fig), ĉenero; (connect, elec), konekti [tr]; (mech), kupli [tr], ligi [tr]; konektilo, kuplilo, ligilo; (joint), artiki [tr]; artiko; linkage, konekt(ad)o; kupl(ad)o, lig(ad)o; konektil(ar)o; kuplil(ar)o; artik(ar)o; downlink, malsuprenkonekto; uplink, suprenkonekto; golf links, golfludejo

Linnaeus, Lineo; Linnaean, ~a

linnet, kanabeno

linoleic, linole/(at)a; linoleate, ~o; linoleic acid, ~a acido

linolenic, linolen/(at)a; linolenate, ~o; linolenic acid, ~a acido

linoleum, linoleumo

linotype, linotipo; linotypist, ~isto

linseed, lin/semo; ~sema; linseed oil, ~oleo

lint, ĉarpio

lintel, lintelo

Linum, lino

lion, leono; lioness, ~ino; ant lion, mirmeleono, formik~o; mountain lion, pumo; sea lion, otario, mar~o

lip, (anat, or similar object), lipo; ~a; ~i [tr] [cp "labium"]; (impertinence), impertinenteco; lip service, malsinceraĵo, ~-servo; give lip service to, malsincere aprobi [tr] (laŭdi, etc.); lipstick, (of any color), ~ŝminko; (red), (~)ruĝigilo; harelip, lepor~o

Lipari (Islands), (Insuloj) Liparoj

lipase, lipazo

lipid, lipido

Li Po, Li Baj

lipoid, lipido; ~eca, grasa

lipoma, lipomo

lipothymia, lipotimio

liquesce, likveski [int]; liquescence, ~(ad)o; liquescent, ~a

liqueur, likvoro

liquid, (fluid), likva; ~o; ~aĵo [cp "fluid"]; (phon), likvido; liquefy, ~igi; ~iĝi

liquidate, (bsns, $: fig: put abrupt end to), likvidi [tr]; liquidation, ~ado; liquidator, ~anto; ~isto

liquor, (alcoholic), likvoro; (juice, liquid), suko, likvaĵo; malt liquor, malt~o

liquorice, [see "licorice"]

lira, liro
Liriodendron tulipifera, tuliparbo
Lisbon, Lisbono
lisp, lispi [tr]; ~o
lissom(e), supla
list, (series written, in cmptr, etc.), listo; (en)~igi; (en)~iĝi; (lean, re ship etc.), kliniĝi; kliniĝo; **blacklist**, nigra ~o; nigra~igi
listel, listelo
listen, listen to, aŭskulti [tr]; ~o; **listen (here)!**, (pay attention!), ~u!; aŭdu!; vidu!
listless, apatia
litany, litanio
litchi, (fruit), liĉio; (tree), ~arbo
Litchi chinensis, liĉiarbo
liter, litro; **milliliter**, mili~o; **deciliter**, deci~o; **decaliter**, deka~o; **hectoliter**, hekto~o; **kiloliter**, kilo~o
literal, (re letters, gen), litera; (word for word), ~a, laŭ~a, laŭvorta
literary, literatura; **literary agent**, ~agento; **literary person**, ~isto, literatoro
literate, (can read and write), legiva, legipova; malanalfabeta; (educated), klera; **literacy**, ~o; klereco; **illiterate**, (cannot read or write), analfabeta; **illiteracy**, analfabeteco; **illiterate person**, analfabeto
literati, literatoroj, literaturistoj
literature, literaturo
litharge, litargiro
lithe, supla
lithiasis, litiazo
lithium, litio; **lithium hydroxide**, litino, ~a hidroksido
lithograph, litografi [tr]; ~o; **lithographic**, ~a; **lithography**, ~io; **lithographer**, ~isto; **photolithograph**, foto~o
lithoplaxy, litotricio
lithopone, litopono
lithoscope, litoskopo
lithotomy, litotomio
lithotrity, litotricio; **lithotrite**, ~ilo
Lithuania, (modern country), Litov/io; (grand duchy including Poland etc. until 1795), Litvo; **Lithuanian**, (modern), ~o; ~a; ~ia; (old), Litvano; Litva
litigate, procesi [tr]; **litigation**, ~(ad)o

litmus, lakmuso; **litmus paper**, ~a papero
litotes, litoto
litre, [see "liter"]
litter, (trash), forĵetaĵo, rubo; (drop trash on ground), disrubi [tr, int]; (disorder), malordo; (strew, scatter), sterni [tr] (stretcher), portlito; (offspring), idaro; **litter box**, katsablujo; **litterbug**, ruboĵetanto; **kitty litter**, katsablo
little, (small), malgranda; (short), mallonga; (not much), malmulte (da), nemulte (da) (e.g.: *know little:* malmulte scii; *the jug had a hole, but little milk leaked:* la botelo havis truon, sed malmulte da lakto likis); **a little**, (some), iom(ete) (da); **little by little**, iom post iom
littoral, borda; ~ejo
Littorina, litorino
liturgy, liturgio; **liturgical**, ~a
live, (be alive, lit or fig, gen), vivi [int]; (reside), loĝi [int]; **living**, (alive, gen), ~a; (livelihood), ~tenado; **live down**, super~i [tr]; **outlive**, (live longer), post~i [tr]; (outlast), postdaŭri [tr]; **livelihood**, ~tenado; **make one's livelihood, make a living**, ~teni sin; **long live ...!**, ~u ...!; **long-lived**, longa~a; **short-lived**, mallonga~a, efemera; **live and let live**, ~i kaj lasi ~i; **live it up**, diboĉi [int]; indulgi sin, ~i larĝe kaj lukse; **live up to**, plenumi la esperojn de; **live with**, (tolerate), toleri [tr]
livedo, livedo
lively, vigla, viv(ec)a, gaja, verva
liver, (organ), hepato; (as food), ~aĵo; **liverwort**, hepatiko; **liverworst**, ~okolbaso
Liverpool, Liverpolo
livery, (dress), livreo; ~ulo; ~ularo; (re horses), ĉevalvartado; **livery stable**, lustablo
livestock, brutaro
Livia, Livia
livid, livida
Livonia, Livon/io; **Livonian**, ~o; ~a; ~ia
Livorno, Livorno
Livy, Livio

Liza, (diminutive of Eliza), Elinjo
lizard, (*Lacerta*), lacerto; **agama lizard,** agamo; **thunder lizard,** brontosaŭro
llama, lamo, ljamo
llano, stepo, prerio
lo, (interj), jen!
loach, kobitido
load, (fill, put on, etc., to be carried; burden; resistance, as on motor, elec circuit, etc.), ŝarĝi [tr]; ~o; (re cmptr, gun, camera, etc.), ŝargi [tr]; ŝargiĝi; **download,** malsuprenŝargi [tr]; **overload,** super~i [tr]; super~o; **payload,** pag~o; **self-loading,** memŝarga; **unload,** mal~i [tr]; senŝargigi; **upload,** suprenŝargi [tr]; **be loaded with,** (fig: have much of), havi abunde da, havi abunda(j)n –o(j)n
loaf, (bread), pano [see "bread"]; (dawdle), lant(ad)i [int]; **loafer,** (person), lantemulo, mallaboremulo; (shoe), lantŝuo
loam, lomo†
loan, prunto; ~(edon)i [tr]; **on loan,** ~a; ~e (e.g.: *I have the book on loan for a month:* mi havas la libron ~e por unu monato)
loath, malinklina, malvolonta
loathe, abomeni [tr]; **loathesome,** ~(ind)a
lob, altpeli [tr]; ~o
lobby, (vestibule etc.), vestiblo; (propagandize), pripropagandi [tr], kampanji [int]; **lobbyist,** propagandisto
lobe, (gen), lobo
lobelia, Lobelia, lobelio
lobotomy, lobotomio
lobster, omaro; **spiny lobster,** palinuro, langusto
local, (gen), loka; (of that place), tiea; (of this place), ĉi-tiea, ĉi-~a; **localize,** (concentrate in a place, as med condition), ~iĝi
locale, lokalo
locality, (place), loko; (district, area), distrikto
locate, (put in a place, gen), loki [tr]; (put relative to surroundings), situigi (e.g.: *locate the office in Washington:* situigi la oficejon en Vaŝingtono; *we located the tent between two large*

oaks: ni situigis la tendon inter du grandaj kverkoj); (take a place), ~iĝi; (find, gen), trovi [tr]; (find position of something or someone), lokalizi [tr] (e.g.: *they located the downed plane 100 km west of Norfolk:* ili lokalizis la falintan avion 100 km–ojn okcidente de Norfolk); **location,** (place), ~o; ~ado; ~iĝo; situo; lokalizo; **located,** ~ita; situanta; **be located,** (situated), situi [int] (e.g.: *the house is well located for the view:* la domo bone situas por la elvido); **dislocate,** (anat joint), elartikigi; (disrupt, upset), malordi [tr], ĥaosigi, disrompi [tr]; **relocate,** re~i [tr]; re~iĝi
locative, lokativo
lochia, lokioj
lock, (w key), ŝlosi [tr]; ~iĝi; (to name type of lock used) -serure ~i (e.g.: *the door was padlocked:* la pordo estis pendserure ~ita); (locking device), seruro [see "key"]; (fasten together as mech parts, lit or fig), kunkupli [tr]; kunkupliĝi; (jam, stick, gen), kunfiksi [tr]; kunfiksiĝi; ("freeze" due to lack of lubrication), rajpi [int]; (of hair), buklo; (in canal), kluzo; **unlock,** mal~i [tr]; mal~iĝi; **locker,** (lockable cabinet), ~oŝranko; (trunk), kofro; (freezer room), frostoĉambro; (cabinet in freezer), frostoŝranko; **locket,** medaliono; **lock away,** for~i [tr]; **lockgate,** kluzpordego; **lockjaw,** tetanoso; **lock on(to),** fiks(iĝ)i al, sur; **lockout,** (e.g., workers from factory), lokaŭto; **locksmith,** seruristo; **air lock,** aerkluzo; **combination lock,** kombinoseruro; **interlock,** (mech), interkupli [tr]; interkupliĝi; interkuplaĵo; **key lock,** ~ilseruro; **padlock,** pendseruro
locomobile, lokomobilo; ~a
locomotive, lokomotivo
locus, lokuso
locust, (insect), lokusto; (tree: *Robinia*), robinio; (tree: *Ceratonia*), karobarbo; **honey locust,** (*Gleditsia*), gledicio; **bristly locust, clammy locust, moss locust,** robinio
Locusta, lokusto
Locustella, lokustelo

locustelle, lokustelo
locution, (expression), esprimo; (speech style), lingvaĵo
lode, gango, vejno
lodge, (reside), loĝi [int]; ~igi, tranoktigi; (stick), fiksi [tr]; fiksiĝi; (deposit, place), deponi [tr]; (register, record), registri [tr]; (inn, hotel), pas~ejo; (meeting place of chapter or organization), loĝio; **lodging(s)**, (permanent residence), ~ejo; (temporary, as in hotel), ~igo, pas~ejo, tranoktejo; **lodging house**, pensiono; **lodger**, pensionulo
lodicule, lodiklo
loess, leŭso, loeso
loft, (attic), subtegmento; (throw high), altĵeti [tr]; altĵeto; **lofty**, (high), alta; (noble), nobla; (arrogant), aroganta; **choir loft**, ĥorejo
log, (entire tree trunk), (arb)trunko; (chopped up for fireplace, construction, sawmill, etc.), ŝtipo; (daily naut, cmptr, or similar record), loglibro; (any daily record), taglibro; (any record), registraĵo; (device to measure ship speed), logo; (record as in a log, gen), registri [tr]; (Bib: unit of volume, about 1/2 liter), log'o; (remove trees from), prisegi [tr]; **logger**, arbsegisto; **log chip**, logo; **log in**, **log on**, (e.g., on cmptr), enregistri sin, enregistriĝi; **logjam**, ŝtipobstaklo; **log off**, elregistri sin, elregistriĝi; **logwood**, (tree: *Haematoxylon*), kampeĉo; (wood), kampeĉa ligno
logarithm, logaritmo; **antilogarithm**, anti~o; **common logarithm**, ordinara ~o; **natural logarithm**, natura ~o
loge, loĝio
loggia, loĝio
logic, (reasoned), logiko; (math, cmptr), logistiko; **logical**, ~a; **illogical**, ne~a
logistic, loĝistika; **logistics**, ~o [note sing]
logo, (symbol of bsns or oth organization), identiga simbolo
logograph, logografo
logotype, [see "logo"]
–logy, [see "–ology"]
loin, **loins**, (anat), lumbo [note sing; plur "~oj" sometimes used as in English, but this should be avoided]; (of animal, as meat), ~aĵo; **loincloth**, pareo; **tenderloin**, mol~aĵo
Loir, Loaro
Loire, Luaro
Loiret, Luareto
Lois, Luisa, Luiza
loiter, (dawdle), lanti [int], malrapidi [int]
Loligo, loligo
Lolium, lolo
loll, (loiter, dawdle), lanti [int]
lollipop, stangobombono
Lombard, Lombardo; ~a; ~ia; Longobardo; **Lombardy**, ~io, ~ujo; **Lombardic**, ~ia [note: "Longobard–" applies generally to early Germanic tribe; "Lombard–" to either ancient or modern]
London, Londono; **Londoner**, ~ano
lone, sola; **loner**, ~(em)ulo; **lonely**, ~eca; **loneliness**, ~eco; **lonesome**, ~eca
long, (of some length or duration, gen), longa; ~e (e.g.: *a long pole:* ~a paliso; *3 meters [or] hours long:* 3 metrojn [or] horojn ~a); (yearn), sopiri [int] (al, pri, je); **longing**, sopirado, saŭdado; **longevity**, (length of life), viv~o; (of work), labor~o; **long enough**, (time), sufiĉe ~e, sufiĉe da tempo; **longhand**, manskribado; manskriba; **longhorn**, ~akorna; ~akornulo; **longshoreman**, stivisto; **longstanding**, ~edaŭra; **how long**, (how much time), kiom ~e, kiom da tempo; **as long as**, (equally long), tiel ~a kiel; (while), dum; **any longer**, (time), plu; **no longer**, (not any more), ne plu, jam ne; **it was not long before**, ne ~e daŭris antaŭ (ol); **the long and the short of** (it), ĉio pri (ĝi)
longe, lonĝo; ~i [tr]
longeron, (muscle), longisimo
longitude, (angle), longitudo; (length), long(ec)o; **longitudinal**, ~a; laŭlonga
Longobard, [see "Lombard"]
Lonicera, lonicero; Lonicera caprifolium, kaprifolio
look, (w eyes; face toward), rigardi [tr]; ~o; (appear, have aspect, mien), aspekti [int], mieni [int]; aspekto, mieno

(e.g.: *you look tired:* vi aspektas [or: mienas] laca); (appear, seem), ŝajni [int]; ŝajno (e.g.: *it looks bigger than it is:* ĝi ŝajnas pli granda ol ĝi estas); (interj: behold!), jen (e.g.: *look, I found it:* jen, mi trovis ĝin); (interj to gain attention), vidu (e.g.: *well, look, let's discuss that tomorrow:* nu, vidu, ni diskutu tion morgaŭ); **looks**, (appearance), aspekto; ŝajno; (good appearance), belaspekto, bonaspekto; **look after**, (care for), prizorgi [tr]; **look after oneself**, fari por si mem, defendi sin mem, prizorgi sin mem; **look alive!**, vigliĝu!; **look as if**, ŝajni ke, ŝajni kvazaŭ [see "look like" below; see "seem", "as"]; **look askance**, strabi [int]; **look at**, ~i [tr] [not "~i al"] (e.g.: *look at the picture:* ~i la bildon); **look away**, forturni la okulojn; **look back**, retro~i [int]; **look down**, (lower eyes), mallevi la okulojn; **look down (upon)**, (disrespect), malrespekti [tr], maladmiri [tr], malestimi [tr]; (view out over), el~i [int] super, sur; **look for**, (search), serĉi [tr] [not "serĉi por"] (e.g.: *look for the dog:* serĉi la hundon); (expect), atendi [tr]; (anticipate), anticipi [tr]; **look forward to**, antaŭĝui [tr]; **look here!**, atentu!, vidu!, ~u!; **look high and low (for)**, serĉi [tr] ĉie; **look in on**, (visit), viziteti [tr]; **look into**, (investigate), kontroli [tr], esplori [tr]; **look like**, (resemble), simili [tr]; (seem, seem likely), ŝajni [int] (ke) (e.g.: *it looks like [it will] rain:* ŝajnas ke pluvos); **look on**, (see), ~i; (consider), konsideri [tr]; (as spectator), spekti [tr]; **look out!**, atentu!, zorgu!; **lookout**, (high place w view), altano, belvidejo; (mil: person), gvatisto; (mil: place), gvatejo; **look out for**, (care for), prizorgi [tr]; **look out (over)**, (have view), el~i [int] (super, al, sur); **be on the lookout for**, serĉadi [tr]; **keep a lookout**, gvati [tr]; **that's your lookout!**, jen via problemo!; **look over**, (check), kontroli [tr]; **look the other way**, ~i alidirekten, ignori [tr]; **look to**, (give attention), atenti [tr]; (approach), aliri [tr]; (consult, refer to), sin turni al

(e.g.: *I looked to him for advice:* mi turnis min al li por konsilo); (expect, anticipate), atendi [tr]; anticipi [tr]; **look up**, (raise eyes), levi la okulojn, ~i supren; (search out, find reference, etc., as in dictionary), serĉi [tr], elserĉi [tr]; (improve), pliboniĝi; (visit), iri viziti [tr]; **look up to**, (respect), respekti [tr], admiri [tr], estimi [tr]; **look upon**, (see), ~i; (consider), konsideri [tr]; **onlooker**, spektanto; **outlook**, (perspective), perspektivo; (expectation), espero, verŝajna rezulto; **overlook**, (not notice), preteratenti [tr]; (look out over), (super)~i [tr] (al); (place w view), altano, belvidejo; **a blank look**, senseprima mieno; **goodlooking**, **nice-looking**, belaspekta, bonaspekta; **not much to look at**, ne tre ~inda, ne tre belaspekta

loom, (operated by hands and feet), teks/ilo; (machine), ~omaŝino, ~atoro; (appear large or menacingly), aperegi [int], ŝvebegi [int]; minaci [tr]; (be half visible), duonaperi [int]; **Jacquard loom**, ĵakardo [cp "weave: Jacquard weave"]

loon, *(Gavia)*, gavio*; *(Colymbus* or *Podiceps)*, kolimbo, podicipo

loony, freneza, lunatika

loop, (as in rope, line, elec circuit, cmptr program, etc.), maŝo; ~igi; (turn back on own path, as plane), lopi [int]; lopo; (sharp turn, as in road, river), serpenti [int]; serpentado; (one turn in coil), volvo; volvi; (wind around, wrap), volvi [tr]; **loophole**, evitilo; (mil), embrazuro; **loop the loop**, lopi [int]; **throw (one) for a loop**, konsterni (iun), malekvilibrigi (iun)

loose, (not fastened, not tight), mal/fiksa; (not compact), ~kompakta, ~firma; (free, not confined), libera; (not packed), loza, nepakita; (baggy), loza, vasta, ~strikta; (irresponsible, careless), ~zorga, nerespondeca; (imprecise), ~preciza; (relaxed), ~streĉa; (re bowels), laksa; (scat tered), disa; (opp "prudish"), ~pruda, ~ĉasta; **loose(n)**, ~fiksi [tr]; ~fiksiĝi; ~kompaktigi; ~kompaktiĝi; liberigi; ~streĉi [tr]; ~streĉiĝi; laksigi; **loose ends**, (tri-

fles), bagatelajoj; **loose-jointed,**
loose-limbed, supla, facilmova;
loose-leaf, liberfolia; **loosestrife,**
(*Lythrum salicaria*), salikario
loot, rab/ajo; pri~i [tr], el~i [tr]
lop, dehaki [tr]
lope, galopeti [int]; ~o
Lophius, lofio
Lophophora williamsii, pejotlo*
loquacious, babilema
Loranthus, loranto
lord, (any master), mastro, sinjoro; (feudal etc.), feŭd~o, senjoro; (English
noble title), lordo; **the Lord,** (God), la
M~o, la Sinjoro, la Eternulo, Dio; **my**
lord, m'lord, (term of address), moŝto
[not "mia moŝto"]; **overlord,** ĉefsen-
joro, feŭdosenjoro; **warlord,** milit-
estro; **lord it over,** diktatori [tr],
moŝtumi [int] (super), supermoŝti [tr],
senjorumi [int] (super)
lordosis, lordozo; **lordotic,** ~a
lore, (folklore), folkloro; (any knowledge, gen), scio
loris, Loris, loriso
lorgnette, lorneto
Lorius, lorio
Lorraine, Loreno
lorry, (Br: truck), kamiono [for varieties, see under "truck"]; (wagon),
platĉarego
lory, lorio
Los Angeles, Los-Anĝeleso
lose, (opp "find"; opp "earn"; cease to
possess; fail to obtain; etc.), perdi [tr];
(be defeated), malvenki [int]; (not
win), malgajni [tr]; [see also "loss"];
lose out, malsukcesi [int]; **lose one's**
way, get lost, (voj)erari [int]; **lose**
oneself in, absorbiĝi en; **have noth-**
ing to lose, riski nenion; **there's**
nothing to lose, estas neniu risko;
what's there to lose?, kiu risko estas?
loss, perdo; malvenko; malgajno; ($:
opp "profit"), malprofito; [see
"lose"]; **take (suffer) a loss,** ($),
suferi malprofiton; **at a loss,** ($), mal-
profite; (puzzled, uncertain), senkomprena, nekapabla (e.g.: *their actions*
leave me at a loss: iliaj agoj lasas min
senkomprena; *the situation leaves me*

at a loss to know what to do: la situacio lasas min nekapabla scii kion fari);
be at a loss to, ne povi [tr] (e.g.: *I am*
at a loss to explain it: mi ne povas
klarigi ĝin); **be at a loss for words,**
esti konsternita ĝis silento, ne povi elpensi kion diri
lot, (piece of land), parcelo, terpeco;
(fate), sorto; (object used to decide by
chance), loto; (decision by lot), lota-
do; [cp "lottery"]; (share), porcio;
(batch, group), aro; **a lot (of), lots**
(of), (much, many), multe (da), multaj
(el) (e.g.: *she reads lots* [or] *a lot:* ŝi
multe legas; *a lot happier:* multe pli
kontenta; *a lot of snow:* multe da
neĝo; *a lot of books:* multaj libroj; *a*
lot of the books were in Esperanto:
multaj el la libroj estis en Esperanto);
the lot, (all), la tuto; **draw lots, cast**
lots, loti [int]; **it fell one's lot,** la loto
falis sur iun
Lot, (Bib; river), Loto
Lota, (zool), lojto
Lothar, Lotario
Lotharingia, Lotaringio
lotion, pomado
lotophagi, lotofagoj
lottery, loterio; ~a [cp "lot"]
lotto, lotludo
lotus, Lotus, lotuso; **lotus-eater,** lotofa-
go; **lotus tree,** ~(arb)o; **Indian lotus,**
Hinda ~o
loud, (re sound), laŭta; (re color), bril-
kolora
Louis, Luiso, Luizo; **Louisa,** ~a, Luiza;
St. Louis, (city), Sankta-Luizo; **Port**
Louis, (capital of Mauritius),
Port–Luizo*
louis d'or, luidoro
Louisiana, Luiziano
lounge, (stand about, loll, sit idle), lanti
[int]; for~i [tr]; (room), sidĉambro;
lounge car, (rr), sidvagono
loupe, lupeo
Lourdes, Lurdo
loukoum, lukumo
louse, (zool, non-specific), laŭso; (*Pedi-*
culus), pediko; (person), aĉulo, fiulo,
kanajlo; **lousewort,** pedikulario;
crab louse, ftiro; **plant louse,** (*Phyl-*
loxera), filoksero, vin~o; **scale louse,**

koĉo; **wood louse**, onisko; **louse up**, fuŝi [tr]
lousy, (bad), fava, aĉa, mizera
lout, krudulo, bubego
Louvain, Loveno
louver, (opening w slats), persieno; (one slat), ~a lato; **louvered**, ~a
Louvre, Luvro
lovage, (*Levisticum*), levistiko
love, (gen), ami [tr]; ~o; (sexual), amori [tr]; amoro; **lover(s)**, (ge)~anto(j); (ge)amoranto(j); **love affair**, ~afero; **love-in-a-mist**, (bot), nigelo; **love-lies-bleeding**, (bot), amaranto; **in love**, en~iĝinta; **be in love with**, ~i; **make love to**, (share sex), amori [tr]; (court), ~indumi [tr]; **fall in love with**, ek~i [tr], en~iĝi al; **fall madly in love with**, arde [or] furore en~iĝi al
lovely, rava, bel(eg)a
low, (not tall or elevated; not great; not advanced; below level; re gear ratio; etc.), mal/alta; ~alte(n); (not primary), ~ĉefa; (re sound pitch), ~akuta, basa; (not loud), ~laŭta; (shallow), ~profunda; (weak), ~vigla, febla; (psych: depressed), deprimita; (not noble), ~nobla; (vulgar), triviala; (indecent), ~deca; (unethical, despicable), fia; (low point, minimum), minimumo; (cow sound), muĝi [int]; muĝo; **lower**, (put down, go down), ~levi [tr]; ~leviĝi; (threaten), minaci [tr]; **lowly**, (humble), humila; **low blow**, (any unfair action), fi~ago; **lowdown**, (information), informo, faktoj; (contemptible), fia, kanajla; **lowland**, ~altejo; **be low on**, (almost out of), esti elĉerpiĝonta de, havi ~multe da, esti sen multe da
lox, (fish), salsalmaĵo; (oxygen), likva oksigeno
Loxia, loksio, krucbekulo
loxodromic, loksodromia; **loxodromics**, ~a velado; **loxodromic line**, ~o
loyal, lojala; **loyalty**, ~eco; **disloyal**, mal~a
lozenge, (gen), lozenĝo
LSD, (abb of "lysergic acid diethylamide"), LZD [abb of "lizergacida dietilamido", more properly "dietilamido de lizergata acido"]

Luan (Ho), Luan
luau, (Havaja) festeno
Lübeck, Lubeko
lubricate, lubriki [tr]; **lubricaion**, ~(ad)o; ~aĵo; **lubricant**, ~aĵo; **lubricator**, ~ilo
Lucan, **Lucanus**, (Roman poet), Lukano
Lucanus, (zool), lukano, cervskarabo
lucerne, luzerno
Lucerne, (city), Lucerno; **Lake (of) Lucerne**, Lago de la Kvar Kantonoj
Lucia, Lucia; **St. Lucia**, (geog), Sankta Lucia†
Lucian, Luciano
lucid, lucida
Lucifer, Lucifero
Lucile, Lucilia
Lucilius, Lucilio
Lucille, Lucilia
Lucina, Lucina
Lucinda, Lucia, Lucinjo
Luciola, luciolo
Lucioperca sandra, sandro
Lucius, Lucio
luck, (chance, gen), ŝanco, hazardo; (good luck), bon~o; (fate), sorto; **lucky, in luck**, bon~a; **luckily**, feliĉe; **luck out**, havi bon~on; **unlucky, out of luck**, **down on one's luck**, malbon~a; **try one's luck**, provi la sorton; **push one's luck**, tenti la sorton; **good luck!**, (wish), bon~on!; **Lady Luck**, (la) Fortuno
Lucknow, Lakno
lucrative, lukr(eg)a
Lucretius, Lukrecio; **Lucretia**, ~a
Lucullus, Lukulo; **Lucull(e)an**, ~a
Lucy, Lucia
ludicrous, ridinda, absurda
Ludwig, Ludoviko
luff, lofi [tr]; ~o
luffa, Luffa, lufo
lug, (carry), port/egi [tr], pene ~i [tr]; (drag), treni [tr]; (mech: projecting piece), buteo
luge, luĝo; ~i [int] [cp "sled"]
luggage, bagaĝot, valizoj
lugger, (boat), lugro
lugubrious, morn(eg)a, melankolia, funebra
Lukas, Lukaso

Luke, Luko
lull, (soothe), luli [tr]; (pause), paŭzo
lullaby, lulkanto
lu-lu, (lulling onom), lu-lu
lumbago, lumbalgio, lumbago
lumbar, lumba
lumber, (wood), ligno, seg~o, ĉar-pent~o, konstru~o; (cut trees), prisegi [tr]; (clutter, junk), fataso, rubo; (move heavily), pezmoviĝi; (walk), pezpaŝi [int]; **lumbering,** prisegado; pezmova; pezpaŝa; **lumberjack,** arb-segisto; **lumberyard,** seg~ejo
lumbo–, (anat root), lumbo–
Lumbricus, lumbriko, termevo
lumen, lumeno
luminary, (ast), lumastro; (person), em-inentulo
luminesce, lumineski [int]; **lumines-cent,** ~a; **luminescence,** ~o; **tribolu-minescence,** tribo~o
luminous, luma; **luminosity,** ~eco, ~–intenso
lump, (hunk, piece), bulo, maso, peco; (in cereal, mashed potatoes, etc.), grumelo; (swelling, bump), tubero; **lump together,** kunamasigi; **lump in one's throat,** ezofaga bulo†
Luna, Luno
lunacy, frenezo
lunar, [see "Luna"]; (re Luna), Luna; (re any moon), luna; **cislunar,** cis–Luna; **translunar,** trans–Luna
Lunaria, lunario
lunatic, freneza, lunatika; ~ulo, lunatiko
lunatum, (bone), lunato
lunch, lunĉo; ~i [int]; **lunch counter,** ~ejo; **luncheon,** (formala) tagmanĝo; **luncheonette,** ~ejo; **lunchroom,** ~oĉambro, ~ejo
lunette, luneto
lung, (organ), pulmo; (as food), ~aĵo; **lungfish,** ~ofiŝo; **lungwort,** pulmo-nario, ~oherbo; **iron lung,** ŝtal~o
lunge, (sudden jump), eksalti [int], im-peti [int]; ~o, impeto; (thrust, as w sword), ekŝovi [tr]; ekŝovo; (horse-training), [see "longe"]
Lungkiang, Kikihar
lungoor, presbito
lunkhead, ŝtipulo
lupine, (bot), lupino; (like wolf),

lup(ec)a
Lupinus, lupino
lupus, lupuso; **lupus erythematosus,** eritema ~o; **lupus vulgaris,** komuna ~o
lurch, (sway), ŝanceliĝi; (jerk), skuiĝi; **leave (someone) in the lurch,** lasi (iun) en embaraso, lasi (iun) senhelpa
lure, (de)logi [tr]; ~o; ~ilo; ~aĵo
lurid, (glowing), nebul-arda; (sensation-al), sensacia
lurk, kaŭri [int]
Luscinia, najtingalo
luscious, (gorgeous), pimpa, rava, bele-ga; (delicious), bongustega; (volup-tuous), volupta
lush, (juicy), sukplena; (luxuriant), abunda; (extravagant), ekstravagan-ca; (drunk), ebriulo
Lushun, Ljuŝun
Lusiad, Luziado
Lusitania, Luzitanio
lust, (gen), avido; (sexual), volupto; **lusty, lustful,** ~a; volupta; **lust after,** ~i [tr]
luster, (gloss, gen), glaceo, brilo, hele-co; (re cloth), katizo; (glory), gloro; (chandelier), lustro; **lustrous,** ~a, bri-la, hela; glora; **lackluster,** senbrila, malbrila; senbrileco
lute, (mus), liuto; (cement), cemento [not "lut–"]; **lutanist,** ~isto
luteo–, (pfx: violet), luteo–
lutetium, lutecio
Luther, Lutero; **Lutheran,** ~ano, ~isto; ~ana; **Lutheranism,** ~anismo
Lutra, lutro; Lutrinae, ~enoj
Lutreola, lutreolo
Lutreolina, lutreolumo
lux, lukso
luxate, luksacii [tr]; **luxation,** ~o; **sub-luxation,** sub~o
Luxemb(o)urg, (city), Luksemburgo; (state, province), ~io
Luxor, Luksoro
luxuriant, (lush), abunda; (fertile), fe-kunda; (extravagant), ekstravaganca; **luxuriate,** (grow luxuriantly), ~i [int]; (live in luxury), luksi [int]
luxury, (condition), lukso; (thing), ~aĵo; **luxurious,** ~a
Luzon, Luzono

Luzula, luzulo
Lvov, Lvovo
–ly, (gen adv sfx), –e (e.g.: *quickly:*
rapide); (adj sfx: like a), –eca (e.g.: *fatherly:* patreca); (per unit of time),
po– [pfx] (e.g.: *hourly, weekly wage:*
pohora, posemajna salajro)
Lycaena, liceno
lyceum, liceo [see "school: high
school"]
Lyceum, Liceo
lychee, [see "litchi"]
Lychnis, liknido
Lycia, Licio; **Lycian**, ~ano; ~a
Lycium, licio
Lycoperdon, likoperdo
Lycopersicon, Lycopersicum, likopersiko [cp "tomato"]
Lycopodium, likopodio
Lycurgus, Likurgo
Lydia, (woman's name), Lidia; (country), ~o; **Lydian**, ~ano; ~a
lye, lesivo; **wash with lye**, ~i [tr]
Lymnaea, limneo
lymph, limfo;   ~a;   **lymphadenitis**,
~adenito; **lymphang(i)itis**, ~angito;
lymphatic, ~ata; **lymphatic temperament**, ~atismo; **lymphatic person**,
~atulo; **lymph node**, ~onodo; **lymphocyte**, ~ocito; **lymphoid**, ~oida;
lymphoma, ~omo; **lymphopoiesis**,
~opoezo
lymphangi(o)–, (med   root),   limfangi(o)–
lynch, linĉi [tr]
lynx, linko; **lynx caracal**, karakalo
Lyon(s), Liono
lyotropic, liotropa
Lyra, (ast), Liro
lyre, liro
lyric, liriko; ~a; **lyric poem**, ~o; **lyrical**, ~a; **lyricism**, ~ismo; **lyricist**, ~isto
Lyrurus tetrix, tetro
Lys, (river in France), Liso
lysergic, lizerg/ata; **lysergic acid**, ~a
acido
lysin, lizenzo
lysine, lisino
Lysippus, Lizipo
lysis, lizo
–lysis, (sfx), –(o)lizo

Lysistrata, Lizistrata
Lythrum salicaria, salikario

M

ma'am, (respectful term for woman), sinjorino
Maas, Mozo
macabre, makabra
Macaca, makako; Macaca sylvana, magoto
macadam, makadamo;   **macadamize**, ~i [tr]
Macao, Makao
macaque, makako
macaroni, makaronio
macaroon, makarono
macaw, arao
Macbeth, (theat), Makbeto
Maccabaeus, Makabeo;   **Maccabean**, ~a; **Maccabees**, ~oj
mace, (club), klabo; (spice), muskatŝelo; **reed mace**, (Br), tifao*
Macedonia, Macedon/io;   **Macedonian**, ~o; ~a; ~ia, ~uja
macerate, maceri [tr]
mach, (speed of sound), maĥo (e.g.: *fly at mach 2:* flugi je 2 ~oj)
Machabees, [see "Maccabaeus"]
machete, maĉeto
Machiavelli, Makiavelo;   **Machiavellian**, ~a; ~ano
machination, maĥinacio
machine, (any apparatus; any complicated arrangement), maŝino; (make, shape, work on), prilabori [tr]; **machinery**, ~aro; **machinist**, ~isto; **machine tool**, il~o;   **war machine**, milit~o
macho, (masculine), maskla, vireca; (he-man), virvira; virviro; **machismo**, ~ismo
Mackenzie (River), (Rivero) Makenzio*
mackerel, skombro;   **mackerel sky**, ~eca ĉielo
mackintosh, pluvmantelo
mackle, (spot), makulo; ~igi; (printing: spoiled sheet), makulaturo
macramé makrameo*
macro–, (pfx), makro–
macrobiotic, makrobiotika; **macrobiotics**, ~o

macrocephalic, **macrocephalous**, makrocefala; **macrocephaly**, ~eco
macrocosm, makrokosmo
macron, superstreko [see § 16(e)]
Macropus, makropo;   Macropodidae, ~edoj; Macropodinae, ~enoj
Macrorhinus, marelefanto
macroscopic, makroskopia
macula, **macule**, makulo; ~igi; ~iĝi; **macular**, ~a; ~hava; **maculate**, ~igi; ~igita; **maculation**, ~igado; ~aĵo
macumba, makumbo†
mad, (crazy), freneza, psikoza; (angry), [see "angry"]; **madcap**, senbridulo, impetemulo; senbrida, impeta; **madman**, ~ulo; **madhouse**, ~ejo; **be mad**, ~i [int]; **go mad**, ~iĝi; **madden**, **drive (one) mad**, ~igi (iun); **be mad about**, (love), amegi [tr], adori [tr]; **like mad**, furioze
Madagascar, Madagaskaro
madam, (respectful term for woman), sinjorino; (in brothel), mastrino
madder, (dye), alizarino; (bot), rubio
madeira, madejro
Madeira, Madejro
Madia, madio
madonna, madono
madras, madraso
Madras, Madraso
Madrepora, madreporo, stelkoralo
madrepore, madreporo, stelkoralo
Madrid, Madrido
madrigal, madrigalo
maduromycosis, perikalo
Maecenas, Mecenaso
maelstrom, malstromo
Maelstrom, Malstromo
maenad, menado
maestoso, (mus), majeste
maestro, majstro
magazine, (publication), revuo, gazeto; (esp of gen, popular interest), magazino; (storehouse; container, as for film, ammunition, etc.), magazeno
Magdalen, **Magdalena**, **Magdalene**, Magdalena; **Magdalenian**, (geol), magdalenio

Magdeburg, Magdeburgo
Magellan, Magelano; **Strait of Magellan**, Markolo ~a
magenta, (fuchsin), fuksino; ~a; (purple-red), purpurruĝa
Maggiore, **(Lake)**, Lago Majora
maggot, (any larva), larvo; (of fly), muŝ~o [not "magoto"]
Maghreb, Magrebo
magi, magoj; **Magi**, M~oj
magic, magio; ~a; **magician**, ~isto; **magic trick**, ~aĵo
magisterial, (authoritative), aŭtoritata; (domineering), tiranema; **magisterium**, ~o
magistrate, (administrative officer), administristo; (judicial official), (loka) juĝisto [not "magistrato"]
magma, magmo
Magna Charta, Granda aĵarto
magna cum laude, [see "cum laude"]
magnanimous, grandanima, malavara; **magnanimity**, ~eco, malavaro
magnate, (gen) magnato
magnesia, magnezo
magnesite, magnezito
magnesium, magnezio; **magnesium flash**, (photo etc.), ~fulmo
magnet, magneto; **magnetic**, ~a; **magnetism**, ~ismo, ~eco; **magnetite**, ~ito; **magnetize**, ~i [tr]; **magnetization**, ~ado; ~iĝo; **magneto**, ~omaŝino; **magneton**, magnetono; **magnetometer**, ~ometro; **magnetostriction**, ~ostringo; **magnetron**, magnetotrono; **demagnetize**, mal~i [tr], sen~igi; **electromagnet**, elektro~o; **electromagnetic**, elektro~a; **electromagnetism**, elektro~ismo; **ferromagnetic**, fer(o)~a; **paramagnet**, para~aĵo, para~a korpo; **paramagnetic**, para~a; **paramagnetism**, para~ismo; **pyromagnetic**, piro~a; **pyromagnetism**, piro~ismo
magnificent, grandioza, belega; **magnificence**, ~eco, belegeco
magnify, (pli)grandigi
magnitude, (size, gen), grand/eco; (extent), amplekso; (of star etc.), magnitudo†
magnolia, Magnolia, magnolio
magnum, dulitra botelo

magpie, pigo
maguey, agavo
magus, mago
Magyar, Madjaro
maha–, (Sanskrit pfx), maha–
Mahabharata(m), Mahabarato
maharaja(h), maharaĝo;   **maharani**, **maharanee**, ~ino
mahatma, mahatmo
Mahavira, Mahaviro
Mahayana, mahajano
mah-jongg, maĝango
mahogany, (tree, wood), mahagono
Mahomet, Mahometo [cp "Mohammed"]
Mahonia, mahonio
mahout, mahuto
maid, (unmarried woman), fraŭlino; (young woman), junulino; (servant), servistino; **barmaid**, verŝknabino, kelnerino; **old maid**, maljuna ~o; **maid of honor**, fianĉinamikino
maiden, (girl), junulino; ~a; (virgin), virgulino; virga; (new, unused), neuzita, nova, freŝa; (first), unua; **maidenhair**, (fern), adianto; **maidenhead**, (hymen), himeno
mail, (postal system), poŝto; (put into mail), en~igi; (letters etc.), ~aĵo; (armor), maŝkiraso; **mailbag**, **mailpouch**, letersako; **mailbox**, (public), leterkesto; (personal, to receive own mail), leterskatolo; **mailman**, leterportisto, ~isto; **air mail**, aer~a, aera; aer~e, aere [see § 22]; **blackmail**, ĉantaĝi [tr]; ĉantaĝo; **surface mail**, surfac~e; **voice mail**, **electronic mail**, **e-mail**, voĉ~o, elektronika ~o; **by return mail**, reven~e
maim, kripligi, lamigi
Maimonides, Majmonido
main, (primary), ĉefa, precipa; (pipe, elec cable, etc.), ~dukto; (sea), oceano; **main-frame (computer)**, centra komputor(eg)o†; **in the main**, plejparte
Main, (river), Majno
Maine, (state; river), Majno; (French province), Mansio
maintain, (keeping in good condition), bontenado; (keep, conserve), konservi [tr]; (keep in good condition), bonteni

[tr]; (support person etc.), vivteni [tr],
subteni [tr]; (assert), aserti [tr]; (do
maintenance on car, machinery, etc.),
revizii [tr]
maintenance, (on car, machinery,
etc.), reviziado; ($ support, gen), viv-
tenado; (alimony, child support), alimento
Mainz, Majenco
maire, oleo(arbo)
maisonette, (house), dometo; (apt),
apartamento
maître d'hôtel, (major-domo), major-
domo; (hotel manager), hotelmastro;
(headwaiter), ĉefkelnero
Maitreya, Majtrejo
maize, maizo
majesty, majesto; (title of respect),
moŝto (e.g.: *your royal majesty:* via
reĝa moŝto); **majestic,** ~a; **lese majesty,** ~atenco
majolica, majoliko
major, (mus; larger; more important),
majôra (e.g.: *major key:* ~a tonalo;
Symphony in D Major: Simfonio en D
M~a; *major success:* ~a sukceso);
(primary, main), ĉefa; (of age), plen-
aĝa, majoritata; plenaĝulo; (main field
of study), ĉefstudo; ĉeffako; (specialize in study), ĉefstudi [tr] [cp "special:
specialize; specialty"]; (mil rank),
majoro; **majority,** (greatest group,
number), plejmulto; (in comparison w
only one oth type), plimulto [cp
"plural: plurality"]; (legal age), majo-
ritato; **major-domo,** majordomo; **semimajor,** (geom), duon~a
Majorana hortensis, majorano
Majorca, Majorko
make, (construct, create, do, fabricate,
form, devise, etc.), fari [tr]; (cause to
do or be), igi, ~igi [sfx] (e.g.: *make it
hot:* varmigi ĝin; *make it much more
difficult:* igi ĝin multe pli malfacila;
make him chop the tree down: igi lin
dehaki la arbon); (force, obligate),
devigi; (catch, as bus, plane, etc.),
trafi [tr]; (destine), destini [tr] (e.g.: *a
day made for picnics:* tago destinita
por piknikoj); (provide), provizi [tr];
(prepare, arrange, as bed), aranĝi [tr],
ordi [tr]; (total), sumi [tr] (e.g.: *100*

centimeters make a meter: 100 centimetroj sumas metron); (constitute),
konsistigi, konstitui [tr]; (establish),
establi [tr]; (acquire), akiri [tr] (e.g.:
make friends: akiri amikojn); (earn),
lukri [tr], gajni [tr]; (reach, arrive at),
atingi [tr]; (do distance, speed), veturi
[tr] (e.g.: *we made 1000 kilometers
yesterday:* ni veturis 1000 kilometrojn
hieraŭ; *the train makes 200 kilometers
per hour:* la trajno veturas po 200 kilometrojn hore); (succeed), sukcesi
[int] (akceptiĝi, atingi, ~i, eniri, etc.)
(e.g.: *she made the team:* ŝi sukcesis
akceptiĝi en la teamon); (cause success), sukcesigi (e.g.: *that book made
him as an author:* tiu libro sukcesigis
lin kiel aŭtoron); (sexual), kuŝigi; (determine), determini [tr] (e.g.: *clothes
make the man:* vestoj determinas la
viron); (style, build), stilo; (brand,
type), (var)speco, (var)modelo; (brand
name), varnomo; **make as if, make
as though, make like,** (act as if), agi
kvazaŭ, ŝajnigi ke; (pretend), ludi ke;
make away with, (steal), ŝteli [tr];
(get rid of), forigi; **make believe
(that),** (pretend), ludi (ke), afekti [tr];
make-believe, ludado; luda (e.g.:
she was a make-believe princess: ŝi
estis luda princino); **make do
with(out),** elteni [int] kun (sen);
make for, (go toward), sin direkti al,
sin turni al, celi [tr]; (attack), ekataki
[tr]; (tend to, help effect), emi [int] al;
make from, ~i el (e.g.: *shoes made
from leather:* ŝuoj faritaj el ledo);
make (it) good (to), make good on,
(compensate), kompensi [tr]; (succeed), sukcesi [int]; (fulfill, as promise), plenumi [tr]; **make it,** (succeed),
sukcesi [int]; **make it with,** (sexual),
kuŝiĝi kun; **make merry,** festiĝi,
amuziĝi, distriĝi; **make of,** (deduce
from), dedukti [tr] el; **make off,**
(flee), fuĝi [int], forkuri [int]; **make
off with,** (carry off), forporti [tr]; (pilfer, steal), marodi [tr], forŝteli [tr];
make or break, sukcesigi aŭ malsukcesigi, decidi ies sorton; **make
out,** (perceive), percepti [tr]; (write,
as check), skribi [tr]; (fill out, as

blank), plenigi, kompletigi; (fare), farti [int]; (make love), kunkaresi [int];
kunamori [int]; (understand), kompreni [tr]; (figure out), diveni [tr]; (decipher), deĉifri [tr]; (imply, affirm),
aserti [tr], implici [tr]; (succeed),
sukcesi [int]; **make out of,** ~i el [see
"make from" above]; **make over,**
(renovate), renovigi; (cede, sign
over), cedi [tr, int]; **makeshift,** improvizita, kunflikita; improvizaĵo;
make up, (put together), kunmeti [tr],
prepari [tr], kun~i [tr]; (untruth), fabriki [tr], inventi [tr]; (form, comprise),
konsistigi, konstitui [tr]; (invent, create, gen), inventi [tr], krei [tr]; (fill in
missing part; complete), kompletigi;
(arrange), aranĝi [tr]; (after quarrel),
repaciĝi, reamikiĝi; (cosmetics),
ŝminki [tr] (sin); (costume, disguise),
alivesti [tr] (sin), kostumi [tr] (sin);
(re-do, as missed exam, course), re~i
[tr], kompletigi; **make-up,** ŝminko;
alivesto, kostumo; konsisto; repaciĝo,
reamikiĝo; kompletigo; **make up
for,** (compensate), kompensi [tr]; **be
made up of,** konsisti [int] el; **make
up one's mind,** decidi [tr]; decidiĝi;
make the best of (it), laŭeble elteni
en (la afero, la situacio); **make the
most of,** laŭeble elprofiti [tr]; **self-
made,** mem~ita
mal–, (pfx: bad, wrong), mis– (e.g.:
malnourished: ~nutrita); (not; opp),
mal– (e.g.: *malcontent:* malkontenta)
Malabar, Malabaro
Malabo, Malabo*
Malacca, Malako; **Strait of Malacca,**
Markolo ~a
Malachi, Malañi
malachite, malakito; **malachite green,**
~a verdo
Malacostraca, malakostrakoj
malady, malsano
Málaga, Malago
Malagasy, (person), Malagaso; (country), ~io
malaise, malsaneto
malapropism, (ŝerca) vorttordo
malaria, malario; **malarial,** ~a
malarkey, blago, sensencaĵo
Malay, (person), Malajo; **Malayan,**

~o; ~a; **Malay Peninsula,** Duoninsulo Malaka
Malaysia, Malajzio
Malawi, Malaviot
Maldives, Maldivojt
male, maskla, virseksa; ~o
Male, (capital of Maldives), Maleo*
malediction, malbeno
malefactor, malbonfar/into; ~anto;
~onto; fiulo, krimulo
maleficence, malbonfaro; **maleficent,**
~(em)a
malevolence, malbonvolo; **malevolent,**
~(em)a
malfeasance, malversacio; mis-
far(ad)o, miskonduko
Mali, Malio
malice, malico; **malicious,** ~a; **with
malice aforethought,** malbonintence
malign, kalumnii [tr]; malica
malignant, maligna; **malignancy,**
~aĵo; ~eco
maline(s), Mefilina punto
Malines, (city), Mefilino; (lace), ~a
punto
malinger, ŝajnigi malsanon
mall, (shopping center), bazaro; (any
walkway, promenade), korso
mallard, sovaĝanaso, platbeka anaso
malleable, maleebla
malleolus, (bone), maleolo
mallet, maleo; ~i [tr]
malleus, (bone), maleo
Malleus, (zool), maleo
Mallorca, Majorko
mallow, (*Malva*), malvo; **Indian mallow,** (herb), abutilo; **marsh mallow,**
(*Althea officinalis*), alteo [cp "marshmallow"]
malmsey, malvazio
malt, (grain), malto; (drink), ~aĵo; ~igi;
~iĝi
Malta, Malto; **Maltese,** ~ano; ~a
maltase, maltazo
Malthus,Maltuso; Malthusian, ~ano;
~ana; ~a; **Malthusianism,** ~anismo
maltose, maltozo
Malus, pom/arbo; Malaceae, ~acoj
Malva, malvo
malvasia, malvazio
malversation, malversacio
Malvina, Malvina

mama, panjo
Mameluke, Mamluko
mamma, (mother), panjo; (anat), mamglando
mammal, mamulo; **mammalian**, ~a Mammalia, mamuloj
mammary, mama; ~glando
mammon, **Mammon**, Mamono
mammoth, mamuto; ~a
man, (male), viro; (any human), homo [see also "person"]; (humanity), la homo, (la) homaro (e.g.: *the nature of man:* la naturo de la homo; *the brotherhood of man:* la frateco de la homaro); (playing piece, for chess or oth game), peco; (provide personnel, staff), stabizi [tr], homekipi [tr], homprovizi [tr]; (work at, take assigned place), postenîĝi ĉe (e.g.: *man the guns:* postenîĝi ĉe la pafiloj); **manned**, (with human operator or crew), stabizita, homekipita (e.g.: *manned spacecraft:* stabizita kosma ŝipo); **unmanned**, senstaba, senhoma; **manly**, ~eca; **man–eater**, (cannibal), kanibalo; (animal, fish), hommanĝulo; **mankind**, la homaro; **man-made**, homfarita, artefarita; **man-of-war**, (ship), militŝipo; **man-of-war bird**, fregato; **Portuguese man-of-war**, (zool), fizalio; **man-to-man**, honesta, sincera; **best man**, (at wedding), fianĉamiko; **cave man**, kavernhomo; **Heidelberg man**, **Java man**, **Peking man**, [note: these early types of human, originally classified as *"Pithecanthropus"* ("pitekantropo") and oth species and genus names, are now all classified as *"Homo erectus"*; use that taxonomic name in Esperanto, or translate locale in common name (e.g.: *Java man:* Java Homo); use upper case "Homo" to distinguish from "Java homo" etc. ("a person from Java" etc.); but cp "Neanderthal", "Cro Magnon"]; **middleman**, peranto, interulo; **minuteman**, (Am), milicano; **superman**, superhomo; **man about town**, restoraciemulo; **man in the street**, ordinarulo; **to a man**, senscepte; **Isle of Man**, Manksinsulo [see also "Manx"]

mana, manao
manacle, mankateni [tr]; ~o
manage, (control), direkti [tr], regi [tr]; (administer), administri [tr]; (re household, estate), mastrumi [tr]; (deal w), trakti [tr]; (get along, succeed in doing, lit or fig), sukcesi [int] (en) (e.g.: *the task was hard, but we managed it:* la tasko estis malfacila, sed ni sukcesis en ĝi; *they managed to mess things up:* ili sukcesis fuŝi aferojn); (fend for self, muddle through), helpi al si (e.g.: *I can't give you a loan; you'll just have to manage:* mi ne povas fari prunton al vi; vi nur devos helpi al vi mem); **manageable**, (can be dealt w), traktebla; **management**, ~ado, regado; administrado; mastrumado; (managers), direkcio, administracio; (of an industry etc. by state, w responsibility to higher authority), regio; [cp "administration"]; **manager**, (gen), ~isto, intendanto, administristo; (of musician, sports figure, etc.), manaĝero†; (of household, estate), ekonomo, intendanto; **managerial**, administra
Manasseh, **Manasses**, Manase
manatee, manato
Mancha, **(La)**, Manĉo
Manche, Maniko
Manchester, Manĉestro
manchineel, mancinelo
Manchu, **Manchoo**, Manĉuro; ~a
Manchuria, Manĉurio
–mancy, (sfx), –mancio
mandala, mandalo*
mandarin, **Mandarin**, (person, language, etc.), Mandareno; ~a; (orange), mandarino
mandate, (commission), mandato; ~igi; (region), ~ejo; (any order, command), ordono, komando; ordoni [tr], komandi [tr]; **mandatory**, deviga
mandible, mandiblo
mandibula, mandiblo
mandola, mandolo
mandolin, mandolino
mandragora, **mandrake**, mandragoro
mandrel, **mandril**, (gen), mandreno
mandrill, mandrilo
Mandrillus, mandrilo

mane, kolhararo
manège, (gen), manego
maneh, mino
manes, (Roman myth), maneso(j)
Manes, (Persian prophet), Manifeo
maneuver, manovri [int]; ~igi; ~o
manganate, manganato
manganese, mangano; manganese
steel, ~stalo
manganic, (valence 3), mangan/ika;
manganic acid, ~ata acido
mange, skabio
mangel(–wurzel), furagbeto
manger, kripo
Mangifera, mangifero; Mangifera indica, mangarbo, mangujo
mangle, (mutilate), kripligi, mutili [tr],
siri [tr]; (cloth press), kalandri [tr]; ka-
landrilo
mango, (fruit), mango; (tree), ~arbo
mangosteen, (fruit or tree), mangostano
mangrove, (fruit), manglo; (tree), ~arbo
Mani, Manifeo
mania, manio; [see separate entries for
varieties]; maniac, ~a; ~ulo; maniac-
depressive, ciklotimia; ciklotimiulo;
maniac-depressive reaction, cikloti-
mio
Manich(a)eus, Manifeo; Manichean,
Manichee, ~ano; ~isma; Mani-
che(an)ism, ~ismo
manicure, manikuri [tr]; ~o; manicur-
ist, ~isto
manifest, manifesti [tr]; ~igi; ~o; ~ita;
(of ship etc.), (sip)~o; manifestation,
~ado; ~ajo
manifesto, manifesto
manifold, (many parts), multobla;
(many-sided, –faceted), multopa;
(make copies), ~igi; (pipe), tubaro, ~a
tubo; manifold paper, kopipapero
Manihot, manihoto; Manihot utilissima, manioko, kasavo
manikin, (dwarf), vireto; (body model), manekeno
Manila, (city), Manilo
manioc, manioko, kasavo
manipulate, manipuli [tr]; manipulation, ~(ad)o
Manis, maniso
Manitoba, Manitobo
Manitou, Manito, Manitou, Manituo

manna, manao
mannequin, (gen), manekeno
manner, (way), maniero; (sort, type),
speco [see "kind"]; (means, method),
rimedo; manners, (etiquette), ~oj,
etiketo; (behavior, gen), konduto;
mannerism, afektajo; (art), ~ismo; in
that manner, tiu~e, tiel; in this manner, ĉi-~e, ĉi tiel, tiel ĉi; in a manner
of speaking, por tiel diri
mannikin, [see "manikin"]
manoeuver, [see "maneuver"]
manometer, manometro
manor, (estate), bieno; (mansion), domego
mansard, mansardo
manse, (parsonage), pastra domo
mansion, domego
mantel, (fireplace facing, w shelf
above), mantelo [cp "fire: fireplace",
"hearth"]; (shelf), kamenbreto; man-
telpiece, kamenbreto
mantilla, mantilo
mantis, Mantis, praying mantis, manto
mantissa, mantiso
mantle, (cloak, cape, lit or fig; geol;
etc.), mantelo; ~igi; ~igi; (of gas
lamp), mufo; (scum, crust), krusto;
krustigi
mantra, mantro
Mantua, Mantuo; Mantuan, ~ano; ~a
Manu, Manuo
manual, (by hand), mana (e.g.: manual
labor: ~a laboro [or] ~laboro); (handbook), ~libro; (mus keyboard), klavaro
Manuel, Manuelo
manufacture, (gen), fabriki [tr]; (large-
scale), ~i, manufakturi [tr]; ~ado,
manufakturado; manufacturing
plant, ~o, manufakturo
manumit, liberigi, malskavigi
manure, sterko
manuscript, manuskripto
Manx, Manksa; Manxman, ~o; Manx
cat, ~a kato [see also "man: Isle of
Man"]
many, multaj, ~e (da) (e.g.: she has
many friends: ŝi havas ~ajn amikojn
[or] ~e da amikoj); a good many, iom
~aj; a great many, ~egaj, ja ~aj;
many a, ~aj, ~e da; as many, (same

number), tiom da (e.g.: *read 5 books
in as many days:* legi 5 librojn en tiom
da tagoj)
manyplies, omaso
Maori, Maorio; ~a
Mao Tse-Tung, Maŭ Ze-dong
map, mapo; ~i [tr]; **map-maker**, ~isto
[cp "cartographer"]; **contour map**,
kontur~o; **road map**, voj~o; **weather
map**, veter~o
maple, (tree), acero; (wood), ~ligno;
flowering maple, abutilo; **sugar maple**, suker~o
Maputo, (capital of Mozambique), Maputo*
mar, difekti [tr]
marabou, marabuo
marabout, (hermit; shrine), marabuto;
(bird), marabuo
Marañón, (river), Maranjo
Maranta, maranto
maraschino, maraskino; **maraschino
cherry**, ~a ĉerizo
marasmus, marasmo; **marasmic**, ~a
marathon, maratono; ~a
Marathon, Maratono
maraud, (raid), prirabi [tr] [not "marodi"]; (at sea), kaperi [tr]
maravedi, maravedo
marble, (stone), marmoro; ~a; ~aĵo;
(glass ball), globeto; (give streaks as
in marble, re cake, steak, paint, etc.),
jaspi [tr], ~umi [tr]
marc, rekremento
Marcel, Marcellus, Marcelo; **Marcel-
la**, ~a
march, (walk w regular steps; mil;
mus), marŝi [int]; ~igi; ~o; (as mil
command), marŝ'!; (border country),
markio; **The Long March**, (by Mao),
la Longa M~ado
March, (month), marto
marchioness, markizino
marchpane, marcipano
Marcia, Marka
Marcus, Marko; **Marcus Aurelius**, ~-
Aŭrelio
Mardi Gras, Karnavala Mardo
mare, (horse), ĉevalino; (donkey),
azenino; **mare's-tail**, (cloud), ciruso;
(bot), hipurido
Margaret, Margareta

margarine, margarino
margin, (gen), marĝeno; **marginal**, ~a;
submarginal, neadekvata, submini-
muma
margosa, melio
margrave, margrafo
marguerite, (daisy), lekanto
Maria, Maria; **black Maria**, ĉelveturilo
Marian, Mariana
Mariana(s) Islands, Insuloj Marianaj
Marie, Maria
marigold, (*Tagetes*), tageto; **bur(r)
marigold**, bidento; **marsh marigold**,
kalto; **pot marigold**, **Scotch marigold**, kalendulo
marihuana, marijuana, (as smoked),
marifiuano; (plant), kanabo
marimba, marimbo
marina, haveneto
marinate, marini [tr]; **marinade, mari-
nated food**, ~aĵo
marine, (re sea, gen), mara; (mil), ~sol-
dato; **mariner**, ~isto; **Marines, Marine Corps**, M~soldataro, M~-
Infanterio; **merchant marine**,
(ships), komercoŝiparo; (personnel),
komerca ~istaro; **submarine**, (under
sea), sub~a; (ship), sub~ŝipo; (sandwich), [see "sub"]
Mario, Mario
Marion, Mariano
marionette, marioneto
marital, geedz/eca; **extramarital**, eks-
ter~eca; **premarital**, antaŭ~iĝa
maritime, mara
Marius, Mario
marjoram, (plant or spice), majorano;
wild marjoram, origano
mark, (scratch, line, symbol; $ unit;
trademark; landmark; school grade;
etc.), marko; ~i [tr]; ~iĝi; (short line),
streko; streki [tr]; (on any calibrated,
graduated measuring device), streketo; (meaningful sign, indicator, etc.),
signo; signi [tr] (e.g.: *mark of success:*
signo de sukceso; *mark a map:* signi
mapon); (indicate), indiki [tr]; indiko;
indikilo; (distinguishing), distingaĵo;
(goal), celo; (dirty spot, blotch), makulo; makuligi; makuliĝi; (notice), rimarki [tr]; **marker**, (to make marks),
~ilo; (sign etc.), indikilo (e.g.: *bound-*

ary marker: limindikilo); (token, counter), ĵetono; (channel marker, runway marker, etc.), balzo†; **felt marker**, felt~ilo; **mark down**, (write), noti [tr]; (reduce price), prezredukti [tr]; **mark off**, (set limits), dislimi [tr]; **marksman**, paflertulo; **marksmanship**, paflerteco; **mark time**, (marching), starmarŝi [int]; (wait), portempe atendi [tr]; **mark up**, (put marks on, gen; e.g., in revising draft), ~i; (increase price), prezaltigi; **birthmark**, haŭtmakulo; **diacritical mark**, (gen), kromsigno [see § 16(e)]; (above letter (e.g.: é)), supersigno; (below letter (e.g.: ç)), subsigno; **exclamation mark**, (symbol: !), krisigno; **paragraph mark**, (¶), alineo–signo; **punctuation mark**, interpunkcia signo [see § 17]; **question mark**, (?), demandosigno; **quotation mark**, (" [or] "), citilo; **open quotation mark**, (at beginning of quote: ["]), malferma citilo; **close quotation mark**, ("), ferma citilo; **section mark**, (§), paragraf-signo; **trademark**, fabrik~o, var~o, komerca ~o; **watermark**, akvo~o; **marked cards**, falsitaj kartoj; **off the mark, wide of the mark**, ekstercela; **toe the mark**, konformiĝi, submetiĝi; **make (someone) toe the mark**, konformigi, submetigi (iun)
Mark, (man's name), Marko
market, (total buying power, offer and demand, etc.; region, group of buyers), merkato; (public marketplace), bazaro; (retail shop), butiko; (sell), vend(ad)i [tr]; **marketing**, (selling), vendado; (art, technique of selling), ~ado; ~ismo; **marketplace**, (public place), bazaro; (abstract market), ~o; **black market**, nigra ~o; **flea market**, pulbazaro; **open market**, (re stock exchange), kuliso; **stock market**, borso; **supermarket**, superbazaro, super~o; **be in the market for**, deziri aĉeti [tr]; **be on the market**, (re mass-produced wares etc.), esti vendata; (re one item, as a house), esti vendota; **put on the market**, vendatigi; vendotigi

markka, marko
marl, (soil), marno; ~i [tr]
marline, marling, merleno
marlin(e)spike, splisilo
marmalade, (oranĝa) marmelado
Marmara, Sea of, Maro Marmora
Marmosa, marmozo
marmoset, hapalo, silksimio
marmot, marmoto
Marmota, marmoto
Marne, Marno
maroon, (abandon), forlasi [tr]; (color), brunkarmezina
marquee, markezo; (Br: tent), tendego
Marquesas (Islands), Markizoj
marquess, markizo
marquetry, marqueterie, marketro; **do marquetry**, ~i [tr]
marquis, markizo; **marquise**, ~ino; (Br: wife of marquis), ~edzino; **marquisate**, ~eco
marriage, (condition), geedz/eco; (ceremony), ~iĝo; **marriage broker**, svatisto; **act as marriage broker (for)**, svati [tr]; **group marriage**, grup~eco; **intermarriage**, inter~ecó; inter~iĝo; **trial marriage**, prov~eco; [see also "marry"]; **by marriage**, (relationship), bo– [pfx] (e.g.: *cousin by marriage:* bokuzo)
marron, marono
marrow, (gen), medolo; **to the marrow**, (thoroughly), ĝisoste
Marrubium, marubio
marry, (by man to woman), edz/inigi (e.g.: *he married her:* li ~inigis ŝin); (by woman to man), ~igi (e.g.: *she married him:* ŝi ~igis lin); (re both together), ge~iĝi (e.g.: *they married on Saturday:* ili ge~iĝis sabate); (by clergy etc.), ge~igi (e.g.: *the minister married them:* la pastro ge~igis ilin); [see also "marriage"]; **married**, ~iĝinta; ~iniĝinta; ge~iĝinta; **marry off**, for~(in)igi; **get married**, ~iĝi; ~iniĝi; ge~iĝi; **intermarry**, interge~iĝi
Mars, (ast; myth), Marso; **Martian**, ~ano; ~a
Marseille(s), Marsejlo; **La Marseillaise**, (anthem), La Marseljezo [note different spelling from "Marsejlo"]

marsh, marĉo
marshall, (mil; official), marŝalo; (arrange, order), aranĝi [tr], vicigi, ordi [tr]; (direct), direkti [tr]; field marshall, feldmarŝalo; Marshall Islands, Insuloj M~aj
marshmallow, (candy), marŝmalo* [cp "mallow"]
marsupial, marsupiulo; ~a Marsupialia, marsupiuloj
marsupium, marsupio
mart, (public market), bazaro; (shop), butik(et)o [cp "market"]
martagon, martagono
marten, (Martes), marteso; stone marten, beech marten, foino, mustelkato Martes, marteso; Martes foina, foino, mustelkato
Martha, Marta
martial, milita
martin, (Progne, Hirundo), hirundo; (Chelidon urbica), urb~o; bank martin, sand martin, (Riparia), bord~o; purple martin, purpura ~o
Martin, (man's name), Marteno; Martinmas, ~festo
martingal(e), (gen), martingalo
martini, martino*
Martinique, Martiniko
martyr, martiro; ~igi; martyrdom, ~eco; ~igo; ~iĝo; martyrize, ~igi; ~iĝi; martyry, ~ejo
marvel, miri [int]; ~(ind)aĵo; marvelous, ~iga, ~inda; marvel-of-Peru, (bot), niktago
Marx, Markso; Marxism, ~ismo; Marxist, ~isma; ~isto
Mary, Maria [nickname: Manjo]
marygold, [see "marigold"]
Maryland, Marilando
marzipan, marcipano
mascara, palpebra ŝminko, okulhara ŝminko
mascon, maskoncentraĵo
mascot, (object), talismano; (person, animal), ~ulo
masculine, (male), maskla, virseksa; (virile), vireca
maser, masero
mash, (any soft mixture, pulp, as of meal), kaĉo, grio, pureot; (crush, make pulp), ~igi, pisti [tr], pulpigi,

pureigit; (potato) masher, ~igilo
mask, (gen), masko
masochism, masoĥismo; masochistic, ~a; masochist, masoĥisto
mason, masoni [tr]; ~isto; masonry, ~ado; ~aĵo; Mason, (Freemason), framasono; Masonic, framasona
Masora(h), masoro; Masorete, Masorite, ~isto; Masoretic(al), ~a; ~ista
Masqat, Maskato
masquerade, maskerado; ~i [int]; masquerade robe, (w hood), domeno
mass, (quantity of material; phys), maso [cp "material", "matter"]; (heap, pile), amaso; (rel service; mus), meso; the masses, (common people), (la) popolamaso; massive, (solid), masiva; (huge), amasa, enorma; mass catcher, ~kaptatoro; mass driver, (linia) mass–akcelatoro; massmeter, ~metro; masspiece, ~aĵo; air mass, aer~o; black mass, nigra meso; center of mass, ~ocentro; counter-mass, kontraŭ~o; high (low) mass, (rel), (mal)alta meso; specific mass, specifa ~o
Massachusetts, Masaĉusecot
massacre, masakri [tr]; ~o
massage, masaĝo; ~i [tr]
masseter, (muscle), masetero
masseur, masaĝisto; masseuse, ~ino
massif, masivo
Massilia, Masilio
mast, masto; masthead, (naut), ~supro; (of newspaper etc.), eldonista angulo; (top of front page), gazetkapo; two-master, three-master, (etc., re ship), du~ulo, tri~ulo (etc.); foremast, front~o; mainmast, ĉef~o; mizzenmast, post~o; topmast, top~o; topgallant mast, bram~o; at half mast, ~meze
mastectomy, mamektomio; radical mastectomy, radika ~o
master, (expert, skilled person; title of respect), majstro; (master of house, landlord, person in charge, boss, etc.), mastro; (be expert in, eminent in), ~i [int] (en, pri); (use, do masterfully), (pri)~i [tr]; (rule, be boss over), mastri [tr], estri [tr]; (university degree), magistro; (holder of degree), magistrulo;

(matrix of metal or oth material, mold, etc.), matrico; (printed or typed original from which copies made), ŝablono; (main, primary), ĉefa, ĉef– [pfx] (e.g.: *master key:* ĉefŝlosilo; *master switch:* ĉefŝaltilo); **masterful,** ~eca; mastreca; **mastery,** ~eco; **mastermind,** (instigator), instiginto; (clever person), lert(eg)ulo; (plan, instigate), instigi [tr], plani [tr], direkti [tr]; **masterpiece,** ~aĵo, ~overko
mastic, (gen), mastiko; **mastic tree,** lentisko
masticate, maĉi [tr]
mastiff, dogo
Mastigophora, flageluloj
mastitis, mamito
mastodon, Mastodon, mastodonto
mastoid, mastoido; ~a; **mastoiditis,** ~ito; **processus mastoideus,** ~a apofizo
masturbate, masturbi sin; **masturbation,** sinmasturbado
mat, (heavy fabric, rubber, etc., as for wiping feet; similar object), mato; (tangle), impliki [tr]; ~igi; implikiĝi, ~iĝi; (naut: to plug leaks), ŝtop~ego; (printing), matrico; (photo etc.: dull finish), malbrila; malbriligi; **sea mat,** flustro
matador, matadoro
match, (firemaking), alumeto; (equal person or animal), egalulo; (equal thing), egalaĵo; (be equal to), egali [tr]; (make equal), egaligi; (pair), paro; (one of a pair), parulo; paraĵo; (pair up), parigi; pariĝi; (contest, game), matĉo; (set against, put in opposition), kontraŭigi; (conform, be similar, etc.), konformigi (sin); konformiĝi; (in accord), akordi [int], kongrui [int] (kun); akordigi; (be appropriate, go w, as colors), konveni [int], deci [int], harmonii [int]; (compare), kompari [tr]; **matchbook,** ~ujo; **matchbox,** ~oskatolo; **matchless,** sen-egala; **matchmaker,** (marriage broker), svatisto; svatanto; **act as matchmaker (for),** svati [tr]; **meet one's match,** trovi sian egalulon; **be a good (poor) match for,** (mal)bone taŭgi [int] (konformi [int], akordi

[int]) al
mate, (one of couple or pair, re people or animals), par/ulo; (of things, as socks), ~aĵo; (pair up), ~igi; ~iĝi; (unite sexually), sekskunigi; sekskuniĝi [cp "copulate"]; (Br colloq: fellow, comrade), kamarado, amiko, kunulo; (naut officer), maato; (maté: tea), mateo; **(check)mate,** (chess), mato; matigi; **be (check)mateed,** mati [tr]; **inmate,** (someone confined, as in prison), enŝlosito; (any resident), enloĝanto [avoid "internulo"; cp "intern"]
maté (tea), mateo
material, (re matter, made of matter), materia (e.g.: *material possessions:* ~aj posedaĵoj); (stuff, substance), materialo (e.g.: *raw materials:* krudaj materialoj); (specific substance), –aĵo [sfx] (e.g.: *flammable material:* brulivaĵo); [cp "matter", "mass"]; (relevant), rilata; (essential), esenca, nepra; (fabric, lit or fig), ŝtofo; **materials,** (tools and equipment), materialo(j); **materialism,** (phil: belief that matter is sole reality), ~ismo; (way of life, seeking material comforts), materialismo; **materialist,** ~isma; ~isto; materialisma; materialisto; **materiality,** ~eco; **materialize,** ~igi; ~iĝi; **dematerialize,** ne~igi; ne~iĝi; **immaterial,** (not of matter, nonmaterial), ne~a; (not important, irrelevant), indiferenta, nerilata; tute egale; **nonmaterial,** ne~a; **packing material,** pakumo; **raw materials,** krudaj materialoj
materiel, materialoj [note plur]
maternal, patrin(ec)a; **maternity,** (motherhood), ~o; (for pregnant woman, as clothes), gravedula; **maternity ward (hospital, home),** akuŝejo
math, matematiko
mathematics, matematiko; **mathematical,** ~a; **mathematician,** ~isto
Mat(h)ilda, Matilda
matin, matutino
matinee, matineo
Mato Grosso, Matogroso
matrass, matraso
matriarch, matriarko;   **matriarchal,**

matriarchic, ~a; matriarchate, ~io;
matriarchy, ~eco; ~io
matricide, patrinmortigo
matriculate, matrikuli [tr]; ~iĝi; ~ito
matrimony, geedzeco; matrimonial,
~a
matrix, (gen), matrico; dot matrix,
punktaro; punktara (e.g.: dot-matrix
printer: punktara presatoro)
matron, (mature, respected woman),
matrono; (woman manager, superintendant, etc.), intendantino; matron-
ly, ~eca; matron of honor, fianĉin~o
matt(e), (dull, as re finish), malbrila;
~aĵo
matter, (phys substance, material), materio [cp "mass", "material"]; (affair,
subject), afero; (be important, make a
difference), gravi [int] (e.g.: will it
matter to you if I'm late?: ĉu gravos al
vi se mi malfruos?; it doesn't matter:
ne gravas; what does it matter?: kiel
tio gravas?); (be wrong), misi [int]
(e.g.: something is the matter with my
car: io misas pri mia aŭto; what's the
matter?: kio misas?; nothing's the
matter: nenio misas); (pus), puso; an-
timatter, anti~o; a matter of, (indefinite number, several), kelkaj, kelke
da (e.g.: we finished it in a matter of
days: ni finis ĝin post kelkaj tagoj);
(approximate number), pli-malpli,
proksimume (e.g.: a matter of a
month: pli-malpli unu monato [or]
proksimume unu monato); a matter
of course, rutina afero; matter-of-
course, rutina; as a matter of fact,
efektive, fakte; matter-of-fact, (factual), efektiva; (serious), serioza, afer-
tona, neŝerca; in the matter of, rilate,
koncerne (–on, al –o); for that matter, tiurilate; no matter, (it doesn't
matter, it's all right), ne gravas, (estas
tute) egale; no matter what, kio ajn
(e.g.: I'm going, no matter what he
says: mi iros, kion ajn li diru); no
matter who, kiu ajn; no matter what
kind of (a), kia ajn; no matter
where, kie(n) ajn; no matter how,
kiel ajn; no matter how much
(many), kiom ajn; no matter whose,
kies ajn; no matter when, kiam ajn;

no matter why, kial ajn; no matter
whether, egale ĉu
Matthew, Matthias, Mateo
Mattiola, levkojo
mattin, matutino
mattock, pioĉo
Matto Grosso, Matogroso
mattrass, matraso
mattress, matraco; innerspring mattress, risorta ~o; air mattress, aer~o,
pneŭmatika ~o; water mattress, ak-
vo~o
mature, matura; ~igi; ~iĝi; maturity,
~eco; immature, ne~a; premature,
(before proper time), antaŭtempa; (re
birth), frunaskita; premature baby,
frunaskito
matutinal, (fru)matena
matzo, maco
Maud(e), Matinjo [not "Manjo"; see
"Mathilda", "Mary"]
maudlin, sentimentalaĉa
maul, (hammer), maleego, martelego;
(injure), kontuzi [tr], bategi [tr]
maunder, deliri [int], ~e babili [int], ~e
paroli [int]; maunderings, ~aĵo(j),
babilaĵo(j)
Mauretania, Magrebo, Maŭrio,
Maŭrlando
Maurice, Maŭrico
Mauritania, Maŭr/io, ~lando
Mauritius, Maŭricio
mausoleum, maŭzoleo
mauve, malvokolora; ~o
maverick, (strayed calf etc.), forvagin-
to; (independent), nekonformulo, sendependulo
maw, stomako; (fig: gaping hole, center), faŭkego (e.g.: into the maw of the
storm: en la faŭkegon de la ŝtormo)
mawkish, (sickeningly sweet), dolĉaĉa;
(sentimental), sentimentalaĉa
Max, (man's name), Makso
maxi–, (pfx: large etc.), –ego [sfx] (e.g.:
maxicoat: paltego)
maxilla, maksilo; maxillary, ~a; sub-
maxilla, sub~o
maxim, maksimo
Maxim, (man's name), Maksimo
Maximilian, Maksimiliano [cp "Max",
"Maxim"]
maximum, maksimumo; ~a; maximal,

~a; **maximize,** ~igi
Maxine, Maksa, ~ina
maxwell, maksvelo
may, (perhaps), eble, povas esti (ke)
(e.g.: *it may rain:* ~e pluvos; *you may be right:* vi ~e pravas); (have permission), rajti [tr] (e.g.: *you may go:* vi rajtas iri; *you may not do that:* tion vi ne rajtas (fari)) [see also "might"] [note: "rajti" is sometimes colloquially replaced by "povi", as in English "may" is sometimes replaced by "can"]; (in subjunctive expression), ~u (e.g.: *they died that we may be free:* ili mortis, ke ni estu liberaj; *may you have good weather:* vi havu bonan veteron); (hawthorn), kratago
May, (month), majo; (woman's name), Maja
Maya, (Native American), Majao; ~a; (Hindu), Maja; **Mayan,** ~o; ~a
maybe, eble, povas esti (ke)
mayhem, (injury), vundado; (any violence), perfortado, tumultado
mayonnaise, majonezo
mayor, urbestro
maypop, pasifloro
Mazama, mazamo
Mazda, (Ahura Mazda), Mazdao; **Mazdaism,** ~ismo; **Mazdaist,** ~isma; ~isto
maze, labirinto
Mazeppa, Mazepo
mazurka, mazurko
mazzard, (fruit), merizo; (tree), ~arbo
Mbabane, Mbabano*
mea culpa, mia kulpo
mead, (drink), medo
meadow, (herbo)kampo   herbejo; **meadowsweet,** (gen), ulmario
meager, magra
meal, (eating), manĝo; (flour), faruno; (unshelled, coarsely milled), grio; **mealies,** (Br: maize), maizo; **mealworm,** tenebria larvo
mean, (signify), signifi [tr] (e.g.: *what does that word mean?:* kion ~as tiu vorto?; *his presence means trouble:* lia ĉeesto ~as ĉagrenon); (want to express), voli diri [tr] (e.g.: *what do you mean by that?:* kion vi volas diri per tio?; *it's the third—I mean, the fourth*

house: ĝi estas la tria—mi volas diri, la kvara domo; *when he calls you a "bastard", he means a compliment:* kiam li nomas vin "bastardo", li volas diri komplimenton); (intend), intenci [tr] (e.g.: *we meant to come earlier:* ni intencis veni pli frue; *what do you mean, running off like that?:* kion vi intencas, forkurante tiel?); (destine), destini [tr] (e.g.: *a rule meant to be broken:* regulo destinita esti rompita); (low, humble, inferior), malsupera, humila; (ignoble), malnobla; (stingy), avara; (bad-tempered), malbonhumora, mishumora; (malicious), malica; (disagreeable), malafabla; (skillful, expert), lerta; (math), mezo, meznombro; **meza; means,** [see "means"]; **meaning,** ~o, senco; intenco; **meaningful,** ~oplena; **meaningless,** sen~a; **mean it,** (be sincere), esti sincera; (be serious, not joking), esti serioza, ne ŝerci [int]; **mean business,** esti serioza; **well-meaning,** bonintenca; **arithmetic mean,** aritmetika meznombro, aritmo; **geometric mean,** geometria meznombro
meander, meandri [int], serpentumi [int], sinui [int]; ~o
means, (agency, method, resources), rimedo(j); (wealth), riĉaĵo(j); **by means of,** per, pere de; **by all means,** nepre, certe, sendube; **by any means,** iel ajn; **by no means,** nepre ne, certe ne, neniel, tute ne
meanwhile, meantime, dume, intertempe
measles, (rubeola), rubeolo; (rubella, German measles), morbilo
measly, (mere), nura, magra, mizera
measure, (extent, dimensions, capacity; standard or system for measurement; mus bar), mezuro; ~i [tr]; (determine quantity, of, gauge), komptit; (procedure, method), rimedo (e.g.: *take stern measures:* uzi striktajn rimedojn); (dance), danco; (statute), statuto; (bill, proposed law), leĝpropono; (mark off, set limits), dislimi [tr]; (appraise, assess), taksi [tr]; (consider), konsideri [tr]; (make rhythmical), ritmi [tr]; **measured,** konsiderita; ritma; **coun-**

termeasure, kontraŭrimedo; **tape-measure**, ~bendo, ~rubando; **for good measure**, kiel kromaĵo; **made to measure**, laŭmende farita; **measure up**, (be judged against standard), taksiĝi; (be suitable), taŭgi [int]; **measure up to**, (meet expectations), plenumi la esperojn de

meat, (as food), viando; (flesh, gen), karno; (kernel, as of nut, story, issue), kerno; **meatball**, knelo, ~obulo; **charcoal-broiled meat**, karbonado; **sweetmeat**, dolĉaĵo, frandaĵo

meatus, (duct), meato; (orifice), orifico

mecca, (bsns center), emporio; (any center), centro, vizitejo (e.g.: *tourist mecca:* turisma centro)

Mecca, (holy city), Mekko

mechanic, meĥanik/isto,   meĥanisto; **mechanical**, ~a; **mechanics**, ~o; **mechanism**, (gen), meĥanismo; **mechanist**, meĥanisto; **mechanize**, meĥanizi [tr]; **mechanotherapy**, meĥanoterapio; **garage mechanic**, garaĝisto; **quantum mechanics**, kvantum~o; **servomechanism**, servomeĥanismo

Mechelen, Meĥlino

Mechlin, (city), Meĥlino; (lace), ~a punto

meconium, mekonio

medal, medalo; ~i [tr]

medallion, (large medal), granda medalo; (oval design etc.), medaliono

meddle, enmiks/iĝi, ~i sin; **meddlesome**, ~iĝema

Mede, Medo [see "Media"]

Medea, Medea

media, [see "medium"]

Media, (kingdom), Medio [see "Mede"]

mediaeval, mezepoka

medial, meza

median, (gen), mediano; ~a; (of triangle), mezanto

mediant, (mus), medianto; **submediant**, sub~o

medianus, (nerve), mediano

mediastinum, mediastino

mediate, mediacii [tr]; **mediation**, ~o; **mediator**, ~into; ~anto; ~onto; ~isto

medic, (med), medicinisto; (bot), medikago; **paramedic**, para~o

Medicago, medikago; Medicago lupulina, lupol~o; Medicago sativa, luzerno

medical, medicina; **paramedical**, para~a; **premedical**, antaŭ~a

medicament, medikamento

medicate, medikamenti [tr]; **medication**, (drug), ~o; (treatment), ~ado

Medici, Mediĉoj

medicine, (sci), medicino; (drug), medikamento; **medicinal**, medikamenta; **social medicine**, sociala ~o

medick, medikago

medico–, (pfx), medicin(o)–

medieval, mezepoka

Medina, Medino

mediocre, mezbona, mezkvalita; **mediocrity**, ~eco

meditate, mediti [int]; **meditation**, ~(ad)o; **meditative**, ~(em)a

Mediterranean, Mediteranea; **Mediterranean Sea**, ~o

medium, (middle), mezo; ~a; ~e; (intervening thing), perilo (e.g.: *a heat-conducting medium:* varmokonduka perilo); (means of communication), komunikilo (e.g.: *the news media:* la novaĵkomunikiloj); (environment, natural or artificial), medio; (psychic), mediumo; **mediumistic**, mediuma; **mediumship**, mediumeco; **mass media**, amaskomunikiloj†

medlar, (fruit), mespilo; (tree), ~arbo

medley, miks/kanzono, ~melodio, ~peco, ~aĵo

medulla, (anat: medulla oblongata; marrow; inner part of any organ; bot: pith), medolo; (spinal cord), mjelo; **medullary**, ~a; **medullary ray**, (gen), ~radio; **medullectomy**, ~ektomio; **medullitis**, ~ito

medusa, meduzo

Medusa, (myth), Meduza

Medusa, (zool), meduzo

meek, humila, milda; submetiĝema

meerschaum, sepiolito, marŝaŭmo

meet, (get together in group for any reason), kunveni [int]; (sit together to discuss etc.), kunsidi [int]; (hold large meeting, as congress, symposium), kongresi [int]; (get acquainted w), konatiĝi kun; (come upon, come to

oth person, animal, or thing), renkonti
[tr]; renkontiĝi; (come across by
chance), trafi [tr]; (fulfill, as requirements, quota), plenumi [tr]; (converge), konverĝi [int]; (decent), deca;
meeting, ~o; kunsido; konatiĝo; renkontiĝo; meeting room, meeting
place, meeting house, ~ejo; mass
meeting, amas~o; (mass pol rally),
mitingo
mega–, (pfx), mega–
megacycle, megaciklo
Megaera, Megera
megahertz, megaherco
megalith, megalito; megalithic, ~a
megalo–, (pfx), megalo–
megaloenteron, megalo/entero;   (re
large intestine), ~kojlo
megaloesophagus, megaloezofago
megalohepatia, megalohepato
megalomania, megalomanio;   megalo-
maniac, ~a; ~ulo
megalopolis, megalourbo
megalosaur, megalosaŭro
Megalosaurus, megalosaŭro
megaphone, megafono; ~i [tr, int]
megathere, megaterio
megatherium, Megatherium,   megaterio
mehari, meharo; meharist, ~isto
Meibom, Mejbomo
meibomian, mejboma;   meibomian
gland, ~a glando; meibomianitis,
~ito
meiosis, mejozo
Mekka, Mekko
Mekong, Mekongo
Melaleuca, kajeputarbo
Melampyrum, melampiro, bovintritiko
melancholy, melancholia, melankolio;
~a; melancholic, ~a; melancholiac,
~ulo
melanemia, melanemio
Melanesia, Melanezio
melange, miks/amaso, ~aĵo
melanin, melanino
melanism, melanismo
Melanocorypha calandra, kalandro
Melanogrammus aeglefinus, eglefino
Melbourne, Melburno
Melchior, Melkioro
Melchizedek, Melchisedec, Melkice-

dek
meld, (cards), deklari [tr]; ~o; (merge,
blend), kunfandi [tr]; kunfandiĝi
Meleager, Meleagro
Meleagrina, meleagreno, perlokonko
Meleagris, meleagro
Meleagros, Meleagro
melee, miksbatalo
melena, meleno
Meles, melo
Melia, melio
melilot, meliloto
Melilotus, meliloto
melinite, melinito
Melissa, (woman's name), Melisa
Melissa, (bot), meliso
melitococcosis, melitokokozo   [see
"brucellosis"]
mellifluous, miel(ton)a
mellow, (ripe, as fruit), matura; ~igi;
~iĝi; (not bitter), malamara, dolĉa;
(mild, gentle, not harsh), milda, malakra
Melocactus, melokakto
Melocanna, bambuso
melodrama, melodramo; melodramat-
ic, ~(ec)a
melody, melodio; melodic, melodious,
~a
Meloe, meloo
Melolontha, melolonto, majskarabo
melomane, melomano;   melomania,
~io
melon, melono; rock melon, (Aus),
kantalupo; watermelon, akvo~o
melongene, melongeno
Melopepo, melopepo
melopoeia, melopeo
Melopsittacus, (Aus),   melopsitako*;
Melopsittacus   undulatus,   (Aus),
buĝerigo
Melos, Meloso
melosa, madio
Melpomene, Melpomena
melt, (re any substance), fandi [tr]; ~iĝi;
(re ice), degeli [int]; degeligi; melt
down, (destroy cast object by melting), re~i [tr]; re~iĝi; meltdown, (nuclear accident), plen~iĝo; melting
point, ~opunkto
Melusina, Meluzina
member, (gen), membro;   member-

ship, ~eco; ~aro; **dismember**, dis~igi
membrane, membrano; **mucous membrane**, mukozo, muk~o; **nictitating membrane**, niktita ~o; **tympanic membrane**, miringo, timpana ~o
Memel, Nemano
memento, memoraĵo
memo, memorando [not "memo"]
memoir, memoraĵo(j) [not "memuaro"]
memorabilia, memoraĵoj
memorable, memorinda
memorandum, memorando   [not "memo"]
memorial, (commemorative), memoriga; ~aĵo; (monument), monumento; (petition), petskribo; **memorialize**, (re)~i
memory, (gen), memoro; **memorize, commit to memory**, parkerigi, lerni [tr] parkere; **memory bank**, (cmptr), (komputora) ~o, storo†; **by memory, from memory**, ~e; **random-access memory**, (cmptr: abb: RAM), ramo†; **read-only memory**, (abb: ROM), romo†
Memphis, (in Tennessee), Memfiso; (in Egypt), Menefro
menace, minaci [tr]; ~o; **menacing**, ~a
menad, menado
ménage, (household), familio, domanaro; (housekeeping), mastrumado; **ménage à trois (quatre, etc.)**, sekstriopo (sekskvaropo, etc.)
menagerie, menaĝerio
Menander, Menandro
menarche, ekmenstruo
mend, (repair), ripari [tr]; (improve), plibonigi; pliboniĝi; (heal, gen), resaniĝi; (knit, as broken bone), kuntiriĝi; (patch clothes), fliki [tr]; **mending**, (things to be mended), ~otaĵo
mendacious, mensoga, ~ema; **mendacity**, ~emo; ~o
Mendel, Mendelo; **Mendelian**, ~a; **Mendel(ian)ism**, ~ismo
mendelevium, mendelevio
mendicant, almoza; ~ulo
Menelaus, Menelao
menhir, menhiro
menial, servista, malalta, malnobela, malprestiĝa

meninges, meningoj
meningitis, meningito
meninx, meningo
meniscus, (gen), menisko
Menispermum, menispermo, lunsemo
Mennonite, Menonito*; ~a
menopause, menopaŭzo, klimaktero
menorah, (Juda) kandelabro
Menorca, Minorko
menses, menstruo
menstrual, menstrua; **menstruate**, ~i [int]; **menstruation**, ~o
mental, mensa; **mentality**, (state), ~ostato; (being), ~ulo
mentation, cerbumado
Mentha, mento
menthane, mentano
menthol, mentolo
mention, mencii [tr]; ~o; **above-mentioned, afore-mentioned**, (supre) ~ita, supre citita, antaŭ~ita, ĉi-supra; **(un)mentionable**, (ne)~inda; **not to mention**, sen ~i; **don't mention it!**, (reply to apology or thanks), ne ~inde!, ne dankinde!, tre volonte!
mentor, mentoro
menu, menuo
Menura, menuro, lirvostulo
Menyanthes, menianto
meow, miaŭi [int]; ~o; (onom), miaŭ!
Mephisto(pheles), Mefisto(felo)
mephitis, (gas), haladzo
Mephitis, (zool), mefito
merbromin, merbromino
mercantile, komerca; **mercantilism**, merkantilismo
mercaptan, merkaptano, tiolo
Mercedes, (woman's name), Mercedesa
mercenary, (hired soldier), soldulo, dungosoldato; (greedy), (mon)avida
mercerize, mercerizi [tr]
merchandise, (goods), komerc/aĵoj, varoj; (deal in), ~i [int] (en) [cp "deal"]
merchant, komerca; ~isto
Mercurialis, merkurialo
Mercurio, (man's name), Merkurio
mercury, (element), hidrargo; **mercurial**, ~(ec)a; **dog's mercury**, (bot), merkurialo
Mercury, (ast; myth), Merkuro
mercy, kompato, korfavoro; **merciful**,

~(em)a; **merciless**, sen~a; **have mercy on**, ~i [tr]; **at one's mercy, at the mercy of**, submetita al ies ~o (la ~o de)

mere, nura; **merely**, nur

meretricious, meretric(ec)a

meretrix, (Roman prostitute), meretrico

merganser, merĝo

merge, (combine, gen; re traffic), kunfandi [tr]; ~iĝi; (re organization, bsns firm, etc.), fuziigi; fuziiĝi; [not "merg–"; not "merĝ–"]; **merger**, ~(iĝ)o; fuzio

Mergus, merĝo

meridian, (of longitude), meridiano; (high point, as of star in sky), kulmino; kulmina; **prime meridian**, (on any world), (la) nul~o; (Earth), (la) nul~o, (la) Grenviĉa ~o

meringue, (gen), meringo; ~a; ~i [tr]

merino, (sheep), merino; (wool), ~lano

meristem, meristemo; **meristematic**, ~a

merit, merito; ~i [tr]; **meritorious**, ~a; **demerit**, (quality), mal~o; (mark etc.), mal~aĵo

merl, merlo

Merlangus, merlango

Merluccius, merluĉo

mermaid, marvir/ino; **merman**, ~o

Merops, meropo

Merovaeus, Merovo; **Merovingian**, ~ido; ~ida

merry, gaja; **merriment, merrymaking**, ~eco; **merry-go-round**, karuselo

Merulus, merulio; Merulus lacrimans, larmofungo

mesa, platmonteto

mésalliance, mezalianco

mesarteritis, mesarteriito

mescal, (cactus), pejotlo*; **mescal button**, ~a butono [cp "mescaline", "peyote"]

mescaline, meskalino

Mesembryanthemum, mesembrianto

mesencephalon, mesoencefalo

mesenchyme, mesenchyma, mezenkimo

mesenteron, mesoo [cp "mesenteron"]

mesh, (of fabric etc.: one loop), maŝo; (many loops), ~aro; (engage, as gears), endentigi; endentiĝi; (inter-

lock), kupli [tr]; kupliĝi; (fig: fit well together, as ideas), (kun)taŭgi [int]; (entangle), impliki [tr]; implikiĝi; implikaĵo; **synchromesh**, sinkrona; sinkrona rapidumo

mesmerism, hipnot/igo; ~ismo; **mesmerize**, ~igi, ~izi [tr]

mes(o)–, (sci, tech pfx), meso– [sometimes absorbed into Esperanto root as "mezo–"; see individual entries]

mesoappendix, mesoapendico

mesocolon, mesokojlo

mesoderm, mesodermo

mesogastrium, mesogastro

mesolithic, mezolitiko

meson, mezono

mesonephros, mesonephron, mesonefro

Mesopotamia, Mezopotamio

mesothorium, mezotorio

Mesozoic, mezozoiko; ~a

Mespilus, mespilarbo

mess, (confusion, disorder), konfuzo, malordo, ĥaoso; (dirty), malpuraĵo; (jumble, hodgepodge), miksamaso; (embarrassment, trouble), embaraso, malfacilaĵo; (gruel, porridge), kaĉo; (anything disagreeable), aĉaĵo; amasaĉo; (meal), manĝo; (botched, bungled), fuŝaĵo; **messy**, ~a, senorda; malpura; embaras(ig)a, malfacila; aĉa; fuŝa; **mess about, mess around**, (dabble, putter), diletanti [int]; (loll, loiter, dawdle), lanti [int]; **mess hall**, manĝejo; **mess kit**, gamelaro; **mess tin**, (item of mess kit), gamelo; **mess up**, ~i [tr], malordi [tr]; malpurigi; fuŝi [tr]; **mess with**, (get involved in), sin enmiski en; (putter), diletanti en, pri

message, mesaĝo

Messalina, Mesalina

messenger, mesaĝisto

messiah, messias, mesio; **messianic**, ~a

Messidor, Mesidoro

Messina, Mesino; **Strait of Messina**, Markolo ~a

mestizo, mestizo

meta–, (pfx), meta–

metabolism, metabolo; **metabolic**, ~a; **metabolize**, ~igi

metacarpus, metakarpo; **metacarpal**, ~a
metacenter, metacentro
metal, metalo; ~a; **metallic**, ~a; **metallography**, ~ografio; **metalloid**, ~oido; **metallurgy**, metalurgio; **metallurgic(al)**, metalurgia; **metallurgist**, metalurgiisto; **metalware**, ~aĵo(j), ~varoj; **metalwork**, ~aĵo; **metalworking**, ~laborado; **Monel(l) metal**, monel~o; **bimetalism**, du~ismo; **monometalism**, mono~ismo; **sheet metal**, lado; **corrugated sheet metal**, ondolado
metamere, metamero; **metamerism**, ~eco
metamorphic, metamorphous, metamorfa
metamorphism, metamorphosis, metamorfozo; **metamorphose**, ~i [int]
metaphor, metaforo; **metaphoric**, ~a
metaphosphate, metafosfato; **metaphosphoric acid**, ~a acido
metaphysics, metafiziko; **metaphysical**, ~a; **metaphysician**, ~isto
metapsychic, metapsikia; **metapsychics**, ~o
metastable, metastabila
metastasis, translokiĝo; **metastasize**, ~i; **metastatic**, ~anta
metatarsus, metatarso; **metatarsal**, ~a
metathesis, metatezo
metaxylene, metaksileno
Metazoa, metazooj
metazoan, metazoo
mete (out), (dis)doni [tr], distribui [tr]
metempsychosis, metempsikozo
metencephalon, metencefalo; **metencephalic**, ~a
meteor, (falling rock in atmosphere), meteoro; (weather phenomenon), meteo; **meteoric**, ~(ec)a; **meteorism**, (med), ~ismo; **meteorite**, (rock after striking ground), ~ŝtono, aerolito; **meteoroid**, (rock in space), ~oido; **meteorology**, meteologio; **meteorologist**, meteologo; **meteorological**, meteologia
meter, (100 cm; poet, mus rhythm), metro; (measure quantity of water, gas, etc.), kompti† [tr]; ~o, komptilo† (e.g.: *water meter:* akvokomptilo) [cp

"compute", "gauge"]; **square meter**, kvadrata ~o, centiaro; **millimeter**, mili~o; **centimeter**, centi~o; **decimeter**, deci~o; **decameter**, deka~o; **hectometer**, hekto~o; **kilometer**, kilo~o; **meter-kilogram**, ~okilogramo, malgranda dinamio; **meter-ton**, granda dinamio; **meter-kilogram-second system**, sistemo ~o-kilogramo-sekundo [abb: sistemo MKS]
methacrylate, metakril/ato; **methacrylic acid**, ~a acido
methadone, metadono*
methanal, metanalo, formaldehido
methane, metano
methanoic acid, metanacido
methanol, metanolo
methene, meteno
method, metodo; **methodical**, ~a; **methodology**, (system of methods), ~aro; (sci of methods), ~ologio, ~iko
Methodism, Metod/ismo; **Methodist**, ~isma; ~isto
methoxy–, (chem root), metoksi–
methoxyl, metoksilo
Methuselah, Metuŝelaĥ
methyl, metilo
methylene, metileno
meticulous, detalema, pedanta, zorgemega
métier, metio
métis, mestizo
metonymy, metonimio
metope, metopo
metopic, frunta
metre, [see "meter"]
metretes, metreto
metric, metra; **metrics**, metriko
–metric, (tech sfx), –metria
metritis, metrito, uterito
metro, (subway or oth urban rr), metroo
metro–, (med pfx: uterus), uter(o)–
metrology, metrologio
metronome, metronomo
metropolis, (city), metropolo; (rel), metropolitejo; **metropolitan**, ~a; metropolito
metroptosis, uteroptozo
Metroxylon, sagu/arbo, ~palmo
–metry, (tech sfx), –metrio
mettle, kuraĝo, spirito
Metz, (city), Messo

Meuse, Mozo
mew, [see "meow"]
mewl, ĝemeti [int], ploreti [int]
mews, stalaleo
Mexico, Meksik/io; **Mexican,** ~iano; ~iana; ~ia; **Mexico City,** ~o; **Mexico Citian,** ~ano; ~ana; ~a; **Gulf of Mexico,** Golfo de ~io; **New Mexico,** Nov-~io
mezcaline, meskalino
mezereon, mezereum, (plant), mezereo; (bark), ~aĵo
mezzanine, mezetaĝo
mezzo–, (pfx), mez(o)– (e.g.: *mezzosoprano:* ~osopranulo)
mezzotint, mezotinto
mho, simenso
mi, (mus), mi
miasma, miasmo
mica, glimo
Micah, Miña
micell, micella, micelle, miĉelo
Michael, (man's name, gen), Mikelo; (Hebrew form), Miñaelo; **Michaela,** ~a; **Michaelmas,** ~festo
Micheas, Miña
Michelangelo, Mikel-Anĝelo
Michelle, Mikela
Michigan, Miĉigano; **Lake Michigan,** Lago ~o
Micky, Miĉjo
micro–, (pfx), mikro–
microbar, barjo
microbe, mikrobo; **microbic, microbial,** ~a; **microbicide,** mikrobicido
microcephaly, mikrocefal/io; **microcephalic, microcephalous,** ~a
micrococcus, mikrokoko
microcosm, mikrokosmo
microfiche, mikrofiĉo*
micrometer, mikrometro
micron, (gen), mikrono
Micronesia, Mikronezio
microphone, mikrofono
Micropus apus, apuso, murhirundo
micropyle, mikropilo; **micropylar,** ~a
microscope, mikroskopo; **microscopic,** ~a; **microscopy,** ~io; **biomicroscope,** bio~o; **submicroscopic,** sub~a; **electron microscope,** elektrona ~o; **ultramicroscope,** ultra~o
Microsporum, mikrosporo

microtome, mikrotomo
microwave, mikroondo†; ~a; **microwave oven,** ~a forno
Microtus, mikroto
mid–, (pfx), mez–; –meza; –mezo (e.g.: *mid-ocean collision:* ~oceana kolizio; *midday:* tag~a; *midland dialect:* land~a dialekto)
Midas, Midaso
middle, mezo; ~a; ~e; **in the middle (of),** ~e (de); **middle voice,** (gram), medialo
middling, mez(bon)a
midge, (imprecise term for any small fly), muŝeto; (gnat: *Culex*), kulo; **biting midge,** simulio; **gall midge,** cecidomio
midget, (person), nano; (tiny, gen), eta
midrash, midraŝo†
midriff, (anat), torsmezo; ~a; (of garment), ~umo
midst, mezo
mien, mieno
miff, (offend), ofendeti [tr]; ~iĝi; (quarrel), kvereleto; kvereleti [int] [cp "pout"]
might, (power), potenco, fort(eg)o; (perhaps will), eble –os (e.g.: *I might go tomorrow:* mi eble iros morgaŭ); (perhaps is), eble –as; povas esti ke (e.g.: *you might be right:* vi eble pravas [or] povas esti ke vi pravas); (perhaps would be), eble –us, povus esti (e.g.: *that might be better:* tio eble estus pli bona [or] tio povus esti pli bona); [see also "may"]; **mighty,** ~a, fortega; **might as well,** povus egale (e.g.: *nothing's happening, so we might as well go home:* nenio okazas, do ni povus egale iri hejmen)
mignon, beleta, delikata
mignonette, (plant), rezedo; (color), ~okolora
migraine, migreno
migrate, migri [int]; **migration,** ~(ad)o; **migratory,** ~a; **migrant,** ~into; ~anto; ~a (e.g.: *migrant worker:* ~a laboristo)
mikado, mikado
mike, (microphone), mikrofono
Mike, (nickname), Miĉjo
mikron, (gen), mikrono

mil, (1/1000 inch), milicolo [25,4 mikronoj (see § 20)]; (milliliter), mililitro
Milan(o), Milano; **Milanese**, ~ano; ~a
mild, milda
mildew, melduo; ~igi; ~iĝi
mile, mejlo [1,609 kilometroj (see § 20)]; **mileage**, (miles traveled; distance in miles), ~aĵo; (distance, not necessarily in miles), kilometraĵo, distanco (e.g.: *a car with low mileage:* aŭto kun malgranda kilometraĵo; *cover lots of mileage:* transiri grandan distancon [or] kilometraĵon); (reimbursement, allotment; cost per distance traveled), por~aĵo; porkilometraĵo; **nautical mile**, mar~o [1,852 kilometroj]
miliaria, miliara erupcio
miliary, miliara
milieu, medio
military, milita; ~eca; **militarism**, militarismo; **militarist**, militaristo; **militaristic**, militarisma; **militarize**, ~ecigi; **demilitarize**, sen~igi, mal~ecigi; **militant**, (at war), ~anta; (aggressive, warlike), ~ema, agresema; **paramilitary**, para~eca
militate, direktiĝi; **militate against**, kontraŭstari [tr]
militia, milicio; **militiaman**, ~ano
milk, (substance, gen), lakto; (remove milk from cow etc.), melki [tr]; **milky**, ~(ec)a; **milkman**, ~isto; **milkshake**, ~oskuaĵo; **milksop**, molaĉulo; **milkweed**, askepiado; **marsh milkweed**, eŭpatorio; **milkwort**, poligalo; **buttermilk**, buter~o; **canned milk**, lad~o; **coconut milk**, kokosa ~o; **condensed milk**, densigita ~o; **goat's milk**, kaprina ~o; **homogenized milk**, homogenigita ~o; **mother's milk**, virina ~o; **one-percent (two-percent) milk**, unu-procenta (du-procenta) ~o; **powdered milk**, pulvorigita ~o; **skim milk**, senkrema ~o; **tinned milk**, lad~o; **whole milk**, kompleta ~o; **milking machine**, melkatoro; **the Milky Way**, (ast), la L~a Vojo
mill, (grind to small pieces), mueli [tr]; (building for this), ~ejo; (apparatus), ~ilo; (machine metal etc.), frezi [tr]; (metal-working plant), uzino; (manufacture by milling), uzini [tr]; (any manufacturing plant), fabriko, manufakturo; (score edge of coin), randostreki [tr]; **miller**, ~isto; **mill's-thumb**, (bot), ĉoto; **milling machine**, frezmaŝino; uzinmaŝino; **mill around**, **mill about**, ĉirkaŭsvarmi [int]; **millrace**, **mill-stream**, ~akvo; **millworker**, ~isto; **millwright**, uzinisto; **watermill**, akvo~ilo; akvo~ejo; **windmill**, vento~ilo; vento~ejo
millenium, jarmilo
millet, milio
milli-, (pfx), mili–
milliard, miliardo [see § 19(b)]
millibar, milibaro [cp "microbar"]
milliner, inĉapel/isto; **millinery**, ~oj, virinaj ĉapeloj
million, miliono [see § 19(b)]; **millionaire**, ~ulo
millipede, miriapodo
Milo, (Melos), Meloso; **Venus of Milo**, la ~a Venero
milt, (fish sperm), laktumo; (gland), ~glando
Miltiades, Miltiado
Milton, Miltono
Milvus, milvo
Milwaukee, Milvokio
mime, mimi [tr]; (actor), ~o; (drama), ~dramo
mimeograph, mimeografo; ~i [tr]
mimetism, mimetismo
mimic, mimi [tr]; mimika; **mimicry**, (gen), ~o; (zool), mimetismo
mimosa, mimozo
Mimosa, mimozo; Mimosa pudica, sentema ~o, sensitivo
Mimulus, mimulo
Mimus polyglottos, mokbirdo
Min, (Rivero) Min
mina, mino
minaret, minareto
mince, (chop), haketi [tr]; (into small pieces), eretigi; (affected expression), afekti [tr], paroli [int] afekte, paroli delikate; **mincemeat**, (frukto)~aĵo; **make mincemeat of**, (lit or fig), dis~i [tr], eretigi; **mince words**, paroli diskrete, nerekte, kaŝeme

mind, (mental entity; mentality), menso; (psyche), psiko; (opinion), opinio (e.g.: *speak one's mind:* diri sian opinion); (pay attention, heed), atenti [tr]; (look after, care for, be careful of), prizorgi [tr], zorgi [int] pri; (object, be against, dislike), kontraŭi [tr] (e.g.: *would you mind if we go?:* ĉu vi kontraŭus se ni iros?; *I don't mind their actions:* mi ne kontraŭas iliajn agojn) [see also "I don't mind" below]; (have concern, negative feelings about), (io) gravi [int] (al iu) (e.g.: *I don't mind the rain, but I do mind the cold:* la pluvo ne gravas al mi, sed la malvarmo ja gravas al mi) [see also "matter"]; (obey), obei [tr]; **mindful,** (attentive), atenta; **be mindful of,** (aware), konscii [int] pri; **mindless,** senpripensa, senintelekta, sen~a; **single-minded,** unucela, neŝancela; **(the) mind's eye,** (la) imagopovo; **be of one mind, be of the same mind,** samopinii [int]; **be of different minds,** malsamopinii [int]; **be of two minds,** esti nedecidiĝinta, ankoraŭ ne decidis; **be in one's right mind,** esti ~e sana; **(something) be on one's mind,** (io) trudi sur ies atenton; io atentadi (ion); **bear (keep) in mind,** memor(ad)i [tr]; **blow one's mind,** (colloq), forpafi la ~on; **mindblowing,** ~opafa; **bring (call) to mind,** rememorigi; **change one's mind,** (re opinion), ŝanĝi ies (sian) opinion (deziron, etc.); (re intention), ŝanĝi ies (sian) intencon; **come to mind, cross one's mind,** veni en ies (sian) kapon, veni al iu en la kapon; **drive one out of one's mind,** frenezigi iun; **fix in one's mind,** encerbigi (al iu); **give someone a piece of one's mind,** kritiki iun, riproĉi iun, koleri [int] kontraŭ iu; **have a (good) mind to, be of a mind to,** (forte) emi [int] (al), (forte) inklini [int] (al), forte intenci [tr]; **have half a mind to,** iom emi [int] al, iom inklini [int] al; **have in mind,** (intend), intenci [tr], celi [tr]; (think about), pripensi [tr]; (remember), memori [tr]; **I don't mind,** (it doesn't matter to me), ne gravas al mi,

estas indiferente al mi, al mi estas tute egale; **keep in mind,** memor(ad)i [tr], konservi en la memoro; **keep one's mind on (something),** ne distriĝi de, resti atenta al; **lose one's mind,** freneziĝi; **make up one's mind,** decidiĝi; decidi (al iu); **meeting of the minds,** konsentiĝo, akordiĝo; **never mind,** ne gravas; negrave; forgesu ĝin, ne domaĝu, ne ĉagreniĝu, ne maltrankviliĝu; **out of one's mind,** (insane; frantic), freneza; **presence of mind,** animvigleco, spiritoĉeesto, spiritopreteco; **put in mind,** rememorigi; **set one's mind on,** firmigi ies (sian) deziron pri; **take one's mind off,** deturni ies atenton de, distri iun de; distriĝi de; **to my mind,** laŭ mia opinio, miaopinie

Mindanao, Mindanao

mine, (source of ore etc.; mil: explosive device), mino; ~a; (remove ore), ~i [tr]; (set mil mines), ~semi [tr]; (block by mines), ~bari [tr]; (entirety of shafts, installations, etc., of a mine), ~ejo; (my), (la) mia (e.g.: *that book is mine:* tiu libro estas mia; *I have your book and you have mine:* mi havas vian libron kaj vi havas la mian); **miner,** ~isto; **mine field,** ~tereno; **minesweep,** ~balai [tr], sen~igi; **coal mine,** karb~o; **iron mine,** fer~o; **undermine,** (gen), sapei [tr], sub~i [tr], subfosi [tr]; sapeo, sub~o

mineral, mineralo; ~a; **mineralize,** ~igi; **mineralogy,** mineralogio; **mineralogist,** mineralogo

Minerva, Minerva

minestrone, minestrono†

minette, mineto

minever, menuvero

mingle, miksi [tr]; ~iĝi; **intermingle,** inter~i [tr]; inter~iĝi

mini–, (pfx), mini–, –et– (e.g.: *miniskirt:* ~jupo)

miniature, miniaturo; ~a; **subminiature,** sub~o; sub~a

minim, (1/60 fluid dram), 0,0616 mililitro, 61,6 mikrolitroj [see § 20]; (drop, approximately), guto; (mus), duonnoto

minimum, minimumo; ~a; **minimal,**

~a; **minimize**, ~igi

minion, (subordinate), subulo; (servile person), lakeo

minister, (government officer), ministro; (rel), pastro; (provide), provizi [tr]; (give, administer), doni [tr]; (serve as rel minister to), pastri [int]; (help, attend to), helpi [tr], atenti [tr]; **ministry**, ~ejo, ministerio; pastreco; atent(ad)o; **ministerial**, ~(ec)a; pastreca; **ministration**, pastreco; atent(ad)o; **prime minister**, premiero, ĉef~o; **minister without portfolio**, senpostena ~o

minium, minio

miniver, menuvero

mink, (zool), vizono; (fur), ~pelto; **European mink**, lutreolo

Minnesota, Minesoto

minnow, fokseno

Minoa, Mino/ujo; **Minoan**, ~a

minor, (lesser, nonmajor, etc.; mus; Bib, re prophets; phil, re syllogism), minora, malĉefa; (not of age), minoritata, neplenaĝa; minoritatulo, neplenaĝulo; (accessory, secondary), akcesora; (second principal university study), subĉefstudo, subĉeffako; subĉefstudi [tr]; **minority**, (smaller group, number), minoritato, malplimulto; (not of age), minoritato, neplenaĝo; **seminor**, (geom), duon~a

Minorca, Minorko

Minos, Minoo

Minotaur, Minotaŭro

minstrel, menestrelo

mint, (make coins etc.), stampi [tr]; (make, gen), fari [tr], fabriki [tr]; (place) mon~ejo; (bot), mento; (candy), mentaĵo; (new), novega; **mountain mint**, **horse mint**, monardo

minuend, malpliigato

minuet, menueto

minus, minus; ~a; ~aĵo; **minus sign**, ~signo

minuscule, (tiny), eta, ~~a, malgrandega; (re letter), minusklo; minuskla

minute, (60 seconds), minuto; (moment), momento (e.g.: *wait a minute!:* atendu momenton!); (tiny), eta, eteta, malgrandega; (detailed), detala; **minutes**, (report of meeting), protokolo

[note sing]

minutia(e), detaleto(j)

minx, koketulino

minyan, kvorumo

Miocene, mioceno

miofibril, miofibretoj

miosis, miozo; **miotic**, ~iga; ~igenzo

mirabelle, (fruit), mirabelo; (tree), ~arbo

Mirabilis jalapa, niktago

miracle, miraklo; **miraculous**, ~a; **miracle-worker**, ~isto

mirage, miraĝo

mire, (bog), marĉo; (mud), koto; **mire down**, en~igi, enkotigi; en~iĝi, enkotiĝi

Miriam, Mirjam

Mirounga, marelefanto

mirror, spegulo; ~i [tr]; **full-length mirror**, piedostara ~o; **rear-view mirror**, (of car etc.), retro~o; **side-view mirror**, flank~o

mirth, ĝojo, gajeco; **mirthful**, ~a, gaja

mis-, (pfx: wrong, improper, poor), mis- (e.g.: *misstep:* ~paŝo); (opp, not), mal- (e.g.: *mistrust:* malfido)

misalliance, mezalianco

mesanthrope, **mesanthropist**, mizantropo; **mesanthropy**, ~eco

misbegotten, misnaskita

miscegenation, rasmiks(ad)o

miscellaneous, diversa; **miscellany**, ~aĵo(j)

mischief, (pranks), petol(ad)o; ~aĵo; (harm, trouble), malutilo; **mischievous**, ~ema, buba; **be mischievous**, ~i [int]

miscible, miksebla; **immiscible**, ne~a

miscreant, fia; ~ulo, kanajlo

misdemeanor, delikto

miser, avar/ulo; **miserly**, ~a

misericord(e), mizerikordo

misery, mizero; **miserable**, ~a; **put one out of one's misery**, liberigi iun de lia (ŝia, ĝia) ~o

misgiving, skrupulo, dubo

mishap, akcidento, misokazo

mishmash, (things), miksamaso; (words), galimatio

misnomer, misnomo

misogyny, mizogen/eco; **misogynist**, ~o; **misogynous**, ~a

miss, (not hit mark or goal; not meet bus, plane, etc.), maltrafi [tr]; ~o; (feel lack due to absence), senti ies mankon (e.g.: *we missed you while you were away:* ni sentis vian mankon dum vi forestis); (woman), fraŭlino [abb: f–ino]; (escape), eskapi [tr, int] (de); (misfire, as engine), misbruli [int]; misbrulo; **missing,** (lacking, absent), mankanta; (disappeared), malaperinta; (soldier, victim of catastrophe, etc.: fate unknown), mankanto
missal, misalo, meslibro
missile, (rocket etc.), misilo; (anything thrown), ĵetaĵo; **antimissile,** anti~o; **air-to-air missile,** aer-aera ~o; **guided missile,** gvidata ~o; **surface-to-air missile (SAM),** ter-aera ~o; **surface-to-surface missile,** ter-tera ~o
mission, (diplomatic etc.; rel), misio; (place, building etc. for same), ~ejo; (expedition), ekspedicio; (errand, task assigned), komisio; **missionary,** ~a; (pol), ~ulo; (rel), ~isto
Mississippi, (river), Misisipo; (state), ~io
missive, letero, mesaĝo
Missouri, (river), Misuro; (state), ~io
mist, (light fog), nebul/eto; (fine drizzle), ~pluvo; ~pluvi [int] [cp "drizzle"]; (light spray), ŝpruceti [int]; ŝprucetaĵo
mistake, (error), eraro, misaĵo; (misunderstand), miskompreni [tr]; (take to be oth person), preni [tr] (por) (e.g.: *I mistook you for a friend of mine:* mi prenis vin por amiko mia); **mistaken,** ~a; **mistakenly,** ~e, pro ~o; **be mistaken,** ~i [int]
mister, sinjoro [abb: s–ro]
mistletoe, visko
mistral, mistralo
mistress, (lover), amorantino; (woman boss, master), mastrino, estrino; (woman superintendant etc.), intendantino; (Br: teacher), instruistino
mistura, miksturo
mite, (zool: any of *Acarina*), akaro; (bit; small thing, animal), peceto, etaĵo; etulo; **follicle mite,** demodekso; **harvest mite,** (*Tunga*), ĉiko; (larva of *Trombiculidae*), lepto; **itch mite,**

(*Sarcoptes*), sarkopto; (Aus: chigger), ĉiko; **a mite,** (slightly), iomete
miter, (saw at angle), geri [tr]; (the cut), ~o; (joint), ~aĵo; (Christian cap), mitro; mitri [tr]; (Jewish), cidaro; **miter box,** ~ilo
Mithra, Mithras, Mitrao; **Mithraism,** ~ismo; **Mithraic,** ~a; ~isma
mithridate, mitridat/aĵo; **mithridatize,** ~izi [tr]
Mithridates, Mitridato
mitigate, moder/igi, mildigi; ~iĝi, mildiĝi
mitosis, kariokinezo, mitozo
mitraille, mitrajlo; **mitrailleur,** ~isto; **mitrailleuse,** ~pafilo
mitral, mitrala; **mitral valve,** ~o
mitre, [see "miter"]
mitt, (glove, gen), ganto; (mitten), muf~o
mitten, mufganto
mix, (gen), miksi [tr]; ~iĝi; ~aĵo; **mixed,** ~ita, miks– [pfx] (e.g.: *of mixed type:* ~ospeca); (of more than one race, gender, etc.), miksta† (e.g.: *a mixed-race society:* miksta–rasa socio) **mixer,** ~ilo; **concrete mixer, cement mixer,** beton~atoro; **mixture,** (gen), ~ado; ~aĵo; (med, pharmacy), miksturo; **mix up,** inter~i [tr], (inter)konfuzi [tr], maldistingi [tr]; **intermix,** inter~i [tr]; inter~iĝi
mnemonic, mnemonika; **mnemonics,** ~o
Mnemosyne, Mnemozina
Moab, (person), Moab; (land), ~io
moan, ĝemi [int]; ~o
moat, ringofosaĵo
mob, (crowd), (hom)amas(aĉ)o; (gang), kanajlaro; (throng, crowd around), svarmi [int] (en, ĉirkaŭ); svarmo; **mobster,** gangstero
mobile, (movable), mov/ebla; (can move), ~a, ~iĝema; (fluid), fluida; (decoration of balanced objects), mobilo; **mobility,** (to be moved), ~ebleco; (to move), ~eco; **mobilize,** (mil etc.), mobilizi [tr]; **mobilization,** mobiliz(ad)o; **demobilize,** malmobilizi [tr]; **immobilize,** fiksi [tr], sen~igi
moccasin, (slipper), mokaseno
mocha, (coffee), mokao

Mocha, (city), Moka
mock, (ridicule), moki [tr]; ~o; (imitation), falsa, imita; **mockery,** ~ado; **mock-up,** postiĉo, modelo
mode, (style, fad), modo; (manner in which thing appears or functions; logic; cmptr; mus; gram), modalo; **modal,** (mus), modala; **modality,** modaleco; **modish,** laŭ~a; **outmoded,** eks~a, ekskutima
model, (gen), modelo; ~a; ~i [tr]; (make), modli [tr], ~i; **remodel,** (redesign, refurbish), redekoracii [tr], redesegni [tr], rekonstrui [tr], renovigi, refari [tr]; **model after,** ~igi laŭ; **scale model,** maketo†
modem, modemo†
moderate, modera; ~igi; ~iĝi; (preside over), prezidi [int] (super, ĉe); **moderation,** ~(ec)o; **moderator,** (person presiding), prezidanto; (phys: substance to absorb radiation), ~enzo; **immoderate,** mal~a, ekscesa
modern, moderna; **modernize,** ~igi; **modernism,** ~ismo; **modernistic,** ~isma; ~a
modest, (humble, unpretentious, small), modesta; (shy, reserved, as re sex, body, etc.), pudora; **modesty,** ~eco; pudoro; **immodest,** mal~a; senpudora
modicum, dozeto, porcieto
modify, modifi [tr]; **modification,** ~(ad)o; ~aĵo
modillion, modilono
modulate, moduli [tr]; **modulation,** ~ado; **amplitude modulation,** amplitud-~ado [abb: AM]; **frequency modulation,** frekvenc-~ado [abb: FM]
module, (math; geom), modulo; (cmptr; tech), modjulo†; **modular,** ~a; modjula†
modulus, modulo
modus operandi, agmaniero, farmaniero, procedo
modus vivendi, (manner of living), vivmaniero; (compromise), kompromiso
Mogadishu, Mogadiŝo*
mogul, (powerful person), potenculo
Mogul, (Mongol), Mogolo [cp "Mongol"]

mohair, mohajro; ~a
Mohammed, Mohamedo, Mahometo; **Mohammedan,** Islama; Islamano; **Mohammedanism,** Islamo
moire, muaraĵo
moiré muaro; ~a; ~i [tr]
moist, malseketa, humida; **moisten,** ~igi; ~iĝi; **moisture,** akvo, ~eco, humideco
molar, (tooth), molaro; (chem), molara; **premolar,** premolaro
molasses, melaso
mold, (cast, reproduce object in same shape), muldi [tr]; ~ilo; (form from soft material), modli [tr]; (shape, gen), formi [tr]; formo; (fungus), ŝimo; ŝimi [int]; **molding,** ~aĵo; modlaĵo; (arch ornament), modluro; (for base of wall), plankoplinto; **moldy,** (w fungus), ŝima; (musty, as odor), mucida
Moldavia, (principality), Moldavujo; (modern), ~io; **Moldavian,** ~o; ~a; ~ia; ~uja
molder, putri [int]
mole, (skin spot), lentugo; (chem), molo; (zool), talpo; (breakwater), moleo; **molehill,** talpejo; **marsupial mole,** (Aus), marsupia talpo; **make a mountain out of a molehill,** fari monton el talpejo, fari elefanton el muso
Molech, Moleĥo
molecule, molekulo; **molecular,** ~a; **gram-molecule,** gram-~o
molest, molesti [tr]
Molière, Moliero
Molinia, molinio
mollah, mulao
mollify, trankviligi, pacigi, mildigi
Mollusca, moluskoj; **Molluscoidea,** ~oidoj
mollycoddle, trodorloti [tr]
moloch, moloko
Moloch, (god), Moleĥo
Moloch, (zool), moloko
molt, (skin), transhaŭtiĝi; (feathers), transplumiĝi
Moluccas, Molucca Islands, Molukoj
Molva, molvo
molybdenate, molibdenato; **molybdenic acid,** ~a acido
molybdenum, molibdeno
mom, panjo

moment, (brief time), momento; (phys: vector product), momanto; (importance), graveco; **momentary,** ~a, maldaŭra, efemera; **momentous,** grav(eg)a; **last-moment,** last~a; **at the last moment,** last~e; **at the moment,** ĝuste nun, nun~e; **for the moment,** provizore, dume, dumtempe; **in a moment,** tre baldaŭ, post ~o; **just a moment!,** ~on!; **moment of force,** momanto de forto, virialo

momentum, impeto

mommy, panjo

Momordica, momordiko

Monaco, Monako

monad, monado

monarch, monarko, monarĥo; **monarchic(al),** ~a; **monarchism,** ~ismo; **monarchist,** ~isma; ~isto; **monarchy,** monarkio

Monarda, monardo

monastery, monaĥejo

monastic, monaĥ(ec)a

monaural, monofonia*

monazite, monazito

Monday, lundo; ~a; ~e

monecious, monoika

monetary, mona

money, mono; ~a; **moneyed,** ~hava; **moneybox,** kaso; **hush money, bribe money,** ŝmir~o; **paper money,** paper~o; **play money,** lud~o; **pin money, pocket money,** poŝ~o

Mongol, Mongolo; ~a; **Mongolia,** ~io; **Inner (Outer) Mongolia,** Interna (Ekstera) ~io; **Mongolian,** ~o; ~a; ~ia, ~uja; **Mongolism,** (med: Down's syndrome), la sindromo de Down, ~ismo; **Mongoloid,** (re Mongolian race), ~(ec)a; ~o; (med), Down-sindromulo, ~ismulo; Down-sindroma, ~isma

mongoose, mungo

mongrel, miksrasa; ~ulo, ~a hundo

Monica, Moniko

Monilla, monilio

monism, monismo; **monist,** ~a; monisto

monitor, (check on, warn, advise, etc.; cmptr†; student assistant; ship), monitoro; ~i [tr]; (lizard), varano

monk, monaĥo; **monkshood,** (bot), na-

pela akonito

monkey, (gen), simio; **monkey puzzle(r),** (tree), araŭkario; **monkey with,** tuŝifuŝi [tr] (e.g.: *the kids have monkeyed with the car:* la infanoj tuŝifuŝis la aŭton); **capuchin monkey,** cebo; **howler monkey,** aluato; **rhesus monkey,** resuso; **saki monkey,** pitecio; **spider monkey,** atelo; **squirrel monkey,** sajmirio; **woolly monkey,** lagotriko

mono, (mononucleosis), mononukleozo; (monophonic), monofonia*

mono–, (pfx), mono–

monochromatic, monokromata; **monochromatic light (generator),** monokromatoro

monochrome, unukolora; ~aĵo

monocle, monoklo

monoclinic, monoclinous, monoklina

Monocotyledones, unukotiledonoj

monocular, (one eye), unuokuleca

Monodelphis, monodelfo

Monodon monoceros, narvalo

monoecious, monoika

monogamy, monogamio; **monogamous,** ~a

monogram, monogramo

monograph, monografio

monolith, monolito; **monolithic,** ~a

monolog(ue), monologo; ~i [int]

monomania, monomanio; **monomaniac,** ~ulo; **monomaniacal,** ~a

monomer, monomero; **monomeric,** ~a

monomial, monoma; ~o

mononucleosis, mononukleozo

monopetalous, (having one petal), monopetala; (gamopetalous), gamopetala

monophonic, monofonia*

monophthong, monoftongo

monophysite, monofizito

monoplane, monoplano

monopole, monopoluso

monopoly, (gen), monopolo; (corner market), trusto; **monopolize,** ~igi, akapari [tr]; trusti [tr] [cp "hoard"]

monorail, unurel(voj)o

monosaccharide, monosakarido, monozo

monosyllabic, unusilaba

monotheism, monoteismo; **monotheist,** ~a; monoteisto

monotone, monotono
monotonous, monotona; monotony, ~eco
Monotremata, kloakuloj, monotremoj
monotreme, kloakulo, monotremo
monotropy, monotropio
monotype, monotipo
monoxide, monooksido
Monrovia, Monrovio*
mons pubis, puba monto, puba elstaraĵo; mons veneris, Venusmonto
monseigneur, monsignor, monsinjoro
monsoon, musono; ~a
monster, monstro; monstrous, ~a; monstrosity, ~aĵo
monstrance, (rel), monstranco†
montage, munt/aĵo; ~ado
montagnard, montarano
Montaigne, Montanjo
Montana, Montano
Monte Carlo, Montekarlo
Monte Christo, Montekristo
Montenegro, Montenegro
Montevideo, Montevideo
month, monato; monthly, (ĉiu)~a; (ĉiu)~e; bimonthly, du~a; semimonthly, duon~a; lunar month, lundaŭro, lun~o; a month from now, de nun post ~o
Montmartre, Montmartro
Montparnasse, Montparnaso
Montpelier, Montpeliero
Montpellier, Montpeliero
Montréal, Montrealo
monument, monumento; monumental, ~a
moo, muĝi [int]; ~o; (onom), muu!
mooch, (beg), depruntaĉi [tr]; (live as parasite), paraziti [int]; (loiter, loaf), lanti [int]; (pilfer), marodi [tr]; moocher, parazito
mood, (state of emotion), humoro; (gram), modo; moody, malgaj(em)a, ŝanĝ~a
moon, (any natural satellite), luno; (lunar month), ~daŭro, ~monato; (wander, daydream), revi [int], gapvagi [int]; (show buttocks), pugumi [tr]; the Moon, (Earth's moon: Luna), L~o; moonlight, [see under "light"]; moonrise, ~leviĝo; moonscape, ~pejzaĝo; moonseed, (bot), meni-

spermo, ~semo; moonshine, (whiskey), kaŝfarita viskio; full moon, plen~o; new moon, nov~o; half moon, duon~o; once in a blue moon, tre malofte
moor, (heath), erikejo; (tie ship to mooring post), albolardigi; (anchor, gen), ankri [tr]; (tie, gen), (al)ligi [tr]; moorfowl, (red grouse, Lagopus), lagopo; (Gallinula), galinolo; moorcock, virlagopo; virgalinolo; moorhen, lagopino; galinolino; moorwort, andromedo; mooring post, bolardo
moose, (Amerika) alko
moot, (irrelevant), nerilata; (debatable), diskutinda; (meaningless, not worth debating), nediskutinda, sensignifa; (propose, bring up), proponi [tr]
mop, ŝvabri [tr]; ~ilo; sponge-mop, spongo~i [tr]; spongo~ilo
mope, malgaji [int]; ~(em)ulo
moped, mopedo
mora, morao
moraine, moreno; terminal moraine, fronta ~o; lateral moraine, flanka ~o; ground moraine, funda ~o
moral, morala; (of fable etc.), ~aĵo, epifonemo; morals, ~o [note sing]; morality, (gen phil), ~o; (of specific situation), ~eco; immoral, mal~a; amoral, sen~a
morale, spirito, entuziasmo [not "moralo"]
morass, marĉo, ŝlimejo
moratorium, moratorio
Morava, (river), Moravo
Moravia, Moravio; Moravian, ~a; ~ano, Moravo
moray, mureno
morbid, morba; morbidity, ~eco; ~okvanto
morbidezza, morbideco
morbilli, morbilo
morbus, morbo
Morchella, morkelo
mordant, (biting, caustic, gen), morda, kaŭstika; ~enzo, kaŭstikaĵo; (to fix dye), tinkturfiksenzo
Mordecai, Mordeĥaj
more, (adv), pli (e.g.: I ate more than you did: mi manĝis pli ol vi; more magnificent: pli grandioza); (adj:

more of), pli da (e.g.: *we saw more
deer than you did:* ni vidis pli da cer-
voj ol vi); (adj: further, additional),
plua, plia (e.g.: *one more guest has
come:* unu plua [or: plia] gasto alvenis); **moreover**, plu, cetere, krome;
more or less, pli-malpli; **not any
more, no more**, (no longer), ne plu,
jam ne; **the more ..., the more (less)**,
ju pli ..., des (mal)pli (e.g.: *the more I
hear, the more impatient I get:* ju pli
mi aŭdas, des pli mi malpacienciĝas;
*the more you tell me about it, the less
I like it:* ju pli vi diras al mi pri ĝi, des
malpli mi ŝatas ĝin; *the sooner, the
better [more soon, more good]:* ju pli
baldaŭ, des pli bone); **all the more**,
des pli [for e.g., see under "all"]
morel, morkelo
morello, grioto
mores, moroj
morganatic, morganata
morgue, (gen), kadavrejo [cp "mortuary"]
moribund, mortanta, kaduka
Mormon, Mormono; ~a; **Mormonism**,
~ismo
morning, mateno; ~a; **good morning!**,
(greeting), bonan ~on!; **in the morning**, ~e; **it is morning**, ~as; **early in
the morning**, fru~e; **mid-morning**,
~meza; ~meze; **the morning after
the night before**, postebrio, la ~o
post la antaŭa nokto
morocco, marokeno
Morocco, Maroko; **Moroccan**, ~ano;
~a
moron, debilulo [cp "idiot", "imbecile",
"retard"]
Moroni, (capital of Comoros), Moronio*
morose, moroza
morpheme, morfemo
Morpheus, Morfeo
morphine, morfino; **morphinism**, (toxic condition), ~ismo; (addiction),
~omanio
morphogenesis, morfogenezo
morphology, morfologio
Morris, Maŭrico
morse, (code), morsa; **signal by morse
code**, ~i [tr]

morsel, mordaĵo
mortal, (re death: dead), morta (e.g.:
mortal remains: ~aj restaĵoj); (that
will die), ~onta, ~ideva; ~onto (e.g.:
our mortal bodies: niaj ~ontaj korpoj;
we mortals: ni ~ontoj); (deadly, fatal),
~iga (e.g.: *mortal wound:* ~iga vundo); **mortality**, (necessity to die),
~emo; (death rate), ~okvanto; **im-
mortal**,   sen~a;   **immortalality**,
sen~eco
mortar, (sand-lime mixture), mortero;
(for grinding), pistujo; (gun), bombo-
kanono; **mortarboard**, (gen), ~tabulo
mortgage, hipoteko; ~i [tr]
mortician, funebraĵisto,   sepult(entrepren)isto
mortify, humiligi, ĉagreni [tr]
mortise, mortezo; ~i [tr]
mortuary, sepultistejo [cp "sepulcher",
"morgue"]
morula, morulo
Morus, moruso
mos, moro
mosaic, (art; plant disease), mozaiko;
~a
Moschus, moskulo; Moschinae, ~enoj
Moscow, Moskvo
Mosel(le), (river), Mozelo; (wine), ~vi-
no
Moses, Moseo; **Mosaic**, ~a
moshav, moŝavo*
Moslem, Islama; ~ano
mosque, moskeo
mosquito, moskito;   **mosquito
net(ting)**, kulvualo, ~o-reto
moss, (gen), musko; **mossy**, ~a; **club
moss**, (*Lycopodium*), likopodio; (*Se-
laginella*), selaginelo; **plume moss**,
hipno; **reindeer moss**, kladonio; **rose
moss**, ĝardena portulako
most, (adv), plej (e.g.: *the most beautiful picture:* la plej bela bildo); (adv:
very), tre (e.g.: *a most fortunate
event:* tre feliĉa evento); (adj, n: most
of, majority), la plejmulto, plejparto
(da, de, el) (e.g.: *most people know
that:* la plejmulto da homoj scias tion;
*we made some errors, but John made
the most:* ni faris kelkajn erarojn, sed
Johano faris la plejmulton; *we finished most of it:* ni finis la plejparton

de ĝi); **mostly, for the most part**, plejparte; **at the (very) most**, maksimume

–most, (sfx), plej– [pfx], plej (e.g.: *northernmost:* plej norda; *uppermost:* plej alta)

Mosul, Mosulo

Motacilla, motacilo, vostskuanto; **Motacillidae**, ~edoj

motel, motelo

motet, moteto

moth, (any small, grayish moth), moteo; (*Phalaena*), faleno; **mothball**, (lit), naftalenbuleto; (fig: store away), stapli [tr]; **in mothballs**, (fig), staplita; **clothes moth**, (*Tinea*), tineo; **emperor moth**, saturnio; **silkworm moth**, bombikso; **tiger moth**, arktio; **underwing moth**, katokalo

mother, (gen), patrino; (act like mother toward), ~umi [tr], ~i [int] al; (give birth to), naski [tr]; **motherhood**, ~eco; **motherly**, ~(ec)a; **mother-in-law**, bo~o; **motherland**, patrio, patrolando; **mother-of-pearl**, perlamoto; perlamota; **mother-of-thousands**, (ivy), cimbalario; **godmother**, bapto~o; **single mother**, sol~o†; **stepmother**, duon~o

Mo Ti, Mozi

motif, motivo

motile, moviĝema

motion, (movement, gen), movo; ~iĝo; (formal proposal in meeting), mocio†; (law: request), peto; (gesture), signi [tr]; gesti [int]; **slow-motion**, (film etc.), lant~a; **on one's own motion**, propra~e, propravole; **go through the motions (of)**, fari la ~ojn (de, por); **in motion**, ~iĝanta; **be in motion**, ~iĝi

motivate, instigi [tr] [not "motivi"]

motive, (reason, incentive, etc.), motivo; (moving), mova; **ulterior motive**, privata ~o

motley, diversa, heterogena

motor, (engine), motoro; ~a; ~ista; (~e) iri [int], veturi [int] (etc.); (anat), mova (e.g.: *motor nerve:* mova nervo); **motoring**, aŭtomobilismo; **motorist**, ~isto; **motorize**, ~izi [tr]; **motorcade**, aŭtokavalkado; **motorcycle**, ~ciklo

mottled, makul(har)a, jaspita

motto, (gen), devizo; (phrase etc. at beginning of book), moto

mouf(f)lon, muflono

mould, [see "mold"]

moulder, putri [int]

moult, [see "molt"]

mound, (gen), altaĵeto; (burial), tumulo

mount, (fix, place, etc., as mech part, jewel, photo), munti [tr]; (climb on, as horse, bicycle), surseliĝi (sur); (climb, as stairs), supreniri [tr]; (get up on, as platform; on animal for copulation), suriri [tr]; (riding animal), rajdbesto; (support, setting, as for jewel etc.), ~umo; (mountain), monto; **mounted**, (as jewel etc.), ~ita; (on horseback), rajda, rajd– [pfx]; **Mountie**, (member of Canadian RCMP), (Kanada) Rajda Ĝendarmo, Rajdpolicisto; **mounting**, (act), ~ado; (setting), ~umo; **dismount**, (from horse, bike, etc.), elseliĝi; elseliĝi; (take apart), mal~i [tr]; **remount**, (mil), remonto

mountain, monto; ~a; **mountaineer**, ~ano; **mountainous**, ~ara, ~eca; **mountain range**, ~aro

mountebank, ĉarlatano

mourn, funebri [tr, int]; lamenti [int] (pri), prilamenti [tr]; **mournful**, ~a, morna; **mourning**, ~o; **be in mourning**, ~i

mouse, (zool; cmptr), muso; **mouse-ear**, (bot), cerastio; **fieldmouse**, kampo~o; **marsupial mouse**, (Aus), marsupia ~o; **sea mouse**, afrodito

mousquetaire, musketero

mousse, ŝaŭm/frandaĵo, ~kaĉo

moustache, lipharoj [note plur]

Moust(i)erian, Musteria; **Mousterian era**, ~o

mouth, (anat. or similar object); buŝo; ~a; (of wild animal, or similar object, as cave, furnace, etc.), faŭko; (of river etc., gen), enfluejo; (into sea), enmariĝo; (utter), el~igi; (form words silently w mouth), ~e mimi [tr]; **mouthpiece**, (of mus instrument, pipe, etc.), ~aĵo; (speaker for), proparolanto; **mouth-to-mouth**, ~-al-~a; **mouthwash**, gargaraĵo; **mouth-watering**, saliviga; **bellmouthed**, kloŝ~a; **mealy-mouthed**, subtilaĉa, malrekt(aĉ)a, malsincera; **down in the mouth**, malgajmiena

mouton, ŝafidopelto

move, (cause or have motion; change position; chess or oth game), movi [tr]; ~iĝi; ~o; (change residence), transloĝigi; transloĝiĝi; transloĝiĝo; (stir to action, instigate), instigi [tr]; (stir feelings), emocii [tr], afekcii [tr]; (offer formal motion in meeting), mocii† [int], fari mocion†; **movement**, (motion), ~iĝ(ad)o; (pol, social cause, campaign), ~ado (e.g.: *the Esperanto movement:* la Esperanta ~ado); (moving parts, as of watch etc.), ~ilaro; (division of mus work), movimento; **mover**, transloĝisto; **move ahead**, (progress), progresi [int], antaŭeniri [int]; progresigi; **move around**, (circulate), cirkul(ad)i [int]; cirkul(ad)igi; **move in**, (residence), enloĝiĝi; **move into**, enloĝiĝi en (~on); **move heaven and earth to**, senlime klopodi [int]

movie, kina; (~)filmo; **movies**, (the art), ~o; **movie theater**, ~ejo, ~teatro

mow, (cut grass from lawn etc.), tondi [tr]; (cut lawn), pri~i [tr]; (cut tall grass, hay, etc.; reap), falĉi [tr]; pri-falĉi [tr]; **lawn mower**, gazon~ilo; **mowing machine**, falĉomaŝino

moxa, mokso

Mozambique, Mozambiko; **Mozambique Channel**, Kanalo ~a

Mozarab, Mozarabo; ~a

Mozart, Mozarto

MP, (abb of "military police"), milit-polico; ~ano, ~isto [no abb in Esperanto]; (member of parliament), parlamentano

Mr. s~ro [abb of "sinjoro"]; **Mr. and Mrs.**, (la) ges~roj [abb of "gesinjoroj"] (e.g.: *I visited Mr. and Mrs. Smith:* mi vizitis la ges-ojn Smith)

Mrs. s~ino [abb of "sinjorino"]

Ms. s~ino [abb of "sinjorino"]

mu, mu [see § 16]

much, multa; ~e (da); ~o (e.g.: *much talk:* ~a parolado; *much hotter:* ~e pli varma; *there was much lightning:* estis ~e da fulmo; *we have done much, but much remains:* ni jam faris ~on,

sed ~o restas); **not much**, mal~a, ne ~a; mal~e, ne ~e, ne~e, ne tre (e.g.: *I don't much like that:* mi ne tre [or: ne ~e] ŝatas tion); **not much of a**, mal~a; **very much**, tre, tre ~e, ~e (e.g.: *I love you very much:* mi tre amas vin; *thank you very much:* ~e dankon [or] mi tre dankas); **too much, much too much**, [see under "too"]; **so much the better**, des pli bone (e.g.: *if the rain stops, so much the better:* se la pluvo ĉesos, des pli bone); **much as one (does something)**, (in spite of how much), malgraŭ (tiom) kiom oni (far-as ion) (e.g.: *much as she tried, she couldn't escape:* malgraŭ kiom ŝi penis, ŝi ne povis eskapi; *I must go home now, much as I would like to stay:* mi devas iri hejmen nun, malgraŭ tiom kiom mi ŝatus resti); **as much as**, (same amount, to same degree), tiom kiom, egale kiel, samkiom (e.g.: *I like jazz as much as classical music:* mi ŝatas ĵazon egale kiel la klasikan muzikon; *pay as much in taxes as one earns:* pagi tiom por impostoj kiom oni lukras); (up to), ĝis (e.g.: *as much as half of it is always wasted:* oni ĉiam malŝparas ĝis duono de ĝi); **how much**, kiom (da); **how much of a**, ki-oma (e.g.: *I don't know how much of a response they'll make:* mi ne scias ki-oman respondon ili faros); **that much, so much**, tiom (da); **that (so) much of a**, tioma

mucid, mucida

mucilage, mucilago; **mucilaginous**, ~a

muck, (ooze), fango; (mud), koto; (dirt, gen), malpuraĵo; (manure), sterko

mucor, mukoro

mucosa, mukozo

mucous, muka; **mucous membrane**, mukozo

mucus, muko

mud, koto; **muddy**, ~a; ~izi [tr]; **mud puddle**, ~ejo; **mud flat**, (tidal), tajd~ejo; (of river, lake, etc.), bor-do~ejo

muddle, konfuzi [tr]; ~iĝi; ~o; **muddle through**, (manage, hold out), (iel) elteni [tr, int]

Mudejar, Mudeharo

muezzin, muezino
muff, (bungle), fuŝi [tr]; ~o; (to warm hands, or similar-shaped object), mufo; (tuft), tufo
muffin, taspano [cp "cupcake"]; **English muffin**, (Angla) tasflano
muffle, (sound), dampi [tr] [cp "damp", "dull", "mute"]; (oven), mufli [tr]; muflo; (wrap in shawl etc.), enŝaligi, ŝalvolvi [tr]; **muffled**, ~ita, obtuza; **muffler**, (for sound, as on car), ~ilo; (scarf), ŝalo
mufti, (rel), muftio; (clothes), civila vesto
mug, (assault), ataki [tr]; (cup), tasego; (make faces), vizaĝaĉi [int]; **mugger**, ~into; ~isto; **mug shot**, vizaĝofoto
muggy, (varm)humida
Mugil, mugilo; Mugiliformes, ~oformaj (fiŝoj)
muguet, mugeto
mugwort, artemizio
Muhammad, Mohamedo
mulatto, mulato
mulberry, (fruit), moruso, ~bero; (tree), ~o, ~arbo; **paper mulberry**, brusonetio
mulch, mulĉo; ~izi [tr]
mule, mulo [see "hinny"]
muleta, muletao†
Mulhausen, Mulhaŭzo
Mulhouse, Mulhaŭzo
mull, (ponder), mediti [int], pens(ad)i [int]; (heat and spice, as wine), spici [tr] kaj varmigi; **mull over**, pripensi [tr], pri~i [tr]
mulla(h), mulao
mullein, verbasko
mullet, (*Mugil*), mugilo; **red mullet**, (*Mullus*), surmuleto
mulligatawney, karea supo
mullion, fenestrokruco
Mullus, surmuleto
multi–, (pfx: many, plural), mult(e)–, plur– (e.g.: *multicolored:* ~kolora; *a multistorey building:* pluretaĝa konstruaĵo)
multifarious, diversspeca, multopa
multiple, (math), oblo (e.g.: *42 is a multiple of 7:* 42 estas ~o de 7); (of many parts, gen), mult~a, plur~a
multiplet, multopo

multiplex, multobla; ~i [int]
multiplicity, multobleco
multiply, (math), multipliki [tr]; (become more numerous), multigi; multiĝi; (breed), brediĝi; **multiplication**, ~o; ~a (e.g.: *multiplication table:* ~a tabelo); **multiplicand**, ~ato; **multiplier**, ~anto
Multituberculata, multetuberuloj
multitude, (of anything), amaso, multego; (people), hom~o, popol~o; **multitudinous**, multegaj, multnombraj
mum, (silent), silenta; (Br: mom), panjo; (chrysanthemum), krizantemo; (theat), maskmimi [tr]
mumble, murmuri [tr, int]; ~o
mumbo-jumbo, (ritual), ritaĉo; (superstition), superstiĉaĉo; (gibberish), (sorĉ)galimatio
mummer, maskmimisto
mummy, mumio; **mummify**, ~igi
mumps, mumpso
munch, maĉ(ad)i [tr]
München, Munkeno
mundane, (ordinary), ĉiutaga, ordinara; (worldly), mond(ec)a
Mungo, (zool), mungoto
Munich, Munkeno
municipal, municipa; **municipality**, ~o
municipium, (Roman town), municipo
munificent, malavarega, grandanimega; **munificence**, ~eco
munition, pafilaĵ/izi [tr]; **munitions**, ~oj [cp "ammunition"]
muon, muono
Muraena, mureno
mural, (re wall), mura; (picture), ~bildo
murder, murdi [tr]; ~o; **murderer**, ~into; ~isto; **murderous**, ~(ec)a
Murex, murekso
Muridae, musedoj
murk, krepusko, malhelo, mallumo; **murky**, ~a, malhela, malluma
murmur, (gen), murmuri [tr, int]; ~o; (as water in brook, on roof), lirli [int]; lirlo; (whisper, rustle, as wind in trees), susuri [int]; susuro
murre, urio
Mus, muso; Mus rattus, rato
Musa, bananarbo
Musca, muŝo
muscardine, muskardino

Muscat, (city), Maskato; **Muscat and Oman**, ~o kaj Omano
muscatel, moskatelo
Musci, musko
muscle, muskolo [for specific anat muscle names, see separate entries]; **muscle fiber**, miono
muscovite, (mineral), muskovito
Muscovite, (of Moscow), Moskva; ~ano
muscular, muskola; **musculature**, ~aro; **intramuscular**, intra~a
musculus, muskolo [see "muscle"]
muse, (ponder), mediti [int] [not "muz–"]
Muse, (myth), Muzo
museum, muzeo
mush, kaĉo
mushroom, (gen), fungo; (any of *Agaricus*), agariko; **mushroom cloud**, fum~o; **milk mushroom**, laktario, lakto~o; **pore mushroom**, poliporo
music, muziko; **musical**, ~a; ~aĵo; **musician**, ~isto; **musicology**, ~ologio; **musicologist**, ~ologo; **play (sing) music**, ~i [int]; **incidental music**, (to accompany play, movie, etc.), scenej~o; **set to music**, ~igi; **face the music**, alfronti la sekvojn
musk, mosko; **musky**, ~(ec)a
muskeg, muskmarĉo
musket, musketo; **musketeer**, (musket user), ~isto; (mousquetaire), musketero
muskmelon, (*Cucumis melo*), melono
muskrat, fibero, ondatro
muslin, muslino
musquash, fibero, ondatro
muss, (disarrange, gen), malaranĝi [tr], malordi [tr]; (tousle hair), taŭzi [tr]
mussel, mitilo
Mussulman, Islamano, Muzulmano [cp "Islam", "Mohammedan"]
must, devas (e.g.: *I must go:* mi ~as iri; *you must be Ms. Jones:* vi ~as esti s–ino Jones) [cp "should", "need"]; (necessity), neprajô (e.g.: *that museum is a must during your visit:* tiu muzeo estas neprajô dum via vizito); (new wine), mosto
mustache, lipharoj [note plur]
Mustagh, Karakorumo

mustang, mustango†
mustard, (food), mustardo; (plant), sinapo; **mustard gas**, iperito, ~a gaso; **treacle mustard, wormseed mustard**, erizimio
Mustela, mustelo; Mustelidae, ~edoj; Mustelinae, ~enoj; Mustela erminea, ermeno; Mustela furo, furo; Mustela lutreola, Mustela foetidus, putoro; Mustela vison, vizono
musteline, mustelana
muster, (mil), apelo; ~i [tr]; ~iĝi; (gather, gen), kolekti [tr]; kolektiĝi; (Aus: re cattle, sheep), bovkunpelo; ŝafkunpelo **muster in**, entrupigi; **muster out**, eltrupigi; **pass muster**, elteni ~on
musty, moska
mutable, ŝanĝebla; **immutable**, ne~a
mutarotation, mutarotacio
mutate, mutacii [int]; ~igi; **mutation**, ~o; **mutant**, ~into; ~a
mute, (unable to speak; silent), muta; ~igi; (mus; muffle sound, gen), dampi [tr], obtuzigi, ~igi; dampilo, ~ilo; (for violin etc.), sordino; **muted**, obtuza, dampita; **deafmute**, surda~ulo
mutilate, (med), mutili [tr]; (gen), kripligi, stumpigi, difekti [tr]
mutiny, ribeli [int]; ~o; **mutinous**, ~ema; **mutineer**, ~anto, ~ulo
mutter, murmuri [tr, int]; ~o
mutton, ŝafaĵo
mutual, (reciprocal), reciproka, inter– [pfx] (e.g.: *mutual admiration:* ~a admiro; *mutual agreement:* interkonsento); (in common), komuna (e.g.: *mutual friend:* komuna amiko); (society, $ etc.), mutuala
muumuu, Havaja robo
muzzle, (snout), muzelo; (strap etc. over snout), ~ingo; (keep quiet, put muzzle on), ~ingizi [tr]; (of gun), buŝo
my, mia; **my –ing**, [see under "her"]
myalgia, mialgio
myasthenia, miastenio
mycelium, micelio
Mycenae, Miceno
mycete, miceto
mycetoma, perikalo
myc(o)–, (pfx), micet(o)–

mycology, micetologio, mikologio
mycomycetes, mikomicetoj
mycor(r)hiza, mikorizo
mycosis, micetozo, mikozo
mydriasis, midriazo; **mydriatic**, ~iga;
~igenzo
myelin, mjelino
myelitis, mjelito
myel(o)–, (anat pfx: spinal cord),
mjel(o)–
myelogram, mjelogramo
myelopathy, mjelopatio
Mygale, (spider: *Avicularia*), migalo
myitis, miito
myna(h), majno*
my(o)–, (anat pfx: muscle), mi(o)–
myocardium, miokardio; **myocardial**,
~a
Myocastor coypus, kojpo
Myogale, miogalo; Myogalinae, ~enoj
myoma, miomo
myopia, miop/eco; **myopic**, ~a
myosote, miozoto, neforgesumino
Myosotis, miozoto, neforgesumino
Myoxus, muskardeno
myria–, (pfx: 10^4), miria–
myriad, miriado (da)
myriapod, miriapodo
Myriapoda, miriapodoj
Myrica, miriko
myricyl, miricilo; **myricyl alcohol**, ~a
alkoholo
myringa, miringo; **myringectomy**,
~ektomio; **myringitis**, ~ito; **myrin-
gotomy**, ~otomio
myristate, mirist/ato; **myristic acid**, ~a
acido
Myristica, miristiko; Myristica fra-
grans, muskatujo, muskatarbo
Myrmecophaga, mirmekofago, formik-
urso
Myrmeleon, mirmeleono, formikleono
Myrmidon, Mirmidono
myrobalan, mirobalano
Myroxylon, balzamarbo
myrrh, mirho
Myrrhis, mirido
myrtle, mirto; **bog myrtle**, menianto
Myrtle, (woman's name), Mirtoa
Myrtus, mirto
Mysore, (city), Majsuro; (state), ~lando
mystery, (gen), mistero; (mysterious

thing), ~o, ~aĵo; **mysterious**, ~a
mystic, mistika; ~ulo; **mystical**, ~a;
mysticism, ~ismo
mystify, perpleksigi [not "mistifiki"]
mystique, mistiko
myth, mito; **mythical**, ~a; **mythology**,
~ologio; **mythological**, ~ologia;
mythologist, ~ologo; **mythomania**,
~omanio
Mytilene, Mytileni, Mitileno
Mytilus, mitilo
myxedema, miksedemo
Myxine, miksino
myxoma, miksomo; **myxomatosis**,
miksomatozo
Myxomycetes, miksomicetoj, mukfun-
goj
Myxophyceae, blualgoj

N

nab, kapti [tr]
nabob, (gen), nabobo
Naboth, Naboto
nacelle, nacelo
nacre, perlamoto; ~a
nadir, nadiro
nag, (annoy), ĉagren(aĉ)i [tr], riproĉaĉi [tr]; ~emulo; (horse), ĉevalaĉo
Nagasaki, Nagasako
Nagoya, Nagojo
Nahuatl, Naŭatlo*; ~a
Nahum, Naĥumo
naiad, najado
nail, (metal fastener), najlo; (al)~i [tr]; fingernail, ungo; toenail, piedungo; (finger)nail polish, ungolako; nail-clippers, ungotondilo [note sing]; nail-puller, ~otirilo; pull nails, mal~i [tr]; hit the nail on the head, ĝuste trafi (la aferon)
naïve, naiva; naïveté, ~eco
Naja, najo; Naja haje, aspido; Naja tripudians, kobro
naked, nuda; nakedness, ~eco; stark naked, tute ~a
namby-pamby, sentimentalaĉa, afekt(aĉ)a
name, nomo; (give name to; describe as), ~i [tr]; (assign to position etc.), ~umi [tr]; namely, ~e; name after, ~i laŭ; nameplate, ~plato; namesake, sam~ulo; Christian name, bapto~o; first name, given name, donita ~o; nickname, neformala ~o, ŝerc~o, mok~o; surname, last name, family name, familia ~o [not "lasta ~o", since surnames are not always last]; place name, lok~o; by name, laŭ~e; by the name of, in the name of, ~e de; call (one) names, ~aĉi [tr] (iun)
Namibia, Namibiot; Namibian Desert, Dezerto ~a
Namur, (city), Namuro; (province), ~io
Nancy, (woman's name), Agnesa; (city), Nancio*
Nanjing, Nankino
nankeen, nankin, nankeno

Nan Ling, Nanlingo
nano–, (pfx), nano– (e.g.: nanosecond: ~sekundo)
Nan Shan, Nanlingo
naos, naoso
nap, (sleep), dormeti [int]; ~o [cp "doze," "siesta"]; (of cloth), vilo
napalm, napalmo; ~i [tr]
nape, nuko
Naphthali, Naftali
naphtha, (petroleum fraction, distillate), petrolo; (crude petroleum), nafto
naphthalene, naftaleno
naphthene, nafteno
naphth(o)–, (chem root), nafto–
naphthol, naftolo
naphthyl, naftilo
napkin, buŝtuko; (Br: diaper), bebtuko
Naples, Napolo
Napoleon, Napoleono; Napoleonic, ~a
Napoli, Napolo
nappie, nappy, bebtuko
Naraka, narako
narcissism, narcisismo; narcissist, ~ulo; narcissistic, ~a
narcissus, narciso
Narcisus, (myth), Narciso
Narcisus, (bot), narciso
narco–, (pfx), narko–
narcoanalysis, narkoanalizo
narcolepsy, narkolepsio; narcoleptic, ~a, ~ulo
narcosis, narkozo
narcotic, narkota; ~aĵo, ~iko; ~ulo; narcotism, ~ismo; narcotize, ~i [tr]; narcotization, ~ado; ~iĝo
narcotine, narkotino
nard, (ointment), nardo; (plant), ~planto
narg(h)ile(h), nargileo
narrate, rakonti [tr]; narration, narrative, ~o; ~a; narrator, ~into; ~anto; ~isto
narrow, mallarĝa; ~igi; ~iĝi; ~o; ~aĵo; (poet), streta; narrows, ~ejo [note sing] [cp "strait"]; narrowness, ~eco
narthex, nartekso
narw(h)al(e), narvalo

nasal, (re nose), naza; (sound; bone), nazalo; nazala; nasalize, nazaligi; postnasal, post~a; postnasal drip, post~a gutado
nascent, naskiĝanta; (chem), naskiĝa
nasturtium, (*Tropaeolum*), tropeolo
Nasturtium officinale, nasturcio, akvokreso
nasty, (filthy), malpurega; (offensive), aĉa, malagrabla; (malicious), malica; (troubling), ĉagrena; (awful, extreme), terura (e.g.: *a nasty cold:* terura malvarmumo)
Nasua, nazuo
natal, (re giving birth), naska; (re being born), ~iĝa; (from birth), de~a; postnatal, post~a; prenatal, antaŭ~a
Natal, Natalo
Natalie, Natalia
Nathan, Natano
nation, (a people), nacio (e.g.: *Indian nations:* Indianaj ~oj); (country), lando, ~o, ŝtato; national, landa, ~a, ŝtata; landano, ~ano, ŝtatano; nationalism, ~ismo; nationalist, ~isma; ~isto; nationality, ~eco; nationalize, (thing, person), ~ecigi; (socialize industry etc.), ŝtatigi, ~igi; nationwide, tutlanda; international, inter~a; (Marxist), Inter~o; supranational, super~a; United Nations, Unuiĝintaj N~oj [abb: UN, UNo]
native, (indigenous), indiĝen; ~a; (innate), denaska (e.g.: *native talent:* denaska talento); (specially characteristic, own), propra (e.g.: *a custom native to the English:* moro propra al la Angloj); (natural, unaltered), natura; nativity, naskiĝo
NATO, (abb of "North Atlantic Treaty Organization"), NATO [abb of "Nord-Atlantika Traktat-Organizo"]
natter, babil(ad)i [int]
natty, eleganta
nature, (gen), naturo, la ~o; natural, ~a; (mus), bekvadrato; bekvadrata, ~a; naturalism, (gen), naturalismo; naturalist, naturalisma; naturalisto; naturalize, (plant etc.), ~igi; (make citizen; adopt word from oth language etc.), naturalizi [tr]; naturism, (nudism), ~ismo, nudismo; naturist, ~is-

ma, nudisma; ~isto, nudisto; denature, de~i [tr]; denaturant, de~enzo; good-natured, afabla, bonhumora, komplezema; preternatural, preter~a; supernature, super~o; super~a; unnatural, kontraŭ~a, ne~a
naugahyde, artledo
naught, nenio
naughty, miskonduta; be naughty, ~i [int]
Nauru, Nauro†
nausea, naŭzo, vomemo; nauseate, ~i [tr]; nauseating, nauseous, ~a
Nausicaa, Naŭsikaa
nautical, naŭtika
nautilus, Nautilus, chambered nautilus, naŭtilo; paper nautilus, argonaŭto
naval, mararmea, militflota
Navarre, Navarra, Navaro
nave, (of church), navo; (hub), nabo
navel, umbiliko
navicular, (in foot), navikulario; (in wrist), skafoido
navigate, navigi [tr, int]; navigation, ~ado; navigational, ~a; navigable, ~ebla; navigator, ~isto; astronavigate, ~i per la steloj [cp "astrogate"]; circumnavigate, ĉirkaŭ~i [tr]
navvy, fosisto, teraĵisto
navy, mararmeo, militfloto
Naxos, Nakso
Nazarene, Nazoreo; ~a
Nazareth, Nazareto
Nazi, nazia; ~o; Nazi(i)sm, ~ismo
N.B. (abb of "nota bene"), N.B. [abb of "notu bone"]
né naskita
Neanderthal, (valley), Neandertalo; (person), ~a homo, ~ulo
neap, morta; ~a tajdo
Neapolitan, Napola; ~ano
near, (close), proksima; ~e(n); al~iĝi (al); (adjacent but not touching), apud [cp "at"]; (adj: almost), preskaŭa (e.g.: *a near miracle:* preskaŭa miraklo); (barely), apenaŭa (e.g.: *a near miss:* apenaŭa maltrafo [or: preskaŭa trafo]); nearby, ~a, apuda; ~e(n), apude(n); nearly, preskaŭ
neat, (w/o corrections etc., re written material; w/o irregularities, re thing

made), neta; (tidy, ordered), ~a, orda;
(orderly, as person), ordema; (good,
okay), bona

Nebraska, Nebrasko

Nebuchadnezzar, Nebuchadrezzar,
Nebukadnecaro

nebula, nebulozo; **nebular,** ~a

nebulous, nebul(ec)a

necessary, necesa; **be necessary,** ~i
[int]; **necessity,** ~o, nepreco; ~aĵo,
nepraĵo; **necessitate,** ~igi

neck, (anat, or similar object), kolo;
(length), ~longo (e.g.: *win by a neck:*
gajni je ~longo); (smooch), amindumi
[tr]; **necking,** amindumado; **neck-
and-neck,** flank-al-flanka; **necklace,**
koliero, ~ĉeno, saltiero; **neckline,**
~linio; **necktie,** kravato; **rubber-
neck,** gapvagi [int]; **rubbernecker,**
gapvagulo; **stiff-necked,** (obstinate),
obstina, malmolnuka; **nape (back) of
the neck,** nuko; **stick one's neck out,**
riski sin

necro–, (pfx), nekro–

necrobiosis, nekrobiozo

necrology, nekrologio

necromancy, nekromancio

necrophilia, necrophilism, nekrofilio

necrophobia, nekrofobio

Necrophorus, nekroforo

necropolis, nekropolo

necropsy, nekropsio; ~i [tr]

necrose, nekrozi [tr]; ~iĝi; **necrosis,**
~o; **necrotic,** ~a

nectar, nektaro; **nectar gland,** ~glando,
nektario

nectarine, (fruit), nektarino; (tree), ~ar-
bo, ~ujo

née, naskita

need, (require, have necessity for), bezoni [tr]; ~o; (poverty), malriĉeco;
needed, needful, ~ata, necesa; **needless,** nenecesa; **needy,** ($), malriĉa,
senhava; (psych etc.), ~hava; mal-
riĉulo(j), senhavulo(j); **as needed,**
laŭ~e; **needless to say,** ne necesas diri (ke); **there's no need to,** ne necesas
~i

needle, (for sewing), kudrilo; (of record
player, compass, carburetor, syringe,
etc.; pointed rock outcropping), nadlo;
(of pine tree etc.), pinglo; (goad, irri-

tate), iriteti [tr]; **needlepoint,** (embroidery), lanbrod/ado; ~aĵo; **needle
valve,** ŝtoppinto; **needlework,** ~ado;
~aĵo; **knitting needle,** trikilo

ne'er-do-well, nenifaranto

nefarious, fi(eg)a, kanajla

negate, (deny), nei [tr]; (make ineffective), senefikigi, malefektivigi [cp
"nullify"]; **negation,** neado; (gram),
negacio

negative, (gen), negativa; ~o; (gram),
negacio; **negativism,** ~ismo; **negativ-
ist,** ~isma; ~isto

negatron, (negative electron), negato-
no; (electron tube), negatrono

Negev, Negeb, Negebo

neglect, neglekti [tr], malatenti [tr];
~(ad)o, malatento, senzorgo; **neglect-
ful,** ~ema, malatenta, malzorgema

negligee, negliĝo

negligent, neglekta; ~ema; **negli-
gence,** ~(ad)o

negligible, nerimarkinda, neatentinda,
nekonsiderinda

negotiate, negoci [int], intertrakti [int];
pri~i [tr], pritrakti [tr]; **negotia-
tion(s),** ~ado, (pri)traktado

Negro, Negro; ~a [cp "black"]; **Ne-
groid,** ~oida; ~oido; **Negritude,** ~eco

Negroponte, Eŭbeo

Negus, Neguso

Nehemiah, Neĥemja

neigh, heni [int]; ~o

neighbor, najbaro; ~a; **neighborhood,**
(area), ~ejo; (approximation), proksimeco; **neighboring,** ~a, apuda;
neighborly, ~eca; **in the neighborhood of,** (approximately), proksimume, ĉirkaŭ

Neisse, Niso

neither, (of two), ambaŭ ne, neniu (e.g.:
neither one of them came: ambaŭ el ili
ne venis [or] neniu el ili venis); (conj:
also not), nek, ankaŭ ne (e.g.: *I didn't
see it, and neither did she:* mi ne vidis
ĝin, kaj nek ŝi [or] kaj ankaŭ ŝi ne);
neither ... nor, nek ... nek (e.g.: *they
chose neither him nor her:* ili elektis
nek lin nek ŝin; *it neither rained nor
snowed:* nek pluvis nek neĝis); **me
neither,** nek mi

Nelumbium speciosum, hinda lotuso

Nelumbo nucifera, hinda lotuso
Neman, Nemano
Nemathelminthes, nematelmintoj, fadenvermoj
Nematoda, nematodoj
nematode, nematodo
Nemea, Nemeo; **Nemean,** ~a
nemesis, nemezo
Nemesis, Nemeza
Nemunas, Nemano
neo–, (pfx), neo–, nov–
neodymium, neodimo
neolithic, neolitiko; ~a
neologism, neologismo; **neologistic(al),** ~a; **neologist,** neologo
neon, neono
neonate, novnaskito
Neophron, neofrono
neophyte, neofito
neoplasia, neoplazio
neoplasm, neoplasmo
neoprene, neopreno
Neopterygii, teleosteoj
Neottia, neotio
Nepal, Nepalo; **Nepalese,** ~ano; ~a
nepenthe(s), nepento
neper, nepero
Nepeta, nepeto; Nepeta cataria, katario
nephew, nevo
nepho–, (pfx), nefo–
nephology, nefologio
nephometer, nefometro
nephoscope, nefoskopo
nephrectomy, nefrektomio
nephridium, nefridio†
nephritis, nefrito
nephr(o)–, (pfx), nefro–
nephrology, nefrologio
nephron, nefrono
nephropathy, nefropatio
nephrosis, nefrozo
nepotism, nepotismo
Neptune, (myth; ast), Neptuno; **Neptunian,** ~a
neptunium, neptunio
Nereid, nereidino
Nereis, nereo
Nereus, Nereo
Nerium, nerio; Nerium oleander, oleandro
Nero, Nerono; **Neronian,** ~a
nerve, (anat, or analogous thing), ner-
vo; (audacity), aŭdaco; (coolness, courage), kuraĝo; **nerves,** (nervousness), ~oj, nervozeco; **unnerving,** konsterna, maltrankviliga; **abducens nerve,** abdukta ~o; **(spinal) accessory nerve,** akcesora ~o; **acoustic nerve,** (stato–)akustika ~o; **cranial nerve,** krania ~o; **facial nerve,** facia ~o; **glossopharyngeal nerve,** glosofaringa ~o; **hypoglossal nerve,** hipoglosa ~o; **oculomotor nerve,** okulmotora ~o; **olfactory nerve,** olfakta ~o; **optic nerve,** optika ~o; **sciatic nerve,** iskiato; **splanchnic nerve,** splankniko; **trigeminal nerve,** triĝemina ~o; **trochlear nerve,** troklea ~o; **vagus nerve,** vaga ~o; **get on (one's) nerves,** agaci [tr] (iun); **have the nerve to,** aŭdaci [tr]
nervous, (re nerves), nerva; (agitated, excitable), nervoza: **nervous system,** (gen), ~a sistemo; **autonomic nervous system,** aŭtonomia ~a sistemo; **sympathetic nervous system,** simpato; **parasympathetic nervous system,** parasimpato
nervure, nervuro
–ness, (sfx), –eco (e.g.: *happiness:* kontenteco)
Nessus, Nesso
nest, nesto; ~i [int]; ~igi; **crow's nest,** (of ship etc.), gvat~o
nestle, (sit, lie as in nest, lit or fig), nesti [int]; (snuggle), premkaresi [tr]; premkaresiĝi
Nestor, (man's name), Nestoro
Nestor notabilis, (zool), keo
Nestorius, Nestorio; **Nestorian,** ~ano; ~a; **Nestorianism,** ~anismo
net, (of mesh, gen), reto; en~igi; (cone-shaped, to catch fish etc.), naso; (re weight, salary etc.: after deductions), neta; netaĵo; **netting,** ~aĵo; **dragnet,** tren~o, sejno; **fishnet,** fiŝ~o; **hairnet,** har~o
nether, suba
Netherlands, Nederlando
nettle, (bot), urtiko; (burn, annoy like a nettle, lit or fig), ~i [int]; **nettle rash,** urtikario; **nettle tree,** (*Celtis*), celtido; **dead nettle,** lamio; **hedge nettle,** stakiso; **hemp nettle,** galeopso; **sea**

nettle, meduzo

network, (radio, TV, roads, colleagues, etc.), reto; (develop, work within a network), ~umi [int]; (object made like a net, netting), ~aĵo

neum(e), neŭmo

neural, nerva

neuralgia, neŭralgio

neurasthenia, neŭrastenio

neuritis, neŭrito

neur(o)–, (pfx), neŭr(o)–

neurology, neŭrolog/io; neurologist, ~o

neuroma, neŭromo

neuron, neŭrono

neuropath, neŭropato; neuropathy, ~io

Neuroptera, neŭropteroj

neurosis, neŭrozo; neurotic, ~a; ~ulo; psychoneurosis, psiko~o

neurotoxin, neŭrotoksino

neurotropic, neŭrotropa

neurula, neŭrulo

neuter, neŭtra; ~aĵo; ~ulo; (castrate), kastri [tr]; (spay), inkastri [tr]

neutral, (pol etc.; re any dispute, issue), neŭtrala; ~ulo (e.g.: *Esperanto is a politically neutral language:* Esperanto estas politike ~a lingvo); (of neither of 2 categories; disengaged vehicle transmission), neŭtra (e.g.: *neutral chemical solution:* neŭtra kemia solvaĵo; *put the car in neutral:* meti la aŭton en la neŭtran (rapidumon)); **neutrality**, ~eco; neŭtreco; **neutralize**, ~igi; neŭtrigi

neutrino, neŭtrino; antineutrino, anti~o

neutrodyne, neŭtrodino

neutron, neŭtrono

Neva, Nevo

Nevada, Nevado

névé (firn), firno; (at head of glacier), nevajo

never, neniam; nevermore, ~ plu; nevertheless, tamen

nevus, nevuso

new, (gen), nova; newfangled, ~moda; renew, (make new), re~igi; (revalidate etc.), re– [pfx] (e.g.: *renew one's subscription:* reaboni); renewal, re~igo; re...o (e.g.: *subscription re-*

newal: reabono)

Newfoundland, Novlando

news, novaĵo(j); newscast, ~elsendo; newscaster, ~komentariisto; newsletter, (~)bulteno; newspaper, ĵurnalo; newspaper boy (girl), ĵurnalportist(in)o; newsprint, ĵurnalpapero; newsreel, ~ofilmo; newsstand, kiosko, gazetbudo

newt, trituro

newton, (unit of force), nutono

Newton, (Isaac), Neŭtono; Newtonian, ~a

next, sekv(ant)a; venonta; posta; ~e; poste; next to, (adjacent), apud; (almost), preskaŭ

nexus, ligo

Nganhui, Anhuj

Niagara, Niagaro; Niagara Falls, (falls or either city), Kaskadoj de ~o

nib, (gen), beko

nibble, (eat), manĝeti [tr]; ~o; (bite), ronĝi [tr], mordeti [tr]; mordeto, ronĝo

Nibelung, Nibelungo

nicad, nikada*

Nicaea, Niceo

Nicaragua, Nikaragvo; Nicaraguan, ~ano; ~a

niccolite, nikelino

nice, (pleasant), agrabla; (refined, delicate), delikata; (good), bona; (subtle), subtila; (well-behaved), bonkonduta; (charming), ĉarma; (affable), afabla, bonkora; (pretty), bel(et)a; (polite), ĝentila; (precise, close), fajna, preciza; nice and, (quite), tute, tre; nicety, delikateco; delikataĵo; subtileco; fajneco, precizeco

Nice, (city), Nico

Nicene, Nicea; Nicene Council, ~a Konsilio; Nicene Creed, ~a Kredo

niche, niĉo; en~igi

Nicholas, Nikolao; St. Nicholas, Sankta ~o [cp "Santa Claus"]

nichrome, nikromo

nick, noĉ(et)i [tr]; ~o; in the nick of time, ĝustamomente

nickel, (metal), nikelo; ~a; ~i [tr]; (coin), kvincendo; chrome nickel, nikromo

nickeline, nikelino

Nicodemus, Nikodemo
Nicolaitan, Nikolaito; ~a
Nicolas, Nikolao
Nicosia, Nikozia
Nicotiana, nikotiano
nicotine, nikotino; **nicotinism**, ~ismo
nictitate, niktiti [int]; **nictitating membrane**, ~a membrano
niece, nevino
niello, nielo; ~i [tr]
Nieman, Nemano
Nietzsche, Niĉeo; **Nietzscheism**, ~ismo
Nigella, nigelo
Niger, (river), Niĝero; (country), ~a Respubliko, ~lando
Nigeria, Niĝerio; **Nigerian**, ~ano; ~a
niggard, avar/ulo; **niggardly**, ~a
night, nokto; ~a; **nightie**, ~orobo; **nightly**, ĉiu~a; ĉiu~e; **night clothes**, ~ovestoj; **nightclub**, ~oklubo; **nightfall**, ~iĝo; **nightgown**, ~orobo; **nightjar**, kaprimulgo; **nightlong**, tut~a, ~odaŭra; **nightmare**, koŝmaro, inkubsonĝo; **(a) night out**, festvespero; **nightshade**, (bot: *Solanum*), solano; **black nightshade**, nigra solano; **deadly nightshade**, beladono; **enchanter's nightshade**, circeo; **woody nightshade**, dolĉamaro; **nightspot**, ~oklubo; **nighttime**, ~o, ~a tempo; dum~a; **night watchman**, ~ogardisto; **midnight**, ~omezo; ~omeza; **overnight**, tra~a; tra~e; **at night**, ~e; **night is falling**, ~iĝas; **spend the night**, tra~i [int]; **last night**, hieraŭ ~e; **night before last**, antaŭhieraŭ ~e; **tomorrow night**, morgaŭ ~e; **in the dead of night**, dum plena ~o
nihilism, nihilismo; **nihilist**, ~a; nihilisto
Nijmegen, Nimego
nil, nul; ~o [see also "zero"]
Nile, Nilo; **White Nile**, Blanka ~o; **Blue Nile**, Blua ~o
nilgai, boselafo
nimble, (agile), facilmova, lertmova; (vigorous), vigla
nimbus, (cloud), nimbuso; (aura), nimbo [cp "aura," "halo"]; **nimbostratus**, ~ostratuso

Nîmes, Nimeso
Nimrod, Nimrodo
Nina, (woman's name), Nina
nincompoop, stultulo, ventkapulo
nine, naŭ; ~o [see § 19]
Nineveh, Ninevo
ninth, (9th), naŭa; (1/9), ~ono [see § 19]; (mus), naŭno
niobate, niobato; **niobateic acid**, ~a acido
Niobe, Nioba
niobium, niobo
nip, (pinch), pinĉi [tr]; ~o; (bite), mordeti [tr]; mordeto; (drink), trinketi [tr]; trinketo; **nip and tuck**, flank-al-flanka, preskaŭ egala
nipple, (human or animal), cico; (artificial, as on baby bottle), ~umo; (pipe coupling), niplo; **nipplewort**, lapsano
Nippon, Nipono; **Nipponese**, ~ano; ~a [cp "Japan"]
Nirvana, nirvano
nisi, provizora
nit, (louse egg), laŭsovo; **nit-picking**, harfend(em)a
nitrate, nitrato; nitroizi [tr]; **nitration**, nitroizo; nitroizado
nitric, (re element nitrogen), nitrogena; (re nitric acid etc.), nitrata; **nitric acid**, nitrata acido
nitride, nitrido
nitrile, nitrilo
nitrite, nitrito
nitr(o)–, (chem sfx), nitr(o)–
nitrogen, nitrogeno; **nitrogenous**, ~a
nitrocellulose, nitrocelulozo
nitroglycerin(e), nitroglicerino
nitroso–, (chem root), nitrozo–
nitrosyl, nitrozilo; ~a
nitrous, nitrita; **nitrous acid**, ~a acido
nitty-gritty, detal(et)a; ~oj
nitwit, stultulo, ventkapulo, sencerbulo
Nivose, Nivozo
nix, (myth), nikso; (turn down), rifuzi [tr], malakcepti [tr]; **nixie**, ~ino
Nizhni Novgorod, Nijni-Novgorodo
no, (adv: opp "yes"), ne; (adj: none, not any), neniu(j), neniom da (e.g.: *no house was damaged:* neniu domo estis difektita [or] neniom da domoj estis difektitaj; *I have no money:* mi havas neniom da mono); (adv: none, not

any, not at all), neniom, ne (e.g.: *that is no better:* tio estas neniom pli bona [or] tio ne estas pli bona); (Japanese play), noo; **say no (to)**, nei [tr, int]; **no one**, [see "nobody"]

Noah, Noa

Nobel, Nobelo; **Nobel prize**, ~a premio

nobelium, nobelio

noble, (rank), nobela; (of high moral character), nobla; **nobility**, ~aro; ~eco; nobleco; **nobleman**, nobelo

noblesse oblige, devigo de nobeleco

nobody, (not anyone), neniu; (unimportant person), neniulo, nulo, malgravulo [see also "one: no one"]

Noctua, noktuo

nocturnal, nokta

nocturne, (mus), nokturno

nod, (sway; bend forward and back, gen), balanci [tr]; ~iĝi; ~o; ("yes" by head), kapjesi [int]; kapjeso; (any sign by head, as greeting etc.), kapsigni [int]; kapsigno

node, (gen), nodo; **lymph node**, limfo~o

nodule, (gen), nodeto; (geol), nodaĵo, konkremento

nodus, nodo

noesis, noetiko; **noetic**, ~o; ~a; ~ulo

no-gaku, noo

noh, noo

nohow, neniel

noise, bruo; **noisy**, ~a; **make noise**, ~i [int]; **background noise**, fon~o; **white noise**, blanka ~o

noisome, (noxious), noca; (malodorous), fiodora, fetora, stinka

nomad, nomado; **wander as a nomad**, ~i [int]; **nomadism**, ~ismo

nomarch, nomarko; **nomarchy**, ~io

nomenclature, nomenklaturo

–nomial, (math sfx), –nomialo (e.g.: *polynomial:* plur~o)

nominal, nominala; **nominalism**, ~ismo; **nominalist**, ~isma; ~isto

nominate, kandidatigi [cp "name"]

nominative, nominativo; ~a

nominee, kandidato

non–, (not), ne– (e.g.: *non-Jewish:* ne-Juda; *nonrenewable:* nerenovigebla) [cp "un–"]

nonagenarian, naŭdekjara; ~ulo

nonagon, naŭangulo

nonahedron, naŭedro

nonane, nonano

nonce, nuno, ~momento; **nonce word**, hapaksot; **for the nonce**, por ~, ~momente

nonchalant, indiferenta, senzorga; **nonchalance**, ~eco

none, neniu(j), neniom (da, de, el) (e.g.: *many people inquired, but none came:* multaj homoj enketis, sed neniuj venis; *none of them:* neniom el ili); **none to speak of**, esence neniu(j), esence neniom

nones, (gen), nonoj

nonet, (any 9), naŭopo; (mus), naŭteto

nonetheless, tamen, malgraŭ ĉio, malgraŭ tio

nonillion, (Am: 10^{30}), kviniliono; (Br: 10^{54}), naŭiliono [see § 19(b)]

nonose, nonozo

nonpareil, (peerless), senegala; ~ulo

nonplus, konsterni [tr], perpleksi [tr]; ~iĝo, perplekseco

nonsense, sensenc/aĵo; **nonsensical**, ~a

non sequitur, nekonsekvenco

noodle, nudelo

nook, angul/eto, kaŝ~o, loketo

noon, tagmezo; ~a; **noontime**, ~a

noose, (ŝnur)maŝo

nopal, nopalo, opuntio

noplace, nenie(n)

nor, nek [see "neither"]

Nordic, Skandinavia, Nord-Eŭropa

noria, norio

norite, gabro [not "norito"]

norm, normo

normal, (gen), normala; ~o; (math: perpendicular), orta; **normality**, ~eco; **abnormal**, ne~a; **paranormal**, para~a; **subnormal**, sub~a

Norman, (man's name), Normano; (member of Scandinavian tribe in 9th-10th Centuries), ~o; (resident of Normandy), Normando

Normandy, Normand/io, ~ujo [see "Norman"]

Norn, Norno

Norse, (Scandinavian), Skandinava; **Old Norse**, (la) Norena (lingvo); **Norseman**, ~o

north, nordo; ~a; ~e(n) [abb: N];

North, (as part of most place names), N~~, N~a [see subentries under separate root names for specific geog names]; **northern**, ~a; **northernmost**, plej ~a; **northerner**, ~ano; **northward**, ~e(n); ~enira; **northerly**, (northern), ~a; (toward north), ~e(n); ~enira; (from north), de~a; de~e; **northbound**, ~enira; **northeast**, ~oriento; ~orienta; ~oriente(n); (esp re compass direction), ~eosto [–a etc.] [abb: NE]; **northwest**, ~okcidenta [–a etc.]; (compass), ~uesto [–a etc.] [abb: NW]; **far north**, alta ~o

Norway, Norveg/io, ~ujo; **Norwegian**, ~o; ~a; ~ia, ~uja

nose, (anat, or similar object), nazo; (pry, snoop), enŝovi sin (en); ŝovi la ~on en fremdan vazon; **nosebleed**, epitakso, ~osangado; **nosegay**, bukedo; **nose out**, (defeat), venki je ~longo; (smell out), elflari [tr]; **beaknosed**, aglo~a; **brown-nose**, (fi)lakei [tr], perflati [tr]; **brown-noser**, (fi)lakeo; **blow one's nose**, mungi [int]; **by a nose**, je ~longo; **look down one's nose at**, maldegni [tr]; **on the nose**, (exactly), precize; **turn up one's nose at**, malestimi [tr]

nostalgia, nostalgio; **nostalgic**, ~a

Nostoc, nostoko

nostril, naztruo

nostrum, (quack medication, lit or fig), ĉarlatan/a medikamento, ~aĵo

nosy, enmiksiĝema, enŝoviĝema

not, ne; **not at all**, tute ne; **I think not**, mi kredas ke ne

nota bene, (abb: N.B.), notu bone [abb: N.B.]

notable, notinda; ~ulo; **notabilia**, ~aĵoj

Notacanthus, notakanto; Notacanthiformes, ~oformaj (fiŝoj)

notary, **notary public**, notario; **notarize**, ~e atesti [tr]

notation, notacio

notch, noĉo; ~i [tr]

note, (mus; brief explanation, reminder, etc.; nuance, quality; jot), noto; ~i [tr]; (take note of, notice), ~i, rimarki [tr]; ($: bill), (mon)bileto; (short letter), ~o, letereto; (detailed comment etc., as biographical note in book),

notico; **noteworthy**, ~inda; **footnote**, pied~o; **whole note**, (mus), plena ~o; **half** (**quarter**, **eighth**, **etc.**) **note**, duon~o (kvaron~o, okon~o, etc.); **grace note**, aĉakaturo*

nothing, nenio; **nothing at all**, nenio ajn; **nothing much**, nemulte, nenio grava; **it's nothing!**, (reply to thanks, apology, etc.), ne menciinde!; **in nothing flat**, preskaŭ tuj; **make nothing of**, (treat as unimportant), malgravigi; (not understand), tute ne kompreni [tr]; **nothing but**, nur, nenio krom; **to say nothing of**, sen mencii [tr]; **there is nothing for it but to**, ne estas alternativo por, oni ne povas eviti [tr], oni ne povas alie ol

notice, (take note of), rimarki [tr]; ~o; (be aware of), konstati [tr], konscii [int] pri; (announcement), avizo, anonco; **noticeable**, ~inda; **serve notice**, avizi [tr]; **take notice (of)**, ~i, observi [tr], ekatenti [tr], ekkonstati [tr], konstatiĝi pri, konsciiĝi [tr]

notify, avizi [tr], informi [tr], sciigi; **notification**, ~o, informo, sciigo

notion, (idea), nocio, koncepto; **notions**, (sewing accessories), mercero, furnituro [note sing]; (cosmetics etc.), galanterio; **preconceived notion**, antaŭkoncepto

notochord, ĥordo

notorious, fifama; **notoriety**, ~eco

Notos, (south wind), Notoso

notwithstanding, malgraŭ [prep: always goes before n (e.g.: *he did it, rules notwithstanding*: li faris ĝin, ~ reguloj)]; (adv), ~e; **notwithstanding (the fact) that**, kvankam, ~ tio ke

nougat, nugato

nought, (nothing), nenio

noumenon, noumeno; **noumenal**, ~a

noun, substantivo

nourish, (feed, gen), nutri [tr]; (fig: keep, conserve, care for), flegi [tr] (e.g.: *nourish a prejudice*: flegi antaŭjuĝon); **nourishing**, ~a; **nourishment**, ~ado; ~aĵo; **malnourished**, mis~ita; **undernourished**, sub~ita

nouveau riche, parvenuo, novriĉulo

nova, novao; **supernova**, super~o†

Nova Scotia, Nov-Skotio

Novaya Zemlya, Novaja Zeml'a, Nova-Zemlo

novel, (fiction book), romano [not "novelo"]; (new), nov(tip)a, originala

novella, novelo

novelty, original/aĵo, novaĵo; ~eco, noveco

November, novembro

novice, (gen), novico

novitiate, (person), novico; (place), ~ejo; (condition), ~eco

novocain(e), novokaino

now, nun [note: may be omitted w participle ending "–ata" or "–anta," unless desired for emphasis (e.g.: *the guests now arriving:* la alvenantaj gastoj)]; **nowadays,** ~tempe; **now that,** ~ kiam (e.g.: *now that the sun is shining:* ~ kiam la suno brilas; *now that I understand the situation:* ~ kiam mi komprenas la situacion); **now and then, now and again,** foje, fojfoje, foje kaj refoje, de tempo al tem po; **now then!,** (interj), nu do!; **now ..., then,** (sometimes one, sometimes another), jen ..., jen (e.g.: *the reaction was now favorable, then unfavorable:* la reago estis jen favora, jen malfavora); **for now,** (temporarily), provizore, dume, por ~; **up to now,** ĝis ~; **ĝis~a; an hour (a day, week, two months, etc.) from now,** de ~ post horo (tago, semajno, du monatoj, etc.)

noxious, noca

nozzle, ajuto

nu, (letter), nu [see § 16]

Nu, (river), (Rivero) Nu

nuance, nuanco; **give nuance(s) to,** ~i [tr]

nub, (bump, lump), tubero; (piece), peceto; (gist, essence), kerno, esenco

Nuba, Nubiano

Nubia, Nubio; **Nubian,** ~ano; ~a

nubile, edzinaĝa

nucha, nuko; **nuchal,** ~a

Nuchiang, (river), (Rivero) Nu

Nucifraga, nucifrago, nuksrompulo

nucleate, nuklea; **nucleatize,** kernigi

nucleo–, (pfx), nukleo–

nucleolus, nucleole, nukleolo

nucleon, nukleono

nucleoside, nukleozido

nucleotide, nukleotido

nucleus, nukleo; **nuclear,** ~a; **polynuclear,** polikerna; **polynucleate,** poli~a; **thermonuclear,** termo~a [see also "nuke"]

nude, nuda; ~ulo; **nudity,** ~eco; **nudism,** ~ismo; **nudist,** ~isma; ~isto; **denude,** ~igi

nudge, (kubut)puŝeti [tr]; ~o

nudibranch, dorido

nugget, (gen), bul(et)o; (gold), or~o

nuisance, ĝenaĵo

nuke, (nuclear, gen), nuklea; (bomb), ~a bombo; ~abombi [tr]; (power plant), ~a centralo [see also "nuclear," "bomb"]; (cook w microwave), mikroondi [tr]

Nukiang, (river), (Rivero) Nu

Nuku'alofa, Nukualofo*

null, nulo; ~a; **null and void,** malvalida

nullify, neniigi, nuligi, malvalidigi

numb, sensenta; ~igi

number, (abstract math quantity; gram [sing, plur]), nombro; ~a; ~i [tr] (e.g.: *the number 5:* la ~o 5; *the membership numbers 30:* la membraro ~as 30); (written figure showing order etc.), numero [abb: n–ro (not "No."; not "#")]; numeri [tr] (e.g.: *account number 1234:* konto numero [n–ro] 1234; *number the pages:* numeri la paĝojn); (numerical figure, symbol), cifero (e.g.: *the number "1" is a single stroke:* la cifero "1" estas unuopa streko); [also see § 19; also cp "numeral," "digit"]; **Numbers,** (Bib), N~oj; **a number of,** (several), pluraj; **a goodly number,** iom multaj; **cardinal number,** kardinala ~o; **even number,** para ~o; **odd number,** nepara ~; **ordinal number,** vicmontra ~o; **outnumber,** super~i [tr]; **page number,** paĝnumero; **prime number,** primo; **quantum-number, q-number,** kvantum-~o, q-~o [pronounce "ku-nombro"]; **real number,** (math), reelo†; **round number,** ronda ~o; **in round numbers,** rondcifere, rond~e; **street number, house number,** domnumero; **telephone number,** telefon-numero; **his number is up,** li estas finota

numen, numeno

Numenius, numenio

numeral, (written figure: 1,2,3...), cifero; (word: one, two...), numeralo [cp "number," "digit"]; **Arabic numerals**, Arabaj ~oj; **Roman numerals**, Romanaj ~oj

numerate, nombri [tr]

numerator, numeratoro, dividato

numerical, nombra; numera; cifera [see "number," "numeral"]

numerology, numerolog/io; **numerological**, ~ia; **numerologist**, ~o

numerous, mult(nombr)aj

Numida, numido

Numidia, Numid/io, ~ujo; **Numidian**, ~o; ~a; ~ia, ~uja

numismatic, numismatika; **numismatics**, ~o; **numismatist**, numismato

nun, monaĥino; **nunnery**, ~ejo

nunatak, nunatako

nuncio, nuncio; **nunciature**, (office), ~ejo

nuptial, nupta

Nuremberg, Nürnberg, Nurenbergo

nurse, (in sickness; fig: harbor, as a feeling), flegi [tr]; ~ist(in)o; (look after, gen; baby-sit), varti [tr]; vartist(in)o; (feed at breast), mamnutri [tr]; mamnutriĝi; (treat, try to cure), kuraci [tr]; **nursemaid**, vartistino; **nursery**, (infant's bedroom), infanĉambro; (nursery school, day nursery), infanvartejo; (for plants), plantovartejo; **nurseryman**, plantovartisto; **nursing home**, (Am: for aged), maljunulejo, ripoz-domo; (Br: for childbirth), akuŝejo; **wet nurse**, mamnutristino

nurture, (feed), nutri [tr]; ~aĵo; (raise, look after), eduki [tr]; edukado

nut, (bot, gen), nukso; (for bolt), boltingo; (enthusiast, fan), adepto; (crazy, lit or fig), maniulo, frenezulo (e.g.: *skiing nut:* skimaniulo); (slang: testicle), kojono; **nuts**, (crazy), freneza; (interj), pa!; **nutcracker**, (device), ~rompilo; (zool), ~rompulo, nucifrago; **nutmeat**, ~kerno; **he's nuts**, mankas klapo en lia kapo; li havas muŝon en la cerbo; **Brazil nut**, Brazila ~o; **butternut**, (blanka) juglando; **can-**

dlenut, (tree), aleŭrito; (nut), aleŭrita ~of; **chestnut**, (*Castanea:* nut). kaŝtano; (tree), kaŝtanarbo; (edible nut), marono; **horse chestnut**, (*Aesculus:* nut), hipokaŝtano; (tree), hipokaŝtanarbo [note: PIV defines "kaŝtano" as the nut but "hipokaŝtano" as the tree]; (*Aesculus hippocastanum*), ordinara hipokaŝtano; ordinara hipokaŝtanarbo; **water chestnut**, (*Trapa*), trapo; **hex nut**, heksagona boltingo; **lock nut**, ŝlosboltingo; **rush nut**, termigdalo; **wing nut**, aletboltingo; [for oth bot nuts, see separate entries]; **hard nut to crack**, malfacila problemo; **in a nutshell**, plej koncize

nutation, (gen), nutacio

nuthatch, sito

nutmeg, (nut, spice), muskato; (tree), ~arbo, ~ujo

nutria, (animal), kojpo; (fur), ~opelto

nutrient, nutra; ~enzo

nutriment, nutrenzo

nutrition, nutr/ado; **nutritious**, ~a; **nutritionist**, ~adisto; **malnutrition**, mis~ado

nux vomica, (tree), strikno; (berry), ~a bero

nuzzle, nazumi [tr]

Nyas(s)a, (Lake), Lago Njasa

nyctalopia, (day blindness), niktalop/eco; (night blindness), mal~eco; **nyctalopic**, (mal)~a

nyct(o)–, (med pfx), nikt(o)–

nylon, nilono

nymph, (gen), nimfo

Nymphaea, nimfeo, akvolilio; Nymphaea lotus, Nymphaea coerulea, Egipta lotuso

nymphomania, nimfomanio; **nymphomaniac**, ~ulino

Nymwegen, Nimego

nystagmus, nistagmo

O, (interj), ho
oaf, bubego, azeno, malspritulo
oak, kverko; **black oak,** nigra ~o; **cork oak,** korko~o; **holm oak,** ileks~o; **red oak,** ruĝa ~o; **silky oak,** (Aus: *Grevillea robusta*), silka ~o; **white oak,** blanka ~o
oakum, stupo
oar, rem/ilo [cp "paddle"]; **oarlock,** ~ilingo; **oarsman,** ~isto; **oarweed,** laminario
oasis, oazo
oat, oats, aveno; **oatmeal,** ~kaĉo, ~grio; **oat flakes,** ~flokoj; **sow one's wild oats,** junule diboĉadi [int]
oath, ĵuro
Ob, (river), Obo
Obadiah, Obadja
obdurate, hardita, obstina, necedema, nekompatema
obedience, obeo, ~ado; **obedient,** ~(em)a; **disobedience,** mal~(ad)o
obeisance, riverenco
obelisk, obelisko
obelus, obeluso; **obelize,** ~izi [tr]
Oberon, (ast), Oberono*
obese, obeza, korpulenta; **obesity,** ~eco
obfuscate, malklarigi, obskurigi
obi, (sash), obio
obituary, nekrologo; ~a
object, (thing; gram), objekto; (goal), celo; (oppose), kontraŭi [tr]; (argue against), objeti [int], kontraŭargumenti [int]; (protest), protesti [tr]; **objection,** objeto, kontraŭ(argument)o; protesto; **objectionable,** kontraŭinda; (offensive), ofenda; **direct object,** (gram), rekta ~o; **indirect object,** nerekta ~o
objective, (opp "subjective"), objektiva; (lens; target etc.), ~o; (gram), akuzativo; akuzativa; (goal), celo; **objectivity,** ~eco; **objectivism,** ~ismo; **objectivist,** ~isma; ~isto
objet d'art, art/objekto, ~aĵo
oblate, platigita
oblation, ofero
obligate, (commit to future action),

dev/ontigi; (compel), ~igi; (law), obligacii [tr]; **obligation,** ~igo; ~o; ($), obligacio; **obligatory,** ~iga
oblige, (do favor), komplezi [tr]; (compel), devigi; **obliging,** ~(em)a; **obliged,** (grateful), dank(em)a; **be obliged to,** (must), (iu) devi [tr], endi [int] al (iu) (e.g.: *I am obliged to tell you this:* mi devas diri al vi ĉi tion [or] endas al mi diri...); **be (much) obliged to (one),** esti (tre) dankema al (iu)
oblique, (gen), oblikva; **go, turn obliquely,** ~i [int]
obliterate, neniigi, forskrapi [tr], forviŝi [tr]
oblivion, forges(itec)o
oblong, oblonga
obloquy, (vituperation), kalumnio; (infamy), fifamo
obnoxious, ofend(eg)a, abomena
Obodenus rosmarus, Obodenus divergens, rosmaro
oboe, hobojo
obolus, obolo
obovate, obovoid, obovala
obscene, obscena; **obscenity,** ~aĵo; ~eco
obscurant, obskuranto*; ~(ism)a; **obscurantism,** ~ismo
obscure, (dim), obskura, malklara; (vague), svaga, malpreciza; (unknown), ~a, nekonata; **obscurity,** ~eco, malklareco, nekonateco
obsequies, funebraĵoj
obsequious, lakea, komplezaĉa, trorespekta, servemaĉa
observatory, (ast etc.), observatorio
observe, (perceive, study; follow, obey), observi [tr]; (celebrate holiday etc.), festi [tr] [cp "celebrate", "solemn: solemnize"]; **observance, observation,** ~ado; fest(ad)o; (ceremony), ceremonio; **observant,** ~(em)a, atenta; **observation deck (tower, look-out, etc.),** ~ejo; **observer,** ~into; ~anto; ~onto; ~isto
obsess, obsedi [tr]; **obsession,** ~o; **ob-**

sessive, ~a
obsidian, obsidiano
obsolete, arkaika; **obsolescent**, ~iĝanta; **obsolescence**, ~ig(ad)o; ~iĝ(ad)o; ~eco
obstacle, obstaklo
obstetric, obstetrika; **obstetrics**, ~o; **obstetrician**, ~isto
obstinate, obstina; **obstinacy**, ~(ec)o
obstreperous, bru-obstina
obstruct, obstrukci [tr]; **obstruction**, (thing), ~o; (act), ~ado; **obstructive**, ~a
obtain, (acquire), akiri [tr], havigi, ricevi [tr]; (derive), derivi [tr]; (exist, be in effect), regi [tr, int], ekzisti [int], validi [int]
obtrude, (push out), elpeli [tr]; (force self on), altrudiĝi, trudi (sin al); **obtrusion**, ~o; sintrudo; **obtrusive**, sintrud(em)a, maldiskreta; **unobtrusive**, nesintruda, diskreta
obturate, obturi [tr]; **obturator**, ~ilo
obtuse, (gen), obtuza
obverse, (of coin, medal, etc.), averso
obviate, (make unnecessary), malnecesigi; (avoid), eviti [tr]
obvious, evidenta, memklara
oca, oksalido
ocarina, okarino
occasion, (happening), okazo; (instance, circumstance, time), ~o, fojo; (cause), kaŭzi [tr], ~igi, estigi. rezultigi; **occasional**, (now and then), (kelk)foja, fojfoja; (for one occasion), por~a; **occasionally, on occasion**, (kelk)foje, fojfoje, de tempo al tempo; **if the occasion should arise (that)**, se eventuale; **rise to the occasion**, plenumi la bezonon, sukcese elproviĝi; **take (advantage of) the occasion**, elprofiti la ~on, elprofiti la oportunon
Occident, Okcidento; **Occidental**, ~a; ~ano
occiput, okcipito; **occipital**, ~a; **occipital bone**, ~osto, okcipitalo
occlude, okluzii [int]; ~igi; **occlusion**, ~o
occult, okulta; ~eco; **occluism**, ~ismo
occupy, (gen), okupi [tr]; **occupant**, ~anto; **occupancy**, ~anteco; ~iteco; **occupation**, (activity), ~(ad)o; (job),

ofico [cp "job", "trade", "profession", "career"]; (mil), okupacio; **occupied**, (in use, not available), ~ita; **preoccupy**, (thoughts), absorbi [tr]; (occupy before), antaŭ~i [tr]; **preoccupation**, absorbigo, absorba zorgo; **unoccupied**, (vacant), vaka, ne~ita, libera; **occupy oneself**, sin ~i, ~iĝi
occur, (happen), okazi [int]; (be found, exist), troviĝi; **occurrence**, ~o; **occur to one**, (come to mind), veni al iu en la kapon
ocean, oceano; ~a; **oceanic**, ~a; **oceanography**, ~ografio; **oceanographer**, ~ografo; **transoceanic**, trans~a
Oceani(c)a, Oceanio
Oceanus, Oceano
ocellus, ocelo; **ocellate(d)**, ~a
ocelot, oceloto
ocher, okro; ~a
Ochroma lagopus, balzo
Ocimum, ocimo; Ocimum basilicum, bazilio
o'clock, la ~a horo, la ~a (e.g.: *it is 3 o'clock in the morning:* estas la 3–a horo matene [or] la 3–a matene; *at 4 o'clock in the afternoon:* je la 4–a (horo) posttagmeze)
octagon, okangulo
octahedron, oktaedro, okedro
octal, okuma
octane, oktano; **octane rating, octane number**, ~a indico, ~a nombro
octant, (gen), oktanto
octave, oktavo
Octavio, Octavius, Oktavio; **Octavia**, ~a
octavo, oktavo
Octavo, Octavus, Octavo
octet, (any 8), okopo; (mus), okteto
octillion, (Am: 10^{27}), kvariliardo; (Br: 10^{48}), okiliono [see § 19(b)]
October, oktobro
Octocorallia, okkoraluloj
octopus, (animal), polpo; (as food), ~aĵo
octuple, okobla; ~igi; ~iĝi; okopa; okopigi; okopiĝi [see § 19]
octyl, oktilo
ocular, (re eye), okula; (lens), okulario
oculist, oftalmologo, okulisto
Ocynum, [see *"Ocimum"*]

odalisk, odalisque, odalisko
odd, (strange, peculiar), stranga, kurioza; (w/o mate, as sock etc.), malpara; (math: not divisible by 2), nepara; (various, diverse), diversa(j); (extra, additional), aldona (e.g.: *a dollar and some odd change:* dolaro kaj aldonaj moneroj); (small amount over round figure), –kelkaj, –kelke (da) (e.g.: *thirty-odd years ago:* antaŭ tridek-kelkaj jaroj [or] tridek-kelke da jaroj; *two hundred odd people came:* ducent-kelkaj homoj venis); **odds,** (probability), probablo, ŝanco; (advantage), avantaĝo; **oddball,** ~a; ~aĵo; ~ulo; **oddity,** ~aĵo; ~eco; ~ulo; **odd man out,** malparulo, ekstrulo; **odds and ends,** diversaĵoj; **at odds with,** en malakordo kun; **lay odds,** veti [int]; **I'll lay long odds (that),** mi vetos je via granda avantaĝo (ke)
ode, odo
Oder, Odro
Odessa, Odeso
Odetta, Odeta
Odin, Odino [cp "Wotan"]
odious, malam/inda, abomena; **odium,** ~o, abomeno
odometer, distancometro   [not "odometro" or "hodometro"]
Odonata, odonatoj
odor, odoro; **have (exude) the odor of,** ~i [int] je (e.g.: *it has the odor of asparagus:* ĝi ~as je asparago); **odoriferous,** ~anta; **odorless,** sen~a; **odorous,** (bon)~a, aroma; **deodorize,** des~igi, sen~igi; **malodorous,** fetora, fi~a, stinka
Odyl(e), (woman's name), Odila
Odysseus, Odiseo
odyssey, odiseado
oe–, [if specific word not listed below, see under "e–"]
Oedipus, Edipo; **Oedipus complex,** ~komplekso
Oenanthe, (zool; bot), enanto; **Oenanthe aquatica,** felandrio
Oenothera, enotero
oersted, orstedo
Oestrus, ojstro; **Oestridae,** ~edoj
Oeta, Ojto
of, (re possession; relationship; authorship; nationality; nature, description, purpose; from; relieved, deprived of), de (e.g.: *assets of the company:* aktivoj de la kompanio; *pages of the book:* paĝoj de la libro; *the square root of 3:* la kvadrata radiko de 3; *the plays of Shakespeare:* la dramoj de Ŝekspiro; *the people of Canada:* la homoj de Kanado; *a piece of wood:* peco de ligno; *a day of rest:* tago de ripozo; *east of the city:* oriente de la urbo; *cured of cancer:* resanigita de kancero; *robbed of one's money:* pri-rabita de sia mono); (re quantity, contents), da (e.g.: *a glass of water:* glaso da akvo; *a liter of milk:* litro da lakto; *a pile of bricks:* amaso da brikoj); (made from; one item or several out of total), el (e.g.: *a ring of gold:* ringo el oro; *made of plastic:* farita el plasto; *one of us:* unu el ni; *some of the trees:* iuj el la arboj); (because of), pro (e.g.: *die of tuberculosis:* morti pro tuberkulozo); (about, concerning), pri (e.g.: *a poem of love:* poemo pri amo; *think of me:* pensu pri mi); (as a kind of), –a (e.g.: *a jewel of a city:* juvela urbo); (specific designation, name, amount), [omit] (e.g.: *the city of Baltimore:* la urbo Baltimoro; *the sum of five dollars:* la sumo kvin dolaroj); (before, in expressions of time), antaŭ (e.g.: *at 10 of 5 [4:50]:* je 10 antaŭ la 5–a); **of late,** lastatempe; **of mine (yours, his, hers, etc.),** mia (via, etc.) [after n; omit prep] (e.g.: *a friend of mine:* amiko mia; *a habit of hers:* kutimo ŝia); **full of,** plena je; **made of,** farita el
off, (away), for, for– [pfx] (e.g.: *off in the distance:* ~ malproksime; *move off:* ~moviĝi); (away from), ~ de (e.g.: *off campus:* ~ de la universitata tereno); (disconnected, re elec circuit, device), malŝaltita (e.g.: *the light [circuit, machine] is off:* la lumo [cirkvito, maŝino] estas malŝaltita); (re closed valve, fluid not flowing, etc.), fermita (e.g.: *the faucet [water, gas] is off:* la krano [akvo, gaso] estas fermita); (away from surface, opp "onto"), de sur (e.g.: *the cat jumped off*

the table: la kato saltis de sur la tablo); (nearby, adjacent), apud (e.g.: *a storm off the coast:* ŝtormo apud la marbordo; *a parking orbit off Mars:* parkorbito apud Marso); (not being worn), demetita (e.g.: *his hat is off:* lia ĉapelo estas demetita); (not attached), malligita, malfiksita (e.g.: *the cover is off the book:* la kovrilo estas malfiksita de la libro); (not in operation), nefunkcianta; (en route), survoja; survoje (e.g.: *we're off for Toronto:* ni estas survoje al Toronto); (less), malpli (e.g.: *sales are off:* vendoj estas malpli); (below normal), subnormala (e.g.: *my singing is off tonight:* mia kantado estas subnormala ĉi-nokte; *an off day:* subnormala tago); (incorrect), malĝusta (e.g.: *their estimate was off:* ilia takso estis malĝusta); (not on target), maltrafa; (outside), ekster (e.g.: *off limits:* eksterlima, ekster limoj); (in future), estontece, en la estonteco (e.g.: *the convention is two months off:* la kongreso estas du monatojn en la estonteco); ($: as rebate), rabate (e.g.: *5% off for cash payment:* 5% rabate por kontanta pago); (away from work, duty, etc.), libera (e.g.: *I'm off on Saturday:* mi estas libera je sabato); (w verb: to measure or divide), dis– [pfx] (e.g.: *mark off:* dislimi); (w verb: to remove, come away), de– [pfx] (e.g.: *the paint rubbed off:* la farbo defrotiĝis); (w verb: by means of), per, pere de (e.g.: *live off an inheritance:* vivi per heredaĵo); **be off**, (free, not on duty), esti libera; havi liberan tempon, tagon; (abstain), abstini [int] (de) (e.g.: *I'm off caffeine:* mi abstinas de kafeino); **we're off!**, ni ekis!; **let's be off!**, ek al!; **(be) off!**, (go away!), for!

offal, (entrails etc.), tripo, visceraĵo

offence, [see "offense"]

offend, ofendi [tr]; **offender**, (guilty person), kulpulo

offense, (act of offending), ofendo; ~ado; (crime), krimo; (attack, sport or mil), ofensivo; **offensive**, ~a; ofensivo; ofensiva; **inoffensive**, ne~a, sen~a; **capital offense**, mortkrimo;

take offense, ~iĝi

offer, (propose, put forth, gen), proponi [tr], elmeti [tr]; ~o; (bsns), oferti [tr]; oferto; (sacrifice), oferi [tr]; ofer(don)o; (present, show), prezenti [tr]; **offering**, (rel donation), monofero

offertory, offertorium, ofertorio

office, (job, position), ofico; (high post), posteno; (place), ~ejo; (of bsns, industry, etc.), kontoro; **officer**, (officeholder, government official, etc.), funkciulo, ~isto; (mil, police, etc.), oficiro; **office boy (girl)**, kurknab(in)o; **office-worker**, ~isto; kontoristo; **box office**, biletejo; **put into office**, en~igi; **come to office**, en~iĝi; **remove from office**, el~igi; **good offices**, komplez(ad)o

official, (authoritative), oficiala; (officeholder), funkciulo; (w judicial or authoritative powers), instanco

officiate, dejori [int], funkcii [int]; **officiate at**, (do ceremony), celebri [tr]

officinal, oficina; ~aĵo

officious, sintruda

offing, malproksimo; **in the offing**, (at some future date), estonta; (iam) estontece

often, ofte

ogee, ogivo; **ogee arch**, ~a kruciĝo

ogive, ogivo

ogle, okulumi [tr]; ~o

Ogmorhinus, marleopardo

ogre, ogro

oh! (gen interj), ho!; (alas!, woe!), oj!, ho ve! [cp "oy!"]

Ohio, (state), Ohio; (river), Rivero ~o

ohm, omo; **megohm**, mega~o, megomo; **ohmmeter**, ~metro

oho! (interj), oho!

–oid, (sfx), –oido; ~a

Oidium albicans, ojdio

oil, (gen), oleo; ~i [tr]; (petroleum), petrolo; (crude petroleum), nafto; (as furnace or diesel fuel etc.), mazuto [cp "diesel"]; (paint), ~ofarbo; (a painting), ~opentraĵo; **oily**, ~(ec)a; **castor oil**, ricin~o; **coal oil**, keroseno; **palm oil**, (chem), palm-~o; (bribe), ŝmirmono

oink, grunti [int]; ~o; (onom), grunt!

ointment, ungvento
Oise, (river), Uazo
OK, [see "okay"]
oka, oksalido
okapi, okapio
Okapia johnstoni, okapio
okay, (all right, good, correct), en ordo, bone (e.g.: *okay, I'll do it:* en ordo, mi faros ĝin; *everything is okay:* ĉio estas en ordo); (approve), aprobi [tr], jesi [tr] (e.g.: *she okayed the proposal:* ŝi aprobis la proponon)
Okhotsk: Sea of Okhotsk, Maro Oñocka
Okinawa, Okinavo
Oklahoma, Oklahomo; **Oklahoma City**, ~-urbo
okra, legomhibisko
–ol, (chem sfx), –olo
old, (not young), maljuna; ~ulo(j); (poet: not young), olda; (not new), malnova; malnovaĵo; (former), antaŭa, eksa; (experienced), sperta; (ancient), antikva; **how old are you?**, kiom aĝa vi estas?, kiom vi aĝas?; **(be) 50 years old**, (esti) 50-jar(aĝ)a, aĝi 50 jarojn; **a 50-year-old**, 50-jarulo; **old age**, ~eco, ~aĝo; **age-old**, antikva, epokojn aĝa; **old-injun, old-squaw, oldwife**, (zool), klangulo, glaci-anaso; **old-man's-beard**, (bot), klematido
Olea, oleo; Olea europaea, olivarbo
oleander, oleandro
oleaster, oleastro
oleate, oleato
olecranon, olekrano
olefin, olefino, alkeno
oleic, (re oil), olea; **oleic acid**, oleata acido
olein, oleino
oleomargarine, margarino
oleum, oleumo
olfactory, olfakta, flara, flar- [pfx]; **olfaction**, ~o
Olga, Olga
olibanum, olibano
oligarch, oligarko; **oligarchy**, ~io; **oligarchic(al)**, ~ia
Oligocene, oligoceno; ~a
Oligochaeta, oligoñetoj
oligochaetous, oligoñeta

oligoclase, oligoklazo
oligopoly, oligopolo†
olive, (fruit), olivo; (tree), ~arbo; (olive-colored), ~kolora, ~(ec)a; **olive oil**, ~oleo; **Mount of Olives**, Monto O~arba; **Russian olive**, oleastro
Oliver, Olivero
Olivet, Monto Olivarba
olivine, oliveno
olm, proteo
–ologer, –ologist, (sfx), –ologo; **–ology**, ~io
Olympia, Olimpio; **Olympian**, (of Olympia), ~ano; ~a; (of Olympus), Olimpano; Olimpa
Olympiad, (ancient), olimpiado; (modern), olimpikoj
Olympic, (re games), Olimpia; (re Olympus, Olympia), [see "Olympia"]; **Olympics, Olympic games**, ~oj
Olympus, Olimpo
–oma, (med sfx), –omo
Oman, Omano; **Gulf of Oman**, Golfo ~a; **Trucial Oman**, ~bordo
Omar, Omaro
omasum, omaso
–omatosis, (med sfx), –omozo
Omayyad, Omajado
ombudsman, rajtoprotektisto
omega, omega [see § 16]
omelet(te), omleto
omen, aŭguro; ~i [tr]
omentum, epiploo, omento
omer, omero
omicron, omikra [see § 16]
ominous, misaŭgura, minaca
omit, ellasi [tr], preterlasi [tr]; **omission**, ~o, preterlaso
Ommiad, Omajado
omni–, (pfx: all), ĉio–, ĉiu– (e.g.: *omnidirectional:* ĉiudirekta; *omnivorous:* ĉiomanĝa)
omnibus, (gen), omnibuso; ~a
omnipotent, ĉiopova; **omnipotence**, ~o
omnipresent, ĉiea; **omnipresence**, ĉie-eco
omniscient, ĉioscia; **omniscience**, ~o
omnivorous, ĉiomanĝa; **omnivore**, ~ulo
Omphale, Omfala
on, (upon), sur (e.g.: *the book is on the*

table: la libro estas ~ la tablo; *the cat jumped on [onto] the sofa:* la kato saltis ~ la sofon; *the fly is on the wall, the ceiling:* la muŝo estas ~ la muro, la plafono); (at, re place), ~, ĉe (e.g.: *on the right side:* ~ [or] ĉe la dekstra flanko); (at same time, re event), ĉe (e.g.: *we succeeded on the third try:* ni sukcesis ĉe la tria provo; *I awoke on her entering:* mi vekiĝis ĉe ŝia eniro [or: kiam ŝi eniris]); (re day of week), –e, je –o (e.g.: *on Thursday:* ĵaŭde [or] je ĵaŭdo); (about, concerning), pri (e.g.: *work on a problem:* labori pri problemo; *a book on trees:* libro pri arboj); (as result of), pro (e.g.: *a profit on the sale:* profito pro la vendo); (by means of), per (e.g.: *live on berries:* vivi per beroj; *I heard on the radio:* mi aŭdis per la radiofono; *she spoke on television:* ŝi parolis per televizio); (repetition), post (e.g.: *wave on wave rolled over us:* ondo post ondo ruliĝis super ni); (after verb: onto), sur– [pfx] (e.g.: *smear the paint on:* surŝmiri la farbon); (after verb: lastingly), daŭre, ade, –ad– [sfx] (e.g.: *they babbled on:* ili daŭre babilis [or] ili babiladis); (connected, re elec light, circuit, device), ŝaltita (e.g.: *the light is on:* la lumo estas ŝaltita); (open, re valve), malfermita (e.g.: *the water, the faucet is on:* la akvo, la krano estas malfermita); (functioning, re any device), funkcianta (e.g.: *I saw two motors on:* mi vidis du funkciantajn motorojn); (planned, going to happen), okazonta (e.g.: *tomorrow's meeting is still on:* la morgaŭa kunveno ankoraŭ estas okazonta); (theat, radio, TV, etc.: presented), prezentata; prezentota (e.g.: *what's on?:* kio estas prezentata?; *the news is on next:* la novaĵoj estas prezentotaj venonte); (at expense of), regale de (e.g.: *drinks are on the house:* trinkaĵoj estas regale de la domo); **onward(s),** antaŭen; **it's on me,** (I will pay), mi regalos; **on and on,** senĉese, senfine, senlime; **on and off,** (intermittent), intermita; intermite; **go (blink, etc.) on and off,** intermiti [int] [cp "blink", "flicker"]

onager, onagro†
Onagraceae, onagracoj
onanism, onanismo
once, (occurring one time), unufoje, unu fojon (e.g.: *eat once a day:* manĝi unufoje [or: unu fojon] tage); (at any time, ever), iam (e.g.: *I'll explain it to him if I once get him to listen:* mi klarigos ĝin al li se mi iam aŭskultigos lin); (at past time), iam, antaŭe (e.g.: *I once lived there:* mi iam [or: antaŭe] loĝis tie); (as soon as), kiam, tuj kiam, kiam jam (e.g.: *we will leave once the rain stops:* ni foriros (tuj) kiam la pluvo (jam) ĉesos); **at once,** (immediately), tuj; **all at once,** (suddenly), subite; (at same time), samtempe; **for once,** (now), ĉi-foje; (then), tiufoje; **once and for all,** unu fojon por ĉiam, definitive; por nun [or: tiam] kaj por ĉiam; **once every three days (etc.),** [see under "every"]; **once in a while,** kelkfoje, fojfoje, de tempo al tempo; **once-over,** rapida ekzamen(et)o; **once upon a time,** iam antaŭ longa tempo
Onchocerca volvulus, onkocerko
onchocerciasis, onchocercosis, onkocerkozo
one–, (med pfx: cancer), onk–†
oncogenic, onkogena†
oncology, onkolog/io†; **oncological,** ~ia; **oncologist,** ~o
Ondatra, fibero; Ondatra zibethica, ondatro
one, (number), unu [see § 19]; (indefinite personal pron), oni (e.g.: *what must one do?:* kion oni devas fari?); (a certain unspecified), iu (e.g.: *I saw her one day last week:* mi vidis ŝin iun tagon la pasintan semajnon); (one and only), sola, nura (e.g.: *the one thing that bothers me:* la nura [or: sola] afero kiu ĝenas min); (after adj, indicating specified one(s) or one(s) of that sort), [not translated] (e.g.: *I finished this one, and I want another one:* mi finis ĉi tiun, kaj mi volas alian; *the green ones are pretty:* la verdaj estas belaj); **one's,** ies; ĉies; sia [note: "onia" is correct but rarely applicable] (e.g.: *one has one's [own] duty:* oni

havas sian devon; *it is (every)one's duty to come:* estas ĉies devo veni; *the Board protected one's (others') right to read their minutes:* la Estraro protektis ies rajton legi iliajn protokolojn); **oneself,** [see "self"]; **oneness,** unueco; **anyone, everyone, someone,** [see "anyone" etc.]; **no one,** neniu [for examples, see "any" and subsequent entries]; **no one at all,** neniu ajn; **no one's (at all),** nenies (ajn); **at one (with),** unueca (kun); **one and the same,** unu sama; **the one ... the other,** unu ... la alia; **one and all,** ĉiu(j) ajn; **one another,** unu la alian; sin reciproke (e.g.: *they hugged one another:* ili brakumis unu la alian [or] brakumis sin reciproke); **one by one,** unuope; **one of those things,** neeviteblaĵo; **one-to-one, one-on-one,** parigita; parigite; **(be) one up on (someone),** (esti) super (iu), (esti) supera al (iu); **one-upmanship,** superemo; **one-way,** (gen), unudirekta

–one, (chem sfx), –ono

Onega, (river), Onego; **Lake Onega,** Lago ~a

onerous, peniga, peza

Onesimus, Onezimo

onion, cepo; **onionskin,** (paper), ~opapero

Oniscus, onisko

only, (adv), nur [must immediately precede word or phrase modified] (e.g.: *I only have five dollars:* mi havas ~ kvin dolarojn); (adj), ~a (e.g.: *the only thing:* la ~a afero); (sole, alone), sola (e.g.: *the only tree in the area:* la sola arbo en la regiono; *only child:* solinfano); (but), sed (e.g.: *I'd come, only I'm too busy:* mi venus, sed mi estas tro okupata); **one and only,** unu~a, unusola, solsola

Onobrychis, onobriko

onomastic, onomastika; ~isto; **onomasticon,** nomaro

onomatology, onomastiko

onomatopoeia, onomatopeo; **onomatopoeic,** ~a

Onopordon, onopordo; Onopordon acanthum, azenkardo

onslaught, atak(eg)o

Ontario, (province), Ontario; **Lake Ontario,** Lago ~o

onto, sur –on (e.g.: *the cat jumped onto the sofa:* la kato saltis sur la sofon); **be onto,** (aware), konscii [int] pri

ontogeny, ontogenesis, ontogenio†; **ontogenetic,** ~a

ontology, ontologio; **ontological,** ~a

onus, (burden), ŝarĝo; (blame), kulpo, respondeco

Onychophora, pratrañeuloj

onyx, onikso

oocyte, oocito*

oodles (of), abunda(j), multega(j), multege da

oof! (interj), uf!

oogenesis, ovogenezo

oolite, oolito

oomycetes, oomicetoj

oophorectomy, ovariektomio

oops! (interj), up!, hup!

oospore, oosporo

ooze, eksudi [int]; ~aĵo; (slime), ŝlimo; (muck), fango

opal, opalo; **opalesce,** ~eski [int]; **opalescence,** ~esko; **opalescent,** ~eska

opaque, opaka; **opacity,** ~eco

open, (opp "close", gen), malfermi [tr]; ~iĝi; ~ita, (neol), aperta [note: "aperta" is useful esp in combined forms (e.g.: *open-heart surgery:* apertakora kirurgio)]; (begin), komenci [tr]; komenciĝi; (inaugurate), inaŭguri [tr]; (make available), disponigi; disponiĝi; (reveal), malkaŝi [tr], riveli [tr]; (spread out, unfold), sterni [tr]; sterniĝi; (outdoors), ekstere(n); eksteraĵo; (public), publika; (free, unrestricted), libera; (broad, clear, unobstructed), vasta, senobstrukca; (not yet decided), decidota, nedecidita; (not prejudiced), senantaŭjuĝa; (not discriminatory), nediskriminacia; (active, in force), aktiva, valida; (not occupied, e.g., seat, job), vaka; (re vowel), vasta; (accessible), alirebla; (known, not secret), konata; (candid, honest), honesta; **opening,** ~(iĝ)o; komenco; inaŭguro; stern(iĝ)o; publikigo; (hole), truo, aperturo; (breach), breĉo; (opportunity), ŝanco, oportuno; (mouth, lit or fig, gen), buŝo; **open-air**, subĉiela; **open-and-shut**, memklara, simpla; **open-ended**, nelimigita; **(out) in the open**, (outdoors), subĉiele, en la eksterajo; (not hidden), malkaŝita; malkaŝite; **open-minded**, senantaŭjuĝa; **open-work**, ajura; aĵuraĵo

opera, opero; **operatic**, ~a; **operetta**, ~eto; **opera house**, ~ejo, ~domo; **soap opera**, populara (televida) dramo

operate, (function), funkcii [int]; ~igi; (med; math), operacii [tr]; (direct, manage), direkti [tr], administri [tr]; **operable**, (feasible), farebla, praktika; (med), operaciebla; **operation**, ~(ig)(ad)o; operacio; direkt(ad)o; (activity, enterprise), agado, aktivaĵo, entrepreno; (mil), operaco; (single step in multiple process), manipulo (e.g.: *the first operation is to engage the machine:* la unua manipulo estas kupli la maŝinon); **go into operation**, (become effective, in force), efektiviĝi; **put into operation**, efektivigi; **operational**, (working), ~anta; (workable), ~iva; (in effect), efektiva; **operative**, ~anta; ~iva; efektiva; (med), operacia; (agent), agento; **inoperative**, ne~anta; ne~iva; (w/o result; invalid), senefika, neefektiva, malvalida; **postoperative**, postoperacia; **preoperative**, antaŭoperacia; **operator**, ~iganto; ~igisto; operacianto; (math; console operator of cmptr; etc.), operatoro; (phone), telefonist(in)o

operculum, (gen), operkulo

Ophelia, Ofelia

ophicleide, ofiklejdo

Ophiura, ofiuro; Ophiuroidea, ~oidoj

ophthalmia, oftalmio

ophthalmic, oftalma

ophthalmitis, oftalmito

ophthalm(o)–, (med pfx), oftalm(o)–

ophthalmology, oftalmolog/io; **ophthalmologist**, ~o

ophthalmometer, oftalmometro

ophthalmoscope, oftalmoskopo; **ophthalmoscopy**, ~io

opiate, opiaĵo

opine, opinii [int]

opinion, opinio; **opinionated**, obstina; **public opinion**, popol~o, publik~o; **have an opinion**, ~i [int]; **in my opinion**, laŭ mia ~o, mia~e, laŭ mi

opium, opio; **opium den**, ~ejo

Oporto, Porto, Oporto

opossum, (zool), didelfo; (pelt, fur), oposumo; **murine opossum**, marmozo

opotherapy, opoterapio

opponent, oponanto; kontraŭulo [see "oppose"]

opportune, oportuna; **opportunism**, ~ismo; **opportunist**, ~isto; **opportunistic**, ~isma; **opportunity**, ~o; **inopportune**, mal~a

oppose, (be against, gen), kontraŭi [tr], ~stari [tr], oponi [int] (al, ke) (e.g.: *he opposed the plan:* li ~is la planon [or] li oponis al la plano); (pol etc.), opozicii [int] (al); (place opposite), ~meti [tr] (e.g.: *opposed thumb:* ~metita polekso); **opposition**, ~(star)o, opon(ad)o; (pol; ast), opozicio; **be opposed to**, ~i, oponi al

opposite, (opposite ideas, antonym), malo; ~a; ~e (e.g.: *"under" is the opposite of "over":* "sub" estas la ~o de "super"; *go in the opposite direction:* iri en la ~a direkto [or] iri ~adirekten; *just the opposite:* tute ~e); (contrary; facing, set against), kontraŭ, kontraŭa (al) (e.g.: *flight opposite to the wind:* flugo kontraŭa al la vento; *their house is opposite ours:* ilia domo estas kontraŭ la nia); (re leaves on stem), kontraŭesidanta; **the opposite gender**, la alia sekso

oppress, (weigh heavily, trouble, gen), premi [tr]; (pol etc.), opresi [tr], tirani [tr]; **oppression**, ~(ad)o; opres(ad)o; **oppressive**, ~a; opresa

opporobrium, (contempt), mallaŭdo; (shame), honto; (infamy), fifamo; **opporobrious**, ~a

opt, opt for, elekti [tr] [cp "option"]; **opt out (of)**, sin retiri (de, el)

optative, optativo; ~a

optic, (re eye), opta

optical, optika

optician, optikisto

optics, optiko [note sing]
optimism, optimismo; **optimist**, optimisto; **optimistic**, ~a
optimum, optimumo; **optimize**, ~igi; **optimal**, ~a
option, (choice, gen), elekto; (bsns, law, etc.), opcio; (alternative), alternativo; **optional**, ~(ebl)a; opcia; (not mandatory), nedeviga, laŭvola, laŭplaĉa, fakultativa
opt(o)–, (pfx), opto–
optometer, optometro
optometry, optometrio; **optometrist**, ~isto
opulent, luksa, riĉa; **opulence**, ~o, riĉeco
Opuntia, opuntio, nopalo; Opuntia ficus-indica, figokakto
opus, verko; **opus number**, (mus), ~numero; **magnum opus**, granda ~o
or, aŭ
–or, (sfx), [see "~er"]
orach(e), atriplo; **garden orache**, ĝarden~o
oracle, (gen), orakolo; **speak as an oracle**, ~i [int]; **oracular**, ~(ec)a
oral, buŝa
Oran, Orano
orange, (fruit), oranĝo; (tree), ~arbo; (color), ~a; ~o; **bergamot orange**, (fruit), bergamoto; (tree), bergamotarbo; **mock orange**, filadelfo; **sour orange**, **bitter orange**, **Seville orange**, bigarado
Orange, (city; river), Oranĝo; **Orange Free State**, ~io
orangery, oranĝerio
orangutan, orangutano
orate, oratori [int]; **orator**, ~o; **oratory**, ~a; ~aĵo; ~ado; **oration**, ~aĵo [not "oracio"]
oratorio, oratorio
orb, (globe), globo; (sphere), sfero; (body in space), astro; (area inside orbit), orbo
orbicular, (spherical), sfera; (anat), orbikula; **orbicular muscle**, **orbiculus**, orbikulo
orbit, (gen), orbito; ~i [int]; ~igi; **orbital**, ~a; **deorbit**, el~igi; el~iĝi; **suborbital**, sub~a; **(geo)stationary orbit**, **(geo)synchronous orbit**, (geo)sink-

rona ~o; **parking orbit**, park~o; **orbital injection**, en~igo; **orbital transfer**, trans~igo; **put into orbit**, en~igi; **go into orbit**, en~iĝi
orchard, fruktarbaro, horto
orchestra, orkestro; **orchestral**, ~a; **orchestrate**, ~i [tr]
orchestrion, orkestriono
orchid, orkideo; **bird's-nest orchid**, neotio
Orchidaceae, orkideoj
orchid(o)–, (med pfx), orkid(o)–
orchidotherapy, orkidoterapio
orchiectomy, orkidektomio
orchil, [see "archil"]
orchi(o)–, (med pfx), orkid(o)–
orchis, orkido
Orchis, (bot), orkido
orchitis, orkidito
Orcinus, orcino
Orcus, Orko
ordain, (destine), destini [tr]; (rel), ordini [tr]; **foreordain**, **preordain**, antaŭ~i [tr], antaŭdekreti [tr]
ordeal, (any severe experience), aflikto, penigo; (ancient legal trial), juĝa ~o
order, (orderliness, opp "chaos"; sequence, rank; bot; zool; math), ordo; ~i [tr]; ~iĝi; (command), ordoni [tr]; ordono; (request sale etc., to pay later), mendi [tr]; mendo (e.g.: *I ordered two books from the book service:* mi mendis du librojn de la libroservo); (rel or honorary society etc.), ordeno; (rel rank, as major or minor order), ordino; (state, condition), stato (e.g.: *in working order:* en funkcianta stato); (sort, type), speco; (food portion, as in restaurant), porcio; (payment order, gen), asigno, mandato; **orderly**, (neat), neta, bon~a, ~(em)a; (well-behaved), bonkonduta; (regular, methodical), regula, laŭmetoda; (mil: servant soldier), servosoldato; (attendant, as in hospital), (hospital)servisto; **disorder**, (chaos), ĥaoso, mal~o, konfuzo; ĥaosigi, mal~i [tr], konfuzi [tr]; (med, tech), perturbo; **disorderly**, sen~a; (chaotic), ĥaosa; (unruly, riotous), malpaca, tumulta; **order form**, **order blank**, mendilo; **order book**, mendolibro; **back-order**, ret-

romendi [tr]; **money order**, mandato; **postal money order**,
poŝtmandato; **tall order**, malfacila
tasko; **out of order**, (not in sequence),
ekster~a; ekster~e; (disordered),
sen~a; (not working), nefunkcianta;
(against rules), kontraŭregula; **call to
order**, (meeting etc.), kunvoki [tr]; **in
order to**, por ~i (e.g.: *she climbed the
tree in order to see better:* ŝi grimpis
la arbon por vidi pli bone); **in order
that**, por ke ~u (e.g.: *I wrote in order
that you might know:* mi skribis por ke
vi sciu); **on order**, mendita; **on the
order of**, (about, approximately), ĉirkaŭ, proksimume, pli-malpli; (similar), (iom) simila al; **to order**, (as ordered), laŭmende (e.g.: *made to
order:* laŭmende farita)
ordinal, (re order), orda; (re ordination),
ordina; ordinlibro
ordinance, (command), komando, ordono; (statute), statuto; (rite), rito
ordinary, (usual, customary), ordinara;
(rel: mass book), meslibro; **out of the
ordinary**, **extraordinary**, ekster~a
ordinate, ordinato
ordination, ordinado, ordinacio
ordnance, artilerio
Ordovician, ordovicio; ~a
ordure, ekskremento
ore, erco
öre, **øre**, ($), oero
oread, oreado
oregano, origano
Oregon, Oregono [note: PIV erroneous-
ly applies the name "Oregono" to the
Columbia River, hence using "~io"
for the state; "~o" can and should be
used for the state w/o confusion or
misunderstanding]
Orestes, Oresto
Öresund, **Øresund**, Sundo
organ, (anat, mech part; organ of communication; etc.), organo; (mus instrument), orgeno; **barrel organ**,
gurdo; **organ grinder**, gurdisto
organdy, **organdie**, organdio
organic, (med: re organs, e.g., organic
pathology), organa; (chem, bio, ecological, etc.), organika; **inorganic**,
ne~a; neorganika

organism, organismo; **microorganism**,
mikro~o
organize, organizi [tr]; ~iĝi; **organization**, (group), ~o; (act), ~ado; **disor-
ganize**, konfuzi [tr], malordi [tr],
mal~i, des~i [tr]; **disorganized**, (w/o
order), senorda, ĥaosa; **reorganize**,
re~i [tr]
orgasm, orgasmo; **orgasmic**, ~a
orgy, orgio; **orgiastic**, ~(ec)a
oriel, orielo
orient, (set in direction; determine direction), orienti [tr]; **orientate**, **orient
oneself**, **get oriented**, ~iĝi, ~i sin;
orientation, ~ado; ~iĝo
Orient, (East), Oriento; **Oriental**, ~a;
~ano; **Orientalism**, orientalismo;
Orientalist, orientalisma; orientalisto
orifice, orifico
oriflamme, oriflamo
Origanum, origano; Origanum majorana, majorano
Origen, Origeno
origin, origino; **original**, (first version;
not copy; new in idea), originala;
originalo; (re origin), ~a; **originality**,
originaleco; **originate**, ~i [int]; ~igi,
iniciati [tr]
Orinoco, Orinoko
oriole, (Eurasian: *Oriolus*), oriolo; (Am:
Icterus), ikteruso*; **Baltimore oriole**, Baltimora ikteruso*; **golden oriole**, ~o
Oriolus, oriolo
Orion, (myth; ast), Oriono
Orkney (Islands), Orkadoj
Orleans, (city), Orleano; (region), ~io;
New Orleans, Nov-~o
orlon, orlono
orlop, orlopo
Ormazd, **Ormuzd**, Ormuzdo [cp "Ahura-Mazda"]
ornament, ornami [tr]; ~aĵo; **ornamental**, ~a; **ornamentation**, ~ado; ~aĵo
ornate, (mult)ornamita
ornery, malafabla, malĝentila, obstina,
kalcitrema
Ornithogalum, ornitogalo
ornithology, ornitolog/io; **ornitholo-
gist**, ~o
Ornithopus, ornitopo
Ornithorhynchus, ornitorinko

Orobanche, ornobanko
orography, orografio;   **orographical**, ~a
Orontium, orontio
orphan, ofro; ~ino; ~igi; **orphaned**, ~a; **orphanage**, ~ejo
Orpheus, Orfeo; **Orphic**, ~(ism)a; **Orphism**, ~ismo
orpine, sedo
orsted, orstedo
orth(o)–, (pfx), ort(o)–
orthochromatic, ortokromata; **orthochromatism**, ~eco, ~ismo
orthoclase, ortoklazo
orthodontic, ortodenta, ~ika; **orthodontics**, ~iko; **orthodontist**, ~isto
orthodox, ortodoksa; ~ulo(j); **orthodoxy**, ~eco; ~ismo; **unorthodox**, mal~a
orthognathous, ortognata
orthogonal, ortangula
orthography, ortografio; **orthographic**, ~a
orthopedic, ortopedia; **orthopedics**, ~o; **orthopedist**, ~isto
Orthoptera, ortopteroj
ortolan, hortulano
Oryctolagus cuniculus, kuniklo
Oryza sativa, rizo
Osaka, Osako
osazone, ozazono
Oscar, (man's name; movie award), Oskaro
oscillate, oscili [int]; **oscillation**, ~ado; **oscillator**, ~ilo
oscilloscope, oscilografo, osciloskopo
oscillograph, oscilografo
osculate, (kiss), kisi [tr]; (math), oskuli [tr]
–ose, (chem sfx), ~ozo
osier, vimeno
Osiris, Oziriso
–osis, (sfx), ~ozo
Oslo, Oslo
Osmerus eperlanus, eperlano
osmium, osmio; **osmic acid**, ~ata acido; **osmate**, ~ato
osmosis, osmozo; **osmotic**, ~a
Osmunda, osmundo, reĝofiliko
osprey, pandiono, fiŝaglo
Ossa, Osso
osseous, ost(ec)a

Ossian, Osiano
ossicle, osteto
ossify, (lit), ost/igi; ~iĝi; (fig), ŝtonigi; ŝtoniĝi
osteal, ost(ec)a
ostealgia, ostalgio
osteitis, ostito
ostensible, (seeming), ŝajna; (claimed), pretendata
ostentatious, pompa; **ostentatiousness**, ~o
oste(o)–, (anat pfx), ost(o)–
osteogenesis, ost/ogenezo; **osteogenetic**, ~ogena
osteology, ostologio
osteoma, ostomo
osteomyelitis, ostomedolito, osteomjelito
osteopath, ostopati/isto; **osteopathy**, ~o; **osteopathic**, ~a
osteotomy, ostotomio
ostracism, ostracismo; **ostracize**, ~i [tr]
Ostrea, ostro
ostrich, struto
Ostrogoth, Ostrogoto
Oswald, Osvaldo
otalgia, otalgio
Otaria, otario, marleono; Otariidae, ~edoj, orelfokoj
Othello, Otelo
other, (different, not same), alia; ~e (e.g.: *John and two others came:* Johano kaj du ~aj venis; *I want the other shirt, not that one:* mi volas la ~an ĉemizon, ne tiun; *other than that, I don't know:* ~e ol tio, mi ne scias); (remaining), cetera (e.g.: *40 members approved, 30 disagreed, and the others abstained:* 40 membroj aprobis, 30 malkonsentis, kaj la ceteraj sin detenis); **otherwise**, (in other circumstances), ~e, ~okaze; (in other manner), ~maniere; **each other**, unu la ~an, unu al la alia, si(n) reciproke (e.g.: *they insulted each other:* ili insultis unu la alian [or] insultis sin reciproke; *they gave each gifts:* ili donis donacojn al si reciproke [or] al si unu al la alia); **every other**, (alternating), ĉiu dua (e.g.: *I cook every other week:* mi kuiras ĉiun duan semajnon); **in other words**, ~vorte; **among other**

things, inter~e [abb: i.a.]; **the other day (week, etc.)**, (a few days etc. ago), antaŭ kelkaj tagoj (semajnoj etc.)
Othin, Odino [cp "Wotan"]
-otic, (med sfx), -oza
Otis, (zool), otido
otitis, otito; **otitis media**, meza ~o, timpanito
ot(o)-, (med pfx: ear), ot(o)-
otology, otologio
otoscope, otoskopo; **otoscopy**, ~io
Ottawa, Otavo
otter, lutro
Ottoman, Otomano; ~a
oubliette, ublieto
ouch! (interj), aj!, aŭ!, huj!
ought, devus (e.g.: *I ought to go:* mi devus iri)
ounce, (weight, volume, gen), unco [avoirdupois: 28,35 gramoj; troy: 31,10 gramoj; fluid: 29,58 mililitroj (see § 20)]; (zool: snow leopard), uncio
our, ours, nia; **ourselves**, [see "self"]; **of our -ing**, [see "her"]
-ous, (chem sfx: lower valence), -oza; (sfx to indicate presence of something, gen), -(hav)a (e.g.: *porous:* porhava [or] pora); ("full of"), -plena
oust, elpeli [tr], elŝovi [tr]; **ouster**, ~o, elŝovo
out, (away), for (e.g.: *we live 60 km out from Washington:* ni loĝas 60 km-ojn ~ de Vaŝingtono; *she is out to lunch:* ŝi estas ~ por lunĉo); (forth from inside or behind; eruption; appearance), el, el- [pfx], ekstere(n) (e.g.: *he fell out:* li elfalis; *the smoke drifted out [outside]:* la fumo drivis eksteren; *the children came out to play:* la infanoj elvenis [or: venis eksteren] por ludi; *the dirt washed out:* la malpuraĵo ellaviĝis); (around, in all directions), dis- [pfx] (e.g.: *give out fliers:* disdoni flugfoliojn; *knock out a wall:* disbati muron; (along), laŭ (e.g.: *drive out Highway 99:* veturi laŭ Ŝoseo 99); (adj: going, leading out etc.), elira (e.g.: *the out door:* la elira pordo); (elec: turned off), malŝaltita; (extinguished, as fire etc.), estingita; (im-

possible, not to be considered), neebla (e.g.: *because of that, our first plan is out:* pro tio, nia unua plano estas neebla); (sports: out of bounds), ekstertaĉa; (out of fashion, passé), eksmoda; (out of the closet, re gay or lesbian), elkameriĝinta; (force gay or lesbian out of closet), elkamerigi; [see also "out-"]; **outer**, ekstera; **outing**, (excursion), ekskurso; (forcing gay or lesbian out of closet), elkamerigo; **be out**, (lose $ etc.), perdi [tr] (e.g.: *I'm out $4:* mi perdis $4); **outback**, (hinterland), landinterno; **outbound**, elira; **outlying**, malproksima; **outspoken**, malkaŝema, kandida [not "elparol-"]; **outward**, ekstera, surfaca; ekstere(n); **out in the open**, (outdoors), subĉiela, en la eksteraĵo; subĉiele; (not hidden), malkaŝita; malkaŝite; **out of**, (beyond), preter; (outside), ekster; (made of), el (e.g.: *made out of wood:* farita el ligno); (because of), pro (e.g.: *out of malice:* pro malico); (from), el (e.g.: *the wind is out of the north:* la vento estas el la nordo) **be out of**, (not have), manki al iu, elĉerpiĝi de (e.g.: *we're out of milk:* mankas al ni lakto [or] ni elĉerpiĝis de lakto; *the store is out of that book:* la butiko elĉerpiĝis de tiu libro); **run out of**, elĉerpiĝi de; **out of it, wiped out**, (colloq: stuporous), stupora, spiritomanka, ellaciĝinta; (unconscious), senkonscia; (out of fashion), eksmoda; **out-and-out**, absoluta, ĝisosta; **out of town**, eksterurba; **all out**, tut(kor)e; **be out for, be out to**, (have as goal), celi [tr] (e.g.: *he's out for blood:* li celas sangon); **out one's way**, (near one), proksima al iu
out-, (pfx: better, to greater degree), super- [pfx] (e.g.: *outfox:* ~ruzi); (external), ekstera, ekster- [pfx] (e.g.: *outboard:* eksterboata); (going outward), el- [pfx] (e.g.: *outbound traffic:* elira trafiko)
ouzel, (any of *Cinclidae*), cinklo
oval, ovalo; ~a
ovary, ovario; **ovariectomy**, ~ektomio; **ovaritis**, ~ito
ovation, ovacio; **give an ovation to**, ~i

[tr]

oven, (gen), forno; (cooking), ~o, bakujo; **Dutch oven,** (cooking pot), bakpoto; (preheated brick oven), (antaŭhejtita) brik~o; **microwave oven,** mikroonda ~o

over, (above), super (e.g.: *fly over the house:* flugi ~ la domo); (upon), sur (e.g.: *snow spread over the plains:* neĝo sterniĝis sur la prerion); (across), trans (e.g.: *walk over the line:* marŝi trans la linion; (at end of 2-way radio transmission), trans (e.g.: *Do you read me? Over!:* ĉu vi aŭdas min? Trans!); (beyond), preter (e.g.: *go over the limit:* iri preter la limon); (through, throughout), (tute) tra (e.g.: *crime increased over the whole city:* krimo pliiĝis tute tra la urbo); (during), dum (e.g.: *they visited me over the holidays:* ili vizitis min dum la libertagoj); (in preference), prefere al (e.g.: *choose blue over red:* elekti bluon prefere al ruĝo); (concerning), pri (e.g.: *argue over money:* disputi pri mono); (by means), per (e.g.: *talk over the telephone, radio, TV:* paroli per la telefono, radiofonio, televizio); (more), pli (ol) (e.g.: *over 200 people came:* pli ol 200 homoj venis; *you must be age 21 or over:* vi devas aĝi 21 jarojn aŭ pli); (finished), finita (e.g.: *the game is over:* la ludo estas finita); (further), plu (e.g.: *stay over for another day:* resti plu dum alia tago); (again), denove, ree, re– [pfx] (e.g.: *write it over:* denove [or] ree verki ĝin [or] reverki ĝin); (here, there), [generally omitted] (e.g.: *it's over there on the shelf:* ĝi estas tie sur la breto; *come over here:* venu ĉi tien); (interj on page, directing reader to turn page), dorsen; [see also "over–"]; **over again,** denove, ree, re– [pfx]; **overall,** tuta, (tut)inkluziva; **overly,** tro, ekscese; **over and above,** aldone al, krom; **over and done with,** nerevokeble finita; **over and out!,** (2-way radio), trans kaj el!; **over and over,** (repeated action), –adi; (more emphatic), –i kaj re...(ad)i (e.g.: *explosions sounded over and over*

through the night: eksplodoj bruis kaj rebruadis tra la nokto; **overlander,** (Aus), brutpelisto; **left over,** restinta; restanta; **be left over,** resti [int]; **get it over with,** tuj [or] senprokraste fini ĝin

over–, (pfx: above, more), super– (e.g.: *overrun:* ~kuri); (too much), tro– (e.g.: *overwork:* trolaborigi); (beyond), preter– (e.g.: *overstep the bounds:* preterpaŝi la limojn)

overalls, supertuto, kombineo [note sing]

overt, nekaŝita, evidenta, malfermita, aperta

overture, (mus), uverturo; (proposal etc.), propono

overweening, (arrogant), aroganta, orgojla; (excessive), troa

overwhelm, (overpower, overcome), dron/igi, subigi, superverŝi [tr]; (stun), stuporigi; **overwhelming,** ~iga, subiga, superverŝa, neeltenebla; **be overwhelmed,** ~i [int], subiĝi; ne (povi) elteni [tr, int] (kontraŭ); stuporiĝi

overwrought, (nervous), nervoz(eg)a, trostreĉita

ovi–, (pfx: egg), ovo–

Ovibos moschatus, ovibovo

Ovid, (Roman poet), Ovidio; (modern man's name), Ovido

oviduct, ovodukto

oviform, ovoida, ovoforma

ovipara, ovonask/uloj; **oviparous,** ~a

Ovis, ovio

ovogenesis, ovogenezo

ovoid, ovoida; ~o

ovolo, kvaroncirkla plinto [not "ovolo"]

ovulate, ovoli [int]; **ovulation,** ~ado, ~ofalo

ovule, ovolo

ovum, ovo

ow! (ouch!), aŭ!, aj!, huj!

owe, (gen), ŝuldi [tr]; **owing,** ~ata; **owing to,** (because of), pro, ~e al

owl, (gen), strigo; (*Athene noctua*), noktuo; (*Asio otus*), otuso, orel~o; **eagle owl,** (*Bubo*), gufo [not "bubo"]

own, (possess), posedi [tr], proprieti [tr]; (re self), propra (e.g.: *my own opinion:* mia propra opinio); (admit), konfesi [tr]; (acknowledge), agnoski

[tr]; **owner**, ~anto, proprietulo; **co-owner**, kun~anto; **ownership**, ~raj-to, ~anteco, proprieto; **disown**, mal-konfesi [tr], malagnoski [tr]; (disinherit), senheredigi; (wife by husband), repudii [tr]; **own up to**, konfesi [tr]; **on one's own**, (by own initiative), propravole; (by own effort), proprapene

ox, (any bovine), bov(in)o; (castrated bull), okso; **oxeye**, (bot: *Buphthalmum*), buftalmo; **oxpecker**, bufago; **musk-ox**, ovibovo; **water ox**, bubalo

oxalate, okzal/ato; **oxalic acid**, ~a acido, etandiacido

Oxalis, oksalido

oxalyl, oksalilo

oxford, (shoe), Oksforda ŝuo

Oxford, (city; university), Oksfordo; ~a

oxidase, oksidazo

oxide, oksido; **oxidize**, ~igi; ~iĝi; **oxidation**, ~igo; ~iĝo

oxim(e), oksimo

Oxonian, Oksforda

oxonium, oksonio

ox(y)‒, (chem pfx), oksi‒

oxyacetylene, oksacetilena

oxycephaly, akrocefal/eco; **oxycephalic**, **oxycephalous**, ~a

Oxycoccus, oksikoko

oxydase, oksidazo

oxygen, oksigeno; **oxygenate**, (water), ~i [tr]; ~iĝi; (chem), ~izi [tr]

oxymoron, oksimoro

oxytocin, oksitocino

oxytone, oksitona; ~o

oxyuria(sis), oksiuriozo

oxyuricide, oksiuricido

Oxyuris vermicularis, oksiuro

oy! (interj), oj!; **oy vey!**, ho ve!, oj ve!

oyster, ostro; **oyster bed**, ~ejo; **pearl oyster**, meleagreno, perlokonko

ozena, ozeno

ozokerite, **ozocerite**, ozokerito

ozone, ozono; **ozonize**, (make ozone), ~igi; (give ozone), ~izi [tr]; **ozonometer**, ~ometro; **ozonosphere**, ~osfero; **ozonotherapy**, ~oterapio

Ozotoceros bezoarticus, venado

P

pa, (dad), paĉjo
pablum, (lit or fig), bebkaĉo
pabulum, (any food), nutraĵo; (pablum), bebkaĉo
pace, (step), paŝi [int]; ~o; (walk on), sur~i [tr], treti [tr]; (speed, rate), rapido; (rhythm, beat), takto; (lead), gvidi [tr]; pacemaker, (in race etc.; pacesetter), rapidogvidanto; (for heart, anat or mech), korritmigilo; set the pace, difini la rapidon (takton); change of pace, rapidoŝanĝo; go (put one) through one's pace, elprovi siajn (ies) kapablojn; keep pace with, ~oteni kun; pace off, (measure w paces), ~mezuri [tr]
pasha, paŝao
pachouli, [see "patchouli"]
pachy–, (pfx), paki– [but see "pachyderm"]
pachyderm, pañidermo
pachydermatous, pakidermia
pacific, (peaceful), paca
Pacific, (ocean), Pacifiko; ~a; trans-Pacific, trans-~a
pacifism, pacifismo; pacifist, ~a; pacifisto
pacify, pacigi; pacifier, (for baby), ~ilo
pacinian, (corpuscle), paĉinia
pack, (put compactly into), paki [tr]; ~iĝi; (things packed, package), ~o; (backpack), tornistro [cp "pannier"]; (oth packing container), ~ujo (e.g.: parachute pack: paraŝuta ~ujo; film pack: film~ujo); (of cigarettes, cards, etc.; packet), ~eto; (group of animals etc.), bando, –aro [sfx] (e.g.: pack of wolves: luparo); (compress), kunpremi [tr]; (med, cosmetic), kompreso; (stuff, lit or fig), farĉi [tr] (e.g.: pack a nose, the jury: farĉi nazon, la ĵurion); [see also "–pack"] packer, ~isto; packing (material), ~umo; backpack, packsack, tornistro; packer, ~isto; daypack, tornistreto; backpacking, tranokta marŝado; go backpacking, take a backpacking trip, fari tranoktan marŝadon; pack

animal (horse etc.), ŝarĝbesto (ŝarĝoĉevalo etc.); packing case (box), ~kesto; ice-pack, pack-ice, (over water, as in Arctic), bankizo; send someone packing, malceremonie forsendi iun
–pack, (sfx: carton), –pako (e.g.: a six-pack of beer: ses~o da biero)
package, pako; ~i [tr]; packaging, ~ado; ~aĵo; prepackage, antaŭ~i [tr]; package store, alkoholaĵa butiko
packet, (package), paketo; (boat), poŝtŝipo
pact, pakto
Pactolus, Paktolo
pad, (cushion; stamp pad, ink pad), kusen/eto; ~i [tr]; (gauze, cotton ball, etc.), vato; vati [tr] (med compress), kompreso; (of paper), (paper)bloko; (stuff, as furniture), remburi [tr]; (walk lightly), paŝeti [int]; (launch pad), lanĉejo; (add wrongfully), farĉi [tr] (e.g.: they padded the expense account, the results of the poll: ili farĉis la elspezokonton, la rezultojn de la opinisondo); padding, remburaĵo; vato
paddle, (for canoe, kayak, table tennis, etc.), pagajo; (propel canoe etc.), ~i [int] (en); ~igi [cp "oar"]; (blade, as of paddlewheel, turbine, oar, etc.), padelo; (splash in water, as w paddle blade; dabble), padeli [int]
paddock, ĉevalkampo
paddy, (rice field), rizejo
Padova, Padovo
padre, (priest), pastro
Padua, Padovo
paean, peano
paed–, [see "ped–"]
Paeonia, peonio
pagan, pagano; ~a; paganism, ~ismo
page, (of book etc.), paĝo; (attendant), paĝio; (call), voki [tr]; paginate, ~onumeri [tr], numeri la ~ojn de; pagination, ~onumerado; pageboy, (haircut), paĝia hararanĝo; page layout, (cmptr preparation of document

for publication), eldon-preparado; eldon-prepara

pageant, spektaklo; **pageantry**, (pageants), ~oj; (pomp), pompo

Pagellus, pagelo

pagoda, pagodo

Pagurus, paguro; Paguridae, ~edoj

pah! (interj), pa!

pail, sitelo

pain, doloro; ~i [tr]; **pains**, (care, effort), klopodo(j), peno(j); **painful**, ~(ig)a; **painkiller**, ~forigenzo, analgeziko; **painstaking**, diligenta, klopodema, penema; **take pains to**, klopodi [tr]; **on pain of**, sub puno de; **pain in the neck**, (bother), ĉagreno

paint, (art), pentri [tr]; (color, gen), farbi [tr]; farbo; (depict, lit or fig), ~i, figuri [tr], desegni [tr]; **painter**, ~isto; farbisto; **painting**, (act), ~ado; farbado; (work of art), ~aĵo; (art form), pikturo; **paintbrush**, peniko; **oilbase paint**, olefarbo; **water-base paint**, akvofarbo; **greasepaint**, ŝminko

pair, paro; ~igi; ~iĝi; **thermoelectric pair**, termoelektrika pilo, termo~o

pajama(s), piĵamo [note sing]; ~a

Pakistan, Pakistano; **Pakistani**, ~ano; ~a

pal, kamarado, amiko; **pal around (with)**, ~i [int] (kun)

palace, palaco; **palatial**, ~a

paladin, paladino

Palaemon, palemono

palaeo–, [see "paleo–"]

Palaeodictyoptera, paleodiktiopteroj

palaestra, palestro

palanquin, palankeen, palankeno

palatable, agrabla, bongusta; **unpalatable**, mal~a, malbongusta

palate, palato; **palatal**, (re palate), ~a; (bone; phon), palatalo; **palatitis**, ~ito

Palatinate, Palatinato

palatine, palatino

Palatine, Palatino

palaver, palavro; ~i [int]

pale, (not bright), pala; ~igi; ~iĝi; (stake), paliso; (limit), limo

palea, paleo

Paleocene, paleoceno; ~a

paleograph/y, paleograf/io; **paleogra-**

pher, ~o

paleolithic, paleolitiko; ~a

paleontology, paleontolog/io; **paleontologist**, ~o

Paleozoic, paleozoiko; ~a

Palermo, Palermo

Palestine, (modern), Palestino; (ancient), Filiŝtujo; **Palestinian**, ~ano; ~a; Filiŝta

palestra, palestro

palette, paletro

Pali, (la) Palia (lingvo)

palimpsest, palimpsesto

palindrome, palindromo

palinode, palinodo

Palinurus, palinuro, langusto

palisade, (pole), paliso; (fence of same), ~aro; (escarpment), krutaĵo

pall, (bore), tedi [tr]; (funeral cloth), ĉerkotuko; (any dark covering, veil, etc.), vualo, mantelo; (dusky gloom), krepusko; **pallbearer**, ĉerkoportanto

palladium, (metal), paladio

Palladium, (statue), Paladio

Pallas, (goddess), Palasa; (man's name; asteroid), ~o

pallet, (bed), litaĉo; (platform for forklift), (tabul)paledo†; (storage chest), (pak)kestego; (potter's tool), platigilo; **palletize**, paledizi† [tr]

palliasse, pajl/matraco, ~olito

palliate, mildigi; **palliative**, paliativo; ~a

pallid, pala

pallium, (gen), paliumo

pallor, paleco

palm, (tree, gen), palmo; (of hand), polmo, manplato; **palm off**, forĵongli [tr], trompdoni [tr]; **palm reading, palmistry**, kiromancio; **palm reader, palmist**, kiromanciisto; **Palm Sunday**, P~odimanĉo, P~festo; **betel palm**, kateĉuareko; **cabbage palm**, (Aus: *Livistona australis*), basikarbo; **coconut palm**, kokosarbo, kokos~o; **date palm**, daktil~o [see "date"]; **jupati palm, raffia palm**, rafio; **sago palm**, cikaso, sagu~o

Palma, (bot), palmo; Palmae, ~acoj

palmetto, palmeto

palmiped, palmipedo

palmitate, palmit/ato; **palmitic acid**, ~a

acido, heksadekan-acido
palomino, kremkolora ĉevalo
palp, ĉiro
palpable, palpebla
palpate, palpi [tr, int]
palpebral, palpebra; **palpebritis**, ~ito, blefarito
palpitate, palpitacii [int]; **palpitation**, ~o
palpus, ĉiro
palsy, paralizo; ~i [tr]
paltry, nura, bagatela
Pamir, Pamira; **Pamiri**, ~ano; **Pamirs**, (Mountains), ~o
pampa, (gen), pampo; **Las Pampas** (of Argentina), la P~oj
pamper, dorloti [tr]
pamphlet, (gen informative), broŝuro; (pol attack, satire), pamfleto, agit-folio; **pamphleteer**, pamfletisto; pamfletadi [int]
Pamplona, Pampluno
pan, (shallow, as frying pan), pato; (deeper pot), poto; (for washing, as dishpan), kuveto, pelvo; (scale tray), pespleto; (wash for gold), orlavi [tr]; (phot), panoram(ad)i [tr, int]; (criticize), mallaŭdi [tr]; **panhandle**, (of pan; strip of land), ~tenilo; (beg), almozi [tr]; **panhandler**, almozulo; **pan out**, (succeed), sukcesi [int]; (have any result), rezulti [int]; **bedpan**, litpelvo; **frying pan**, (frit)~o
Pan, (myth), Pajno; **Panpipes, pipes of Pan**, ~oŝalmo [note sing]
Pan troglodytes, (zool), ĉimpanzo
pan–, (pfx: all), tut– (e.g.: *Pan-American:* tut-Amerika) [note: sometimes absorbed into Esperanto root as "pan–"; see separate entries below]
panacea, panaceo
panache, (plume), plumaro; (flair), brilo, puceco
Panama, (country), Panam/io; **Panama Canal**, Kanalo de ~o; **Panama City**, ~o
Panax, panako; Panax schinseng, Panax ginseng, ginsengo
panchromatic, pankromata
pancratium, (sport), pankraco
Pancratium, (bot), pankracio
pancreas, pankreato; **pancreatic**, ~a;

pancreatectomy, ~ektomio; **pancreatitis**, ~ito
pancreatin, pankreatino
panda, (gen), pando; **lesser panda**, *(Ailurus fulgens)*, malgranda ~o; **giant panda**, *(Ailuropoda melanoleucus)*, granda ~o
Pandalus, pandalo; Pandalidae, ~edoj
Pandava, Pandavo(j)
pandemic, (prevalent everywhere, gen), ĉiea, universala; (disease), pandemio*
pandemonium, Pandemonium, pandemonio
pander, prostituisto, parigisto; **pander to**, fiflati [tr]
Pandion, pandiono, fiŝaglo; Pandionidae, ~edoj
Pandora, Pandora
pane, (glass), vitro(panel)o; (wood panel etc.), panelo
panegyric, panegiro; **panegyrical**, ~a; **panegyrize**, ~i [int]
panel, (covering of wood etc.; instrument panel etc.), panelo; ~i [tr]; (group), grupo, –aro [sfx] (e.g.: *panel of judges:* juĝistaro)
pang, ekdoloro
panga, maĉeto
pangolin, maniso
panic, (fear; grass), paniko; ~i [tr]; ~iĝi
panicle, paniklo
Panicum, paniko; Panicum miliaceum, milio
pannier, (modern pack for bicycle, horse, etc.), flanktornistro; (basket on back), dorskorbo
Pannonia, Panonio
panoply, panoplio; **panoplied**, ~izita
panoptic, panoptika; ~o
panorama, panoramo; **panoramic**, ~a
pansy, violego, trikoloreto
pant, (gasp), anheli [int]; ~o
Pantagruel, Pantagruelo
pantechnicon, (truck), meblokamiono
pantheism, panteismo; **pantheist**, ~a; panteisto
pantheon, panteono
Pantheon, Panteono
panther, leopardo, pantero
pantof(f)le, pantoflo
pantograph, (gen), pantografo
pantomime, pantomimo [cp "mime",

"mummer"]
pantothenic, pantotena;   **pantothenic acid,** ~a acido
pantoum, pantumo
pantry, mangôsranko
pants, pantalono [note sing]; **panty, panties,** kalsoneto [note sing]; **underpants,** (modern briefs), kalsoneto; (old-fashioned, long), kalsono
Panurge, Panurgo
panus, panuso
pap, (nipple), cico; (mush), kaĉo
papa, paĉjo
papacy, papeco
papain, papino
papal, papa
Papaver, papavo;   Papaver rhoeas, ~eto; Papaver somniferum, opio~o
papaverine, papaverino
papaw, (tree), papaŭo; (fruit), ~frukto
papaya, papaia, (tree), papajo; (fruit), ~bero, ~frukto
paper, (material, gen), papero; ~a; (newspaper), ĵurnalo; (scholarly treatise), referaĵo; (treatise presented at symposium, conference, etc.), memuaro; **paperback,** poŝlibro; poŝlibra; **paperbound,** ~e bindita; **paperboy, papergirl,** ĵurnalportist(in)o; **paper clip,** vinkto; **paperhanger,** tapetisto; **paper nautilus, paper sailor,** argonaŭto; **paperweight,** ~premilo; **blotter paper,** sorbo~o; **carbon paper,** karbo~o; **crêpe paper,** krepa ~o; **curlpaper,** papiloto; **drawing paper,** desegno~o; **filter paper,** filtro~o; **fly paper,** muŝ~o; **incense paper,** incens~o†; **sandpaper,** sablo~o; sablo~i [tr], sabli [tr]; **tissue paper,** silko~o; **toilet paper,** klozet~o; **tracing paper,** paŭs~o; **wallpaper,** tapet~o; tapeti [tr]; **wastepaper,** rubo~o; **put (get) down on paper,** sur~igi; **present a paper (on),** referi [int] (pri)
Paphos, Pafoso
papier-mâché muldokartono, papermaĉaĵo; ~a
Papilio, papiliono; Papilio machaon, makaono, hirundovostulo; Papilionidae, ~edoj
Papilionaceae, legumenacoj

papilla, papilo; **papillary,** ~a; **papilloma,** ~omo; **papillomatosis,** ~omatozo
papillote, papiloto
Papio, paviano
papoose, (Indiana) bebo
paprika, paprica, papriko
Papua, Papu/lando; **Papuan,** ~o; ~a; ~landa; **Papua New Guinea,** Novgvinea—~lando†
papule, papulo
papyr-, (sci pfx: papyrus), papir/(o)– (e.g.: *papyrology:* ~ologio)
papyrus, papiruso
par, ($), alparo; (norm; golf), normo; **on a par with,** egala al, samnivela kun
para-, (sci pfx), para–
parable, parabolo
parabola, parabolo; **parabolic,** ~a; **paraboloid,** ~oido
paracentesis, paracentezo
parachor, parakoro
parachute, paraŝuto; ~a; ~i [int]; ~igi; **parachutist,** ~isto
paraclete, parakleto
Paraclete, Parakleto
parade, (gen), parado; ~i [int]; (to display mil troops, equipment, etc.), revuo
paradigm, paradigmo
paradise, paradizo; **fool's paradise,** iluzia ~o
Paradisea, paradizeo, paradizbirdo
parados, paradoso
paradox, paradokso; **paradoxical,** ~a
paragoge, paragogo; **paragogic,** ~a
paraffin, (wax, or any saturated hydrocarbon), parafino; (Br: kerosene), keroseno
paragon, perfekta modelo
paragraph, (gen), alineo; (in legal text etc.), paragrafo
Paraguay, Paragvajo; **Paraguayan,** ~ano; ~a
parakeet, (*Melopsittacus*), melopsitako*
paraldehyde, paraldehido
Paralipomenon, Paralipomenoj   [cp "chronicle; Chronicles"]
parallax, paralakso
parallel, (gen), paralela; ~e; ~o; ~i [int] (al, kun); **make, show a parallel (be-**

tween), ~igi (ion kun io)
parallelepiped, paralelepipedo
parallelogram, paralelogramo
paralogism, paralogismo
paralyze, paralizi [tr]; **paralysis**, ~o;
paralytic, ~(ig)a; ~ulo; **infantile paralysis**, infana ~o, poliomjelito
Paramaribo, Paramaribo*
paramecium, Paramecium, paramecio*
parameter, parametro
paramount, unuaranga, ĉefa
paramour, amorant(in)o
paramyoclonus, paramioklonio
paranoia, paranojo; **paranoid**, ~a; ~ulo
parapet, parapeto
paraph, parafo
paraphernalia, (tools, equipment), ilaro, ekipaĵo; (things, gen), aĵaro, akcesoraĵoj
paraphrase, parafrazo; ~i [tr]
paraphysis, parafizo
paraplegia, paraplegio; **paraplegic**, ~a; ~ulo
parasite, (gen), parazito; **parasitic**, ~a; **parasiticide**, ~icido; **parasitism**, ~ismo; **parasitosis**, ~ozo; **parasitology**, ~ologio; **parasitologist**, ~ologo; **live as a parasite**, ~i [int]
parasol, sunombrelo
Parastacidae, (Aus), parastacedoj*
parataxis, paratakso
parbuckle, tiravivo
Parca(e), Parco(j)
parcel, (package), pako; (of land), parcelo, terpeco; **parcel out**, disdividi [tr], distribui [tr]
parch, sekeg/igi; **parched**, ~a
parchment, pergameno
pardon, pardoni [tr]; ~o; **pardon me!**, ~u min!, ~u!; **beg one's pardon**, ~peti [int] (e.g.: *I beg your pardon!:* mi ~petas!)
pare, (fruit etc.), senŝeligi; **pare down**, (reduce, gen), malpliigi, ĉirkaŭtondi [tr], detranĉ(et)i [tr]
paregoric, paregorika; ~a eliksiro, ~aĵo
parenchyma, parenkimo; **parenchymatous**, ~a; **palisade parenchyma**, palisadaj ĉeloj
parent, (bio), patr/(in)o, ge~o; (re organization), filiiga, origina, ge~a; par-

ents, ge~oj; **parental**, ge~a;
parentage, deveno; **parents-in-law**, boge~oj; **godparents**, baptoge~oj;
stepparent, duon~(in)o, duonge~o;
duon~(in)a, duonge~a; **stepparents**, duonge~oj
parenthesis, parentezo; **parenthetical**, ~a; **parenthetical phrase**, ~o
paresis, parezo
par excellence, senkompara, elstara
parfait, parfeo
pariah, pario
paries, parieto
parietal, (re paries), parieta; (bone), parietalo
Parietaria, parietario; Parietaria officinalis, mura ~o
Paris, (city), Parizo; (myth), Pariso; **Parisian**, ~ano; ~a
parish, paroĥo, paroko; **parishioner**, ~ano; **parish house**, ~estrejo
parity, ($), alparo; (equality, gen), egaleco
park, (gen), parko; ~i [tr]; **parking lot**, ~ejo; **parking meter**, ~ometro; **parking orbit**, ~orbito; **parking place (space)**, ~spaco; **parkway**, ~vojo
parka, kapuĉpalto
parkinsonism, Parkinson's disease, Parkinsona morbo
parlance, lingvaĵo
parlay, (bet), kromveti [tr]; ~o; (exploit), ekspluati [tr]
parley, konferenci [int], konsultiĝi, diskuti [tr]; ~o, diskuto
parliament, parlamento; **parliamentary**, (re parliament), ~a; **parliamentarian**, ~isto; **parliamentarianism**, ~ismo; **member of parliament**, ~ano; **parliament house**, ~ejo
parlo(u)r, (gen), salono
Parma, Parmo
Parmenides, Parmenido
Parmesan, Parma; ~ano; ~a fromaĝo
Parnassus, Parnaso; **Parnassian**, ~ano; ~a
parochial, (gen), paroĥa, paroka; **parochialism**, ~ismo
parody, parodio; ~i [tr]
parole, (release), honorliberigi; ~o; (word of honor), parolo; **on parole**,

~ita; ~ite; **parolee,** ~ito
paronomasia, paronomazio
paronychia, paroniñio
paronym, paronimo; **paronymous,** ~a
Paros, Paroso
parotid, parotido; ~a
parot(id)itis, parotidito, mumpso
paroxysm, paroksismo; ~ajo
paroxytone, paroksitona; ~ajo
parquet, (floor), pargeto; (one tile), ~ero; **parquetry,** ~ajo
parricide, (act), gepatromortigo; (person), ~into
parrot, papago; ~umi [tr, int]; **gray parrot,** psitako
parry, deturni [tr]; ~o
parsec, parseko
Parsee, Parsi, Parsio; ~a [cp "Farsi"]; **Parseeism,** ~ismo
parsimony, avar/eco; **parsimonious,** ~a
parsley, petroselo; **beaked parsley,** cerefolio; **fool's parsley,** etuzo; **poison parsley,** makula konio
parsnip, pastikano; **cow parsnip,** herakleo; **water parsnip,** siumo
parson, (any clergy), pastro; (in charge of parish), parofiestro; **parsonage,** ~odomo; parofiestrejo
part, (division of whole; mus; share), parto; ~a; ~e; (partition), (dis)~igi; (dis)~iĝi; (break up), disigi; disiĝi; (separate), apartigi; apartiĝi; (role etc.), rolo; (replacement part, spare part), vicpeco; (hair), dividi [tr], dislimi [tr]; hardivido, hardislimo; **partly, in part,** ~e; **partway,** ~e, iom; **part and parcel of,** esenca ~o de; **part of speech,** ~o de parolo; **part with,** (separate), apartiĝi de; (give away), fordoni [tr]; **take part in,** ~opreni [int] en; **play the part (of),** roli [int] (kiel); **for my part,** miaflanke; **on the part of,** flanke de; **for the most part,** plej~e
partake, (participate), partopreni [int] (en); (take), preni [tr] (iom da), kundividi [tr]
parterre, (gen), partero
Parthenocissus quinquefolia, ampelopso
parthenogenesis, partenogenezo

Parthenon, Partenono
Parthia, Part/io; **Parthian,** ~o; ~a; ~ia
partial, (in part), parta; (biased), partia; (inclined to), inklina, tendenca; **partiality,** partieco, antaŭjuĝ(em)o; **impartial,** senpartia, justa; **impartiality,** senpartieco, justeco
participate, partopreni [int] (en); **participant,** ~into; ~anto
participle, participo; **active, passive, past, present, future participle,** aktiva, pasiva, preterita, prezenca, futura ~o
particle, (tiny piece, thing), korpusklo, peceto, ereto; (subatomic), ~o, partiklo; (gram), partikulo; **alpha-particle,** alfa-~o; **antiparticle,** anti~o; **virtual particle,** efektiva ~o
particular, (distinct, separate, specific), aparta, specifa; (certain, definite), difinita; (special), speciala; (choosy, preferring own way), partikulara, elektema, precioza; (one's own), propra; (detail), detalo; **particularism,** partikularismo; **particularly, in particular,** ~e, specife; **particularize,** detali [tr]
particulate, korpuskla, partikla [see "particle"]
partisan, (re pol party, faction, etc.), partia; (sam)~ano; (mil; fervent adherent), partizano; **nonpartisan,** sen~a
partition, (divide), part/igi; ~iĝi; ~igo; ~iĝo; (room divider etc.), vando, septo
partitive, (gram), partitiva; ~ajo
partner, (gen), partnero; **partnership,** ~eco; **silent partner, sleeping partner,** (bsns), komanditanto; **silent (sleeping) partnership,** komandito
partridge, perdriko; **black partridge,** frankolino
parturition, akuŝo
party, (gathering for fun), festo; (more formal reception etc.), akcepto; (group), bando, grupo; (pol organization etc.; individual in contract, lawsuit, etc.), partio; partia; (traveling group), karavano; **party line,** (telephone), komuna linio; (pol), partia dogmo; **party wall,** komuna muro;

third party, krompersono, krompartio, tria partio; be a party to, (law), esti partio en; (be involved, gen), sin miksi en; hen party, in-~o [not "in~o"; see "infest"]; housewarming party, fajrej–inaŭguro; stag party, vir~o
Parus, paruo; Paridae, ~edoj
Parvati, Parvatia
parvenu, parvenuo; ~(ec)a
Pascal, (man's name), Paskalo
pascal, (unit of pressure), paskalo*
pasha, paŝao
Pashto, (la) Puŝtua† (lingvo)
Pasiphae, Pazifaa
pasquil, pasquinade, paskvilo, pamfleto
pass, (go, send, put from one point to oth, in space or time; disappear, cease; get through; etc.), pasi [tr, int]; ~igi (e.g.: the crisis passed: la krizo ~is; we passed the crisis: ni ~is la krizon; pass over the river: ~i trans [or] trans~i la riveron; we passed 3 days there: ni ~igis 3 tagojn tie); (succeed in exam, class, etc.), sukcesi [int] (ĉe, en) (e.g.: I passed physics: mi sukcesis en la fiziko); (occur), okazi [int]; (approve law etc.), promulgi [tr]; promulgiĝi; (ratify treaty etc.), ratifiki [tr]; ratifikiĝi; (excrete), eligi, ekskrecii [tr]; eliĝi, ekskreciiĝi; (go past), preter~i [tr]; (overtake, as one car by oth), devanci [tr]; (die, pass away), for~i [int]; (penetrate), penetri [tr]; (give over), (trans)doni [tr]; (trans)doniĝi (e.g.: please pass the salt: bonvolu doni la salon; the throne passed to his son: la trono transdoniĝis al lia filo); (meet, come across), renkonti [tr]; (way through mountains), monto~ejo, intermonto; (steep gorge etc.), gorĝo; (situation), situacio; (entry, exit permit), ~ilo; passable, (can go along, through, as re road), veturebla, trairebla, irebla; (acceptable), (apenaŭ) akceptebla, adekvata, mezbona; impassable, neveturebla, netrairebla, neirebla; passing, ~anta, ~ema, efemera; pass as, pass for, akceptiĝi kiel; pass away, (die), for~i [int]; pass by, (beyond),

preter~i [tr]; devanci [tr]; (along, to), ~i laŭ; passer-by, ~anto; pass off, (by trick), forĵongli [tr], trompdoni [tr]; pass on, (tell), transdiri [tr]; (give), transdoni [tr]; (bequeath), heredigi; (as tradition), tradicii [tr]; (judge), juĝi [tr]; (die, pass away), for~i [int]; pass out, (give), disdoni [tr]; (faint), senkonsciiĝi; pass over, (go over), super~i [tr]; sur~i [tr]; (omit), preterlasi [tr]; pass up, malakcepti [tr], ellasi [tr], preterlasi [tr]; bypass, (go past, beyond), preter~i [tr]; (gen), ĉirkaŭiri [tr]; (gen), preter~ejo; (road), pretervojo; (med etc.: any tubing), pretertub(et)o; (elec: shunt), ŝunto; ŝunti [tr]; (avoid), eviti [tr]; overpass, super~ejo; underpass, sub~ejo, strattunelo; in passing, ~ante; bring to pass, okazigi; come to pass, okazi [int]; make a pass at, provi amindumi [tr]
passage, pas/ado; ~ejo; (excerpt), ekstrakto, partaĵo; passageway, ~ejo
passé eks/moda, ~kutima
passementerie, pasamento
passenger, pasaĝero; ~a
passe-partout, (gen), paspartuo
Passer, pasero; Passeriformes, ~oformaj (birdoj); Passer domesticus, dom~o; Passer montanus, monto~o
Passiflora, pasifloro; Passiflora edulis, grenadilo
passim, diversloke
passion, (emotion), pasio; (ardor), ardo; passionate, impassioned, ~(plen)a; arda; be(come) impassioned, ~iĝi; dispassionate, sen~a, nepartizana
Passion, (rel; mus), Pasiono
passive, (gen), pasiva; ~o
Passover, Pesaño*, Pasko [note: "Easter" is also "Pasko"; "Pesaño" is recommended to avoid ambiguity]
passport, pasporto
past, (re time), pasinta; ~eco (e.g.: past history: ~a historio; forget the past: forgesu la ~econ); (former), eksa, eks– [pfx], ~a (e.g.: past president: eksprezidento); (by, beyond), preter, preter– [pfx] (e.g.: walk past the house: marŝi preter la domon; they

flew past: ili preterflugis); (after), post (e.g.: *it is past your bedtime:* estas post via enlitiĝa tempo; *ten past three (o'clock):* dek post la tria (horo); *half past six:* duono post la sesa); (gram: preterite tense ["–is"]), preterito; preterita; **past event, past thing,** ~aĵo; **I wouldn't put it past him to (do something),** mi kredas ke li ja povus (fari ion)

pasta, (flour), pasto; (food), ~aĵo(j)

paste, (gen), pasto; ~i [tr]; **pasty,** ~eca; **Turkish paste,** lukumo

pastel, (gen), paŝtelo; ~a

pastern, pasterno

Pasteur, Pasteŭro

pasteurize, pasteŭrizi [tr]

pasticcio, pastiche, (pie), pasteĉo; (art, mus), pastiĉo; pastiĉi [tr]

pasties, cicaĵoj [cp "nipple"]

pastil(le), (pastel), paŝtelo; ~a; (pill etc.), pastelo

pastime, distraĵo, tempopasigo; **favorite pastime,** maroto

Pastinaca, pastinako

pastor, (rel; zool), pastoro [cp "priest"] Pastor, pastoro

pastoral, (rural), kampar(ec)a, paŝtista; (rel), pastora

pastorale, pastoralo

pastry, (dough), pasto; (food), kukaĵo(j)

pasture, paŝti [tr]; ~ejo

pasty, (Br: meat pie), pasteĉo

pat, (touch, tap), frapeti [tr]; ~o; (piece of butter etc.), peceto, buleto; (apt, opportune), oportuna, tujpreta; (suitable, good), taŭga; **have down pat,** scii [tr] parkere; **stand pat,** stari [int] senmove

Patagonia, Patagon/io; **Patagonian,** ~o; ~a; ~ia

patch, (mend), fliki [tr]; ~aĵo; (med dressing), pansaĵo; (spot, small area), makulo; (piece), peco; (garden bed), bedo; (mil etc. insignia), ŝultrosigno; (elec cord), (konekto)ŝnuro; **patchwork,** miksaĵo, miksaranĝo

patchouli, patchouly, (plant or perfume), paĉulo

paté (meat paste, pie), pasteĉo; **paté de foie gras,** anser~o

patella, patelo; **patellar,** ~a

Patella, (zool), patelo

paten, pateno

patent, (on invention etc.), patento; ~i [tr]; ~ita; (obvious), memklara, (mem)evidenta; **patent pending,** ~ota

paterfamilias, familipatro

paternal, patr(ec)a; **paternalism,** paternalismo

paternity, patreco

paternoster, Pater Noster, Patro Nia, Patronia (e.g.: *he said a paternoster:* li diris Patro-Nian [or] Patronian) [cp "prayer: Lord's Prayer"]

path, (footpath, lit or fig), pado; (way, gen), vojo; **pathfinder,** vojtrovanto; **pathway,** ~o; vojo; **flight-path,** flugitinero

Pathan, Patano; ~a

pathetic, (pitiful), mizera, kompatinda, korŝira

pathogen, patogen/enzo; **pathogen(et)ic,** ~a; **pathogenesis,** patogenezo

pathology, patolog/io; **pathologist,** ~o; **pathological,** ~ia

pathos, patoso

patience, pacienco; **impatience,** mal~o; **have patience,** ~i [int]; **patience!,** (be patient!), ~u! [see also "patient"]

patient, (having patience), pacienca; (med), paciento; **impatient,** mal~a; **be patient,** ~i [int]; **inpatient,** interna paciento; **outpatient,** ambulatoria paciento; **outpatient clinic,** ambulatorio; [see also "patience"]

patina, patine, (paten), pateno; (coating), patino

patio, korteto

Patmos, Patmo

patois, dialekto

patriarch, patriarko; **patriarchal,** ~a; **patriarchy,** ~eco; ~ujo

Patricia, Patrika

patrician, patricio; ~a

patricide, patromortigo

Patrick, Patriko

patrimony, hereda posedaĵo

patriot, patrioto; **patriotic,** ~a; **patriotism,** ~ismo

patristic(al), patrologia, patristika

Patroclus, Patroclos, Patroklo
patrol, (group of police or soldiers), patrolo; (act of patrolling), ~ado; ~i [int] (en, ĉe); **patrolman,** ~isto
patron, (sponsor, donor), patrono; ~ino; ~a; (client, customer), kliento; **patronize,** (as protector etc.), ~i [tr]; (treat condescendingly), ~aĉi [tr]; (do bsns w), negoci [int] (kun); **patronage,** ~ado; ~eco; negoco [cp "sponsor"]
patronymic, patronoma; ~o
patsy, dupo
patter, (any light tapping), frapetadi [tr, int]; ~o; (as rain), plaŭdet(ad)i [int]; plaŭdet(ad)o; (chatter), babili [int]; babil(ad)o; (jargon), ĵargono
pattern, (model, gen), modelo; ~i [tr]; (from which oth objects made, as mold etc.; matrix, orderly arrangement), matrico [cp "mold"]; (of cardboard, plastic, etc., for drawing, lettering, etc.; template), ŝablono; (for sewing), patroneo†; (design), desegno; (custom, habit), kutimo, moro (e.g.: *behavior patterns:* kondutaj kutimoj [or] moroj); (movement), moviĝado (e.g.: *traffic patterns:* trafikaj moviĝadoj); **pattern after,** ~igi laŭ
patty, (disk of ground meat etc.), diskbulo; (small meat pie), pasteĉeto
Pau, Paŭo
paucity, (few), malmult(ec)o; (insufficiency), nesufiĉo
Paul, Paŭlo; **Paula,** ~a; **Pauline,** ~ino; **Paulist,** ~ano; ~ana
paunch, (belly), ventr/ego, ŝvel~o; (rumen), rumeno; **paunchy,** ~ega, ŝvel~a
pauper, malriĉ/ulo; **pauperism,** (re one person), ~eco; (social phenomenon), paŭperismo
Pausanias, Paŭzanio
pause, paŭzi [int]; ~o; (mus), fermato; **give one pause,** hezitigi iun
pavan(e), pavano
pave, pavimi [tr]; **pavement,** ~o; **paving stone,** ~ero
Pavia, Pavio
pavilion, (gen), pavilono
pavin, pavano
Pavo, (zool), pavo

paw, (animal foot), piedo; (dig, claw, etc.), ~umi [tr] [cp "claw"]; (handle awkwardly, roughly), fuŝpalpi [tr]; (caress roughly), fuŝkaresi [tr]
pawl, kliko
pawn, (hock), lombardi [tr]; (peon, person as tool), peono, servutulo; (chess), peono; **pawnbroker,** ~isto; **pawnshop,** ~ejo
pawpaw, [see "papaw"]
pay, (give $ etc.), pagi [tr]; ~o (e.g.: *I will pay you a dollar:* mi ~os al vi dolaron); (be worthwhile), profiti [int], valori la penon (e.g.: *it will pay you to listen:* profitos al vi aŭskulti [or] valoros al vi la penon aŭskulti); (wages, salary), salajro; (operable by payment), ~a, pag– [pfx] (e.g.: *pay telephone:* ~telefono); **payable,** (due, to be paid), ~enda; **payee,** al~ato; **representative payee,** (guardian), kuratoro; **payment,** ~o; ~aĵo; **down payment,** ek~o; **paid,** (re extra charge), fri [prep] (e.g.: *for $15, postpaid:* kontraŭ $15, fri afranko); **paycheck,** salajroĉeko; **payday,** ~tago; **payload,** ~ŝarĝo; **paymaster,** ~estro; **payola,** ŝmirmono; **pay off,** (settle debt), kvitigi; (repay, compensate), re~i [tr], rekompenci [tr]; **payoff,** kvitigo; rekompenco; (bribe), subaĉeto; (climax), kulmino; **payroll,** (list), salajrolisto, salajr-etato; ($ sum), salajromono; **overpay,** tro~i [tr]; **postpay,** (pay after), post~i [tr]; **prepay,** antaŭ~i [tr]; **repay,** ($), re~i [tr], ristorni [tr]; (compensate, gen), kompensi [tr], re~i [tr]; **pay through the nose,** ~i tro, ~egi [tr]; **pay the piper,** ~i la koston; **there'll be hell to pay,** al infero ŝuldiĝos; estos gravaj sekvoj
pea, (seed or plant, gen), pizo; (any of *Lathyrus*), latiro; **pea-shooter,** cerbatano; **butterfly pea,** (*Clitoria*), klitorio; **chickpea, dwarf pea,** kikero; **field pea,** kampa ~o; **garden pea,** ĝardena ~o; **Sturt's desert pea,** (Aus: *Clianthus formosus*), dezerta ~o; **sweet pea,** bonodor~o
peace, paco; (calm, quiet), ~o, kvieto, trankvilo; **peaceable, peaceful,**

~(em)a; trankvila, kvieta; **peace-time**, ~tempo; dum~a; **peace of mind**, trankvilo; **hold one's peace**, silentadi [int]; **keep the peace**, konservi la ~on; **make peace with**, ~iĝi kun

peach, (fruit), persiko; (tree), ~arbo

peacock, peafowl, pavo; **peahen**, ~ino; **peachick**, ~ido

peak, (maximum), maksimumo, kulmino, zenito; ~a; ~igi; ~iĝi; (any sharp, high point), pinto; pintigi; pintiĝi; (mountain), pint(mont)o

peal, sonor/adi [int]; ~iĝadi; ~ado

pean, peano

peanut, arakido; **peanut butter**, ~aĵo

pear, (fruit, gen), piro; (tree, gen), ~arbo; **pear-shaped**, ~forma; **balsam pear**, momordiko; **bergamot pear**, bergamot~o; bergamot~a arbo; **prickly pear (cactus)**, opuntio, nopalo

pearl, perlo; **cultured pearl**, kultur~o; **mother-of-pearl**, perlamoto

peasant, kamparano; **peasantry**, ~aro

peat, torfo; **peat moss**, sfagno

peba, dazipo

pebble, ŝtoneto, gruzero

pecan, (nut), pekano; (tree), ~arbo

peccadillo, peketo

peccary, pekario

peck, (as by bird), beki [tr], pikpluki† [tr], (~)piki [tr]; (~)piko; (kiss), kiseti [tr]; kiseto; (unit of volume), kvaronbuŝelo [(Am), 8,81 litroj; (Br), 9,09 litroj (see § 20)]

Pecten, pekteno

pectin, pektino

pectineus, (muscle), pektineo

pectoral, (re chest), brusta; (muscle), pektoralo

peculiar, (strange), kurioza, stranga; (characteristic, distinctive), propra (e.g.: *a custom peculiar to the Germans:* moro propra al la Germanoj); (special, unique), aparta; **peculiarity**, ~aĵo; ~eco; propraĵo

pecuniary, mona

–ped, (sfx: –footed), –pieda; –piedulo (e.g.: *quadruped:* kvar~ulo)

pedagog(ue), pedagogo; **pedagogy, pedagogics**, ~io

pedal, (part moved by foot), pedalo; ~i [tr]; (re foot), pieda

pedant, pedanto; **pedantic**, ~a; **pedantry**, ~eco

peddle, kolporti [tr]; **peddler**, ~isto

–pede, [see "–ped"]

pederast, pederasti/ulo; **pederasty**, ~o

pedestal, piedestalo; **put (someone) on a pedestal**, apoteozi [tr]

pedestrian, (walking), piedira; ~anto; (dull, uninteresting), malinteresa, malsprita

pediatrics, pediatr/io; **pediatrician**, ~o

pedicel, pedicle, (bot), pedicelo; (zool), pediklo [cp "peduncle"]

Pedicularis, pedikulario

Pediculus, pediko

pedicure, pedikuri [tr]; ~o

pedigree, (lineage, ancestry), deveno; (record of ancestry), genealogio; **pedigreed**, (purebred), purrasa

pediment, frontono

pedometer, hodometro, odometro

peduncle, pedunklo

pee, (colloq: piss, urinate), pisi [int]; ~aĵo

peek, gvati [tr]; ~o; **peek at**, ~i

peel, (re fruit, tree, etc.), ŝelo; sen~igi; sen~iĝi; (re skin), senhaŭtiĝi; (flake off, as paint, skin, etc.), deskvamiĝi; **peeling**, ~o

peen, martelbeko [see "hammer"]

peep, (chirp), pepi [int]; ~o; (peek), gvati [tr]; gvato; **peeping-tom**, gvatanto; **spring peeper**, (frog), hilo

peer, (equal), egala; ~ulo; ~aĵo; ~ula (e.g.: *peer pressure:* ~ula premo [or] premo de ~uloj); (noble), nobelo; (look), strabi [int]; **peerless**, sen~a, senkompara

peeve, ĝeni [tr]; ~aĵo; **peeved**, ~ita, kolereta; **peevish**, malafabla, malbonhumora, iritiĝema; **pet peeve**, plej granda ~aĵo

peg, (of wood etc.), kejlo; ~i [tr]; (metal pin), stifto; stifti [tr]; (degree, step), grado; (maintain, hold), konservi [tr], fiksi [tr]; **tuning peg**, agorda ~o

Pegasus, (myth; ast), Pegazo

Peipus, Pejpuso

Peiraeus, Pireo

pejorative, (derogatory), mallaŭda; ~o

Peking, Pekino; **Pekingese**, ~ano; ~a;

(dog), ~a hundo
pelada, pelade, pelado
Pelagianism, pelagianismo†
pelagic, pelaga
Pelargonium, pelargonio
Pelasgi, Pelasgoj; **Pelasgian,** ~o; ~a
Pelecanus, pelikano; Pelecaniformes, ~oformaj (birdoj)
pelerine, pelerino
Peleus, Peleo
pelf, monaĉo
pelican, pelikano
Pelion, Peliono
pellagra, pelagro
pellet, granulo, grajno
pellitory, (*Parietaria*), parietario
pell-mell, iele trapele, pelmele; pelmelo
pellucid, (clear, gen), klara; (transparent), diafana
Peloponnesus, Peloponnesos, Peloponezo; **Peloponnesian,** ~a
Pelops, Pelopso
pelota, (jai alai), peloto†
pelt, (skin and fur), felo; (proceed), pelto; (bombard), bombardi [tr]; (beat), batadi [tr]
pelvis, pelvo; **pelvic,** ~a; **pelvimetry,** ~ometrio; **pelvis renalis, pelvis of the kidney,** pielo
pem(m)ican, pemikano
pemphigus, pemfigo
pen, (writing), plumo; (enclosure), enfermejo; enfermi [tr]; (write), skribi [tr]; **penmanship,** manskribado; **pen pal, pen friend,** ~amiko, korespondamiko; **pen name,** ~nomo, pseŭdonimo; **ball-point pen,** globkrajono, bulpinta ~o; **felt-tip pen,** felt~o; **fountain pen,** fonto~o
penal, puna; **penal code,** ~kodo; **penal servitude,** ~laboro
penalty, (disadvantage), malavantaĝo; ~igo; (punishment), puno; (sports), penalo†; **penalize,** ~igi; puni [tr]; penali† [tr]; **death penalty,** mortpuno, mortkondamno
penance, pentofarado
penates, Penatoj
pence, pencoj [see "penny"]; **sixpence,** (coin), ses~o
penchant, inklino, emo, tendenco
pencil, krajono; ~i [tr]

pendant, (for chain etc.), breloko; (anything hanging), pendaĵo
pendentive, pendentivo
pending, (yet to be decided), decidota; (yet to be dealt with), pritraktota; (about to happen, impending), okazonta; (during), dum; (until), ĝis
pendulous, pendanta
pendulum, pendolo
Penelope, Penelopa
peneplain, peneplane, peneplano
penetrate, penetri [tr, int]; **impenetrable,** ne~ebla
penguin, (gen), pingveno; (*Spheniscus*), sfenisko
penicillin, penicilino
Penicillium, penicilio
peninsula, duoninsulo
penis, peniso; (colloq), kaco
penitent, penta, ~ema, ~ofara; ~(ofar)anto; **penitence,** ~ofarado
penitentiary, pundomo
pennant, pennon, flageto
Pennsylvania, Pensilvanio
penny, (Am), cendo; (Br), penco; **new penny,** (Br), novpenco; **sixpenny,** sespenca; **pennycress,** (bot), tlaspo; **pennyless,** (tute) senmona; **pennywort,** (bot: *Hydrocotyle*), hidrokotilo, akvotelero; **a pretty penny,** konsiderinda sumo, multe da mono, granda monsumo; **penny wise and pound foolish,** ete ŝparema sed ege malŝparema
Penny, (woman's name), Penjo [see "Penelope"]
pension, (annuity), pensio; ~i [tr]; (lodging), pensiono; **pensioned,** ~iĝinta; **pensioner,** ~ulo
pensive, pensema
pent (up), (enclosed), enfermita; (plugged), ŝtopita; (controlled), bridita
penta-, (pfx), penta-, kvin–
pentagon, pentagono
Pentagon, Pentagono
pentagram, pentagramo
pentahedron, kvinedro
pentameter, pentametro
pentane, pentano
Pentateuch, Pentateŭko
pentathlon, pentatlono†

Pentatoma, pentatomo
Pentecost, Pentekosto
penthouse, tegment/-apartamento, ~o-
loĝejo
pentode, pentodo
pentosan, pentozano
pentose, pentozo
pentothal, pentotalo
penultimate, antaŭlasta
penumbra, duonombro
penurious, (miserly), avara; (poor),
malriĉa, senhava
peon, peonot, servutulo [cp "pawn"]
peony, peonio
people, (persons, plur), homoj; (sing:
ethnic group etc.; population), popolo,
gento; (impersonal), oni (e.g.: *what
will people think?:* kion oni pensos?)
pep, vigl/eco, vervo; **pep up,** ~igi, stimuli [tr]
peplos, peplo
peplum, falbalo
peplus, peplo
pepper, (gen), pipro; ~a; ~i [tr]; **pep-
percorn,** ~ograjno; **peppergrass,** lepidio; **pepper mill,** ~omuelilo;
peppermint, (plant or spice), ~omen-
to; ~omenta; (candy etc.), ~omentaĵo;
pepper shaker, ~ujo; **black pepper,**
nigra ~o; **cayenne pepper,** (spice),
papriko, kajena ~o, ruĝa ~o; (plant),
kapsiko; **Java pepper,** kubebo; **wall
pepper,** sedo
pepperoni, kajenkolbaso
pepsin, pepsino
peptic, (re digestion), digesta; ~iga
peptidase, peptidazo
peptide, peptido
peptize, peptizi [tr]; **peptization,** ~ado
peptone, peptono
per, (at rate of, "@"), en, por, je, per–,
–e (e.g.: *mix 2 spoonfuls per liter of
water:* miksu 2 kulerplenojn en litro
da akvo; *2 spoonfuls per liter is
enough:* 2 kulerplenoj en litro sufiĉas;
they cost $5 per dozen: ili kostas kvin
dolarojn por dekduo; *go 90 kilometers
per hour:* iri 90 kilometrojn en horo
[or] kilometrojn hore); (in accord w),
laŭ (e.g.: *per your request:* laŭ via peto)
per–, (chem sfx), per–

perambulator, bebĉareto, infanĉareto
per annum, (po)jare
Perca, perko; Percidae. ~edoj; Perci-
formes, ~oformaj (fiŝoj)
percale, perkalo
per capita, pohoma, popersona; ~e
perceive, percepti [tr]
percent, procento(j); ~a; ~e (e.g.: *3% of
the students:* 3% [tri ~oj] el la studentoj; *at 15% interest:* je 15%–a [dek-
kvin-~a] interezo [or] je interezo de
15%; *the price is 5% higher:* la prezo
estas 5% [kvin ~ojn] pli alta; *that is
100% better:* tio estas 100% [cent–~e]
pli bona; *the cost of living increased
8.7%:* la vivkosto pliiĝis (je) 8,7% [ok
komo sep ~ojn [or] je ok komo sep
~oj]); **percentage,** ~o (e.g.: *a high
percentage of the students:* alta ~o el
la studentoj); (profit, use), profito;
percentile, centilo
perception, percepto; ~aĵo; **(im)per-
ceptible,** (ne)~ebla; **perceptive,** ~a
Perceval, Percevalo
perch, (fish), perko; (sit), sidi [int];
(pole for bird to sit), sidstango; (unit
of linear measure), 5,03 metroj [see
§ 20]; (of area), 25,3 m²; (of volume),
0,701 m³; **pike perch,** (*Lucioperca*),
sandro
perchlorate, perklorato
percipient, percept(em)a
Percival(e), Percevalo
percolate, perkoli [tr]; ~iĝi; **percola-
tor,** ~ilo
percuss, perkuti [tr]; **percussion,**
~(ad)o; (mus), ~instrumento(j); **per-
cussive,** ~a
per diem, portaga; ~aĵo
perdition, (rel), damniĝo
Perdix, perdriko
peregrinate, vag(ad)i [int]
peremptory, (decisive), decida, absoluta, fina; (dictatorial), diktator(ec)a, ordonema
perennial, (long-lasting), daŭra; (lasting through year), jar~a; (plant),
staŭdo
perestroika, rekonstruo
perfect, perfekta; ~igi; **perfection,**
~igo; ~iĝo; ~eco; **perfectionist,** ~is-

tot; **imperfect**, (not perfect), ne~a; (gram), imperfekto; imperfekta; **imperfection**, (flaw), difekt(et)o, ne~aĵo
perfervid, ard(eg)a
perfidy, perfido; ~aĵo; **perfidious**, ~a
perforate, (gen), trueti [tr]; (med), perfori [tr]; **perforation**, ~ado; ~iĝo; (of stamps etc.), ~aro; (med), perforado; perforaĵo; **perforated**, (w many holes), aĵura
perform, (mus, theat, etc.: present before audience), prezenti [tr]; (play mus, gen), ludi [tr]; (sing), kanti [tr]; (act role, gen), roli [int] (en, kiel); (carry out), efektivigi; (do), fari [tr]; (fulfill), plenumi [tr]; (do ceremony etc.), celebri [tr]; **performance**, ~o; ludado; kantado; rolado; efektivigo; plenum(ad)o; celebr(ad)o; **performer**, (gen), ~isto; (specific), ludanto; kantanto; muzikisto; rolanto, aktoro
perfume, parfumo; ~i [tr]
perfunctory, supraĵa, indiferenta
perfuse, perfuzi [tr]
Pergamum, Pergamus, Pergamo
pergola, pergolo
perhaps, eble, povas esti (ke)
peri–, (tech pfx), ĉirkaŭ– [note: often absorbed into Esperanto root as "peri–"; see separate entries]
perianth, perianto
periaster, periastro*
perical, perikalo
pericardium, perikardio; **pericarditis**, ~ito
pericarp, perikarpo
Pericles, Periklo
peridium, peridio
peridot, peridoto; **peridotic**, ~eca
perigee, perigeo
perigynous, perigina
perihelion, perihelio
peril, danĝero; **perilous**, ~a; **imperil**, en~igi
perimeter, perimetro
perineum, perineo; **perineal**, ~a
period, (of cycle or oth measure of time), periodo; (punctuation: "."), punkto [see § 17]; (menses), menstruo; (menses, colloq), monataĵo; **periodic**, ~a; **periodicity**, ~eco
periodate, perjodato; **periodic acid**,

~a acido
periodical, (publication), periodaĵo, gazeto
periosteum, periosto; **periosteal**, ~a; **periostitis**, ~ito
peripeteia, peripetia, peripety, peripetiot
peripatetic, migra
periphery, periferio; **peripheral**, ~a
periphrase, periphrasis, perifrazo; **periphrastic**, ~a
periscope, periskopo
perish, perei [int]; **perishable**, (can spoil, as food), putrema; putremaĵo; (fragile), difektiĝema, rompiĝema, pereema
Periodissodactyla, neparhufuloj
peristalsis, peristalto; **peristaltic**, ~a; **antiperistaltic**, anti~a; anti~aĵo
peristyle, peristilo
perithecium, peritecio
peritoneum, peritoneo; **peritoneal**, ~a
peritonitis, peritoneito
periwinkle, (zool: *Littorina*), litorino; (bot: *Vinca*), vinko
perjury, ĵurrompo; **commit perjury, perjure oneself**, ĵurrompi [int]
perk, perk up, revigl/igi; ~iĝi; (perquisite), kromprivilegio; **perky**, vigla, gaja
perleche, perleĉo
permafrost, daŭrofrosto
permalloy, permalojo
permanent, konstanta, daŭra; **permanence, permanency**, ~eco; **permanent wave**, ~a frizo
permanganate, permanganato
permapress, neĉifebla
permeable, permeabla, tralas(iv)a; **permeability**, ~eco, tralasivo; **impermeable**, ne~a; **semipermeable**, duon~a
permeance, (elec: inverse of reluctance), permeanco; (permeability, gen), permeablo
permeate, (tra)penetri [tr, int]
Permian, permio
permission, permeso; **permissible**, ~ebla; **permissive**, ~ema
permit, (allow, consent), permesi [tr]; (allow, let, enable), ebligi, (al)lasi [tr]; (license), licenco, ~ilo
permute, permuti [tr]; **permutation**,

~ado; ~aĵo
Pernambuco, Pernambuko [see "Recife"]
pernicious, pernicioza
pernio, pernio
Pernis apivorus, perniso, vespobuteo
peroxide, peroksido; ~i [tr]
perpendicular, (math, geom), orta; ~anto; (non-tech), ~a, perpendikulara; ~anto, perpendikularo
perpetrate, (fi)fari [tr]
perpetual, eterna, konstanta, ĉiama; **perpetuity,** ~eco; **perpetuate,** daŭrigi, ~igi; **self-perpetuating,** sindaŭriga
Perpignan, Perpinjano
perplex, perpleks/igi, konfuzi [tr]; **perplexed,** ~a; **be(come) perplexed,** ~iĝi; **perplexity,** ~eco
perquisite, kromprivilegio
perry, pirvino
per se, per si mem
Persea americana, Persea gratissima, avokadarbo
persecute, persekuti [tr]; **persecution,** ~(ad)o; ~iĝo
Perseids, Perseidoj
Persephone, Persefona
Persepolis, Persepolo
Perseus, (myth; ast), Perseo
persevere, persisti [int]; **perseverance,** ~(ad)o
Persia, Pers/io; **Persian,** ~o; ~a; ~ia; **Persian Gulf,** Golfo ~a
Persica vulgaris, persikarbo
persien(nes), (shutter), persieno(j)
persimmon, (fruit or tree), persimono
persist, persisti [int]; **persistent,** ~a; **persistence,** ~ado; ~eco
persnickety, precioza, elektema, neplaĉiĝema
person, (gen), persono [cp "human"]; (describing personal attribute), –ulo [sfx] (e.g.: *common person:* ordinarulo; *modern person:* modernulo); (describing occupation, profession), –isto (e.g.: *telephone person:* telefonisto); **personable,** bonaspekta; **personage,** (notable), notindulo, eminentulo; **personal,** ~a; (own), propra; (private), privata; **personality,** (personal characteristics), ~eco; (individual person,

as a famous personality), ~ulo; **personalize,** ~ecigi; **personify,** ~igi; **personification,** ~igo, prozopopeo; **impersonal,** ne~a
persona, (theat), rolo; (psych), (ekstera) personeco; **persona (non) grata,** (ne)bonvenigito
personnel, personaro, personalo; **antipersonnel,** (mil), kontraŭhoma
perspective, perspektivo; **in perspective,** ~e; **put into perspective,** ~igi
perspicacious, sagaca; **perspicacity,** ~eco
perspicuous, klara, evidenta
perspire, ŝviti [int], transpiri [int]; **perspiration,** ~o; ~ado; **antiperspirant,** kontraŭ~a; kontraŭ~enzo
persuade, persvadi [tr]; **persuasion,** ~(ad)o; **persuasive,** ~(em)a
pert, (bold), impertinenta, aŭdaca
pertain, (belong), aparteni [int]; (be suitable), deci [int], taŭgi [int]; (relate), rilati [int]
Perth, (gen), Perto*
pertinacious, obstina
pertinent, rilata, trafa; **pertinence,** ~o; **impertinent,** ~a; (disrespectful), impertinenta; **impertinence,** ne~eco; impertinenteco
perturb, perturbi [tr]; **perturbation,** ~(ad)o; **imperturbable,** ne~ebla, neĝenebla, nekonsternebla
pertussis, kokluŝo
Peru, Peruo; **Peruvian,** ~ano; ~a
Perugia, Peruĝo
peruse, tralegi [tr], studi [tr], trarigardi [tr]
pervade, trapenetri [tr, int]; **pervasive,** ~ema
perverse, perversa; **perversity,** ~eco; **perverssion,** (med, psych), perversio
pervert, perversi/ulo; **perverted,** ~a
Pesach, Pesaĥo*, Pasko [see "Passover"]
peseta, peseto
Peshawar, Peŝavaro
pesky, ĉagrena, ĝena, plageta
peso, peso
pessary, pesario
pessimism, pesimismo; **pessimist,** pesimisto; **pessimistic,** ~a
pest, (animal), trud/besto; (weed), ~her-

bo; (person), ~ulo, ĝenulo [not "pesto"]; **pesticide**, ~bestmortigenzo;
~herbomortigenzo
pestle, pistilo
pester, ĝen(ad)i [tr], turmenti [tr], plag-
eti [tr]
pestilence, pesto; **pestilent(ial)**, ~a;
~odona
pet, (pamper, indulge), dorloti [tr]; (caress), karesi [tr]; (animal), ~besto; ~a
petal, petalo
petard, (small firecracker), petardo;
(larger explosive), ~ego
petasos, petasus, petazo
Petaurista, flugsciuro
petcock, kraneto
peter (out), (be used up), elĉerpiĝi;
(disappear), forvelki [int], malaperi
[int]
Peter, (man's name), Petro; **St. Petersburg**, (any city), ~oburgo
petiole, petiolo
petite, svelta, maldika
petit four, spongokuko
petition, (formal request), peticio; ~i
[tr]; (request, gen), peti [tr]; peto
Petrarch, Petrarko
petrel, petrelo; **fulmar petrel**, fulmaro;
stormy petrel, (*Oceanites oceani-
cus*), butpieda ŝtorm~o; (fig), an-
taŭvenanto de malfacilaĵoj; **white-
chinned petrel**, procelario
petrify, ŝton/igi; ~iĝi
petro–, (sci pfx: rock), petro–; (petroleum), petrol–
Petrogale, valabio
petrography, petrografio, petrologio
[see "petrology"]
petrol, benzino [not "petrolo"] [see also
"gasoline"]
petrolatum, vazelino, petrol-ĝelo
petroleum, petrolo; ~a; **petroleum jelly**, vazelino
petrology, petrolog/io; **petrologist**, ~o
Petromyzon, petromizo
Petronius, Petronio
Petroselinum, petroselo
petticoat, (underskirt), subjupo
petty, (trivial), bagatela, malgrava;
(small-minded), etanima
petulent, (immodest), malmodesta; (insolent), impertinenta; (irritable), ofen-

diĝema, kolereta, iritiĝema
petunia, Petunia, petunio
Peumus, boldo
pew, (preĝeja, kirka, etc.) benko
pewit, (lapwing), vanelo
pewter, stanalojo; ~a
pexis, pexia, peksio
–pexy, (med sfx), –peksio
peyote, (plant), pejotlo*; (drug), meskalino
pfennig, pfenigo
pH, pH [pronounce "po-ho"]
Phaeacian, Feako; ~a
Phaedra, Fedra
Phaedrus, Federo
Phaeophyceae, Phaeophyta, brunalgoj
phaeophytin, feofitino; **alpha-phaeo-
phytin**, alfa~o; **beta-phaeophytin**,
beta~o
Phaethon, Faetono
phaeton, faetono
phagocyte, fagocito
Phalacrocorax, kormorano
Phalaena, faleno
Phalangium, falangio;   Phalangida,
~uloj
phalanstery, falanstero
phalanx, (gen), falango
Phalaris, falaro
phalarope, falaropo
Phalaropus, falaropo
phallus, (anat), peniso; (as symbol), fa-
luso† **phallic**, ~a
Phanariot, Fanarioto
phaner(o)–, (anat pfx), faner(o)–
phanerogam, fanerogamo
phantasm, fantomo
phantasmagoria, fantasmagorio
phantom, fantomo
pharaoh, faraono
Pharisee, Fariseo
pharmaceutics, farmacio; **pharmaceutical**, ~a; ~aĵo
pharmacology, farmakolog/io;   **phar-
macologist**, ~o
pharmacop(o)eia, farmakopeo
pharmacy, (sci), farmacio; (drug store,
chemist shop), apoteko; **pharmacist**,
~isto; apotekisto
Pharomacrus, kecalo
Pharos, Faroso
Pharsalus, Farsalo; **Pharsalia**, ~io

pharynx, faringo; **pharyngeal**, ~a
Phascolarctos cinereus, koalo
Phascolomys, vombato
phase, (gen), fazo; **phase in**, laŭgrade
enkonduki [tr]; **phase out**, laŭgrade
elkonduki [tr], laŭgrade forigi; **in
phase**, sam~a; sam~e; **out of phase**,
mal~a; mal~e
Phaseolus, fazeolo
Phasianus, fazano; Phasianus pictus,
or~o; Phasianidae, ~edoj
Phasma, fasmo; Phasmidae, ~edoj
pheasant, fazano; **peacock pheasant**,
poliplektro, pavo~~o; **pheasant's-
eye**, (bot), adonido
Phebe, Feba
Phellandrium, felandrio
phenacetin(e), fenacetino
phenanthrene, fenantreno
phenetol, fenetolo
Phenicia, [see "Phoenicia"]
phen(o)–, (chem pfx), fen(o)–
phenobarbital, fenobarbitalo*
phenol, (C_6H_5OH), fenolo
phenolphthalein, fenolftaleino
phenomenon, fenomeno; **phenome-
nal**, ~a; **phenomenalism**, ~ismo;
phenomenology, ~ologio; **Hall's,
Joule's (etc.) phenomen**, la ~o de
Hall, Joule (etc.)
phenotype, fenotipo
phenyl, fenilo
phenylene, fenileno, feneno
phew! (interj), pu!
phi, fi [see § 16]
phial, flakoneto, fiolo
Phidias, Fidio
Philadelphia, Filadelfio
Philadelphus, filadelfo
philander, (leĝere) amoradi [tr]; **phi-
landerer**, amoremulo
philanthropy, filantrop/io, mecenateco; **philanthropic**, ~ia, mecenata;
philanthropist, ~o, mecenato
philately, filatelo; **philatelist**, ~isto
Philemon, Filemono
philharmonic, filharmonio; ~a
Philip, Filipo
Philippi, Filipio; **Philippians**, (Bib),
~anoj
philippic, filipiko
Philippine, Filipina; ~ano; **Philippines**,

Philippine Islands, ~oj
Philister, filistro
Philistia, Filiŝtujo
Philistine, (re ancient people), Filiŝto;
~a; (uncultured person), filistro; ~eca;
Philistinism, filistreco
Phillip, Filipo
Philo (Judaeus), Filono
Philoctetes, Filokteto
philology, filolog/io; **philologist**, ~o
Philomela, Filomela
philosemite, filosemito; **philosemit-
ism**, ~o
philosophy, (re ancient people), filozof/io; **philosopher**,
~o; **philosophize**, ~ii [int]
philter, (love potion), ampocio
philtrum, filtrumo
phimosis, fimozo
phlebitis, flebito
phlebotome, flebotomo
Phlebotomus, (zool), flebotomo
phlebotomy, flebotomio
Phlegethon, Flegetono
phlegm, (mucus), muko; (calmness),
flegmo; **phlegmatic**, flegma
phlegmasia, flegmazio
Phleum, fleo
phloem, floemo
phlogiston, flogistono
phloroglucinol, floroglucinolo
phlox, Phlox, flokso
phlyctena, flikteno
Phnom-Penh, Pnompeno
–phobe, (sfx), –fobiulo
phobia, fobio
–phobia, (sfx), –fobio
Phobos, (ast), Foboso*
Phoca, foko, marhundo; Phocidae, ~ed-
oj
Phocaena, foceno, marporko
Phocis, Focido
Phoebe, Feba
Phoebus, Febo
Phoenicia, Fenic/io; **Phoenician**, ~o;
~a; ~ia
Phoenicopterus, fenikoptero, flamengo
phoenix, (myth etc.), fenikso
Phoenix, (city; ast), Fenikso
Phoenix dactylifera, (bot), daktilarbo
Pholas, folado; Pholadidae, ~edoj, bor-
konkoj
Pholidota, manisuloj

phone, [see "telephone"]

phoneme, fonemo; **phonemic**, ~a

phonetic, fonetika; **phonetics**, ~o; **phonetician**, ~isto

phonetist, (advocate of phonetic spelling), fonetisto; (phonetician), fonetikisto

phonic, (re phonics), akustika; (of sound), sona; **phonics**, ~o

phonograph, gramofono; (old cylinder-type), fonografo; **phonograph record**, (~)disko

phonology, fonolog/io; **phonologist**, ~o

phonometer, fonometro; **phonometry**, ~io

phonoscope, fonoskopo

phony, falsa; ~aĵo; ~ulo

phooey, (interj), pa!

Phormium, formio

phosgene, fosgeno

phosphate, fosfato;   **phosphatemia**, ~emio; **phosphatide**, ~ido; **phosphaturia**, ~urio; **superphosphate**, super~o

phosphene, fosfeno

phosphide, fosfido

phosphine, fosfino

phosphite, fosfito

phosph(o)–, (chem pfx), fosf(o)–

phosphonium, fosfonio

phosphoresce, fosforeski [int]; **phosphorescence**, ~o; **phosphorescet**, ~a

phosphorite, fosforito

phosphorus, fosforo

photo, foto [see "photograph"]; **telephoto**, (re telescopic photography), tele~o; tele~a; (photo transmitted electronically), telebildo; telebilda; **telephoto lens**, teleobjektivo

photo–, (pfx), foto–

photochromy, fotokromio; **photochromic**, ~a

photocopy, fotokopii [tr]; ~o; **photocopy machine**, (gen), ~atoro; (by any dry process), ~atoro, kserografiatoro

photogrammetry, fotogrametrio†

photogenic, fotoplaĉa

photograph, fotografi [tr], foti [tr]; ~aĵo, foto; **photographer**, ~isto; **photography**, (the art), ~io; **telephotograph**, telefoto, tele~aĵo; telebildo; telefoti [tr], tele~i; telebildigi [see

"photo: telephoto"]; **telephotographic**, tele~ia; telebildiga; **telephotography**, tele~io; telebildigo

photogravure, fotogravuri [tr]; ~(ad)o; ~aĵo

photometer, fotometro;   **photometry**, fotometrio

photon, fotono

photosphere, fotosfero

photostat, (machine), fotostato; (copy), ~aĵo; **photostatic**, ~a

phototropism, fototropismo

phototropy, fototropio

phototype, fototipo; **phototypy**, ~io

Phoxinus, fokseno

phrase, (part of sentence), propozicio (e.g.: *subordinate phrase:* subordita ~o [or] sub~o); (express in words), vortigi (e.g.: *try to phrase the idea better:* peni vortigi la ideon pli bone); (non-literal expression), idiotismo; (mus), frazo; **phrasing**, (mus), frazado

phraseology, frazeologio

phratria, **phratry**, fratrio

phrenology, frenolog/io; **phrenologist**, ~o

Phrine, Frina

Phrygia, Frigio; **Phrygian**, ~a; ~ano

phthalein, ftaleino

phthalic, ftal/ata; **phthalic acid**, ~a acido

Phthir(i)us, ftiro

phthisis, ftizo

phycomycete, fikomiceto

Phycomycetes, fikomicetoj

phylactery, filakterio

phyle, fratriaro

Phyllanthus, filanto

Phyllis, Filisa

phyllite, filito

Phyllitis scolopendrium, skolopendrio

Phylloscopus, filoskopo;   Phylloscopus collybita, ĉifĉafo; Phylloscopus trochilus, fitiso

Phyllostoma, filostomo;   Phyllostomatidae, ~edoj

Phylloxera, filoksero

phylogenesis, **phylogeny**, (group evolution), filogenezo; (history and sci of), filogenio

phylum, filono†

Physalia, fizalio
physalis, fizalido
Physalis, fizalido; Physalis alkekengi, alkekengo
Physeter catodon, Physeter macrocephalus, makrocefalo, kaĉaloto
physical, fizika
physician, kuracisto
physics, fiziko; **physicist,** ~isto; **astrophysics,** astro~o; **biophysics,** bio~o; **nuclear physics,** nuklea ~o; **quantum physics,** kvantum~o
physiognomy, fiziognomiko
physiography, fiziografio
physiology, fiziolog/io; **physiologist,** ~o; **psychophysiology,** psiko~io
psysique, korp/formo, ~strukturo, ~naturo [not "fiziko"]
Phyteuma, fiteŭmo
phyt(o)–, (pfx), fito–
phytogenic, fitogena
phytol, fitolo
pi, (Greek letter), pi [see § 16]; (printing), tipmiksaĵo
Piacenza, Plaĉenzo
pia mater, piamatro
piano, (instrument), piano; (not loud), mallaŭte; **pianissimo,** mallaŭtege; **pianist,** ~isto; **grand piano,** horizontala ~o; **upright pian,** vertikala ~o; **player pian,** pianolo
pianoforte, piano
pianolo, pianolo
piaster, piastre, piastro
piazza, (plaza), placo; (arcade), arkado; (veranda), verando
pibroch, pibroño*
pica, (type), cicero; ~a
Pica, (zool), pigo
picador, pikadoro†
Picard, Pikardo; **Picardy,** ~io
picaresque, pikareska
picayune, bagatela, malgrandioza
piccalilli, legomspicaĵo
piccolo, fluteto
Picea, piceo; Picea glauca, Picea alba, Picea canadensis, blanka ~o; Picea abies, Picea excelsa, ordinara ~o
pick, (choose, select), elekti [tr], selekti [tr]; ~(aĵ)o, selekt(aĵ)o; (prick, jab), piki [tr]; pikilo; (digging tool), pioĉi [tr]; pioĉo [cp "hoe"]; (small, as for

mountain-climbing), pioĉeto; (pluck, as flower, fruit, mus instrument), pluki [tr]; (mus: plectrum; strum w plectrum), plektro; plektri [tr, int]; (instigate, as fight), instigi [tr]; (unlock w wire etc.), kroĉe malŝlosi [tr]; (steal from, as pocket), priŝteli [tr], primarodi [tr]; (choice, favorite one), plej ~inda; favorito; **picky,** precioza, (tro) ~ema; **pick at,** (food), ~eme manĝeti [tr]; **pick on,** (choose), ~i; (tease), ĉagren(ad)i [tr], mokŝerc(ad)i [tr]; **pick one's way,** zorge progresi [int]; **pick out,** (choose), ~i; (distinguish), distingi [tr]; (play mus by ear), ludi [tr] laŭ orelo, ludi orele; **pick up,** (take), (al)preni [tr]; (get), havigi, akiri [tr]; (raise something fallen), (re)levi [tr]; (find), trovi [tr]; (learn), lerni [tr]; (arrest), aresti [tr]; (accelerate), akceli [tr]; akceliĝi; (improve), plibonigi; pliboniĝi; (resume), rekomenci [tr]; rekomenciĝi; (receive by radio, TV, etc.), ricevi [tr]; (perceive by ear etc.), percepti [tr]; (clean, make tidy), purigi, ordi [tr]; (give ride, as to hitchhiker), veturigi; (make acquaintance), ekkonatiĝi kun; **pickup,** (acceleration), akceliĝo; (truck), aperta kamioneto; (tone arm of record player etc.), sonprenilo, pikupo; (acquaintance), ekkonato; (stimulant), stimulenzo; (radio, TV reception), ricevado; **finger pick,** fingroplektro; fingroplektri [tr]; **flat pick,** platplektro; platplektri [tr]; **toothpick,** dentopikilo; **pick and choose,** fari ~ojn. ~(ad)i
pickerel, ezoketo
picket, (fence stake), paliso; (strike), strik-postenulo; strik-stari [int], strik-posteniĝi (ĉe, antaŭ); (demonstration), manifestacia postenulo; manifestacie posteniĝi (ĉe, antaŭ); (mil: guard), pikedo
pickle, pekli [tr]; (vegetable), ~aĵo, piklo; (chem bath), ~akvo
picnic, pikniko; ~i [int]
picoline, pikolino
picrate, pikr/ato; **picric acid,** ~a acido
pictograph, piktogramo
picture, bildo; ~igi; (imagine), ~igi al

si; **pictorial**, ~a; ~ogazeto; **pictur-esque**, pitoreska
Picus, pego; Picidae, ~edoj; Picifor-mes, ~oformaj (birdoj); Picoides, ~oi-doj
piddle, (dawdle), lanti [int]; (do little work), laboreti [int]; **piddling**, bag-atela, etgrava
piddock, folado
pidgin, piĝino; ~a; **pidgin English**, (la) ~-Angla (lingvo, dialekto)
pie, (gen), torto (e.g.: *apple pie:* pom~o); (pasticcio), pasteĉo; (print-ing), tipmiksaĵo; **pieplant**, rabarbo; **as easy as pie**, facilega
piebald, piga
piece, (gen), peco; (coin), monero; (ba-sic component), ~ero [sfx] (e.g.: *piece of dust:* polvero); **piecemeal**, po~a; po~e; **piecework**, po~a (laboro); po~aĵo; **one-piece**, unu~a; **cross-piece**, (beam etc., fastened in middle, as in balance scales), vekto; **piece to-gether**, po~e kunmeti [tr]; **go to piec-es**, dis~iĝi
pièce de résistance, (dish) ĉef/manĝo; (oth), ~aĵo
pied, (piebald), piga ·
piedmont, (gen), montopiedo; (of Ita-ly), Piemonto
Piemonte, Piemonto
pier, (wharf, for fishing, etc.), varfo; (bridge etc. support), piliero
pierce, trapiki [tr], (tra)penetri [tr, int]
Pieris, (zool), pieriso
Pierrot, pieroto
pietism, pietismo; **pietist**, piestisto
piety, pieco
piezoelectric, piezoelektra; **piezoelec-tricity**, ~o
piezometer, piezometro
piezometry, piezometrio; **piezomet-ric**, ~a
piffle, sensencaĵo
pig, (zool, gen), porko; (of iron), ferbri-ko; **piggyback**, surŝultra; surdorsa; **piglet**, ~ido; **pig-sty**, ~ejo; **pigtail**, (braid), harplektaĵo; **pigweed**, ama-ranto; **guinea pig**, (lit or fig), kobajo; **sea pig**, (porpoise), foceno, mar~o; (dolphin), delfeno; **suckling pig**, suĉ~ido

pigeon, (gen), kolombo; **pigeonhole**, (for pigeons), ~ejo; (compartment), fak(et)o; enfakigi; **carrier pigeon**, kurier~o, leter~o; **homing pigeon**, hejmenira ~o, kurier-~o; **rock pi-geon**, livio, rok~o; **wood pigeon**, pa-lumbo, arbo~o
pigment, pigmento; ~i [tr]; **pigmenta-tion**, ~ado; ~iĝo; ~aĵo; ~eco
pigmey, pigmeo; ~a
pike, (fish), ezoko; (spear), pikstango; (spear tip), stangopinto
pilaf(f), pilafo
pilaster, pilastro
Pilate, Pilato [see "Pontius"]
pilau, pilaw, pilafo
pilchard, pilĉardo [cp "sardine"]
pile, (mass, heap), amaso; ~igi; ~iĝi [cp "stack"]; (of rug, hook and pile fas-tener, etc.), vilo; (piling), palafito; (structure to support bridge span etc.), piliero; (elec), pilo; (hemorrhoid), hemoroido; **pile-driver**, rammaŝino; **pilewort**, fikario; **atomic pile**, atom-pilo
pilfer, marodi [tr], ŝteleti [tr] [cp "ma-raud"]
pilgrim, pilgrim/anto, ~ulo; **pilgrim-age**, ~(ad)o; **go on a pilgrimage**, ~i [int]
piling, (supporting beams over water etc.), palafito
Pilipino, Filipino; (la) ~a (lingvo)
pill, pilolo; **pillbox**, (for pills), ~ujo; (mil), kirasita pafilejo; **a bitter pill to swallow**, amara afero akcepti
pillage, rab/ado; ~aĵo; pri~i [tr]
pillar, piliero, kolono; **pillar box**, (Br), [see "mail: mailbox"]
pillion, kromselo
pillory, pilorio; en~igi
pillow, kuseno, kap~o; ~i [tr]; **pillow-case**, ~tego
Pilocarpus, jaborando
pilot, piloto; ~i [tr]; (test, experimental), prova, prov- [pfx] (e.g.: pilot project: provprojekto); **pilothouse**, navigejo; **pilot light**, ekbruliga flamo; **auto-matic pilot**, aŭtomata ~ilo
Pimenta dioica, pimento
pimento, (allspice), pimento; (capsicum pepper), kapsiko

pimp, prostitui [tr]; ~isto, parigisto [not "pimp–"]

pimpernel, anagalo; **scarlet pimpernel**, kamp~o; (w red flowers), ruĝa kamp~o; **water pimpernel**, (brook weed), samolo

Pimpinella, pimpinelo; Pimpinella anisum, anizujo

pimple, akno [cp "acne"]; **goose pimples**, ansera haŭto

pin, (sharp, as for sewing), pinglo; (al)~i [tr]; (metal rod for holding parts together etc.), stifto; stifti [tr]; (peg for fastening, wedging, etc.), kejlo; kejli [tr] [cp "wedge"]; (clothing ornament), broĉo [see "brooch"]; (badge etc.), insigno; (bowling), keglo; **pincushion**, ~okuseneto; **pinup**, (woman, man), allogul(in)o; (picture), allogul(in)a bildo; **belaying pin**, bito; **Cotter pin**, duobla stifto; **firing pin**, perkut~o; **hairpin, bobby pin**, har~o; **hatpin**, ĉapel~o; **linchpin**, radfiksilo; **safety pin**, fibolo, sendanĝera ~o; **ninepins, tenpins**, (game), (naŭkegla, dekkegla) kegloludo [see "bowl"]; **pins and needles**, (skin sensation), piketado; **on pins and needles**, (anxious), nervoza

pinafore, antaŭtuko

pinaster, pinastro

pinball, kejlpilka; ~a ludo; **pinball machine**, ~a maŝino

pince-nez, nazumo

pincers, tenajlo, pinĉiloj; **pincers movement (maneuver, operation)**, (mil), ~a manovro

pinch, pinĉi [tr]; ~o; (small amount), ~ajo; **pinchcock**, ~krano; **in a pinch**, (in case of need), okaze de neceso; (in difficulty), en embaraso

Pinctada, meleagreno, perlokonko

Pindar, Pindaro

Pindus, Pindo

pine, (tree or wood, gen), pino; (yearn), sopiri [int]; **pine away**, forvelki de sopirado; **arolla pine, cembra pine, Swiss pine**, cembro; **Austrian pine, black pine**, nigra ~o; **cluster pine, maritime pine**, pinastro; **dammar pine**, damaro; **ground pine**, likopodio; **kauri pine**, [also various oth

spellings], kaŭrio; **mountain pine, mug(h)o pine**, monta ~o; **Norfolk Island pine**, araŭkario; **red pine**, ruĝa ~o; **resinous pinewood**, keno; **Scotch pine, Scots pine**, ordinara ~o; **stone pine, umbrella pine**, pinio; **white pine, American white pine, eastern white pine**, blanka ~o

pineal, pinealo, ~a korpo, ~a glando

pineapple, ananaso

pinene, pineno

ping, tinti [int]; ~igi; ~o

ping-pong, tabloteniso; **ping-pong ball**, ~a pilketo; **ping-pong paddle**, ~a pagajo

Pinicola, pinikolo

pinion, (gear), pinjono, dentradeto; (wing), flugilo; (bind wings, arms), ligi (la flugilojn, brakojn de)

pink, (color), roza, ~kolora, ruĝeta; ~koloro, ruĝeto [not "~o"]; (bot), dianto; (notch cloth), noĉi [tr]; **clove pink, carnation pink**, kariofildianto; **in the pink**, en bona sanstato, bonstata

pinnace, pinaso

pinnacle, kulmino, pinto; (arch: small turret, spire), pinaklo

pinnate, pinata

pinniped, fokulo

Pinnipedia, fokuloj

pint, pindo [(Am: liquid), 473 mililitroj; (Br), 568 mililitroj; (dry pint: see "quart"); see § 20]

pintle, spindelo

pinto, piga (ĉevalo)

Pinus, pino; Pinus cembra, cembro; Pinus mugo, Pinus montana, monta ~o; Pinus nigra, Pinus laricio austriaca, nigra ~o; Pinus pinaster, Pinus maritima, pinastro; Pinus pinea, pinio; Pinus strobus, blanka ~o; Pinus sylvestris, ordinara ~o

pion, piono

pioneer, pioniro; ~a; ~i [int]

pious, pia; ~ulo(j); **impious**, mal~a

pip, (spot), punkto; (seed), semo; (Br army insignia), stelinsigno; (bird disease), pipso; (blip), pulso; (peep, chirp), pepi [int]; pepo

pipe, (tube, gen), tubo; ~i [tr]; (smoking), pipo; (mus: simple flute), ŝalmo;

(play on), ŝalmi [tr, int], fluti [tr, int]; (bagpipe), sakŝalmo; (panpipes), Pajnoŝalmo; **piper**, (bagpipe player), sakŝalmisto; **pipe cleaner**, pippurigilo; **pipe down**, kvietiĝi; **pipe fitter**, ~instalisto; **pipe in**, (gen), enpumpi [tr]; **pipeline**, dukto, ~linio; **pipe rack**, piprako; **bagpipe**, sakŝalmo; **blowpipe**, (pipe), blov~o; (blowgun), blovpafilo; **drainpipe**, pluv~o; **exhaust pipe**, ellas~o; **peacepipe**, pacpipo; **panpipe(s)**, **pipes of Pan**, Pajnoŝalmo; **standpipe**, rezervocisterno; **stovepipe**, stov~o; **tailpipe**, ellas~o; **uillen pipe**, kubutŝalmo; **waterpipe**, akvopipo, nargileo

Piper, (bot), piprarbedo; Piper betel, betelo; Piper cubeba, kubebo; Piper methysticum, Piper excelsum, kavao

pipet(te), pipeto
pipistrel(le), pipistrelo
Pipistrellus, pipistrelo
pipit, pipio
piquant, (gen), spica, pika
pique, ofendi [tr]; ~iĝo
Piraeus, Pireo
piragua, pirogo
piranha, piraña, piranjo
pirate, pirato; ~a; ~i [tr, int]; **piracy**, ~ado; **air piracy**, aer~ado; **pirated**, (unauthorized copy), ~a†
Pirithous, Piritoo
pirogue, pirogo
pirouette, pirueto; ~i [int]
Pisa, Pizo
Pisces, (ast), Fiŝoj
Pisistratus, Pizistrato
piss, (colloq), pisi [int]; ~aĵo; **piss-pot**, ~poto
pistachio, (nut or tree), pistako
Pistacia, pistako; Pistacia lentiscus, lentisko, mastikarbo; Pistacia terebinthus, terebintarbo
pistil, pistilo
pistol, pistolo
pistole, piŝtolo
piston, piŝto
Pisum, pizo; Pisum sativum, Pisum hortense, ĝardena ~o; Pisum arvense, kampa ~o
pit, (cavity), kavo, ~eto; ~igi; (hole), truo; (dug out), fosaĵo; (alveolus), al-

veolo [cp "pock"]; (trap), enfalujo; (enclosed area, as for animals), ~ejo [sfx] (e.g.: *bear pit:* ursejo); (mine), minejo; (at auto racetrack etc.), reviziejo; (date seed), amando; (any seed etc.), kerno; (theat), partero; (set against, make fight), bataligi; **pitted**, (w cavities), ~igita; **pitfall**, (lit or fig), enfalujo; **pit stop**, (in auto race), revizihalto; (bathroom stop while traveling), neceseja halto, (colloq), pishalto

pitch, (resin extract), peĉo; ~a; ~i [tr]; (asphalt), asfalto, ter~o; (of screwthread; type size), paŝo; (erect, as tent), starigi; (mus), pitĉo; pitĉigi; (throw), ĵeti [tr]; ĵeto; (plunge, lunge ahead), impeti [int]; impeto; (rise and fall, re front and rear of boat, plane, etc.), tangi [int]; tang(ad)o; (rock up and down, gen), balanciĝi; (degree), grado (e.g.: *a high pitch of emotion:* alta grado de emocio); (sales line), (vendo)propagando; (slope angle), inklinangulo; (angle of propeller blade, plane wing, etc.), klinangulo; **pitch in**, kunhelpi [tr]; **pitchman**, prikriisto, ĉarlatano; **pitch pipe**, diapazono; **standard pitch**, (A 440), pitĉ-normo; **make a pitch for**, propagandi [int] por, pripropagandi [tr]
pitchblende, peĉblendo
pitcher, kruĉo [cp "jug"]
piteous, kompatinda, korŝira, povra
pith, (center tissue of plant stem etc.), medolo; (core, kernel, gist), kerno; **pithy**, (concise, profound), trafa, konciza, sentencoplena; **pithy statement**, sentenco
Pithecanthropus, pitekantropo [note: term now obsolete; see "man: Heidelberg man", *"Homo"*, *"Australopithecus"*]
Pithecia, pitecio
Pithecus, piteko, makako
pithiatic, pitiata; **pithiatism**, ~ismo
pitiful, pitiable, kompatinda, korŝira, mizera
piton, kroĉnajlo
pittance, sumeto
pitter-patter, (feet etc.), frapetado; (rain etc.), plaŭdetado

Pittsburgh, Pitsburgo
pituita, pituito
pituitary, **pituitary gland**, pituitario,
  hipofazo; **pituitary extract**, pituitrino
pity, kompato; ~i [tr, int]: **have pity on**,
  ~i [tr]; **what a pity!**, domaĝe!, kia
  domaĝo!; **it's a pity (that)**, estas
  domaĝe (ke)
pityriasis, pitiriazo
Pius, (popes), Pio
pivot, pivoto; ~i [int]; ~igi; **pivotal**, ~a
pixel, bildopunkto
pixie, (fairy), koboldo, fe(in)o
pizza, pico†; **pizzeria**, ~ejo
pizzazz, ĵazaĵ', ~o
pizzicato, plukita; ~e
placard, afiŝo
placate, (re)pacigi,   malkolerigi,
  (re)trankviligi
place, (position, location, part of a
  space, gen), loko; (having specified
  purpose), ejo, –ejo [sfx] (e.g.: *place of*
  amusement: amuzejo); (put, locate),
  ~i [tr], meti [tr]; (turn, position in series), vico; (rank), rango; (plaza, city
  square), placo; (space, room), spaco;
  (situation), situacio; (residence),
  loĝejo; (location relative to oth objects, numbers, etc.), situo; (hire),
  dungi [tr]; (find employment for),
  dungigi; (make ready for given treatment), pretigi (e.g.: *place a child for*
  adoption: pretigi infanon por adopto);
  (finish, as in race), finiĝi; **placement**,
  ~ado; ~iĝo; vicigo; arranĝo; loĝigo;
  situo; situigo; dung(ig)o; pretigo; fin-
  iĝo; **displace**, de~i [tr], dismeti [tr];
  displacement, de~o, dismeto; **mis-**
  place, mis~i [tr], perdi [tr]; **replace**,
  (substitute, take place of), anstataŭi
  [tr]; (put in place of), anstataŭigi; (put
  back), remeti [tr], re~i [tr]; **replace-**
  ment, anstataŭ(ig)(ad)o; anstataŭaĵo;
  anstataŭanto; anstataŭulo; remeto; **re-**
  placement part, vicpeco; **take place**,
  okazi [int], efektiviĝi; **go places**,
  (progress), progresi [int]; **in place of**,
  anstataŭ; **in the first (second etc.)**
  place, unu(avic)e du(avic)e, etc.);
  know one's place, scii sian rangon;
  out of place, (inappropriate), malkonvena; (misplaced), mis~ita; **be out of**

place, malkonveni [int]; **all over the**
  place, ĉie kaj dise; **of that place**, tiea;
  take the place of, anstataŭi [tr]
placebo, placebo
placenta, (gen), placento
Placentalia, placentuloj
placid, trankvila, kvieta, serena
Placido, Placidus, (man's name), Placido
plagiarism, plagiary, plagiato; **plagia-**
  rize, ~i [tr]; **plagiarist**, ~into; ~anto;
  ~isto
plagioclase, plagioklazo
Plagiostomi, Plagiostomata,   plagiosto-
  moj
plague, (gen), pesto; (any long-term catastrophe, esp viewed as punishment
  by God etc.; extreme bother), plago;
  plagi [tr]; (torment, gen), turmenti
  [tr]; **black plague**, nigra ~o; **bubonic**
  plague, bubona ~o
plaice, plateso
plaid, plejdo; ~a
plain, (clear), klara; (simple), simpla;
  (obvious), evidenta, mem~a; (frank,
  candid), kandida; (downright, thorough), ĝisosta, kompleta; (not ornamented),   neornamita,   ordinara;
  (homely),   nebela,   ordinar(aspekt)a;
  (pure, unmixed), pura; (level land),
  ebenaĵo [cp "prairie", "pampa",
  "steppe"]; **coastal plain**, apudmara
  ebenaĵo; (esp formed by sea sedi-
  ment), marsko
plaintiff, plendanto
plaintive, plenda, morna, melankolia
plaise, plateso
plait, (braid), plekti [tr]; ~aĵo
plan, (gen), plani [tr]; ~o [cp "scheme",
  "schema", "diagram"]; (pol etc.), ~izi
  [tr] (e.g.: *planned economy:* ~izita
  ekonomio); **plan on**, (plan to), ~i
  (e.g.: *I plan on going:* mi ~as iri);
  (count on, trust), fidi [tr, int] (al, je,
  ~n)
planchette, tabuleto
plane, (flat), ebena; (surface), ~o; (level, stage), nivelo, stadio; (airplane),
  avio, aer(o)plano; (soar, glide, re aircraft, hydroplane, etc.), sori [int];
  (smooth wood), raboti [tr]; rabotilo;
  (machine), rabotmaŝino; (tree: *Plata-*

nus), platano; **sailplane**, (sor)glisilo; **seaplane**, hidroplano; **spaceplane**, kosmo–avio

planet, planedo; **planetary**, ~a; **planetarium**, ~planetario†; **planetoid, minor planet**, (asteroid), asteroido; **extraplanetary**, ekster~a; **off-planet**, ekster~a; ekster~e(n)

planimeter, planimetro; **planimetry**, planimetrio

plank, (any board; pol), tabulo; (for crossing stream; gangplank from ship to shore; etc.), pas~o; (board w cross-section between 5x10 and 8x30 cm), dilo

plankton, planktono; **phytoplankton**, fito~o

plant, (bot organism), planto; (put plant in soil, or similar action), ~i [tr]; (cover area w plants), pri~i [tr] (e.g.: *plant a hill with cedars:* pri~i monteton per cedroj); (re cuttings of plant, as leaf, shoot, etc.), stiki [tr]; (factory), fabriko; (metal-working factory), uzino; (large manufacturing plant), manufakturo; (for production of energy, as hydroelectric plant), centralo; (set of machinery etc.), maŝinaro; (any installation), instalaĵo; (fix firmly), fiksi [tr]; (settle, establish), establi [tr] [cp "settle"]; **planter**, (plant container), ~ingo; **cast-iron plant**, (bot), aspidistro; **castor-oil plant**, ricino; **century plant**, agavo; **chalk plant**, gipsofilo; **Chinese lantern plant**, alkekengo; **flamingo plant**, flamengofloro; **gas plant**, fraksinelo; **house-plant**, ĉambro~o; **implant**, en~i [tr], establi [tr], fiksi [tr]; en~aĵo; **indigo plant**, indigujo, indigo~o; **money plant**, (*Lunaria*), lunario; **pilot plant**, prov-instalaĵo; **sensitive plant**, sentema mimozo, sensitivo; **sunplant**, (*Portulaca*), portulako; **telegraph plant**, telegraf~o; **tobacco plant**, nikotiano; **transplant**, trans~i [tr]; trans~o; trans~aĵo [cp "graft"]

Plantago, plantago

plantain, (weed: *Plantago*), plantago; (banana plant: *Musa paradisiaca*), bananujo; **water plantain**, alismo

plantation, (estate), bien/ego, grand~o,

latifundio; (cultivated area), kultivejo

Planuloidea, planuloidoj†

plaque, (tablet etc.), ŝildo

–plasia, (med sfx), –plazio

plasis, plazio

plasma, plasmo; **bioplasma**, bio~o; **nuclear plasma**, nukleo~o

plasmodium, Plasmodium, plasmodio

plaster, (for walls etc.), gipso; ~i [tr] [cp "stucco"]; (medication), plastro; **plaster of Paris**, Pariza ~o

plastic, (gen: moldable etc.; any of variety of substances thus named), plasto; ~a; (3-dimensional, re art, sculpture, etc.), plastiko; plastika; (med: reparatory), plastia (e.g.: *plastic surgery:* plastia kirurgio); (med: re tissue building), plazia (e.g.: *neoplastic:* neoplazia); **plasticity**, ~eco; **plasticize**, ~igi; ~iĝi; **plasticizer**, ~igenzo

–plasty, (med sfx: reparatory surgery), –plastio; (re tissue building), –plazio (e.g.: *neoplasty:* neoplazio)

plat, (piece of ground), teren/(et)o; (map), ~mapo

Plata, (river), Rivero Plata

Platalea, plataleo

Platanus, platano

plate, (any flat surface or object, as in printing, med, elec, etc.), plato; (for food; or contents of; or similar-shaped object), telero; (thin layer of any metal on oth metal etc.), plaki [tr]; plak(aĵ)o; (specified metal), –izi [tr sfx]; –izaĵo (e.g.: *silver-plate:* arĝentizi; arĝentizaĵo); (phot), plako; (engraving), gravuraĵo; (any illustration), ilustraĵo; (lamina), lameno; (of capacitor), armaturo; (anode), anodo; **armor-plate**, kiras~o; **breast-plate**, brustkiraso; **electroplate**, galvanizi [tr], elektroplaki [tr]; **hot plate**, hejt~o; **license plate**, licenco~o, numer~o; **name-plate**, nom~o

plateau, (any level place or period), ebenaĵo, plataĵo; (tableland), alt~o

platelet, (of blood), trombocito

platen, platino

platform, (raised support), podio; (pol etc.), platformo; (at rr station etc.), kajo

platinum, plateno; **platinate**, ~ato; **pla-**

tinic (acid), ~ata (acido); platinize, ~i [tr]

platitude, banal/ajo; platitudinous, ~a

Plato, Platono; Platonic, ~a; Platonism, ~ismo; neo-Platonism, novplatonismo†

platonic, platona

platoon, plotono

platter, plado

Platyhelminthes, platvermoj

platypus, ornitorinko

platysma, (muscle), platismo

plaudit, (applause), aplaŭdo; (praise), laŭdo

plausible, kredinda

Plautus, Plaŭto

play, (recreational activity; play game; play mus instrument, radio, TV, etc.), ludi [tr, int]; (such activity; moving space, as re mech part), ~o; (theat: act role), roli [int] (kiel), ~i; (frolic, romp), petoli [int], kaprioli [int]; (gamble), vet~i [tr, int]; (drama), dramo, teatraĵo; (be directed, as spot light, water, etc.), direktiĝi; (oppose in game), ~i kontraŭ, kontraŭi [tr]; (put, use, as card in game), elmeti [tr], ~i; (pretend to be), ~i kiel (e.g.: *play teacher:* ~i kiel instruisto); (motion, gen), moviĝado; player, ~anto; ~isto; (theat), aktoro, rolanto; playful, ~ema; petolema; play around, frivole ~adi [int]; playback, re~o; playbill, (poster), dramafiŝo; (program), programo; playboy, (playgirl), amoremul(in)o; play-by-play, detala; play down, malemfazi [tr], minimumigi; play hooky, lernejeviti [int], eviti la lernejon; playground, ~ejo, ~okorto; playhouse, (theat), dramteatro; (for child's play), ~dometo; playmate, kun~anto; play-off, post~o; play on words, vort~o [cp "pun"]; playpen, ~okaĝo; playsuit, ~kompleto; plaything, ~ilo; play up, emfazi [tr], substreki [tr], naksimumigi; play up to, (flatter), flati [tr]; playwright, dram(verk)isto; child's play, (easy task), simplegaĵo; foul play, perforto; interplay, interefik(ad)o; miracle play, mystery play, miraklo~o [not "miraklodramo"]; overplay, troigi,

troknedi [tr]; bring into play, alvoki [tr], aktivigi; come into play, alvokiĝi, aktiviĝi; make a play for, provi amindumi [tr]

plaza, placo

plea, (law), pledo; (request), peto; (pretext), preteksto

plead, (implore), pet(eg)i [tr]; (law), pledi [tr]; (as pretext), preteksti [tr]; plead guilty (innocent), (mal)konfesi [tr] (kulpon)

pleasant, (gen), agrabla, plaĉa, plezura; (re person), afabla, ~a, ĉarma

please, (satisfy, make content), plaĉi [tr] (e.g.: *the results pleased us:* la rezultoj nin ~is); (polite request), bonvole ~u, bonvolu ~i, mi (ni) petas [note: "mi petas" goes after main clause, "bonvol~" generally before (e.g.: *please come:* bonvole venu [or] bonvolu veni [or] venu, mi petas)] [abb of "bonvol~": bv., bv~u, bv~e]; pleased, (contented), kontenta; pleasing, ~a; displease, mal~i [tr]; as you please, laŭ~e, laŭ via ~o

pleasure, plezuro; pleasurable, ~a, agrabla, plaĉa; displeasure, mal~o; my pleasure, (response after "thank you"), mia ~o; ne menciinde; with pleasure, (willingly), volonte

pleat, plisi [tr]; ~(aĵ)o

plebeian, pleba; ~eca; ~ano

plebiscite, plebiscito

plebs, plebo

Plectrophenax nivalis, neĝemberizo

plectrum, plektro [see also "pick"]

pledge, (promise), promesi [tr], devontigi sin; ~o; (security, as on loan), garantii [tr]; garanti(aĵ)o; (toast), tosti [tr]; tosto; (trial member, as in fraternity), provmembro; provmembrigi; provmembriĝi

–plegi/a, (med sfx), –plegio; –plegic, ~a; ~ulo

pleiad, Pleiad, Pleiade, plejado

Pleiades, (ast), Plejado

Pleistocene, plejstoceno; ~a

plenary, plena

plenipotentiary, plenrajta; ~ulo, ~igito

plenty, (abundance), abundo; plenty (of), ~a(j); (many), multaj, multe da; plentiful, ~a

plenum, (full meeting), plen/kunsido; (full space), ~eco; ~ejo
pleonasm, pleonasmo; **pleonastic**, ~a
Plesiosaurus, plesiosaŭro
plethora, pletoro
pleura, pleŭro; **pleurisy**, ~ito; **pleuritic**, ~ita
Pleuronectes, pleŭronekto; Pleuronectes flesus, fleso; Pleuronectes limanda, limando; Pleuronectes platessa, plateso; Pleuronectidae, ~edoj
plexiglass, plastovitro
plexus, plekso; **solar plexus**, suna ~o, stomaka ~o
pliable, pliant, fleksebla
plica, faldo; **plica umbilicalis medi(an)a**, urako
plié genuelturno
pliers, pair of pliers, tenajlo [note sing]
plight, (misfortune), malfeliĉo; (pledge), promesi [tr]
plimsoll, (shoe), tolŝuo; **Plimsoll mark, Plimsoll line**, floslinio
plink, (tinkle), tinti [int]; ~igi; ~o
plinth, plinth course, plinto
Pliny, Plinio; **Pliny the Elder**, ~o la Maljuna; **Pliny the Younger**, ~o la Juna
Pliocene, plioceno; ~a
plod, pezpaŝi [int]; ~o
plop, (sound of flat surface hitting water etc.), plaŭdi [int]; ~o; (onom), plaŭd!; (fall), fal(eg)i [int]; (fall, onom), pum!
plosive, plozivo; ~a
plot, (scheme), komploto; ~i [int]; pri~i [tr]; (small piece of land), tereneto; (garden), bedo; (story line), intrigo; (draw chart, graph, etc.), grafiki [tr]; grafikaĵo
plough, [see "plow"]
plover, pluvio; **golden plover**, or~o; **green plover**, (lapwing), vanelo; **piping plover**, ĥaradrio
plow, plugi [tr]; ~ilo; **plowshare**, soko; **snowplow**, neĝ~ilo
ploy, artifiko, ruzo
pluck, (pick, pull off; mus), pluki [tr]; (courage), kuraĝo; **plucky**, kuraĝa
plug, (stop up; elec), ŝtopi [tr]; ~ilo; (peg etc.), kejlo; (for anchor bolt), dubelo; **plug in**, (elec and fig), konekti [tr], eningigi; **fireplug**, fajrokran-

ego; **spark plug**, sparkilo; **pull the plug**, malkonekti [tr], elingigi
plum, pruno [cp "prune"]; **plum tree**, ~arbo; **cherry plum**, mirobalano; **governor('s) plum**, flakurtio; **greengage plum**, renklodo
plumage, plumaro
plumb, (provide plumbing, work w pipes), tub/izi [tr]; (vertical), vertikala; (test depth, fathom, lit or fig), sondi [tr]; (plumb bob and line), lodo, vertikalilo; **plumber**, ~isto; **plumbing**, (pipes), ~aro; (work), ~izado; **plumb bob**, (weight), lodpezilo; **plumb line**, (string), lodfadeno
plumbago, (gen), plumbago
Plumbago, plumbago
plumbate, plumbato; **plumbic**, ~a
plumbite, plumbito; **plumbous**, ~a
plume, plumo; ~i [tr]; ~iĝi; ~aĵo, ~tufo
plummet, (fall), plonĝi [int]; (plumb), [see "plumb"]
plump, (fat), dika [not "plumpa"]; (drop), falegi [int], peze fali [int]; peze faligi; **plump for**, (support), forte apogi [tr]
plumule, plumulo
plunder, (steal items), rabi [tr]; (re person or place), pri~i [tr]; (pri)~ado; ~aĵo, kaptaĵo
plunge, plonĝi [int]; ~igi; ~o; **plunger**, (of pump, syringe, etc.), piŝto; (to unclog drain), malŝtopilo
plunk, (sound), klaktinti [int]; ~o; (put down), (de)meti [tr]; (strum, as on banjo), plektri [tr]; (fall heavily), peze fali [int]
pluperfect, pluskvamperfekto; ~a
plural, (gram), pluralo; ~a; (several), pluropa; **pluralism**, plurismo; **plurality**, (plural condition), plureco; (margin, as of highest vote), plimulto [cp "majority"]
plus, (math), plus; pluso; plusa, plus– [pfx] (e.g.: *plus sign:* plussigno); (besides), krome, aldone
plusfours, golfkuloto, pufpantalono [note sing]
plush, (luxurious), pluŝ/eca, luksa; (fabric), ~o; ~a
Plutarch, Plutarko
Pluto, (myth; ast), Plutono

plutocrat, plutokrato; **plutocracy**, ~io
Plutonian, Plutona
plutonic, plutona
plutonium, plutonio
Plutus, Pluto
Pluvialis, pluvio; Pluvialis apricarius,
    or~o
Pluviôse, Pluviozo
ply, (layer), lameno; (strand, as of rope),
    ŝnurero; (use), uzi [tr], utiligi; (work
    as at trade), labori [int] (kiel); (give,
    supply), donadi [tr], donacadi [tr],
    direktadi [tr], provizadi [tr] (al) (etc.)
    (e.g.: *they plied me with questions:* ili
    direktadis demandojn al mi; *he plied
    her with wine:* li donadis vinon al ŝi);
    (follow route), trafiki [int], iradi [int]
    (laŭ, trans, etc.), laŭiradi [tr], transira-
    di [tr] (etc.) (e.g.: *the ferries ply the
    channel every summer:* la pramoj
    transiradas la markolon ĉiun somer-
    on); **four-ply (six-ply, etc.)**, kvar~a
    (ses~a, etc.)
p.m. (abb of "post meridiem"), ptm.
    [abb of "posttagmeze"]
pneumatic, (worked by air), pneŭmata;
    (re sci of pneumatics), pneŭmatika;
    pneumatics, pneŭmatiko
pneum(o)–, (pfx: re anything pneu-
    matic),   pneŭmo–;   (re   lungs),
    pneŭmon(o)–
pneumococcus, pneŭmokoko
pneumoconiosis, pneŭmokoniozo   [cp
    "pneumonoconiosis"];   (caused   by
    cork), suberozo
pneumogastric, vaga, pneŭmogastra
pneumology, pneŭmologio
pneumonectomy, pneŭmonektomio
pneumonia, pneŭmonito, pneŭmonio
pneumon(o)–, (med pfx), pneŭmono–
    [for specific words beginning thus,
    not listed, see under "pneumo–"]
pneumonoconiosis, pneŭmonokoniozo
    [cp "pneumoconiosis"]
pneumonopathy, pneŭmonopatio
Pnom-Penh, Pnompeno
Po, (river), Pado
poach, (cook in water), poĉi [tr]; (hunt
    illegally), ŝtelĉasi [tr]
pochard, merganaso; **tufted pochard**,
    fuligulo
pock, (pustule),   pustulo   [cp "pock-

mark"]
pocket, (clothing etc.), poŝo; en~igi;
    (hollow), kavo; **air pocket**, aerkavo;
    pickpocket, ~oŝtelisto; **pick one's
    pocket**, ~oŝteli [tr]; **pull from one's
    pocket**, el~igi; **pay out-of-pocket**,
    pagi [tr] propra~e; **out-of-pocket ex-
    pense**, propra~a elspezo
pockmark, (from disease), variolmar-
    ko; ~i [tr]; (w hollows, craters, etc., as
    on Luna and oth airless worlds), kav-
    igita
pod, (pea, bean, etc., or any similar ob-
    ject), guŝo; **locust pod**, (fruit), karo-
    bo; (tree), karobarbo
–pod, (sfx: foot), –piedo (e.g.: *pseudo-
    pod:* pseŭdo~o)
podagra, podagro
podgy, diketa
podiatry, pied/medicino;   **podiatrist**,
    ~kuracisto
Podiceps, podicipo
podium, (gen), podio
Podocarpus, podokarpo
Poephagus grunniens, poefago,   grunt-
    bovo
poem, poemo
poet, poeto; **poetaster**, ~aĉo; **poetic**,
    poezia; **poetics**, poetiko; **poetry**, (po-
    ems), poezio; (poetic quality), poezi-
    eco
Pogostemon cablin, Pogostemon
    patchouli, paĉulo
pogrom, pogromo
–poie/sis, (med sfx), –poezo; –**poietic**,
    ~a
poignant, pika, akra, korŝira
poinsettia, ruĝa eŭforbio
point, (spot, dot; geom; punctuation;
    theme, idea; degree; type size; etc.),
    punkto; ~i [tr]; (sharp end etc.; ex-
    tremity), pinto; pintigi; (indicate,
    point at), indiki [tr], montri [tr]; (of
    joke), pintumo; (unit of score in
    game; of mark in school, on test; etc.),
    poento; (purpose), celo (e.g.: *pointless
    argument:* sencela disputo); (utility),
    utilo; (moment), momento; (item, ele-
    ment), ero; (suggestion), sugesto;
    (elec contact point as in distributor
    etc.), kontakto~o; (Br: elec outlet,
    socket), (konekt)ingo; (of compass),

rumbo; (punctuate), interpunkcii [tr]; (aim), celi [tr]; (decimal marker), komo, decimalo [see § 19(e)] (e.g.: *twelve point four three [12.43]:* dek du komo [or: decimalo] kvar tri [12,43]); (matter), afero; (issue, question), demando; **pointed**, (sharp), pinta; (remark etc.), pika, trafa; **pointer**, (stick, needle, etc.), montrilo; (dog), montrohundo; **pointless**, sencela; **point at, point to**, (indicate, show), indiki [tr], montri [tr]; (aim), celi [tr]; **point-blank**, (direct), rekta, tuj apuda, je nula distanco; **point of honor**, afero de honoro; **point of information**, interpelacio; **ask a point of information (of)**, interpelacii [tr]; **point of land**, terpinto [cp "promontory"]; **point of no return**, nerevena ~o; **point of order**, demando pri ordo; **point of time**, tempo~o, momento; **point of view**, vid~o; **point out**, (show), montri [tr]; (call attention), atentigi (iun pri io); **boiling point**, bol~o; **exclamation point**, kri~o; **freezing point**, frosto~o; **Lagrange point, libration point**, oscilo~o; **melting point**, fando~o; **midpoint**, mez~o; **pinpoint**, (locate), (precize) trovi [tr]; (define), (precize) di fini [tr]; (point of pin), pinglopinto; **starting point**, deir~o; **strong point**, ĉefa talento, ĉefa forto; **turning point**, turno~o, krizo; **vantage point**, ~o de elvido, elvida ~o; **viewpoint**, vid~o; **weak point**, (weakness), (ĉefa) malforto; (vulnerable spot), vundebla loko; **zero point**, nul~o; **to the point**, (relevant, concise), rilata, trafa, alcela, lakona, konciza; **beside the point**, nerilata, ekstercela; **be beside the point**, ne rilati [int]; **get (come) to the point**, ekatenti la celon (temon, demandon); **(be) on the point of**, esti tuj –onta (e.g.: *we were on the point of leaving:* ni estis tuj forirontaj); **in point of fact**, efektive, fakte; **make a point of**, (be sure to), certiĝi ke, nepre, certe (e.g.: *we made a point of inviting her:* ni certiĝis ke ni invitis ŝin; *I'll make a point of going:* mi nepre iros); (emphasize), emfazi [tr],

substreki [tr] (e.g.: *he made a point of his opposition:* li emfazis [or] substrekis sian kontraŭon); **up to a point**, ĝis iu ~o (limo, grado); **what's the point of ...?**, kiel utilas ...?; **you've got a point**, vi pravas, vi havas pravan (konsiderindan) ~on

poise, (balance), ekvilibro; ~i [int]; ~igi; (composure, aplomb), aplombo; (unit of viscosity), puazo; **centipoise**, centipuazo

poison, veneno; ~i [tr]; **poisonous**, ~a

Poitiers, (French town), Puatiero

Poitou, Puatuo

poke, (jab), piki [tr]; ~o; (hit), frapi [tr]; frapo; (stir up, as fire), inciti [tr]; (thrust), ĵeti [tr]; (intrude), sin trudi [tr]; (stick out), etendiĝi, elstari [tr]; (loiter, dawdle), lanti [int]; (push), puŝ(et)i [tr]; puŝ(et)o

poker, (game), pokero; (for fire), fajrostango; **poker-face**, ~vizaĝo; **poker-faced**, ~vizaĝa

Poland, Pol/io, ~lando; **Pole**, ~o; **Polish**, ~a; ~ia

polar, (tech: re radiation), polara; (re planetary, magnetic, chem, math etc. pole or oth opposites), polusa; (math: section of conic), polajro [see "pole"]; **polarimeter**, polarimetro; **polarity**, ~eco; poluseco; **polarize**, (elec, magnetic, etc.; divide opinions etc. into opposites, gen), ~igi; ~iĝi; polusigi; polusiĝi; (light), ~izi [tr]; **polarograph**, ~ografo; **bipolar**, dupolusa

Polaris, (star), la Polusa Stelo

polder, poldero

pole, (rod etc.), stango; ~i [tr]; (stake), paliso; (of planet etc.; elec; magnetic; of battery; etc.), poluso [see also "polar"]; (post, as fence, telephone, etc.), fosto; **May pole**, majarbo, majfosto; **totem pole**, totemfosto

Pole, [see under "Poland"]

polemic, polemika; **polemics**, ~o; **polemize, polemicize**, ~i [int]; **polemist, polemicist**, ~isto

polenta, polento

Polianthes, polianto; Polianthes tuberosa, tuberoso

police, polico; ~i [tr]; **police(wo)man, police officer**, ~isto, ~ano; **police**

chief, ~estro; **police station**, ~ejo;
plain-clothes police officer, kaŝ~isto
Policlitus, Policleitus, Poliklito†
policy, (plan, way of doing), politiko;
(insurance contract), poliso
polio, poliomjelito
polio-, (anat pfx), polio–
polioencephalitis, polioencefalito
poliomyelitis, poliomjelito
polish, (gen), poluri [tr]; ~o; (wax for
shoes etc.), ciri [tr]; ciro; (wood etc.,
by covering w shellac and polishing),
polituri [tr]; **(finger)nail polish,** ungolako; laki [tr] (la ungojn); **polish
off,** (consume), forkonsumi [tr]
Politburo, Politikburoo
polite, ĝentila
politic, politiki [int]; (prudent), prudenta
politics, politiko [note sing]; **political,**
~a; **politician,** ~isto; **political science,** ~ologio†; **political scientist,**
~ologo†
polka, polko; ~i [int]
poll, (vote), baloti [int]; ~igi; ~o; ~ejo;
(opinion survey), opinisondi [tr];
opinisondo; **pollster,** opinisondisto;
polling booth, ~budo; **poll tax,** (per
head), kapimposto; (to vote), ~impos-
to
pollan, koregono
pollen, poleno; **pollinate,** ~i [tr]; **pol-
linization,** ~ado; **pollen grain,** ~ero;
pollen sac, ~ujo, ~sako
pollex, polekso
pollute, polui† [tr]; **pollution,** (act, process), ~(ad)o; (substance), ~aĵo; **pol-
lutant,** ~anto; ~enzo
Pollux, (myth; ast), Polukso
pollywog, ranido
polo, (game), poloo; **water polo,** ak-
vo~o
polonaise, polonezo
polonium, polonio
Polonius, Polonio
Poltava, Poltavo
poltergeist, bru/fantomo, ~spirito
poltroon, poltrono
poly-, (tech pfx), poli– [see also
"multi–"]
polyandry, poliandrio
Polybius, Polibio
Polychaeta, poliĥetoj

polychrome, polikromio; ~aĵo; **poly-
chromic,** ~a
polyclinic, polikliniko
polyconic, polikonusa
Polycrates, Polikrato
polyene, polieno
polyester, poliestero; ~a
polyethylene, polietileno; ~a
polygamy, poligamio; **polygamist,**
~ulo; **polygamous,** ~a
polyglot, poligloto; ~a, plurlingva
polygon, poligono
Polygonum, poligono; Polygonum bis-
torta, Polygonum bistortoides, bistorto
polygraph, mensogodetektatoro
polygyny, poligamio
polyhedron, poliedro, pluredro
Polyhymnia, Polimnia
polymath, ĉioklerulo
polymer, polimero; **polymeric,** ~a; **po-
lymerize,** ~igi; ~iĝi
polymorph, polimorf/aĵo; ~ulo; **poly-
morphous,** ~a; **polymorphism,** ~is-
mo
Polynesia, Polinezio; **Polynesian,**
~ano; ~a
Polynices, Poliniko
polynomial, polinomo; ~a
polyp, (gen), polipo; **polyposis,** ~ozo
Polyphemus, Polifemo
polyphony, polifonio; **polyphonic,** ~a
Polyplectron, poliplektro, pavo-fazano
polypore, poliporo
Polyporus, poliporo; Polyporus fomentarius, tindrofungo, fajrofungo; Poly-
poraceae, ~acoj, porofungoj
Polypterus, poliptero
polyptych, poliptiko
Polypus, polpo
Polystichum, polistiko
polysyndeton, polisindeto
polytechnic, politekniko; ~a; **polytech-
nical,** ~a, plurfaka
Polyxena, Poliksena
pomace, rekremento
Pomaceae, pomacoj
pomade, pomado; ~i [tr]
pomegranate, (fruit), granato; (tree),
~arbo
pomelo, [see "shaddock"]
Pomerania, Pomer/io; **Pomeranian,**

(person), ~o; ~ia; (dog), ~hundo, ŝpico
pommel, (gen), pomelo
pomology, pomolog/io; **pomologist**, ~o
pomp, pompo
Pompeii, Pompejo; **Pompeian**, ~ano; ~a
Pompey, Pompeius, Pompeo
pom-pom, bulkvasto
pompous, pompa
poncho, ponĉo
pond, lageto; **millpond**, muel~o
ponder, mediti [int] (pri), pri~i [tr], cerbumi [int] (pri)
ponderous, (heavy), peza; (ungraceful), malgracia; (unwieldy), nemanovrebla, maloportuna; (dull), malsprita
Pondicherry, Pondiĉero
pongee, ponĝeo
poniard, ponardo; ~i [tr]
pontifex, pontifiko
pontiff, pontifiko; **supreme pontiff**, ĉef~o
pontifical, pontifika; **pontificate**, ~i [int]
Pontine Marshes, Marĉoj Pontinaj
Pontius, Poncio; **Pontius Pilate**, ~o Pilato
pontoon, pontono
Pontus, Ponto; **Pontus Euxinus**, ~- Eŭksino
pony, poneo, ĉevaleto; **ponytail**, ~vosto; **on shank's pony**, (Aus colloq), piede
pood, pudo
poodle, pudelo
poof! (onom), puf!
pool, (pond), lageto; (puddle), flako; (of fountain; reflecting; etc.), baseno; (swimming), naĝejo; (game), poŝbilardo; (combine), kunigi, komunigi; kuniĝi; kunig(aĵ)o, komunaĵo (e.g.: *carpool:* aŭtokuniĝi; aŭtokomunaĵo); ($ bet), vetaĵo, vetmono, ludmono; (group of persons), kunigitaro; (collective set), provizo, ~provizo (e.g.: *gene pool:* genprovizo); ($: arrangement to fix prices or provide common market), pullo; **pool hall, poolroom**, bilardejo; **whirlpool**, kirlakvo
poop, (naut), pobo, poŭpo; (fatigue), (el)lacigi; **pooped**, (el)laciĝinta

poor, (lacking $ or oth thing), malriĉa; (pitiable), povra, kompatinda (e.g.: *oh, you poor little thing!:* ho, vi povruleto!); (low quality etc.), malbona, senvalora; (not abundant), malabunda; (contemptible), aĉa; (not skillful), mallerta
pop, (noise of balloon, whip, etc.), knali [int]; ~igi; ~o; (onom), krak!, paf!, klak!; (burst, crack apart), krevi [int]; krevigi; krev(ig)o; (do suddenly), ek– [pfx] (e.g.: *he popped a question at them:* li ekĵetis demandon al ili; *she popped into the room:* ŝi ekvenis en la ĉambron; *a fish popped out of the water:* fiŝo ekeliĝis el la akvo; *the weeds popped up from nowhere:* la trudherboj ekaperis el nenie); (dad), paĉjo; (popular, gen), popa*, populara, (laŭ)moda; **pop music**, popmuziko*†
pope, (Catholic), papo; (Greek Orthodox priest), popo; (zool), perĉo
poplar, poplo; **tulip poplar**, tuliparbo
poples, poplito
poplin, poplino
popliteal, poplita; **popliteal cavity**, ~a kavo
poppy, papavo; **poppy red**, punca; **corn poppy, field poppy**, ~eto; **horned poppy**, glaŭcio; **opium poppy**, opio~o; **prickly poppy, Mexican poppy**, argemono
poppycock, sensencaĵo
populace, popol(amas)o
popular, (known, used, liked, admired by many), populara; (pop), ~a, popa* (re a people or peoples), popola (e.g.: *popular plebiscite:* popola plebiscito); **popularity**, ~eco; **popularize**, ~igi; **unpopular**, ne~a
populate, loĝ/igi; popoli [tr] [cp "settle"]; **populated**, ~ata; **population**, (re density etc.), ~ateco; (total residents), ~antaro; (statistical sample), populacio; **depopulate**, senpopoligi; **overpopulate**, tro~atigi; **overpopulation**, tro~ateco; **underpopulation**, sub~ateco
populism, popol/ismo; **populist**, ~isma; ~isto
populous, multloĝata, dense loĝata, homplena

Populus, poplo; Populus tremula, tremolo
porbeagle, lamno
porcelain, (substance), porcelano; ~a; (object made of), ~aĵo
porch, verando, porĉo, antaŭpordo
porcine, pork(ec)a
porcupine, histriko; **tree porcupine**, koenduo
pore, (hole), poro; **pore over**, absorbiĝi en, atente stud(ad)i [tr]
Porifera, sponguloj
pork, pork/aĵo; **pork chop**, ~kotleto
pornography, pornograf/io; **pornographic**, ~ia; **pornographer**, ~o
porous, pora, ~oza; **porosity**, ~eco
porphyry, porfiro; **porphyrize**, ~izi [tr]
porpoise, foceno, marporko
porridge, poriĝo
port, (harbor), haveno; (city), ~urbo; (naut: left), babordo; baborda; (wine), portovino; **Port**, (in place names), Porto, Port– [see subentries under main name]; **port of entry**, doganejo; **airport**, flug~o; **gun-port**, embrazuro; **seaport**, mar~o; **spaceport**, kosmo~o
portable, portebla
portage, (carrying), port/ado; (place), ~ejo
portal, portalo
portcullis, barokrado
portend, aŭguri [tr]; **portent**, ~o; **portentous**, (ominous), mis~a; (self-important), pompa, mem grava; (impressive), impona
porter, (carrier), portisto; (doorkeeper), pordisto; (servant, as on train etc.), servisto; (beer), portero
portfolio, (briefcase), teko; (for state documents etc.), aktujo; (office of minister etc.), posteno, ministrejo; (stock list), akcilisto; **without portfolio**, sen ofico
portico, portiko
portion, porcio; **portion out**, (ration), ~umi [tr], disdividi [tr]
Portland, (gen), Portlando
portly, korpulenta
portmanteau, valizo
Porto, Porto, Oporto
portrait, portreto; ~i [tr]; **portraiture**,

~arto; ~aro; ~o; **portrait artist**, ~isto; **self-portrait**, mem~o
portray, (lit or fig), portreti [tr], bildigi [tr]; **portrayal**, bildigo, ~ado
Portugal, Portugal/io; **Portuguese**, ~o; ~a; ~ia
Portulaca, portulako; Portulaca grandiflora, ĝardena ~o; Portulaca oleracea, legoma ~o
pose, (as for artist, lit or fig), pozo; ~i [int]; ~igi; (put question), fari [tr] (demandon); (assert), aserti [tr]; (pretense), pretendo; **pose as**, (impersonate), fraŭdimiti [tr]
Poseidon, Pozidono
posh, luksa [cp "plush"]
posit, (place), pozicii [tr], situigi; (postulate), postulati [tr]
position, (place, gen), pozicio; ~i [tr], loki [tr]; (site, relative to surroundings), situo; (job), ofico; (rank), rango; **positioned**, situanta; **be positioned**, situi [int] (e.g.: *the house is well positioned for the view:* la domo bone situas por la elvido)
positive, (definite; plus), pozitiva; ~o; ~aĵo; (specific), specifa; (firm, resolute), firma, rezoluta; (real, concrete), konkreta; (certain), certa; (absolute), absoluta; **positivism**, ~ismo; **positivist**, ~isma; ~isto
positron, pozitrono
posse, deputitaro
possess, posedi [tr]; **possession**, (act, state), ~o; (thing possessed), ~aĵo; (right to possess), ~rajto; **possessive**, (acquisitive), ~ema; (gram), posesivo; posesiva; **possessor**, ~anto; **dispossess**, evikcii [tr], sen~igi; **repossess**, reproprietigi; **self-possessed**, aplomba; **self-possession**, aplombo; **take possession of**, ek~i [tr]; (re land etc.), okupi [tr]
possible, (that could happen in present), ebla, ~i [int] (e.g.: *success is still possible:* sukceso ankoraŭ estas ~a [or] ankoraŭ ~as); (that might happen in future), eventuala; **possibly**, ~e; (there is a slight chance that), ~ete; **possibility**, ~(ec)o; **impossible**, ne~a; **as much (far) as possible**, laŭ~e; **as ... as possible**, [see under "as"]

possum, didelfo; **ring-tailed possum**, (Aus), ringvostulo; **play possum**, ŝajnigi morton

post, (pole), fosto; (any duty station), posteno, deĵorejo; (mil; high office etc.), posteno; postenigi; (mail), poŝto; enpoŝtigi; (starting point), komencejo; (put up poster etc.), afiŝi [tr]; (announce, gen), anonci [tr]; (enter, as in books, record), registri [tr], enskribi [tr]; (inform), informi [tr]; **be posted**, (assign person to given post), posteni [int]; **postal**, poŝta; **postbox**, [see "mail: mailbox"]; **postcard**, poŝtkarto; **postman**, leter(port)isto; **postmark**, poŝtstampo, poŝta stampo; **postmaster**, poŝtestro; **post office**, poŝtoficejo; **post office box**, poŝtkesto [see § 22]; **postpaid**, afrankita; afrankite; fri afranko; **Postal Service**, Poŝta Servo; **Postal Union**, Poŝtunuiĝo; **bedpost**, lit~o; **milepost**, (specifically of miles), mejlfosto; (if miles not specifically indicated; or fig), kilometrofosto [see § 20]; **outpost**, (gen), antaŭposteno

post–, (pfx: after, behind), post–

postage, afranko; **postage due**, poŝtrepage; **postage meter**, stampmaŝino; **postage stamp**, poŝtmarko; **pay (the) postage (on)**, ~i [tr]

poster, afiŝo

poste restante, poŝtrestante [see § 22]

posterior, posta; (buttocks), ~aĵo, (colloq), pugo

postern, posterno

posthumous, postmorta

postiche, postiĉo; ~a

postil(l)ion, postiljono

postlude, postludo

post meridiem, (abb: p.m.), posttagmeze [abb: ptm]

post-mortem, postmorta; (med exam), nekropsio

postpartum, postnaska

postpone, prokrasti [tr]

postposition, (gram), postpozicio

postscript, (abb: P.S.), postskribo [abb: P.S.]

postulate, (demand), postuli [tr]; ~o; (phil, sci, math), postulato; postulati [tr]

posture, (gen), pozo, sinteno; ~i [int]

pot, (container, gen), poto; (w spout, as coffee pot), kruĉo; (metal cooking pot w 2 handles and lid), marmito; (jar), ĵaro; (clay), argilaĵo; (ceramic), ceramikaĵo; **potter**, ~isto; (Br: putter), lanti [int], nenifaradi [int]; **pottery**, ~aro; **piece of pottery**, ~aĵo; **potty**, ~eto; **pot-luck meal**, kooperativa manĝo; **take pot-luck**, (accept whatever), akcepti kion ajn; **pot-pourri**, miks~o; **potsherd**, ~peco; **chamber pot**, noktovazo; (colloq), pis~o; **cooking pot**, kuir~o; **flower pot**, flor~o; **melting pot**, fando~o; **smudge pot**, fum~o

potable, trinkebla

Potamobius, astako, kankro

potash, potaso; **caustic potash**, kaŭstika ~o

potassium, kalio

potato, terpomo; **potato chip**, (Am), ~floko [cp "chip"]; **French-fried potatoes**, ~fingroj; **mashed potatoes**, ~a kaĉo; **small potatoes**, (fig), bagatelaĵo(j); **sweet potato**, batato [cp "yam"]

potent, potenca; **potency**, ~o; **impotent**, (powerless), sen~a; (sexually), impotenta; **impotence**, sen~o; impotenteco

potentate, potenculo

potential, (possible), eventuala, ebla; ebleco(j); (latent), latenta; (elec, magnetic, etc.), potencialo; potenciala; **equipotential**, ekvipotenciala; ekvipotencialo

potentiate, potencigi

Potentilla, potentilo

potentiometer, potenciometro

pother, (uproar), bruado, malpaco

potion, pocio

Potomac, Potomako*

pouch, (any sack, as mail pouch), sako; (small), ~eto; (pocket), poŝo; (of marsupial), marsupio

poulard(e), pulardo

poultice, kataplasmo; ~i [tr] [cp "compress"]

poultry, (animals), kortobirdoj [note plur]; ~aro; (as meat), ~aĵo

pounce, kaptosalti [int]; ~o

pound, ($), pundo; (beat), bat(ad)i [tr]; (stamp feet, fist, etc.), stamfi [int] (sur); (grind by pounding), pisti [tr]; (weight, gen), funto [avoirdupois: 0,454 kilogramoj; troy: 0,373 kilogramoj (see § 20)]; (enclosure), gardejo (e.g.: *dog pound:* hundogardejo); **poundage**, (commission etc.), makleraĵo; **pound sterling**, sterlinga ~o

pour, (liquids), verŝi [tr]; ~iĝi; (solids, as grains, gravel, etc.), ŝuti [tr]; ŝutiĝi; **(down)pour**, (rain), (pluv)torenti [int]; (pluv)torento; **outpour**, el~i [tr]; el~iĝi; **outpouring**, el~(iĝ)o

pout, paŭti [int]; ~o

poverty, (lack of $ or oth thing), malriĉeco, senhaveco; **poverty-stricken**, senhava, malriĉa, trafita de ~o; mizera

powder, (any powdered substance), pulvoro; (pulverize), ~igi; (dust w), pudri [tr]; (cosmetic), pudro; pudri [tr] [cp "dust"]; **powdered**, ~a; **talcum powder**, talka ~o, talka pudro; **powder-keg**, pulvujo; **powder puff**, pudrilo, pudrokvasto; **gunpowder**, pulvo

power, (force, potency, gen; optics; math), potenco; ~izi [tr], movi [tr] (e.g.: *electric power:* elektra ~o; *powered by electricity:* ~izita per elektro; *a steam-powered ship,* ŝipo movata de vaporo; x^5: [pronounce] ikso ~o kvin [or] ikso al la kvina ~o [or] la kvina ~o de ikso); (being able, gen; tech, phys, etc.), povo (e.g.: *have the power [be able] to do something:* havi la povon fari ion; *buying power:* aĉetpovo); (right), rajto; (person), ~ulo; (nation etc.), ~aĵo, ~lando; **powerful**, ~a; **powerless**, sen~a; **powerhouse**, (elec), centralo; (person etc.), ~ulo; **empower**, (give right to), rajtigi; **all-powerful**, ĉiopova; **horsepower**, ĉevalpovo [see § 20]; **manpower**, (human workforce), homlaboro; **overpower**, superforti [tr], subigi; **superpower**, (pol etc.), super~o; **have power over**, ~i [tr], havi ~on super; **everything in one's power**, ĉio laŭ sia povo (e.g.: *they did everything in their power to save him:* ili faris ĉion laŭ sia povo por savi lin)

pox, (disease, gen), pokso; (syphilis), sifiliso; **chicken pox**, varicelo, kokina ~o; **cow pox**, kaŭpokso, bova ~o

pozzolan, **pozzuolana**, pozolano

practicable, efektivigebla; **impracticable**, ne~a

practical, praktika; **practicality**, ~eco; ~emo; **practically**, (almost), preskaŭ

practice, **practise**, (do for learning), ekzerci [tr]; sin ~i, ~iĝi (en. al); ~(ad)o (e.g.: *practice the piano:* sin ~i al la piano [not "~i la pianon"]; *I must practice writing with my left hand:* mi devas ~i mian maldekstran manon en skribado); (apply, use, follow, perform), praktiki [tr]; praktik(ad)o (e.g.: *practice medicine, thrift, vegetarianism:* praktiki medicinon, ŝparemon, vegetalismon); (usage, custom), kutimo, moro; **practitioner**, praktikisto; praktikanto; **malpractice**, mispraktik(ad)o, misag(ad)o; **put into practice**, apliki [tr], ekpraktiki [tr], efektivigi

praetor, pretoro; **praetorian**, ~a; ~ano

pragmatic, pragmata; **pragmatism**, ~ismo; **pragmatist**, ~isto

Prague, Prago

Prairial, Prerialo

prairie, prerio; **Prairie Provinces**, P~aj Provincoj

praise, laŭdi [tr]; ~o; **praiseworthy**, ~inda

Prakrit, Prakrito; ~a

praline, pralino

pram, (carriage), bebĉareto, infanĉareto; (boat), pramo

prance, pranci [int], kaprioli [int]

prank, petol/aĵo; **play pranks**, **pull a prank**, ~i [int]

praseodymium, prazeodimo

prate, klaĉi [int], babilaĉi [int]

pratincole, glareolo, marhirundo

prattle, klaĉi [int], babilaĉi [int]; ~(ad)o

prawn, (*Palaemon*), palemono; (*Pandalus*), pandalo [cp "shrimp"]

Praxiteles, Praksitelo

pray, preĝi [tr, int]; **prayer**, ~o; **prayerful**, ~ema; **Lord's Pprayer**, P~o de la Sinjoro [cp "Pater Noster"]

pre‑, (pfx: before, in front, gen), antaŭ‑ (e.g.: *prearrange:* ~aranĝi); (very early, primeval), pra– (e.g.: *prehistoric:* prahistoria) [note: sometimes absorbed into Esperanto root as "pre–"; see separate entries]

preach, prediki [tr, int]; **preacher,** ~anto; ~isto

preamble, antaŭparolo, antaŭvorto

prebend, prebendo

Precambrian, antaŭkambrio; ~a

precarious, nestabila, nesekura, necerta, nefirma

precede, antaŭi [tr]; ~iri [tr]; ~veni [tr]; **preceding,** ~a, jama

precedence, (coming before, gen), antaŭ/eco; (right), ~rajto; (priority), prioritato; **take precedence over,** havi prioritaton ~, super

precedent, precedento; **unprecedented,** sen~a

precentor, kantoro

precept, precepto

precess, precesii [int]; **precession,** ~o

precinct, (district), distrikto; (yard), korto, tereno

precious, (valuable), valor/ega, alt~a, mult~a; (beloved), amata, karega; (fastidious), precioza; **semiprecious,** duonjuvela

precipice, klif(eg)o

precipitate, (chem; weather; etc.), precipiti [tr]; ~iĝi; ~aĵo; (bring on, hasten), rapidigi, ~i; (headlong, rushing), impeta, hasta; (sudden, abrupt), subita, abrupta; **precipitation,** ~aĵo; ~ado; ~iĝado

precipitous, (steep), krutega; (hasty, impetuous), impeta, hasta

précis, epitomo

precise, (gen), preciza; **precision,** ~eco

preclude, malebligi

precocious, frumatura

precognition, antaŭsci/ado; **precognitive,** ~a

precordial, antaŭkora

precursor, antaŭ/(ven)anto; **precursory,** enkonduka, ~a, anonca

predator, (animal), rab/obesto; (person), ~ulo, ~anto; **predatory,** ~a; **predation,** ~ado

predecessor, antaŭulo

predicament, embaraso, malfacilaĵo

predicate, (base on), bazi [tr]; (assert),

aserti [tr]; (gram, logic), predikato; **predicate noun, predicate adjective,** predikativo

predict, prognozi [tr], antaŭdiri [tr]; **prediction,** ~o, antaŭdiro

predilection, prefero

preempt, (acquire), antaŭ/akiri [tr]; (buy), ~aĉeti [tr]; (appropriate exclusively, hoard), akapari [tr]; (replace, as re radio, TV program), anstataŭi [tr]; **preemptive,** ~evita

preen, netigi (sin)

prefab, pretkonstru/ita; ~aĵo, pretdomo

preface, prefaco, antaŭparolo; ~i [tr]; **prefatory,** ~a, antaŭa

prefect, prefekto; **prefecture,** (building), ~ejo; (job), ~eco; (territory), ~io

prefer, preferi [tr]; **preferable,** ~inda; **preferably,** ~e; **preference,** ~o; **preferential,** ~a, favora

prefix, prefikso; ~a

pregnant, graveda; **pregnancy,** ~eco

prehensile, pren/iva, ~ipova

prejudice, antaŭjuĝo; (cause prejudice), ~igi; (hinder), malhelpi [tr], malutili [int] (al); **prejudiced,** ~a; **prejudicial,** ~iga; malhelpa, malutila

prelate, prelato

preliminary, prepara; ~aĵo, ~a laboro (diskuto, diraĵoj, etc.)

prelude, (gen), preludo; (serve as prelude), esti ~o al, enkonduki [tr]

premeditate, antaŭ/pensi [tr], ~plani [tr], ~intenci [tr]

premier, première, premiere, (first show; prime minister; head of Canadian province), premiero; ~i [int]; (first, leading), ĉefa

premise, (assert, assume, base on), premiso; ~i [tr]; **premises,** (place), lokalo [note sing]

premium, (insurance payment), premiumo; (prize), premio; (any extra payment), krompago; (any extra), ekstraĵo, kromaĵo; (high value), altvaloro; altvalora; (high quality), altkvalita; **at a premium,** (high price), altpreze

premonition, (feeling), antaŭ/sento; (forewarning), ~averto

prep, (prepare), prepari [tr]; (preparatory), ~a

prepare, prepari [tr]; ~i sin; **preparation**, (act), ~o; (thing), ~aĵo; **preparatory**, ~a; **unprepared**, sen~a
preponderant, supera, precipa; **preponderance**, ~eco
preposition, prepozicio
prepositive, prepozitivo; ~a
prepositor, preposto
prepossessing, alloga, plaĉa, ĉarma
preposterous, absurda
prepotent, plipotenca, superrega; **prepotency**, ~o
prepuce, prepucio
prerequisite, antaŭrekvizito, antaŭkondiĉo; ~a
prerogative, prerogativo
presage, aŭguri [tr], antaŭsigni [tr]; ~o, antaŭsigno
presbyopia, presbiop/eco; **presbyopic**, ~a
presbyter, presbitero; **presbyterian**, ~a; **presbytery**, ~aro; ~ejo
Presbyterian, Presbiteriano; ~a; ~isma; **Presbyterianism**, ~ismo
Presbytis, presbito; Presbytis entellus, entelo
prescience, antaŭsci/(ad)o; **prescient**, ~a
prescribe, (order; med), preskribi [tr]; (law), preskripti [tr]; **prescript(ion)**, ~o; preskripto
presence, (attending, being present), ĉeesto; (existence), ekzisto; (person, spirit, etc., felt to be present), ~anto, ~ulo; (imposing person), eminentulo, imponulo; [see also "present"]; **presence of mind**, spirito~o, spiritopreteco; **stage presence**, scenejpreteco
present, (show, introduce, etc.), prezenti [tr] (e.g.: *present a plan:* ~i planon; *let me present Mr. Jones:* permesu al mi ~i s–ron Jones; *a Shakespeare tragedy was presented:* oni ~is tragedion de Ŝekspiro); (give, gen), doni [tr]; (give gift, donate), donaci [tr]; (gift), donaco; (now), nuna; nuntempo; (gram: verb tense ["–as"]), prezenco; prezenca; (in attendance), ĉeestanta; (existing), ekzistanta (e.g.: *the gases present in air:* la gasoj ekzistantaj en aero); [see also "presence"]; **be present (at)**, ĉeesti [tr];

ekzisti [int] (ĉe, en); **presentable**, ~inda, bonaspekta, respektinda; **presentation**, ~(ad)o; **present-day**, nuntempa, aktuala, hodiaŭa; **at present**, nun(tempe), aktuale; **one who is present, those present**, (la) ĉeestanto(j)
preserve, (keep, gen), konservi [tr]; (keep fresh, in good condition), ~i, prezervi [tr]; ~aĵo; (fruit), konfiti [tr]; konfitaĵo; (marmelade etc.), marmelado; (land for animals, etc.), ~ejo (e.g.: *game preserve:* ĉasbesta ~ejo); (any special domain), faktereno; **preservation**, ~o; prezervo; **self-preservation**, mem~ado; **preservative**, ~a; prezerva; prezervenzo
preside, prezidi [tr]
president, (formal title), prezidento; (less formal; one who presides, as over small group), prezidanto; **presidency**, ~eco; **vice president**, vico~o; vicoprezidanto; **president-elect**, elektita ~o; elektita prezidanto
presidium, prezidio
press, (apply pressure, force, gen), premi [tr]; ~(ad)o; ~ilo; (printed news media), (la) gazetaro; (iron clothing), gladi [tr]; gladeco; (urge), urĝi [tr], insisti [int] (al iu pri io); (bother), ĝeni [tr], ĉagreni [tr]; (make by pressing), ~formi [tr]; (flatten flower in book etc.), ~platigi; (criticism), gazeta kritikado (e.g.: *the campaign received a bad press:* la kampanjo ricevis malbonan gazetan kritikadon); (closet), ŝranko; **pressing**, ~a; urĝa; **printing press**, presmaŝino; **go to press**, ekpresiĝi
pressure, premo; ~i [tr]; ~ado (e.g.: *atmospheric pressure:* atmosfera ~o; *they pressured her to accept:* ili ~is ŝin ke ŝi akceptu); **pressurize**, (build pressure-tight), (prem)hermetikigi; (pump pressure into), aerizi [tr]; **depressurize**, malaerizi [tr]; **pressure cooker**, ~kuirilo; **pressure gauge**, ~metro, manometro; **pressure group**, ~grupo; **high blood pressure**, hipertensio; **low blood pressure**, hipotensio
prestidigitate, prestidigiti [int]; **presti-**

digitation, ~ado; **prestidigitator**, ~isto

prestige, prestiĝo; **prestigious**, ~a

presto, (mus), rapide; **prestissimo**, ~ege

presume, (suppose), supozi [tr]; (arrogate), arogi [tr] (al si); **presumably**, ~eble; **presumed**, (according to presumption), ~a; **presumption**, ~o; arogo; (arrogance), aroganteco; **presumptive**, ~inda; ~ita; ~a; **presumptuous**, aroganta; **presuming that**, ~e ke

pretend, (claim, assert), pretendi [tr], aserti [tr]; (feign, simulate), ŝajnigi; (play as, as in child's game), ludi [tr, int] (kiel; **pretense, pretence, pretension**, ~o, aserto; ŝajnigo; (pretext), preteksto; (false claim), fi~o; **pretender**, (as to throne), ~anto

pretentious, pompaĉa, paradaĉa

preterit(e), preterito; ~a

pretext, preteksto; **give as a pretext**, ~i [tr]; **on the pretext that**, ~e ke

pretor, pretoro

Pretoria, Pretorio

pretty, bela, ~eta; (poet), linda; ~igi; (rather), iom, sufiĉe; (very), tre

pretzel, breco*

prevail, (overcome), superi [tr], ~forti [tr], venki [tr]; (succeed), sukcesi [int]; (be prevalent), regi [int], ofti [int], ~i, vaste troviĝi; **prevailing**, reganta, plej ofta; **prevalent**, plej ofta, reganta, vaste trovata

prevaricate, (equivocate, evade), hipokriti [tr]; ŝanceliĝi; (lie), mensogi [int]

prevent, (make impossible), malebligi; (avoid), eviti [tr]; (prohibit), malpermesi [tr]; (med), preventi [tr]; **prevent(at)ive**, evitiga; evitigaĵo; preventa; preventilo; (chem), evitigenzo; **prevention**, ~o; evit(ad)o; malpermes(ad)o; prevent(ad)o

previous, antaŭa, jama, ĝisnuna

prey, predo, ~aĵo; **prey (up)on**, ~i [tr]; **animal of prey**, ~besto

Priam, Priamo

priapic, priapa; **priapism**, ~ismo

Priapus, Priapo

price, prezo, ~i [tr]; **priceless**, sen~a, valorega; **price list**, ~aro, ~listo;

price control, ~oregado; **price index**, ~indico

prick, (as by pin etc.), piki [tr]; ~o; (slang: penis), kaco; **prick up**, (as animal's ears), starigi; stariĝi

prickle, dorno, ~eto, pikil(et)o; piki [tr] [not "prikl–"]; **prickly**, ~a, pika

pride, fiero, ~eco; ~aĵo; ~ulo; (false pride, vanity), orgojlo; **pride oneself on**, ~i pri

priest, (gen), pastro; (Roman Catholic), sacerdoto; **priestess**, ~ino; **priestly**, ~(ec)a; sacerdot(ec)a; **priesthood**, ~aro; ~eco; sacerdotaro; sacerdoteco

prig, virt/ulaĉo, ~afektulo; **priggish**, ~aĉa, ~afekta

prim, precioza, modesta, rigida, formalema, ceremoniema

primacy, (supremacy), unuarangeco, supereco; (rel: rank of primate), primaseco

primadonna, primadono

primaeval, [see "primeval"]

prima facie, unuavida; ~e

primal, praa, origina

primary, (of top degree, gen; chem; re elec current; etc.), primara; ~aĵo; (election), ~a balotado; (chief, main), ĉefa, precipa; (original, primitive), praa; (preparatory), prepara; (direct), rekta, senpera

primate, (zool), primato; (rel), primaso

prime, (first rank), unuaranga; (chief, main), ĉefa, precipa; (highest quality), unuakvalita; (fundamental, basic), fundamenta, baza; (number; rel: first canonical hour), primo; (best, most vigorous etc. time), ĉeftempo; (prepare, gen), prepari [tr]; (re gun), prajmi [tr]; (re pump, carburetor), priverŝi [tr]; (math etc.: mark ['] after quantity), (vertikala) streketo; strekita (e.g.: x': [pronounce] ikso strekita); (paint), subfarbi [tr]; (inform), antaŭinformi [tr]

primer, (text), abocolibro, krestomatio; (for gun), prajmo; (paint), subfarbo

primeval, praa, ~epoka; pra– [pfx] (e.g.: *primeval forest:* ~arbaro)

primitive, (gen), primitiva; ~ulo; ~aĵo

primordial, (primeval), praa; (original), origina

primp, netigi (sin)
primrose, primolo; evening primrose, enotero
Primula, primolo; Primula auricula, aŭrikulo
primus, Primus, (stove), primuso
prince, (gen), princo; princess, ~ino; princely, ~(ec)a; crown prince, kron~o
principal, (primary, main), precipa, ĉefa; (first rank), unuaranga; (school head), lemejestro; (any head: primary person), ĉefo, estro; ĉef– [pfx] (e.g.: principal bassoonist: ĉeffagotisto); ($), kapitalo
principality, princlando
principle, (gen), principo
print, (cmptr etc.; phot), printi† [tr]; ~(ad)o; ~aĵo; (mass-produce, as for publication), presi [tr]; pres(ad)o; presaĵo; (art copy or oth picture), presita bildo; (fabric), presita tolo; (track, as footprint), spuro; (phot), printi* [tr]; printo*; (block letters, not cursive), blokliteroj; skribi [tr] bloklitere; printer, (cmptr), ~atoro†; (person), presisto; printing, (block letters), blokliterado; printing press, presatoro; print out, (by cmptr, word processor, etc.), el~i [tr]; printout, el~aĵo; blueprint, blukopio; in print, liverebla, aĉetebla; misprint, (keying error), misklavi [tr] klavararo, misklavo; offprint, depresi [tr]; depresaĵo; out of print, elĉerpita; overprint, surpresi [tr]; surpres(aĵ)o; reprint, represi [tr]; repres(aĵ)o; daisy-wheel printer, petalrada ~atoro; dot-matrix printer, punktara ~atoro; ink-jet printer, ink-ŝpruca ~atoro; laser printer, lasera ~atoro; teleprinter, tele~atoro
prior, (previous), antaŭa; (rel), prioro; prioress, priorino; priory, priorejo; priority, (right of precedence), prioritato; (being prior), ~eco
prism, prismo; prismatic, ~a
prison, prizono, malliberejo; prisoner, ~ulo, malliberulo, kaptito; prisoner of war, militkaptito; imprison, en~igi, enkarcerigi, malliberigi
pristine, (pure), pura, nemakulita; (ori-

ginal), origina, praa
private, (closed; personal), privata; (mil), simpla soldato; (as mil rank), soldato (e.g.: Private Smith: Soldato Smith); privacy, ~eco; semiprivate, duon~a
privateer, (private armed ship), kaper/ŝipo; ~i [tr]; ~isto; (corsair), korsaro
privation, sen/ig(ad)o; ~eco, manko
privet, ligustro
privilege, privilegio; ~i [tr] [cp "license", "permit"]; privileged, ~a; ~ita
privy, (private), privata; (outhouse), ekstera necesejo; privy to, ~e informita pri; privy council, ~a konsilio
prize, (award), premio; (value), altestimi [tr], alte taksi [tr]; (awarded prize), ~ita (e.g.: a prize novel: ~ita romano); (worthy of prize), ~inda; (captured), kaptaĵo; (pry), levstangumi [tr]; prize-winner, ~ito; Nobel Prize, Nobela P~o; award a prize to, ~i [tr]
pro, (professional), profesia; ~isto, ~ulo; (in favor), favora; favoranta; por; the pros and the cons, la por kaj la kontraŭ
pro–, (pfx: in favor, for), –favora [sfx] (e.g.: pro-labor: laborist-~a)
proa, praho
proactive, antaŭaga, anticipa
probable, probabla, verŝajna; probably, kredeble, ~e; probability, (math, statistics), ~o; (abstract), ~eco; probability theory, stokastiko; improbable, ne~a, neverŝajna; in all probability, plej ~e
probate, (authentication, as of will), aŭtentik/igi; ~igo; (copy), ~a kopio
probation, (trial period), prov/tempo; ~libereco; (probating), aŭtentikigo; probationer, ~ato; ~liberigito
probative, (evidence), pruvema
probe, (explore, as wound, space, depths), sondi [tr], esplori [tr]; ~o, esploro; ~ilo; (check on), kontroli [tr]; kontrolo; (inquire, investigate), enketi [int] (en, pri); enketo
probity, honesteco
problem, problemo; ~a; problematic, ~a

Proboscidea, rostruloj
proboscis, rostro
procaine (hydrochloride), novokaino
Procavia, prokavio
procedure, (any proceeding; method to obtain a result), procedo (e.g.: *the procedure for manufacturing plastic:* la ~o por fabriki plaston); (method per custom, law, rule, etc.), proceduro (e.g.: *the proceduree for electing the president:* la proceduro por elekti la prezidenton; *our usual procedure in that situation:* nia kutima proceduro en tiu situacio); **procedural,** ~a; procedura
proceed, procedi [int]; **proceeding,** ~o; **proceeds,** ($), enspezo [note sing]; **proceeds of the Assembly,** (Aus), funkciado de la Asambleo
Procellaria, procelario; Procellariidae, ~edoj; Procellariiformes, ~oformaj (birdoj)
process, (sequence of occurrences, phenomena, etc.), procezo; (anat), proceso; (work, subject to a process), trakti [tr], prilabori [tr], ~i [tr]; (procedure, method), **processor,** (cmptr), procesoro†; **electronic data processing,** elektronika daten–traktado; **microprocessor,** mikroprocesoro†; **word-processing,** teksto–prilaborado†; **word processor,** teksto–prilaborilo†; **word-processing program,** teksto–prilabora programo†; **xiphoid process,** (anat), ksifoido
procession, procesio; **processional,** ~a; ~o
proclaim, proklami [tr]; **proclamation,** ~o; ~ado [cp "declare"]; **self-proclaimed,** memdeklarita, mem~ita
proclitic, proklitika; ~o
proclivity, inklino, emo, tendenco
Procne, Prokna
proconsul, prokonsulo
procrastinate, prokrasti [tr]; ~iĝi; **procrastination,** ~(ad)o
procreate, (give birth), naski [tr]; (beget, gen, including by males), ~igi, generi [tr]
Procrustes, Prokrusto; **Procrustean,** ~a
proctitis, rektumito

proct(o)–, (anat, med pfx), rektum(o)–
proctor, (agent), prokuristo; (university), intendanto
proctoscope, rektumoskopo; **proctoscopy,** ~io
procurator, (Roman or similar official), prokuratoro; (agent), prokuristo
procure, (acquire), akiri [tr], havigi; (arrange, bring about), aranĝi [tr], estigi, okazigi
Procyon, (ast), Prociono
Procyon, (zool), prociono; Procyonidae, ~edoj
prod, (jab, incite), piki [tr], sproni [tr]; ~o; ~ilo; (shove), ~puŝi [tr]
prodigal, (lavish), malavarega, (poet), prodiga; (abundant), abundega; **the prodigal son,** (Bib), la erarinta filo
prodigious, (wonderful), mir/iga, ~inda; (huge), enorma, grandega
prodigy, mirind/ulo; ~aĵo
prodrome, prodroma, prodromo
produce, (make, gen), produkti [tr]; ~o(j); (give forth), doni [tr], eligi; (cause), kaŭzi [tr], rezultigi; (theat etc.), enscenigi; (show), montri [tr]; **producer,** ~isto; enscenigisto; **mass-produce,** amas~i [tr] [see also "product"]
product, (thing produced), produkto; (math), produto; **production,** ~ado; enscenigo [see "produce"]; **productive,** ~iva; **productivity,** ~ivo; **byproduct,** krom~o; **counterproductive,** kontraŭefik(ig)a; **mass-production,** amas~ado; **overproduction,** super~ado; **underproduction,** sub~ado; **gross national product,** malneta nacia ~o
profane, profana; ~i [tr]; (person), ~o; **profanity,** ~eco; (cursing), sakrado; sakraĵo; **utter profanities,** sakri [int]
profess, (state openly), konfesi [tr], deklari [tr]
profession, (vocation), profesio; (avowal), konfeso, deklaro; **professional,** ~a; ~isto, ~ulo; **professional education,** por~a edukado
professor, profesoro
proffer, proponi [tr]
proficient, kompetenta, kapabla, lerta; **proficiency,** ~eco, kapablo, lerteco

profile, profilo; ~a; ~i [tr]; **half-profile**, (3/4-full face), duon~o

profit, profito; ~i [int]; **profitable**, ~odona, rentabilitata; **profitability**, rentabilitato; **profiteer**, ~aĉi [int]; ~aĉanto, ~aĉemulo; **nonprofit**, sen~cela; sen~cele

profligate, diboĉa; ~ulo

pro forma, proforma

profound, profunda; **profundity**, ~eco

profuse, abunda, riĉa; **profusion**, ~aĵo; ~eco

progenitor, pra/patro; **progenitors**, ~gepatroj

progeny, idaro

progesterone, progesterono

prognathous, prognata

prognosis, prognozo

prognosticate, prognozi [tr]

program(me), (gen), programo; ~a; ~i [tr]; **programmer**, ~isto; **programmatic**, ~a

progress, progresi [int]; ~o; **progression**, ~ado; (math), progresio; **arithmetic progression**, aritmetika progresio; **geometric progression**, geometria progresio; **progressive**, ~ema; ~emulo; (gradual), laŭgrada, iompostioma; ($, math: gradually increasing), progresiva (e.g.: *progressive tax:* progresiva imposto)

prohibit, (not allow), malpermesi [tr]; (make impossible), malebligi; **prohibition**, ~o; malebligo; (law), prohibicio; **prohibitive**, malebliga, ekscesa

project, (as image on screen, lit or fig), projekcii [tr] (e.g.: *project a trend into the future:* ~i tendencon estontecen); (plan; idea), projekto; projekti [tr]; (stick out), elstari [int]; elstarigi; **projection**, ~(ad)o; ~aĵo; projektado; elstar(aĵ)o; **projective**, projektiva; **projector**, ~ilo, ~atoro; **movie projector**, kin~ilo; **slide projector**, diaskopo; **pilot project**, provprojekto

projectile, (gen), ĵetaĵo; (shot), pafaĵo

prolactin, prolaktino

prolamine, prolamino

prolan, prolano; **prolanemia**, ~emio; **prolan A**, ~o A; **prolan B**, ~o B

prolapse, prolapso, ptozo; **prolapsed**, ~iĝinta, ptoza

prolate, etendita

prole, [see "proletarian"]

prolegomenon, prolegomenono†

prolepsis, prolepso

proletarian, proleto; ~a; **proletariat**, ~aro; **proletarianize**, ~anigi

proliferate, (gen), multiĝi, dis~i; (bot, zool), proliferi [int]; **proliferation**, (dis)~o; proliferado; **proliferous**, ~a; prolifera

prolific, fekunda

proline, prolino

prolix, malkonciza

prologue, prologo

prolong, daŭr/igi, pli~igi, plilongigi; **prolonged**, longe~a

prom, balo

promenade, (stroll), promeni [int]; ~(ad)o; (place for), ~ejo

Prometheus, Prometio; **Promethean**, ~a

promethium, prometio; (former name), ilinio

prominent, elstara; (eminent), eminenta; **prominence**, (gen), ~aĵo; ~eco; eminenteco; (anat), prominenco

promiscuous, dismalĉasta; **promiscuity**, ~eco

promise, promesi [tr]; ~o; **promising**, ~plena, multe~a; **promisory**, ~a; **promisory note**, ŝuldatesto

promontory, (gen), promontoro

promote, (to higher position, rank), promocii [tr]; (further), antaŭenigi; (develop), evoluigi; (advertise), propagandi [tr], reklami [tr]; **promotion**, ~o; antaŭenigo; propagandado, reklamado

prompt, (w/o delay), senprokrasta, senhezita, baldaŭa; (quick), rapida; (poet), prompta; (give lines to actor etc.), suflori [tr]; (urge), instigi [tr]; **prompter**, (person), sufloro; (machine), suflorilo; **teleprompter**, telesuflorilo; **prompting**, suflorado; instigo; **promptly**, ~e, baldaŭ; rapide

promulgate, (law), promulgi [tr]; (spread, make known), disvastigi, publikigi, diskonigi; **promulgation**, (law), ~o

pronate, proni [tr]; ~iĝi

pronator, (muscle), pronatoro

prone, vizaĝaltera; (inclined), inklina, ema, –ema [sfx] (e.g.: *prone to cry:* plorema); [not "pron–"]

prong, (of fork etc.), dento; (sharp), pikilo; (of elec plug etc.), stifto; (of creek etc.), branĉo

pronoun, pronomo;   **demonstrative pronoun**, montra ~o; **indefinite pronoun**, nedifina ~o; **interrogative pronoun**, demanda ~o; **personal pronoun**, personalo, persona ~o; **possessive pronoun**, poseda ~o; **relative pronoun**, rilativo, rilata ~o

pronounce, (articulate), prononci [tr], elparoli [tr]; (utter, state), deklari [tr], eldiri [tr]; **mispronounce**, mis~i [tr]; **pronounced**, forta, elstara; **pronouncement**, deklaro

pronunciamento, deklaro

pronunciation, prononco, elparolo [see "pronounce"]

proof, (that proves), pruvo; (test, trial), provo; (of alcohol), provnormo; provnorma (e.g.: *80-proof whiskey:* 80-provnorma viskio); (printing), presprovaĵo, gale-provaĵo [see "galley"]; (phot), provprinto*; (coin), fajnstampita; (impervious), imuna; imunigi (e.g.: *waterproof:* akvimuna; akvimunigi; *proof against chemical corrosion:* imuna kontraŭ kemia korodo); (proofread), provlegi [tr]

prop, (support), apogi [tr], subteni [tr]; ~ilo, ~stango; (propeller), helico; (object used in drama etc.), rekvizito; **prop manager**, rekvizitoro; **turboprop**, (engine), turbinhelico; (plane), turbinavio

propaedeutic, propedeŭtika;   **propaedeutics**, ~o

propaganda, propagando;   **propagandize**, ~i [tr]; **means of propaganda**, ~ilo

propagate, (elec etc.; bio: reproduce), propagi [tr]; ~iĝi; (spread, gen), disvastigi; disvastiĝi; (breed), bredi [tr]; **propagation**, ~(iĝ)ado; bredado

propane, propano

proparoxytone, proparoksitona; ~aĵo

propel, propulsi [tr]; **propellant**, ~ilo, pelilo; (chem), ~enzo; **propeller**, (of plane etc.), helico; **self-propelled**,

mempela, mem~a

propene, propeno

propensity, inklino, emo, tendenco

proper, (fitting, decent), konvena, deca; (suitable), taŭga; (correct), ĝusta; (naturally belonging to), propra (e.g.: *weather proper to October:* vetero propra al oktobro); (in strict sense), strikta; strikte (e.g.: *there are two million people in greater Baltimore, but one million in Baltimore proper:* estas du milionoj da homoj en la ĉirkaŭaĵo de Baltimoro, sed unu miliono strikte en Baltimoro); **improper**, mal~a, maldeca; **be proper**, ~i [int], deci [int]; taŭgi [int]

property, (possession), propraĵo, proprietaĵo, posedaĵo, havaĵo; (estate, land), bieno [note: not a collective n (e.g.: *I have some property in Pennsylvania:* mi havas bienon [or: iom da grundo; but not: "iom da bieno"] en Pensilvanio); (native characteristic), ~eco, eco (e.g.: *fluidity is a property of liquids:* fluivo estas ~eco [or: eco] de likvaĵoj); (theat etc.: props), [see "prop"]

prophet, profeto; **prophetess**, ~ino; **prophecy**, ~aĵo; **prophesy**, ~i [tr]; **prophetic**, ~a

prophylactic, (treatment etc.), profilakta; ~iko; (condom), kondomo; **prophylaxis**, ~ado, preventado

propinquity, (nearness), proksimeco; (kinship), parenceco

propionate, propion/ato; **propionic acid**, ~a acido, propanacido

propitiate, favor/igi, (re)pacigi, (re)kvietigi; **propitious**, ~a

propolis, propoliso

proponent, proponanto, favoranto

proportion, proporcio; ~igi; **proportional**, **proportionate**, ~a; **disproportion**, mis~o, dis~o; **disproportionate**, mis~a

propose, proponi [tr]; **proposal**, ~o; **counterproposal**, kontraŭ~o; **proposition**, (any proposal), ~o; (phil, logic), propozicio; (invite sex), seks~i [int] (al iu)

propound, prezenti [tr], elmeti [tr], proponi [tr]

proprietor, propriet/ulo; **proprietor-ship**, ~o; **have proprietorship over**, ~i [tr]; **proprietary**, ~a
propriety, deco, konveneco; taŭgeco [see "proper"]
proprioceptive, propriocepta; **perceive proprioceptively**, ~i [tr]; **proprioceptor**, ~ilo
propulsion, propulso
propyl, propilo
propylaeum, propileo
propylene, propeno, propileno
pro rata, proporcia
prorate, proporciigi
prorogue, fini [tr]
prosaic, (mundane, commonplace), ĉiutaga, mondeca, ordinara, vulgara; (of prose), proza
proscenium, proscenio, rivalto, antaŭscenejo
proscribe, (forbid), malpermesi [tr]; (banish), proskribi [tr]; (condemn), kondamni [tr]; **proscription**, ~o; proskribo, proskripcio; kondamno
prose, prozo; ~a; **prose work**, ~aĵo
prosector, prosektoro
prosecute, (law), procesi [int] (kontraŭ, pri), (juĝe) persekuti [tr]; (effectuate), efektivigi; **prosecution**, ~ado, persekut(ad)o; efektivig(ad)o; **prosecutor**, persekutisto
proselyte, prozelito; **proselyt(iz)e**, varbi ~ojn; **proselytism**, ~ismo
Proserpina, Prozerpina
Prosimiae, prasimioj
prosody, prozodio
prosopopoeia, prozopopeo
prospect, (view, perspective), perspektivo; (anticipation), anticipo; (expectation), espero; (chance, as for success), ŝanco; (likely person, as for sale, office, etc.), probablulo, verŝajnulo [not "prospekt–"]; (search for ore, oil, etc.), prospektori [tr]; **prospector**, prospektoro
prospective, (future, looking to future), anticipa, estonta; (anticipated), ~ita; (possible in future), eventuala
prospectus, prospekto
prosper, prosperi [int]; **prosperity**, ~o; **prosperous**, ~a
Prospero, Prospero

prostate (gland), prostato; **prostatectomy**, ~ektomio; **prostatitis**, ~ito
prosthesis, (artificial limb, organ, etc.), protezo [cp "prothesis"]; **prosthetic**, ~a; prosteta
prostitute, prostitui [tr]; ~it(in)o; (colloq), putino; **male prostitute**, ~ito; **prostitution**, ~(ad)o
prostrate, sterni [tr]; ~ita; (from humility, submission), humil~ita; (exhausted), ellaciĝinta; **prostration**, (humil)~iteco; ellaciĝo; (med, as heat prostration), prostracio
protactinium, protaktinio
protagonist, protagonisto
Protagoras, Protagoro
protamine, protamino
protasis, (theat), protazo
Protea, proteo
protean, protea
protect, protekti [tr]; **protection**, ~(ad)o; **protectionism**, ~ismo; **protective**, (for purpose of protecting), ~a; (inclined to protect), ~ema; **protector**, ~anto; **protectorate**, protektorato; **self-protection**, sin~ado
protégé protektato
protein, (nitrogen-hydrogen compound, gen), proteino; (amino acid and oth group), proteido; **proteinase**, ~azo; **mucoprotein**, mukoproteido; **nucleoprotein**, nukleoproteido; **scleroprotein**, sklero~o; **silver protein**, kolargolo; **xanthoprotein**, ksanto~o
proteolysis, proteolizo; **proteolytic**, ~a
protest, protesti [tr, int]; ~o; **protestation**, ~o; **thou dost protest too much**, ju pli da ĵuroj, des pli da suspekto
Protestant, Protestanto; ~a; **Protestantism**, ~ismo
Proteus, (myth), Proteo
Proteus, (zool), proteo
prothesis, prostezo [cp "prosthesis"]
proto–, (pfx), proto–
protocol, (document), protokolo; (etiquette, custom), ceremoniaro; **make (write) a protocol**, ~i [int]
proton, protono; **antiproton**, anti~o
protoplasm, protoplasmo
prototype, prototipo
Protozoa, protozooj

protozoan, protozoon, protozoo; ~a; protozoiasis, protozoosis, ~ozo
Protracheata, pratrañeuloj
protract, daŭr/igi, plilongigi; protracted, longe~a
protractor, angulmezurilo
protrude, (gen), elŝovi [tr], elŝveligi; ~iĝi, elŝveli [int], elstari [int]; (anat), protrudi [int]; protruding, elstaranta; protruda; protrusion, ~o; elstaraĵo; protrud(aĵ)o
protuberance, (anat), protuberanco; (any bulge), tubero, ŝvelaĵo; protuberant, ~a; tubera, ŝvela
Protungulata, prahufuloj
proud, (gen), fiera; (haughty), orgojla, aroganta; be proud of, ~i [int] pri; (something) to be proud of, (io) pri~inda
prove, (establish proof), pruvi [tr]; (turn out, result as), montriĝi; (test), provi [tr]; disprove, mal~i [tr] [cp "refute"]
Provence, Provenco; Provençal, ~a
provender, (fodder), furaĝo
proverb, proverbo; proverbial, ~a; proverbs, (collection), ~aro; Proverbs, (Bib), Sentencoj
provide, (make available), provizi [tr] (iun per io) [not "ion al iu"] (e.g.: we provided chairs for the guests: ni ~is la gastojn per seĝoj); (give, gen), doni [tr]; (require, as in law), postuli [tr]; (stipulate), kondiĉi [tr]; provided (that), providing (that), (on condition), kondiĉe ke
providence, (divine, natural), providenco; (prudence), prudento, antaŭzorgo [cp "thrift"]; providential, ~a; prudenta, antaŭzorga; improvident, neantaŭzorga
province, (gen), provinco; provincial, (of a province), ~ano; ~a; (narrow-minded), ~isma; (head of rel province), provincialo; provincialism, (narrow thinking), ~ismo; (word etc. peculiar to certain area), provincialismo
provision, (supply, gen), provizi [tr] [see "provide"]; ~ado; ~aĵo; (food), provianti [tr]; (requirement, as in law), postulo; (stipulation), kondiĉo; provisions, (food), provianto [note

sing]; provisional, (temporary), provizora
proviso, kondiĉo; provisory, ~a
provoke, provoki [tr]; provocation, ~o; provocative, ~(em)a
provost, (pol), provosto; (rel), preposto
prow, pruo
prowess, (skill), lerteco; (bravery), braveco, kuraĝo
prowl, (after prey), predvagi [int]; ~o; (stealthily, for any reason), ŝtelvagi [int]; ŝtelvago; prowler, ŝtelvaganto
proximal, proximate, proksima, apuda; proximity, ~eco
proxy, prokura; ~anto; ~isto; by proxy, ~e
prude, prud/ulo; prudish, ~a; prudery, ~eco
prudent, prudenta; prudence, ~o; imprudent, mal~a; sen~a; prudential, ~a; (advisory), konsila
prune, (fruit), sekpruno [cp "plum"]; (trim plant, or analogous fig action), stuci [tr]; Japanese prune, (Prunus mume), umeo; pruning shears, stucilo; pruning knife, pruning hook, hipo
Prunella, (bot: selfheal), brunelo; (zool: hedge sparrow), pronelo
Prunus, prunuso; Prunus amygdalus, Prunus communis, migdalarbo; Prunus armeniaca, abrikotarbo; Prunus avium, ĉerizarbo; Prunus cerasifera, mirobalano; Prunus cerasus, grioto; Prunus domestica, prunarbo; Prunus donarium spontanea, sakuro; Prunus instititia, prunarbo; Prunus instititia syriaca, mirabelarbo; Prunus mume, umeo; Prunus padus, paduso, grapolĉerizarbo; Prunus persica, persikarbo; Prunus persica nectarina, nektarinarbo; Prunus spinosa, prunelarbo; Prunus subhirtella, Prunus yedoensis, sakuro
prurient, lasciva
prurigo, prurigo
pruritus, prurito; pruritic, ~a
Prussia, Prus/io; Prussian, ~o; ~a; ~ia
prussiate, cianido; prussic acid, ~a acido
pry, (lever), levstango; ~umi [tr]; (snoop), enŝovi sin, ŝovi la nazon en

fremdan vazon; spioni [tr]; **prying,**
enŝoviĝema
P.S. (abb of "postscript"), P.S. [abb of
"postskribo"]
Psalliota, ĉampinjono [cp "Agaricus"]
psalm, psalmo; ~i [tr]; **Psalms,** (Bib),
P~aro
psalmody, (singing), psalm/okantado;
(collection), ~aro
psalterium, omaso
psaltery, psalterio
pschent, pŝento
pseudarthrosis, pseŭdartro
pseudo, (sham, fake), falsa, strasa;
~ajo, straso; ~ulo
pseudo–, (pfx), pseŭdo– [cp "quasi–"]
pseudonym, pseŭdonimo
pseudopod(ium), pseŭdopodo
Pseudotsuga, (speco de) abio
psi, (Greek letter), psi [see § 16]; (psychic), psika
Psidium, psidio
psittacosis, psitakozo
Psittacus, psitako; Psittacidae, ~edoj;
Psittaciformes, ~oformaj (birdoj), pa-
paguloj
psoas, (muscle), psoaso; **greater psoas,**
psoas major, granda ~o; **smaller**
psoas, psoas minor, eta ~o
Psocus, psoko
Psophia, agamio
Psophodes, vipobirdo
psoriasis, psoriazo
psych, (excite), eksciti [tr], inciti [tr];
(disturb), ĉagreni [tr]
psychasthenia, psikastenio
psyche, (mind), psiko
Psyche, (myth), Psiĥa
psychedelic, psikedela†
psychiatry, psikiatr/io; **psychiatric,**
~ia; **psychiatrist,** ~o; **neuropsychia-**
try, neŭro~io
psychic, (gen), psika; ~ulo; **psychics,**
(study of psychic phenomena), meta-
psikio
psycho–, (pfx), psik(o)–
psychokinesis, psikokinezo, telekinezo
psychology, psikolog/io; **psychological,**
~ia; **psychologist,** ~o; **parapsycholo-**
gy, para~io; **technopsychology,** tek-
no~o
psychometry, (measure, study of men-

tal phenomena), psikotekniko; (perceiving information re object or
person psychically by touching object), psikometrio*
psychopath, psikopato; **psychopathy,**
~io; **psychopathology,** ~ologio
psychosis, psikozo; **psychotic,** ~a; ~ulo
psychosomatic, psikosomata
psychrometer, psikrometro
ptarmica, ptarmiko
ptarmigan, lagopo
Pteranodon, pteranodonto†
Pteridium, pterido
Pteris, pterido
Pterocarpus, pterokarpo
pterodactyl, pterodaktilo†
Pterodactylus, pterodaktilo†
Pteropus, pteropo
Pterygota, pteriguloj†
ptisan, tizano
Ptolemy, Ptolemeo; **Ptolemaic,** ~a
ptomaine, ptomaino
ptosis, ptozo
ptyalin, ptialazo
pub, drinkejo; (also serving food), taverno
puberty, pubereco
pubes, pubo
pubescent, pubera
pubic, puba; **pubic region,** ~o
pubiotomy, pubiotomio
pubis, pubio
public, (gen), publiko; ~a; **in public,**
~e; **public house,** [see "pub"]
publican, (ancient), impostkolektisto;
(Br), drinkejmastro
publication, (printing), eldono; ~ado;
(thing printed), ~ajo [cp "periodical"];
(public notice), publikigo
publicist, (writer), publicisto
publicity, publikig/(ad)o, reklam(ad)o;
publicize, ~i
publish, (print), eldoni [tr]; (make
known), publikigi; **publisher,** ~isto;
publishing house, ~ejo; **desk-top**
publishing, skribtabla ~ado
puce, pulkolora; ~o
puck, (hockey), (hoke)disko; (elf), koboldo
pucker, faldeti [tr]; ~iĝi; ~o [cp "wrinkle", "curl"]; **puckered,** ~a; **pucker**
up, (for kiss), ~i la lipojn

pud, pudo
pudding, pudingo
puddle, (water), flako; (treat iron to make soft), pudli [tr]; **mud puddle**, kotejo; **puddling**, (metal treatment), pudlado
pudendum, pudendo
pudgy, diketa, kompakta
pudu, Pudu, Pudua, puduo
pueblo, (indiana) vilaĝo
puerile, infaneca
puerperium, puerper/eco; **puerperal**, ~a; **puerpera**, ~ulino
Puerto Ric/o, Porto-Riko; **Puerto Rican**, Porto-Rikano; Porto-Rika
puff, (blow), ekblovi [tr, int]; ~o; (gasp), anheli [int]; anhelo; (fluff), floko; (candy), pufaĵo; (cotton pad etc.), kvasto; **puffball**, (bot: *Lycoperdon*), likoperdo; (*Bovista*), bovisteo; **puff up, puff out**, pufigi, ŝveligi; pufiĝi, ŝveli [int]; **powder puff**, pudrilo; **puffy**, ŝvelmola
puffin, fraterkulo
pug, (dog), mopso; (clay), (plastika) argilo, knedargilo; argilizi [tr]; (knead, mix clay etc.), knedi [tr]; **pug-nosed**, ~naza
pugilism, boks/ado; **pugilist**, ~isto
pugnacious, pugnema, batalema
puke, (colloq), vomi [tr]; ~aĵo
pukka, (good), bona; (real), vera, aŭtentika
pulchritude, beleco
Pulex, pulo
pull, (apply traction force, gen; opp "push"), tiri [tr]; ~iĝi; ~o; (extract), el~i [tr]; (strain, as muscle), trostreĉi [tr]; (carry out, perform, do), fari [tr], efektivigi; (drag), treni [tr]; treniĝi; tren(iĝ)o; (hold back, restrain), bridi [tr]; (take out, off), elpreni [tr], demeti [tr]; (suck in, as drink, cigarette), (en)suĉi [tr]; (en)suĉo; (come), veni [int]; (go), iri [int]; (drive car etc.), veturigi; (effort), klopodo; (handle etc.), ~ilo, anso; (influence), influo; **pull back**, re~i [tr]; re~iĝi; **pull down**, (overthrow), renversi [tr]; (humble), humiligi; (reduce), redukti [tr], malpliigi; **pull for**, subteni [tr]; **pull in**, (arrive), alveni [int]; (stop, pause),

halti [int], paŭzi [int]; (hold back), (sin) bridi; (retract, withdraw), re~i [tr]; re~iĝi; **pull off**, efektivigi, sukcesigi; **pull out**, (leave), ekiri [int]; (withdraw self), sin el~i, sin re~~i; (move over into traffic), entrafikiĝi; **pull over**, flankenigi; flankeniĝi; **pullover**, (sweater), pulovero; **pull through**, (live through), travivi [tr], elturniĝi; (recover health), resaniĝi; **pull together**, kun~i [tr]; kun~iĝi; **pull oneself together**, sin ekregi; **pull up**, (stop), halti [int]; haltigi; (drive up to), veturigi antaŭen, veturigi ĝis; (uproot), elradikigi; elradikiĝi; (re own body, aircraft, etc.), (sin) levi [tr], leviĝi; **pull oneself up by one's bootstraps**, sukcesigi sin mem
pullet, kokidino
pulley, pulio
Pullman, (rr car), pulmano
pullulate, pululi [tr], svarmi [int]
Pulmonaria, (bot), pulmonario, pulmoherbo
pulmonary, pulma
pulp, (gen), pulpo; ~igi; (any pasty mixture, as wood pulp), pasto; (of fruit etc. after squeezing, boiling, etc.), rekremento; **pulpy**, ~(ec)a
pulpit, predik/ejo, ~pupitro
pulpitis, pulpito
pulque, pulkvo
Pulsatilla, pulsatilo
pulse, pulso; ~i [int]; (legume), legumeno; **pulse(beat)**, (one beat), ~obato
pultaceous, pultacea
pulverize, pulvorigi
puma, pumo
pumice, pumiko; ~i [tr]
pummel, pugn(ad)i [tr]
pump, (mech, or analogous process), pumpi [tr]; ~ilo; (shoe), balŝuo; **pump out**, (re substance pumped), el~i [tr] (e.g.: *pump out the water from the basement:* el~i la akvon el la kelo); (re region pumped), pri~i [tr] (e.g.: *pump out the basement:* pri~i la kelon)
pumpernickel, Vestfalia sekalpano
pumpkin, kukurbo
pun, kalemburo; ~i [int]

punch, (jab, poke), piki [tr]; ~o; (tool, as for punching leather), aleno; aleni [tr]; (mark metal), punktofrapi [tr]; punktofrapilo; (stamp), stampi [tr]; (w fist), pugni [tr]; pugnado; (make any hole), trui [tr]; (drink), punĉo; **punchdrunk**, boksebria; **punching bag**, boksbalono; **punch line**, frapfrazo, pintumo; **punch in**, **punch out**, **punch a (time) clock**, registri sian tempon, enregistri sin, elregistri sin; **pull one's punches**, sin bridi

Punch, (puppet etc.), Pulĉinelo

punchinello, pulĉinelo

punctilio, punktilio; **punctilious**, ~a, ceremoniema, precizema

punctual, akurata

punctuate, interpunkcii [tr]; **punctuation (marks)**, ~o [see § 17(f)]

puncture, (gen), (tra)piki [tr], trui [tr]; ~o; (med: to enter cavity), punkcii [tr]; punkcio; (med: through skin or oth tissue), punkturo

pundit, saĝulo

pungent, (taste), pik/agusta; (smell), ~odora; (biting, gen), morda

Punic, Punika

punish, puni [tr]; **punishable**, ~enda; **punishment**, ~o; **punitive**, ~a; **capital punishment**, mort~o

Punjab, Panĝabo; **Punjabi**, ~a; ~ano

punk, (tinder), tindro; (hoodlum), fiulo, misulo, fripono

punt, (kick), demane (pied)bati [tr]; demana (pied)bato; (boat), prameto; (propel boat w pole), stangumi [tr]; (Br, Aus: bet), veti [tr]

puny, duonkreska, malforta, eta

pup, hundido

pupa, pupo

pupil, (student), lernanto, studento; (of eye), pupilo

puppet, (gen), pupo; (as glove), gant~o; (marionette), marioneto; **puppet show**, ~teatro

puppy, hundido

Purana, Purano(j)

purchase, (buy), aĉeti [tr]; ~o; ~aĵo; (hold), teno

pure, (gen), pura; **purify**, ~igi; **purist**, ~isto; **purity**, ~eco; **impure**, mal~a; **impurity**, mal~aĵo; mal~eco

purée, pureo†

purgative, laksiga; ~enzo

purgatory, purgatorio

purge, (clean out; pol), elpurigi; ~o; (law), senkulpigi; (med), laksigi

Purim, Purim

puritan, puritano; ~a; ~isma; **puritanism**, ~ismo; **puritanical**, ~a, rigidmora

Purkinje, (in med names), Purkinje

purl, (knitting), inverse triki [tr]

purloin, ŝteli [tr]

purple, purpura; ~o

purport, (claim, profess), pretendi [tr]; (falsely), ŝajnigi; (meaning), signifo

purpose, motivo, intenco, celo; ~i [tr], intenci [tr], celi [tr]; **purposeful**, intenca; **purposely**, **on purpose**, intence; **all-purpose**, ĉia~a, ĉiu~a; **for that purpose**, tiucele; **for what purpose**, kiucele; **serve a purpose**, havi utilon; **serve the purpose**, taŭgi [int], sufiĉi [int]; **defeat the purpose (of)**, kontraŭi la ~on (de), agi [int] kontraŭ; **to good purpose**, avantaĝe, profite; **to no purpose**, senprofite, senrezulte; **to the purpose**, (relevant), rilata; **be at cross-purposes**, malsame intenci, kontraŭintenci (unu la alian)

purpura, purpurao

purr, (as cat), ronroni [int]; ~o; (onom), ron!, ronron!

purse, ($ container, gen), mon/ujo; (pouch tied to belt), burso; (handbag), retikulo; ($ itself), ~o; (as prize), (~)premio; (pucker), faltigi; **purser**, kasisto

purslane, portulako

pursuant (to), laŭ, konforme al

pursue, (chase), postkuri [tr]; (follow, as plan etc.), sekvi [tr]; (search, strive for), serĉi [tr], strebi akiri [tr]; (have as occupation, devote self to), sin dediĉi al, okupiĝi pri; **pursuit**, ~ado; sekvado; serĉado; okupo; strebado; **pursue efforts**, (Aus), disvolvi klopodojn

purulent, pusa

purvey, (esp food), provianti [tr]; (supply, gen), provizi [tr]

purview, amplekso

pus, puso; **produce pus**, **exude pus**, ~i

[int]

push, (gen), puŝi [tr]; ~iĝi; ~o; (deal in illegal drugs), ŝakri [tr]; **pusher,** ŝakristo; **pushy,** trudema; **push-out,** (student etc.), el~ito; **push-pull,** (gen), ~tira; **push-up,** (exercise), lev~o

Pushtu, (la) Puŝtua† (lingvo)

pusillanimous, malkuraĝa, timema; **pusillanimity,** ~o

puss, (cat), kato; ~ĉjo; **pussy,** (cat), ~(ĉj)o; (vulg: vagina), piĉo; **pussyfoot,** (walk cautiously), etpaŝi [int], ~paŝi [int]; (vacillate), ŝanceliĝi

pustule, pustulo; **pustular,** ~a; **pustulosis,** ~ozo

put, (place, locate, set, subject, impose, etc.), meti [tr], loki [tr] (e.g.: *put the book on the table:* ~i la libron sur la tablon; *put a tax on tobacco:* ~i imposton sur tabakon; *put it under pressure:* ~i ĝin sub premon); (express), esprimi [tr] (e.g.: *I'll put it to you this way:* mi esprimos ĝin al vi ĉi-maniere; *put it in simple language:* esprimi ĝin per simpla lingvaĵo); (cause to be in specified condition), ~igi [sfx] (e.g.: *put your mind at ease:* trankviligu vian menson; *put a stop to that:* haltigi tion); (make do), igi, ~igi [sfx] (e.g.: *put the dog through his tricks:* igi la hundon fari siajn lertaĵojn); (attribute, ascribe), atribui [tr], imputi [tr] (e.g.: *put the blame on him:* imputi la kulpon al li); (translate), traduki [tr] (e.g.: *put it into Esperanto:* traduki ĝin en Esperanton); (estimate, assess), taksi [tr] (e.g.: *put the attendance at 200:* taksi la ĉeestantaron je 200); (fix, establish), fiksi [tr] (e.g.: *we put the price at \$50:* ni fiksis la prezon je \$50); (bet), veti [tr] (e.g.: *put \$10 on a horse:* veti \$10 pri ĉevalo); **put about,** (naut: change course), ĝiri [tr]; ĝiriĝi; **put across,** (communicate), komuniki [tr]; (get accepted), akceptiĝi; (make succeed), sukcesigi; (by trickery), (ruze) altrudi [tr], tromptrudi [tr]; **put aside,** flanken~i [tr], flanklasi [tr]; **put away,** for~i [tr]; **put back,** (replace), re~i [tr]; (backwards), retro~i [tr]; **put down,** (suppress, squelch, repress), subigi,

subpremi [tr] [not "sub~i"]; (on paper), surpaperigi; (record, gen), registri [tr]; (make stop), ĉesigi; (attribute), atribui [tr], imputi [tr]; (classify), klasifiki [tr]; (land, re aircraft etc.), surteriĝi; (humiliate, belittle), humiligi; **put-down,** humiligo; **put forth,** (extend, gen), el~i [tr], etendi [tr]; (assert), aserti [tr]; (propose), proponi [tr]; (bud, sprout), burĝoni [int] (je); **put forward,** (propose), proponi [tr]; **put in,** (install), instali [tr]; (into port), enhavenigi; enhaveniĝi; (submit, as claim, request, etc.), sub~i [tr]; (insert, interpose), inter~i [tr], en~i [tr]; (spend time), pasigi; **put in for,** (request), peti [tr]; **put off,** (delay), prokrasti [tr]; (discourage), malkuraĝigi; (evade, turn away), eviti [tr], forturni [tr]; (upset, distress), ĉagreni [tr], maltrankviligi, malplaĉi [tr]; (repel), mallogi [tr]; (turn off, re elec, water, etc.), [see "turn: turn off"]; **put on,** (clothes etc.), sur~i [tr]; (pretend), ŝajnigi; (concert, play, etc.), prezenti [tr]; (bring about, as party, celebration, etc.), okazigi; (trick, fool), trompi [tr]; (take on), alpreni [tr]; (apply, as brakes), apliki [tr]; (turn on, re elec, water, etc.), [see "turn: turn on"]; **put it on,** troigi; troiĝi; **put out,** (expel, as animal), elpeli [tr]; (dismiss from job), maldungi [tr]; (extinguish fire, light, etc.), estingi [tr]; (spend \$), elspezi [tr]; (confuse), konfuzi [tr]; (distress, bother), ĝeni [tr], ĉagreni, malplaĉi [tr]; (inconvenience), ĝeni [tr] (e.g.: *don't put yourself out because of me:* ne ĝenu vin pro mi); (publish), eldoni [tr]; (produce, gen), produkti [tr]; (display), montri [tr]; (spread out, as flatware on table, roots, etc.), dis~i [tr]; **put over,** [see "put across" above]; **put (something) over on,** superruzi [tr], trompi [tr]; **put through,** (carry out, effectuate), efektivigi; (connect, as by phone), konekti [tr]; (make undergo), sub~i [tr] (al) (e.g.: *put a car through the tests:* sub~i aŭton al la provoj); (make do), igi fari [tr] (e.g.: *put a dog through his tricks:* igi hundon fari sia-

jn lertaĵojn); **put together**, kun~i [tr];
put up, (offer, propose, gen), proponi
[tr]; (bsns offer), oferti [tr]; (invest,
provide $), investi [tr]; (as candidate),
kandidatigi; (preserve, can, re foods),
prezervi [tr], enladigi, konservi [tr];
(prepare, gen), prepari [tr]; (build),
konstrui [tr]; (give lodging to, gen),
loĝigi; (to guest for short time), gastigi; (stay as guest), gasti [int]; (arrange, re hair), aranĝi [tr]; (carry on),
starigi, efektivigi, estigi (e.g.: *put up a*
struggle: starigi lukton); (put away),
for~i [tr]; **put (someone) up to**, instigi (iun) al; **put up with**, (tolerate), toleri [tr]; (resignedly), rezignacii [int]
(pri); **put upon**, sin trudi al; **put-up-**
on, altrudita; **input**, (gen), en~i [tr];
en~o; (cmptr), enigi; **input device**,
(cmptr), enigatoro; **output**, (gen), el~i
[tr]; el~o; (cmptr), eligi; (production), produktaĵo; produktado; (esp in
relation to energy etc. input), rendimento [see "efficient"]; **output de-**
vice, (cmptr), eligatoro; **I wouldn't**
put it past (someone to do some-
thing), mi ne opinias (iun) nekapabla
(de io, fari ion); **be hard put to**, malfacile povi [tr]

putative, supozata

putrefy, putri [int]; ~igi; **putrefaction**,
~(ad)o; **putrescent**, ~anta

putrid, putra

putsch, puĉo

putt, (golf), ruli [tr]; ~o

putter, (dabble), diletanti [int], lanti
[int], nenifaradi [int]; (golf), rulklabo

putt-putt, (motor sound), knaladi [int];
~o; (onom), krak-krak-krak!

putty, mastiko; ~i [tr]

puzzle, (enigma; problem for amusement), enigmo [cp "charade", "logo-
griph", "rebus", "cryptogram"];
(perplex), mistifiki [tr], konfuzi [tr],
embarasi [tr], perpleksigi; konfuziĝi,
embarasiĝi, perpleksiĝi; **puzzling**, ~a,
konfuza, embarasa, perpleksiga; **puz-**
zlement, embaraso, konfuziĝo; **puz-**
zle out, deĉifri [tr], solvi [tr]; **puzzle**
over, pripensi [tr], stud(ad)i [tr];
crossword puzzle, krucvorto; **jigsaw**
puzzle, puzlo, ĵigo; **jigsaw puzzle**

    piece, puzlero
pycnidium, piknido
pycnometer, piknometro
pyelitis, pielito
pyemia, pioemio
Pygmalion, Pigmaliono
pygmy, **Pygmy**, Pigmeo; ~a
pyjama(s), piĵamo [note sing]
pylon, (gen), pilono
pylorus, piloro; **pyloric**, ~a
py(o)-, (med pfx), pio-
pyogenic, piogena
pyorrhea, pioreo
Pyralis, piralo, lum-moteo
pyramid, piramido
pyramidale, piramidalo, triketro
Pyramus, Piramo
pyran, pirano
pyranose, piranozo
pyre, funebra ŝtiparo
Pyrenees, Pireneoj; **Pyrenean**, ~a
Pyrenomycetes, pirenomicetoj
pyrethrum, (plant), krizantemo; (insec-
    ticide), piretro
pyrheliometer, pirheliometro
pyridine, piridino
pyridoxin, piridoksino
pyrite, iron pyrites, pirito
pyr(o)-, (pfx), piro-
pyrogallol, pyrogallic acid, pirogaĵlo
pyrolusite, piroluzito
pyromania, piromanio;   **pyromaniac**,
    ~a; ~ulo
pyrometer, pirometro
pyrophoric, pirofora; **pyrophoric sub-**
stance, ~o
pyrophosphate, pirofosfato; **pyrophos-**
phoric acid, ~a acido
pyrosis, pirozo
pyrosulfate, pirosulfato;   **pyrosulfuric**
acid, ~a acido
pyrotechnic, piroteknika;   **pyrotech-**
nics, ~o [note sing]
pyroxene, pirokseno
Pyrrhic, Pirra
Pyrrho, Pirono; **Pyrrhonism**, ~ismo
Pyrrhocorax, pirokorako, montkorvo
Pyrrhula, pirolo
pyrrole, pirolo
Pyrrhus, Pirro
Pyrus, Pyrus communis, pirarbo; Pyrus
    aria, alizarbo

Pythagoras, Pitagoro;   **Pythagorean**,
~a; **Pythagoreanism**, ~ismo
Pythia, Pitia
Pythian, Pitia
Pytho, Pitio
python, pitono
Python, (myth), Pitono
Python, (zool), pitono
pyx, ciborio, hostiujo
pyxidium, piksidio

Q

Q, (elec: energy ratio), ŝarganco [symbol "Q" also in Esperanto; pronounce "kuo" (see § 16)]

Qaraqoram, Karakorumo

Qatar, Kataro†

Q.E.D. (abb of "quod erat demonstrandum"), kio estis pruvenda; jen la pruvo [no abb in Esperanto]

Qingdao, Kingdaŭ

Qiqihar, Kikihar

qua, (as), kiel

quack, (duck sound), kvaki [int]; ~o; (onom), gik–gak!, kvak-kvak!; (charlatan), ĉarlatano, fuŝ-kuracisto; **quackery,** ĉarlatanaĵo

quad, (yard), korto; (quadruplet), kvarnaskito; (printing), kadrato

quadrangle, (geom), kvar/angulo, ~latero; (yard), korto

quadrant, kvadranto

quadraphonic, kvadrafonia*

quadrat, kadrato

quadrate, (90° out of phase), kvadratura; (square), kvadrata

quadratic, kvadrata; **biquadratic,** kvaragrada

quadrature, (gen), kvadraturo

quadrennium, jarkvaro; **quadrennial,** ~a

quadric, (math: 2nd degree), kvadrata

quadriceps, kvadricepso

quadriga, kvadrigo

quadrilateral, kvar/latero, ~angulo; ~latera, ~angula

quadrille, (dance), kvadrilo

quadrillion, (Am: 10^{15}), duiliardo; (Br: 10^{24}), kvariliono [see § 19(b)]

quadriplegia, kvadriplegio; **quadriplegic,** ~a; ~ulo

quadrireme, kvadriremo

quadroon, kvarterono

quadruped, kvarpiedulo

quadruple, kvar/obla; ~oblo; ~oble; ~obligi; ~obliĝi; ~opa; ~opo; ~ope; ~opigi; ~opiĝi [see "double"]

quadruplet, kvarnaskito

quadruplex, kvadruplekso; ~a

quadruplicate, kvaroblo; ~a; ~igi; **in**

quadruplicate, ~e

quaestor, kvestoro; **quaestorship,** ~eco; ~ejo; kvesturo

quaff, trink(eg)i [tr]; ~o

quagmire, ŝlimejo, marĉo

quail, (zool), koturno; (lose courage), senkuraĝiĝi

quaint, (agrable) kurioza

quake, (tremble, gen), tremi [int]; ~o; (earthquake), ter~o, sismo

Quaker, (rel), Kvakero; ~a [cp "friend"]

qualify, (define qualities of, characterize), kvalifiki [tr]; ~iĝi; (make fit for), taŭgigi, kompetentigi; (give right to), rajtigi; (meet requirements for), taŭgi [int], kompetenti [int], rajti [int]; (limit, restrict), kondiĉi [tr]; (moderate), moderigi; **qualification,** ~(iĝ)o; taŭgigo, kompetentigo; kompetenteco; rajt(ig)o; kondiĉo; moderigo; **qualified,** (fit; meeting requirements), taŭga, kompetenta; **disqualify,** senrajtigi

quality, (feature, attribute), kvalito, eco; (degree of excellence), ~o; (excellent), alt~a; **qualitative,** ~(ec)a

qualm, (scruple, misgiving), skrupulo; (nausea), eknaŭzo

quandary, dilemo, perplekseco

quantity, (amount, gen), kvanto; (quality of measurability), ~eco; **quantify,** ~igi; **quantitative,** ~a

quantum, kvantumo; ~a; **quantum mechanics,** ~meĥaniko; **quantum theory,** ~teorio

quarantine, kvaranteno; ~igi; **be in quarantine,** ~i [int]

quark, kvarko†

quarrel, kvereli [int]; ~o; **quarrelsome,** ~ema

quarry, (stone), mini [tr]; ŝton~ejo; (hunted animal), ĉasaĵo

quart, kvarto [dry quart (Am): 1,101 litroj; liquid quart (Am), 0,946 litroj; Imperial quart (Br): 1,137 litroj] [note that PIV gives erroneous equivalent in definition of "kvarto"; convert to "lit-

roj" to avoid confusion (see § 20)]
quartan, kvartana
quarter, (1/4), kvarono, kvaron– [pfx];
~igi (e.g.: *quarter hour:* ~horo) [see
§ 19(d)]; (of year), trimestro, jar~o;
(section of city), kvartalo [cp "ghetto"]; (moon phase), ~luno; ($), ~dola-
ro; (indulgence, mercy), indulgi [tr],
kompati [tr]; (give lodging), loĝigi;
quarters, (any lodging), loĝejo; (barracks), barak(ar)o; kazerno [see "barracks"]; (overnight), tranoktejo;
(source, as of information), fonto;
quarterly, trimestra; trimestre; **quar-
termaster,** (mil, gen), furiero; (naut),
kvartirmastro; **bachelor's quarters,**
fraŭlobarak(ar)o; **show no quarter,**
esti senkompata
quartet, (any 4), kvaropo; (mus), kvarteto
quartile, kvarilo; ~a
quarto, kvarto, folianto
quartz, kvarco; **quartzite,** ~ito
quasar, kvazaro
quash, (law), kasacii [tr]; (quell, suppress), subpremi [tr]
quasi, kvazaŭa
quasi–, (pfx), kvazaŭ– [cp "pseudo–"]
quass, kvaso
quassia, (drug), kvasio; (tree), ~arbo;
(wood), ~ligno
quaternary, Quaternary, (chem: 4 va-
lences; geol), kvaternaro; ~a; (in 4
parts), kvaropa
quaver, (tremble), tremi [int]; ~o; (Br:
8th note), okonnoto; **semiquaver,**
deksesonnoto
quay, kajo
queasy, naŭza; ~eta; ~iga; ~iĝema
Québec, (city), Kebeko; (province),
~io; **Québecois,** ~a; ~ia; ~ano; ~iano
quebracho, kebraĉo; **white quebracho,** blanka ~o; **red quebracho,** ruĝa
~o
Quechua, Keĉuo; (la) ~a (lingvo)
queen, (royal), reĝino; (games), damo;
queen of the meadow, (bot), ulmario
Queensland, Kvinslando
queer, (strange), stranga, kurioza; (ill),
malsaneta, misfarta
quell, sub/premi [tr]; ~iĝi
quench, (fire), estingi [tr]; (thirst), sati-

gi; (hot metal), trempi [tr]; (subdue),
subigi, superi [tr]
Quercus, kverko; Quercus ilex,
ileks~o, verda ~o; Quercus suber,
korko~o
querulous, plendema
query, demando; pri~i [tr], dubi [tr]
quest, serĉo [not "kvesto"]
question, (gen), demando; (ask question
of), pri~i [tr] [see "ask"]; (doubt),
pri~i, dubi [tr]; dubo; (casuistic, moral), kazuo; (interrogate), ekzameni
[tr], pri~i; (dispute), kontesti [tr];
questionable, dubinda; **question
mark,** ~osigno; **questionnaire,**
~aro; **ask a question,** fari ~on [not
"~i ~on"]; **beg the question,** an-
taŭsupozi la pruvotaĵon; **beyond
question,** preterdube; **call into question,** dubindigi, pridubi [tr], disputi
[tr]; **pop the question,** proponi ge-
edziĝon; **raise the question,** (for discussion), diskutigi; **a question of
(honor etc.),** ~o pri (honoro etc.); **a
question of whether,** ~o ĉu; **in question,** (presently discussed), koncerna
[goes before n (e.g.: *the subject in
question:* la koncerna temo)]; **out of
the question,** tute neebla; nediskuteb-
la; **leading question, loaded question,** sugesta ~o; **without question,**
sendube
questor, [see "quaestor"]
quetzal, kvezalo†
queue, (line of people), starvico; vicigi; viciĝi; (cmptr), sekvovico; (pigtail), harplektaĵo
quibble, ĉikani [tr]; ~o
quiche, fromaĝotorto
quick, (rapid), rapida; ~e; (prompt),
baldaŭa, senprokrasta; (witty), sprita;
(excitable, volatile), ekscitiĝema; (in-
nervated flesh), karno (e.g.: *cut to the
quick:* tranĉi ĝiskarne); (vigorous),
vigla; **quicken,** (accelerate), akceli
[tr]; akceliĝi; (liven up), vigligi; vigliĝi; **quickie,** ~a; ~aĵo; **quick on the
uptake,** viglanima
quid, (tobacco), (tabak)maĉaĵo; ($),
pundo
quid pro quo, (thing in return), recipro-
kaĵo; (substitute), anstataŭaĵo

quiescent, kvieta
quiet, (silent), silenta; ~o; ~igi; (tranquil), trankvila: trankvil(ec)o; (calm), kvieta: kvietigi; kviet(ec)o; (soft, not loud), mallaŭta; **quietude,** trankvil(ec)o; kviet(ec)o; **disquiet,** maltrankvil(ec)o; maltrankviligi; **be quiet,** ~i [int]; **(be) quiet!,** ~u!
quietus, (discharge from debt or oth duty), kvitigo
quiff, (frunto)buklo
quill, (feather), plumo; (of porcupine), pikilo
quilt, peplomo; **quilted,** ~a
quince, (fruit), cidonio; (tree), ~arbo
quinine, kinino; **quininism,** ~ismo
quinoid, kinoida; ~ajo
quinoline, kinolino
quinone, kinono
quinquennium, jarkvino; **quinquennial,** ~a
quintal, kvintalo [(Am), 45,36 kilogramoj; (Br), 50,80 kilogramoj; (metric), 100 kilogramoj (see § 20)]
quintessence, kvintesenco
quintet, (any 5), kvinopo; (mus), kvinteto
quintile, kvinilo
Quintilian, Kvintiliano
quintillion, (Am; 10^{18}), triiliono; (Br; 10^{30}), kviniliono [see § 19(b)]
quintuple, kvin/oblo; ~obla; ~obligi; ~obliĝi; ~opa; ~opigi; ~opiĝi [see "double"]
quintuplet, kvinnaskito
Quintus Curtius (Rufus), Kvinto-Kurcio
quip, spriti [int]; ~ajo
quire, (24-folia [or] 25-folia) kajero
Quirinal, Kvirinalo
quirk, (peculiarity, idiosyncrasy), idiosinkrazio; (caprice, twist of fate etc.), kaprico
quirt, rajdvipo
quit, (give up, resign, leave), rezigni [tr], forlasi [tr]; (relieve of debt), kvita; kvitigi; kvitiĝi; (stop), ĉesi [int]; ĉesigi; (totally leave a movement or cause), kabei [int]; **quits,** ($: even), kvita; **quitclaim,** (act), pretendokvitigo; (document), pretendokvitilo; **quittance,** kvitigo; **call it quits,** ~i

quitch, kviko
quite, (very, rather), tre (e.g.: *it is quite hot:* estas tre varme); (entirely), tute (e.g.: *you are quite right:* vi tute pravas); **quite a,** (a remarkable), rimarkinda; kia (rimarkinda) ...! (e.g.: *That was quite a storm yesterday evening!:* Tio estis rimarkinda ŝtormo hieraŭ vespere! [or] Kia ŝtormo hieraŭ vespere!); **quite a few, quite some,** (many), ne malmulte da, iom multe da, iom multaj (e.g.: *there were quite a few newcomers at the dance:* estis iom multaj nov-venintoj ĉe la danco); **not quite,** ne tute
Quito, Kito
quiver, (tremble), tremeti [int]; ~o; (arrow holder), sagujo
quixotic, donkiĥota
quiz, (test), testeto; (interrogate), pridemandi [tr]; **quizzical,** (perplexed), perpleksa, demanda; (teasing), mokŝerca
quodlibet, kvodlibeto
quoin, (in building corner), angulŝtono; (any wedge), kojno
quoit, ĵetringo; **quoits,** (game), ~oludo
quondam, iama
quorum, kvorumo
quota, kvoto
quote, (repeat statement etc.), citi [tr]; ~ajo; (bsns, $), kvoti [tr]; **quotation,** ~ado; ~ajo; kvotajo [avoid "kvoto" in this sense; see "quota"]; **quotation mark,** ~ilo [see § 17]; **misquote,** mis~i [tr]; **quote, end quote (unquote),** (in reading a quotation aloud), cit', malcit' (e.g.: *the message says, quote, we will come tomorrow, unquote:* la mesaĝo diras, cit', ni venos morgaŭ, malcit'; *they claimed that the problem was due to a quote-unquote clerical error:* ili pretendis ke la problemo ŝuldiĝis al cit'-malcit' komizeraro)
quotidian, (gen), ĉiutaga
quotient, kvociento; **intelligence quotient,** intelekta ~o†

R

Ra, (sun god), Reo
rabbet, rabeto; ~igi; ~iĝi
rabbi, (gen), rabeno; (title of address, respect), Rabbi; **rabbinic(al),** ~a
rabbit, (domestic or common wild), kuniklo; (*Lepus*; any hare), leporo; **rabbiter,** (Aus), ~oĉasisto; **snowshoe rabbit,** nordlanda leporo; **rabbit ears,** (antenna), ~–orela anteno
rabble, kanajlaro; **rabble-rouser,** tumultincitanto
Rabelais, Rabelezo; **Rabelaisian,** ~a
rabies, rabio; **rabid,** ~a; **anti-rabies,** kontraŭ~a
raccoon, prociono
race, (any contest), konkurso; ~i [int] (kontraŭ); ~igi; (of speed, gen), vetkuro; vetkuri [int] (kontraŭ); vetkurigi; (run, go very fast), kuregi [int]; kuregigi; (species or variety of human, animal, plant), raso; (ethnic group), gento; (of water), kurento; (water channel), kurentejo; (mech: groove etc. for moving parts), kurujo; **racial,** rasa; **racism,** rasismo; **racist,** rasisma; rasisto; **race course, race track,** ĉevalkurejo, hipodromo; **arms race,** armil~o, vetarmado; **auto race,** aŭto~o; **drag race,** akcel~o; **foot race,** kur~o; **horse race,** ĉeval~o; **relay race,** stafetkurado; **tailrace,** postmuela fluejo; **biracial,** durasa; **multiracial,** plurrasa
raceme, grapolo [not "racem–"]; **racemose,** ~a
racemic, (chem), racema; **racemic acid,** ~a acido, tartra acido; **racemization,** ~igo
Rachel, Raĥel
Racine, (city; French writer), Racino
rack, (frame, holder, etc., as for bicycles, hay, pipes, etc.), rako; en~igi; (for torture), torturkadro; **rack one's brains,** streĉi la cerbon; **go to rack and ruin,** komplete ruiniĝi
racket, (tennis etc.), rakedo; (noise), bruego; (illegal bsns, scheme etc.), fikomerco, fiafero; **racketeer,** ŝakris-

to, fikomercisto, gangstero; **racketeering,** ŝakrado **make a racket,** bruegi [int]
raconteur, rakontisto
racy, (lively, spirited), verva, spica, pika
rad, (unit of radiation), rado*
radar, radaro
radial, radiala
radian, radiano
radiant, radianta, brila; **radiance,** ~eco, brilo
radiate, (gen), radii [int]; ~igi; **radiation,** ~ado; **corpuscular radiation,** korpuskla ~ado; **wave radiation,** onda ~ado; **irradiate,** sur~i [tr]; **irradiation,** sur~ado; [see also "ray"]
radiatio, (anat), radiacio
radiator, radiatoro
radical, (re plant's or analogous root), radika [see "root"]; (extreme), radikala; radikalulo; (chem; word part), radikalo; (math sign indicating square root), ~ilo, ~signo
radicle, (anat: nerve root), radiklo
radicula, radiklo
radio, (system), radiofonio; ~a; ~i [int] (al); (receiver), radiofono, radioricevilo [not "radio"]
radio–, (sci pfx: radio or radiation), radio–
radiogram, (message sent by radio), radiogramo; **radiogram, radiograph,** (X-ray), radiografaĵo; **make a radiograph,** radiografi [tr]; **radiography,** radiografio; **radiographer,** radiografisto [see also "X: X-ray"]
Radiolaria, radiolarioj
radiology, radiolog/io; **radiologist,** ~o
radiometer, radiometro
radiophone, radiotelefono
radioscopy, radioskopio; **radioscopic,** ~a
radiosonde, radiosondilo
radish, rafano
radium, radiumo
radius, radiuso
radix, (gen), radiko

radome, radarkupolo
radon, radono
Raetia, Retio
raffia, (tree), rafio; (fiber from), ~aĵo
raffinose, rafinozo
raffish, (licentious), diboĉa; (vulgar), triviala
raffle, lotumi [tr]; ~o, loterio
Rafflesia, raflezio
raft, floso
rafter, ĉevrono
rag, ĉifono; **ragged**, ~a; (type: margin not justified), neĝustigita; **ragweed**, ambrosio; **ragwort**, senecio
raga, rago*
ragamuffin, ĉifonulo
rage, (fury, gen), furiozo, rabio; ~i [int]; (fad), furoro; **raging**, ~a; **outrage**, (anger), kolerego, ~o; koleregigi, ~igi; (insult), insultegi [tr], insultego; (offend), ofendegi [tr]; ofendego; (violent act), perforti [tr], atenci [tr]; perfort(aĵ)o, atenco; **outrageous**, insultega; ofendega, ŝoka; **be (all) the rage**, furori [int]
raglan, raglano; ~a
Ragnarok, Ragnarok
ragout, raguo
ragtime, ragtimo†
Raia, rajo
raid, (attack, gen), ataki [tr]; ~o; (by police), kapt~i [tr]; kapt~o; (plunder etc.), rab~i [tr]; rab~o
rail, (one side of rr track; similar object), relo; (fence, barrier), barilo; (support, railing), apog~o, (man)apogilo; (a railroad), fervojo (e.g.: *travel by rail:* veturi per fervojo); (rim, as of billiard table), rando; (complain), plendegi [int]; riproĉegi [tr]; (zool), ralo; **railing**, apog~o, (man)apogilo; (bannister), balustrado; **railroad, railway**, fervojo; fervoja; **railway car, railway coach**, vagono; **derail**, de~igi; de~iĝi; **bedrail**, lit~o; **guardrail**, gard~o; **monorail**, unu~a (trajno, fervojo); **sliprail**, glitotrabo; **water rail**, (zool), akvoralo
raiment, vesto
rain, (gen), pluvo; ~i [int]; ~igi (e.g.: *the volcano rained ashes on the village:* la vulkano ~igis cindrojn sur la vilaĝon); **rainy**, ~(em)a; **it's raining**, ~as; **it looks like rain**, ŝajnas ~eme, aspektas ~eme; **rainbow**, ĉielarko; **rain check**, ~bileto; **raincoat**, ~mantelo; **raindrop**, ~ero; **rainfall**, (as total rain in given area), ~okvanto; (condition of rain), ~ado; **rain forest**, ~arbaro; **rain gauge**, ~ometro; **rainstorm**, ~oŝtormo; **rainwater**, ~akvo; **rainwear**, ~ovestoj; **freezing rain**, glaci~o; **golden rain**, (bot), laburno, or~o
raise, (make higher, elevate, bring up [question etc.], lit or fig), levi [tr]; ~o; (erect, set upright, as tent, structure), starigi; (build), konstrui [tr]; (educate children), eduki [tr]; (breed animals), bredi [tr]; (waken), veki [tr]; (incite), inciti [tr]; (increase), pliigi; pliigo; (advance, enhance), antaŭenigi; (bring about), estigi, rezultigi; (collect $ etc.), kolekti [tr]; (make relief, surface), reliefigi; (put nap on cloth etc.), vilizi [tr]; (bet more, as in poker), pliveti [tr]; pliveto; (in salary), pagopliigo, salajropliigo; **raised**, (surface in relief), reliefa; **raise hell, raise the roof**, ~i tumulton; **rais one's voice**, laŭtigi la voĉon; **hairraising**, hirtiga, harstariga
raisin, rosino, sekvinbero
raison d'être, estkialo, ekzistkialo
raja, raĝo
Raja, (zool), rajo
rake, (tool), rasti [tr]; ~ilo; (debauched), diboĉulo; (gunfire), enfili [tr]
rakish, galanta, verva, gaja
rale, raslo; ~i [int] [cp "rattle"]
Rallus, ralo; Rallus aquaticus, akvo~o; Rallus pectoralis, mallonga akvo~o; Rallidae, ~edoj
rally, (bring, come together), kunven/igi; ~iĝi; (revive spirits), revigligi; revigliĝi; (group for common purpose), solidarigi, grupigi, alianci [tr]; solidariĝi, grupiĝi, allianciĝi; (mass pol meeting), mitingo; (contest, rallye), ralio
rallye, ralio
Ralph, Raulo
ram, (battering), ramo, murrompilo; ~i

[tr]; (sheep), virŝafo; (beak on ancient ship), rostro; (such a ship), rostroŝipo

RAM, (cmptr: abb of "random-access memory"), ramo‡

Rama, Ramo

Ramadan, Ramadano

Ramayana, Ramajano

ramble, vagi [int]; ~(ad)o

rambunctious, senbrida, senorda, kapriol(eg)a

Rameses, Ramseso

ramie, **ramee**, ramio

ramify, disbranĉ/igi; ~iĝi; **ramification**, (branching), ~igo; ~iĝo; (consequence), sekvo, rezulto, konsekvenco

ramontchi, flakurtio

ramp, (sloping surface, walk, road, etc.), ramplo; (bot: *Allium tricoccum*), trikarpela ajlo; **off ramp**, **exit ramp**, (in highway interchange), elirejo; **on ramp**, **entrance ramp**, alirejo

rampage, furiozi [int]; ~o; **on a rampage**, ~anta

rampant, (unchecked, widespread), furiozanta, svarmanta, nebridita; (luxuriant, lush), abunda

rampart, remparo; ~i [tr]

rampion, rapunkolo

Ramses, Ramseso

ramshackle, kaduka

Rana, rano; Ranidae, ~edoj

ranch, ranĉo; **rancher**, (person), ~isto; (house), ~odomo

rancid, ranca

rancor, rankoro

rand, ($), rando

random, (statistics), aleatora, loteca; (haphazard, aimless), hazarda; **random sample**, ~a samplo; **at random**, ~e; hazarde, arbitre

randy, amorema, seksema, lasciva

range, (reach, gen), atingo, ~opovo; etendi [int]; etendo; (extent), amplekso; (tech: spectrum), gamo, spektro; (of mus instrument, voice), tonetendo; (of gun etc.), pafdistanco, pafkampo, (traf)distanco (e.g.: *medium-range rocket:* mez-distanca raketo); (of radio, TV station), ricevdistanco; (of hearing), aŭdodistanco; (distance which plane, vehicle etc. can go w/o refueling), aŭtonomio; (in row), vici-

gi; vico; (systematize), klasifiki [tr], sistemigi; (aim gun, telescope, etc.), celumi [tr]; (roam through), travagi [tr]; (vary), varii [int]; (habitat of plant), kreskejo; (habitat of animal), loĝloko; (type), speco; (for shooting practice or sport), pafejo; (test area, as for rockets), provkampo; (for animal grazing), paŝtejo; (cooking stove), fornelo; **range finder**, telemetro; **mountain range**, montaro, montoĉeno

ranger, (park police), arbar(polic)isto

Rangifer, rangifero

Rangoon, Ranguno

rani, raĝino

Ranidae, ranedoj

rank, (position in hierarchy, status, etc.; any relative position), rango; ~i [int]; ~igi; (any row), vico; (to distinguish from file, as in mil formation), transvico [cp "file"]; (rancid), ranca; (bad odor), fetora; (luxuriant), abunda; (fertile), fekund(eg)a; (complete, utter), kompleta; **ranking**, (of highest rank), plej alt~a; **close ranks**, (lit or fig), fermi vicojn; **first-rank**, **top-rank**, unua~a; **high-ranking**, alt~a; **outrank**, super~i [tr], el~i [tr]; **second-rank**, dua~a; **rank and file**, (common soldiers; ordinary people), plebo; **pull rank on**, aserti sian ~on super

rankle, rankorigi

ransack, (pillage), disrabi [tr]; (search thoroughly), ĝisfunde traserĉi [tr]

ransom, elaĉeti [tr]; ~a; ~o; ($), ~a mono

rant, furiozi [int], ~e deklamadi [int]; ~a deklamado

Ranunculus, ranunkolo

Raoul, Raulo

rap, (knock), frapi [tr], perkuti [tr]; ~iĝi, perkutiĝi; ~o, perkuto

rapacious, (greedy), avara; (plundering), rabema

rape, (sex attack), seksatenci [tr]; ~o; (bot: *Brassica napus*, gen), napo; (*B. napus rapifera* [or] *B. napus esculenta*), brasiknapo; (*B. napus sativa biennis*), kolzo; (grape pulp), rekremento; **broomrape**, orobanko

Raphael, Rafaelo
rapid, rapida; **rapidity**, ~eco; **rapids**, (of river), kaskadeto(j)
rapier, rapiro
rappel, varapo; ~i [int]
rapport, harmonio, akordo
rapprochement, (re)akordiĝo
rapt, ravita
rapture, ravo, ekstazo; **enrapture**, ~i [tr]
rare, (infrequent), malofta; (good, fine), rara; (tenuous, thin), maldensa; (cooked little), subkuirita; **rarity**, ~aĵo; ~eco; raraĵo; rareco; **rarefy**, maldensigi; **rarefied**, maldensa
rarebit, fromaĝofandaĵo
rascal, kanajlo, fripono
rash, (on skin), raŝo; (reckless), temerara, malprudenta, troriskema, maldiskreta
rasher, trançaĵo
rasp, raspi [tr]; ~ilo; **raspy**, ~a, raŭka
raspatory, rugino
rat, rato
ratafia, (drink), ratafio
ratchet, (pawl), kliko; (wheel, w or w/o pawl), ~rado; (shaft), ~stango
rate, (measure of amount), kvanto (e.g.: *birth rate:* nasko~o; *rate of acceleration:* ~o de akcelo); (ratio), rejŝo; (speed), rapido; (price, fare), tarifo; (rank), rango; rangi [int]; rangigi; (Br: tax), loka imposto; (appraise), taksi [tr]; (classify), klasifiki [tr]; (consider), konsideri [tr], opinii [tr]; (deserve), meriti [tr]; **rating**, takso; klasifiko; rango; **overrate**, trotaksi [tr], tro alte taksi [tr]; **birth rate**, nasko~o, natalitato; **at the rate of**, po (e.g.: *use fuel at the rate of 2 liters per hour:* uzi brulaĵon po 2 litroj en horo) [see also "per", "each"]; **rate of exchange**, ($), kurzo; **first-rate**, unuaranga, unuagrada; **second-rate**, duaranga, mezkvalita, mezgrada; **at any rate**, ĉiuokaze, almenaŭ
rather, (prefer), preferi [tr] (e.g.: *I would rather swim than bicycle:* mi ~us naĝi ol bicikli); (instead), antataŭe, male (e.g.: *I don't like swimming; rather, I enjoy bicycling:* mi ne ŝatas naĝadon; anstataŭe, mi ĝuas

bicikladon; *it's not too hot; rather, it's a little chilly:* ne estas tro varme; male, estas iom malvarmete); (more precisely), pli ĝuste (e.g.: *his mother, or rather, his stepmother:* lia patrino, aŭ pli ĝuste, lia duonpatrino); (somewhat), iom (e.g.: *a rather long story:* iom longa rakonto; *I'm rather tired:* mi iom lacas); **rather than**, anstataŭ, prefere al
ratify, ratifiki [tr]
ratio, rejŝo†; **gear ratio**, ~o de transmisio [cp "gear"]
ration, (limit on quantity), porci/umi [tr]; ~olimigo; (food, gen), nutraĵo~o; **ration book**, ~olibreto; **ration coupon**, ~okupono
rational, (in accord w human reason, gen; not emotional; sensible), racia; (math; phil etc.; deduced by logic, sci rules, etc.), racionala; **rationalism**, racionalismo; **rationalist**, racionalisma; racionalisto; **rationalize**, (reason), rezoni [int]; prirezoni [tr]; (make reasonable), ~igi; (invent spurious reason for deed, opinion, etc.), mispravigi
rationale, raciigo
Ratitae, senkarinuloj
rattan, rotango
rattle, klak/adi [int], ~etadi [int]; ~ig(ad)i; ~ado; ~ilo; (disconcert), konfuzi [tr]; (breathing sound), stertori [int]; stertoro [cp "rale"]; (bot: *Rhinanthus*), rinanto; **(red) rattle**, (*Pedicularis*), pedikularo; **rattlesnake**, krotalo, sonserpento; **rattletrap**, kadukaĵo
Rattus, rato
raucous, raŭka
raunchy, (re sex), lasciva; (bad), aĉa
ravage, ruinigi
rave, (talk incoherently), deliri [int]; (enthusiastically), entuziasmiĝi; (rage, as storm etc.), furiozi [int] [not "ravi"]
ravel, unravel, (lit or fig), malplekti [tr], dismaŝigi, malimpliki [tr], disfadenigi; ~iĝi, dismaŝiĝi, malimplikiĝi, disfadeniĝi
raven, korako; **Australian raven**, Aŭstralia korniko
ravening, rabanta, predanta

ravenous, malsat/ega; **be ravenous**, ~egi [int], lupe ~i [int] [see "hunger"]
ravine, ravino
ravioli, raviolo
ravish, (rape), seksatenci [tr]; (carry off, plunder), forrabi [tr]; (enrapture), ravi [tr]; **ravishing**, rava
raw, (gen), kruda; **raw material(s)**, ~materialo(j), ~aĵo(j)
ray, (of light etc.; math), radio; (stripe), strio; (fish), rajo; **alpha-rays**, alfa~oj; **beta-rays**, beta~oj; **gamma-rays**, gama~oj; **X-rays**, **Roentgen rays**, [see under "X"]; **electric ray**, (fish: *Torpedo*), torpedo
Raymond, Rajmondo; **Raymonda**, ~a
rayon, rajono, art-silko
raze, malkonstrui [tr], (fin)detrui [tr]
razor, razilo
razz, moki [tr]
razzia, razio; **go on a razzia (against)**, ~i [tr]
razzmatazz, ĵazaĵ', ~o, sprito, vigleco
re, (regarding, about), pri; (mus), re
re–, (pfx: again, back, etc.), re–
reach, (attain; come up to, out to, down to), atingi [tr]; ~o (e.g.: *we reached Boston yesterday:* ni ~is Bostonon hieraŭ; *the ladder won't reach that branch:* la eskalo ne ~os tiun branĉon; *the temperature reached 30:* la temperaturo ~is 30); (extend, thrust toward, not attaining), etendi [tr] (al); etendiĝi; etend(iĝ)o (e.g.: *she reached her hand out to them:* ŝi etendis sian manon al ili; *he reached for the salt:* li etendis la manon al la salo; *mountains reaching toward the sky:* montoj etendiĝantaj al la ĉielo); (ability to attain), ~o, ~opovo (e.g.: *beyond one's reach:* preter ies ~opovo); (add up to), sumi [int] (ĝis) (e.g.: *our expenses reached $500:* niaj elspezoj sumis ĝis $500 [kvincent dolaroj]); (affect, impress), tuŝi [tr], impresi [tr]; (penetrate), penetri [tr]; (area), etendaĵo (e.g.: *vast reaches of water:* vastaj etendaĵoj de akvo); **within reach of**, ~ebla de; **unreachable**, **beyond reach**, ne~ebla, preter ~(opov)o; **far-reaching**, vast(etend)a, grandampleksa, vastampleksa; **outreach**, etendiĝi, etendi sin;

etendo; etenda; (reach farther), super(etend)i [tr], preteretendi [tr]
react, (gen), reakcii [int], reagi [int]; **reactance**, reaktanco; **reactant**, ~anto; **reaction**, (gen), ~o, reago; **reactionary**, ~a; ~ulo; **chain reaction**, ĉen~o; **reactor**, reaktoro
read, (follow written words, or perceive in analogous manner, re person, machine, cmptr, etc.), legi [tr] (e.g.: *read a book:* ~i libron; *can you read music?:* ĉu vi povas ~i muzikon?; *read one's mind:* ~i ies menson; *the computer reads magnetic input:* la komputoro ~as magnetan enmeton); (have as text, be worded), teksti [int] (e.g.: *the sentence reads as follows:* la frazo tekstas jene); (show, register), montri [tr] (e.g.: *the thermometer reads 20:* la termometro montras 20); **reader**, (book, esp elementary text), ~olibro, krestomatio; **reading**, ~o (e.g.: *on first reading:* ĉe unua ~o); (text to be read), ~aĵo; **read aloud**, laŭt~i [tr], voĉ~i [tr]; **read in(to)**, entekstigi; atribui [tr]; **read out**, (register on instrument, gauge), (el)montri [tr]; (cmptr printout etc.), elpresi [tr]; **readout**, (el)montro; (el)preso; **read up on**, studi [tr] (pri); **sight-read**, senstude ~i; **sight-reading**, senstuda ~(ad)o; **well-read**, mult~inta, klera
ready, (prepared), preta; ~igi; ~iĝi; (willing), volonta; (about to, likely to), ema, –ema [sfx] (e.g.: *he's ready to cry:* li emas plori; *it looks ready to snow:* ŝajnas neĝeme); (prompt), baldaŭa, akurata, senprokrasta (e.g.: *a ready answer:* senprokrasta respondo); (available), disponebla, uzebla; **be ready**, ~i [int]; **readiness**, ~eco; **ready-made**, antaŭfarita, konfekcia; **ready-made garment**, konfekcio
reagent, reagenzo
real, (actual, not imaginary), reala, efektiva, vera; (law; re phys possession), ~a; (math: re number), reelat† ($), ~o; **realism**, ~ismo; **realist**, ~isto; **realistic**, ~isma; **reality**, ~aĵo; ~eco; **really**, efektive, vere, ~e; (is that so?), ĉu vere?; **real estate**, bienaĵo, terenaĵo [see also "realtor"]; **the**

real McCoy, la aŭtentikulo; la aŭtentikaĵo

realgar, realgaro

realize, (be aware), konstati [tr], konscii [int] (pri), kompreni [tr]; (make real), efektivigi, realigi; (cash), monigi; (make profit, earn), lukri [tr], gajni [tr]; **realization**, ~o, konsciiĝo; **self-realization**, sinrealigo, sinefektivigo

realm, (gen), regno

realtor, bien/makleristo; **realty**, ~aĵo

ream, (bore, smooth hole), alezi [tr]; (paper), rismo; **reamer**, ~ilo

reap, (harvest), rikolti [tr]; (mow, as w scythe or reaper), falĉi [tr]; **reaper**, ~maŝino; falĉatoro, falĉomaŝino [cp "combine", "scythe", "sickle"]; **reaper and binder**, rikolt-garbiga kombajno

rear, (back, hind), malantaŭo; ~a; (educate children etc.), eduki [tr]; (breed animals), bredi [tr]; (stand on hind legs, as horse), baŭmi [int]; (mil; sport; etc.), ariero; (buttocks), postaĵo. (colloq), pugo; **at (to) the rear**, **rearward**, ~e(n), poste(n); retroira; retroen

reason, (think, argue logically), rezoni [int]; ~ado; (logic, rational process), racio; (explanation), kialo; (cause), kialo, kaŭzo; (purpose), motivo; **reasonable**, (sensible), bonsenca, senchava; (moderate), modera; (not expensive), nemultekosta; (able to reason), ~iva; **reasoning**, ~ado; **for some reason**, ial; **for any reason (at all)**, ial (ajn); **for what(ever) reason**, kial (ajn); **for that reason**, tial, pro tio; **for this reason**, ĉi tial, tial ĉi; **for every reason (at all)**, ĉial (ajn); **for no reason (at all)**, nenial (ajn); **for the same (a different) reason**, (mal)samkial, pro la (mal)sama kialo; **there is no reason not to, there is no reason why one should not**, nenial oni ne ~u (e.g.: *there is no reason not to tell you what happened:* nenial mi ne diru al vi kio okazis); **the reason why**, la kialo kial, la kialo pro kio; **that is the reason why**, jen kial; **by reason of**, (because of), pro; **without rhyme or reason**, tute senkiale, tute

nenial; **within reason**, laŭ modereco; **it stands to reason (that)**, ĝi logike sekvas (logike sekvas ke)

Reaumur, Reaŭmura

rebate, rabati [tr]; ~o

rebec, ribeko

Rebecca, Rebeka

rebeck, ribeko

rebel, ribeli [int]; ~anto; ~ulo; **rebellion**, ~o; **rebellious**, ~ema

rebound, resalto; ~iĝi

rebuff, rifuzi [tr], malakcepti [tr], repuŝi [tr]; ~o, malakcepto, repuŝo

rebuke, riproĉi [tr]; ~o

rebus, rebuso

rebut, refuti [tr]; **rebuttal**, ~o

recalcitrant, kontumaca, kalcitr(em)a, ribelema; **recalcitrance**, ~o, kalcitremo, ribelemo

recall, (remember), (re)memori [tr]; ~o; (call back, revoke), revoki [tr]; revoko

recant, forkonfesi [tr]; **recantation**, ~o

recap, (tire), retegi [tr]; ~ita pneŭo, ~itaĵo; (recapitulate), resumi [tr]; resumo

recapitulate, resumi [tr]; **recapitulation**, ~o

recede, retiriĝi

receipt, (written acknowledgement of receipt of $ or object), kvitanco; (receiving), ricev(ad)o; (recipe), recepto; ($ received), enspezo; **give a receipt (for)**, ~i [tr] (ion al iu) (e.g.: *he gave me a receipt for my payment:* li ~is al mi mian pagon)

receive, (gen), ricevi [tr]; ($ income), enspezi [tr]; (guests), akcepti [tr]; (stolen goods), riceli [tr]; **receiver**, (person etc.), ~anto; (elec: radio etc.), ~ilo; ($ agent, as in bankruptcy), sindiko; (of stolen goods), ricelisto

recent, lasta, ~atempa, freŝdata; **recently**, ~(atemp)e, antaŭ nelonge; **recent times**, ~aj tempoj

receptacle, (any container), ujo; (elec or oth socket), ingo; (bot), receptaklo, toruso

reception, (receiving, gen), ricev(ad)o; (formal party), akcepto; **receptive**, ~(em)a, akcept(em)a; **receptionist**, akceptist(in)o [see "receive"]

recess, (pause, break in activity), paŭzi [int]; ~igi; ~o; (close meeting etc.), fermi [tr]; fermiĝi; (niche), niĉo; (nook, alcove), alkovo, kaŝangulo, anguleto; (anat), receso; (any cavity), kav(et)o; (set back, as into niche), enniĉigi, malelstarigi; **recessed**, fermita; malelstara

recession, (going back, receding, regression), regreso, retroiro; ($, bsns), recesio†

recessive, recesivo; ~a

recessus, receso

recherche, (rare, choice), rara

recidivation, recidivo;   **recidivism**, ~emo; **recidivist**, ~ulo

Recife, Recifo

recipe, recepto

recipient, ricev/into; ~anto; ~onto

reciprocal, (gen), reciproka; ~o; **reciprocate**, ~i [tr]; **reciprocity**, ~eco

recitative, recitativo

recite, reciti [tr]; **recitation**, ~(ad)o; **recital**, (mus), recitalo

reckless, malprudenta,   sendisciplina, temerara, troriskema

reckon, (compute), kalkuli [tr]; (consider), konsideri [tr]; (think, suppose), supozi [tr]; **reckoning**, (accounting, lit or fig), konto; **reckon on**, (rely on), kalkuli je, fidi [tr]

reclaim, (gen), regajni [tr], revalorigi, reutiligi; **reclamation**, ~(ad)o, revalorigo, reutiligo

recline, kuŝ/igi, klini [tr]; ~iĝi, kliniĝi; **recliner**, (chair), klinseĝo

recluse, ermito

recognizance, kaŭcio

recognize, (know),   rekoni   [tr]; (acknowledge; pol), agnoski [tr]; (officially approve), aprobi [tr]; **recognition**, ~o; agnosko; aprobo

recoil, (draw back, retreat), retir/iĝi, sin ~i; sin~o; (as gun, spring), repuŝi [tr]; repuŝiĝi; repuŝo; **recoilless**, senrepuŝa

recollect, (re)memori [tr]; **recollection**, ~(ad)o

recommend, rekomendi [tr]; **recommendation**, ~o; **recommendable**, ~inda; **letter of recommendation**, ~oletero

recompense, rekompenci [tr]

reconcile, (make agree, gen), akordigi;

(pacify), repacigi; **reconciliation**, ~o; repacigo; **irreconcilable**, ne~ebla

recondite, profunda

reconnaissance, rekognosko; ~a

reconnoiter, rekognoski [tr]

record, (put in writing, register, gen), registri [tr]; ~iĝi; ~o; (chronicle), kroniki [tr]; (show, as on instrument dial), montri [tr]; (phonograph), (gramofon)disko; (sound or video onto tape), ~i, surbendigi; (greatest amount achieved), rekordo; rekorda (e.g.: *a record high temperature:* rekorda maksimuma temperaturo; *break, tie the record:* rompi, egali la rekordon); **recordation**, ~ado; **recorder**, (one who records), ~isto; (machine, oth than sound or video tape recorder), ~ilo; (audio tape), magnetofono; (flute), bekfluto; **recording**, ~aĵo; surbendigo; disko; bendo; **records**, (archive), arkivo; **record player**, gramofono; **prerecord**, antaŭsurbendigi; antaŭ~i [tr]; **self-recording**,   mem~a;   **tape-record**, surbendigi; **tape recorder**, (using magnetic tape), magnetofono; **digital audio tape recorder**, cifera aŭdben-domaŝino; **videocassette recorder**, **videotape recorder**, aŭdvida magnetofono; [see also "tape"] **off the record**, malpublika, konfidenca; malpublike, konfidence; **on the record**, publika, oficiala; publike, oficiale; **go on record**, oficiale [or] publike deklari [tr]

recount, (count again), renombri [tr]; ~o; (narrate, relate), rakonti [tr]

recoup, (recover, gen), rekuperi† [tr], regajni [tr], reakiri [tr]; ($), reenspezi [tr]

recourse, (means), rimedo; **have recourse to**, sin turni al

recover, (get back), reakiri [tr], regajni [tr]; (compensate), rekompenci [tr]; (regain health), resaniĝi [cp "convalesce"]; (regain self-control etc.), reekregi sin; (normalize), renormaliĝi; **recovery**, ~o, regajno; rekompenco; resaniĝo; reekrego; renormaliĝo

recreation, distr/iĝo; ~aĵo; **recreational**, ~a

recrement, rekremento
recriminate, kontraŭriproĉi [tr]; **re-crimination**, ~(ad)o
recrudesce, reelrompiĝi, reintensiĝi
recruit, (mil), rekruti [tr]; ~o; (oth), varbi [tr]; varbito; **recruitment**, ~ado; varbado; **recruiter, recruiting officer**, ~isto
rectangle, ortangulo; **rectangular**, ~a
rectenna, rekteno*
rectify, (correct), korekti [tr]; (chem, elec, etc.), rektifiki [tr]; **rectifier**, (elec), rektifikilo
rectilinear, rektlinia
rectitude, honesteco, ĝusteco
rector, (rel: head of parish), paroĥestro; (in univ etc.), rektoro; **rectory**, ~ejo; (benefice), benefico
rectum, rektumo; **rectal**, ~a; **rectitis**, ~ito
rectus, rekta muskolo
recumbent, kuŝ(ant)a
recuperate, (health), konvaleski [int], resaniĝi; (strength), refortiĝi; ($ losses etc.), regajni [tr]; **recuperation**, ~o, resaniĝo; refortiĝo; regajno
recur, ripetiĝi, reokazi [int]; **recurrence**, ~o, reokazo; **recurrent**, ~anta, perioda, ripetiĝema; (anat), rekuranta
Recurvirostra avoceta, avoceto
recusant, neobe/anto; ~(em)a
rec-vee, [see "vehicle"]
red, ruĝa; ~o; **redden**, ~igi; ~iĝi; **Red Sea**, Maro R~a; **redstart**, (*Phoenicurus*), fenikuro; **redwood**, (tree: *Sequoia sempervirens*), sekvojo; (wood), sekvoja ligno [see "sequoia"]; **infrared**, infra~a; infra~o; **Congo red**, Kongo-~a; Kongo-~o; **poppy red**, punca; punco; see **red**, koleregi [int]
redeem, (buy back, recover, exchange), reaĉeti [tr]; (pay off), kvitigi; (convert stocks etc. to cash), monigi; (ransom), elaĉeti [tr]; (rel: free from sin etc.), redempti† [tr]; (make amends), kompensi [tr]; (justify), pravigi; **redemption**, ~o; kvitigo; monigo; redempt(iĝ)o†; kompenso; pravigo; **Redeemer**, (rel), Redemptoro, Elaĉetinto

redingote, redingoto
redolent, odor/anta; **redolence**, ~o
redouble, (intensify, as effects), intensigi; (bridge), reduobligo
redoubt, reduto
redound, (have effect), efikiĝi; (react), reagi [int], reakcii [int]
redox, redoksa; ~o
redress, (rectify, set right), reĝustigi, rebonigi, kompensi [tr]; ~o, rebonigo, kompenso
reduce, (lessen, gen; chem: downgrade), redukti [tr]; ~iĝi; (moderate), moderigi; moderiĝi; (order, systematize), ordi [tr], sistemigi; (change form), aliformigi; (break up), disrompi [tr], disigi; (pulverize), pulvorigi; (thin, dilute), dilui [tr]; **reducer**, (phot), ~enzo; (pipe fitting), ~a peco; **reduction**, ~(iĝ)(ad)o; moderigo; moderiĝo; ordado, sistemigo; aliformigo; disrompo, disigo; pulvorigo; dilu(ad)o; **reducing agent**, (chem), ~enzo; **irreducible**, ne~ebla
redundant, (gen), pleonasma, superflua; (gram; tech), redundanca†; **redundancy**, ~o; redundanco†
reed, (bot: *Phragmites*), fragmito; (cane, gen), kano; (of mus instrument), anĉo; **sand reed**, amofilo; **reed instrument**, anĉ–instrumento
reef, (of coral etc.), rifo; (re sail), refo; refi [tr]
reek, fetori [int], stinki [int], haladzi [int], odoraĉi [int]; ~o, stinko, haladzo, odoraĉo
reel, (spool), bobeno; (large, as for cable), ~ego; (wind onto), ~i [tr]; (stagger, sway), ŝanceliĝi; (be dizzy), kapturniĝi; (dance; tune), rilo*; **reel off**, (lit or fig), el~igi; **take-off reel**, malvolva ~o; **take-up reel**, volva ~o
refectory, refektorio
refer, refer to, (allude to), aludi [tr], mencii [tr] (e.g.: *I refer to your letter:* mi ~as vian leteron); (submit, as for determination), submeti [tr], prezenti [tr]; (return), resendi [tr] (e.g.: *refer the proposal to the committee for clarification:* resendi la proponon al la komitato por klarigo); (direct someone for aid etc.), direkti [tr] (al); (con-

sult, go to for aid etc.), konsulti [tr], sin turni (al); (relate), rilati [int] (al); (deal w, have to do w), temi [int] pri; (give as reference in book, scholarly work, etc.), referenci [tr]; (describe topic etc. before sci meeting etc.), referi [tr]; **reference,** ~o; referenco; **referral,** submeto; resendo; direkta-do; konsulto, sinturno; **cross-refer,** krucreferenci [tr]; **cross-reference,** krucreferenco; **with reference to,** koncerne (~on, al ~o), rilate (~on, al ~o), pri (~o) (e.g.: *I am writing with reference to your proposal:* mi skribas koncerne vian proponon [or] pri via propono)

referee, (gen), arbitracii [tr]; ~anto; ~isto

referendary, referendario

referendum, referendumo

refine, rafini [tr]; **refinement,** ~ado; ~aĵo; ~iteco; (manners etc.), bonedu-kiteco; **refined,** ~ita; bonedukita; **re-finery,** ~ejo

reflect, (bounce radiation back; repro-duce image or idea, lit or fig), reflekti [tr], speguli [tr]; ~iĝi; (ponder, think), pensi [int] (pri); kontempli [tr], konsideri [tr]; **reflection,** ~o; ~ado, spegulado; kontemplado, pensado, konsiderado; **reflector,** (gen), ~ilo; (esp to focus light etc. into beam), re-flektoro; **reflect on,** (think about), pripensi [tr], kontempli [tr]; (have ef-fect, influence), reefiki [int] sur

reflex, reflekso; ~a; **conditioned re-flex,** influita ~o

reflexive, (gram), refleksivo; ~a

reform, reformi [tr]; ~o; ~ado; ~iĝo; **Reformation,** (rel), Reformacio; **re-formatory,** ~ejo

refract, refrakti [tr]; **refraction,** ~o; **re-fractive,** ~a; **refractor,** ~ilo; (esp ast), ~oro; **refractometer,** ~ometro; **refractive index,** ~indico

refractory, (heat-resistant), refraktara; (obstinate), obstina, kalcitr(em)a

refrain, (hold back), sin deteni; (mus), refreno, rekantaĵo

refresh, refreŝigi; **refresher,** (e.g., course), renoviga (kurso)

refrigerate, frid/igi; **refrigerator,** ~ujo; **refrigeration,** ~igado; **refrig-eration unit,** (motor, coils, etc.), ~igi-lo; **refrigerant,** ~igenzo

refuge, (protection), rifuĝo; (place of), ~ejo; **take refuge,** ~i [int]; **refugee,** ~into

refulgent, brilega, radianta

refund, repagi [tr], ristorni [tr]; ~o, ris-torno

refurbish, renovigi, refreŝigi

refuse, (reject, decline, etc.), rifuzi [tr]; (rubbish), rubo; **refusal,** ~o

refute, refuti [tr]; **refutation,** ~o; **irre-futable,** ne~ebla

regal, reĝeca

regale, regali [tr]

regalia, (any insignia), insignaro; (of king, queen), reĝ(in)a ~o

regard, (look at), rigardi [tr]; ~o; (con-sider, view), ~i, konsideri [tr]; ~o; (at-tention, concern), atento; (respect), respekto; (relation), rilato; (esteem), estimi [tr]; estimo; **regarding, as re-gards, with regard to,** koncerne, rilate (~on, al ~o), pri (~o) (e.g.: *your letter regarding [with regard to] our up-coming visit:* via letero koncerne nian baldaŭan viziton [or] pri nia bal-daŭa vizito); **regardless,** malgraŭe, malgraŭ tio, malgraŭ ĉio; **regardless of,** malgraŭ, senkonsidere al, sen-rigarde al; **disregard,** malatenti [tr], ignori [tr]; malatento, ignoro; **kind regards,** bondeziroj; **self-regard,** digno, memrespekto; **give her my re-gards,** salutu ŝin por mi

regatta, regatto

Regensburg, (city in Bavaria), Ratis-bono

regent, (substitute for monarch), re-gento; (member of ruling board etc.), reganto; **regency,** (condition), ~eco; (country under regent), ~ujo; reganta-ro; reganteco

reggae, regeo†

regicide, (act), reĝomortigo; (person), ~into

regime, reĝimo

regimen, (diet), dieto

regiment, (mil), regimento; (organize), ~igi

Regina, (woman's name), Reĝina;

(city), ~o
Reginald, Rejnaldo
region, (gen), regiono; **regional**, ~a;
  regionalism, ~ismo
register, (written or oth record of;
  mus), registri [tr]; ~iĝi; ~o; (show,
  make or be visible or perceived),
  montri [tr]; montriĝi; (enter name, enroll, gen), enskribi [tr]; enskribiĝi; (in
  school or oth organization), matrikuli
  [tr]; matrikuliĝi; matrikulo; (any list),
  listo, ~o; enlistigi; (book), ~olibro;
  (registrar), arkivisto, aktisto; (one
  who registers), ~isto; matrikulisto;
  (grating, air duct cover), krado
registrar, (in university etc.), matrikulisto; (any keeper of records), arkivisto, aktisto
registry, (list, register), registro, matrikulo; (office), ~ejo, arkivo; (certificate re nationality of ship), landatesto
rego, (Aus), (aŭtomobila) registrajo
regolith, mantelroko
regress, regresi [int]; **regression**,
  ~(ad)o; **regressive**, ~(em)a
regret, bedaŭri [tr]; ~o; **regrettable**,
  ~inda
regular, (conforming to rule, norm,
  etc.; symmetrical, harmonious, etc.;
  geom; gram), regula; (on time), akurata; (usual), kutima; (ordinary), ordinara; **regularize**, ~igi [cp "regulate"];
  irregular, ne~a; neakurata; nekutima;
  neordinara; (uneven), malebena; **ir-
  regularity**, ne~aĵo; ne~eco; male-
  benaĵo
regulate, (control, govern), reguli [tr],
  regi [tr, int]; (regularize), ~igi; (subject to rules and regulations), ~igi,
  reglamenti [tr]; **regulation**, ~(ig)ado;
  (a rule), reglamento; **rules and regulations**, ~oj kaj reglamentoj; **regulator**, ~ilo, ~atoro, ~ilo; **regulatory**,
  ~iga, reglamenta; **self-regulating**,
  memrega; **thermoregulate**, termore-
  gi [tr]; **thermoregulator**, termoregilo
Regulus, (man's name), Regulo; (ast),
  Reguluso
Regulus, (zool), regolo
regurgitate, regurgiti [int]; pri~i [tr]
rehabilitate, (restore person's work
  ability), rekapabligi; (restore good

condition of person or thing), rebonstatigi; (reinstate to rank etc.), rerangi-
  gi, reinstali [tr]; (pol), rehabiliti†
rehash, re(pri)trakti [tr]; ~o
rehearse, (mus), provludi [tr]; (singing), provkanti [tr] (e.g.: *we rehearsed
  the Beethoven symphony:* ni ~is la
  simfonion de Betoveno); (drill, train),
  trejni [tr]; trejniĝi (e.g.: *the conductor
  rehearsed the orchestra on Beethoven:* la kondukisto trejnis la or-
  kestron pri Betoveno); (theat), provrolado; (recite), reciti [tr]; (narrate),
  rakonti [tr]; **rehearsal**, ~(ad)o; prov-
  kant(ad)o; provrolado; trejn(iĝ)(ad)o;
  recit(ad)o; rakont(ad)o; **dress rehearsal**, fina ~o (provkanto, provrolado), kostuma provrolado
Reich, regno, R~o
reign, reĝi [int]; ~ado, rego
reimburse, ristorni [tr], kompensi [tr]
Reims, Remso
rein, brid/rimeno; **rein in**, **draw rein**,
  ~i [tr]; **give (free) rein to**, mal~i [tr];
  take the reins, alpreni la regon; **keep
  a (close, tight) rein on**, konservi regon super
reindeer, boaco
reinette, (apple), renedo
reinforce, (make stronger), plifortikigi;
  plifortigi [see "strong"]; (re concrete
  etc.), armaturi [tr]; **reinforcement**,
  ~o; plifortigo; armaturo; **reinforce-
  ments**, (mil etc.), helpotrupoj; **reinforced concrete**, armaturita betono,
  ferbetono
reis, rejso
reiterate, ripeti [tr]
reject, (refuse), rifuzi [tr], malakcepti
  [tr]; ~aĵo; (throw away), elĵeti [tr];
  elĵetaĵo; difektaĵo
rejoice, jubili [int], ĝoji [int]
rejuvenate, rejun/igi; **become rejuve-
  nated**, ~iĝi
relapse, recidivi [int]; ~o
relate, (be connected w, have relationship), rilati [int]; ~igi; (concern), koncerni [tr]; (tell), rakonti [tr]; **related**,
  ~a; (kin, re person, word, idea, etc.),
  parenca; (analogous), analoga, koneksa; **related by blood**, sangoparenca;
  related by marriage, boparenca; **re-

lation, (related person), parenco [see "relative"]; (relationship), ~o; **in relation to**, (about, concerning), koncerne (–on, al –o), pri (–o) [see "regard"], ~e al; **relationship**, (any relating), ~o; relatedness), parenceco

relative, (not absolute; comparative), relativa; (related person etc.), parenco [cp "agnate", "cognate"]; (that relates), rilata; **relativity**, ~eco; **relativism**, ~ismo; **relativistic**, ~eca; ~isma; **relative to**, (about, concerning), koncerne, rilate (–on, al –o), pri (–o) [see "regard"]; **blood relative**, sangoparenco; **relative by marriage**, boparenco

relax, (gen), malstreĉi [tr]; ~iĝi, ~i sin; (med, psych), relaksi† [tr]; relaksiĝi†; (moderate), moderigi; [cp "relief"]

relay, mech, elec, etc.), relajso; (crew, shift), skipo; (pass on, give over), transdoni [tr], transsendi [tr], resendi [tr]; **relay race**, stafetkurado; **relay runner**, stafetkuranto

release, (let loose), delasi [tr]; ~iĝi; ~o; (free), liberigi; liberiĝi; liberigo; (let out), ellasi [tr]; ellasiĝi; ellaso; (fastener, hook, etc.), ellasilo; (mech: disconnect), malkupli [tr]; malkupliĝi; malkuplo; malkuplilo; (unhook), malhoki [tr]; malhokiĝi; (unfasten), malfiksi [tr]; malfiksiĝi; (untie), malligi [tr]; malligiĝi; (unblock), malbloki [tr]; malblokiĝi; (relieve of debt, duty), kvitigi; (of worry, care, etc.), senzorgigi, senĉagrenigi; (allow back to original state or position, as action, pressure), relasi [tr]; relasiĝi; (unhire), maldungi [tr]; (allow or cause publication), eldonigi; (put into circulation), cirkuligi; (document giving up right etc.; quitclaim), kvit-atesto; **quick-release**, rapid~a; rapidmalfiksa

relegate, relegacii [tr]; **relegation**, ~o

relent, (give in, yield), cedi [tr, int]; (become less severe), mildiĝi, malobstiniĝi; **relentless**, senkompata, sen~a; (unremitting), senĉesa, persista

relevant, rilata, koncerna; **irrelevant**, ne~a, indiferenta; **relevance**, ~eco; **be (ir)relevant**, (ne) ~i [int]

reliable, fid/inda; **reliance**, ~o; **reliant**, ~a; **be reliant on**, ~i (–on, je –o); (be dependent), dependi [int] de; **self-reliance**, mem~o; sindependado

relic, relikvo

relief, (easing of pain, burden, etc.), malŝarĝo, faciligo; (of tension, strain, etc., gen), trankviligo, senzorgigo, senĉagrenigo, malstreĉ(iĝ)o; (of tension, tech), senŝarĝiĝo; (from debt, duty), kvitigo; (help, gen), helpo; (official help or assistance, as for welfare, disaster, etc.), asisto; (person(s) who relieve), helpant(ar)o; asistant(ar)o; (replacement), anstataŭanto, anstataŭulo; anstataŭajo; (legal redress), kompenso; (difference in height, depth, color, light and darkness, or oth contrast, as in arch, sculpture, geog area, etc.; analogous distinction), reliefo; reliefa (e.g.: *the temple was ornamented with reliefs, with sculptures in relief:* la templo estis ornamita per reliefoj, per reliefaj skulptajoj; *relief map:* reliefmapo; *the disaster put the problem into relief:* la katastrofo reliefigis la problemon); **relieve**, ~i [tr], faciligi; trankviligi, senzorgigi, senĉagrenigi, malstreĉi [tr]; kvitigi; helpi [tr]; asisti [tr]; anstataŭi [tr]; kompensi [tr]; reliefigi; [cp "relax"]

religion, (abstract, or a religious sect, system, etc.), religio; **religious**, ~a; (member of religious order), ~ulo; **state religion**, ŝtat~o†

relinquish, rezigni [tr], cedi [tr]

reliquary, relikvujo

relish, (flavor), saporo; (food), frandaĵo; (eat for enjoyment, flavor), frandi [tr]; (zest, enjoyment), vervo, entuziasmo, ĝuo; (enjoy), ĝui [tr], ŝati [tr], entuziasmiĝi pri

reluctant, malvolonta, malinklina, hezit(em)a; **reluctance**, ~eco, malinklino, hezit(em)o; (elec), relŭktanco

rely, rely on, (trust), fidi (–on, je –o); (depend on), dependi [int] de, kalkuli kun

remain, resti [int]; **remains**, ~aĵo(j); (ruins), ruino(j); **remaining**, (the rest), cetera(j), ~(ant)a(j); **remainder**, cetero, ~o; (sell), rabatvendi [tr]; **remaindered**, (bsns: re left-over stock), ekssortimenta†

remand, resendi [tr]; ~o; **on remand**, ~ita; ~ite

remanence, remanenco

remark, (notice), rimarki [tr]; ~o; (comment), ~i, ~igi; ~o; **remarkable**, ~inda

Rembrandt, Rembranto

remedy, (correct, relieve), reĝustigi, rebonigi; (med), kuracenzo; (means), rimedo; **remediable**, ~ebla, rebonigebla; kuracebla; **remedial**, ~a, reboniga; kuraca

remember, memori [tr]; **remembrance**, ~(ad)o; ~aĵo; **remember me to (someone)**, salutu (iun) por mi

Remijo, Remiĝo

remind, (re)memorigi; **reminder**, ~aĵo, ~ilo

reminisce, rememor/adi [tr]; **reminiscence**, ~ado; **reminiscent**, ~iga

remiss, malatenta, malzorga, neglekta; **be remiss in**, ~i [tr], malzorgi [tr], neglekti [tr]

remission, (med), remito; intermito; (pardon), pardono

remit, (pay), (trans)pagi [tr]; (pardon), pardoni [tr]; (slacken, relax, as efforts), malstreĉi [tr], moderigi; malstreĉiĝi, moderiĝi; (submit), submeti [tr]; (put back), remeti [tr]; (postpone), prokrasti [tr]; (med), remitiĝi; **remittance**, ~o, rimeso; **unremitting**, senĉesa, persista

remnant, restaĵo

remolade, remolado

remonstrate, protesti [tr]; **remonstrance**, ~o

remorse, rimorso; **remorseful**, ~a; **remorseless**, sen~a; **feel remorse**, ~i [int]

remote, (distant), malproksima, fora; (indirect), nerekta; (aloof), indiferenta; **remote control**, telekomandi [tr]; telekomand(ad)o

remoulade, remolado

remount, (mil), remonto

remove, (take away, do away w. gen), for/igi, ~preni [tr]; ~iĝi; (take off clothing), demeti [tr]; (person from

office etc.), eksigi; (from job), maldungi [tr]; (move away), ~movi [tr]; ~moviĝi; (change residence), transloĝiĝi; transloĝiĝo; **removal**, ~igo, ~preno; ~iĝo; demeto; eksigo; maldungo; ~mov(iĝ)o; transloĝiĝo

remunerate, kompensi [tr]; **remuneration**, ~(ad)o; ~aĵo; **remunerative**, ~a [cp "earn", "salary", "pay"]

Remus, Remo

renaissance, renesanco; **Renaissance**, R~o

renal, rena; **suprarenal**, super~a

renascent, renaskiĝanta

Renato, (man's name), Renato; **Renata**, (woman's name), ~a

rend, (rip), ŝiri [tr]; ~iĝi; **heart-rending**, kor~a

render, (give), doni [tr]; (hand over), trans~i [tr]; (give back), re~i [tr]; (make, cause to be), igi, ~igi [sfx], fari [tr] (e.g.: _render something harmless:_ sendanĝerigi ion [or] igi (fari) ion sendanĝera); (provide), provizi [tr]; (represent, show), prezenti [tr], montri [tr]; (perform mus etc.), ludi [tr], prezenti [tr]; kanti [tr]; (act theat role etc.), roli [int] (kiel); (translate), traduki [tr]; (melt fat from), sengrasigi; (declare, as verdict), deklari [tr]; (plaster), stuki [tr]

rendezvous, rendevui [tr]; ~iĝi; (meeting), ~o; (place of meeting), ~ejo

rendition, (mus), prezento, ludo; (theat), ~o, rolado

renegade, renegato

renege, (not fulfill), malplenumi [tr] (promeson, konsenton); (cards), misludi [tr]; missekvi [int]

renitent, renit/anta; **renitence**, ~ado; **be renitent**, ~i [int]

rennet, (curdling substance), kazeigenzo

rennin, ĉimozino

renounce, (give up thing, claim, etc.), rezigni [tr] [cp "abdicate"]; (belief, activity, etc.), forkonfesi [tr]; (disown, disinherit), malkonfesi [tr], senheredigi; (cards), renonci [tr]; **renunciation**, ~o; forkonfeso; malkonfeso; renonco

renovate, (renew), renovigi, refari [tr]; (remodel), redekoracii [tr], ~i

renown, renomo; **renowned,** ~a; **become renowned,** ~iĝi

rent, (receive for $), lui [tr]; (give for $), ~igi; ($ paid), ~prezo, ~pago; (tear), ŝiro; **rental,** ~a: ~(ig)ado; ~prezo, ~pago; (place, e.g., apartment), ~ejo; (thing, e.g., car), ~aĵo; **for rent,** ~igota

renunciation, [see "renounce"]

rep, (fabric), repso

repair, (mend, fix), ripari [tr]; ~(ad)o; ~a; (renew, restore), renovigi; (remedy, set right), reĝustigi, rebonigi; (compensate, make amends), kompensi [tr]; (go), iri [int]; **disrepair,** kadukeco, malbona stato; **in good (bad, poor) repair,** en (mal)bona stato

reparation, (repairing), ripar(ad)o; renovigo; reĝustigo, rebonigo; (compensation), kompenso; [see "repair"]; (for legal or war damages), reparacio

repartee, sprita respond(ad)o, sprita replik(ad)o

repast, manĝo

repatriate, repatrujigi

repeal, nuligi, revoki [tr]; ~o, revoko

repeat, ripeti [tr]; ~iĝi; ~ita; ~(aĵ)o; (symbol, as in mus), ~osigno

repel, (ward off), repeli [tr], forpeli [tr], forpuŝi [tr]; (re magnets), repuŝi (sin), repuŝiĝi; (reject), malakcepti [tr], rifuzi [tr]; (opp "attract"), mallogi [tr]; (be resistant to), ne tralasi [tr] [cp "proof"]; **repellent,** ~a, forpela; malloga; netralasema (e.g.: *a water-repellent coat:* palto netralasema al akvo); (solution for fabrics etc.), netralasaĵo; (for insects etc.), forpelenzo

repent, penti [int]; **repentance,** ~(ad)o, rimorso

repercussion, (reaction, result), reakcio, reago, sekvo, konsekvenco, postefiko(j); (reflection, echo), (re)eĥo, reflekto

repertoire, repertory, (theat, mus, etc.), repertuaro

repetition, ripeto; ~ado; **repetitious,** ~ada

replenish, replenigi

replete, sata, plena

replica, repliko, kopio; (imitation), straso

replicate, (repeat), ripeti [tr]; (make replica), repliki [tr], kopii [tr]; **replication,** (reply; reproduction), repliko; (echo), eĥo; (copying), replikado, kopiado; (biol), memreplikiĝo

reply, (answer, gen), respondi [tr, int]; ~o; (in answer to demand or assertion), repliki [tr, int]; repliko

report, (account, information, etc., gen), raporti [tr]; ~o; (present self, as for duty), prezenti sin; (be responsible to), esti respondeca al; (rumor), [see "rumor"]; (noise, as of gun etc.), knalo, (paf)bruo; **reporter,** ~isto; (journalist), reportero; **reportedly,** laŭ~e, laŭdire; **report card, school report,** lernej-atesto

repose, ripozi [int]; ~o

repository, (box, chest, etc.), ten/ujo; (room, building, etc.), ~ejo

repp, repso

reprehend, riproĉi [tr]; **reprehensible,** ~inda; **reprehension,** ~o

represent, (go, act in place of; stand for, symbolize), reprezenti [tr]; (show, claim to be), prezenti [tr] (e.g.: *he represents himself as [to be] a great actor:* li prezentas sin kiel [esti] granda aktoro); (depict, portray), pentri [tr], figuri [tr], prezenti [tr], bildigi; **representation,** ~(ad)o; prezent(ad)o; prezentaĵo, figuraĵo, bildigo; **representational,** ~a; figura; **representative,** ~anto; ~isto; ~a; figura; **misrepresent,** mis~i [tr]; misprezenti [tr]

repress, (gen), repuŝi [tr], repremi [tr] [cp "suppress"]; (restrain), bridi [tr]; (stifle), sufoki [tr]; **repressive,** ~(em)a; subprema; **repression,** ~(ad)o; ~aĵo; subpremo

reprieve, (dumtempe) prokrasti [tr]; (dumtempa) prokrasto

reprimand, riproĉi [tr]; ~o

reprisal, reprezalio

reprise, (mus), ripeto, reludo; rekanto

reproach, riproĉi [tr]; ~o

reprobate, (scoundrel), kanajlo, depravaciulo; (depraved), depravacia, ~a, fia; (condemn), kondamni [tr]

reproduce, (gen), reprodukti [tr]; ~iĝi;

(copy printed material etc.), kopii [tr], multobligi; **reproduction**, ~(ad)o; ~aĵo; multoblaĵo, kopio
reprographic, reprografa†; **reprographics**, ~ado
reprove, riproĉi [tr]; **reproof**, ~o
reptile, reptilio, rampulo
Reptilia, reptiluloj, rampuloj
republic, respubliko; **republican**, ~a; ~ano; ~isto; **republicanism**, ~ismo; **Republican**, R~ano; R~ana; **People's Democratic Republic**, (communist nomenclature), Popoldemokratia R~o, Popoldemokratio
repudiate, (reject), forkonfesi [tr]; (disown), malkonfesi [tr], malagnoski [tr]; (divorce by repudiation, as per Arab etc. custom), repudii [tr]
repugnant, antipatia; **repugnance**, **repugnancy**, ~o
repulse, forpuŝi [tr], forpeli [tr]; ~o, forpelo; **repulsion**, (magnetic etc.), ~o; (distaste), antipatio; **repulsive**, (phys), ~a, forpela; (very unpleasant), malloga, naŭziga, ~a
reputable, respekt/ata, ~inda, prestiĝa
reputation, reputacio
repute, (consider), supozi [tr], konsideri [tr]; (reputation), reputacio; **reputed**, ~ata; **disrepute**, malestimo, fireputacio; **disreputable**, **of ill repute**, malestiminda, fifama, fireputacia; **of good repute**, bonfama
request, peti [tr]; ~o; **on request**, je ~o
requiem, rekviemo
require, (demand, call for), postuli [tr]; (need), bezoni [tr]; **requirement**, ~o; bezono; **as may be required**, laŭbezone, kiel necesas
requisite, necesa, postulita; ~aĵo, postulo, bezono
requisition, rekvizicii [tr]; ~o
requite, (compensate), kompensi [tr]; (give back, return, gen), redoni [tr]; **requital**, ~o; re dono
reredos, altarekrano
rescind, nuligi, malvalidigi; **rescission**, ~o, malvalidigo
rescript, reskripto
rescue, savi [tr]; ~(iĝ)o; ~a
research, reserĉi [tr], espłori [tr]; ~(ad)o, esplorado; **researcher**, ~isto,

esploristo; **research and development**, (abb: R&D), esploro kaj disvolvo [no abb in Esperanto]
resect, desekci [tr]
reseda, (color), rezedokolora
Reseda, (bot), rezedo
resemble, simili [tr]; **resemblance**, ~eco
resent, indigni [int] (pri), senti rankoron pri; **resentful**, ~a, rankora; **resentment**, ~o; rankoro
reserve, (set aside, hold), rezervi [tr]; ~o; ~a; (mood, personality), diskretemo, deteniĝemo, distancemo; (retain), reteni [tr]; (mil), ~istaro; ~ista (e.g.: *reserve officer*: ~ista oficiro; *army reserve*: armea ~istaro, ~armeo); (land area for animals, indigenous peoples, etc.), ~ejo; **reservation**, ~(ad)o; sindeteno; reteno; ~ejo; (hesitancy), hezit(em)o; (doubt), dubo; **reserves**, (supplies held back), ~aĵoj; (mil), ~oj, ~istaro; **reservist, member of the (military) reserves**, ~isto; **in reserve**, en ~iteco; **unreserved**, sen~a; **with reservations**, ~e
reservoir, (gen), rezervujo, akvo-tenejo
reside, rezidi [int], loĝi [int]; **residence**, loĝejo, ~ejo; loĝado, ~ado; **residential**, loĝeja, ~eja; **resident**, ~anto; ~anta; (government official in protectorate), rezidento; **take up residence**, ekloĝi [int]
residual, rest/anta; ~aĵo
residue, (gen), reziduo
resign, (give up, quit), rezigni [tr]; (from office, job, etc.), demisii [int], eksiĝi (el, de); **resign oneself**, (accept w/o protest), rezignacii [int]; **resignation**, ~o; demisio, eksiĝo; rezignacio; **with resignation**, **resignedly**, rezignacie
resilient, elasta; **resilience**, ~eco
resin, (gen), rezino; (for violin etc. bows), kolofono; **resinous**, ~eca; **gum resin**, gum~o
resist, rezisti [tr, int] (al), kontraŭstari [tr, int] (al); **resistant**, ~a; **resistance**, ~(ad)o; ~emo; (elec), rezistanco; (tech: resistance to push, pull, bend, etc.), ~eco; **resistor**, (elec), ~ilo; **variable resistor**, variigebla ~ilo,

reostato; **resistivity,** ~iv(ec)o; **irre-sistible,** ne~ebla

res judicata, juĝitaĵo

resolute, rezoluta; **irresolute,** ŝancel-iĝema, nedecidema, malfirma, molaĉa

resolution, (resolving), solv(iĝ)o; decido; rezolutiĝo; rezoluteco; fokusiĝo; fokusivo; apartigo; elnodiĝo; [see "resolve"]; (expression of opinion by parliament, organization, etc.), rezolucio; (med: subsidence of inflammation, muscle contraction, etc.; phot etc.: sharpness of picture; mech: replacement of one force by several equivalent; replacement of long syllable by 2 short), resolucio

resolve, (solve problem etc.), solvi [tr]; ~iĝi; (unravel story line etc.), elnodigi; elnodiĝi; (decide), decidi [tr]; (become resolute, firm), rezolutiĝi; (separate, as visual image), fokusi [tr], apartigi; fokusiĝi, apartiĝi; (intent), rezoluteco, intenco; (med: subside swelling etc.; phys; show equivalent forces), resoluciigi

resonate, resonanci [int]; **resonance,** ~o; **resonator,** resonatoro; **magnetic resonance,** (nuklea) magneta ~o†

resorcinol, rezorcinolo

resort, (for recreation etc.), feri/ejo; (means, as for help), rimedo (e.g.: *this is our last resort:* jen nia lasta rimedo); (have recourse, turn to), sin turni (al) (e.g.: *resort to violence:* sin turni al perforto); **resort town,** ~urbo; **health resort,** kuracejo; **resort resort,** lasta rimedo

resound, resoni [int], reeĥiĝi

resource, (material; means), rimedo; **resourceful,** elturniĝema, trovema

respect, (honor, esteem), respekti [tr]; ~o; (relate), rilati [int] (al); rilato; **respectable,** ~inda, deca, oportuna; **respectful,** ~(em)a; **respects,** (good wishes), bondeziroj; **disrespect,** mal~i [tr]; mal~~o; **disrespectful,** mal~(em)a, malĝentila; **pay one's respects,** prezenti sian ~on; **self-respect,** mem~o; **in some respects,** iurilate; **in that (those) respect(s),** tiurilate; **in this (these) respect(s),** ĉi-rilate; **in what respect(s),** kiuri-late; **in every (all) respect(s),** ĉiuri-late; **with all due respect,** kiu ĉiu deca ~o

respective, respektiva; **respectively,** ~e

respire, spiri [tr, int]; **respiration,** ~ado; **respirator,** (gen), en~atoro; **respiratory,** ~a

respite, ripozo

resplendence, splend/ado†, brilego; **resplendent.** ~a; **be resplendent,** ~i [int]

respond, (answer, gen), respondi [tr, int]; (react), reagi [int]; **response,** ~o; reago; (rel, mus: responsory), responsorio

responsible, (accountable; can be charged as cause, doer), responsa, respond(ec)a (e.g.: *a staff responsible only to the president:* stabo ~a nur al la prezidento; *a responsible position:* ~a posteno; *every person is responsible for the situation in which he finds himself:* ĉiu estas ~a [or: ĉiu ~as] pro la situacio en kiu li trovas sin; *water was responsible for the rust:* akvo estis ~a pro la rusto); (guilty), kulpa, ~a; (reliable), fidinda; **be responsible,** ~i [int], respondi [int]; kulpi [int]; **responsibility,** respondeco, ~eco; kulpo; **jointly responsible,** (for debts etc.), solidara

responsive, respondema, reagema

responsory, responsorio

rest, (repose, lie quietly, not move), ripozi [int]; ~igi; ~o; (from fatigue), ~igi, mallacigi; ~i, mallaciĝi; ~o, mallaciĝo; (lie, recline, be on), kuŝi [int]; kuŝigi; (tranquility), trankviligi; trankviliĝi; trankvil(ec)o; (support), apogi [tr]; sin apogi; apogilo; (remainder), cetero, rest(aĵ)o; (mus), silento; silenti [int]; (depend), dependi [int] (de); **restless,** maltrankvila, agitita, sen~a; **rest on,** (base on), bazi [tr] sur; baziĝi sur; **rest home,** ~domo; **at rest,** en ~o, senmova; **come to rest,** halti [int]; **unrest,** malpaco, malkvieteco, tumultemo, agitiĝo; **whole rest,** (mus), plensilento; **half rest,** duon-silento; **quarter rest,** kvaronsilento; **let rest,** (leave alone), lasi [tr]; **lay to**

rest, (bury), enterigi; **set to rest**, (ease, calm), trankviligi, kvietigi

restaurant, restoracio; **restaurateur**, ~isto; **fast-food restaurant**, krakmanĝejo

restitution, restitu/ado; ~aĵo; **make restitution (to)**, ~i [tr]

restive, (unruly), ribelema; (restless), maltrankvila, malkvieta

restore, (to original condition, state, rank), restaŭri [tr]; (put back), remeti [tr]; (make restitution), restitui [tr]; (revive), revigligi, revivigi; (reestablish), reestabli [tr], restarigi

restrain, (hold back, curb), bridi [tr], bremsi [tr]; (deprive of freedom), malliberigi, deteni [tr]; (stifle), sufoki [tr]; (tie), ligi [tr]; (moderate), moderigi; (limit), limigi; **restraint**, (act), (sin)~ado; malliberigo, deteno; sufoko; moderigo; modereco; limigo; (device), ~ilo, detenilo, ligilo; limigilo; **self-restraint**, memregado, sinbrid(ad)o

restrict, restrikti [tr], limigi; **restriction**, ~o; **restrictive**, ~a

result, rezulti [int]; ~o; **resultant**, ~a; (math, phys: sum of vectors), ~anto; **result in**, ~igi; **as a result of**, ~e de

resume, rekomenci [tr]; ~iĝi; **resumption**, ~(iĝ)o

résumé (viv)resumo; **give (write) a résumé (of)**, ~i [tr]

resurge, releviĝi, reviviĝi; **resurgence**, ~o, reviviĝo; **resurgent**, ~anta

resurrect, (rel), resurekti [int]; ~igi; (gen), relevi [tr]; **resurrection**, ~(ig)o; relev(iĝ)o; **resurrection plant**, anastatiko, jerikorozo

resuscitate, reanimi† [tr]; ~iĝi; **resuscitation**, ~ado; **resuscitator**, ~igilo

ret, rui [tr]

retable, retablo

retail, detali [tr]; ~iĝi; ~ado; po~a; po~e; **retailer**, ~isto

retain, (hold back), reteni [tr]; (keep, conserve), konservi [tr]; (hire), dungi [tr]; **retainer**, (fee), dungopago, antaŭhonorario; (device), ~ilo, ~framo

retaliate, kontraŭataki [tr], fari reprezalio(j)n (kontraŭ); **retaliation**, ~o, reprezalio

retard, malakceli [tr]; ~iĝi; ~(iĝ)o; **retarded**, (person), malfruiĝinta; **retardation**, ~(iĝ)o; **mental retardation**, intelekta malfruiĝo; **retardate**, malfruiĝinto

retch, duonvomi [int]

retention, reteno; konserv(ad)o; dungo; [see "retain"]; **retentive**, ~(em)a

reticent, silentema, malkomunikema, malparolema

reticle, reteto

reticule, (handbag), retikulo; (reticle), reteto; **reticular**, ~a; **reticulate**, ~hava

reticulum, retikulo; **reticulosis**, ~ozo; **reticuloendothelial**, ~oendotelia

retina, retino; **retinal**, ~a; **retinaculum**, retinaklo; **retinitis**, ~ito; **retinopathy**, ~opatio

retinue, sekvantaro

retire, (cease career for pension), pensii [tr]; ~iĝi, emeritiĝi; (withdraw), retiri [tr]; sin retiri, retiriĝi; (to bed), enlitiĝi; (pay off debt etc.), kvitigi; **retired**, emerita, ~iĝinta; **retiree**, **retired person**, emerito, ~ulo; **retirement**, emeritiĝo, ~iĝo; retir(iĝ)o; enlitiĝo; kvitigo; **retiring**, (reserved, modest), modesta, retiriĝema

retort, (reply), repliki [tr, int]; ~o; (chem), retorto

retract, (pull back), retiri [tr]; (disavow statement etc.), malkonfesi [tr]

retreat, (pull back, withdraw, gen), retiri [tr]; ~iĝi; ~(iĝ)o; (mil), retreti [int]; retreto; (quiet, secluded place), retretejo†, izolejo; (refuge), rifuĝejo; (withdrawal to secluded place), retreto†; (gathering), retretkuniĝo†

retribution, venĝo, (meritita) puno

retrieve, (get back), repreni [tr], reakiri [tr]; (find), retrovi [tr]; **retrieval**, ~o, reakiro; retrovo; **retriever**, (dog), trovhundo; **information retrieval**, informa retrovo

retro, (adj: rear, back), retroa; (rocket), ~raketo

retro–, (pfx), retro– (e.g.: *retroactive*: ~aktiva)

retroflex, retrofleks/ita; **retroflexion**, ~iĝo

retrograde, retroira

retrogress, regresi [int], malprogresi [int]; **retrogression,** ~o, malprogreso

retrorse, retrofleksita

retrospect, retrospektivo; **retrospective,** ~a; **retrospection,** retrorigard(ad)o; **in retrospect,** ~e

retroversion, retroturniĝo

return, (come back), reveni [int]; ~o; ~a; (go back), reiri [int]; reiro; (send back), resendi [tr]; resendo; resendaĵo; (give back), redoni [tr]; redono; (put back), remeti [tr]; remeto; (reciprocate), reciproki [tr]; reciproka (e.g.: *a return visit:* reciproka vizito); (compensate), kompensi [tr]; kompenso; (profit), profito; (sum repaid, as on investment, for rebate, etc.), ristorno; ristorni [tr]; (report), raporti [tr]; raporto; (sports: hit back), rebati [tr]; rebato; (retort), repliki [tr, int]; repliko; **return address,** resend-adreso, sendinto-adreso [see § 22]; **return ticket,** ~bileto; **in return,** kompense; **tax return,** impostraporto; **by return mail (post),** ~poŝte, per ~poŝto

reunion, (gathering), rekuniĝo

Réunion, (country), Reunio

rev, (speed up), akceli [tr]; ~iĝi; (revolution), rivoluo

revamp, (revise), revizii [tr]

reveal, (make appear, gen), riveli [tr], malkaŝi [tr]; (rel), revelacii [tr]

reveille, veksignalo

revel, festi [int], ĝoji [int]; ĝoj~o

revelation, rivelo, malkaŝo; revelacio [see "reveal"]; **Revelations,** (Bib), Apokalipso

revelry, festado, ĝojado

revenge, venĝi [tr]; ~o; **revengeful,** ~ema

revenue, enspezo; **Internal Revenue Service,** (Am), Enlanda Imposta Servo

reverberate, reeĥi [tr]; ~iĝi

revere, respekt/egi [tr]; **reverent,** ~ega; **reverence,** ~e go; (piety), pietato; **your Reverence,** (title of respect), via (Pastra) Moŝto; **reverend,** ~inda; (clergy), pastro [no abb in Esperanto] (e.g.: *Rev. John Jones:* Pastro John Jones); **irreverent,** mal~a,

mal~oplena; **irreverence,** mal~o

reverie, rev/ado; ~o(j)

reverse, (backward, in opp order or direction), inversa; ~o; ~igi; ~iĝi (e.g.: *reverse the direction of flow:* ~igi la direkton de fluo); (opp), malo; mala; maligi; maliĝi (e.g.: *the reverse situation:* la mala situacio); (go backwards), regresi [int], retroiri [int]; (auto gear etc.), retrorapidumo; (back side, as of coin, fabric, etc.), reverso; reversa; reversi [tr]; (judicial decision by higher court etc.), kasacii [tr]; (misfortune), sortobato, misfortuno, malfeliĉo; (defeat), malvenko; **reversal,** ~igo; ~iĝo; maligo, maliĝo; regreso, retroiro; kasacio; sortobato, misfortuno, malfeliĉo; malvenko; **reversible,** ~igebla; (cloth), reversigebla

reversion, (reverting), reveno; (property), transproprietiĝo, transposedigo; (disease of currant plant), reversio

revert, (return, gen), reveni [int]; (property to former owner), transproprietiĝi, transposediĝi

revest, reinvesti [tr]

review, (look over again; check over persons, text, etc., for fitness, accuracy, etc.; reopen court decision on appeal), revizii [tr]; ~(ad)o; (look back on), retrorigardi [tr]; retrorigardo; (reexamine), reekzameni [tr], restudi [tr]; reekzameno, restudo; (critique book, movie, etc.), recenzi [tr]; recenzo; (a magazine; revue; mil parade etc.; written article covering highlights), revuo; revui [tr]; **reviewer,** (critic), recenzisto

revile, insulti [tr]

revise, (modify), modifi [tr]; (Br: look over, check out, correct as needed), revizii [tr]; **revision,** ~o; revizio; **revisionism,** reviziiismo; **revisionist,** reviziiisma; reviziiisto

revise, reviv/igi; ~iĝi; **revisal,** (gen), ~(ig)o

revoke, (cancel etc.), revoki [tr], nuligi; (cards), missekvi [tr]; **revocation,** ~o, nuligo

revolt, (rebel), ribeli [int]; ~o; (disgust), naŭzigi; naŭziĝi; indigni [int]; in-

dignigi; **revolting**, ~anta; naŭziga, indigniga, aboneninda
revolution, (pol), revolucio; (one turn),
rivoluo, giro; (act of revolving), rotacio [cp "revolve", "rotate"]; **revolu-
tionary, revolutionist**, ~a; ~ulo,
~isto; **revolutionize, cause (bring
about) a revolution (in)**, ~i [tr]
revolve, rotacii [int], giri [int]; ~igi,
girigi [cp "rotate"]
revolver, (gun), revolvero
revue, revuo
revulsion, abomeno, naŭzo; (med), re-
vulsio
reward, rekompenci [tr]; ~o; **reward-
ing**, ~a
Reynard, Renardo
Reynold, Rejnaldo, Rinaldo†
Rh, (blood factor), resusfaktoro, Rh-
faktoro; **Rh-positive**, Rh-pozitiva
(Rh+); **Rh-negative**, Rh-negativa
(Rh–)
rhabdomancy, rabdismo, rabdomancio
Rhadamanthus, Rhadamanthys, Rad-
amantiso
Rhaetia, Retio
Rhamnus, ramno; Rhamnus alater-
nus, alaterno; Rhamnus **frangula**,
frangolo
Rhamphastus, tukano
Rhamphorhyncus, ramforinko†
rhapsody, (mus, poet), rapsodio; **rhap-
sodize**, ~i [int]; ekstazi [int]; **rhapso-
dist, rhapsode**, rapsodo
Rhea, (ast), Reo*; (myth), Rea
Rhea, (zool), reao; Rheaformes, reafor-
maj (birdoj)
Rheims, Remso
Rhein, [see "Rhine"]
rhenium, renio
rheobase, reobazo
rheology, reologio
rheostat, reostato
rhesus, resuso; **rhesus factor**, ~faktoro,
Rh-faktoro [see "Rh"]
rhetor, retoro
rhetoric, (theory of speaking), retoriko;
(specific e.g.), retorajo; **rhetorical**,
~a
Rheum, (bot), rabarbo
rheumatic, reŭmata
rheumatism, reŭmatismo

rheumatoid, reŭmatoida
rheumatology, reŭmatolog/io; **rheu-
matologist**, ~o
rheumatosis, reŭmato
Rhinanthus, rinanto
Rhine, Rejno; **Rhineland**, ~lando;
North Rhine-Westphalia, Nordrej-
no-Vestfalio
rhinestone, diamantoido
rhinitis, rinito
rhin(o)–, (anat, med pfx: nose), rin(o)–
rhinoceros, Rhinoceros, rinocero; Rhi-
nocerotidae, ~edoj
rhinology, rinolog/io; **rhinologist**, ~o
rhinoplasty, rinoplastio
rhinoscope, rinoskopo; **rhinoscopy**,
~io
Rhiptoglossa, vermolanguloj
rhizome, rizomo
rhizomorph, rizomorfo; **rhizomor-
phous**, ~a
Rhizophora mangle, manglarbo
rhizopod, rizopodo
Rhizopoda, rizopodoj
rho, rota [see § 16
], **Rhode Island**, Rod-Insulo
Rhodes, Rodiso
Rhodesia, Rodezio [cp "Zimbabwe"]
rhodium, rodio
rhododendron, Rhododendron, rodo-
dendro
Rhodope, Rodopo
Rhodophyceae, Rhodophyta, ruĝalgoj
rhomb, [see "rhombus"]
rhombohedron, romboedro
rhomboid, romboido; ~a
rhombus, rombo; **rhombic**, ~(oform)a
Rhombus laevis, (zool), rombo
rhonchus, ronko
Rhône, Rodano
rhotacism, rotaismo
rhubarb, (plant), rabarbo
rhumb, rhumb line, loksodromio
rhumba, rumbo
Rhus, sumako; Rhus radicans, Rhus
toxodendron radicans, venena ~o;
Rhus vernicicflua, Rhus vernicifera,
uruŝio
rhyme, rimo; ~i [tr]; ~iĝi; **rhymoid**,
~oido
Rhynchocephalia, rinñocefaloj
rhythm, ritmo; **rhythmic(al)**, ~a;

rhythm and blues, (mus), ritmenblusot

rib, (bone, or any similar object, stripe, etc.), ripo; (as food), ~aĵo; (tease), mokŝerci [tr]; **ribbed,** ~a, stria; **spareribs,** (porkaj) ~aĵoj

ribald, triviala; **ribaldry,** ~aĵo; ~eco

ribbon, (gen), rubando; **ink ribbon,** (for cmptr printer, etc.), ink~o

Ribes, ribo; Ribes glossularia, grosarbusto; Ribes nigrum, nigra ~o; Ribes rubrum, ruĝa ~o

ribo–, (chem pfx), ribo–

riboflavin(e), riboflavino

ribonucleic, ribonukleata

ribose, ribozo

ribosome, ribosomo*

rice, (plant or food), rizo; (reduce food to granules), grajnigi; **rice paddy,** ~ejo

rich, (gen), riĉa; **riches,** ~aĵoj; ~eco; **enrich,** ~igi

Richard, Rikardo

Richmond, Riĉmondo*

Richmondena cardinalis, kardinalbirdo

ricinoleate, ricinol/ato; **ricinoleic acid,** ~a acido

Ricinus, ricino

rick, (stack, as hay etc.), stako; ~igi; (Br: sprain, wrench), tordi [tr]; tordo

rickets, (disease), rakit/ismo; (deformation of bones resulting from), ~o

rickettsemia, rikeciemio

rickettsia, Rickettsia, rikecio; **rickettsiosis,** ~ozo

rickety, (decrepit, shaky), kaduka, disfalema

rickrack, zigzagaĵo

ricksha(w), rikiŝo

ricochet, karamboli [int]; ~o

rictus, (gaping mouth), gap/faŭko; (grin), ~grimaco

rid, senigi, liberigi; **get rid of, rid oneself of,** sin ~i je, forigi; **be rid of,** esti libera de; **riddance,** ~o, liberigo; **good riddance!,** bonvena ~o!

riddle, (puzzle), enigmo; (make holes), distrui [tr]; (sieve), kribrilo

ride, (on something, as horse, bicycle), rajdi [int] (sur); ~o; (in something, as car, train, plane; travel, gen), veturi [int] (en, sur); veturigi; veturo; (depend on), dependi [int] (de); (control, dominate), regi [tr]; (torment, tease), turmenti [tr], moki [tr]; (device to ride on, as at amusement park), ~ilo; **rider,** ~into; ~anto; ~onto; ~isto; veturinto (etc.); (codicil, attachment to document etc.), alpendaĵot, kodicilo, krom– [type of document] (e.g.: [on bill in Congress, Parliament]: kromakto; [on insurance policy]: krompoliso; [on any contract]: kromkontrakto) [cp "codicil"]; **ride out,** (go through storm etc.), trapasi [tr], trasuferi [tr]; **override,** (suppress, overcome), superi [tr], subpremi [tr]; (be more (most) important), pli (plej) gravi [int] ol; (overrule), renversi [tr], nuligi, kasacii [tr]; (prevail over), superregi [tr], superinflui [tr]; **dispatch rider,** (mil), stafeto; **take for a ride,** (give ride to), ~igi; veturigi; (trick), tromplogi [tr]; **ride herd on,** regadi [tr]

ridge, (of roof), firsto; (mountain), ~o, kresto; (any crest, edge), kresto, eĝo, spino; ~izi [tr], krestizi [tr]; **ridgepole,** ~otrabo; **Blue Ridge Mountains,** Montoj Bluaj

ridiculous, ridinda; **ridicule,** moki [tr], ~igi

rife, abunda; **be rife,** ~i [int], svarmi [int]

riffle, (choppy water), kirlakvejo; (groove), kanelo

riff-raff, kanajlaro

rifle, (gun), fusilo; (gun groove), kanelo; kaneli [tr]; (ransack), (dis)rabi [tr]; **rifling,** kanelaĵo; **rifleman,** ~isto; **rifle range,** (~)pafejo

rift, fendo; ~i [tr]; ~iĝi; **Great Rift Valley,** Valo Grand~a

rig, (equip, gen), ekipi [tr]; ~aĵo; (ship etc.), rigi [tr]; (arrange), aranĝi [tr]; (fraudulently fix), fifiksi [tr]; (drilling apparatus), borstacio; (tractor-trailer truck), kamionego; (truck tractor alone), traktoro; (carriage), ĉaro [see "carriage"]; **rigging,** (on ship), rigo; **jerry-rig,** improvizi [tr], konstruaĉi [tr], fuŝkonstrui [tr]; **outrigger,** (support), balanciero; (canoe w this), balanciera kanuo

Riga, Rigo
rigatoni, kanelpastaĵo
right, (right-handed; at or toward that side; pol), dekstra; ~e(n); ~o; (correct; exactly), ĝusta; ĝuste (e.g.: *the right answer:* la ĝusta respondo; *You are John, aren't you?* *Right:* Vi estas Johano, ĉu ne? Ĝuste; *right now:* ĝuste nun); (make correct), korekti [tr], ĝustigi; (correct, re opinion, statement of fact, etc.), prava; (just, fair), justa; justeco; (freedom, permission), rajto (e.g.: *basic human rights:* bazaj homaj rajtoj); (decent, proper), deca, konvena; (convenient), oportuna; (clockwise), ~uma; ~ume(n); (right-angled), orta; (immediately; w no separation), tuj (e.g.: *right in front of your nose:* tuj antaŭ via nazo; *I'll be right there:* mi estos tie tuj); (rather, very), tre; (quite, thoroughly, totally), tute; (outside, as of cloth), ekstera; (straight, directly), rekte (e.g.: *go right home:* iri rekte hejmen); (set upright), (re)starigi; **be right**, (correct in opinion, action, etc.), pravi [int] (e.g.: *she is right in what she is doing:* ŝi pravas en tio kion ŝi faras); **(isn't that) right?**, ĉu ne? (e.g.: *Mozart wrote that, right?:* Mozart verkis tion, ĉu ne?); **righteous**, virta, justa; **self-righteous**, virtaĉa, aroganta, sankt~afekta; **rightful**, justa, rajta; **rightist**, ~ano; ~ana [not "~ulo"]; **righto**, jes, jes ja, certe; **right angle**, orto; **right-angled**, orta; **right away, right now**, ĝuste nun, tuj, senprokraste, jam nun; **right-handed**, ~ula; **right-handed person**, ~ulo; **right-minded**, prav(pens)a; **right-of-way**, (re traffic), pasrajto, vojrajto, prioritato; (strip of land which road traverses), vojlinio; **right to work**, (Am: right not to join union), laborlibereco; **birthright**, (right due to birth in family, nation, etc.), naskiĝrajto; (as oldest son), majorato; **by rights**, laŭ justo, laŭ rajto; **just right**, ĝustega, precize ĝusta; **make right, set right**, (re)ĝustigi, korekti [tr]; justigi; (recom pense), rekompenci [tr]; **outright**, absoluta, senrezerva; absolute; **upright**, (standing, vertical),

staranta, vertikala, rekta; (support, post, strut, etc.), apogfosto; (honest), honesta, justa; **take a right**, turniĝi ~en; **have the right (to)**, rajti [tr]; **give the right (to)**, rajtigi; **in one's right mind**, mense sana; **in one's own right**, mem, propre, proprarajte
rigid, rigida; **rigidity**, ~eco
rigmarole, (nonsense), galimatio; (foolish procedures), proceduraĉo
rigor, rigor/eco; ~aĵo; **rigorous**, ~a, severa; **rigorism**, ~ismo; **rigor mortis**, morta rigidiĝo
Rig-Veda, Rigvedo
rile, agaci [tr]
rill, (brook), roj(et)o
rille, (groove, trench worn in rock), lapiezo†
rillettes, rijeto
rim, (edge), rando; ~izi [tr]; (for mounting tire), radrondo
rime, (frost), prujno; (rhyme), [see "rhyme"]
rind, (as of fruit), ŝelo; **bacon rind**, lardhaŭto
ring, (any circular object), ringo; (encircle), ĉirkaŭi [tr], en~igi; (place ring(s), band(s) around), ~izi [tr]; (circle, as of people, stones, etc.), rondo; (sound, as re bell, telephone, etc.), soni [int]; sonigi; sono; sonori [int]; sonorigi; sonoro [see "sound"]; (boxing, circus), areno; (telephone call), telefoni [tr], (telefone) voki [tr]; (telefon)voko; (impress), impreso; impresi [tr] (e.g.: *her story rings false to me:* ŝia rakonto impresas min kiel falsa); (resound, reverberate), resoni [int], reeĥiĝi; resonigi, reeĥi [tr]; (signal), signali [tr]; **ringer**, (bell etc.), solino; (fraudulent substitute), fisubstituito; (Aus: shearer), ĉampiontondisto; **ringlet**, (hair), buklo; **ringbark**, (a tree), ĉirkaŭhaki [tr]; **ring a bell**, (seem familiar), ŝajni konata, impresi kiel konata; **ring box**, ~ujo; **ring down the curtain (on)**, anonci la finon (de); **ring in**, (introduce), enkonduki [tr]; **ringleader**, kanajlestro, ĉefkanajlo, figvidanto; **ringmaster**, arenestro; **ring off**, (Br: hang up phone), remeti la aŭdilon, malŝalti [tr,

int]; **ring out**, elkonduki [tr]; **ring up**, (Br: call on phone), telefoni [tr], (telefone) voki [tr]; **annual ring**, (of tree), jar~o; **earring**, orel~o; **piston ring**, piŝto~o; **signet ring**, sigel~o; **wedding ring**, geedziĝa ~o; **run rings around**, ege superi [tr]

rink, (for ice skating), sketejo; (for roller skating), rul~o

rinse, gargari [tr], tralavi [tr], akvolavi [tr]; ~(ad)o, tralav(ad)o; ~aĵo, tralavaĵo

Rio de Janeiro, Rio-de-Ĵanejro

Río de la Plata, Rivero Plata

Rio Grande, Rivero Granda

Río Negro, Rivero Negra

riot, tumulto; ~i [int]; **riotous**, ~a; (debauched), diboĉa; **riot of color**, bunt(ec)o; **run riot**, ~i

rip, ŝiri [tr]; ~iĝi; ~(iĝ)o; ~aĵo; (onom: ripping sound), riĉ-raĉ!; **rip apart**, dis~i [tr]; dis~iĝi; **rip into**, (attack), atakegi [tr]; **rip off**, de~i [tr]; de~iĝi; (colloq: steal), ŝteli [tr]; (cheat), friponi [tr]; **rip out**, el~i [tr]; el~iĝi

Riparia riparia, bordhirundo

riparian, laŭborda

ripe, matura; **ripen**, ~igi; ~iĝi; **overripe**, tro~a; **the time is ripe**, la tempo estas ĝusta, estas la ĝusta tempo

ripost(e), repliki [tr, int]; ~o

ripple, (little wave, gen), krisp/aĵo; ~igi; ~iĝi; (sound, light, etc.), plaŭd(et)i [int]; plaŭd(et)igi; plaŭd(et)ado; **rippled**, ~a

rise, (get up, be raised, gen), leviĝi; ~o; (increase), pliiĝi; pliiĝo; (dough w yeast), fermenti [int]; (hill), altaĵeto; (Br: pay raise), pagopliigo; **riser**, (vertical piece in stairway), interŝtupo; **risers**, (platform for choral group etc. to stand on), ŝtuppodio; **rise up**, **uprise**, (rise), ~i; ~o; **uprising**, (revolt), ribelo, (popol–)~o; **self-rising**, memfermenta; **give rise to**, okazigi, estigi, rezultigi, kaŭzi [tr]; **get a rise out of**, reagigi, replikigi

risk, (gen), riski [tr]; ~o; **risky**, ~(oplen)a; ~eca; **at the risk of**, je ~o de; **run the risk of, run a risk, take a risk**, ~i

risorius, (muscle), rizorio

risotto, rizoto

risqué maldeceta, sugesta

Rissa tridactyla, kitio

rissole, risolo

ritardando, (mus), malrapidante

rite, rito; **rite of passage**, ~o de maturiĝo

ritornello, ritornelo [cp "refrain"]

ritual, rita; ~o; **ritualism**, ~ismo; **ritualistic**, ~isma

rival, rivalo; ~i [int] (kun); **rivalry**, ~eco; ~ado

river, rivero

rivet, nito; ~i [tr]; **riveter**, ~isto; ~maŝino

Riviera, Riviero

rivulet, rojo

RNA, [abb of "ribonucleic acid"), RNA [abb of "ribonukleata acido"]

roach, (cockroach), blato; (fish), ploto

road, (gen), vojo [cp "street", "highway"]; **roads**, (naut), rodo; **roadblock**, ~obstrukco; **roadhouse**, (Am: tavern), apud~a taverno; (Aus: inn), apud~a hotelo; **roadkill**, ~mortigito; **road plant**, (Aus), ~maŝinaro; **roadside**, ~flanko; apud~a, ĉe~a; **roadstead**, rodo; **roadway**, (traveled part of road), vetur~o [cp "lane", "shoulder"; **road workers, road crew**, ~istaro; **paved road, sealed road**, (Aus), pavimita ~o; **on the road to**, sur~e al

roam, vagi [int], nomadi [int]

roan, (color), ruana; (animal), ~ulo

roar, (gen), rorit [int]; ~(ad)o; **uproar**, tumulto; bruego; **uproarious**, tumulta, bruega

roast, (cook, or subject to heat in similar way), rosti [tr]; ~iĝi; (roasted meat), ~aĵo; (party, picnic, etc.), ~festo; **roast beef**, rostbefo

rob, (w violence, re thing robbed), rabi [tr]; (re place or person robbed), pri~i [tr] (e.g.: *he robbed $5000 from the bank:* li ~is $5000 de la banko; *he robbed the bank of $5000:* li pri~is la bankon de $5000); (steal, gen: re thing stolen), ŝteli [tr]; (re person or place), priŝteli [tr]; (thickened fruit juice), robbo; **robber**, ~into; ~anto; ~isto; ŝtelinto (etc.); (extreme), latrono; **robbery**, ~(ad)o; ŝtel(ad)o

robe, (gen), robo; (ceremonial, as worn by judge, university official, clergy, etc.), talaro; (dress in robes), en~iĝi; en~iĝi [cp "dress"]; **bathrobe**, ban~o, ĉambra ~o; **disrobe**, malvesti [tr], senvestigi; malvesti sin, malvestiĝi, senvestiĝi

Robert, Roberto; **Roberta**, ~a

robin, (Am: *Turdus migratorius*), migra turdo; (Aus: *Petroika goodenovii*), ruĝkapa turdo; (European: *Erithracus rubecula*), rubekolo; **ragged robin**, (bot), liknido

Robinia, robinio

Robinson, Robinsono

robot, roboto; **robotic**, ~ika; **robotics**, ~iko

robust, fortika

Roccella, rocelo; Roccella tinctoria, lakmusa ~o

rock, (a stone), ŝtono; (boulder; large rock outcropping or underground geol mass), roko; (mineral substance), roko, ~o; (mus), rok~muziko; (swing up and down), balanci [tr]; balanciĝi; (back and forth), ŝanceli [tr]; ŝanceliĝi; (side to side, as ship), rul(ad)i [tr]; ruliĝ(ad)i; (swing as arms, pendulum), pendoligi, svingi [tr]; pendoli [int], svingiĝi; (gently back and forth, as to lull baby), luli [tr]; **rocky**, ~(plen)a; rok(plen)a; ŝanceliĝema, nestabila; **rock-bottom**, absoluta minimumo; absolute minimuma; **rockclimbing**, varapo, rokgrimpado; **rock-'n'-roll**, (mus), rokenrolo†; **bedrock**, (geol), bazoroko; (basics), fundamentoj; **Rocky Mountains**, Montaro R~a

rocker, (rocking chair), lulseĝo; (its curved piece), balancarko; (rocker arm; any rocking mech part on pivot), baskulo

rocket, (gen), raketo; ~i [int]; ~igi; **rocketsonde**, sond~o; **booster rocket**, port~o; **garden rocket**, (bot), eruko; **skyrocket**, (fireworks), piroteknika ~o; (rise rapidly), ~i; **sweet rocket**, (bot), hesperido; **retrorocket**, retro~o

rococo, rokoko; ~a

rod, (pole, gen), stango; (stick, as for punishment), vergo, bastono; vergi [tr], bastoni [tr]; **Aaron's rod**, (bot), verbasko; **connecting rod**, (for piston etc.), bielo; **lightning rod**, fulmosuĉilo; **ramrod**, ŝargo~o; **surveyor's rod**, cel~o; **welding rod**, veldodrato

Rod, (man's nickname), Roĉjo

rodent, ronĝulo

Rodentia, ronĝuloj

rodeo, rodeo†

Roderick, Rodrigo

Rodrigo, Rodrigo

roe, (eggs of fish etc.), frajo; (deer), kapreolo

roebuck, virkapreolo

roentgen, rentgeno; **roentgenography**, ~fotografio, X-radia fotografio [pronounce "iks-radia"]

rogation, rogacio

Roger, Roĝero

rogue, fripono, kanajlo

roil, (gen), agiti [tr]

roister, (boast), fanfaroni [int]; (be boisterous), bruadi [int]

Roland, Rolando

role, rolo; **lead role, title role**, ĉef~o; **play a (the) role (of)**, ~i [int] (kiel)

roll, (rotate and move, as wheel; travel in wheeled vehicle; rock side to side, re ship; rotate on same axis, re aircraft or spacecraft; wave motion; any analogous motion; sound of thunder, drum, etc.), ruli [tr]; ~iĝi; ~(iĝ)(ad)o; (roll up, as fabric, cigarette, etc.), volvi [tr]; volviĝi; (thing rolled up), volvaĵo; (spool), bobeno; (wind onto spool), bobeni [tr]; bobeniĝi; (flatten by rollers etc., gen), ~premi [tr]; ~premiĝi; (make metal sheeting, tubing, etc.), lamenati [tr]; lamenatiĝi; (advance, progress), antaŭeniri [int], progresi [int]; (start operating), ekfunkcii [int]; ekfunkciiĝi; (bread), bulko; (list of members, students, etc.), matrikulo, registro, etato; (scroll), [see "scroll"]; **roller**, (any rolling device, cylinder, platen), ~o; (cylinder for flattening), ~premilo, ~cilindro; (wave), ~o; (bird), koracio; **roller bearing**, ~lagro; **roller coaster**, ondanta fervojo; **leaf roller**, (larva of *Tortrix*), tortrika larvo; **road roller**, (for smoothing asphalt etc.), ŝose~ilo; **rolling**, ~(iĝ)anta; (undulating, as countryside etc.), ondanta; **rolling mill**, (machine), lamenatilo; (series of such machines), lamenatilaro; (factory), lamenatejo; **rolling pin**, ~premilo; **rolling stock**, (rr etc.), ~iĝantaĵoj; **roll call**, kontrolvoko; **call the roll (of)**, kontrolvoki [tr]; **roll one's R's**, (trill), ~i la R-ojn; (in throat), kartavi [int]; **roll out**, (unroll), [see "unroll" below]; (flatten etc. w roller), ~premi [tr]; **roll up**, kun~i [tr]; kun~iĝi; kunvolvi [tr]; kunvolviĝi; (arrive, as in vehicle), al~iĝi; (sleeve, pants cuff, etc.), kuspi [tr]; **bedroll**, litaĵo; **enroll**, matrikuli [tr], enmatrikuligi; matrikuliĝi; **unroll**, el~i [tr], dis~i [tr]; el~iĝi, dis~iĝi; malvolvi [tr]; malvolviĝi; **strike from the rolls**, elmatrikuligi

rollick, petoli [int], kaprioli [int]; **rollicking**, (lively), gajega, festega, verva

roly-poly, (plump), dikmalalta; (Br: pudding), rulpudingo

roman, (narrative), romano

Roman, [see "Rome"]

romance, (romantic quality), romantikeco; (love affair), amafero; (court, woo), amindumi [tr]; (narrative), romano; (song form), romanco

Romance, (re language), Latinida; **Romance language(s)**, ~a(j) lingvo(j)

romancero, (collection of Spanish romances), romancero

Romand(e), (re French Switzerland), Romanda

Romanesque, (re romance [lit fantasy]), romaneska; (re style of arch, lit, etc., arising in Europe around 1000 C.E.), romanika

Romania, [see "Rumania"]

Romans(c)h, Romanĉo; ~a

romantic, (gen), romantika; ~isto, ~ulo; **romanticism**, ~ismo

Romany, Cigano, Romo*; ~a, Roma*

Rome, Romo; **Roman**, (of city of Rome), ~a; ~ano; ~ana; (of Roman Empire), ~(an)ia; **Roman Empire**, ~(an)io; **Holy Roman Empire**, (Sankta) ~-Germana Imperio

Romeo, Romeo

romp, (frolic), kaprioli [int], petoli [int]; ~o, petolo; **romper**, (garment), (beba) kombineo, (beba) ludvesto

Romulus, Romulo

Ronald, Rejnaldo

rondeau, rondaŭo

rondel, rondelo

rondelet, rondeleto

rondo, rondelo

Ronsard, Ronsardo

roo, kanguruido

rood, (crucifix), krucifikso; (unit of linear or square measure), [imprecise; see § 20]

roof, tegmento; ~i [tr]

rook, (zool), frugilego; (cheat), friponi [tr], trompi [tr]; (chess piece), turo

rookie, novico

room, (any chamber, as in building, cave, etc.), ĉambro; (rented), lu~o; (space, gen), spaco (e.g.: *there is not enough room on the shelf for these books:* mankas sufiĉa spaco sur la breto por ĉi tiuj libroj); (reside), loĝi [int]; (provide lodging), loĝigi; **roomy**, vasta; **roomer**, pensionulo; **roommate**, sam~ano; **anteroom**, antaŭ~o; **bathroom**, ban~o, necesejo; **bedroom**, dorm~o; **bed-sitting room**, (Br), unu~a apartamento; **classroom**, klas~o; **control room**, komando~o; **courtroom**, tribunalejo, kortumejo [see "court"]; **darkroom**, mallum~o; **dining room**, manĝo~o; **dressing room**, vestiĝo~o; **elbow room**, vivospaco; movospaco; **guest room**, gasto~o; **living room**, loĝo~o, vivo~o, salono; **powder room**, pudrejo; **reading room**, lego~o; **recovery room**, (in hospital), postoperaciejo; **restroom**, necesejo; **schoolroom**, klas~o; **showroom**, montrejo, montrosalono; **sickroom**, malsan~o; **steamroom**, vaporbanejo; **storeroom, storage room**, staplo~o; **supply room**, provizejo; **taproom**, trink~o; **waiting room**, antaŭ~o; **wardroom**, oficirejo; **rooming house**, pensiono; **room and board**, pensionado

roost, (sit), sidi [int]; (rest), ripozi [int];
(pole), ~stango

rooster, (colloq), koko; (more precise),
vir~o

root, (of plant; similar or analogous
thing; basic word part; math), radiko;
(core, basic part), kerno (e.g.: *get to
the root of the matter:* atingi la kernon
de la afero); (source), fonto; (dig w
snout), nazfosi [tr], serĉfosi [tr];
(cheer), hurai [tr, int], subteni [tr];
root out, root up, el~igi; **rootstock,**
(rhizome), rizomo; (for grafting), al-
greftaĵo; **taproot,** pivot~o; **uproot,**
el~igi; **grass roots,** popolbazo; popol-
baza; **take root,** en~iĝi, ek~i [int];
square (cube, fourth, etc.**) root,**
(math), kvadrata (kuba [or: tria], kvara, etc.) ~o; **be rooted in, have roots
(in),** ~i [int] (en)

rope, ŝnuro; ~i [tr]; **rope off,** for~i [tr],
~e rezervi [tr]; **boltrope,** raliko; **jump
rope,** ~salti [int]; **jumprope,** salto~o;
tightrope, danco~o; **learn the ropes,**
spertiĝi; **know the ropes,** esti sperta;
be at the end of one's rope, ne plu
povi elteni [tr]; **walk a tightrope,** (lit
or fig), ~danci [int]; **tightrope walker,** ~dancisto; **on the ropes,** fraka-
sonta

Roquefort, (cheese), Rokforto

rorqual, balenoptero, rorkvalo

rort, (Aus), brua festo, aferaĉo

Rosa, (woman's name), Roza

Rosa, (bot), rozo; Rosa centifolia, cen-
tifolio; Rosa centifolia muscosa,
Rosa moschata, musko~o; Rosa eg-
lanteria, eglanterio; Rosaceae, ~acoj

rosacea, (med). kuperozo, rozacea akneo

rosaniline, rozanilino

rosary, rozario

rose, (flower, plant; similar-shaped object), rozo; (color), ~(kolor)a; ~koloro;
rosy, (color), ~kolora; (cheerful),
gaja; (promising, optimistic), bonaŭgura; **rose mallow,** hibisko; **rose of
Jericho,** jeriko~o; **rosewood,**
(wood), palisandro; **Brazilian rosewood,** jakarando; **cliff rose,** armerio;
Guelder rose, opulo; **musk rose,**
musko~o; **rockrose,** cisto; **sunrose,**

heliantemo; **wild rose,** eglanterio

Rose, (woman's name), Roza

rosé (wine), rozvino

roseate, (color), rozkolora; (cheerful),
gaja

rossella, (Aus: *Platycercus eximus*),
Aŭstralia psitako

rosemary, (plant or spice), rosmareno;
bog rosemary, andromedo

roseola, rozeolo

rosette, kokardo

Rosicrucian, Ruzkruca; ~ano; **Rosicru-
cianism,** ~ismo

rosin, kolofono [cp "resin"]

Rosmarinus, rosmareno

roster, matrikulo, etato

rostrum, (podium), tribuno, podio;
(beak of ancient ship; [bot, zool]
beaklike part), rostro; (platform in ancient Roman Forum), Ros troj

rot, (decompose), putri [int]; ~igi;
~ado; ~aĵo; ~iĝo; (nonsense), sensencaĵo; (blarney), blago; **rotten,** ~a; **dry
rot,** (rotten condition), larmofunga
~o; ~i de larmofungo; (fungus causing this), larmofungo; **tommy rot,**
sensencaĵo; blago

rota, (Br: roster), deĵoretato

rotary, (rotating), rotacia; (traffic circle), trafikcirklo; **Rotary International,** Rotario

rotate, (gen), rotacii [int], turniĝi; ~igi
[cp "revolve"]; **rotation,** ~o; (game of
bridge etc.), rondiro; **rotational,** ~a;
rotator, (tech; anat), rotatoro

Rotatoria, rotaciuloj

rote, parkera; **learn by rote,** ~igi, lerni
[tr] ~e

rotisserie, rostostango; (machine), ~a
maŝino; (shop), ~a butiko

rotogravure, rotacigravura; ~ado; ~aĵo

rotor, rotoro

Rotterdam, Roterdamo

rotund, ronda

rotunda, rotondo

rouble, rublo

rouche, krispo

roué diboĉulo

Rouen, Rueno

rouge, (make-up), ruĵo; (polish for jewelry etc.), ferika oksido

rough, (not smooth), mal/glata; (not

level), ~ebena; (not delicate, gen), ~delikata; (not tender), ~tenera; (coarse, not fine), ~fajna; (approximate), proksimuma, ~preciza; (like rasp), aspra; (primitive), primitiva; (crude, raw, unworked), kruda; (first draft of written material etc.), ~neta; ~neto; (re adjustment of microscope etc.), makrometra; (stormy), ŝtorma, tempesta; (disorderly), senorda, ~orda; (harsh), ~milda, severa; (discordant, grating), agaca; (unrefined), nerafinita; (difficult), ~facila; (treat roughly), ~delikate trakti [tr], ~karesi [tr], ~dorloti [tr]; (Br: rough person), krudulo, kanajlo; **roughage**, (as in food), fibraĵo; **roughen**, ~glatigi; ~glatiĝi; ~ebenigi; ~delikatigi; asprigi; ~mildigi, severigi; **roughhouse**, tumulte ludi [int]; **roughneck**, krudulo; **roughshod**, butee hufferita; **ride roughshod over**, tirani [tr]; **rough-and-ready**, krudpreta; **rough-and-tumble**, senorda, ĉiolibera; **rough it**, primitive vivi [int]
roulade, (gen), rulado
rouleau, rulaĵo
roulette, (gen), ruleto
Roumania, [see "Rumania"]
round, (circular; re number), ronda; ~e; ~o; ~igi; (full, complete), plena, kompleta; (series), serio; (any round-about route, as of police officer, letter-carrier, etc.), rundo [cp "route"]; (of boxing match etc.), rundo†, raŭndo; (cycle), ciklo; (song), ~kanto; (gunfire), salvo; (around, about), ĉirkaŭ; (go around, turn, as corner), ĉirkaŭiri [tr], ĉirkaŭi [tr]; (here and there), diversloke(n); [see also "around", "about"]; (meat), femuraĵo; **rounder**, ~igilo; (dissolute person), diboĉulo; **rounders**, (Br game), ~kuro; **round about**, ĉirkaŭ, ĉirkaŭe (de); **roundabout**, (indirect), nerekta; (Br: merry-go-round, carousel), karuselo; (Br: traffic circle), trafikcirklo; **roundhouse**, (rr), ~domo; **round off**, (make round, as number), ~igi; (finish), fini [tr]; **round out**, (el)~igi; (el)~iĝi; (complete), kompletigi, fini [tr]; **round trip**, ~veturo; **round-trip tick-**

et, revenbileto; **round up**, kolekti [tr], kunigi, kunpeli [tr]; **go the rounds**, (follow route), sekvi la rundon; (circulate), cirkuli [int]; **the year round**, tute tra la jaro, tutjare; **year-round**, tutjara; **out of round**, ne perfekte ~a
roundel, (round window, ornament, etc.), rondaĵo, disk(et)o
roundelay, rondelo
rouse, (stir, excite), eksciti [tr], vigligi, stimuli [tr]; ~iĝi, vigliĝi; (awaken), veki [tr]; vekiĝi
Roussillon, Rusiljono
roust, (rouse), eksciti [tr], stimuli [tr]; (rout, drive out), elpeli [tr]; **roustabout**, (naut), stivisto; (any laborer), laboristo
rout, (thoroughly beat), disvenki [tr]; disvenko; (dig, root), nazfosi [tr], serĉfosi [tr]; (force out), elpeli [tr]; (band, group), bando
route, (course for travel), itinero (e.g.: *the scenic route:* la pejzaĝa ~o); (regular scheduled, as mail route etc.), kurso [cp "round"]; (send by specified route), ~igi; **air route**, flugvojo, flug~o; **en route (to)**, survoja (al); survoje (al); **stock route**, (Aus), vojo por brutpelado
routine, rutino; ~a; **subroutine**, sub~o
rove, vagi [int]; **rover**, ~ulo; (scout), rovero; (Aus football), malgranda vaganta ludanto
row, (series, column, queue), vico; ~igi; (boat), remi [tr] [cp "paddle"]; (brawl), tumulto, kverelego; **in a row**, laŭ~a(j); laŭ~e; sinsekva(j); sinsekve; **kick up a row**, levi tu multon
rowan, monta sorpo
rowdy, tumulta; ~(em)ulo
rowel, spronradeto
royal, reĝa; **royalism**, rojalismo; **royalist**, rojalisma; rojalisto; **royalty**, (rank), ~eco; (person), ~ul(ar)o, ~familiano(j); (kingdom), ~lando; ($ paid to author, composer, etc.), tantiemo
rub, (friction), froti [tr]; ~iĝi; ~o; (problem, difficulty), problemo, malfacilaĵo; **rub down**, (massage), masaĝi [tr]; masaĝo; **rub it in**, troemfazi [tr] ĝin; **rub off on**, de~(iĝ)i sur; **rub out**, for~i [tr], forskrapi [tr]; **rub the**

wrong way, (lit, as cat fur), kuspi [tr]; (irritate), iriti [tr]
rubber, (substance), kaŭĉuko; ~a; (eraser), skrapgumo; (galosh), galoŝo; (condom), kondomo; (cards), robro; (that rubs), frotilo; **rubberize**, ~izi [tr]; **rubber band**, ~a ringo; **crêpe rubber**, krepa ~o; **foam rubber**, ŝaŭm~o; **sponge rubber**, spongo~o
rubbish, (trash), rubo; (nonsense), sensencaĵo; (Aus), moki [tr]
rubble, rubo; **rubblework**, rablo
rube, kamparanaĉo
rubella, morbilo
rubeola, rubeolo
Rubia, rubio
Rubicon, Rubikono
rubicund, ruĝ/vanga, ~vizaĝa
rubidium, rubidio
ruble, rublo
rubric, (gen), rubriko
Rubus, rubuso; Rubus idaeus, Rubus strigosus, Rubus caesius, Rubus hispidis, Rubus flagellaris, Rubus trivialis, frambujo; Rubus loganobaccus, loganberujo
ruby, rubeno
ruche, ruŝo
ruck, (Aus football), miksbatalo; **ruckman**, alta vaganta ludanto
ruckus, ruction, tumulto, bru(ad)o, kverelego
rudder, (of boat), rudro; ~i [tr]; (plane), direkterono; **rudder bar**, stirstango; **rudder-chain, rudder-rope**, droso; **rudder lines**, stirŝnuroj; **rudder-post**, ~ostango
ruddle, ruĝokro; ~a; ~igi
ruddy, (red), ruĝa; (Br colloq: bloody, damn), diabla
rude, (impolite), malĝentila; (crude, rough, gen), kruda; nerafinita [see "rough"]; (vulgar), triviala; (harsh), malmilda, severa
rudiment, (gen), rudimento; **rudimentary**, ~a
Rudolph, Rudolfo
rue, (regret), bedaŭri [tr]; (bot), ruto; **meadow rue**, taliktro; **wall rue**, (spleenwort), mororuto
ruff, (collar), krispo; (fish), perĉo;

(bird), duelbirdo; (cards), atuti [int]; atutado
ruffe, (fish), perĉo
ruffian, brutulo, bandito
ruffle, (regular folds), krispo; ~igi; ~iĝi; (disarray, as hair, clothing, etc.), taŭzi [tr]; (annoy), ĉagreni [tr], malserenigi, maltrankviligi; (clothing trim), falbalo; **ruffled**, ~a; taŭzita; ĉagrenita, malserena, maltrankvila; **unruffled**, (calm), serena, kvieta, trankvila
rufous, rufa
rug, tapiŝo; **shag rug**, vila ~o; **throw rug, scatter rug**, (or any small rug), ~eto; **pull the rug out from under**, (fig), renversi [tr], perfidi [tr], lasi (iun) senhelpa
rugby, rugbeo
rugged, (rough, uneven), mal/ebena, ~glata; (strong), fortika; (stormy), ŝtorma, tempesta; (harsh, severe), severa, ~milda; (difficult), ~facila; (crude), kruda [see also "rough"]
rugine, rugino
rugous, rugose, rug/inta; **be rugous**, ~i [int]
Ruhr, (river), Ruro; **Ruhr Valley, Ruhr Basin**, ~valo
ruin, ruino; ~igi; **ruins**, ~oj; **ruinous**, (ruined), ~a; (causing ruin), ~iga; **ruination**, ~igo; ~iĝo
rule, (regulation), regulo [cp "regulate"]; (principle), principo; (govern, control, prevail, hold sway), regi [tr, int]; reg(ad)o; (dominate, give orders), mastri [tr]; (right to rule), mastreco; (draw lines), linii [tr], streki [tr]; (decree, judge, decide), dekreti [tr], juĝi [tr], decidi [tr]; (ruler, straightedge), liniilo; **ruler**, (straightedge), liniilo; (for measuring), mezurilo; (one who rules), reganto; **rule on**, decidi [tr], juĝi [tr]; **rule out**, elimini [tr]; **rule of thumb**, empirio, praktika ~o; **rule the roost**, mastri [tr]; **ground rule**, specifa ~o; **home-rule, self-rule**, memregado, aŭtonomio; **overrule**, renversi [tr], nuligi, kasacii [tr]; (prevail), superinflui [tr]; **as a rule**, ĝenerale, kutime, ordinare; **the Golden Rule**, la Ora R~o
rum, rumo

Rumania, Ruman/io; **Rumanian,** ~o; ~a; ~ia

rumba, rumbo

rumble, (noise etc.), muĝi [int]; ~(ad)o; **rumble seat,** postsidejo

rumen, rumeno

Rumex,rumekso; Rumex acetosa, okzalo; Rumex patientia, patienco

ruminate, (chew cud), remaĉi [tr]; (ponder), mediti [int], ~i, pensi [int]; **ruminant,** ~a; ~ulo

rummage, (miscellany), diversaĵo(j); (dig through), serĉfosi [tr]; **rummage sale,** ~a vendo

rummy, (game), rumio*

rumo(u)r, famo, onidiro; **rumormonger,** ~emulo; **he is rumored to be, it is rumored that he is,** oni diras ke li estas

rump, (of animal), gropo; (as meat), ~aĵo; (buttocks), pugo, postaĵo; (remnant), restaĵo

rumple, (wrinkle, crumple), ĉifi [tr]; ~aĵo; (ruffle, as hair), taŭzi [tr]

run, (go fast on foot; any analogous motion, lit or fig; continuous going or activity), kuri [int]; ~igi; ~(ig)(ad)o (e.g.: *they ran down the street:* ili ~is laŭ la strato; *he ran his horse until it was exhausted:* li ~igis sian ĉevalon ĝis ĝi ellaciĝis; *flames ran up the wall:* flamoj ~is supren laŭ la muro; *a rumor ran through the crowd:* famo ~is tra la homamaso); (go, gen), iri [int] (e.g.: *I'll run to the store for more eggs:* mi iros al la butiko por pli da ovoj); (trip), veturi [int]; veturo; (flee), fuĝi [int]; fuĝigi; fuĝo; (compete in race, contest), konkursi [int]; konkursigi; konkursado [see "race"]; (function, operate), funkcii [int]; funkciigi (e.g.: *the motor (the club, the plan) is running smoothly:* la motoro (la klubo, la plano) funkcias glate; *don't run the motor without oil:* ne funkciigu la motoron sen oleo); (manage, direct), direkti [tr], administri [tr]; (control, rule), regi [tr]; (flow), flui [int]; fluigi; fluo; (gutter), defluilo; (continue), daŭri [int]; daŭrigi; daŭro; (follow regular route), kursadi [int]; kursado (e.g.: *that train runs*

only on Saturday: tiu trajno kursadas nur sabate); (in stocking), ŝtupetaro, dismaŝaĵo; ŝtupetari, dismaŝiĝi; (spread, as dye), difuzi [int]; difuz(aĵ)o; (be a candidate), esti kandidato, kandidatiĝi; kandidatigi; (finish, as in race), finiĝi (e.g.: *my horse ran third:* mia ĉevalo finiĝis la tria); (swim upstream, re fish), suprennaĝi [int]; suprennaĝado; (many fish migrating together), kunnaĝado (e.g.: *the salmon run:* la salma kunnaĝado); (circulate), cirkuli [int]; cirkuligi; (climb, creep, as plants), grimpi [tr], rampi [int]; (give mucus, re nose), muki [int]; (give tears, re eyes), larmi [int]; (leak, re faucet etc.), liki [int]; (elapse), pasi [int]; pas(ad)o (e.g.: *days ran into weeks:* tagoj pasis en semajnojn); (print, publish), eldoni [tr], publikigi; eldoniĝi, publikiĝi; eldono, publikigo (e.g.: *the paper ran the story yesterday:* la ĵurnalo eldonis [or: publikigis] la rakonton hieraŭ; *the article ran for three consecutive days:* la artikolo eldoniĝis tri sinsekvajn tagojn); (appear regularly, as special feature, play, etc.), prezentadi [tr]; prezentiĝadi, aperi [int]; prezentado (e.g.: *the chess column runs once every week:* la ŝakrubriko aperas unufoje ĉiun semajnon; *that play was run for a year:* oni prezentis tiun dramon dum unu jaro; *during its one-year run:* dum ĝia unujara prezentado); (remain in effect), validi [int], resti valida, resti efektiva; (be inclined toward), inklini [int], emi [int], tendenci [int] (e.g.: *her musical taste runs to jazz:* ŝia muziko prefero inklinas al la ĵazo); (extend), etendi [tr]; etendiĝi, ~i (e.g.: *that road runs from coast to coast:* tiu vojo ~as [or: etendiĝas] de marbordo al marbordo); (be expressed, worded), teksti [int] (e.g.: *the poem runs like this:* la poemo tekstas jene); (cost), kosti [int] (e.g.: *it usually runs 2 dollars a kilo:* ĝi kutime kostas 2 dolarojn por kilogramo); (incur), akiri [tr], altiri sur sin (e.g.: *you'll run a risk of losing:* vi altiros sur vin riskon de perdo); (run through,

escape through), tra~i [tr] (e.g.: *they
ran the blockade:* ili tra~is la bloka-
don; *you ran a red light:* vi tra~is
ruĝan lumon); (hunt), ĉasi [tr]; ĉaso;
(compete, gen), konkuri [int] [see
"compete"]; (transport), transporti
[tr]; transportiĝi; (drive, force, thrust),
peli [tr]; (uninterrupted series), sinsekvo, serio; (consecutive cards etc.),
sekvenco; (progression), progreso,
sinsekvo; (brook), rojo, rivereto;
(type, kind), speco; (usual, ordinary
type), kutima (ordinara) speco, kuti-
maĵo, ordinaraĵo; (pathway, course),
kurso (e.g.: *ski run:* skikurso); (path,
as by animals), pado (e.g.: *deer run:*
cervopado); (enclosed area where animals can run), ~ejo; (Aus: ranch),
ranĉo; (baseball, cricket score), poen-
to; **runner,** (one who runs), ~anto;
(courier), kuriero, ~isto; (on sled etc.),
glitilo; (bot: stolon), stolono; (such a
plant, e.g. strawberry), stolonplanto;
(smuggler), kontrabandisto; (ship),
kontrabandoŝipo; (stocking run), eskalo; (channel), kanelo; **runner-up,**
(2nd in contest etc.), dua gajninto; due
gajninta; **running,** (cursive), kursiva;
(pustulent), pusanta; (linear), linia
(e.g.: *ten running meters of wood:* dek
liniaj metroj da ligno); (simultaneous), samtempa (e.g.: *a running
translation:* samtempa traduko); (consecutively), sinsekve (e.g.: *for 3 days
running:* dum 3 tagoj sinsekve); **run
across,** (come upon), (hazarde) renkonti [tr], (hazarde) trovi [tr]; **run after,** post~i [tr]; ~ĉasi [tr]; **run along,**
(leave), foriri [int]; (follow), laŭiri
[tr], iri [int] laŭ (e.g.: *the road runs
along the river:* la vojo laŭiras la riveron); **run around with,** asociiĝ(ad)i
kun; **run away,** for~i [int], fuĝi [int];
runaway, for~inta, fuĝinta; for~into,
fuĝinto; (uncontrolled), nebridita
(e.g.: *runaway inflation:* nebridita inflacio); **run away with,** for~i [int]
kun; (steal), forŝteli [tr]; (carry out of
control), forporti [tr] (e.g.: *her enthusiasm ran away with her:* ŝia entuziasmo forportis ŝin [or] ŝi forportiĝis de
entuziasmo); **run down,** (battery or

mech device: run out of energy),
elĉerpi [tr]; elĉerpiĝi; elĉerpiĝinta;
(clock spring etc.), malstreĉiĝi; mal-
streĉiĝinta; (knock down, run over),
faligi, super~i [tr]; (chase and catch),
ĉaskapti [tr]; (search out), elserĉi [tr];
(disparage, decry, impugn), mallaŭdi
[tr]; (slander, libel), kalumnii [tr];
(read through), tralegi [tr]; (look over,
review), trarigardi [tr], kontroli [tr];
(summarize), resumi [tr]; (recite list),
listigi; (decrepit), kaduka; kadukigi;
kadukiĝi; (poor health), malbonsana;
malbonsanigi; (fatigued), lac(iĝint)a;
rundown, (summary), resumo; **run
for it,** fuĝ(~)i [int]; **run in,** (insert),
enmeti [tr]; **run-in,** (quarrel), kverelo;
have a run-in (with), kvereli [int]
(kun); **run into,** (come across), (hazarde) renkonti [tr]; (encounter as obstacle; hit, run up against), trafi [tr];
(collide), kolizii [int] (kun); (add up
to), sumi [tr] (ĝis); **run off,** for~i [int];
for~igi; (print), presi [tr]; (type), tajpi
[tr]; (copy), kopii [tr]; (flow), forflui
[int]; **run-off,** (contest, election, etc.),
decidiga (konkurso, balotado, etc.);
(flow), forflu(ad)o; forfluaĵo; **run on,**
(continue), daŭri [int]; daŭrigi; (babble), babil(ad)i [int]; **run out,** (expire), malvalidiĝi; (end, stop), ĉesi
[int], finiĝi; ĉesigi, fini [tr]; (use up),
eluziĝi, forkonsumiĝi, elĉerpiĝi; (expel), elpeli [tr], forpeli [tr]; **run out
of,** (use up), elĉerpi [tr], elĉerpiĝi de,
seniĝi de, je; **run out on,** (abandon),
forlasi [tr]; **run over,** (knock down
and drive over etc.), super~i [tr];
(overflow), superflui [int]; (exceed
limit), superi [tr], transpasi [tr] (limon, tempon, etc.); (summarize), resumi [tr]; (check on), kontroli [tr];
(rehearse), provi [tr], provludi [tr];
provkanti [tr] [see "rehearse"]; **run-
proof,** (stocking), eskalimuna, nedis-
maŝiĝa; (re dyes), difuzimuna; **run
through,** tra~i [tr]; (use up), elĉerpi
[tr], eluzi [tr]; ($), forspezi [tr];
(waste, gen), malŝpari [tr]; (pierce),
trapiki [tr], trapenetri [tr]; (rehearse),
[see "run over" above]; (examine),
kontroli [tr], espleri [tr]; **run up,**

(amass, total), amasigi; amasiĝi (e.g.:
we ran up a huge deficit: ni amasigis
grandegan deficiton); **run up against,**
(hazarde) renkonti [tr]; trafi [tr];
kolízii [int] (kun) [see "run into"
above]; **runway,** (for planes etc.),
~ejo; **run-of-the-mill,** ordinara; **dry
run,** provo [see "rehearse"]; **end-run,**
ĉirkaŭevito; **do an end-run around,**
ĉirkaŭeviti [tr]; **forerunner,** (person),
antaŭiranto, antaŭsignanto; (thing),
antaŭsigno; **overrun,** (lit), super~i
[tr]; super~o (e.g.: *cost overrun:* kos-
tosuper~o); (invade), invadi [tr]; (conquer), venki [tr]; (infest), supersvarmi
[tr], trasvarmi [tr], svarmi [int] tra;
(overflow), superflui [int] (sur, en);
(go beyond limit), translimiĝi, transpasi la limo(j)n; translimiĝo; **rerun,**
(TV etc.), re-prezento; **a run for
one's money,** (powerful competition), potenca konkuro [see "compete"]; **in the long run,** fine, finfine,
longadaŭre, en la longa daŭro; **in the
short run,** mallongadaŭre, en la mallonga daŭro; **on the run,** ~anta; (hur-
rying), hast(em)a; hastanta; **give one
the runaround,** (intence) devojigadi
iun; **get the runaround,** esti (intence)
devojigita; **be in (out of) the running,** (ne) esti en la konkuro; **have
the run of,** disponi libere de; **it runs
in the family,** ĝi estas familia trajto
runcinate, runcinata
rune, (gen), runo; **runic,** ~a
rung, (of ladder, chair, etc.), rungo
runnel, (stream), rojo, rivereto; (channel, watercourse), kaneleto, defluileto
runt, nano
rupee, rupia, rupio; **rupiah,** (Indone-
zia) ~o
Rupicapra, ĉamo
rupture, (break, gen), rompi [tr]; ~iĝi;
~iĝo; (hernia), hernio; herniiĝi; **rup-
turewort,** herniario
rural, kampara, (poet), rura
Ruscus, rusko
ruse, ruzo, artifiko
rush, (hurry), hasti [int]; ~igi; ~(ig)o;
~eco; (dash on, move impetuously),
impeti [int]; impetigi; impeto; (attack), sturmi [tr], ekataki [tr]; (run etc.

fast), kuregi [int]; kuregigi; kurego
[see "run"]; (lavish attention, as in
courting), superŝuti [tr] per atentado;
(urgent), urĝa (e.g.: *a rush order:* urĝa
mendo); (expedite), urĝekspedi [tr];
(heavy workload, traffic, etc.), premo,
troabundo, superŝuto; (bot: *Juncus*),
junko; **rush hour,** pinthoro(j), prem-
periodo; **bulrush, bullrush,** (*Scirpus*), skirpo; **flowering rush,** butomo;
gold rush, orĉaso; **hare's-tail rush,**
erioforo; **inrush,** enflu(eg)o, invado,
enrompo; **onrush,** impeto; **outrush,**
elflu(eg)o, elrompo; **wood rush,** luzulo
rusk, biskoto
russet, (color), rufa; ~o
Russia, Rus/io; **Russian,** ~o; ~a; ~ia
Russo-, (pfx: Russian), Rus(o)– [see
"Russia"]
rust, rusto; ~i [int]; ~igi; **rusty,** (gen),
~a; **rustproof,** ~imuna; ~imunigi;
rust-colored, ~kolora; rufa
rustic, (simple, unrefined), rustika; (rural), kampara
rusticate, (send, go to rural area), alka-
mpar/igi; ~iĝi; (Br: suspend student),
provizore eksigi
rustle, (sound), susuri [int]; ~o; (steal),
ŝteli [tr], marodi [tr]
rut, (in a road, or similar groove, lit or
fig), vojsulko; (voj)sulkigi; (routine),
rutin(aĉ)o; (sexual), seksardo; seksar-
di [int]; **in a rut,** rutiniĝinta; **get into
a rut,** rutiniĝi
Ruta, ruto
rutabaga, flava rapo
Ruth, Rut
ruthenate, rutenato; **ruthenic acid,** ~a
acido
Ruthenia, Ruten/io; **Ruthenian,** ~o;
~a; ~ia
ruthenium, rutenio
ruthless, senkompata,   senindulga;
ruthlessness, ~o, senindulgemo
rutile, rutilo
Rutilus, ploto
Rwanda, Ruando†
rye, (grain; its plant), sekalo; (bread),
~pano; (whiskey), ~viskio

S

Saar, (river), Saaro; (region), ~lando
Saarbrucken, Saarbruko
Saba, (in Yemen), Ŝebao
sabbat, sabatorgio
sabbath, sabato; witch's sabbath, ~orgio
sabbatical, sabata jaro; sabata periodo
saber, sabro
Sabina, (woman's name), Sabina
Sabine, Sabeno; ~a
sable, (zool: animal), zibelo; (fur), ~aĵo; (bird), marteso
sabot, lignoboto [not "sabot–"]
sabotage, saboti [tr]; ~ado; saboteur, ~into; ~anto; ~isto
sabre, sabro
saburra, saburo
sac, (anat), receso [not "sako"]
saccharate, sakarato
saccharide, sakarido; polysaccharide, poli~o
saccharimeter, [see "saccharometer"]
saccharin(e), (chem), sakarino; (fig: sweet, syrupy), dolĉ-afekta, dolĉ(aĉ)a; soluble saccharin, kristalozo, natria ~o
sacchar(o)–, (chem pfx), sakar(o)–
saccharometer, sakarometro; saccharometry, ~io
saccharomycetes, sakaromicetoj
Saccharum officinarum, sukerkano
sacerdotal, sacerdota
sachet, parfumsaketo
sack, (any bag etc.), sako; en~igi; (dismiss from job), maldungi [tr], eksigi; (from government post etc.), malpostenigi, eksigi; (plunder), disrabi [tr]; disrabo; sacking, (cloth for sacks), ~ŝtofo; sackcloth, (for penitence etc.), ~aĵo; packsack, tornistro [see "pack"]; rucksack, ŝultrotornistro
sackbut, (early trombone), pratrombono; (erroneous synonym for "sambuke"), sabeko
sacral, (rel), sakralat, sakramenta [cp "sacred"; (anat), sakra
sacrament, sakramento; sacramental, ~a

Sacramento, Sakramento
sacred, sankta [cp "sacral"]
sacrifice, (gen), oferi [tr]; ~o; ~aĵo; (by slaughter), ~buĉi [tr]; ~buĉo; sacrificial, ~a; self-sacrifice, sin~o, sindono; self-sacrificing, sin~a, sindona
sacrilege, sakrilegio; sacrilegious, ~a; commit sacrilege, ~i [int]
sacrist(an), sakristiano
sacristy, sakristio
sacro–, (anat pfx), sakro–
sacroiliac, sakroiliaka; ~o
sacrosanct, sanktega
sacrum, sakro
sad, malĝoja, malgaja, trista, morna; sadness, ~o, malgajo, trist(ec)o
saddle, (seat for horse, bike, etc.), selo; ~i [tr]; (burden), ŝarĝi [tr]; saddlebacked, malĝiba; saddlebag, ~sako; saddlecloth, ĉabrako; Dryad's saddle, (bot), poliporo; packsaddle, pak~o, ŝarĝo~o [cp "pannier"]; sidesaddle, flank~o; flank~e
Sadducee, Sadukeo
sadhu, saduo
Sadi, Sadio
sadism, sadismo; sadist, sadisto; sadistic, ~a
safari, ĉasekspedicio
safe, (secure, unharmed, out of danger, sure), sekura; (lockable container), monŝranko; safety, (safe condition), ~eco; ~eca; (device, as on gun), ~ilo; safety catch, safety lock, ~ilo, ~butono; make safe, ~igi; safe and sound, (re person, animal), ~a kaj sana; (gen), ~a kaj bonstata; safe-conduct, paspermeso, pasgarantio; safe-deposit box, ŝloskesto; safe-deposit vault, ŝloskelo; safeguard, (protect), protekti [tr], ~igi; protekto, ~igo; (person, thing), protektanto; protektilo, sekurigilo; (guarantee), garantio; (safe passage permit), paspermeso, pasgarantio; safekeeping, protektado
safflower, kartamo
saffron, (plant or spice), safrano; (flavor w saffron), ~i [tr]; (color), ~a; mead-

ow **saffron**, kolĉiko

sag, (bend of cable, beam, etc., due to weight), sago; ~igi, defleksigi; ~iĝi, defleksiĝi; (any deflection), subfleksiĝi, derektiĝi; (droop, wane, lose vigor), velki [int], malvigliĝi [cp "sink", "bend"]

saga, sagao

sage, (wise), saĝa; ~ulo; (plant or spice), salvio; **sagebrush**, artemizio; **Bethlehem sage**, pulmonario; **red sage**, **wild sage**, lantano; **wood sage**, teŭkrio

sagittal, (arrow-shaped), sagoforma; (anat, med), sagitala

Sagittaria, sagitario

Sagittarius, (ast), Sagitario

sagittate, sagoforma

sago, (starch), saguo; **sago (palm)**, ~arbo, ~palmo

Sahara, Saharo; ~a

sahib, sahibo

said, (as adj: aforementioned), menciita

Said: Port Said, Port-Saido

Saigon, Sajgono [see "Ho Ĉi Min City"]

sail, velo; (go by sail), ~(ad)i [int]; (navigate, gen), navigi [tr]; (glide smoothly), glisi [int]; glisigi; **sailing**, (art of navigation), naŭtiko; **sailor**, maristo; (ordinary, of low rank), matroso; **lugsail**, lugro~o; **mainsail**, ĉef~o; **royal sail**, reĝ~o; **set sail**, ek~i [int]; **solar sail**, suna ~o; **topsail**, top~o; **topgallant sail**, bram~o; **have plain sailing**, senĝene progresi [int]

saimiri, Saimiri, sajmirio

sainfoin, *(Onobrychis)*, onobriko

saint, sank/ul(in)o; ~uligi, kanonizi [tr]; **saintly**, ~uleca; **Saint**, (as title), S~a; (in place names), S~a– [sometimes absorbed into Esperanto root as "San–" etc.; see below and under primary part of name; also see "St.", "San", "São"]

Saint Got(t)hard, San-Gotardo

Saintpaulia, (bot), sanktapaŭlio*

sake, (purpose, motive), motivo; (rice drink), sakeo; **for (someone's) sake**, **for the sake of (someone)**, por (la bono de) (iu) (e.g.: *I'll do it for your sake:* mi faros ĝin por vi; *for the sake of completeness:* por kompleteco); **for**

heaven's sake!, je l' ĉielo!; **for old times' sake**, pro malnovaj memoroj

Sakhalin, Saĥaleno

saki, sakeo

Sakti, Ŝaktio

Sakyamuni, Ŝakjamunio

sal, salo; **sal ammoniac**, ~amoniako, amonia klorido

salaam, (bow), riverenci [int]; ~o

salacious, (lecherous), lasciva, malĉasta, diboĉa; (pornographic), ~a, pornografia

salad, salato; **salad bowl**, ~ujo; **salad dressing**, ~osaŭco; **corn salad**, (bot: *Valerianella*), valerianelo; **fruit salad**, frukto~o; **potato salad**, terpom~o

Saladin, Saladino†

salamander, (zool; myth), salamandro

Salamandra, salamandro; **Salamandridae**, ~edoj; **Salamandrinae**, ~enoj

salami, salamo

Salamis, Salamiso

salary, salajro; **salaried**, ~ata

sale, (act of selling), vend/(ad)o; (selling event, as by store), (rabat)~ado; **sales**, (re selling, gen), ~a; **salable**, ~ebla; **salesclerk**, **salesperson**, **saleman**, komizo, ~isto; **salesmanship**, ~arto; **for sale**, ~ota; **offer for sale**, ~e pro poni [tr]; **yard sale**, **garage sale**, **rummage sale**, **jumble sale**, **white-elephant sale**, brokantobazaro

salicin, salicino

salicylate, salicil/ato; **salicylic acid**, ~a acido

salient, elstara, okulfrapa; ~aĵo

Salientia, batrakoj

saline, sala; (salt lick, marsh, etc.), ~ejo; **salinity**, ~eco; **salinometer**, ~ometro; **desalinate**, sen~igi

saliva, salivo; **salivary**, ~a; **salivate**, ~i [int]

Salix, saliko; **Salix viminalis**, vimeno

sallow, (color), palflava; (bot), saliketo

sally, (rush out), ekeliri [int], atakeliri [int]; ~o, atakeliro; (quip), spritaĵo; (jaunt, excursion), ekskurso; ekskursi [int]

Sally, (woman's nickname), Sanjo

Salmo, salmo; **Salmo trutta**, truto; **Salmonidae**, ~edoj

salmon, salmo

salmonella, Salmonella, salmonelo;
salmonellosis, ~ozo
Salome, Salomea
salon, salono
Salokina, Saloniko [cp "Thessaloniki"]
saloon, (bar, pub), drinkejo; (any salon, large hall), salono
salpingectomy, salpingektomio
salpingitis, salpingito
salping(o)–, (anat pfx), salping(o)–
salsify, tragopogo; **black salsify,** skorzonero
Salsola, salsolo
salt, (gen), salo; ~i [tr]; ~a; **salty,** ~a; **salt away, salt down,** forpaki [tr]; **(Great) Salt Lake,** S~lago; **Salt Lake City,** S~laga Urbo; **saltpeter,** (KNO_3), salpetro, kalia nitrato; **Chilean saltpeter,** ($NaNO_3$), Ĉilia salpetro, natria nitrato; **saltwort,** salsolo; **Epsom salt,** magnezia sulfato; **old salt,** (sailor), marhundo; **rock salt,** rok~o; **smelling salt,** odor~o(j); **take something with a grain of salt,** preni (akcepti) ion rezerve [or] kun iom da rezervo; **be the salt of the earth,** valori pli ol oro
saltarello, saltodanco
saltine, salbiskvito
salubrious, salubra
salutary, saniga, salubra
salute, saluti [tr]; ~o; **salutation,** ~o
Salvador(i)an, Salvadoreño, Salvadora; ~ano
salvage, (rescue, save), savi [tr]; ~(ad)o; ~ajo; (recover after disaster, damage, etc.), post~i [tr]; post~(ad)o; post~ajo, rekuperajo†
salvarsan, Salvarsan, salvarsano
salvation, savo; ~iĝo
salve, (ointment), ungvento; ~i [tr]; (salvage), [see "salvage"]
salver, pleto
Salvia, salvio; Salvia sclarea, sklareo
salvo, (gunfire etc.), salvo
Salween, Salveno
Sam, Samêjo
samara, samaro
Samaria, Samario; **Samaritan,** (gen), ~ano
samarium, samario
Samarkand, Samarkando

samba, sambo†
Sambucus, sambuko; Sambucus ebulus, ebulo; Sambucus nigra, nigra ~o
sambuke, sabeko [not "sambuko"]
same, sama; ~e; ~o; **sameness,** ~eco; **the same thing,** la ~o; **the very same, the selfsame,** la tut~a; **all the same,** (nevertheless), tamen, malgraŭ tio, malgraŭ ĉio; (it doesn't matter), tute egale, negrave, ne gravas; **same kind of,** ~speca; **for the same reason,** ~kial; **at the same time,** ~tempe; **in the same place,** ~loke; **in the same way,** ~maniere, ~kiel
samisen, ŝamiseno
Samoa, Insularo Samoa; **Samoan,** Samoano; Samoa
Samolus, samolo
Samos, Samoso
Samothrace, Samotraco
samovar, samovaro
Samoyed(e), (person), Samojedo; (dog), ~a hundo
sampan, sampano
samphire, (*Salsola*), salsolo; **golden samphire,** inulo
sample, (specimen), specimeno, provaĵo; ~i [tr]; (test small piece), provi [tr]; (statistics), muestro†, samplo; sampli [tr]; **sampler,** (collection of samples), ~aro; (concert), ~koncerto
Samson, Ŝimŝon
Samuel, Samuelo
samurai, samurajo
San, ("Saint", in place names), San– (e.g.: *San Francisco:* ~-Francisko) [see also separate entries below; see "saint", "St.", "São"]
sanatorium, sanatorio
San Bernardino, San-Bernardino
Sancho, Sanĉo
sanctify, sanktigi, konsekri [tr]
sanctimonious, sanktafekta, piafekta
sanction, (gen), sankcio; ~i [tr]
sanctity, sankteco
sanctuary, (holy place), sanktejo; (refuge, asylum), azilo, rifuĝejo; (animal reservation), rezervejo
sanctum, sanktejo; **sanctum sanctorum, inner sanctum,** plej~o
sand, sablo; ~a; ~i [tr]; (color), ~okolora; **sandbag,** ~osako; ~osakizi [tr];

sandbank, (sand bar), ~obenko, ~aĵo; (embankment), ~odeklivo; sand bar, ~obenko, ~aĵo; sandblast, ~oŝprucigi; ~oŝpruc(ad)o; sandblaster, ~oŝprucilo; sandbox, ~oskatolo; sandgroper, (Aus colloq), Okcident-Aŭstraliano; sandhopper, (zool), talitro; sandpiper, tringo; (Aus), pintvosta kalidro; sandwort, arenario; grain of sand, ~ero; quicksand, flu~o

sandal, (shoe), sandalo; sandalwood, (wood), santalligno; (tree), santalo

sandarac, sandarako

sandwich, (gen), sandviĉo; ~igi; Sandwich Islands, Insuloj S~aj [cp "Hawaii"]; sandwich man, ~ulo, afiŝportanto; open-face sandwich, (on one slice of bread), ~eto

sane, (mentally healthy), mense sana; (sensible), bonsenca, prudenta, saĝa, racia; sanity, mensa sano; insane, mense malsana, aliena, freneza; insanity, mensa malsano, alieneco, frenezo; insane asylum, frenezulejo; insane person, alienulo, frenezulo [cp "psychosis: psychotic"]

sanfoin, [see "sainfoin"]

San Francisco, San-Francisko

sangha, samgo

sanguine, sangvina; (drawing in ruddy colors), ~o

Sanguisorba, sangvisorbo

Sanhedrin, sinedrino, S~o

sanicle, saniklo

Sanicula, saniklo

sanitarium, sanatorio

sanitary, (clean, hygienic), higiena; (re public health), sanitara, san-protekta; sanitary napkin, sanitary towel, menstrua tuko

sanitation, (re public health, as sewage system etc.), sanitar/aĵo; ~eco; ~a servo; ~aj instalaĵoj; (hygiene), higieno

sanitize, higienigi

sanity, [see under "sane"]

San Marino, San–Marino†

San Remo, San–Remo

sans-serif, senornama

Sanskrit, Sanskrito; ~a

Santa, (in place names), Sankta [see "saint", "St.", "San"]

Santa Claus, Sankta Klaŭso [cp "Nicholas: St. Nicholas"]

Santalum, santalo

Santiago, (cities), Santiago

Santo Domingo, San-Domingo

Santolina, santolino

Saône, Saono

São Paulo, (city or state), San-Paŭlo

São Tomé and Principe, San–Tomeo kaj Principeo†

sap, (of tree, plant), suko; (undermine, weaken), sapei [tr], subfosi [tr]; sapeo

sapek, sapec, sapeko

saphenous, safena; saphena, ~a vejno

Sapindus, sapindo

sapling, arbido

sapodilla, (fruit), sapoto; (tree), ~arbo

Saponaria, saponario; Saponaria vaccaria, vakario

saponify, sapigi; saponification, ~o

saponin, saponino

Sapphic, Sapfa

sapphire, safiro

Sappho, Sapfoa

sapropel, sapropelio

saprophyte, (plant), saprofito; (animal), saprozoo

saprozoic, saprozoa

sapucaia, sapucaja, sapucaya, lecitido

Sara, Sara

saraband, sarabando

Saraca indica, aŝoko

Saracen, Saraceno; ~a

Saragossa, Zaragozo

Sarah, Sara

sarcasm, sarkasmo; sarcastic, ~a

sarcina, sarcino; sarcine, (sarcina cube), ~a kubo [note: PIV does not clearly distinguish between the bacterium and the cube of 8 cells]

sarcocarp, sarkokarpo

Sarcodina, rizopodoj

sarcoma, sarkomo; sarcomosis, ~ozo

sarcophagus, sarkofago

Sarcopsylla, sarkopsilo

Sarcoptes, sarkopto

sard, sardio

Sardanapalos, Sardanapalus, Sardanapalo

sardine, sardino [cp "pilchard"]

Sardinella pilchardus, pilĉardo

Sardinia, Sardinio, Sardio, Sardujo;

Sardinian, ~a, Sarda; Sardo
Sardis, Sarto
sardonic, sardona
sardonyx, sardionikso
Sargasso Sea, Maro Sargasa
sargassum, sargasso, sargaso
sari, sario
Sarmatia, Sarmat/io; **Sarmatian,** ~o; ~a; ~ia
sarong, sarongo
sarsaparilla, (plant), smilako; (root, extract, drink), ~aĵo
sartorial, tajlora
sartorius, (muscle), satorio
Sartre, (Jean-Paul), Sartro
sash, (over shoulder), balteo; (window), fenestroklapo [cp "shutter"]
Saskatchewan, Saskaĉevano*
sass, repliki [tr, int]; ~(ad)o; ~emo; **sassy,** ~ema
sassafras, Sassafras, sasafraso; **sassafras tea,** ~a teo
Sassan, Sasano; **Sassanid,** ~ido; ~ida
Satan, Satano; **Satanic,** ~a; **Satanism,** ~ismo
satchel, tornistro [cp "pack", "pannier"]
sate, sat/igi; **sated,** ~a
sateen, sateneto
satellite, (gen), satelito; ~a; **artificial satellite,** art~o; **communications satellite,** komunika ~o; **solar power satellite,** sunpotenca ~o; **spy satellite,** spiona ~o
sati, [see "suttee"]
satiate, satigi; **satiable,** ~ebla; **insatiable,** ne~ebla; **satiated,** sata
satiety, sateco
satin, sateno; **satinet(te),** ~eto; **satinpod,** lunario
satire, satiro; **satiric(al),** ~a; **satirist,** ~isto; **satirize,** ~i [tr]
satisfy, (gratify, content, fulfill desire), kontent/igi; (fulfill, gen, as requirements, expectations), plenumi [tr]; (fulfill debt or duty), kvitigi; (convince), konvinki [tr]; **satisfied,** ~a; plenumita; kvita; konvinkita; **be(come) satisfied,** ~iĝi; plenumiĝi; kvitiĝi; konvinkiĝi; **satisfaction,** ~igo; ~iĝo; ~eco; plenumo; kvitigo; kvitiĝo; konvinko; (re duel; rel recompense for sin), satisfakcio; **satisfacto-**

ry, ~iga, adekvata, sufiĉa; **dissatisfy,** mal~igi, malplaĉi [tr]; **self-satisfied,** mem~a; **to one's satisfaction,** ~ige al iu, ĝis ies ~igo
satrap, satrapo; **satrapy,** (land of a satrap), ~io
saturate, saturi [tr]; **saturation,** (process), ~ado; (saturated state), ~eco; **saturated,** ~ita; **saturation point,** ~punkto; **supersaturate,** super~i [tr]; **unsaturatd,** ne~a; **polyunsaturated,** poline~a
Saturday, sabato; ~a; ~e
Satureia, satureo
Satureja, kalaminto
Saturn, (ast; myth), Saturno
Saturnalia, Saturnalioj
Saturnia, saturnio
saturnine, malvigla, malgaja, moroza
satyr, satiruso
satyriasis, satiriazo
sauce, saŭco; **sauce dish,** ~ujo; **saucepan,** kuirpoto
saucer, pladeto, subtaso
sauerkraut, saŭrkraŭto
Saul, Saul
sauna, saŭno
saunter, promen(et)i [int]; ~o
–saur(us), (sfx: lizard, dinosaur), –saŭro [see separate entries]
Saururae, saŭrovostuloj
sausage, (gen), kolbaso; (small), ~eto; **blood sausage,** budeno; **link sausage,** ĉen~o
sauté malprofunde friti [tr]; malprofunde fritita
savage, sovaĝa; ~ulo; **savagery,** ~eco
savanna(h), savano
Savannah, Savano
savant, multesciulo, klerulo [cp "polymath"]
save, (conserve, not spend or use), ŝpari [tr]; (rescue; rel: free from damnation, degeneracy, etc.), savi [tr]; (set aside, reserve), rezervi [tr]; (avoid), eviti [tr]; (except), [see "except"]; **savings,** ~aĵo; **savings account,** ~konto
saveloy, (Br, Aus), ruĝhaŭta (spicita) kolbaso
savio(u)r, sav/into; ~anto; ~onto; **Savior,** (rel), S~anto
savoir-faire, farscio, takto

savoir-vivre, bonedukiteco [cp "joie de vivre"]

savor, (taste), saporo; (have taste of), ~i [int], gusti [int]; (perceive taste), gustumi [tr]; **savory,** (tasty), ~plena, bongusta; (herb), satureo

savoy, (cabbage), sabeliko

Savoy, (geog), Savojo; **Savoyard,** ~ano; ~a

savvy, kompreno, povoscio, lerteco; mult~a, lerta; ~i [tr]

saw, (cut), segi [tr]; ~ilo; (saying, maxim), popoldiro, aforismo, sentenco; **sawbuck, sawhorse,** ~boko; **sawdust,** ~aĵo; **sawmill,** ~ejo; **sawtoothed,** ~ildenta; **sawwort,** (bot: *Serratula*), seratulo; **sawyer,** (person), ~isto; **band saw,** bend~ilo, senfina ~ilo; **bucksaw,** fram~ilo; **buzz saw,** ~maŝino; **chain saw,** ĉen~ilo; **circular saw,** disk~ilo; **coping saw,** kurb~ilo; **crosscut saw,** transtranĉa ~ilo; **hacksaw,** metal~ilo; **hand saw,** man~ilo, trapeza ~ilo; **jigsaw,** ĵig~ilo; **power saw,** ~maŝino; **rip saw,** laŭvejna ~ilo

sax, (saxophone), saksofono

saxhorn, buglo

Saxicola, saksikolo

Saxifraga, saksifrago

saxifrage, saksifrago; **burnet saxifrage,** pimpinelo

Saxon, (gen), Sakso; ~a; ~ia; **Saxony,** ~io

saxophone, saksofono

say, diri [tr]; (for example), ni ~u (e.g.: *if the class has, say, 30 students:* se la klaso havas, ni ~u, 30 studentojn); **say!,** (interj to get attention), vidu!, he!; [see also "said"]; **saying,** popol~o, aforismo, sentenco; **say-so,** (statement, assurance, opinion), ~o, deklaro, opinio, certigo; (authority), aŭtoritato; **aforesaid,** supre ~ita, antaŭ~ita; **he said so (no, not),** li ~is ke jes (ne); **they say that, it is said that,** laŭ~e, oni ~as ke; **so to say,** por tiel ~i; **you don't say!,** (really?, is that right? [showing some surprise or doubt]), ĉu vere?; **it goes without saying, needless to say,** ne necesas ~i (ke); **(you can) say what you like,**

kion ajn vi opinias; **easier said than done,** pli facile ~i ol fari; **no sooner said than done,** ~ite, tuj farite; **have a say in,** havi voĉon pri, en; **have the last say in,** paroli la lasta pri, havi la lastan voĉon pri; **there is something (much) to be said for,** estas io (multe) laŭdinda pri

scab, (on wound), krusto; ~iĝi; [cp "scar"]; (plant disease), skabo [cp "scabies"]; (strike-breaker), strikrompanto

scabbard, glavingo

scabies, skabio [cp "scab"]

scabinus, skabeno

Scabiosa, skabiozo

scabious, (scabby), krusta; (re scabies), skabia; (bot: *Scabiosa*), skabiozo

scabrous, (rough), malglata; (scabby, crusty), krusta; (indecent), maldeca, malkonvena, skandala

scaffold, (for construction, painting, etc.), skafaldo; (of oil well etc.), ŝakto~o; (for hanging), eŝafodo, pendingo; **scaffolding,** ~aĵo; ~aro

scalar, (math), skalaro; ~a

scald, (heat, burn), brogi [tr]; ~(vund)o; (skald), skaldo

scale, (series of degrees, divisions, marks, levels, etc.; reduction ratio on map, drawing, etc.); skalo; ~igi; (mus), ~o, gamo; (scope, degree of inclusiveness etc.), amplekso; (table of previously calculated values), baremo; (on fish etc.), skvamo; (weighing device), pesilo; (any measuring device), mezurilo [cp "gauge", "meter"]; (pan on balance scale), pespleto; (insect), koĉo; (climb), grimpi [tr]; **scaly,** skvama; **boiler scale,** kaldronkrusto; **(according) to scale,** laŭ~a; laŭ~e; **full-scale,** plen~a; **large-scale,** grand~a, grandampleksa (e.g.: *large-scale destruction:* grandampleksa detruado); **on a large scale,** grand~e, grandampleksa; **small-scale,** malgrand~a, et~a, malgrandampleksa; **scale down (up),** laŭ~e redukti [tr] (pliigi); **scale model,** ~modelo; **tip the scales,** klini la vekton

scalene, (gen), skaleno; ~a

scalenus, (muscle), skaleno

scallion, askalono
scallop, (zool), pekteno; (as food), ~aĵo; (curved edge as on fabric), kurbrandaĵo; (escallop, cook brown w bread crumbs), panerbrunigi
scalp, (cranial skin and hair), kranihaŭto; (cut off, as war trophy etc.), skalpo; skalpi [tr]
scalpel, skalpelo
scam, ruzo
Scamander, Skamandro
scamp, (rascal), kanajlo; (botch, do badly), fuŝi [tr], fuŝfini [tr], faraĉi [tr]
scamper, impeti [int], kuri [int], peliĝi
scampi, verdaj salikokoj
scan, (TV, cmptr, radar, etc.), skani† [tr]; **scanner**, ~ilo†; (divide verse by meter etc.), skandi [tr]; ~iĝi; ~o; (scrutinize), ekzameni [tr], (okul)esplori [tr]; (look over or read over lightly), fluglegi [tr], flugekzameni [tr]; (re TV screen, cmptr, radar, etc., or analogous action), balai [tr]; balaado
scandal, skandalo; **scandalous**, ~a; **scandalize**, ~i [tr]
Scandinavia, Skandinav/io; **Scandinavian**, ~o; ~a; ~ia
scandium, skandio
Scandix, skandiko
scansion, skandado
scant(y), magra, malabunda
scape, (flower stalk), skapo
~scape, (sfx: view of), ~pejzaĝo (e.g.: *moonscape:* lun~o; *cityscape:* urbo~o)
scaphoid, skafoido
scaphopod, skafopodo
Scaphopoda, skafopodoj
scapula, skapolo; **scapulalgia**, ~algio; **scapular**, (re scapular), ~a; (rel mantle, cloth), skapulario
scar, cikatro; ~igi; ~iĝi [cp "scab"]
scarab, skarabo
Scarabaeus, skarabo
scarce, (rare), mal/ofta, ~abunda; (hardly as much as), apenaŭa; **scarcely**, apenaŭ; **scarcity**, ~ofteco, ~abundo
scare, timigi; ~o [cp "fear", "alarm"]; **scarecrow**, birdo~ilo, ĉifonfiguro
scarf, (head or neck wrap; sash), skarpo; (joint), fiksita duonuma junto

scarify, (gen), skarifiki [tr]; **scarification**, ~(ad)o; **scarificator**, ~ilo
scarlatina, skarlatino; **scarlatiniform**, **scarlatinoid**, ~oforma
scarlet, skarlata; ~o
scarp, (geol), krutaĵo; (of mil rampart etc.), kontraŭeskarpo
scat, (interj to scare off small animal etc.), huŝ!; (jazz), galimatia kantado
scathe, denuncegi [tr]; **scathing**, ~a, kaŭstik(eg)a
scatol, skatolo
scatology, fekologio
scatter, (flee, as crowd, birds, etc.), dis/igi, ~peli [tr]; ~iĝi, ~kuri [int], ~peliĝi, ~fuĝi [int]; (throw about, as seeds, papers, etc.), ~ĵeti [tr], ~ŝuti [tr]; ~ĵetiĝi, ~ŝutiĝi; (phys etc.: disperse), dispersi [tr]; dispersiĝi; dispersado; **scattered**, (sporadic, here and there), sporada, ~a; **scatterbrain**, facilanimulo, ventkapulo; **scatterbrained**, facilanima, ventkapa, malatent(em)a
scavenge, (salvage from refuse), rubsavi [tr], postrikolti [tr]; (clean streets etc.), purigi (la stratojn); **scavenger**, (animal, bird, etc., feeding after others), postpredanto
scenario, scenaro
scene, (theat; any event; location or description of event), sceno; (view, landscape), vidaĵo, pejzaĝo; **scenery**, (theat), dekoracio [cp "prop"]; **scenic**, (re landscapes etc.), pejzaĝa, pitoreska; (re drama, gen), teatra; (re stage scenery), dekoracia, ~a; **make a scene**, krei malpacon; **behind the scens**, (lit or fig), post la kulisoj; postkulisa
scent, (aroma), aromo, odoro; parfumo; (exude aroma), ~i [int], odori [int]; (give aroma to, perfume), parfumi [tr], ~igi; (smell, gen), flari [tr]; (footprints, trail, etc., left by animal or person, lit or fig), spuro; (hunt by scenting), spuri [tr]; (suspect), suspekti [tr]; **scent out**, elspuri [tr]
scepter, sceptro
sceptic, [see "skeptic"]
sceptre, sceptro
schedule, (list of times), horaro (e.g.:

bus schedule: busa ~o; *the TV schedule lists a play at 9:30 p.m.:* la televizia ~o listigas dramon je la 9.30 ptm); (plan, gen), plani [tr]; plano (e.g.: *we scheduled a meeting for tomorrow:* ni planis kunvenon por morgaŭ); (table, list, etc.), tabelo; tabeligi (e.g.: *schedule of expenses:* tabelo de elspezoj); (table of taxes, prices, etc.), tarifo; tarifi [tr]; **on schedule**, akurata, ĝustatempa; **ahead of schedule**, antaŭtempa; **behind schedule**, malakurata

Scheherezade, Ŝarazada

Scheldt, Skeldo

schema, skemo

schematic, skema; **schematic (diagram)**, ~o, konekto~o

schematism, aranĝoskemo

scheme, (plot), insidi [int], komploti [int]; ~o, komploto [not "skem–"; cp "plot"]; (plan, project), plano, projekto; (arrangement, as color scheme), aranĝo

scherzo, skerco

Schiller, Ŝillero

schilling, ŝilingo [abb: ŝ.]

Schinopsis lorentzii, Schinopsis balansae, ruĝa kebraĉo

schism, skismo; **schismatic**, ~a; ~ulo

schist, skisto; **schistous, schistose**, ~a

Schistosoma, skistosomo

schistosome, skistosomo; **schistosomiasis**, ~ozo

schizoid, skizoida; ~ulo

schizomycete, skizomiceto, bakterio

Schizomycetes,skizomicetoj, bakterioj

schizophrenia, skizofrenio; **schizophrenic**, ~a; ~ulo

Schleswig, Ŝlesvigo; **Schleswig-Holstein**, ~-Holstinio

schmaltz, sentimental/aĵo; ~eco; **schmaltzy**, ~a, siropa

schnap(p)s, (Nederlanda) ĝino

schnitzel, (any cutlet), kotleto; (veal), ~o, eskalopo

scholar, (learned person), kler/ulo, erudiciulo; (any student), studento, lernanto; (student w $ scholarship), stipendiulo; **scholarly**, (learned), ~a, erudicia; (studious), studema, erudicia; **scholarship**, (learning), erudicio,

~eco; (stipend), stipendio

scholastic, (phil: re scholasticism), skolastika; ~ulo; (re schools, gen), lerneja; **scholasticism**, (phil), ~o; **interscholastic**, interlerneja

scholium, skolio; **scholiast**, ~isto

school, (place for learning), lernejo; ~a; (phil, art, lit, etc.: style, manner), skolo (e.g.: *the Epicurean school:* la skolo de Epikuro; *that school of thought:* tiu skolo de pensado); (of fish), benko: (teach), instrui [tr]; **schooling**, lernado; **schoolboy**, **(schoolgirl)**, **schoolchild**, ~an(in)o, lernant(in)o: **schoolmaster**, (Br: school head), ~estro; **School of Arts**, (Aus), komuna kunvenejo; **School of the Air**, (Aus), Radio–~o; **nursery school**, varto~o; **elementary school**, **primary school**, elementa ~o; **grammar school**, (Am), elementa ~o; (Aus), eklezia ~o; **middle school, junior high school**, submez~o, submezklasa ~o; **high school**, secondary school, mez~o, liceo, gimnazio; **public school**, (Am), publika ~o; (Br, Aus), privata ~o; **reform school**, **approved school**, pun~o; **night school**, vesper~o; **business school**, komerca ~o

schooner, (boat), skuno; (glass), glasego

schottische, ŝotiŝo*; ~i [int]

schuss, ŝusi [int]; ~o

schwa, neŭtrovokalo

Schwaben, [see "Swabia"]

Schwann, (in anat names), ŝvanna (e.g.: *white substance of Schwann:* ~a ingo)

schwannoma, ŝvannomo; **schwannosis**, ~ozo

Schwartzwald, Ŝvarcvaldo

schyphozoa, skifozooj†

sciatic, iskiata; **sciatica**, ~algio

science, scienco; **scientific**, ~a; **scientist**, ~isto, ~ulo; **scientism**, ~ismo

Scilla, scilo

scimitar, cimitaro†

Scincus, skinko; Scincidae, ~edoj

scintigram, scintil/ogramo†; **scintigraphy**, ~ografio†

scintilla, ereto, joto

scintillate, scintili [int]; ~igi; **scintillation**, ~ado; **scintillation counter**,

~ometro
scintillometer, scintilometro
scintiscan, scintil/ogramo†: **scintiscan-ner,** ~oskanilo†
scion, (shoot, bud, for grafting), greft-aĵo; (offspring), ido
Scipio, Scipiono
Scirpus, skirpo
scirrus, skiro
scissor, tondi [tr]: **(pair of) scissors,** ~ilo [note sing]
Sciuropterus, flugsciuro
Sciurus, sciuro; Sciuridae, ~edoj
sclera, skleroto
Scleranthus, skleranto
sclerenchyma, sklerenkimo*
scler(o)–, (pfx), skler(o)–
scleroderma, sklerodermo
sclerometer, sklerometro
sclerosis, sklerozo; **sclerotic, scler-osed,** ~a; **multiple sclerosis,** multob-la ~o
sclerotium, skleroto
sclerotomy, sklerotomio
scoff, (mock), moki [tr], priridi [tr], ridindigi; ~o, prirido, ridindigo; (eat), manĝegi [tr], vori [tr]
scold, riproĉi [tr], skoldi [tr]; ~emulo, skoldemulo; **scolding,** ~o, skoldo
scolex, sklolekso
scoliosis, skoliozo
Scolopax, skolopo; Scolopacidae, ~ed-oj
Scolopendra, skolopendro
Scolopendrium, skolopendrio
Scomber, skombro; Scombriformes, ~oformaj (fiŝoj)
sconce, (for candles), (mura) kandelin-go
scone, skono*
scoop, (bucket-sized and ~shaped, as for dipping water from boat etc.), ŝkopo; ~i [tr]: (small, as for kitchen use), ~eto; ~eti [tr]; (large, as on power shovel etc.), ~ego; ~egi [tr]; (scoop-ful), ~opleno; (news), novaĵakaparo
scoot, hasti [int]; **scooter,** (child's vehi-cle), skutilo; **motorscooter,** skotero, motorskutilo; **go scooting off,** for~i [int]; (go on child's scooter), skuti [int]
scope, (extent), amplekso, kadro

–scope, (sfx), –skopo
scopolamine, skopolamino
scopophilia, skopofilio; **scopophiliac,** ~a; ~ulo
–scopy, (sfx), –skopio
scorbutic, skorbuta
scorch, (burn), surfac/bruli [int], ~e bru-li [int]; ~bruligi, ~e bruligi; ~brulo, ~a brulo; (wither), velki [int]; velkigi; (assail, caustic attack), riproĉegi [tr]; **scorching,** (very hot), arda, varmega; (fig: caustic), kaŭstika, vitriola; **scorched-earth policy,** politiko de bruligita tero
score, (make a point in game etc.), poenti [tr, int]; (total points in game etc.), ~aro; (mark line), streki [tr]; streko; (on edge of coin), randostreki [tr]; randostreko; (amount due, ac-count, lit or fig), konto (e.g.: *settle the score:* reguligi la konton); (twenty), dudeko; (mus part), partituro; (orches-trate, arrange), orkestri [tr], aranĝi [tr]; (win, gain), gajni [tr] (poentojn); (succeed), sukcesi [int]; **out-score,** (gain more points), el~i [tr]; **under-score,** (lit or fig), substreki [tr]; sub-streko; **know the score,** (colloq: know the situation), scii [or] kompre-ni la situacion; **what's the score?,** (colloq), kiel statas la afero?
scoria, skorio
scorn, malestimi [tr]; ~o; **scornful,** ~a
Scorpaena, skorpeno; Scorpaenifor-mes, ~oformaj (fiŝoj)
Scorpio, (ast), Skorpio
Scorpio, (zool), skorpio; Scorpionidae, ~edoj
scorpion, skorpio; **scorpion fish,** skor-peno
Scorpiurus, skorpiuro
Scorzonera, skorzonero
Scot, Skoto; **Scotland,** ~lando, ~io; **Scots, Scottish,** ~a; ~landa, ~ia; (dia-lect of English), (la) ~–Angla (dialek-to); **Scots Gaelic,** (la) ~–Gaela (lingvo)
scotch, (whiskey), skotviskio; (scratch), streki [tr], ekskorii [tr]; (wound), vundi [tr]; (end), fini [tr], forigi; (wedge), kojno; kojni [tr]
Scott, Walter, Valtero Skot

scoundrel, kanajlo

scour, (clean w scrubbing), frotpurigi; (wash, clear, by water current; flush), akvumi [tr]; (purge intestines), elpurigi [cp "enema"]; (get rid of), forigi; (search through), traserĉi [tr]; (run about), kuri [int] tra, trakuri [tr]

scourge, (whip), skurĝo; ~i [tr]; (plague etc.), plago

scout, (gen), skolto; ~i [int]; ~a; **scout out,** pri~i [tr]; **boy scout,** ~o; **girl scout,** ~ino; **explorer scout,** rover(in)o; **scouting,** (movement), ~ismo; **scoutmaster,** ~estro

scow, barĝo

scowl, (koler)grimaci [int]; ~o

scrabble, (scrape, scratch), skrapi [tr]; ~o; (struggle), lukti [int], barakti [int]; lukto, barakto

scrag, (lean, scrawny person or animal), magr/ulo, malgrasulo; duonkreskulo; (tree, plant), ~aĵo, duonkreskaĵo

scraggly, malabunda, malgrasa, osta [see "scrag", "scrub"]

scraggy, (rough, jagged), malglata, neregula; (lean, skinny), magra, malgrasa, duonkreska [see "scrag", "scrub"]

scram, (colloq interj: go!), for!; (leave), ~kuri [int], ~iri [int]

scramble, (climb, clamber), grimpi [tr]; ~o; (struggle, scuffle), barakti [int]; barakto; (throw together), kunĵeti [tr]; (mix up), malaranĝi [tr], malordi [tr]; (plane takeoff), (rapida) ekflugo; (rapide) ekflugi [int]; (rapide) ekflugigi; (cook eggs), kirl(kuir)i [tr]; **scrambled eggs,** ovkirlaĵo, kirlitaj ovoj

scrap, (small piece), peceto, fragmento; (of paper etc.), ĉifaĵo; (discard), forĵeti [tr]; forĵetaĵo, rubo; forĵetita, ~rubo [sfx] (e.g.: *scrap iron:* ferrubo) [cp "junk"]; (fight), batali [int], lukti [int], barakti [int]; batalo, lukto, barakto; (quarrel), kvereli [int]; kverelo

scrape, (scratch, abrade, rub), skrapi [tr]; ~o; (wound), ~vundo; [see "scratch"]; (sound), knari [int]; knaro; (difficult situation), embaraso; **scrapings,** ~aĵo(j); **scrape along,** (live w difficulty), elten(ad)i iele trapele

scrapple, maizporkaĵo

scratch, (scrape, cut surface etc.; rub itch), grati [tr]; ~iĝi; ~o; (wound), ekskorii [tr]; ekskoriaĵo; (sound), knari [int]; knaro; [see "scrape"]; (dig), ~fosi [tr]; (scribble), skribaĉi [tr]; (strike out, line through), forstreki [tr]; (billiards, pool), misludi [tr]; misludo; (starting line, point, as in race), komenclinio, komencopunkto, nulpunkto; (w/o handicap), senhandikapa; senhandikapulo; **scratchy,** ~a, malglata; **from scratch,** (from very beginning), (tute) dekomence; **start from scratch,** komenci (tute) de la komenco; **(just) scratch the surface,** (nur) supraĵe trakti [tr] (priatenti [tr], fari [tr], etc.); nur ~i la surfacon

scrawl, skribaĉi [tr]; ~o

scrawny, malgrasega, magrega, osta

scream, kriegi [tr, int]; ~o [cp "screech"]

scree, klifrubo

screech, kriĉi [int]; ~o

screen, (shield; TV, cmptr, movie, etc.), ekrano; (be a screen), ~i [int] (kontraŭ); (provide screen), ~umi [tr]; (hide, conceal), kaŝi [tr], ŝirmi [tr]; (room divider), septo, ~ego [see "partition"]; (show), sur~igi; (wire mesh), dratgazo; (sift), kribri [tr]; (sieve), kribrilo; **screen out,** elkribri [tr] [cp "cull"]; **screenplay,** filmdialogo, scenaro; **fire screen,** fendro, fajr~o; **off-screen,** (movie etc.), ekster~a†; ekster~e†

screw, (threaded shaft, gen; turn), ŝraŭbo; ~i [tr]; ~iĝi; (propeller etc.), helico; (twist), tordi [tr]; (vulg: fuck), fiki [tr]; fiko; (colloq: cheat, swindle), trompi [tr], superruzi [tr]; **unscrew,** mal~i [tr]; **screwdriver,** ~ilo; **Phillips screwdriver,** kruckapa ~ilo; **adjusting screw,** ĝustiga ~o; **Archimedean screw,** Arkimeda ~o; **female (internal) screw,** ~ino; **male (external) screw,** maskla ~o, ekstera ~o; **metal screw,** metal~o; **Phillips screw,** kruckapa ~o; **setscrew,** blokanta ~o; **thumbscrew,** alet~o; **wood screw,** ligno~o; **put the screws to,** premegi [tr]; **he has a screw loose,** mankas klapo en lia kapo; li ha-

vas mušon en la cerbo
scribble, skribaĉi [tr]; ~o
scribe, (person who professionally
writes, copies), skribisto [cp "write"];
(scratching tool), gratilo
scrimmage, (fight), tumulto, miksbatalo; (football play), ludero; (football
practice), ludekzerciĝi; ludek-
zerc(ad)o
scrimp, (make too small, skimp), nesu-
fiĉigi; (economize), ŝpari [tr];
scrimpy, magra, nesufiĉa
scrip, (any certificate), atestilo; (stock),
akci~o
script, (handwriting), (man)skribado;
~aĵo [cp "cursive"]; (manuscript),
manuskripto; (theat etc.), teksto, dialogo
scriptorium, skribejo
scripture, (sankta) skrib(aĵ)o
scrofula, skrofolo
scroll, (roll cmptr screen image, scrolled
book, etc.), volvo-ruli [tr]; ~iĝi;
(book, e.g. Torah), volvlibro, skribrul-
aĵo; (volute), voluto
Scrophularia, skrofulario
scrotum, skroto; **scrotal,** ~a
scrounge, (mooch), depruntaĉi [tr];
(scavenge, hunt out), elserĉi [tr]; (pilfer), marodi [tr]
scrub, (wash), bros/lavi [tr], frotlavi
[tr]; (scrabbly undergrowth), vep-
ro(j); vepra; (land covered by such),
veprejo, makiso; [see "scraggly",
"scraggy"]; (delete, eliminate), nuligi;
(get rid of), forigi; (waste gases), el-
lavi [tr]; (strike out), forstreki [tr];
scrubbrush, frot~o, lav~o; **scrub-
ber,** (Aus), sovaĝiĝinta bruto; **scrub-
by,** vepra, duonkreska
scruff, nuko
scruffy, malneta, senorda
scrumptious, delica, bongustega
scruple, (qualm, moral doubt), skrupulo; (unit of weight), 1,30 gramoj [see
§ 20]; (hesitate), heziti [int]
scrupulous, skrupula; **scrupulousness,**
~o
scrutiny, skrutinio; **scrutinize,** ~i [tr]
scuba, akvopulmo; **scuba diver,** ~a
plonĝisto; **go scuba-diving,** ~e plonĝi
[int]

scud, drivi [int], peliĝi
scuff, (scrape), skrapi [tr]; ~iĝi; ~aĵo;
(shuffling walk), ~paŝi [int]
scuffle, (fight), lukti [int], barakti [int];
~o, barakto; (drag feet, shuffle), sk-
rappaŝi [int]; skrappaŝ(ad)o
scull, (any oar), rem/ilo; (at rear), julo;
juladi [int]; (boat), (vetkura) ~boato
scullery, vaz-lavejo
sculpin, ĉoto
sculpt, skulpti [tr]; **sculptor,** ~isto;
sculpture, (something sculpted),
~aĵo; (art form), skulpturo
scum, (on water etc.), (flos)rekremento;
(dross; fig: anything worthless), skorio; (person), pleb(an)aĉo, sen-
taŭgul(ar)o, aĉul(ar)o
scupper, defluilo
scurf, dartro
scurrilous, (vulgar), triviala, filingva,
maldeca; (libelous), kalumnia
scurry, hasti [int], rapidi [int]; ~(ad)o,
rapidado
scurvy, (disease), skorbuto; (vile), fia,
aĉa
scut, stumpvosto
scuttle, (coal), karbujo; (scurry, run),
kuri [int], hasti [int], rapidi [int];
(hatch), luko; (abandon), forlasi [tr];
(sink), fundenigi, sinkigi; **scuttlebutt,**
klaĉo
Scylla, Scila
Scyphozoa, grandmeduzoj
scythe, falĉi [tr]; ~ilo
Scythia, Skit/io; **Scythian,** ~o; ~a; ~ia
sea, (gen), maro; ~a; **seafarer,** ~isto;
seafaring, ~a; **seagoing,** ~vetura;
seaman, (sailor, gen), ~isto; (ordinary
sailor of lowest rank), matroso; **sea-
mount,** ~monto; **seascape,** ~pej-
zaĝo; **seashore,** ~bordo; ~borda;
seasick, ~naŭza, ~malsana; **seasickness,** ~naŭzo, ~malsano; **seaside,**
~bordo; ~borda, apud~a; **seaward,**
~en; ~ena; **seaway,** ~kanalo; **seawor-
thy,** ~taŭga; **North Sea,** M~o Norda;
oversea(s), (foreign), eksterlanda;
eksterlande(n); (across ocean), trans-
mara; transmare(n); **South Seas,** (la)
Sudaj M~oj [cp "Zuider Zee"]; **put to
sea,** sur~iĝi
seal, (mark, stamp for authenticity

etc.), sigelo; ~i [tr]; (device), ~ilo;
(brand mark etc.), (kontrol)marko;
(close off), obturi [tr]; obturo; (re
roads), bitumi [tr]; (zool), foko;
(glued sticker), glumarko; glumarki
[tr]; (confirm), konfirmi [tr]; konfir-
mo; (settle, determine), determini
[tr], fiksi [tr], dediĉi [tr]; **hermetically seal**, hermetikigi; **sealer**, (Aus:
seal hunter), fokĉasisto; **hermetically sealed**, hermetika; **eared seal**,
(*Otaria*), otario; **elephant seal**, marelefanto; **fur seal**, (*Arctocephalus* or
Callorhinus), marurso; **gray seal**, haliñero, grizfoko; **Solomon's seal**,
(bot), poligonato, Salomon~o

seam, (sewn etc.), kunkudro; ~i [tr] [cp
"hem"]; (in metal, stone, etc.), junto;
(wrinkle, groove, etc.), sulk(et)o;
sulk(et)igi, fald(eg)igi; (of ore, coal,
etc.), vejno; (geol: similar narrow
mass of any substance), gango; **seam-
stress**, tajlorino, kudristino; **seamy**,
(sordid), malagrabla, aĉa, malpura,
(poet), sordida; **inseam**, ingvenuma
~o

séance, seanco

sear, (wither), velki [int]; ~igi; (scorch),
[see "scorch"]; (cauterize), kaŭterizi
[tr]

search, search for, serĉi [tr]; ~o;
search (a place) for, pri~i [tr], tra~i
[tr] (por); (pri)~o (e.g.: *search for the
book:* ~i la libron; *search the room for
the book:* pri~i la ĉambron por la libro); **searching**, (thorough), penetra;
in search of, ~e de; **search me!**, mi
tute ne scias!

season, (time), sezono; (spice), spici
[tr]; **seasonable**, laŭ~a; **seasonal**, ~a;
seasoning, spicaĵo; **in season**, (main
season, as for tourism etc.), ĉef~o;
ĉef~a; **preseason**, antaŭ~a; **out-of-
season**, ekster~a; ekster~e

seat, (any place to sit; headquarters),
sid/ejo, ~loko (e.g.: *the county seat:* la
kontea* ~ejo; *the flat boulder made a
good seat:* la plata roko prezentis bonan ~ejon); (chair-like, for one person, as in theater, plane, etc.), seĝo;
(in car, full-width), benko; (buttocks), postaĵo, (colloq), pugo; (that

part of pants etc.), postaĵumo; (right to
sit, as in governing body), ~rajto; (any
base part), bazo; bazi [tr]; baziĝi;
(socket etc.), ingo; eningigi; eningiĝi;
(make sit), ~igi (e.g.: *seat the child at
the table:* ~igi la infanon ĉe la tablo;
the hall seats 750: la halo ~igas 750);
seated, (sitting), ~anta; (resting, as
mech part), kuŝanta; **seating**,
~ig(ad)o; (arrangement), ~aranĝo;
(total seats), ~lokoj; **ejection seat**,
(for plane pilot), elĵetseĝo; **have a
seat, take a seat**, ~iĝi, ek~i [int];
one-seater, **two-seater**, (etc.),
unu~a, du~a (etc.)

Seattle, Seatlo*

sebacate, sebac/ato; **sebacic acid**, ~a
acido, dekandiacido

sebaceous, (re tallow), seba; (re sebum; sebaceous gland), sebuma

Sebastes, sebasto

Sebastian, Sebastiano

Sebastodes, sebasto

Sebastopol, Sebastopolo

sebum, sebumo

Secale, sekalo

secant, sekanto; **cosecant**, kosekanto

secateurs, stucilo [note sing]

secede, secesii [int]; **secession**, ~o

seclude, izoli [tr]; **secluded**, ~ita, privata, kaŝita; **seclusion**, ~(it)eco

second, (in sequence, order), dua; (another), alia; (article below standard
quality), ~aranĝaĵo; (unit of time; of
angle; mus interval), sekundo; (duel-
ing), sekundanto; (aid, assist), asisti
[tr], helpi [tr]; (support formal motion), subteni [tr]; subteno; **seconds**,
(food serving), ~a(j) porcio(j); **secondary**, (gen), sekundara, duaranga;
sekundarulo; sekundaraĵo

seconde, sekundo

secpar, parseko

secret, sekreto; ~a; ~i [int]; pri~i [tr];
secrecy, ~eco; **secretive**, ~ema;
keep secret, kaŝi [tr], konservi [tr]
~a; **top secre**, strikte ~a, plej alte ~a,
~ega

secretary, (gen), sekretari(in)o; **secre-
tarial**, ~a; **secretariat**, ~ato

secrete, (give off), sekrecii [tr]; (hide),
kaŝi [tr]; **secretion**, ~o

secretin, sekretino
sect, sekto [cp "faith", "religion"]; **sectarian,** ~a; ~ano; **sectarianism,** ~ismo
section, (division), dividaĵo; (any group), grupo; (admin or oth subdivision), sekcio; (division of law, regulation, or similar text), paragrafo; (part of city, as business section), kvartalo [cp "ghetto"]; (of newspaper, magazine, etc., devoted to one topic), rubriko; (math: bisecting line, plane, etc.), sekco; (med: piece excised), sekcaĵo; **section mark,** (symbol "§"), paragrafo–signo; **Caesarian section,** C-**section,** Cezara operacio; **midsection,** mezo, mezparto
sector, (gen), sektoro; **government sector,** ($), registara ~o; **private sector,** privata ~o; (esp in Communist terminology), priseko
secular, sekulara; **secularize,** ~igi
secure, (safe), sekura; ~igi; (obtain), akiri [tr], havigi; (firm, stable), firma, stabila; firmigi, stabiligi; (reliable), fidinda; (ensure, make certain), certigi; (give collateral for loan etc.), garantii [tr], ~igi (per ristorno) [cp "collateral", "hypothecate"]; (capture), kapti [tr]; (insure), asekuri [tr]; **security,** ~eco; firmeco, stabileco; fidindeco; (collateral), ristorno; **insecure,** (not safe, not firm), mal~a, malfirma; (not confident), nememfida; **insecurity,** mal~eco, malfirmeco; nememfido
sedan, fermita aŭto; **sedan chair,** portoseĝo [cp "palanquin"]
sedate, sobra
sedative, sedativo; ~a; **sedation,** ~igo
sedentary, (sitting), sida; (not migratory), nemigra
seder, Pesaĥomanĝo*
sedge, karekso
sediment, sedimento; **sedimentary,** ~a; **sedimentation,** ~iĝo
sedition, ribelincito; **seditious,** ~(em)a
seduce, delogi [tr]; **seduction,** ~o; **seductive,** ~a, ĉarma
sedulous, diligenta
Sedum, sedo
see, (re sense of sight, gen), vidi [tr];

(understand), kompreni [tr], ~i; (see psychic vision), vizii [tr]; (imagine), imagi [tr]; (consider), konsideri [tr]; (find out, learn), sciiĝi, lerni [tr]; (make sure), certiĝi; (accompany), akompani [tr]; (date regularly), akompanadi [tr], rendevuadi [int] (kun); (visit), viziti [tr]; (accept visitor), akcepti [tr]; (meet bet, as in poker), egali [tr]; (behold!, look!), ~u!, rigardu!; (interj preceding statement, explanation, etc.), ~u (e.g.: *well, see, I didn't have enough time:* nu, ~u, mi ne havis sufiĉan tempon); (rel), diocezo; **seer,** (prophet), profeto; (psychic), psikulo viziulo; **see about,** (investigate), kontroli [tr], esplori [tr], enketi [int] (pri); (attend to), prizorgi [tr], zorgi [int] pri; **see after,** prizorgi [tr], zorgi [int] pri; **see fit to (do something),** konsideri ke indas (fari ion); **see into,** (check on), kontroli [tr], esplori [tr], enketi [int] (pri); (understand), kompreni [tr]; **see (someone) off,** akompani (iun) al la foriro; iri kun (iu) por adiaŭi [tr]; **see through,** (lit), tra~i [tr]; (persist), persisti [int] (en, kun); (help), trahelpi [tr]; (penetrate problem, ruse, etc.), penetri [tr]; **see to,** (take care of), prizorgi [tr], zorgi [int] pri; **see (to it) that,** (make sure that), certiĝi ke; **seeing that,** (since, because), pro tio ke, ĉar; **foresee,** antaŭ~i [tr]; **oversee,** (watch over), superrigardi [tr], kontroli [tr]; **overseer,** (work foreman), vokto, laborestro; **see you later!,** ĝis re~o!, ĝis poste!, ĝis!; **see you tomorrow (next week, etc.),** ĝis morgaŭ (la venonta semajno, etc.); **see if you can,** provu ĉu vi povas; **seeing is believing,** kiam mi ~os, tiam mi kredos; **let me see,** (wait while I think), mi pensu iomete; **that remains to be seen,** tio restas ~ota; tio restas konstatota; **as far as the eye can see,** ĝis la limo de la ~atingo; ĝis la ~limo; **as one sees fit,** laŭ ies plaĉo, laŭ ies bontrovo
seed, (reproductive elements, collectively, gen), semo; (one grain), ~ero; (sow, spread seed), ~i [tr]; (spread seed on field etc., or analogous action,

as seeding clouds to induce rain), pri~i [tr]; (remove seed), sen~igi; (go to seed, form seeds), ~iĝi; **seeder**, ~ilo; **seedy**, (shabby), ĉifona; **seedbed**, ~bedo; **seedling**, ~plantido; **go to seed**, (lit), ~iĝi; (fig: deteriorate), kadukiĝi, degeneri [int]

seek, (search), serĉi [tr]; (try), peni [tr]; (request), peti [tr]; (have as goal), celi [tr]; **self-seeking**, sincela

seem, ŝajni [int]; **seeming**, ~a, kvazaŭa; **seemingly**, ~e [cp "likely"]; **seemly**, (proper), konvena, deca

seep, (ooze out), eksudi [int], ŝviti [int]; (through), traliki [int]; **seepage**, ~ado; ~aĵo; tralikado; tralikaĵo

seersucker, krisptolo

seesaw, baskulo

seethe, (boil, bubble), boli [int]; (be agitated), agitiĝi; (swarm), svarmi [int]

segment, segmento; ~i [tr]; ~iĝi; **segmented**, ~ita

segregate, (separate, gen), apartigi; (as social system), segregacii [tr]; **segregation**, ~o; segregacio; **segregationist**, segregacia; segregaciisto

seine, sejno

Seine, Sejno

seismic, sisma; **seismogram**, ~ogramo; **seismograph**, ~ografo; **seismology**, ~ologio; **seismologist**, ~ologo; **seismometer**, ~ometro, ~ografo

seism(o)–, (pfx), sism(o)–

seize, (capture, gen), kapti [tr]; (confiscate), konfiski [tr]; (property of debtor to settle debt), tradi [tr]; **seizure**, ~o; konfisko; trado; (med: attack, fit, as of epilepsy), ikto

seldom, malofte

select, selekti [tr], elekti [tr]; ~ita; **selection**, ~(ad)o, elekt(ad)o; (assortment of goods etc.), sortimento; (Aus: settlement), setlejo†, pionirbieno; **natural selection**, natura ~ado; **selective**, (re radio etc.), ~iva; (choosy), ~ema; **selectivity**, ~iveco; **selector**, (switch), elektilo; (Aus: settler), setlinto†, pionirbienulo

selenate, selenato; **selenic (acid)**, ~a (acido)

Selene, Selena

selenide, selenido

selenite, selenito; **selenious (acid)**, ~a (acido)

selenium, seleno; **selenide**, ~ido; **selenite**, ~ito; **selenium cell**, ~ĉelo; **selenious (acid)**, ~ita (acido)

selen(o)–, (pfx: Lunar), lun(o)–, L~–

self, (n), memo (e.g.: *deny the self:* nei la ~on); (reflexive, w my–, your–, him–, etc.), mi, vi, si (etc.) (e.g.: *he washed himself:* li lavis sin; *I hurt myself:* mi vundis min); (emphasizing oneself, not someone else), mi mem, vi mem, si mem (etc.) (e.g.: *he washed himself* [emphasizing that no one else washed him, or that he washed no one else]: li lavis sin mem); (myself, etc., for emphasis but not reflexive), mem (e.g.: *George built it himself:* Georgo mem konstruis ĝin; *you must do it yourself:* vi mem devas fari ĝin) [note: in this usage, "mem" must always immediately follow n or pron it refers to; "Georgo konstruis ĝin mem" would mean, "George built it itself", "George built that very thing"] [see also "self–"]; **selfheal**, (bot: *Prunella*), brunelo; **selfish**, egoisma, nesindon(em)a; **selfishness**, egoismo, nesindonemo; **unselfish**, sindon(em)a, malegoisma

self–, (pfx: indicating reflexive action), sin–, mem– [note: in this sense, "sin–" is used regardless of subject (e.g.: *your self-sacrifice:* via sindono)]; (emphasizing action by or regarding oneself), mem– (e.g.: *self-employed:* memdungita) [see separate entries for subentries with "self–"]

sell, (for $), vendi [tr]; ~iĝi; (convince), konvinki [tr]; **sell out**, elĉerpi [tr]; elĉerpiĝi; elĉerpiĝo; (betray), perfidi [tr]; perfido; **sell short**, (underestimate), subtaksi [tr]; **bestseller**, (book etc.), furora (libro, varo, etc.)

Seltzer (water), Selters-akvo

selvage, **selvedge**, ŝtofrando

semanteme, semantemo

semantic, semantika; **semantics**, ~o

semaphore, (gen), semaforo; ~i [tr, int]

semblance, ŝajno

Semele, Semela

semen, spermo [cp "sperm"]; (colloq), ĉuro

semester, semestro

semi–, (pfx: half), duon– (e.g.: *semiannual:* ~jara); (approximately half; partly similar), semi–, duon– (e.g.: *semivowel:* semivokalo)

seminal, (re semen), sperma; (re seed), sema; (fig), ĝerma, fundamenta **seminal duct**, spermatodukto

seminar, seminario

seminary, seminario

semiology, semiologio

Semiramis, Semirama

Semite, Semido; **Semitic**, ~a; **antisemite**, antisemito; **antisemitic**, antisemita

Semnopithecus entellus, entelo

semolina, semolo

Sempervivum, sempervivo

sen, ($), seno

senate, (institution), senato; ~a; (place where senate meets), ~ejo; **senator**, ~ano

send, (gen), sendi [tr]; **sender**, (person who sent), ~into (e.g. [on mail]: *return to sender:* re~u al ~into [see § 22]); (radio etc.), ~ilo; **send away**, for~i [tr]; **send away for**, (order), mendi [tr]; **send for**, (call person), voki [tr], venigi; (order), mendi [tr]; **send-off**, adiaŭo; **send out**, (to various destinations), dis~i [tr] (e.g.: *send out invitations:* dis~i invitojn); (from one place), el~i [tr] (e.g.: *send someone out for beer:* el~i iun por biero)

Seneca, (native American), Seneko; ~a; (Roman), ~o

Senecio, senecio; Senecio cruentus, cinerario

senega, senega root, poligalo

Senegal, (river), Senegalo; (country), ~io; **Senegalese**, ~ia; ~iano

Senegambia, Senegambio†

senescent, maljuniĝa; **senescence**, ~o

seneschal, seneskalo

senile, senila; **senility**, ~eco

senior, (older), pliaĝa; ~ulo; (after name), la Maljuna (e.g.: *John Smith, Sr.:* John Smith (la) Maljuna); (oldest), plejaĝa; plejaĝulo; (higher, as in hierarchy), supera; **seniority**, ~eco;

plejaĝeco; super(rang)eco, rango; **senior citizen**, ~ulo

senna, (leaves), senao; (plant), kasio; **bladder senna**, koluteo; **scorpion senna**, koronilo

Sennacherib, Sanĥerib

sensate, sensiva; **insensate**, (not feeling), ne~a, sensenta; (senseless), sensenca; (insensitive), nesentiva

sensation, (subjective experience through senses etc.), sensaco; (feeling), sento; (event causing gen excitement), sensacio; **sensational**, sensacia; **sensationalism**, sensaciismo, sensaciemo

sense, (action of organ of perception), senso; ~i [tr]; (meaning of word, phrase; math and geom), senco; (prudence), prudento; **senseless**, (pointless), sensenca, senrezulta, senmotiva; (unconscious), senkonscia; **sense datum**, ~itaĵo; **sense organ**, ~organo; **sense of humor**, ~o de humuro; **common sense**, prudento

sensible, (perceivable), sens/ebla; (able to perceive), ~iva; (of good sense), bonsenca; (prudent), prudenta; **sensibility**, (ability to perceive), ~ivo; (sensitivity to impression, feeling, etc.), sentemo, impresiĝemo; **insensible**, (not perceiving), nepercepta; (imperceptible), neperceptebla; (unconscious), senkonscia; (unfeeling), nesentiva

sensitive, (able to feel, respond to stimuli), sent/iva, ~ema [note: "~ema" may be confused w "sen-tema"]; (re senses), sensa; (able to sense), sensiva; (psychic), psikulo [cp "medium", "psychic"]; (easily hurt), doloriĝema; (easily affected emotionally), tuŝiĝema, impresiĝema; (easily offended, shocked, etc.), ofendiĝema, ŝokiĝema, ĝeniĝema, iritiĝema; (powerful, as radio receiver), ~iva, forta, potenca; (delicate, as re situation, diplomacy), delikata; (phot etc.), impresiĝema; **sensitivity**, ~ivo, ~emo; sensivo; doloriĝemo; tuŝiĝemo; ofendiĝemo, ŝokiĝemo, ĝeniĝemo, iritiĝemo; forto, potenco; impresiĝemo; **insensitive**, ne~iva, ne~ema; nesensema; nedoloriĝema, nedolorebla; netuŝiĝema, netuŝebla, apatia; neofendiĝema, neofendebla; malforta; neimpresiĝema; **supersensitive**, sensivega, supersensiva; ~ivega, ~emega, super~ema

sensitize, sentiv/igi; sensivigi; impresiĝemigi; iritiĝemigi [see "sensitive"]; **desensitize**, maliritiĝemigi (etc.); **be(come) sensitized**, ~iĝi (etc.)

sensitometer, sensometro; **sensitometry**, ~io

sensor, sensilo

sensorium, sensorio

sensory, (re senses, gen), sensa; (anat: re nervous system etc.), sensora; **extrasensory**, ekster~a

sensual, volupta; sensama; **sensualism**, sensismo

sensuous, (re senses), sensa; (sensual), volupta, ~ama

sentence, (gram), frazo; (decree punishment), kondamni [tr]; kondamno [not "sentenco"]; **death sentence**, mortkondamno

sententious, sentenca

sentient, sensiva, konscia; **sentience**, ~o, konscio

sentiment, (feeling, gen), sento; (sentimentality; appeal to emotion etc.), sentimentaleco; **presentiment**, antaŭ~o

sentimental, sentimentala; **sentimentality**, ~eco

sentinel, **sentry**, gard/isto, ~ostaranto, (poet), sentinelo; **sentry box**, ~obudo

Seoul, Seulo

sepal, sepalo

separate, (gen), aparta; ~igi; ~iĝi; (into pieces; move way, as in various directions), disigi, erigi; disiĝi, eriĝi; (spouses w/o divorce), separi [tr]; separiĝi; (release from job), maldungi [tr]; (from mil service), malsoldatigi; (various), diversa(j); **separable**, ~igebla; disigebla, erigebla; **separation**, ~igo; ~iĝo; disigo, erigo; disiĝo, eriĝo; separiĝo; maldungo; malsoldatigo; **separatism**, (pol), separatismo; **separatist**, (pol), separatisma; separatisto

Sephard, Sefardo; **Sephardim**, ~oj;

Sephardic, ~a

sepia, (dye; color), sepio; ~a; (drawing, photo in sepia), ~aĵo

Sepia, (zool), sepio

sepiolite, sepiolito, marŝaŭmo

sepoy, sipajo

sepsis, sepseco

September, septembro

septet, (any 7), sepopo; (mus), septeto

septic, sepsa; **septicemia**, ~emio; **septic tank**, ~ujo; **antiseptic**, anti~a; anti~enzo; **antisepticize**, anti~i [tr] [cp "asepsis"]

septillion, (Am: 10^{24}), kvariliono; (Br: 10^{42}), sepiliono [see § 19(b)]

septime, (fencing position), septimo

septuagenarian, sepdekjara; ~ulo

Septuagint, Septuaginto

septum, septo

septuple, sep/obla; ~oblo; ~oble; ~obligi; ~obliĝi; ~opo; ~ope; ~opigi; ~opiĝi [see "double"]

septuplet, sepnaskito

sepulcher, (for burial), sepult/ejo; (for relics), relikvujo; **sepulchral**, ~eca

sepulture, sepult(ad)o

sequel, (subsequent item, continuation), sekv/aĵo; (consequence, result), ~o, rezulto, konsekvenco

sequence, (any series of 2 or more items), sekvenco, sinsekvo (e.g.: *arrange the cards in sequence*: aranĝi la kartojn ~e [or] laŭ ~o; *a sequence of events*: ~o [or] sinsekvo de eventoj); (mus), ~o; (any row), vico; vicigi; **sequential**, ~a, sinsekva; (laŭ)vica; **sequencer**, ~igilo

sequester, (hide), kaŝi [tr]; (set aside, separate), apartigi, flankenmeti [tr]; (law: entrust disputed property pending judicial decision), sekvestri [tr]; **sequestration**, ~o; apartigo; flankenmeto; sekvestro

sequin, (gen), zekineto

sequoia, (*Sequoia sempervirens*), sekvojo; **giant sequoia**, (*Sequoiadendron*), sekvojadendro

serac, serako

seraglio, serajlo

serail, serajlo

seraph, serafo; **seraphim**, ~oj

Serapis, Serapo

Serb, Serbo; Serbia, ~io; Serbian, ~a; ~ia; Serbo-Croatian, (la) ~kroata (lingvo)
serenade, serenado; ~i [tr]
serendipity, serendip/ecot; serendipitous, ~a
serene, serena; serenity, ~eco
serf, servut/ulo; serfdom, serfhood, ~eco; work as a serf, ~i [int]
serge, serĝo; ~igi; serging, ~aĵo
sergeant, serĝento; sergeant at arms, ordokonservisto; staff sergeant, ĉef~o
serial, seria; ~aĵo
series, (gen), serio; ~a; (column, row), vico; (elec connection), ~a (konekto)
serif, literstreketo, ornamstreketo; sansserif, senornama
Serinus canaria, kanario
serious, (earnest, sincere, not joking), serioza; (grave, important, not trifling), grava
serjeant, [see "sergeant"]
sermon, prediko; sermonize, ~i [tr, int]; the Sermon on the Mount, la P~o sur la Monto
serology, ser/ologio; ~umologio [see "serum"]
serous, (re serum), sera; ~uma [see "serum"]; (re serous membrane), seroza; serous membrane, serozo
serpent, (gen), serpento; sea serpent, mar~o; serpentine, ~(oform)a; (stone), serpenteno
Serpentarius, serpentario
serpiginous, serpigina
serpigo, serpiginaĵo
Serranus, serano*; Serranidae, ~edoj
Serrasalmus, piranjo
serrate(d), segil-denta
Serratula, seratulo
serratus, (muscle), serato
serum, (of blood), sero; (as medication), ~umo; (liquid in serous membrane), serozaĵo
serval, servalo
servant, servist(in)o; bondservant, servutulo; domestic servant, dom~o
serve, (work for; provide; assist; be useful; suffice; etc.), servi [tr, int]; (set food or drink; deliver), prezenti [tr]; (tennis etc.), serviri† [int]; serviro†;

server, (waiter or waitress), kelner(in)o; (tennis etc.), serviranto†; serve in the military, milit~i [int]; it serves you right, vi ja meritas tion; serving, (food portion), porcio; self-serving, sin~a
service, (serving), servo; ~ado; ~a; (rel), di~o; (mil), militistaro; militista; (car maintenance etc.), revizii [tr]; revizia; reviziado; (tennis etc.), serviro†; (presenting), prezent(ad)o; (tree), sorparbo; serviceable, utila, utiligebla, praktika; serviceberry, (fruit), sorpo; (tree), sorparbo; serviceman, servicewoman, (in mil service), militist(in)o, soldat(in)o; service station, benzinstacio; disservice, malutilo; conditions of service, laborkondiĉoj; do a disservice to, esti malutila al, malutili [int] al; military service, milit~o; self-service, (re store, gas station, etc.), mem~a; self-service store, mem~ejo; (I am) at your service, (mi estas) je via ~o [or] dispono
serviette, buŝtuko
servile, lakea, sklav(ec)a, servut(ec)a, servemaĉa, (poet), servila
servitude, servitudo, sklaveco, servuteco
servo, servomechanism, servomeĥanismo
sesame, sezamo
sesamoid, sezamoido; ~a
Sesamum, sezamo
sesqui-, (pfx), seskvi~
sesquicentennial, centkvindekjara; ~a datreveno, ~a jubileo
sesquioxide, seskvioksido
sesquipedalian, (very long, as re words), seskvimetr/olonga; (inclined to use long words), ~avortutiligema
sessile, sesila
session, sesio, kunsido; be in session, sidi [int] (e.g.: Parliament is not now in session: Parlamento ne sidas nun)
sesterce, sesterco
sestet, (mus), sesteto [cp "sextet"]
sestina, sestino
set, (place, put, gen), meti [tr], loki [tr]; (fasten), fiksi [tr]; (make sit), sidigi; (place to, as a match to paper), al~i

[tr]; (put out items, as dishes on table), pri~i [tr] [cp "set out" below]; (cause to be in condition or relation), –igi [sfx] (e.g.: *set on fire:* ekbruligi; *set the table on edge:* surrandigi la tablon); (fix in position, adjust, set up, as trap, sail, etc.), starigi, ĝustigi, aranĝi [tr], prepari [tr]; (regulate, as radio, thermostat, etc.), ĝustigi, reguligi; (adjust timepiece to right time), akuratigi, ĝustigi, altempigi; (ready), pretigi; preta; (sawteeth angle), dentklinigi; dentklino; (sink nail, screw), subnajli [tr]; subŝraŭbi [tr]; subnajlilo; (position fractured bone), reloki [tr], repoziciigi; (grow together, knit, re bone etc.), kuntrikiĝi, kuntiriĝi; (position dislocated joint), enartikigi; (rigid, settled, firm), rigida, firma; rigidigi, firmigi; rigidiĝi, firmiĝi; (reserve fixed time, purpose, etc.), destini [tr], aranĝi [tr]; (establish, decide), establi [tr], difini [tr], decidi [tr] (e.g.: *set a date for the meeting:* decidi daton por la kunveno); (make colorfast), palimunigi; palimuniĝi; (go down, re sun, moon, etc.), subiri [int]; subiro (e.g.: *sunset:* sunsubiro); (math; any group considered as unit, whole), aro, –aro [sfx], kompleto (e.g.: *set of tools:* ilaro; *woodworking set:* lignolabora kompleto; *the set of whole numbers:* la aro de entjeroj); (accessories), garnituro (e.g.: *desk set* [pen, pencil, notepad, etc.]: skribtabla garnituro); (set metal type for printing, or analogous computerized process), komposti [tr]; (mount, as gems), munti [tr] [see "setting" below]; (incrust, as w gems), inkrusti [tr]; (arrange hair etc.), aranĝi (la hararon); (har)aranĝo; (transplant), transplanti [tr]; transplantaĵo; (post guards etc.), posteni [tr]; (point, re hunting dog), indiki [tr] [see "setter" below]; (theat: scene, locale), sceno, lokalo; (sit on eggs), kovi [tr]; (obstinate), obstina; (tendency), tendenco, inklino, emo; (clique, coterie), kliko, koterio; (service of dishes etc.), servico; (mus selections between intermissions), prezentero; (apparatus), aparato (e.g.: *television*

set: televidaparato); (tennis), ludaro, serio; (bridge: defeat contract), faligi; **setter**, (dog), setero; **setting**, (position of dial etc.), pozicio; (gem mounting), muntumo; (locale, as of story, event, etc.), lokalo; **place setting**, (dishes), (unuloka) servico; **set about**, komenci [tr]; **set against**, (balance), ekvilibrigi; (compare), kompari [tr]; (make hostile, make oppose), malamikigi, kontraŭigi; **set one against**, instigi iun kontraŭ; **be set against**, (oppose), kontraŭi [tr]; **be dead set against**, senmove kontraŭi [tr]; **set apart**, (separate), apartigi; (reserve), rezervi [tr]; (designate, assign), destini [tr], asigni [tr]; **set aside**, (separate), apartigi; (put to side), flanken~i [tr]; (reject, dismiss), malakcepti [tr]; (law: reverse lower court or admin decision), kasacii [tr]; (annul), nuligi; (hold back, reserve), rezervi [tr]; **set back**, (move backwards, as clock), retro~i [tr]; (hinder; reverse progress), malhelpi [tr], regresigi, malprogresigi, malantaŭenigi; **set-back**, malhelpo, regreso, malprogreso; **set down**, (put down, release), de~i [tr], mallevi [tr], kuŝigi; (on paper), surpaperigi; (land plane etc.), surterigi, alterigi; (establish, as rules etc.), fiksi [tr], establi [tr]; (ascribe, attribute), atribui [tr]; **set forth**, (express, state), deklari [tr], esprimi [tr], antaŭ~i [tr]; (define, formulate), difini [tr], formuli [tr]; (present, make known), prezenti [tr], sciigi; **set in**, (begin), komenci [tr]; komenciĝi; (direct ship etc. toward shore), terenigi; tereniĝi; (insert), en~i [tr]; (become established), establiĝi; **set off**, (leave, start), ekiri [int]; ekirigi; (make function), ekfunkciigi; (set in relief), reliefigi; (show in good light), plibeligi; (make explode), eksplodigi, knaligi; **setoff**, (offset, compensation), kompenso; **set on**, (attack), ataki [tr]; (incite to attack), atakigi, inciti [tr] al atako; **be set on**, (determined to do, firmly decided upon), esti rezoluta, esti (firme) decidinta; firme intenci [tr]; **set out**, (define),

difini [tr]; (establish limits), dislimi [tr]; (display), el~i [tr], elmontri [tr]; (plant), planti [tr]; (leave, go), ekiri [int]; (undertake goal), preni al si (la taskon), klopodi [tr], sin dediĉi al; (arrange), aranĝi [tr]; (spread out, as flatware etc.), dis~i [tr]; (state), deklari [tr], detali [tr], prezenti [tr]; **set straight**, ĝustigi (iun, ion); ĝuste informi (iun pri io); **set to**, (apply self), sin dediĉi al, sin apliki al; (begin), ek–[pfx] (e.g.: *set to work:* eklabori); **set to**, (fight), barakto, lukto, batalo; **set up**, (set upright), starigi; (raise, gen), levi [tr]; (represent self), prezenti (sin kiel, sin esti); (arrange), aranĝi [tr]; (put together, assemble, as machine, apparatus), munti [tr]; (establish, found), fondi [tr], starigi, establi [tr]; (provide, fit out), provizi [tr]; (prepare), prepari [tr], pretigi; (cause), kaŭzi [tr], starigi, estigi; (serve drinks etc. before customers in bar), servi [tr]; **set-up**, (arrangement), aranĝo; (circumstance), cirkonstanco; (drink mix), (trink)miksaĵo; **set up shop**, establi sin; **set upon**, (attack), ataki [tr]; **all set**, tute preta, ĉio preta; **inset**, en~aĵo; **jet set**, mondumanaro; **null set**, nula aro; **offset**, (printing), ofseti [tr]; ofseto; ofseta; (compensate), kompensi [tr]; kompenso; **onset**, (beginning), komenco; (attack), atako; **outset**, komenco; **subset**, subaro, subkompleto; **thickset**, kompakta, dikmalalta; **upset**, (overturn, overthrow), renversi [tr]; renversiĝi; renvers(iĝ)o; (disturb emotions, bother), ĉagreni [tr]; ĉagreno; (disturb, gen), malkvietigi, maltrankviligi; malkvieto, maltrankvilo; (disorder), malaranĝi [tr], malordi [tr]; malaranĝo, malordo; **set oneself the task of,** [see "set out" above]
seta, fieto; **setaceous**, fiet/ohava; ~eca
Seth, Set
seton, setono
settee, kanapo
settle, (put in order, arrange), reguligi, aranĝi [tr]; (sink; become comfortably set), sinki [int], sin komfortigi (e.g.: *settle into a chair:* sinki [or] sin kom-

fortigi en seĝon); (onto bottom of liquid or oth surface), surfundiĝi (e.g.: *the leaves settled to the bottom of the lake, to the forest floor:* la folioj surfundiĝis al la fundo de la lago, al la arbara fundo); (sediment), sedimenti [int]; sedimentigi; (establish residence, gen), loĝigi; ekloĝi [int] (e.g.: *he settled his family in the city:* li loĝigis sian familion en la urbo; *they settled in the city:* ili ekloĝis en la urbo); (in uninhabited area, region), setli† [int] (en) (e.g.: *Virginians settled Kentucky:* Virginianoj setlis en Kentukio); (colonize), kolonii [tr]; (make, become dense and compact), kompaktigi; kompaktiĝi (e.g.: *the rain settled the dust:* la pluvo kompaktigis la polvon); (calm nerves, stomach, etc.), kvietigi; kvietiĝi; (establish), establi [tr]; establiĝi; (decide, determine), decidi [tr], fin-aranĝi [tr], fiksi [tr], determini [tr]; (pay debt, relieve obligation), kvitigi; (transfer property), transproprietigi, transposedigi; (decide legal issue out of court), decidi (akordiĝi) ekstertribunale [or] ekster la tribunalo; (come to rest, halt), halti [int], senmoviĝi; (bench, sofa), kanapo; **settler**, setlinto†; koloniano, koloniinto; **settlement,** setlado; (village), setlejo†, setlemento; kolonio; **settle down,** sinki [int]; kompaktiĝi; kvietiĝi; establiĝi; halti [int], senmoviĝi; (start to work etc.), ekdediĉi sin; **settle for,** (accept), akcepti [tr]; **settle up,** (settle accounts, lit or fig), ~i la konton
Sevastopol, Sebastopolo
seven, sep [see § 19]; **seventh,** (7th), ~a; (1/7), ~ono; (mus interval), septimo
sever, tranĉi [tr], rompi [tr]; (more emphatic: cut through, cut off), tra~i [tr], dis~i [tr], for~i [tr]; **severance,** (for)~o, (for)rompo; (from job), maldungo
several, (a few), pluraj; (separate, diverse, individual), diversa(j), aparta(j)
severe, severa; **severity,** ~(ec)o
Seville, Sevilla, Sevilo
sew, (gen), kudri [tr] [cp "stitch"];

(booklet pages), broŝuri [tr]; **sewing supplies**, mercero [note sing]
sewer, kloako; **sewage**, ~aĵo; **storm sewer**, (drainage pipes), tubkulverto; (opening w grating), ~faŭko
sex, gen), sekso; ~a; **sexed**, ~hava; **sexism**, ~ismo; **sexist**, ~isma; ~isto; **sexless**, (asexual), sen~a; **sexology**, ~ologio; **sexologist**, ~ologo; **sexpot**, erotul(in)o; **sexual**, ~a; **sexuality**, ~eco; **sex appeal**, ~allogo; **bisexual**, ambaŭ~a; ambaŭ~ema; ambaŭ~emulo; **heterosexual, homosexual**, [see "heterosexual", "homosexual"]; **transsexual**, trans~a; trans~ulo; **transsexualism**, trans~ismo; **unisex**, ambaŭgenra; **sex urge, sex desire**, ~urĝo, eroto; **share sex, have sex**, ~kuniĝi
sexagenarian, sesdekjara; ~ulo
sextant, sekstanto
sextet, (any group of 6), sesopo [cp "sestet"]
sextile, sesilo; ~a
sextillion, (Am: 10^{21}), triiliardo; (Br: 10^{36}), sesiliono [see § 19(b)]
sexton, sakristiano
sextuple, ses/obla; ~oblo; ~oble; ~obligi; ~obliĝi; ~opa; ~opo; ~ope; ~opigi; ~opiĝi [see "double"]
sextuplet, sesnaskito
Seychelles, Sejĉelojt
sforzando, (mus), akcentite
sh! (interj to order quiet), ŝŝ!, ĉit!
Shaanxi, Ŝenhi
shabby, (dilapidated), kaduka; (ragged, worn), ĉifona; (disgraceful), hontinda, fia
shack, domaĉo, kaban(aĉ)o
shackle, ŝeklo; en~igi
shad, alozo
shaddock, (fruit), pampelmuso; (tree), ~arbo
shade, (shadow), ombro; (cast shadow on), ~i [tr]; (depict shadow in painting etc.), ~umi [tr]; (color gradation), kolor(helec)o [cp "hue"]; (nuance, small amount or degree), nuanco; (influence), influi [tr]; (ghost), ~o, fantomo; (light cover, as lamp shade), ŝirmilo; ŝirmi [tr]; **shaded**, ~a; **shady**, (shaded), ~a; (dishonest), fia, suspek-

tinda, malhonesta; **lamp shade**, lampŝirmilo; **sunshade**, (as in car, to shield eyes), viziero; **window shade**, rulkurteno
shadoof, ŝadufo
shadow, (shade), ombro; ~i [tr]; (follow), gvatsekvi [tr]; (ghost), ~o, fantomo; **shadowed, shadowy**, ~a; **foreshadow**, aŭguri [tr], antaŭsigni [tr]; **overshadow**, super~i [tr]
shaft, (of arrow, spear, etc.; any rod, pole), stango; (center length of column, of rod, axle, etc.), fusto; (mech: entire rod or axle), ŝafto; (of mine, elevator, stairwell, etc.), ŝakto; (of light etc.), fasko; (pole to harness horse to wagon etc.), timono; **cam shaft**, kamŝafto; **crankshaft**, krankŝafto
shag, (heavy nap), vil/ego, dik~o; (tobacco), malfajna tabako; (zool), tufa kormorano; **shaggy**, ~a
shagreen, ŝagrino
shah, ŝaho
shake, (gen), skui [tr]; ~iĝi; ~(iĝ)o; (agitate), agiti [tr]; (rock back and forth), ŝanceli [tr]; ŝanceliĝi; **shaky**, (uncertain), necerta; (weak, unstable), kaduka, malstabila, ŝanceliĝema; **(milk)shake**, laktokoktelo; **shake down**, (make fall), ~faligi; (compress), kun~i [tr]; **shakedown**, (bed), litaĉo; (blackmail), ĉantaĝo; (search), traserĉo; (test-run), prova; provo; **shake up**, (mix), ~miksi [tr]; (disturb, rouse), ~veki [tr], ~stimuli [tr], ~inciti [tr]; (jar, shock), ~ŝoki [tr]; (disconcert), konsterni [tr]; **shake (hands)**, manpremi [tr, int]; **handshake**, manpremo; **shake one's head**, (to indicate "no"), kapnei [int]; (slower motion, indicating wonder, uncertainty, etc.), ŝanceli la kapon; **a fair shake**, justa trakt(ad)o; **salt shaker**, salujo; **pepper shak**, piprujo
Shakespeare, Ŝekspiro; **Shakespearean**, ~a
shako, ĉako
Shakti, Ŝaktio
Shakyamuni, Ŝakjamunio
shale, skisto; **oil shale**, petrol~o
shall, (future tense; compulsion), ~os [sfx] (e.g.: *we shall leave:* ni foriros;

this door shall remain closed at all times: ĉi tiu pordo restos ĉiam fermita); (in question), ĉu –u (e.g.: *shall we leave now?:* ĉu ni foriru nun?)

shallop, ŝalupo

shallot, askalono, ŝaloto

shallow, (gen), malprofunda; (superficial), ~a, supraĵa; **shallow(s),** ~aĵo [note sing]

sham, falsa; ~igi, artifiki [tr]; ~aĵo, artifiko

shaman, ŝamano

shamble, (shuffle), trenmarŝi [int]; ~(ad)o; **shambles,** (disorder), ĥaoso; (slaughterhouse), buĉejo

shame, honto; ~igi; **feel shame, be ashamed,** ~i [int]; **shameful,** ~inda; **shameless,** sen~a, cinika; **for shame!, shame on you!,** ~u!, fi al vi!; **put (one) to shame,** ~igi (iun); **what a shame!,** kia domaĝo!. domaĝe!; **it's a shame that,** estas domaĝe ke

shammy, [see "chamois"]

shampoo, ŝampui [tr]; (soap), ~o; (action), ~ado

shamrock, (Irlanda) trifolio

Shandong, Ŝandongo

shanghai, (capture), forkapti [tr]

Shanghai, (city), Ŝanhajo

Shangri-La, paradizo, utopio

shank, (lower leg), tibio; (calf muscle etc.), suro; (as meat), suraĵo; (of shaft), fusto [see "shaft"]

Shansi, Ŝanhi

shantey, marista kanto

Shantung, Ŝandongo

shanty, (hut), domaĉo; (song), marista kanto; **shanty-town,** ladvilaĝo

Shanxi, Ŝanhi

shape, (form, gen), formo, figuro; ~i [tr]; (cut out, as from rock etc.), tajli [tr]; (state, condition), stato (e.g.: *what kind of shape is that car in?:* en kia stato estas tiu aŭto?); [see also "–shaped"]; **shapeless,** sen~a; **shapely,** bel~a; **shape up,** (take shape), ~iĝi; (get into good shape), bonstatiĝi; bonstatiĝi; **in (good) shape,** bonstata, en bona stato; **in bad shape, out of shape,** malbonstata, en malbona stato; **misshape,** mis~i [tr]; **misshapen,** mis~(it)a; **take shape,** ~iĝi

–shaped, (sfx: having shape of), –forma (e.g.: *pear-shaped:* pir~a)

shard, (broken piece, gen), peco; (potsherd), pot~o

share, (divide among), dividi [tr], dis~i [tr]; (distribute), distribui [tr]; (portion), porcio; (have share in, have jointly), kunhavi [tr], ~i; (participate), partopreni [tr]; (of stocks), akcio; **sharecrop,** farmi [tr] [cp "farm"]; **sharecropper,** farmanto, farmisto; **shareholder,** akciulo; **plowshare,** soko; **the lion's share,** la plej granda parto, superporcio

Shari, (river), Ŝario

shark, (fish, gen), ŝarko; (*Squalus acanthias*), akantiaso; (tricky, unscrupulous person), ruzulo, fikomercisto (e.g.: *loan shark:* pruntruzulo); (expert), lertulo (e.g.: *card shark:* kartlertulo); **angel shark,** skvateno

Sharon, (woman's name), Ŝarona; (plain of), ~o

sharp, (re knife, pick, etc.; re feelings, eyes, ears, etc.), akra; (penetrating, as voice), akuta; (witty, sprightly), sprita; (sagacious, sharp-witted), sagaca; (tricky), ruza; (brusque), bruska; (abrupt), abrupta; (clear, distinct), klara; (harsh), severa, malmilda, maldorlota; (mus), dieso; diesa; diesigi; diesiĝi (e.g.: *C-sharp [C#] Major:* C-diesa [C#] Maĵora; *my guitar is sharp:* mia gitaro estas diesa); (exactly, re time), akurate (e.g.: *at two o'clock sharp:* akurate je la dua horo); **sharpen,** ~igi; ~iĝi; **double-sharp,** (mus), dudiesa

shatter, frakasi [tr]; ~iĝi

shave, razi [tr]; ~o; (re self), ~i sin (e.g.: *I shave every day:* mi ~as min ĉiun tagon); **shaver,** (razor), ~ilo; **shavings,** (as from wood plane), rabotaĵo(j); **clean-shaven,** ~ita; **close shave,** apenaŭa eskapo

shawl, ŝalo

shawm, ŝalmo

she, ŝi; (pfx to indicate female gender), –ino [sfx] (e.g.: *she-bear:* ursino)

shear, (cut w shears or scissors), tondi [tr]; (re animal etc. sheared), pri~i [tr] (e.g.: *shear the wool from a sheep:* ~i

la lanon de ŝafo; *shear a sheep:* pri~i
ŝafon); (cut w tin-snips), ĉizoji [tr];
(cut w pruning shears), stuci [tr]; pri-
stuci [tr]; (rip, tear, break from shear
stress), ŝiri [tr]; ŝiriĝi; **shears,**
~il(eg)o [note sing]; (tin-snips), ĉizojo; **pinking shears,** breĉetilo; **pruning shears,** stucilo; **shearwater,**
(zool: *Puffinus, Fratercula*), fraterkulo; (*Procellaria*), procelario
sheath, (case, receptacle), ingo; (skin,
husk, shell, etc.), ŝelo; (dress), gaino;
sheath(e), (put into sheath), en~igi;
cable sheath, kablomantelo
Sheba, Ŝebao
Shechem, Ŝeĥem
shed, (crude building for shelter, storage, animals, etc.), ŝedo [cp "garage",
"barn"]; (lose, make fall, etc.), as
tears, skin, fur), delasi [tr], defaligi,
perdi [tr]; (give out, emit), ellasi [tr],
elsendi [tr], dissendi [tr]; (pour out),
elverŝi [tr]; (repel), forpeli [tr]; **shear-
ing shed,** ŝaftondejo
sheen, brilo, poluro
sheep, ŝafo; **sheepish,** ~(ec)a; **sheep's-
bit,** (bot), jaziono; **sheep dip,**
~trempaĵo **sheepskin,** ~felo; ~fela
sheer, (pure), pura; (downright, absolute, utter), ~a, kompleta, absoluta,
tutsimpla; (diaphanous), diafana;
(steep, vertical), apika; (swerve, deviate), devii [int]; deviiĝi; devio
sheet, (for bed), littuko; (paper), folio;
(lamina), lameno; (layer; broad surface, expanse), tavolo (e.g.: *sheet of
ice, of flames:* tavolo de glacio, de
flamoj); (sail), velo; (naut: rope or
chain), ŝkopo; **sheet anchor,** sav-ank-
ro; **broadsheet,** flugfolio; **three
sheets to the wind,** ebriega
sheik(h), ŝejko
shekel, siklo
sheldrake, (*Tadorna*), tadorno
shelf, (gen), breto; **shelve,** (provide
shelves), ~izi [tr]; (put on shelf),
sur~igi; (defer), prokrasti [tr], flankenmeti [tr]; (slope), dekl.iviĝi; **on the
shelf,** (not active), ekster la fluo
shell, (any hard outer covering etc., lit
or fig), ŝelo; sen~igi; (of mollusk etc.,
or similar object), konko; (shellfish),

konkulo; (of turtle, armadillo, etc.),
karapaco; (armor), kiraso; (pod),
guŝo; elguŝigi; (small-arms cartridge),
kartoĉo; (projectile for larger artillery,
cannon), obuso; (bombard), bombar-
di [tr]; **file shell,** (zool), limao; **hammer shell,** maleo
shellac(k), (resin, varnish), lako; ~i [tr];
(in layers or shells, as elec insulation
etc.), ŝelako
shelter, (gen), ŝirmi [tr]; ~ilo; ~ejo;
(shed etc.), ŝedo; (in mountains for
hikers etc.), rifuĝejo; **tax shelter,** imposta ~ejo
Shem, Ŝem
Shenandoah, Ŝenandoo*
shenanigans, petolaĵoj
Shensi, Ŝenhi
Shenyang, Ŝenjang
Sheol, Ŝeolo
shepherd, (sheepherder), ŝaf/isto,
paŝtisto; (lead), ~peli [tr], konduki
[tr]; **shepherd's-purse,** (bot), paŝtista kapselo
sherbet, (Br: drink), ŝorbeto; (Am: frozen), ~glaciaĵo
sherif, ŝarifo
sheriff, ŝerifo
Sherpa, Ŝerpo; ~a
sherry, ŝereo
Shetland, Ŝetlando; ~a; **Shetland Islands,** ~oj, Insuloj ~aj; **Shetland pony,** ~a poneo
shibboleth, ŝiboleto
shield, (protect, guard, gen), ŝirmi [tr];
~ilo; (armor of ancient warrior, or
similar-shaped object or design), ŝildo; (cover elec wire etc.), armi [tr];
(cable covering), kablomantelo; **he-
raldic shield,** blazono; **windshield,**
vento~ilo
shift, (group of workers at same time;
time worked), skipo (e.g.: *day shift:*
tag~o; *night shift:* nokto~o; *work a 4-
hour shift:* labori 4-horan ~on);
(move), movi [tr]; moviĝi; mov(iĝ)o;
(press shift key on cmptr keyboard or
typewriter for upper case), majuskligi;
(change, gen), ŝanĝi [tr]; ŝanĝiĝi;
ŝanĝ(iĝ)o (e.g.: *shift gears:* ŝanĝi rapidumon); (exchange), interŝanĝi [tr],
anstataŭi [tr]; interŝanĝo, anstataŭo;

(means, expedient), rimedo; (ruse, trick), ruzo, artifiko; (dress), gaino; (phys: frequency change, Doppler effect), ŝoviĝo (e.g.: *red shift:* ruĝenŝoviĝo); **shifting**, moviĝema; ŝanĝiĝema; **shiftless**, mallaborema, maldiligenta; **shifty**, ruza; **shift key**, (as on cmptr keyboard, typewriter), majuskla klavo; **shift for oneself**, helpi al si mem; **gear-shift lever**, kluĉostango

Shiism, Ŝijaismo; **Shiite**, ~a; Ŝijaisto

shillelagh, (Irlanda) klabo

shilling, (Br etc. $), ŝilingo [abb: ŝ.]

shilly-shally, ŝanceliĝi; ~a, malrezoluta; ~(ad)o, malrezoluteco

Shiloah, Ŝiloaĥ

Shiloh, Ŝilo

shim, kojneto; ~i [tr]

shimmer, trembrili [int]; ~o

shimmy, (wobble), vobli [int]; ~o

shin, tibio; **shin (up)**, krurkroĉe grimpi [tr]

shine, brili [int]; ~igi, poluri [tr]; ~o; (wax shoes etc.), ciri [tr]; **shining**, **shiny**, ~a; **take a shine to**, ekŝati [tr]

shingle, (for roof or wall), ŝindo; (sign), ŝildo; **shingles**, (disease), zostero [note sing]; (gravel), gruzo

Shinto, Shintoism, Ŝintoo; **Shintoist**, ~a; ~ano

shinny (up), krurkroĉe grimpi [tr]

ship, (ocean vessel, aircraft, spacecraft, gen), ŝipo; (transport freight, gen), ekspedi [tr]; (by any kind of ship), per~i [tr]; (take into ship), en~igi; **shipment**, ekspedado; ekspedaĵo; [cp "freight"]; **shipping**, (for ships), ~a; (re freight, gen), ekspeda; ekspedado; **ship out**, (serve on a ship), ~servi [int]; **shipshape**, bonorda, (tute) neta; **shipworm**, teredo; **shipwreck**, ~rompi [int]; ~rompiĝo; ~rompaĵo, vrako; **shipyard**, ~konstruejo; **airship**, aer~o; **battleship**, batal~o; **flagship**, flag~o; **hospital ship**, hospital~o; **lightship**, lum~o; **merchant ship**, komerco~o; **midshipman**, midŝipmano; **sailing ship**, vel~o; **slave ship**, sklavo~o; **spaceship**, kosmo~o; **steamship**, vapor~o; **torpedo ship**, torpedo~o; **transship**, transŝarĝi [tr];

transport ship, transporto~o

-ship, (sfx: state, condition, status; -ness), -eco (e.g.: *friendship:* amikeco); (all individuals together), -aro (e.g.: *readership:* legantaro)

shire, graflando, distrikto

shirk, ruzeviti [tr], neglekti [tr]

shirr, (sewing), krisp/igi; **shirring**, ~aĵo

shirt, ĉemizo; **shirt-sleeves**. (w/o coat), senpalta (e.g.: *shirt-sleeves weather:* senpalta vetero); **in one's shirt-sleeves**, senpalte; **shirttail**, basko; **T-shirt, tee-shirt**, T-ĉemizo; **stuffed shirt**, egoisto; **keep your shirt on!**, paciencu!

shish kebab, (pecigita) pikilrostaĵo

shit, (vulg, lit or fig), merdo; (vulg), kaki* [int]; **bullshit**, taŭr~o

Shiva, [see "Siva"]

shiver, (tremble, gen), tremi [int], ~eti [int]; ~(et)o; (from cold), frosto~i [int]; frosto~o; (fragment, splinter), split(et)o, fragmento; **shivery**, ~(et)ema; **give one the shivers**, ~etigi iun

shlemiel, ŝlemilo

shlock, tombaka

shoal, (shallows), malprofundaĵo; (school of fish), benko; (any mass, crowd), amaso

shochet, [see "shohet"]

shock, (elec etc.; disturb, disgust, etc.; med), ŝoki [tr]; ~iĝi; ~o; (bump, jar), skui [tr]; skuo; (of grain), fasko; faskigi; (hair), haramaso, hararaĉo, tufego; **shocking**, ~a; **shock absorber**, skusorbilo; **aftershock**, (earthquake), posttremo; **electroshock**, (therapy), elektro~o; elektro~a

shoddy, (poor quality), aĉa, tombaka, miskvalita, malbonkvalita; (contemptible), fia, kanajla

shoe, (gen), ŝuo; (horse etc.), huferi [tr]; **shoehorn**, ~korno; **shoelace**, **shoestring**, (~)laĉo; **shoemaker**, ~isto; (repair), ~flikisto; **shoeshine**, ~cirado; ~ciraĵo; ~cira; **brake shoe**, bremsa ~o; **high-heeled shoe**, altkalkanuma ~o; **horseshoe**, huffero; **overshoe**, (low, covering shoe only), sur~o [cp "galosh"]; **sandshoe**, (Aus), tol~o; **snowshoe**, neĝo~o, rakedo; **tennis shoe**, (canvas, rubber-soled shoe, gen), tol~o

shofar, ŝofaro*

shogun, ŝoguno

shohet, ŝoĥt/isto; **act (slaughter) as shohet**, ~i [tr]

shoji, ŝoĵio

shoo, huŝi [tr]; (interj), huŝ!; **shoo-in**, (certain winner), certa gajnonto

shoot, (fire gun, oth weapon, or analogous device; strike w bullet, arrow, etc.), pafi [tr]; ~iĝi; (kill), mort~i [tr]; (move quickly, surge), sin ~i, impeti [int] (e.g.: *the car shot away:* la aŭto sin ~is for); (move through), trakuri [tr] (e.g.: *shoot the rapids in a canoe:* trakuri la rapidejon en kanuo); (chute), ŝuti [tr]; ŝutiĝi; ŝutilo [cp "slide"]; (throw (out)), (el)ĵeti [tr]; (use up, waste), foruzi [tr], forkonsumi [tr], (for)malŝpari [tr]; (hunt), ĉasi [tr]; (aim at w transit, sextant), celi [tr]; (phot), fotografi [tr], foti [tr]; (movie), filmi [tr]; (videotape), vidbendigi; (inject drug etc.), injekti [tr]; (sports: attempt score by throwing ball etc.), ŝoti [int]; (play, as pool, craps, etc.), ludi [tr]; [see also "shot"]; (spurt, gush), ŝpruc(eg)i [int]; (young twig, stem), ŝoso; (interj: begin talking!, go ahead!), ek!; **shoot through**, (Aus), forrapidi [int], tuj foriri [int], senpermese eliri [int]; **shoot with**, (streak), strii [tr] (e.g.: *black hair shot through with gray:* nigra hararo trastriita de griza) [cp "mottled"]; **shooting range**, ~ejo; **offshoot**, branĉo; **overshoot**, (w gun etc.), preter~i [tr]; (pass beyond, gen), transpasi [tr], preterpasi [tr]; **pea-shooter**, cerbatano; **sharpshooter**, lert~isto, tiraljoro; **six-shooter**, (seskamera) revolvero

shop, (small retail store, or department of large store), butiko; (go shopping), ~umi [int]; (workshop, gen), laborejo; (place for particular type of item, work, etc.), –ejo [sfx] (e.g.: *printing shop:* presejo); **shopkeeper**, ~isto; **shoplift**, ~ŝteli [tr]; **shopping bag**, ~umsako; **shopping center**, ~centro; **shoptalk**, metia ĵargono; **talk shop**, metie paroli [int], fakparoli [int], fak-

babili [int]; **shopworn**, ~erodita; **butcher shop**, viandejo; **second-hand shop**, brokantejo; **sweat-shop**, ŝvitlaborejo; **workshop**, [see under "work"]

shore, (of ocean, lake), bordo; (beach), plaĝo; (prop up), apogi [tr]; apogilo; **offshore**, apud~a; de~e(n); **onshore**, sur~a; sur~e(n)

short, (opp "long", gen), mallonga; (esp in combined forms), kurta, kurt– (e.g.: *shortwave radio:* kurtonda radiofono); (opp "tall"), malalta; (concise), konciza, lakona; (abrupt), abrupta; (quickly angered), koleriĝema, iritiĝema; (insufficient), nesufiĉa (e.g.: *a short measure:* nesufiĉa mezuro); (lacking), manka [see "be short on" below]; (not far enough), tro proksime (e.g.: *the shot fell short:* la pafo falis tro proksime) [see "short of" below]; (give less than wanted, required), nesufiĉe doni [tr] [cp "change: short-change"]; **shortage**, nesufiĉo, manko, deficito; **shorten**, ~igi; ~iĝi; malaltigi; malaltiĝi; koncizigi; **shortening**, (fat), graso; **shortly**, ~e; koncize; (soon), baldaŭ; **shortly thereafter**, post nelonge; **shorts**, (short pants), ŝorto [note sing]; (underpants), kalsoneto; **short for**, ~e por; ~igo por (e.g.: *"auto" is short for "automobile":* "aŭto" estas ~igo por "aŭtomobilo"); **short of**, (less), malpli ol (e.g.: *little short of a miracle:* malmulte malpli ol miraklo); (lacking), sen (sufiĉa), al kiu mankas (e.g.: *a city short of water:* urbo sen sufiĉa akvo [or] urbo al kiu mankas akvo); (not far enough), ne atinginta (e.g.: *we gathered up the arrows short of the target:* ni kunkolektis la sagojn ne atingintajn [or: kiuj ne atingis] la celon); (except, w/o resorting to), krom, malpli ol (e.g.: *use all methods short of murder:* uzi ĉiujn rimedojn krom [or: malpli ol] murdo); (on this side, not beyond), cis, ĉi-flanke de (e.g.: *we stopped for the night short of the Canadian border:* ni haltis por la nokto cis la Kanada landlimo); **be short of**, (be less), esti malpli ol; (lack), manki [int] (al iu), ne havi [tr] (sufiĉe da) (e.g.: *we are short of bread:* mankas al ni pano [or] ni ne havas sufiĉe da pano); (not reach), ne atingi [tr]; **fall short,** (be insufficient), ne sufiĉi [int]; (not reach goal etc.), ne atingi (la celon); (not succeed), ne sukcesi [int]; **for short,** ~e, kiel ~igo; **foreshorten,** kurtigi†; **in short,** ~e, resume; **run short (of),** (not have or be enough), trafi nesufiĉon (da); elĉerpiĝi (de), ne sufiĉi [int]; **short and sweet,** agrable ~a; **short-circuit,** (elec), kurta cirkvito, fuŝkontakto; kurtcirkvitigi; (resulting high current), superkurento; (bypass any obstacle etc.), preterpasi [tr]; (impede, thwart), obstrukci [tr]; **short-lived,** maldaŭra, kurtviva, efemera; **short-order,** (re food), krakmanĝa; **short-order restaurant,** krakmanĝejo; **short-term,** ~atempa, kurttempa; **undershorts,** kalsoneto [note sing]; **catch one short,** kapti (trafi) iun surprizita

shot, (act of shooting), pafo; impeto; trakuro; ŝuto; (el)ĵeto; celado, celiĝo; fotado; foto; filmado; vidbendigado; injekto; injektaĵo; ŝoto; ludo, movo; striita; [see "shoot"]; (range, reach), atingo (e.g.: *within earshot:* en aŭdatingo); (attempt, try), provo; (guess), konjekto; (metal pellet(s)), kugletaĵo; (sport, for shotput), ĵetglobo; (movie, TV, etc.: one sequence w/o moving camera), plano; (marksman), pafisto (e.g.: *a poor shot:* malbona pafisto) [cp "shoot: sharpshooter"]; (drink), trinko; (thing etc. to be bet on), privetaĵo; privetulo (e.g.: *that horse is a ten-to-one shot:* tiu ĉevalo estas privetaĵo dek-al-unu; *a long shot:* malprobabla privetaĵo); **shot put,** (sport), globĵeto; **put the shot,** globĵeti [int]; **big shot,** gravulo, dignulo; **buckshot,** kugletaĵo; **good shot,** [see "shoot: sharpshooter"]; **Indian shot,** (bot), kanao; **potshot,** (random or haphazard shot, attack, try), hazarda ~o; **take potshots at,** far hazardajn ~ojn al; **snapshot,** tuja foto, momenta foto; **take a snapshot of,** kodaki [tr]; **upshot,** (consequence), rezulto, konse-

kvenco; **a shot in the arm,** (fig), reviglilo, stimulilo, rekuraĝigilo; **have (take) a shot at,** (try), provi [tr]; **call the shots,** ordoni [tr], mastri [tr]

should, (ought to), devus (e.g.: *you should go:* vi devus iri; *they should have gone:* ili devus esti irintaj); (if), se (e.g.: *should it rain, we won't go:* se pluvos, ni ne iros); (Br: would), [see "would"]

shoulder, (anat), ŝultro; (of garment), ~umo; (place, carry on shoulders), sur~igi; (push through, shove w shoulders), ~umi [tr]; (meat), ~aĵo; (of road), vojrando, vojflanko; **shoulder blade,** skapolo; **shoulder harness,** ~ozono; **shoulder strap,** ~orimeno, ŝelketo; **shoulder-to-shoulder,** ~on ĉe ~o; **cold-shoulder treatment,** malvarma traktado; **shoulder the responsibility,** akcepti la respondecon; **give one a cold shoulder,** malvarme trakti iun; **put one's shoulder to the wheel,** plendediĉi sin al la tasko; **straight from the shoulder,** rekte kaj klare

shout, krii [tr, int]; ~o; **shout down,** ~e silentigi

shove, ŝovi [tr]; ~iĝi; ~o; **shove off,** for~i sin; (colloq: leave), ekiri [int]

shovel, ŝoveli [tr]; ~ilo [cp "spade"]; **shovel(l)er, shovelbill,** (zool), spatulo, kuleranaso; **power shovel, steam shovel,** ~maŝino

show, (demonstrate; make or be visible or noticeable; display reading, re instrument, gauge, etc.), montri [tr]; ~iĝi, aperi [int]; ~(ad)o (e.g.: *she showed me the report:* ŝi ~is al mi la raporton; *your unpreparedness shows:* via nepreteco ~iĝas; *a show of force:* ~o de potenco); (manifest, make visible), manifesti [tr], aperigi, videbligi; manifest(ad)o; manifestaĵo; (public display, exposition, exhibition), el~aĵo, ekspozicio; ekspozicii [tr], eksponi [tr] (e.g.: *art show:* artekspozicio); (movie), filmo; (theat etc.), teatraĵo, prezento; (spectacle), spektaklo; (appearance, semblance, not real), ŝajno; (guide, conduct), konduki [tr], gvidi [tr]; (demonstrate, explain, prove), klarigi, pruvi [tr], ~i; (finish 3rd in race), finiĝi la tria; **showy**, (gaudy), puca; (show-off), el~iĝema, pavema, paradema; **show (one) around (a place)**, ĉirkaŭ~i (al iu) (lokon); **showcase**, vitrino, vitroŝranko; **showdown**, klimaksa alfronto, decidiga alfronto; **show in**, enkonduki [tr]; **show off**, (display), el~i [tr]; (be vainly flashy), pavi [int], paradi [int]; **show-off**, pavulo; **show out**, elkonduki [tr]; **showpiece**, ~(ind)aĵo, vitrinaĵo; **showroom**, ~ejo, ~osalono; **show up**, (appear), aperi [int], ~iĝi; (expose), eksponi [tr], malkaŝi [tr]; (arrive), alveni [int]; (surpass), superi [tr]; (humble), humiligi; **for show**, por bonaspekto; **good show!**, bonege!, gratulon!, brave!; **sideshow**, flankspektaklo; **that goes to show that**, tio servas por ~i ke

shower, (bath; any analogous abundant flow, fall, etc.), duŝo; ~i [tr]; ~iĝi; ~ilo; ~ejo; (rain), ekpluvo, pluv~o; (gift party, as bridal, baby shower), donacofesto

shrapnel, ŝrapnelo

shred, (piece, fragment), er(et)o, peceto, fragmento; (narrow torn strip), ŝirstrio; **shredder**, (paper)disŝirilo; **(tear to) shred(s)**, disŝiri [tr], dispecigi, ĉifonigi

shrew, (zool), soriko; (woman), megero, drakino, diablino

shrewd, (clever, astute), sagaca; (cunning, wily), ruza

shriek, ŝirkrii [int], (poet), ŝriki [int], kriĉi [int]; ~o, ŝriko, kriĉo

shrike, lanio

shrill, strida, akra(tona)

shrimp, salikoko

shrine, sanktejo

shrink, (opp "grow"), mal/kreski [int]; ~kreskigi; (decrease), ~pliigi; ~pliiĝi; (opp "expand"), ~ŝveli [int], ~ekspansii [int]; ~ŝveligi, ~ekspansiigi; (opp "dilate"), ~dilati [tr]; ~dilatiĝi; (shrivel), ŝrumpi [int]; ŝrumpigi; **shrinkage**, ~kresk(ad)o; ~pliigo; ~pliiĝo; ~ekspansi(ig)(ad)o; ~dilat(iĝ)(ad)o; ŝrump(ig)(ad)o; **shrink from (doing something)**, ne kuraĝi (fari ion), re

tiriĝi de (io, fari ion)

shrivel, ŝrumpi [int]; ~igi

shroud, (veil), vuali [tr]; ~o; (for corpse), mortotuko; (naut: mast rope, cable), stajo; (wrap), envolvi [tr]

shrub, arbedo [see "bush"]; **shrubbery**, ~aro; **mastic shrub**, lentisko, mastikarbo

shrug, ŝultrolevi [int], levi la ŝultrojn; ~o; **shrug off**, forskui [tr]

shuck, ŝelo; sen~igi; (get rid of), senigi sin de

shudder, tremi [int]; ~o

shuffle, (walk), tren/marŝi [int], sin ~i; ~marŝ(ad)o; (mix, as cards), miksi [tr]; mikso; **shuffleboard**, ŝovludo; **get lost in the shuffle**, perdiĝi en la konfuzo

Shulamite, Ŝulamit

shun, eviti [tr]

Shunem, Ŝunemo; **Shunammite**, ~a; ~ano

shunt, (elec), ŝunti [tr]; ~iĝi; ~o; (rr), komuti [tr]; komuto; (move aside, divert, gen), flankigi, flankenŝovi [tr]

shush, (hush, quiet), silentigi [not "ŝuŝ-"]; (interj), ŝŝ!, ĉit!

Shushan, Ŝuŝan

shut, (gen), fermi [tr]; ~iĝi; ~ita; ~iĝinta; **shut down**, (machine etc.), malfunkciigi; malfunkciiĝi; (office, any operation, etc.), ~i; ~iĝi; **shut in**, (enclose), en~i [tr]; (close off), enbari [tr]; **shut-in**, (confined to home etc.), en~ito; **shut off**, (close off), for~i [tr]; (stop), ĉesigi; (elec), malŝalti [tr]; (water, gas, etc.), ~i; **shut out**, elbari [tr]; **shut up**, (enclose), en~i [tr]; (close entrances), ~i; (silence), silentigi; **shut up!**, silentu!, ŝtopu la buŝon!

shutter, (covering for window), ŝutro; ~izi [tr] [cp "persien"]; (over any opening), klapo; klapizi [tr]; (phot), obturilo

shuttle, (weaving; bus, plane, etc., traveling back and forth; commute), naveto; ~a; ~i [int], kuradi [int] (e.g.: *shuttle bus*: ~a buso; *she shuttles to Chicago for the monthly meetings*: ŝi ~as al Ĉikago por la monataj kunvenoj); **shuttlecock**, volano; **space shuttle**, kosma pramo

shy, (bashful), modesta; (lacking self-confidence), singena; (timid, easily frightened), timida, timema; (distrustful, wary), nefidema; (jump, recoil), (flanken) salti [int]; (throw), ĵeti [tr]; (short, short of, not enough), [see "short"]; **shy away from**, sin retiri (de), retiriĝi (de)

shyster, fiadvokato

si, (mus: ti), si

sial, sialot

Sialia, sialio*

sialitis, sialito

sial(o)–, (med pfx), sial(o)–

sialogenous, sialogena

Siam, Siamo [cp "Thai"]; **Siamese**, ~a; ~ano; ~ana; **Gulf of Siam**, Golfo ~a

Siberia, Siberio; **Siberian**, ~a; ~ano; ~ana

sibilant, sibla; (gram), ~anto

sibling, frat/(in)o, ge~o; ge~a; **siblings**, ge~oj

sibyl, (prophetess), sibilo; **sibylline**, ~a

Sibyl, (woman's name), Sibila

sic, (thus), tiel; (attack), ataki [tr]; (make attack), atakigi

siccative, sekiga; ~enzo

Sicily, Sicilio; **Sicilian**, ~a; ~ano; ~ana

sick, (ill), malsana; (nauseated), naŭzita; (distressed), ĉagrenita, maltrankvila; **be sick**, ~i [int]; esti naŭzita; (vomit), vomi [int]; **be sick of**, (disgusted, exasperated), laciĝi de, tedi [int] de; **sicken**, (make, become ill), ~iĝi; ~iĝi; (nauseate), naŭzigi; **sickening**, ~iga; naŭziga; **sickie**, (Aus), forpermeso pro malsano; **sickly**, ~eca; **sickness**, ~o [cp "disease"]; **sick leave**, ~foresto; **carsick**, **motionsick**, vetur~a; **carsickness**, **motion sickness**, vetur~o; **greensickness**, klorozo; **homesick**, hejmsopira, hejmvea; **homesickness**, hejmsopiro, hejmveo; **make one sick**, ~igi; naŭzigi; **seasick**, mar~a; **seasickness**, mar~o; **sleeping sickness**, dormo~o, tripanosomozo; **deathly sick**, mort~a

sickle, rikolti [tr]; falĉileto

Siddartha Gauthama, Sidarto Gotamo*

side, (flank, lateral part; aspect, facet; point of view; etc.), flanko; ~a; (of geom fig), latero; (faction, party), partio; (accessory, secondary), akcesora, ~a; (separate), aparta; **sideburns**, vangoharoj; **sidelong**, (to side), oblikva; oblikve(n); ~en; (sloping), dekliva; (indirect, subtle), nerekta, subtila; **cast a sidelong glance**, strabi [int]; **sideperson**, **sideman**, ~ulo; **sideswipe**, ~frapi [tr]; ~frapo; **sideways**, ~en; ~en(ir)a; **side with**, **take sides (with)**, partiiĝi (kun); **alongside**, ~e de; **back side**, (gen), dors~o; dors~a; (rump), postajo; (reverse side of coin, fabric, etc.), reverso; **offside(s)**, (sports), eksterluda; eksterlude(n); **outside**, (gen), ekster; ekstera; ekstere(n); eksterajo; **outsider**, eksterulo; **at the outside**, (at most, maximum), maksimume; **upside**, [see under "up"]; **by the side of**, apud; **on the other side of**, (across), trans; (beyond), preter; **on this (the near) side of**, cis; **lopsided**, nesimetria; **this side up!**, ĉi-~e supre!; **side by side**, ~-al-~e

sideling, (Aus), krutajo, monteĝo

sidereal, sidera

siderite, siderito

siding, (covering), (mur)tegajo, murŝindo; (rr), flanktrako

sidle, flankeniri [int], krabri [int]

Sidon, Cidono

Sidonius, Sidonio

siege, sieĝo; **besiege**, **lay siege to**, ~i [tr]

Siegfried, Sigfrido

siemen, (elec), simenso

Siena, Sieno

sienna, sieno; ~(kolor)a

sierra, (segil)montaro; **Sierra Leone**, Siera-Leono; **Sierra Madre**, Montaro Patrina; **Sierra Nevada**, Montaro Neĝa

siesta, siesto; **take a siesta**, ~i [int]

sieve, (large), kribrilo; (kitchen strainer), ~eto

sift, kribri [tr]

sigh, (breath), suspiri [tr, int]; ~o; (yearn), sopiri [int]; sopiro

sight, (act of seeing), vido; (sense of), ~ado; (scenic view), ~indajo; (spectacle), spektaklo; (on gun, sextant, etc.), celilo; (aim gun etc.), celumi [tr]; (aim at, bring into gunsight etc.), celi [tr]; (opinion), opinio, ~punkto; (look), rigardi [tr]; **far-sighted,** (lit, re eyes), malmiopa; (planning well ahead), longa~a, antaŭzorga; **near-sighted,** miopa; **oversight,** (omission), preteratento; (supervision), kontrolado; **shortsighted,** (lit or fig), miopa; **at first sight,** unua~a; unua~e; **by sight,** laŭ~e; **catch sight of,** ek~i [tr]; **foresight,** antaŭ~(ad)o, antaŭzorgo; **lose sight of,** (not see), perdi [tr] el la ~o; (forget), forgesi [tr]; **on sight,** je ~o; **out of sight,** preter ~ebleco(n), preter ~odistanco(n); **out of sight, out of mind,** for de l' okulo, for de l' koro; **unsightly,** malbela, okul-ofenda, malpitoreska; **(with)in sight of,** en ~odistanco de; **sightseeing,** ~vizita; ~vizitado (e.g.: *sightseeing bus:* ~vizita buso); **go sightseeing,** viziti la ~indaĵojn; **sightseer,** ~vizitanto

sigil, sigelo

Sigismund, Sigismundo

sigma, sigma [see § 16]

sigmoid, sigmoida; **sigmoid colon,** ~o

Sigmund, Sigmundo

sign, (words or symbols on board; any symbol; zodiac), signo; ~i [tr] (e.g.: *street sign:* strat~o; *sign of peace:* ~o de paco); (indicator), indikilo; (mark), marko; marki [tr]; (portent, omen), aŭguro; (write name, gen), subskribi [tr]; (to authenticate), signaturi [tr]; signaturo; (track, as footprint, dung, etc.), spuro; (engage by contract, sign on), kontraktigi, dungi [tr]; **sign in,** enskribi [tr]; enskribiĝi, sin enskribi; **sign off,** (radio), ĉesigi dissendadon; (TV), ĉesigi telesendadon; **sign on,** ekdissendi [int]; ektelesendi; (hire; be hired), dungi [tr]; dungiĝi; **sign out,** elskribi [tr]; elskribiĝi, sin elskribi; **signpost,** (sign on post), voj~o; (any indicator, clue, etc.), indikilo, ~o; **sign up,** enskribi [tr], matrikuli [tr]; enskribiĝi; **countersign,** kromsubskribi [tr]; **radical sign,** (math, to show square root), radik~o; **undersign,** subskribi [tr]; **sign of the cross,** kruco~o

signal, (gen), signali [tr]; ~o; ~a; **signalize,** (make noteworthy), rimarkindigi, notindigi; (signal, draw attention), ~i, atentigi; **signal corps,** (mil), ~servo; **carrier signal,** (radio, TV), portanta ondo

signatory, subskribinta; ~o

signature, (signed name), subskribo; (mark at bottom of printed page), signaturo; **countersignature,** krom~o; **time signature,** (mus), taktosigno; **key signature,** (mus), gamsigno

signet, (seal mark), sigelo; ~i [tr]; (device), ~ilo; **signet ring,** ~ringo

significance, signifo; **significant,** (meaningful), ~oplena; (math, statistics; precise; not by chance), signifika; **significant figures,** (math), signifikaj ciferoj; **significant difference,** signifika diferenco; **insignificant,** sen~a, malgrava, bagatela

signify, signifi [tr]

Sikh, Siko

Sikkim, Sikimo

silage, silaĵo, insilaĵo

silane, silano

silence, silento; ~igi; **silent,** ~a; **be silent,** ~i [int]; **dead silence,** morta ~o; **stony silence,** glacia ~o; **silencer,** ~igilo

Silene, Sileno

Silenus, Sileno

Silesia, Silezio; **Silesian,** ~a; ~ano; ~ana

silhouette, silueto; ~igi; **be silhouetted,** ~iĝi

silica, siliko

silicate, (from silica), silikato; (from silicic acid), siliciato

siliceous, silika; ~hava; ~eca

silicic, (from silica), silika; (from silicon), silicia; **silicic acid,** ~ata acido

silicide, siliciido

siliciferous, silikhava

silicle, silikveto

silicon, silicio

silicone, silikono

silicosis, silikozo

silique, silikvo

silk, silko; ~a; **silky,** ~eca; **artificial silk,** art~o

sill, (of door, window), sojlo

silly, (foolish), fola, malracia, stulta
silo, silo
Silpha, silfo
silt, ŝlimo; (deposit silt), ~i [int]; ~igi
Silurian, Silurio; ~a
Silurus, siluro; Siluridae, ~edoj
silver, arĝento; ~a; **silvery**, ~(ec)a; **silverberry**, (bot), eleagro; **silverfish**, (insect), lepismo; **silver-plate**, ~i [tr]; **silverware**, (flatware: forks, spoons, etc.), manĝilaro; **nickel silver, German silver**, nikelino; **quicksilver**, hidrargo
silviculture, silvikulturo
Silybum, kardo; Silybum marianum, marikardo
sima, simaot
Simeon, Simeono
Simia, simio; Simia satyrus, orangutano
simian, simiulo; ~(ec)a
similar, simila; **similarity**, ~aĵo; ~eco; **dissimilar**, mal~a; **be similar to**, ~i [tr]
simile, komparfiguro
simmer, boleti [int]; ~igi; ~ado; **simmer down**, (calm down), malkoleriĝi, kvietiĝi, trankviliĝi
Simon, Simono; **Saint-Simon**, (French philosopher), Sansimono
Simone, Simona
Simonides, Simonido
simony, simonio
simoom, simoon, samumo
simpatico, simpatia [cp "sympathy: sympathetic"]
simper, afekte rideti [int]; afekta rideto
simple, (of one or few parts; not complex; easy; mere, only; unadorned; natural, innocent; $: not compound, as re interest), simpla; (not luxurious or elegant), neluksa; (pure), ~a, pura; (ordinary), ordinara, ĉiutaga; (ignorant), malklera, fola, trompiĝema; (unceremonious), senceremonia; **simpleton**, ~ulo, folulo, stultulo; **simplicity**, ~eco; **simplify**, ~igi; **simplistic**, naiva
simplex, (one part), simpla; (telegraphy etc.), unukanala
Simplon, Simplono
simulacrum, simul/aĵo, faksimilo; ~ita
simulate, simuli [tr]; **simulation**, ~ado;

~aĵo; **simulator**, ~ilot; ~atoro
simulcast, radiovidsendi [tr]; ~o
Simulium, simulio
simultaneous, simultana, samtempa, sammomenta
sin, peki [int]; ~o; ~ado; **sinful**, ~a; **sinner**, ~into; ~anto; ~ulo; **original sin**, pra~o
Sinai, Sinajo; **Sinai Peninsula**, Duoninsulo ~a
Sinanthropus, sinantropot [see "man: Peking man"]
Sinapsis, sinapo
since, (prep: starting w time given), ekde, ek de, de (e.g.: *we've been here since Thursday:* ni estas ĉi tie ekde jaŭdo); (prep: starting after time given), de post (e.g.: *he has been more careful since the accident:* li estas pli zorgema de post la akcidento) [note: avoid writing "depost", since spoken stress falls on "post"]; [note: distinction between "ekde" and "de post" not always made]; (conj), ekde kiam; de post kiam (e.g.: *we've been more careful since you warned us:* ni estas pli zorgemaj ekde kiam vi avertis nin; *changes since the war ended:* ŝanĝoj de post kiam finiĝis la milito); (because), ĉar; (ago), antaŭ (e.g.: *they have long since left:* ili antaŭ longe foriris)
sincere, sincera; **sincerity**, ~eco; **insincere**, mal~a
sine, sinuso; **cosine**, kosinuso; **sine curve, sine wave**, ~oido
sinecure, sinekuro
sine qua non, nepraĵo
sinew, tendeno; **sinewy**, ~eca
sing, kanti [tr]; **sing out**, elkrii [tr, int]; **singsong**, ritmaĉa, ~aĉa; **sing-along, open sing**, kun~ado; **sing a different tune**, (fig), alimaniere konduti [int]
Singapore, (state and city), Singapuro
singe, brul/eti [int]; surfac~i [int]; ~etigi, surfac~igi; ~eto, surfac~o
Singhalese, [see "Sinhalese"]
single, (one alone, not multiple), unuopa; ~aĵo; ~ulo (e.g.: *a single house among the trees:* ~a domo inter la arboj); (sole, solitary), sola (e.g.: *one single drop of water:* unu sola guto de

akvo; *the single thing I object to:* la
sola afero kiun mi kontraŭas); (unmarried), fraŭla; fraŭl(in)o; gefraŭloj;
(baseball), unubaza bato; (cricket),
unupoenta bato; **single out,** elelekti
[tr], elpluki [tr]; **single–space,** [see
under "space"]; **not a single,** (not
even one), eĉ ne unu (e.g.: *we didn't
see a single tree:* ni vidis eĉ ne unu arbon)
singlet, singuleto
singular, (single), unuopa; (unique),
unika; (strange), stranga, kurioza;
(remarkable), aparta, rimarkinda;
(gram), singularo; singulara
Sinhalese, (language), Sinhalo; ~a;
(person of Ceylon etc.), Cejlona; Cej-
lonano
Sining, Hining
sinister, (ominous), sinistra; (evil), fia
sinistr(o)–, (pfx: left-handed), liv(o)–
[see "left"]
sinistrorse, livuma
sinistrosis, sinistrozo
sink, (go down slowly), sinki [int]; ~igi;
(submerge), mergi [tr]; mergiĝi; (lower, gen), mallevi [tr]; malleviĝi; (diminish, decrease, subside, lessen),
malpliigi, redukti [tr]; malpliiĝi, re-
duktiĝi; (weaken), malfortiĝi; (dig, as
well, mine, etc.), fosi [tr]; (invest), investi [tr]; (defeat), venki [tr]; (basin w
faucets and drain), lavabo; (hollow),
kavo; (geol: low region w/o drainage),
ŝoto; **sinkage,** ~ado; **sink in,** (on
mind), fari impreson, enpenetriĝi,
en~i [int]
Sinkiang, Hingiang
Sino–, (pfx), ĉin(o)–
Sinology, Ĉinolog/io; **Sinologist,** ~o
sinople, sinoplo
sinter, (metallurgy), sintri [tr]; ~aĵo
sinuate, sinui [int]; ~a
sinuous, sinua
sinus, sinuso; **sinusitis,** ~ito; **sinusoid,**
~oido
Sioux, (individual), Siuo; ~a; (plur; entire tribe), ~oj, ~a tribo; **Sioux City,**
~-Urbo
sip, trinketi [tr]; ~o
siphon, sifono; ~i [tr]
Siphonaptera, afanipteroj

sir, (respectful address for man), sinjoro; (knight), kavaliro
sire, (father), patro; (beget), generi [tr];
(title of respect for king etc.), Siro
siren, Siren, (gen), sireno; S~o; ~(ec)a
Sirena, sireno
Sirenia, sirenoj
sirenian, sireno
Sirius, Siriuso
sirloin, sirloin steak, (bov)lumbaĵo
sirocco, siroko
sirup, [see "syrup"]
sis, (short for "sister"), franjo
sisal, sisalo
siskin, fringelo
sissy, (effeminate), inaĉa; ~ulo; (coward), malkuraĝa; malkuraĝulo
sister, (sibling), fratino; (intimate
form), franjo; (nun), monaĥino; **sis-
terhood,** (sisterliness), ~eco; (organization), ~aro; **sisterly,** ~eca; **sister-
in-law,** bo~o; **half-sister,** duon~o;
brother(s) and sister(s), gefratoj
Sistine, siksta; **Sistine Chapel,** S~a
Kapelo
sistrum, sistro
Sisymbrium, sisimbrio
Sisyphus, Sizifo; **Sisyphean,** ~a
sit, (be seated, occupy seat, etc.; be in a
position, location), sidi [int] [cp "situate"]; (on eggs), kovi [tr]; (pose), pozi
[int]; (babysit), (infan)varti [tr]; **sitting,** (session of assembly, of model
posing, etc.), kun~o, seanco [cp "session"]; **sit back,** (relax, make self
comfortable), malstreĉiĝi, komfortiĝi; (remain passive), resti pasiva; **sit
down,** ~iĝi, ek~i [int]; **sit in (on),** partopreni [tr], ĉeesti [tr]; **sit on,** (participate), partopreni [tr]; (suppress),
subpremi [tr]; **sit (something) out,**
traatendi (ion); **sit pretty,** favore troviĝi; **sit tight,** (not move), ne moviĝi,
ne leviĝi; (be patient), pacienci [int];
sit up, (rise to sitting position), ~iĝi,
ek~i [int]; (sit erect), rekte ~i; (not
sleep), maldormi [int], resti maldorma; (take notice), ekatenti [tr]; (sit on
haunches, re 4-legged animal),
baŭm~i [int]; **sit well with,** plaĉi [tr];
esti akceptebla (taŭga, agrabla, etc.) al
Sita, Sita

sitar, setaro*
site, (location, gen), situo; (archeology, geog), sito†
Sitophilus, kalandrao
Sitta, sito
situate, loki [tr]; (relative to surroundings), situigi; **situated**, ~ita; situanta; **be situated**, situi [int] (e.g.: *the house is well situated for the view:* la domo bone situas por la elvido)
situation, (gen), situacio
Sium, siumo
Siva, Ŝivao; **Sivaism**, ~ismo
six, ses [see § 19]; **sixth**, (1/6), ~ono; (6th), ~a; **six of one and a half dozen of the other**, tute egale; tute ne gravas; kiel averso, tiel reverso
sixpence, (coin), sespenco; (sum), ses pencoj; **sixpenny**, ~a
sixte, (fencing), seksto
Sixtus, Siksto
size, (magnitude, quantity), grando; (of a given size, usually as sfx), –formata, –dimensia (e.g.: *a child-size table:* infan-formata tablo); (relative extent), ~eco (e.g.: *person of normal size:* homo de normala ~eco) [cp "extent"]; (index for clothing, shoes, etc.), ~onumero (e.g.: *size 9 shoes:* ŝuoj de ~onumero 9); (status), stato; (glue, glaze, etc.), apreti [tr]; apreturo; **size up**, (appraise), (okule, mense) taksi [tr]; **sizable**, iom ~a; **sizing**, apretado; apreturo; **large-sized**, **of large size**, grand-formata [not "de ~a ~o"]; **outsized**, **oversize(d)**, super~a
sizzle, sibli [int]; ~o
skål! je via sano!
skald, skaldo
skat, skato
skate, (on ice), sketi [int]; (shoe for skating), ~ŝuo; (fish), rajo; **skating**, ~ado; **skate blade**, ~ilo; **in-line skate**, linia ~ŝuo; **roller-skate**, rul~i [int]; rul~ŝuo
skatole, skatolo
skedaddle, fuĝi [int], forkuri [int]
skeet, **skeet shooting**, argilpafado
skein, (coil of yarn etc.), buklaro
skeleton, skeleto; **skeletal**, ~a; **endoskeleton**, endoskeleto; **exoskeleton**, ekzoskeleto*

skep, (basket), korbo; (beehive), abel~o
skeptic, skeptik/ulo; **skeptical**, ~a; **skepticism**, (condition), ~eco; (doctrine), ~ismo
skerrick, (Aus), peceto, joto
sketch, (draw or describe in gen outline), skizi [tr]; ~o; (drawing etc. as trial, study), studo; (esp w no intent to do more complete picture), krokizi [tr]; krokizo; (short movie scene etc.), skeĉo; **sketchy**, ~(ec)a; **sketch book**, **sketch pad**, ~bloko
skew, (oblique, slanted, not direct), oblikva; ~igi; (go in oblique direction, swerve), ~i [int] [cp "skid"]; (glance sideways), strabi [int]
skewbald, blankmakula
skewer, rostostango; surstangigi
ski, skii [int]; ~o; **skier**, ~anto; ~isto; **skiing**, ~ado; **ski-lift**, ~-lifto; **ski slope**, ~deklivo; **ski pole**, ~bastono; **cross-country ski**, transgrunde ~i; transgrunda ~o; **cross-country skiing**, transgrunda ~ado; **downhill ski**, malsupren~i [int]; malsuprena ~o; **water-ski**, akvo~i [int]; akvo~o
skid, (slip, as car on ice; move sideways, re plane in turn etc.), jori [int]; joro; (plank etc. for sliding heavy objects), glittabulo; (runner, as for plane landing on snow etc.), glitilo
skiff, (rowboat), (malpeza) remboato; (w sail), velboato
skill, lert/eco; ~aĵo; **skillful**, **skilled**, ~a; **semiskilled**, duon~a
skillet, (frying pan), pato; (Br: pot, kettle), kaserolo
skim, (read, look over fast), flug/legi [tr], tuŝlegi [tr], ~rigardi [tr], ~tuŝi [tr]; (remove cream), senkrenigi; (remove scum etc.), deĉerpi [tr]; (touch surface lightly), tanĝi [tr]; (throw etc. so as to skim), tanĝigi (e.g.: *skim rocks across the river:* tanĝigi ŝtonojn trans la riveron) [cp "skip"]; **skimmer**, (dragonfly), libelo; **skim milk**, senkrema lakto
skimp, (give, allow too little; be stingy), magri [int]; esti avara; doni [tr] malabunde; (save, economize), ŝpari [tr]; (do poorly), fuŝi [tr], faraĉi [tr]; **skimpy**, ~a, malabunda, nesufiĉa

skin, (of person or animal, or similar thing), haŭto; sen~igi; (animal hide, esp unprocessed), felo; (processed hide), pelto; (of fruit; any similar covering), ŝelo; senŝeligi; (abrade, scrape), skrapi [tr], ekskoriacii [tr]; **skinny**, malgrasa, magrega, senkarna; **skin-deep**, supraĵa; **foreskin**, prepucio; **thick-skinned**, neofendiĝema; **thin-skinned**, ofendiĝema; **skinnydip**, **go skinny-dipping**, nudnaĝi [int]; nudnaĝo; **get under one's skin**, inciti iun, kolerigi iun; **by the skin of one's teeth**, apenaŭege; **that's no skin off my back**, tio tute ne tuŝas min, tio tute ne estas mia problemo

skink, skinko

skip, (hop), salteti [int]; ~o; (ricochet), karamboli [int]; karamboligi; karambolo; (bounce lightly, as flat rock on water), tanĝi [int]; tanĝigi; tanĝo; (omit), ellasi [tr], preterpasi [tr], transpasi [tr], preteratenti [tr]; (Aus: beehive), abelujo; (Aus: container for rubbish), rubujego; **skipjack**, (fish: gen, imprecise term), saltfiŝo; **skip it!**, forgesu ĝin!, tute egale!

skipper, (naut), ŝipestro; (sport), teamestro

skirl, (pik)soni [int], trili [int]; ~igi, triligi; ~o, trilo

skirmish, bataleto; ~i [int]

skirt, (garment), jupo; (edge), rando; (move along edge), randiri [tr]; (avoid), eviti [tr]; **miniskirt**, mini~o; **outskirts**, (edge of city), antaŭurbo; **sheath skirt**, **tight skirt**, gain~o

skit, (theat etc.), skeĉo; (satire), satiro

skite, (Aus), fanfaroni [int]

skittle, (pin), keglo; **skittles**, (game), ~aro

skitter, saltetadi [int]

skittish, (easily frightened), timema; (playful), petola

skoal! je via sano!

skua, rabmevo

skulduggery, ruzaĵo(j), fiaĵo(j), kanajlaĵo(j)

skulk, kaŭri [int] [cp "slink"]

skull, kranio

skunk, (animal), mefito; (its fur), skunko

sky, ĉielo; **sky-high**, altega; **skyjack**, aerpirati [tr, int]; **skyjacker**, aerpirato; **skyscraper**, ~skrapanto; **out of a clear blue sky**, tute sen averto, tute subite

slab, (gen), slabo

slack, (loose, not taut), mal/streĉita, loza; ~streĉi [tr]; (not rigid), ~rigida; (idle, sluggish, not busy), ~vigla, ~aktiva; (careless), ~zorga; (not diligent), ~diligenta; (coal), karbogruzo; **slacken**, ~streĉi [tr]; ~streĉiĝi; ~vigligi; ~vigliĝi; (slow), ~akceli [tr]; ~akceliĝi; (moderate), moderigi; moderiĝi; **slacks**, pantalono

slag, skorio; **slag-heap**, ~amaso, ~ejo

slake, (sate), satigi (soifon etc.), sensoifigi; (make fire etc. die down), kvietigi; (extinguish fire), estingi [tr]; (hydrate), hidrati [tr]

slalom, slalomo

slam, (close), brufermi [tr], klakigi; ~iĝi, klakiĝi; ~o; (cards), ŝlemo; **grand slam**, granda ŝlemo; **little slam**, malgranda ŝlemo

slander, kalumnii [tr]; ~o; **slanderous**, ~a

slang, slango; ~a; **slang word**, **slang expression**, ~aĵo

slant, (incline), klini [tr]; ~iĝi; ~o; (oblique; distort writing etc. to give bias), oblikvi [int]; oblikvigi; oblikveco; (slope), deklivo; (attitude), sinteno, vidpunkto; (Br: symbol "/"), oblikva streko; **slanted**, **slanting**, **aslant**, ~ita; oblikva; dekliva

slap, (hit as w palm of hand), polmobati [tr]; ~o; (sound), klaki [int]; klako; (onom), klak!; (put, throw, etc., w force), ĵeti [tr] (e.g.: *he slapped his hat on his head:* li ĵetis sian ĉapelon sur la kapon); (splash), plaŭdi [int]; plaŭdo (e.g.: *waves slapped against the boat:* ondoj plaŭdis kontraŭ la boato); **slapdash**, malzorga, trohasta; **slap down**, forbati [tr]; **slap-happy**, (punch-drunk), boksebria; **slapstick**, farso; farsa

slash, (cut), strektranĉi [tr]; ~o; (reduce sharply), reduktegi [tr], onigi; (symbol "/"), oblikva streko; **backslash**, ("\"), retroa oblikva streko

slat, (thin, narrow piece), lato

slate, (stone), ardezo; (as writing tablet), tabelo; (color), ~kolora; (list of candidates), kandidataro; (cover w slate), ~izi [tr]; (designate, choose, schedule), elekti [tr], nomumi [tr], specifi [tr]; plani [tr]; **start with a clean slate**, komenc(iĝ)i kun glata tabelo; senmakule komenc(iĝ)i; **wipe the slate clean**, glatviŝi la tabelon

slater, (zool), onisko

slather, ŝmiregi [tr] [cp "spread"]

slattern, (slut), malĉastulino, diboĉulino; (sloppy woman), malpurulino

slaughter, (butcher animals; kill recklessly), buĉi [tr]; ~(ad)o; (massacre), masakri [tr]; masakro; [cp "shohet"]; **slaughterhouse**, ~ejo; **manslaughter**, hommortigo

Slav, Slavo; **Slavic**, ~a; **Slavism**, ~ismo; **Pan-Slavism**, tut-~ismo

slave, sklav/(in)o; ~a; (work hard, do drudgery), servuti [int]; **slavery**, ~eco; **slavedriver**, ~pelisto; **slave trade**, ~komerco

slaver, bavi [int], salivumi [int]

Slavonia, Slavonio

Slavonic, (rel language), Slavono; (la) ~a (lingvo); (Slavic), Slava

slaw, brasiksalato

slay, mortigi

sleazy, (flimsy), malfirma, malfortika; (shabby, shoddy), tombaka, kaduka; ĉifona

sled, sledo; ~i [int] [cp "luge", "sleigh"]; **bobsled**, bobo†

sledge, (sled), sledo [cp "sled", "sleigh"]; **sledgehammer**, martelego

sleek, (smooth, polished), glata, polurita

sleep, (gen), dormi [int]; ~o; (drug-induced), hipnozo; **sleepy**, ~ema; **sleeper**, (Br: rr tie), ŝpalo; (rr car), litvagono; **go to sleep**, ek~i [int], en~iĝi; **put to sleep**, (lit), (en)~iĝi; (kill), mortigi; **sleep away**, (time etc.), for~i [tr]; **sleep in**, (sleep where employed, e.g. as servant), ~i surloke; (sleep late), ~i malfrue; **sleep off**, for~i [tr]; **sleep over**, tranokti [int]; **sleep through**, tra~i [tr]; **sleep deeply**, ~egi [int]; **sleep lightly**, (doze), ~eti [int], somnoli [int]; **sleeping bag**, ~osako; **sleeping car**, (rr), litvagono; **sleeping partner**, [see under "partner"]; **sleeping pill**, ~igenzo; **sleepwalk**, [see under "walk"]; **sleep on it**, lasi tion ĝis morgaŭ; **oversleep**, tro~i [int]; **my foot (etc.) has gone to sleep**, al mi pingletas en la piedo (etc.)

sleet, (frozen rain), grajlo; ~i [int]; (ice glaze from rain freezing on surface), glatiso; **it's sleeting**, ~as

sleeve, (of garment or similar object), maniko; (of pipe; elec), mufo; **have something up one's sleeve**, kaŝi ion en la ~o; rezervi ion, reteni ion

sleigh, sledoĉaro [cp "sled", "troika"]

sleight, ruzo, jonglado; **sleight of hand**, prestidigitado; **perform sleight of hand**, prestidigiti [int]

slender, (thin), maldika; (svelte), svelta; (weak), malforta, febla; (narrow, as margin), mallarĝa

sleuth, (detective), detektivo; (dog), spurhundo

slice, (cut), tranĉi [tr]; ~aĵo; (curve, as hit ball), rekurbiĝi; rekurbiĝo; (spatula etc.), spatelo

slick, (slippery), glitiga; fari ~a [avoid "~i"; see "slide"]; (smooth), glata; glatigi; (neat), neta; netigi; (adept, clever), lerta; (deceptive), ruz(lert)a; (re paper etc.), glacea; (oil on water), oleglataĵo, oleverŝaĵo; **slicker**, (raincoat), pluvmantelo

slide, (slip, glide, move along surface), gliti [int]; ~igi; ~(ig)o; ~ejo; (push, shove), ŝovi [tr]; ŝoviĝi; ŝov(iĝ)o; (film), diapozitivo, diafilmo*; (projected image), lumbildo; (sliding mech part), ~peco; (playground equipment, or analogous device for packages etc.), tobogano; (for microscope), muntovitro; (landslide, snowslide), lavango; **slide fastener**, ~zipo; **slide rule**, ~kalkulilo, kalkulbastono; **sliding scale**, varianta tarifo; **let (matters) slide**, malatenti (aferojn)

slight, (small), malgranda, (iom)eta; (slender), maldika, svelta; (mild), milda; (disrespect), malrespekti [tr]; malrespekto; (neglect), neglekti [tr]; neglekto; **slightly**, iomete

slim, svelta, maldika

slime, ŝlimo; ~i [int]; **slimy**, ~a, muka

sling, (throw), ĵeti [tr]; ~o; (hang), pendigi; (for broken arm etc.), skarpo; (slingshot), katapulto; katapulti [tr]; (of rope etc., as on dock), ŝarĝoŝnurego; **slingers**, (Aus), kolbasetoj; **slingshot**, katapulto

slink, ŝtel/iri [int], ~vagi [int] [cp "skulk"]

slip, (slide), gliti [int]; ~igi; ~o; (stumble), stumbli [int]; stumblo; (on slippery surface), ~fali [int]; (go stealthily), ŝteliri [int]; (go, move, pass), pasi [int]; (escape), eskapi [int] (de); (mistake), erar(et)i [int]; erar(et)o; (become worse; regress; weaken etc.), regresi [int], malpliboniĝi; malfortiĝi; mallertiĝi; malvigliĝi; (decline, become less), malpliiĝi; (sideslip, re plane), flanken~i [int]; flanken~o; (put), meti [tr]; (insert), enmeti [tr], en~igi; (piece of paper), slipo; (woman's undergarment), subrobo; (ramp for ship launching), lanĉejo; (water channel between piers), intervarfo; (stem etc. for grafting), greftaĵo; (for planting), stiki [tr]; stikaĵo; **slippery**, (slick), ~iga; (tricky), ruzema; **slip up**, erari [int]; **slipshod**, (careless), malzorga; **slipway**, lanĉejo; **slip a disk**, herniigi diskon; **slipped disk**, diska hernio; **slip of the tongue**, misparolo; **let slip**, senintence malkaŝi [tr], lasi [tr] fali; **sideslip**, flanken~o; **give (someone) the slip**, ŝteleviti (iun)

slipper, (house shoe), pantoflo; **slipperwort**, kalceolario

slit, fendeto; ~i [tr]

slither, (crawl like snake), glit/rampi [int]; (slip, slide, as on loose surface), stumblo~i [int]; **slithery**, ŝlim~a

sliver, (wood etc.), spliteto; ~i [tr]; (any fragment), fragmento

slob, krudulo, bubego

slobber, bavi [int], salivumi [int]; ~aĵo, salivo

sloe, prunelo

slog, (plod), penpaŝi [int]; (slug), pugni [tr]; (toil), penlabori [int], servuti [int]

slogan, slogano

slöjd, slojdo

sloop, slupo

slop, (spill), verŝaĉi [tr]; ~iĝi; (gruel), kaĉaĉo; (mud), kot(aĉ)o; (slush), neĝakvo, neĝkoto; (sludge, slime), ŝlimo; (waste water etc.), forĵetakvo, rubakvo; (hog swill), porkokaĉo; (feed hogs), nutri, kaĉizi (la porkojn); **sloppy**, kaĉa; kota; neĝkota; ŝlima; (not neat), senorda, malneta; (careless), malzorga; **slop over**, superverŝi [tr]; superverŝiĝi

slope, deklivo; ~i [int]; ~igi

slosh, (splash), plaŭdi [int]; ~igi; ~o; (shake, agitate), skui [tr], agiti [tr]

slot, (groove), foldo; ~i [tr]; (notch), noĉo; noĉi [tr]; (position), pozicio; **slot machine**, vetaŭtomato

sloth, (zool), bradipo; (laziness), pigreco, maldiligenteco; (person), pigrulo, maldiligentulo; **slothful**, pigra, maldiligenta; **two-toed sloth**, unaŭo

slouch, (droop, bend forward, standing), malrekt/e stari [int]; ~a staro; (sitting), ~e sidi [int]; ~a sido; (sag, gen), sagiĝi, velki [int]; (awkward, inept), mallerta; mallertulo

slough, (cast off, discard), forĵeti [tr], forigi; (med: separate, as dead tissue from living), disigi, apartigi; (outer skin of snake), ekstera haŭto; (be shed, re snake skin etc.), senhaŭtiĝi; (quagmire), ŝlimejo

Slovak, Slovako; **Slovakia**, ~io; **Slovakian**, ~a; ~ia

Slovenia, Sloven/io; **Slovenian**, **Slovene**, ~o; ~a; ~ia

slovenly, mal/zorga, ~diligenta, ~ordema

slow, (not rapid), malrapida; ~igi; ~iĝi; (esp in compound forms), lanta, lant~ (e.g.: *slow-moving:* lantmova; (re clock), malfrua; (not clever), mallerta; (sluggish), malenergia, malvigla; **slow down**, **slow up**, ~igi; ~iĝi; **go slowly**, ~i [int], lanti [int]; **slowly**, ~e; (mus), adaĝe; **slowpoke**, lantemulo; **slow on the uptake**, malviglanima

sloyd, slojdo

sludge, ŝlimo, feĉo

slug, (zool), limako; (token), ĵetono; (bullet), kuglo; (swallow), gluto; (hit), pugni [tr]; pugnado; **sea slug**, dorido

sluggard, maldiligentulo, lantemulo, mallaboremulo, pigrulo

sluggish, malvigla, malenergia, malrapida

sluice, (channel), kluzo; ~i [tr]; **sluice (gate)**, herso, ~opordo

slum, kvartalaĉo, domaĉaro; (of tin shacks, as in some cities), ladvilaĝo; **go slumming**, viziti la ~on

slumber, dormi [int]; ~o

slump, (bsns decline), malprospero; ~iĝi; (any decline, fall), ekfali [int], malvigliĝi; ekfalo, malvigliĝo; (droop, as in posture), sagiĝi; sagiĝo

slur, (pronounce indistinctly), malklare prononci [tr], fuŝprononci [tr]; malklara prononco, fuŝprononco; (disparage), diskrediti [tr], mallaŭdi [tr]; diskredito, mallaŭdo; (mus), ligaturi* [tr]; ligaturo

slurb, suburbaĉo

slurry, flukoto

slush, (snow and water), neĝakvo; (snow and mud), neĝokoto; (mud, mire), koto, ŝlimo

slut, (promiscuous), diboĉulino, malĉastulino; (slovenly), malpurulino

sly, ruza; **on the sly**, kaŝe

smack, (sound of smacking lips etc.), ŝmaci [int]; ~igi; ~o; (onom), ŝmac!; (slight flavor, hint, suggestion), gusteto, nuanco, sugesteto [see "smack of" below]; (any slight amount), iometo da; iometo, gusteto, nuanco; (loud kiss), ~kisi [tr]; ~kiso; (hit, slap), manfrapi [tr]; manfrapo; (hitting sound), klaki [int]; klako; (onom), klak!; (squarely, precisely), rekte (e.g.: *I ran smack into the wall:* mi kuris rekte kontraŭ la muron); (sloop), slupo; (fishing boat), fiŝboato; **smack of**, gusti de, (fig), odori de (e.g.: *the ice cream smacks of mint:* la glaciaĵo gustas de mento; *his tone of voice smacks of sarcasm:* lia voĉtono odoras de sarkasmo)

small, (little, gen), malgranda; (lowercase type, not capitalized), minuskla; (narrow part, as of back), mallarĝaĵo; **smallpox**, variolo

smallage, apio

smalt, smalto

smart, (intelligent), inteligenta; (clever, alert), lerta; (witty), sprita; (neat, trim), neta; (stylish), laŭmoda; (impertinent, flippant), impertinenta, replik(em)a; (pain), dolori [tr]; doloro; **smart aleck**, impertinentulo, replikemulo; **smart-alecky**, impertinenta; **outsmart**, superruzi [tr]

smash, (shatter), frakasi [tr]; ~iĝi; ~o; (hit), bategi [tr]; batego; (ruin), ruiniĝi; ruiniĝi; (break up), disrompi [tr], disbati [tr] disrompiĝi; (collide), kolizi(eg)i [int]; kolizi(eg)igi; kolizi(eg)o; (success), sukcesego

smattering, (slight knowledge), sci/eto, iometa ~o; (small number), malmulto, iometo

smear, (spread, daub, etc.), ŝmiri [tr]; ~iĝi; ~o [cp "dab"]; (blot, streak, as wet ink etc.), makuli [tr]; makuliĝi; makulo; (malign, slander, libel), kalumnii [tr]; kalumnio

smearcase, kazea fromaĝo

smell, (perceive odor; test by smelling), flari [tr]; ~o (e.g.: *I smell smoke:* mi ~as fumon; *smell the milk to see if it's sour:* ~u la lakton por vidi ĉu ĝi estas acida); (one of the 5 senses), ~ado; (an odor), odoro; (have, emit odor), odori [int] (e.g.: *the milk smells sour:* la lakto odoras acida); (stink, bad odor), fetori [int], stinki [int]; fetoro, stinko; (aroma), aromo; (trace, suggestion), indiko, spureto; **smelly**, fetora, odoraĉa, stinka; **smell out**, el~i [tr]; **smell up**, odorigi; fetorigi; **smelling salts**, odorsaloj

smelt, (metal), gisi [tr], fandi [tr]; (zool: any of *Osmerus*), osmero; (European: *O. eperlanus*), eperlano; (Am: *O. mordax*), Amerika osmero, mordako*; **smelter**, ~isto; ~ejo

smidgen, iometo

Smilax, smilako

smile, rideti [int]; ~o; **smile on**, (favor), favori [tr]

smirch, (gen), makuli [tr]; ~o

smirk, ridetaĉi [int]; ~o

smite, frapegi [tr], bategi [tr]

smith, (forge worker, gen), forĝisto; (craftworker in specified metal), –me-

tiisto [sfx] (e.g.: *coppersmith:* kupro-
metîisto; *tinsmith:* stanmetiisto);
smithy, ~ejo; **blacksmith,** huffer~is-
to
smithereens, pecetoj, eretoj, frag-
ment(et)oj
smithsonite, zinkospato
smock, kitelo
smog, fumnebulo; **smoggy,** ~a
smoke, (substance), fumo; (give off
smoke; smoke tobacco etc.), ~i [tr,
int]; (act of), ~ado; (treat w smoke,
gen), ~aĵi [tr]; (re meat or fish), bu-
kani [tr]; **smoker,** (person), ~anto; (rr
car), ~vagono; (compartment of rr car
etc.), ~kupeo; **smoke bomb,** ~bom-
bo; **smokehouse,** ~aĵejo; **smoke
jumper,** fajroparaŝutisto; **smoke out,**
(drive out animal or person by
smoke), ~peli [tr]; **smokescreen,**
~ŝirmilo; **smokestack,** ~tubo;
smoked meat, smoked fish, bukano;
no smoking, ne ~u, ~ado malperme-
sata; **(non)smoking section,** sekcio
por (ne)~antoj; **go up in smoke,** (burn
up), forbruli [int]; (be in vain), esti vana, forvaporiĝi
smolder, subbruli [int]
smooch, kunkaresi [int]
smooth, (gen), glata; ~igi; **smooth-
shaven,** senbarba; **smooth-spoken,
smooth-talking,** ~parola
smorgasbord, bufedo
smother, sufoki [tr]; ~iĝi; ~aĵo
smoulder, subbruli [int]
smudge, (stain, spot), makuli [tr]; ~o;
(fire), fumfajro; **smudgy,** ~a; fuma;
smudge pot, fumpoto
smug, memkontent(aĉ)a; **smugness,** ~o
smuggle, (across borders), kontrabandi
[tr]; **smuggling,** (act of), ~o; **smuggler,** ~isto; **smuggled goods,** ~aĵo;
smuggle in, (fig: bring thing hidden
to any place), kaŝ–enporti [tr] (e.g.:
*cameras were not permitted, but we
smuggled one into the room:* fotiloj
estis malpermesitaj, sed ni kaŝ–enpor-
tis unu en la ĉambron); **smuggle out,**
(fig), kaŝelporti [tr]
smut, (pornography etc.), pornografio;
(plant disease), smuto; (soot), fulgo;
(particle of soot), fulgero; **smutty,** ~a,

maldeca; smuta; fulga; **loose smut,**
(bot: *Ustilago*), ustilago
Smyrna, Smirno
snack, manĝeti [tr, int], kolazioni [int];
~o, kolaziono; **snack bar,** ~ejo
snaffle, (simpla) mordaĵo
snafu, konfuzi [tr], malordi [tr], ħaosigi;
(normale) ~ita (malorda, ħaosa)
snag, (obstacle), obstrukco, obstaklo;
(tear), ŝiri [tr]; ŝiraĵo; (catch, hook),
kroĉi [tr]; kroĉiĝi; kroĉo; kroĉaĵo;
(fig: any hazard), rifo
snail, heliko; **snail-paced,** ~rapida;
move at a snail's pace, moviĝi je ~a
rapido
snake, (gen), serpento; **snake-charm-
er,** ~dresisto; **snakeroot,** cimicifugo;
black snakeroot, saniklo; **snake-
weed,** (bistort), bistorto; **snakewood,**
(*Strychnos*), strikno; **blacksnake,** kolubro; **coral snake,** koral~o; **garter
snake,** (*Elaps*), elapo; **glass snake,**
angviso, vitro~o; **rattlesnake,** krotalo, son~o; **wart snake,** akroħordo;
snake-in-the-grass, perfidulo
snap, (sound, as crack, clack, etc.), klaki [int]; ~igi; ~o; (sound as whip etc.),
knali [int]; knaligi; knalo; (onom),
klak!, krak!; (shut), ~fermi [tr]; ~fer-
miĝi; (bite), ~mordi [tr]; ~mordo;
(grab), ekkapti [tr]; (speak sharply),
knal(parol)i [int], ~(parol)i [int];
(break), ekrompi [tr]; ekrompiĝi;
(phot), kapti [tr] (foton de), foti [tr];
(clothing fastener), ~fiksilo; ~fiksi
[tr]; (easy task), facilaĵo; (sudden),
subita, senpripensa (e.g.: *a snap decision:* senpripensa decido); **snappy,**
(concise), lakona, konciza; (witty),
sprita; (retort), replika; (stylish),
laŭmoda; **snap back, snap out of it,**
(recover), (subite, rapide) resaniĝi, renormaliĝi; (rapide) reakiri (bonhumo-
ron, sanon, ekvilibron, etc.);
snapdragon, antirino; **snap off,** de-
rompi [tr]; derompiĝi; **snapweed,** netuŝumino, ĝardena balzamino; **snap
one's fingers,** ~igi la fingrojn; **cold
snap,** malvarma periodo
snare, (trap), kapti [tr]; ~ilo; (wire for
snare drum), tamburdrato; **snare
drum,** drattamburo

snarl, (growl), grumbl/egi [int], knari [int], minac~i [int]; ~ego, minac~o; (tangle), impliki [tr]; implikiĝi; implik(aĵ)o

snatch, (grab), ekkapti [tr], forkapti [tr]; (jerk), ektiri [tr]; ~o, forkapto; ektiro; (small amount, fragment), fragmento; (brief time), periodeto

snazzy, puca, ŝika

sneak, (move stealthily), ŝtel/iri [int], ~paŝi [int]; (take), ~preni [tr]; (put), ~meti [tr]; (pilfer), marodi [tr]; (tricky person), ruzulo; (w/o warning), senaverta, ŝtel– [pfx] (e.g.: *sneak attack:* senaverta atako [or] ~atako); **sneaker,** (shoe), tolŝuo; **sneaky,** ruza; **sneak one over on,** superruzi [tr]; **sneak out of,** ~eviti [tr]; **sneak up on,** ~atingi [tr], ~veni al

sneer, rikani [int]; ~o

sneeze, terni [int]; ~o; **sneezewort,** ptarmiko

snick, (notch, nick), noĉi [tr]; ~o; (cricket: glancing blow), tuŝeti [tr]; tuŝeto

snicker, subrid(aĉ)i [int]; ~o

snide, malica

sniff, snufi [tr, int]; ~o; **sniff out,** (find by smelling, lit or fig), elflari [tr], el~i [tr]

sniffle, snufeti [int]; ~o; **the sniffles,** ~ado

snifter, snufpokalo

snigger, subrid(aĉ)i [int]; ~o

snip, (cut), tond/eti [tr]; ~etaĵo; (impudent person), impertinentulo; **snips,** (metal shears), ĉizojo [note sing]

snipe, (shoot), kaŝpafi [tr]; (zool), galinago; **sniper,** ~into; ~anto; ~isto

snippet, peceto

snitch, (inform on, tattle), denunci [tr]; ~into; ~anto; (pilfer), marodi [tr]

snivel, (cry and sniffle), snufplori [int]

snob, klasafekt/ulo [not "snobo"]; **snobbish, snobby,** ~a; **snobbery,** ~ado

snood, (hairnet), harneto

snooker, 21-pilka bilardo

snoop, (spy), spioni [tr]; ~emulo; **snoopy,** ~ema

snooty, aroganta, fieraĉa

snooze, somnoli [int], dormeti [int]; ~o, dormeto

snore, ronki [int]; ~o

snorkel, (breathing tube), spirtubo; (hydraulic crane), korbogruo

snort, (ek)ronki [int]; ~o

snot, muk(aĉ)o; **snotty,** ~a; (offensive), aĉa; (impudent), impertinenta

snout, muzelo, rostro

snow, (precipitation), neĝo; ~i [int]; (deceive, flatter), flattrompi [tr]; **snowy,** ~(em)a; **it's snowing,** ~as; **it looks like snow,** ŝajnas ~eme, ŝajnas ke ~os, aspektas ~eme; **snowball,** ~bulo; (bot), opulo; **snowbound,** ~kaptita, ~-blokita; **snowcapped,** ~(o)verta; **snowdrift,** ~duno, ~drivaĵo; **snowdrop,** (bot: *Galanthus*), galanto; **common snowdrop,** (*G. nivalis*), ~borulo; **snowfall,** ~ado; (as total snow in given area), ~okvanto; **snowfield,** ~okampo; **snowflake,** (snow), ~ero; (bot), leŭkojo; **snow-in-summer, snow-in-harvest,** (bot), cerastio; **snow job,** flattrompo; **snowman, snowperson,** ~homo; **snowmobile,** ~aŭto; **snowplow,** ~plugilo; **snowshoe,** rakedo, ~oŝuo; **snowslide,** ~olavango; **snowstorm,** ~oŝtormo; **snowsuit,** ~kostumo; **Snow-White,** (in fairy tale), N~ulino; **be snowed under (with),** droni (en); **mixed rain and snow,** pluv~o

snub, (scorn, disdain), mal/degni [tr], ~estimi [tr]; ~degno, ~estimo; (slight, ignore), ~rekoni [tr]; ~rekono; **snub-nosed,** platnaza, mopsnaza

snuff, (sniff), snufi [tr]; ~o; (tobacco), ~tabako, flartabako; (put out candle etc.), sufokestingi [tr]; (trim wick), tondi (la meĉon); **dip snuff,** ~i tabakon; **snuff out,** sufokestingi [tr]; (extinguish, gen), estingi [tr]; **up to snuff,** laŭnorma

snuffle, snufadi [tr, int]; ~o

snug, (comfortable), komforta, gemutaț; (compact, not roomy), malvasta, kompakta

snuggle, premkaresi [tr], alpremi [tr]; ~iĝi, alpremiĝi, kunvolvi sin

so, (as; in that way; to that extent), tiel (e.g.: *stand just so:* staru ĝuste ~; *why are you so nervous?:* kial vi estas ~ nervoza?; *I am not so tall as you:* mi ne estas ~ alta kiel vi); (therefore; colloq conj), do (e.g.: *it rained, so we stayed home:* pluvis, do ni restis hejme; *so, as I was saying:* do, kiel mi diris); (so that), [see "so that" below]; (likewise), same (e.g.: *she speaks Esperanto, and so does he:* ŝi parolas Esperanton, kaj same li); (true), vera, prava (e.g.: *that's not so:* tio ne estas vera [or] tio ne pravas); (in proper order etc.), ĝuste en ordo (e.g.: *everything in the room was just so:* ĉio en la ĉambro estis ĝuste en ordo); **if so**, se jes; **I think so**, mi kredas ke jes; **she said so**, ŝi diris ke jes; **so-called**, ~ nomata [abb: t.n.]; **and so on, and so forth**, kaj ~ plu [abb: ktp.]; **so as to**, por ~i (e.g.: *he came near so as to hear better:* li proksimiĝis por pli bone aŭdi); **so that**, por ke ~u (e.g.: *she came so [that] we could discuss it:* ŝi venis por ke ni povu diskuti ĝin); **so what?**, kio do?; **so-so**, meza; meze (bone), mezbone, sufiĉe bone; **so-and-so**, (gen, to indicate unknown or nonspecific person), ajnulo, umulo; (insult), ulaĉo (e.g.: *start each letter with "Dear Mr. or Ms. so-and-so":* komencu ĉiun leteron per "Kara s–ro aŭ s–ino Ajnulo"; *that so-and-so borrowed a book and didn't return it:* tiu ulaĉo prunteprenis libron kaj ne redonis ĝin); **so far**, (up to now), ĝis nun; ĝisnuna; **so far so good**, ĝis nun ĉio en ordo; **so much**, (unspecified amount), iom (e.g.: *the workers are paid so much a day:* oni pagas al la laboristoj iom en tago); **so much for**, (no need to consider further), jen ĉio pri (e.g.: *well, so much for that idea!:* nu, jen ĉio pri tiu ideo!); **not so much as**, (not even), eĉ ne (e.g.: *they didn't so much as acknowledge my letter:* ili eĉ ne agnoskis mian leteron); **or so**, (approximately), ĉirkaŭ [abb: ĉ.], proksimume (e.g.: *a hundred or so people came:* ĉirkaŭ [ĉ.] cent homoj venis)

soak, tremp/(ad)i [tr]; ~iĝi; ~(iĝ)o; **soak up**, sorbi [tr]; sorbiĝi

soap, sapo; ~i [tr]; ~a; **soapy**, ~eca; **soapberry**, (tree), sapindo; **soap-**
dish, ~ujo; **soap flakes**, ~flokoj; **soapstone**, ~ŝtono; **soapwort**, saponario; **bar soap**, blok~o; **bar of soap**, ~bloko; **soft soap**, ŝmir~o; **softsoap**, (flatter), flati [tr]; flatado; flataĵo

soar, (rise high), sori [int]; ~ado; (float, glide), ŝvebi [int]; ŝvebado

sob, plorsingulti [int], ploreti [int]; ~o, ploreto

sober, (not drunk), malebria; (of moderate habits, sedate), sobra; **sobriety**, ~o; sobreco; **sober up**, ~igi; ~iĝi

soccer, futbalo [cp "football"]

sociable, amikema, gregema, afabla, societema, ariĝema

social, (re society, gen), socia (e.g.: *social sciences:* ~aj sciencoj; *social gathering:* ~a kuniĝo); (socialistic, pol, etc.), sociala (e.g.: *social insurance:* sociala asekuro; *Social Democratic Party:* Socialdemokratia Partio); (sociable, gregarious), [see "sociable"]; (party), (~a) fest(et)o; **socialism**, socialismo; **socialist**, socialisma; socialisto; **socialize**, ~igi; socialigi; ~etumi [int]; **social security**, sociala sekureco; **antisocial**, kontraŭ~a

society, (at large), socio; (organization, club, etc.), ~eto; **societal**, ~a, tut~a [cp "social"]; **Society of Friends**, S~eto de Amikoj [cp "Quaker"]; **Society of Jesus**, Kompanio de Jesuo [cp "Jesuit"]

Socinus, Socinio; **Socinianism**, ~anismo

socio–, (pfx: society), soci(o)–

sociology, sociolog/io; **sociologist**, ~o

sociopath, psikopato; **sociopathic**, ~ia

sock, (foot garment), ŝtrumpeto; (hit w fist), pugni [tr]; pugnado; (hit, gen), bati [tr]; bato; **sock away**, forŝpari [tr]; **sock in**, enfermi [tr] (pro nebulo); **windsock**, maniko

socket, (gen), ingo; (for elec bulb), lamp~o; **threaded socket**, ŝraŭb~o; **ball and socket joint**, globartiko

socle, soklo

Socrates, Sokrato; **Socratic**, ~a

sod, gazonbulo; ~izi [tr]

soda, (Na_2CO_3), sodo; ($NaHCO_3$), natria hidrokarbonato; (Na_2O), natria oksido; (NaOH), natro, kaŭstika ~o; (carbonated drink), ~aĵo, karbonata trinkaĵo; **soda cracker**, salbiskvito; **soda fountain**, refreŝigejo, ~akvejo; **soda water**, ~-akvo, ŝaŭm-akvo; **caustic soda**, natro, kaŭstika ~o; **ice cream soda**, karbonata glaciaĵo

sodium, natrio; **sodium hydroxide**, ~a hidroksido, natro

sodoku, sodokuo

Sodom, Sodomo; **Sodomite**, ~ano

sodomy, sodomio; **sodomize**, ~i [tr], bugri [tr]

sofa, sofo; **sofa bed**, ~olito

soffit, sofito

Sofia, Sofio

soft, (yielding to pressure; not hard; not sharp, re contours, shadows, etc.; re coal, water, etc.; gram. re consonant sound etc.), mola; (not loud), mallaŭta; (poet: not loud), softa; (mild, gentle), milda, delikata, malakra, dolĉa; (moderate), modera; (re food: easy to digest, w/o roughage), senfibra; (re drink: w/o alcohol), senalkohola; (weak, flabby), ~aĉa; (easy), facila; (lenient, pampering), dorlota; (re paintings), morbida; **be soft on**, (pamper, be lenient), dorloti [tr], milde trakti [tr]

softball, (ball), molpilko; (game), ~ado

software, (cmptr), softvaro†

soggy, saturita

soil, (earth), grundo; (dirty), malpurigi; **subsoil**, sub~o; **topsoil**, supraĵa ~o

soirée, vesperfesto

sojourn, resti [int], gasti [int]; ~o; **sojourner**, pasloĝanto

sol, (mus), sol; (colloidal suspension), solo

Sol, (sun), Suno

solace, konsoli [tr]; ~o

Solanum, solano; Solanum dulcamara, dolĉamaro; Solanum lycopersicum, tomato; Solanum melongena, melongeno

solar, suna

solarium, sunum/ejo, ~ĉambro

Soldanella, soldanelo

solder, luti [tr]; ~aĵo; **soldering gun**, (pistola) ~ilo; **soldering iron**, (mar-

tela) ~ilo

soldier, soldato; ~i [int]

soldo, soldo

sole, (foot), plando; (shoe), ~umo; (alone, only, single), sola; (fish), soleo; **re-sole**, re~umi [tr]; **half-sole**, duon~umo; duon~umi [tr]; **fillet of sole**, solea fileo

Solea, soleo

solecism, solecismo

solemn, solena; **solemnize**, ~i [tr]; **solemnify**, ~igi; **solemnity**, ~aĵo; ~eco

solenoid, solenoido

soleus, (muscle), soleo

sol-fa, solfeĝo

solfatara, solfataro

solfeggio, solfeĝo

solicit, (request), peti [tr]; (as by prostitute), putine ~i, putin~i [tr]; **solicitor**, (Br: legal advisor), solicitoro

solicitous, (attentive, having care for), atenta, zorga; (desirous, gen), dezira

solid, (gen), solida; ~o; (not hollow), ~a, masiva; **solidify**, ~igi; ~iĝi; **solidity**, ~eco

Solidago, solidago

solidarity, solidareco

soliloquy, monologo; **soliloquize**, ~i [int]

solipsism, solipsismo

solitaire, (gem; game), solitero

solitary, sola

solitude, soleco

solmization, solfeĝo

solo, (mus etc.), solo; ~i [int]; (adj or adv: alone), ~e; **soloist**, ~isto

Solomon, Salomono; **Solomon Islands**, ~-Insuloj

Solon, Solono

solstice, solstico

soluble, solvebla; **solubility**, ~eco; **insolubble**, ne~a

solute, solvitaĵo [not "solvaĵo"]

solution, (gen), solvo; (chem), ~aĵo

Solutrean, Solutrian, solutreo, ~a periodo

solvate, solvati [tr]; ~aĵo; **solvation**, ~iĝo; **heat of solvation**, ~iĝa varmo

solve, (gen), solvi [tr]

solvent, ($), solventa; (chem), solvenzo; **solvency**, ~eco; **insolvent**, ne~a

soma, (body), somato [cp "body"]

Somali, Somalia; ~ano; **Somalia**, ~o
Somateria mollissima, somaterio,
molanaso
somatic, somata; **psychosomatic**, psi-
ko~a
somat(o)–, (med pfx), somat(o)–,
somatology, somatologio
somber, sombra
sombrero, Meksikia ĉapelo, larĝranda
ĉapelo
some, (certain unspecified one(s)), iu(j)
(e.g.: *we are busy some days:* ni estas
okupataj iujn tagojn; *some rogue stole
my bicycle:* iu kanajlo ŝtelis mian
biciklon); (unspecified amount), iom
(da) (e.g.: *I have some milk, some
books:* mi havas iom da lakto, iom da
libroj; *do you want some?:* ĉu vi volas
iom?; *we slept some in the car:* ni dor-
mis iom en la aŭto) [cp "several",
"few"]; (approximately), ĉirkaŭ [abb:
ĉ.], proksimume (e.g.: *there were
some twenty people at the meeting:*
estis ĉirkaŭ [ĉ.] dudek homoj ĉe la
kunveno); (of an unspecified sort), ia
(e.g.: *some bug bit me:* ia besteto min
mordis)
–some, (sfx: causing), –iga (e.g.: *tiresome:* laciga); (in a group of given
number), –opo (e.g.: *a threesome:* triopo)
somebody, iu [see "anyone"]; (important person), gravulo; **somebody's**,
ies
somehow, iel [see "anyhow"]; **somehow or other**, iel aŭ tiel
someday, iun tagon, iam
someone, [see "somebody"]
someplace, [see "somewhere"]
somersault, transkapiĝi; ~o
something, io [see "anything"]; **something of a**, ioma (e.g.: *he is something
of an expert:* li estas ioma spertulo);
something or other, io aŭ tio
sometime, (adv), iam; (adj), ~a;
(former), ~a, antaŭa; **sometimes**, (on
various occasions), (kelk)foje;
(kelk)foja; **sometimes ..., sometimes,
jen ...,** jen (e.g.: *the weather was
sometimes sunny, sometimes rainy:* la
vetero estis jen suna, jen pluva)
somewhat, iom

somewhere, (at some place), ie; (to
some place), ien [see "anywhere"];
get somewhere, (progress), progresi
[int]; **somewhere or other**, ie aŭ tie
Somme, Sommo
somnambulate, somnambuli   [int];
somnambulator, **somnambulist**,
~o; **somnambulation**, ~ado; **som-
nambulism**, ~ismo
somniferous, dormiga
somniloquy, dormparolo; **somnilo-
quist**, ~anto
somnolent, (drowsy), somnola; (soporific), ~iga, dormiga
son, filo; **son-in-law**, bo~o; **stepson**,
duon~o; **godson**, bapto~o
sonant, sona; ~anto; ~anta
sonar, (method), eĥosond/ado; (device),
~ilo
sonata, sonato; **sonatina**, ~eto
sonde, sondilo
song, (gen), kanto; (light, merry, or sa-
tirical), kanzono; **songfest**, ~festo;
Song of Solomon, Song of Songs,
(Bib), (Alta) K~o de Salomono, K~o
de K~oj; **night song**, kompletorio;
plainsong, Gregoria ĉantado; **swan-
song**, cigno~o, ~o de cigno; **theme
song**, tem~o, temkanzono; **buy (sell)
for a song**, aĉeti [tr] (vendi [tr]) kontraŭ bagatelo
sonic, sona; **sonic boom**, ~tondro; **in-
frasonic**, infra~a; **subsonic**, sub~a;
supersonic, super~a; **ultrasonic**, ul-
tra~a
sonnet, soneto
sonny, knabêjo
sonorous, sonora; **sonority**, ~eco
Sonya, Sonjo, ~a
Soochow, Suĝoŭ
soon, baldaŭ; **as soon as**, [see under
"as"]; **no sooner**, (immediately
when), apenaŭ (e.g.: *no sooner had
they done it when:* apenaŭ ili faris ĝin
kiam); **sooner or later**, pli-malpli ~;
would sooner, (rather), preferus (e.g.:
she would sooner die than quit: ŝi
preferus morti ol rezigni)
soot, fulgo
soothe, (ease), kvietigi, trankviligi; (relieve pain etc.), mildigi, malakrigi;
(console), konsoli [tr]

soothsayer, aŭguristo
sop, (soak), trempi [tr]; ~iĝi; (absorb), sorbi [tr]; sorbiĝi; (bread), ~pano; (appeasement), pacigilo; **soppy,** (wet), saturita, gutanta; (sentimental), sentimental(aĉ)a
Sophia, Sofia; **Sophie,** Sonjo, Sonja
sophism, sofismo; **sophist,** sofisto
sophisticate, (make more complex), kompleks/igi; (make worldly, nonnaïve), malnaivigi, mondumigi; **sophisticated,** (re person), ~a: malnaiva, monduma, multscia, klera; (refined), rafinita; (tech), (alte) disvolvita, alt-kapabla, kompleksa; **sophistication,** ~eco; malnaiveco, mondumeco; rafiniteco; disvolviteco, alta kapablo, komplekseco
sophistry, sofistiko
Sophocles, Sofoklo
sophomore, duajara; ~ulo, ~a studento; **sophomoric,** tromemfida
Sophora, soforo
sopor, soporo
soporific, dormiga, somnoliga
soprano, (voice range), soprano; (singer), ~ulo
Sorbonne, Sorbono
Sorbus, sorparbo; Sorbus aria, alizarbo
sorcery, sorĉ/ado; ~aĵo; ~arto; **sorcerer,** ~isto; **sorceress,** ~istino
sordes, saburo
sordid, malpura, (poet), sordida
sordino, sordino
sore, (painful), dolora; (offended), ofendita; (distressed), ĉagrenita; (ulcer, boil, etc.), ulcero; **be sore,** (feel pain), ~iĝi; (re specific body part), ~i min (vin, etc.) (e.g.: *my foot is sore:* mia piedo ~as min); **bedsore,** kuŝeskaro
Sorex, soriko; Soricidae, ~edoj
sorghum, Sorghum, sorgo
Soricidae, [see *"Sorex"*]
sorites, sorito
sororicide, fratinmortigo
sorority, fratinaro
sorrel, (*Rumex*), rumekso; (color), ruĝbruneta; **wood sorrel,** (*Oxalis*), oksalido
sorrow, (sadness), malĝojo; ~i [int]; (grief, affliction), aflikto, ĉagreno, doloro; afliktiĝi, ĉagreniĝi, doloriĝi; **sor-**

rowful, ~a; aflikta, ĉagrena, dolora
sorry, (feeling regret), bedaŭr/anta; (regrettable, unfortunate), ~inda; (poor, inferior), aĉa, tombaka; (miserable), mizera; **I'm sorry,** (apology), mi ~as; mi pardonpetas; pardonu; (regret), mi ~as; **feel sorry for, be sorry for,** (have sympathy), kompati [tr]
sort, (type, kind), speco; (sort out, classify), ~igi, ordigi, klasifiki [tr]; **sort of,** (somewhat), iom; **sort of a,** kvazaŭa, ia, ioma; **sort out,** (classify), ~igi, klasifiki [tr]; (disentangle), malimpliki [tr]; **of sorts, of a sort,** ia; **out of sorts,** (slightly ill), malsaneta
sortie, atakeliro
sorus, soro
S.O.S. S.O.S.
Sosia, Sozio
sot, drink(em)ulo
sotto voce, subvoĉe
sou, soldo
soubrette, subreto
soufflé sufleo
sough, susuri [int]; ~o
soul, animo; **oversoul,** super~o
sound, (audible, gen), sono; ~i [tr, int] (e.g.: *the whistle sounded:* la fajfilo ~is; *sound the alarm:* ~i (la) alarmon; *the sound of thunder:* la ~o de tondro); (vibrate, resonate after initial impulse ceased, as bell, gong, etc.), sonori [int]; sonorigi; sonoro; (range of sound, earshot), aŭdatingo (e.g.: *within sound of my voice:* en la aŭdatingo de mia voĉo); (seem, appear), ŝajni [int], aspekti [int]; ŝajno, aspekto (e.g.: *you sound bothered:* vi ŝajnas ĉagrenita; *it sounds like [as if] dogs [are] barking:* ŝajnas kvazaŭ hundoj bojas [or: ŝajnas ke hundoj bojas]; *I don't like the sound of his report:* mi ne ŝatas la aspekton de lia raporto); (signal), signali [tr]; (proclaim), proklami [tr]; (undamaged, in good condition), sendifekta, bonstata; (healthy), sana; (firm, secure), firma, sekura, stabila; (correct, accurate), prava; (deep, as sleep), profunda; (valid), valida; (sea arm), markolo [cp "fjord"]; (measure depth or height; explore, probe, etc., lit or fig), sondi

[tr]; **sound out**, (fig), sondi [tr]; **ultra-sound**, ultra~o; **unsound**, malfirma, malstabila; malbonstata; malprava; malvalida; **the Sound**, (Øresund), Sundo; **sound track**, ~streko
soup, supo; **soup bowl**, ~ujo; **soup up**, (pli)potencigi; **in the soup**, (in difficulty), en embaraso, en malfacilaĵo
soupçon, (hint, trace), nuanco, gusteto, sugesteto; (suspicion), suspekteto
sour, (acid, as lemon etc.), acida; ~igi; ~iĝi; (bitter), amara; amarigi; amariĝi; (fig: not sweet, gen), maldolĉa; maldolĉigi; maldolĉiĝi (e.g.: *their relationship soured:* ilia rilato maldolĉiĝis)
source, (gen), fonto
sousaphone, kojltubjo
souse, (plunge into liquid), mergi [tr]; (brine), salakvo; (pickle), pekli [tr]; (wet), saturi [tr]; (drunk), ebriigi; ebriulo
souslik, zizelo
south, sudo [abb: S]; ~a; ~e(n); **South**, (as part of most place names), Sud-, Suda [see subentries under main part of each name for specific geog names]; **southern**, ~a; **southernmost**, plej ~a; **southerner**, ~ano; **southward**, ~e(n); ~enira; **southerly**, (southern), ~a; (toward south), ~e(n); ~enira; (from south), de~a; de~e; **southbound**, ~enira; **southeast**, ~oriento; ~orienta; ~oriente(n); (esp re compass direction), ~eosto [–a etc.] [abb: SE]; **southwest**, ~okcidento [–a etc.]; (compass), ~uesto [abb: SW]
souvenir, memoraĵo
sovereign, (supreme), suverena; ~ulo; (independent), sendependa; **sovereignty**, ~eco; sendependeco
soviet, (council or governing body during the time of the Soviet Union), soveto; ~a; **Soviet**, (re Soviet Union), S~ia; S~iano; **the (former) Soviet Union**, (la eksa) S~io, S~unio; **(the) Union of Soviet Socialist Republics**, (complete formal name), (la) Unio de S~aj Socialistaj Respublikoj [abb: USSR]
sovkhoz, sovĥozo

sow, (spread seed, or analogous action), semi [tr] (e.g.: *sow wheat in the field:* ~i tritikon en la kampo; *sow discontent:* ~i malkontenton); (re land seeded etc.), pri~i [tr] (e.g.: *sow ten hectares with wheat:* pri~i dek hektarojn per tritiko); (pig), porkino; **as you sow, so shall you reap**, kia la ~o, tia la rikolto
soy, soy sauce, sojo; **soybean**, (bean or plant), ~fabo
spa, banurbo, banloko; **health spa**, kuracejo
space, (volume, distance, room, etc.; math), spaco; (free space, cosmos), kosmo; kosma, spaciala, ~a; (blank between words etc.), ~eto; (locate w space between), inter~igi; **spacing**, (space between 2 printed lines), interlinio; **spacecraft**, (any apparatus used in space), ~a aparato; **spaceflight**, kosma flugo; **spaceport**, kosmohaveno; **spaceship**, kosmoŝipo; **spacesuit**, (kosma) skafandro; **aerospace**, aerokosmo; aerokosma; **space-time (continuum)**, ~tempo; **free space, outer space**, (libera) kosmo; **single–space**, klavumi [tr], printi [tr], tajpi [tr] sen interlinio; **single–spaced**, sen interlinio; **double–space**, interlinii [tr], printi kun interlinio; **triple–space**, duoble interlinii [tr]; **space-and-a-half, one-and-a-half space**, sesqviinterlinii [tr]; **single-spaced, double-spaced**, (etc.), sen (kun) interlinio (etc.); **interspace**, inter~o
spacious, vasta, spacoplena, grandspaca
spade, (tool), ŝpato; ~i [tr]; (card emblem), piko; **call a spade a spade**, malkaŝe paroli, uzi la ĝustan vorton
spadix, spadiko
spaghetti, spagetoj [note plur]
Spain, Hispanio
span, (of bridge etc.; length unit of 9 inches), spano [see § 20]; ~izi [tr]; (stretch across, jump), transsalti [tr], transetendi [tr], transponti [tr]; (duration), daŭri [int]; daŭro (e.g.: *attention span:* atentodaŭro; *over a span of centuries:* dum daŭro de jarcentoj; *their culture spanned centuries:* ilia kulturo daŭris jarcentojn); (spatial extent),

etendiĝi; etendo (e.g.: *wingspan:* flug-iletendo); (team of animals), jungaĵo; **screw-spanner,** [see "wrench"]; **outspan,** (draft animals), maljungi [tr]; maljungo; maljungejo

spandrel, timpano

spangle, bril/aĵeto, zekineto; (sprinkle spangles), ~aspergi [tr]; (shine, glitter), ~eti [int], scintili [int]; **star-spangled,** stel-sternita, stel-semita

Spaniard, Hispano

spaniel, cocker spaniel, spanielo

Spanish, Hispana; ~ia; **Spanish-American,** ~–Amerikana; ~–Amerikano; **Spanish needles,** (bot), bidento

spank, (hit), pugfrapi [tr]; ~o; (move swiftly), impeti [int]

spanner, [see "wrench"]

spar, (of airplane wing or similar structural piece), sparo; (any pole for sail), velstango [cp "mast"]; (mineral), spato; (boxing), trejnboksi [int]; (dispute), disputi [int]

sparadrap, sparadrapo

spare, (be lenient), indulgi [tr]; (save). savi [tr]; (free), liberigi; (refrain from using), ne uzi [tr], domaĝi [tr], sin deteni de uzi (e.g.: *we won't spare any means:* ni domaĝos neniun ajn rimedon; *I'll spare the rod this time:* mi ne uzos la vergon ĉi-foje); (give up, do w/o), fordoni [tr], esti sen (e.g.: *can you spare a cup of sugar?:* ĉu vi povas fordoni tasplenon da sukero?; *the trip would be useful, but we can't spare your services here:* la vojaĝo estus utila, sed ni ne povas esti sen viaj servoj ĉi tie); (use, devote), dediĉi [tr] (e.g.: *we can't spare the time for that:* ni ne povas dediĉi la tempon por tio); (use frugally, save), ŝpari [tr]; (extra), ekstra; ekstraĵo; (in reserve), rezerva, anstataŭa, vic- [pfx]; rezervaĵo; (replacement part), vicpeco; (not occupied), libera (e.g.: *spare time:* libera tempo); (lean, scant, meager), magra, malabunda; (sparse, thin), maldensa, magra; **sparingly,** magre, malabunde, ŝpareme; **(something) to spar,** (io) ekstra (e.g.: *we can all fit in here with room to spare:* ni ĉiuj povas taŭgi ĉi tie kun ekstra spaco); **spare**

one's feelings, ~i ies sentojn

spark, (of fire, from flint, grinding wheel, etc.; fig, as of life, interest, etc.), fajrero; ~i [int]; ~igi; (elec), sparko; sparki [int]; sparkigi; (liveliness), vigleco, animeco, gajeco; **spark plug,** sparkilo

sparkle, (glitter), scintili [int], brileti [int], fajreri [int]; ~ado, briletado, fajrerado; (efferversce), eferveski [int], ŝaŭmi [int]; (liveliness), vigleco, animeco, gajeco; **sparkler,** (firework), fuzo-stangeto

sparling, eperlano

sparrow, (any of *Passer*), pasero; **hedge sparrow,** pronelo; **house sparrow,** dom~o; **tree sparrow, mountain sparrow,** mont~o; **willow sparrow,** fitiso

sparse, maldensa, malabunda, disa, magra

Sparta, Sparto; **Spartan,** ~a; ~ano

Spartacus, Spartako

Spartium, spartio

spasm, spasmo; **spasmodic, spastic,** ~a; ~ulo; **antispasmodic,** anti~a; anti~aĵo

spat, (quarrel), kvereleto; (for foot), gamaŝeto

spate, elverŝo; (Br: flood), ekinundo

spathe, spato

spatial, (re math space), spaca; (re cosmos), kosma, spaciala [cp "space"]

spatter, surŝpruci [int]; ~igi; ~ado; ~aĵo; **bespatter,** makuli [tr], kotizi [tr], ŝprucmakuli [tr]

spatterdock, nufaro, flava akvolilio, flava nimfeo

spatula, (in kitchen; chem), spatelo

Spatula, (zool), spatulo, kuleranaso

spavin, spavino; **spavined,** ~hava

spawn, (fish, frog, etc.), fraji [int]; ~o; (produce, gen), produkti [tr], generi [tr]; (mycelium), micelio

spay, inkastri [tr] [cp "castrate"]

speak, (talk, gen), paroli [tr, int]; (long or extended; give a speech), ~adi [int]; (speak ethnic language w oth Esperantist), krokodili [int]; **speaker,** (person), ~into; ~anto; ~onto; (elec), ~ilo; **loudspeaker,** laŭt~ilo; **English-speaker, French-speak, (etc.),** Anglalingvano, Angla~anto; Franclingvano, Franc~anto (etc.); **speak out, speak up,** (speak loudly), (pli) laŭte ~i; (express self), esprimi sin; **bespeak,** (reserve), rezervi [tr]; (show), montri [tr], indiki [tr]; (foreshadow), aŭguri [tr]; **speak for itself,** (needs no explanation), esti memstara, esti memklara; **speak well for,** favore atesti pri; **speak well (ill) of,** (mal)laŭdi [tr], ~i (mal)laŭde [or] (mal)favore pri; **be well spoken of,** esti laŭde (favore) pri~ata; **so to speak,** por tiel diri; **strictly speaking,** ĝustadire

spear, lanco; ~i [tr]; **spearhead,** (head of spear), ~pinto; (leading group or person, as in mil operation, pol campaign, etc.), avano; (lead), avani [tr], gvidi [tr]; **spearmint,** spikmento; spikmenta; **spearwort,** ranunkolo

special, (for certain purpose; of certain sort; highly regarded), speciala (e.g.: *call a special meeting:* kunvoki ~an kunvenon; *one must use a special oil for that:* oni devas uzi ~an oleon por tio; *you are very special to me:* vi estas tre ~a ĉe mi); (set apart, thought of separately, as because of being remarkable etc.), aparta (e.g.: *an item of special interest:* ero de aparta intereso); **specialist,** (in branch of study or activity), ~isto, fakulo; **specialize,** ~igi; ~iĝi [cp "major"]; **specialization,** ~igado; ~iĝado; (field of study etc.), fako, ĉeffako; **specialty,** ~aĵo; ~eco; fako; **special delivery,** (mail), aparta livero [see § 22]

specie, metalmono

species, (bio), specio; (any sort, type), speco; **speciation,** ~iĝado; **subspecies,** sub~o

specific, specifa, konkreta (e.g.: *specific example:* konkreta ekzemplo); ~aĵo; **specification,** ~o

specify, specifi [tr]

specimen, specimeno

specious, falslogika, mislogika, ŝajniga

speck, (spot), punkto, makuleto; ~i [tr]; (particle), grajno, peceto, ereto; (of specific substance), ~ero [sfx] (e.g.: *a speck of dust:* polvero)

specs, (specifications), specifoj, ~aro;

(glasses), okulvitroj

spectacle, spektaklo;   **spectacles,** (glasses), okulvitroj; **spectacular,** ~a; ~o; **make a spectacle of oneself,** ridindigi sin

spectator, spektatoro, spektanto

specter, fantomo [not "spektro"]

spectro–, (sci pfx), spektro–

spectrometer, spektrometro

spectroscope, spektroskopo; **spectroscopy,** ~io

spectrum, spektro; **spectral,** ~a Specularia, spekulario

speculate, (conjecture, ponder), spekulativi [int]; ($), spekuli [int]; **speculation,** ~ado; spekulado; spekulaĵo; **speculative,** ~a; spekula; **speculator,** spekulanto

speculum, (med), spegulumo [cp "mirror"]

speech, (talking, gen), parolo; (long or extended), ~ado; (oration), ~ado, prelego, oratoraĵo; **figure of speech,** ~figuro; **part of speech,** parto de ~o, ~-elemento

speed, (gen), rapido; ~i [int] (e.g.: *the speed of light:* la ~o de lumo); (gear ratio), ~umo (e.g.: *a four-speed car:* kvar~uma aŭto); **speedy,** ~a; **speed up,** akceli [tr], ~igi; akceliĝi, ~iĝi; **speed limit,** ~limo; **speedometer,** ~ometro; **speedway,** aŭkurejo, aŭta vetkurejo; **speedwell,** (bot: *Veronica*), veroniko; **fast (slow) speed,** (mal)alta ~o [avoid "~a ~o"]

speleology, speleolog/io; **speleologist,** ~o [cp "spe lunker"]

spell, (sound letters of word; form a word, re letters), literumi [tr] (e.g.: *please spell your name:* bonvolu ~i vian nomon; *L-I-G-H-T spells "light":* L-I-G-H-T ~as "light"); (signify), signifi [tr] (e.g.: *the flood spelled the end of prosperity:* la inundo signifis la finon de prospero); (bewitching, magic formula etc.), sorĉo; (relieve, replace from work or duty), anstataŭi [tr]; (rest), ripozi [int]; ripoziĝi; ripozo; (turn at working), vico [cp "shift"]; (period of time), periodo (e.g.: *a warm spell in January:* varmeta periodo en januaro); **spelling,** (act), ~ado

spelunker › 489 ‹ **spin**

(e.g.: *he is good at spelling:* li estas
lerta en ~ado); (manner, system; orthography), ortografio (e.g.: *English
spelling is irregular:* la Angla ortografio estas neregula); **spell out,**
(read letters), ~i; (detail), detali [tr];
misspell, mis~i [tr]; **spellbind, cast a
spell on,** (bewitch), sorĉi [tr]; (fascinate), ravi [tr]; **spellbound, under a
spell,** sorĉita; ravita; **spelling checker,** (cmptr), literum–kontrolilo
spelunker, kavernesplor/anto; **spe-
lunking,** ~ado [cp "speleology"]
spend, ($), elspezi [tr]; (pass time),
pasigi (e.g.: *we spent three days there:*
ni pasigis tri tagojn tie); (consume),
konsumi [tr]; (use up), elĉerpi [tr],
eluzi [tr]; **spendthrift,** malŝparulo;
spendthrifty, malŝparema
Spergula, spergulo
sperm, (semen), spermo; ~a; (spermatozoon), spermatozoo; **spermicide,**
~icido; **sperm cell,** spermatozoo;
sperm duct, spermatodukto
spermaceti, spermaceto
spermagonium, spermogonio
spermatic, sperma
spermatium, spermatio
spermat(o)–, (pfx: sperm), spermat(o)–
spermatocyte, spermatocito
spermatogenesis, spermatogenezo
spermatogonium, spermogonio
spermatophore, spermogonio
spermatophyte, spermatofito, fanerogamo
spermatorrhea, spermatoreo
spermatospore, spermogonio
spermatozoid, spermatoido
spermatozoon, spermatozoo
spermogonium, spermogonio
spermospore, spermogonio
spes(o)–, (fictional $ unit), speso
spew, elvomi [tr], (el)sputi [tr]
sphacelus, sfacelo
sphagnum, Sphagnum, sfagno
sphalerite, zinkoblendo
Sphecidae, [see *"Sphex"]*
Sphecotheres, figbirdo
Spheniscus, sfenisko; Sphenisciformes,
~oformaj (birdoj)
Sphenodon, sfenodonto
sphenoid, (bone), sfenoido

sphere, (gen), sfero; **spherical,** ~a;
spheroid, ~oido; ~oida; **spherome-
ter,** ~ometro; **biosphere, ecospher,**
bio~o; **lithosphere,** lito~o; **magneto-
sphere,** magneto~o
Sphex, sfego; Sphecidae, ~edoj
sphincter, sfinktero
sphinx, (myth beast), sfinkso
Sphinx, (statue), (la) Sfinkso
Sphinx, (zool), sfingo; Sphingidae,
~edoj
sphygm(o)–, (med pfx), sfigm(o)–
sphygmomanometer, sfigmografo;
sphygmomanometry, ~io
spica, (bot), spiko
spice, spico; **spicy,** ~a
spick-and-span, purega, netega
spicule, (gen), spiketo
spider, araneo; **spiderweb,** ~aĵo; **spi-
dery,** ~eca; **bird spider,** avikulario,
bird~o; **black widow spider,** nigra
~o; **house spider,** (*Tegenaria*), tegenario
spiel, blago, bombasto, rakonto; ~i [int],
bombasti [int], rakonti [tr]
spigot, (faucet), krano; (bung plug),
ŝtopkejlo
spike, (of plant or any pointed object,
graph curve, etc.), spiko; ~iĝi (e.g.:
his fever spiked to 40°: lia febro ~iĝis
ĝis 40°); (impale on spike), sur~igi;
(prong, barb), pikilo, ~o; (big nail),
najlego; (thwart), obstrukci [tr], malhelpi [tr]; (add alcohol to drink), alko-
holizi [tr]; (cleat), buteo; **handspike,**
manlevstango
spikenard, (ointment), nardo; **plow-
man's spikenard,** (bot), inulo
spile, (tap barrel, tree, etc., to draw liquid), spili [tr]; ~ilo
spill, (flow, pour out), disverŝi [tr]; ~iĝi;
~ado; ~aĵo; (fall), falo; faligi; (for
lighting candle, pipe, etc.), brulŝtipe-
to; (bung plug), ŝtopkejlo; (divulge, as
secret), malkaŝi [tr]; **spill out,** elverŝi
[tr]; elverŝiĝi; **spill over,** (out of container etc.), superverŝi [tr]; superverŝiĝi; (over surface, as flood
waters), surverŝi [tr]; surverŝiĝi; **spill-
way,** verŝkanalo
spin, (rotate), giri [int], rotacii [int];
~igi; rotaciigi; ~o; rotacio; (make

thread; [fig], tell stories etc.), ŝpini
[tr]; (be dizzy), kapturniĝi; (pleasure
trip), ekskurso; (phys: angular momentum), spino; **spin off,** (as byproduct), kromprodukti [tr]; **spinoff,**
kromprodukto; **spinning wheel,** ŝpin-
rado; **tailspin,** spiralplonĝo, vostoglit-
ado
spinach, spinaco; **mountain spinach,**
ĝardenatriplo; **New Zealand spinach,** Novzelanda ~o
Spinacia, spinaco
spindle, (gen), spindelo; ~iĝi; sur~igi;
~izi [tr]; (onto which thread is wound
from spinning wheel), ŝpinilo
spine, (anat, or similar object), spino;
(thorn), dorno; **spinal,** ~a
spinel, spinelo
spinet, spineto
spinnaker, spinako
spinneret, (gen), ŝpinileto
spinn(e)y, (Br: grove), bosko
Spinoza, Spinozo; **Spinozism,** ~ismo
spinster, (maljuna) fraŭlino
Spinus spinus, fringelo
spiracle, spirtruo
Spiraea, spireo*; Spiraea ulmaria, ulmario
spiral, spiralo; ~a; ~i [int]
spirant, frikativo
Spiranthes, spiranto
spire, (arch), spajro; (bot: spike), spiko;
(point, peak, as of mountain etc.), pinto
spirea, spireo*
spirillosis, spirilozo
spirillum, Spirillum, spirilo
spirit, (gen), spirito [cp "ghost",
"soul", "mood", "courage", "verve",
"enthusiasm"]; **spirited,** vigla, verva;
disspirited, sen~a; **spiritual,** (re spirit, gen), ~a; ~eca; (song), ~a kanto;
spirituality, ~eco; **spiritualism,** (re
communication w dead), ~ismo; (phil:
that mind, spirit is more basic than
matter), spiritualismo; **spiritualist,**
~isma; ~isto; spiritualisma; spiritual-
isto; **(the) Holy Spirit,** (rel), (la)
Sankta S~o; **in good spirits,** bonhumora; **the spirit is willing but the
flesh is weak,** la ~o volontas sed la
karno malfortas

Spirochaeta, spiroketo
spirochete, spiroketo; **spirochetosis,**
~ozo
spirograph, spirografo
spirometer, spirometro; **spirometry,**
~io
spit, (rod for roasting meat), rostostango; (point of land), terpinto; (saliva),
salivo; (eject saliva), kraĉi [int];
kraĉaĵo; (eject any substance from
mouth, as blood etc., due to illness;
oth analogous process), sputi [tr];
sputaĵo; **spittle,** salivo; **spittoon,**
kraĉujo
spite, (defy), spiti [tr]; ~ado [cp "malice"]; **spiteful,** ~ema; **in spite of (the
fact that),** (against adverse conditions), malgraŭ (tio ke) (e.g.: *he came
in spite of the weather:* li venis malgraŭ la vetero; *he came in spite of the
fact that it was snowing:* li venis malgraŭ tio ke neĝis); (against willful opposition), ~e de (tio ke) (e.g.: *he left in
spite of her request that he stay:* li foriris ~e de ŝia peto ke li restu; *he left in
spite of the fact that she asked him to
stay:* li foriris ~e de to, ke ŝi petis lin
resti)
Spitsbergen, Spicbergo
spitz, ŝpico
spiv, (Br: engaged in shady dealings),
ŝakristo
splanchnic, viscera; **splanchnic nerve,**
splankniko
splanchnology, splanknologio
splash, (audible disturbance in water
etc.), plaŭdi [int]; ~igi; ~(ad)o (e.g.:
the waves splashed against the rocks:
la ondoj ~is kontraŭ la rokoj); (splatter water on etc.), ŝpruci [tr]; ŝpruciĝi;
surŝprucigi; ŝpruco; ŝprucaĵo (e.g.: *the
car splashed mud on me:* la aŭto ŝpru-
cigis [or] surŝprucigis koton sur min;
the car splashed me with mud: la aŭto
surŝprucigis min per koto); (onom),
plaŭd!; ŝpruc!; **splashy,** (multicolored), bunta; (gaudy, showy), puca;
splashdown, surakviĝo
splat, plaŭdo; (onom: splatter), plaŭd!
splatter, (splash, spatter), [see "splash"]
splay, (bevel), beveli [tr]; ~iĝi; ~o;
splayfeet, dispiedoj; **splayfooted,**

dispieda

spleen, (anat), lieno [see "splen(o)–"]; (melancholy), spleno [cp "melancholy", "lethargy"]; (malice), malico; (bad humor), malbonhumoro, mishumoro; **spleenwort**, asplenio; **wall rue spleenwort**, mororuto; **vent one's spleen**, esprimi sian malbonhumoron (mishumoron)

splendid, grandioza, belega; **splendor**, ~o, pompo

splenectomy, splenektomio

splenitis, splenito

splenius, (muscle), splenio

splen(o)–, (med root), splen(o)–

splice, splisi [tr]; ~aĵo; **splicer**, ~ilo

splint, splinto; ~i [tr]

splinter, splito; ~i [tr]; ~iĝi; **splinter group**, frakcio

split, (burst), krevi [int]; ~igi; ~o; (crack), fendi [tr]; fendiĝi; fend(iĝ)o; (break apart, gen), disrompi [tr]; disrompiĝi; disromp(iĝ)o; (separate, gen, as individuals from group, parts from whole), apartigi, disigi; apartiĝi, disiĝi; apartigo, disigo; apartiĝo, disiĝo; (into splinters), spliti [tr]; splitiĝi; splitiĝo; (cleave along natural lines), klivi [tr]; kliviĝi; kliv(iĝ)o; (share, divide), dividi [tr]; divid(ad)o; divid(aĵ)o; (flat on floor, legs 180° apart), krur~o; **split hairs**, spliti harojn; **hair-splitting**, harsplita; harsplitado; **banana split**, banano kun siropglaciaĵo; **split-level**, (re house etc.), disnivela; **split shift**, dividita skipo

splotch, makulo, ~ego; ~i [tr]; ~iĝi; **splotchy**, ~(eg)a

splurge, ekstravaganci [int]; ~o

splutter, (stutter, stammer), ŝpruc/balbuti [int]; ~balbut(ad)o; (like something frying), ~osibli [int]; ~osibl(ad)o

spoil, (damage), difekti [tr]; ~iĝi; (decay, rot), putri [tr]; putriĝi; (overindulge), troindulgi [tr], trodorloti [tr]; **spoils**, (loot), trofeo(j), kaptaĵo, rabaĵo; **spoilsport**, ĝojfuŝanto; **spoiled paper**, (printed badly), makulaturo

spoke, spoko; **spokeshave**, kurbrabotilo

spokesperson, spokesman, proparo-

lanto

spoliate, (as re ships), prirabi [tr]; **spoliation**, ~ado; (spoiling, damaging), difektado; (alteration of document), falsado

spondee, spondeo; **spondaic**, ~a

spondylitis, spondilito

spondyl(o)–, (med, anat root), spondil(o)–

spondylosis, spondilozo

sponge, (zool; artificial, as for washing), spongo; ~i [tr]; (mooch), parazito; paraziti [int]; **spongy**, ~eca; **sponge on, sponge off (of)**, paraziti sur; **spongecake**, ~okuko; **throw in the sponge**, rezigni [tr]

Spongiaria, sponguloj

sponsor, (pay for, as radio, TV program etc.; provide means, auspices), aŭspicii [tr]; ~into; ~anto; ~onto; (patron, as of arts or mus by wealthy person etc.), patroni [tr]; mecenato, patrono; (godparent), baptopatr(in)o; baptogepatro; (propose bill in legislature), proponi [tr]; proponanto (e.g.: *this bill has ten cosponsors:* ĉi tiu leĝpropono havas dek kunproponantojn); **sponsorship**, (bsns; auspices), ~o; (patronage), mecenateco, patroneco

spontaneous, spontanea; **spontaneity**, ~eco

spontoon, spontono

spoof, mistifiki [tr]

spook, (ghost), fantomo; (startle), ektimigi

spool, bobeno; ~i [tr]

spoon, (gen), kulero; (dip out), ~i [tr]; ĉerpi [tr]; **spoonbill**, (zool), plataleo; **teaspoon**, (spoon or unit of measure), kaf~o [5 mililitroj; see § 20]; **tablespoon, soupspoon**, sup~o [15 mililitroj]

spoonerism, kontraŭknalo

spoor, spuro; ~i [tr]

sporadic, sporada, intermita

sporangium, sporangio; **sporangiospore**, ~osporo

spore, sporo; **spore case, spore sac**, ~ujo [cp "sporangium"]; **microspore**, mikro~o; **microsporosis**, mikro~ozo

sporidium, sporidio

sporophyte, sporofito
sporotrichosis, sporotrikozo
Sporotrichum, sporotriko
Sporozoa, sporozooj
sporozoan, sporozoo
sport, (esp organized, requiring skill, etc.), sporto; ~a; ~i [tr, int]; (any play, fun), ludi [int]; ludo; luda; (sportsmanlike person), ~ulo; (bio: variant), varianto; (wear, display), porti [tr], montri [tr]; **sporting**, (gen), ~a; **sports**, ~oj; ~a; **sportsperson**, **sportsman**, ~ulo; **sportsmanlike**, ~inda; **sportsmanship**, ~(ind)eco; **sportscast**, ~dissendo; ~telesendo [see "broadcast"]; **sportive**, ~a; lud(em)a; **sportswear**, ~vesto(j); **sportswriter**, ~reportero; **in sport**, **for sport**, ŝerca; ŝerce; **make sport of**, moki [tr]; **be a (good) sport (about)**, (accept in good humor), esti bonhumora (pri)
spot, (stain, blotch), makulo; ~igi; ~iĝi; (place), loko; loki [tr]; situigi; (find), trovi [tr]; (small amount, bit), iometo, iomete da (e.g.: *a spot of tea:* iomete da teo); (ready immediately), tutpreta (e.g.: *spot cash:* tutpreta mono); (random sampling), specimena, aleatora (e.g.: *make a spot check for accuracy:* fari specimenan [or] aleatoran kontrolon por precizeco [or] specimene kontroli la precizecon); (brief radio or TV announcement), anonceto; **spotcheck**, specimene kontroli [tr], aleatore kontroli [tr]; specimena (aleatora) kontrolo; **hit the high spots**, supraĵe pritrakti [tr]; **in a (bad) spot**, en embaraso, en malfacilaĵo; **on the spot**, (at location), surloka; surloke; (immediate(ly)), tuj; tuja; (in difficulty), en embaraso, en malfacilaĵo
spouse, edz/(in)o, ge~o; **spouses**, ge~oj
spout, (tube, pipe), verŝtubo; (lip of pitcher etc.), beko; (downspout for drainage etc.), pluvodukto; (stream emerging from tube etc.), elfluo; (pour, spew, as unpleasant substance, pompous talk, etc.), sputi [tr]; sputiĝi; (spray), ŝpruci [tr]; ŝpruciĝi; **spout off**, eksputi [tr]
sprain, tordi [tr]; ~o

sprat, sproto
sprawl, dissterniĝi; ~o
spray, (mist of water etc.), ŝpruci [int]; ~igi; ~o; ~aĵo; (nozzle for spraying), ~igilo; (sprig, branch), (flor)branĉeto; (med), sprajit [tr]; sprajaĵo; **spray can**, ~ladaĵo; **spray(er)**, **spray gun**, (apparatus to spray liquid under pressure), pistolo (e.g.: *paint sprayer:* farbopistolo)
spread, (stretch out, over; lay out flatly or thinly, as blanket, dust, etc.; cover surface), sterni [tr]; ~iĝi; ~(iĝ)o; ~aĵo (e.g.: *spread the blanket on the bed:* ~i la litkovrilon sur la liton; *snow spread across the valley:* neĝo ~iĝis trans la valon); (smear, slather, as butter), ŝmiri [tr]; ŝmiriĝi; ŝmiraĵo; (put out in all directions, as news, sun's rays, etc.), disvastigi; disvastiĝi; disvastigo; disvastiĝo; (re disease etc.), propagi [tr]; propagiĝi; propag(iĝ)ado; (circulate), cirkuli [int]; cirkuligi; cirkulado; (diffuse), difuzi [int]; difuzigi; difuzo; (disperse), dispersi [tr]; dispersiĝi; disperso; (extend), etendi [tr]; etendiĝi; etendo; (grow outwards), diskreski [int]; (branch), disbranĉiĝi; (interval, distance, as between highest and lowest), intervalo; (printed matter across columns, 2 pages, etc.), transpresaĵo; **spread out**, dis~i [tr]; dis~iĝi; **spread-eagle**, (limbs extended), dis~ita; **spreadsheet**, ($ tables etc. on paper), ~aĵo; (cmptr software), ~programo; **bedspread**, supra littuko [cp "sheet"]; **outspread**, ~i; ~iĝi; ~(iĝ)o; ~ita; **spread the word**, **spread the news**, **(about)**, diskonigi
spree, (frolic; period of specified activity), festado, petolado (e.g.: *go on a shopping spree:* fari butikum~on); (drunkenness), drink~o
sprig, branĉeto
sprightly, vigla, gaja
spring, (season), printempo; ~a; (poet: season), primavero; (water source or [fig] any source; arise from), fonto; deveni [int], fonti [int] (e.g.: *revolution springs from discontent:* revolucio fontas el malkontenteco); (elastic

object), risorto; (jump, bounce), salti [int]; salto; (surge forward), impeti [int]; impeto; (become warped, sprung, misshapen), misformi [tr]; misformiĝi; (resume original shape, like a spring), risorti [int]; (release trap etc.), relasi [tr]; (make known, reveal), malkaŝi [tr], riveli [tr]; (resilience, springiness), risorteco, elasteco; **springy**, risorteca, elasta; **spring up**, (arise, appear), leviĝi, aperi [int]; **spring-cleaning**, ~a purigado; **springtime**, ~o; **box spring**, (of bed), somiero; **bedspring**, (one spring), litrisorto; (frame), risortokadro; **coil spring**, spiralrisorto; **leaf spring**, elipsa risorto; **mainspring**, (spring), ĉefrisorto; (fig: instigator), ĉefinstiganto; ĉefinstigilo; **offspring**, (one), ido; (collective), idaro, idoj

springbok, saltantilopo

sprinkle, (gen), aspergi [tr]; ~iĝi; (rain), pluveti [int]; **sprinkler**, ~ilo

sprint, (gen), sprinto; ~i [int]; (spurt at end of race etc.), spurto†; spurti† [int]

sprite, elfo, koboldo

sprocket, (one tooth), rad/odento; **sprocket (wheel)**, ĉen~o

sprout, (new shoot, twig, etc.), ŝoso; ~i [int]; ~igi; (poet), sproso; sprosi [int]; (bud), burĝono; burĝoni [int]; burĝonigi; **Brussels sprout(s)**, burĝonbrasiko(j)

spruce, (tree), piceo; (trim, neat), neta, pimpa; **spruce up**, netigi, pimpigi; netiĝi, pimpiĝi; **white spruce**, blanka ~o; **Norway spruce**, **spruce fir**, ordinara ~o

sprung, misformita [see "spring"]

spry, vigla

spume, ŝaŭmo; ~i [int]

spunk, (courage, spirit), animo, spirito, kuraĝo; (tinder), tindro; **spunky**, ~a, spirita, kuraĝa

spur, (for goading horse; any similar projecting or pointed object), sprono; (goad, incite), ~i [tr]; (of bird, rye), ergoto; (rouse, stimulate), ~i, stimuli [tr]; vigligi; **spur-of-the-moment**, senpripensa, impulsa; **on the spur of the moment**, senpripense, impulse

spurge, eŭforbio

spurious, falsa, malaŭtentika, apokrifa

spurn, forpuŝi [tr], repuŝi [tr], rifuzi [tr]

spurry, spergulo; **(common) corn spurry**, kampa ~o

spurt, (gen), ŝpruci [int]; ~igi; ~o

sputnik, (esp any of early Soviet satellites), sputniko; (any artificial satellite), (artefarita) satelito

sputter, (spit, splutter), sputeti [tr, int]; ~(ad)o; (as re fuse), fuzi [int]; fuz(ad)o

sputum, sputaĵo

spy, (gen), spioni [tr]; ~o; (spy on, keep a look-out), gvati [tr]; gvatanto; gvatisto

squabble, kvereli [int], disputaĉi [int]; ~o, disputaĉo

squad, roto

squadron, (ships, planes), eskadro; (cavalry), skadro

squalid, (wretched), mizera, aĉa; (dirty), malhigiena, malpura; **squalor**, ~o; malhigieneco, malpureco

squall, (weather), skualo; (cry), kriegi [int]; kriego

squalor, [see "squalid"]

Squalus, skvalo; Squalus acanthias, akantiaso

squama, skvamo

Squamata, skvamuloj

squamous, skvama; **squamous-cell carcinoma**, ~ĉela karcinomo

squander, malŝpari [tr], prodigi [tr]

square, (geom figure or object of this shape; product of number and itself), kvadrato (e.g.: *a square of cloth:* ~o da tolo; *the square of 3 is 9:* la ~o de 3 estas 9; *5 square meters:* 5 ~aj metroj); ~a; (draw squares, as on map), ~i [tr]; (multiply by self), ~igi; (geom: draw square equal in area to oth shape), kvadraturigi; kradraturo; (right angle), orta; (make a right angle), ortigi; (tool to make right angle), ortilo; (open area at street intersection), placo (e.g.: *Times Square:* Placo Times); (settle, as account), kvitigi; (settled, even, no balance), kvita; (make right), ĝustigi; (conform), konformigi; konformiĝi; (agree), akordigi; akordiĝi; (fair, honest), honesta, justa; (direct, straight), rekta; (firm, solid), firma, solida; **square away**, (naut), ortigi (la velojn); **square off**, pretigi sin (por atako, batalo); **square oneself**, (make amends), rekompenci [tr], kvitigi sin; **T-square**, T-ortilo

squash, (any fruit or plant of *Cucurbita*), kukurbo; (crush), premfrakasi [tr]; (press hard), prem(eg)i [tr]; (suppress), subpremi [tr]; (game), skvaŝo* (Aus); (Br: fruit drink), suk(trink)aĵo

squat, (crouch), kaŭri [int]; ~o; (short and heavy), dikmalalta, kompakta; (settle on unoccupied land to obtain title; homestead), setliĝi† [cp "settle"]; (occupy any property, as vacant house, w/o legal right), uzurpi [tr]; **squatter**, (settler), setlinto†; (illegal occupier of vacant house etc.), uzurpanto, enkrakinto†; (Aus), ŝafbienulo, bienposedanto; **squat down**, ~iĝi; **squat on**, setli* [tr]; uzurpi [tr]

Squatina, skvateno

squaw, Indianino

squawk, graki [int], kvaki [int], raŭki [int]; ~o, kvako

squeak, (sound), grinci [tr, int], knari [tr, int]; ~o, knaro; (onom), grinc!; **squeak by**, apenaŭ sukcesi [int] (trairi [int], etc.)

squeal, grincadi [tr, int], knaradi [int]; ~o, knarado; **squeal on**, (colloq: inform on, betray), denunci [tr], perfidi [tr]; fifajfi [int]

squeamish, (queasy, easily nauseated), naŭziĝema; (easily offended), ofendiĝema, ŝokiĝema, pruda; (fastidious), elektema, precioza

squeegee, gumviŝi [tr]; ~ilo

squeeze, (press, gen), premi [tr]; ~iĝi; ~o; (squeeze together, compress), kun~i [tr]; kun~iĝi; kun~o; (squeeze out, as juice), el~i [tr]; el~iĝi; el~o; (constrict, press on all sides), stringi [tr]; stringo

squelch, (suppress, silence), subpremi [tr], silentigi; (smash), frakasi [tr]; (squish; sound as walking in mud etc.), ŝmaci [int]; ŝmaco

squib, (firecracker), petardo; (lampoon), satiro; satiri [tr]

squid, (any of *Loligo*), loligo; (*L. vulgaris*), kalmaro

squiggle, (short curvy line), tord/streko, zigzageto; (wriggle, squirm), ~iĝi; ~iĝo

squill, (*Scilla*), scilo

squint, (peer; look askance), strabi [int]; ~o

squire, (knight attendant), eskviro; (Br: landowner), bienulo

squirm, tordiĝadi; ~o

squirrel, sciuro; **flying squirrel**, flug~o; **squirrel away**, forkaŝi [tr]; (hoard), hamstri [tr]

squirt, ŝpruci [int]; ~igi; ~o

squish, (sound of walking in mud etc.), ŝmaci [int]; ~igi; ~o; (onom), ŝmac!; (squash, squeeze), [see "squeeze"]; **squishy**, mol(aĉ)a, ~a

Sri Lanka, Sri Lanko†

stab, (jab, gen), piki [tr]; (w knife etc.), ponardi [tr]; ponardado; ponardovundo, pikvundo; (sudden pain), ekdoloro; **make a stab at**, provi [tr]; **stab in the back**, perfidi [tr]; perfido

stable, (firm, steady, enduring, in equilibrium), stabila; (animal shelter), stalo [cp "stall"]; enstaligi; **stability**, ~eco; **stabilize**, ~igi; **instability**, mal~eco; **unstable**, mal~a; (re equilibrium), labila

staccato, stakato; ~a; ~e

Stachys, stakiso

stack, (of bricks, wood, hay, dishes, etc.; cmptr), stako; ~igi; ~iĝi; (smokestack), fumtubo; **stacks**, (library shelves), bretaro

stacte, stakto

stadium, (for sport event), stadiono; (Greek unit of measure), stadio

staff, (officers, administrators), stabo; (employees, total work force in an office etc.), oficistaro, personaro; (provide personnel), ~izi [tr]; personarizi [tr]; (work at), labori [int] (ĉe, en) (e.g.: *we need a volunteer to staff our booth at the fair:* ni bezonas volontulon por labori ĉe nia stando ĉe la foiro); (rod, pole), bastono, stango; (mus), liniaro [cp "clef"]; **member of (a, the) staff**, ~ano; oficisto; **chief of staff**, ~estro

stag, (male deer), vir/cervo; (for or re men), ~a, vir~ [pfx] (e.g.: *stag party:*

~festo); (man w/o escort), sol~o; **staghead**, (bot: witches'-broom), fefasko

stage, (theat. mus, etc.), scen/ejo; (put on stage, arrange for stage, theat or fig), en~igi; (period, level, part; degree of development, journey, etc.), etapo, stadio [cp "level"]; (phase), fazo; (stagecoach), diliĝenco; (of microscope), muntejo; **stage effect**, ~ejefekto; **stage fright**, kulistimo; **stagehand**, kulisisto; **stage manager**, reĝisoro; **downstage**, ~ejantaŭa; ~ejantaŭe(n); **offstage**, postkulisa; postkulise; **upstage**, (theat), ~ejmalantaŭa; ~ejmalantaŭe(n); (fig: draw attention from someone else to self), fimalantaŭigi

stagger, (sway, totter, waver), ŝanceli [tr]; ~iĝi; ~(iĝ)o; (astonish, dismay), konsterni [tr], kapskui [tr]; (separate), apartigi

stagnate, stagni [int]; **stagnant**, ~anta; **stagnation**, ~(ad)o

staid, sobra, serioza

stain, (blot, spot; taint, dishonor), makulo; ~igi; ~iĝi; (dye, pigment), tinkturo; tinkturi [tr]; tinkturiĝi; **stainless**, (corrosion-proof), korodimuna; **stained glass**, vitralvitro; **stained-glass window**, vitralo

stair, (one step), ŝtupo; (flight of steps), ~aro; **stairs, staircase, stairway**, ~aro; **stairwell**, (~ar)ŝakto; **downstairs, upstairs**, [see under "up"]

stake, (large pole, as for barricade etc.), paliso; ~igi; (small, to support vegetable plant, fasten tent, mark boundary, etc.), ~eto; ~etigi; (bet $), veti [tr]; vetaĵo; (provide $ for bsns venture or oth project; underwrite), monprovizi [tr]; (interest, share, as in bsns venture or oth activity), intereso; **at stake**, (being risked), riskata; (to be decided), decidota; **stake out**, (post police etc. at a place), priposteni [tr]; (mark plot etc. w stakes), ~ete dislimi [tr], ~etigi; **burn at the stake**, ŝtiparumi [tr]

Stakhanovism, Staĥanovismo; **Stakhanovite**, Staĥanovisto*

stalactite, stalaktito

stalagmite, stalagmito

stale, (not fresh), malfreŝa; (musty odor), mucida; (trite, banal, hackneyed), banala, malsprita; **stalemate**, (chess, or [fig] any contest, struggle), pato; pati [int]; patigi; (interj in chess), pat!; (any deadlock), plenhalto, ~o

Stalin, Stalino; **Stalinism**, ~ismo; **Stalinist**, ~isma; ~isto

stalk, (follow stealthily), ŝtel/sekvi [tr], ~ĉasi [tr], gvatsekvi [tr]; (walk or advance grimly, fearfully), terurpaŝi [int]; (fleshy plant stem, as of flower; analogous anat part), tigo; (stiff plant stem, as corn, cane, bamboo), trunketo

stall, (booth etc.), budo, kiosko; (display stand at fair, exhibition, etc.), stando; (of animal in barn etc.), stalfako [cp "barn", "stable"]; (stop, re motor or any activity etc.), panei [int]; paneigi; paneo; (lose lift, re airplane), staŭli [int]; staŭligi; staŭlo; (delay, evade), prokrasti [tr]; prokrasto; (Br: theat seat), fotelo; **stall angle**, staŭlangulo, staŭla angulo

stallion, virĉevalo; (poet), stalono

stalwart, (brave, valiant), brava; ~ulo; (resolute), rezoluta; (strong, robust), forta; (partisan), partizano

stamen, stameno

stamina, eltenivo, rezistivo

staminal, stamena; **staminate**, ~hava

stammer, balbuti [int]; el~i [tr]; ~o

stamp, (make printed, embossed etc. impression; fig, impress into memory, on consciousness, etc.), stampi [tr]; ~o; (seal, mark of authenticity), sigelo; sigeli [tr] (e.g.: *her manner bears the stamp of truth*: ŝia mieno prezentas la sigelon de la vero); (postage), poŝtmarko; (pay postage on), afranki [tr]; (glued sticker similar to postage stamp), glumarko; (stomp, pound feet), stamfi [int]; pristamfi [tr], piedbati [tr] (e.g.: *stamp the grass into the ground*: piedbati la herbon en la grundon); **stamp out**, (get rid of), ekstermi [tr]; (extinguish, as fire etc., lit or fig), stamfestingi [tr]; (mark by stamping feet etc.), elstamfi [tr] (e.g.: *an S.O.S.*

stamped out in the snow: S.O.S. elstamfita en la neĝo); (shape metal part by stamping w dies etc.), pregi [tr]; (emboss, print), (el)~i [tr]; **date stamp**, dat~i [tr]; dat~ilo; **food stamp**, nutromarko; **rubber stamp**, (lit or fig), ~i; ~ilo

stampede, stampedi† [int]; ~igi; ~o

stance, (posture), pozo, star~o; (attitude), ~o, sinteno; [not "stanco"]

stand, (be erect, on one's or its feet or oth support, vertical, etc.; be located; have a position; remain; etc.), stari [int]; ~igi; (be situated), situi [int] [see "situate"]; (remain valid, in effect), ~i, resti valida, resti efektiva; (remain resolute), resti rezoluta; (resist), rezisti [tr]; rezist(ad)o; (halt), halti [int]; halto; haltejo (e.g.: *taxi stand:* taksia haltejo); (be candidate), kandidatiĝi; kandidatiĝo; (tolerate), toleri [tr]; (undergo, be subjected to), submetiĝi al; (pay, bear cost of, treat), regali [tr] (ion al iu) (e.g.: *I'll stand you to dinner:* mi regalos al vi vespermanĝon); (position), ~ejo, ~punkto; (display stall at fair, exhibition, etc.), stando; (booth), budo; (to hold lab equipment etc.), stativo; (base for statue, vase, etc.), soklo; (for music etc.), apogilo; (theat presentation), prezento (e.g.: *a two-week stand:* dusemajna prezento); (post, station, as of guard), posteno; (place for witness in courtroom), atestejo; (copse of trees etc.), bosko; (of any plant), kreskejo; **standee**, ~anto; **standing**, ~anta; (constant), konstanta (e.g.: *standing committee:* konstanta komitato); (motionless), senmova; (stagnant), stagna; (enduring), konstanta, daŭra (e.g.: *long-standing:* longadaŭra); (rank), rango; (reputation), reputacio; **standing room**, (as in theat), ~ejo; **stands**, (for spectators etc.), benkaro; **stand against**, (oppose), kontraŭ(~)i [tr], oponi [tr]; **stand back!**, dorsen!; **stand by**, (be ready), ~i preta; (wait), atendi [tr, int]; (support), subteni [tr], resti fidela al, resti ĉe; **stand by!**, (be ready!), pretiĝu!; **stand-by**, (ready), preta; (waiting), atendanta; atendanto; (in reserve),

rezerva; rezervaĵo; rezervulo; **stand for**, (replace), anstataŭi [tr]; (tolerate), toleri [tr]; (signify), signifi [tr], signi [tr]; **stand good for**, garantii [tr]; **stand in (for)**, (substitute), anstataŭi [tr]; **stand-in**, anstataŭulo; **stand in the way of**, obstrukci [tr]; **stand-off**, (deadlock), senvenko, plenhalto, pato; **stand-offish**, retiriĝema, distanca, malafabla; **stand on**, (be based on), baziĝi sur; (insist on, demand), insisti pri, postuli [tr]; **stand on end**, (re hair), hirtigi; hirtiĝi; **standing on end**, (re hair), hirta; **stand one's ground**, defendi sian pozicion [or] terenon; rezisti [tr] (kontraŭ); **stand out**, el~i [int], distingiĝi, reliefiĝi; **stand pat**, ~i senmova; **standpoint**, vidpunkto, ~punkto; **standstill**, plenhalto; **stand up**, (arise, become standing), ~iĝi, ek~i [int]; (hold out, be durable), elteni [int], daŭri [int]; (not keep engagement), forlasi [tr]; **stand-up**, (standing), ~anta; (to stand at), ~a, star– [pfx] (e.g.: *a stand-up lunch counter:* ~lunĉejo); **stand up for**, (support), subteni [tr]; (assert), aserti [tr]; (defend), defendi [tr]; **stand up to**, (face), alfronti [tr]; **bystander**, apud~anto; **outstanding**, (excellent), el~a; ($: debt balance), repagenda; **upstanding**, honesta, nobla, honora; **stand one in good stead**, utili [int] al iu; **stand a chance**, havi ŝancon; **take the stand**, (in courtroom), eniri la atestejon; **put (someone) on the stand**, meti (iun) en la atestejon

standard, (norm), normo; ~a; [cp "normal"]; (flag), standardo; (base, support, stand), soklo, apogilo; **standardize**, ~igi; **standard-bearer**, standardisto; **standard of living**, vivnivelo

Stanisław, Stanislav, Stalislao

stannate, stan/ato; **stannic**, ~ata; **stannous**, (containing tin), ~a; (w valence 2), ~oza; **stannous acid**, ~ita acido

stanza, stanco

Stapelia, stapelio, kadavrofloro

stapes, stapedo

staph, stafilokoko

staphyl(o)–, (med root), stafil(o)–

staphylococcia, stafilokokozo
staphylococcus, Staphylococcus, stafilokoko
staphyloma, stafilomo
staple, (fastener), vinkto; ~i [tr]; (primary), ĉefa; ĉefaĵo; [not "staplo"]; **stapler**, (device), ~ilo
star, (gen), stelo; (actor, singer, etc.), ~(in)o, ~ul(in)o; ~a; (play chief role), ~i [int], ĉefroli [int]; **starlet**, ~etulino; **star-of-Bethlehem**, (bot), ornitogalo; **star-spangled**, ~semita; **starwort**, (aster), astero; **water starwort**, kalitriko; **Dog Star**, (Sirius), Siriuso; **evening star**, vesper~o; **morning star**, maten~o; **falling star**, **shooting star**, (meteor), fal~o, meteoro; **brittle star**, **sand star**, (zool), ofiuro
starboard, (of ship), tribordo; ~a
starch, amelo; ~i [tr]
stare (at), fiksrigardi [tr]; ~o
stark, (harsh, rigorous), severa, maldelikata, akra; (bleak, barren), malfekunda; (utter, downright), absoluta; absolute, tut~ [pfx] (e.g.: *stark naked:* tutnuda; *stark terror:* absoluta teruro)
starling, sturno; **rose-colored starling**, pastoro
starost(a), starosto
start, (begin, gen), komenci [tr]; ~iĝi; ~o; ek– (e.g.: *he started to cry:* li ~is plori [or] li ekploris; *the start of the shooting:* la ekpafado); (start to go, move), ekiri [int]; (re race, sport; motor, machine, etc.), starti [int]; startigi; starto; (initiate), iniciati [tr]; iniciato; (jump, as when startled), eksalti [int]; eksalto; (starting place), deirpunkto; (in race etc.), startejo; (headstart, lead), antaŭeco; **starter**, (for car motor etc.), startigilo; **start out**, **start off**, ~i; ~iĝi; ek–; ekiri [int]; **start up**, (begin), ~i; ~iĝi; (motor), starti [int]; startigi (jump), eksalti [int]; **upstart**, parvenuo; parvenu(ec)a; **starting from**, (date, time), ekde [see "since"]; **start from scratch**, ~i de la ~o
startle, (sudden fright), ektimi [int], ekkonsterniĝi; ~igi, ekkonsterni [tr]; ~o, ekkonsterniĝo; (surprise), surprizegi [tr]; surprizegiĝi; **startling**, ~iga, ekkonsterna; surprizega; **be startled**,

~i, ekkonsterniĝi; surprizegiĝi
starve, malsatmorti [int]; ~igi; **starvation**, ~(iĝ)o
stash, stapli [tr]; ~ejo, kaŝejo; ~aĵo, kaŝaĵo
stasis, (med: flow stop etc.), stazo; (any static condition), senmoveco
state, (country; division of USA, Australia, etc.; civil government), ŝtato; ~a (e.g.: *there are 50 states in the United States:* estas 50 ~oj en Usono; *separation of church and state:* aparteco de religio kaj ~o; *state capital:* ~a ĉefurbo); (w connotation of sovereignty and power), regno; (condition; division of government function, as in France etc.), stato (e.g.: *a good state of mind:* bona mensa stato; *a state of confusion:* stato de konfuzo); (declare), deklari [tr], aserti [tr], diri [tr]; **statecraft**, ~isteco; **stately**, digna, majesta; **statement**, (thing said), deklaro, aserto, diro; (itemized list of $ or oth quantities, as bank statement, statement of assets, etc.), etato [cp "table", "sched ule"]; (bill, invoice), fakturo; **stateroom**, (privata) kajuto; **stateside**, Usona; Usone(n); **statesman**, ~isto; **statesmanship**, ~isteco; **buffer state**, bufro~o; **chief of state**, regnestro; **interstate**, inter~a; (Am: highway), inter~a ŝoseo, inter~o; **mainland state**, (Aus), kontinenta ~o; **overstate**, troigi; **solid-state**, (elec), ic(hav)a, icizita; **understate**, maltroigi; **upstate**, ~interna; ~interne(n); **lie in state**, kuŝi elmontrata; **State Department**, (Am), Departemento pri Fremdaj Aferoj
static, (elec), statika; ~a elektro, ~aĵo; (radio noise etc.), perturbo; (unmoving), senmova, staranta; **statics**, (sci of static forces), ~o; **electrostatic**, elektro~a
station, (base, place, etc.; radio, TV, etc.), stacio; (for specific purpose), ~ejo [sfx] (e.g.: *police station:* policejo; *first aid station:* sukurejo); (ranch), ranĉo, brutbieno; (post, as guard), posteno; posteni [tr]; (rank), rango, stato; **station break**, ~a identi-

go; **gas station, service station,** benzin~o, aŭtoservejo; **radio station,** radiofonia ~o; **relay station,** redissenda ~o; **space station,** kosmo~o; **television station,** televizia ~o; **tracking station,** spur~o; **train station, bus station,** (trajna, busa) ~domo [cp "stop: bus stop"]
stationary, senmova, staranta
stationer, papervar/isto; **stationery,** ~oj [note plur]
statistic, statistik/ero; **statistics,** (collective data, or sci of), ~o [note sing]; **statistical,** ~a; **statistician,** ~isto
stator, statoro
statue, statuo; **statuary,** (statues), ~aro; (art of), ~arto; **statuesque,** ~eska; **statuette,** ~eto
stature, staturo
status, (state, condition), stato; (legal, as citizen, heir, guardian, etc.), statuso; (rank, standing), rango; **the status quo,** la nuna (tiama) ~o; **the status quo ante,** la antaŭ~o; **status symbol,** simbolo de rango
statute, statuto; **statutory,** ~a; **statute of limitations,** limiga ~o
staunch, (stop flow or leak), ŝtopi [tr]; (loyal, firm), lojala, fidela
stave, (of barrel etc.), daŭbo; (mus: staff), liniaro; **stave in,** enrompi [tr]; **stave off,** forteni [tr], deflankigi
stay, (remain), resti [int]; ~(ad)o; (dwell as guest), gasti [int]; (halt), halti [int]; haltigi; halt(ig)o; (wait), atendi [tr, int]; atendo; (pause), paŭzi [int]; paŭzo; (hinder, restrain), bridi [tr]; (postpone), prokrasti [tr]; prokrasto; (support, gen), subtenilo, apogilo; (naut: mast rope etc.), stajo; **stay put,** ~i senmova; **stay up,** (not go to bed), ~i sendorma, maldormi [int], ne dormi [int]; **stay-at-home,** hejmsidulo; **bobstay,** buspritstajo; **mainstay,** (naut), ĉefstajo; (support, gen), ĉefapoganto; ĉefapogilo; **overstay,** preter~i [tr]
stead, loko; **in (someone's, something's) stead,** anstataŭ (iu, io) [see "instead"]; **stand (one) in good stead,** multe utili [int] [or] servi [int] al (iu)

steadfast, (firm, settled), firma, establita; (loyal, constant), lojala, konstanta, rezoluta
steady, (stable), stabila, firma; ~igi, firmigi; ~iĝi, firmiĝi; (constant, regular), konstanta, regula; (continuous), daŭra, seninterrompa; (calm, not excitable; grave, staid, sober), sobra; (person dated regularly; sweetheart), konstantul(in)o; **go steady (with),** konstante rendevuadi [int] (kun); **steady-state,** (phys), konstantastata
steak, (any thick meat slice), steko; (beef), bifsteko, bov~o; **sirloin steak,** (bov)lumbaĵo; **steak tartare,** Tatara ~o
steal, (take), ŝteli [tr]; (move stealthily), ~iri [int], en~iĝi; **stealth,** ~eco; **stealthy,** ~eca; **steal away,** for~iĝi; **steal in,** (enter stealthily), en~iĝi
steam, vaporo; ~a; (give off steam), ~i [int]; (become steam, vaporize), ~iĝi; (treat w steam), ~izi [tr]; (cook by steam), ~kuiri [tr]; ~kuiriĝi; (go via steam, as train or ship), ~iri [int]; **steamer,** (ship), ~ŝipo; (cooker), ~kuirilo; **steam bath,** (bath), ~bano; (room), ~banejo [cp "sauna"]; **steamboat,** ~boato; **steam boiler,** ~kaldrono; **steam engine,** ~motoro; **steam fitter,** ~tubisto; **steamfitting,** ~tubizado; **steam heat,** ~hejtado; **steam iron,** ~gladilo; **steamroller,** (road roller, or [fig] any overwhelming power like a road roller), ŝoserulilo; (use such power, crush), premfrakasi [tr], superruli [tr]; (force through), traŝovi [tr], trapuŝegi [tr]; **steamship,** ~ŝipo; **steam shovel,** ŝovelmaŝino; **steam table,** ~tablo; **let off steam,** (emotions), liberigi la emociojn
stearate, stear/ato; **stearic acid,** ~a acido
stearin, stearino
stear(o)–, (pfx: fat), steat(o)–
stearrhea, steatoreo
steatite, steatito, sapŝtono
steat(o)–, (pfx: fat), steat(o)–
steatolysis, steatolizo
steatopygic, steatopygous, steatopuga; **steatopygia,** ~eco

steatorrhea, steatoreo
steatosis, steatozo
steed, ĉevalo
steel, (metal), ŝtalo; ~a; (harden), hardi [tr]; **steel mill**, ~ejo, ~-uzino; **steelyard**, stangopesilo; **manganese steel**, mangan~o; **steel oneself**, alvoki sian kuraĝon, firmigi sin
steep, (re slope), kruta; (excessive, as price etc.), ekscesa; (soak, gen, as tea), trempi [tr]; trempiĝi; (to dissolve substance), maceri [tr]; maceriĝi; (to soften, as flax), rui [tr]; ruiĝi; (saturate), saturi [tr]; (absorb, imbue), prisorbi [tr] (e.g.: *he is steeped in folklore:* li estas prisorbita en la folkloro)
steeple, spajro; **steeplechase**, (obstacle race), obstaklovetkuro; **steeplejack**, turlaboristo [not "turisto"]
steer, (guide vehicle), stiri [tr] [cp "drive"]; (guide, direct, gen), gvidi [tr]; (young of cattle), virbovido; (castrated), kastrita bovo; **steerage**, (steering), ~ado; (low class), tria klaso, plej malalta klaso; **steerageway**, (minimuma) ~rapido; **steering wheel**, ~ilo; **steer clear of**, (nepre, zorge) eviti [tr]
steeve, (stow), stivi [tr]
Stefania, (woman's name), Stefania
Stegocephali, stegocefaloj
stegosaurus, stegosaŭro
stein, tasego
stele, stela, (arch), steleo
Stella, (woman's name), Stela
stellar, (re star), stela; (outstanding), el-stara
Stellaria, stelario
stem, (of plant, or similar-shaped object), tigo; (of wineglass etc.), fusto; (of ship), steveno; (of spring-wound watch, clock, etc.), streĉilo; (word root, to which gram endings are attached), radikalo; (dam up), digi [tr]; (stop, plug up), ŝtopi [tr]; (originate, derive from), deveni [int] (de), rezulti [int] (de); **stemware**, fustoglasaro
stench, fetoro, stinko
stencil, (w cut-out letters, design, etc., as for inking, painting, silk-screening; any analogous pattern), ŝablono; ~i [tr]; (for mimeograph etc.), stencilo; stencili [tr]
steno, (stenographer), sten(ografi)/isto [see "stenograph"]; (stenography), ~o
stenograph, (write in shorthand), stenografi [tr]; (machine), stenotipo, stenmaŝino; **stenographer**, ~iisto, stenisto; **stenography**, ~io, steno; **stenographic**, ~ia, stena
stenosis, stenozo
stenotype, stenotipi [tr]; ~o; **stenotypy**, ~io
Stentor, Stentoro
stentorian, Stentora, laŭtega
step, (move foot; one footfall; gait; distance of one pace), paŝi [int]; ~o; (one level of stairs), ŝtupo; (one stage of multiple process etc.), manipulo, ~o, ŝtupo (e.g.: *the first step is to stir the paint:* la unua manipulo estas kirli la farbon; *the instruction is in several steps:* la instruado estas en pluraj ŝtupoj); **step by step**, ~on post ~o, ~ope; **step down**, (resign), eksiĝi (el, de), rezigni [tr]; (elec: reduce voltage), malaltigi (la tension); **step in**, (intervene), interveni [int]; **step on it**, hasti [int], rapidi [int]; **step on the gas**, plirapidiĝi; **step up**, (increase), pliigi, (pli)intensigi; (elec: increase voltage), plialtigi (la tension); (progress), progresi [int]; **break step**, elkadenciĝi; **goose-step**, anser~i [int]; anser~o; **in step**, laŭkadenca; **misstep**, mis~o; **out of step**, eksterkadenca, nekonforma; **overstep**, preterpasi [tr] (la limojn de); **sidestep**, eviti [tr]; **take steps (to)**, (adopt measures, make effort), klopodi [tr], preni rimedojn (por)
step–, (pfx: related by remarriage of parent), duon– (e.g.: *stepmother:* ~patrino)
Stephen, Stefano
steppe, stepo
–ster, (sfx: one who is, does), –ulo (e.g.: *youngster:* junulo; *jokester:* ŝercemulo)
steradian, steradiano
Stercorarius, sterkorario, rabmevo, lestro
Sterculia, sterkulio

stere, stero; **decastere,** deka~o
stereo, (stereophonic sound), stereofo-
nio; ~a; (stereo music system), ~ilo,
stereoilo
stere(o)–, (pfx: spatial), stereo–
stereography, stereografio
stereoisomer, stereoizomero
stereometry, stereometrio
stereophonic, stereofonia; **stereophonic sound,** ~o
stereoscop/e, stereoskopo; **stereosco-
py,** ~io
stereotomy, stereotomio
stereotype, (gen), stereotipo; ~i [tr];
stereotypical, stereotyped, ~a
sterile, (gen), sterila; **sterility,** ~eco;
sterilize, (kill microbes), ~izi [tr];
(make unable to reproduce), ~igi;
sterilizer, ~izilo, ~izatoro
sterlet, sterledo
sterling, (re Br $), sterlinga; ~a valuto;
(excellent), bonega, unuaranga
stern, (severe), severa; (of ship), pobo;
astern, pobe(n); **sternpost,** posta steveno
Sterna, ŝterno; Sterna bergii, tuf~o;
Sterna albifrons, malgranda ~o; Sterna nereis, feina ~o
sterno–, (anat pfx: sternum), sterno–
sternum, sternumo
steroid, steroido
sterol, sterolo
stertor, stertoro [cp "snore"]
stet, restu
stethoscope, stetoskopo; **stethoscopy,**
~io; **examine by stethoscope,** ~i [tr]
stevedore, stivisto
Steven, Stefano
stew, stufi [tr]; ~aĵo; **stew(ing) pan
(pot),** ~ujo, kaserolo; **mulligan stew,**
miks~aĵo
steward, (on plane, ship), stevardo;
(manager, as on estate, or fig), intendanto
Stewart, Stuarto
stichometry, stikometrio
stick, (of wood, gen; similar object;
sports: for striking ball, puck, etc.),
bastono; (small pole, rod), stang(et)o;
(esp for punishment), vergo; vergi
[tr]; (piece, as of chewing gum,
chalk), peco; (car shift lever), kluĉos-

tango; (to steer plane), stirilo, stirstango; (fasten), fiksi [tr]; fiksiĝi; (fasten
w glue etc.), alglui [tr]; algluiĝi; (jab,
pierce), piki [tr]; (thrust, shove), ŝovi
[tr] (e.g.: *stick one's finger in a hole:*
ŝovi la fingron en truon); (put, place,
gen), meti [tr]; (bog down, become
stuck or entangled), fiksiĝi, implikiĝi;
(impose on), trudi [tr] (ion al iu) (e.g.:
*they stuck me with cleaning up, with
the bill:* ili trudis al mi la purigadon,
la fakturon); (remain), resti [int]; (persist, persevere), persisti [int]; [see also
"stuck"]; **sticker,** (gummed label),
gluetikedo, glumarko; **sticky,** (gluey), glueca; (difficult), malfacila;
stickbeak, (Aus), scivolemulo; **sticky
wicket,** (Br colloq), malfacilaĵo, embaraso; **the sticks,** (colloq), la (fora)
kamparo; **stick around,** resti proksima, ne foriri [int]; **stick by,** (remain
loyal), resti fidela [or] lojala al; **stick-
in-the-mud,** ĝojfuŝanto; **stick out,**
(protrude), elstari [int]; (push out),
elŝovi [tr]; (persevere through), persisti [int] (tra), elteni [tr]; **stick shift,**
kluĉostango; **stick to,** (persist), persisti [int] (en); **stick-to-it-iveness,** per-
sistemo; **stick up,** (rob), prirabi [tr];
(put up), starigi; (fasten), fiksi [tr];
stick up for, defendi [tr], subteni [tr];
chopstick, manĝo~o; **dipstick,** (to
measure depth of liquid), stangogaŭĝo; **pogo stick,** salt~o
stickleback, gasterosteo, dornfiŝo
stickler, insist/emulo, pedanto; **be a
stickler for,** ~i [int] pri
stiff, (rigid), rigida; (not easily moved
or moving), nefacilmova; (strong, as
re current, alcoholic drink, opposition,
etc.), forta; (harsh), severa, malmilda;
(difficult), malfacila; (too formal,
constrained), troformala, (tro)~a, tro-
bridita; (excessive, as price), ekscesa;
stiffen, ~igi; ~iĝi; (pli)fortigi;
(pli)fortiĝi; (pli)severigi
stifle, sufoki [tr]; ~iĝi
stigma, (mark, sign), stigmato; (bot,
anat), stigmo; **stigmatic,** (gen), ~a;
stigmatize, ~izi [tr]; **stigmatism,** ~is-
mo
stilb, stilbo

stile, (steps over fence, wall), murŝtuparo; **(turn)stile**, turnbariero

stiletto, stileto

still, (motionless), senmova; ~e; (tranquil, calm), trankvila, kvieta; trankviligi, kvietigi; (phot), ~a foto; (silent), silenta; silentigi; (for distilling), distililo; (chem retort), retorto; (however), tamen (e.g.: *it's long; still, it's not tedious:* ĝi estas longa; tamen, ĝi ne estas teda); (yet), ankoraŭ (e.g.: *it's still raining:* ankoraŭ pluvas; *it's raining, but I still want to go:* pluvas, sed mi ankoraŭ volas iri); (even more), eê (pli) (e.g.: *it was cold yesterday, and is still colder today:* estis malvarme hieraŭ, kaj estas eê pli malvarme hodiaŭ); **stillness**, ~eco; trankvil(ec)o, kviet(ec)o; silento; **still life**, (as objects for painting), ~aĵo

stilt, stilzo; **stilted**, (rigid, pompous), rigida, pompa, afekta, (tro)formala; **walk on stilts**, ~iri [int]

stimulate, stimuli [tr]; **stimulnt**, ~anto; ~enzo; **stimulus**, ~o; ~ilo; ~enzo; **stimulator**, (med: e.g., for heart), ~atoro†

stimulin, stimulino

stimy, obstrukci [tr]

sting, (gen), piki [tr]; ~o; **stinger**, ~ilo

stingray, rajo

stingy, avara

stink, fetoro, stinko, odoraĉo; ~i [int], stinki [int], odoraĉi [int]; **stinkbug**, (*Pentatoma*), pentatomo; **stink to high heaven**, ~egi [int], ~i ĝis la ĉielo

stint, (limit), limigi; ~o; (be sparing, miserly), avari [tr]; (task), tasko; (period, shift of work), skipo

Stipa, stipo; Stipa tenacissima, alfo

stipe, stipo

stipend, (any salary), salajro; (scholarship, allowance, subsidy), stipendio; [cp "pension"]; **stipendiary**, ~a; ~ato; stipendia; stipendiulo; **pay a stipend to**, ~i [tr]; stipendii [tr]

stipes, stipo

stipulate, kondiĉi [tr]; **stipulation**, ~o

stipule, stipulo

stir, (mix, re liquid etc.), kirli [tr], agiti [tr]; ~iĝi; ~o; (move slightly, displace), ekmovi [tr]; ekmoviĝi; ekmov-

iĝo; (rouse), eksciti [tr], veki [tr], vigligi; ekscitiĝi, vekiĝi, vigliĝi; (feelings), emocii [tr]; (commotion, tumult), bruo, ekscitiĝo, tumulto; **stir up**, (agitate, gen), agiti [tr]; **bestir**, vigligi

stirrup, (for riding), piedingo; (bone), stapedo; (beam reinforcement), U-stango

stitch, (in sewing etc.), stebi [tr]; ~o; (knitting), maŝo; (suture), suturi [tr]; suturo; [cp "sew"; "knit"]; (pain), ekdoloro; **stitchwort**, stelario

stoat, ermeno

stochastic, stokasta

stock, (provide, equip, gen), provizi [tr] (per); ~aĵo(j) (e.g.: *stock the shelves with cans:* ~i la bretojn per ladaĵoj; *stock a lake with fish:* ~i lagon per fiŝoj); (supply commercial goods etc.), stoki [tr]; stoko (e.g.: *that store stocks all types of shoes:* tiu butiko stokas ĉiajn ŝuojn); (extra, reserve supplies), rezervaĵoj; (bsns, $: capital shares collectively), akcioj; (one share), akcio; (bot: plant onto which graft is inserted), algreftaĵo; (rhizome, rootstock), rizomo; (bot: *Mathiola*), levkojo; (progenitor), prapatro; (line of descent), deveno; (race, strain), raso; (domestic animals), brutaro; (for breeding), breda; (handle, part held, as of tool), tenilo; (of gun etc.), fusto; (of anchor), ŝtoko; (trunk, as of tree), trunko; (frame, as of plow), framo; (raw material), krudaĵo; (paper), papero (e.g.: *print on heavy (glossy) stock:* presi sur peza (glacea) papero); (cards, dominoes, etc., not dealt out), talono; (partial interest, concern), intereso (e.g.: *I have a stock in the outcome of the venture:* mi havas intereson en la rezulto de la entrepreno); (ordinary, usual), ordinara, kutima; (hackneyed, trite), banala; **stocks**, (for punishment), piedpilorio; (for ship construction), kilblokoj; **stockbreeder**, brutbredisto; **stockbroker**, akcimakleristo, borsagento [see "broker"]; **stock car**, (rr), brutvagono; (auto), norma aŭto, seri-aŭto; **stock certificate**, akcio; **stock exchange, stock**

market, borso; **stockholder,** (bsns), akciulo; **stock in trade,** (goods), (stok)varoj; (tools etc.), iloj kaj materialoj; (resources, devices), (kutimaj) rimedoj; **stockman,** (Aus), vakero; **stockpile,** rezervi [tr], stapli [tr]; rezervo, staplaĵo; **stockroom,** stokejo, ~ejo; **stock up (on),** plen~i [tr] (sin per); plenstoki [tr]; **stockyard,** brutokorto, brut-enfermejo; **in stock,** stokata, en stoko, dispona; **out of stock,** (sold out, used up), elĉerpita; **put stock in,** (trust), fidi [tr]; **rolling stock,** (rr), surrelaĵoj; (any vehicles), veturilaro; **tailstock,** postĉuko; **take stock in,** ($, bsns), aĝioti [int] (en), aĉeti akciojn (en, de); (trust, give credence to), fidi [tr]; **take stock of,** (inventory), inventari [tr]; (assess), taksi [tr]; **speculate in stocks,** aĝioti [int]

stockade, palisaro; ~izi [tr]

Stockholm, Stokholmo

stocking, ŝtrumpo

stocky, dikmalalta, kompakta

stodgy, (heavy, slow), peza, lantmova; (dull, tedious), teda, malsprita; (old-fashioned, narrow), malnovemaĉa, malvastanima

stof, stofo

stoic, stoika; ~ulo; **stoicism,** ~ismo; **stoicist,** ~isma; ~isto

stoke, hejti [tr]

stole, (garment, gen), stolo

stolid, flegma

stolon, stolono

stoma, stomo

stomach, stomako; ~a; en~igi; (tolerate), toleri [tr]; **stomachache,** ~odoloro

stomatitis, stomatito

stomat(o)–, (sci root), stomat(o)–

stomatology, stomatolog/io; **stomatologist,** ~o

stomatoscope, stomatoskopo

stomp, (stamp, pound feet), stamfi [int]; ~o; (trample), treti [tr]

–stomy, (med sfx), –stomio

stone, (rocky substance, or a piece of this), ŝtono; ~a [cp "rock", "boulder", "gravel"]; (of fruit), kerno; (of kidney etc.), kalkuluso; (gem), gemo; (Br: unit of weight), 6,35 kilogramoj [see § 20]; (throw stones at, kill w stones), ~umi [tr]; (remove fruit stones), senkernigi; [see also "stone–"]; **stoned,** (intoxicated), ebria; **stonechat,** (zool), saksikolo; **stonecrop,** (bot), sedo; **stonecutter,** (one who cuts stones from quarry), ~hakisto; (one who shapes, engraves, etc.), ~tajlisto; **stonemason,** ~masonisto; **stonewall,** (obstruct), obstrukci [tr]; **stonework,** ~masonaĵo; **brimstone,** sulfuro; **brownstone,** brun~o; brun~a domo; **chalkstone,** tofo; **cobblestone,** pavim~o; **cobblestone street,** ~pavimita strato; **cornerstone,** angul~o; **gallstone,** (gala) kalkuluso, gal~o; **grindstone,** akriga disko; **keystone,** ŝlosil~o; **limestone,** kalk~o; **lodestone, loadstone,** magnetito; **milestone,** (lit: specifically indicating miles), mejl~o; (if miles not specifically indicated; or fig), kilometro~o [see § 20]; **millstone,** muel~o; **moonstone,** lun~o; **rhinestone,** diamantoido; **rolling stone,** (fig: wanderer), vagemulo; **sandstone,** grejso, sablo~o; **soapstone,** steatito, sap~o; **stepping-stone,** (lit), paŝo~~o; (fig), helpilo; **touchstone,** tuŝ~o; **whetstone,** akriga ~o; **leave no stone unturned,** provi ĉion: domaĝi nenion; **stone the crows!, stone the lizards!,** (Aus colloq), nekredeble!

stone–, (pfx: completely), tut–, tute (e.g.: *stone-deaf:* ~surda [or] ~e surda)

stooge, pajl(o)homo, subul(aĉ)o

stool, (any low, backless chair), skabelo, tabureto; (feces), fekaĵo; **footstool,** (pied)~o

stoop, (bend down), kliniĝi; (condescend, deign), degni [tr]; (small porch), peron(et)o

stop, (motion), halti [int]; ~igi; ~(ig)o; ~(ig)a; ~ejo (e.g.: *the car stopped:* la aŭto ~is; *stop the car:* ~igi la aŭton); (activity: condition), ĉesi [int]; ĉesigi; ĉes(ig)o; ĉes(ig)a (e.g.: *the noise stopped:* la bruo ĉesis; *stop the noise:* ĉesigi la bruon; *we stopped trying:* ni ĉesis provi; *stop that!:* ĉesigu tion!); (plug up; close, as bottle w cork or

cap), ŝtopi [tr]; (bar, hinder), bari [tr],
malhelpi [tr]; (prevent), malebligi;
(mus: finger string, as on violin, guitar, to produce higher pitch), fingri
[tr]; (set of organ pipes), tubaro;
(stay), resti [int]; (any mech piece to
stop motion), ~peco; (mech: projecting lug etc.), buteo; (Br: period [.]),
punkto; (phot: aperture), aperturo; (f-
number), aperturnumero, f–numero;
(interj: naut or oth command to stop
machine etc.; as period in telegram),
stop!; stopi [tr]; stopo; **stopper**, (plug,
cork, etc.), ŝtopilo; **stop bath**, (phot),
~iga bano; **stop down**, (phot), mal-
larĝigi la aperturon; **stopgap**, provizora, dumtempa; provizoraĵo; pro-
vizorulo; **stop off, stop over, stop by,
stop in**, (to visit), veni [int], (viziti
[tr], vidi [tr], etc.); (pause in journey),
paŭzi [int]; ~i; (go by), pasi laŭ; **stop
up**, (plug), ŝtopi [tr]; ŝtopiĝi; **bus
stop**, busa stacio [cp "station"];
f–stop, (phot), aperturnumero, f–numero; **nonstop**, sen~a; sen~e; **short-
stop**, (baseball), interbazulo; **put a
stop to**, ĉesigi; **pull out all the stops**,
(lit, re organ), funkciigi ĉiujn tubar-
ojn; (fig: use everything possible), uzi
ĉiujn rimedojn

storage, (room, building, etc.), staplo,
provizejo [not "~ejo"]; (act), ~ado;
[see also "store"]; (cmptr), storo†
storax, (resin), storako; (tree), stirako
store, (put away in storage, warehouse,
etc.), stapli [tr]; (amass), amasigi;
(hoard), akumuli [tr]; (save up), ŝpari
[tr]; (reserve), rezervi [tr]; rezervaĵoj,
ŝparaĵoj; (furnish w), pri~i [tr] (e.g.: *a
book stored with facts:* libro pri~ita de
faktoj); (put into cmptr memory),
stori† [tr], enmemorigi; (retail shop),
butiko; (warehouse), ~o, magazeno;
storefront, butikantaŭo; butikantaŭa;
storehouse, ~o, magazeno; **store-
keeper**, butikisto; **storewise**, tutbuti-
ka, tutmagazena; **chain store**,
ĉenmagazeno; **convenience store**,
(oportun–)butiketo; **department
store**, magazeno; **drugstore**, apoteko, drogejo; **second-hand store**, brokantejo; **set much (little) store by**,

(mal)multe taksi [tr], (mal)multe valori [tr]; **be in store for one**, atendi iun;
iu esti ricevonta, iu ricevos (e.g.: *a
surprise is in store for you:* surprizo
atendas vin [or] vi estas ricevonta sur-
prizon)
storey, etaĝo
stork, cikonio;   **stork's-bill**,   (bot),
erodio; **marabou stork**, marabuo
storm, (weather, or analogous out-
break), ŝtormo; ~i [int]; [cp "furor"];
(attack), sturmi [tr]; **stormy**, ~a;
storm-trooper,   sturmanto;   **sand-
storm**,   sablo~o;   **snowstorm**,
neĝo~o; **thunderstorm**, fulmotondro;
windstorm, (gen, w rain or snow),
burasko; **take by storm**, sturmkapti
[tr]
stornello, stornelo
story, (tale), rakonto, historio; (history), historio; (lie), fablaĵo, mensogo;
(floor of building, storey), etaĝo;
fairy story, fabelo; **short story**, (lit),
novelo; **shaggy dog story**, kalem-
bur~o; **sob story**, ve-~o
stotinka, stotinko
stout, (strong), forta; fortika [see
"strong"]; (fat), korpulenta, dika; (solid, firm), solida, firma; (brave), kuraĝa, brava; (drink), portero
stove, (gen), forno; (for heating), stovo,
hejto~o; (for cooking), fornelo; [cp
"oven", "furnace"];   **pot-bellied
stove**, ŝvelventra stovo; **wood stove**,
lignostovo
stow, (put away), stivi [tr]; (pack, gen),
paki [tr]; **stow away**, (travel hidden),
kaŝvojaĝi [int]; **stowaway**, kaŝvo-
jaĝanto
St. (as element in geog names), [see
"saint"]
St. Petersburg, (gen), Peterburgo
strabismometer, strabometro
strabismus, strabismo;   **convergent
strabismus**, konverĝa ~o; **divergent
strabismus**, diverĝa ~o
Strabo, Strabono
strabometer, strabometro
strabotomy, strabotomio
straddle, (stand w legs apart; analogous
action), disstari [int] (sur, super,
trans); (sit astride, as horse, fence;

analogous action), ambaŭflanki [tr],
sidi rajde sur, situi rajde sur, rajdi [tr]
(e.g.: *he straddled the fence:* li rajdis
[or] ambaŭflankis la barilon; *Bristol
straddles the Tennessee-Virginia
boundary:* Bristolo ambaŭflankas la
ŝtatlimon Tenesian-Virginian [or] situas rajde sur la ŝtatlimo)

strafe, mitrali [tr], (~)bombardi [tr]

straggle, (wander), disvagi [int]; (lag
behind), postlanti [int]; (arrive, leave,
etc., at irregular intervals), neregule
(alveni, foriri, etc.)

straight, (not curved or angular; direct),
rekta; ~e; (straight up, erect, vertical),
~a, vertikala; (in order, arranged,
neat), orda, neta, aranĝita; (honest,
sincere), honesta, sincera; (undiluted,
as re alcoholic drink), nediluita, pura;
(w/o ice, re drink), senglacia; (cards:
series in order in same suit), sekvenco; (colloq: normal, not homosexual,
not drug addict, etc.), normala, ~a;
normalulo, ~ulo; **straighten,** (gen),
~igi; ~iĝi; (re hair), malbukli [tr];
straighten out, (put in order), ordi
[tr], malkonfuzi [tr], malimpliki [tr];
straight ahead, ~e antaŭe(n);
straight angle, ~a angulo; **straight-
away,** ~vojo; **straight down,** apika,
apike malsupra; apike (malsupre(n));
straightedge, ~ilo, liniilo; **straight
face,** pokervizaĝo; **straightforward,**
~a, honesta; ~e, honeste; **straight
line,** ~o; **straight man,** komediista
helpanto; **straight-out,** ~a; ~e;
straight up, apika, apike supra; apike
(supre(n)); **straightway,** tuj, senprokraste

strain, (stretch, create stress), streĉi [tr];
~(ad)o [cp "stress"]; (tech: change of
length under stress), (mal)plilongigo;
(overtax, overstretch, as muscle),
tro~i [tr]; tro~o; (sift), kribri [tr]; (filter), filtri [tr]; (strive), strebi [int]; (genetic), stamo; (manner, tone, style),
tono, maniero; **strains,** (mus), sono(j),
tono(j); **strainer,** (for kitchen), kribri-
leto

strait, markolo; **straits,** (difficulty), embaraso; **strait-laced,** pruda, strikta-
kondukta, severmora, maldiboĉa; **in

dire straits, urĝe senmona

strand, (run aground), grundi [tr], ter-
fiksiĝi; ~igi, terfiksi [tr]; (abandon in
difficulty), forlasi [tr] (embarasita,
senhelpa, etc.) (e.g.: *we were stranded
penniless in Chicago:* ni estis forlasi-
taj senmone en Ĉikago; *the flood
stranded us on the hill:* la inundo for-
lasis nin embarasitaj sur la monteto);
(shore), strando; (of string or rope),
ŝnurero; (of wire), dratero; (of cable),
kablero

strange, (odd, peculiar), stranga, kurioza; (foreign), fremda; (unknown),
nekonata; **stranger,** nekonato, frem-
dulo; **strange as it may seem,** malgraŭ la ŝajno

strangle, strangulate, strangoli [tr] [cp
"suffocate"]; **stranglulation,** ~o

strangury, strangurio

strap, (gen), rimeno; ~i [tr]; (of garment, over shoulder), ŝelko (e.g.:
strapless bra: senŝelka mamzono);
(metal, for packing crates etc.), lad-
bendo, ŝtalrubando

Strasbourg, Strasburgo

stratagem, ruzo, taktiko

strategos, (Greek mil general), stratego

stragegy, strategio; **stragegic,** ~a;
stragegist, ~isto

stratify, tavol/igi; ~iĝi

stratigraphy, stratigrafio

Stratiotes aloides, stratioto, akvosoldato

stratosphere, stratosfero

stratum, (geol etc.), stratumo; (any layer), tavolo; **substratum,** sub~o; **stratum corneum,** kerato

stratus, stratuso

straw, (collective), pajlo; (one strand),
~ero; (drinking), ŝalmo, ~ero; **straw
boss,** submastro, vokto; **straw-stack,**
~amaso; **bedstraw,** (bot), galio;
broomstraw, fragmito; **grasp at
straws,** alkroĉi sin al ~ero; **the last
straw,** la troiga ~ero; **man of straw,**
~ohomo

stray, (wander off), forvagi [int], erar-
vagi [int], erarforiĝi; ~inta; ~into; (incidental, random, isolated), hazarda

streak, (stripe), strio; ~i [tr]; ~iĝi; (of
lightning; line, mark, etc.), streko;
streki [tr]; (layer), tavolo; tavoligi; ta-

voliĝi; (marbled layers), jaspi [tr]; jaspaĵo; (tendency, element, as of beha vior), tendenco; (period of time), periodo; (series, spell), serio, sinsekvo; (rush, go fast), flugi [int], kuregi [int], impeti [int]

stream, (flow, current), flui [int]; ~o; (creek), rivereto; (rivulet), rojo; **streamer,** (strip of cloth or paper, etc.), flagrubando; **streamline,** (path of flow), ~linio; (design for easy flow), ~igi; (simplify), simpligi; **streamlined,** ~linia; simpligita; **Black Stream,** Kuroŝio; **downstream,** laŭ~e; **Gulf Stream,** Golfa F~o; **midstream,** rivermeze, ~meze; **slipstream,** post~o; **upstream,** kontraŭ~a; kontraŭ~e(n)

street, strato; ~a; **main street,** ĉef~o; **one-way street,** unudirekta ~o; **dead-end street,** sak~o

strength, forto; fortiko; potenco [see "strong"]; **strengthen,** (pli)~igi; (pli)~iĝi; (pli)fortikigi; (pli)fortikiĝi; (pli)potencigi; (pli)potenciĝi; **tensile strength,** tir-fortiko; **on the strength of,** (based on), surbaze de

strenuous, pen/iga, ~plena, energia

Strepsiptera, strepsipteroj

strepsipteron, strepsipteran, strepsiptero

streptococcus, streptokoko; **streptococcicosis,** ~ozo

streptomycin, streptomicino

Streptopelia turtur, turto

stress, (compression), premi [tr]; ~o; (tech, gen), streĉi [tr]; streĉo; (shear), tondi [tr]; (tension), tiri [tr]; streĉo; (psych), streso; (emphasis), emfazi [tr], substreki [tr], akcenti [tr]; emfazo, substreko, akcento; (mus, phon: accent), akcenti [tr]; akcento; **stressful,** ~a; streĉa; stresiga; **prestressed,** antaŭstreĉita; **compression stress,** (kun)~a streĉo; **shear stress,** ŝira streĉo; **tensile stress,** tira streĉo

stretch, (lengthen as from strain), streĉi [tr]; ~iĝi; ~(iĝ)o; (extend, reach out; expanse), etendi [tr]; etendiĝi; etendo; (extend own limbs, as while yawning), sin ~i, sin etendi; (spread over area), sterni [tr]; sterniĝi; (period, se-

quence), periodo, sinsekvo; **stretcher,** (to carry injured), brankardo; (Aus: bed), faldebla lito; **stretch out,** (self), kuŝiĝi, sin etendi [tr]; (prolong), plilongigi; plilongiĝi; **stretch to,** (reach to, attain), atingi [tr]; **outstretch,** etendi [tr]; etendiĝi; etend(iĝ)o; **the home stretch,** la fina parto; **at a stretch,** seninterrompe

strew, disŝuti [tr], dissterni [tr]; **bestrew,** surŝuti [tr], ĉirkaŭŝuti [tr]

stria, strio

striate, strii [tr]; **striated,** ~ita; **striation,** ~oj, ~iteco

stricken, trafita, afliktita

strict, (rigorous; not lax or loose), strikta, rigora; (severe), severa; (precise), preciza

striction, stringo

stricture, (restriction, limitation), limigo; (censure), malaprobo, mallaŭdo, kritiko; (med: stenosis), stenozo; (any narrowing), mallarĝigo

stride, paŝegi [int], vigle marŝi [int]; ~o, vigla marŝado; **make strides (toward),** (progress), progresi [int] (al); **take (something) in stride,** akcepti (ion) sen ĝeno

strident, knara, akrasona

strife, kverel(ad)o, malpaco, konflikto; **in strife,** (Aus), en malfacilaĵo, en embaraso

Strigidae, Strigiformes. [see "Strix"]

strike, (hit), frapi [tr]; ~iĝi (kontraŭ); ~o (e.g.: *the wind struck me in the face:* la vento min ~is kontraŭ la vizaĝo); (hit w force, beat), bati [tr]; bato (e.g.: *the hammer strikes the nail:* la martelo batas la najlon); (hit mark or target; wound; collide w; connect w; come upon), trafi [tr]; trafo (e.g.: *the bullet struck him in the arm:* la kuglo trafis lin ĉe la brako; *our car struck a tree:* nia aŭto trafis arbon; *strike oil:* trafi nafton); (afflict), aflikti [tr] (e.g.: *misfortune struck him:* malfeliĉo afliktis lin); (stamp, press, as coin, etc.), stampi [tr]; stampo; (ring bell, as re clock), sonori [tr, int] (e.g.: *the clock struck three:* la horloĝo sonoris la trian (horon)); (ignite match), ekflamigi; ekflami [int]; (stop work), striki [int] (kontraŭ); striko [see also "–in"]; (attack), ataki [tr]; atako; (impress), imponi [int] (al); impresi [tr] [see "impress"]; (draw line), streki [tr]; streko; (line out, delete, remove), forstreki [tr]; (make, as bargain, agreement), fari [tr], starigi; (lower, as flag, sails), mallevi [tr]; (take down, dismantle, as tent, theat scenery, etc.), malstarigi; (baseball), maltrafo; (bowling), plentrafo; **striking**, (impressive), impona; (eye-catching), okul~a; **strike down**, (knock down), (~)faligi, forbati [tr]; **strike dumb**, (render speechless w surprise etc.), konsterni [tr]; **strike home**, (hit the mark, lit or fig), trafi la celon; **strike off**, (remove, delete), forstreki [tr], forigi; (print), presi [tr]; **strike out**, (delete), forstreki [tr]; (hit at), ekbati [tr]; (start off), ekiri [int], komenciĝi; **strike up**, (begin), komenci [tr]; (mus), ekludi [tr]; **strike it rich**, trafi riĉaĵojn; **be struck with**, esti imponita de, esti trafita de; **on strike**, strikanta; **go on strike**, ekstriki [int] (kontraŭ); **strike-breaker**, strikrompanto; **have two strikes against one**, esti je malavantaĝo

Strine, (Aus), la Aŭstralia dialekto [or] lingvo

string, (cord, twine, etc.), ŝnuro; ~i [tr]; (thin, light), ~eto; [cp "thread", "rope"]; (for mus instrument), kordo; (lace for shoe etc.), laĉo; laĉi [tr]; (beads etc.), surfadenigi; (beads on string, or any series, row), serio, vico; (colloq: restriction, condition), kondiĉo; [see also "strung"]; **drawstring**, stringo~eto; **superstring**, super~o **pull strings**, subinflui [tr]; (**with**) **no strings attached**, senkondiĉe

strip, (undress), malvesti [tr], senvestigi, nudigi; ~iĝi, sin ~i, senvestiĝi, nudiĝi; (deprive of, remove), senigi (je) (e.g.: *strip one of authority:* senigi iun je aŭtoritato); (remove layer, as paint, veneer, etc.), maltegi [tr]; (plunder, rob), prirabi [tr]; (break, damage screw threads or gear teeth), rompi [tr] (la ŝraŭbrelojn, la radodentojn);

(stripe; any narrow piece, part, place, area), strio; (band, zone, belt), zono; (lath), lato; (of iron), ferlato; (of steel), ŝtallato; **striptease**, striptizo; **stripper**, **striptease artist**, striptizist(in)o; **strip off**, (clothes etc.), demeti (la vestojn etc.); (rip off), forŝiri [tr]; **airstrip**, **landing strip**, surteriĝejo [cp "airport"]; **comic strip**, bildstrio; **outstrip**, superi [tr], devanci [tr]

stripe, (gen), strio; ~i [tr]; (indicating rank on uniform), galono; **striped**, ~(it)a

stripling, junulo, adoleskanto

strive, strebi [int]

Strix, strigo; Strigidae, ~edoj; Strigiformes, ~oformaj (birdoj)

strobe, stroboskopo; ~a

stroboscope, stroboskopo; **stroboscopic**, ~a

stroke, (hit, strike), bati [tr], frapi [tr]; ~o, frapo [see "strike", "hit"]; (med: attack), (cerbarteria) ikto; (caress), karesi [tr]; kareso; (line, dash), streko; streki [tr]; (effect, touch), tuŝo (e.g.: *her book shows a stroke of genius:* ŝia libro montras tuŝon de la genio); (sound of clock chime etc.), sonoro (e.g.: *at the stroke of midnight:* ĉe la sonoro de noktomezo); (one movement or pass, as of tool), tiro, movo (e.g.: *a stroke of the (paint)brush:* peniktiro; *a stroke of the pen:* plumtiro); (type of swimming), naĝado; **backstroke**, dorsnaĝado; **breaststroke**, brustnaĝado; **sidestroke**, flanknaĝado; **sunstroke**, suna ikto, sunfrapo, insolacio; **stroke of (good) luck**, feliĉaĵo; **stroke of bad luck**, sorto~o; **at a single stroke**, per unu ~o

stroll, promeni [int]; ~(ad)o; **stroller**, (one who strolls), ~anto; (for baby), (beba) ~ilo

stroma, stromo

Stromboli, Strombolo

strong, (having great energy, power, effect, forcefulness), forta (e.g.: *strong arm:* ~a brako; *strong transmitter:* ~a dissendilo; *strong coffee:* ~a kafo); (sturdy; durable; having great resistance to pressure, force, etc.), fortika (e.g.: *strong wall:* fortika muro;

strong rope: fortika ŝnuro); (power-ful), potenca; (numbering), sumanta (e.g.: *a membership 2000 strong:* membraro sumanta 2000); **strong-hold**, fortikaĵo [cp "fort", "fortress"]; **be going strong**, bone farti [int], bone progresi [int]; **come on strong**, ~e impresi [tr]
strongyle, strongilo
Strongylus, strongilo
strontianite, stroncianito
strontium, stroncio
strop, akrigi; ~a ledo
strophanthin, strofantino
strophanthus, (seed of *Strophanthus*), strofanta semo
Strophanthus, strofanto
strophe, strofo
structure, (manner of building; arrangement of parts; etc.), strukturo; (a building; something built; something consisting of interrelated parts), konstru(aĵ)o; **structural**, ~a; **structuralism**, ~ismo; **structuralist**, ~isma; **infrastructure**, sub~o; **substructure**, subkonstruaĵo; **superstructure**, superkonstruaĵo
strudel, spiral-kukaĵo
struggle, lukti [int], barakti [int]; ~o, barakto
strum, plektri [tr]; ~ado
struma, (goiter), strumo; **strumectomy**, ~ektomio
strumpet, prostituitino, putino
strung, [see "string"]; **high-strung**, nervoza, ekscitiĝema; **strung-out**, maltrankvil(iĝint)a
strut, (swagger, showy walk), pavi [int], paradi [int]; ~ado; (support), apogilo, apogstango, fosto
Struthidea cinerea, (Aus), apostolbirdo
Struthio, struto; Struthioniformes, ~oformaj (birdoj)
strychnine, striknino; **strychninism**, ~ozo
Strychnos, strikno
Stuart, (man's name; Scots royal family), Stuarto
stub, (stump of pencil, bristle, etc.), stumpo; (hit toe etc.), frapi [tr]; (one stalk of stubble), stoplo; **stub out**, (put out cigarette etc.), (prem)estingi

[tr]; **check stub**, talono; **ticket stub**, kontramarko
stubble, stopl/aro, ~oj [note: "stoplo" is one plant stump, not "stubble" collectively]; **stubblefield**, ~ejo
stubborn, obstina
stucco, stuko; ~i [tr]
stuck, [see "stick"]; **stuck-up**, fieraĉa, egoisma; **get stuck into**, (Aus: busy oneself with), okupiĝi pri; (Aus: eat), ekmanĝi [tr]
stud, (vertical beam), fost(et)o; (short metal or wood rod), ŝtudo; (small peg, pin), stifto, kejlo; (small knob, rounded nailhead), anskapa najlo; (be scattered over), dissterniĝi (sur, tra, en) (e.g.: *rocks studded the field:* ŝtonoj dissterniĝis tra la kampo); (male animal for breeding), bredbesto; (group of these), bredbestaro [or the animal may be specified: bredoĉeval(ar)o; bredobov(ar)o; etc.]; (place for these), bredejo; (man), virviro; **studded**, (covered w), sternita (de), kovrita (de) (e.g.: *a crown studded with jewels:* krono sternita de juveloj; *a star-studded sky:* stelsternita ĉielo); **at stud**, bredopreta
student, (formally enrolled in institution of higher learning), studento; ~a (e.g.: *medical student:* medicina ~o; *student housing:* ~aj loĝejoj); (in elementary, middle, or high school), lernanto; (re particular course), kursano; (casual, informal), studanto (e.g.: *student of the passing scene:* studanto de la pasantaĵo); **student body**, ~aro
studio, (TV, movie, etc.), studio; (private study), studejo; (of artist etc.), ateliero; (workshop), laborejo; (apartment), kombinita apartamento
study, (examine, research, learn about, etc.), studi [tr]; ~(ad)o; (room for), ~ejo, kabineto; (sketch, étude), etudo; (ponder), pripensi [tr]; **studious**, ~ema; **self-study**, mem~ado; mem~a, aŭtodidakta; **understudy**, (for actor etc.), dubli [tr]; dublanto; dublisto; **study up on**, (zorge) ~adi [tr]
stuff, (substance, material, gen), materialo (e.g.: *stuff to make plastic from:* ~o el kiu fari plaston; *what's that stuff*

on the floor?: kio estas tiu ~o sur la planko?); (of specific sort), –aĵo(j) [sfx] (e.g.: *a box of gardening stuff:* skatolo de ĝardenaĵoj); (cloth; fig, any component substance), ŝtofo; (possessions), posedaĵoj, havaĵoj; (fill, plug up), ŝtopi [tr]; (shove in), (en)ŝovi [tr]; (re food; oth analogous action), farĉi [tr] (e.g.: *stuffed turkey:* farĉita meleagraĵo; *the report was stuffed with errors:* la raporto estis farĉita de eraroj); (pad, as re furniture), remburi [tr]; (re taxidermy), remburi [tr], pajloŝtopi [tr]; **stuffing**, ŝtopaĵo; farĉo; remburaĵo; **stuffing box**, ŝtopaĵujo; **stuffed shirt**, egoisto; **overstuff**, (furniture etc.), troremburi [tr]

stuffy, (air), sufoka, malfreŝa; (dull, unimaginative), malsprita, maloriginala; (pompous), pompa

stultify, (make stupid, dull), stultigi [cp "stupefy"]; (make futile), vanigi

stumble, stumbli [int]; ~o; **stumble on**, hazarde renkonti [tr], hazarde al~i [tr]; **stumbling block**, obstaklo, falilo

stump, (of tree, candle, pencil, etc.), stumpo; ~igi; (pointed roll for shading drawings), stompo; stompi [tr]; (baffle), perpleksigi, mistifiki [tr]; (cricket post), fosteto; (end of cricket period), fino de ludperiodo

stun, (knock out), senkonsciigi; (stupefy), stuporigi; (shock), ŝok(eg)i [tr]; (astound), konsterni [tr], mirfrapi [tr]

stunt, (acrobatic or oth feat), akrobataĵo; (hinder growth), nanigi

stupa, stupao

stupefy, (stun, make dull), stuporigi [cp "stultify"]; (astound), konsterni [tr]; **stupefaction**, ~o

stupendous, kolosa

stupid, stulta; **stupidity**, ~eco

stupor, stuporo; **stuporous**, ~a; **be stuporous**, ~i [int]

sturdy, fortika

sturgeon, sturgo

Sturnus, sturno; Sturnus roseus, pastoro

stutter, balbuti [int]; ~o

Stuttgart, Stutgarto

sty, (for pigs), pork/ejo, ~ostalo; (on eye), hordeolo

stye, hordeolo

Stygian, Stiksa

style, (manner of expression, doing, etc.), stilo; ~igi; (mode, fashion), modo; modigi; (pattern, form of clothes, etc.), fasono; (originality), originaleco; (pattern after), fasoni [tr] (laŭ); (name, call), nomi [tr]; (law: title), titoli [tr]; (sort, type), speco; (of flower), stiluso; (stylus, marker), grifelo; **stylish, in style**, laŭmoda; **out of style**, eksmoda; **go out of style**, eksmodiĝi; **stylize**, ~igi; **stylistic**, ~eca; **live in style**, vivi lukse; **self-styled**, memdeklarita, memnomita

stylite, stilito†

stylobate, stilobato

stylus, (pointed tool), grifelo; (phonograph needle), nadlo

stymie, obstrukci [tr]

Stymphais, Stymphaus, Stimfalo

styptic, adstringa; ~enzo

Styrax, stirako

styrene, stireno

Styria, Stirio

styrofoam, ŝaŭmplasto, stirenplasto

Styx, Stikso

suave, miela, dolĉa

sub, (substitute), anstataŭi [tr]; ~iĝi; ~aĵo; ~ulo; (ship), submarŝipo; (sandwich), bulsandviĉo [or for brevity: bulo, –bulo (e.g.: *steak sub:* bifsteka bulo, stekbulo)] [cp "burger", "hamburger", "cheeseburger"]

sub–, (pfx), sub–

subaltern, subalterna; ~ulo, subulo

subdue, (overcome), subigi; (conquer, vanquish), venki [tr]; (reduce, diminish), mildigi, malintensigi, trankviligi, delikatigi, dolĉigi; **subdued**, (soft, gentle), delikata, milda, dolĉa

suber, subero

suberate, suber/ato; **suberic acid**, ~a acido, oktandiacido

subgum, mikslegoma

subject, (gram; phil; object of med study or experiment etc.), subjekto; (object of study or action etc.), fako, (stud)objekto; (topic, theme), temo [cp "field"]; (citizen, national), regnano, naciano, regato; (expose to, present to, make liable, cause to un-

dergo), submeti [tr], elmeti [tr]; sub-metita, elmetita (e.g.: *subject it to heat:* elmeti ĝin al varmo; *subject oneself to criticism:* submeti [or] el-meti sin al kritikado); **subject to,** (on condition of), kondiĉe (–a) de (e.g.: *closed subject to further notice:* fer-mita kondiĉe de posta avizo; *her ap-proval is subject to higher authority:* ŝia aprobo estas kondiĉa de pli alta aŭtoritato); (prone to, inclined to), in-klina al, ema al (e.g.: *he is subject to outbursts of anger:* li estas ema al ek-splodoj de kolero); (exposed to), el-metita al, submetita al; (under authority of), regata de; **subject mat-ter,** (studo)temo, (stud)objekto
subjective, subjektiva; **subjectivity,** ~eco; **subjectivism,** ~ismo
subjugate, subjugigi
subjunctive, subjunktivo; ~a
sublimate, sublimi [tr]; ~iĝi; (sublimat-ed substance), sublimato
sublime, sublima; (vaporize), ~i [tr]; ~iĝi
subliminal, subliminala
submerge, submerse, mergi [tr]; ~iĝi; **submersion,** ~(iĝ)o; **submersible,** ~ebla
submit, (present, subject, refer), subme-ti [tr]; ~iĝi; (yield), cedi [int]; (pro-pose, suggest), sugesti [tr], prezenti [tr], proponi [tr]; **submission,** ~(iĝ)o; cedo; sugesto, propono; **submissive,** cedema
subordinate, (inferior, secondary, gen), suba, ~ranga, malĉefa; ~ordigi; (person in hierarchy etc.), subalterna; subalternulo, ~ulo, ~rangulo; **insub-ordinate,** malobeema, sendisciplina; **insubordination,** malobeemo
subpoena, juĝalvoki [tr]; ~o
subrogate, anstataŭi [tr]; ~o
sub rosa, sekreta, kaŝa, postkulisa
subscribe, (sign name), subskribi [tr]; (pledge $ contribution), promesi kon-tribui [tr]; **subscribe to,** (periodical, service, etc.), aboni [tr] (e.g.: *sub-scribe to the magazine "Monato":* aboni la revuon "Monato"); (support, endorse, approve), ~i, apogi [tr], apro-bi [tr], subteni [tr], akcepti [tr], kon-

senti [int] (kun, pri); **subscription,** ~o; abono; **subscriber,** abonanto
subscript, indico
subsequent, posta, sekvanta
subservient, (submissive), cedema; (servile), sklav(ec)a; (useful), utila, helpa; **subservience,** ~o; sklaveco; utilo, helpo
subside, (abate, become less active), mildiĝi, moderiĝi, malvigliĝi, malak-tiviĝi, kvietiĝi; (settle, sink, as sedi-ment), sedimenti [int], surfundiĝi; (lower, sink, gen), malleviĝi, sinki [int]
subsidiary, (auxiliary, accessory), akce-sora; (bsns, as re company controlled by another), filio; (subordinate, sec-ondary), sub(rang)a, duaranga
subsidy, subvencio; **subsidize,** ~i [tr] [cp "write: underwrite"]
subsist, (continue), daŭri [int], ~i ekzisti [int], ekzistadi [int]; (maintain own life), sin vivteni (e.g.: *we subsisted on berries:* ni nin vivtenis per beroj); **subsistence,** ~ado, ekzistado; (ap-enaŭa) vivteno (e.g.: *they receive only a subsistence income:* ili ricevas en-spezon nur por apenaŭa vivteno [or] enspezon kiu apenaŭ vivtenas ilin)
substance, (essence, gen), substanco, esenco, elemento; (matter), materio; (chem; specific type of matter), ~o; (solidity), solideco; (possessions), havaĵoj; **substantial, substantive,** (solid, real), ~a; (considerable), konsiderinda, signifa, malbagatela, grava; (gram: n), substantivo; **insub-stantial,** sen~a, malsolida, nereala, febla, malfortika; **in substance,** es-ence, ~e; **white substane of Schwann,** Ŝvanna ingo
substantiate, pruvi [tr], konfirmi [tr]; **transsubstantiate,** transsubstancigi
substitute, anstataŭi [tr] (A–on per B), substitui (B–on al A) [in either case, B replaces A]; ~a, substitua; ~ulo, ~in-to; ~aĵo, substituito, substituajo [cp "surrogate"]; **substitution,** ~(ad)o
substrate, substrato†
subsume, subkuŝ/igi; **be subsumed,** ~i [int]
subtend, substreĉi [tr]

subterfuge, artifiko, ruzo
subterranean, subtera
subtle, subtila; **subtlety,** ~aĵo; ~eco
subtract, subtrahi [tr]; **subtraction,**
~(ad)o
subtrahend, subtrahato
suburb, antaŭurbo, suburbo; **suburban,**
~a; **suburbanite,** ~ano; **suburbia,**
(la) ~aro
subvention, subvencio
subvert, (undermine), subfosi [tr], sub-
mini [tr]; (overthrow), renversi [tr];
subversion, ~(ad)o; renvers(ad)o;
subversive, ~(em)a; renvers(em)a;
~emulo, renversemulo
subway, (urban trains), metroo; ~a; (Br:
underpass), subvojo
succeed, (work well, achieve goal),
sukcesi [int]; (follow, come after),
sukcedi† [tr]; **success,** ~o; **successful,**
~a; **succession,** sinsekvo, serio; suk-
cedo; **successive,** sinsekva; **succes-
sor,** sekvinto; sekvanto; sekvonto;
sukcedanto
succinate, sukcen/ato; **succinic acid,** ~a
acido, butandiacido
succinct, konciza
succor, helpi [tr]; ~o
succory, cikorio
succotash, sukotaŝo*
Succoth, Tendofesto, Festo de Laŭboj
succour, helpi [tr]; ~o
succubus, sukubo
succulent, sukulenta
succumb, cedi [int], fali [int], venkiĝi
such, (of that sort), tia (e.g.: *swimming,
bicycling, and such things:* naĝado,
biciklado, kaj tiaj aferoj; *some such
story:* iu tia rakonto); (in such a way;
to such a degree, extent), tiel (e.g.: *it
is such a nice day:* estas tiel agrabla
tago); **suchlike,** tia, simila; simile;
such as, (for example), ekzemple
[abb: ekz–e], (tia) kiel (e.g.: *find a flat
stone, such as this one:* trovu platan
ŝtonon, ekz–e ĉi tiun [or] trovu platan
ŝtonon kiel ĉi tiun); (of the sort that),
tia kia (e.g.: *a symmetrical tree, such
as grow in open fields:* simetria arbo,
tia kia kreskas en malplenaj kampoj;
such a group as may exist there: tia
grupo kia povus ekzisti tie); **such as**

that (this), (ĉi) tia (e.g.: *there has
never been such a day as this before:*
neniam antaŭe estis ĉi tia tago); **such
as it is,** tia kia ĝi estas; **and such,** kaj
simile [abb: k.s.] [cp "et cetera"]; **as
such,** (as being such a thing), kiel tia
(e.g.: *our argument was not a fight as
such:* nia disputo ne estis batalo kiel
tia); (in itself, per se), en si mem, per
si mem (e.g.: *an organization, as
such, is not enough:* organizo, en si
mem, ne sufiĉas); **at such time,** (at
whatever time, at a certain but unspecified time), tiam kiam (e.g.: *to be
delivered at such time as you choose:*
liverota tiam kiam vi elektos); **at such
place,** tie kie; **for such reason,** tial
kial; **in such manner, in such way,**
tiel kiel; **in such amount,** tiom kiom;
is such that, estas tia ke; estas tiel ke;
such and such, iu aŭ alia (e.g.: *he
lives on such and such a street:* li
loĝas en iu aŭ alia strato)
suck, suĉi [tr]; **sucker,** (one who sucks),
~anto; (device, organ, etc., for sucking), ~ilo; (lollipop), stangobombono; (dupe), dupo; dupigi
suckle, (take milk at breast), mam/suĉi
[int], ~nutriĝi; (give milk), ~nutri [tr],
~suĉigi; **suckling,** suĉinfano
Sucre, Sukro
sucrose, sakarozo
suction, suĉo, ~ado; **suction cup,** ~teni-
lo; **suction pump,** ~pumpilo
Sudan, Sudano; **Sudanese,** ~a; ~ano
sudden, subita
Sudra, ŝudr/ulo; **Sudra caste,** ~o
suds, (sap)ŝaŭmo; **suds (up),** ~igi; ~iĝi;
sudsy, ~a
sue, (law), procesi [int] (kontraŭ, pri)
Sue, (woman's name), Sunjo
suede, Svedledo; ~a
suet, sebo
Suetonius, Suetonio
Suez, (city), Suezo; **Suez Canal,** Kanalo ~a; **Isthmus of Suez,** Istmo ~a
suffer, (undergo unpleasantness), suferi
[tr, int]; (tolerate), toleri [tr]; (allow),
lasi [tr], permesi [tr]; **suffering,** ~ado;
insufferable, netolerebla
suffice, sufiĉi [int]; **sufficient,** ~a; **sufficiency,** ~eco; **insufficient,** ne~a; **in-**

sufficiency, ne~o; (med), insuficienco; **self-sufficient,** sendependa, mem~a; **suffice it to say that,** ~u diri ke

suffix, sufikso

suffocate, sufoki [tr]; ~iĝi [cp "asphyxia: asphyxiate"]

suffragan, sufragano

suffrage, (right to vote), balotrajto, voĉdonrajto; **suffragette,** sufrageto

suffuse, sufuzi [int]; ~iĝi; **suffusion,** ~o

Sufi, Sufio*: **Sufism,** ~ismo; **Sufic,** ~a; ~isma

sugar, (gen), sukero; ~a; **sugarberry,** celtido; **sugar bowl,** ~ujo; **sugarcane,** ~kano; **sugarplum,** bombono; **beet sugar,** bet~o; **blood sugar,** glukozemio, sango~o; **high blood sugar,** hiperglukozemio; **low blood sugar,** hipoglukozemio; **brown sugar,** bruna ~o; **cane sugar,** kan~o, sukrozo; **fruit sugar,** levulozo; **granulated sugar,** kristal~o; **maple sugar,** acer~o; **powdered sugar,** **confectioner's sugar,** pulvor-~o, frandaĵa ~o; **refined sugar,** rafinita ~o

suggest, (propose idea, gen), sugesti [tr]; (hint), duondiri [tr], kvazaŭdiri [tr]; (influence person under hypnosis etc.), sugestii [tr]; **suggestion,** ~(ad)o; sugesti(ad)o; **suggestive,** ~a; sugestia; **suggestible,** sugestiebla; **autosuggestion,** aŭtosugestiado

suicide, suicido, memmortigo, sinmortigo; **suicidal,** ~(em)a; **commit suicide,** mortigi sin, ~iĝi

sui generis, unika

suit, (clothes), kompleto; (legal action), proceso; (cards), emblemo; (be appropriate, acceptable), konveni [int] (al); (be fit, satisfactory), taŭgi [int] (al); (adapt), adapti [tr], taŭgigi; (provide clothes, dress), vesti [tr]; **suitable,** konvena; taŭga, laŭcela; **suitor,** (wooer), amindumanto; (one who sues), procesanto; **suitcase,** valizo; **diving suit,** skafandro; **flying suit, jump suit,** kombineo; **lawsuit,** proceso; **pantsuit,** pantalon~o; **pressure suit,** premokombineo; **side suit,** (bridge), neatuta emblemo; **spacesuit,** (kosma)

skafandro; **swimsuit,** (bottom only, for man or woman), banŝorto; (full, for woman), bankostumo, naĝkostumo; **follow suit,** (cards), sekvi laŭembleme; (act similarly, gen), simile fari [tr], simile agi [int]; **be (one's) strong suit,** (fig), (iu) superi en (e.g.: *math is his strong suit:* li superas en la matematiko)

suite, (of rooms), ĉambraro; (furniture etc.), ensemblo; (mus), suito; (servants, retinue), sekvantaro

sukiyaki, sukijako

Sukkoth, Sukkos, Tendofesto, Festo de Laŭboj

Sula, sulo

Suleiman, Solimano

sulf-, (sulfur, in chem names), sulf(o)–

sulfa, sulfanilamida; **sulfa drug,** ~a drogo

sulfate, sulfato

sulfide, sulfido

sulfinate, sulfinato

sulfinyl, sulfinilo

sulfite, sulfito

sulf(o)–, (sulfur, in chem names), sulf(o)–

sulfonamide, sulfonamido

sulfonate, sulfonato

sulfone, sulfono

sulfonic, sulfona; **sulfonic acid,** ~a acido

sulfonium, sulfonio

sulfonyl, sulfurilo, sulfonilo

sulfoxide, sulfoksido

sulfur, sulfuro; ~a [see also "sulf(o)–"]; **sulfurize,** (treat w sulfur), ~izi [tr]

sulfuric, sulfata; **sulfuric acid,** ~a acido; **fuming sulfuric acid,** oleumo

sulfurous, (containing sulfur), sulfura; **sulfurous acid,** sulfita acido

sulfuryl, sulfurilo, sulfonilo

sulk, paŭti [int]; ~o; **sulky, in a sulk,** ~a

sulky, (light carriage), sulkio‡

Sulla, Sullo

sullen, moroza, malafabla, paŭta

sulphur, (and derivations), [see "sulfur" etc.]

Sulpicius, (Roman name), Sulpicio

sultan, sultano; **sultana, sultaness,** ~ino; **sultanate,** (office), ~eco;

(land), ~ejo
sultry, (hot and humid), sufoke varma, humidvarma; (passionate), pasi(em)a
sum, (any total), sumo; ~igi; ($), mon~o; **sum up**, (total), ~igi; (summarize), resumi [tr]; **lump-sum**, ~pago; ~paga; **in sum**, resume
sumac, sumako; **Japanese sumac**, uruŝio; **poison sumac**, venena ~o
Sumatra, Sumatro; **Sumatran**, ~a; ~ano; ~ana
Sumer, Sumero; **Sumerian**, ~a; ~ano
summa cum laude, [see "cum laude"]
summary, resumo; **summarize**, ~i [tr]
summer, somero; ~a; (pass the summer), (tra)~i [tr]; **summertime**, ~o; ~a; **summer place, summer house, summer residence**, ~domo, ~loĝejo; **midsummer**, ~mezo; ~meza
summit, supro; **summit conference**, (land)estra konferenco
summon, (call), voki [tr]; (to come), al~i [tr]; (to meet), kun~i [tr]
summons, (any request to come), alvoki [tr]; ~o; (by court etc.), juĝ~i [tr]; juĝ~o
sump, (drain pit, cistern, etc.), cisterno; (Br: oilpan), olekuveto; **sump pump**, ~pumpilo
sumptuary, priluksa, kontraŭluksa
sumptuous, luksa
sun, (ast, gen), suno; (expose to sun), ~umi [tr]; (bot), krotalario; **sunny**, ~(plen)a; **sunbath**, ~umado, ~bano; **sunbake, sunbathe**, ~umi (sin), ~baniĝi; **sunburn**, ~bruli [int]; ~brul-igi; ~brulo; **sundial**, ~horloĝo; **sundown, sunset**, ~subiĝo; **sunrise, sunup**, ~leviĝo; **sunshade**, (gen), ~ombrilo; (parasol), ~ombrelo; **sunshine**, ~brilo; **sunspot**, ~makulo
sundae, siropglaciaĵo
Sunda Islands, Insuloj Sundaj; **Sunda Strait**, Sundo
Sunday, dimanĉo
sunder, dis/igi; ~iĝi
sundew, drozero
sundowner, (Aus), nomado, vagulo
sundry, diversaj; **all and sundry**, (senescepte) ĉiuj
sunken, (below adjoining level), subnivela; (underwater), subakva; (hollow),

kava; (pressed down), deprimita
sunn, krotalario
Sunna, Sunnah, Sunao; **Sunni, Sunnite**, ~isto; **Sunnism**, ~ismo
Sun Yat-Sen, Sun Jatsen
Suomi, Suomio, Finnlando
sup, (sip), trinketi [tr]; ~o; (eat supper), vespermanĝi [int]
super, (greater, more, etc.), supera; (excellent), bonega, superba; (excessive), ekscesa; (superintendent), intendanto
super–, (pfx), super–
superannuate, pensi/igi, emeritigi; ~iĝi, emeritiĝi; **superannuation**, (act), ~igo, emeritigo; (pension), ~o
superb, superba, elstara
supercilious, orgojla, aroganta
supererogatory, preterdeva; **supererogation**, ~o
superficial, supraĵa, surfaca
superfluous, superflua
superheterodyne, superheterodino; ~a
superintend, direkti [tr], superrigardi [tr], kontroli [tr]; **superintendent**, intendanto
superior, (better), pli bona; (higher), supera; (person in hierarchy etc.), superulo; **superiority**, pliboneco; supereco; **Lake Superior**, Lago Supera
superlative, superlativo; ~a
supermarket, superbazaro [not "supermerka to"]
supernal, ĉiela
supernova, supernovao†
supernumerary, supernumera; ~ulo
superpose, supermeti [tr]
superscript, superskribo; **superscription**, surskribo
supersede, anstataŭi [tr]
superstition, superstiĉo; **superstitious**, ~a
supervene, okazi [int]
supervise, superrigardi [tr], kontroli [tr], direkti [tr]; **supervision**, ~o, kontrolo, direkto; **supervisor**, superulo, intendanto, vokto, kontrolisto
supinate, supini [tr]; **supination**, ~ado; **supinator**, (muscle), supinatoro
supine, (lying on back), surdorse kuŝanta; (re hand), supinita; (gram form), supino
supper, vespermanĝo; ~i [int]; (light),

supeo; **the Last Supper**, (rel), la Sankta Manĝo
supplant, anstataŭi [tr]
supple, supla
supplement, suplementi [tr]; ~o; **supplemental**, **supplementary**, ~a
suppliant, **supplicant**, petega; ~anto; **supplicate**, ~i [tr]; **supplication**, ~o
supply, provizi (iun per io) (e.g.: *they supplied information to us:* ili ~is nin per informoj); ~o; ~ado; ~aĵo; (deliver), liveri [tr]; liver(ad)o; liver(aĵ)o; (bsns, $: total of goods offered in a market), ofertado (e.g.: *supply and demand:* ofertado kaj mendado); **in short supply**, malabunda, nesufiĉe abunda
support, (bear, hold, brace, uphold, etc.), apogi [tr], subteni [tr]; ~o, subteno; ~ilo (e.g.: *floor supports:* plankaj ~iloj; *support a candidate:* ~i kandidaton); (bear weight), subporti [tr]; (for holding lab equipment), stativo; (provide life needs), vivteni [tr] (e.g.: *he supports his mother:* li vivtenas sian patrinon; *she supports herself by carpentry:* ŝi vivtenas sin per ĉarpentado; *child-support payments:* infanvivtenaj pagoj); (tolerate), toleri [tr]; **supporter**, ~anto, subtenanto; ~ilo, subtenilo; (jockstrap), ingvenzono; **support for**, subteno al
suppose, supozi [tr], premisi [tr]; **supposition**, ~o; **supposed**, (according to supposition), ~a; **supposedly**, ~eble; **presuppose**, antaŭ~i [tr]; **presupposition**, antaŭ~o; **supposing that**, (under the supposition that), ~e ke; **be supposed to**, (must), devi [tr] (e.g.: *we're supposed to finish it by tomorrow:* ni devas fini ĝin ĝis morgaŭ)
suppository, supozitorio
suppress, subpremi [tr]; **suppression**, ~(ad)o; **suppressive**, ~a; **insuppressible**, nebridebla
suppurate, pusi [int]; **suppuration**, ~ado; **suppurative**, ~anta
supra–, (pfx), super–
supreme, (of highest degree, gen), suverena, plej supera, superega (e.g.: *supreme court:* ~a kortumo; *supreme contempt:* ~a malestimo); **suprema-**

cy, ~eco; **supremacist**, ~isto (e.g.: *white supremacist:* blankula ~isto)
sura, (anat), suro; (rel: division of Koran), surao; **sural**, ~a
surcease, ĉeso
surcoat, kuto
surd, (math), neracionala; ~aĵo; (phon), senvoĉa
sure, (certain), certa; ~e; (reliable), fidinda; **sure enough**, tute~e, ja; **to be sure**, **for sure**, (certainly), ~e, sendube; **make sure (of, that)**, sureiĝi (pri, ke); **sure-fire**, sukces~a, ~e sukcesonta; **sure-footed**, firmpieda, nestumblema
surety, (certainty), cert/eco; ~aĵo, garantiaĵo; ($: bond), kaŭcio
surf, surfo; ~(otabul)i [int]; **surfing**, ~(otabul)ado
surface, surfaco; ~a; (emerge), malmergi [tr]; malmergiĝi; **subsurface**, sub~a; **equipotential surface**, (tech), nivoo
surfactant, surfac-aga; ~enzo
surfeit, supersato, eksceso; ~igi
surge, (wave, swell), ŝveli [int], ondi [int]; ~o, ondo; (rush ahead), impeti [int]; impeto; (sudden increase, as elec), impulso; impulsiĝi; **upsurge**, ekkresko, ek~o, ekpliiĝo; **surge protector**, (elec), impuls-blokilo
surgery, kirurg/io; **surgical**, ~ia; **surgeon**, ~o; **plastic surgery**, plastia ~io; **psychosurgery**, psiko~io
Surinam, Surinamo
surly, malafabla, mishumora
surmise, konjekti [tr], supozi [tr]; ~o, supozo
surmount, (overcome, get over), superi [tr]; (conquer), venki [tr]; **insurmountable**, ne~ebla; nevenkebla
surmullet, surmuleto
surpass, superi [tr]
surplice, surpliso
surplus, (bsns), supergajno; (excess), eksceso; ekscesa; troa; (extra), ekstra, nebezonata; ekstraĵo
surprise, surprizi [tr]; ~o; ~a; **surprising**, ~a; **be(come) surprised**, ~iĝi (e.g.: *I'm surprised that he didn't tell me:* mi ~iĝas ke li ne diris al mi)
surrealism, surreal/ismo; **surrealist**,

~isto; **surrealistic,** ~isma
surrender, (capitulate), kapitulaci [int]; ~o; (give up, quit, gen), rezigni [tr]; ~i (pri); (give up, give over), cedi [tr, int], transdoni [tr]; cedo, transdono
surreptitious, ŝtela, kaŝa
surrey, kaleŝo
surrogate, surogato; ~a
surround, (encircle, encompass), ĉirkaŭi [tr]; (Br: border), bordero; **surrounding,** ~a; **surroundings,** ~aĵo(j)
surtout, surtuto
surveillance, kontrolado, gvatado, observado; **keep under surveillance, maintain surveillance over,** ~i [tr], observadi [tr]
survey, (examine, inspect, research), esplori [tr], reserĉi [tr], superrigardi [tr], ekzameni [tr]; ~o, reserĉo, superrigardo, ekzameno; (measure land etc.), termezuri [tr]; termezuro; (study), studi [tr]; studo; (inquire, investigate), enketi [int] (pri); (public opinion), opiniosondi [tr]; opiniosondo; (look around), ĉirkaŭrigardi [tr]; ĉirkaŭrigardo; (act as consultant, use expertise), ekspertizi [int]; **surveying,** termezura; termezurado; **surveyor,** termezuristo
survive, postvivi [tr], transvivi [tr]; **survival,** ~(ad)o; **survivor,** ~into; ~anto; (person rescued, saved), savito
Sus, suso*; Sus scrofa, Sus aper, apro; Sus scrofa domesticus, porko
Susa, Suzo
Susan, Susanna, Susanne, Suzana
suscept, suscepto
susceptance, susceptanco
susceptible, (impressed by), impres/ebla, ~iĝema, afekciiĝema, sentema (e.g.: *susceptible to persuasion:* ~iĝema de persvado); (prone to), ema, inklina (e.g.: *an analysis susceptible to error:* analizo ema al eraro); (can be affected by), influiĝema, influebla, tuŝebla; (to disease), trafiĝema; (phys: affected by magnetism), susceptibla; **susceptibility,** ~ebleco, ~iĝemo, afekciiĝemo, sentemo; emo, inklino, tendenco; influiĝemo; trafiĝemo; susceptibleco

sushi, suŝio
suslik, zizelo
suspect, suspekti [tr]; ~inda; (person), ~ato
suspend, (temporarily remove from position, job; make rule, law etc. inoperative), suspendi [tr]; (hang), pendi [int]; pendigi; (solid particles in liquid or gas), suspensiigi; (keep in suspense, wonder), suspensigi; **suspenders,** (to hold up pants, skirt, etc.), ŝelko [note sing]; **suspension,** ~o; pend(iĝ)o; (condition of solid particles suspended in fluid; any supporting device or framework, as of car, bridge, etc.), suspensio; (the suspended particles), suspensiaĵo; **suspensoid,** suspensoido
suspense, (tense moment), suspenso
suspensory, (ligament, bandage, etc.), suspensorio; ~a
suspicion, suspekto; **suspicious,** (arousing suspicion), ~inda; (feeling suspicion), ~a; (inclined to suspect), ~ema; **beyond suspicion,** ne~ebla
Susquehanna, Suskvehano*
sustain, (continue, maintain, keep up), daŭrigi; (support, gen), subteni [tr]; (provide food, livelihood), vivteni [tr]; (bear weight), subporti [tr]; (encourage, strengthen spirits), kuraĝigi; (endure, suffer, withstand), suferi [tr]; (confirm, corroborate), konfirmi [tr]
sustenance, (food), nutraĵo; (livelihood, support), vivtenado
sutra, sutro
suttee, (custom), satio; (widow), ~ulino; **sutteeism,** ~o
suturarum, ossa suturarum, vormiano
suture, suturo; ~i [tr]
Suva, Suvo*
suzerain, suzerano; **suzerainty,** ~eco
svelte, svelta
swab, (mop), ŝvabri [tr]; ~ilo; (small piece of cotton etc. on stick), tamponeto
Swabia, Ŝvab/io; **Swabian,** ~o; ~a
swaddle, vindi [tr]; **swaddling clothes,** ~otuko
swag, (festoon), festono; ~i [tr]; (lurch, sway), ŝanceliĝi; ŝanceliĝo; (loot), ra-

baĵo; (bundle of belongings), (vag)pako; **swagman**, (Aus), vagpakulo, vagulo, vagabondo
swagger, pavi [int], paradi [int]; ~ado, paradado
Swahili, Svahilo; (la) ~a (lingvo)
swain, amanto
swallow, (down throat, or oth analogous action), gluti [tr]; ~o; ~aĵo; (bird), hirundo; **swallowtail**, hirundovost(aĵ)o; (butterfly), papiliono; **swallow up**, en~i [tr]; **bank swallow**, bordhirundo; **barn swallow**, kamphirundo; **swallow (something) whole**, (lit or fig), en~i (ion) tuta; **hard to swallow**, malfacila akcepti [tr]
swami, (Hindua) majstro
swamp, (gen), marĉo; en~igi; en~iĝi; (overwhelm, inundate), inundi [tr]; inundiĝi; **swampland**, ~ejo
swan, cigno; **black swan**, (*Cygnus stratus*), nigra ~o
swank, (luxurious), luksa; ~o; (brag, swagger), fanfaroni [int]; fanfaronado; **swanky**, ~a
swap, interŝanĝi [tr]; ~o
sward, gazono, herbotapiŝo
swarm, (throng, teem, gen), svarmi [int]; ~o; (bees), esameno; esameni [int]; (climb), grimpi [tr]
swarthy, nigreta, malhela
swash, (splash), plaŭdi [int]; ~o
swashbuckler, fanfaron/ulo; **swashbuckling**, ~a; ~ado
swastika, svastiko
swat, frapi [tr]; **flyswatter**, muŝ~ilo
swatch, (ŝtof)specimeno
swath, falĉolarĝo; **cut a wide swath**, (fig), forte impresi [tr], fari fortan impreson
swathe, vindi [tr]
sway, (reel, rock back and forth), ŝanceli [tr]; ~iĝi; ~(iĝ)o; (up and down), balanci [tr]; balanciĝi; balanc(iĝ)o; (incline; influence), inklinigi, influi [tr]; inklini [int]; influo; (power, control), rego; **swaybacked**, malĝiba; **hold sway**, regi [tr, int]
Swaziland, Svazio†, ~lando†
swear, (vow, make oath), ĵuri [tr, int] (e.g.: *I swear it's true:* mi ~as ke ĝi es-

tas vera); (administer oath to, as in legal proceeding), ~igi; (use obscene language), sakri [int] [see "word: 'four-letter' word"]; **swear by**, ~i je; **swear in**, ~igi; **swear off, forswear**, for~i [tr], forkonfesi [tr]; **swearword**, sakraĵo
sweat, (gen), ŝviti [int]; ~igi; ~o; ~ado; **sweat off**, (weight etc.), for~igi; **sweat out**, (get through difficulty), trasuferi [tr], tra-elteni [tr]; **sweatband**, ~rubando; **sweat shirt**, ~oĵerzo; **sweat pants**, ~pantalono [note sing]; **sweat suit**, ~kompleto
sweater, svetero
Sweden, Sved/io; **Swede**, ~o; **Swedish**, ~a; ~ia
sweep, (w broom; scan, re TV, cmptr, radar screen etc.; or any analogous action of moving through or over), balai [tr]; ~iĝi; ~o; (extend), etendi [tr]; etendiĝi; **sweepstakes**, (any lottery), loterio; (prize), loteria premio; **chimney sweep**, kamen~isto, kamenskrapisto; **(carpet) sweeper**, (tapiŝ)~ilo; **clean sweep**, (win all), kompleta venko; **make a clean sweep (of)**, komplete venki [tr]; **upsweep**, suprenkurbigi; suprenkurbiĝi; suprenkurb(iĝ)o; **upswept**, suprenkurba
sweet, (gen), dolĉa; ~aĵo; ~eco; (candy), ~aĵo, frandaĵo, bombono; **sweeten**, ~igi; ~iĝi; **sweetener**, ~igenzo; **sweetsop**, (fruit), sukerpomo; (tree), sukerpomarbo
swell, (expand, increase, dilate, gen), ŝveli [int]; ~igi; (puff up, distend), pufigi; pufiĝi; (wave), hulo; **swelling**, ~(ad)o; ~aĵo; puf(iĝ)o; (bump, protuberance, as in flesh), tubero
swelter, varmego; ~i [int], esti (ŝvite) ~a; **sweltering**, (ŝvite) ~a
swerve, (subite) devii [int]; (subite) deviigi; (subita) devio
Swietenia mahagoni, mahagono
swift, rapida, fluga; (zool), apuso, murhirundo
swig, gluti [tr]; ~o
swill, (drink), trinkegi [int]; (wash, rinse), tralavi [tr]; (pig slop), porkokaĉo

swim, (move in water), naĝi [tr, int]; ~o; (be dizzy), (kap)turniĝi (e.g.: *my head is swimming:* mia kapo turniĝas) [cp "swirl"]; **swimming pool,** ~ejo; **swimsuit,** [see under "suit"]
swindle, friponi [tr], defraŭdi [tr]; ~aĵo, defraŭdo; **swindler,** ~o
swine, (ge)porko(j)
swing, (like pendulum or arm; pivot), svingi [tr]; ~iĝi; ~(ad)o; ~iĝo; (child's ~ing seat), ~ilo, pendolo; (rock up and down), balanci [tr]; balanciĝi; balanc(iĝ)o; [cp "pendulum", "rock"]; (mus style), ~omuziko; **swing out,** el~i [tr]; el~iĝi; **upswing,** supren~iĝi, suprentendenci [int]; supren~iĝo, suprentendenco; **in full swing,** plene vigla, en plena fervoro
swipe, (steal), ŝteli [tr]; (hit), bati [tr]; bato
swirl, turbuli [int]; ~o; **swirling,** ~a
swish, susuri [int], sibli [int]; ~igi; ~o
Swiss, Sviso; ~a
switch, (elec: to turn on and off), ŝalt/ilo; (elec: from one circuit to another; rr: train from one track to another; etc.), komuti [tr]; komutilo; (rr), trakforko; (exchange, swap), interŝanĝi [tr]; interŝanĝiĝi; interŝanĝo; (change), ŝanĝi [tr]; ŝanĝiĝi; ŝanĝo; (stick, as for whipping), vergo; vergi [tr]; (lash out, whip), vipi [tr]; **switchback,** (zigzag, as in road up steep grade), zigzago; (such a road), zigzagvojo; (rr), zigzagtrako; (Br: roller coaster), ondanta fervojo; **switch off,** mal~i [tr]; mal~iĝi; **switch on,** ~i [tr]; ~iĝi; **gang switch,** ar~ilo; **microswitch,** mikro~ilo; **on-off switch,** tramal~~ilo; **toggle switch,** baskul~ilo, stifto~ilo
Switzerland, Svis/io, ~lando
swivel, (turn), giri [int]; ~igi; (coupling), ~artiko
swizzle, trinkaĵo; **swizzle stick,** kirlileto
swollen, [see "swell"]
swoon, sveni [int]; ~o
swoop, swoop down, falflugi [int]; ~o; **swoop down on,** (to attack), falataki [tr]; **in one fell swoop,** per unuopa svingo
swoosh, ŝuŝi [int]; ~o; (onom), ŝuŝ!

sword, (gen), glavo [cp "saber"]; (long, narrow, straight), spado; **broadsword,** larĝa ~o
sybarite, sibarito; **sybaritic,** ~o; **sybaritism,** ~ismo
Sybil, (woman's name), Sibila
sycamore, (Platanus), platano; (*Acer pseudoplatanus*), ~acero, pseŭdo~a acero; (*Ficus sycamorus*), sikamoro
sycophant, lakeo, jesul(aĉ)o; **sycophancy,** ~eco
Sydney, (man's name or city), Sidnejo
syenite, sienito
syllable, silabo; **syllabic,** ~a; **syllabify,** ~i [tr]; **syllabary,** ~aro; **monosyllabic,** unu~a; **polysyllabic,** plur~a
syllabus, (of course of instruction), instruplano, temaro; (law; any summary), resumo
syllepsis, silepso
syllogism, silogismo; **syllogize,** ~i [int]
sylph, silf(in)o
sylvan, arbar(ec)a
Sylvester, Silvestro
Sylvia, (woman's name), Silvia
Sylvia, (zool), silvio; Sylvia curruca, kuruko; Sylvidae, ~edoj
sylvian, (in anat names), silvia
sylviculture, silvikulturo
sylvite, silvino
Sylvius, Silvio
symbiont, simbioto
symbiosis, simbiozo; **symbiotic,** ~a
symbol, (gen), simbolo; **symbolic,** ~a; **symbolism,** ~ismo; **symbolist,** ~isto; **symbolize,** (be symbol of), ~i [tr] (e.g.: *a white flag symbolizes neutrality:* blanka standardo ~as neŭtralecon); (represent by symbol), ~igi (e.g.: *we symbolized our commitment by exchanging flowers:* ni ~igis nian interdediĉon per interŝanĝi florojn); **symbology,** (study of symbols), ~iko; (use of symbols; symbolism), ~ismo
Symbranchus, simbranko; **Symbranchiformes,** ~oformaj (fiŝoj)
symmetry, simetrio; **symmetrical,** ~a; **symmetrize,** ~igi; **asymmetry,** ne~o
sympathectomy, simpatektomio
sympathetic, (re sympathy), simpatia; (re sympathetic nervous system), sim-

pata; **sympathetic nervous system,** simpato; **parasympathetic,** parasimpata; **parasympathetic nervous system,** parasimpato
sympathicus, simpato
sympathy, (mutual liking, affinity of feelings, harmony, etc.), simpatio; (compassion), kompato; (condolence), kondolenco; **sympathize (with),** ~i [int] (kun); kompati [tr]; kondolenci [tr]
symphony, simfonio; **symphonic,** ~a
symphysis, simfizo
Symphytum,simfito
sympodium, simpodio
symposium, (gen), simpozio
symptom, simptomo; **symptomatic,** ~a; **asymptomatic,** sen~a; **symptomatology,** (all symptoms), ~aro; (study of symptoms), ~ologio
synagogue, sinagogo
synapse, sinapso
synarthrosis, sinartro
sync(h), sinkron/igi; ~iĝi; ~eco; **in (out of) sync,** (ne)~a
synchronous, synchronal, synchronic, sinkrona; **synchronize,** ~igi; ~iĝi; **synchronism,** (synchronous condition), ~eco; (synchronous table), ~ajo, ~a tabelo
synchroscope, sinkroskopo
synchrotron, sinkrotrono
syncline, sinklinalo
syncopate, (gen), sinkop/igi; **syncopated,** ~a; **syncopation,** ~o
syncope, sinkopo
syncretism, sinkretismo; **syncretistic,** ~a; **syncretize,** ~igi
syncytium, sincitio
syndic, sindiko
syndical, (re syndic), sindika; (re syndicalism), sindikatisma; **syndicalism,** ~o
syndicate, (organization, union, etc.), sindikato; (have published in many newspapers etc.), amaspublikigi
syndrome, sindromo; **acquired immune deficiency syndrome,** (abb: AIDS), aideso; **crash syndrome,** kraŝ~o; **Down's syndrome,** la ~o de Down; **Moliere's syndrome,** la ~o de Moliere

synecdoche, sinekdoko
syneresis, sinerezo
synergy, synergism, sinergio; **synergistic,** ~a
synesis, sinetio
synod, sinodo; **synodic(al),** ~a
synonym, sinonimo; **synonymous,** ~a; **synonymy,** (study of synonyms), ~iko; (list of), ~aro [cp "thesaurus"]; (condition of synonymity), ~eco
synopsis, resumo; **synopsize,** ~i [tr]
synoptic, sinoptika
synost(e)o/sis, sinosto; **synosteotic,** ~a
synovia, sinovio; **synovial,** ~a; **synovial fluid,** ~o; **synovial membrane,** ~a membrano
synovitis, sinovito
syntagma, sintagmo
syntax, sintakso; **syntactic,** ~a
synthesis, (gen), sintezo; **synthetic,** ~a; ~aĵo; **synthesize,** ~i [tr]; **synthesizer,** (mus), (muzik)~atoro†; **photosynthesis,** foto~o
syphil–, (med: "syphilis" as combining form), sifil– [cp "syphilis"]
syphilis, sifiliso; **syphilitic,** ~a; ~ulo [see also "syphil–"]
syphiloid, sifiloida
syphilology, sifilologio
syphiloma, sifilomo
syphon, sifono; ~i [tr]
Syracuse, (gen), Sirakuzo
Syria, Sirio; **Syrian,** ~a; ~ano
Syringa, siringo
syringe, injektilo [not "siringo"]; **Pravaz's syringe,** ~o de Pravaz
syringeal, sirinksa
syringectomy, siringektomio
syring(o)–, (med pfx), siring(o)–
syringobulbia, siringobulbio
syringomyelia, siringomjelio
syrinx, (gen), sirinkso
Syrrhaptes, sirapto
Syrtis, (bays, "Major" and "Minor"), Sirtoj
syrup, (gen), siropo; (syrupy medication), looko; **cough syrup,** kontraŭtusa ~o
Sysa, Suzo
system, (gen), sistemo; **systematic, systemic,** ~a; **systematize,** ~igi; **systematics,** sistematiko; **CGS system,** ~o

CGS; **MKS system,** ~o MKS; **MK-SA system,** ~o MKSA; **SI system,** ~o SI; **subsystem,** sub~o; **operating system,** (cmptr), mastruma ~o†

Système International, (abb: SI), Sistemo Internacia (de Unuoj) [abb: SI]

systole, sistolo; **systolic,** ~a; **extrasystole,** krom~o

Syzygium aromaticum, kariofil/arbo, ~mirto

syzygy, sizigio

Szechwan, Siĉuan

T

T, (letter); (suit, fit) to a T, (taŭgi) perfekte; [see also "tee"]
tab, (small projection, as on card for filing), langeto; ~izi [tr]; (small loop), maŝeto; maŝetizi [tr]; (extra airfoil), kromplaneo; (bill, restaurant check, etc.), kalkulo; pick up the tab, pay the tab, pagi la kalkulon; keep tabs on, kontroladi [tr]
Tabanus, tabano; Tabanidae, ~edoj
tabby, (cat), kat(in)o; (striped), (tigro)stria ~o
tabernacle, tabernaklo; Feast of Tabernacles, (rel), Tendofesto, Festo de Laŭboj
tabes, atrofio; tabes (dorsalis), tabeto; tabetic, ~a; ~ulo
tabi, tabio
table, (furniture, or similar-shaped object), tablo; (list of names, values, or oth information), tabelo; (list of previously calculated values), baremo; (official list or statement of $, names, etc.), etato; (Am: postpone a motion, bill, etc.), prokrasti [tr]; (Br: consider motion, bill, etc., now), konsiderigi; roundtable, (rr, to turn locomotive), turnoplato; (discussion group), diskutgrupo, diskut-rondo; turntable, (as in record player), girplato; turn the tables on, renversi la rolojn al; under the table, (covertly), sekrete, kaŝe, postkulise
tableau, (striking scene), (okulfrapa, drameca) sceno; tableau vivant, vivanta bildo
tablet, (pad of paper), paperbloko; (plaque), ŝildo; (panel, board), tabulo; (of clay, etc., as for inscriptions), tabelo; (pill), tablojdo
tabloid, (newspaper), (bild)jurnaleto [not "tablojdo"]; (condensed), kondensita
taboo, tabu, tabuo; ~a
tabular, (flat), plata; (tabulated, re data etc.), tabela
tabula rasa, blanka tabelo
tabulate, (arrange data etc. in table), ta-

beligi; tabulator, ~ilo
tacet, (mus), silentu
tachometer, rivolumetro [not "takimetro"]; tachometry, ~io
tachy–, (tech pfx), taki–
tachycardia, takikardio
Tachyglossus, eñidno
tachymeter, takeometro [not "takimetro"]; tachymetry, ~io
tachyon, takiono
tachypnea, takipneo
tacit, (not expressed), neesprimita, subkomprenita; (silent), silenta
taciturn, silentema, neparolema
Tacitus, Tacito
tack, (small nail), najleto; ~i [tr]; (sewing), duonkudri [tr]; duonkudro; (attach, gen), alfiksi [tr]; (naut: sail against wind by zigzagging), boardi [int], taki [int]; boardigi, takigi; boardo, tako [cp "luff"]; (naut: sail rope), halso; thumbtack, prempinglo [cp "pin: pushpin"]; get down to brass tacks, ekatenti la praktikaĵojn
tackle, (attack, gen. as a task, problem), ataki [tr]; ~o; (sport: throw down, as in football), faligi; ~igisto; (begin dealing w), ektrakti [tr]; (rope and pulleys), takelo; (apparatus, equipment), ilaro, ekipaĵo; block and tackle, [see under "block"]
tacky, (sticky), glueta; (shabby), tombaka, ĉifona; (disgraceful), hontinda
tact, takto; tactful, ~oplena; tactless, sen~a
tactic, taktiko; tactical, ~a
tactile, (re sense of touch), tuŝa; (touchable, tangible), ~ebla
tactual, tuŝa
Tad, (short for "Thaddeus"), Taĉjo
Tadorna, tadorno
tadpole, ranido
Tadzhik, [see "Tajik"]
tael, taelo
taenia, (anat; zool), tenio; taeniasis, ~ozo
Taenia, (zool), tenio
taffeta, tafto; ~a

taffy, tofeo*
tag, (label), etikedo; ~i [tr] (e.g.: *price tag:* prez~o); (piece hanging), pendantaĵo; (tab, small projecting piece), langeto; (hard tip, as on shoelace), laĉferaĵo; (loop for hanging garment), (pendo)maŝo; (child's game of catching and touching), tuŝludo; (touch, as in baseball or game of tag), tuŝi [tr]; tuŝo; **tag along, tag after**, kuniri [int] (kun), postiri [int] (post); **play tag**, tuŝludi [int]
Tagalog, (person), Tagalogo*; (language), (la) ~a (lingvo)
Tagetes, tageto
Tagus, (river), Taño
Tahiti, Tahitio; **Tahitian**, ~a; ~ano
taiga, tajgo
Taihang (Shan), (Montaro) Tajhang
tail, (anat, or similar object), vosto; (of shirt, coat), basko; (of plane), empeno; (reverse side of coin etc.), reverso; (rear part, gen), postaĵo; (follow and spy), gvatsekvi [tr]; gvatsekvanto; **tail off, tail away**, malpliiĝi, malfortiĝi, estingiĝi (iom post iom); **tail end**, ~finaĵo; **tailpiece**, (any end piece), postpeco; (printed design), (fina) vinjeto; **tailwind**, postvento; **bobtail**, tond~a; tond~ulo; **broadtail**, (sheep), astrakana ŝafo; (pelt), astrakano; **wag one's tail**, ~umi [int]; **turn tail (and run)**, senkuraĝiĝi kaj forkuri [int]
tailor, (re clothes), tajloro; ~a; ~i [tr]; (form, fashion, gen), fasoni [tr]; **tailor-made**, (lit or fig), aparte fasonita, speciale fasonita, almezurita, laŭmezura
taint, (infect), infekti [tr]; ~iĝi; ~(ad)o; (contaminate), malpurigi; (putrefy), putrigi; putriĝi; (corrupt), deprave), korupti [tr]; korupto; (disgrace, sully), makuli [tr]; makulo
Taipei, Tajpeo
Taiwan, Tajvan
Taiyuan, Tajjuan
Tajik, Taĝiko; **Tajiki**, ~a; **Tajikistan**, ~io, ~lando
Taj Mahal, Taĝ-Mahalo
Tajo, Taño
take, (get, catch, grasp, hold, choose, derive, buy, rent, acquire, etc.; ingest food, drink, medication; understand, consider, assume; etc.), preni [tr]; ~iĝi; ~(iĝ)o; ~aĵo (e.g.: *take a book from the shelf:* ~i libron de la breto; *take my hand:* ~u mian manon; [making purchase], *I'll take that one:* mi ~os tiun; *take a pill after supper:* ~i pilolon post la vespermanĝo; *it takes its name from:* ĝi ~as sian nomon de; *I took you for an intruder:* mi ~is vin por enŝtelinto; *don't take it so seriously:* ne ~u ĝin tiel serioze; *the give and take:* la dono kaj ~o); (capture, seize), ~i, kapti [tr]; (win, as trick at cards), ~i, gajni [tr]; (charm), ĉarmi [tr] (e.g.: *I was taken by their friendliness:* mi estis ĉarmita de [or: min ĉarmis] ilia amikeco); (subscribe to), aboni [tr] (e.g.: *we take the Post:* ni abonas la Post-on); (accept), ~i, akcepti [tr] (e.g.: *take the blame:* akcepti la kulpon); (withstand, tolerate), toleri [tr], elteni [tr, int] (e.g.: *I can't take the cold weather there:* mi ne povas toleri [or] elteni la malvarman veteron tie); (apply, use on), apliki [tr], utiligi (e.g.: *take a broom to the floor:* apliki balailon al la planko); (travel by), ~i, veturi [int] per, iri [int] per (etc.) (e.g.: *take an S-2 bus to my house:* ~u buson S-2 al mia domo; *will you take a train or plane to Boston?:* ĉu vi veturos al Bostono per trajno aŭ avio?); (follow, as road), sekvi [tr] (e.g.: *take Highway 29:* sekvu Ŝoseon 29; *we took the scenic route:* ni sekvis la pejzaĝan itineron); (spend time), pasigi (e.g.: *don't take all day in the bathroom:* ne pasigu la tutan tagon en la banĉambro); (require), postuli [tr] (e.g.: *travel takes money:* vojaĝado postulas monon; *the project took years:* la projekto postulis jarojn); (last through time), daŭri [int] (e.g.: *how long will the trip take?:* kiom longe la vojaĝo daŭros?; *it will take a week:* ĝi daŭros unu semajnon); (be necessary), necesi [int] (e.g.: *it takes time to do that:* necesas tempo por fari tion); (be enrolled in course), studi [tr], matrikuliĝi en (e.g.: *she's taking physics and history:* ŝi studas la fiz-

ikon kaj historion); (do, make), fari [tr] (e.g.: *take notes:* fari notojn; *take a walk:* fari promenon) [note: "taking" an action is often expressed in Esperanto by the simple verb (e.g.: *take a bath, a nap, a walk:* bani sin, dormeti, promeni); see subentries below]; (lead, be the way to), konduki [tr] (e.g.: *this road takes you to the lake:* ĉi tiu vojo kondukas vin al la lago); (draw out), ĉerpi [tr] (e.g.: *take water from the well:* ĉerpi akvon el la puto; *take sand from the box:* ĉerpi sablon el la skatolo); (escort, accompany), akompani [tr] (e.g.: *he took her to the dance:* li akompanis ŝin al la danco); (subtract), de~i [tr], subtrahi [tr] (e.g.: *take 2 from 8:* de~i [or] subtrahi 2 de 8); (take root, as re plant, movement, campaign; become established), enradikiĝi; establiĝi; (be effective, have effect), efektiviĝi, ekefiki [int] (e.g.: *the vaccination didn't take:* la vakcinado ne efektiviĝis); ($ received), enspezo; **take aback,** konsterni [tr]; **take after,** (resemble), simili [tr]; (chase), postkuri [tr]; **take apart,** (into pieces), dis(pec)igi; (dismantle, disassemble), malmulti [tr]; **take away,** for~i [tr]; **take back,** (retract statement), maldiri [tr], re~i [tr] sian diraĵon; (get or carry object back), re~i [tr]; **take a bath,** sin bani, baniĝi; **take cover,** sin kaŝi, kaŝiĝi; **take down,** (something set up), malstarigi; (dismantle, disassemble), malmunti [tr]; (lower, bring down), mallevi [tr]; (put in writing), surpaperigi; (take note of), noti [tr]; (record, gen), registri [tr]; **take effect,** ekefiki [int], ekvalidi [int]; **take exception to,** protesti [tr]; **take five (ten, etc.),** (short break, pause), paŭzi [int] kvin (dek, etc.) (minutojn); **take for,** (regard as, mistake for), ~i por; **take hold,** (take effect), ekefiki [int]; (grasp), ekkroĉi [tr]; **take in,** (admit, receive), en~i [tr], ricevi [tr]; (accept, receive in home), akcepti [tr]; (include, comprise), inkludi [tr]; (understand), kompreni [tr]; (cheat, trick), superruzi [tr], trompi [tr]; (by inhal-

ing, sucking, osmosis, etc.), sorbi [tr]; (visit), viziti [tr]; **take it,** (suppose, conclude), supozi [tr], konkludi [tr] (e.g.: *I take it you're hungry:* mi supozas ke vi malsatas); (tolerate), elteni [tr, int], toleri (ĝin) (e.g.: *I can't take it any more:* mi ne plu povas elteni); **take it easy,** (relax), malstreĉiĝi; (not hurry), ne hasti [int], ne urĝi sin; **take it from,** (believe, rely on), kredi [tr], fidi [tr]; **take (it) lying down,** senreziste akcepti (ĝin); **take it or leave it,** tio aŭ nenio; akceptu ĝin aŭ ne; **take it out of one,** ellacigi; **take it out on,** venĝi sin kontraŭ; **take it upon oneself,** ~i al si [or] doni al si la devon [or] taskon; **take a nap,** dormeti [int]; **take off,** (clothing etc.), demeti [tr]; (remove, gen), for~i [tr], forigi; (leave, gen), foriri [int] (e.g.: *the meeting was boring, so I took off:* la kunveno estis enuiga, do mi foriris); (depart from certain place), deiri [int] (e.g.: *the plane took off from Rome:* la avio deiris de Romo); (in many directions), disiri [int] (e.g.: *after the meeting we all took off:* post la kunveno ni ĉiuj disiris); (fly), ekflugi [int] (e.g.: *the bird took off at the noise:* la birdo ekflugis ĉe la bruo); (start going, gen), ekiri [int]; (remain absent, as from work), resti for, forresti [int] (e.g.: *I took off sick yesterday:* mi forrestis pro malsano hieraŭ; *I'll take off a week for vacation:* mi forrestos unu semajnon por ferio); (deduct, subtract), subtrahi [tr], de~i [tr]; ($), depagi [tr]; dekalkuli [tr] [see "deduct"]; **take-off,** (caricature), karikaturo; **take on,** (assume, get), al~i [tr]; (receive), ricevi [tr]; (acquire), akiri [tr]; (employ person), dungi [tr]; (undertake), entrepreni [tr]; **take out,** (take away), for~i [tr], forigi; (take out of), el~i [tr]; (carry out, as food from restaurant), elporti [tr]; (obtain, acquire, as insurance), akiri [tr]; (escort, have date w), akompani [tr], rendevui [int] kun; **take over,** (take control), akiri regon super, ekregi [tr]; (acquire possession), trans~i [tr], ekposedi [tr]; **take pity on,** (ek)kompati [tr]; **take**

possession of, ekposedi [tr], trans~i [tr]; **take a shower,** sin duŝi, duŝiĝi; **take to,** (develop habit of), ek...adi, komenci ~adi (e.g.: *he took to smoking:* li ekfumadis; *she took to staying up late:* ŝi komencis restadi maldorma malfrue); (like), ekŝati [tr] (e.g.: *the cat quickly took to its new master:* la kato rapide ekŝatis sian novan mastron); (go to, into), iri al, iri en, aliri [tr], eniri [tr] (e.g.: *he took to the woods to hide:* li eniris la arbaron por sin kaŝi); **take up,** ~i, al~i [tr]; (raise, lift), levi [tr]; (make shorter, as garment), mallongigi; (constrict, as drawstring), stringi [tr]; (absorb), ensorbi [tr]; (accept, as task, offer, challenge, etc.), akcepti [tr]; (undertake), entrepreni [tr]; (begin to deal w), ektrakti [tr]; (start), komenci [tr]; (occupy, as volume, space, time), okupi [tr] (e.g.: *the water takes up 3 liters:* la akvo okupas 3 litrojn; *the discussion took up 2 hours:* la diskuto okupis 2 horojn); (resume something interrupted), rekomenci [tr]; rekomenciĝi; (become interested in), interesiĝi pri, ekdediĉi sin al; **take up with,** (as friend, companion), kunuliĝi kun; **take someone up on,** akcepti ies (proponon, oferton, sugeston, etc.); **take one's time,** lanti [int], malhasti [int], ne rapidi [int], senhaste ~i; **take one for a ride,** (deceive, trick), tromplogi [tr]; **intake,** en~o; en~ejo; **overtake,** devanci [tr]; **uptake,** (taking up, drawing up, etc.), al~o; **quick (slow) on the uptake,** (mal)rapida kompreni [tr], (mal)rapide komprenanta; **be taken with,** esti ĉarmita de

talc, talko; ~i [tr]

talcum, talcum powder, talk/a pulvoro, ~a pudro

tale, (story), rakonto; (lie), mensogo, fablaĵo; **fairy tale,** (fe)fabelo; **tall tale,** blago; **tell a tall tale,** blagi [int]

talent, (skill), talento [cp "skill"]; (ancient weight and $), talanto; **talented,** ~a

taler, talero

Talien, Dajren

talipes, bulpiedo

talisman, talismano

Talitrus, talitro

talk, (gen), paroli [int]; ~o; (long; informal lecture), ~adi [int], prelegi [int]; ~ado, prelego; (chat, babble), babili [int]; babil(ad)o; (gossip), klaĉi [int]; klaĉo; (manner of speech, dialect), lingvaĵo, dialekto; **talkative, talky,** babilema; **talk back (to),** (sass, answer rudely), repliki [tr, int] (al); **talk big,** (boast), fanfaroni [int]; **talk down,** (silence by talking louder etc.), superkrii [tr]; **talk down to,** fieraĉe al~i [tr]; **talk (one) into,** (persuade), persvadi [tr] (iun) (pri io, fari ion); **talk out,** (discuss), diskut(ad)i [tr, int] (pri); **talk (one) out of,** (dissuade), malpersvadi [tr] (iun) (pri io, pri fari ion); **talk over,** (discuss), diskuti [tr, int] (pri), pri~i [tr], (pri)diskuti [tr]; **small talk,** babilado; **sweet-talk,** (flatter), flati [tr]; flat(ad)o; **the talk of the town,** ĉies klaĉo

tall, alta (e.g.: *a tall tree, person:* ~a arbo, homo; *two meters tall:* du metrojn ~a)

tallow, sebo

tally, (count), kalkuli [tr]; ~o; (conform, be in accord), akordi [int], konformiĝi; akordigi, konformigi; **stroke tally,** strek~i [tr]; strek~o

Talmud, Talmudo; **Talmudical,** ~a; **Talmudist,** ~isto

talon, (claw), ungego; (cards), talono

Talpa, talpo; **Talpidae,** ~edoj; **Talpinae,** ~enoj

talus, (bone), talo; (slope), taluso; (rock debris, as at base of cliff), rubo

tamandua, Tamandua, tamanduo

tamarind, (tree or fruit), tamarindo; **Tamarindus,** tamarindo

tamarisk, tamarisko; **Tamarix,** tamariko

tambour, (any drum), tamburo; (embroidery frame), brodoframo

tambourin, tamburino

tambourine, tamburino

tame, malsovaĝa; ~igi

Tamerlane, Timur

Tamil, (person), Tamilo; (gen), ~a; (la) ~a (lingvo)

tam-o'-shanter, skota ĉapo

tamp, (compact, pack down), kompakti-gi; (pack, plug drill hole for blasting etc.), ŝtopi [tr]
tamper (with), (mess w, so as to damage), tuŝaĉi [tr], tuŝi-fuŝi [tr]; (meddle, get involved), miksiĝi en, sin miksi en
tampon, tampono; ~i [tr]
tan, (color), brun/eta; ~eto; (treat hide), tani [tr]; **tanner**, tanisto; **tannery**, tanejo; **suntan**, sun~o; sun~a; sun~igi; sun~iĝi
Tanacetum, tanaceto
tanager, tanagro
Tanagra, Tanagro
Tanagris, tanagro
tandem, tandemo; ~a; ~e; **in tandem**, ~e
tang, (taste), (akra) gusto, (akra) saporo; **tangy**, akragusta
Tanganyika, (region; former country), Tanganjik/io; **Lake Tanganyika**, Lago ~o
tangent, (sine_ cosine), tangento [abb: tan]; (touching but not intersecting), tanĝanta; tanĝanto; **cotangent**, kotangento; **be tangent to**, tanĝi [tr]
tangential, (touching, as tangent), tanĝanta; (superficial), surfaca, supra-ĵa
tangerine, mandarino
tangible, palpebla, sentebla, materia
Tangier, Tanĝero
tangle, (snarl, disorder, knot, etc.), impliki [tr]; ~iĝi; ~aĵo; (seaweed: *Laminaria*), laminario; **disentangle**, mal~i [tr]; mal~iĝi
tango, tango
Tangshan, Tangŝan
tank, (large container), cisterno [cp "contain: container"]; (armed mil vehicle), tanko; **tanker**, (ship), ~ŝipo; (truck), ~kamiono; (rr car), ~vagono; **antitank**, (mil), kontraŭtanka; **tank sinker**, (Aus), lagetfosisto; **gas tank**, (of car etc.), benzinujo, kanistro; **think tank**, cerbumkomitato
tanka, tankao
tankard, tasego, trinkpoto
tannic, tan/acida; **tannic acid**, ~a acido
tannin, tanino
tansy, tanaceto

tantalate, tantalato; **tantalic acid**, ~a acido
tantalize, tantaligi; **tantalizing**, ~a
tantalum, tantalo
Tantalus, Tantalo
tantamount, ekvivalenta, egalvalora, samvalora
tantra, **Tantra**, tantro, T~o; **tantric**, ~a
tantrum, koleroŝtormo
Tanzania, Tanzanio
Tao, Tao; **Taoism**, Taoismo; **Taoisto**, Taoisma; Taoisto
tap, (knock lightly), frapeti [tr]; ~iĝi; ~(iĝ)o; (touch lightly), tuŝeti [tr]; tuŝetiĝi; tuŝet(iĝ)o; (click, clack), klaki [int]; klako; (onom), klak!; (metal piece on shoe), klakilo; (faucet), krano; (stopper), ŝtopilo, ŝtopkejlo; (make hole in barrel etc.), spili [tr]; (draw liquid off from container or pipe; fig: any drawing from), deĉerpi [tr] (e.g.: *tap one's expertise:* deĉerpi ies ekspertizon); (threaded hole in metal part), ŝraŭbino; (thread w such a hole), ŝraŭbinizi [tr]; (make elec connection), konekti [tr] (kun); konektiĝi (kun); konekto; **on tap**, (as draft beer), ĉerpebla
tapa, brusonetiŝelo; **tapa cloth**, ~a ŝtofo
tape, (gen), bendo; (adhesive), glu~o; (fasten w tape), (glu)~i [tr]; (taperecord, audio or video), sur~igi; **tape deck**, ~okompleto; **tape measure**, mezur~o, mezurrubando; **taperecord**, sur~igi; **tape recorder**, (magnetic), magnetofono; (digital), (diĝita†) aŭdbendomaŝino; **adhesive tape**, (cloth, as for bandages), tol~o; **cellophane tape**, (or similar transparent tape), glu~o; **digital audio tape**, diĝita† aŭdbendo; **electrical tape**, **friction tape**, **insulating tape**, izol~o, izolrubando; **magnetic tape**, son~o; **red tape**, burokrataĵoj; **tickertape**, paper~o; **videotape**, vid~o; vid~igi; **videotape machine**, **videotape recorder**, vidomagnetofono [see also "record"]
taper, (narrow), mallarĝ/igi; ~iĝi; ~igo; ~iĝo; (lessen), malpliigi; malpliiĝi; malpliigo; malpliiĝo; (to a point), pintiĝi; (candle), kandeleto

tapestry, tapiserio
tapioca, tapioko; ~a
tapir, tapiro
Tapirus, tapiro
tappa, [see "tapa"]
tappet, levbuteo, puŝbuteo
taps, (bugle call), dormsignalo
tar, gudro; ~a; ~i [tr]; tar boy, (Aus), helpanto (en ŝaftondejo)
tarantella, (dance, mus), tarantelo
Taranto, Tarento
tarantula, tarantulo
Taraxacum, leontodo, buterfloro
Tardigrada, tardigradoj
tardigrade, tardigrado
tardy, (late), malfrua; (slow), malrapida
tare, (weight of container, vehicle), taro; ~a; ~i [tr]; (Bib: weed), lolo
Tarentula, tarantulo
Tarentum, Tarento
target, (anything aimed at; any goal), celo; (concentric rings etc. for shooting practice), ~tabulo
tariff, tarifo; ~i [tr]
Tarim (River), (Rivero) Tarim
tarmac, (gudro)makadamo
Tarn (River), (Rivero) Tarno
tarnish, malbril/igi; ~iĝi; ~aĵo
taro, kolokasio
tarot, tarot card, (each card), taroko; tarot deck, ~a kartaro, ~aro
tarp(aulin), baŝo†
Tarpeia, Tarpeian, tarpeja
Tarquin(ius), Tarkvinio
tarragon, drakunkolo
tarry, resti [int], atendi [tr, int]
tarsal, [see "tarsus"]
tarsalgia, tarsalgio
Tarshish, Tarŝiŝo
tarsier, tarsio
tarsus, (bone), tarso; (of eyelid), tarzo; tarsal, ~a; tarza
Tarsus, (city), Tarzo
tart, (sharp taste), akr(agust)a; (pie etc.), torteto; (whore), putino
tartan, (plaid; boat), tartano
tartar, (gen), tartro; tartar sauce, tatara saŭco
Tartar, Tataro
tartaric, tartra; tartaric acid, ~a acido
Tartarus, Tartaro
tartrate, tartrato

Tartuffe, Tartufo
task, tasko; task force, laborgrupo; take to task, call to task, riproĉi [tr]
Tasmania, Tasmanio
tassel, kvasto
Tasso, Tasso
taste, (flavor; preference, judgment, as for music, style, etc.), gusto (e.g.: the taste of onion: la ~o de cepo; a house furnished with good taste: domo meblita kun bona ~o) [cp "flavor"]; (have flavor of), ~i [int] (–e, je –o) (e.g.: the soup tastes good, bitter, salty: la supo ~as bone, amare, sale; the eggs tasted of burned butter: la ovoj ~is je bruligita butero); (perceive flavor; try, test; one of 5 senses; fig: experience), ~umi [tr]; ~umo (e.g.: I taste sugar in the coffee: mi ~umas sukeron en la kafo; a taste of freedom: ~umo de libereco; taste it to see if it is done: ~umi ĝin por vidi ĉu ĝi estas kuirita); tasty, bon~a; taster, (wine etc.), ~umisto; tasteful, in good taste, ~oplena; tasteless, in bad taste, mis~a†, ~omanka, sen~a; aftertaste, post~o; distasteful, malagrabla; foretaste, antaŭ~o; taste bud, ~oburĝono; to (one's) taste, laŭ~e, laŭ (ies) ~o; each to his own taste, there's no accounting for taste, it's a matter of taste, al ĉiu sia ~o
ta-ta! (onom: trumpets etc.), trateratra!
tatami, tatamo
Tatar, Tataro; ~a
tatter, ĉifono; ~igi; ~iĝi; tattered, ~a
tatterdemalion, ĉifonulo
tattle, klaĉi [int]; ~o; tattler, ~emulo
tattoo, (skin design), tatui [tr]; ~aĵo; (drumming), tamburado; (mil spectacle), (militeca) spektaklo, procesio; tattooing, ~(ad)o
tau, taŭ [see § 16]
taunt, moki [tr], ~inciti [tr], ~riproĉi [tr]; ~(incit)o, ~riproĉo
Taurus, (ast), Taŭro; Taurus Mountains, Montaro Taŭruso
taut, streĉita
tautology, taŭtologio; tautological, ~a
tautomer, taŭtomero; tautomerism, ~io
tavern, drinkejo; (also serving food), ta-

verno
tawdry, puca, pava, ornamaĉa
tawny, flavbruna
tax, ($), imposti [tr]; ~o; (burden), ŝarĝi [tr]; ŝarĝo (e.g.: *the task taxed all her abilities:* la tasko ŝarĝis ĉiujn ŝiajn kapablojn); **taxation**, ~ado; **taxable**, ~ebla; **tax-free**, sen~a; sen~e; **tax-deductible**, ~e dekalkulebla; **tax-exempt**, ne~ebla; **excise tax**, akciso; **income tax**, enspez~o; **(in)direct tax**, (ne)rekta ~o; **luxury tax**, luksaĵ~o; **overtax**, ($), tro~i [tr]; (demand), tropostuli [tr]; **property tax**, bien~o; **surtax**, sur~i [tr]; super~o
taxi, (taxicab), taksio; (move on runway, re plane), rulkuri [int]; rulkurigi
taxidermy, bestrembur/ado; **taxidermist**, ~isto
taximeter, taksimetro
taxis, (tropism), taksio, tropismo; (manipulation to reorient displaced organ etc.), taksiso
taxon, taksono
taxonomy, taksonomio; **taxonomic**, ~a
Tbilisi, Tifliso
tea, (plant; drink), teo; (gathering to drink tea and converse), ~kunveno; (Aus: evening meal), vespermanĝo **teabag**, ~saketo; **teapot**, ~kruĉo; **Oswego tea**, monardo; **Paraguay tea**, mateo; **sassafras tea**, sasafrasa ~o
teach, (gen), instrui [tr]; (in complete detail), erudi [tr]; **teacher**, ~isto; **self-taught**, memlerninta, aŭtodidakta; **self-taught person**, aŭtodidakto
teak, (tree), tektono; (wood), ~a ligno
team, (sport etc.; [fig], any work group), teamo; ~a; (draft animals), jungitaro; (kun)jungi [tr]; **team up**, ~iĝi; **teammate**, sam~ano; **teamster**, kamionisto; **teamwork**, ~laboro, kunlaboro; **bullock team**, (Aus), tirbovaro
tear, (rip), ŝiri [tr]; ~iĝi; ~(iĝ)o; (run, dash), kuregi [int], impeti [int]; (eye fluid), larmo; larmi [int]; (causing tears, as tear gas), larmiga; **tear apart**, dis~i [tr]; dis~iĝi; **tear down**, (demolish), disbati [tr], malkonstrui [tr]; (dismantle machine etc.), malmunti [tr]; (take down something set

up), malstarigi; (make disintegrate), diserigi; **teardrop**, larmero, larmoguto; **tearful**, larmoplena, plorema; **tear gas**, larmiga gaso; **tear jerker**, larmigilo; larmiga; **crocodile tears**, hipokritaj larmoj; **burst into tears**, ekplori [int]
tease, (mock mildly), moketi [tr]; ~emulo; (annoy, harass), turmenteti [tr]; (excite, arouse), inciteti [tr]; (flirt), koketi [int] (al); koketul(in)o; (comb hair back), retrokombi [tr]; (card wool etc.), kardi [tr]
teasel, teasle, dipsako
teat, (on breast, udder), cico; (any nipple-shaped object, as of rubber), ~umo
teazel, teazle, dipsako
tech, (in school name: polytechnic), politekniko; ~a; **high-tech**, alt-teknika
technetium, teknecio
technical, teknika; **technicality**, ~aĵo; ~eco [cp "technique"]
technician, teknikisto
technicolor, teknikoloro; ~a
technique, tekniko, metodo
technocrat, teknokrato; **technocracy**, ~io; **technocratic**, ~ia
technology, (study, sci of), teknologio; (practice; artifacts), tekniko; **technological**, ~a; teknika
technopathy, teknopatio
Tectona, tektono
tectonic, (re global crust), tektona; (re construction), konstrua; (re arch), arkitektura; **tectonics**, tektoniko
Ted(dy), Teĉjo
Te Deum, tedeumo
tedium, tedo; **tedious**, ~a
tee, (golf or football), konus/eto, apogo~o; sur~igi; **tee off**, (de~e) komenciĝi; **to a tee**, precize [see also "T"]
teem, svarmi [int], pululi [int]
teen, teenager, dekkelk/jarulo, adoleskanto; **teenage(d)**, ~jara; **teens**, (teenagers), ~jaruloj; (teenage years), ~aj jaroj; (second decade of a century), dekaj jaroj; (numbers 13 to 19), (la) dekoj [note: in Esperanto "la dekoj" include 10–19] (e.g.: *the temperature was in the teens:* la temperaturo estis en la dekoj)

teeny, teeny-weeny, eteta
teepee, [see "tepee"]
teeter, ŝanceli [tr]; ~iĝi; **teeter-totter,** baskulo
teethe, dentopuŝi [int]; **teething ring,** mordoringo
Tegenaria, tegenario
tegument, tegumento
Teh(e)ran, Teherano
Tejo, (river), Taño
telautograph, teleaŭtografo; ~i [tr]
Tel Aviv, Tel-Avivo
tele–, (pfx), tele–
telecast, vidsendi [tr]; ~(ad)o
telecommute, telenaveti [int]
telegram, telegramo
telegraph, telegrafo; ~i [tr]; **telegraphy,** ~io; **phototelegraph,** foto~i [tr]
telekinesis, telekinezo
Telemachus, Telemaño
telemark, telemarko
telemeter, telemetro; ~i [tr]; **telemetry,** ~io
telencephalon, telencefalo
teleology, teologio; **teleological,** ~a
teleost, teleosto
Teleostei, teleosteoj
telepath, telepati/ulo; **telepathy,** ~o; **telepathic,** ~a
telephone, telefono; ~i [tr]; **telephonic,** (by telephone), ~a; (re telephony), ~ia; **telephony,** ~io; **telephone book,** ~libro; **telephone booth,** ~budo; **telephone exchange,** (network), ~reto; **telephone number,** ~numero; **cellular telephone,** ĉela ~o; **cordless telephone,** senŝnura ~o; **dial telephone,** disko~o; **push-button telephone,** prembutona ~o; **rotary telephone,** rotacia ~o; **touch-tone telephone,** sonbutona ~o; **video telephone, videophone,** vido~o, bildo~o; vido~i [tr], bildo~i [tr]; **play telephone tag,** ludi ~an tuŝludon
teleport, teleporti [tr]; **teleportation,** ~ado
telescope, teleskopo; **telescopic,** ~a; **telescopy,** ~io; **radiotelescope,** radio~o
telesthesia, teleestezo
teleutospore, teleŭtosporo
televise, telesendi [tr]; **television,** (re-

ceiving set), televidilo; (act of viewing television), televidado; (gen technique; medium), televizio
telex, teleksot; ~i [tr]
telfer, telfero; ~i [tr]
teliospore, teleŭtosporo
tell, (say), diri [tr] (ion al iu) (e.g.: *tell me the truth:* ~u al mi la veron); (relate), rakonti [tr] (ion al iu) (e.g.: *tell me about your trip:* rakontu al mi pri via vojaĝo); (notify, inform), sciigi (iun pri io, al iu pri io), informi [tr] (iun pri io); (distinguish), distingi [tr] (e.g.: *I can't tell which is my umbrella:* mi ne povas distingi kiu estas mia ombrelo); (order), ordoni [tr] (ion al iu) (e.g.: *they told us to leave:* ili ordonis al ni foriri); (assure, state emphatically), certigi (ion al iu); (have effect), efiki [int] (sur); (mound of ancient ruins), ruinmonteto; **teller,** (bank clerk), komizo, giĉetisto; (vote counter), (voĉdon)nombristo; (of tales), rakontisto; **telling,** (meaningful), signifoplena; (forceful), frapa, efika; **tell of,** (indicate), indiki [tr]; **tell off,** (rebuke), riproĉi [tr]; **tell on,** (affect), efiki [int] sur; (denounce, tattle), denunci [tr]; (gossip about), klaĉi [int] pri; **telltale,** (tattler), disbabilanto, denuncemulo, klaĉemulo; (revealing), rivela, malkaŝa; **foretell,** antaŭ~i [tr], profeti [int] (pri), priprofeti [tr]; **I told you so!,** mi ja avertis vin!, tiel mi ja diris!
tellurate, telurato; **telluric acid,** ~a acido
tellurite, telurito
tellurium, teluro
telly, [see "televise"]
telpher, telfero; ~i [tr]
temblor, tertremo, sismo
temerity, temerar/eco, malzorgemo; **temerarious,** ~a
temper, (mood, disposition), temperamento, humoro (e.g.: *have a calm temper:* havi trankvilan ~on); (anger), kolero; (tendency to anger), koleremo; (moderate, make mild), moderigi, mildigi; (harden steel; toughen, gen), hardi [tr]; harditeco; (mus), tempero; temperi [tr]; **even-tempered,**

egal–anima; **hot-tempered, short-tempered**, kolerema; **hold (keep) one's temper**, konservi sian trankvilon, resti trankvila; **lose one's temper**, koleriĝi, perdi sian trankvilon
tempera, tempero; ~i [tr]
temperament, (disposition), temperamento; (mus: temper), tempero; **temperamental**, ~a
temperance, modereco, sinbridado
temperate, (moderate), modera; (weather, climate), mezvarma, ~klimata; **intemperate**, mal~a, ekscesa
temperature, (measure of heat), temperaturo; (fever), febro; **take one's temperature**, kontroli ies ~on
tempest, tempesto; **tempestuous**, ~a
template, ŝablono
temple, (rel building, lit or fig), templo; (anat), tempio
tempo, tempo
temporal, (re time), tempa; (transitory), dum~a, efemera; (worldly), monda; (anat: re temple), tempia; **temporal bone**, temporalo
temporary, provizora, dumtempa, intertempa
temporize, (stall for time), prokrastadi [tr], evitadi [tr]
tempt, tenti [tr]; **temptation**, ~(iĝ)o; **tempting**, ~a
tempura, tempuro
ten, dek [see § 19]
tenable, defendebla
tenacious, tenaca; **tenacity**, ~eco
tenant, (of rented space etc.), luanto; **tenancy**, okupado; **subtenant**, sub~o
tench, tinko
tend, (be inclined to), emi [int], inklini [int], tendenci [int]; (look after, care for, gen), prizorgi [tr], zorgi [int] pri; (care for child etc.), varti [tr]; (care for sick etc.), flegi [tr]; (care for herd, flock, etc.), paŝti [tr]
tendency, tendenco, emo, inklino
tendentious, tendenca
tender, (gentle, loving), tenera; (delicate, light), delikata; (painful), dolo– rema; (soft), mola; (frail, feeble), malfortika, febla, malhardita; (compassionate), kompata; (of train), tendro; (offer), proponi [tr]; propono;

tenderize, moligi; **legal tender**, ($), (laŭleĝa) valuto
tendon, tendeno; **tendonitis**, ~ito; **tendonotomy**, ~otomio **Achilles tendon**, Aĥila ~o
tendril, ĉiro
Tenebrio, tenebrio
tenebrous, tenebra
Tenedos, Tenedo
tenement, (one apartment), apartamento; (tenement house), ~aro; (run-down, slummy), ~aĉo; ~araĉo
Tenerife, Tenerifo
tenesmus, tenesmo
tenet, doktrino, dogmo
tenia, (anat; zool), tenio
teniasis, teniozo
Tennessee, Tenesio; **Tennessee River**, Rivero ~a; **Tennessee Valley**, Valo ~o; **Tennessee Valley Authority**, ~vala Aŭtoritato
tennis, teniso; ~a; **play tennis**, ludi ~on, ~i [int]; **tennis court**, ~ejo; **lawn tennis**, gazon~o, laŭteniso; **paddle tennis**, pagajo~o; **platform tennis**, podio~o; **table tennis**, tablo~o
tenon, tenono
tenor, (voice range), tenoro; (singer), ~ulo; (direction), direkto; (meaning), signifo; **countertenor**, kontra~o; kontra~ulo
tense, (tight, alert, unrelaxed, etc.), streĉi [tr]; ~ita; (nervous), nervoza, ~ita; (verb time), tenso
tensile, tira
tensimeter, gas-tensiometro [cp "tensiometer"]
tensiometer, tensiometro; **tensiometry**, ~io
tension, (psych or phys: stress, unrelaxedness), streĉ(itec)o; [cp "stress"]; (pressure, gen; elec voltage), tensio
tensor, (muscle; math), tensoro
tent, tendo
tentacle, tentaklo
Tentaculata, tentakluloj
tentative, provizora
tentorium, tendo; **tentorium cerebelli, tentorium of cerebellum**, cerebela ~o
tenuous, (not dense), maldensa; (slen-

der, as fiber), maldika, fajna; (flimsy, insubstantial), malfortika

tenure, (length of service), servodaŭro; (right to permanent position), postenrajto; (act of holding, as property), tenado; (feudal), tenuro

tenuto, (mus), tenate

tepee, tipio* [cp "wigwam"]

tepid, tepida, varmeta; **tepidarium,** ~ejo

tequila, pulkvolikvoro

tera-, (pfx: 10^{12}), tera–

teratism, teratulo

terat(o)-, (pfx), terat(o)–

teratogenic, teratogena

teratology, teratologio

teratoma, teratomo

terbium, terbio

terce, (gen), tercio

tercentennial, tercentenary, [see "tricentennial"]

tercet, terceto

terebinth, terebintarbo

Teredo, teredo

Terence, (man's name), Terencio

Teresa, (woman's name), Tereza

tergiversate, kabei [int]; **tergiversation,** ~ado

term, (expression, phrase, word, etc.), termino; (math, logic), termo; (condition), kondiĉo; (provision, as in contract, treaty), preskribo; (semester), semestro; (quarter year), trimestro; (period for holding office etc.), oficoperiodo, deĵorperiodo; (gestation period), gravedperiodo; (any time period), periodo; (termination, end of time period), fino; (name, call), nomi [tr]; **midterm,** (of class), kursmeza; (of term of office, duty, etc.), deĵormeza; **bring to terms,** (cause agreement), akordigi; (cause surrender), kapitulacigi; **in terms of,** (w regard to, in relation to), rilate al (e.g.: *interpret her opposition in terms of her previous experiences:* interpreti ŝian kontraŭon rilate al ŝiaj antaŭaj spertoj); **come to terms,** akordiĝi; **on equal terms with,** sur egala bazo kun; **be on good (friendly) terms with,** havi amikan rilaton kun; **in no uncertain terms,** per nedubeblaj ~oj

termagant, megero. diablino

Termes, termito

terminal, (station, gen), stacio; (train, bus, etc. station), ~domo; (at end of line), fin~o; (city at such station), ~urbo; (cmptr), terminalo†; (final; at any end), fina; (fatal), mortiga; (elec: connection point), klemo

terminate, (finish, end), fini [tr]; ~iĝi; (stop, cease), ĉesi [int]; ĉesigi; **termination,** ~o; ĉeso; (gram ending), ~aĵo; **terminator,** (ast), terminatoro; **interminable,** sen~a, senĉesa

terminative, finitivo

terminology, (sci), terminologio; (collection of tgerms), terminaro

terminus, (boundary, limit), limo; (station), finstacio; (city), staciurbo

Terminus, Termino

termite, termito

tern, ŝterno; **crested tern,** (*Sterna bergii*), tuf~o; **fairy tern,** (*S. nereis*), feina ~o; **little tern,** (*S. albifrons*), malgranda ~o

ternary, ternate, (3–fold), ternara; (math: base 3), triaria†

terpene, terpeno

Terpsichore, Terpsikora

Terra, (planet), Tero; (goddess), ~a

terrace, (flat ground strip etc.; balcony), teraso; ~igi; (line of row houses), domvico; **terraced,** ~a

terracotta, terakoto; ~a

terra firma, firma tero

terraform, terformi [tr]

terrain, tereno

terra incognita, nekonata tero

terrapin, akvotestudo

terrarium, vazoĝardeneto

terrestrial, tera; **extraterrestrial,** ekster~a

terrible, terura

terrier, terhundo

terrific, (great, extreme, etc.), kolosa, grandega; (terrible, frightful), terura

terrify, teruri [tr]

territory, (gen), teritorio; **territorial,** ~a; **territoriality,** ~eco; **Territorian,** (Aus), Nord–T~ano; **extraterritorial,** ekster~a; **Australian Capital Territory,** Aŭstralia Ĉefurba T~o; **Northern Territory,** (Aus), Norda

T~o; **Northwest Territories**, (Canada), Nordokcidentaj T~oj

terror, (great fear; person creating same), teruro; (terrible thing), ~aĵo (e.g.: *the terrors of war:* la ~aĵoj de milito); (repression by terrorizing), teroro; **terrorism**, terorismo; **terrorist**, terorisma; teroristo; **terrorize**, terorizi† [tr]

Terry, (man's name), Teĉjo; (woman's), Tenjo

terse, lakona, konciza

tertian, terciana

tertiary, (gen), terciara; (geol age), ~o

Tertullian, Tertuliano

tesla, teslo

test, (try out), provi [tr]; ~iĝi; ~o (e.g.: *test milk to see if it is fresh:* ~i lakton por vidi ĉu ĝi estas freŝa; *a test of courage:* ~o de kuraĝo); (determine person's knowledge, IQ, etc., as in class; check functioning of machine, demand for product, etc.), testi [tr]; testiĝi; testo; (examine), ekzameni [tr]; ekzameno; (standard, criterion), normo, kriterio; **acid test**, decida ~o; **put to the test**, submeti [tr] al la ~o, el~i [tr, int]; **take a test**, testiĝi, ricevi teston; **Wasserman test**, reago de Vaserman

Testacella, testacelo

testament, (gen), testamento; **Old Testament**, (Bib), Malnova T~o; **New Testament**, Nova T~o

testate, testament/inta; **testator**, ~into; **intestate**, sen~a

testicle, testiko; (tech name, as in compound med terms), orkido [see "orchid(o)–"]; (colloq), kojono

testify, atesti [tr]

testimony, atesto; **testimonial**, ~a; ~o

testis, [see "testicle"]

testitis, testikito

testosterone, testosterono

testudo, testudo

Testudo, testudo; Testudinata, ~uloj

–tet, (sfx: number in any group), –opo (e.g.: *a quartet of friends:* kvaropo da amikoj); (mus: work for specified number, or that number of musicians), –teto (e.g.: *string quartet:* korda kvarteto) [see "solo", "duet", "trio",

"quartet", "quintet", etc.]

tetania, tetanio

tetanize, tetanizi [tr]

tetanus, (disease), tetanoso; (muscular contraction), tetano

tatany, tatanio

tête-à-tête, duopa konversacio

tether, (tie animal etc. by rope), ŝnuri [tr]; (lig)~o; (in space, for attaching), kabli [tr]; kablo; (in space: orbital catapult), (orbita) katapulto; **be at the end of one's tether**, (fig), ne plu povi elteni

Tethys, (ast), Tetiso*; (myth), ~a†

tetra–, (pfx), tetra–

tetradecanoic, miristata [see "myristate"]

Tetragonia, tetragonio; Tetragonia expansa, Novzelanda spinaco

Tetragrammaton, tetragramo

tetrahedron, tetraedro; **tetrahedral**, ~a

tetra(kis)hexahedron, tetrakisheksaedro

tetraline, tetraleno

tetralogy, tetralogio

tetrameter, tetrametro

Tetrao, tetraono [not "tetrao"; see *"Tetrastes"*]; Tetrao urogallus, urogalo; Tetraonidae, ~edoj

tetrarch, tetrarko; **tetrarchy**, (land area), ~ejo; (system), ~io

Tetrastes bonasia, tetrao, bonazio

tetrastyle, tetrastila

tetrathionate, tetration/ato; **tetrathionic acid**, ~a acido

tetrode, tetrodo

tetryl, tetrilo

Teucrium, teŭkrio

Teuton, Teŭtono; **Teutonic**, ~a [cp "Germanic"]

tewel, duzo

Texas, Teksaso

text, (written material), teksto; **text(book)**, lernolibro

textile, tekstila; ~aĵo, teksaĵo

texture, teksturo; ~igi

–th, (sfx: in fractions), –ono (e.g.: *three-fourths of a cake:* tri kvaronoj de kuko); (in ordinal numbers), –a (e.g.: *the fourth floor:* la kvara (4–a) etaĝo) [see § 19(c) and (d)]

Thad(d)eus, Tadeo
Thai, Tajo; ~a; ~landa; **Thailand,** ~lando
Thaïs, Taisa
thalamus, talamo
thaler, talero
Thales, Taleso
Thalia, Talia
Thalictrium, taliktro
thallium, taliumo
Thallophyta, talofitoj
thallophyte, talofito
thallus, talo
thalweg, talvego
Thames, (river), Tamizo
than, (gen), ol (e.g.: *more than five:* pli ~ kvin; *less than perfect:* malpli ~ perfekta)
thank, danki [tr]; **thank you!, thanks!,** ~on!; **thank you very much!, thanks a lot!, many thanks,** multan ~on!; **thankful,** ~ema; **thankless,** sen~a; **thanks to,** dank' al (e.g.: *we finished, thanks to your help:* ni finis, dank' al via helpo); **thanksgiving,** (expression of thanks), ~esprimo; **Thanksgiving Day,** D~festo; **give thanks (to),** ~i; **thanks just the same,** tamen ~on; **thank in advance,** antaŭ~i [tr]
Thapsia, tapsio
that, (pron: that thing), tio (e.g.: *that is my car:* tio estas mia aŭto); (pron: that person or animal; adj re that person, animal, or thing), tiu (e.g.: *that is my brother:* tiu estas mia frato; *that car is mine:* tiu aŭto estas mia); (who, whom, which), kiu(j) (e.g.: *the movie that we saw:* la filmo kiun ni vidis; *the people that came:* la homoj kiuj venis); (when), kiam (e.g.: *the year that we were married:* la jaro kiam ni geedziĝis); (conj before indicative mood; before n phrase), ke (e.g.: *I know that you're right:* mi scias ke vi pravas [note: comma often used before "ke", as in German, Russian, etc., though not required]; *that the task is hard is well known:* ke la tasko estas malfacila estas bone konate) [note: although "that" in these senses may be omitted in English ("the movie we saw", "the year we were married", "I

know you're right"), the Esperanto equivalents may never be omitted ("la kino kiun ni vidis")]; (conj before subjunctive clause), por ke ~u [no comma before "ke"] (e.g.: *they died that we might be free:* ili mortis por ke ni estu liberaj); (to that extent), tiom (e.g.: *the day was hot, but not that hot:* la tago estis varma, sed ne tiom varma); **that is,** (in oth words), alivorte; (to be specific), nome, specife; (pointing out existence; indicating one of several), jen (e.g.: *Look, that's an eagle:* Rigardu, jen aglo; *that's the biggest lie I've ever heard:* Jen la plej granda mensogo kiun mi iam ajn aŭdis); **that's that!,** (that is done, all, finished), jen ĉio!, kaj punkto!, kaj fino! (e.g.: *you may not go, and that's that!:* vi ne rajtas iri, kaj jen ĉio!; *I have sewn on the buttons, and that's that:* mi alkudris la butonojn, kaj jen ĉio!); **that kind of (a), such as that (one), like that (one),** tia (e.g.: *I don't like that kind of music:* mi ne ŝatas tian muzikon; *there was never a day such as that before:* neniam antaŭe estis tia tago); **that way, like that,** (in that manner), tiel, tiumaniere (e.g.: *do it like that:* faru ĝin tiel [or] tiumaniere); **that much,** tiom; **that one,** tiu [see "one"]; **that one's, that person's,** (possessive), ties; **all that,** (so very), tiom (e.g.: *he's not all that smart:* li ne estas tiom inteligenta); (everything of that sort), ĉio tio (e.g.: *crime and all that:* krimo kaj ĉio tio; *he did all that today:* li faris ĉion tion hodiaŭ); (adj: that entire amount of), ĉiom tiom (da) (e.g.: *all that water spilled:* ĉiom tiom da akvo renversiĝis; *who spilled all that water?:* kiu renversis ĉiom tiom da akvo?); **for all that,** (in spite of it all), malgraŭ ĉio tio
thatch, pajlo; **thatched,** (roof, hut, etc.), ~a; **thatching,** ~aĵo; **thatched hut,** ~obudo
thaw, degeli [int]; ~igi; ~o
the, la [note: form does not change, sing or plur, nominative or accusative (e.g.: *I have the books:* mi havas la librojn)]

Thea, teo

theater, teatro; **theatrical**, ~a; **theater piece, theatrical work**, ~ajo [cp "drama"]; **movie theater**, kinejo, kin~o; **drive–in theater**, parkokinejo†

Thebaid, Tebaido

thebaine, tebino

thebaism, tebaismo

Thebes, Tebo

theca, teko

thee, ci(n) [see "thou"]

theft, ŝtel(ad)o

theine, teino

their, ilia [see "they"]; (reflexive), sia (e.g.: *they found their cat:* ili trovis sian katon); **theirs**, ~a; sia; **(of) their –ing, (of) their being –ed**, [see "her"]

theism, teismo; **theist**, ~a; teisto; **monotheism**, mono~o; **polytheism**, poli~o

theme, (gen), temo; **thematic**, ~a

Themis, Temisa

Themistocles, Temistoklo

themself, themselves, [see "self", "they"]

then, (at that time, gen; next in time; in that case), tiam (e.g.: *then we went home:* ~ ni iris hejmen; *if you are Mr. Smith, then I am in the right place:* se vi estas s–ro Smith, ~ mi estas en la ĝusta loko); (adj: at that time), ~a (e.g.: *the then president:* la ~a prezidento); (subsequently, afterwards), poste, tiam (e.g.: *first it rained and then it snowed:* unue pluvis kaj poste neĝis); (so, therefore), do (e.g.: *then you were right after all:* do vi pravis post cio; **thence**, (from that place), de tie; (from that time), de tiam; **thenceforth**, de tiam; **but then**, (however, on the oth hand), tamen, aliflanke; **now then!, so then!**, nu do!

thenar, (palm of hand), polmo; (bulge at base of thumb), tenaro

Theobroma, kakaoarbo

theobromine, teobromino

theocrat, teokrato; **theocratic**, ~ia; **theocracy**, ~io

Theocritus, Teokrito

theodicy, teodiceo

theodolite, teodolito

Theodore, Teodoro; **Theodora**, ~a

Theodosius, Teodozio; **Theodosia**, ~a

Theognis, Teognizo

theogony, teogonio

theology, teolog/io; **theological**, ~ia; **theologian**, ~o

Theophilus, Teofilo

theorbo, teorbo

theorem, teoremo

theory, teorio; **theoretical**, ~a; **in theory, theoretically**, ~e; **theorize**, ~adi [int]; **theoretician**, ~isto, ~ulo

theosophy, teozof/io; **theosophical**, ~ia; **theosophist**. ~o; **Theosophical Society**, T~a Societo

therapy, terapio; **therapeutic**, (curative), ~a; (re therapeutics), terapeŭtika; **therapeutics**, terapeŭtiko; **therapist**, terapeŭto; **chemotherapy**, kemi(o)~o; **electrotherapy**, elektro~o; **heliotherapy**, helio~o; **hydrotherapy**, hidro~o; **hypnotherapy**, hipno~o; **opotherapy**, opo~o; **phototherapy**, foto~o; **phytotherapy**, fito~o; **psychotherapy**, psiko~o; **radiotherapy**, **roentgenotherapy**, radio~o, rentgen~o; **serotherapy**, sero~o; **shock therapy, convulsive therapy**, konvulsio~o; **thermotherapy**, termo~o

there, (in that place), tie; (to that place), tien; (interj: behold!, aha!), jen! (e.g.: *there, I finished!:* jen, mi finis!; *oh yes, there it is:* ho jes, jen ĝi estas; *there goes the bell:* jen sonoras la sonorilo); (before verb when subject follows), [not translated] (e.g.: *there is a fly in my soup:* estas muŝo en mia supo; *there were ten people in the room:* estis dek homoj en la ĉambro; *there arose a great shout:* leviĝis granda krio); **thereabouts**, ĉirkaŭe; **thereafter**, poste, post tio, post tiam; **thereby**, per tio, tiel, tiumaniere; **therefor**, por tio; **therefore**, tial, pro tio, sekve (de tio) [see also "so"]; **therefrom**, (from there), de tie; (from that), de tio; **therein**, (in that), en tio; (in that place), tie, en tie; (into, to that place), tien; (in that regard), tiurilate; **thereof**, de tio, de ĝi; **thereon**, (upon that),

sur tio(n); (about that), pri tio; **thereto,** (to that), al tio; (to that place), tien; **theretofore,** ĝis tiam; **thereunder,** sub tio; **thereupon,** (when that happened), tiam, post tio, je tio, ĉe tio; (on that), sur tio(n); **therewith,** (accompanied w that), kun tio; (by means of that), per tio
Theresa, (woman's name), Tereza
thermal, termika, termo– [pfx] (e.g.: *thermal bath:* termobanejo; *thermal underwear:* termokalsono); **electrothermal,** elektro~a
thermic, termika;   **electrothermic,** elektro~a
Thermidor, Termidoro
thermistor, termistoro
thermit, termito
thermo–, (pfx: heat), termo–, varmo–
thermocauter, termokaŭteri [tr]; **thermocautery,** ~ado
thermocouple, termoparo
thermogram, termografaĵo
thermograph, termografo
thermometer, termometro; **maximumminimum thermometer,** minimummaksimum(–indik)a ~o; **recording thermometer,** registra ~o
thermopile, termopilo
Thermopylae, Termopiloj
thermos, termoso; ~a
thermoscope, termoskopo;   **thermoscopic,** ~a
thermosiphon, termosifono
thermostat, termostato
thermotropic, termotropa; **thermotropism,** ~ismo
Theromorpha, teromorfoj
thesaurus, tezaŭro*
these, [see "this"]
Theseus, Tezeo
thesis, (proposition, idea; dissertation, paper), tezo; (poet: accented syllable), ikto; (unaccented syllable), senikto
thespian, drama; ~ulo, ~isto
Thespis, Tespiso
Thessalonian, Tesalonika; ~ano; **Thessalonians,** (Bib), ~anoj
Thessaloniki, Thessalonike, Tesaloniko [cp "Salonika"]
Thessaly, Tesalio
theta, teta [see § 16]

Thetis, Tetisa
thews, (muscles), muskoloj; (strength), forto
they, (3rd person plur pron; colloq: 3rd sing of either gender), ili (e.g.: *two people came, and they liked it:* du homoj venis, kaj ili ŝatis ĝin; *someone phoned, but they had hung up when I answered:* iu telefonis, sed ili estis remetinta [note sing] la aŭdilon kiam mi respondis); (impersonal, one, someone), oni (e.g.: *why don't they fix the street?:* kial oni ne riparas la straton?; *they say that:* oni diras ke)
thiamine, tiamino
thiazole, tiazolo
thick, (large depth), dika (e.g.: *a thick wall:* ~a muro); (dense), densa; (abundant, luxurious), abunda; (viscous), viskoza; **thicken,** ~igi; ~iĝi; densigi; densiĝi; abundigi; abundiĝi; viskozigi; viskoziĝi; **thickness,** ~o; denso; abundo; viskozo; (layer), tavolo; **through thick and thin,** en ĝojo kaj malĝojo; okazu kio ajn
thicket, vepro, densejo
thief, ŝtel/into; ~isto; (extreme), latrono
thieve, ŝteladi [tr]; **thievery,** ~o
thigh, (anat), femuro; (as meat), ~aĵo
thimble, (for finger), fingringo; (grooved rope ring), koŝo
Thimphu, Timbuo*
thin, (little depth), maldika; ~igi; ~iĝi (e.g.: *a thin wall:* ~a muro); (poet: little depth), minca; (not dense), maldensa; maldensigi; maldensiĝi; (not abundant, not luxurious), malabunda; malabundigi; malabundiĝi; (not viscous), malviskoza; malviskozigi; malviskoziĝi; (dilute), dilui [tr] diluiĝi; diluita; (lean, gaunt), magra; magrigi; magriĝi; (insubstantial, weak, unconvincing), malforta, nesubstanca
thine, cia [see "thou"]
thing, (gen), afero; (concrete object), ~o, aĵo, objekto; **thingamajig,** umo; **the thing is that,** temas pri tio ke; **all things considered,** ĉion konsiderinte; **there is no such thing (as a),** ne ekzistas tia ~ (kia); **carry a (good) thing too far,** troigi ~on, preterpasi la limojn; **do one's own thing,** plugi la

propran sulkon

think, (cerebrate, have thought), pensi [tr]; (have opinion, consider, view), opinii [int], ~i, kredi [tr], konsideri [tr]; [see also "thought"]; **think about,** ~i pri, pri~i [tr]; **think better of,** ŝanĝi sian opinion [or] intencon pri; **think much (little) of,** (mal)alte taksi [tr]; **think of,** (think about), ~i pri, pri~i [tr]; (remember), memori [tr]; (consider, view as), rigardi [tr], konsideri [tr] (e.g.: *I think of her as a family member:* mi rigardas ŝin kiel familianon); **think out,** el~i [tr]; **think over,** (re)pri~i [tr]; **think to,** (remember), memori [tr]; **think through,** tra~i [tr]; **think twice,** re~i [int]; repri~i [tr], rekonsideri [tr]; **think up,** el~i [tr]; **unthinkable,** ne~ebla; **free-thinking,** liber~a; **wishful thinking,** dezirfantazio; **something to think about,** io pri~in-da

thio–, (chem pfx), tio–

thiocyanate, tiocianato; **potassium thiocyanate,** kalia ~o

thiol, tiolo

thionyl, tionilo

thiophene, tiofeno

thiosulfate, tiosulfato

thiosulfite, tiosulfito

thiosulfuric, tiosulfata; **thiosulfuric acid,** ~a acido

thiosulfurous, tiosulfita; **thiosulfurous acid,** ~a acido

third, (3rd), tria; (1/3), ~ono [see § 19]; (mus), tercio

thirst, soifo; ~i [int]; **thirsty,** ~a; **be thirsty,** ~i; **quench (one's) thirst,** sen~igi, mal~igi (sin, iun)

this, (this thing), ĉi tio, tio ĉi (e.g.: *this is my car:* ĉi tio [or] tio ĉi estas mia aŭto) [note: if the antecedent does not directly precede "this" or is not expressly mentioned, "ĉi" is sometimes omitted]; (this person or animal; adj re this person, animal, or thing), ĉi tiu, tiu ĉi (e.g.: *this car is mine:* ĉi tiu aŭto estas mia); (to this extent), (ĉi) tiom, tiom (ĉi) (e.g.: *the day was hot, but not this hot:* la tago estis varma, sed ne (ĉi) tiom varma); [note: in adj and adv phrases, esp re time, "this" is often expressed as "ĉi–" attached (with hyphen) to the word modified (e.g.: *in this month's issue:* en la ĉi-monata numero; *I will stay home this week:* mi restos hejme ĉi-semajne; *it's my turn this time:* estas mia vico ĉi-foje)]; **this kind of (a), such as this (one), like this (one),** (ĉi) tia, tia (ĉi) (e.g.: *I don't like this kind of music:* mi ne ŝatas (ĉi) tian muzikon; *there was never a day such as this* [or] *like this before:* neniam antaŭe estis (ĉi) tia tago; **this way, like this,** (in this manner), (ĉi) tiel, tiel (ĉi) (e.g.: *do it like this:* faru ĝin tiel (ĉi)); **this much,** (ĉi) tiom, tiom (ĉi); **this one,** (ĉi) tiu, tiu (ĉi) [see "one"]; **this one's, this person's,** (possessive), (ĉi) ties; **all this,** (everything of this sort), ĉio ĉi [not "ĉi ĉio"] (e.g.: *he did all this today:* li faris ĉion ĉi hodiaŭ); (adj: this entire amount of), ĉiom ĉi (da) (e.g.: *all this water spilled:* ĉiom ĉi da akvo renversiĝis; *who spilled all this water?:* kiu renversis ĉiom ĉi da akvo?)

Thisbe, Tisba

thistle, (gen, unspecific name), kardo; (*Cirsium*), cirsio; (*Cnicus*), kniko; (*Onopordum*), onopordo; **blessed thistle,** kniko; **blue thistle,** ekio; **bull thistle,** cirsio; **carline thistle,** karlino; **globe thistle,** ~o; **holy thistle,** kniko; **musk thistle, nodding thistle,** karduo; **plume(d) thistle,** cirsio; **Russian thistle,** salsolo; **Scotch thistle, cotton thistle,** (*Onopordum acanthicum*), azen~o; **star thistle,** stel~o

thither, tien

thixotropy, tiksotrop.io; **thixotropic,** ~a

Thlaspi, tlaspo

thole, (remil)forketo

Thomas, Tomaso

Thomism, Tom/ismo; **Thomist,** ~isma; ~isto

thong, (leather lace), (leda) laĉo; (sandal), rimensandalo

Thor, Toro

thoracic, toraka

thoracoplasty, torakoplastio

thorax, (gen), torako

thorium, torio
thorn, dorno; **thorny,** ~a; **blackthorn,** (fruit), prunelo; (tree), prunelarbo; **boxthorn,** lico; **buckthorn,** (*Rhamnus*), ramno; **alder buckthorn,** frangolo
thorough, (complete), kompleta; (exact, detailed, painstaking), ĝisosta, ĝisfunda; (conscientious), konscienca; **thoroughbred,** purrasa; purrasulo; **thoroughfare,** (main road), ĉefvojo; (way through), trairejo, trapasejo; **thoroughwort,** eŭpatorio
Thoth, Tot
thou, ci [note: In Esperanto as in English, used only for archaic or special effect]
though, (conj: although), kvankam; (adv: however), tamen; **as though,** (as if), kvazaŭ
thought, penso [see also "think"]; **thoughtful,** ~ema; **thoughtless,** senpri~a; **thought-provoking,** ~iga; **aforethought,** antaŭ~ita; **afterthought,** post~o; **forethought,** antaŭ~(ad)o, antaŭvido, antaŭzorgo; antaŭ~ita; **on second thought,** je dua ~o; **train of thought,** ~fadeno; **collect one's thoughts,** ordi siajn ~ojn; **give a (any) thought to,** konsideri [tr]; **with malice aforethought,** malbonintence
thousand, mil [see § 19]
Thrace, Trac/ujo; **Thracian,** ~o; ~a
thrall, (slave, serf), servut/ulo; (serfdom), ~eco; **thralldom,** ~eco
Thrasaetus harpya, harpio
thrash, (thresh), [see "thresh"]; (beat), bategi [tr], (tra)draŝi [tr]; **thrash out,** eldiskuti [tr]
Thraupis, tanagro
thread, (light string, or any analogous thing), fadeno (e.g.: *nylon thread:* nilona ~o; *the thread of a story:* la ~o de rakonto); (poke thread through needle, or analogous action), tredi [tr] (e.g.: *we threaded our way through traffic:* ni tredis nin tra la trafiko); (string objects, as beads, onto thread), sur~igi; (of screw etc.), (ŝraŭb)kanelo; (make screwthreads on), ŝraŭbigi; **threader,** (machine for making

screwthreads), ŝraŭbigilo; **threadbare,** ~montra; **female thread,** ina ŝraŭbkanelo; **male thread,** vira ŝraŭbkanelo; **hang by a thread,** esti tre minacata, esti en granda danĝero, pendi per ~o; **take up the thread,** daŭrigi la aferon (rakonton)
threat, minaco; **threaten,** ~i [tr]; **threatening,** ~a
three, tri [see § 19]
thresh, draŝi [tr]; **thresher, threshing machine,** ~maŝino
threshold, (gen), sojlo; (of perception), limino; **on the threshold of,** ĉe la ~o de, ~e de
thrice, trifoje, tri fojojn
thrift, (frugality), ŝparemo, ekonomio; (bot: *Armeria*), armerio; **thrifty,** ~a
thrill, (excite), eksciti [tr], entuziasmigi; ~iĝi, entuziasmiĝi; ~o; (vibration, quiver), tremeti [int]; tremetigi; tremeto; **thriller,** ~ilo; **thrilling,** ~a, rava
thrips, tizanoptero, tripso
thrive, prosperi [int], flori [int]
throat, gorĝo; **bluethroat,** (zool), blu~ulo; **rubythroat,** (zool), ruĝ~ulo, rubekolo; **back of the throat,** (behind tonsils), ~fundo; **clear one's throat,** tuseti [int]; **cut each other's throats,** ruinigi sin reciproke; tranĉi la ~ojn unu al la alia; **cut one's own throat,** tranĉi al si la ~on, ruinigi sin mem; **jump down (someone's) throat,** akre riproĉi (iun); **stick in the throat,** esti malfacila gluti (diri, akcepti, etc.)
throb, pulsadi [int]; ~o
throes, agonio [note sing]
thrombase, trombazo
thrombectomy, trombektomio
thrombin, trombazo
thromb(o)–, (med pfx), tromb(o)–
thrombocyte, trombocito
thrombosis, trombozo
thrombus, trombo
throne, trono; **enthrone,** sur~igi; **dethrone,** de~igi
throng, svarmo, (popol)amaso; ~i [int] (en), amasiĝi (en)
throttle, (valve), obturilo; stringi [tr]; (hand knob or foot pedal), akcelilo; (strangle), strangoli [tr]

through, (from one side to oth; throughout, among; here and there in), tra
(e.g.: *go through the door:* iri ~ la
pordo; *read through a book:* legi ~ libro [or] tralegi libron; *a vacation trip
through Canada:* feria vojaĝo ~ Kanado; *watch through a telescope:*
rigardi ~ teleskopo) [note: accusative
is not usually used, but may be for
greater clarity (e.g.: *sweep the dust
through the door:* "balai la polvon ~
la pordon" [instead of "pordo"] shows
that person sweeping is not on oth
side of door)]; (by means of), per,
pere de, far (e.g.: *speak through an interpreter:* paroli far [or] pere de inter-
pretisto; (because of), pro (e.g.: *done
through error:* farita pro eraro); (adv:
completely to end, conclusion), ĝis fino, ĝisfine (e.g.: *work the problem
through:* trakti la problemon ĝis fino);
(thoroughly, completely), komplete,
ĝisoste, ĝisfunde; (adj: finished), finita (e.g.: *the program is through:* la
programo estas finita; *after the scandal, he's through in politics:* post la
skandalo, li estas finita en la politiko);
(no longer dealing w each oth), finin-
ta(j), ne plu interrilati [int] (e.g.: *he
and she are through:* li kaj ŝi estas fin-
intaj [or] li kaj ŝi ne plu interrilatas);
(open through), ~ira (e.g.: *a through
street:* ~ira strato); (traveling through,
nonstop), senhalta (e.g.: *a through
flight:* senhalta flugo); **throughout,**
(tute) ~, ~ la tuta; ~ la tuto; **through-
put,** ~meto; **throughway,** aŭtovojo;
am, is, are through with, finis (e.g.:
are you through with supper?: ĉu vi
finis la vespermanĝon?); **was, were
through with,** esti fininta(j); **get
through with,** fini [tr]; **through and
through,** komplete, ĝisoste, ĝisfunde
throw, (cast, hurl, put forcibly, project,
etc.), ĵeti [tr]; ~iĝi; ~o; (give party
etc.), okazigi; (pottery), torni [tr];
(confuse), konfuzi [tr]; **throw away,**
for~i [tr]; **throwaway,** for~aĵo;
for~enda; (leaflet, handbill), flugfolio; **throw back,** (stop), re~i [tr];
throwback, (reversion), atavismo, reveno; **throw in,** (connect mech parts),

kupli [tr]; (add), aldoni [tr] (senpage);
(cards), abandoni [tr]; **throw in with,**
(join), aliĝi al; **throw off,** (get rid of),
forigi, for~i [tr]; (give off, emit), eligi;
(deceive), erarigi; (evade), eviti [tr];
(confuse), konfuzi [tr]; **throw oneself
into,** fervore dediĉi sin al; **throw
open,** (open suddenly), subite malfermi [tr]; (make available), disponigi,
prezenti [tr]; **throw out,** (throw
away), for~i [tr]; (put forth), elmeti
[tr]; (disengage mech parts), malkupli
[tr]; **throw over,** (give up), rezigni
[tr]; (abandon), forlasi [tr]; **throw up,**
(vomit), vomi [int]; elvomi [tr]; (give
up), rezigni [tr]; (abandon), forlasi
[tr]; (mention repeatedly, as in reproach), al~adi [tr]; **overthrow,**
(gen), renversi [tr]; renvers(iĝ)o;
throw cold water on, malkuraĝigi,
senentuziasmigi
thrum, (on loom), varpfinaĵo; (fringe),
franĝo
thrush, (zool), turdo; (med), mugeto;
song thrush, kanto~o
thrust, (shove, push), ŝovi [tr], puŝi [tr];
~iĝi, puŝiĝi; ~o, puŝo; (continuous
force, as of rocket engine), puŝforto;
(basic meaning, import), signifo;
thruster, (rocket, jet, etc.), reaktoro,
puŝ-motoro; (Aus: pushy person), sin-
trudemulo; **upthrust,** supren~ita; su-
pren~iĝo; **thrust oneself on,** tru di sin
al
Thucydides, Tucidido
thud, obtuz/a bruo; ~e brui [int]; (onom), bum!
thug, gangstero, bandito
Thuja, tujo
Thule, Tuleo
thulium, tulio
thumb, (anat), polekso; (of glove etc.),
~umo; (handle, finger), fingrumi [tr];
(leaf through pages), foliumi [tr];
(hitchhike), petveturi [int]; **thumb-
nail,** (anat), ~ungo; (brief, miniature), miniatura; **under the thumb of,**
sub la rego de; **thumb a ride,** peti veturon; **twiddle one's thumbs,** turnadi
la ~ojn
thump, (hit), bru/bati [tr]; ~bato;
(noise), obtuza ~o; obtuze ~i [int];

(onom), bum!

thunder, (gen), tondro; ~i [int]; el~i [tr]; **thunderous,** ~a; **thunderbolt,** fulmofrapo, fulmosago; **thunderclap,** ~okrako; **thundercloud,** fulmonubo; **thunderhead,** fulmokumuluso; **thunderstorm,** fulmo~o; **thunderstruck,** konsternita

Thunnus thynnus, tinuso

Thuringia, Turingio

Thursday, ĵaŭdo

thus, (in that way), tiel; (in this way), ĉi tiel, tiel ĉi; (so, accordingly), do, sekve

Thuya, tujo

thwack, frapegi [tr]; ~o

thwart, (hinder), malhelpi [tr], obstrukci [tr]; (rower's seat), rembenko

thy, cia [see "thou"]

Thyestes, Tiesto

Thymallis, timalo

thyme, timiano; **wild thyme, creeping thyme,** serpilo

thymol, timolo

thymus, timuso

Thymus,(bot), timiano; Thymus serpyllum, serpilo

thyratron, tiratrono

thyr(e)o–, (anat and med pfx: re thyroid gland), tiro–; (re thyroid cartilege), tireo– (e.g.: thyrotomy: tirotomio; tireotomio)

thyroarytenoid, (muscle), tireoaritenoida muskolo

thyrogenous, thyrogenic, tirogeneza

thyroid, (gland), tiroido; ~a; ~aĵo; (cartilege), tireoido; tireoida; **thyroidectomy,** ~ektomio; **thyroidism,** ~ismo; **thyroiditis,** ~ito; **parathyroid,** para~o; para~a

thyrotropic, tirotropa

thyroxin(e), tiroksino

thyrsus, tirso

Thysanoptera, tizanopteroj

ti, (mus), si

Tian Shan, Tianŝan

tiara, (gen), tiaro

Tiber, Tibero

Tiberias, (town), Tiberiado; **Lake Tiberias,** Lago ~a

Tiberius, Tiberio

Tibesti, Tibestio

Tibet, Tibeto; **Tibetan,** ~a; ~ano

tibia, tibio

Tibullus, Tibulo

tic, tiko, klono

tick, (sound as of spring-wound clock), tiktaki [int]; ~o; (zool), iksodo; (check mark), streki [tr]; streko; (mattress cover), tikaĵo; (cloth for mattress cover), tiko; (colloq: function), funkcii [int]; **ticking,** (fabric), tiko; **tick-tock,** ~o; (onom), tiktak!

ticket, (for theater, plane, etc.), bileto; (list of candidates), kandidataro; **ticket window,** giĉeto; **commutation ticket,** navetado~o; **season ticket(s),** abon~o(j); **that's the ticket!,** bone farite!

tickle, (excite sensitive nerves), tikli [tr]; ~o; (pin and needle sensation, tingle, etc., as in throat), piketadi [tr, int]; piketado; **tickling,** ~a; ~(ad)o; **ticklish,** (sensitive, easily tickled), ~iĝema; (delicate), delikata; **tickled pink,** ravita; **tickle (one's fancy),** amuzi (iun)

tickseed, koreopso

tick-tack-toe, krucvicludo

tidbit, frandaĵeto

tiddlywink, (disk), saltodisko; **tiddlywinks,** (game), ~oj

tide, tajdo; **tideland,** ~lando; **tidewater,** (water), ~akvo; (area), ~akvejo; **tideway,** ~ovojo; **ebb tide,** malleviĝa ~o; **flood tide,** leviĝa ~o; **high tide,** alta ~o; **low tide,** malalta ~o; **neap tide,** morta ~o; **riptide,** kontraŭ~o; **spring tide,** sizigia ~o; **stem the tide,** ŝtopi la fluon, bari la fluon; **tide (one) over,** portempe helpi (iun), ebligi (iun) travivi [tr]

tidings, novaĵo(j), sciigo(j)

tidy, (neat), neta, ord(em)a; (large), konsiderinda, iom granda

tie, (fasten, connect, gen), ligi [tr]; ~iĝi ~o; ~ilo; (with a knot), nodi [tr]; (equal points, votes, etc., gen), egaligi; egaliĝi; egaliĝo; (in game, contest, etc.), egalgajno, egalvenko; (vote), egalvoĉdono; (stalemate), pato; (of rr tracks), ŝpalo; (necktie), kravato; **tie down,** fiksi [tr], limigi, malhelpi [tr], bridi [tr]; **tie in,** (have connection), ~i, konekti [tr], rilatigi; ~iĝi, konektiĝi, rilati [int], esti koneksa; **tie off,** ferm~i [tr]; **tie up,** (by wrapping ropes etc.), ĉirkaŭ~i [tr]; (make busy, occupy, etc.), okupi [tr] (e.g.: *the meeting tied me up all morning:* la kunveno min okupis la tutan matenon; *they kept the phone tied up for an hour:* ili tenis la telefonon okupita dum unu horo); (block, obstruct), obstrukci [tr], ŝtopi [tr] (e.g.: *commuter traffic tied up the expressway:* naveta trafiko obstrukcis la aŭtovojon); (moor ship), albolardigi; albolardiĝi; **bowtie,** bantokravato; **necktie,** kravato

Tien Shan, Tianŝan
Tientsin, Tiangin
tier, vico; ~igi
tierce, (gen), tercio
Tierra del Fuego, Fuegio
tiff, kverel(et)o
Tiflis, Tifliso
tiger, tigro
tight, (taught, drawn, tense), streĉ/ita; (strict), strikta; (rigid), rigida; (firm, well-fastened), firma; (close-fitting), strikta, malloza, malvasta; (difficult), malfacila; (sharp, short radius, as re curve etc.), akuta; (scarce, hard to get), malabunda; [see also "-tight"]; **tighten,** ~i [tr]; ~iĝi; striktigi; rigidigi; firmigi; **tights,** (tight pants), striktaĵo(j); **uptight,** (colloq: upset), ĉagrenita, maltrankvila, nervoza, ~ita **–tight,** (sfx: impervious), –imuna, hermetika (al) (e.g.: *watertight:* akv~a [or] hermetika al akvo)
Tigris, Tigriso
tilbury, tilburo
tilde, tildo
tile, (small, glazed, etc., as for interior use, or for games: one piece; math; window arrangement on cmptr screen), kahelo; ~a; (collectively), ~oj, ~aro; (put tile on), ~i [tr]; (roofing), tegolo; tegola; tegolaro; tegoli [tr]; **pantile,** kurb~o(j)
Tilia, tilio
till, (until), ĝis; (work land), erpi [tr]; (moneybox), kaso; **till-chain, till-rope,** droso; **tillable field,** agro

tiller, (of boat), rudr/ilo [not "~ostango"; see "rudder"]; (machine to till field), erpilo
tilt, (lean), klini [tr]; ~iĝi; ~(iĝ)o; (joust), turniri [int]; turniro; **at full tilt,** impete, plenrapide
Tim, Timĉjo
timbal, (drum), timbalo
timbale, (food), timbalo
timber, (wood, lumber), ligno, seg~o, ĉarpent~o, konstru~o; (cut trees), prisegi [tr]; (beam), trabo; (trees, forest), arbaro; **timbered,** (covered w trees), arbara; **timberline,** arbolimo
timbre, tembro
Timbuktu, Timbuktuo
time, (duration, gen; period, span of time; mus etc.: tempo), tempo; ~a (e.g.: *time and space:* ~o kaj spaco; *sidereal time:* sidera ~o; *the time of the French Revolution:* la ~o de la Franca Revolucio; *I don't have [enough] time to go there:* mi ne havas la ~on [sufiĉe da ~o] por iri tien; *chemical reaction time:* ~o de kemia reago; *harvest time:* rikolta ~o; *it's time to leave:* estas la ~o foriri); (instance, occasion), fojo (e.g.: *I've been there many times:* mi estis tie multajn fojojn; *that's the third time it's happened:* jen la tria fojo kiam ĝi okazis; *one time is not enough:* unu fojo ne sufiĉas; *three times:* tri fojojn [or] trifoje); (multiplication), oble (e.g.: *2 times 3 is 6:* 2 oble 3 estas 6); (clock hour), horo (e.g.: *starting time is 8 o'clock:* la komenca horo estas la 8–a); (turn in sequence), vico (e.g.: *it's my time to sit there:* estas mia vico sidi tie); (set, establish the clock time of an event), fiksi la ~on [or] horon de (e.g.: *time the attack to coincide with the holiday:* fiksi la ~on de la atako por koincidi kun la libertago; *time the meeting to be convenient to everyone's schedule:* fiksi la horon de la kunveno por esti oportuna por ĉies horaro); (measure duration, gen; set to last certain duration), ~omezuri [tr], mezuri la daŭron de (e.g.: *we timed the trip there at 5 hours:* ni ~omezuris la vojaĝon tien je 5 horoj); (measure

duration accurately), kronometri [tr] (e.g.: *he was timed in the 1000-meter run at 2 minutes, 43.7 seconds:* li estis kronometrita en la 1000-metra kuro je 2 minutoj, 43,7 sekundoj); (regulate spark timing of motor), reguligi la spark~on (de); **timeless,** eterna, senĉesa, senfina; **timely,** (on time, at right time), akurata, ĝusta~a; akurate, ĝusta~e; (opportune, well-timed), oportuna; **timer,** (device that times), ~omezurilo [cp "chronometer"]; (in motor, for timing spark), spark~a regilo; **times,** (multiplied by), oble, multiplikita de; **time-consuming,** ~oraba, ~opostula; **timekeeper,** ~oregistristo; **time-lapse,** (phot), ~opasa; **time limit,** ~limo; **time out,** (sport etc.), paŭzo; **timepiece,** (any clock, watch), horloĝo; **timesaving,** ~oŝpara; **time sharing,** ~odividado; ~odivida; **time sheet,** ~oregistrilo; **time signature,** (mus), taktosigno; **timetable,** horaro, ~otabelo; **time zone,** hordaŭbo, horzono [see names of zones under "standard time" below]; **time and again,** ree kaj ree, refoje; **time of life,** viv~o, aĝo; **time of year,** jar~o, sezono; **time will tell,** la ~o malkaŝos; **abreast of the times,** (up-to-date, informed), ĝisdata, aktuala; (modern, fashionable), moderna, laŭmoda; **ahead of time,** frua, antaŭ~a; frue, antaŭ~e; **any time, anytime,** (whenever), kiam ajn (e.g.: *come anytime you want:* venu kiam ajn vi volas); (adv: at any time), iam ajn (e.g.: *you may go anytime:* vi rajtas iri iam ajn; *any other time you wish:* iam ajn alie kiam vi deziras); **at a time,** ope, ~ope [sfx] (e.g.: *they crossed the road 5 at a time:* ili transiris la vojon kvinope [5–ope]; *climb the stairs two steps at a time:* grimpi la ŝtuparon duŝtupope [or] du ŝtupojn ope); **at times,** foje, kelkfoje; **at all times (whatever),** ĉiam (ajn); **at any time,** en kiu ajn momento; **at no time (whatever),** neniam (ajn); **at one time,** iam, foje; **at one time or another,** iam aŭ tiam, fojfoje; **at the same time,** sam~e; **behind time,**

malfrua, malakurata; malfrue; malakurate; **behind the times,** eksmoda, neĝisdata; **betimes,** (early), frue; **bide one's time,** atendi sian ŝancon; **by the time (that),** ĝis (kiam) (e.g.: *by the time they got there, it was too late:* ĝis kiam [or] ĝis ili alvenis, estis tro malfrue); **daylight (savings) time,** taglumŝpara ~o [avoid "somera ~o", since such time is sometimes observed year-round] [see "standard time" below for zones]; **do time,** resti en la prizono; **every time, everytime,** (adv), ĉiam, ĉiun fojon (e.g.: *I botch it every time:* mi ĉiam fuŝas ĝin); (conj), ĉiam kiam (e.g.: *I see him every time I come:* mi vidas lin ĉiam kiam mi venas); **for a long (short) time,** dum (mal)longa ~o, (mal)longa~e; **for a long time past,** jam delonge; **for the time being,** provizore, dum~e, por~e; **for the first (second etc.) time,** unuafoje (duafoje etc.); **from time to time,** de ~o al ~o; **gain time,** (re clock etc.), fruiĝi; (stall, delay), prokrastiĝi, evitadi [tr], gajni ~on; **have a good time,** havi bonan ~on, ĝui sin; **in time,** (eventually), fin(fin)e; (at right time, before too late), akurate, ĝusta~e, antaŭ ol estas (–is, –os) tro malfrue; (w mus or marching beat), laŭtakta; laŭtakte; **in good time,** (at proper time), sia~e; (quickly), rapide; **in no time,** tre baldaŭ, tre rapide, tuj; **in one's own (good, proper) time,** sia~e; **in three days' (etc.) time,** post tri tagoj (etc.); **it's about time!,** estas ja la ~o!; **just in time,** ĝusta~e; **keep good (poor) time,** (re clock etc.), (mal)akurate funkcii [int]; **kill time,** forpasigi la ~on; **lose time,** (re clock etc.), malfruiĝi; (lit, as from delays), perdi ~on (e.g.: *we lost two days' time because of the snow:* ni perdis du tagojn da ~o pro la neĝo); **make (good) time,** (go fast), rapidi [int]; (progress), (bone) progresi [int]; **make poor time,** prokrastiĝi, malbone progresi [int]; **make time with,** sukcese amindumi [tr]; **make up (for lost) time,** regajni (la perditan) ~on; **many a time,** many times, ofte, multfoje, multajn fojojn; **mark time**, starmarŝi [int]; (wait), por~e atendi [tr, int]; **mean time**, [see "standard time" below]; **Greenwich Mean Time**, Grenviĉa Meza T~o [abb: GMT] [also see "Universal Coordinated Time" below; for oth time zones, see following "standard time" below]; **next time**, la venontan fojon, venontfoje; **on time**, (punctual), akurata; akurate; (to be paid in installments), partopaga; partopage; **on one's own time**, dum sia libera ~o; **one-time**, (former), iama, antaŭa, eksa; (on one occasion only), unufoja; **overtime**, (pay for overtime work), krompago, kromsalajro; (the work), krom~o, kromlaboro; **pass the time of day**, saluti (sin reciproke); **prime-time**, ĉef-hora; **real time**, reala ~o; **serve (one's) time**, resti en prizono; **since time immemorial**, de post ~o nememorebla; **standard time**, meza ~o; **Newfoundland, Atlantic, Eastern, Central, Mountain, Pacific, Alaska, Hawaii, Bering Standard Time**, Novlanda, Atlantika, Orienta, Centra, Montara, Pacifika, Alaska, Havaja, Beringa Meza T~o [note: abbreviations for these North American time zones are not universally understood in Esperanto and hence should be avoided]; **Universal Coordinated Time**, Universala T~o; **Chicago time, Moscow time, Sydney time, (etc.)**, (clock time in specified place w/o naming zone), ~o de Ĉikago, Moskvo, Sidnejo (etc.); **summer time**, [see "daylight savings time" above]; **take up someone's time**, okupi ies ~on; **the time has come (for, to)**, la ~o jam venis (por, ke); **the time is ripe**, jam estas la ĝusta tempo; **there's a time for everything**, al ĉio sia ~o; **there's no time like the present**, nun estas la plej bona momento; **three (etc.) times running**, tri (etc.) fojojn sinsekve; **what time is it?**, kioma horo estas?; (colloq), kiomas? [see also "o'clock"]; **while away the time**, forpasigi la ~on

timid, timida; **timidity**, ~eco
Timor, Timoro
timorous, timida, timema
timothy, (bot), fleo
Timothy, (man's name), Timoteo
timpano, (kettledrum), timbalo [not "timpano"]; **timpani**, ~oj; **timpanist**, ~isto
Timur, Timuro
tin, (metal), stano; (coat w tin), ~i [tr]; (Br: seal in cans, or the can), [see "can"]; **tinsmith**, ~isto; **tin-snips**, ĉizojo [note sing]
tinamou, tinamo
Tinamus, tinamo;   Tinamiformes, ~oformaj (birdoj)
Tinca, tinko
tincture, (gen), tinkturo; ~a; ~i [tr]
tinder, tindro
tine, dento
tinea, (skin infection), tinio; **tinea amiantacea**, amianteca ~o; **tinea favosa**, fava ~o, favo
Tinea, (zool), tineo; Tineidae, ~edoj
ting, tinti [int]; ~igi; ~o
ting-a-ling, ting-ting, (etc.), (jingling sound, onom), tin tin tin, giling-gilang
tinge, nuanco; ~i [tr]
tingle, piketadi [tr, int]; ~o
tinker, (putter, work w), laboreti [int], amatori [int]; pri~i [tr]; (tinsmith), ladisto
tinkle, tinti [int]; ~igi; ~(ad)o
tinsel, brilaĵeto; ~a
tint, (kolor)nuanco; ~i [tr]
tintinnabulation, sonorado
tintype, (process), ferotipio; (product), ~aĵo
tiny, eta
tip, (gratuity), gratifiko, trinkmono; ~i [tr], trinkmonigi; (top, apex; point, end, as of pencil), pinto; pintigi; (hit glancing blow), tanĝe frapi [tr]; tanĝa frapo; (suggestion), sugesto; (secret information), kaŝinformo; (raise slightly), leveti [tr]; levetiĝi; (tilt, lean), klini [tr]; kliniĝi; **tip off**, malkaŝi [tr], riveli [tr] (la sekreton al); **tip over**, (overturn), renversi [tr]; renversiĝi; **tiptop**, (highest), (plej alta) pinto; (best), plej bona
tippet, pelerino

tipple, (drink), drinkadi [int]; (mining), malŝarĝilo

tipsy, (unsteady), malstabila, ŝanceliĝema; (drunk), ebri(et)a

Tipula, tipulo

tirade, riproĉ/(eg)o, ~bombasto, ~deklamado

tirailleur, tiraljoro

Tirana, Tirano*

tire, (pneumatic, for car, bicycle, etc.), pneŭo, pneŭmatiko; (fatigue), lacigi; laciĝi; (bore), enuigi; enuiĝi; **tired,** laca; enua; **be tired,** laci [int]; enui [int]; **dead tired,** lacega, ellaciĝinta; **tiring,** laciga; teda, enuiga; **tireless,** senlaca; **tiresome,** (boring), teda, enuiga; **tire chain,** ~ĉeno; **tire tool,** (to remove tire from rim), ~levilo; **all-weather tire,** ĉiavetera ~o; **flat tire,** malŝvela ~o; **snow tire,** neĝo~o; **spare tire,** krom~o, vic~o; **tube-type tire,** ~o kun interna aertubo; **tubeless tire,** sentuba ~o

Tiresias, Tirezio

Tisa, (river), Tiso

tisane, tizano

tissue, (soft paper, as toilet tissue, facial tissue), tualetpapero; (firmer, for wrapping, protecting pictures, etc.), silkopapero; (gauze), gazo; (organic, as flesh, bone, etc.), histo; **connective tissue,** konektivo

Tisza, (river), Tiso

tit, (titmouse), paruo; (teat), cico; (breast), mamo; **tit for tat,** bato por bato

Titan, (myth; ast), Titano

titanate, titanato

Titania, (ast), Titanio*; (myth), ~a

titanic, (gigantic), titana, kolosa; (chem: re titanium), ~a; (w valence 4), ~ata; **titanic acid,** ~ata acido

titanium, titano†

titbit, frandaĵeto

titer, titro

tithe, dekonaĵo; kontribui per ~o

titi, kalicebo, titio

Titian, Ticiano

Titicaca, (Lake), Lago Titikako

titillate, tikli [tr]

titivate, beligi (sin), pimpigi (sin)

titlark, pipio

title, (name of book etc.; term of address, as "doctor" etc.; section of law etc.), titolo; ~a; ~i [tr]; (claim, right), rajto; (right of ownership), posedrajto; (document, deed), posedakto; **subtitle,** (gen), sub~o; sub~i [tr]; **titled (person),** ~ulo

titmouse, paruo

titrate, titri [tr]; **titration,** ~ado

titre, titro

titter, subridi [int]; ~o

tittle, joto, streketo

titular, (re title; titled), titol(it)a; (nominal, in name only), titulara

Titus, Tito

tizzy, ekscit/iĝo; **in a tizzy,** ~ita

tmesis, tmezo

TNT, (abb of "trinitrotoluene"), TNT [abb of "trinitrotolueno"]

to, (motion or direction toward; gen relation, possession, etc.; addition or completion; etc.), al (e.g.: *we were flying to London:* ni flugis ~ Londono; *a ticket to the play:* bileto al la dramo; *it seems to me:* ŝajnas ~ mi; *it belongs to him:* ĝi apartenas ~ li; *add 3 to 5:* adicii 3 ~ 5); (motion reaching goal, completing action, achieving state; until), ĝis (e.g.: *we flew to London:* ni flugis ĝis Londono; *a fight to the death:* batalo ĝis la morto; *wet to the skin:* malseka ĝis la haŭto; *open from 9 to 6:* malfermita de la 9–a ĝis la 6–a); (in conformity, according to), laŭ (e.g.: *it's too sweet to my taste:* ĝi estas tro dolĉa laŭ mia gusto); (in order to), por (–i) (e.g.: *I went there [in order] to visit a friend:* mi iris tien por viziti amikon); (before infinitive), [not translated] (e.g.: *I want to go:* mi volas iri; *to err is human:* erari estas home); **to and fro,** tien kaj reen

toad, bufo; **toadflax,** linario; **ivy-leaved toadflax,** cimbalario; **toadstool,** (venena) fungo; **toady,** lakeo; **tree toad,** hilo

toast, (bread: each slice), toasto (e.g.: *two slices of toast:* du ~oj); (heat, cook), rosti [tr]; (drink to health etc.), tosto; tosti [tr]; **toaster,** panrostilo; **toastmaster, toastmistress,** prelegestr(in)o; **French toast,** ovaĵpano

tobacco, tabako; ~a; **tobacconist**, ~isto;
tobacco plant, nikotiano; **chewing
tobacco**, maĉ~o; **chew tobacco**,
~maĉi [int]
Tobiah, Tobias, Tobio
Tobit, Tobio
toboggan, tobogano
Toby, Tobio
toccata, tokato
Tocharian, toĥaro; ~a
tocology, obstetriko, tokologio
tocopherol, tokoferolo; **alpha-toco-
pherol**, alfa-~o; **beta-tocopherol**,
beta-~o
tocsin, (bell), alarmsonor/ilo; (sound),
~ado
today, (adv), hodiaŭ (e.g.: *it arrived today:* ĝi alvenis ~; *today is hot:* ~ estas
varme; **today's**, la ~a (e.g.: *today's
newspaper:* la ~a ĵurnalo)
toddle, paŝeti [int]; **toddler**, ~anto,
~ulo
toddy, grogo
toe, (of foot), pied/fingro; ~umi [tr]; (of
shoe etc.), (ŝu)antaŭo; **toehold**, ~ote-
no; **toe-in**, (re car wheels etc.), kon-
verĝeco; **toenail**, ~ungo; **tiptoe**,
~pinto; ~pinta; ~pinte; marŝi [int]
~pinte; **on tiptoe(s)**, ~pinte; **on one's
toes**, viglega; **tread on one's toes**,
ofendi iun
toffee, tofeo*
tofu, tohuo
toga, togo
together, kune(n); ~a; kun– [pfx] (e.g.:
he pushed the books together: li
~puŝis la librojn [or] li puŝis la librojn
~en); **togetherness**, ~eco; **together
with**, ~e ~; **"alone together"**, (man
and woman together), gesolaj; gesole
toggle, (rod, pin, etc.), stifto; (elec:
switch back and forth), reŝaltiĝ(ad)i
Togo(land), Togolando
toil, labor/adi [int], ~egi [int]; ~ado,
~ego; **toilsome**, ~iga, peniga
toilet, (flushable fixture for excretion),
klozeto; ~a; (any toilet facility, including nonflushable), fekseĝo;
(room), necesejo; (grooming, toiletry), tualeto; tualeta: **toiletry, toilette**,
tualeto; **toiletries, toilet articles**, tu-
aletaĵoj; **toilet bowl**, klozeta pelvo;

toilet paper, ~papero; **toiletries
case**, tualetaĵujo
Tokay, (region in Hungary). Tokajo†;
(re wine), ~a
token, (for bus, tolls, games, etc.), ĵetono; (sign, mark), signo, simbolo;
(slight, nominal), nominala; **beto-
ken**, (show), signi [tr], montri [tr];
(presage), aŭguri [tr]; **by the same token**, (in same way), sammaniere; (for
same reason), samkiale
Tokharian, Tokharic, toĥaro; ~a
Tokyo, Tokio
Toledo, (gen), Toledo
tolerate, toleri [tr]; **tolerable**, ~ebla;
tolerance, (ability to tolerate, as re
disease), ~ateco; (inclination to tolerate, as re differing opinions), ~emo,
~o; (mech: tolerable variation), ~o;
tolerant, ~ema; **intolerable**, ne~eb-
la; **intolerance**, ne~emo; ne~ateco;
intolerant, ne~ema
toll, (any tax), imposto; (bridge),
pont~o; (road), voj~o; (adj: requiring
toll), pag– [pfx] (e.g.: *toll bridge:*
pagponto; *toll road:* pagvojo; *toll
call:* pagvoko); (number, sum lost
etc.), (perdo)sumo (e.g.: *the storm's
death toll reached 23:* la mortosumo
de la ŝtormo atingis 23); (ring bell),
(mort)sonori [int]; (mort)sonorigis
tolu, (resin), toluo; **toluene**, ~eno; **tolu-
idine**, ~idino; **toluol**, toluolo, tolueno;
toluyl, ~ilo **tolu balsam, balsam of
Tolu**, ~balzamo
Tom, Tom(ĉj)o, Toĉjo
tomahawk, tomahoko
toman, tomano
tomato, (plant or fruit), tomato; **cherry
tomato**, ~eto; **strawberry tomato**, fizalido
tomb, tombo; **entomb**, en~igi; **tomb-
stone**, ~oŝtono
tombac, tombak, tombako
tombola, tombolo
tome, volumo
–tome, (med sfx), –tomo; **–tomic**, ~a;
–tomize, ~izi [tr]; **–tomy**, ~io
tomography, tomografio
tomorrow, (adv), morgaŭ (e.g.: *we will
arrive tomorrow:* ni alvenos ~; *tomorrow will be hot:* ~ estos varme); **to-**

morrow's, la ~a (e.g.: *tomorrow's newspaper:* la ~a ĵurnalo); **day after tomorrow**, post~; **a week from tomorrow**, ~ post semajno
tomtit, (titmouse), paruo
tomtom, tamtamo; ~i [int]
ton, (unit of weight, gen), tuno [note: unless context is clear, avoid confusion by using "tuno" only in the metric sense (see § 20); see subentries below; however, since the American ton and British ton are each close in size to the metric ton, one can translate either of those tons as "tuno" when an exact weight is not expressed (e.g.: *large trucks weighing several tons:* grandaj kamionoj pezantaj plurajn ~ojn)]; (unit of ship volume, register ton [2,83 m³ or 100 ft³]), tonelo; (unit of air-conditioner capacity [12 000 BTU]), 3024 (grandaj) kalorioj; **kiloton**, kilo~o; **tonage**, (weight), ~aro; (capacity), tonelaro; **short ton**, (Am: 2000 pounds), 0,7072 (metra) ~o; **long ton**, (Br: 2240 pounds), 1,016 (metraj) ~oj; **register ton**, tonelo; **measurement ton, freight ton**, (40 ft³), 2,5 toneloj; **displacement ton**, (35 ft³), 2,86 toneloj
tonal, (re any tone), tona; (re mus tonality), tonala; **atonal**, netona; netonala; **tonality**, ~eco; (key), tonalo
tone, (mus, sound, color, nuance, manner, etc.), tono; ~igi; (of muscle or oth organ), tonio; (elasticity, as of rubber), elasteco; **toner**, (phot; for photocopy machine, laser printer, etc.), ~enzo; ~iga bano; **tone cluster**, ~fasko; **tone down**, moderigi, mildigi; **half-tone**, (mus, art), duon~o; duon~a; **overtone**, (gen), krom~o; **semitone**, duon~o; **two-tone**, (2 colors), du~a; **twelve-tone**, (mus), dekdu~a
toneme, tonemo
Tonga, Tongo†
tongs, prenilo [note sing]; **fireplace tongs**, fajro~o
tongue, (anat, or any similar object), lango; (of land), ter~o; (small piece, as on oboe; tab, as for soldered connection; etc.), ~eto; (mus: act on by tongue, as re wind instrument), ~i [tr, int]; (language, gen), lingvo; (local language), idiomo [cp "dialect", "language"]; **tongue and groove**, ~o kaj foldo; **tongue-in-cheek**, ~-en-vanga; ~-en-vange; **with tongue in cheek**, kun ~o en la vango, ~-en-vange; **tongue-lash**, riproĉegi [tr]; **tongue-tied**, (as from fear etc.), konsternita; **tongue-twister**, ~otordilo; **mother tongue**, gepatra lingvo; **hold one's tongue**, regi la ~on, bridi la buŝon; **be on the tip of one's tongue**, ŝvebi sur la ~o, esti sur la pinto de la ~o
–tonia, (med sfx: tone), –tonio
tonic, (mus; med), toniko; ~a; **subtonic**, sub~o
tonight, ĉi–nokte,   hodiaŭ   vespere, ĉi–vespere; **tonight's**, la ĉi–nokta, la ĉi–vespera
tonka, (bean), tonka* fabo
Tonkin, Tonkino; **Gulf of Tonkin**, Golfo de ~o
tonolysis, tonolizo
tonsil, tonsilo; **tonsillectomy**, ~ektomio; **tonsillitis**, ~ito
tonsilla, tonsilla palatina, tonsilo
tonsorial, barbira
tonsure, tonsuro; ~i [tr]
tonus, tonio
Tony, (man's nickname), Tonĉjo
too, (excessively), tro (e.g.: *it is too big:* ĝi estas ~ granda; *you speak too fast:* vi parolas ~ rapide); (also), ankaŭ [see "also"]; (indeed), ja (e.g.: *he said I couldn't bicycle that far, but I can too do it!:* li diris ke mi ne povas bicikli tiel malproksimen, sed mi ja povas fari ĝin!); **too much, too many**, ~ (da), ~ multe (da) (e.g.: *you talk too much:* vi babilas ~ [or: ~ multe]; *he put in too much salt:* li enmetis tro (multe) da salo); **much too much, much too many**, multe ~ (da)
tool, (gen), ilo; (specified type), –ilo [sfx] (e.g.: *sharpening tool:* akrigilo); (form, work w a tool), prilabori [tr]; **tool up**, ilarizi [tr]; ilariziĝi; **hand tool**, mana ~o [not "manilo"]; **power tool**, pova ilo, povo–ilo [not "potenca ilo"; not "povilo"]

toot, (whistle etc.), fajfi [int]; ~igi; ~o; (car horn etc.), hupi [int]; hupigi; hupado; (onom, gen), hup!

tooth, (anat, or similar object), dento; (of gearwheel), noĉo†; (provide w teeth), ~izi [tr]; (notch, make jagged), noĉi [tr]; **toothache**, ~odoloro; **toothbrush**, ~obroso; **toothpaste**, ~opasto; **toothpick**, ~opikilo; **toothwort**, (*Lathraea*), latreo; **eye-tooth**, (canine), kanino; **false teeth**, ~a protezo, artefarita ~aro [note sing]; **sweet tooth**, dolĉavido; **wisdom tooth**, saĝo~o; **tooth and nail**, furioze; **in the teeth of**, plene kontraŭ; **sink one's teeth into**, (fig), (plene) sin miksi en, plen~e mordi [tr]

tootle, (whistle), fajfeti [int]; ~o; (car horn etc.), hupeti [int]; hupetado

top, (highest point, summit; lid, cover; etc.), supro; (surface), ~aĵo; (of convertible car, camper top for pickup truck, etc.), kovrumo, kapuĉo; (seats on top of bus etc.), imperialo; (child's spinning toy), turbo; (platform on ship mast), topo; (primary, main), ĉefa; (exceed, surpass), superi [tr]; (cross top of rise of ground etc.), suriri [tr]; (be at head of, lead), estri [tr]; **topless**, sen~a; sen~e; **top-notch**, unuaranga; **topping**, sur(verŝ)aĵo; **on top**, ~e; **on top of**, sur; **on top of that**, ne nur tio; aldone al tio, krom tio; **top off**, kompletigi, fini [tr]; **top up**, replenigi; **blacktop**, asfalto; asfalti [tr]; **blow one's top**, perdi sian sinregon, ekkoleriĝi

topaz, topazo

topee, sunkasko

topgallant, bramo; ~a; **topgallant sail**, ~velo

tophus, tofo

topiary, (the art), arbotondarto; ~a; (topiary work), ~aĵo

topic, (theme, subject), temo; (rhetorical category), topiko; **subtopic**, sub~o; **topical**, (local), loka; (arranged by topic), laŭ~a; (current), aktuala

topinamb(o)ur, topinamburo

topography, topograf/io; **topographic(al)**, ~ia; **topographer**, ~o

topology, topologio; **topological**, ~a

toponymy, toponimio

topple, (overturn, fall), renversi [tr], faligi; ~iĝi; (totter), ŝanceli [tr]; ŝanceliĝi

topsy-turvy, tohuvabohuo; ~a, renversita; ~e

toque, ĉapo

tor, pintmonteto

Torah, Torao

torch, (flaming stick etc.; for welding etc.), torĉo; (Br: flashlight), poŝlampo; **blowtorch**, blov~o; **cutting torch**, tranĉ~o

toreador, toreisto, toreadoro

torii, torijo

Torino, Torino

torment, turmenti [tr]; ~o

tornado, (gen), tornado; (whirlwind), trombo

toroid, toroido

Toronto, Toronto

torpedo, torpedo; ~i [tr]

Torpedo, torpedo

torpid, torpora; **torpor**, ~o

torque, tordo

Torquemada, Torkemado

torrent, torento; **torrential**, ~a

torrid, varm/ega, brul~a, arda

torsion, tord/ado; **torsion bar**, ~ostango

torso, torso

tort, delikt/eto; (more precise), nekontrakta civila ~o

torticollis, tortikolo

tortilla, maizpaneto

tortoise, (land tortoise, *Testudo*), testudo; (sea tortoise, *Chelonia*), ĥelonio

Tortrix, tortriko

tortuous, serpenta, sinua; **tortuosity**, ~eco, sinueco

torture, torturi [tr]; ~(ad)o

torus, (math; geom), toro; (of flower), toruso, receptaklo

toss, (throw), ĵeti [tr]; ~iĝi; ~(iĝ)o; (flip coin etc.), frapeti [tr]; frapeto; **toss about**, (knock, bump), ŝanceladi [tr], skuadi [tr]; ŝanceliĝadi, skuiĝadi; **toss-up**, (equal chance), egalŝanco; **toss and turn**, (be restless), ~iĝadi

tot, (child), etulo; (Br: add up), sumigi

total, totalo, tuto; ~a, tuta; ~igi, sumigi; **totality**, ~eco; ~aĵo; **totalizator**, **totalizater**, (gen), totalizatoro; **subto-**

tal, sub~o; sub~igi; **teetotal**, tuttuta, absoluta; **teetotaler**, abstinulo
totalitarian, total/isma; ~isto; **totalitarianism**, ~ismo
tote, (carry), porti [tr]; **tote bag**, ~osaketo
totem, totemo; ~a; **totemism**, ~ismo; **totem pole**, ~fosto
totter, ŝanceliĝi; ~o
toucan, tukano
touch, (contact, feel, make impression on, etc., gen), tuŝi [tr]; ~iĝi; ~(iĝ)o; (sense of feel), ~ado; (palpate), palpi [tr, int]; (concern), koncerni [tr]; (relate to, have to do w), aludi [tr], temi pri, rilati al; (stir feelings), emocii [tr], afekcii [tr], kor~i [tr]; (skill), lerteco (e.g.: *I've lost my touch with tennis:* mi perdis mian lertecon ĉe teniso); (small amount, trace), nuanco, gusteto (e.g.: *a touch of sadness in her voice:* nuanco de malĝojo en ŝia voĉo); (child's game), ~ludo; **touching**, (impressing emotions), kor~a; **touchy**, (taking offense), ofendiĝema; (delicate), delikata; **touch down**, (plane etc.), surterigi, alterigi; surteriĝi, alteriĝi; **touchdown**, (landing), surteriĝo; (football), celtrafo; **touchline**, ~linio; **touch-me-not**, (bot), ne~umino, ĝardena balzamino; **touch off**, (set off, detonate, lit or fig), eksplodigi; **touch on**, (supraĵe) rilati al, aludi [tr], trakti [tr]; **touchstone**, ~ŝtono; **touch up**, (photo etc.), re~i [tr]; **touch upon**, aludi [tr], koncerni [tr]; **touchwood**, tindro; **retouch**, (phot etc.), re~i [tr]; **a touch of**, (slight amount), iomete da, nuanco da, gusteto da; **touch-and-go**, necerta, kriza, delikata; **in touch (with)**, en kontakto (kun); **keep in touch (with)**, resti en kontakto (kun); **lose touch (with)**, perdi kontakton (kun); **get in touch (with)**, kontaktiĝi (kun)
touché trafite
tough, (resistant), rezista; (strong), fortika; forta [see "strong"]; (firm), firma; (hard), malmola, hardita; (tenacious), tenaca; (difficult), malfacila; (unfortunate), malfeliĉa; (hoodlum), gangstero, bandito; **toughen**, fortiki-

gi; fortikiĝi; fortigi; fortiĝi; firmigi; firmiĝi; hardi [tr]; hardiĝi
Toulon, Tulono
Toulouse, Tuluzo
toupee, peruketo
tour, (trip), veturo, vojaĝo; ~i [int], vojaĝi [int] (tra, al, en, ĉirkaŭ); (as by performing group to various cities), turneo; fari turneon (tra, al, etc.); **tourism**, turismo; **tourist**, turisma; turisto; **tour of duty**, deĵorperiodo; **on tour**, (re performer etc.), en turneo
Touraine, Tureno, Turlando
tourmaline, turmalino
tournament, turniro; ~i [int]
tournedos, turnedoso
tourney, turniro; ~i [int]
tourniquet, turniketo
Tours, (city), Turo
tousle, taŭzi [tr]
tout, (praise), laŭdi [tr], paradigi; (solicit), varb(aĉ)i [tr]
touzle, taŭzi [tr]
tow, (pull behind, drag), treni [tr]; ~iĝi; ~(iĝ)o; (pull as trailer), remorki [tr]; remorkiĝi (e.g.: *we drove to the beach towing a boat:* ni veturis al la strando remorkante boaton); (fiber), stupo; **in tow**, ~ata; remorkata; **undertow**, kontraŭfluo; **tow-headed**, stup-hara
toward(s), (in direction of), al (e.g.: *walk toward town:* marŝi al la urbo; *steps toward peace:* paŝoj al la paco) [cp "to"]; (more emphatic), cele al, direkte al; (concerning, about), pri, al (e.g.: *antipathy toward new music:* antipatio pri nova muziko); (close to), ĉirkaŭ (e.g.: *toward sunset:* ĉirkaŭ la sunsubiro); (for; as goal), por, cele ~ (e.g.: *save toward a new car:* ŝpari por [or] cele ~ nova aŭto)
towel, (gen), viŝtuko; ~i [tr]; (for bath), bantuko; (any small towel), mantuko; **throw in the towel**, kapitulaci [int]
tower, (structure, gen), turo; (rise high, stand high over), ~i [int], alte leviĝi, alte stari [int]; (high-voltage elec transmission tower, pylon tower), latismasto; **conning tower**, rekognoska ~o; **watchtower**, gvato~o
town, (small city), urb/eto; (re any urban area), ~o; ~a (e.g.: *town plan-*

ning; ~a planado; *I'm going to town:* mi iras al la ~o); **town hall,** ~domo; **townhouse,** (in continuous row), vicdomo; **township,** komunumo; **downtown,** (town center), ~centro; ~centra; ~centre(n); **uptown,** ekster~centra; ekster~centre(n)

toxemia, toksemio

toxic, toksa; **toxicity,** ~eco; **toxicology,** ~ologio; **toxicologist,** ~ologo; **detoxify, detoxicate,** sen~igi

toxin, (any toxic substance), tokso; (specific toxin from microbe etc.), toksino; **antitoxin,** anti~a; antitoksino

toy, (for play), ludilo; (toy copy of specified thing), ludil– [pfx] (e.g.: *toy giraffe:* ~-ĝirafo); **toy with,** (play w), ludi [int] per; (dabble), diletanti [int] kun; (consider, as idea), konsideri [tr], pripensi [tr]

trabecula, trabeklo

trace, (copy drawing etc.), paŭsi [tr]; ~iĝi; (track, footprint, etc., left behind), spuro; (follow same; track, search for), spuri [tr]; (follow, gen), sekvi [tr]; (any sign, mark), signo; (mark route of future road etc. on map or ground), tracei [tr]; traceo; (outline), konturo; konturi [tr]; (sketch briefly), skizi [tr]; (path, trail), pado, vojeto; (tiny amount), iometo, sugesto, nuanco; (record, register), registri [tr]; (harness strap), tirrimeno; **tracer,** (tracking inquiry), spurenketo; **tracer bullet, tracer shell,** spurkuglo; **tracing,** (traced drawing etc.), ~aĵo; **tracing paper,** ~papero; **tracery,** aĵuraĵo, retaĵo; **retrace,** resekvi [tr], respuri [tr]; **kick over the traces,** plene ribeli [int]

trachea, trafieo; **tracheitis,** ~ito; **tracheotomy,** ~otomio

Tracheata, trafieuloj

trache(o)–, (anat root), trafie(o)–

Trachinus, trafiino

trachoma, trakomo

track, (footprints, scent, wake of boat, or oth sign left by passing person, animal, object), spuro; (follow same; follow star, spaceship, satellite, etc., by telescope, radar, etc.), ~i [tr]; (path of moving object; re magnetic tape, movie film, etc.; 2 parallel rr rails; etc.), trako (e.g.: 4–track stereo recording: 4–traka stereoa registraĵo); (one rr rail), relo; (go, follow, run along a track or course), kuri [int] (e.g.: *in turning, the rear wheels track inside the front ones:* turniĝante, la postaj radoj kuras interne de la antaŭaj); (trail, path), pado, vojeto; (racetrack etc.), vego†; (distance between wheels on one axle of vehicle), ŝpuro (e.g.: *a wide-track car:* larĝaŝpura aŭto); (roller belt on which caterpillar vehicle moves), raŭpo; (track sports, as running, high jump, pole vault, etc.), traksportoj; (leave behind, as dirt, snow, etc.), postlasi [tr] (e.g.: *the children tracked mud on the rug:* la infanoj postlasis koton sur la tapiŝo); **track down,** ~kapti [tr]; **track up,** (leave dirty tracks), ~malpurigi; **tracking station,** ~stacio; **beaten track,** batita vojo; **racetrack,** kurejo; **sidetrack,** (lit or fig), flanktrako; flanktrakigi; **get sidetracked,** flanktrakiĝi; **soundtrack,** (of movie, video), sonstreko; **spur track,** (rr), sprona trako; **the Wool Track,** (Aus), la Tondista Vojo; **in one's tracks,** (where one is), kie oni staras (–is, –os) (e.g.: *the sight stopped him in his tracks:* la vido haltigis lin kie li staris); **keep track of,** (maintain control, check on), kontroladi [tr], teni kalkulon de; (follow, gen; keep informed about, etc.), sekvi [tr] (e.g.: *keep track of new discoveries:* sekvi novajn malkovrojn); (keep, hold), konservi [tr] (e.g.: *a cabinet to keep track of my papers:* ŝranko por konservi miajn paperojn); **lose track of,** perdi (kontakton kun, kontrolon sur); **be on the right (wrong) track,** sekvi la (mal)ĝustan ~on; **be (get) off the track, jump the tracks,** (lit or fig), elreliĝi, devojiĝi; **you're off the track,** vi elreliĝis

tract, (anat, zool), traktuso; (treatise, short work), traktaĵo; (pamphlet, leaflet), pamfleto, flugfolio; (stretch, expanse, area), regiono, etendaĵo, vastaĵo

tractable, (docile), obeema; (malleable, easily worked), maleebla, prilaborebla

traction, (pulling, gen), tirado; (of train etc.), trakcio†; (friction, as of tire on road), (rul)frotado, malglito

tractor, (gen), traktoro; **tractor-trailer (truck, rig)**, tir-kamiono, kamionego

tractus, (anat), traktuso

trade, (bsns), komerco; ~a; ~i [int]; (occupation), metio; metia; (swap, exchange), interŝanĝi [tr]; interŝanĝo; (deal in used or cheap items), brokanti [int]; **trade in**, (resell car etc. in buying new one), revendi [tr]; **trade-in**, revend(aĵ)o; **trademark**, varnomo; **trade off**, (compromise), kompromisi [int]; kompromisigi; **trade-off**, kompromiso; **trade on**, **trade upon**, (exploit), ekspluati [tr]; **tradesperson**, **tradesman**, metiisto

tradition, tradicio; **traditional**, ~a; **traditionalism**, ~ismo; **traditionalist**, ~isma; ~isto

traduce, kalumnii [tr] [not "traduki"]

traffic, (movement of vehicles, people, goods), trafiko; ~a; (re illegal commerce), ŝakri [tr]; ŝakrado (e.g.: *drug traffic:* narkot-ŝakrado); **trafficker**, ŝakristo (e.g.: *drug trafficker:* narkot-ŝakristo)

tragacanth, (gum), traganto; (plant), astragalo

tragedy, tragedio; **tragedian**, ~isto

tragic, tragika; (esp re theat tragedy), tragedia

tragicomedy, tragikomedio

Tragopogon, tragopogo, bokbarbo

Tragulus, tragolo

tragus, trago

trail, (footpath etc.), pado; vojeto; (footprints, track, etc., left by person, animal, or object), spuro; (follow same), spuri [tr]; (drag, pull behind), treni [tr]; treniĝi (e.g.: *a rope trailed behind the car:* ŝnuro treniĝis malantaŭ la aŭto); (pull behind, as trailer), remorki [tr] (e.g.: *we drove to the shore trailing a boat:* ni veturis al la marbordo remorkante boaton); (leave behind), postlasi [tr] (e.g.: *a car trailing smoke:* aŭto postlasanta fumon);

(grow along ground, re plants), rampi [int]; (follow, lag behind), postsekvi [tr]; posteniĝi; **trailer**, (towed vehicle), remorko (e.g.: *camper trailer:* kampada remorko, (w canvas top), tendoremorko); (large mobile home), ruldomo; (movie preview), antaŭfilmo; **trailer park**, **trailer court**, ruldomejo; **semitrailer**, duonremorko

train, (rr), trajno; (hang behind; thing hanging down, trailing), treni [int]; trenaĵo; (retinue), sekvantaro; (procession), procesio; (caravan), karavano; (series), serio; (subway or el), metroo [cp "subway", "tram"]; (coach, teach, rehearse, etc.), trejni [tr]; trejniĝi; (rear, bring up, educate), eduki [tr]; (study), studi [tr, int]; (teach animals behavior, tricks, etc.), dresi [tr]; dresiĝi (e.g.: *that dog is not house-trained:* tiu hundo ne estas hejmdresita); (aim, direct), celumi [tr]; **trainee**, trejnato; **trainer**, trejnisto; dresisto; **training**, trejnado; trejniĝo; dresado; dresiĝo; (received by professionals etc. to update knowledge, for new position, etc.), staĝo; **train of events**, eventserio; **freight train**, var~o; **passenger train**, pasaĝer~o; **power train**, (mech linkage from motor to load), transmisiilaro; **train of thought**, pensfadeno

traipse, promeni [int], vagi [int]

trait, trajto

traitor, (gen), perfid/ulo; (pol), ŝtat~ulo; **traitorous**, (ŝtat)~a

Trajan, Trajano

trajectory, trajektorio

tram, (trolley; mine train), tramo; **tramroad**, ~vojo; **tramway**, (on rails), ~vojo; (on overhead cables), telfero

trammel, (shackle), ŝeklo; en~igi, kateni [tr]; (fishnet), tramelo

tramontane, (beyond mountains), transmonta; (wind), tramontano; tramontana

tramp, (hobo; unscheduled ship, plane, etc.), trampo; ~i [int]; (trample, stomp), treti [tr, int]; tret(ad)o

trample, **trample on**, treti [tr, int]

trampoline, trampolino

trance, tranco; **be in trance**, ~i [int]; **go**

into trance, ek~i [int]; **come out of trance**, el~iĝi; **entrance**, (bewitch), ensorĉi [tr]

tranquil, trankvila; **tranquility**, ~(ec)o; **tranquilize**, ~igi; **tranquilizer**, (drug etc.), ~igenzo

trans–, (pfx), trans–

transact, (any transfer of $), spezi [tr]; (carry on, conduct, do), fari [tr], konduki [tr]; **transaction**, ~o, negoco, transakcio; **transactions**, (written record), aktoj; **transact business**, negoci [int]

transceiver, ricevosendilo [cp "transponder"]

transcend, transcendi [tr]; **transcendent**, **transcendental**, (gen), ~a; **transcendentalism**, ~ismo; **transcendentalist**, ~isma; ~isto

transcribe, transskribi [tr]; **transcript**, ~o; **transcription**, ~o; ~ado

transducer, transduktoro

transect, transsekci [tr]

transept, transepto

transfer, (give, convey, put over, change over, gen), trans/igi, ~doni [tr]; ~iĝi, ~doniĝi; ~igo, ~dono; ~igaĵo; ~iĝinto; (coupon, as for bus transfer), ~igilo; (any $ transaction), spezi [tr]; spezo; (psych: transfer feelings, reactions, etc., from person or self to oth), ~ŝovi [tr]; ~ŝovo; **transference**, ~igo; ~iĝo; ~dono; spezo; ~ŝovo

transfix, (make motionless, gen), senmovigi; (impale), trapiki [tr]

transform, transformi [tr], aliformi [tr], ŝanĝi [tr]; **transformation**, ~iĝo; **transformer**, ~ilo

transfuse, transfuzi [tr]; **transfusion**, ~o

transgress, transpaŝi [tr], peki [int]; **transgression**, ~o, peko

transient, (fleeting, momentary), maldaŭra, efemera; (elec), ~a kurento; (person), trapasanto

transistor, transistoro; **transistorize**, ~izi [tr]

transit, (any going across), transiri [tr]; ~o; ~a; (bsns: goods crossing country w/o paying import tax), transiti [int]; transito; transite; (public transportation system), (publika) vetursistemo

(e.g.: *rapid transit*: rapida vetursistemo); (surveying), (horizontala) teodolito; (ast: passage across, as of sun by Venus), transpaso; transpasi [tr]; **in transit**, survoja; survoje

transition, (change), ŝanĝo; (passing over, between), transiro, transpaso; **in transition**, ~iĝanta

transitive, transitiva; **intransitive**, ne~a

transitory, efemera, pasanta, maldaŭra

Transjordan, Transjordanio

translate, (from one language or form to another), traduki [tr]; ~iĝi; (move object; transfer legal right to), translacii [tr]; **translation**, ~o; ~ado; translacio; **translator**, ~into; ~anto; ~isto; **mistranslate**, ~i [tr]; **mistranslation**, mis~o

transliterate, transliteri [tr]

translucent, diafana; **translucence**, ~eco

transmigrate, transmigri [int]; **transmigration**, ~ado

transmit, (send, gen), sendi [tr] (e.g.: *transmit the information by mail:* poŝte ~i la informon); (broadcast by radio), dis~i [tr]; (TV), tele~i [tr]; (transfer, move substance across), transdoni [tr], transmeti [tr]; (transfer energy, force, motion), transmisii [tr]; (transfer disease), kontaĝi [tr], transmisii [tr]; (impart, communicate), komuniki [tr]; (give over), transigi, transdoni [tr]; (lead), konduki [tr]; **transmission**, ~(ad)o; dis~(ad)o; tele~(ad)o; transdon(ad)o, transmet(ad)o; transmisii(ad)o; kontaĝado; komunikado; transigo; (machinery, power train), transmisiilo; **transmittal**, ~aĵo; **transmitter**, dis~ilo; tele~ilo

transmute, (transform, gen), transformi [tr]; (chem: from one element to another), transmutacii [tr]; **transmutation**, ~(ad)o; transmutaci(ad)o

transom, (crosspiece, lintel), lintelo; (small window above door etc.), vazistaso

transparent, travidebla; **transparency**, ~eco; ~aĵo; (film, slide), diapozitivo, diafilmo*; **semitransparent**, duon~a

transpir/e, (perspire, re plant or animal), transpiri [int]; (breathe, pass gas through leaves, membranes, etc.), transpiri [tr, int]; (through skin), perspiri [int]; (occur), okazi [int]; (become known), evidentiĝi, aperi [int], riveliĝi

transponder, respondosendilo   [cp "transceiver"]

transport, transporti [tr]; ~ado; ~a; (ship, train, etc.), ~a ŝipo (trajno, etc.)

transpose, (gen), transponi [tr]; (math: transposed matrix), ~ato; **transposition,** ~o; (of words, as in poetry), inversio

Transvaal, Transvalo

transverse, transversa; ~e; ~o

transversus, transversalis, (in anat names), transversa; ~o

transvestite, transvestulo

Transylvania, Transilvanio

trap, (catch), kapti [tr]; ~ilo; (pit), enfalujo; (in drainpipe), U–tubo; (carriage), kabrioleto; **trapper,** ~ilisto; **trappings,** (accouterments), garnituro, akcesoraĵoj; **trapdoor,** klap(pord)o

Trapa, trapo

trapeze, trapezo

trapezium, (Am: no sides parallel), (neregula) kvarlatero; (Br: 2 sides parallel; anat: bone), trapezo

trapezius, (muscle), trapezo

trapezoid, (Am: 2 sides parallel), trapezo; (Br: no sides parallel), (neregula) kvarlatero; (anat: bone), trapezoido

Trappe, (abbey), Trapo; **Trappist (monk),** ~isto

trash, rubo, forĵetaĵo; ~igi

Trasimeno, Trasimenus, (Lake), Trazimeno

trauma, traŭmato; **traumatic,** ~a; **traumatism,** (gen state caused by trauma), ~ismo; **traumatize,** ~izi [tr]; **traumatology,** ~ologio

travail, (difficulty, bother), ĉagreno; (agony), agonio; (toil), laborego, peno; (pains of childbirth), akuŝodoloro

travel, (gen), veturi [int]; ~(ad)o; (voyage, connoting set itinerary), vojaĝi [int]; vojaĝ(ad)o; (move, as re mech parts), movi [int]; moviĝi; mov-iĝ(ad)o; **travel(l)er,** ~anto, vojaĝanto; **travel agent,** vojaĝagento; **travel agency,** vojaĝagentejo; **air travel,** aer~ado; **space travel,** kosmo~ado; **traveller's-joy,** (bot), klematido; **travelog(ue),** vojaĝprelego

traverse, (go across), trans/iri [tr]; ~pasi [tr]; ~iro, ~paso; (go through), trairi [tr], trapasi [tr]; trairo, trapaso; (way across, passage), ~pasejo; trapasejo; (crossbar), ~stango; (beam), ~trabo; **traverse rod,** ~stango

travertine, travertino

travesty, travestio; ~i [tr]

trawl, troli [int]; **trawl(net),** ~o; **trawler,** (boat), ~barko

tray, pleto; **warming tray,** hejto~o

treachery, (perfidy), perfido; **treacherous,** ~a; (dangerous), danĝera

treacle, (remedy), rimedo; (Br: molasses), melaso

tread, (walk on, tromp), treti [tr]; ~o; (outer layer, as of tire, shoe, etc.), tegaĵo; (stairstep or analogous thing), ŝtupo; **treadmill,** (lit or fig), paŝrado; **tread water,** akvo~i [int]; **retread,** (tire etc.), retegi [tr]; retegaĵo

treadle, pedalo

treason, ŝtatperfido; **treasonous,** ~a

treasure, (wealth; anything treasured), trezoro; (greatly appreciate), ŝategi [tr], estimegi [tr]; (save), zorge konservi [tr], ~igi; **treasurer,** (of government), ~isto; (of club, organization, etc.), kasisto; **treasury,** (storage place of treasurer; government department; $ held by government), ~ejo, fisko; ($ of club etc.), kaso

treat, (deal w; subject to some process; etc.), trakti [tr]; (med), kuraci [tr] [cp "cure"]; (pay for food, drink, etc., of oth person), regali (iun per io); regalo (e.g.: *I'll treat you to supper:* mi regalos al vi per vespermanĝo); (delightful thing, experience), delekto; **treatment,** ~ado; kurac(ad)o; (one session, as for therapy etc.), seanco; **treat of,** (have to do w), temi pri; **mistreat,** mis~i [tr]

treaty, traktato

Trebizond, Trebizondo

treble, (mus: high range), soprano; ~a; (singer), ~ulo; (instrument), ~aĵo; (triple), triobla; trioblig¡; triobliĝi
tree, (gen), arbo; ~a [note: in names of specific trees, "arbo" is usually omitted (e.g.: *oak tree:* kverko) unless tree is named for fruit or nut (e.g.: *orange tree:* oranĝ~o)]; if specific tree name not found below, check individual tree name]; (chase up a tree), en~igi; **tree of heaven, tree of the gods,** ailanto; **allspice tree,** pimento; **apple tree,** pom~o; **bay tree,** laŭro; **big tree,** (*Sequoiadendron*), sekvojadendro; **blackthorn tree,** prunel~o; **bottle tree,** (Aus: *Brachychiton*), brakikito*; **Brazil-nut tree,** brazilnuksa ~o; **camphor tree,** kamfor~o; **ceiba tree,** kapok~o; **chinaberry tree,** melio; **chocolate tree,** kakao~o; **Christmas tree,** Krist(nask)~o; **clothes tree,** veststango; **clove tree,** kariofil~o, kariofilmirto; **cocoa tree,** kakao~o; **cranberry tree,** viburno; **deciduous tree,** falfolia ~o; **dragon tree,** draceno, drak~o; **ebony tree,** ebon~o; **evergreen tree,** ĉiamverda ~o; **family tree,** genealogio; **fruit tree,** frukt~o; **God tree,** kapok~o; **gum tree,** eŭkalipto; **gum arabic tree,** Senegalia akacio; **Japanese lacquer tree, Japanese varnish tree,** uruŝio; **mastic tree,** lentisko, mastik~o; **mealy tree,** viburno; **nutmeg tree,** miristiko; **oak tree,** kverko [for varieties, see "oak" or "*Quercus*"]; **orange tree,** oranĝ~o; **palm tree,** palmo [for varieties, see "palm"]; **pea tree,** karagano; **pear tree,** pir~o; **pimento tree,** pimento; **pine tree,** pino [for varieties, see "pine" or "*Pinus*"]; **plane tree,** platano; **plum tree,** prun~o; **silk-cotton tree,** kapok~o; **singletree,** timono; **spindle tree,** evonimo; **strawberry tree,** arbut~o; **tea tree,** kajeput~o; **tulip tree,** tulip~o; **wayfaring tree,** viburno; (**be**) **up a tree,** (esti) en embaraso, en malfacilajo, en dilemo; (sidi) en amaso de embaraso
trefoil, (plant or design), trifolio; **bean trefoil,** laburno, orpluvo; **marsh tre-**

foil, menianto
trek, (in wagon), ĉar/vojaĝi [int], ~iri [int]; ~vojaĝo, ~iro; (on foot), piedovojaĝi [int], piediri [int]; piedvojaĝo, piediro; (migrate), migri [int]; migr(ad)o
trellis, pergolo [cp "bower", "lattice"]
Trematoda, trematodoj
trematode, trematodo
tremble, tremi [int]; ~o; (med: as from disease), trepidi [int]
tremendous, (huge), enorma, kolosa, grandega; (dreadful), tremiga; (to any extreme degree), ega
tremolo, tremado [not "tremolo"]
tremor, (trembling, gen), tremo
tremulous, tremeta
trench, (gen), tranĉeo; ~igi; **retrench,** (economize), ŝpari [tr]; ekonomiiĝi, limigi elspezojn
trenchant, (incisive), morda, tranĉa, akra; (forceful), forta, vigla; (effective), efika; (clear-cut), klara
trend, tendenco; ~i [int]; **trendy,** (following fads), furorema
Trent, (Italian or oth city; English river), Trento; (Italian region), ~io
Trento, [see "Trent"]
trepan, (med: trephine), trepano; ~i [tr]; (well-driller etc.), drilego
trepang, tripango
trephine, trepano; ~i [tr]
trepidation, trepidado
treponema. Treponema, treponemo; **treponematosis, treponemiasis,** ~ozo; **treponemicide,** ~icido
trespass, (go on property w/o right), transpaŝi [tr]; (transgress, sin), ~i, peki [int]; ~o, peko; (intrude, encroach), entrudi sin
tress, buklo
trestle, (bridge), trusponto; (sawhorse), stablo
Treves, Treviro
trey, (Aus), tripenca monero
tri–, (pfx), tri–
triad, triopo
trial, (any test), provo, testo; ~a, testa; (hardship, affliction), aflikto; (law), proceso; procesa; **mistrial,** misproceso; **on trial,** ~ata, testata; priprocesata; **time trial,** (sport), tempokurumo†;

trial and error, (per) ~o kaj eraro
triangle, triangulo; **triangular**, ~a; **triangulate**, ~i [tr]; **triangulation**, ~ado
Triassic, triaso; ~a
tribe, tribo; **tribal**, ~a; **tribesman**, ~ano; **tribalism**, ~ismo
tribo–, (pfx: friction), tribo–
Tribonema, konfervo
tribrach, tribrako
tribulation, mízero, aflikt(eg)o, malfelič(eg)o
tribunal, (gen), tribunalo
tribune, (Roman official etc.), tribunuso; (dais), tribuno
tributary, (river), flankrivero, enflurivero; (paying tribute), tributanta; (re tributes), tributa
tribute, (gen), tributo; **pay as tribute**, ~i [tr]
trice, momento
tricentennial, tricentenary, tricentjara; ~a datreveno, ~a jubileo
triceps, (muscle), tricepso
Trichecus, manato
trichiasis, triñozo, trikozo
trichina, triñino, trikino
Trichinella, triñino, trikino
trichinosis, triñinozo, trikinozo
trich(o)–, (med pfx: hair), triñ(o)–, trik(o)–
trichomycosis, trichomycetosis, triñomicetozo, trikomicetozo
trichopathy, triñopatio, trikopatio
Trichophyton, triñofito
trichophytosis, triñofitozo
trichoplasia, triñoplazio, trikoplazio
Trichoptera, triñopteroj
trichromatic, trikromia; **trichromatism**, ~o
trick, (ruse, deceit, artifice), ruzo, artifiko, trompo; ~i [int] (kontraŭ), super~i [tr], friponi [tr], trompi [tr]; (joke), ŝerci [int] (kontraŭ), priŝerci [tr]; (clever, skillful act; knack), lertaĵo; (expedient), rimedo (e.g.: *the tricks of the trade:* la rimedoj de l' metio); (cards won in game), preno; (uncertain, unreliable, as injured knee or back), nefidinda; **trickery**, ~ado, artifikado, friponado, trompado; **trickster**, ~emulo, fripono; **tricky**, (inclined to trick; deceive, fool),

~ema, artifikema; (difficult), tikla, malfacila, delikata; **dirty trick**, fitrompo, fi~o; **play a trick on**, (joke), priŝerci [tr]; **do the trick**, atingi la rezulton
trickle, flueti [int]; ~igi; ~o
triclinic, triklina
tricot, (fabric), trikoto; (garment), ~aĵo
trictrac, triktrako
tricycle, triciklo
Tridacna, tridakno
trident, tridento
Tridentine, trenta
Tridentum, Tridentino [cp "Trent"]
triennium, jar/trio; **triennial**, tri~a
Trier, Treviro
Trieste, Triesto; **Gulf of Trieste**, Golfo de ~o
trifle, (trivial, unimportant), bagatelo; (small amount), ~o, iometo; (of $), (mon)sumeto; **trifling**, ~a; **trifle with**, ludi per, frivole trakti [tr], priŝerci [tr]
Trifolium, trifolio
triforium, triforio
trigeminal, trigemina; **trigeminal nerve**, ~o
trigger, (of gun etc.), ellasilo; (set off, gen), ekagigi; **trigger-happy**, **quick on the trigger**, pafema; (fig), tuj agema
Trigla, triglo; Trigla gurnardus, gurnardo; Triglidae, ~edoj
triglyph, triglifo
trigon, trigone, trigonum, (ast; naut), trigono; **trigonal**, (re trigon, gen), trigona; (3–sided symmetry), trigonala
Trigonella foenumgraecum, fenugreko
trigonometry, trigonometrio; **trigonometric**, ~a; **trigonometric function**, ~a funkcio
trill, (gen), trili [tr, int]; ~o
trillion, (Am: 10^{12}), duiliono; (Br: 10^{18}), triiliono [see § 19(b)]
trilobate, triloba
Trilobita, trilobuloj
trilobite, trilobulo
trilogy, trilogio
trim, (clip, cut, as hair, grass, etc.), tond(et)i [tr]; ~o; (prune tree or similar action), stuci [tr]; (decorate, garnish), ornami [tr], garni [tr];

ornamaĵo, garnaĵo; (balance), ekvilibrigi; (in good order; neat), neta, bonorda; netigi; bonordigi, ordi [tr];
trimming(s), garnaĵo(j)
trimaran, trimaran†
trimester, trimestro
trimeter, trimetro
trine, (threefold), triopa; (triad), ~o
Tringa, tringo; Tringa totanus, ruĝkrura ~o
Trinidad, Trinidado; **Trinidad and Tobago**, ~o kaj Tobago
trinitrotoluene, trinitrotolueno   [abb: TNT]
trinity, (gen), triunuo; **Trinity**, (Christian), T~o, Trinitato; **Ttrinitarian**, trinitatano; trinitatana
trinket, breloko
trinomial, tritermo; ~a
trio, (any group of 3), triopo; (mus: work for 3 voices or instruments), terceto
triode, triodo
triolet, trioleto
trip, (any travel), veturo (e.g.: *a trip to the store:* ~o al la butiko); (esp w specific itinerary; voyage), vojaĝo (e.g.: *a trip to Bolivia:* vojaĝo al Bolivio); (any going), iro (e.g.: *three trips to the kitchen:* tri iroj al la kuirejo); (excursion, pleasure trip), ekskurso; (stumble, make misstep, err), stumbli [int]; stumblo; (make person or animal stumble), krurfalĉi [tr], stumbligi; krurfalĉo, stumbligo; (skip, caper), kaprioli [int]; kapriolado; (release mech part, as from pawl), elklikigi; (pawl), kliko; (start to operate), ekagigi, funkciigi; (drug experience or analogous experience), revego; revegi [int]; **round-trip**, rondvojaĝo, iroreiro; rondvojaĝa, ira-reira
tripartite, (w 3 parties), tripartia; (3 parts), triobla, triparta
tripe, (animal organs), tripo; (nonsense), sensencaĵo; **rock tripe**, rok~o
triphthong, triftongo
triple, triobla; ~e; ~o; ~igi; ~iĝi; triopa; triope [see "double"]
triplet, (any group of 3, triad), triopo; (one of 3 born together), trinaskito; (mus: 3 notes in time of 2), trioleto

triplicate, (threefold), triobla; ~e; ~aĵo; (3rd copy), triplikato; **in triplicate**, ~e
tripod, (gen), tripiedo
Tripoli, (any of several cities), Tripolo; (region), ~io
Tripolitania, Tripolio
triptych, triptiko
triquetrum, (bone), triketro
trireme, triremo
trisect, trisekci [tr]
triskaidekaphobia, dektrifobio
Trismegistus, Trismegisto
trismus, trismo
Tristan, Tristano
trite, banala
Triticum, tritiko; Triticum spelta, spelto
tritium, tricio
triton, (phys), tritono
Triton, (ast; myth), Tritono
Triton, (zool), trituro
triumph, triumfo; ~i [int]; **triumphal**, **triumphant**, ~a
triumvir, triumviro;   **triumvirate**, ~aro; **triumviral**, ~(ar)a
triune, triunueca [see "trinity"]
trivet, tripiedeto
trivia, bagateloj; **trivial**, ~a [not "triviala"]
Troas, the Troad, Troado
trocar, trokaro
trochaic, trokea
trochanter, (anat), trokantero
trochar, trokaro
trochee, trokeo
Trochillidae, kolibroj, muŝbirdoj
trochiter, (trochanter major), granda trokantero; (tuberculum majus humeri), granda trokitero
trochlea, trokeo; **trochlear**, ~a
troglodyte, troglodito
Troglodytes, troglodito
troika, trojko*
Troilus, Troilo
Trojan, Troja; ~ano
troll, (myth), trolo; (fish w moving bait), trenlogi [tr] [not "troli"; cp "trawl"]; (fishing line), trenlogilo
trolley, (vehicle), tramo, ~veturilo; (pulley etc. on pole, for directing elec to troley car), troleo; (carriage etc.

rolling on overhead cable or track; Br: various small carts or trucks), ĉareto; **trolley bus, trackless trolley,** trolebuso; **trolley car,** ~(veturil)o
Trollius europaeus, trolio
trollop, putino
Trombicula, trombidio
trombiculiasis, trombidiozo
trombidiasis, trombidiosis, trombidiozo
Trombidium, trombidio
trombone, trombono
trommel, tromelo
trompe l'œil, okultromp/aĵo†; ~a; ~e
troop, (mil, scouting, theat, etc., group), trupo; (any organized band), bando, brigado, roto; (walk), marŝi [int]; **troops,** (soldiers, gen), ~oj, soldatoj, soldataro; (those left in garrison), depoto; **trooper,** (soldier), soldato; (police), policano, policisto; (on horseback), rajdpolicisto; **paratroop,** paraŝuta; **paratrooper,** paraŝutsoldato, paraŝutisto; **paratroops,** paraŝut~o, paraŝutsoldataro, paraŝutistaro; **storm-trooper,** sturmanto
Tropaeolum, tropeolo
trope, tropo
trophic, trofia
troph(o)–, (med pfx), trof(o)–
trophoneurosis, trofoneŭrozo
trophy, trofeo
tropic, tropiko; ~a; **tropical,** ~a; **semitropical,** duon~a; **subtropical,** sub~a; **(the) tropics,** (la) ~oj, ~landoj; **Tropic of Cancer,** T~o de Kankro; **Tropic of Capricorn,** T~o de Kaprikorno
–tropic, (sci sfx: showing affinity), –tropa†
Tropidonotus, tropidonoto
tropism, tropismo
tropopause, tropopaŭzo
troposphere, troposfero
trot, troti [int]; ~igi; ~(ad)o; **trot out,** (for presentation), elporti [tr]; **the trots,** (colloq: diarrhea), diareo
Trotsky, Trocki; **Trotskyism,** ~ismo; **Trotskyist, Trotskyite,** ~isma; ~isto
troubador, trobadoro
trouble, (bother), ĝeni [tr]; ~o (e.g.: *may I trouble you for a glass of wa-*

ter?: ĉu mi povas ~i vin por glaso da akvo?; *I can do that with no trouble:* mi povas fari tion sen ~o); (annoy; inconvenience, cause difficulty), ĉagreni [tr]; ĉagreno; (afflict), aflikti [tr]; aflikto; (perturb), perturbi [tr], maltrankviligi, malkvietigi, malserenigi; perturbo, maltrankvilo, malkvieteco, malsereneco; (agitate), agiti [tr]; agiteco, agitiĝo; (problem), problemo; (misfortune), malfeliĉo; (difficulty, misfunction, etc.), malfacilaĵo (e.g.: *I have some sort of trouble with my car:* mi havas ian malfacilaĵon kun mia aŭto; *I've got engine trouble:* mi havas motoran malfacilaĵon [or] mia motoro misfunkcias); (inconvenient, embarrassing situation), embaraso; (civil disturbance), malpaco, tumulto; **troubled,** ~ita; ĉagrenita; afliktita; perturbita, maltrankvila, malkvieta, malserena; agitita; malfeliĉa; malpaca; **untroubled,** trankvila, kvieta, serena; **troublemaker,** incitemulo, agitemulo; **trouble-shoot,** spuri problemojn; **trouble-shooter,** problemspuranto; problemspuristo; **troubleshooting,** problemspurado; **troublesome,** ~a; ĉagrena; malfacila; embarasiga; problema; malpaca; **in trouble,** (gen), en embaraso, en malfacilaĵo; **get into trouble,** embarasiĝi; **ask for (look for, invite) trouble,** inviti embarason; **be too much trouble,** tro ~i. esti tro da ~o; **be worth the trouble,** valori la penon, penvalori [int]; **go to the trouble,** fari al si la ~on, fari la klopodon; **go to a lot of trouble (for nothing),** multe sin ~i (por nenio); **it's no trouble,** (ĝi, tio) ne ~as; **put someone to (the) trouble,** fari al iu (la) ~on, ~i iun; **save oneself the trouble,** eviti al si la ~on; **take the trouble,** fari al si la ~on; **with no trouble,** sen~e, senprobleme; **without too much trouble,** sen tro da ~o

trough, trogo; (small, as for feeding birds), ~eto; (between waves), kavo, interondo
trounce, bategi [tr], draŝi [tr]
troupe, trupo

trousers, pantalono [note sing]
trousseau, dotaĵo
trout, (*Salmo*), truto
trowel, trulo; ~i [tr]; **lay it on with a trowel,** (exaggerate), ŝmiri ĝin per ~o; troigi
troy, (weight), [see "ounce", "pound"; see § 20]
Troy, (city), Trojo
truant, forvag/anto, lernejevitanto; ~i, lernejeviti [int], eviti la lernejon; **truancy,** ~(ad)o, lernejevitado
truce, batalhalto
truck, (motor vehicle, gen), kamiono; (light, as panel truck), ~eto; (heavy, as tractor-trailer), ~ego; (transport by truck), ~i [tr]; (wheel assembly under rr car), boĝio; (Br: rr flatcar), platvagono; (dealings, bsns), negoco; **trucker,** ~isto; **trucking,** ~ado; **dump truck,** baskul~o; **flat-bed truck,** plat~o; **hand truck,** rulframo [cp "dolly"]; **panel truck,** (fermita) ~eto; **pickup truck,** (aperta) ~eto; **sprinkler (street-washer) truck,** ŝpruc~o; **stake truck,** palis~o; **tank truck,** cistern~o; **taxi truck,** (Aus), luebla ~o; **tow truck,** tren~o; **tractor-trailer truck,** ~ego; **utility truck,** (Aus), ĉiucela ~eto
truckle, lakei [int]; **truckle bed,** subŝovebla lito
truculent, sovaĝa, kruda, malafabl(eg)a
trudge, pezpaŝ(ad)i [int]; ~o
true, (factual, real), vera; ~e; (correct), ~a, ĝusta, prava; (reliable, faithful), fidela, fidinda; (rightful), rajt(hav)a; (authentc), ~a, aŭtentika; **truism,** aksiomo, ~aĵo; **true-hearted,** lojala, fidela; **true-life,** ~viva; **true up,** ĝustaformigi; **come true,** efektiviĝi, realiĝi; **true to form,** konforma (~e) al la atendo, kiel oni atendas
truffle, trufo; ~i [tr]
trump, (cards), atuto; ~i [tr]; **crosstrump,** kruc~i [tr]; **overtrump, trump higher,** super~i [tr]; **undertrump,** sub~i [tr]; **no trumps,** sen ~oj; **trump up,** (devise), fiinventi [tr]
trumpery, senvaloraĵo, sensencaĵo
trumpet, trumpeto; ~i [tr, int]; **ear trumpet,** korneto

truncate, trunki [tr]
truncheon, klabo
trundle, (roll), ruli [tr]; ~iĝi; (roller), ~ilo; **trundle bed,** subŝovebla lito
trunk, (of car; large chest), kofro; (of tree, body, artery, pipeline, elec or phone line, geom form, etc.), trunko; (of elephant), rostro; **trunks,** (pants), pantaloneto [note sing]; **trunk line,** (gen), trunklinio; **swimming trunks,** naĝo-ŝorto, naĝkalsoneto, (vira) naĝkostumo
trunnion, pivoto
truss, (any framework for support, as of bridge, roof, etc.), truso; ~izi [tr]; (tie up), kunligi [tr]; (bundle), fasko; (for hernia), hernia bandaĝo
trust, (faith, reliance), fido; ~a; ~i [tr]; (care, custody), zorgo; (entrust), konfidi [tr]; konfido; (bsns; credit), kredito; kredita; (cartel, monopoly), trusto; trusta; (trusteeship), kuratoreco; (property legally entrusted to a trustee), fideikomiso; (expect, hope), esperi [tr]; **trustee,** (commissioner), komisiito; (guardian of person etc.), kuratoro; (guardian of property), fideikomisulo; (of bankrupt bsns etc.), sindiko; **trusteeship,** (over person etc.), kuratoreco; (territory, as under UN), kuratorejo; **trusting,** ~ema; **trusty, trustworthy,** ~inda; **antitrust,** kontraŭtrusta; **distrust, mistrust,** mal~i [tr]; mal~o; **sacred trust,** sankta misiono; **put one's trust in, have trust in,** ~i (al); **trust territory,** kuratorejo
truth, (abstract), vero; (a fact), ~aĵo; **truthful,** honesta, ~(em)a, ~dira; **to tell the truth, the truth (of the matter) is,** ~dire, efektive, fakte; **the naked truth,** la nuda ~o, la senŝminka ~o; **the truth will out,** la ~o sin elŝovos
try, (attempt), peni [tr]; ~o (e.g.: *try to do something:* ~i fari ion; *a second try:* dua ~o); (try hard, endeavor, strive), klopodi [tr], strebi [tr]; klopodo; (test), provi [tr]; provo; (hear court case), juĝi [tr] [cp "trial"]; (afflict), aflikti [tr], suferigi [cp "trouble"]; **trying,** (difficult), ~iga; (troublesome), ĝena, ĉagrena, mal-

facila, aflikta; **try on,** (clothes etc.), surprovi [tr]; **try out,** (test), elprovi [tr]; (apply for mus, theat role etc.), elprovi sin; **tryout,** (gen), elprovo; **try one's hand (at),** provi sin (ĉe, kun)

Trypanosoma, tripanosomo

trypanosome, tripanosomo

trypsin, tripsino

tryptophan(e), triptofano

tryst, amrendevuo

tsar, caro; **tsarina,** ~ino

tsetse, [see under "fly"]

Tsingtao, Kingdaŭ

Tsitsihar, Kikihar

Tsuga, cugo

tsunami, cunamo

Tuareg, Tuarego; ~a

tuatara, tuatera, sfendono

tub, kuvo, tino; **bathtub,** banujo, ban~o; **washtub,** lav~o, lavtino

tuba, tubjo

tube, (any pipe; for toothpaste etc.; elec vacuum tube), tubo; (tunnel), tunelo; (dress), gaino; (skirt), gainjupo; **blow-tube,** (blowpipe), blov~o; (blowgun), blovpafilo; **cathode ray tube,** katodradia ~o; **discharge tube,** malŝargo~o; **Fallopian tube, uterine tube,** salpingo; **inner-tube,** (for tire), interna aer~o; **mailing tube,** (of stiff cardboard etc.), poŝto~o [cp "wrap: wrapper"]; **picture tube,** (TV), bildo~o; **test-tube,** prov~o; **vacuum tube,** vaku~o; **go down the tubes,** (colloq), fiaski [int], ruiniĝi

tuber, (gen), tubero; **tuberous,** ~a

Tuber, (bot: truffle), trufo

tubercle, (of tuberculosis), tuberkulo; (any small nodule), tubereto; **tubercle bacillus,** ~a bacilo

tuberculin, tuberkulino; **tuberculinization,** ~izado

tuberculization, tuberkulizado

tuberculosis, tuberkulozo; (of the lungs; popular term), ftizo; **(acute) miliary tuberculosis,** tuberkulgranulozo; **tuberculotic,** ~a; ~ulo

tuberculum, [see "tubercle"]; **tuberculum majus humeri,** granda trokitero; **tuberculum minus humeri,** eta trokitero

tuberose, tuberoso

tuberositas, (anat), tuberaĵo

tuberous, tubera

Tubitella, tubitelo

tubular, (tube-shaped), tubforma

tubule, tubeto; **seminiferous tubule,** spermatotubo

Tubulidentata, tubetodentuloj

tuck, (thrust, put in, under, etc.), ŝovi [tr], en~i [tr], meti [tr]; ~iĝi; ~o; (pull togethor, up), altiri [tr]; altiriĝi; (fold), faldeti [tr]; faldetiĝi; faldeto; (make snug), nestigi (e.g.: *tuck a baby into bed:* nestigi bebon en la liton; *a cabin tucked into the hills:* kabano nestigita [or: nestanta] en la montetoj); **tuck away,** for~i [tr], formeti [tr]; **tuck in,** (pull in, as chin etc.), entiri [tr]

tucker, (Aus: food), manĝaĵo; **tucker bag,** ~osako; **tucker box,** ~okesto

tuco-tuco, tucu-tucu, tukuo

Tudor, Tudoro; ~a

Tuesday, mardo; **Shrove Tuesday,** Karnavala M~o

tuff, tofo

tuft, (bunch of hair, feathers, etc.), tufo; (fine, delicate), hufo; (aigrette), egreto

Tu Fu, Du Fu

tug, (pull), tiri [tr]; ~o; **tug-of-war,** ~konkuro

Tuileries, Tuilerioj

tuition, ($), (universitata, lerneja) abonpago; (teaching), instruado

tularemia, tularemio

tule, skirpo

tulip, tulipo; **tulip tree, tulip poplar,** ~arbo

Tulipa, tulipo

tulle, tulo

Tullius, Tully, Tulio

tumble, (fall), fali [int], rul~i [int]; ~igi; ~o; (suddenly), ek~(ig)i; ek~o; (stumble), stumbli [int]; stumbligi; stumblo; (ruin), ruinigi; ruiniĝi; ruiniĝo; (somersault), transkapiĝi; transkapiĝo; (disarrange, jumble), malaranĝi [tr], malordi [tr]; malordo; **tumbler,** (acrobat), transkapisto; (glass), glaso; **tumbledown,** kaduka

tumbrel, tumbril, (tiltable cart), baskulĉaro

tummy, ventro

tumor, tumoro; **tumorous,** ~a

tumult, tumulto; **tumultuous**, ~a
tumulus, tumulo
tun, barelego
tuna, tunafish, (fish or its meat), tinuso
tundra, tundro
tune, (adjust mus pitch, radio frequency, etc.; make analogous adjustment, as of machine, motor), agordi [tr]; (melody), melodio; **tuner**, (radio), ricevilo; (mus), ~ilo; ~isto; **tuning**, ~o; **tuning fork**, ~ilforko, ~ila forko, diapazono; **tune in**, al~i [tr]; **tune out**, el~i [tr]; **tune up**, ~i; ~iĝi, ~i sin; **in (out of) tune**, (mal)~ita; (mal)~ite; **change one's tune, sing a different tune**, ŝanĝi sian sintenon, ŝanĝi sian rakonton; **to the tune of**, ($), ĝis la sumo de
Tunga penetrans, ĉiko
tungsten, volframo
Tungus, Tunguz, Tunguzo; ~a
tunic, tuniko; **tunic testis**, testika vaginalo; **tunic vaginalis**, vaginalo; **tunic vasculosa bulbi**, uveo
Tunis, Tunizo; **Tunisia**, ~io; **Tunisian**, ~a; ~ano
tunnel, tunelo; ~i [tr, int]; **wind tunnel**, vent~o
tunny, tinuso
turban, turbano
turbid, (unclear), malklara, nuba
turbine, turbino
turbo–, (pfx: turbine), turbin(o)–, turbina (e.g.: *turbogenerator:* ~a generatoro, ~generatoro)
turbot, rombo
turbulent, (gen), turbula; (re crowd, situation, etc.), turbulenta; **turbulence**, ~(ad)o; **be turbulent**, ~i [int]
turd, (vulg), kako*, merd(aĵ)o
Turdus, turdo; Turdus ericetorum philomelus, kanto~o; Turdus merula, merlo; Turdus pilaris, litorno; Turdidae, ~edoj
tureen, sup/ujo, ~vazo
turf, (lawn, sod), gazono; (piece), ~ero, ~peco; (peat), torfo; (racetrack), ĉevalkurejo
turgescent, turgeska; **turgescence**, ~o
turgid, turgora; **turgor**, ~o
Turin, Torino
Turk, (of Turkey), Turko; (any of

Turkic tribe, people), Tjurko; **Turkey**, ~io; **Turkic**, Tjurka; **Turkish**, ~a
Turkestan, Turkestano
turkey, (animal, gen), meleagro; (meat), ~aĵo; **brush turkey**, (Aus: *Alectura lathami*), arbustara ~o; **plain turkey**, (Aus: *Eupodotis australis*), Aŭstralia otido
Turkey, [see "Turk"]
Turkman, Turkmeno
Turkmen, Turkmena; **Turkmenistan**, ~io
Turkoman, Turkomeno; ~a
turmeric, kurkumo
turmoil, tumulto, agiteco
turn, (re any change in direction), turni [tr]; ~iĝi; ~(iĝ)o; (change in direction, esp of vehicle, ship, etc.), ĝiri [tr]; ĝiriĝi; ĝir(iĝ)o (e.g.: *turn the car to the right:* ~u [or: ĝiru] la aŭton dekstren; *the car turned right:* la aŭto ~iĝis (ĝiriĝis) dekstren); (re any circular motion, rotation, gyration), ~i, girigi; ~iĝi, giri [int] [cp "revolve", "revolution", "rotate", "gyrate", "pivot"]; (work wood or metal on lathe, pot on wheel, etc.; give any rounded shape, lit or fig), torni [tr]; torniĝi; (cause to be any specified condition), igi, –igi [sfx] (e.g.: *the sun turned the paper yellow:* la suno flavigis la paperon); (become any specified condition), (far)iĝi, –iĝi [sfx] (e.g.: *the paper turned yellow in the sun:* la papero flaviĝis en la suno; *the leaves turned pale, delicate yellow:* la folioj fariĝis pale, delikate flavaj); (bend), fleksi [tr]; fleksiĝi; fleks(iĝ)o; (fold), faldi [tr]; faldiĝi; fald(iĝ)o; (twist, wrench), tordi [tr]; tordiĝi; tord(iĝ)o; (invert), inversigi; inversiĝi; (reverse, turn over), renversi [tr]; renversiĝi; renvers(iĝ)o; (deflect), for~i [tr], de~i [tr]; (reach, attain, as age), atingi [tr], fariĝi (e.g.: *she turned 50 yesterday:* ŝi fariĝis 50–jara [or: atingis 50 jarojn] hieraŭ); (recoil), resalti [int]; resaltigi; resalto; (direct, aim), direkti [tr], celumi [tr]; direktiĝi, celumiĝi; (change, convert), ŝanĝi [tr]; ŝanĝiĝi; ŝanĝ(iĝ)o (e.g.: *turn cream to butter:*

ŝanĝi kremon en buteron; *leaves turn in the fall:* folioj ŝanĝiĝas en la aŭtuno); devii [int]; deviigi; (alternation, sequence of activity), vico (e.g.: *it's your turn at bat:* estas via vico bati; *my turn to wash dishes:* mia vico lavi la telerojn); (wind, as re coil), volvi [tr]; volviĝi; volvo; (tendency, trend), tendenco; **turn (and turn) about**, (in turn), laŭvice; **turn about is fair play**, ĉiu laŭ sia vico; **turn against**, kontraŭigi (kontraŭ) (e.g.: *she turned the children against me:* ŝi kontraŭigis la infanojn kontraŭ min); **turn around**, re~i [tr], reĝiri [tr]; re~iĝi, reĝiriĝi; **turn-around**, (return), respondo; resendo; **turn aside**, **turn away**, for~i [tr], forklini [tr], flankenigi, deviigi; for~iĝi, forkliniĝi, flankeniĝi, devii [int]; **turn back**, (not proceed further), re~iĝi, reĝiriĝi; (fold back, as sheet etc.), refaldi [tr]; refaldiĝi; **turn down**, (reject), rifuzi [tr], malakcepti [tr]; (lessen intensity of sound, light, flow, etc.), malpliigi, malintensigi; (re sound), mallaŭtigi; (re light), malheligi; (fold back), refaldi [tr]; refaldiĝi; **turn in**, (enter, make turn into), en~i [tr], enĝiri [tr]; en~iĝi, enĝiriĝi (e.g.: *turn in at the red mailbox:* enĝiriĝu ĉe la ruĝa leterskatolo); (deliver, hand in, submit), submeti [tr], liveri [tr]; (give back), redoni [tr]; (denounce, inform on), denunci [tr]; (go to bed), enlitiĝi; **turn (something) inside out**, eksterigi la internon (de io); (ies) interno eksteriĝi; **turn into**, (cause to be), igi, –igi [sfx], fari [tr], ŝanĝi en (–on) (e.g.: *the magician turned the black cat into a white rabbit:* la magiisto igis la nigran katon blanka kuniklo [or] ŝanĝis la nigran katon en blankan kuniklon); (become), (far)iĝi, –iĝi [sfx], ŝanĝiĝi en (–on); **turn loose**, delasi [tr], liberigi; **turn off**, (elec; fig: repel one), malŝalti [tr]; malŝaltiĝi; mallogi [tr], de~i [tr]; mallogiĝi, deturniĝi (e.g.: *turn the light off:* malŝalti la lumon; *his egotism turns me off:* lia egoismo min malŝaltas); (re gas, liquid), fermi [tr]; fermiĝi (e.g.: *turn off the water:*

fermi la akvon); (re vehicle, road, person, etc.; leave road), devojiĝi (de); devojiĝi (de) (e.g.: *turn off Highway 32 at Highway 108:* devojiĝu de Ŝoseo 32 ĉe Ŝoseo 108; *the road to our house turns off there:* la vojo al nia domo devojiĝas tie); (stop functioning, gen), malfunkciiĝi; ĉesi funkcii [int]; **turn on**, ŝalti [tr]; ŝaltiĝi; malfermi [tr]; malfermiĝi; funkciigi; ekfunkcii [int]; [see "turn off" above]; (attack), ekataki [tr]; **turn out**, (result), rezulti [int], montriĝi; rezultigi (e.g.: *how did the cake turn out?:* kiel rezultis la kuko?); (drive out), elpeli [tr]; (throw out), elĵeti [tr]; (appear), aperi [int]; (produce), produkti [tr]; **turn out well**, bone sukcesi [int]; **turn over**, (turn on side or top, reverse, roll over), renversi [tr]; renversiĝi; (start, re motor etc.), starti [int]; startigi; (ponder), pripensi [tr]; (give over, transfer), transdoni [tr]; (delegate), delegi [tr]; ($ transaction), spezi [tr]; speziĝi; **turnover**, renvers(iĝ)o; transdono; delego; spez(ad)o; (pie), torteto, benjeto; (rate of selling and replenishing stock, as in store), restokokvanto; (rate of replenishment of employees, members, etc.), anstataŭiĝa kvanto; anstataŭiĝa kvanto; **turnpike**, (any expressway), aŭtovojo; (toll road), pagvojo; **turn round**, [see "turn around" above]; **turn signal**, ĝirindikilo; **turnstile**, ~kruco; **turn one's stomach**, malkvietigi (la, ies) stomakon; **turn to**, (refer to), sin ~i al; **turn up**, (fold back), refaldi [tr]; refaldiĝi; (turn face up, as card etc.), ~i supren; (appear, come to light), aperi [int], eltroviĝi; (bring to light), aperigi, eltrovi [tr]; (arrive), alveni [int]; (increase intensity of sound, light, flow, etc.), pliigi, (pli)intensigi; (re sound), (pli)laŭtigi; (re light), (pli)heligi; **turn upon**, (attack), ekataki [tr]; **turn upside down**, renversi [tr]; renversiĝi; **ampere-turn**, ampervolvo; **good turn**, bonfaro; **one good turn deserves another**, razisto raziston razas; **in turn**, (taking turns), laŭvice; (in exchange), kompense (e.g.: *she mowed her neighbor's lawn, and in turn, the neighbor looked after her cat:* ŝi tondis la gazonon de sia najbaro, kaj kompense, la najbaro prizorgis ŝian katon); (in further sequence), siavice (e.g.: *they helped her, and she in turn helped him:* ili helpis ŝin, kaj ŝi siavice helpis lin) [note: "siavice" used also for first and second persons (e.g.: *you in your turn:* vi siavice)]; **out of turn**, ekstervice; **overturn**, (gen), renversi [tr]; renversiĝi; renvers(iĝ)o; **take turns**, iri (ludi etc.) laŭvice; **(cooked, done) to a turn**, perfekte (kuirita); **U–turn**, U–ĝiro; **as it turned out**, rezultis ke; hazarde

turnip, napo, rapo
turpentine, terebinto
turpitude, malmoraleco, malnobleco
turquoise, turkiso; ~a
turret, tureto
turtle, (land turtle: *Testudo*), testudo; (sea turtle, green turtle: *Chelonia*), ĥelonio; **turtledove**, turto; **spotted turtledove**, (*Streptopelia chinensis*), punktata turto; **turtleneck**, striktakoluma (svetero); **loggerhead turtle**, kareto
Tuscan, Toskano; ~a; **Tuscany**, ~io
tusk, dentego
Tussilago, tusilago
tussle, (struggle), lukti [int], barakti [int]; ~o, barakto
tut! tut-tut!, (interj), ta ta ta!
tutelage, (function of guardian), kurator/eco; (any protection), protekt(ad)o; (teaching), instru(ad)o; **tutelary**, ~a; protekta
tutor, (private teacher), repetitoro; ~i [tr]; (guardian), kuratoro; (Br: university official in charge of studies), studdirektoro; **tutorial**, ~a; kuratora
tutoyer, ci-diri [int] (al iu)
tutu, (danc)jupeto
Tuvalu, Tuvalo†
tux(edo), frako
tuyère, duzo
TV, [see "televise"]
twaddle, sensencaĵo, stultaĵo
twang, (vibrate), ekvibri [int]; ~igi; ~(ig)o; (nasal voice tone), naza

voĉtono; naze paroli [tr, int]
tweak, ektordi [tr], ekpinĉi [tr]; ~o, ekpinĉo
tweed, tvido†
tweet, (bird sound), kviviti [int], kviki [int], pepeti [int]; ~o, kviko, pepeto; (onom), kvivit!; **tweeter**, (speaker), pepilo
tweezer(s), pinĉileto [note sing]
twelvemo, dozavo†
twice, (2 times), dufoje, du fojojn; (double), duoble; **twice as much (many)**, duoble tiom (da)
twiddle, (twirl, as thumbs), turneti [tr]
twig, branĉeto, vergeto
twilight, krepusko; ~a
twill, kepro; ~a
twin, (gen), ĝemelo; ~a; **Siamese twins**, Siamaj ~oj
twine, (cord), ŝnureto; **(inter)twine**, interplekti [tr], intertordi [tr]; interplektiĝi, intertordiĝi
twinge, ekdoloro
twinkle, scintili [int], trembrili [int]; ~igi, trembriligi; ~o, trembrilo
twirl, (spin, rotate), giri [int], rotacii [int]; ~igi, rotaciigi; ~ado, rotaciado; (twist, coil), tordi [tr]; tordiĝi; tordado; (stir), kirli [tr]; kirliĝi; kirl(iĝ)ado
twist, (contort, distort, wrench, apply torsion, lit or fig), tordi [tr]; ~iĝi; ~(iĝ)o; ~aĵo; (wind, wrap), volvi [tr]; volviĝi; volv(iĝ)o; volvaĵo; (bend, wind, as road etc.), sinui [int], serpenti [int], kurbiĝadi [int]; sinuo, kurbiĝo; (pervert), perversigi; (squirm, writhe), ~iĝadi; **twisted**, ~a; **twisting**, (sinuous), sinua; **twist off**, (break off by twisting), ~orompi [tr]; ~orompiĝi; (unscrew), de~i [tr]; de~iĝi
twit, (reproach, tease), inciteti [tr]; ~o
twitch, (tic, jerk), tiko, klono; ~i [int], kloni [int]; (twinge of pain), ekdoloro
twitter, [see "tweet"]
two, du [see § 19]; **put two and two together**, fari logikan konkludon; bone rezoni [int]
tycoon, magnato
tympan, (gen), timpano
tympanic, timpana; **tympanic membrane**, ~a membrano; **tympanic bone**, timpanalo

tympanites, timpanismo, meteorismo
tympanitis, timpanito, meza otito
tympano, [see "timpano"]
tympanum, (gen), timpano
type, (ideal; model; printing letter; bot,
zool; typical sample), tipo; (printing
characters collectively), ~aro [cp
"character", "font"]; (sort, kind), speco; (write on typewriter, cmptr, etc.),
tajpi [tr] [cp "key"]; (classify), klasifiki [tr]; **typist,** tajpisto; **type face,**
(karaktro)~o* [cp "font"]; **type
founder,** ~fandisto; **type foundry,**
~fandejo; **typescript,** tajpskribo,
tajpaĵo; **typeset, set type (for),** komposti [tr]; **typesetter,** (person), kompostisto; (machine), kompostilo;
typewriter, tajpilo; **teletype,** teletaj-
pi [tr]; teletajpado; **teletypewriter,**
teletajpilo; **by teletype,** teletajpe
typhlitis, tiflito
typhoid, tifoida; **typhoid fever,** ~a
febro; **paratyphoid,** paratifo; paratifa
typhoon, tajfuno
typhus, tifo; **scrub typhus,** cucugamuŝio
typical, tipa
typify, tipigi
typo, (typing, keying error), misklavo,
klaveraro, mistajpo, tajperaro; (printing), mispreso, preseraro
typography, tipograf/io; **typograph-
ic(al),** ~ia; **typographer,** ~o
typology, tipologio
tyrant, tirano, despoto; **tyranny,** ~eco;
tyrannize, ~i [tr]; **tyrannic(al), tyr-
annous,** ~a
tyre, [see "tire"]
Tyre, (city), Tiro; **Tyrian,** ~a; ~ano
tyro, novico
Tyrol, Tirolo; **Tyrolean, Tyrolese,** ~a;
~ano
tyrosine, tirozino
Tyrrhenian Sea, Maro Tirena
tzar, caro; **tzarina,** ~ino

U

ubiquitous, ĉiea; **ubiquity**, ĉieeco
udder, mam(ar)o
UFO, (abb of "unidentified flying object"), NIFO [abb of "neidentigita fluganta objekto"]
Uganda, Ugando†
ugly, malbela; (poet), turpa
Ugric, Ugrican, Ugro; ~a
uh, (interj: pause in speech), aa, ah
uhlan, ulano
Uig(h)ur, Ujguro; ~a
ukase, ukazo
Ukraine, Ukrajno; **Ukrainian**, ~a; ~ano
ukulele, ukulelo
ulama, ulemo
ulan, ulano
Ulan Bator, Ulan-Bator*
ulcer, ulcero; **ulcerous**, ~a; **ulcerate**, ~igi; ~iĝi
ulema, ulemo
Ulex, ulekso
ullage, nepleneco
Ulmus, ulmo
ulna, ulno; **ulnar**, ~a
ulterior, (undisclosed, additional), kaŝita, kroma; (beyond), pretera
ultimate, lasta, fina; ~aĵo; **ultimately**, fin(fin)e; **penultimate**, antaŭ~a; **antepenultimate**, praantaŭ~a
ultimatum, ultimato
ultra-, (pfx), ultra–
ultramarine, (color), ultramara; ~o
ululate, ululi [int]
Ulysses, Uliso
umbel, umbelo
Umbelliferae, umbeliferacoj
umber, sieno; ~a
Umbilicaria, roktripo
umbilicus, umbiliko; **umbilical**, ~a; **umbilical cord**, ~a ŝnuro
umbra, ombro; **penumbra**, duon~o
umbrage, (offense), ofendiĝo; (foliage), foliaro; **take umbrage at**, ~i pro
umbrella, ombrelo; **umbrella stand**, ~ujo
Umbria, Umbrio; **Umbrian**, ~a; ~ano

Umbriel, Umbrielo*
umiak, umjako
umlaut, (vowel change), umlaŭto; (symbol " ¨ "), surdupunkto [see § 16(e)]
umpire, (gen), arbitracii [tr]; ~anto; ~isto
umpteen, dek um [cp "jillion"]
UN, (abb of "United Nations"), UN, UNo [abb of "Unuiĝintaj Nacioj"]
un-, (pfx: opp), mal– (e.g.: *unfortunate:* ~feliĉa; *unfasten:* ~ligi); (not), ne– (e.g.: *unwashed:* nelavita)
unanimous, unuanima
unau, unaŭo
uncanny, mistera, strang(eg)a
Uncia, uncio
uncial, uncialo; ~a
uncle, onklo; (pet name, "unk"), oĉjo; **great-uncle**, pra~o
uncouth, triviala, kruda, maldelikata, malkonvena
unction, sanktole(ad)o; (poet), unkto, unktado [see "anoint"]
unctuous, (gen), oleeca
undecahedron, dekunuedro
undecane, undekano
under, (gen), sub; ~e(n); (in the presence of, with), en, kun (e.g.: *under conditions of equality:* en kondiĉoj de egaleco); (according to), laŭ (e.g.: *under the present Charter:* laŭ la nuna Ĉarto); (presently being –ed), –ata (e.g.: *the subject under discussion:* la diskutata temo; *under construction:* konstruata); **underling**, ~ulo; **underneath**, sub; ~e(n)
under-, (pfx, gen), sub–
understand, (gen), kompreni [tr]; (assume something not expressed), sub~i [tr]; **understanding**, ~o; (ability), ~ivo; **mutual understanding**, (agreement), inter~o, interkonsento; **misunderstand**, mis~i [tr]; **give one to understand**, lasi iun ~i, igi iun ~i
undertake, entrepreni [tr]; **undertaker**, funebraĵisto
undine, undino†

undulate, ondi [int], ~adi; **undulant,** ~anta; **undulation,** ~ado

UNESCO, Unesko [full Esperanto name: Eduka, Scienca, kaj Kultura Organizo de la Unuiĝintaj Nacioj; Esperanto short name derived from (universally understood) English acronym]

ungainly, malgracia, mallerta

unguent, ungvento

unguis, (bot), ungolo; (zool: claw), ungego

ungula, ungolo

Ungulata, hufuloj

uni–, (pfx: one), unu– (e.g.: *unicellular:* unuĉela) [note: sometimes absorbed into Esperanto root as "uni–"; see separate entries]

unicorn, unikorno

unicycle, unuciklo

uniform, (mil or oth standard dress), uniformo; (of one shape or type; unvarying), unuforma, senvaria; **uniformity,** unuformeco

unify, unuigi; **reunify,** re~i; **unification,** ~o

union, (any uniting or thing united), unuiĝo; (pol), unio (e.g.: *Postal Union:* Poŝta Unio); (labor etc.: syndicate), (labor)sindikato; **(labor) unionism,** (labor)sindikatismo; **unionize,** sindikatigi; **reunion,** (meeting), rekuniĝo; (reuniting), reunuigo; re~o; **Union of Soviet Socialist Republics,** [see under "soviet"]

unique, unika

unison, unisono; ~a; **in unison,** ~e

unit, (basic number or quantity; one; basic administrative division; etc.), unuo; unuo– [pfx; note: in adj use in this sense, avoid "unua" = "first" (e.g.: *unit chief:* unuoestro)]; (basic unit of measurement), unito, ~o (e.g.: *a unit of weight:* unito de pezo); (single item), ~aĵo, ero (e.g.: *that factory produces 2000 units a week:* tiu fabriko produktas 2000 ~aĵojn [or] erojn semajne); (tech: assembly; parts etc. in one whole, replaceable as such), bloko (e.g.: *steering unit:* stirila bloko); (mil: of troops), trup~o; **unitize,** (tech), blokigi

Unitarian, Unitariano; ~a; **Unitarianism,** ~ismo; **Unitarian-Universalist,** ~-Universalisma; ~-Universalisto

unitary, unara

unite, unu/igi; ~iĝi [cp "union"]; **reunite,** re~igi; re~iĝi; **United Arab Emirates,** Unuiĝintaj Arabaj Emirlandoj; **United Kingdom,** Unuiĝinta Regno, Unuiĝinta Reĝlando [cp "Britain"]; **United Nations,** Unuiĝintaj Nacioj [abb: UN, UNo]; **United States (of America),** Usono; Usona [no abb in Esperanto]

unity, unu/igo; ~iĝo; ~aĵo; ~eco [cp "one", "unit"]

universal, (applicable, relating to all), universala; (re universe), universa; **universality,** ~aĵo; ~eco; **universalize,** ~igi; **(U)niversalism,** (U)~ismo; **(U)niversalist,** (U)~isma; (U)~isto

universe, universo

university, universitato; ~a

unk, (short for "uncle"), oĉjo

unkempt, taŭzita, malneta, senorda

unless, krom se (e.g.: *I won't go unless she does:* mi ne iros krom se ŝi iros)

unruly, tumultema, nebridebla, malobeema, sendisciplina

unscathed, (not damaged), sendifekta; (not injured), senvunda

until, ĝis (e.g.: *I'll be here until tomorrow:* mi estos ĉi tie ~ morgaŭ); **not until,** (not before), ne antaŭ (e.g.: *I won't come until tomorrow:* mi ne venos antaŭ morgaŭ)

unto, (to), [see "to"]; (until), [see "until"]

untold, (re discrete objects), sennombraj (e.g.: *untold millions of people:* ~aj milionoj da homoj); (collective), nemezurebla (e.g.: *untold misery:* nemezurebla mizero)

untoward, (improper), malkonvena; (adverse, unfavorable), malfavora, malfeliĉa

unwieldy, maloportuna, nemanipulebla

up, (at or to higher position), supre, ~en (e.g.: *go up:* iri ~en; *it's up there:* ĝi estas tie ~e); [note: in expressions like "go upstairs", "go uphill", etc., "stairs" etc. is usually omitted ("iri ~en"), but may be included for emphasis or to be specific ("iri ~en la ŝtuparon", "iri ~en la deklivon")]; (after verb: completely), fin– [pfx], tute (e.g.: *we ate the pie up:* ni finmanĝis la torton); (apart), dis– [pfx] (e.g.: *the police broke up the gathering:* la polico disrompis la homamason); (away), for– [pfx] (e.g.: *the house burned up:* la domo forbrulis); (exhausting or removing the whole), el– [pfx] (e.g.: *use up:* eluzi; *buy up:* elaĉeti); (toward, up to), al– [pfx] (e.g.: *the courier ran up:* la kuriero alkuris); [note: "up" after a verb often adds nothing to meaning of verb and serves no function; in such cases it is not translated (e.g.: *he woke me up:* li vekis min; *light up a cigarette:* bruligi cigaredon; *cook up a meal:* kuiri manĝon)]; (w/o ice, re drink), sen glacio, senglacia; (prep: following along), laŭ (e.g.: *go up that road:* iri laŭ tiu vojo); (adj: directed upward), ~enira (e.g.: *the up escalator:* la ~enira eskalatoro); (more, bigger, higher, etc.), pli (granda, alta, etc.) (e.g.: *prices are up:* prezoj estas pli altaj); (over, finished), finita, pasinta, jam –is (e.g.: *the time is up:* la tempo estas finita [or] jam pasis la tempo); (interj: jump, hop up!), hop!; (out of bed), (esti) el la lito, ellitiĝinta; ellitiĝis (e.g.: *go see if George is up yet:* iru por vidi ĉu Georgo ankoraŭ ellitiĝis); (above horizon, re sun, moon, etc.), (esti) leviĝinta, (jam) leviĝis (e.g.: *the sun is up:* la suno jam leviĝis; (have one's turn), (esti) ies vico (e.g.: *you're up next:* estos via vico la venonta); **upper,** [see "upper"]; **uppity, uppish,** aroganta; **up above,** ~e(n), tie(n) ~e(n); **up against,** alfrontanta; **be up against,** alfronti [tr]; **(be) up against it,** (esti) en embaraso, en malfacilaĵo; **up and,** (colloq: suddenly), subite [or not translated] (e.g.: *he up and left:* li (subite) foriris); **(be) up for,** (as candidate), esti kandidato por; kandidatiĝi por; (to be acted on in specified way), –ota [sfx] (e.g.: *up for sale:* vendota; *up for reelection:* reelektota); (be presented for), (esti) prezentita (–ata) por, prezentiĝi por,

–enda (e.g.: *the subject now up for discussion:* la temo nun prezentata por diskuto [or] la temo nun diskutenda); **up here,** ĉi tie(n) ~e(n); **up on,** (well-informed), (bone) informita pri (e.g.: *I'm not up on ancient history:* mi ne estas bone informita pri la antikva historio); **up there,** tie(n) ~e(n); **up to,** (until; as far as; as much (many) as), ĝis (e.g.: *the bus will hold up to 40 people:* la buso entenos ĝis 40 homoj); **be up to,** (responsibility), la devo (tasko) esti de (iu) (e.g.: *it's up to you to finish the job:* la devo estas via fini la taskon; *it was up to the police to inform them:* la tasko estis de la polico informi ilin); (concern), esti ies afero (e.g.: *it's up to you whether or not you come:* estas via afero ĉu vi venos aŭ ne); (do), fari [tr] (e.g.: *what are you up to?:* kion vi faras?); (plot), komploti [tr] (e.g.: *they're up to something:* ili komplotas ion); (be adequate; equal to task), esti adekvata (kapabla) por, sufiĉi por (e.g.: *that car isn't up to a transcontinental trip:* tiu aŭto ne estas adekvata por transkontinenta vojaĝo); (feel inclined to), inklini [int] (al) (e.g.: *I'm not up to doing that now:* mi ne inklinas fari tion nun); **up until,** ĝis; **upward(s),** (adv), ~en (e.g.: *the road leads upward:* la vojo kondukas ~en); (adj: leading up), ~ena (e.g.: *the upward path:* la ~ena pado); **upwards of,** (more than), pli ol; **up and down,** (along), laŭ; **ups and downs,** sortoŝanĝoj, la feliĉoj kaj malfeliĉoj; **upside down,** renversita, kun la kapo mal~a; renversite; **turn upside down,** renversi [tr], starigi sur la kapon; renversiĝi; **right side up,** kun la ĝusta flanko ~en, kun la kapo ~e; **turn (something) right side up,** turni la kapon (de io) ~en; **what's up?,** kio okazas?; **on the up and up,** honesta, nekaŝita; **up and about,** ellitiĝinta kaj aktiva; **up-and-coming,** promesplena, sukcesonta, entreprenema, agema; **up-to-date,** ĝisdata; **bring up-to-date,** ĝisdatigi, aktualigi; **up the stairs (the mountain, etc.),** ~en la ŝtuparon (monton, etc.), laŭ la

ŝtuparo (monto, etc.)
Upanishad, Upaniŝado
upas, (poison), upaso; (tree), ~arbo
upholster, remburi [tr]; **upholsterer,** ~isto; **upholstery,** ~ado; ~aĵo
–uple, (sfx), –obla; –~igi; –~iĝi (e.g.: *quadruple:* kvar~a; kvar~igi; kvar~iĝi)
upon, [see "on"]
upper, supra; ~aĵo
Uppsala, Upsalo
upshot, rezulto; **in the upshot,** fine, ~e
upsilon, upsila [cp "Y"; see § 16]
Upupa, upupo
uraemia, uremio; **uraemic,** ~a
uraeus, ureuso
Ural, Urals, (mountains), Uralo(j); ~a
Urania, Urania
uranium, uranio; **transuraniic,** trans~a
Uranus, (myth; ast), Urano
uranyl, uranilo
urate, urato
urban, urba; **urbanite,** ~ano; **urbanity,** ~(an)eco; **urbanize,** urbecigi [tr]; **urbanization,** urbecigado; **interurban,** inter~a
urbane, rafinita, ĝentila, polurita, kulturita
urchin, bubo; **sea urchin,** eĥino
Urdu, Urduo; ~a
urea, ureo; **ureameter,** ~ometro; **urease,** ~azo; **ureide,** ~ido
Uredinales, uredinaloj, rustfungoj
Uredo, uredo
uremia, uremio; **uremic,** ~a
ureter, uretero; **ureteritis,** ~ito
urethane, uretano; **polyurethane,** poli~o
urethra, uretro; **urethritis,** ~ito; **urethroscope,** ~oskopo
uretic, urina
urge, urĝi [tr]; ~o; (instinctual), apetenco
urgent, urĝa; **urgency,** ~eco
Uria, urio
–uria, (med sfx), –urio
Uriah, Urias, Urija
uric, (re urine), urina; **uric acid,** ura acido
urine, urino; (colloq), pisaĵo; **urinal,** ~ujo; **urinalysis,** ~analizo; **urinary,** ~a; **urinate,** ~i [int]; (colloq), pisi

[int]; **urinometer,** ~ometro
urn, urno
uro–, (med pfx: urine), uro–
Urodeli, urodeloj
urogenital, urogenera
urogram, urografi/aĵo; **urography,** ~o
urology, urolog/io; **urologist,** ~o
uroscopy, urinoskopio
urotropin, urotropino
Ursa, (ast), Ursino; **Ursa Major,** Granda ~o; **Ursa Minor,** Malgranda ~o
ursine, urs(ec)a
Ursula, Ursula
Ursuline, Ursulanino
Ursus, (zool), urso
Urtica, urtiko
urticaria, urtikario
Uruguay, Urugvajo; **Uruguayan,** ~a; ~ano
Urumchi, Urumĉi
urus, uro
U.S. U.S.A., (abb of "United States of America"), Usono; Usona [no abb in Esperanto]
usage, (custom, manner of speaking, doing), uzanco, uzado [cp "mores"]; (language), lingv-uzo
use, (employ, put into action; consume, spend, take; etc.), uzi [tr]; ~(ad)o; (utilize), utiligi, ~i; utiligo, ~o; (utility, usefulness), utilo; (exploit, use badly), ekspluati [tr], mis~i [tr], mistrakti [tr]; (need), bezono; **useful,** utila; **usefulness,** utilo; **useless,** (not useful), senutila; (w/o result, in vain), senrezulta, vana; **disuse,** ne~ateco; **misuse,** (use wrongly), mis~i [tr]; mis~(ad)o; (mistreat, as person), mistrakti [tr]; mistrakt(ad)o; **use up,** el~i [tr], elĉerpi [tr], forkonsumi [tr]; **used to,** (accustomed to), alkutimiĝinta al (e.g.: *I am used to cold weather:* mi estas alkutimiĝinta al malvarma vetero); (formerly), antaŭe –is, iam –is (e.g.: *I used to live in Tennessee:* mi antaŭe loĝis [or] iam mi loĝis en Tenesio); **be used to,** (customarily), kutime –as, kutimas –i (e.g.: *he's used to walking to work:* li kutimas marŝi al la laboro); **get (become) used to,** alkutimiĝi (e.g.: *he couldn't get used to the thin air of La Paz:* li ne povis

alkutimiĝi al la maldensa aero en La-
Pazo); **in use,** ~ata; **be of use (to,
for),** utili [int] (al, por) (e.g.: *is that of
any use to you?:* ĉu tio iel utilas al
vi?); **have (any) use for,** povi utiligi;
have no use for, ne bezoni [tr], ne
povi utiligi; **make use of, put to use,**
utiligi; **it's no use,** (in vain), estas
vane; **what's the use (of something)?,** kiel utilas (io)?
usher, (in theater etc.), konduk/isto; ~i
[tr]; **usher in,** (lit), en~i [tr]; (bring in,
fig), inaŭguri [tr]
USSR, USSR [abb of "Unio de Sovetaj
Socialistaj Respublikoj"] [see also
"soviet"]
Ustilaginales, ustilaginaloj
Ustilago, ustilago
usual, kutima; **usually,** ~e (~is, ~as,
~os); ~is, ~as, ~os (~i) (e.g.: *she usually came:* ŝi ~e venis [or] ŝi ~is veni)
usufruct, fruktuzo; **usufructuary,** ~an-
to; ~a
usurp, uzurpi [tr]; **usurpation,** ~(ad)o;
usurper, ~into; ~anto; ~onto; ~isto;
(gen), uzurpatoro
usury, uzuro; **usurer,** ~isto; **usurious,**
~a
uta, utao
Utah, Utaho
utensil, ilo, ~ilo [sfx] (e.g.: *cooking
utensil:* kuirilo)
uterus, utero; **uterine,** ~a; **uteritis,**
~ito; **uterine tube,** salpingo; **extrau-
terine,** ekster~a; **intrauterine,** in-
tra~a; **intrauterine device,** intra~a
(kontraŭkoncip)ilo
Utica, (gen), Utiko
utility, (usefulness), utilo, ~eco; (utilitarian), ~(cel)a; (public services, as
gas, elec, etc.), publik~aĵo; pub-
lik~aĵa; **utilitarian,** (useful), ~(cel)a;
(re utilitarianism), ~isma; ~isto; **utilitarianism,** ~ismo; **utilise, utilize,**
~igi
utmost, (greatest, extreme), ekstrema,
pleja; ~(aĵ)o, plejo; ~eco; **do one's utmost,** fari sian plejeblon; **to the utmost,** ĝis la limo (de ebleco)
utopia, utopio; **utopian,** ~a
utricle, utriklo [see "utriculus"]
Utricularia, utrikulario

utriculus, (gen), utriklo; **utriculus ves-
tibuli,** (utriculus of ear), intern-orela
~o; **utriculus prostaticus,** prostata
~o
utter, (absolute), absoluta, kompleta;
(say, speak), eldiri [tr], esprimi [tr];
(give forth, as nonspeech sounds), eligi; **utterance,** eldiro
uvea, uveo; **uveitis,** ~ito
uvula, uvulo; **uvular,** ~a
Uvularia, uvulario*
uxoricide, edzinmortigo
Uzbek, Uzbeko; ~a; **Uzbekistan,** ~io,
~lando

V

vacant, vaka; (in lists, tables, etc., showing unoccupied position etc.), ~as; vacancy, ~eco; be vacan, ~i [int]

vacate, (make vacant), vakigi; (leave), forlasi [tr], foriri de

Vaccaria, vakario

vaccine, vakcino; vaccinate, ~i [tr]; vaccination, ~ado

Vaccinium, vakcinio; Vaccinium myrtillus, mirtelo

vacillate, (waver, oscillate, etc.), ŝanceliĝi; (hesitate), heziti [int], ~i

vacuity, vakueco

vacuole, vakuolo

vacuous, (empty), vaka; (inane, stupid), ~mensa

vacuum, vakuo; ~a; (clean), polvosuĉi [tr]; vacuum bottle, vacuum flask, termoso; vacuum cleaner, polvosuĉilo

vagabond, vagabondo

vagary, kaprico

vagina, vagino; (vulg), piĉo; vaginal, ~a; vaginismus, ~ismo, ~algio; vaginitis, ~ito

vaginalitis, vaginalito

vagotomy, vagotomio

vagrant, (wanderer), vag/anto; ~isto [cp "hobo", "vagabond"]; vagrancy, ~anteco

vague, svaga, malpreciza

vagus, (nerve), vago

vain, (empty, worthless, idle, etc.), vanta; (conceited), orgojla, ~a; (futile, to no avail), vana; in vain, (futile), vana; take in vain, profani [tr]

vainglory, orgojlo, vanteco; vainglorious, ~a, vanta

vair, vajro

Vaisya, (caste), vaiŝjo; (person), ~ulo

Valais, Valezo

valance, drapeto, pendbordero

Valdemar, Valdemaro

vale, valo

valediction, adiaŭo; valedictory, ~a

valence, (chem), valento [see also "~valent"]; valent, ~a; monovalent, uni-

valent, unu~a; bivalent, du~a; covalence, kovalento; covalent, kovalenta; electrovalence, polar valence, elektro~o

Valence, (city), Valenco

Valencia, Valenco

Valenciennes, Valencieno

−valent, (chem sfx), −valenta [see "valence"]

valentine, (card), valentena karto

Valentine, (man's name), Valenteno

Valentinian, Valentiniano

valerate, valerato; valeric acid, valer(i)a acido, pentanacido

valerian, (plant), valeriano; (drug), ~aĵo; Greek valerian, polemonio; red valerian, centranto

Valeriana, (bot), valeriano

Valerianella, valerianelo

valeric, [see "valerate"]

Valerie, Valeria, (woman's name), Valeria

Valerio, (man's name), Valerio

valet, valeto; ~a

valgus, valga; ~aĵo

Valhalla, Valhalo

valiant, brava, kuraĝa, sentima

valid,valida; validate, ~igi; validity, ~eco; invalid, ne~a; invalidate, mal~igi

valise, valizo

Valkyrie, Valkirio

valley, valo

Valois, (region), Valezio; (family), ~ano(j)

valor, kuraĝo, braveco [not "valoro"]; valorous, ~a, brava

Valparaíso, Valparaiso†

value, (worth, gen), valoro; (think highly of), estimi [tr], alte taksi [tr]; (like), ŝati [tr]; [cp "appraise"]; valuable, ~a; ~aĵo; invaluable, ~ega, netaksebla; valuate, (appraise), taksi [tr] [not "~igi"]; valuation, (appraisal), takso; (worth, value), ~o; revaluate, ($), re~igi; devalue, devaluti [tr]; face value, nominala ~o; take at face value, akcepti [tr] laŭ nominala ~o, ak-

cepti laŭ ŝajnoj
valuta, valuto
valve, (for any fluid, gen), valvo; (Br: electron tube), (elektron)tubo, (elektron)~o; (zool: of mollusk etc.), klapo; **bivalve**, duklapa; duklapulo; **needle valve**, ŝtoppinto; **safety valve**, sekur~o; **univalve**, unuklapa; unuklapulo
vamp, (of shoe), ŝudorso; (mus: improvise), improvizi [tr]
vampire, (gen), vampiro; **vampire bat**, (*Desmodus*), desmodo
Vampirus, vampiro
van, (box-like car), vano*; (truck), (fermita) kamion(et)o [see "truck"]; (mil: front line), avano [cp "vanguard"]; (Br: rr car), (fermita) varvagono; **vanpool**, ~komunaĵo
vanadium, vanadio
Vancouver, Vankuvero; **Vancouver Island**, Insulo ~o
vandal, vandalo; **Vandal**, V~o; **vandalize**, ~i [tr]; **vandalism**, ~ismo
Van Dyck, (the painter), Van-Dajk
Vandyke, (re beard etc.), Van-Dajka
vane, (of turbine, windmill, etc.), padelo, alo; **weathervane**, ventoflago
Vanellus, vanelo
vanessa, (zool), vaneso
Vanessa, (woman's name), Vanesa
Vanessa, (zool), vaneso
vanguard, avangardo [cp "van"]
vanilla, (plant or spice), vanilo; ~a
Vanilla, vanilo
vanillin, vanilino
vanish, malaperi [int]
vanity, (conceit), orgojlo, vant(ec)o; vantaĵo; (pointlessness, futility), vaneco, vanaĵo; (dressing table), tualeta tablo; **vanity case**, tualetujo
vanquish, venki [tr]
vantage, vantage point, favora pozicio, elvidejo
Vanuatu, Vanuatuo†
vapid, sengusta, seninteresa, malsprita, teda
vapor, vaporo; **vaporize**, ~igi; ~iĝi; (disappear in vapor), el~iĝi, for~iĝi; **vaporizer**, (atomizer), ŝprucflakono; **vaporous**, ~(ec)a
vaquero, vakero

Varangian, varengo; ~a
Varanus, varano; Varanidae, ~edoj
variable, (changing, gen), varia; ~anto (e.g.: *variable star:* ~a stelo); (changeable), ~igebla (e.g.: *variable capacitor:* ~igebla kondensilo); (math: any changing factor), variablo; **invariable**, ne~a, senŝanĝa, konstanta; (math), invarianto
variance, (varying state, condition), vario; ~ado; (statistics: square of deviation), varianco; (law: exception), escepto; **be at variance**, malakordi [int]
variant, (different), malsama, diferenca; (different version), varianto; (sci), varietato† **invariant**, nevaria, senŝanĝa, konstanta
varicella, varicelo
varicocele, skrotovariko
varicose, varika; **varicosity**, ~o
variegate, (diversify), variigi; **variegated**, ~(igit)a; (multicolored), bunta
variety, (one of several varying types), vario; (changeable condition, state), ~ado; (show), varieteo; (sort, kind), speco, sortimento; (of bio species, e.g., winesap as variety of apple), kultivaro
variform, variforma
variola, variolo
variole, kaveto [not "variolo"]
varioloid, varioloido
variometer, variometro
various, diversa(j); **at various times**, ~foje; ~tempe; [see "time"]; **in various places**, ~loke
varlet, (attendant), varleto; (scoundrel), kanajlo
varnish, verniso; ~i [tr]; **unvarnished**, (story, truth), negarnita, senŝminka, nuda
varsity, (re main team), ĉefa (teamo), ĉefteamo; ĉefteama
Varuna, Varuno
varus, varo; ~a
vary, varii [int]; ~igi; **varied**, diversa, ~(igit)a; **variation**, (one of several varying types), ~o; (changeable condition, state), ~ado; (% change), ~ero; (mus), variacio
vas, vaskulo [cp "vaso~"]; **vas defer-**

ens, spermatodukto
vascular, vaskula; **vascularize**, vaskularizi [tr]
vasculature, vaskularo
vasculitis, vaskulito
vase, vazo
vasectomy, vazektomio
vaseline, vazelino, petrol-ĝelo
Vashti, Vaŝti
vasitis, vaskulito
vas(o)–, (anat, med pfx: vascular), vaz(o)– [cp "vas"]
vasoconstriction, vazokonstrikto; **vasoconstrictor**, ~enzo
vasodilation, vazodilato; **vasodilator**, ~enzo
vasomotor, vazomotora
vasopressin, vazopresino
vassal, vasalo; **vassalage**, (condition), ~eco; (land), ~lando; (all vassals), ~aro
vast, vasta
vat, kuvego, tinego
Vatican, Vatikano; ~a
Vaud, Vaŭdo
vaudeville, vodevilo; ~a
vault, (arched roof etc.; anat), volbo; (chamber, cellar, etc.), kelo; (lockable, as in bank), ŝloskelo; (burial), kripto; (jump), salti [int] (trans); transsalti [tr]; (trans)salto; **vaulted**, (arched), ~a; **pole vault**, (sport), stangosalto†
vaunt, fanfaroni [int] (pri)
veal, bovidaĵo
vector, vektoro; ~a
Veda, (each), Vedo; (all), ~oj; **Vedic**, ~a
Vedanta, vedanto, V~o
veer, (turn, change direction), turni [tr], ĝiri [tr]; ~iĝi, ĝiriĝi; ~iĝo, ĝiriĝo [cp "turn", "careen", "deflect"]; (naut), mallofi [tr]; mallofiĝi; mallofo; **veer off**, oblikvi [int]
Vega, (ast), Vego
vegetable, (any plant), veget/aĵo, vegetalo; (re vegetables), vegetala; (food), legomo; **vegetable garden**, legomĝardeno; **vegetate**, (gen), ~i [int]; **vegetation**, (act of vegetating), ~ado; (plant growth), ~aĵo; (flora of region etc.), flaŭro, vegetalaro; **vege-**

tative, (re vegetation), planta, vegetala; ([capable of] growing; reproducing by growing, not seed), vegetativa
vegetarian, (allowing meat products, as milk, eggs, etc.), vegetara; ~ano; (absolute), vegetalisma; vegetalisto; **vegetarianism**, ~ismo; vegetalismo
vehement, pasia, fervora, arda, impeta
vehicle, (means of travel, as car, plane, etc.), veturilo; (med, chem, phil, etc.: carrier of disease, medium of creative thought, etc.), vehiklo; **vehicular**, ~a; **extravehicular**, (ast), eksterŝipa; **recreational vehicle**, kampadaŭto, kampada ~o
veil, (gen), vualo; ~i [tr]; ~iĝi; (bot, zool, anat: velum), velo; **unveil**, sen~igi
vein, (anat; geol; streak etc., gen), vejno; ~i [tr] [cp "marble", "streak"]; (line of thought), (pens)linio; (style), stilo, maniero; **portal vein**, pileo, porda ~o; **in the same (a different) vein**, laŭ (mal)sama stilo, (mal)samstile
velar, velaro; ~a
veld(t), stepo
vellum, veleno
velocipede, velocipedo
velocity, rapido; **escape velocity**, liberiga ~o
velum, velo
velure, veluro
velvet, veluro; ~a; **velvety**, ~a
velveteen, felpo; ~a
venal, korupt(ebl)a
venation, vejnaro
vend, vendi [tr]; (peddle), kolporti [tr]; **vendor**, (person), ~isto; **vending machine**, ~aŭtomato
Vendée, Vendeo; **Vendean**, ~a; ~ano
vendetta, vendetto
veneer, plaki [tr]; ~(aĵ)o; (fig: false appearance), ŝajno, fasado; **cross-veneer**, kruc~i [tr]; kruc~aĵo
venerate, (respect), respekti [tr]; **venerable**, (respectable), ~inda; (impressive), impona; **veneration**, ~o
venereal, venerea; **venereology**, ~ologio
venesection, flebotomio
venetian, **Venetian**, Venecia

Veneto, Venecilando
Venezuela, Venezuelo; **Venezuelan,** ~a; ~ano
vengeance, venĝo, ~ado; **vengeful,** ~ema; **with a vengeance,** furioze
venial, veniala
Venice, Venecio
venison, cervaĵo
venom, veneno; **venomous,** ~a
venous, vejna
vent, (give off or escape, re gas etc.), eligi, ellasi; eliĝi; (airhole to ventilate room, machine, etc.), aertruo [cp "ventilate"]; (window, as in car), ventolfenestro; (any aperture), aperturo; (fumarole), fumarolo; **vent one's feelings,** elverŝi siajn sentojn
ventilate, ventoli [tr]; **ventilation,** ~ado; **ventilator,** ~ilo; **hyperventilate,** hiper~i [tr]; hiper~iĝi; **hyperventilation,** hiper~(iĝ)ado
ventral, ventra
ventricle, ventriklo
ventriloquy, ventriloquism, ventroparol/(ad)o; **ventriloquist,** ~isto
venture, (risk), riski [tr]; ~o; (enterprise), entrepreno; (adventure), aventuro; (dare), kuraĝi [int]; **nothing ventured, nothing gained,** kiu ne ~as, tiu ne gajnas
venue, (proces)loko
Venus, (myth), Venera; (ast), Venuso; (statue, painting), ~o; **Venus's-comb,** (bot), murekso; **Venus's-fly-trap,** (bot), dioneo, muŝkaptulo; **Venus's-looking-glass,** (bot), spekulario; **Venus of Milo,** la Melosa ~o
veracity, vereco
Veracruz, Verakruco
veranda, verando
Veratrum, veratro; **Veratrum album,** blanka ~o; **Veratrum nigrum,** nigra ~o
verb, verbo
verbal, (in words), vorta; (re verb), verba; (oral), buŝa; **verbalize,** ~igi
Verbascum, verbasko
verbatim, laŭvorta; ~e
verbena, Verbena, verbeno; ~(kolor)a
Verbesina, verbesino
verbiage, vorteksceso, malkoncizeco
verbose, malkonciza

verdant, verda
Verde, [see under "Cape"]
verdict, verdikto; **issue a verdict,** ~i [int]
verdigris, verdigro; ~a
Verdun, Verduno
verdure, verdaĵo
verge, (edge, brink), rando; (approach), proksimiĝi al; (Br: road edge), voj~o, vojbordero; **be on the verge of –ing,** sojli ĉe, esti tuj –onta (e.g.: *we were on the verge of leaving:* ni estis tuj forirontaj)
verger, pedelo
Vergil, [see "Virgil"]
verify, (confirm), konfirmi [tr]; (check on), kontroli [tr]; **verification,** ~o; kontrolo
verisimilar, verŝajna; **verisimilitude,** ~o
veritable, efektiva, vera
verity, veraĵo
Verlaine, Verleno
Vermes, vermoj
vermicelli, vermiĉeloj
vermicular, vermoforma
vermiform, vermoforma
vermifuge, vermifugo
Vermilinguia, (lizards), vermolanguloj
vermillion, vermiljono; ~a
vermin, bestetaĉo(j), insektaĉo(j)
vermis, vermiso
Vermont, Vermonto
vermouth, vermuto
vernacular, vulgara; ~aĵo; ~eco
vernal, printempa
vernalize, vernalizi [tr]
vernation, vernacio
vernier, verniero; ~a
Verona, Verono
veronal, veronalo
Veronese, Veronezo
Veronica, (woman's name), Veronika
Veronica, (bot), veroniko; **Veronica beccabunga,** bekabungo
verruca, veruko
Versailles, Versajlo
versatile, divers/kapabla, ~talenta, ~utila, ~flanka
verse, verso; ~a; **in verse,** ~a; ~e; **versify,** ~i [int]; **(well) versed in,** spert(oplen)a pri

version, (gen), versio, varianto; (med: turning, as of fetus), ~o
verst, versto
versus, kontraŭ
vertebra, vertebro; **vertebral**, ~a; **intervertebral**, inter~a Vertebrata, vertebruloj
vertebrate, vertebra; ~ulo; **invertebrate**, sen~a; sen~ulo
vertex, (math etc.: apex), vertico; (anat: crown of head), verto
vertical, vertikala, apika; ~o
verticil, verticilo
vertigo, vertiĝo; **vertiginous**, ~iga
verumontanum, verumontano
vervain, verbeno; ~(kolor)a
verve, vervo
very, (to high degree), tre (e.g.: *very large trees:* tre grandaj arboj); (the selfsame, real one(s)), mem [adv which must follow n] (e.g.: *there is the very tree we sat under:* jen la arbo mem sub kiu ni sidis); (right), ĝusta (e.g.: *the very person for the job:* la ĝusta homo por la tasko); (precise, exact), preciza, ĝusta (e.g.: *at the very moment when:* je la preciza [or] ĝusta momento kiam [or] precize (ĝuste) (je la momento) kiam); **very much**, tre multe, tre (e.g.: *I would very much like to go:* mi tre ŝatus iri; *that text is somewhat useful, but not very much:* tiu lernolibro estas iom utila, sed ne tre [or] ne tre multe)
vesica, (anat), veziko; **vesical**, ~a
vesicant, vezikiga; ~enzo
vesicle, veziketo
Vespa, (zool), vespo; ~a; Vespa crabro, krabro; Vespidae, ~edoj
Vespasian, Vespaziano
vesper, vespera; **vespers**, (rel), vesproj Vespertilio, vesperto; Vespertilionidae, ~edoj
vessel, (any container), ujo, vazo [cp "contain: container"]; (ship), ŝipo; (anat: for blood, lymph, etc.), angio
vest, (short, tight coat), veŝto; (Br: undershirt), subĉemizo; (clothe, dress), vesti [tr]; **vest in**, (place power, property, etc., in control of), komisii [tr] al, konfidi [tr] (al) (e.g.: *the right to perform weddings is vested in the*

clergy: la rajto geedzigi estas komisiita al la klerikaro); (having earned right, as to pension), rajtiĝinta; **vest with**, (put person in control, invest person w authority), investi (iun per); **vested interest**, privata intereso, persona intereso
Vesta, Vesta
vestal, **vestal virgin**, vestalo
vestibule, vestiblo
vestige, vestiĝo, (post)restaĵo; **vestigial**, ~a; (biol), rudimenta†
vestment, ornato
vestry, sakristio
Vesuvius, Vezuvio
vet, (veteran), veterano; (veterinarian), veterinaro
vetch, vicio; **crown vetch**, koronilo; **kidney vetch**, antilido; **milk vetch**, astragalo
vetchling, latiro
veteran, veterano
veterinarian, veterinaro; ~a; **veterinary**, ~a
veto, vetoo; ~i [tr]
vex, ĉagreni [tr]; **vexation**, ~(ad)o; **vexatious**, ~a
via, (routed through, along), tra, laŭ; (by means of), per
viable, viv/iva, ~kapabla
viaduct, viadukto
vial, flakono
viaticum, (rite for dying person), viatiko
vibes, (colloq: vibrations), vibroj
vibraphone, vibrafono†
vibrate, vibri [int]; ~igi; **vibrant**, (vibrating), ~anta; (vigorous, lively), vigla; **vibration**, ~(ad)o; **vibrator**, ~ilo; **vibratory**, ~a
vibrato, vibr/ado; ~ate
vibrio, Vibrio, vibrio
vibrissa, vibriso
Viburnum, viburno; Viburnum opulus, opulo
vicar, vikario
vicarious, anstataŭa, aliula, malrekta, surogata
vice, (opp "virtue"), malvirto; (subordinate), vic– [pfx] (e.g.: *vice president:* vicprezidento); (Br: vise), ŝraŭbtenilo
vicennial, dudekjara

viceroy, vicrêĝo
vice versa, inverse
Vicia, vicio; Vicia faba, fabo
vicinity, najbar/eco; ~aĵo
vicious, (causing corruption), korupta;
(corrupt, depraved), ~ita, malvirta,
depravacia; (malicious), malic(eg)a,
atakema; (forceful), fort(eg)a
vicissitude, sortoŝanĝo
victim, viktimo; **victimize**, ~igi
victor, venkinto
Victor, (man's name), Viktoro
Victoria, (city in BC, Canada, and elsewhere; lake and falls in Australia; lake and
falls in Africa), Viktorio; (woman's
name), ~a; **Victorian**, (re time of
Queen Victoria), ~ana
Victorio, Victorius, Viktorio
victory, venko; **victorious**, (having
won), ~inta; (triumphant), triumfa
victual, nutroprovizo, (neol), viktualio
Vicugna, vikuno
vicuña, (animal), vikuno; (fur), ~lano
video, (re TV), televida [see "televise"];
(re TV picture, as distinguished from
audio), vida, bilda, vid– [pfx]; vidaĵo
video–, (gen pfx), video–† (e.g.: *videotape:* videobendo)
vie, konkuri [int], rivali [int]
vielle, vjelo
Vienna, Vieno
Vienne, (city and river), Vieno
Vientiane, Vjentiano*
Vietnam, Vjetnamo; **Vietnamese**, ~a;
~o
view, (act of seeing), vido; (thing, scene
viewed; picture), ~aĵo; (scenic sight),
~indaĵo; (out over area, as from
height), el~o; (look at, visually or
mentally), rigardi [tr]; rigardo; (consider, regard), rigardi [tr], konsideri
[tr]; rigardo, konsidero; (opinion),
opinio; (inspect, examine visually),
spekti [tr]; **viewer**, (device), rigardilo;
viewfinder, celilo, rigardilo, serĉilo;
viewpoint, ~punkto; **in view**, (visible), ~ebla; (as goal), celata; **in view
of (something)**, pro (io), konsiderante
(ion); **on view**, elmontrata; **overview**,
superrigardo; **preview**, (view), an-
taŭ~i [tr]; antaŭ~o; (show), an-
taŭmontri [tr]; antaŭmontro; **with a**

view to(ward), cele al [–o], celanta
(–e) [–on], kun la celo [infl], por [
infl]; **take a dim view of**, malaprobi
[tr], malfavori [tr]
vigil, gard/ado, ~maldormo
vigilant, atenta; **vigilance**, ~(ad)o; **vigilance committee**, privata milico; **vi-
gilante**, privatmilica; privatmilicano
vignette, vinjeto
vigor, vigl/eco; **vigorous**, ~a; **invigorate**, (pli)~igi
viking, vikingo
Vila, Vilao*
vile, (gen), fia, aĉa, abomena [not "vila"]
vilify, kalumnii [tr]
villa, villo, vilao
village, vilaĝo
villain, kanajlo; **villainous**, ~a, fia
villus, vilo
Vilnius, Vilna, Vilno
vim, energio, vigleco
vinaigrette, aromujo;   **vinaigrette
sauce**, vinagrosaŭco
Vinca, vinko
Vince, Vinĉjo
Vincent, (man's name), Vincento; **St.
Vincent and Grenadines**, Sankta ~o
kaj Grenadinoj
Vinci, (Leonardo da), Vinĉi
vinculum, vinkulo
vindicate, (justify), pravigi; (remove
blame), senkulpigi
vindictive, venĝema
vine, grimpoplanto; **vineyard**, vinbere-
jo, vitejo [see "grape"]; **cup-and-sau-
cer vine**, kobeo; **grapevine**, [see
under "grape"]; **love vine**, kuskuto;
matrimony vine, licio
vinegar, vinagro
vintage, (year of harvest), rikolt/ojaro;
(particular grape crop), vin~o; (age,
gen), aĝo; (choice, of good vintage),
bon~a, bondata; (old), malnova
vintner, vin(komerc)isto
vinyl, vinilo; ~a
viol, vjolo
viola, (mus), aldo; (flower), violo; **vio-
laist**, ~isto; **viola da gamba**, gambov-
jolo
Viola, (woman's name), Viola
Viola, (bot), violo; Viola tricolor, ~ego,

trikoloreto

violate, (go against, as law etc.), malobservi [tr], malobei [tr]; (treat improperly or disrespectfully), profani [tr]; (intrude, overpower, do violence to, gen), perforti [tr]; (criminally attack person), atenci [tr]; (rape), seksatenci [tr]; **violation,** ~(ad)o; profanado; perfort(ad)o; (seks)atenc(ad)o

violence, (great force, as of storm), fort/ego; (force against justice, right, etc.), per~o, violento† [cp "fury", "violate"]; **violent,** ~ega; violenta; **nonviolent,** neviolenta†

violet, (bot; color), violo; ~a; **African violet,** (*Saintpaulia*), sanktapaŭlio*; **corn violet,** (bot), spekulario; **dame's violet,** hesperido; **dogtooth violet,** eritronio; **ultraviolet,** ultra~o; ultra~a

violin, violono; **violinist,** ~isto

violoncello, violonĉelo

V.I.P. (abb of "very important person"), gravegulo, eminentulo [no abb in Esperanto]

viper, (zool: *Vipera*), vipuro; **horned viper,** cerasto; **pit viper,** botropo

Vipera, vipuro; Viperidae, ~edoj

virago, megero

viral, virusa; viroza [see "virus"]

Virgil, (man's name), Virgilo; (Latin poet), Virgilio

virgin, (gen), virga; ~ul(in)o; **virginal,** ~a; **virginity,** ~eco; **Virgin Islands,** Insuloj V~aj; **vestal virgin,** vestalo

Virginia, (woman's name), Virginia; (state), ~o; **West Virginia,** Okcident-~o

Virgo, (ast), Virgo

virgule, diagonalo, oblikva streketo

virile, vireca; **virility,** ~o

virology, virjolog/io†; **virologist,** ~o

virtual, (effective, practical, almost), efektiva, preskaŭa (e.g.: *a virtual certainty:* preskaŭa certaĵo); (phil; quantum phys; optics), virtuala (e.g.: *virtual particle:* virtuala korpusklo); **virtually,** ~e, preskaŭ

virtue, virto; **virtuous,** ~a; **by virtue of,** (because of), pro; (by authority of), laŭ rajto de, laŭ aŭtoritato de

virtuoso, virtuozo; ~a; **virtuosity,** ~eco

virulent, virulenta; **virulence,** ~eco

virus, (pathogen), virjo†; (disease), ~ozo†, virozo

visa, vizo

visage, (face), vizaĝo; (appearance), aspekto, mieno

vis-à-vis, vidalvide al

visacha, lagostomo

viscera, visceroj; **visceral,** ~a

viscount, vicgrafo

viscous, viskoza; **viscosity,** ~(ec)o; **viscometer,** ~ometro

Viscum, visko

viscus, viscero

vise, ŝraŭbtenilo

Vishnu, Viŝnuo

visible, videbla; **invisible,** ne~a; **(in)visibility,** (ne)~eco

Visigoth, Visigoto

vision, (act of seeing), vido; (sense of sight), ~ado; (mental or psychic image), vizio; **visionary,** vizia; viziulo

visit, (go to see, for any reason), viziti [tr]; ~o; (afflict), aflikti [tr] (iun per io); (inflict), trudi [tr] (ion al iu); (punish), puni [tr] (iun per io); **visitation,** ~o; aflikto; trudo; puno; **visitor,** ~into; ~anto; ~onto; (would-be), ~unto (e.g.: *no visitors allowed:* ~untoj malpermesataj) [see "would"]

visor, viziero

vista, (view out), elvido [see "view"]; (perspective), perspektivo

Vistula, Vistulo

visual, vida

Vitaceae, vitacoj

vital, (re life), vitala, viv– [pfx] (e.g.: *vital process:* vivprocezo); (essential to life), vivesenca; (active, vigorous), vigla; (important), gravega, krize grava, krizgrava; **vitalism,** ~ismo; **vitality,** (vital force), ~eco; (vigor), vigleco; **vitalize,** ~igi; vigligi; **revitalize,** reviĝligi

Vitallium, vitalio†

vitamin, vitamino; ~a; **vitaminology,** ~ologio; **avitaminosis,** avitaminozo; **vitamin A, B$_6$, C, (etc.),** ~o A, B$_6$, C (etc.)

vitellus, vitelo

vitiate, (corrupt), korupti [tr]; (make faulty), difekti [tr]; (invalidate, as contract), malvalidigi

viticulture, vitokulturado
vitiligo, vitiligo
Vitis, vito, vinberujo
vitreous, (glassy), vitreca; **vitreous humor, vitreous body,** (anat), vitreo
vitreum, vitreo
vitrify, vitrigi
vitrine, vitrôŝranko
vitriol, vitriolo; **vitriolic,** (chem: re vitriol), ~a; (fig: biting, caustic), acidega, kaŭstika, ~a
Vitruvius, Vitruvio
vituperate, insultegi [tr], vortvipi [tr]; **vituperative,** ~a
Vitus, (man's name), Vito
viva, (inter: long live ...!), vivu ...!
vivace, (mus), vigle, vivece
vivacious, vigla, viveca, vivplena
vive, [see "viva"]
Viverra, vivero; Viverra civetta, civeto; Viverra genetta, genoto; Viverra zibetha, zibeto; Viverridae, ~edoj
vivid, (bright), bril(eg)a; (lively), vigla; (lifelike), viv(plen)a, viveca
vivify, vivigi
vivipara, vivonask/uloj; **viviparous,** ~a
vivisect, vivosekci [tr]; **vivisection,** ~(ad)o, vivisekcio
vixen, (fox), vulpino; (woman), megero
viz, nome, tio estas [abb: t.e.]
vizier, veziro
Vladimir, Vladimiro
Vladivostok, Vladivostoko
Voandzeia, voandzeo
vocabulary, (all words in a language), leksiko†; (that a person knows), vort/stoko; (word list, as in one lesson of language course), vortlisto; (short dictionary, as at back of language text), vortareto
vocal, (re voice, spoken, oral), voĉa; (vociferous), laŭt~a, bru(em)a; (mus: song or part to be sung, not played), kantaĵo; **vocalic,** vokala; **vocalist,** kantisto; **vocalize,** (use voice, express vocally), ~igi; (add vowel marks, as in Hebrew), vokalizi [tr]; (change into vowel), vokaligi
vocation, kariero, profesio, metio; **vocational,** ~a, profesia, metia
vocative, vokativo
vociferous, laŭtvoĉa,   bru(em)a,

kri(em)a
vocoid, vokoido
vodka, vodko
vogue, (fashion, style), modo; (craze, fad), furoro; **in vogue,** laŭ~a; **out of vogue,** eks~a
voice, (gen), voĉo; ~i [int] (pri); ~igi; **voiced,** (gram, re consonant, as b, d, g, etc.), ~a; **unvoiced,** (p, t, k, etc.), sen~a; **active voice,** (gram), aktivo; **middle voice,** medialo; **passive voice,** pasivo; **raise one's voice,** laŭtigi la ~on; **at the top of one's voice,** plen~e
void, (invalid), malvalida; ~igi, nuligi; (lapsed), ~a, kaduka; (empty), malplena; malplenaĵo; malpleneco; (discharge, excrete), eligi, ekskrecii [tr]
voilà, jen
Volapük, Volapuko
volatile, (easily vaporizing), volatila; (re cmptr or oth elec memory), forstrekiĝa; (unstable, explosive), nestabila, eksplodema; (fickle), facilanima, ŝanĝiĝema
volcano, vulkano; **volcanic,** ~a; **volcanism,** ~ado
vole, mikroto; **water vole,** arvikolo
Volga, Volgo
volition, volo
volitive, volitivo
volley, (weapon firing etc.), salvo; (sports: hit ball etc. back), (sensalte) rebati [tr]; (sensalta) rebat(ad)o
volleyball, (game), volejbalo†; (ball), ~pilko
volt, (elec), volto; (horse turn), volteo; (place for this), volteejo; (fencing leap), salto; **voltage,** tensio; **voltmeter,** ~metro; **abvolt,** ab~o; **electron volt,** elektron~o
Volta, (river), Voltao
voltaic, (elec), voltaa
Voltaire, Voltero; **Voltairean,** ~a; ~ano
voluble, parolema, babilema, malkonciza
volume, (space), volumeno; (tome; series of magazines etc.), volumo; (amount), kvanto; (loudness), laŭto; **volumeter,** ~metro; **volumetric,** ~a; **voluminous,**   multampleksa,

grand~a; **have a volume of,** (capacity), kubi [tr, int] (e.g.: *the bottle has a volume of 2 liters:* la botelo kubas 2 litrojn); **automatic volume control,** (elec), aŭtomata fadkompensilo

voluntary, (of free will, not obligatory), volonta, laŭvola, libervola, propravola; (intentional, not accidental), intenca; **involuntary,** ne~a, nevola, senintenca; **volunteer,** ~ulo; ~ula; (offer self), sin proponi; (voluntarily give), memvole doni [tr]; (ironic usage: order oth person to "offer self", as in mil), "~igi", "sinproponigi"

voluptuous, volupta; ~ama, ~avida; **voluptuousness,** ~eco; ~aĵo; (pleasure), ~o

volute, (arch), voluto; (spiral, gen), spirala

volvulus, volvulo

vomer, (bone), vomero

vomit, vomi [tr, int]; ~aĵo; **vomitus,** ~aĵo

voodoo, envultoreligio; ~a; sorĉi [tr], envulti [tr]

voracious, vorema

–vorous, (sfx: eating), –vora (e.g.: *carnivorous:* karno~a); **–vore,** –~ulo

vortex, (gen), vortico; **vortical,** ~a

votary, (person bound by vow, as monk, nun), votul(in)o; (worshipper), adorant(in)o

vote, voĉdoni [int]; ~o [cp "ballot", "elect"]; (suffrage, right to vote), ~rajto; (total votes cast, or specified group of votes or voters), ~aro; **voter,** ~into; ~anto; ~onto; **vote down,** ~e rifuzi [tr], ~e malakcepti [tr]; **vote in,** elekti [tr]; **vote out,** ~e eksigi; **voting machine,** balotmaŝino; **vote of no confidence,** ~o de malaprobo; **vote of thanks,** dankesprimo; **put to a vote,** ~igi

votive, vota

vouch, (support), subteni [tr], atesti [tr]; (assure, guarantee), garantii [tr], certigi

voucher, atestilo, kreditilo

vow, (oath, gen), ĵuri [tr]; ~o; (rel), voto; voti [tr]

vowel, vokalo; ~a; **semivowel,** (in English: w, y), duon~o

voyage, vojaĝo; ~i [int]; **voyager,** ~into; ~anto; ~onto; ~isto; **maiden voyage,** prov~o

voyeur, skopofili/ulo; **voyeurism,** ~o, vuajerismo

Vulcan, Vulkano

vulcanite, ebonito

vulcanize, vulkanizi [tr]

vulgar, (common, ordinary), vulgara; (uncouth, boorish), triviala, ~aĉa; (crude), kruda; **vulgarism,** ~ismo; **vulgarity,** ~eco; trivialeco; krudeco

Vulgate, Vulgato

vulnerable, vundebla, difektebla, atakebla

Vulpes, vulpo

Vultur, vulturo

vulture, vulturo; **bearded vulture,** gipaeto; **Egyptian vulture,** neofrono; **griffin vulture** gipo; **turkey vulture,** katarto

vulva, vulvo; **vulvitis,** ~ito

W

wacky, frenez(et)a [cp "zany"]

wad, (of cotton etc.), vato; ~i [tr]; (oth, as clothing etc.), bulo; buligi; (crumple, wrinkle), ĉifi [tr]; ĉifaĵo, ĉifbulo

waddle, anas/paŝi [int], ~iri [int]; ~paŝo

wade, vadi [tr, int]

wadi, uedo

wafer, (for rel communion; sealing; med), oblato; (food), vafleto

waffle, (food), vaflo; (waver, be indecisive), ŝanceliĝadi; (Aus: talk long), blagadi [int]; **waffle iron,** ~ofero

waft, (float, as on wind), ŝvebi [int]; ~o; (blow gently, as breeze), bloveti [int]

wag, (tail), vostumi [int]; ~o; (analogous swinging, as tongue), svingi [tr]; svingiĝi; sving(iĝ)o; (jokester), ŝerc(em)ulo; **wagtail,** (zool), motacilo

wage, ($), salajro; (carry on), faradi [tr], estigi, efektivigi; **wage-earner,** ~ulo; **wage war,** militi [int]

wager, veti [tr]; ~o [see "bet"]

waggish, ŝerc(em)a

waggle, svingeti [tr]; ~iĝi; ~o

waggon, [see "wagon"]

Wagner, Vagnero; **Wagnerian,** ~a

wagon, (as for farm or gen use), ĉaro; (4 wheels, pulled by animals), ~ego; (small, for child), ~eto; (Br: rr car), (ŝarĝ)vagono; **paddy wagon,** ĉelveturilo; **station wagon,** postsideja aŭto [cp "hatch: hatchback", "van"]

wah! (onom: cry, as by baby), ŭa!

waif, senhejmulo

wail, ploregi [int], ululi [int]; ~(ad)o, ulul(ad)o

wainscot, (paneling), panelaĵo; (any wall finish), murtegaĵo [cp "mold: molding"]

waist, waistline, talio

wait, (await, be ready; be delayed; etc.), atendi [tr, int]; ~o (e.g.: *wait for the train:* ~i la trajnon); (act as restaurant server), kelneri [int]; **wait for,** ~i; **wait on,** ~i; kelneri al; **wait out,** tra~i [tr]; **waiter, waitress,** (restaurant server), kelner(in)o; **wait table,** kelneri [int]; **wait up,** (stay awake, wait-

ing). ~i sendorme; **lie in wait,** (ambush), ~i en embusko

waive, rezigni [tr]; **waiver,** ~o

wake, (awaken, wake up), veki [tr]; ~iĝi; (funeral vigil), mortfesto; (boat track etc., lit or fig), poststrio, postsulko, trenstrio, disondo; **waken,** ~i; ~iĝi; **wakeful,** maldorma; **wakefulness,** maldormeco; **wake-robin,** (Br), arumo; **in the wake of,** post, rezulte de

Walachia, Valaĥio; **Walachian,** ~a; ~o

Waldemar, Valdemaro

Waldenses, Valdano(j)

waldo, (remote manipulator), telemanipulilo

Waldo, (man's name), Valdo

wale, (welt), vipstrio; (ridge, as on cloth), kresteto

Wales, Kimrio; **New South Wales,** Nova Sud-~o (abb: N.S.K.)

Walhalla, Valhalo

walk, (go on foot, or analogous action), marŝi [int], piediri [int]; ~igi; ~(ad)o; (walk along), laŭ~i [tr], ~i laŭ (e.g.: *walk the streets:* laŭ~i la stratojn); (stroll), promeni [int] (laŭ); promeno; (take for a walk), promenigi (e.g.: *walk the dog:* promenigi la hundon); (walk, pushing bicycle etc.), ~puŝi [tr] (e.g.: *walk the bicycle across the street:* ~puŝi la biciklon trans la straton); (walk, accompanying), ~i kun (e.g.: *I'll walk you home:* mi ~os kun vi hejmen); (walkway, path, etc.), ~ejo, promenejo [cp "path"]; (gait), irmaniero, ~maniero; **walker,** (device for toddlers or handicapped), ~ilo; **walk-in,** en~ebla; **walkway,** ~ejo, promenejo; (for crossing street), pasejo; **walkie-talkie,** (portebla) sendricevilo; **walk of life,** vivokupo; **walk off with,** forporti [tr]; **walk out on,** forlasi [tr]; **jaywalk,** mis~i [int], kontraŭ~i [int]; **sleepwalk,** [see "somnambulate"]

Walkyrie, Valkirio

wall, (gen), muro; ~a; ~igi; ĉirkaŭ~igi,

en~igi; (large, as around city), ~ego; (membrane), parieto; **wall in**, en~igi; **wall off**, dis~igi; **wall up**, ~fermi [tr]; **wall-to-wall**, ~-al-~a; **wall rue (spleenwort)**, harasplenio, ~a asplenio; **firewall**, ferkurteno; **retaining wall**, (low stone wall by road etc.), randbenko; **sidewall**, pneûoflanko; **sea wall**, digo; **supporting wall**, apog~o

wallaby, valabio; **rock wallaby**, rok~o; **tree wallaby**, dendrolago

Wallachia, [see "Walachia"]

wallet, biletujo, monbilujo

walleye, ezoka perko

Walloon, Valono; ~a

wallop, (beat, thrash), bategi [tr], draŝi [tr]; ~o, draŝo; (power, as to strike), potenco

wallow, (flounder, as ship), barakti [int]; (indulge in fully, roll about in, lit or fig), vadi [int] (en, tra), sin ruli (en)

walnut, (nut), juglando; (tree), ~arbo; (wood), ~oligno

Walpurgis, Valpurga; **Walpurgis Night**, ~a Nokto

walrus, rosmaro

Walter, Valtero

waltz, valso; ~i [int]

wan, pala

wand, vergo

wander, vagi [int], nomadi [int]; **wanderer**, ~anto, ~emulo; **wanderlust**, ~emo, migremo; **my mind wandered**, mi distriĝis; **let one's mind wander**, lasi sin distriĝi

wane, (shrink), malkreski [int]; ~(ad)o; (deteriorate), dekadenci [int]; **on the wane**, ~anta; dekadencanta

wangle, perruzi [tr], elruzi [tr]

want, (desire), voli [tr], deziri [tr]; ~o, deziro (e.g.: *I want that:* mi ~as tion; *I want to go:* mi ~as iri); (lack), manko (e.g.: *for want of a nail the shoe was lost:* pro manko de najlo la huffero perdiĝis); (Br: need, require), bezoni [tr]; bezono; (poverty), malriĉeco; (search by police for arrest etc.), serĉi [tr] (e.g.: *wanted for murder:* serĉata pro murdo); **wanting**, (lacking), mankanta; **be wanting, want for**, (lack), (io) manki [int] al (iu, io) (e.g.:

the stew is wanting in salt: mankas salo al la stufo); **want in (out, off, etc.)**, ~i enveni (eliri, deiri, etc.) (e.g.: *the cat wants out:* la kato ~as eliri)

wanton, (senseless, malicious), sensenc(aĉ)a, malica, kapric(aĉ)a; (debauched), diboĉa; diboĉulo; (reckless), senpripensa, aroganta

wapiti, Kanada cervo

war, milito; ~a; ~i [int]; **warfare**, ~ado; **warhead**, ŝargokapo; **warlord**, ~estro, tirano; **warmonger**, ~emulo; **warmongering**, ~ema, ~-incita; **warrior**, batalisto, ~isto; **civil war**, enlanda ~o; **guerrilla war**, gerilo [cp "guerrilla"]; **guerrilla warfare**, gerilado; **postwar**, post~a; **prewar**, antaŭ~a; **wage war**, ~i; **on the warpath**, ~-avida, ~ema; **war of attrition**, forfrot~o; **World War I (II)**, Unua (Dua) Mond~o

warble, tril(ad)i [int]; el~i [tr]; ~o; **warbler**, (bird: gen, unspecific term), ~birdo; (*Hippolais*), hipolao; (*Phylloscopus*), filoskopo; (*Sylvia*), silvio; **grasshopper warbler**, lokustelo; **willow warbler**, fitiso

ward, (division of hospital, jail, etc.), fako; (division of city etc.), kvartalo; (child etc. in custody, as of court or guardian), zorgato; **ward off**, forturni [tr], antaŭforigi

–ward, (adv sfx: toward), –en (e.g.: *homeward:* hejmen; *climb upward:* grimpi supren); (adj), ~ena (e.g.: *an upward climb:* suprena grimpo)

warden, warder, (guard, custodian), gardisto; (in prison), provoso; (chief official of prison), prizonestro; **game warden**, best~o

wardrobe, (clothes), vest/aro; (cabinet), ~oŝranko; (room), ~oĉambro

–wards, [see "–ward"]

ware, (commercial item), varo; (of specific type), –aĵo(j) [sfx] (e.g.: *glassware:* vitraĵoj); **warehouse**, staplo, tenejo; stapli [tr]; **second-hand wares**, brokantaĵoj

warlock, sorĉisto

warm, (not cold, gen), varma; ~igi; ~iĝi; (less than hot), ~eta (e.g.: *during warm weather* [not winter]: dum ~a vetero; *if the soup is too hot, let it cool, but eat it while it is still warm:* se la supo estas tro ~a, lasu ĝin mal~iĝi, sed manĝu ĝin dum ĝi ankoraŭ estas ~eta; *it cooled too much, so I will warm it again:* ĝi tro mal~iĝis, do mi re~igos ĝin); **warmth,** ~(et)o; **lukewarm,** tepida, ~eta

warn, averti [tr]; **warning,** ~o; ~a

warp, (distort), distordi [tr]; ~iĝi; ~(iĝ)o; (weaving), varpo; varpi [tr]; (naut), gerleno

warrant, (written authority to act, pay $, etc.), mandato (e.g.: *search warrant:* traserĉa ~o; *arrest warrant:* arest-~o); (guarantee), garantii [tr]; garantio; (authorize), rajtigi; (justify), motivi [tr], pravigi; **warranty,** ~o, rajtigo; garantio

warren, (of rabbits), gareno, kuniklejo

Warsaw, Varsovio

wart, veruko

wary, singarda

wasabi, vasabio
Wasabia japonica, vasabio

wash, (clean, rinse, etc., gen), lavi [tr]; ~iĝi; (act), ~o; (items washed), ~itaĵo; ~ataĵo; ~otaĵo; (backflow, eddy, etc., as behind propeller), kirlfluo; **washer,** (disk for bolt etc.), ringeto, platringo; (washing machine), ~maŝino, ~atoro; **dishwasher,** teler~atoro; **washing,** (laundry etc.), ~itaĵo; ~ataĵo; ~otaĵo; **washing machine,** ~maŝino, ~atoro; **wash out,** el~i [tr], for~i [tr]; el~iĝi, for~iĝi; (pale colors), paligi; paliĝi; (erode ground, as by run-off water or flood), forerozii [tr]; foreroziiĝi; **wash-out,** (fiasco), fiasko; (erosion), erozio; **wash up,** ~i (sin, la telerojn, etc.); (finish), fini [tr]; **come out in the wash,** finfine malkaŝiĝi

Washington, (city), Vaŝingtono; (state), ~io; (man), Vaŝington

wasp, vespo; **digger wasp,** terloĝanta ~o; **gall wasp,** cinipo; **sea wasp,** (Aus: *Chironex fleckeri*), mar~o

wassail, (toast), tosti [tr]; ~o; (ale etc.), ~trinkaĵo; (celebration), ~festo

Wasserman test (reaction), reago de Vaserman

waste, (squander, not save), malŝpari

[tr]; ~(ad)o; (misuse), miskonsumi [tr], misuzi [tr]; miskonsum(ad)o, misuz(ad)o; (desert), dezerta; dezerto; dezertigi; (excretory), ekskrecia; ekskrecio; (refuse, unusable), forĵetinda, ruba; forĵetaĵo, rubo; **wasted,** (in vain, futile), vana; **wasteful,** ~(em)a; **waste away,** (atrophy), atrofiiĝi, forvelki [int]; **lay waste to,** dezertigi; **go to waste,** ~iĝi; dezertiĝi

watch, (timepiece, gen), horloĝo [see subentries for types]; (observe), rigardi [tr], observi [tr], spekti [tr]; rigard(ad)o, observ(ad)o, spekt(ad)o; (on TV), televidi [tr]; (spy on), gvati [tr]; (look-out), gvatisto; (guard), gardi [tr]; gardisto; (guard duty), vaĉo; vaĉi [int]; (duty shift, period), deĵoro; (look after, take care of), prizorgi [tr]; **watchful,** atenta, gardema; **watchband,** ~obraceleto; **watchman,** gardisto; **watch out!,** zorgu!, atentu!; **watch out for, watch after,** prizorgi [tr]; **watch oneself,** zorgi [int]; **analog watch,** analoga (brak)~o; **digital watch,** cifera (brak)~o; **pocketwatch,** poŝ~o; **stopwatch,** klik~o; **wind-up watch,** risorta (brak)~o; **wristwatch,** brak~o; **officer of the watch,** vaĉoficiro; **keep watch on,** observadi [tr]; gardadi [tr]; atentadi [tr]

water, akvo; ~a; (give water to; pour water on, over, through; flush), ~umi [tr], ~i [tr]; (sprinkle), aspergi [tr]; (salivate), salivi [int]; (tear), larmi [int]; **waters,** ~aro, ~oj; **watercolor,** (painting), akvarelo; (paint), akvarela farbo; **watercourse,** ~ofluejo; **watercress,** ~okreso, nasturcio; **water down,** (lit or fig), dilui [tr]; **waterfall,** ~ofalo; **waterfront,** havenkvartalo; havenkvartala; **waterline,** (of ship etc.), floslinio; (of river, lake, etc.), ~orando [cp "watermark" below]; (pipe), ~odukto; **waterlogged,** ~osaturita; **watermark,** (on paper), filigrano; filigrani [tr]; (high water line, as of flood), ~olinio; **watermelon,** ~omelono; **waterproof,** ~imuna; ~imunigi; **waterproofing,** ~imunigenzo; **watershed,** ~odislimo; **waterspout,** (tornado over water), (mara) trombo;

(drainpipe etc.), [see "spout"]; **water- way**, ~oirejo, ~ovojo; **waterworks**, ~ocentralo; **waterwort**, elatino; **breakwater**, (in harbor), moleo; **break water**, (in childbirth), rompi la amnion; **her water broke**, ŝia amnio rompiĝis; **carbonated water**, sod~o, gas~~o; **fresh water**, (not saline), dolĉ~o; dolĉ~a; **running water**, fluanta ~o; **salt water**, sal~o; sal~a; **Seltzer water**, Selters~~o; **soda water**, sod~o; **underwater**, sub~a; **throw cold water on**, malkuraĝigi; senentuziasmigi

watt, vatto, ŭato [abb: W]; **wattage**, ~aro, ŭataro; **watt-hour**, ~horo [etc.]; **wattmeter**, ~metro; **kilowatt**, kilo~o

wattle, (of turkey etc.), gorĝpendaĵo; (woven sticks etc.), hurdo; hurdigi; (acacia tree), akacio

wave, (as on ocean, lit or fig; electromagnetic etc.), ondo; ~(ad)i [int]; (rolling, w/o foam), hulo; (swing arm etc.), svingi [tr]; svingiĝi; (flutter, as flag), flirti [int]; flirtigi; **wavy**, ~(ec)a; ~olinia; (curly, as hair), krispa; **wave band**, (radio etc.), ~obendo; **wavelength**, ~olongo; **heat (cold) wave**, (weather), (mal)varm~o; **longwave**, (radio), longa ~o; long~a; **microwave**, mikro~o; mikro~a; (oven), mikro~a forno; **shortwave**, mallonga ~o, kurt~o; kurt~a; **shock wave**, (as from sonic boom), klak~o; (from earthquake, bomb, etc.), ŝok~o; **tidal wave**, cunamo

waver, (sway, vacillate, falter), ŝanceliĝi; ~o; (tremble), tremi [int]; tremo

wax, (from bees, or any similar substance), vakso; ~a; ~i [tr]; (polish, as for leather), ciro; ciri [tr]; (grow), kreski [int]; kresk(ad)o; **waxer**, (waxing machine), ~imaŝino; **waxwing**, bombicilo; **wax museum**, **waxworks**, ~muzeo; **earwax**, orel~o, cerumeno; **sealing wax**, sigel~o

way, (manner), maniero (e.g.: *the easiest way to do it:* la plej facila maniero fari ĝin); (means of passing), pasejo, irejo (e.g.: *hack a way through the jungle:* haki pasejon tra la ĝangalo);

(route, road), vojo (e.g.: *which way to San Francisco?:* kiun vojon al San-Francisko?; *railway:* fervojo); (direction), direkto (e.g.: *which way is north?:* kiu direkto estas nordo?); (long *way*, distance), distanco (e.g.: *it's a long way home:* estas longa distanco hejmen); (means, method), rimedo, metodo; (custom), kutimo, moro; (respect, relationship), rilato (e.g.: *you are right in some ways:* vi pravas kelkrilate [or] laŭ kelkaj rilatoj); (area, locality), regiono; (colloq: very, quite), tre, multe (e.g.: *you're way beyond me:* vi estas multe preter mi); **the way**, (as), kiel (e.g.: *leave things the way they are:* lasi aferojn kiel ili estas); **wayfarer**, vaganto; **wayfaring**, vaganta; **way in**, (entrance), enirejo; **waylay**, embuski [tr, int] (por, kontraŭ); **way out**, (exit, lit or fig), elirejo; **wayside**, vojflanko; vojflanka; **go by the wayside**, flankeniĝi, forjetiĝi; **wayward**, (capricious), kaprica, neregula; (obstinate), obstina; **midway**, (middle), meza; meze; (half-way, as along road), vojmeza; vojmeze; (of carnival etc.), spektakl-aleo; **(in) some way**, (somehow), iel, iu~e; **(in) any way**, iel ajn; **(in) that way**, tiel, tiu~e; (such, in such a condition), [see "such"]; **(in) this way**, ĉi tiel, tiel ĉi, ĉi-~e; **(in) what way**, kiel, kiu~e; **(in) whatever way**, kiel ajn; **(in) all ways**, **(in) every way**, ĉiel; **(in) all ways whatever**, ĉiel ajn; **(in) no way (whatever)**, neniel (ajn); **which way**, (road, direction), kiu(n) vojo(n); kiudirekte(n); **(go) the right way**, (iri) ĝustadirekten; **(go) the wrong way**, (iri) misdirekten; **half-way (to)**, duonvoje (al), duone (la distancon) (al); **all the way (to)**, tute (la distancon) (al), la tutan distancon (al); **Appian Way**, Appia* Vojo; **Milky Way**, Lakta Vojo; **way of life**, viv~o; **ways and means**, rimedoj; **be in the way (of)**, obstrukci [tr], bari la vojon (al, de); **by way of**, (via), laŭ; (by means of), pere de, per; (purpose), cele al, por motivo de; **by the way**, parenteze, flanke; **come**

one's way, veni al iu; **feel one's way**, (lit or fig), elpalpi la vojon; **force one's way in (out)**, trude eniri [tr, int] (eliri [tr. int]), perforte eniri (eliri); **give way**, (yield), cedi [tr, int] (al); (collapse), disfali [int]; **go one's way**, foriri [int]; **go out of one's way (to)**, (lit), sin devojigi (por); (fig), sin ĝeni (por); **have one's (own) way**, **get one's (own) way**, trudi sian volon; **in a way**, iusence, iel, iu~e; **in a bad way**, (in bad condition), en malbona stato; (in difficulty), en embaraso, en malfacilaĵo; **in the way**, obstrukca; **get in the way**, obstrukciĝi; **get in the way of (someone, something)**, ekobstrukci [tr] (iun, ion); **know (learn) one's way around (a place)**, koni (lerni) la vojon ĉirkaŭe (ĉirkaŭ loko); **lead the way**, (go first), antaŭiri [int]; (show direction), montri la vojon; (show how), montri kiel, montri la vojon; **lose the way**, perdiĝi, devojiĝi, perdi la vojon; **make way**, (open a space), malfermi vojon, lasi vojon; (yield), cedi [tr, int] (al); **make way!**, lasu vojon!, flanken!; **make one's way**, (prosper), prosperi [int]; **make one's way through**, (move through, as crowd etc.), trairi [tr], tredi sin tra; **mend one's ways**, ĝustigi (korekti) siajn morojn; **one-way (street, traffic)**, unudirekta (strato, trafiko); **two-way**, ambaŭdirekta, dudirekta; **on one's way (to)**, (lit or fig), survoje (al); **well on the way to(ward)**, longe sur la vojo al; **on the way out**, (going out of style, becoming obsolescent), eksmodiĝanta, arkaiĝanta; **the other way around**, inversa; inverse; **out of the way**, (not blocking way), neobstrukca; (off beaten path), fora, malofte vizitata; **get out of the way**, malobstrukciĝi; **pave the way**, prepari la vojon; **pay one's own way**, pagi por si mem; **see one's way clear to**, trovi eble ke ~u (e.g.: *I can't see my way clear to come:* mi ne trovas eble ke mi venu); **stand in the way of**, obstrukci [tr], malhelpi, malebligi; **thread one's way (through)**, serpenti [int] (tra), tredi sin (tra),

(tra)penetri [tr]; **underway**, (being done), farata, komenciĝinta, komencita; (moving), survoja, moviĝanta; **be underway**, moviĝi; **get underway**, komenci [tr]; komenciĝi, ekmoviĝi [see "start"]

W.C. (Br: abb of "water closet"), klozeto, necesejo

we, ni

weak, (little strength), malforta, debila; malfortika; malpotenca; [see "strong"]; (dilute), diluita; (in character), molaĉa; **weaken**, ~igi, debiligi; ~iĝi, debiliĝi; malfortikigi; malfortikiĝi; malpotencigi; malpotenciĝi; dilui [tr]; molaĉigi; molaĉiĝi; **weakling**, ~ulo, debilulo; **weakly**, (feeble), febla, ~a

weal, (welt, wale), vipstrio; (welfare), bonfarto, prospero

wealth, (richness, gen), riĉ/(ec)o; ~aĵo(j); (abundance), abundo; **wealthy**, ~a; **a wealth of**, abund(aĵ)o da, abunde da, abunda

wean, demamigi

weapon, armilo, batalilo; **weaponry**, ~aro

wear, (have clothes on body etc.), porti [tr] (e.g.: *I wore my blue shirt:* mi ~is mian bluan ĉemizon; *wear a smile:* ~i rideton); (clothing), vestoj (e.g.: *men's wear:* viraj vestoj); (erode, grind away, as from use, friction), erodi [tr], ŝlifi [tr]; erodiĝi, ŝlifiĝi; erod(iĝ)o, ŝlif(iĝ)o (e.g.: *that tire is worn:* tiu pneŭo estas ŝlifita); (last), daŭri [int] (e.g.: *those shoes wore well:* tiuj ŝuoj bone daŭris); (naut: veer), mallofi [tr]; mallofo; **wear down**, erodi [tr], ŝlifi [tr]; erodiĝi, ŝlifiĝi; **wear out**, [see "wear down" above]; (use up, wear away), eluzi [tr]; eluziĝi; (fatigue), ellacigi; ellaciĝi; **underwear**, subvesto(j); **wear and tear**, uzdifektoj, uzdifektado; erodado, ŝlifado

weary, (fatigue), laca, ~igi; ~iĝi; (bore), tedi [tr]; **weariness**, ~eco; **wearisome**, ~iga; (tedious), teda

weasel, mustelo; **weasel out of**, evitaĉi [tr], eltordi sin el

weather, vetero; ~a; (come through), travivi [tr]; (wear down land, structure, etc. by weather or analogous erosion), (~)ŝlifi [tr]; (~)ŝlifiĝi; **weathered, weather-beaten**, ~kaduka; **weathercock, weathervane**, ventoflago; **weather report, weather forecast**, ~prognozo, ~informo(j); **weatherstrip(ping)**, ~strio(j); **(a little) under the weather**, malsan(et)a

weave, (fabric, or analogous action), teksi [tr]; ~iĝi; ~aĵo; ~aranĝo (e.g.: *weave a tale:* ~i rakonton); (braid), plekti [tr]; **weave through**, (move through crowd, congestion), tredi sin tra, sinui [int] tra; **interweave**, inter~i [tr]; interplekti [tr]; inter~iĝi; interplektiĝi; **Jacquard weave**, ĵakarda ~o [cp "loom: Jacquard loom"]

web, (fabric), teksaĵo, ŝtofo; (oth woven thing or concept), ~o, plektaĵo (e.g.: *a web of lies:* plektaĵo de mensogoj) [see "weave"]; (of spider), araneaĵo; (of I–beam etc.), almo; (of duck etc.), naĝhaŭto; **webbing**, plektaĵo; **webfoot**, palmopieda; palmopiedulo

weber, vebero

wed, edz/inigi; ~igi; ge~iĝi; ge~igi [see "marry"]; **wedded**, ~(in)iĝinta; ge~iĝinta(j); ge~eca; **wedding**, nupto, ge~iĝ(osolen)o; nupta; **wedding cake**, nupta kuko; **wedding ring**, ge~eca ringo; **wedlock**, ge~eco; **newlywed**, nov~(in)o; novge~a; **newlyweds**, novge~oj

wedge, kojno; ~i [tr]

Wednesday, merkredo; **Ash Wednesday**, Cindro~o

weed, (gen), herb/aĉo, trud~o; (remove weeds), sarki [tr]; **weed out**, (lit or fig), elsarki [tr]; **weed-killer**, herbicido; **beggarweed**, (*Desmodium*), desmodio; **bindweed**, (any of *Convolvulus*), konvolvulo; **bishop('s)-weed**, amio; **blueweed**, ekio; **brookweed**, samolo; **chickweed**, (*Stellaria*), stelario; **mouse-ear(ed) chickweed, clammy chickweed, field chickweed**, (*Cerastium*), cerastio; **jimsonweed**, stramonio; **Joe-Pye weed**, eŭpatorio; **locoweed**, astragalo; **seaweed**, (gen), mar~o; (*Fucus*), fuko; (*Zostera*), zostero; **tarweed**, madio; **tumbleweed**, salsolo

week, semajno; **weekly**, (ĉiu)~a; (ĉiu)~e; (periodical), ~gazeto; **biweekly**, (once every 2 weeks), du~a; du~e; **weekday**, labortago; labortaga; **weekend**, ~fino; **midweek**, ~mezo; ~meza; **a week from Tuesday (etc.), next Tuesday week**, la venontan mardon (etc.) post ~o

weep, plori [int]; **weepy**, ~ema

weever, trañino

weevil, kurkulio

weft, vefto

weigh, (have weight, be heavy, lit or fig), pezi [tr, int] (e.g.: *it weighs 5 kilos:* ĝi ~as 5 kilogramojn); (measure weight of, as on a scale), pesi [tr]; [see also "weight"]; **outweigh**, super~i [tr]; **weigh anchor**, levi la ankron; **weigh station**, pesadejo; **weigh heavily on**, ~e ŝarĝi [tr]; **weigh one's words carefully**, zorge elekti siajn vortojn

weight, (heaviness, gravitational or artificial gravitational [centrifugal] force), pezo [cp "mass"]; (heavy object), ~aĵo; (for purpose of weighing down, making heavier), ~ilo; (importance), graveco; (influence), influo; (load, burden), ŝarĝo; (make heavier), ~igi; (load, add weight to; oppress), ŝarĝi [tr]; [see also "weigh"]; **weightless**, sen~a; **weightlessness**, sen~eco, nulgravito; **weighty**, ~a; **atomic weight**, atommaso; **by weight**, laŭ~e; **carry weight**, (have influence), havi influon; **counterweight**, kontraŭ~o; kontraŭ~i [tr]; **gain (lose) weight**, (mal)pli~iĝi; **gross weight**, brutta ~o; **heavyweight**, ~ega; ~egulo; **lightweight**, et~a; et~ulo; **molecular weight**, molekulmaso; **net weight**, neta ~o; **overweight**, tro~a; super~eco, tro~eco; **tare weight**, tara ~o; **underweight**, sub~a, tro mal~a; sub~eco; **pull one's weight**, fari sian parton

weir, digeto

weird, strang(eg)a, mistera, kurioz(eg)a

welcome, (gladly receive), bonvena; ~igi (en —on); ~igo (e.g.: *a welcome sight:* ~a vido; *we welcome you to our city:* ni ~igas vin en nian urbon); (in-

terj, as a greeting, on a sign, etc.), ~on
(en –on)! (e.g.: *welcome to Toronto!:*
~on en Toronton!); **you're welcome,**
(in reply to "thank you"), mia plezuro;
(ĝi estas) nenio; ne menciinde; **wear
out one's welcome,** trotrudi sian ~on

weld, veldi [tr]; ~iĝi; ~aĵo; **welding
machine,** ~omaŝino; **welding rod,**
~odrato

welfare, (well-being), bonfarto; ~a;
(public assistance), ~a; ~aj pagoj; **be
on welfare,** ricevi ~ajn pagojn; **welfare state,** ~oŝtato

well, (adv of "good"), bone; (not sick),
sana, bonfarta; (gen interj), nu (e.g.:
well, I don't know: nu, mi ne scias; *if
you say so, well, okay:* se vi tion diras,
nu, en ordo); (indeed), ja (e.g.: *that
may well be so:* tio ja povus esti);
(much), multe, mult– [pfx] (e.g.: *well-
used:* multe uzita [or] multuzita); (in
ground, source of water, oil, etc.), puto; (container), –ujo [sfx] (e.g.: *inkwell:* inkujo) [cp "tank"]; (flow up,
gush, spring up), fonti [int], elverŝiĝi;
well-being, ~farto, ~stato; **well-dig-
ger,** putisto; **well-formed,** belforma;
well then!, nu do!; **well-to-do, well-
off,** multhava, riĉa; **as well,** ankaŭ,
krome, aldone; **as well as,** krom, aldone al; **it is just as well,** estas ~e
(post ĉio); **all's well that ends well,**
fino ~a, ĉio ~a; **wish (someone) well,**
~deziri [tr] (iun)

Wellington, Velingtono

welsh, welsh on, (evade debt etc.), ŝul-
deviti [tr] (al), fortroti [int] (de)

Welsh, (of Wales), kimra; ~o; **Welsh-
man,** ~o

welt, (raised wound, as from whip;
weal), vipstrio; ~i [tr]; (bump, as from
insect bite), tubereto; (cording, as on
cushion), (ŝnur)bordero

Weltanschauung, mondrigardo

welter, (confusion, turmoil), konfuzo,
tumulto; (wallow), vadi [int] (en, tra),
sin ruli (en)

wen, kisto

Wenceslas, Venceslao†

wench, knabino, fraŭlino, bubino

wend, wend one's way, iri [int]

werewolf, lupfantomo

west, okcidento; ~a; ~e(n); (esp re compass point), uesto [abb: W]; **western,**
~a; **westerner,** ~ano; **westward,**
~e(n); ~enira; **westerly,** (western),
~a; (toward west), ~e(n); ~enira;
(from west), de~a; de~e; **westbound,**
~enira; **Midwest,** Mez~o; mez~a

Westphalia, Vestfalio; **Westphalian,**
~a; **North Rhine-Westphalia,** Nord-
rejno-~o

wet, malseka; ~igi; ~iĝi; ~(ec)o; **soak-
ing wet, sopping wet, wet to the
skin,** (re person or animal), ĝisoste
trempita; (oth), trempe ~a, ~ega, saturita; **bed-wetting,** enurezo, liturina-
do; (colloq), litpisado

wether, kastrita ŝafo

whack, bati [tr]; ~o; **at a whack,**
samtempe; **take a whack at,** (try),
provi [tr]; **out of whack,** misa; **be out
of whack,** misi [int]; **whack off,** dishaki [tr]

whale, baleno; **whalebone,** barto; **blue
whale,** blua ~o; **finback whale,** balenoptero; **killer whale,** orcino; **sperm
whale, black whale,** makrocefalo,
kaĉaloto

wharf, varfo; ~i [int]; al~iĝi; al~igi;
wharfy, (Aus), doklaboristo

what, (pron; interj, standing alone, to
express surprise or ask speaker to repeat), kio (e.g.: *what is that?:* kio estas tio?; *It's starting to snow. What?!:*
Ekneĝas. Kio?!); (adj), kiu (e.g.: *what
tree is that?:* kiu arbo estas tiu?; *I
don't know what tree that is:* mi ne
scias kiu arbo tiu estas); (adj, in exclamation), kia (e.g.: *what nonsense!:* kia
sensencaĵo!; *what a bother!:* kia
ĝeno!; *what big teeth you have!:* kiajn
grandajn dentojn vi havas!); (in what
way), kiel (e.g.: *what does it matter?:*
kiel ĝi gravas?); **whatchamacallit,
whatnot, whatsit,** (nondescript
thing), umo; **whatever, whatsoever,**
(pron), kio ajn; (adj), kiu ajn; (to emphasize), ajn (e.g.: *in whatever way:*
kiel ajn; *none whatever:* neniom ajn;
at no time whatever: neniam ajn);
what for, (for what reason), kial, pro
kio (e.g.: *what did you do that for?:*
kial [or] pro kio vi faris tion?); (for

what purpose), kial, por kio (e.g.: *what is that stick for?:* por kio estas tiu bastono? [or] kial vi havas tiun bastonon?); **what have you,** (whatever else), kio ajn; **what it takes,** tio kio necesas, tio necesa; **what kind of,** kia (e.g.: *what kind of tree is that?:* kia arbo estas tiu?); **whatnot,** (shelves), etaĝero; **and what not,** kaj tiel plu [abb: ktp.]; **what of it?,** kio do?, ĉu gravas?; **what's it to you?,** kiel tio koncernas vin?

whaup, (zool), numenio, kurlo

wheal, (welt, weal), vipstrio

wheat, tritiko; ~a; **wheatear,** (plant or bird), enanto; **buckwheat,** fagopiro

wheedle, (cajole person), kaĵoli [tr]; (get something by cajoling), perflati [tr], el~i [tr]

wheel, (gen), rado; ~iri [int]; ~irigi; (steering wheel), stirilo, stir~o; (pivot), pivoti [int]; pivotado; **wheels,** (set of wheels, as in mechanism), ~oaro [not "~aro"; see "radar"]; **wheelbarrow,** ĉarumo; **wheelbase,** interaksa distanco; **wheelwright,** ~faristo; **two-wheeled, three-wheeled, (etc.),** du~a, tri~a (etc.); **balance wheel,** balanc~o; **control wheel,** (for valve, mechanism, etc.), reg~o; **daisy wheel,** (for cmptr printer, typewriter), petalrado; **drive wheel,** (of rr locomotive, car, etc.), pel~o; **flywheel,** inerci~o; **front wheel,** (of car etc.), front~o (e.g.: *front-wheel drive:* front~a pelado); **gear wheel,** dent~o; **planetary gear wheel,** planeda dent~oaro; **millwheel,** muel~o; **paddlewheel,** padel~o; **paddlewheel boat,** ~ŝipo; **pinwheel,** pinglo~o; **potter's wheel,** tornostablo; **ratchet wheel,** klik~o; **spare wheel,** (for car etc.), vic~o; **spinning wheel,** ŝpin~o; **sprocket wheel,** ĉen~o; **steering wheel,** stirilo, stir~o; **waterwheel,** (wheel moved by water), akvo~o; (wheel w buckets for lifting water), trog~o

wheeze, raslo; ~i [int]

whelk, bukceno

whelp, ido [or species may be identified: hundido, ursido, leonido, etc.]

when, kiam; **whenever,** (at any time), ~ ajn (e.g.: *come whenever you want:* venu ~ ajn vi volas); (always when), ĉiam ~ (e.g.: *whenever I'm in the shower, the phone rings:* ĉiam kiam mi estas en la duŝo, la telefono sonoras)

whence, de kie

where, (at what place), kie; (to what place), kien; (from what place), de kie; **whereabouts,** (where), (proksimume) kie; (location), kieo, situo, trovloko [note sing], kie iu estas (e.g.: *his whereabouts are unknown:* lia situo (trovloko, kieo) ne estas konata [or] oni ne scias kie li estas); **whereas,** (because, in view of the fact that), ĉar, pro tio ke, konsidere ke; (on contrary, although), kvankam; (while), dum; **whereby,** (by means of which), per kio; per kiu; (according to which), laŭ kio; laŭ kiu; **wherefore,** (because of which), pro kio; pro kiu; **wherefrom,** de kio; de kiu; **wherein,** en kio; en kiu; **whereof,** pri kio, de kio; pri kiu, de kiu; **whereon,** sur kio(n); sur kiu(n); **whereto,** kie(n); al kiu; **whereunder,** sub kio; sub kiu; **whereupon,** (at which time), kiam, je kio, ĉe kio; (after which time), post kiam, post kio; (on which place), sur kio(n); **wherever,** kie(n) ajn; **wherewith,** (accompanied w which, whom), kun kio; kun kiu; (by means of which, whom), per kio; per kiu; **wherewithal,** (mon)rimedoj; **anywhere,** ie(n) ajn; **everywhere,** ĉie(n); **somewhere,** ie(n); **nowhere,** nenie(n)

whet, akrigi; **whetstone,** ~a ŝtono

whether, ĉu; **whether ... or,** (in parallel or alternative clauses), ĉu ... ĉu (e.g.: *whether from error or deceit, his answer was wrong:* ĉu pro eraro, ĉu pro ruzo, lia respondo malpravis); (whether or not), ĉu ... aŭ ne (e.g.: *I'll come, whether it rains or not:* mi venos, ĉu pluvos aŭ ne)

whew, (interj), pu!, uf!, fu!

whey, selakto

which, (pron, adj), kiu(j) (e.g.: *which car is yours?:* kiu aŭto estas via?; *which is your car?:* kiu estas via aŭto?; *the story which we heard:* la rakonto kiun ni aŭdis); (referring to entire clause), kio (e.g.: *they were the best ones, which is why we chose them:* ili estis la plej bonaj, kio estas kial ni elektis ilin; *you are late, which reminds me, where is John?:* vi malfruas, kio min rememorigas, kie estas Johano?); **whichever**, kiu ajn

whiff, (puff, as of breeze), (ek)bloveto; (of odor), odoreto

while, whilst, (during time that), dum, –ante (e.g.: *we talked while we ate:* ni parolis ~ ni manĝis [or] manĝante, ni parolis); (although), kvankam; (period of time), tempo (e.g.: *we waited a little while:* ni atendis mallongan tempon [or] iom da tempo); **while away**, forpasigi; **in a little while**, baldaŭ, post nelonge; **be worth (one's) while**, valori la penon

whim, kaprico

whimbrel, numenio, kurlo

whimper, plor/eti [int], ~pepi [int]; ~eto, ~pepo

whimsy, kaprico; **whimsical**, ~a

whin, (bot), ulekso; **petty whin**, genisto

whine, (cry), plor/aĉi [int], ~plendi [int]; ~aĉo, ~plendo; (long, hi-pitched sound, as of jet engine), grincadi [int]; grincado

whinny, heni [int]; ~o

whip, (snap, beat, flog, etc.; analogous action), vipi [tr]; ~iĝi; (act), ~ado; ~iĝo; (device), ~o; (stir, as eggs), kirli [tr]; (defeat, outdo), venki [tr]; (go quickly), rapidi [int]; (dessert w whipped cream, fruit, etc.), kirlaĵo; (pol official, as in Congress, Parliament), instigisto; **whiplash**, ~iĝo; ~iĝa; **whip up**, (concoct), fabriki [tr], kunmiksi [tr], kunkirli [tr]; **potato whip**, kaĉigilo; **riding whip**, rajd~o; **stock whip**, (Aus), brut~o

whippersnapper, impertinentulo, malgravuleto

whippet, grejhundeto

whippoorwill, (zool), kaprimulgo

whir, zum(ad)i [int]; ~o

whirl, (spin), kirli [tr], girigi; ~iĝi, giri [int]; ~o, giro; **whirlpool**, ~akvo, turnakvo; (fig), ~aĵo (e.g.: *whirlpool*

of stars: ~aĵo da steloj)

whirr, zum(ad)i [int]; ~o

whisk, (whip eggs etc.), kirli [tr]; ~ilo; (sweep), balai [tr]; **whisk away, whisk off**, (carry, sweep, wipe, etc., quickly), (rapide) forporti [tr], forbalai [tr], forviŝi [tr] (etc.); **whisk broom**, balaileto, man-balailo

whisker, vangharo

whiskey, viskio

whisper, flustri [tr, int]; ~o

whist, (game), visto

whistle, fajfi [tr, int]; (sound), ~o; (device), ~ilo; (large, as on ship, factory), ~ilego; (like hiss, as wind), sibli [int]; sibl(ad)o; **wolf whistle**, flirt~o

whit, joto; **not a whit**, (tute) neniom, (tute) neniel, tute ne

white, (color), blanka; ~o; ~aĵo; (Caucasian), ~ulo; ~ula; (of egg), albumeno, ovo~o; **whiten**, ~igi; ~iĝi; **whitish, off-white**, ~eta; **whitebeam**, alizarbo; **white elephant**, nevolataĵo, senutilaĵo; **white-hot**, ~arda; **white-out**, ~umo; **white person**, ~ulo; **whitethorn**, (hawthorn), kratago; **whitewall**, (tire), ~flanka; ~flanka pneŭo, ~flankaĵo; **whitewash**, (lit or fig), kalkolakto; kalkolakti [tr]

whither, kien

whiting, (zool), merlango

Whitsunday, Pentekosto

whittle, (lit or fig), ĉizi [tr]

whiz(z), (hiss, buzz), sibli [int], zumi [int]; ~o, zumo; (colloq: expert), spertulo, lertulo, cerbulo

who, kiu; **whodunit**, murdomistero; **whoever**, kiu ajn; **who cares?**, al kiu gravas?; **who's who**, (who are important), kiuj estas gravaj (e.g.: *one must know who's who in the organization:* oni devas scii kiu estas grava en la organizo); (list), gravularo

whoa, (interj), halt(u)!

whole, (entire), tuta; ~o; (complete), kompleta, integra; (undamaged), sendifekta; (unwounded), senvunda; **wholesale**, (bsns), pogranda; pogrande; vendi [tr] pogrande; vendiĝi pogrande; (massive), amasa; amase (e.g.: *wholesale slaughter:* amasa buĉado); **wholesaler**, pograndisto, grocisto; **wholesome**, (healthy, sound), sana; (promoting health), saniga; **as a whole**, en~e; la ~a (e.g.: *in the world as a whole:* en la ~a mondo); **on the whole**, ĝenerale, plejparte, ĉion konsiderinte

whomp, (beat), bategi [tr]; ~o; (onom), bum!

whoop, krii [int], ~egi [int]; ~(eg)o, ĝoj~o

whoops, (interj), up!, hup!

whoosh, ŝuŝi [int]; ~o; (onom), ŝuŝ!

whop, bategi [tr]; ~o

whopper, kolos/aĵo; **whopping**, ~a

whore, putino, prostituitino

whorl, (verticil), verticilo; (spiral etc.), spiralo

whose,kies; whosever, kies ajn

why, (for what reason), kial, pro kio; (for what purpose), por kio; (interj: surprise etc.), nu, ja, fakte (e.g.: *why, I didn't know that!:* nu, mi (ja) ne sciis tion!)

wick, meĉo

wicked, (evil), fia, malvirta; (malicious), malica; (terrible, unpleasant, etc.), malbon(eg)a, terura, abomena; (mischievous), petola

wicker, (willow branch(es) etc.), vimen/tigo(j); ~(tig)a; **wickerwork**, ~aĵo

wicket, (door), pord/eto; (window, as in bank, box office), giĉeto; (gate in canal, watercourse, etc.), kluz~o; (cricket), palisetaro; **sticky wicket**, malfacila situacio; (said sarcastically), jen via problemo!

wide, (re extent side to side), larĝa (e.g.: *a wide road:* ~a vojo; *5 meters wide:* 5 metrojn ~a); (vast, broad, over large area), vasta (e.g.: *a widely known fact:* vaste konata fakto); (roomy, loose, as re clothing), loza; (off to one side, gen), flanka; flanke(n) (e.g.: *her response was wide of the mark:* ŝia respondo estis flanka de la celo); [see also "width"]; **widen**, ~igi; ~iĝi [cp "dilate"]; **widespread**, vasta, disvastiĝinta, ĝenerala

widget, umilo

widow, vidv/ino; ~(in)igi; **widower**, ~o; **widow's walk**, altano

width, larĝo, ~eco; ~aĵo; [see also "wide"]; **finger-width, hand-width**, (etc.), fingro~o, man~o (etc.)

wield, manipuli [tr], uzi [tr], svingi [tr]

wiener, kolbaseto

wife, edzino; **co-wife**, kun~o; **midwife**, akuŝist(in)o; **midwifery**, akuŝigado [cp "obstetrics"]

wig, peruko; **bigwig**, dignulo, gravulo

wiggle, tordeti [tr], vibrigi; ~iĝi, vibri [int]; ~o, vibro

Wight, Isle of, Vajt-Insulo*

wigwam, vigvamo [cp "tepee"]

wild, (not tame; savage; not domesticated), sovaĝa; (unrestrained, frenetic), furioza, senbrida, freneza; (debauched), diboĉa; (extravagant), ekstravaganca; (cards etc.: no set value), libervalora; **wilds**, ~ejo(j); **wilderness**, (uninhabited, uncultivated land), ~ejo, senloĝatejo; (desert, wasteland), dezerto; [cp "scrub"]

wildebeest, gnuo

wile, artifiko, ruzo

Wilhelm, Vilhelmo; **Wilhelmina**, ~ina, ~ino

will, (future tense), ~os [sfx] (e.g.: *I will go:* mi iros); (volition), pervoli [tr]; pervolo (e.g.: *he willed himself to be happy:* li pervolis sin esti kontenta); (wishes, desire), volo (e.g.: *the will of the people:* la volo de la popolo); (testament), testamento; (bequeath), testamenti [tr]; **willful**, (deliberate), intenca; (stubborn), obstina; **will-o'-the-wisp**, vaglumo, erarlumo; **willpower**, volrego, memrego; **at will**, laŭvole; **against one's will**, kontraŭvole; **free will**, libera volo, libervolo; libervola; **good (bad) will**, (mal)bonvolo; (mal)bonvola; **where there's a will, there's a way**, kiu volas, tiu povas

willing, volonta; **be willing to**, volonte ~i, volonti [int] (e.g.: *would you be willing to help me?:* ĉu vi volontus helpi min?; *I am willing and able:* mi ~as kaj kapablas)

willow, saliko; **willowy**, (graceful, supple), supla; **weeping willow**, plor~o

willy-nilly, vole-nevole; vola-nevola

Wilma, Vilhelmina

wilt, velki [int]; ~igi; (disease), ~ozo; **wilted**, ~a
wily, ruza
wimble, borilo
wimp, malbrav/ulo, senspinulo; **wimpy**, ~a, senspina
wimple, kapvualo
win, (in game, battle, contest, etc.; acquire, earn, achieve), gajni [tr, int]; ~o; (conquer), venki [tr]; venko; (attain, reach), atingi [tr]; **winning**, ~a; (attractive), (al)loga, simpatia; **win over**, (convince), konvinki [tr]; (recruit, convert), varbi [tr]
wince, (ek)kuntiriĝi, ekspasmi [int]; ~o, ekspasmo
winch, vinĉo; ~i [tr]
wind, (blowing air), vento; (crank), kranki [tr]; krankiĝi; (wrap, as into coil etc.), volvi [tr]; volviĝi; (one wound turn, as of wire), volv(aĵ)o; (onto spool), volvi [tr], bobeni [tr]; volviĝi, bobeniĝi; (wrap, bind up, as a wound), vindi [tr]; (bend, twist, as road, river, etc.), sinui [int], serpenti [int], tordiĝi; sinuo, tordiĝo; (breath), spiro; senspirigi; (tighten spring of watch etc.), streĉi [tr]; streĉiĝi; **winded**, senspir(igit)a; **winding**, volvaĵo; vindo; (sinuous), sinua, serpenta; **windy**, ~a; **windbreak**, ~rompilo; **windbreaker**, (jacket), ~ojaketo; **windfall**, (something blown down, as fruits, trees), deblovaĵo; (good luck), bonŝancaĵo; **windjammer**, velŝipo; **windscreen**, **windshield**, ~ŝirmilo, antaŭa glaco; **windshield wiper**, glacoviŝilo; **windsock**, maniko; **windswept**, ~oblovata; **wind up**, (re spring etc.), streĉi [tr]; streĉiĝi; (conclude, finish), kompletigi, fini [tr]; (end up), fine esti [int], fine troviĝi; **windward**, al~a; al~e(n); **downwind**, laŭ~a; laŭ~e(n); **unwind**, malvolvi [tr], disvolvi [tr]; malbobeni [tr], disbobeni [tr]; malbobeniĝi, disbobeniĝi; malvindi [tr]; malvindiĝi; **upwind**, kontraŭ~a; kontraŭ~e(n); **whirlwind**, (wind), kirl~o [cp "tornado"]; (impetuous), impeta; **woodwind**, (mus), ligna blovinstrumento; **wind instrument**, (mus), blovinstrumento; **long-**

winded, malkonciza, mallakona; **self-winding**, memstreĉa; **trade wind**, alizeo; **the wind is blowing**, ~as; **get wind of**, aŭdi sufloron de, sciiĝi pri; **in the wind**, okazonta
Windhoek, Vindhuko*
windlass, (any winch), vinĉo; (of anchor), vindaso
window, (gen), fenestro; **window dressing**, (~)ornamaĵo; **window frame**, ~oframo; **windowpane**, vitro; **bay window**, orielo; **French window**, ~opordo; **show window**, **display window**, montro~o, montra ~o; **ticket window**, giĉeto
wine, vino; ~izi [tr]; **wineoh**, (Aus), ~drinkemulo; **winery**, ~farejo; **wine press**, (tub etc.), ~premejo; (modern machine), ~premilo; **fortified wine**, fortigita ~o, alkoholizita ~o; **red wine**, ruĝa ~o; **rosé wine**, roza ~o; **sparkling wine**, ŝaŭma ~o [cp "champagne"]; **white wine**, blanka ~o
wing, (of bird etc.), flug/ilo, alo†; (of plane etc.), ~ilo, alo, planeo; (extremity of building, pol faction, etc.), alo; (of stage), kuliso; (fly), ~i [int]; (wound in wing), ~ilvundi [tr]; **wingspan**, enverguro; **in the wings**, (of stage, lit or fig), en la kulisoj; **on the wing**, ~anta; ~ante; **take wing**, ek~i [int], for~i [int]; **under one's wing**, (protected), sub ies protekto
wink, (re eye), palpebrumi [int]; ~igi; ~o; (twinkle, as star), scintili [int], trembrili [int]; (moment), momento; **wink at**, (ignore), fermi la okulojn ĉe; **in the wink of an eye**, (short time), en ~a daŭro
winkle, (periwinkle), litorino; (ferret out), elanguligi, elserĉi [tr]
Winnipeg, Vinipego*
winnow, ventumi [tr]; ~ilo
wino, vindrinkemulo
winsome, ĉarma, alloga
winter, vintro; ~a; (tra)~i [int]; **wintertime**, ~o; ~a; **midwinter**, ~omezo; ~omeza; **wintergreen**, (*Gaultheria*), gaŭlterio; **flowering wintergreen**, (*Polygala*), poligalo
wipe, viŝi [tr]; ~o; **wipe off**, (clean, as

table), ~i; (remove, as dust from table), for~i [tr]; **wipe out**, (exterminate), ekstermi [tr]; (nullify), nuligi, neniigi, for~i [tr]; (lit), for~i [tr]; **windshield wiper**, glaco~ilo

wire, (gen), drato; (install wiring), ~i [tr]; (2– or 3–strand, insulated, elec: one piece, as for any elec device), (ŝnur)konduktilo; (telegram), telegramo; telegrafi [tr]; (fasten w wire), ~ligi [tr], ~fiksi [tr]; **wiring**, (elec), ~aro, konduktilaro; **wireless**, sen~a; (Br: radio), [see "radio"]; wiry, ~eca, malfajna; **wiretap**, kaŝkonekti [tr]; kaŝkonekto; kaŝkonektilo; **barbed wire**, pik~o; **guy-wire**, stajo; **live wire**, (energetic person), energiulo, viglulo; **down to the wire**, ĝis la fino, proksimiĝanta al la fino; **get in under the wire**, apenaŭ eniri (atingi, sukcesi, etc.)

Wisconsin, Viskonsino

wisdom, saĝo, ~eco [see also "wise"]; **Wisdom (of Solomon)**, (Bib), la S~o de Salomono; **Wisdom of Jesus, Son of Sirach**, (Bib), la S~o de Jesuo, filo de Siraĥ

wise, saĝa [see also "wisdom", "–wise"]; **wiseacre**, ~oŝajnulo; **be wise to**, konscii [int] pri

–wise, (sfx: regarding), pri (e.g.: *we have problems budgetwise:* ni havas problemojn pri la buĝeto)

wisent, Eŭropa bizono

wish, deziri [tr]; ~o; **wishful**, ~a; **wish for**, ~i; **wishful thinking**, ~pensado; **as you wish**, laŭ via plaĉo, laŭvole; **good wishes, best wishes**, bon~oj; **wish one well**, bon~i iun

wisp, (of hair), bukleto; (of smoke etc.; any filament-like thing), filamento; (bundle of twigs etc.), fasketo; (will-o'-the-wisp), vaglumo, erarlumo

Wisteria, Wistaria, visterio

wistful, sopira

wit, (humor), humuro; ~ulo; (cleverness), sprito; spritulo; **wits**, (intellectual, perceptive powers), intelekto, perceptivo, rezonivo; **witty, quick-witted, sharp-witted**, ~a, sprita, inteligenta; **slow-witted**, malinteligenta, stulta; **half-wit**, sencerbulo,

malinteligentulo, stultulo, ventkapulo; **witticism**, spritaĵo, ~aĵo; **outwit**, superruzi [tr]; **to wit**, (that is), nome, tio estas; **unwitting**, senscia; **be at wit's end**, ne scii kion fari; **keep one's wits about one**, resti spiritopreta, resti vigla

witch, sorĉ/istino; **witchcraft**, ~arto; **witches'-broom**, (bot), fefasko; **witchhazel**, hamamelido; **waterwitch**, rabdisto [see "divine"]

with, (in company of, together, including), kun, kun– [pfx] (e.g.: *he came with Ann:* li venis ~ Anna; *he took the book with him:* li portis la libron ~ si [or] li ~portis la libron); (by means of), per (e.g.: *write with a pencil:* skribi per krajono); (along, not against, as wind, flow, etc.), laŭ (e.g.: *we sailed with the wind:* ni velis laŭ la vento); (in proportion to), kun, laŭ, proporcie kun, laŭmezure kiel (e.g.: *the pressure in the container increases with increasing temperature:* la premo en la ujo pligrandiĝas laŭ pliiĝanta temperaturo); (showing relationship; in the case of), ĉe (e.g.: *it doesn't matter with me:* ne gravas ĉe mi; *things are better with us now:* aferoj estas pli bonaj ĉe ni nun); **within**, (adv: inside place), interne(n); (prep), interne de (e.g.: *within the limits:* interne de la limoj); (within specified time), ĝis post, en la daŭro de (e.g.: *we'll finish it within two months:* ni finos ĝis ĝis post du monatoj); **with it**, (colloq: snappy, witty), sprita; (alert, having presence of mind), spiritopreta; (up to date), ĝisdata, freŝdata; (in fashion), laŭmoda; **without**, (lacking, not w), sen; (outside), ekstere(n); (not doing), ne –inte, ne –ante, sen –i (e.g.: *he left without saying good-bye:* li foriris, ne adiaŭinte nin [or] li foriris sen adiaŭi nin)

withal, (besides), krome, aldone; (notwithstanding), malgraŭe, malgraŭ tio

withdraw, (pull back, take back, retreat), retiri [tr]; ~iĝi; (draw out, as water), ĉerpi [tr]; (extract), elpreni [tr]; ($ from bank etc.), retrati [tr]; (retract statement), maldiri [tr]; (waive,

forego), rezigni [tr]; **withdrawal**, ~(iĝ)o; ĉerpo; elpreno; retrato; retrataĵo; maldiro; rezigno; **withdrawn**, (psych), ~iĝema
wither, velki [int]; ~igi [cp "wizen"]; **withered**, ~a
withers, postkolo [cp "nape"]
withstand, kontraŭstari [tr], rezisti [tr]
witness, (testify), atesti [tr]; (person), ~into; ~anto; ~onto; (testimony), ~o; (observe), observi [tr], vidi [tr]; observinto; observanto; **eye-witness**, vidinto, vid~anto; vid~a; **bear witness to**, ~i; **witness stand**, **witnessbox**, ~antejo
wizard, (magician), magi/isto, sorĉisto; (expert, clever person), lertulo; **wizardry**, ~o, sorĉado, sorĉarto
wizen, ŝrumpi [int], velki [int]; ~igi, velkigi; **wizened**, ~(int)a, velka
woad, izatido
wobble, vobli [int]; ~igi; ~(ad)o; **wobbly**, ~ema, nestabila, ŝanceliĝema
Woden, **Wodan**, Votano [cp "Odin"]
woe, (misfortune), malfeliĉo, ĉagreno, mizero, aflikto, doloro; (interj), ve!, ho ve!; **woeful**, ~a, mizera; **woe is me!**, ho ve!; **woe unto**, ve al
woebegone, veaspekta, mizer(aspekt)a
wok, uako*
wolf, (zool), lupo; (flirtatious man), flirtemulo, amoremulo; (gulp food), vori [tr], manĝegi [tr]; **wolfsbane**, akonito; **cry wolf**, false alarmi [tr]; **prairie wolf**, kojoto, preri~o
Wolfgang, Volfgango
wolfram, volframo
wolverine, (*Gulo*), gulo; (*Icticyon*), mustelvulpo
woman, virino; (adj, to show that person described by n is a woman), ~ino [sfx] [e.g.: *a woman physicist*: fizikistino]; **womanly**, ~eca
womb, utero
wombat, vombato
wonder, (marvel, amazement), miro; ~i [int] (e.g.: *we watched with wonder*: ni rigardis kun ~o; *they wondered at the tall buildings*: ili ~is pri [or: pro] la altaj konstruaĵoj); (thing), ~(ind)aĵo; [cp "amaze", "miracle"]; (wish to know, be curious), scivoli

[tr], demandi sin (ĉu) (e.g.: *I wonder who she is*: mi scivolas [or: demandas min] kiu ŝi estas; *I wonder if it's going to rain*: mi scivolas ĉu pluvos); **wonderful**, ~inda; **wonderland**, ~lando; **wonderment**, ~o; **wonder-struck**, ~trafita; **it's no wonder (that)**, ne ~indas (ke); ne surprize (ke)
wondrous, miriga
wont, (custom), kutimo; **be wont to**, ~i [tr]
won ton, vantano*; ~a
woo, amindumi [tr]
wood, (substance, gen), ligno; ~a [cp "xylem"]; (forest), arbaro; **wooded**, arbara; **wooden**, ~a; **woods**, arbaro; **woodsy**, arbareca; **woodbine**, (*Lonicera*), lonicero; **woodchuck**, marmoto; **woodcock**, (*Scolopax*), skolopo; **woodcut**, (print), ksilografaĵo; ~ogravuraĵo; **make woodcuts**, ksilografi [tr]; **woodland**, arbaro; arbara; **woodpecker**, pego; **woodpile**, ŝtiparo; **woodruff**, asperulo; **woodwax(en)**, genisto; **woodwork**, ~aĵo; **woodworker**, ~aĵisto; **woodworking**, ~laborado; ~labora; **blackwood**, (Aus: *Acacia menaloxylon*), nigra akacio; **campeachy wood**, kampeĉa ~o; **dogwood**, (tree), kornuso; (wood), kornusa ~o; **alder dogwood**, frangolo; **driftwood**, flos~o; **firewood**, ŝtipoj, brul~o; **heartwood**, kern~o; **plywood**, tavol~o, krucoplakaĵo; **sapwood**, alburno; **touchwood**, tindro; **wormwood**, absinto, vermartemizio
woof, (weft), vefto; (dog bark), boji [int]; bojo; **woofer**, (bass speaker), bojilo
wool, lano; ~a; **woollen**, ~a; ~aĵo; **woollens**, (clothing), ~aĵoj; **woollen fabric**, (for clothing), drapo; **woolly**, ~(ec)a; (confused), konfuza; **wool shed**, (Aus), ~tondejo; **glass wool**, vitro~o; **wool classer**, (Aus), ~klasigisto; **steel wool**, ŝtal~o; **pull the wool over one's eyes**, mistifiki iun; **be woolgathering**, vagpensi [int]
woozy, kapturniĝa, nespiritopreta, neplenkonscia
word, (element of language), vorto; (form in words, choose wording),

~igi, formuli [tr]; (esp re written material), tekstigi (e.g.: *reword a sentence for clarity:* re~igi [or: retekstigi] frazon por klareco); (promise), promeso; (fame), famo; (news, information), sciigo, informo; (order, authorization), rajtigo, ordono; **worded**, ~igita, tekstigita; **be worded**, teksti [int] (e.g.: *the sentence is worded poorly:* la frazo tekstas malbone); **words**, (mus: lyrics, text), teksto (e.g.: *learn the words of a song:* lerni la tekston de kanto); **wordy**, mallakona, vort-ekscesa; **word-for-word**, laŭ~a, ~opa; laŭ~e, ~ope; **word of honor**, (solena) promeso, ĵuro; **word-of-mouth**, perbuŝa; **by word of mouth**, (per)buŝe; **word order**, ~ordo; **wordplay, play on words**, ~ludo; **buzzword**, fulmĵargonaĵo; **buzzwords**, fulmĵargono; **byword**, proverbo; **catchword**, (catchy word in advertising etc.), frap~o; **crossword (puzzle)**, kruc~(enigm)o; **foreword**, antaŭ~o; **"four-letter" word**, sakraĵo [not "kvarlitera ~o", since most equivalent roots in Esperanto do not have 4 letters]; **headword**, kap~o†; **password**, pas~o [cp "shibboleth"]; **eat one's words**, konfesi sian eraron [cp "recant", "withdraw"]; **watchword**, signal~o; **give one's word**, doni sian promeson; **go back on one's word**, rompi sian promeson; **have a word with**, paroli [int] kun; **have words with**, kvereli [int] kun, disputi [int] kun; **in other words**, ali~e; **put in a good word for**, rekomendi [tr], laŭdi [tr]; **take one's word for, take at one's word**, fidi ies parolon; **upon my word**, je mia ~o; mi ĵuras; **you took the words right out of my mouth**, mi ĵus estis dironta tion
work, (labor, gen, re person or machine; phys; ferment, re wine etc.), labori [int]; ~igi; ~a; ~(ad)o; (process, work on, shape, sculpt, etc.), pri~i [tr] [cp "turn"]; (material to be worked on), pri~ataĵo; pri~otaĵo; (work out, elaborate), el~i [tr]; (as job, occupation), ofici [int] (e.g.: *she works as an ac-*

countant: ŝi oficas kiel kontisto; *his work is outdoors:* lia ofico estas subĉiela); (task), tasko; (piece of lit, mus, poetry, etc.), verko; (function), funkcii [int]; funkciigi (e.g.: *the clock doesn't work:* la horloĝo ne funkcias); (solve problem, puzzle, etc.), solvi [tr]; (have effect, be efficacious), efiki [int] (e.g.: *antibiotics don't work on viruses:* antibiotikoj ne efikas sur virusojn); (succeed, re plan, project, etc.), sukcesi [int]; (do, make), fari [tr] (e.g.: *work miracles:* fari miraklojn); (thing done, made), faraĵo; (knead), knedi [tr]; (become, come into specified condition), ~iĝi [sfx] (e.g.: *the screw worked loose:* la ŝraŭbo malfiksiĝis); (cultivate, till), kultivi [tr], erpi [tr]; **workable**, praktika, efektivigebla, farebla; **working**, (active), aktiva; (functioning; for current use, not back-up copy or original), funkcianta (e.g.: *the working copy of the computer program:* la funkcianta kopio de la komputora programo), (re, for work), ~a, labor– [pfx] (e.g.: *working clothes:* ~vestoj); (provisional), provizora (e.g.: *working hypothesis:* provizora hipotezo); **works**, (plant, factory), [see "plant"]; (things made, built), konstruitaĵoj, ~aĵoj, faraĵoj; **workaday**, ĉiutaga, ordinara; **workaholic**, ~maniulo; **workbench**, (~)benko; **workbook**, [see under "book"]; **workday**, ~tago; ~taga; **worker, workman**, ~isto; **waterside worker**, (Aus), doklaboristo; **workforce**, ~istaro; **work in**, (introduce), enkonduki [tr]; (insert), enmeti [tr]; **workload**, ~ŝarĝo; **workmanlike**, lerta, bonkvalita; **workmanship**, bonkvalito, lerteco; **work off**, (debt), for~i [tr], ~amortizi [tr], per~e amortizi (ŝuldon); (weight), forekzerci [tr]; **work on**, (influence), influi [tr]; (try to persuade), provi persvadi [tr]; (try to do), provi [tr] (fari [tr]), ~i pri (e.g.: *work on a project:* ~i pri projekto; *I'm working on improving my singing:* mi provas plibonigi mian kantadon); **work out**, (work outside home), ~i [or: ofici [int] eksterdome; (make its way out, re imbedded object), (iom post iom) eliĝi; (exhaust mine, soil, etc.), elĉerpi [tr]; (debt), [see "work off" above]; (arrange, accomplish), aranĝi [tr]; (solve), solvi [tr]; (calculate), kalkuli [tr]; (result okay), rezulti [int] bone; (develop, elaborate), el~i [tr], evoluigi [tr]; evolu(ad)i [int]; (physical exercise), ekzerc(ad)i [tr] (sin); ekzerciĝ(ad)i; **workout,** (sin) ekzercado; **work over,** pri~i [tr]; **workshop,** (meeting to discuss, deal w, or teach particular subject, skill, etc.), kunsido, kuniĝo, ~kunsido, diskutkunsido, instrukunsido [cp "seminar"]; (place for gen work, as at home), ~ejo; (of skilled tradesperson), metiejo; **work up,** (prepare), prepari [tr]; (advance, rise), sin antaŭenigi; (elaborate), el~i [tr], evoluigi; (arouse, excite), eksciti [tr], inciti [tr]; (raise, bring about by activity), levi [tr] (e.g.: *work up a sweat:* levi ŝviton; *work up a cloud of dust:* levi pulvonubon); **workweek,** ~semajno; **domestic work,** hejm~o; **guest worker,** gast~isto†; **hard-working,** ~ema; **homework,** (as for school), hejmtasko(j); **housework,** mastrumado; **officework,** ofic~o; **office-worker,** kontoristo, oficisto; **overwork,** tro~i [int]; tro~igi; tro~ado; **piecework,** popeca ~o; **public works,** publikaj vorkoj†; **go to work,** (start a job), ek~i [int], ekofici [int]; (go to place of work), iri al la ~o; **out of work,** sendunga, senofica; **have one's work cut out (for one),** havi sian ~on antaŭeltondita, havi ja grandan taskon; **work on an assembly line,** ĉen~i [int]

world, (gen), mondo; ~a; **worldly,** ~(ec)a; **worldwide,** tut~a; **afterworld,** trans~o; trans~a; **underworld,** (criminal), krima, kanajla; krimularo, krim-medio; (myth), infero; **for all the world,** (indeed), ja (e.g.: *he looks for all the world like my brother:* li ja aspektas kiel mia frato); **worldview,** ~rigardo

worm, (zool, gen; any analogous object), vermo; (insinuate self into), enŝovi sin (en ion); (extract by cajol-

ery, subtle remarks, etc.), elkaĵoli [tr], eltordi [tr]; (purge intestinal worms), sen~igi; **wormy, worm-eaten,** (containing worms, as a fruit), ~ohava; (containing worm-holes, as wood), ~borita, ~trua; **wormhole,** ~truo; **blindworm,** angviso; **clam worm,** nereo; **pinworm,** oksiuro; **ringworm,** ringodartro; **roundworm,** (any nematode), nematodo; (*Ascaris*), askarido; **silkworm,** silkraŭpo; **silkworm moth,** bombikso; **slowworm,** angviso; **tapeworm,** tenio; **wireworm,** elaterido; **worm out of,** eltordi sin de, el

worry, ĉagreni [tr], maltrankviligi; ~iĝi; ~o (e.g.: *the financial report worries me:* la financa raporto min ~as; *don't worry about that:* ne ~iĝu pri tio); **worrisome,** (causing worry), ~a; (tending to worry), ~iĝema; **worrywart,** ~iĝemulo

worse, pli malbona; pli malbone; [see also "worst"]; **worsen,** plimalbonigi; plimalboniĝi; **worse off,** en pli malbona [or: malfavora] stato; **if worse comes to worst,** je l' plej malbona okazo; **change (take a turn) for the worse,** (pli)malbonigi, (pli)malfavoriĝi; (pli)malboniĝi, (pli)malfavoriĝi

worship, (esp rel), kulti [tr]; ~a; ~o; (adore, gen), adori [tr]; **worshipful,** ~anta; adoranta; (Br: honorable), honorinda; **worship service,** (rel), diservo; **your worship,** (title of respect), via (juĝista) moŝto

worst, plej malbona; plej malbone; [see also "worse"]; (conquer), venki [tr]; **at worst,** plej malfavore, en la plej malbona okazo; **the worst of it,** la plejmalbono

worsted, (fabric), glatdrapo; ~a; (yarn), ~a fadeno

worth, (value), valoro; ~i [tr]; ~anta (e.g.: *the book is well worth the price:* la libro bone ~as la prezon; *ten dollars' worth of gas:* benzino ĝis ~o de [or: benzino ~anta] dek dolaroj[n]); (dignity, personal worth), digno; (worthiness), indeco; (merit), merito; **worthless,** sen~a; **worthwhile,** (worthy), inda; (worth the effort), pen~a;

be worthwhile, be worth it, ~i la penon (e.g.: *I could keep protesting, but it's not worth it [not worthwhile]:* mi povus daŭri protesti, sed ĝi ne ~as la penon); **worthy,** (dignified), digna; (having merit, worthwhile), inda, pen~a (e.g.: *a worthy project:* inda [or] pen~a projekto); (person), indulo; dignulo; (fit for), taŭga (e.g.: *sea-worthy:* martaŭga); **worthy of,** inda je, –inda [sfx] (e.g.: *worthy of respect:* respektinda); **for all one is worth,** per ĉiuj ies (siaj) fortoj

Wotan, Votano [cp "Odin"]

would, (conditional tense), –us [sfx] (e.g.: *they would not go even if I ask them:* ili ne irus eĉ se mi petos ilin; *would you please do that?:* ĉu vi bonvole farus tion?); (past habitual action), –adis, kutimis –i, kutime –is (e.g.: *in summer she would walk home:* dum somero ŝi marŝadis [or] kutimis marŝi [or] kutime marŝis hejmen); **would-be,** estunta; **would that,** mi deziras ke –us

wound, vundi [tr]; ~o; **wounded,** (person(s)), ~ito(j); **woundwort,** (*Betonica*), betoniko; (*Stachys*), stakiso

wow, (distortion of sound), oscildistordo; (marvel), mirindaĵo; mirindulo; (arouse enthusiasm), entuziasmigi; (interj), nu!, ha!

wrack, (convulse, torture), torturi [tr]; **grass wrack,** (bot), zostero

wraith, fantomo

wrangle, kvereli [int], disput(aĉ)i [int]; ~o, disput(aĉ)o

wrap, (envelop, fold covering around, etc.), volvi [tr]; ~iĝi; ~aĵo (e.g.: *wrap a package:* ~i pakon; *she wrapped her arms around him:* ŝi volvis siajn brakojn ĉirkaŭ lin); (wind, as bandage), vindi [tr]; (overcoat), surtuto, palto; (shawl), ŝalo; **wrapper,** ~aĵo; (cylindrical, of paper, for mailing magazines etc.), banderolo [cp "tube: mailing tube"]; **wrapping,** ~aĵo; **wraparound,** ĉirkaŭ~a; **wrap up,** (en)~i [tr]; (finish), fini [tr]; **keep under wraps,** konservi kaŝita, konservi sekreta

wrasse, labro

wrath, kolero; **wrathful,** ~a

wreak, fari [tr], kaŭzi [tr], trudi [tr], okazigi

wreath, (flor)krono

wreck, (damage), difekti [tr]; ~iĝi; (accident, as car, train wreck), akcidenti [int]; akcidento; (wreck totally, demolish, destroy), frakasi [tr], detrui [tr], pereigi; frakasiĝi, detruiĝi, perei [int]; frakas(iĝ)o, detru(iĝ)o, pere(ig)o; (wrecked remains), vrakot; (fig: person), frakasulo, ruinulo, kadukulo; (remains of wrecked ship, plane, etc.), vrako; **wreckage,** frakasaĵo; vrako; (debris), disrompaĵo; **wrecker,** (tow truck), trenkamiono; (rr), tirvagono, gruvagono; (person who demolishes buildings etc.), domfrakasisto

wren, (*Troglodytes*), troglodito; **grass wren,** (Aus: *Amytornis textilis*), grandvosta herbopipio

wrench, (tool for turning bolt etc., gen), klevo*; (turn with a wrench), ~i [tr]; (twist, gen), tordi [tr]; tordiĝi; tord(iĝ)o (e.g.: *I wrenched my ankle:* mi tordis la maleolon); **adjustable wrench,** ĝustigebla ~o; **monkey wrench, pipe wrench,** tub~o; **socket wrench,** ingo~o; **torque wrench,** tord~o; **throw a monkey wrench into the works,** ĵeti bastonon en la radon

wrest, eltordi [tr], elvringi [tr]

wrestle, lukti [int]; (as sport), ~(olud)i [int]; ~(olud)o

wretch, mizer/ulo; **wretched,** ~a; **wretchedness,** ~o

wrick, tordi [tr]; ~o

wriggle, tord(et)iĝi; ~o; **wriggler,** (mosquito larva), moskitido

wring, wring out, vringi [tr], prem-tordi [tr]; **wringer,** ~ilo

wrinkle, (wad up, as paper, clothes), ĉifi [tr]; ~iĝi; ~aĵo; (pucker, furrow, as in skin), falto; falti [tr]; faltiĝi; (trick, idea), ideo, artifiko

wrist, (anat), pojno; (of garment), ~umo

writ, mandato, akto

write, (inscribe, put down written words, mus notes, etc., gen, on paper or in cmptr), skribi [tr] (e.g.: *write a* *check, a letter:* ~i ĉekon, leteron); (create lit, mus, poet work etc.), verki [tr] (e.g.: *write a novel, a symphony:* verki romanon, simfonion); **writer**, verkisto; **writing**, ~ado; ~aĵo; verkado; **in writing**, ~e; **handwriting**, man~(ad)o; **write by hand**, man~i [tr]; **writing utensil(s)**, ~il(ar)o; **write down**, surpaperigi; **write in**, en~i [tr]; **write off**, (cancel), nuligi; (debt), amortizi [tr]; (stop considering), ĉesi konsideri [tr]; **write out**, ~i, surpaperigi; (in full), plen~i [tr]; **write up**, (write record, account of), registri [tr]; (complete in writing), (fin)~i [tr]; (describe in writing), pri~i [tr]; **write-up**, (press article etc.), artikolo, pri~o; **skywriting**, ĉiel~ado; **underwrite**, (finance, pay for), subskripcii [tr] [cp "subsidy: subsidize"]; (insure), asekuri [tr]; (guarantee), garantii [tr]; (write under, sign), sub~i [tr]; **underwriter**, subskripciinto; subskripciisto; asekurinto; asekuristo; garantiinto; sub~into; **handwriting on the wall**, antaŭaverto

writhe, barakti [int]

wrong, (opp "right": incorrect, unjust, indecent, etc.), mal/ĝusta; ~prava; ~justa; ~deca, ~konvena [see "right"]; (erroneous), erara; (amiss), misa, mis– [pfx] (e.g.: *you did it wrong:* vi faris ĝin mise [or] vi misfaris ĝin); (mistreat), mistrakti [tr], ofendi [tr]; (misdeed), misfaro; **wrongful**, ~justa; **wrongdoer**, misfaranto, ~bonfaranto; **wrongdoing**, misfarado, ~bonfarado; **be wrong**, (amiss), misi [int] (e.g.: *what's wrong?:* kio misas?; *something's wrong with the motor:* io misas pri la motoro); (err), erari [int]; **go wrong**, misiĝi; **in the wrong**, ~prava; **be in the wrong**, ~pravi [int]; **do (someone) wrong**, mistrakti [tr] (iun); **get (someone) wrong**, miskompreni [tr] (iun)

wrought, (formed, fashioned, shaped), prilaborita, fasonita; **wrought-up**, maltrankvila, ekscitita

wry, (twisted), tordita; (distorted), dis~a; (perverse), perversa; **wryneck**, (zool), jingo

Wucheria bancrofti, Wucheria sanguinis-hominis, filario de la sango

Wuhan, Vuhan

Wuhsi, Vusi

wurst, kolbaso

Württemberg, Vurtemburgo

Wusih, Vusi

Wyoming, Vajomingo

wyvern, (dukrura) drako

X

X, (letter), ikso [see § 16]; **X out**, (delete by drawing X through), trastreki [tr], el~i [tr]; **X-ray**, (a ray), X-radio, ~-radio, Rentgena radio; (phot process), radiografio; radiografi [tr]; (a phot plate), radiografajo; **X-radiation**, X-radiado, Rentgena radiado
xanthelasma, ksantelasmo
xanthine, ksantino
Xantippe, Ksantipa
Xanthium, ksantio
xanthoma, ksantomo; **xanthomatosis**, ~ozo
xanthophyl(l), ksantofilo
Xanthosoma, ksantosomo
Xanthus, Ksanto
Xavier, Ksavero
xebec, korsaro
Xenarthra, ksenartroj
xenon, ksenono
xenophobia, ksenofob/io; **xenophobe**, ~o
Xenophon, Ksenofono
xeroderma, kserodermo
xerography, kserografio; **xerographic**, ~a
xerophilous, kserofita; **xerophilous plant**, ~o
xerophthalmia, kseroftalmio
xerophyte, kserofito
Xerxes, Kserkso
xi, ksi [see § 16]
Xiphias, ksifio
xiphoid, ksifoida; **xiphoid process**, ~o
Xuzhou, Suĝoŭ
xylem, ksilemo
xylene, ksileno; **metaxylene**, meta~o; **orthoxylene**, orto~o; **paraxylene**, para~o
xylograph, ksilografi [tr]; ~ajo; **xylographer**, ~o; **xylographic(al)**, ~ia; **xylography**, ~io
xylophone, ksilofono
xylose, ksilozo
xyster, rugino

Y

Y, (letter), ipsilono [see § 16; cp "upsilon"]
–y, (sfx: having, characterized by), –a (e.g.: *muddy:* kota; *healthy:* sana); (having quality of; somewhat), –eca (e.g.: *springy:* risorteca; *yellowy:* flaveca); (inclined to), –ema (e.g.: *drowsy:* dormema); ("full of"), –plena (e.g.: *a branchy tree:* brancôplena arbo)
yabber, babil(ad)i [int]
yacht, jakto; **yachtsman**, ~isto
Yahwe(h), **Yahve(h)**, Javeo
yak, (zool), poefago, gruntbovo; (babble), babili [int]; babil(ad)o
yakka, **yakker**, (Aus), laborego
Yakut, Jakuto; ~a
Yalta, Jalto
yam, (tuber, as food), ignamo; (any plant of *Dioscorea*), dioskoreo [cp "potato: sweet potato"]
yammer, (plend)kriadi [tr, int]; ~o
Yangtze, Jangzi
yank, ektiri [tr]; ~o
yankee, jankio; ~a
Yaoundé Jaunde
yap, (bark), bojeti [int]; ~o
yapok, ĥironekto
yarborough, (cards), nenobela mano
yard, (lawn), gazono; (enclosed courtyard), korto; (for specified purpose), –ejo [sfx] (e.g.: *lumber yard:* seglignejo); (length: 3 feet; naut: sail support), jardo [0,9144 metro (see § 20)]; **yardage**, (distance), metraro; (if unit "yard" must be specified), jardaro; **yardarm**, jardbrako; **yard goods**, ŝtofoj; **yardstick**, (lit or fig), mezurstango; **barnyard**, stalkorto
yarmulke, (Juda) vertoĉapo
yarn, (thread), (trik)fadeno; (tale), (blag)rakonto
yarrow, akileo
yashmak, vizaĝvualo
yatag(h)an, jatagano
yatter, babiladi [int]; ~o
yautia, ksantosomo
yaw, jori [int]; ~igi; ~o

yawl, (gen), jolo [cp "ketch"]
yawn, (open mouth), oscedi [int]; ~o; (gape wide, as re hole etc.), faŭki [int]
yaws, frambezio
ye, (archaic: you), vi; (the), la
yea, (yes), jes; ~o; (indeed), ja; (interj: hurrah!), hura!
year, jaro; **yearly**, (ĉiu)~a; (ĉiu)~e; jar– [pfx] (e.g.: *yearly report:* ~raporto); **yearling**, unu~a; unu~ulo; **common year**, ordinara ~o; **leap year**, super~o; **light-year**, lum~o; **lunar year**, lun~o; **midyear**, ~meza; **yesteryear**, pasint~e; **New Year's Day**, (la) Nov~tago; **New Year's Eve**, (la) Nov~a Antaŭvespero; **happy new year!**, feliĉan nov~on!; **year after year**, **year by year**, **year in**, **year out**, ~on post ~o; **a year from now**, de nun post ~o
yearn, sopiri [tr, int] (al, pri, –on); **yearning**, ~(ad)o; (for something past or lost), saŭdado
yeast, gisto
yell, kriegi [int]; ~o
yellow, flava; ~o; ~igi; ~iĝi
yelp, jelpi [int]; ~o
Yemen, Jemeno; **Yemeni**, **Yemenite**, ~ano; ~a; **Southern Yemen**, Sud–~o
yen, ($), eno; (longing), sopiro, deziro [cp "yearn"]
Yenisei, (river), Jenisejo
yenta, klaĉemulino
yeoman, (Am: naval officer), kontoroficiro; (Br: land-owner), etbienulo; (member of Br cavalry), rajdmilicano; (good, useful), bonega, utilega, valorega; **yeomanry**, ~aro; rajdmilico
yerba mate, mateo
yes, jes; ~o; **say yes to**, ~i [tr, int]; **yesperson**, ~(em)ulo
yesterday, (adv), hieraŭ (e.g.: *yesterday was hot:* ~ estis varme); **yesterday's**, la ~a (e.g.: *yesterday's newspaper:* la ~a ĵurnalo)
yet, (still; thus far), ankoraŭ (e.g.: *she may yet come:* ŝi ~ eble venos); (already), jam (e.g.: *have they gone yet?:*

ĉu ili jam iris?); (eventually, sooner or later), finfine, pli-malpli baldaŭ (e.g.: *we'll win a game yet:* finfine ni gajnos ludon); (however, nevertheless), tamen (e.g.: *poor, yet happy:* malriĉa, tamen kontenta; *they seem carefree, yet they have troubles:* ili ŝajnas senzorgaj, tamen ili havas ĉagrenojn); (even more, even less), eĉ (e.g.: *he began crying yet louder:* li komencis plori eĉ pli laŭte); **as yet**, (up to now), ĝis nun; **not yet**, ankoraŭ ne

yew, (tree), taksuso; (wood), ~a ligno

Yezo, Jezo [cp "Hokkaido"]

Yiddish, Jido; ~a

yield, (surrender, concede, relinquish), cedi [tr, int] (e.g. [re traffic]: *yield right-of-way:* ~i la pasrajton); (produce, give forth), produkti [tr], liveri [tr], doni [tr], naski [tr]; produkto, livero, dono; ($ etc.), redoni [tr]; redono; (output of factory, mine, etc.), rendimento; (chem), rikolto; **unyielding**, ne~ema, rezista, rigida

~yl, (chem sfx), ~ilo

yodel, jodli [int]; ~o

yoga, jogo; **yogi**, ~ano

yogurt, jahurto, jogurto

yohimbe, **yohimbi**, **yohimbihi**, johimbo

yoke, (gen), jugo; ~i [tr]

yokel, kamparanaĉo

Yokohama, Jokohamo

yolk, vitelo, ovoflavo

yonder, (that one), tiu fora; (over there), tie for

yoni, jonio

yoo-hoo, (interj), uhu!

yore, antaŭ longe

York, Jorko; **Cape York**, Kabo ~a; **New York**, (city), Nov-~o; (state), Nov-~io

you, (sing or plur, formal or familiar, as in English), vi [cp "thou"]

young, juna; (young person(s)), ~ul(ar)o; (offspring), id(ar)o; **youngster**, ~ulo; **with young**, (pregnant), graveda

your, **yours**, via; **yourself**, **yourselves**, [see "self"]; (**of**) **your being –d**, [see "her"]

youth, (young age), jun/eco; (young

person(s)), ~ul(ar)o; **youthful**, ~a

yowl, hojli [int], hurli [int], ululi [int]; ~o, hurlo, ululo

yo-yo, ludbobeno

yperite, iperito

Yser, Izero

ytterbium, iterbio

yttrium, itrio

yuan, ($), juano†

Yucatán, (peninsula), Jukatano; (state), ~io

yucca, Yucca, jukao

Yugoslav, Jugoslavo; ~a; ~ia; **Yugoslavia**, ~io; **Yugoslavian Federation**, ~a Federacio

Yukon, (river), Jukono; (territory), ~io

Yule, Julo

Yunnan, Junnan

yurt, jurto

Yvonne, Ivona

Z

zac, (Aus), sespenca monero
Zachariah, Zacharias, (Bib), Zeĥarja;
  (modern name), Zakario
Zachary, (man's name), Zakario
Zagreb, Zagrebo
Zaïre, Zairo†; **Zaïrian**, ~ano; ~a
Zakynthos, [see "Zante"]
Zambezi, (river), Zambezo
Zambia, Zambio; **Zambian**, ~ano; ~a
Zamenhof, Zamenhof;   **Zamenhofan**,
  ~a
Zante, (city or island), Zakinto
zany, harlekena, bufona, pajaca; ~o, bu-
  fono, pajaco [cp "wacky"]
Zanzibar, Zanzibaro
Zaporozhets, Zaporogo
Zaragoza, Zaragozo
Zarathustra, Zaratuŝtro [cp "Zoroas-
  ter"]
Zea mays, maizo
zeal, fervoro; **zealous**, ~a; [cp "zealot"]
Zealand, Zelando; **New Zealand**, Nov-
  ~o; **New Zealander**, Nov-~a; Nov-
  ~ano
zealot, Zealot, zeloto [cp "zeal"]
zeaxanthin, zeaksantolo
zebec(k), korsaro
zebra, zebro
zebu, zebuo
zecchino, zekino
Zechariah, [see "Zachariah"]
zechin, zekino
zedoary, kurkumaĵo
Zeeland, Zelando
Zeidae, [see "Zeus"]
zein, zeino
Zeke, Ezeĉjo [cp "Ezekiel"]
zemstvo, zemstvo
Zen, zeno; ~a
zenana, zenano
Zend, (language), Zendo;   ~a;   **Zend-**
  Avesta, ~o [cp "Avesta"]
zenith, zenito; ~a
Zeno, Zenono
Zeorhombiformes, [see "Zeus"]
Zephaniah, Cefanja
zephyr, (gen), zefiro; ~a
Zephyrus, Zefiro

zeppelin, zepelino
zequin, zekino
zero, (as numeral), nul [see § 19]; (n),
  ~o; ~a (e.g.: *Area Code 301:* Regionkodo 301 [pronounce: tri nul unu];
  10° below zero: 10° sub ~; *"million"
  is written as one followed by 6 zeros:*
  "miliono" estas skribata kiel unu sek-
  vata de 6 ~oj; *the zero column,* la ~a
  kolumno); **zero in on**, alceliri [int] al,
  alceliĝi al
zest, (gen), vervo, entuziasmo, gusto
zeta, zeta [see § 16]
zeugma, zeŭgmo
Zeus, (myth), Zeŭso
Zeus, (zool), zeo; Zeidae, zeedoj; Zeorhombiformes,   zeoromboformaj
  (fiŝoj)
Zeuxis, Zeŭksiso
zibel(l)ine, [see "sable"]
zibet(h), zibeto
ziff, (Aus), barbo
ziggurat, zigurato
zigzag, zigzago; ~a; ~i [int]
zik(k)urat, zigurato
zillion, umiliono
Zimbabwe, Zimbabvo†;   **Zimbabwe-**
  an, ~ano; ~a
zimbalon, zimbalono
zinc, zinko; **zinc blende**, ~oblendo;
  zinc spar, ~ospato; **zinc white**,
  ~oblanko
zincate, zinkato
zincography, zinkogravuro
zing, (sound), zumi [int]; ~o; (onom),
  zum!; (zest), vervo
Zingiber, zingibro
zinnia, Zinnia, zinio
Zion, Ciono; **Zionism**, c~ismo; **Zionist**,
  c~isma; c~isto
zip, (w zipper), zipi [tr]; (whiz, go fast),
  impeti [int], hasti [int]; (vigor), vigleco; (Br: zipper), ~o; **zipper**, ~o; **zip-**
  py, vigla; **ZIP Code**, poŝta kodo [not
  "ZIP-kodo"]
zircon, zirkono
zirconium, zirkonio
zither, citro

Ziziphus, zizifo; Ziziphus jujuba, Ziziphus vulgaris, jujub-arbo; Ziziphus lotus, lotus(arb)o
zloty, zloto
zo–, (pfx: animal), zo(o)–
Zoantharia, seskoraluloj
Zoarces, zoarco
zodiac, zodiako; **zodiacal**, ~a
Zoe, Zoa
Zohar, Zoharo
–zoic, (zool sfx), –zoa
zombi(e), (animated corpse), sorĉkadavro; (snake god), serpentodio
zone, (gen), zono; ~a; dis~i [tr], distrikti [tr]; **zoning**, dis~ado; dis~a; **time zone**, [see under "time"]
zonule, zonula, zonulo
zoo, zoo, zoologia ĝardeno
zoology, zoolog/io; **zoological**, ~ia; **zoologist**, ~o; **protozoology**, proto~io
zoom, (buzz, hum), zumi [int]; ~o; (onom), zum!; (re plane: climb, using kinetic energy; any analogous quick motion; enlarge view, as in camera or cmptr screen), zomi [int]; zomo; **zoom in**, zomi; **zoom out**, malzomi [int]; **zoom lens**, zomobjektivo
zoomorph, zoomorf/aĵo; **zoomorphic**, ~a; **zoomorphism**, ~ismo
Zoophyta, zoofitoj
zoophyte, zoofito
zoospore, zoosporo, sporangiosporo
zoosterol, zoosterolo
zootechny, zootekniko
Zoroaster, Zoroastro [cp "Zarathustra"]; **Zoroastrian**, ~ano; ~ana; **Zoroastrianism**, ~anismo
zoster, zostero
Zostera, zostero
Zouave, Zuavo
zucchini, kukurbeto, Italaj kukurboj
Zuider Zee, [see "Zuyder Zee"]
Zulu, Zuluo; ~a; **Zululand**, ~lando
Zurich, Zuriko
Zuyder Zee, Suda Maro [cp "south: South Seas"]
zwieback, rebakaĵo
zwitterion, ambaŭjono
zygomatic, (anat), zigoma; **zygomatic bone**, ~o
zygomycete, zigomiceto
Zygomycetes, zigomicetoj

Zygophyllaceae, zigofilacoj
zygospore, zigosporo
zygote, zigoto
zymase, zimazo
zyme, zimo
–zyme, (chem sfx: fermentation), –zimo
zymology, zimologio
zymosis, zimozo
zymotic, (re fermentation), fermenta
zymurgy, zimologio

Glossary of Neologisms

The Introduction at the beginning of this book contains a discussion of Esperanto neologisms used as translations in the body of this dictionary (see § 12). Not all Esperanto words listed in this Glossary are strictly "neologisms", since some have been established in Esperanto usage for many years, although, for whatever reason, they do not appear in the *Plena Ilustrita Vortaro de Esperanto* (PIV) nor the *Plena Ilustrita Vortaro, Suplemento* (PIVS).

That section of the Introduction mentioned that Esperanto translations in the body of this dictionary which are taken from the PIVS are marked by "†". This Glossary lists only those roots and affixes which are used as translations herein, *and* which appear in *neither* the PIV nor PIVS. A few of the terms in this Glossary are newly coined by the author in accordance with the 15th Fundamental Rule of Esperanto; most have been taken from existing written or spoken Esperanto. Glossary entries adopted from the *Australian-Esperanto Dictionary* (AED), by R. L. Harry and V. Gueltling, are marked "(Aus)" in the main body of the CEED, which also indicates that the term is particular to Australian English.

Newly coined neologisms are used in the CEED only when there appears to be no satisfactory way to translate an English word or expression using the existing Esperanto wordstock, for example if several words would be required in Esperanto where English uses only one or two.

In many instances, the author has felt that a neologism would better express a sense than the existing wordstock. Those who reviewed this dictionary before publication proposed many more neologisms. Nevertheless, the author believes strongly in two linguistic principles: first, that the introduction of neologisms as a substitute for preexisting terms should be kept to a bare minimum, for the sake of stability and uniformity in the language; and second, that a dictionary should generally not seek to mold a language, but should reflect the language that is spoken and written. Accordingly, in most cases the author has resisted the temptation to adopt neologisms. Fortunately, resort to a neologism in Esperanto is rarely necessary.

Although the PIV lists all planets of our Solar System, neither the PIV nor the PIVS lists any of the moons except Earth's own moon, Luna, and (curiously) one of Saturn's moons, Dione. The CEED partially fills this gap by giving Esperanto names for the two moons of Mars plus those moons of the outer planets (besides Dione) with diameters over 500 kilometers.

Analogous to the latitude and longitude given for each geographical name in the PIV and PIVS, the location of each moon named in this Glossary is specified by the moon's mean orbital radius (semimajor axis) as well as its parent planet.

Following each keyword below, a brief etymological note in parentheses is also given, to show the source of each Esperanto neologism from English and/or other ethnic languages. These etymological notes also serve to cross-refer back to the English keyword in the body of this dictionary (or one of the keywords) under which the Esperanto neologism is used as a translation.

Abiĝano, (nacilingve, "Abidjan"), la ĉefurbo de Eburio (4°W, 5°N)

Abudabo, (nacilingve, "Abu Dhabi"), la ĉefurbo de la Unuiĝintaj Arabaj Emirlandoj (54°E, 24°N)

aĉakaturo, (Itale kaj Angle, "acciacatura"), tre mallonga muzika noto, sonata ĵus antaŭ ĉefa noto, skribata kiel malgranda trastrekita okonnoto

Adelajdo, (Angle, "Adelaide"), la ĉefurbo de Sud-Aŭstralio [la AED donas ĉi tiun formon, kvankam la PIV donas la malpli taŭgan formon "Adelaido"]

Adirondakoj, (Angle, "Adirondacks"), montoĉeno en nord-orienta Nov-Jorkio (74°W, 44°N)

afganio, (nacilingve, "afghani"), la monunuo de Afganlando

Agano, (nacilingve, "Agana"), la ĉefurbo de Gvamo* (146°E, 14°N)

agistrodono, (Angla komuna nomo, "copperhead"), genro de venena serpento (*Agkistrodon contortrix*), ofta en Nord-Ameriko, kun kuprokolora kapo kaj malhelbrunaj iks-formaj strioj sur la dorso

Ajo, (nacilingve, "Io", laŭ la Greka diino Esperante nomata "Ioa"), la plej proksima el la ĉefaj lunoj de Jupitero (meza orbita radiuso 422 000 km)

akantropagro, (Aŭstrali-Angla komuna nomo, "bream"), Aŭstralia marfiŝo iom simila al la bramo (*Acanthopagrus*)

Akapulko, (nacilingve, "Acapulco"), feriurbo ĉe la Pacifika bordo de Meksikio (100°W, 17°N)

Akrao, (nacilingve, "Accra"), la ĉefurbo de Ganao (0°, 5°N)

aktinono, (Angle, "actinon"), izotopo (atommaso 217) de radono, estigata de la radioaktiva malkomponiĝo de aktinio

Albeno, (Angle, "Albany"), la ĉefurbo de Nov-Jorkio, ĉe la Rivero Hudsona (74°W, 43°N)

Algonkena, (Angle kaj Algonkenlingve, "Algonquin"), karakterizanta iom grandan aron da Indianaj triboj kaj la familion de iliaj lingvoj, en centra Nord-Ameriko

algoritmo, (Angle, "algorithm"), speciala metodo por solvi ian matematikan problemon; serio de kalkuloj kiun faras komputoro por atingi iun celon

alniko, (Angle, "alnico"; el la komencaj silaboj de la alojantaj metaloj), alojo de fero kun aluminio, nikelo, kaj kobalto, kaj kelkfoje kupro kaj aliaj metaloj; uzata por fabriki potencajn magnetojn

ambiverti, [tr], (Angle, "ambivert"), doni al homo la trajtojn kaj de introverteco kaj de ekstraverteco, tiamaniere estigante ekvilibron en la personeco; **ambivertito,** tia homo

amniocentezo, (Angle, "amniocentesis"; formo ankaŭ vidata en "paracentezo" en PIV), eltiro de specimeno de amnia fluido el la utero de gravedulino, por esplori la staton de la feto aŭ por aliaj medicinaj motivoj

aneroida, (Angle, "aneroid"), senlikva (aparte kiel rilatas al neelektronikaj barometroj) [menciita en PIV sub "barometro", sed ne mem difinita]

angoforo, (Angle, "angophora"), Aŭstralia arbo parenca al la eŭkalipto

Apalaĉoj, (Angle, "Appalachians", el Indiana vorto "Apalaĉi"), granda montoĉeno en orienta Nord-Ameriko, etendiĝanta ĉ. 2500 kilometrojn de Alabamo ĝis Kebekio (87°W, 34°N ĝis 66°W, 49°N); **Apalaĉio,** la montareca regiono de Alabamo ĝis Pensilvanio, kaj ĝia kulturo

apastro, (Angle, "apaster", el Grekaj elementoj por "for de" + "astro"), punkto en orbito plej malproksima de la ĉirkaŭorbitata astro [ĝeneralaĵo de la terminoj "afelio" (= "ap–helios" = "for de suno") kaj "apogeo"; cp "periastro"*]

Apio, (nacilingve, "Apia"), la ĉefurbo de la Okcidenta Insularo Samoa† (172°W, 14°S) [menciita en PIVS sub "Samoa" sed ne mem difinita]

Appia, (Itale, "Appia"), nomo de fama Romia vojo (Vojo Appia) en Italio [menciita en PIV sub "vojo", sed ne mem difinita]

Arielo, (nacilingve, "Ariel"), la plej proksima ĉefa luno de Urano (meza orbita radiuso 191 800 km)

askoto, (Angle, "ascot"), speco de larĝa kravato, origininta en Anglio

aŝramo, (Angle, "ashram", el la Sanskrita, "aŝrama"), izola loko por komunumo de Hinduoj sekvantaj vivon de simpleco kaj religia meditado

Atlanto, (Angle, "Atlanta"), urbego kaj plej grava komercocentro en sudorienta Usono, la ĉefurbo de Georgio (84°W, 34°N)

aŭtoharpo, (Angle, "autoharp"), 36-korda muzik-instrumento, iom simila al la citro (de kiu ĝi devenas), sed kun butonoj por aŭtomate elekti akordojn; ofta en Nord-Amerika folklora muziko

Bahaa, (nacilingve, "Baha'i", "Bahai"),

rilata al Bahaismo; **Bahaismo,** religio fondita de Baha'u'llah en Irano en la 19–a Jarcento, emfazanta universalan gefratecon kaj socian egalecon; **Bahaano,** ano de Bahaismo

balaklavo, (Angle, "balaclava", el la urbo Balaklava en Krimeo), ŝtofa ĉapo kiu etendiĝas malsupren por kovri la tutan kapon ĝis la kolo, kun truoj por la okuloj kaj nazo; portata por protekti kontraŭ ekstrema malvarmo

Bandar-Seri-Begavano, (nacilingve, "Bandar Seri Begawan"), la ĉefurbo de Brunejo† (115°E, 5°N) [menciita en PIVS sub "Brunejo" sed ne mem difinita]

bandikoto, (Angle, "bandicoot"), tre granda rato trovata en Hindio kaj Cejlono (*Bandicota*)

Bangvio, (nacilingve, "Bangui"), la ĉefurbo de la Centrafrika Respubliko† (19°E, 4°N) [menciita en PIVS sub "Centrafrika Respubliko" sed ne mem difinita]

banksio, (Angla komuna nomo, "banksia"), Aŭstralia ĉiamverda planto kun helaj flavaj floroj (*Banksia*)

baramundo, (Aŭstralia komuna nomo, "barramunda", "barramundi", el aborigena nomo), manĝebla Aŭstralia freŝakva fiŝo (*Neoceratodus forsteri*)

barmicvo, (Hebree, "bar micva", t.e., "filo de la leĝo"), Juda rito por 13-jaraĝaj knaboj, kiuj tiam atingas religian plenaĝon; **barmicvulo,** tia knabo

batmicvo, (Hebree, "bat micva", t.e., "filino de la leĝo"), Juda rito por 13-jaraĝaj knabinoj, kiuj tiam atingas religian plenaĝon; **batmicvulino,** tia knabino

behavioristo, (Angle, "behaviorist"), ano de behaviorismo

Biafro, (nacilingve, "Biafra"), orienta regiono de Niĝerio, kiu sensukcese klopodis starigi sian sendependecon en 1967—70)

bilabongo, (Aŭstrali-Angle, "billabong", el aborigena nomo), lageto distranĉita de rivero kiam la rivero tranĉas novan ŝanelon

bingo, (Angle, "bingo"), vetludo en kiu vokisto elvokas numerojn, kaj ĉiu ludanto metas ĵetonojn sur la samnumerajn kvadratojn aleatore presitajn sur kartona tabulo; la gajnanto estas la unua kiu faras rektan vicon da kvin ĵetonoj, aŭ alian antaŭanoncitan aranĝon

bolonjo, (Angle, "bologna"; el la samnoma Itala regiono—vidu sube), speco de granda, fumaĵita kolbaso el bovaĵo, porkaĵo, aŭ bovidaĵo, aŭ miksaĵo de tiuj; ofte manĝata en maldikaj trancaĵoj en sandviĉoj

Bolonjo, (nacilingve, "Bologna"), regiono kaj urbo en norda Italio, apud la Apeninoj (11°E, 44°N)

botulismo, (Angle, "botulism"), veneniĝo kaŭzata de la toksino produktata de iu bacilo foje trovata en nutraĵoj mishermetikigitaj

brakikito, (Aŭstrali-Angla komuna nomo, "bottle tree"), Aŭstralia speco de arbo (*Brachychiton*), kun ŝvela, botelforma trunko

Brazavilo, (Angle, "Brazzaville"), ĉefurbo de Kongolo (15°E, 4°S) [menciita en PIV sub "Kongolo", sed ne mem difinita]

breco, (Germane, "Bretzel"; Angle, "pretzel"), German-devena speco de malmola kaj seka (aŭ foje mola), forte salita biskvito, en formo de vergeto ordinare fleksita kvazaŭ krucitaj brakoj

brevo, (nacilingve, "breve"), la suprenkurba diakrita signo uzata sur la Esperanta litero "ŭ", kaj internacie uzata por indiki mallongecon de vokalo kaj por aliaj motivoj [en PIV nomata "hoksigno", sed la brevo devus esti distingita disde la vere hokforma (angula) diakritaĵo "dukorno", uzata en kelkaj orient-Eŭropaj lingvoj (ekz-e, "č", "ř", "š")]

Briĝtaŭno, (nacilingve, "Bridgetown"), la nomo de diversaj urboj, i.a. la ĉefurbo de Barbadot (60°W, 13°N) [menciita en PIVS sub "Barbado" sed ne mem difinita]

briofitoj, (Latine, "*Bryophyta*"), divizio botanika, kiun konsistigas la muskoj kaj hepatikoj [menciita en PIV sub "musko", sed ne mem difini-

ta]

brolgo, (Aŭstrali-Angla komuna nomo, "brolga"), granda arĝentogriza gruo de norda kaj orienta Aŭstralio (*Grus rubicunda*)

buĝerigo, (Angla komuna nomo, "budgerigar", "budgie"), speco de melopsitako* kun verdflava korpo, bluo sur la vangoj kaj vostoplumoj, kaj brune striitaj flugiloj (*Melopsittacus undulatus*)

Bujumburo, (nacilingve, "Bujumbura"), la ĉefurbo de Burundot (29°E, 3°S) [menciita en PIVS sub "Burundo" sed ne mem difinita]

burgo, (vortelemento el Angla "hamburger", "cheeseburger", k.s.), sandviĉo el bulko plenigita je ia hakviando, kun aŭ sen aliaj saporaĵoj kiel fromaĝo, laktuko, saŭco, peklaĵoj, k.s.; specifajn burgojn oni nomu laŭ la fontbesto de la viando, ekz–e, bovburgo (Angle, "hamburger"), fromaĝobovburgo (Angle, "cheeseburger"), kokinburgo, k.s.

centrarkedoj, (Angla komuna nomo, "bass"), familio (*Centrarchidae*) de oftaj Nord-Amerikaj karnovoraj perkoidaj sensalakvaj fiŝoj

codoroma, (Angle, "CD–ROM", siglo por "compact disk, read-only memory", t.e., "kompakta disko, neredaktebla memoro"), karakterizanta diskon sur kiu estas registrita teksto aŭ datenoj en duaria kodo lase re legata

ĉakro, (Angle, "chakra", el la Sanskrita), laŭ iuj orientaj religiaj filozofioj, unu el la sep centroj aŭ vorticoj de spirita energio en la fizika korpo, proksimume respondaj al sep fizikaj glandoj

Ĉarlestono, (Angle "Charleston"), (1) ĉefurbo de Okcident-Virginio (82°W, 38°N); (2) havenurbo en Sud-Karolinio (80°W, 33°N) [menciita en PIV sub "Virginio", sed ne mem difinita]

ĉatnio, (Angle, "chutney"; Hindie, "ĉatni"), Hindedevena frandaĵo el fruktoj, spicaĵoj, kaj aromherboj, ofte manĝata kun kareoj

ĉaŭo, (Angle, "chow"), speco de mezgranda Ĉindevena hundo, kun kompakta, muskola korpo, dika bruna aŭ nigra felo, kaj nigre-bruna lango

Ĉesapika, (Angle, "Chesapeake"), nomo de granda golfo en orienta Usono, etendiĝanta ĉ. 350 kilometrojn tra Marilando kaj Virginio (76°W, 37°N)

dajkirio, (nacilingve, "daiquiri"), alkohola trinkaĵo farita el rumo, sukero, kaj limeta aŭ limona suko

Dakaro, (nacilingve, "Dakar"), ĉefurbo de Senegalio kaj ĉefa komercocentro en okcidenta Afriko (17°W, 15°N) [menciita en PIV sub "Senegalo", sed ne mem difinita]

Dar-es-salamo, (nacilingve, "Dar es Salaam"), ĉefurbo de Tanzanio (39°E, 7°S) [menciita en PIV sub "Tanzanio", sed ne mem difinita]

daŝiko, (Angle, "dashiki", el la Svahila), Afrikdevena, loza, helkolora ĉemizo aŭ mallonga robo

dekstrozo, (Angle, "dextrose"), dekstroglukozo, $C_6H_{12}O_6$

Dejmoso, (nacilingve, "Deimos"), la pli malgranda kaj pli malproksima el la du lunoj de Marso (meza orbita radiuso 23 000 km)

demografo, (Angle, "demographer"), demografiisto

Denpasaro, (nacilingve, "Denpasar"), la ĉefurbo de Balio† (115°E, 9°S) [menciita en PIVS sub "Balio" sed ne mem difinita]

Denvero, (Angle, "Denver"), urbego kaj grava komercocentro en centra Usono, la ĉefurbo de Koloradio (105°W, 40°N)

diafilmo, (Angle, "slide"; el internaciaj vortelementoj "dia–" [tra] + "filmo"), diapozitivo

diĝeriduo, (Aŭstrali-Angle, "digeridoo", el aborigena nomo), unutona blovinstrumento de la Aŭstraliaj aborigenoj

distrofio, (Angle, "dystrophy"), (med), misformiĝo aŭ morba degenerado de organo aŭ histo

dobro, (Angle, "dobro"), Usona speco de gitaro, kun kaŭĉuka membrano kovranta la resonanc-aperturon, pro tio havanta pli malakutan sonon ol ordinara gitaro

Dohao, (nacilingve, "Doha"), la ĉefurbo de Kataro† (52°E, 25°N) [menciita en PIVS sub "Kataro" sed ne mem difinita]

dulcimero, (Angle, "[hammered] dulcimer"), kord-instrumento, en formo de malprofunda trapeza skatolo kun la kordoj streĉitaj horizontale trans (ordinare) du pontoj, ludata per frapi la kordojn per du malgrandaj marteloj (la cimbalono estas pli granda parenco); **fretodulcimero**, (Angle, "mountain dulcimer", "fretted dulcimer"), kord-instrumento, origininta en Apalaĉio* sed kredeble kun radikoj en Eŭropo, ordinare kun vespoforma (foje larmoforma) sonkesto, fretoj, kaj tri ĝis kvin kordoj, unu el kiuj estas unutona zumkordo; oni plektras ĝin sidante kaj kuŝiganta ĝin sur la femuro; ofta en Nord-Amerika folklora muziko

ekosistemo, (Angle, "ecosystem"), ekologia sistemo

ekstroverti, [tr], (Angle, "extrovert"), direkti ies libidon aŭ personecon eksteren; estigi iun sociema [PIV listigas la participon, "ekstrovertito": tia homo]

ekzo–, (Angle, "exo–", el la Greka), teknika prefikso kun la signifo "ekstera"; la malo de "endo–"

ekzobiologio, (Angle, "exobiology"), branĉo de la biologio, kiu koncernas sin pri la ebleco de vivo origininta ekster Tero

ekzoskeleto, (Angle, "exoskeleton"), ekstera skeleto, kiel havas kraboj, iuj insektoj, k.a.

–enzo, (nacilingve, "–ence" k.s.), teknika sufikso indikanta substancon kiu plenumas la agon de la radiko (ekz-e: halucinenzo, solvenzo, rivelenzo)

epiciklo, (Angle, "epicycle"), cirklo, kiu ruliĝas sur la ekstera aŭ interna flanko de fiksa cirklo, tiel naskanta respektive epicikloidon aŭ hipocikloidon

esceto, (Germane, "Eszett", t.e., "s-z"), litero ("ß") uzata en la Germana lingvo, ligaturo* de "ss"

eŭgenio, (Angle, "eugenia", el la Greka), granda genro (*Eugenia*) de tropikaj arboj kaj arbustoj, el la familio de mirtacoj; ĝiaj specioj inkludas la grumiksamarbon, la kariofilarbon, la jamboson, la pimenton, kaj la pitangarbon

Eŭropao, (nacilingve, "Europa"), la dua ĉefa luno de Jupitero (meza orbita radiuso 671 000 km)

eŭtamio, (Angla komuna nomo, "chipmunk"), genro (*Eutamias*) de oftaj malgrandaj Nord-Amerikaj sciuroj, kun strioj sur la kapo kaj dorso, vivantaj ĉefe sur la grundo

faksi [tr], (Angle kaj internacie, "fax", mallongigo de "faksimilo"), sendi faksimilon (faksaĵon) de dokumento per faksilo; **faksaĵo**, ricevita faksimilo transmisiita fakse; **faksilo**, aparato kiu skanas dokumenton kaj transmisiias la tiel kodigitan signalon telefone kaj ricevas tiajn signalojn el alia faksilo kaj elprintas faksimilon (faksaĵon) de la aliloke transmisiita dokumento

Fanafutio, (nacilingve, "Funafuti"), la ĉefurbo de Tuvalo† (178°E, 8°S) [menciita en PIVS sub "Tuvalo" sed ne mem difinita]

fenobarbitalo, (Angle, "phenobarbital"), kristalaĵo ($C_{12}O_3N_2H_{12}$), uzata kiel sedativo kaj antispasmaĵo

filibustri, [int], (Angle, "filibuster"), en parlamento, kunveno, k.s., intence prokrasti voĉdonon pri leĝopropono k.s. per longa kaj ofte nerilata prelegado; **filibustro**, tia ago

flamenko, (Angle kaj Hispane, "flamenco"), speco de Hispana muziko kaj dancado, tre vigla kaj ritma

Foboso, (nacilingve, "Phobos"), la pli granda kaj pli proksima el la du lunoj de Marso (meza orbita radiuso 9000 km)

fonduo, (Angle kaj France, "fondue", t.e., "fanditaĵo"), manĝaĵo ordinare el fandita fromaĝo kun vino, varmigata en poteto super kandelo k.s., uzata kiel trempaĵo por pecetoj de viando, pano, k.s.

fraktalo, (Angle, "fractal"), matematika kurbo, surfaco, volumeno, k.t.p., kies ĉiu parto konsistas en pli malgrand-

skalaj kurbiĝoj, kaj simile ĝis infinito

frankfurto, (Angle, "frankfurter", "hot dog"), maldika, mildgusta kolbaso, ofte rostata super fajro ĉe pikniko k.s. kaj manĝata sandviĉe en bulko kun mustardo ili keĉupo*, hakita cepo, fromaĝo, k.s.; **frankfurta bulko**, tia sandviĉo

frusto, (Angle kaj Latine, "frustum"), geometria solido formita sub ebeno kiu tranĉas konuson aŭ piramidon paralele al ĝia bazo

gajlusaco, (Angla komuna nomo, "huckleberry"), genro (*Gaylussacia*, el erikacoj) de plantoj, kun bluaj beroj iom similaj al mirtelberoj, sed kun dek grandaj semoj; la beroj estas ofte uzataj por tortoj, benjetoj, k.s.

Ganimedo, (nacilingve, "Ganymede"), la tria el la ĉefaj lunoj de Jupitero (meza orbita radiuso 1 070 000 km) [difino aldona al tiu en PIV]

Gaspeo, (nacilingve, "Gaspé"), granda duoninsulo en sudorienta Kebekio, ĉe la enmariĝo de la Rivero Sankta-Laŭrenco (65°W, 49°N)

gavio, (Angla komuna nomo, "loon"), genro (*Gavia*) de relative grandaj, primitivaj akvobirdoj kun la kruroj situantaj ĵus antaŭ la vosto, kaj kun naĝhaŭto inter la piedfingroj; parenca al la kolimbo, sed distingita disde ĉi tiu per tio ke la kolimbo estas malpli granda kaj ne havas piedfingran naĝhaŭton [PIV erare diras ke la kolimbo ja havas naĝhaŭton kaj erare indikas ke la kolimbo (*Colymbus*) kaj podicipo (*Podiceps*) ne estas identaj]

Georgtaŭno, (nacilingve, "Georgetown"), urbnomo, i.a. de la ĉefurbo de Brita Gvajanio† (58°W, 7°N) [menciita en PIVS sub "Gvajano" sed ne mem difinita]

gerontokratio, (Angle, "gerontocracy"), regado far maljunuloj

gerontologo, (Angle, "gerontologist"), specialisto pri gerontologio; **gerontologio**, la medicina scienco pri maljuniĝado kaj la problemoj de maljunuloj

gingamo, (Angle, "gingham"), speco de katuno teksita en strioj, kvadratoj, aŭ plejdoj

granolo, (Angle, "granola"), manĝaĵo farita el la kernoj de diversaj grenoj kaj mielo kunbakitaj; manĝata kun lakto ĉe matenmanĝo aŭ uzata kiel ingredienco en kuketoj k.s.

gupio, (Angle, "guppy"), malgranda tropika nesalakva fiŝo (*Lebistes reticulatus*), ofta en akvarioj

Gvamo, (Angle, "Guam"), la plej granda el la Insuloj Marianaj, posedata de Usono; ĉefurbo, Agano* (146°E, 14°N)

ĝinzo, (Angle, kaj nun internacie, "jeans"), pantalono el drelika ŝtofo, plej ofte blua

halioto, (Angla komuna nomo, "abalone"), genro (*Haliotis*) de mara molusko, kun ovala, iom spirala konko kun vico de truoj proksimaj al la rando kaj tegita de perlamoto

Halovino, (Angle, "Halloween", el "All Hallows' Evening", t.e., "Vespero de Ĉiuj Sanktuloj"), festo je la 31–a de oktobro, origine asociita kun la Kelta Novjar-Tago je la 1–a de novembro, poste asociita kun la Tago de Ĉiuj Sanktuloj ĉe Kristanoj ankaŭ je la 1–a de novembro, nun nereligia festo en Nord-Ameriko por distriĝado kaj petolado, ĉefe ĉe infanoj

Hampŝiro, (Angle, "Hampshire"), graflando en suda Anglio (1°W, 51°N) [en PIV aparte listiĝas "Nov-Hampŝiro", la Usona ŝtato, sed mankas "Hampŝiro"]

Hobarto, (Angle, "Hobart"), la ĉefurbo de Tasmanio (147°E, 42°S)

holokaŭsto, (Angle, "holocaust", el Grekaj radikoj kun la signifo "plenbruligo"), grandskala, amasa genocido, ekz-e de la Judoj far la Nazioj antaŭ kaj dum la Dua Mondmilito

Honiaro, (nacilingve, "Honiara"), la ĉefurbo de la Salomon-Insuloj† (160°E, 8°S) [menciita en PIVS sub "Salomon-Insuloj" sed ne mem difinita]

Ĥanukao, (Angle, "Chanukah", "Hanuka"; Hebree, "Ĥanukah"), ok-taga Juda festo, komenciĝanta je la 25–a de la monato Kislev (ordinare meze de decembro), por rememorigi la redediĉon de la Templo en 165 a.K.

ikteruso, (Angla komuna nomo, "oriole"), genro (*Icterus*) de Nord-Amerikaj birdoj, kiuj similas laŭ koloraĵo al la oriolo, kaj kiuj konstruas pendantajn nestojn

introverti, [tr], (Angle, "introvert"), direkti ies libidon aŭ personecon internen; estigi iun introspektema [PIV listigas la participon, "introvertito:" tia homo]

Islamabado, (nacilingve, "Islamabad"), la ĉefurbo de Pakistano† (73°E, 34°N) [menciita en PIVS sub "Pakistano" sed ne mem difinita]

Jafeto, (Angle kaj Latine, "Iapetus", el la Hebrea "Jafeth"), unu el la lunoj de Saturno (meza orbita radiuso 3 560 800 km) [difino aldona al tiu en PIV]

Jaundeo, (nacilingve, "Yaoundé"), la ĉefurbo de la Kamerunia Respubliko (11°38E, 3°50N) [PIV donas la ne-Esperantan literumon "Jaunde" sub "Kameruno"]

kaki, [int], (triviala slango, el Ĝermanaj lingvoj), feki; **kako**, fekaĵo

kalipso, (Angle, "calypso"), speco de muziko origininta en Trinidado, satiraj baladoj kun forte sinkopa ritmo

Kalisto, (nacilingve, "Callisto", laŭ la Greka mitologia figuro Esperante nomata "Kalistoa"), la kvara el la ĉefaj lunoj de Jupitero (meza orbita radiuso 1 880 000 km)

Kampalo, (nacilingve, "Kampala"), la ĉefurbo de Ugando† (32°E, 0°) [menciita en PIVS sub "Ugando" sed ne mem difinita]

kandlo, (nacilingve, "candela"), unuo de lumintenso, 1/60 de la lumintenso de unu kvadrata centimetro de nigra korpo je la temperaturo de solidiĝo de plateno

kardio, (Angla komuna nomo, "cockle"), genro (*Cardium*) de duklapaj moluskoj, kun granda piedo por surrampi la marfundon, vaste ŝatata kiel marmanĝaĵo

Karono, (nacilingve, "Charon", laŭ la Greka mitologia figuro "Ĥarōn"), la sola luno de Plutono, preskaŭ ĝemela planedo kun Plutono (meza orbita radiuso 653 600 km) [difino aldona al tiu en PIV]

Kastrio, (nacilingve, "Castries"), la ĉefurbo de Sankta Lucia† (61°W, 14°N) [menciita en PIVS sub "Sankta Lucia" sed ne mem difinita]

keĉupo, (Angle, "catsup", "ketchup", el la Ĉina, "kecjap"), speco de tomata saŭco, saporizita per cepo, salo, sukero, kaj spicaĵoj; ofte uzata sur viandoj

Kingstaŭno, (nacilingve, "Kingstown"), urbnomo, i.a. de la ĉefurbo de Sankta Vincento kaj Grenadinoj† (61°W, 13°N) [menciita en PIVS sub "Sankta Vincento kaj Grenadinoj" sed ne mem difinita]

Kigalo, (nacilingve, "Kigali"), la ĉefurbo de Ruando† (30°E, 2°S) [menciita en PIVS sub "Ruando" sed ne mem difinita]

klevo, [tr], (French, "clef", "clé"; Usone, "wrench"; Brite, "screwspanner"), simpla ilo kun du makzeloj kaj tenilo, uzata por streĉi aŭ malstreĉi bolton aŭ boltingon, turni aŭ teni tubon, k.s.; ankaŭ nomata "ŝraŭbŝlosilo"; **klevi,** [tr], streĉi, malstreĉi, turni, teni, k.s., per tia ilo

kniki, [int], (Angle, "buckle"; Germane, "knicken"), fleksiĝi, tordiĝi, aŭ frakasiĝi pro troa laŭlonga premforto, parolante pri fertrabo, tubo, betono, genuoj, k.s.

kolacii, [tr], (Angle, "collate"), meti (paĝojn, ekz–e de bindota libro) en ĝustan ordon, prepare al bindado

komjuno, (Angle, "commune"), speco de kolektiva komunumo, formita far kelkaj ĝis pli ol cent homoj, por sia komuna ekonomia kaj spirita bonfarto; loĝantaj sur unu terpeco, ofte en unu konstruaĵo, kun kompleta aŭ parta komuneco de laboro, mono, manĝaĵo, posedaĵoj, ĉefaj celoj kaj motivoj, seksrilataj, religiaj kaj/aŭ politikaj konvinkoj, k.s.

Konektikuto, (Angle, "Connecticut", el Indiana nomo), (1) unu el la ŝtatoj de Usono; ĉefurbo, Hartford (73°W, 42°N); (2) rivero en nordorienta Usono, originanta inter Vermonto kaj Nov-Hampŝiro kaj finiĝanta en la

Markolo Long-Insula (72°W, 41°N)

Konjako, (France, "Cognac"), Franca urbo en la regiono kie oni faras konjakon (0°, 45°N)

konteo, (Angle, "county"; France, "comté"), la plej granda subdivizio de Usona ŝtato aŭ Kanada provinco [Esperanta formo ankaŭ vidata en "Franĉkonteo" en PIV; "konteo" distingiĝas de la Brita graflando (ankaŭ "county" en la Angla) per tio ke en Nord-Ameriko neniam estis grafoj, sekve ne povas esti graflandoj]

kontragitaro, (Hispane, "guitarrón", t.e., "gitarego", basa gitaro), muzikinstrumento similforma al gitaro sed pli granda, kun pli profunda sonkesto, kaj kun pli basa tonetendo; ofta en Meksikia populara muziko

kontratenoro, (Angle, "countertenor"), la plej alta rango de matura vira kantvoĉo, super la tenoro; **kontratenorulo,** tia kantisto

koroborio, (Aŭstrali-Angle, "corroboree", el aborigena nomo), dancfesto de Aŭstraliaj aborigenoj

kribaĝo, (Angle, "cribbage"), kartludo en kiu oni registras la poentaron per meti pinglojn en truitan tabuleton

krisopogono, (Aŭstralia komuna nomo, "beard grass"), Aŭstralia speco de herbo (Chrysopogon)

kulabao, (Aŭstrali-Angla komuna nomo, "coolabah", "coolibah"), Aŭstralia speco de eŭkalipto, ofta en la Aŭstralia landinterno (Eucalyptus microtheca)

kundalina, (Angle kaj Sanskrite, "kundalini"), karakterizanta forton kiu, laŭ Hindua psikologio kaj jogo, situas ĉe la bazo de la spino kaj estas intime asociita kun la seksa forto kaj ĝenerale kun la krea potenco; kiam ekscitita (ekz–e dum meditado), ĝi moviĝas supren laŭ la spino ĝis la supraj ĉakroj*

Kuracao, (nacilingve, "Curaçao"), antaŭe, la Nederlandaj Antiloj; nun, la plej granda insulo de la Nederlandaj Antiloj; originejo de kuracao (69°W, 12°N)

kurio, (nacilingve, "curie", laŭ Marie

Curie), unuo de radioaktiveco, egala la la kvanto de iu ajn radioaktiva substanco en kiu la nombro da malkombiniĝoj en sekundo egalas 3,7 x 10^{10})

kvadrafonia, (Angle, "quadraphonic"), karakterizanta sistemon de sonreproduktado en kiu estas kvar apartaj kanaloj, tiamaniere ke aŭskultanto meze de ili aŭdas sonojn el ĉiu direkto, kvazaŭ sidante meze de la orkestro aŭ alia sonfonto

labruskano, (Angla komuna nomo, "catawba"), variaĵo de vinberujo (*Vitis labruscana*), vaste kultivata en orienta Nord-Ameriko por la vinberoj kaj vino

leno, (Angle, "lane"), unu el la paralelaj irejoj (koridoroj) de ŝoseo aŭ larĝa strato, laŭ kiu veturas unu vico de veturiloj

ligaturo, (Angle, "ligature"), (1) kunŝoviĝo de du literoj en unu karaktron (ekz-e, "æ", "œ", "ß"); (2) kurba linio super aŭ sub du aŭ pli da skribitaj muzikaj notoj, por indiki ke la notoj estu ludataj aŭ kantataj glate, senrompe [difinoj aldonaj al tiu en PIV]; **ligaturi,** [tr], (Angle, "slur"), ludi aŭ kanti sinsekvajn muzikajn notojn glate kaj senrompe

Lilongvo, (nacilingve, "Lilongwe"), la ĉefurbo de Malavio† (34°E, 14°S) [menciita en PIVS sub "Malavio" sed ne mem difinita]

Limeriko, (Angle, "Limerick"), provinco (kaj ĝia ĉefurbo) en Irlando, el kiu eble originis la poezia formo "limeriko" (6°W, 53°N)

limetado, (Angle, "limeade"), trinkaĵo farita el limeta suko, akvo, kaj sukero, analoge al limonado

majno, (Angle, "myna"; Hindie, "majna"), iu el la grupo de Aziaj birdoj (aparte *Eulabes religiosa*), parenca al la sturno, kapabla imiti homan parolon; konservata kiel kaĝbirdo

Makenzio, (nacilingve, "Mackenzie"), granda rivero en nord-okcidenta Kanado, originanta ĉe Lago Grand-Sklava, fluanta tra la Teritorioj Nord-Okcidentaj, kaj finiĝanta en la Maro Boforta (135°W, 69°)

makrameo, (Angle kaj France, "macramé"; el la Araba, "mikramah"), speco de malfajna punto el ŝnuro, kun nodoj kaj maŝoj en diversaj aranĝoj, ofte uzata por ornamado

Malabo, (nacilingve, "Malabo"), la ĉefurbo de Ekvatora Gvineo† (9°E, 4°N) [menciita en PIVS sub "Gvineo" sed ne mem difinita]

Maleo, (nacilingve, "Male"), la ĉefurbo de Maldivoj† (74°E, 4°N) [menciita en PIVS sub "Maldivoj" sed ne mem difinita]

mandalo, (Angle kaj Sanskrite, "mandala"), cirkla desegnaĵo kun samcentraj geometriaj formoj, bildoj, k.s., simbolanta en Hinduismo kaj Budhismo la universon aŭ tutecon

Maputo, (nacilingve, "Maputo"), la ĉefurbo de Mozambiko† (32°E, 26°S) [menciita en PIVS sub "Mozambiko" sed ne mem difinita]

marŝmalo, (Angle, "marshmallow"), speco de mola, spongeca bombono, kutime en malgrandaj blankaj buloj, farita el sukero, amelo, maizosiropo, kaj gelateno; ofte rostata super fajro ĉe pikniko k.s.

martino, (Angle, "martini"), alkohola trinkaĵo el ĝino aŭ vodko kun vermuto, ofte servata kun verda olivo en la glaso

Mbabano, (nacilingve, "Mbabane"), la ĉefurbo de Svazio† (31°E, 26°S) [menciita en PIVS sub "Svazio" sed ne mem difinita]

melopsitako, (Angla komuna nomo, "parakeet"), familio de Aŭstraliaj papagetoj inkludante la buĝerigo* (*Melopsittacus*)

Menonito, (Angle, "Mennonite", laŭ la fondinto, Menno Simons), ano de Protestanta Kristana sekto kontraŭanta ĵurojn kaj baptadon de infanoj, favorantan simplajn vestojn kaj vivstilon

metadono, (Angle, "methadone"), sinteza narkotaĵo ($C_{21}H_{27}ON$), ofte uzata i.a. por kuraci heroinmanion

mikrofiĉo, (nacilingve, "microfiche"), mikrofilma karto enhavanta mikroskope malpligrandigitajn kopiojn de pluraj normgrandaj dokumentoj aŭ paĝoj, kiujn oni legas per aparato kiu projekcias repligrandigitan imagon sur ekranon

Mogadiŝo, (nacilingve, "Mogadishu"), ĉefurbo de Somalio (45°E, 2°N) [menciita en PIV sub "Somalio", sed ne mem difinita]

monofonia, (Angle, "monophonic"), karakterizanta sistemon de sonreproduktado en kiu estas nur unu sonfonto aŭ kanalo (kontraste al "stereofonia" kaj "kvadrafonia")

Monrovio, (nacilingve, "Monrovia"), la ĉefurbo de Liberio (11°W, 6°N)

mordako, (Angla komuna nomo, "American smelt"), Amerika genro de osmero (*Osmerus mordax*), nun vivanta nur en nesalakvo

Moronio, (nacilingve, "Moroni"), la ĉefurbo de Komoroj† (44°E, 12°S) [menciita en PIVS sub "Komoroj" sed ne mem difinita]

moŝavo, (Angle, "moshav", el la Hebrea, "moŝav"), speco de Israela vilaĝo, kun agroj kooperative kultivataj sed kun individuaj loĝejoj (kontraste al "kibuco")

Nancio, (France, "Nancy"), urbo en Loreno, Francio (6°E, 49°N) [menciita en PIV sub "Loreno", sed ne mem difinita]

Naŭatlo, (nacilingve, "Náhuatl"), ano de unu el granda familio de gentoj indiĝenaj al Meksikio kaj Centra Ameriko, inkluzive la Aztekoj; **Naŭatla,** karakterizanta la lingvon de la Aztekoj kaj parencaj gentoj, trovatan en pluraj dialektoj

nikada, (Angle, "nicad"; mallongigo en ambaŭ lingvoj de la du metaloj), karakterizanta baterion kies elektra tensio ŝuldiĝas al kemia interago inter nikelo kaj kadmio

Nukualofo, (nacilingve, "Nuku'alofa"), la ĉefurbo de Tongo† (175°W, 21°S) [menciita en PIVS sub "Tongo" sed ne mem difinita]

Oberono, (nacilingve, "Oberon"), unu el la ĉefaj lunoj de Urano (meza orbita radiuso 586 600 km)

obskuranto, (Angle, "obscurantist"), ano de obskurantismo ["obskurantismo" troviĝas en PIV, sed ne "obskuranto"]

oocito, (Angle, "oocyte"), la unua, nematura stadio de ovo (la femala analogo de "spermatocito")

pandemio, (Angle, "pandemic"), epidemio okazanta ĉie

Paramaribo, (nacilingve, "Paramaribo"), la ĉefurbo de Surinamo† (55°W, 6°N) [menciita en PIVS sub "Surinamo" sed ne mem difinita]

paramecio, (Angle, "paramecium"), genro (*Paramecium*) de unuĉelaj, pantofloformaj protozooj, moviĝantaj per cilioj

paramelo, (Aŭstralia komuna nomo, "bandicoot"), iu el diversaj Aŭstraliaj marsupiuloj, iom similaj al la bandikoto*

parastacedo, (Aŭstrali-Angla komuna nomo, "crayfish"), Aŭstralia familio de krustuloj similaj al la astako (*Parastacidae*)

paskalo, (nacilingve, "pascal", laŭ Blaise Pascal), unuo de premo, egala al la premo de unu nutono de forto sur unu kvadrata metro; 100 000 paskaloj egalas unu baron; simbolo: Pa

pejotlo, (Angle kaj Hispane, "peyote", el la Naŭatla* "peyotl"), malgranda kaktaco (*Lophophora williamsii*) de norda Meksikio kaj sudokcidenta Usono, sur kiu kreskas "butonoj" entenantaj meskalinon [menciita en PIV sub "meskalino", sed ne mem difinita]

periastro, (Angle, "periaster", el Grekaj elementoj por "ĉirkaŭ" "astro"), punkto en orbito plej proksima al la ĉirkaŭorbitata astro [ĝeneralaĵo de la terminoj "perihelio" kaj "perigeo"; cp "apastro"]

Perto, (Angle, "Perth"), (1) urbo en Skotlando (3°W, 56°N); (2) la ĉefurbo de Okcidenta-Aŭstralio (116°E, 32°S)

Pesaño, (Hebree, "pesaĥ"; Angle, "Passover"), la Hebrea Pasko; vorto uzata por eviti konfuzon kun la Kristana Pasko

pibroño, (Angle, "pibroch", el la Skotgaela, "piobaireachd"), Skota muzikpeco por la sakŝalmo, ĝenerale en ritmo de funebra marŝo

popa, (Angle, "pop"), populara, laŭmoda (pri muziko, arto, k.s.); celata al
laikoj aŭ la ĝenerala publiko (pri scienca verko k.s.)

Port-Luizo, (nacilingve, "Port Louis"),
la ĉefurbo de Maŭricio† (58°E, 20°S)
[menciita en PIVS sub "Maŭricio" sed
ne mem difinita]

Potomako, (Angle, "Potomac", el Indiana nomo), granda rivero en mez-
orienta Usono, inter Marilando, Okcident-Virginio, kaj Virginio, fluanta
preter Vaŝingtono kaj finiĝanta en la
Golfo Ĉesapika* (76°W, 38°N)

psikometrio, (Angle, "psychometry"),
la supozata psika kapablo percepti informon pri homo aŭ objekto, aŭ pri
homo asociita kun objekto, per tuŝi la
homon aŭ objekton

rado, (nacilingve, "rad"; difino aldona
al tiuj en PIV), unuo de dozo de en-
sorbita radiado, egala al la ensorbo de
100 ergoj da energio en unu gramo da
materio

rago, (Angle kaj Sanskrite, "raga"),
tradicia Hinda muzikformo, kun ka-
rakterizaj intervaloj, ritmoj, ktp., uzata kiel matrico aŭ fontomaterialo por
improvizado

Reo, (nacilingve, "Rhea", laŭ la Greka
mitologia figuro Esperante nomata
"Rea"), unu el la ĉefaj lunoj de Saturno (meza orbita radiuso 527 070
km)

rekteno, (Angle, "rectenna", el "recti-
fying antenna array", t.e., "rektiga an-
tenaro"), aranĝo de tre multaj antenoj
kovrantaj plurajn kvadratajn kilometrojn de la tersurfaco aŭ marsurfa-
co, uzata (ankoraŭ "–ota") por ricevi
kaj retransformi mikroondajn transmi-
siojn de elektro generata (–ota) per
sunenergiaj potencosatelitoj

ribosomo, (Angle, "ribosome"), malgrandega, sferforma korpusklo, kon-
sistanta en ribonuklea acido (RNA)
kaj proteinoj kaj multnombre trovata
en la citoplasmo de ĉeloj

Riĉmondo, (Angle, "Richmond"), ĉefurbo de Virginio (77°W, 38°N)
[menciita en PIV sub "Virginio", sed

ne mem difinita]

rilo, (Angle kaj France, "reel"), (1) vigla folklora paŝdanco origininta en
Keltaj landoj, ankaŭ ofta en Usono,
Kanado, ktp.; (2) la akompananta muziko, en rapida duopa takto kaj la formo AABB

rumio, (Angle, "rummy"), speco de
kartludo, ludata laŭ multaj varioj; la
celo estas kunmeti kartojn laŭ difinitaj
aroj

sanktapaŭlio, (Angla komuna nomo,
"African violet"), genro (*Saintpaulia*)
de Afrikdevenaj plantoj, kun violaj,
blankaj, aŭ ruĝetaj floroj kaj malhel-
verdaj, vilaj folioj; ofta endoma or-
namplanto

Saskaĉevano, (Angle, "Saskatchewan"), preria provinco en centra Kanado; ĉefurbo, Regina (105°W, 50°N)

Seatlo, (Angle, "Seattle"), urbo en
Vaŝingtonio, la plej granda urbo kaj
ĉefa haveno de nord-okcidenta Usono
(122°W, 47°N)

seranio, (Angla komuna nomo, "bass"),
genro (*Serranus*) de Pacifikaj salakvaj
fiŝoj; **seraniedoj,** familio (*Serranidae*), el kiu la seranio estas la tipo

setaro, (Angle kaj Hindie, "sitar"), Hinda kord-instrumento, iom simila al
granda liuto, kun kutime ses plukataj
kordoj kaj pluraj kunresonantaj zum-
kordoj

sialio, (Angla komuna nomo, "bluebird"), genro (*Sialia*) de oftaj Nord-
Amerikaj kantbirdoj; la virbirdo kutime havas bluan dorson

Sidarto Gotamo, (nacilingve, "Sid-
dhartha Gautama"), denaska nomo de
la Budho [menciita en PIVS sub
"Kapilavasto" sed ne mem difinita]

sklerenkimo, (Angle, "sclerenchyma"), planta histo el malmolaj, dik-
septaj, mortintaj ĉeloj, kiel ekz–e
trunkligno, nuksoŝelo, k.s. [cp "parenkimo" en PIV]

skono, (Angle, "scone"), Britdevena
sensukera kekso, ofte manĝata en Britio kaj Britidaj landoj kun butero ĉe
te-manĝo

skvaŝo, (Angle, "squash"), iu el du lud-
oj, iom similaj al teniso sed ludataj en

kvar-mura endoma tereno
sociopato, (Angle, "sociopath"), psikopato kies konduto estas agreseme kon-
traŭsocia
spireo, (Angla komuna nomo, "spirea"), genro (*Spiraea*) de plantoj el
rozacoj, kun densaj amasoj de malgrandaj ruĝetaj aŭ blankaj floroj
[menciita en PIV ĉe "ulmario", kiu estas unu el ĝiaj specioj, sed ne mem di-
finita]
Srilanko, (nacilingve, "Sri Lanka"),
lando sur la insulo Cejlono; ĉefurbo,
Kolombo (80°E, 7°N)
staĥanovisto, (Angle, "Stakhanovite"),
ano de staĥanovismo
Sufio, (Angle kaj Perse, "Sufi"), ano de
Persdevena Islama mistikismo (Sufi-
ismo)
sukotaŝo, (Angle, "succotash", el Indiana origino), limaj fazeoloj kaj maizk-
ernoj kune bolkuiritaj
suso, (Latine, "sus"), genro (*Sus*) de mamuloj el la subordo de parhufuloj, al
kiu apartenas la porko kaj apro
Suskvehano, (Angle, "Susquehanna",
el Indiana nomo), granda rivero en
orienta Usono, fluanta tra Nov-Jorkio,
Pensilvanio, kaj Marilando; ĝia enmariĝo formas la Golfon Ĉesapikan*
(76°W, 39°30N)
Suvo, (nacilingve, "Suva"), la ĉefurbo
de Fiĝioj† (178°E, 18°S) [menciita en
PIVS sub "Fiĝioj" sed ne mem difini-
ta]
ŝablizo, (Angle kaj France, "chablis"),
speco de seka, blanka, burgonja vino,
origininta en samnoma Franca regiono (proksimume 4°E, 48°N)
Ŝenandoo, (Angle, "Shenandoah", el
Indiana nomo), rivero kaj larĝa intermonta valo en Virginio, finiĝanta en
la Rivero Potomako* (77°45W,
39°20N)
ŝofaro, (Angle, "shofar", el la Hebrea,
"ŝofar"), virkapra korno kiun la Judoj
rite uzas kiel trumpeton
ŝotiŝo, (Angle, "schottische"; Svede,
"schottis"; Hispane, "chotis"), popoldanco por geparoj en duopa takto, iom
simila al la polko sed iom pli malrapida; ofta en Skandinavio, Irlando,

Nord-Ameriko, Meksikio, kaj aliloke
ŝusi, [int], Germane kaj Angle,
"schuss", t.e., "pafo"), en skiado,
rapide kuri rekte malsupren deklivon;
ŝuso, tia kuro
Tagalogo, (nacilingve, "Tagalog"), ano
de Malaja gento en la Filipinoj; la Ta-
galoga lingvo estas la ĉefa indiĝena
lingvo de la Filipinoj
tempro, (Angle, "distemper"), kontaĝa,
febra, virusa malsano ĉe bestoj, aparte
ĉe hundoj [PIV krucreferencas de "de-
tempro" al "tempro", sed "tempro"
mem mankas]
Tetiso, (nacilingve, "Tethys"), unu el la
ĉefaj lunoj de Saturno (meza orbita radiuso 294 670 km)
tezaŭro, (Angle, "thesaurus"), speco de
vortaro kiu konsistas en listoj da si-
nonimoj kaj antonimoj
tifao, (Usona komuna nomo, "cattail";
Brita komuna nomo, "reed mace"),
genro (*Typha*) de altaj marĉaj plantoj,
kun longaj, brunaj, vilaj spikoj, kiuj
similas katvostojn; la fragmitecajn fo-
liojn oni uzas por fari korbojn, mat-
aĵojn, k.s.
Timbuo, (nacilingve, "Thimphu"), la
ĉefurbo de Butano† (90°E, 27°N)
[menciita en PIVS sub "Butano" sed
ne mem difinita]
tipio, (Angle, "tepee", el la Siua), ko-
nusforma Indiana tendo, tegita de
feloj
Tirano, (Angle, "Tirana"; Albane, "Ti-
ranë"), ĉefurbo de Albanio (20°E,
41°N) [menciita en PIV sub "Alba-
no", sed ne mem difinita]
Titano, (nacilingve, "Titan"), la plej
granda luno de Saturno kaj unu el la
malmultaj lunoj kun atmosfero (meza
orbita radiuso 1 221 860 km) [difino
aldona al tiu en PIV]
tofeo, (Angle, "taffy" aŭ "toffee"), karameleca, glueca dolĉaĵo farita el sukero
aŭ melaso, tirita en longajn ŝnurojn
kaj dishakita en oportunajn pecojn
tonka, (Angle, "tonka"), karakterizanta
specon de fabo (*Dipteryx odorata, D.*
oppositifolia), fonto de kumarino
[menciita en PIV sub "kumarino", sed
ne mem difinita]

Tritono, (nacilingve, "Triton"), la pli granda kaj pli proksima el la du ĉefaj lunoj de Neptuno (meza orbita radiuso 653 600) [difino aldona al tiu en PIV]

trojko, (Angle, "troika", el la Rusa, "trojka"), (1) veturilo tirata de tri ĉevaloj; (2) (analoge), alispeca triopo, ekz–e de regantoj

uako, (Angle, "wok", el la Ĉina). Ĉindevena pato kun konkava fundo, uzata por fritado, vaporkuirado, k.s.

Ulan-Bator, (nacilingve, "Ulan Bator"), ĉefurbo de Mongolio (107°E, 47°N) [menciita en PIV sub "Mongolo", sed ne mem difinita]

Umbrielo, (nacilingve, "Umbriel"), unu el la ĉefaj lunoj de Urano (meza orbita radiuso 267 300 km)

uvulario, (Angla komuna nomo, "bellwort"), genro (*Uvularia*) de arbaraj staŭdoj, de la familio de liliacoj, ofta en Nord-Ameriko

Vajt-Insulo, (Angle, "Isle of Wight"), Brita insulo en Maniko, apud la suda Angla marbordo (1°W, 51°N)

vano, (Angle, "van"), aŭtomobilo plimalpli skatolforma por maksimumigi la internan spacon rilate al la eksteraj dimensioj

Vilao, (nacilingve, "Vila"), la ĉefurbo de Vanatuo† (168°E, 18°S) [menciita en PIVS sub "Vanatuo" sed ne mem difinita]

Vindhuko, (nacilingve, "Windhoek"), la ĉefurbo de Namibio† (17°E, 22°S) [menciita en PIVS sub "Namibio" sed ne mem difinita]

Vinipego, (nacilingve, "Winnipeg"), (1) la ĉefurbo de Manitobo (97°W, 50°N); (2), granda lago en centra Manitobo (98°W, 53°N)

Vjentiano, (nacilingve, "Vientiane"), la ĉefurbo de Laoso (103°E, 18°N)

75406520R00340

Made in the USA
Middletown, DE
05 June 2018